economics

THE MCGRAW HILL SERIES: ECONOMICS

ESSENTIALS OF ECONOMICS

Brue, McConnell, and Flynn
Essentials of Economics
Fifth Edition

Mandel
M: Economics, The Basics
Fourth Edition

McConnell, Brue, and Flynn
Economics: Brief Edition.
Macroeconomics: Brief Edition, and
Macroeconomics: Brief Edition
Third Edition

Schiller and Gebhardt
Essentials of Economics
Twelfth Edition

PRINCIPLES OF ECONOMICS

Asarta and Butters
Connect Master: Principles of Economics

Colander
Economics, Microeconomics, and Macroeconomics
Twelfth Edition

Frank, Bernanke, Antonovics, and Heffetz
Principles of Economics, Principles of Microeconomics, Principles of Macroeconomics
Eighth Edition

Frank, Bernanke, Antonovics, and Heffetz
Streamlined Editions: Principles of Economics, Principles of Microeconomics, Principles of Macroeconomics
Fourth Edition

Karlan and Morduch
Economics, Microeconomics, and Macroeconomics
Third Edition

McConnell, Brue, and Flynn
Economics, Microeconomics, and Macroeconomics
Twenty-Third Edition

Schiller and Gebhardt
The Economy Today, The Micro Economy Today, and The Macro Economy Today
Sixteenth Edition

Slavin
Economics, Microeconomics, and Macroeconomics
Twelfth Edition

ECONOMICS OF SOCIAL ISSUES

Guell
Issues in Economics Today
Tenth Edition

Register and Grimes
Economics of Social Issues
Twenty-First Edition

DATA ANALYTICS FOR ECONOMICS

Jaggia, Kelly, Lertwachara, and Chen
Business Analytics: Communicating with Numbers
Second Edition

Prince
Predictive Analytics for Business Strategy
First Edition

Richardson and Weidenmier-Watson
Introduction to Business Analytics
First Edition

Taddy, Hendrix, and Harding
Modern Business Analytics
First Edition

MANAGERIAL ECONOMICS

Baye and Prince
Managerial Economics and Business Strategy
Tenth Edition

Brickley, Smith, and Zimmerman
Managerial Economics and Organizational Architecture
Seventh Edition

Thomas and Maurice
Managerial Economics
Thirteenth Edition

INTERMEDIATE ECONOMICS

Bernheim and Whinston
Microeconomics
Second Edition

Dornbusch, Fischer, and Startz
Macroeconomics
Thirteenth Edition

Frank
Microeconomics and Behavior
Tenth Edition

ADVANCED ECONOMICS

Romer
Advanced Macroeconomics
Fifth Edition

MONEY AND BANKING

Cecchetti and Schoenholtz
Money, Banking, and Financial Markets
Sixth Edition

URBAN ECONOMICS

O'Sullivan
Urban Economics
Nineth Edition

LABOR ECONOMICS

Borjas
Labor Economics
Nineth Edition

McConnell, Brue, and Macpherson
Contemporary Labor Economics
Twelfth Edition

PUBLIC FINANCE

Rosen and Gayer
Public Finance
Tenth Edition

ENVIRONMENTAL ECONOMICS

Field and Field
Environmental Economics: An Introduction
Eighth Edition

INTERNATIONAL ECONOMICS

Appleyard and Field
International Economics
Ninth Edition

Pugel
International Economics
Eighteenth Edition

THE FOUR VERSIONS OF MCCONNELL, BRUE, FLYNN

Economics 23e Chapter Title	Economics 23e	Microeconomics 23e	Macroeconomics 23e	Essentials of Economics 5e
Limits, Alternatives, and Choices	X	X	X	X
The Market System and the Circular Flow	X	X	X	X
Demand, Supply, and Market Equilibrium	X	X	X	X
Market Failures Caused by Externalities & Asymmetric Information	X	X	X	X
Public Goods, Public Choice, and Government Failure	X	X	X	X
Elasticity	X	X		X
Utility Maximization	X	X		X
Behavioral Economics	X	X		
Businesses and the Costs of Production	X	X		X
Pure Competition	X	X		X
Pure Monopoly	X	X		X
Monopolistic Competition	X	X		X
Oligopoly and Strategic Behavior	X	X		X
Internet Oligopoly: Networks and Platforms	X	X		
Technology, R&D, and Efficiency	X	X		
The Demand for Resources	X	X		
Wage Determination	X	X		
Rent, Interest, and Profit	X	X		
Environmental Economics	X	X		
Public Finance: Expenditures and Taxes	X	X		
Antitrust Policy and Regulation	X	X		
Agriculture: Economics and Policy	X	X		X
Income Inequality, Poverty, and Discrimination	X	X		
Health Care	X	X		
Immigration	X	X		
An Introduction to Macroeconomics	X		X	X
Measuring Domestic Output and National Income	X		X	X
Economic Growth	X		X	X
Business Cycles, Unemployment, and Inflation	X		X	X
Basic Macroeconomic Relationships	X		X	X
The Aggregate Expenditures Model	X		X	X
Aggregate Demand and Aggregate Supply	X		X	X
Fiscal Policy, Deficits, and Debt	X		X	X
Money, the Federal Reserve, and Interest Rates	X		X	X
Monetary Policy, GDP, and the Price Level	X		X	
Financial Economics	X		X	
Extending the Analysis of Aggregate Supply	X		X	X
Current Issues in Macro Theory and Policy	X		X	
International Trade	X	X	X	X
The Balance of Payments, Exchange Rates, and Trade Deficits	X	X	X	X
The Economics of Developing Countries	X	X	X	

A red "**X**" indicates chapters that combine or consolidate content from two or more *Economics* chapters.

economics

Twenty-Third Edition

Campbell R. McConnell
University of Nebraska

Stanley L. Brue
Pacific Lutheran University

Sean M. Flynn
Scripps College

ECONOMICS

Published by McGraw Hill LLC, 1325 Avenue of the Americas, New York, NY 10019. Copyright ©2024 by McGraw Hill LLC. All rights reserved. Printed in the United States of America. No part of this publication may be reproduced or distributed in any form or by any means, or stored in a database or retrieval system, without the prior written consent of McGraw Hill LLC, including, but not limited to, in any network or other electronic storage or transmission, or broadcast for distance learning.

Some ancillaries, including electronic and print components, may not be available to customers outside the United States.

This book is printed on acid-free paper.

1 2 3 4 5 6 7 8 9 LWI 28 27 26 25 24 23

ISBN 978-1-266-10684-2
MHID 1-266-10684-7

Cover Image: *vchal/Shutterstock*

To Mac and Mem, Terri and Craig, and past instructors.

Campbell R. McConnell/McGraw Hill

CAMPBELL R. MCCONNELL earned his Ph.D. at the University of Iowa after receiving degrees from Cornell College and the University of Illinois. He taught at the University of Nebraska–Lincoln from 1953 until his retirement in 1990. He was also coauthor of *Contemporary Labor Economics* and *Essentials of Economics*. He was a recipient of both the University of Nebraska Distinguished Teaching Award and the James A. Lake Academic Freedom Award and served as president of the Midwest Economics Association. Professor McConnell was awarded an honorary Doctor of Laws degree from Cornell College in 1973 and received its Distinguished Achievement Award in 1994. He was also a jazz expert and aficionado until his passing in 2019.

Stanley L. Brue/McGraw Hill

STANLEY L. BRUE did his undergraduate work at Augustana College (South Dakota) and received its Distinguished Achievement Award in 1991. He received his Ph.D. from the University of Nebraska–Lincoln. He is retired from a long career at Pacific Lutheran University, where he was honored as a recipient of the Burlington Northern Faculty Achievement Award. Professor Brue has also received the national Leavey Award for excellence in economics education. He has served as national president and chair of the Board of Trustees of Omicron Delta Epsilon International Economics Honorary. He is coauthor of *Economic Scenes,* fifth edition (Prentice-Hall); *Contemporary Labor Economics,* twelfth edition; *Essentials of Economics,* fourth edition; and *The Evolution of Economic Thought,* eighth edition (Cengage Learning). For relaxation, he enjoys international travel, attending sporting events, and going on fishing trips.

Sean M. Flynn/McGraw Hill

SEAN M. FLYNN did his undergraduate work at the University of Southern California before completing his Ph.D. at U.C. Berkeley, where he served as the Head Graduate Student Instructor for the Department of Economics after receiving the Outstanding Graduate Student Instructor Award. He teaches at Scripps College (of the Claremont Colleges) and is the author of *Economics for Dummies,* third edition (Wiley); *Essentials of Economics,* fourth edition; and *The Cure That Works: How to Have the World's Best Healthcare—at a Quarter of the Price* (Regnery). His research interests include behavioral finance, behavioral economics, and health care economics. An accomplished martial artist, Sean has coached five of his students to national championships and is the author of *Understanding Shodokan Aikido.* Other hobbies include running, traveling, and cooking.

KEY GRAPHS

Welcome to the 23rd edition of *Economics*, America's most innovative—and popular—economics learning resource.

We are pleased to present faculty and students with comprehensive revisions, insightful new content, and significant improvements to both our online learning system and our industry-leading ancillary materials.

From real-life examples to cutting-edge learning resources, our modern approach makes learning and applying economics easier for both students and instructors.

- For students, *Economics* **offers a student-centered learning environment that presents the subject matter in new and engaging ways.**

- For instructors, **a full and supportive teaching package does the heavy lifting with regard to basic concepts and ideas so that instructors can focus their attention on helping students achieve the highest levels of Bloom's taxonomy of learning,** including being able to analyze, apply, and create based on economics concepts and ideas.

Optimize your outcomes
MORE Student-Centered

McConnell has always put students at the center of every revision and the new edition is no exception. Extensive market feedback and a keen focus on optimizing student outcomes drove this revision. Nearly every element—from the work itself to the digital tools and resources—has been updated and optimized for today's learners.

- **An all-new chapter, "Internet Oligopoly: Networks and Platforms,"** provides an intuitive presentation of the Nobel Prize-winning economic theories that explain why Internet industries are highly concentrated due to network effects but at the same time often deliver their main products for free, as though the firms in those industries had no pricing power at all. This innovative chapter also explains why Internet platforms that bring together different groups of users typically charge one those groups nothing while charging other groups (like advertisers) heavily. We have found that this material is highly popular with both students and instructors.

- **We have consolidated our previous two chapters on pure competition into a single chapter** in response to extensive faculty feedback that there is too much material to cover in the principles course and to give more room for other material, like the new chapter on Internet Oligopoly.

- **We have updated and enhanced SmartBook,** making our adaptive reading experience more personal, more accessible, and more productive, in addition to making it fully mobile across devices for students who, for example, begin a SmartBook assignment on their laptop but then want to finish it on their smartphone.

- **We have created additional Concept Overview and Guided Examples videos** to help students with challenging concepts and to offer immediate feedback and assistance as students work through difficult problems.

- **We have developed additional Application-Based Activities (ABAs)** that immerse students in real-time interactive role playing scenarios in order to hone problem-solving skills and sharpen economics intuition.

- **We have updated our Adaptive Econ Prep: Math and Graphing tool** that gives students just-in-time math remediation as well as experience with the graphing fundamentals that are a prerequisite to success in principles of economics courses.

- **We have extended our ongoing efforts to accommodate the fast-paced, nonlinear learning style of contemporary students** by streamlining paragraphs, highlighting key examples, and introducing additional Key Graphs. These changes will help digital natives quickly scan for key concepts and core material. Scores of newly added headers, Quick Review boxes, and bullet points will assist them in rapidly identifying the most important ideas and information.

MORE Accessible

We are proud that our publisher, McGraw Hill, is fully committed to Accessibility, as is made clear by McGraw Hill's Accessibility Statement:

> At McGraw Hill, we're committed to unlocking the potential of all learners. We believe that the best learning materials should be accessible to students of all abilities, and are building an inclusive culture that considers the needs of every learner from the outset. We achieve this through a comprehensive strategy that starts with planning and research. We seek to create learning materials that are accessible to all learners. McGraw Hill is making every effort to ensure that all new educational content and technology follows the WCAG (Web Content Accessibility Guidelines) version 2.1 AA guidelines and best practices. To achieve this and continuously improve the accessibility of our products, our internal product teams regularly engage with external experts and solicit user feedback.

One aspect of Accessibility is the ability of students from all backgrounds to instantly and immediately open, use, and benefit from every learning tool available to them no matter what device they are using to access the Internet and our content.

- **We are consequently very happy to announce that** *Economics* **takes full advantage of McGraw Hill's free ReadAnywhere app.** Available for both iOS and Android smartphones and tablets, ReadAnywhere gives students access to all of the McGraw Hill learning tools, including

SmartBook 2.0, Recharge, and our Adaptive Learning Assignments. Students using ReadAnywhere can even take notes, highlight key material, and complete assignments *offline* knowing that all of their work will sync the next time they connect to the Internet.

Another key aspect of Accessibility is affordability. Our goal is an "education of value" for each and every student regardless of background or circumstance. **Therefore, we are very appreciative of McGraw Hill's commitment to improving access by providing institutions and instructors with a wide range of options to lower costs and thereby clear more paths that can help to achieve equity across campuses and learners.**

MORE Current

- *Incorporating the Pandemic* For the current generation of traditional-aged college students, the COVID-19 pandemic has been the most extreme and long-lasting economic event of their lives. We have thus striven in this edition to use examples from the pandemic to illustrate economics principles and to explain the economic logic behind various government efforts to moderate the harm caused by the pandemic. To that end, the new edition features extensive coverage of the effects that the pandemic had on everything from labor markets to chip shortages. We also detail the government's various fiscal and monetary policy responses, many of which directly affected our students, their families, and their employers.

- *Consolidating our Presentation of Monetary Policy* We have consolidated what were formerly three chapters on central banking, monetary policy, and money creation into two succinct chapters on the Federal Reserve, interest rates, and monetary policy. This major consolidation was a response both to faculty surveys and to the Fed's elimination of reserve requirements, which rendered concepts like the monetary multiplier irrelevant to the conduct of monetary policy.

- *Enhancing our Discussion of the Fed's Policy Tools* We have fully revised our discussion of the Fed's current set of monetary policy tools so as to emphasize (1) the Fed's use of the so-called administered rates—especially the IORB and ON RRP rates—to control short-term interest rates in every segment of the money market, including the federal funds market; (2) the Fed's ability to use open-market purchases and sales of longer-term bonds to influence medium- and long-term interest rates through quantitative easing or tightening; and (3) the Fed's ability to use forward guidance to shape expectations. This presentation is pithy, intuitive, and has been met with very positive responses from both students and faculty.

MORE Examples

The 23rd edition abounds with new examples on many topics, including pandemic-induced labor shortages, the supply-chain problems caused by the COVID-19 pandemic, economies of scale in cloud computing, how firms in various industries implemented the short-run shutdown condition during the pandemic, the strategies employed by pharmaceutical companies when attempting to extend their patents past the normal 20-year expiration date, nonprice competition among oligopoly credit-card issuers, and the various ways that governments are seeking to regulate oligopoly Internet firms that enjoy network effects and platform externalities.

We have also added seventeen new "Consider This" and "Last Word" boxed features. These short, stand-alone essays convey key ideas in an accessible, student-oriented manner. New additions include, "The COVID Inflation," "The Great Resignation," and "A New Inflationary Era?"

MORE Faculty Tools, Resources, and Support

Faculty time is precious. To preserve as much of it as possible for faculty adopting *Economics*, we went sentence-by-sentence and section-by-section, pulling out extraneous examples, eliminating unnecessary paragraphs, and—in some cases—removing entire sections that faculty reported they didn't have time to teach.

These changes have been reviewed positively by faculty and **we are excited that our streamlined presentation frees up faculty time for more advanced classroom activities,** including experiments, debates, simulations, and various forms of peer instruction and team-based learning. (Instructors can find more information about our Guided Peer Instruction resources below and, if interested, should reach out to their reps for access.)

Accelerating Student Achievement via Adaptive Learning and Innovative Ancillary Materials

Would you as a faculty member enjoy spending less time on definitions and more time on theory, applications, and enrichment material? Most faculty say YES!—which is why **we continue to make large annual improvements to what is already the most effective digital learning platform in higher education: Connect Economics.**

Before Class

You can use Connect Economics and its built-in adaptive reading technology, SmartBook, to ensure that students know all the basics before class starts. Simply assign your selected chapter readings in SmartBook and have students complete related problems and questions before lecture. The Connect Economics platform will automatically probe for misunderstandings and then fix them with instant feedback and remediation.

To further enhance the ability of instructors to "get students up to speed" before class, **we also offer adaptive economics preparedness tutorials for math and graphing as well as a large bank of custom-made videos covering real-world examples.** All are assignable within Connect Economics, and each includes assessment questions that offer instant feedback whenever students give incorrect answers.

During Class

You can then proceed, during class, to higher-level learning activities that build correct intuitions and the ability to apply models, theories, and concepts to new situations that have not already been covered in your class.

Creating higher-level classroom activities is no easy task, and we know from personal experience that faculty often find themselves with too little time left over at the end of a long day of teaching, service, and research to create the high-quality enrichment materials that they would like to use in class.

To that end, we have gone out of our way to develop three major in-class enrichment tools that instructors can use to "flip the classroom" and engage students at a higher level.

Guided Peer Instruction

With the help of Todd Fitch of U.C. Berkeley, we have authored and field-tested hundreds of in-class questions and answers that can be used to facilitate the peer-instruction teaching method pioneered by Eric Mazur of Harvard University. Our version, which we call Guided Peer Instruction, is a student-focused, interactive teaching method that has been shown to more than double student understanding relative to lecture-based presentation formats like "chalk and talk." We are proud to be the first to offer Guided Peer Instruction.

Interactive Graphs

Easier to use than going directly to the St. Louis Fed's FRED site, our Interactive Graphs provide instructors with quick access to visual displays of real-world data that can be used to immediately illustrate important economic concepts and relationships. These Interactive Graphs are also available for students to play with and learn from. To that end, each Interactive Graph is accompanied by assignable assessment questions as well as feedback and tutorials to guide students through the experience of learning to read and interpret graphs and data.

ECON Everyday

Our ECON Everyday Blog saves instructors time by bringing current, student-centered content into their courses all semester long. Short articles written for principles-level students are tagged by topic to make them easily searchable. We also provide discussion questions to help instructors drive the conversation forward. Visit www.econeveryday.com and subscribe for updates.

After Class

Our Application-Based Activities (ABAs) are immersive decision-making simulations that put students into the role of everyday economists. Students practice their economics thinking and problem-solving skills as they apply course concepts to interactive digital scenarios that are delivered within Connect Economics. Each simulation was designed as a 15-minute experience that instructors can set to be replayed repeatedly.

Hundreds of problems with algorithmic variations provide ample opportunities for students to practice quantitative skills outside the classroom, while scores of graphing exercises give students the opportunity to draw, interact with, and analyze graphs even when studying alone.

Remote Proctoring & Browser-Locking Capabilities

Remote proctoring and browser-locking capabilities, curated by Proctorio, provide faculty with control of the assessment environment by enabling security options and verifying the identity of each student. Seamlessly integrated within Connect, these services allow instructors to control the assessment experience by verifying identification, restricting browser activity, and monitoring student actions. Instant and detailed reporting gives instructors an at-a-glance view of potential academic integrity concerns, thereby avoiding personal bias and supporting evidence-based claims.

High-Quality Instruction and Assessment through Preconfigured, OLC-Aligned Courseware

In consultation with the Online Learning Consortium (OLC) and our Certified Faculty Consultants, McGraw Hill has created preconfigured courseware using the OLC's quality scorecard to align with best practices in online course delivery. This turnkey courseware contains a combination of formative assessments, summative assessments, homework, and application activities, and can easily be customized to meet an individual instructor's needs and desired course outcomes. For more information, visit https://www.mheducation.com/highered/olc.

Support at Every Step

To ensure that it will continue providing the best faculty support services in higher education, McGraw Hill interviewed hundreds of faculty, who helped to identify the most common and problematic pain points with respect to the successful implementation and use of digital courseware.

Based on that information, McGraw Hill teamed up with faculty consultants to design and build higher-education's leading faculty support portal, Support at Every Step.

From initial training to implementing new tools, Support at Every Step is ready to help. If you're looking for a prebuilt course, or a tool to help design your own course, or you just want to talk to another McConnell user, please visit www.supportateverystep.com.

Reflecting the Diverse World around Us

McGraw Hill believes in unlocking the potential of every learner at every stage of life. To accomplish that, we are dedicated to creating products that reflect, and are accessible to, all the diverse global customers that McGraw Hill serves. Within McGraw Hill, we foster a culture of belonging, and we work with partners who share our commitment to equity, inclusion, and diversity in all forms. This includes, but is not limited to:

- Refreshing and implementing inclusive content guidelines around topics including generalizations and stereotypes, gender, abilities/disabilities, race/ethnicity, sexual orientation, diversity of names, and age.

- Enhancing best practices in assessment creation to eliminate cultural, cognitive, and affective biases.

- Maintaining and continually updating a robust photo library of diverse images that reflect our student populations.

- Including more diverse voices in the development and review of our content.

- Strengthening art guidelines to improve accessibility both by ensuring meaningful text and by ensuring that images are distinguishable and perceivable by users with limited color vision as well as by users with moderately low vision.

A 23rd Edition for the 21st Century

Economics **has maintained its position as the world's best-selling economics textbook for over six decades by continually updating its coverage and its pedagogy.** We weren't just the first with adaptive learning and instant remediation, but first also with everything from student study guides to computerized test banks.

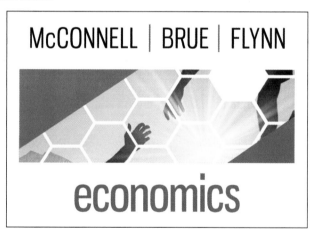

MCCONNELL | BRUE | FLYNN

economics

McConnell Is/Was/and Will Remain the Innovation Champion:
- The first with a student study guide.
- The first with test banks.
- The first with multi-color graphs.
- The first with televised economics lectures.
- The first with overhead projector slides.
- The first with an instructors' manual.
- The first with a computerized test bank.
- The first with PowerPoint slides.
- The first with algorithmic problem sets.

- The first with an adaptive-learning system.
- The first optimized for smartphones.

It is our sincere hope that our 23rd edition will continue to promote rapid learning and deep understanding as the 21st century approaches its 25th birthday. We have worked hard to ensure that *Economics* and all of its ancillary materials are comprehensive, analytical, and challenging—yet fully accessible to a wide range of students. **Where needed, an extra sentence of explanation is provided. Brevity at the expense of clarity is false economy.**

Sean M. Flynn
Stanley L. Brue

Chapter-by-Chapter Changes

Each chapter of *Economics,* 23rd edition, contains data updates and numerous revised examples that will be fresh and relevant for today's students. Chapter-specific updates include new boxed pieces, additional Key Graphs, and substantial revisions to the core content. The content and examples were also revised with a keen eye toward diversity, equity and inclusion.

As mentioned earlier, the largest changes are a completely new Chapter 14, "Internet Oligopoly: Networks and Platforms," as well as a new consolidated, intuitive, and state-of-the-art presentation of monetary policy as the Fed now conducts it (Chapters 34 and 35). Other changes include the following:

Chapter 1: Limits, Alternatives, and Choices features updated examples and a revised presentation of capital (and, thus, investment) that highlights the fact that "capital" includes intangible intellectual capital as well as physical capital. By popular demand, we have also brought back the Last Word about faulty economic reasoning that appeared in several earlier editions.

Chapter 2: The Market System and the Circular Flow contains two new Key Words (*coordination problem* and *incentive problem*), revised examples, increased clarity on the benefits of property rights, and a streamlined presentation of the circular flow model.

Chapter 3: Demand, Supply, and Market Equilibrium includes several new examples, new material on how network and congestion effects shift demand curves, a new Key Word (*rent control*), and a new Last Word on how rapid shifts in supply and demand prompted dramatic price changes as well as shortages during the COVID-19 pandemic.

Chapter 4: Market Failures Caused by Externalities and Asymmetric Information contains two new Key Words (*deadweight loss* and *private information*) as well as several updates in both the text and in figures to emphasize the concepts of maximum willingness to pay (demand curve) and minimum willingness to accept (supply curve), thereby enhancing student understanding of both consumer and producer surplus as well as the efficiency losses that result from over- and under-production.

Chapter 5: Public Goods, Public Choice, and Government Failure contains data updates as well as revisions that clarify the necessity that a good or service be excludable if private firms are going to be willing to provide it; the fact that the collective demand schedule used for valuing public goods is a collective willingness-to-pay curve; and the strength and generalizability of the median voter theorem. We also introduce a new Key Word (*collective demand for a public good*).

Chapter 6: Elasticity contains a new Discussion Question, refreshed examples, and several wording changes to improve clarity.

Chapter 7: Utility Maximization contains several new examples as well as revisions of existing material for clarity and concision. Additionally, a new Last Word presents some famous examples of excise taxes that resulted in very peculiar architecture.

Chapter 8: Behavioral Economics has data updates, updated examples, and a new Last Word on using behavioral economics to help people save more for retirement.

Chapter 9: Businesses and the Costs of Production includes an improved definition of explicit costs, several updated examples, a more intuitive explanation of sunk costs, a new Review Question, and a new Last Word on cloud computing and economies of scale.

Chapter 10: Pure Competition responds to faculty requests that we consolidate our two previous pure-competition chapters ("Pure Competition in the Short Run" and "Pure Competition in the Long Run") into a single chapter. The new, consolidated chapter features several new examples, a clarified explanation of the $P = MC$ rule for competitive profit maximization, and a new Consider This about the decreasing-cost characteristics of the lithium-ion battery industry on which electric cars depend. There is also a new Last Word on how firms in various industries implemented the short-run shutdown condition during the COVID-19 pandemic.

Chapter 11: Pure Monopoly has several new examples, an expanded treatment of network effects as a cause of monopoly power, a revised Summary section, a new end-of-chapter problem on how the size of social networks can serve as a barrier to entry, and a new Last Word on the computer-chip supply chain disruptions caused by the COVID-19 pandemic.

Chapter 12: Monopolistic Competition contains new examples, a new end-of-chapter Discussion Question, a new Key Word (*pricing power*), and brief clarifications of the role of advertising in shifting and tilting the demand curves of monopolistically competitive firms.

Chapter 13: Oligopoly and Strategic Behavior contains several new examples, revised Key Word definitions, and a new Last Word on how the worldwide credit-card oligopoly engages in nonprice competition via credit-card rewards programs. For instructors who do not have enough time to teach our new Chapter 14 on *Internet Oligopoly*, we incorporate into this existing chapter a short new discussion of how network effects can give first-mover advantages to Internet companies as well as concise material that explains the role of network effects in creating and maintaining Internet oligopolies.

Chapter 14: Internet Oligopoly: Networks and Platforms is an all-new chapter that delivers an intuitive presentation of how network effects and platform competition drive the high concentration found in many Internet industries, including social media and gaming. Other topics include network switching costs, contestable industries, technological lock-in, and why so many Internet firms give away their main products for free.

Chapter 15: Technology, R&D, and Efficiency contains numerous updated examples, extensive data updates, and a new Last Word on drug makers' attempts to extend patent protections beyond the normal 20-year expiration date.

Chapter 16: The Demand for Resources contains data updates, new examples, and wording improvements to enhance clarity.

Chapter 17: Wage Determination has extensive data updates as well as increases in the example wages used in Figure 17.3, Table 17.1, and Table 17.2. The appendix on unions also contains a brief reference to the Supreme Court's 2018 *Janus* decision, which made agency shops illegal for public sector employees.

Chapter 18: Rent, Interest, and Profit incorporates wording improvements, data updates, a new Key Word (*interest income*), and a very brief application of the loanable funds model to explain why interest rates fell dramatically during the COVID-19 pandemic. We also in passing reference cryptocurrencies as a form of money.

Chapter 19: Environmental Economics was previously titled, "Environmental and Natural Resource Economics." In addition to updating the name, we have provided extensive data updates, a new application involving conflict minerals, a new section on how the growth of commercial aquaculture has assisted wildlife conservation efforts, and a new Key Word (*aquaculture*).

Chapter 20: Public Finance: Expenditures and Taxes contains extensive data updates plus substantial new coverage of how the COVID-19 pandemic dramatically increased government expenditures, especially with respect to transfer payments.

Chapter 21: Antitrust Policy and Regulation includes increased clarity about the perverse incentives that can be generated by fair-return rate regulation and a richer explanation of the differences between *structural remedies* and *behavioral remedies*. We have also elevated those two concepts to Key Word status, so that they now have definitions that appear in the Glossary and in the margins of the printed book.

Chapter 22: Agriculture: Economics and Policy delivers numerous data updates and several wording changes to improve clarity.

Chapter 23: Income Inequality, Poverty, and Discrimination has new material that distinguishes clearly between average and median household income, a revised discussion of the long-term effects of the 1996 welfare reform, and a synopsis of how unemployment benefits were 20 times larger in 2020 relative to previous years due to the enhanced unemployment benefits that Congress approved when the COVID-19 pandemic started. This chapter's Last Word on Universal Basic Income has also been heavily revised in light of the natural experiment provided by those enhanced and extended unemployment benefits.

Chapter 24: Health Care features a short new section near the start of the chapter called Basic Insurance Terminology that explains, right up front, how premiums, deductibles, copays, and coinsurance work (rather than having the explanations for those items given in passing throughout the chapter, as was the case in prior editions). As part of those changes, *coinsurance* is a now Key Word.

Chapter 25: Immigration contains new data on immigrant remittances as a percentage of GDP as well as various small wording changes to improve student comprehension.

Chapter 26: An Introduction to Macroeconomics features a new Consider This boxed piece about the COVID-19 recession, a more efficient summary section, and various updates and wording improvements.

Chapter 27: Measuring Domestic Output and National Income benefits from data updates, revisions to our presentation of the income and allocation approaches to totaling up GDP, and a revised presentation of why financial transactions are excluded from GDP.

Chapter 28: Economic Growth contains numerous data updates and several wording improvements for clarity. (As an aside, we would like to mention the recently available extensions to Angus Maddison's historical tables of long-run economic growth that are now being maintained by the Maddison Project at the University of Groningen. Kudos to them for extending Professor Maddison's groundbreaking data tables after his passing.)

Chapter 29: Business Cycles, Unemployment, and Inflation has extensive data updates, new material that relates the chapter's key concepts to the COVID-19 recession, and a new Last Word on the highly unusual behavior of labor markets and unemployment over the course of the pandemic.

Chapter 30: Basic Macroeconomic Relationships features a revised Consider This, a new example about 3-D printers, and a revised Discussion Question.

Chapter 31: The Aggregate Expenditures Model contains new material that relates the aggregate expenditure model to the COVID-19 recession, as well as several small but meaningful wording improvements.

Chapter 32: Aggregate Demand and Aggregate Supply contains improved definitions of two Key Words (*short-run aggregate supply* and *long-run aggregate supply*) as well as substantial new material relating the AD-AS model to the COVID-19 recession, including a new Last Word explaining how unusual it was to have a recession and then a recovery in which inflation rose due to *simultaneous* shifts of AD (to the right, due to

stimulus funds) and AS (to the left, due to supply chain disruptions and labor shortages).

Chapter 33: Fiscal Policy, Deficits, and Debt incorporates several discussions of fiscal policy before and during the COVID-19 pandemic, especially with respect to the sheer magnitude of the stimulus but also with respect to other things, like how unusual the stimulus was in not having any recognition lag and, compared with typical recessions, hardly any administrative or operational lag, either.

Chapter 34: Money, the Federal Reserve, and Interest Rates is the first of two monetary policy chapters that respond to faculty feedback that we should consolidate what had previously been three monetary policy chapters into two. Much of the consolidation was also necessitated by the Federal Reserve's decision to eliminate reserve requirements for banks, thereby rendering irrelevant for policy purposes concepts like the monetary multiplier. This chapter contains much of the material that was previously in our chapter titled "Money, Banking, and Financial Institutions" (which was Chapter 34 in the previous edition). We have added to it the material on interest rate determination (that appeared in the previous edition's Chapter 36, "Interest Rates and Monetary Policy") in addition to adding discussions of debit cards as a means of accessing checkable deposits, electronic cash-transfer systems like PayPal and Venmo, and a new Last Word about cryptocurrencies, including Bitcoin and central-bank digital currencies. Please also note the subtle but profound revisions that were necessitated by the Fed's changing the definitions of the $M1$ and $M2$ measures of the money supply such that noncheckable savings deposits are now part of $M1$ rather than $M2$. That definitional adjustment has produced the strange result that $M2$ is now only about 5 percent larger than $M1$ (whereas, previously, $M2$ had always been at least triple the size of $M1$).

Chapter 35: Monetary Policy, GDP, and Price Level is the second of our two monetary policy chapters that respond to faculty feedback that we should consolidate what had previously been three monetary policy chapters into two. In making those consolidations, we completely eliminated the previous edition's Chapter 35 ("Money Creation") both in response to faculty feedback and in response to the Federal Reserve's decision to eliminate bank reserve requirements in March 2020. The Fed is now opting to control bank lending (and thus bank money creation) through other channels, especially its ability to modulate the interest rate on reserve balances (IORB). Much of the material in this chapter is brand new, including an innovative presentation of the Fed's current set of monetary policy tools. Along those lines, we explain how the modern Fed uses IORB and the overnight reverse repo rate (ON RRP) to control short-run interest rates, including the effective federal funds rate, independently of longer-run rates, which it can manipulate with quantitative easing and quantitative tightening. Other new topics include the Fed's ability, through the payment of IORB to banks and ON RRP to nonbanks, to use the banking and financial system as a giant anti-inflationary "money sponge" that can be used to help offset the massive increases in the money supply that have been generated by the Fed's massive quantitative-easing asset purchases. The Dual-Mandate Bullseye Chart has also been expanded into a Key Graph with an embedded Quick Quiz.

Chapter 36: Financial Economics contains data updates; a new Key Word (*securities*); improved presentations of present value and the inverse relationship between asset prices and rates of return; and a discussion of how time-varying risk premiums can explain the initial stock market crash at the very start of the COVID-19 pandemic as well as the subsequent recovery in stock prices over the following six months.

Chapter 37: Extending the Analysis of Aggregate Supply delivers data updates, several new or revised Key Words (*short run*, *long run*, *short-run downward sloping Phillips Curve*), and a new Consider This on how the COVID-19 supply shocks contributed to rising inflation.

Chapter 38: Current Issues in Macro Theory and Policy includes data updates, new examples, and a brief summary of the successful policy actions that the Fed took between March and June 2020 in order to prevent the COVID-19 pandemic from causing a major financial crisis.

Chapter 39: International Trade contains extensive data updates, a new Key Word (*trade*), a streamlined Summary, and a highly revised and substantially more intuitive presentation of absolute and comparative advantage.

Chapter 40: The Balance of Payments, Exchange Rates, and Trade Deficits offers extensive data updates, various edits for concision and clarity, and a new Last Word describing the Exchange Rate Trilemma.

Chapter 41: The Economics of Developing Countries includes data updates, a new Global Perspective on the high cost of legally registering a new business in many developing countries, and an integration of the concepts of *state capacity* and *failed states* into our discussion of the economic factors that can hinder or help economic development. *State capacity* and *failed states* have also been made into Key Words, with glossary and margin entries.

Historical Data We have added four rows to the macroeconomic historical data that appears after the final chapter of both *Economics* and *Macroeconomics*. The new rows show historical data for, respectively, (1) real GDP per capita, (2) the annual percentage growth rate of real GDP per capita, (3) the federal budget deficit or surplus, and (4) the federal budget deficit or surplus as a percentage of GDP. By contrast, the microeconomic historical data that appears after the final chapter of *Microeconomics* remains unchanged.

Acknowledgments

We give special thanks to Peggy Dalton and Peter Staples for their hard work updating and accuracy checking the questions and problems in *Connect*, as well as the material they created for the additional Connect Problems.

A big thank you to Stephanie Campbell and Randy Grant for all of their efforts updating and accuracy checking the test bank.

We thank Tom Barbiero (the coauthor of our Canadian edition) for helpful ideas and insights.

We are greatly indebted to an all-star group of professionals at McGraw Hill—in particular, Kelly Pekelder, Anke Weekes, Bobby Pearson, Harvey Yep, and Jackie Higgason—for their publishing and marketing expertise. We would also like to thank the talented McGraw Hill Learning Technology Representatives and Implementation Teams.

The 23rd edition has also greatly benefited from a number of perceptive faculty reviews. The reviewers, listed in the next section, were a rich source of suggestions for this revision. To each of you, and to any others we may have inadvertently overlooked, thank you for your considerable help in improving *Economics*.

REVIEWERS SUPPORTING THE 23RD EDITION:

Carlos Aguilar, *El Paso Community College*
Barbara Baer, *Palomar College*
Kuntal Banerjee, *Florida Atlantic University*
Jill M. Beccaris-Pescatore, *Montgomery County Community College*
Lee A. Bertman, *Indian River State College*
Roberta Biby, *Grand Valley State University*
Melissa Blankenship, *North Central Texas College*
Stephanie Lyn Blowe, *Lone Star College*
Andrea Borchard, *Hillsborough Community College*
Greg Burge, *University of Oklahoma*
Mark L. Burkey, *North Carolina A&T State University*
William Byrd, *Troy University*
Joab Corey, *University of California-Riverside*
Norman Cure, *Macomb Community College*
Sonia Dalmia, *Grand Valley State University*
Maria S. Davis, *Indian River State College*
Irani DeAraujo, *Pace University*
Carter Doyle, *University of Virginia*
Sheryl Dusek, *Nashville State Community College*
Lynne Elkes, *Loyola University Maryland*
Tammie Fischer, *University of Nebraska-Lincoln*
Robert J. Foran, *Miami Dade College-Wolfson Campus*
Michael G. Goode, *Central Piedmont Community College*
Joseph Guider, *Essex County College*
Gabriela Hamilton, *Hillsborough Community College*
Christiana Hilmer, *San Diego State University*
Michael Hilmer, *San Diego State University*
Daniel Hoffman, *University of Nebraska-Lincoln*
Liang Hu, *Wayne State University*
Zagros Madjd-Sadjadi, *Winston-Salem State University*
Laura Maghoney, *Solano Community College*
Marilyn Markel, *Western Michigan University*
Erika Martinez, *University of South Florida*
Jesse D. Melvin, *Rowan University*
Victoria Miller, *Piedmont Technical College*
Phillip Mixon, *Troy University*
Alex Obiya, *San Diego City College*
Larry Olanrewaju, *John Tyler Community College*
Andre Luis Oliveira, *Utah Valley University*
Samuel Olowu, *Lone Star College*
Grace Onodipe, *Georgia Gwinnett College*
Louis A. Palombit, *Macomb Community College*
Marina Rubenkov, *Milwaukee Area Technical College*
Dustin J. Rumbaugh, *Belmont University*
Thomas Sahajdack, *Kent State University*
Mark Scanlan, *Stephen F. Austin State University*
Anne Shugars, *Harford Community College*
Thomas W. Stone, *Penn State Abington*
Eric C. Taylor, *Central Piedmont Community College*
Veronica N. Udeogalanya, *Fashion Institute of Technology*
Philip Vinson, *Georgia Gwinnett College*
Christine Wathen, *Middlesex County College*
Anne Williams, *Gateway Community College*
Karen Yancey, *Community College of Philadelphia*
Joseph Zitka, *Pellissippi State Community College*

REVIEWERS SUPPORTING PREVIOUS EDITIONS:

Alison J. Adderley, *Valencia College*
Richard Agesa, *Marshall University*
Carlos Aguilar, *El Paso Community College*
Yamin Ahmad, *University of Wisconsin-Whitewater*
Eun Ahn, *University of Hawaii-West Oahu*
Miki Anderson, *Pikes Peak Community College*
Giuliana Andreopoulos, *William Paterson University*
Thomas Andrews, *West Chester University of Pennsylvania*
Fatma Antar, *Manchester Community College*
Len Anyanwu, *Union County College*
Kathleen Arano, *Indiana University Southeast*
Emmanuel Asigbee, *Kirkwood Community College*
John Atkins, *Pensacola State College*
Moses Ayiku, *Essex County College*
Barbara Baer, *Palomar College*
Wendy Bailey, *Troy University*
Dean Baim, *Pepperdine University*
Herman Baine, *Broward College*
Kuntal Banerjee, *Florida Atlantic University*
Tyra Barrett, *Pellissippi State Community College*
David Barrus, *Brigham Young University-Idaho*
Leon Battista, *CUNY Bronx Community College*
Jill M. Beccaris-Pescatore, *Montgomery County Community College*
Kevin Beckwith, *Salem State University*
Christian Beer, *Cape Fear Community College*
Robert Belsterling, *Pennsylvania State University-Altoona*
Lee A. Bertman, *Indian River State College*
Laura Jean Bhadra, *Northern Virginia Community College-Manassas*
Roberta Biby, *Grand Valley State University*
David Black, *University of Toledo*
Melissa Blankenship, *North Central Texas College*
Priscilla Block, *Broward College*
Stephanie Lyn Blowe, *Lone Star College*
Augustine Boakye, *Essex County College*
Andrea Borchard, *Hillsborough Community College*
Greg Burge, *University of Oklahoma*
Mark L. Burkey, *North Carolina A&T State University*
William Byrd, *Troy University*
Stephanie Campbell, *Mineral Area College*
Bruce Carpenter, *Mansfield University*
Tom Cate, *Northern Kentucky University*
Semih Emre Çekin, *Texas Tech University*
Suparna Chakraborty, *University of San Francisco*
Claude Chang, *Johnson & Wales University*
Amy Chataginer, *Mississippi Gulf Coast Community College-Gautier*
Shuo Chen, *State University of New York-Geneseo*
Jon Chesbro, *Montana Tech of the University of Montana*
Amod Choudhary, *Lehman College*
Constantinos Christofides, *East Stroudsburg University*
Kathy Clark, *Edison College-Fort Myers*
Wes Clark, *Midlands Technical College*
Jane Clary, *College of Charleston*
Jane Cline, *Forsyth Technical Community College*
Joab Corey, *University of California-Riverside*
Ana Carolina Corrales, *Miami Dade College-Wolfson Campus*

Norman Cure, *Macomb Community College*

Patricia Daigle, *Mount Wachusett Community College*

Sonia Dalmia, *Grand Valley State University*

Anthony Daniele, *St. Petersburg College-Gibbs*

Rosa Lee Danielson, *College of DuPage*

Ribhi Daoud, *Sinclair Community College*

Maria S. Davis, *Indian River State College*

William L. Davis, *University of Tennessee-Martin*

Irani DeAraujo, *Pace University*

Richard Dixon, *Thomas Nelson Community College*

Tanya Downing, *Cuesta College*

Carter Doyle, *University of Virginia*

Scott Dressler, *Villanova University*

Brad Duerson, *Des Moines Area Community College*

Sheryl Dusek, *Nashville State Community College*

Lynne Elkes, *Loyola University Maryland*

Mark J. Eschenfelder, *Robert Morris University*

Maxwell Eseonu, *Virginia State University*

Michael Fenick, *Broward College*

Tyrone Ferdnance, *Hampton University*

Tammie Fischer, *University of Nebraska-Lincoln*

Mary Flannery, *University of Notre Dame*

Robert J. Foran, *Miami Dade College-Wolfson Campus*

Jeffrey Forrest, *St. Louis Community College-Florissant Valley*

Richard Fowles, *University of Utah, Salt Lake City*

Mark Frascatore, *Clarkson University*

Shelby Frost, *Georgia State University*

Connel Fullenkamp, *Duke University*

Sudip Ghosh, *Penn State University-Berks*

Alex Gialanella, *Fordham University*

Daniel Giedeman, *Grand Valley State University*

Scott Gilbert, *Southern Illinois University*

James Giordano, *Villanova University*

Susan Glanz, *St. John's University*

Lowell Glenn, *Utah Valley University*

Randy Glover, *Brevard Community College-Melbourne*

Terri Gonzales, *Delgado Community College*

Michael G. Goode, *Central Piedmont Community College*

Paul Graf, *Indiana University-Bloomington*

Joseph Guider, *Essex County College*

Cole Gustafson, *North Dakota State University-Fargo*

Sheryl Hadley, *Johnson County Community College*

Gabriela Hamilton, *Hillsborough Community College*

Moonsu Han, *North Shore Community College*

Charlie Harrington, *Nova Southeastern University-Main*

Virden Harrison, *Modesto Junior College*

Darcy Hartman, *Ohio State University*

Richard R. Hawkins, *University of West Florida*

Kim Hawtrey, *Hope College*

Glenn Haynes, *Western Illinois University*

Mark Healy, *Harper College*

Dennis Heiner, *College of Southern Idaho*

Michael Heslop, *Northern Virginia Community College-Annandale*

Jesse Hoyt Hill, *Tarrant County College*

Christiana Hilmer, *San Diego State University*

Michael Hilmer, *San Diego State University*

Daniel Hoffman, *University of Nebraska-Lincoln*

Calvin Hoy, *County College of Morris*

Liang Hu, *Wayne State University*

Jim Hubert, *Seattle Central Community College*

Greg W. Hunter, *California State Polytechnic University-Pomona*

Christos Ioannou, *University of Minnesota-Minneapolis*

Faridul Islam, *Utah Valley University*

Mahshid Jalilvand, *University of Wisconsin-Stout*

Ricot Jean, *Valencia Community College-Osceola*

Jonatan Jelen, *City College of New York*

Stephen Kaifa, *County College of Morris*

Brad Kamp, *University of South Florida, Sarasota-Manatee*

Robert Kao, *Park University*

Gus Karam, *Pace University-Pleasantville*

Kevin Kelley, *Northwest Vista College*

Chris Klein, *Middle Tennessee State University*

Barry Kotlove, *Edmonds Community College*

Richard Kramer, *New England College*

Felix Kwan, *Maryville University*

Ted Labay, *Bishop State Community College*

Alex Lancaster, *Tallahassee Community College*

Tina Lance, *Germanna Community College-Fredericksburg*

Sarah Leahy, *Brookdale Community College*

Yu-Feng Lee, *New Mexico State University-Las Cruces*

Jim Lee, *Texas A&M University-Corpus Christi*

Adam Y. C. Lei, *Midwestern State University*

Phillip Letting, *Harrisburg Area Community College*

Hank Lewis, *Lone Star College*

Brian Lynch, *Lake Land College*

Zagros Madjd-Sadjadi, *Winston-Salem State University*

Laura Maghoney, *Solano Community College*

Svitlana Maksymenko, *University of Pittsburgh*

Christine Lucy Malakar, *Lorain County Community College*

Vincent Mangum, *Grambling State University*

Marilyn Markel, *Western Michigan University*

Erika Martinez, *University of South Florida*

Benjamin Matta, *New Mexico State University-Las Cruces*

Pete Mavrokordatos, *Tarrant County College-Northeast Campus*

Frederick May, *Trident Technical College*

Katherine McClain, *University of Georgia*

Michael McIntyre, *Copiah-Lincoln Community College*

Robert McKizzie, *Tarrant County College-Southeast Campus*

Kevin McWoodson, *Moraine Valley Community College*

Jesse D. Melvin, *Rowan University*

Edwin Mensah, *University of North Carolina at Pembroke*

Randy Methenitis, *Richland College*

Victoria Miller, *Piedmont Technical College*

Ida Mirzaie, *The Ohio State University*

David Mitch, *University of Maryland-Baltimore County*

Phillip Mixon, *Troy University*

Ramesh Mohan, *Bryant University*

Daniel Morvey, *Piedmont Technical College*

Tina Mosleh, *Ohlone College*

Shahriar Mostashari, *Campbell University*

Richard Mount, *Monmouth University*

Stefan Mullinax, *College of Lake County*

Ted Muzio, *St. John's University*

Pattabiraman Neelakantan, *East Stroudsburg University of Pennsylvania*

John A. Neri, *University of Maryland*

Cliff Nowell, *Weber State University*

Alex Obiya, *San Diego City College*

Constantin Ogloblin, *Georgia Southern University*

Albert Okunade, *University of Memphis*
Larry Olanrewaju, *John Tyler Community College*
Andre Luis Oliveira, *Utah Valley University*
Samuel Olowu, *Lone Star College*
Grace Onodipe, *Georgia Gwinnett College*
Mary Ellen Overbay, *Seton Hall University*
Louis A. Palombit, *Macomb Community College*
Tammy Parker, *University of Louisiana at Monroe*
Alberto Alexander Perez, *Harford Community College*
David Petersen, *American River College*
Mary Anne Pettit, *Southern Illinois University-Edwardsville*
Jeff Phillips, *Morrisville State College*
William Piper, *Piedmont College*
Robert Poulton, *Graceland University*
Dezzie Prewitt, *Rio Hondo College*
Joe Prinzinger, *Lynchburg College*
Jaishankar Raman, *Valparaiso University*
Gregory Randolph, *Southern New Hampshire University*
Natalie Reaves, *Rowan University*
Virginia Reilly, *Ocean County College*
Tim Reynolds, *Alvin Community College*
Jose Rafael Rodriguez-Solis, *Nova Community College-Annandale*
John Romps, *Saint Anselm College*
Marina Rubenkov, *Milwaukee Area Technical College*
Melissa Rueterbusch, *Mott Community College*
Dustin J. Rumbaugh, *Belmont University*
Thomas Sahajdack, *Kent State University*
Mark Scanlan, *Stephen F. Austin State University*
Tom Scheiding, *Elizabethtown College*
Amy Schmidt, *Saint Anselm College*
Ron Schuelke, *Santa Rosa Junior College*
Richard Alan Seals, Jr., *Auburn University*
James K. Self, *Indiana University-Bloomington Campus*
Sangheon Shin, *Alabama State University*
Alexandra Shiu, *McLennan Community College*
Anne Shugars, *Harford Community College*
Dorothy Siden, *Salem State University*

Robert Simonson, *Minnesota State University-Mankato*
Timothy Simpson, *Central New Mexico Community College*
Jonathan Sleeper, *Indian River State College*
Jose Rodriguez Solis, *Northern Virginia Community College*
Camille Soltau-Nelson, *Oregon State University*
Robert Sonora, *Fort Lewis College*
Maritza Sotomayor, *Utah Valley University-Orem*
Nick Spangenberg, *Ozarks Technical Community College*
Dennis Spector, *Naugatuck Valley Community College*
Thomas Stevens, *University of Massachusetts-Amherst*
Tamika Steward, *Tarrant County College-Southeast*
Thomas W. Stone, *Penn State Abington*
Robin Sturik, *Cuyahoga Community College Western-Parma*
Regina Tawah, *Bowie State University*
Eric C. Taylor, *Central Piedmont Community College*
Travis Taylor, *Christopher Newport University*
Ross Thomas, *Central New Mexico Community College*
Mark Thompson, *Augusta State University*
Owen Thompson, *University of Wisconsin-Milwaukee*
Deborah Thorsen, *Palm Beach State College*
Michael Toma, *Armstrong Atlantic State University*
Dosse Toulaboe, *Fort Hays State University*
Veronica N. Udeogalanya, *Fashion Institute of Technology*
Adriana Vamosiu, *University of San Diego*
Jeff Vance, *Sinclair Community College*
Philip Vinson, *Georgia Gwinnett College*
Cheryl Wachenheim, *North Dakota State University-Fargo*
Brandon Walcutt, *Mohawk Valley Community College*
Christine Wathen, *Middlesex County College*
Anne Williams, *Gateway Community College*
Scott Williams, *Winston-Salem State University*
Wendy Wysocki, *Monroe County Community College*
Karen Yancey, *Community College of Philadelphia*
Edward Zajicek, *Winston-Salem State University*
Sourushe Zandvakili, *University of Cincinnati*
Joseph Zitka, *Pellissippi State Community College*

Instructors
Student Success Starts with You

Tools to enhance your unique voice

Want to build your own course? No problem. Prefer to use an OLC-aligned, prebuilt course? Easy. Want to make changes throughout the semester? Sure. And you'll save time with Connect's auto-grading, too.

65%
Less Time Grading

Laptop: Getty Images; Woman/dog: George Doyle/Getty Images

A unique path for each student

In Connect, instructors can assign an adaptive reading experience with SmartBook® 2.0. Rooted in advanced learning science principles, SmartBook 2.0 delivers each student a personalized experience, focusing students on their learning gaps, ensuring that the time they spend studying is time well-spent.
mheducation.com/highered/connect/smartbook

Affordable solutions, added value

Make technology work for you with LMS integration for single sign-on access, mobile access to the digital textbook, and reports to quickly show you how each of your students is doing. And with our Inclusive Access program, you can provide all these tools at the lowest available market price to your students. Ask your McGraw Hill representative for more information.

Solutions for your challenges

A product isn't a solution. Real solutions are affordable, reliable, and come with training and ongoing support when you need it and how you want it. Visit **supportateverystep.com** for videos and resources both you and your students can use throughout the term.

Students
Get Learning that Fits You

Effective tools for efficient studying

Connect is designed to help you be more productive with simple, flexible, intuitive tools that maximize your study time and meet your individual learning needs. Get learning that works for you with Connect.

Study anytime, anywhere

Download the free ReadAnywhere® app and access your online eBook, SmartBook® 2.0, or Adaptive Learning Assignments when it's convenient, even if you're offline. And since the app automatically syncs with your Connect account, all of your work is available every time you open it. Find out more at **mheducation.com/readanywhere**

"I really liked this app—it made it easy to study when you don't have your text-book in front of you."

- Jordan Cunningham, Eastern Washington University

iPhone: Getty Images

Everything you need in one place

Your Connect course has everything you need—whether reading your digital eBook or completing assignments for class, Connect makes it easy to get your work done.

Learning for everyone

McGraw Hill works directly with Accessibility Services Departments and faculty to meet the learning needs of all students. Please contact your Accessibility Services Office and ask them to email accessibility@mheducation.com, or visit **mheducation.com/about/accessibility** for more information.

BRIEF CONTENTS

Blue: Core Chapter
Black: Topics Chapter

Roschetzky Photography/Shutterstock

Limits, Alternatives, and Choices

>> **LEARNING OBJECTIVES**

LO1.1 Define economics and explain the economic perspective.

LO1.2 Describe the role of economic theory in economics.

LO1.3 Distinguish microeconomics from macroeconomics and positive economics from normative economics.

LO1.4 Explain the individual's economizing problem and illustrate trade-offs, opportunity costs, and attainable combinations with budget lines.

LO1.5 List the categories of scarce resources and explain society's economizing problem.

LO1.6 Apply production possibilities analysis.

LO1.7 Explain how economic growth and international trade increase consumption possibilities.

LO1.8 (Appendix) Understand graphs, curves, and slopes as they relate to economics.

People's wants are numerous and varied. Biologically, people need only air, water, food, clothing, and shelter. But in modern societies, people also desire goods and services that provide a more comfortable or affluent standard of living. We want bottled water, soft drinks, and fruit juices, not just water from the creek. We want salads, burgers, and pizzas, not just berries and nuts. We also want flat-panel TVs, Internet service, education, national defense, smartphones, health care, and much more.

Fortunately, society possesses productive resources, such as labor and managerial talent, tools and machinery, and land and mineral deposits. These resources, employed in the economic system (or simply the economy), help us produce goods and services that satisfy many of our economic wants. But in reality, our economic wants far exceed the productive capacity of our scarce (limited) resources. We are forced to make choices. This unyielding truth underlies the definition of **economics** as the social science concerned with how individuals, institutions, and society make optimal (best) choices under conditions of scarcity.

economics The social science concerned with how individuals, institutions, and society make optimal (best) choices under conditions of scarcity.

1

The Economic Perspective

>> **LO1.1** Define economics and explain the economic perspective.

economic perspective A viewpoint that envisions individuals and institutions making rational decisions by comparing the *marginal benefits* and *marginal costs* associated with their actions.

scarcity The limits placed on the amounts and types of *goods* and *services* available for consumption as the result of there being only limited *economic resources* from which to produce output; the fundamental economic constraint that creates *opportunity costs* and that necessitates the use of *marginal analysis* (*cost-benefit analysis*) to make optimal choices.

opportunity cost The amount of other products that must be forgone or sacrificed to produce a unit of a given product.

utility The want-satisfying power of a *good* or *service*; the satisfaction or pleasure a consumer obtains from the consumption of a good or service (or from the consumption of a collection of *goods* and *services*).

Economists view things from a unique perspective. This **economic perspective** has several critical and closely interrelated features.

Scarcity and Choice

The economic resources needed to make goods and services are in limited supply. This **scarcity** restricts options and demands choices. Because we "can't have it all," we must decide what we will have and what we must forgo.

At the core of economics is the idea that "there is no free lunch." You may be treated to lunch, making it "free" from your perspective, but someone must bear the cost. The scarce inputs involved in creating the lunch include land, equipment, and farm labor. Because society could have used these resources to produce other things, it sacrifices those other goods and services in making the lunch available. Economists call such sacrifices **opportunity costs:** To obtain more of one thing, society sacrifices the opportunity of getting the next best thing that could have been created with those resources.

The nearby Consider This story about Facebook discusses yet another example of a "free" product that is anything but.

Purposeful Behavior

Economics assumes that human behavior reflects "rational self-interest." Individuals and institutions look for and pursue opportunities to increase their **utility**—the pleasure, happiness, or satisfaction obtained from consuming goods and services. They allocate their time, energy, and money to maximize their satisfaction. Because they weigh costs and benefits, their economic decisions are purposeful or rational, not random or chaotic.

"Purposeful behavior" does not assume that people and institutions are immune from faulty logic and therefore are perfect decision makers. They sometimes make mistakes. Nor does it mean that people's decisions are unaffected by emotion or the decisions of those around them. Indeed, economists acknowledge that people are sometimes impulsive or irrational. "Purposeful behavior" simply means that people make decisions with some desired outcome in mind.

Please note that rational self-interest is not the same as selfishness. To begin with, increasing one's own wage, rent, interest, or profit normally requires identifying and satisfying somebody else's wants! In addition, self-interested people routinely make personal sacrifices for others. They, for example, contribute time and money to charities because they derive pleasure from doing so. And parents help pay for their children's education for the same reason. These self-interested, but unselfish, acts help maximize the givers' satisfaction as much as any personal purchase of goods or services.

Marginal Analysis: Comparing Benefits and Costs

The economic perspective focuses largely on **marginal analysis**—comparisons of marginal benefits and marginal costs, usually for decision making. To economists, "marginal" means "extra," "additional," or "a change in." Most choices or decisions involve changes in the existing state of affairs.

CONSIDER THIS . . .

Is Facebook Free?

Facebook spends over $50 billion every year updating its platform, running server farms, and paying its employees. It also gives away its product for free to more than 3 billion users. Has Facebook figured out a way to overcome scarcity?

No, it hasn't. Scarcity is permanent. But Facebook *has* figured out a way to more than cover its costs without charging its users a penny. Facebook's trick is to charge advertisers instead. They pay Facebook over

rvlsoft/Shutterstock

$100 billion per year to boost content and target ads to specific individuals.

Lesson One: If you are consuming a good or service and not paying for it, the cost is being borne by someone else.

Lesson Two: Companies don't usually give freebies to be nice; they do it as part of their business model. Facebook grants users free access to its platform to make sure that it has as many "eyeballs" as possible to sell to advertisers.

Should you attend school for another year? Should you study an extra hour for an exam? Should a business expand or reduce its output? Should government increase or decrease its funding for a missile defense system?

Each option involves marginal benefits and marginal costs. In making choices rationally, the decision maker must compare those two amounts. Example: You and your significant other are shopping for an engagement ring. Should you buy a $\frac{1}{2}$-carat diamond or a 1-carat diamond? The marginal cost of the larger diamond is the added expense beyond the cost of the smaller diamond. The marginal benefit is the perceived lifetime pleasure (utility) from the larger stone. If the marginal benefit of the larger diamond exceeds its marginal cost (and you can afford it), buy the larger stone. But if the marginal cost is more than the marginal benefit, you should buy the smaller diamond instead—even if you can afford the larger stone!

In a world of scarcity, the decision to obtain the marginal benefit associated with some specific option always includes the marginal cost of giving up something else. The money spent on the larger diamond means forgoing some other product. An opportunity cost—the value of the next best thing given up—is always present whenever a choice is made.

> **marginal analysis** The comparison of *marginal* ("extra" or "additional") *benefits* and *marginal costs,* usually for decision making.

Theories, Principles, and Models

Like the other sciences, economics relies on the **scientific method** to transform specific observations of real-world activity into general explanations of how the world works. That procedure consists of several elements:

> **>> LO1.2** Describe the role of economic theory in economics.

- Observing real-world behavior and outcomes.

- Based on those observations, formulating a possible explanation (hypothesis) of cause and effect.

- Testing this explanation by comparing the outcomes of specific events to the outcome predicted by the hypothesis.

- Accepting, rejecting, and modifying the hypothesis, based on these comparisons.

- Continuing to test the hypothesis against the facts. If favorable results accumulate, the hypothesis evolves into a theory. A very well-tested and widely accepted theory is called an economic law or an **economic principle**—a statement about economic behavior or the economy that enables prediction of the probable effects of certain actions. Combinations of such laws or principles are incorporated into models, which are simplified representations of how something works, such as a market or segment of the economy.

> **scientific method** The procedure for the systematic pursuit of knowledge involving the observation of facts and the formulation and testing of hypotheses to obtain theories, principles, and laws.

> **economic principle** A widely accepted generalization about the economic behavior of individuals or institutions.

Theories, principles, and models are "purposeful simplifications." The full scope of economic reality itself is too complex to be fully understood. In developing theories, principles, and models, economists remove the clutter and simplify. Despite their simplifications, good theories do a good job of explaining and predicting how individuals and institutions actually behave in producing, exchanging, and consuming goods and services.

There are some other things you should know about economic principles.

- *Generalizations* Economic principles are generalizations. Economic principles are expressed as the tendencies of typical or average consumers, workers, or business firms. For example, economists say that consumers buy more of a particular product when its price falls. Economists recognize that some consumers may increase their purchases by a large amount, others by a small amount, and a few not at all. This "price-quantity" principle, however, holds for the typical consumer and for consumers as a group.

- *Other-things-equal assumption* In constructing theories, economists use the *ceteris paribus* or **other-things-equal assumption**—the assumption that factors other than those being considered do not change. They assume that all variables except those under immediate consideration are held constant for a particular analysis. For example, when considering the relationship between the price of Pepsi and the amount of Pepsi purchased, economists ignore all of the other factors that might influence the amount of Pepsi purchased (for example, the price of Coca-Cola and consumer incomes and preferences). Holding all of those other things equal is helpful because the economist can then focus on the relationship between the price of Pepsi and purchases of Pepsi without being confused by changes in other variables.

> **other-things-equal assumption** The assumption that factors other than those being considered are held constant. Also known as the *ceteris paribus* assumption.

- *Graphical expression* Many economic models are expressed graphically. Be sure to read the appendix at the end of this chapter as a review of graphs.

Microeconomics and Macroeconomics

Economists develop economic principles and models at two levels.

>> **LO1.3** Distinguish microeconomics from macroeconomics and positive economics from normative economics.

Microeconomics

Microeconomics is concerned with decision making by individual customers, workers, households, and business firms. At this level of analysis, we observe the details of their behavior under a figurative microscope. We measure the price of a specific product, the revenue or income of a particular firm or household, or the expenditures of a specific firm, government entity, or family.

Macroeconomics

Macroeconomics examines the performance and behavior of the economy as a whole. It focuses on economic growth, the business cycle, interest rates, inflation, and the behavior of major economic aggregates such as the government, household, and business sectors. An **aggregate** is a collection of specific economic units treated as if they were one unit. Therefore, we might lump together the millions of consumers in the U.S. economy and treat them as one huge unit called "consumers."

In using aggregates, macroeconomics seeks to obtain an overview of the economy and the relationships of its major aggregates. Macroeconomics speaks of such economic measures as total output, total employment, total income, aggregate expenditures, and the general level of prices. Very little attention is given to the specific units making up the various aggregates.

The micro–macro distinction does not mean that economics is so highly compartmentalized that every topic can be readily labeled as either micro or macro; many topics and subdivisions of economics are rooted in both. Example: While unemployment is usually treated as a macroeconomic topic (because unemployment relates to aggregate production), economists recognize that the decisions made by *individual* workers and the way *specific* labor markets encourage or impede hiring are also critical in determining the unemployment rate.

Positive and Normative Economics

Positive economics focuses on facts and cause-and-effect relationships. It avoids value judgments and tries to establish scientific statements about economic behavior. Such scientific analysis is critical to good policy analysis.

In contrast, **normative economics** incorporates value judgments about what the economy should be like or what policy actions should be recommended. Normative economics underlies expressions of support for, or opposition to, particular economic policies.

Positive economics concerns *what is,* whereas normative economics embodies subjective feelings about *what ought to be.* Examples: Positive statement: "The unemployment rate in France is higher than that in the United States." Normative statement: "France ought to undertake policies to make its labor market more flexible to reduce unemployment rates." Whenever words such as "ought" or "should" appear in a sentence, you are likely encountering a normative statement. Most of the disagreement among economists involves normative, value-based policy questions.

microeconomics The part of economics concerned with (1) decision making by individual units such as a *household*, a *firm*, or an *industry* and (2) individual markets, specific *goods* and *services*, and product and resource *prices*.

macroeconomics The part of *economics* concerned with the performance and behavior of the economy as a whole. Focuses on *economic growth*, the *business cycle, interest rates, inflation*, and the behavior of major economic *aggregates* such as the household, business, and government sectors.

aggregate A collection of specific economic units treated as if they were one unit.

positive economics The analysis of facts or data to establish scientific generalizations about economic behavior.

normative economics The part of economics involving value judgments about what the economy should be like; focused on which economic goals and policies should be implemented; policy economics.

**QUICK REVIEW
1.1**

▶ Economics examines how individuals, institutions, and society make choices under conditions of scarcity.

▶ The economic perspective stresses (a) resource scarcity and the necessity of making choices, (b) the assumption of purposeful (or rational) behavior, and (c) comparisons of marginal benefit and marginal cost.

▶ In choosing the best option, people incur an opportunity cost—the value of the next-best option.

▶ Economists use the scientific method to establish economic theories—cause-effect generalizations about the economic behavior of individuals and institutions.

▶ Microeconomics focuses on specific decision-making units within the economy. Macroeconomics examines the economy as a whole.

▶ Positive economics deals with factual statements ("what is"); normative economics involves value judgments ("what ought to be").

Individual's Economizing Problem

A close examination of the **economizing problem**—the need to make choices because economic wants exceed economic means—will enhance your understanding of economic models and the difference between microeconomics and macroeconomics.

To that end, let's first build a microeconomic model of the economizing problem faced by an individual. We will then, later in this chapter, build a macroeconomic model of the economizing problem faced by an entire nation or society.

Limited Income

We all have a finite amount of income, even the wealthiest among us. Even Jeff Bezos must decide how to spend his money! Our income comes in the form of wages, interest, rent, and profit, although we may also receive money from government programs or family members. As Global Perspective 1.1 shows, the average income of Americans in 2020 was $65,280 after adjusting for international differences in the cost of living. In the poorest nations, it was less than $500.

Unlimited Wants

Most people have virtually unlimited wants. Our wants extend over a wide range of products, from *necessities* (food, shelter, clothing) to *luxuries* (perfumes, yachts, sports cars).

Over time, as new and improved products are introduced, economic wants tend to change and multiply. Only recently have people wanted wi-fi connections, tablet computers, and flying drones—products that did not exist a generation ago. Also, the satisfaction of certain wants may trigger others: The acquisition of a Chevy Spark or a Nissan Versa has been known to whet the appetite for a Lexus or a Mercedes.

Like goods, services also satisfy our wants. Car repair work, legal and accounting advice, and haircuts all satisfy human wants. Actually, we buy many goods, such as automobiles and washing machines, for the services they render.

Most people's desires for goods and services cannot be fully satisfied, though our desires for a particular good or service can be satisfied; over a short period of time, we can surely get enough toothpaste or pasta. But our broader desire for more goods and services and higher-quality goods and services seems to be another story.

Because we have only limited income (usually through our work) but seemingly insatiable wants, it is in our self-interest to economize: to pick and choose goods and services that maximize our satisfaction given the limitations we face.

>> **LO1.4** Explain the individual's economizing problem and illustrate trade-offs, opportunity costs, and attainable combinations with budget lines.

economizing problem The choices necessitated because society's economic wants for *goods* and *services* are unlimited but the resources available to satisfy these wants are limited (scarce).

🌐 GLOBAL PERSPECTIVE 1.1

AVERAGE INCOME PER PERSON, SELECTED NATIONS

Average income per capita, and therefore typical individual budget constraints, vary greatly from one country to another, even after adjusting for international differences in the cost of living.

Country	Country Per Capita Income, 2020 (PPP-adjusted international dollars)
Switzerland	$70,277
Norway	67,979
United States	65,280
Germany	55,891
Canada	50,511
Japan	42,338
Poland	34,131
Mexico	20,447
China	16,847
Guatemala	8,983
India	6,994
Burundi	783
Zimbabwe	411

Source: The World Bank, data.worldbank.org. Cost of living adjustments are based on purchasing power parity (PPP).

A Budget Line

budget line A line that shows the different combinations of two products a consumer can purchase with a specific money income, given the products' prices.

We can clarify the economizing problem facing consumers by visualizing a **budget line** or *budget constraint,* which is a schedule or curve that shows various combinations of two products a consumer can purchase with a specific income. Although we assume two products, the analysis generalizes to the full range of products available to consumers.

To understand what a budget line shows, suppose that you receive an Amazon gift card as a birthday present. The $120 card will soon expire. You go to Amazon.com and confine your purchase decisions to two alternatives: t-shirts and paperback books. T-shirts are $20 each and paperback books are $10 each. The table in Figure 1.1 shows your purchase options.

At one extreme, you might spend all of your $120 "income" on 6 t-shirts at $20 each and have nothing left to spend on books. Or, by giving up 2 t-shirts and thereby gaining $40, you can buy 4 t-shirts at $20 each and 4 books at $10 each. At the other extreme, you could buy 12 books at $10 each, spending your entire gift card on books with nothing left to spend on t-shirts.

The graph in Figure 1.1 shows the budget line. Every point on the graph represents a possible combination of t-shirts and books, including fractional quantities. The slope of the graphed budget line measures the ratio of the price of books (P_b) to the price of t-shirts (P_t); more precisely, the slope is $P_b/P_t = \$-10/\$+20 = -\frac{1}{2}$. So you must forgo 1 t-shirt (measured on the vertical axis) to buy 2 books (measured on the horizontal axis). This yields a slope of $-\frac{1}{2}$ or $-.5$.

The budget line illustrates several ideas.

Attainable and Unattainable Combinations All the combinations of t-shirts and books on or inside the budget line are *attainable* with $120 of income. You can afford to buy, for example, 3 t-shirts at $20 each and 6 books at $10 each. You also can afford to buy 2 t-shirts and 5 books, thereby using up only $90 of the $120 available on your gift card. But to achieve maximum utility, you will want to spend the full $120. The budget line shows all of the combinations that cost exactly the full $120.

In contrast, all combinations beyond the budget line are *unattainable.* The $120 limit simply does not allow you to purchase, for example, 5 t-shirts at $20 each and 5 books at $10 each. That $150 expenditure would clearly exceed the $120 limit.

Trade-Offs and Opportunity Costs The budget line in Figure 1.1 illustrates the idea of trade-offs arising from limited income. To obtain more t-shirts, you have to give up some books. For example, to obtain the first t-shirt, you trade off 2 books. So the opportunity cost of the first t-shirt is 2 books. To obtain the second t-shirt, the opportunity cost is also 2 books. The straight-line budget constraint, with its constant slope, indicates constant opportunity cost. That is, the opportunity cost of 1 extra t-shirt remains the same (= 2 books) as you purchase more t-shirts. Likewise, the opportunity cost of 1 extra book does not change ($= \frac{1}{2}$ t-shirt) as you purchase more books.

FIGURE 1.1 A consumer's budget line.

A consumer's budget line (or budget constraint) shows all the combinations of any two products that can be purchased, given the prices of the products and the consumer's income.

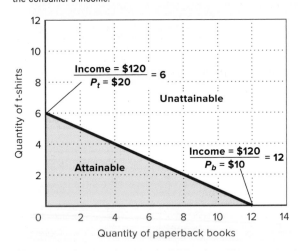

Units of T-shirts (Price = $20)	Units of Books (Price = $10)	Total Expenditure
6	0	$120 (= $120 + $0)
5	2	$120 (= $100 + $20)
4	4	$120 (= $80 + $40)
3	6	$120 (= $60 + $60)
2	8	$120 (= $40 + $80)
1	10	$120 (= $20 + $100)
0	12	$120 (= $0 + $120)

The Budget Line: Whole-Unit Combinations of T-shirts and Paperback Books Attainable with an Income of $120

CONSIDER THIS . . .

Did Zuckerberg, Durant, and Grande Make Bad Choices?

Opportunity costs come into play in decisions well beyond simple buying decisions. Consider the different choices people make with respect to college. The average salaries earned by college graduates are nearly twice as high as those earned by persons with just high school diplomas. For most capable students, "Go to college, stay in college, and earn a degree" is very sound advice.

Yet Facebook founder Mark Zuckerberg and basketball superstar Kevin Durant both dropped out of college, while pop singer Ariana Grande never even bothered to start classes. What were they thinking?

Unlike most students, Zuckerberg faced enormous opportunity costs for staying in college. He had a vision for

Swen Pförtner/dpa/Alamy Stock Photo

his company, and dropping out helped to ensure Facebook's success.

Durant was the college basketball player of the year as a freshman. So it was a natural for him to head to the NBA the next year and begin earning millions of dollars rather than stay in school for zero pay.

Grande knew that staying on top in the world of pop takes unceasing work. So after her first album became a massive hit, it made sense for her to skip college in order to relentlessly pursue continuing success.

Zuckerberg, Durant, and Grande understood opportunity costs and made their choices accordingly. They knew that size matters when it comes to opportunity costs and individual decisions.

Choice Limited income forces people to choose what to buy and what to forgo. You will select the combination of t-shirts and paperback books that you think is "best." That is, you will evaluate your marginal benefits and marginal costs (here, product price) to make choices that maximize your satisfaction. Other people, with the same $120 gift card, would undoubtedly make different choices.

Income Changes The budget line varies with income. An increase in income shifts the budget line to the right; a decrease in income shifts it to the left. To verify this, recalculate the table in Figure 1.1, assuming the card value (income) is (a) $240 and (b) $60, and plot the new budget lines in the graph. No wonder people like to have more income: It shifts their budget lines outward and enables them to buy more goods and services. But even with more income, people still face spending trade-offs, choices, and opportunity costs.

QUICK REVIEW

1.2

▶ Because wants exceed incomes, individuals face an economizing problem; they must decide what to buy and what to forgo.

▶ A budget line (budget constraint) shows the various combinations of two goods that a consumer can purchase with a specific income.

▶ Straight-line budget constraints imply constant opportunity costs for both goods.

Society's Economizing Problem

Society also faces an economizing problem. Should it devote more of its limited resources to the criminal justice system (police, courts, and prisons) or to education (teachers, books, and schools)? If it decides to devote more resources to both, what other goods and services does it forgo?

Scarce Resources

Society has limited or scarce **economic resources,** meaning all natural, human, and manufactured resources that go into the production of goods and services.

Resource Categories

Economists classify economic resources into four general categories.

>> **LO1.5** List the categories of scarce resources and explain society's economizing problem.

economic resources The *land, labor, capital,* and *entrepreneurial ability* that are used to produce *goods* and *services.* Also known as the *factors of production.*

land In addition to the part of the earth's surface not covered by water, this term refers to any and all natural resources ("free gifts of nature") that are used to produce *goods* and *services.* Thus, it includes the oceans, sunshine, coal deposits, forests, the electromagnetic spectrum, and *fisheries.* Note that land is one of the four *economic resources.*

labor Any mental or physical exertion on the part of a human being that is used in the production of a *good* or *service.* One of the four *economic resources.*

capital Man-made physical objects (factories, roads) and intangible ideas (the recipe for cement) that do not directly satisfy human wants but which help to produce *goods* and *services* that do satisfy human wants. One of the four *economic resources.*

consumer goods Products and *services* that satisfy human wants directly.

investment Expenditures that increase the volume of physical *capital* (roads, factories, wireless networks) and intangible ideas (formulas, processes, algorithms) that help to produce goods and services. Also known as *economic investment.* Not to be confused with *financial investment.*

entrepreneurial ability The human resource that combines the other *economic resources* of *land, labor,* and *capital* to produce new products or make innovations in the production of existing products; provided by *entrepreneurs.*

>> **LO1.6** Apply production possibilities analysis.

Land **Land** includes all natural resources used in the production process. These include forests, mineral and oil deposits, water resources, wind power, sunlight, and arable land.

Labor The **labor** resource consists of the physical actions and mental activities that people contribute to the production of goods and services. The work-related activities of a retail clerk, teacher, professional football player, and nuclear physicist all fall under the general heading "labor."

Capital For economists, **capital** includes all human-produced physical objects and intangible ideas used to produce consumer goods and services.

- The physical objects, or *capital goods*, include all factory, storage, transportation, and distribution facilities, as well as tools and machinery, electrical grids, and communication satellites.
- The intangible ideas, or intellectual property, include inventions, recipes, designs, blueprints, instructions, and software.

Note that while **consumer goods** satisfy wants directly, *capital* does so indirectly by aiding in the production of consumer goods. For example, a large commercial baking oven (a capital good) combined with a particular recipe (an intangible idea) helps make loaves of bread (a consumer good).

Also understand that the term "capital" as used by economists does *not* refer to money. Because money produces nothing, economists do not consider it an economic resource.

Finally, please also note that while the words *capital* and *investment* are related, economists have a very restrictive definition of the word **investment.** When an economist uses the word investment, she is referring to spending that pays for the production of *new* physical or intangible capital. Thus Bill Gates spending a billion dollars to invent a cure for malaria is investment (since it pays for the creation of a *new* vaccine recipe) but his purchasing an old factory is not (because that capital good already existed and thus no new capital is created as a result of his purchase).

Entrepreneurial Ability Finally, there is the very special human resource, distinct from labor, that is known as entrepreneurial ability. **Entrepreneurial ability** combines the other economic resources of land, labor, and capital to produce new products or make *innovations* in the production of existing products.

Entrepreneurial ability is supplied by **entrepreneurs,** who perform several important economic functions that are not performed by ordinary labor, which engages in routine functions and does not innovate.

The unique contributions of entrepreneurs include:

- Taking the initiative in combining resources to produce a good or a service—entrepreneurs are the creative force behind production.
- Making the strategic business decisions that set the course of an enterprise.
- Innovating by commercializing new products, new production techniques, and new forms of business organization.
- Bearing risk. Because innovation is risky, progress would cease without entrepreneurs willing to bear risk by devoting their time, effort, and ability—as well as their own money and the money of others—to commercializing new products and ideas.

In closing, note that because land, labor, capital, and entrepreneurial ability are combined to produce goods and services, they are called the **factors of production,** or simply "inputs."

Production Possibilities Model

Society uses its scarce resources to produce goods and services. The alternatives it faces can best be understood through a macroeconomic model of production possibilities. To keep things simple, let's initially assume:

- *Full employment* The economy is employing all of its available resources.
- *Fixed resources* The quantity and quality of the factors of production are fixed.
- *Fixed technology* The state of technology (the methods used to produce output) is constant.

TABLE 1.1 Production Possibilities of Pizzas and Industrial Robots

	Production Alternatives				
Type of Product	**A**	**B**	**C**	**D**	**E**
Pizzas (in hundred thousands)	0	1	2	3	4
Robots (in thousands)	10	9	7	4	0

- *Two goods* The economy is producing only two goods: pizzas and industrial robots. Pizzas symbolize **consumer goods,** products that satisfy our wants directly; industrial robots (for example, the kind used to weld automobile frames) symbolize *capital*, physical objects or intangible ideas that satisfy our wants indirectly by making possible more efficient production of consumer goods.

Production Possibilities Table

A production possibilities table lists the different combinations of two products that can be produced with a specific set of resources, assuming full employment. Table 1.1 presents a simple hypothetical economy that is producing pizzas and industrial robots. At alternative A, this economy would be devoting all its resources to the production of industrial robots (capital). At alternative E, all resources would go to pizza production (consumer goods). Those alternatives are unrealistic extremes; an economy typically produces both capital goods and consumer goods, as in B, C, and D. As we move from alternative A to E, we increase the production of pizzas at the expense of the production of industrial robots.

Because consumer goods satisfy our wants directly, any movement toward E looks tempting. In producing more pizzas, society increases the satisfaction of its current wants. But there is a cost: More pizzas mean fewer industrial robots. This shift to consumer goods catches up with society over time because the stock of capital expands more slowly, thereby reducing potential future production. By moving toward alternative E, society chooses "more now" at the expense of "much more later."

In contrast, by moving toward A, society chooses to forgo current consumption, thereby freeing up resources to increase the production of capital. By choosing to build up its stock of capital, society will have greater future production and, therefore, greater future consumption. By moving toward A, society is choosing "more later" at the cost of "less now."

Generalization: At any point in time, a fully employed economy must sacrifice some of one good to obtain more of another good. Scarce resources prohibit a fully employed economy from having more of both goods. Having more of one thing means having less of something else.

Production Possibilities Curve

The data presented in a production possibilities table are shown graphically as a **production possibilities curve.** This curve displays the different combinations of goods and services that society can produce in a fully employed economy, assuming a fixed availability of supplies of resources and fixed technology.

In **Figure 1.2 (Key Graph),** each point on the production possibilities curve represents a maximum output combination of the two products. Consequently, the entire length of the curve can be thought of as a "constraint" because it shows the limit of attainable outputs given current resources and technology.

- Points on the curve are attainable as long as the economy uses all its available resources and technology.

- Points inside the curve are also attainable, but are associated with less than full employment of resources and technology. These inside points reflect less total output than points on the curve and are therefore not as desirable as points on the curve.

- Points lying beyond the production possibilities curve, like *W*, represent a greater output than the output at any point on the curve. Such points, however, are unattainable with current resources and technology.

entrepreneurs Individuals who provide *entrepreneurial ability* to *firms* by setting strategy, advancing innovations, and bearing the financial risk if their firms do poorly.

factors of production The four *economic resources: land, labor, capital*, and *entrepreneurial ability*.

consumer goods Products and services that satisfy human wants directly.

production possibilities curve A curve showing the different combinations of two goods or *services* that can be produced in a *full-employment, full-production* economy where the available supplies of *resources* and technology are fixed.

..∎l KEY GRAPH

FIGURE 1.2 **The production possibilities curve.**

Each point on the production possibilities curve represents some maximum combination of two products that can be produced if resources are fully employed. When an economy is operating on the curve, more industrial robots means fewer pizzas, and vice versa. Limited resources and a fixed technology make any combination of industrial robots and pizzas lying outside the curve (such as at *W*) unattainable. Points inside the curve are attainable, but they indicate that full employment is not being realized.

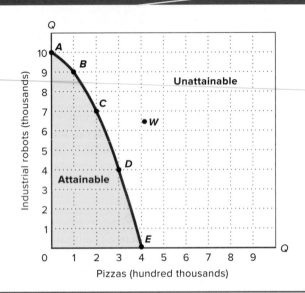

QUICK QUIZ FOR FIGURE 1.2

1. **Production possibilities curve *ABCDE* is bowed out from the origin because:**
   a. the marginal benefit of pizzas declines as more pizzas are consumed.
   b. the curve gets steeper as we move from *E* to *A*.
   c. it reflects the law of increasing opportunity costs.
   d. resources are scarce.

2. **The marginal opportunity cost of the second unit of pizza is:**
   a. 2 units of robots.
   b. 3 units of robots.
   c. 7 units of robots.
   d. 9 units of robots.

3. **The total opportunity cost of 7 units of robots is:**
   a. 1 unit of pizza.
   b. 2 units of pizza.
   c. 3 units of pizza.
   d. 4 units of pizza.

4. **All points on this production possibilities curve necessarily represent:**
   a. society's optimal choice.
   b. less than full use of resources.
   c. unattainable levels of output.
   d. full employment.

Answers: 1. c; 2. a; 3. b; 4. d

Law of Increasing Opportunity Costs

Figure 1.2 clearly shows that more pizzas mean fewer industrial robots. The number of industrial robots that must be given up to obtain another pizza is the opportunity cost of pizza.

In moving from alternative *A* to alternative *B* in Table 1.1, the cost of 1 additional pizza is 1 fewer robot. As we move from *B* to *C*, *C* to *D*, and *D* to *E*, an important economic principle is revealed: For society, the opportunity cost of each additional pizza is greater than the opportunity cost of the preceding pizza. When we move from *A* to *B*, just 1 industrial robot is sacrificed for 1 more pizza; but in going from *B* to *C*, we sacrifice 2 industrial robots for 1 more pizza; then 3 industrial robots for 1 more pizza; and finally 4 for 1. Conversely, confirm that as we move from *E* to *A*, the cost of an additional industrial robot (on average) is $\frac{1}{4}$, $\frac{1}{3}$, $\frac{1}{2}$, and 1 pizzas, respectively, for the four successive moves.

law of increasing opportunity costs The principle that as the production of a good increases, the *opportunity cost* of producing an additional unit rises.

Our example illustrates the **law of increasing opportunity costs.** As we increase the production of a particular good, the opportunity cost of producing an additional unit rises.

Shape of the Curve The law of increasing opportunity costs is reflected in the shape of the production possibilities curve: The curve is bowed out from the origin of the graph. As Figure 1.2 shows, when the economy moves from *A* to *E*, it must give up successively larger amounts of industrial robots (1, 2, 3, and 4) to acquire equal increments of pizzas (1, 1, 1, and 1). Thus the slope of the production possibilities curve becomes steeper as we move from *A* to *E*.

Economic Rationale The economic rationale for the law of increasing opportunity costs is that economic resources are not completely adaptable to alternative uses. Many resources are better at producing one type of good than at producing others. Some land, for example, is highly suited to growing the ingredients necessary for pizza production, but as pizza production expands, society has to start using land that is less bountiful for farming. Other land, by contrast, is rich in mineral deposits and therefore well-suited to producing the materials needed to make industrial robots. As society steps up the production of robots, it must use land that is less and less adaptable to making their components.

If we start at *A* and move to *B* in Figure 1.2, we can shift resources whose productivity is relatively high in pizza production and low in industrial robots. But as we move from *B* to *C*, *C* to *D*, and so on, resources highly productive of pizzas become increasingly scarce. To get more pizzas, resources whose productivity in industrial robots is relatively great will be needed. Increasingly more of such resources, and hence greater sacrifices of industrial robots, will be needed to achieve each 1-unit increase in pizzas. This lack of perfect flexibility, or interchangeability, on the part of resources is the cause of increasing opportunity costs for society.

Optimal Allocation

Of all the attainable combinations of pizzas and industrial robots along the production possibilities curve in Figure 1.2, which one is optimal (best)? That is, which quantities of pizzas and industrial robots will maximize satisfaction?

Recall that economic decisions center on comparisons of marginal benefit (MB) and marginal cost (MC): Any economic activity should be expanded as long as marginal benefit exceeds marginal cost; and any economic activity should be reduced as long as marginal cost exceeds marginal benefit. The optimal amount of the activity occurs where MB = MC.

The Optimum Quantity of Pizza Society can use the same logic to decide which output combination to produce among all the output combinations available along the production possibilities curve in Figure 1.2.

Consider pizzas. We know from the law of increasing opportunity costs that the marginal cost of additional pizzas will rise as more pizzas are produced. At the same time, we need to recognize that the extra, or marginal, benefits that come from consuming pizza decline with each additional pizza because as consumers eat more and more pizza, they begin to get fed up with it and, as they do, the value they place on each additional pizza decreases. Consequently, each additional pizza brings both increasing marginal costs and decreasing marginal benefits.

The optimal quantity of pizza production—200,000 pizzas—is indicated in Figure 1.3 by point *e* at the intersection of the MB and MC curves.

Why is 200,000 pizzas the optimal quantity?

- If only 100,000 pizzas were produced, the marginal benefit of an extra pizza (point *a*) would exceed its marginal cost (point *b*). In money terms, MB is $15, while MC is only $5. When society gains something worth $15 at a marginal cost of only $5, it is better off. In Figure 1.3, net gains continue to be realized until pizza production has been increased to 200,000 pizzas.

- In contrast, the production of 300,000 pizzas is excessive. At that quantity, the MC of an added pizza is $15 (point *c*) and its MB is only $5 (point *d*). This is a losing proposition for society, as would be any output level above 200,000 pizzas.

You can see from this analysis that the optimal (utility maximizing) amount of this society's limited resources will be allocated to pizza production when

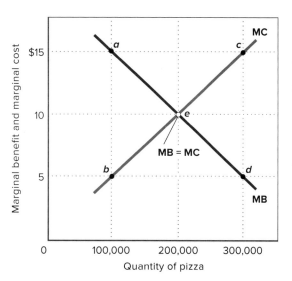

FIGURE 1.3
Optimal output: MB = MC.

Achieving the optimal output requires the expansion of a good's output until its marginal benefit (MB) and marginal cost (MC) are equal. No resources beyond that point should be allocated to the product. Here, optimal output occurs at point *e*, where 200,000 pizzas are produced.

exactly 200,000 pizzas are produced. The remainder of society's resources will then flow toward the production of industrial robots. That would put us at point C on the production possibilities curve in Figure 1.2, with 200,000 pizzas and 7,000 robots being produced simultaneously by fully employing all of this society's limited supplies of land, labor, capital, and entrepreneurial ability.

QUICK REVIEW
1.3

▶ Economists categorize economic resources as land, labor, capital, and entrepreneurial ability.

▶ The production possibilities curve illustrates several ideas: (a) scarcity of resources is implied by the area of unattainable combinations of output lying outside the production possibilities curve; (b) choice among outputs is reflected in the variety of attainable combinations of goods lying along

the curve; (c) opportunity cost is illustrated by the downward slope of the curve; (d) the law of increasing opportunity costs is reflected in the bowed-outward shape of the curve.

▶ A comparison of marginal benefits and marginal costs is needed to determine the best or optimal output mix on a production possibilities curve.

Unemployment, Growth, and the Future

>> **LO1.7** Explain how economic growth and international trade increase consumption possibilities.

In the depths of the Great Depression of the 1930s, one-quarter of U.S. workers were unemployed and one-third of U.S. production capacity was idle. Subsequent downturns have been much less severe. During the brief but sharp COVID-19 recession of 2020, for instance, 1 in 7 workers was without a job while production fell by a comparably small 10 percent.

Almost all nations have experienced widespread unemployment and unused production capacity from business downturns. Since 2020, for example, Brazil, Italy, Russia, Japan, and France have had economic downturns and elevated unemployment. How do these realities relate to the production possibilities model?

Our analysis and conclusions change if we relax the assumption that all available resources are fully employed. The five alternatives in Table 1.1 represent maximum outputs; they illustrate the combinations of pizzas and industrial robots that can be produced when the economy is operating at full employment. With unemployment, this economy would produce less than each alternative shown in the table.

Graphically, we represent situations of unemployment by points inside the original production possibilities curve (reproduced here in Figure 1.4). Point U is one such point. At point U, the economy is falling short of the various maximum combinations of pizzas and industrial robots represented by the points on the production possibilities curve. Movement toward full employment would yield a greater output of one or both products.

A Growing Economy

When we drop the assumption that the quantity and quality of resources and technology are fixed, the production possibilities curve shifts positions, and the economy's potential maximum output changes.

FIGURE 1.4
Unemployment and the production possibilities curve.

Any point inside the production possibilities curve, such as U, represents unemployment or a failure to achieve full employment. The arrows indicate that by realizing full employment, the economy could operate on the curve. This means it could produce more of one or both products than it is producing at point U.

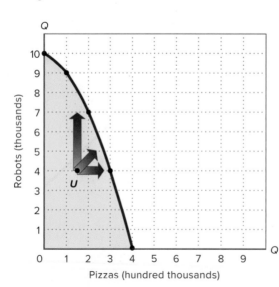

Pizzas (hundred thousands)

Increases in Resource Supplies Although resource supplies are fixed at any specific moment, they change over time. For example, a nation's growing population increases the supplies of labor and entrepreneurial ability. Also, labor quality usually improves over time via more education and training. And although some of our energy and mineral resources are being depleted, new sources are also being discovered. The development of irrigation systems, for example, adds to the supply of arable land.

The net result of these increases in the factors of production is society's ability to produce more consumer goods and more capital goods. The new production possibilities might look like those in the table in

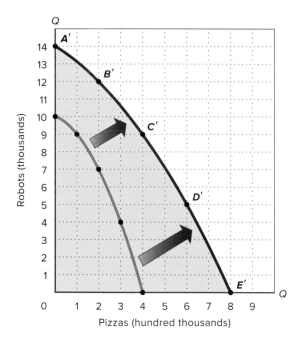

FIGURE 1.5 Economic growth and the production possibilities curve.

The increase in supplies of resources, improvements in resource quality, and technological advances that occur in a dynamic economy move the production possibilities curve outward and to the right, allowing the economy to have larger quantities of both types of goods.

| | **Production Alternatives** | | | | |
Type of Product	A′	B′	C′	D′	E′
Pizzas (in hundred thousands)	0	2	4	6	8
Robots (in thousands)	14	12	9	5	0

Figure 1.5. The greater abundance of resources will result in a greater potential output of one or both products. The economy will have achieved economic growth in the form of expanded potential output. Graphically, the production possibilities curve shifts outward and to the right, as illustrated in Figure 1.5 by the move from the original, inner, curve to curve *A′B′C′D′E′*. This shift represents increased productive capacity, which, if used, will result in **economic growth** and a larger total output.

Advances in Technology Improvements in technology bring both new and better goods and improved ways of producing them. For now, let's focus on one type of technological advance: improvements in the methods of production—for example, the introduction of computerized artificial intelligence (AI) systems to manage inventories and schedule production. These advances allow society to produce more goods with available resources. They make possible the production of more industrial robots *and* more pizzas.

Conclusion: Economic growth is the result of (1) increases in supplies of resources, (2) improvements in resource quality, and (3) technological advances. Whereas static, no-growth economies must sacrifice some of one good to obtain more of another, dynamic, growing economies can produce larger quantities of both goods.

Present Choices and Future Possibilities

An economy's current choice of its position on its production possibilities curve helps determine the curve's future location. Let's designate the two axes of the production possibilities curve as "goods for the future" and "goods for the present," as in Figure 1.6. Goods for the future include capital goods, research, education, and preventive medicine; they are the ingredients of economic growth. Goods for the present are consumer goods such as food, clothing, and entertainment.

Now suppose there are two hypothetical economies, Presentville and Futureville, that are initially identical in every respect except one: Presentville's current choice of positions on its production possibilities curve (point *P* in Figure 1.6a) strongly favors present goods over future goods. Futureville, in contrast, makes a current choice that stresses larger amounts of future goods and smaller amounts of present goods, as shown by point *F* in Figure 1.6b.

Now, other things equal, we can expect Futureville's future production possibilities curve to be farther to the right than Presentville's. By currently choosing an output more favorable to technological advances and to increases in the quantity and quality of resources, Futureville will achieve greater economic growth than Presentville. In terms of capital goods, Futureville is choosing to make larger current additions to its "national factory" by devoting more of its current output to capital than Presentville. The payoff for Futureville is greater future production capacity and economic growth. The opportunity cost is fewer consumer goods in the present.

economic growth (1) An outward shift in the *production possibilities curve* that results from an increase in resource supplies or quality or an improvement in *technology*; (2) an increase of real output (*gross domestic product*) or real output per capita.

Pitfalls to Sound Economic Reasoning

Because They Affect Us So Personally, We Often Have Trouble Thinking Accurately and Objectively about Economic Issues.

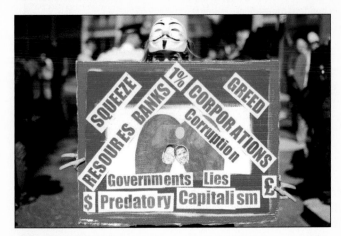

LEON NEAL/AFP/GettyImages

Here are some common pitfalls to avoid in successfully applying the economic perspective.

Biases Most people bring a bundle of biases and preconceptions to the field of economics. For example, some might think that corporate profits are excessive or that lending money is always superior to borrowing money. Others might believe that government is necessarily less efficient than businesses, or that more government regulation is always better than less. Biases distort thinking and interfere with objective analysis. All of us must be willing to shed biases and preconceptions that are not supported by facts.

Loaded Terminology The economic terminology used in newspapers and broadcast media is sometimes emotionally biased, or loaded. The writer or spokesperson may have a cause to promote or an ax to grind, and may slant comments accordingly. High profits may be labeled "obscene," low wages may be called "exploitative," or self-interested behavior may be "greed." Government workers may be referred to as "mindless bureaucrats" and those favoring stronger government regulations may be called "socialists." To objectively analyze economic issues, you must be prepared to reject or discount such terminology.

Fallacy of Composition Another pitfall in economic thinking is the assumption that what is true for one individual or part of a whole is necessarily true for a group of individuals or the whole. This is a logical fallacy called the *fallacy of composition*; the assumption is not correct. A statement that is valid for an individual or part is not necessarily valid for the larger group or whole.

FIGURE 1.6 Present choices and future locations of production possibilities curves.

(a) Presentville's current choice to produce more "present goods" and fewer "future goods," as represented by point *P*, will result in a modest outward shift of the production possibilities curve in the future. (b) Futureville's current choice of producing fewer "present goods" and more "future goods," as depicted by point *F*, will lead to a greater outward shift of the production possibilities curve in the future.

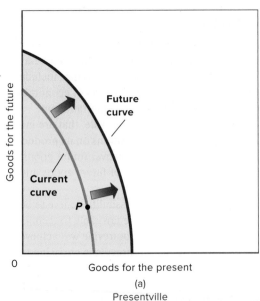

Goods for the future

Goods for the present

(a)
Presentville

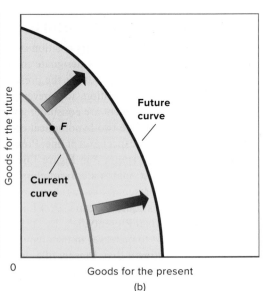

Goods for the future

Goods for the present

(b)
Futureville

Noneconomic example:

- You may see the action better if you leap to your feet to see an outstanding play at a football game. But if all the spectators leap to their feet at the same time, nobody—including you—will have a better view than when all remained seated.

Economic examples:

- An individual stockholder can sell shares of, say, Tesla stock without affecting the price of the stock. The individual's sale will not noticeably reduce the share price because the sale is a negligible fraction of the total shares of Tesla being bought and sold. But if all the Tesla shareholders decide to sell their shares the same day, the market will be flooded with shares and the stock price will fall precipitously.

- A single cattle ranch can increase its revenue by expanding the size of its livestock herd. The extra cattle will not affect the price of cattle when they are brought to market. But if all ranchers as a group expand their herds, the total output of cattle will increase so much that the price of cattle will decline when the cattle are sold. If the price reduction is relatively large, ranchers as a group might find that their income has fallen despite their having sold a greater number of cattle because the fall in price overwhelms the increase in quantity.

Post Hoc Fallacy You must think very carefully before concluding that because event A precedes event B, A is the cause of B. This kind of faulty reasoning is known as the *post hoc, ergo propter hoc,* or "after this, therefore because of this," fallacy.

Noneconomic example:

- A professional football team hires a new coach and the team's record improves. Is the new coach the cause? Maybe. Perhaps the presence of more experienced and talented players or an easier schedule is the true cause. The rooster crows before dawn, but does not cause the sunrise.

Economic example:

- Many people blamed the Great Depression of the 1930s on the stock market crash of 1929. But the crash did not cause the Great Depression. The same severe weaknesses in the economy that caused the crash caused the Great Depression. The depression would have occurred even without the preceding stock market crash.

Correlation but Not Causation Do not confuse correlation, or connection, with causation. Correlation between two events or two sets of data indicates only that they are associated in some systematic and dependable way. For example, we may find that when variable X increases, Y also increases. But this correlation does not necessarily mean that there is causation—that increases in X cause increases in Y. The relationship could be purely coincidental or dependent on some other factor, Z, not included in the analysis.

Here is an example: Economists have found a positive correlation between education and income. In general, people with more education earn higher incomes than those with less education. Common sense suggests education is the cause and higher incomes are the effect; more education implies a more knowledgeable and productive worker, and such workers receive larger salaries.

But might the relationship be explainable in other ways? Are education and income correlated because the characteristics required for succeeding in education—ability and motivation— are the same ones required to be a productive and highly paid worker? If so, then people with those traits will probably both obtain more education and earn higher incomes. But greater education will not be the sole cause of the higher income.

Is Futureville's choice necessarily "better" than Presentville's? We cannot say. The different outcomes simply reflect different preferences and priorities in the two countries.

Global Perspective 1.2 indicates that nations differ substantially in how large a fraction of their respective *national incomes* they choose to devote to investments in capital ("goods for the future") as opposed to expenditures on consumer goods ("goods for the present").

A Qualification: International Trade

Production possibilities analysis implies that an individual nation is limited to the combinations of output indicated by its production possibilities curve. But we must modify this principle when international specialization and trade exist.

You will see in later chapters that an economy can circumvent, through international specialization and trade, the output limits imposed by its domestic production possibilities curve. With international specialization and trade, each nation specializes in the production of those items for which it has the lowest opportunity costs. Countries then engage in trade, with each country exchanging the items that it can produce at the lowest opportunity costs for the items that other countries can produce at their lowest opportunity costs.

International specialization and trade allow a nation to get more of a desired good at less sacrifice of some other good. Rather than sacrifice three units of domestically produced robots to get a third domestically produced pizza, as in Table 1.1, a nation that engages in specialization and trade might be able to do much better. If it specializes in robots while another country specializes in pizza, then it may be able to obtain the third unit of pizza by trading only two domestically

GLOBAL PERSPECTIVE 1.2

GROSS FIXED CAPITAL FORMATION AS A PERCENTAGE OF NATIONAL INCOME, SELECTED NATIONS, 2020

Countries vary widely in the percentage of their respective national incomes that they devote to investments in capital goods ("gross fixed capital formation") rather than on purchases of consumer goods. Only the former generates increases in future production capacity.

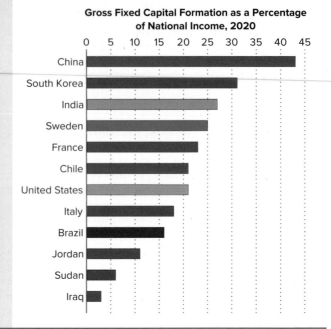

Gross Fixed Capital Formation as a Percentage of National Income, 2020

Source: The World Bank, www.worldbank.org.

produced robots for one foreign-produced pizza. Specialization and trade have the same effect as having more and better resources or discovering improved production techniques; both increase the quantities of capital and consumer goods available to society. Expansion of domestic production possibilities and international trade are two separate routes for obtaining greater output.

QUICK REVIEW

1.4

▶ Unemployment causes an economy to operate at a point inside its production possibilities curve.

▶ Increases in resource supplies, improvements in resource quality, and technological advance cause economic growth, which shifts the production possibilities curve outward.

▶ An economy's present choice of capital and consumer goods helps determine its future production possibilities curve.

▶ International specialization and trade enable a nation to obtain more goods than its production possibilities curve indicates.

Summary

LO1.1 Define economics and explain the economic perspective.

Economics is the social science that examines how individuals, institutions, and society make optimal choices under conditions of scarcity. Central to economics is the idea of opportunity cost: the value of the next-best good or service forgone to obtain something.

The economic perspective includes three elements: scarcity and choice, purposeful behavior, and marginal analysis. It sees individuals and institutions as making rational decisions based on comparisons of marginal costs and marginal benefits.

LO1.2 Describe the role of economic theory in economics.

Economists employ the scientific method, in which they form and test hypotheses of cause-and-effect relationships to generate theories, laws, and principles. Economists often combine theories into representations called models.

LO1.3 Distinguish microeconomics from macroeconomics and positive economics from normative economics.

Microeconomics examines the decision making of specific economic units or institutions. Macroeconomics looks at the economy as a whole or its major aggregates.

Positive economic analysis deals with facts; normative economics reflects value judgments.

LO1.4 Explain the individual's economizing problem and illustrate trade-offs, opportunity costs, and attainable combinations with budget lines.

Individuals face an economizing problem. Because their wants exceed their incomes, they must decide what to purchase and what to forgo. Society also faces an economizing problem. Societal wants exceed the available resources necessary to fulfill them. Society therefore must decide what to produce and what to forgo.

Graphically, a budget line (or budget constraint) illustrates the economizing problem for individuals. The line shows the various combinations of two products that a consumer can purchase with a specific money income, given the prices of the two products.

LO1.5 List the categories of scarce resources and explain society's economizing problem.

Economic resources are inputs into the production process and can be classified as land, labor, capital, or entrepreneurial ability. Economic resources are also known as factors of production or inputs.

Economists illustrate society's economizing problem through production possibilities analysis. Production possibilities tables and curves show the different combinations of goods and services that can be produced in a fully employed economy, assuming that resource quantity, resource quality, and technology are fixed.

LO1.6 Apply production possibilities analysis.

An economy that is fully employed and thus operating on its production possibilities curve must sacrifice the output of some types of goods and services to increase the production of others. The gain of one type of good or service is always accompanied by an opportunity cost in the form of the loss of some of the other type of good or service.

Because resources are not equally productive in all possible uses, shifting resources from one use to another creates increasing opportunity costs. The production of additional units of one product requires the sacrifice of increasing amounts of the other product.

The optimal (best) point on the production possibilities curve represents the most desirable mix of goods. It requires the expanded production of each good until its marginal benefit (MB) equals its marginal cost (MC).

LO1.7 Explain how economic growth and international trade increase consumption possibilities.

Over time, technological advances and increases in the quantity and quality of resources enable the economy to produce more of all goods and services—that is, to experience economic growth. Society's choice regarding the mix of consumer goods and capital goods in current output determines the future location of the production possibilities curve and the extent of economic growth.

International trade enables a nation to obtain more goods from its limited resources than its production possibilities curve indicates.

Terms and Concepts

economics	macroeconomics	investment
economic perspective	aggregate	consumer goods
scarcity	positive economics	entrepreneurial ability
opportunity cost	normative economics	entrepreneurs
utility	economizing problem	factors of production
marginal analysis	budget line	production possibilities curve
scientific method	economic resources	law of increasing opportunity costs
economic principle	land	economic growth
other-things-equal assumption	labor	
microeconomics	capital	

Discussion Questions

1. What is an opportunity cost? How does the idea relate to the definition of economics? Which of the following decisions would entail the greater opportunity cost: allocating a square block in the heart of New York City for a surface parking lot or allocating a square block at the edge of a typical suburb for such a lot? Explain. **LO1.1**

2. Cite three examples of recent decisions that you made in which you, at least implicitly, weighed marginal cost and marginal benefit. **LO1.1**

3. What is "utility" and how does it relate to purposeful behavior? **LO1.1**

4. What are the key elements of the scientific method, and how does this method relate to economic principles and laws? **LO1.2**

5. Make (a) a positive economic statement of your choice, and then (b) a normative economic statement relating to your first statement. **LO1.3**

6. How does the slope of a budget line illustrate opportunity costs and trade-offs? How does a budget line illustrate scarcity and the effect of limited incomes? **LO1.4**

7. What are economic resources? What categories do economists use to classify them? Why are resources also called factors of production? Why are they called inputs? **LO1.5**

8. Why is money not considered to be a capital resource in economics? Why is entrepreneurial ability considered a category of economic resource, distinct from labor? What roles do entrepreneurs play in the economy? **LO1.5**

9. Explain the typical shapes of marginal-benefit and marginal-cost curves. How are these curves used to determine the optimal allocation of resources to a particular product? If current output is such that marginal cost exceeds marginal benefit, should more or fewer resources be allocated to this product? Explain. **LO1.6**

10. Suppose that, on the basis of a nation's production possibilities curve, an economy must sacrifice 10,000 pizzas domestically to get the 1 additional industrial robot it desires, but it can get the robot from another country in exchange for 9,000 pizzas. Relate this information to the following statement: "Through international specialization and trade, a nation can reduce its opportunity cost of obtaining goods and thus move outside its production possibilities curve." **LO1.7**

11. **LAST WORD** Studies indicate that married men on average earn more income than unmarried men of the same age and education level. Why must we be cautious in concluding that marriage is the cause and higher income is the effect?

Review Questions

1. Match each term with the correct definition. **LO1.1**
   economics
   opportunity cost
   marginal analysis
   utility
   a. The next-best thing that must be forgone in order to produce one more unit of a given product.
   b. The pleasure, happiness, or satisfaction obtained from consuming a good or service.
   c. The social science concerned with how individuals, institutions, and society make optimal (best) choices under conditions of scarcity.
   d. Making choices based on comparing marginal benefits with marginal costs.

2. Indicate whether each of the following statements applies to microeconomics or macroeconomics: **LO1.3**
   a. The unemployment rate in the United States was 5.2 percent in August 2021.
   b. A U.S. software firm laid off 15 workers last month and transferred the work to India.
   c. An unexpected freeze in central Florida reduced the citrus crop and caused the price of oranges to rise.
   d. U.S. output, adjusted for inflation, decreased by 3.5 percent in 2020.
   e. Last week Wells Fargo Bank lowered its interest rate on business loans by one-half of 1 percentage point.
   f. The consumer price index rose by 0.3 percent from July 2021 to August 2021.

3. Suppose that you initially have $100 to spend on books or movie tickets. The books start off costing $25 each and the movie tickets start off costing $10 each. For each of the following situations, would the attainable set of combinations that you can afford increase or decrease? **LO1.4**
   a. Your budget increases from $100 to $150 while the prices stay the same.
   b. Your budget remains $100, and the price of books remains $25, but the price of movie tickets rises to $20.
   c. Your budget remains $100, and the price of movie tickets remains $10, but the price of a book falls to $15.

4. Suppose that you are given a $100 budget at work that can be spent only on two items: staplers and pens. If staplers cost $10 each and pens cost $2.50 each, then the opportunity cost of purchasing one stapler is: **LO1.4**
   a. 10 pens.
   b. 5 pens.
   c. zero pens.
   d. 4 pens.

5. As economists use the terms, investment is related to capital in the same way that: **LO1.5**
   a. MB is to MC.
   b. practice is to acquiring skill.
   c. color is to sound.
   d. positive economics is to normative economics.

6. For each of the following situations involving marginal cost (MC) and marginal benefit (MB), indicate whether it would be best to produce more, fewer, or the current number of units. **LO1.6**
   a. 3,000 units at which MC = $10 and MB = $13.
   b. 11 units at which MC = $4 and MB = $3.
   c. 43,277 units at which MC = $99 and MB = $99.
   d. 82 units at which MC < MB.
   e. 5 units at which MB < MC.

7. Explain how (if at all) each of the following events affects the location of a country's production possibilities curve. **LO1.6**
   a. The quality of education increases.
   b. The number of unemployed workers increases.
   c. A new technique improves the efficiency of extracting copper from ore.
   d. A devastating earthquake destroys numerous production facilities.

8. What are the two major ways in which an economy can grow and push out its production possibilities curve? **LO1.7**
   a. Better weather and nicer cars
   b. Higher taxes and lower spending
   c. Increases in resource supplies and advances in technology
   d. Decreases in scarcity and advances in auditing

9. To obtain greater output, a nation can: **LO1.7**
   a. invest in more goods for the future (capital).
   b. increase the quantity and quality of its resources.
   c. engage in international specialization and trade.
   d. all of the above.

Problems

1. Potatoes cost Janice $1 per pound, and she has $5.00 that she could possibly spend on potatoes or other items. If she feels that the first pound of potatoes is worth $1.50, the second pound is worth $1.14, the third pound is worth $1.05, and all subsequent pounds are worth $0.30 per pound, how many pounds of potatoes will she purchase? How many pounds will she purchase if she has only $2 to spend? **LO1.1**

2. Pham can work as many or as few hours as she wants at the college bookstore for $12 per hour. But due to her hectic schedule, she has just 15 hours per week that she can spend working at either the bookstore or other potential jobs. One potential job, at a café, will pay her $15 per hour for up to 6 hours per week. She has another job offer at a garage that will pay her $13 an hour for up to 5 hours per week. And she has a potential job at a daycare center that will pay her $11.50 per hour for as many hours as she can work. If her goal is to maximize the amount of money she can make each week, how many hours will she work at the bookstore? **LO1.1**

3. Suppose you won $15 on a lotto ticket at the local 7-Eleven and decided to spend all the winnings on candy bars and bags of peanuts. Candy bars cost $0.75 each while bags of peanuts cost $1.50 each. **LO1.4**
   a. Construct a table showing the alternative combinations of the two products that are available.
   b. Plot the data in your table as a budget line in a graph. What is the slope of the budget line? What is the opportunity cost of one more candy bar? Of one more bag of peanuts? Do these opportunity costs rise, fall, or remain constant as additional units are purchased?
   c. Does the budget line tell you which of the available combinations of candy bars and bags of peanuts to buy?
   d. Suppose that you had won $30 on your ticket, not $15. Show the $30 budget line in your diagram. Has the number of available combinations increased or decreased?

4. Suppose that you are on a desert island and possess exactly 20 coconuts. Your neighbor, Friday, is a fisherman, and he is willing to trade 2 fish for every 1 coconut that you are willing to give him. Another neighbor, Kwame, is also a fisherman, and he is willing to trade 3 fish for every 1 coconut. **LO1.5**
   a. On a single figure, draw budget lines for trading with Friday and for trading with Kwame. (Put coconuts on the vertical axis.)
   b. What is the slope of the budget line from trading with Friday?
   c. What is the slope of the budget line from trading with Kwame?
   d. Which budget line features a larger set of attainable combinations of coconuts and fish?
   e. If you are going to trade coconuts for fish, would you rather trade with Friday or Kwame? Why?

5. Refer to the following production possibilities table for consumer goods (automobiles) and capital goods (forklifts): **LO1.6**
   a. Show these data graphically. Upon what specific assumptions is this production possibilities curve based?
   b. If the economy is at point C, what is the cost of one more automobile? Of one more forklift? Which characteristic of the production possibilities curve reflects the law of increasing opportunity costs: its shape or its length?

   c. If the economy characterized by this production possibilities table and curve is producing 3 automobiles and 20 forklifts, what could you conclude about its use of its available resources?
   d. Is production at a point outside the production possibilities curve currently possible? Could a future advance in technology allow production beyond the current production possibilities curve? Could international trade allow a country to consume beyond its current production possibilities curve?

	Production Alternatives				
Type of Production	**A**	**B**	**C**	**D**	**E**
Automobiles	0	2	4	6	8
Forklifts	30	27	21	12	0

6. Refer to Figure 1.3. Suppose that the cost of cheese falls, so that the marginal cost of producing pizza decreases. Will the MC curve shift up or down? Will the optimal amount of pizza increase or decrease? Explain. **LO1.6**

7. Referring to the table in problem 5, suppose improvement occurs in the technology of producing forklifts but not in the technology of producing automobiles. Draw the new production possibilities curve. Now assume that a technological advance occurs in producing automobiles but not in producing forklifts. Draw the new production possibilities curve. Now draw a production possibilities curve that reflects technological improvement in the production of both goods. **LO1.7**

8. Because investment and capital goods are paid for with savings, higher savings rates reflect a decision to consume fewer goods in the present so as to invest in more goods for the future. Households in China save about 35 percent of their annual incomes each year, whereas U.S. households save only around 7 percent. At the same time, production possibilities are growing at roughly 6 percent per year in China but only about 2 percent per year in the United States. Use graphical analysis of "present goods" versus "future goods" to explain the difference between China's growth rate and the U.S. growth rate. **LO1.7**

Graphs and Their Meanings

LO1.8 Understand graphs, curves, and slopes as they relate to economics.

Economists often use graphs to illustrate economic models. By understanding these "pictures," you will more readily comprehend economic relationships.

Constructing a Graph

A *graph* is a visual representation of the relationship between two economic quantities, or variables. The table in Figure 1 is a hypothetical illustration showing the relationship between income and consumption for the economy as a whole. We logically expect that people will buy more goods and services when their incomes go up. Thus, it is not surprising to find in the table that total consumption in the economy increases as total income increases.

The information in the table is expressed graphically in Figure 1. Here is how it is done: We want to show visually how consumption changes as income changes. We therefore represent income on the **horizontal axis** of the graph and consumption on the **vertical axis.**

FIGURE 1 Graphing the direct relationship between consumption and income.
Two sets of data that are positively or directly related, such as consumption and income, graph as an upward sloping line.

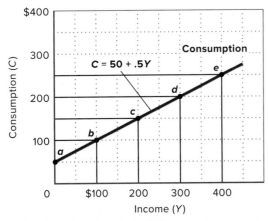

Income per Week	Consumption per Week	Point
$ 0	$ 50	a
100	100	b
200	150	c
300	200	d
400	250	e

horizontal axis The "left-right" or "west-east" measurement line on a graph or grid.

vertical axis The "up-down" or "north-south" measurement line on a graph or grid.

Now we arrange the vertical and horizontal scales of the graph to reflect the ranges of values for consumption and income and mark the scales in convenient increments. As you can see, the values marked on the graph cover all the values in the table. The increments on both scales are $100.

Because the graph has two dimensions, each point within it represents an income value and its associated consumption value. To find a point that represents one of the five income-consumption combinations in the table in Figure 1, we draw straight lines from the appropriate values on the vertical and horizontal axes. For example, to plot point *c* (the $200 income–$150 consumption point), we draw straight lines up from the horizontal (income) axis at $200 and across from the vertical (consumption) axis at $150. These lines intersect at point *c*, which represents this particular income-consumption combination. You should verify that the other income-consumption combinations shown in the table are properly located in the graph in Figure 1. Finally, by assuming that the same general relationship between income and consumption prevails for all other incomes, we draw a line or smooth curve to connect these points. That line or curve represents the income-consumption relationship.

If the curve is a straight line, as in Figure 1, we say the relationship is *linear*. (It is permissible, and even customary, to refer to straight lines in graphs as "curves.")

Direct and Inverse Relationships

The line in Figure 1 slopes upward to the right, so it depicts a direct (or positive) relationship between income and consumption. When two variables (in this case, consumption and income) have a **direct relationship** (or positive relationship), they change in the *same* direction. An increase in consumption is associated with an increase in income; a decrease in consumption accompanies a decrease in income. When two sets of data are directly (or positively) related, they always graph as an *upward sloping* line, as in Figure 1.

In contrast, two sets of data may be inversely (or negatively) related. Consider the table in Figure 2, which shows the relationship between the price of basketball tickets and game attendance at Gigantic State University (GSU). Here we have an **inverse relationship** (or negative relationship) because the two variables change in *opposite* directions. When ticket prices decrease, attendance increases. When ticket prices increase, attendance decreases. The six data points in the table in Figure 2 are plotted in the graph. An inverse (or negative) relationship always graphs as a *downward sloping* line.

direct relationship The relationship between two variables that change in the same direction, for example, product *price* and quantity supplied; a positive relationship.

inverse relationship The relationship between two variables that change in opposite directions, for example, product *price* and quantity demanded; a negative relationship.

FIGURE 2 Graphing the inverse relationship between ticket prices and game attendance.

Two sets of data that are negatively or inversely related, such as ticket price and the attendance at basketball games, graph as a downward sloping line.

Ticket Price	Attendance, Thousands	Point
$50	0	a
40	4	b
30	8	c
20	12	d
10	16	e
0	20	f

Dependent and Independent Variables

Economists often seek to determine which variable is the "cause" and which is the "effect." The **independent variable** is the cause or source; it is the variable that changes first. The **dependent variable** is the effect or outcome; it is the variable that changes as a result of the change in the independent variable. In our income-consumption example, income is the independent variable while consumption is the dependent variable. Income causes consumption to be what it is rather than the other way around. Similarly, ticket prices (set in advance of the season and printed on the ticket) determine attendance at GSU basketball games; attendance at games does not determine the printed ticket prices for those games. Ticket price is the independent variable and the quantity of tickets purchased is the dependent variable.

---

independent variable The variable causing a change in some other (dependent) variable.

dependent variable A variable that changes as a consequence of a change in some other (independent) variable; the "effect" or outcome.

Axis Placement of Dependent and Independent Variables

Your may recall from your high school math courses that mathematicians are in the habit of putting the independent variable (cause) on the horizontal axis and the dependent variable (effect) on the vertical axis. Economists are less tidy; their graphing of independent and dependent variables is more arbitrary. For example, economists' graphing of the income-consumption relationship is consistent with mathematical convention, but, contrariwise, economists put price and cost data (which are both cause variables) on the vertical axis, as we did in Figure 2.

This does not present any sort of fundamental difficulty, but we want you to be aware of this fact to avoid any possible confusion. Independent variables are the "cause" variables and dependent variables are the "effect" variables. But their axis placement varies in economics.

Other Things Equal

Our simple two-variable graphs purposely ignore many other factors that might affect the amount of consumption occurring at each income level or the number of people who attend GSU basketball games at each possible ticket price. When economists plot the relationship between any two variables, they employ the *ceteris paribus* (other-things-equal) assumption. Thus, in Figure 1 all factors other than income that might affect the amount of consumption are presumed to be constant or unchanged. Similarly, in Figure 2 all factors other than ticket price that might influence attendance at GSU basketball games are assumed constant. In reality, "other things" are not equal; they often change, and when they do, the relationship represented in our two tables and graphs will change. Specifically, the lines we have plotted would *shift* to new locations.

Consider a stock market "crash." The dramatic drop in the value of stocks might make people less willing to consume at each level of income. The result might be a downward shift of the consumption line. To see this, you should plot a new consumption line in Figure 1, assuming that consumption is, say, $20 less at each income level. Note that the relationship remains direct; the line merely shifts downward to reflect less consumption spending at each income level.

Similarly, factors other than ticket prices might affect GSU game attendance. If GSU loses most of its games, attendance at GSU games might be less at each ticket price. To see this, redraw Figure 2 assuming that 2,000 fewer fans attend GSU games at each ticket price.

Slope of a Line

Lines can be described in terms of their slopes. The **slope of a straight line** is the ratio of the vertical change (the rise or

---

slope of a straight line The ratio of the vertical change (the rise or fall) to the horizontal change (the run) between any two points on a straight line. The slope of an upward-sloping line is positive, reflecting a direct relationship between two variables; the slope of a downward-sloping line is negative, reflecting an inverse relationship between two variables.

drop) to the horizontal change (the run) between any two points on the line.

Positive Slope

Between point b and point c in Figure 1, the rise or vertical change (the change in consumption) is +$50 and the run or horizontal change (the change in income) is +$100. Therefore:

$$\text{slope} = \frac{\text{vertical change}}{\text{horizontal change}} = \frac{+50}{+100} = \frac{1}{2} = .5$$

Note that our slope of .5 is positive because consumption and income change in the same direction; that is, consumption and income are directly or positively related.

The slope of .5 tells us there will be a $0.50 increase in consumption for every $1 increase in income. Similarly, there will be a $0.50 decrease in consumption for every $1 decrease in income.

Negative Slope

Between any two of the identified points in Figure 2, say, point c and point d, the vertical change is −10 (the drop) and the horizontal change is +4 (the run).

Therefore:

$$\text{slope} = \frac{\text{vertical change}}{\text{horizontal change}} = \frac{-10}{+4} = -2\frac{1}{2} = -2.5$$

This slope is negative because ticket price and attendance have an inverse relationship.

Note that the values on the horizontal axis are stated in thousands of people. So the slope of −10 / +4 or −2.5 means that lowering the price by $10 will increase attendance by 4,000 people. That ratio also implies that a $2.50 price reduction will increase attendance by 1,000 persons.

Slopes and Measurement Units

The slope of a line will be affected by the choice of units for either variable. In our ticket-price illustration, if we had chosen to measure attendance in individual people rather than in thousands of people, our horizontal change would have been 4,000 and the slope would have been

$$\text{slope} = \frac{-10}{+4,000} = \frac{-1}{+400} = -.0025$$

Slopes and Marginal Analysis

The concept of slope is important in economics because it reflects marginal changes—those involving 1 more (or 1 fewer) unit. For example, in Figure 1 the .5 slope shows that $0.50 of extra or marginal consumption is associated with each $1 change in income. In that example, people collectively will consume $0.50 of any $1 increase in their incomes and reduce their consumption by $0.50 for each $1 decline in income.

Infinite and Zero Slopes

Many variables are unrelated (or "independent") of one another. For example, the quantity of wristwatches purchased is not related to the price of bananas. Figure 3a represents the

FIGURE 3 Infinite and zero slopes.
(a) A line parallel to the vertical axis has an infinite slope. Here, purchases of watches remain the same no matter what happens to the price of bananas. (b) A line parallel to the horizontal axis has a slope of zero. In this case, consumption remains the same no matter what happens to the divorce rate. In both (a) and (b), the two variables are totally unrelated to each other.

(a)

(b)

price of bananas on the vertical axis and the quantity of watches demanded on the horizontal axis. The graph of their relationship is the line parallel to the vertical axis. The line's vertical slope indicates that the same quantity of watches is purchased no matter what the price of bananas. The slope of vertical lines is *infinite*.

Similarly, aggregate consumption is completely unrelated to the nation's divorce rate. Figure 3b places consumption on the vertical axis and the divorce rate on the horizontal axis. The line parallel to the horizontal axis represents this lack of relatedness because the amount of consumption remains the same no matter what happens to the divorce rate. The slope of horizontal lines is *zero*.

Absolute Value of Slopes

The demand curves and production possibilities curves that you will encounter in subsequent chapters will typically have negative slopes because they plot inverse relationships. But it is sometimes useful to drop the negative sign and speak only of the **absolute value** of the slope. Thus a slope of −8/2 would equal 8/2 = 4 once you took its absolute value and dispensed with the negative sign.

---

absolute value The magnitude of a number without regard to its sign. For any number x, the absolute value of x is denoted $|x|$, and $|x| = +x$ no matter whether x itself is a positive or negative number. Thus, $|-3| = +3$ and $|+3| = +3$.

Vertical Intercept

Any line can be positioned on a graph (without plotting points) if we know just two things: its slope and its vertical intercept. We have already discussed slope. The **vertical intercept** of a line is the point where the line meets the vertical axis. In Figure 1 the vertical intercept is $50. This intercept means that if current income were zero, consumers would still spend $50. They might do this by borrowing or by selling some of their assets. Similarly, the $50 vertical intercept in Figure 2 shows that at a $50 ticket price, GSU's basketball team would be playing in an empty arena.

Equation of a Linear Relationship

If we know the vertical intercept and slope, we can describe a line in equation form. When the independent variable is on the horizontal axis, the equation of a straight line is

$$y = a + bx$$

where y = dependent variable
a = vertical intercept
b = slope of line
x = independent variable

For our income-consumption example, if C represents consumption (the dependent variable) and Y represents income (the independent variable), we can write $C = a + bY$. By substituting the known values of the intercept and the slope, we get

$$C = 50 + .5Y$$

This equation also allows us to determine the amount of consumption C at any specific level of income. You should use it to confirm that at the $250 income level, consumption is $175.

When economists put the independent variable on the vertical axis and the dependent variable on the horizontal axis, then y stands for the independent variable. Look again at our GSU ticket price–attendance data. If P represents the ticket price (independent variable) and Q represents attendance (dependent variable), their relationship is given by

$$P = 50 - 2.5Q$$

where the vertical intercept is 50 and the negative slope is $-2\frac{1}{2}$, or -2.5. Knowing the value of P lets us solve for Q, our

---

vertical intercept The point at which a line meets the vertical axis of a graph.

dependent variable. You should use this equation to predict GSU ticket sales when the ticket price is $15.

Slope of a Nonlinear Curve

We now move from the simple world of linear relationships (straight lines) to the more complex world of nonlinear relationships (curved lines). The slope of a straight line is the same at all its points. The slope of a line representing a nonlinear relationship changes from one point to another. Such lines are always called *curves*.

Consider the downward sloping curve in Figure 4. Its slope is negative throughout, but the curve flattens as we move down along it. Thus, its slope constantly changes; the curve has a different slope at each point.

To measure the slope at a specific point, we draw a straight line tangent to the curve at that point. A straight line is *tangent* at a point if it touches, but does not intersect, the curve at that point. Thus, line aa is tangent to the curve in Figure 4 at point A. The slope of the curve at that point is equal to the slope of the tangent line. Specifically, the total vertical change (drop) in the tangent line aa is -20 and the total horizontal change (run) is $+5$. Because the slope of the tangent line aa is $-20/+5$, or -4, the slope of the curve at point A is also -4.

Line bb in Figure 4 is tangent to the curve at point B. Following the same procedure, we find the slope at B to be $-5/+15$, or $-\frac{1}{3}$. Thus, in this flatter part of the curve, the slope is less negative.

FIGURE 4 Determining the slopes of curves.
The slope of a nonlinear curve changes from point to point on the curve. The slope at any point (say, B) can be determined by drawing a straight line that is tangent to that point (line bb) and calculating the slope of that line.

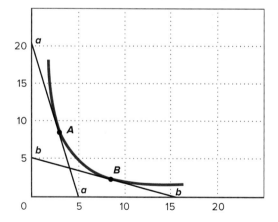

Appendix Summary

LO1.8 Understand graphs, curves, and slopes as they relate to economics.

Graphs are a convenient and revealing way to represent economic relationships.

Two variables are positively (or directly) related when their values change in the same direction. The line or curve representing two directly related variables slopes upward.

Two variables are negatively (or inversely) related when their values change in opposite directions. The line or curve representing two inversely related variables slopes downward.

The value of the dependent variable (the "effect") is determined by the value of the independent variable (the "cause").

When the "other factors" that might affect a two-variable relationship are allowed to change, the graph of the relationship will likely shift to a new location.

The slope of a straight line is the ratio of the vertical change to the horizontal change between any two points. The slope of an upward sloping line is positive; the slope of a downward sloping line is negative.

The slope of a line or curve depends on the units used in measuring the variables. The slope is especially relevant for economics because it measures marginal changes.

The slope of a horizontal line is zero; the slope of a vertical line is infinite.

Together, the vertical intercept and slope of a line determine its location; they are used in expressing the line—and the relationship between the two variables—as an equation.

The slope of a curve at any point is determined by calculating the slope of a straight line tangent to the curve at that point.

Appendix Terms and Concepts

horizontal axis

vertical axis

direct (positive) relationship

inverse (negative) relationship

independent variable

dependent variable

slope of a straight line

absolute value

vertical intercept

Appendix Discussion Questions   Mc Graw Hill connect

1. What is an inverse relationship? How does it graph? What is a direct relationship? How does it graph? **LO1.8**
2. Describe the graphical relationship between ticket prices and the number of people choosing to visit amusement parks. Is that relationship consistent with the fact that, historically, park attendance and ticket prices have both risen? Explain. **LO1.8**
3. Look back at Figure 2, which shows the inverse relationship between ticket prices and game attendance at Gigantic State

University. (a) Interpret the meaning of both the slope and the intercept. (b) If the slope of the line were steeper, what would that say about the amount by which ticket sales respond to increases in ticket prices? (c) If the slope of the line stayed the same but the intercept increased, what could you say about the amount by which ticket sales respond to increases in ticket prices? **LO1.8**

Appendix Review Questions   Mc Graw Hill connect

1. Indicate whether each of the following relationships is usually a direct relationship or an inverse relationship. **LO1.8**
   a. A sports team's winning percentage and attendance at its home games
   b. Higher temperatures and sweater sales
   c. A person's income and how often he or she shops at discount stores
   d. Higher gasoline prices and miles driven in automobiles
2. Erin grows pecans. The number of bushels (B) that she can produce depends on the number of inches of rainfall (R) that her

orchards get. The relationship is given by the following equation: $B = 3,000 + 800R$. Match each part of this equation with the correct term. **LO1.8**

B	slope
3,000	dependent variable
800	vertical intercept
R	independent variable

Appendix Problems   Mc Graw Hill connect

1. Graph and label as either direct or indirect the relationships you would expect to find between (a) the number of inches of rainfall per month and the sale of umbrellas, (b) the amount of tuition and the level of enrollment at a university, and (c) the popularity of an entertainer and the price of her concert tickets. **LO1.8**
2. Indicate how each of the following might affect the data shown in the table and graph in Figure 2 of this appendix: **LO1.8**
   a. GSU's athletic director schedules higher-quality opponents.
   b. An NBA team locates in the city where GSU plays.
   c. GSU contracts to have all its home games televised.
3. The table at the top of the next page contains data on the relationship between saving and income. Rearrange these data into a meaningful order and graph them on the grid displayed for this problem. What is the slope of the line? The vertical intercept? Write the equation that represents this line. What

would you predict saving to be at the $12,500 level of income? **LO1.8**

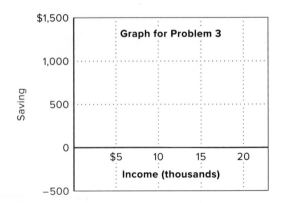

Income per Year	Saving per Year
$15,000	$1,000
0	−500
10,000	500
5,000	0
20,000	1,500

4. Construct a table from the data shown in the accompanying graph. Which is the dependent variable and which is the independent variable? Summarize the data in equation form. **LO1.8**

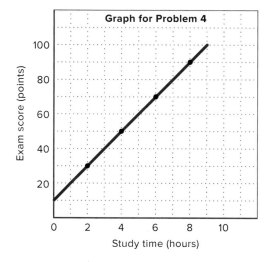

Graph for Problem 4

5. Suppose that when the interest rate on loans is 16 percent, businesses find it unprofitable to invest in machinery and equipment. However, when the interest rate is 14 percent, $5 billion worth of investment is profitable. At 12 percent interest, a total of $10 billion of investment is profitable. Similarly, total investment increases by $5 billion for each successive 2-percentage-point decline in the interest rate. Describe the relevant relationship between the interest rate and investment in a table, on a graph, and as an equation. Put the interest rate on the vertical axis and investment on the horizontal axis. In your equation use the form $i = a + bI$, where i is the interest rate, a is the vertical intercept, b is the slope of the line (which is negative), and I is the level of investment. **LO1.8**

6. Suppose that $C = a + bY$, where C = consumption, a = consumption at zero income, b = slope, and Y = income. **LO1.8**
   a. Are C and Y positively related, or are they negatively related?
   b. If graphed, would the curve for this equation slope upward or slope downward?

c. Are the variables C and Y inversely related or directly related?
d. What is the value of C if $a = 10$, $b = 0.50$, and $Y = 200$?
e. What is the value of Y if $C = 100$, $a = 10$, and $b = 0.25$?

7. The accompanying graph shows curve XX' and tangents at points A, B, and C. Calculate the slope of the curve at these three points. **LO1.8**

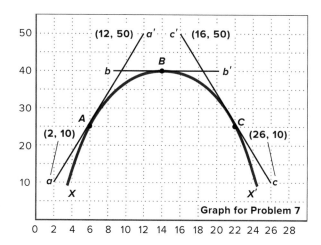

Graph for Problem 7

8. In the accompanying graph, is the slope of curve AA' positive or negative? Does the slope increase or decrease as we move along the curve from A to A'? Answer the same two questions for curve BB'. **LO1.8**

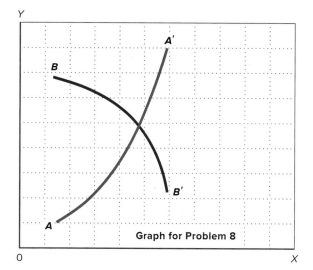

Graph for Problem 8

The Market System and the Circular Flow

>> LEARNING OBJECTIVES

LO2.1 Define and explain laissez-faire capitalism, the command system, and the market system.

LO2.2 List the main characteristics of the market system.

LO2.3 Explain how the market system answers the five fundamental questions of what to produce, how to produce, who obtains the output, how to adjust to change, and how to promote technological progress.

LO2.4 Explain the operation of the "invisible hand."

LO2.5 Describe the mechanics of the circular flow model.

LO2.6 Explain how the market system deals with risk.

Frustrated with shopping online, you decide to go to the local mall, where you can touch and feel products before deciding what to buy. There are fewer products at the mall than online, but suppose you tried to compile a list of all the individual goods and services available at the mall. That task would be daunting, but your list could prompt some fundamental questions about the economy, such as:

- Who decides which goods and services should be produced?
- How do the producers determine which technologies and resources to use in producing these goods?
- Who will obtain these products?
- What accounts for new and improved products?

This chapter answers all of these questions.

>> **LO2.1** Define and explain laissez-faire capitalism, the command system, and the market system.

economic system A particular set of institutional arrangements and a coordinating mechanism for solving the *economizing problem;* a method of organizing an economy, of which the *market system* and the *command system* are the two general types.

Economic Systems

Every society needs to develop an **economic system**—a particular set of institutional arrangements and a coordinating mechanism—to respond to the economizing problem. The economic system determines what goods are produced, how they are produced, who gets them, how to accommodate change, and how to promote technological progress.

Economic systems differ as to (1) who owns the factors of production and (2) the methods used to motivate, coordinate, and direct economic activity.

Economics systems can be classified by their degree of centralized or decentralized decision making. At one extreme lies *laissez-faire capitalism,* in which government intervention is minimal and markets and prices direct nearly all economic activity. At the other extreme lie *command systems,* in which governments have total control over all economic activity. The vast majority of national economies lie somewhere in the middle. These economies have *market systems* or *mixed economies.*

Laissez-Faire Capitalism

In **laissez-faire capitalism**—or "pure capitalism"—the government's role is limited to protecting private property and establishing a legal environment in which contracts are enforced and people interact in markets to buy and sell goods, services, and resources.

The term "laissez-faire" is French for "let it be," meaning that the government should leave entrepreneurs and businesspeople unmolested so that they can make their own decisions about what to produce and how to produce it. Proponents of laissez-faire believe that any interference in the economy on the part of government reduces human welfare. They maintain that governments are corrupted by special interests that use the government's economic influence to benefit themselves rather than society at large.

To prevent that from happening, the proponents of laissez-faire argue that government's only role should be preventing individuals and firms from coercing each other, thus ensuring that only mutually beneficial economic transactions are negotiated and completed. The result should be the highest possible level of human satisfaction because, after all, who knows better what people want than the people themselves?

In reality, no society has ever employed a pure laissez-faire system. In fact, no government has *ever* limited its economic actions to the short list of functions permitted under laissez-faire. Instead, every government in history has undertaken a wider range of economic activities, including industrial safety regulations, taxes and subsidies, occupational licensing requirements, and income redistribution.

laissez-faire capitalism A hypothetical *economic system* in which the government's economic role is limited to protecting private property and establishing a legal environment appropriate to the operation of *markets* in which only mutually agreeable transactions take place between buyers and sellers; sometimes referred to as "pure capitalism."

The Command System

The polar opposite of laissez-faire capitalism is the **command system,** in which government owns most property resources, and economic decision making is set by a central economic plan created and enforced by the government. The command system has been utilized by several countries with socialist or communist governments, including the Soviet Union, Cuba, and China.

Under the command system, the government owns most of the business firms, which produce according to government directives. A central planning board determines production goals for each enterprise and specifies the amount of resources allocated to each enterprise so that it can reach its production goals. The division of output between capital and consumer goods is centrally decided, and capital goods are allocated among industries based on the central planning board's long-term priorities.

A pure command economy would rely exclusively on a central plan. But, in reality, even the preeminent command economy—the Soviet Union—tolerated some private ownership before its collapse in 1992. Subsequent reforms in Russia and most of the eastern European nations have, to one degree or another, transformed their command economies to capitalistic, market-oriented systems. China's reforms have not gone as far, but they have greatly reduced China's reliance on central planning. Although government ownership of resources and capital in China is still extensive, the nation has increasingly relied on markets to organize and coordinate its economy. North Korea and Cuba are the last prominent remaining examples of largely centrally planned economies. Other countries using mainly the command system include Turkmenistan, Laos, Belarus, Myanmar, Venezuela, and Iran.

command system A method of organizing an economy in which property resources are publicly owned and government uses *central economic planning* to direct and coordinate economic activities; *socialism; communism.* Compare with *market system.*

The Market System

The vast majority of the world's economies utilize the **market system,** also known as *capitalism, the mixed economy,* or the market economy.

The market system is characterized by a mixture of centralized government economic initiatives and decentralized actions taken by individuals and firms. The precise mixture varies by country, but in each case the system features the private ownership of resources and the use of markets and prices to coordinate and direct economic activity.

In the market system, individuals and businesses seek to achieve their economic goals through their own decisions regarding work, consumption, or production. The system allows for the private ownership of capital, communicates through prices, and coordinates economic activity through **markets**—places where buyers and sellers come together to buy and sell goods, services, and resources.

market system (1) An *economic system* in which individuals own most *economic resources* and in which *markets* and *prices* serve as the dominant coordinating mechanism used to allocate those resources; *capitalism.* Compare with *command system.* (2) All the product and resource markets of a *market economy* and the relationships among them.

market Any institution or mechanism that brings together buyers (demanders) and sellers (suppliers) of a particular *good* or *service.*

Participants pursue their own self-interest, and goods and services are produced and resources are supplied by whoever is willing and able to do so. The result is competition among independently acting buyers and sellers and an economic system in which decision making is widely dispersed.

The market system offers high potential monetary rewards that create powerful incentives for existing firms to innovate and for entrepreneurs to pioneer new products and processes.

It is true, however, that in the capitalism practiced in the United States and most other countries, the government plays a substantial role in the economy. It not only sets the rules for economic activity but also promotes economic stability and growth, provides certain goods and services that would otherwise be underproduced or not produced at all, and modifies the distribution of income. The government, however, is not the dominant economic force in deciding what to produce, how to produce it, and who will get it. That force is the market and the individuals participating in it.

Characteristics of the Market System

>> **LO2.2** List the main characteristics of the market system.

Let's examine the key features of the market system.

Private Property

In addition to providing individuals with the freedom to engage in the economic activities of their choice, the market system is characterized by the private ownership of most property resources, including capital. That extensive private ownership of capital is what gives capitalism its name.

private property The right of private persons and *firms* to obtain, own, control, employ, dispose of, and bequeath *land, capital,* and other property.

More broadly speaking, the legal right to **private property,** coupled with the freedom to negotiate binding legal contracts, enables individuals and businesses to obtain, use, and dispose of property resources as they see fit.

Property rights encourage people to cooperate by helping to ensure that only *mutually agreeable* economic transactions take place. To understand why this is true, imagine a world without legally enforceable property rights. In that world, the strong could simply take whatever they wanted from the weak without compensating them. But in a world with legally enforceable property rights, any person who wants something must pay for it. If a person really wants something you have, they must offer you something that you value in return. That is, the person must offer you a mutually agreeable economic transaction—one that benefits both of you. Thus property rights facilitate exchange.

Property rights also:

- Encourage investment, innovation, and economic growth. Nobody would stock a store, build a factory, or clear land for farming if someone else, or the government itself, could take away that property at any moment.

- Encourage owners to maintain or improve their property so as to preserve or increase its value.

- Enable people to spend their time and resources increasing the production of goods and services, rather than having to devote money and time to protecting and retaining the property they already possess.

freedom of enterprise The freedom of *firms* to obtain economic resources, to use those resources to produce products of the firms' own choosing, and to sell their products in markets of their choice.

- Protect intellectual property through patents, copyrights, and trademarks. Such long-term protection encourages people to write books, compose music, create social media platforms, and invent new products and production processes.

Freedom of Enterprise and Choice

Closely related to private property is freedom of enterprise and freedom of choice.

- **Freedom of enterprise** ensures that entrepreneurs and private businesses are free to obtain and use economic resources to produce their choice of goods and services and to sell them in their chosen markets.

freedom of choice The freedom of owners of property resources to employ or dispose of them as they see fit, of workers to enter any line of work for which they are qualified, and of consumers to spend their incomes in the manner that they prefer.

- **Freedom of choice** allows owners to employ or dispose of their property and money as they see fit. It also allows workers to try to enter any line of work for which they are qualified. Finally, it ensures that consumers are free to buy the goods and services that best satisfy their wants and that their budgets allow.

These choices are free only within legal limitations, however. Illegal choices such as human trafficking and drug trafficking are punished through fines or imprisonment. (As Global Perspective 2.1 shows, the degree of economic freedom varies greatly from country to country.)

GLOBAL PERSPECTIVE 2.1

INDEX OF ECONOMIC FREEDOM, SELECTED ECONOMIES, 2021

The Index of Economic Freedom measures economic freedom using 10 major groupings such as trade policy, property rights, and government intervention, with each category containing more than 50 specific criteria. The index then ranks 178 economies according to their degree of economic freedom. Those freedom rankings are used to place each country into one of five categories: Free, Mostly Free, Moderately Free, Mostly Unfree, and Repressed. We present three countries from each category as well as their respective overall ranks (from 1, most free, to 178, least free).

Source: The Heritage Foundation, www.heritage.org.

FREE
1 Singapore
2 New Zealand
3 Australia

MOSTLY FREE
14 United Arab Emirates
20 United States
29 Germany

MODERATELY FREE
39 Spain
68 Italy
92 Russia

MOSTLY UNFREE
105 Nigeria
121 India
143 Brazil

REPRESSED
168 Iran
177 Venezuela
178 North Korea

Self-Interest

In the market system, **self-interest** is the motivating force. Self-interest simply means that each economic unit tries to achieve its own particular goal. Entrepreneurs try to maximize profit or minimize loss. Property owners try to get the highest price for the sale or rent of their resources. Workers try to maximize their utility (satisfaction) by finding jobs that offer the best combination of wages, hours, benefits, and working conditions. Consumers try to obtain products at the lowest possible price. Self-interest provides direction and consistency to what might otherwise be a chaotic economy.

self-interest That which each *firm*, property owner, worker, and consumer believes is best for itself and seeks to obtain.

Competition

The market system depends on **competition** among economic units. Very broadly defined, competition requires

- Two or more buyers and two or more sellers acting independently in a particular product or resource market. (Usually there are many more than two buyers and two sellers.)
- Freedom of sellers and buyers to enter or leave (exit) markets, on the basis of their economic self-interest.

competition The effort and striving between two or more independent rivals to secure the business of one or more third parties by offering the best possible terms.

Competition among buyers and sellers diffuses economic power throughout the economy. When many buyers and many sellers act independently of each other in a market, no single buyer or seller can dictate the price of the product or resource because other buyers and sellers can undercut that price.

In a competitive system, producers can enter or leave an industry; no insurmountable barriers prevent an industry from expanding or contracting. This freedom to expand or contract provides the economy with the flexibility needed to remain efficient over time. Freedom of entry and exit enables the economy to adjust to changes in consumer tastes, technology, and resource availability.

The diffusion of economic power inherent in competition limits the potential abuse of that power. A producer that charges more than the competitive market price will lose sales to other producers. An employer who pays less than the competitive market wage rate will lose workers to other employers. Competition is the key regulatory force in the market system.

Markets and Prices

You may wonder why an economy based on self-interest does not collapse into chaos. If consumers want breakfast cereal, but businesses choose to produce running shoes, the economy could become deadlocked by the inconsistencies between what consumers and producers desire.

In reality, the billions of decisions made by households and businesses each day are highly coordinated by markets, prices, and profits. The preferences of buyers and the production costs of sellers are brought together in markets, where prices rise and fall in response to changing demands by consumers and the changing resource and opportunity costs facing producers.

Those changes guide resource owners, entrepreneurs, and consumers as they make and revise their choices and pursue their self-interest. Businesses, in particular, react strongly to how changes in prices affect their profitability and thus whether they should continue doing what they have been doing or make changes and adjustments.

Just as competition is the regulatory mechanism of the market system, the system of markets and prices is the coordinating mechanism. It is an elaborate communication network through which innumerable individual choices are recorded, summarized, and balanced. Those who respond to market signals are rewarded with greater profit or increased *utility* (satisfaction). Those who ignore or do not respond to those signals are penalized with losses or decreased utility.

QUICK REVIEW

2.1

- ▶ The market system rests on the private ownership of property and on freedom of enterprise and freedom of choice.

- ▶ Property rights encourage people to cooperate and make mutually agreeable economic transactions.

- ▶ The market system permits consumers, resource suppliers, and businesses to pursue their self-interest.

- ▶ Competition diffuses economic power and limits the actions of any single seller or buyer.

- ▶ The coordinating mechanism of capitalism is a system of markets and prices.

Technology and Capital Goods

In the market system, the monetary rewards for creating new products or production techniques accrue directly to the innovator. The market system therefore encourages extensive use and rapid development of complex capital goods, including wireless networks, the Global Positioning System (GPS), highly automated warehouse distribution centers, and the software necessary to run nuclear power plants and self-driving cars.

Advanced technology and capital goods are important because the most direct methods of production are often the least efficient. The only way to avoid that inefficiency is to rely on capital goods. It would be ridiculous for a farmer to go at production with bare hands. Huge benefits can be derived from creating and using even simple capital equipment such as horse-drawn plows, let alone modern farm equipment like self-driving tractors and AI-guided pollination drones. More efficient production means much more output.

Specialization

specialization The use of the *resources* of an individual, a *firm*, a region, or a nation to concentrate production on one or a small number of *goods* and *services*.

Market economies rely on specialization. **Specialization** means using the resources of an individual, firm, region, or nation to produce one or a few goods or services rather than the entire range of desired goods and services. The economic unit then exchanges those goods and services for a wide range of desired products. The majority of consumers produce virtually none of the goods and services they consume, and they consume little or nothing of the items they produce. The person working nine to five installing windows in commercial aircraft may rarely fly. Some dairy farmers sell their milk to the local or regional dairy cooperative and then buy energy drinks at the local grocery store.

division of labor The separation of the work required to produce a product into a number of different tasks that are performed by different workers; *specialization* of workers.

Division of Labor Human specialization—called the **division of labor**—contributes to society's output in several ways:

- *Human specialization makes use of differences in ability.* Human specialization enables individuals to take advantage of the differences in their abilities and skills. If LeBron is good at shooting a basketball and Beyoncé can sing and dance, their talents are most efficiently used if LeBron plays professional basketball while Beyoncé records songs and gives concerts.

- ***Human specialization fosters learning by doing.*** Even if two people have identical abilities, specialization may still be advantageous. By devoting time to a single task, people are more likely to develop the skills required and to improve their techniques. You learn to be a good lawyer by studying, practicing, and specializing in law.

- ***Human specialization saves time.*** By devoting time to a single task, a person avoids the loss of time incurred in shifting from one job to another. Also, time is saved by not "fumbling around" with tasks that one is not trained to do.

For all these reasons, human specialization increases the total output society derives from limited resources.

Geographic Specialization Specialization also works on a regional and international basis. Oranges could be grown in Nebraska, but because of the unsuitability of the land, rainfall, and temperature, the cost would be very high. And wheat could be grown in Florida, but it would be costly for similar geographical reasons. So Nebraskans produce the wheat for which their resources are best suited, and Floridians produce oranges. By specializing, both economies produce more than is needed locally. Then, very sensibly, Nebraskans and Floridians swap some of their surpluses—wheat for oranges, oranges for wheat.

Similarly, on an international scale, the United States specializes in producing such items as commercial aircraft and software, which it sells abroad in exchange for machinery from Mexico, mobile phones from China, and footwear from Vietnam. Both human specialization and geographic specialization increase efficiency in the use of our limited resources.

Use of Money

Any economic system makes extensive use of money. Money performs several functions, but first and foremost it is a **medium of exchange.** It makes trade easier.

Specialization requires exchange. Exchange can, and sometimes does, occur through **barter**—swapping goods for goods, say, wheat for oranges. But barter poses serious problems because it requires a *coincidence of wants* between the buyer and the seller. In our example, we assumed that Nebraskans had excess wheat to trade and wanted oranges. And we assumed that Floridians had excess oranges to trade and wanted wheat. So an exchange occurred. But if this coincidence of wants is missing, trade is stymied.

Suppose that Nebraska has no interest in Florida's oranges but wants potatoes from Idaho. And suppose that Idaho wants Florida's oranges but not Nebraska's wheat. And, to complicate matters, suppose that Florida wants some of Nebraska's wheat but none of Idaho's potatoes. Figure 2.1 summarizes the situation.

In none of the cases shown in the figure is there a coincidence of wants. Trade by barter clearly would be difficult. Instead, people in each state use **money,** which is simply a convenient social invention to facilitate the exchange of goods and services. To serve as money, an item needs to pass only one test: Sellers must be willing to accept it as payment for their goods and services.

medium of exchange Any item sellers generally accept and buyers generally use to pay for a *good* or *service; money;* a convenient means of exchanging goods and *services* without engaging in *barter*.

barter The direct exchange of one *good* or *service* for another good or service.

money Any item that is generally acceptable to sellers in exchange for *goods* and *services*.

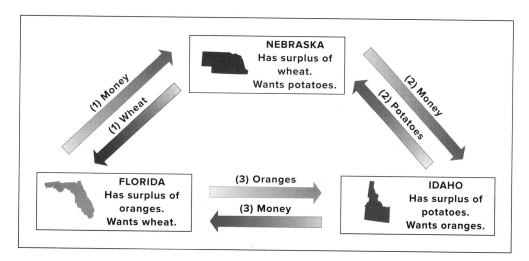

FIGURE 2.1
Money facilitates trade when wants do not coincide.

The use of money as a medium of exchange permits trade to be accomplished despite a noncoincidence of wants. (1) Nebraska trades the wheat that Florida wants for money from Floridians; (2) Nebraska trades the money it receives from Florida for the potatoes it wants from Idaho; (3) Idaho trades the money it receives from Nebraska for the oranges it wants from Florida.

Money is socially defined; whatever society accepts as a medium of exchange *is* money. Today, most economies use pieces of paper as money in addition to checking account balances and, recently, electronic "cryptocurrencies" like Bitcoin.

On a global basis, specialization and exchange are complicated by the fact that different nations have different currencies. But markets in which currencies are bought and sold make it possible for people living in different countries to exchange goods and services without resorting to barter.

Active, but Limited, Government

An active, but limited, government is the final characteristic of modern market systems. Although a market system promotes a high degree of efficiency in the use of its resources, it has certain inherent shortcomings, called "market failures." We will discover in later chapters that governments can often increase the overall effectiveness of a market system. That said, governments have their own set of shortcomings that can cause substantial misallocations of resources. Consequently, we will also investigate several types of "government failure."

QUICK REVIEW 2.2

▶ The market systems of modern industrial economies are characterized by extensive use of technologically advanced capital goods. Such goods help these economies achieve greater efficiency in production.

▶ Specialization is extensive in market systems; it enhances efficiency and output by enabling individuals, regions, and nations to produce the goods and services for which their resources are best suited.

▶ The use of money in market systems facilitates the exchange of goods and services that specialization requires.

Five Fundamental Questions

>> **LO2.3** Explain how the market system answers the five fundamental questions of what to produce, how to produce, who obtains the output, how to adjust to change, and how to promote technological progress.

The key features of the market system help explain how market economies respond to five fundamental questions:

- What goods and services will be produced?
- How will the goods and services be produced?
- Who will get the output?
- How will the system accommodate change?
- How will the system promote technological progress?

These five questions highlight the economic choices underlying the production possibilities curve discussed in Chapter 1. They reflect the constraints that scarce resources impose on a world of unlimited wants.

What Will Be Produced?

How does a market system decide on the specific types and quantities of goods to be produced? The simple answer is this: The goods and services that can be produced at a continuing profit will be produced, while those whose production generates a continuing loss will be discontinued. Profits and losses are the difference between the total revenue (TR) a firm receives from the sale of its products and the total cost (TC) of producing those products.

Continuing economic profit (TR > TC) in an industry results in expanded production and the movement of resources toward that industry. Existing firms grow and new firms enter. The industry expands. Continuing losses (TC > TR) in an industry lead to reduced production and the exit of resources from that industry. Some existing firms shrink; others go out of business. The industry contracts.

In the market system, consumers are sovereign (in command). **Consumer sovereignty** is crucial in determining the types and quantities of goods produced. Consumers spend their income on the goods they are most willing and able to buy. Through these "**dollar votes**," they register their wants in the market. If the dollar votes for a certain product are great enough to create a profit, businesses will produce and sell that product. In contrast, if the dollar votes do not create sufficient revenues to cover costs, businesses will not produce the product. Thus consumers collectively direct resources to industries that are meeting their wants and away from industries that are not meeting their wants.

consumer sovereignty The determination by consumers of the types and quantities of *goods* and *services* that will be produced with the scarce resources of the economy; consumers' direction of production through their *dollar votes.*

dollar votes The "votes" that consumers cast for the production of preferred products when they purchase those products rather than the alternatives that were also available.

CONSIDER THIS . . .

Bitcoin and Cheap Electrons

Bitcoin is an electronic "cryptocurrency" accepted as payment for goods and services by millions of people around the world. It has several novel characteristics, including not being issued by any government and existing and transacting entirely in cyberspace.

The creation of additional Bitcoins (units of Bitcoin currency) is also done entirely electronically, with anyone in the world able to download a free piece of software and start "mining" for Bitcoins by having their computers solve some of the difficult mathematical

Valery Bond/123RF

calculations required to maintain the Bitcoin payments system.

Since computers operate on electricity, mining Bitcoins is at its most profitable when Bitcoin miners utilize the least costly electricity. So it should be no surprise that large-scale Bitcoin mining operations have tended to cluster around low-cost sources of electricity, including hydroelectric dams in the United States and geothermal electricity plants in Iceland.

Market forces encourage low-cost production, even for intangible items like Bitcoin.

How Will the Goods and Services Be Produced?

What combinations of resources and technologies will be used to produce goods and services? How will the production be organized? The answer: in combinations and ways that minimize the cost per unit of output. Inefficiency drives up costs and lowers profits. As a result, any firm wishing to maximize its profits will make great efforts to minimize production costs. These efforts include using the right mix of labor and capital. They also mean locating production facilities optimally to hold down production and transportation expenses (as in the nearby Consider This story about Bitcoin mining).

These efforts will be intensified if the firm faces competition, as consumers strongly prefer low prices and will shift their purchases to the firms that can produce and sell a quality product for the lowest possible price. Any firm foolish enough to use higher-cost production methods will go bankrupt as it is undersold by more efficient competitors who can still make a profit when selling at a lower price. Simply stated: Competition eliminates high-cost producers.

To see how competition favors the lowest-cost combination of resources to produce a given product, suppose there are three possible techniques for producing $15 worth of bars of soap. Table 2.1 shows the quantity of each resource required by each production technique and the prices of those resources. By multiplying the required quantities of each resource by its price in each of the three techniques, we can determine the total cost of producing $15 worth of soap by means of each technique.

Technique 2 is economically the most efficient because it is the least costly. It enables society to obtain $15 worth of output by using a smaller amount of resources—$13 worth—than the $15 worth required by the two other techniques. Competition will dictate that producers use technique 2. Thus, the question of how goods will be produced is answered: They will be produced in the least-costly way.

A change in either technology or resource prices may cause a firm to shift from the technology it is using. Firms will find they can lower their costs by shifting to a technology that uses more of the resource whose price has fallen. For example, if the price of labor falls to $0.50, technique 1 becomes more desirable than technique 2.

TABLE 2.1 Three Techniques for Producing $15 Worth of Bar Soap

Resource	Price per Unit of Resource	Units of Resource					
		Technique 1		Technique 2		Technique 3	
		Units	Cost	Units	Cost	Units	Cost
Labor	$2	4	$ 8	2	$ 4	1	$ 2
Land	1	1	1	3	3	4	4
Capital	3	1	3	1	3	2	6
Entrepreneurial ability	3	1	3	1	3	1	3
Total cost of $15 worth of bar soap			$15		$13		$15

Who Will Get the Output?

In a market economy, a good or service is distributed to consumers on the basis of their ability and willingness to pay the market price. If the price of some product (say, a small sailboat) is $3,000, then buyers who are willing and able to pay that price will "sail, sail away." Consumers who are unwilling or unable to pay the price will be "sitting on the dock of the bay."

The ability to pay the market price for sailboats and other products depends for the most part on the amount of income that consumers have at their disposal. The amount of income they possess depends, in turn, on (1) the quantities of the property resources (land and capital) and human resources (labor and entrepreneurship) that they supply and (2) the prices that those resources command in the resource markets. The more income a consumer can generate from selling resources, the more output they will be able to purchase and consume.

How Will the System Accommodate Change?

Market systems are dynamic: Consumer preferences, technologies, and resource supplies all change. Thus the allocation of resources that is now the most efficient for a specific pattern of consumer tastes, range of technological alternatives, and amount of available resources will become inefficient as consumer preferences change, new production techniques are discovered, and resource supplies change. Can a market economy adjust to such changes?

Suppose consumer tastes change. For instance, assume that consumers decide they want more fruit juice and less milk than the economy currently provides. They communicate these changes in consumer tastes to producers by spending more on fruit juice and less on milk. Other things equal, prices and profits in the fruit-juice industry will rise, and those in the milk industry will fall. Self-interest will induce existing fruit-juice producers to expand output and entice new competitors to enter the prosperous fruit-juice industry. At the same time, firms in the milk industry will scale down, or exit the industry entirely.

The higher prices and greater economic profit in the fruit-juice industry will not only cause that industry to expand but also give it the revenue needed to obtain the resources essential to its growth. Higher prices and profits will permit fruit producers to attract more resources from less-urgent alternative uses. The reverse occurs in the milk industry, where fewer workers and other resources are employed. These adjustments in the economy are appropriate responses to the changes in consumer tastes. This is consumer sovereignty at work.

This directing or guiding function of prices and profits is a core element of the market system. Without such a system, a government planning board or some other administrative agency would have to direct businesses and resources into the appropriate industries.

How Will the System Promote Technological Progress?

Society desires economic growth (greater output) and higher standards of living (greater output per person). How does the market system promote technological improvements and capital accumulation, which both contribute to a higher standard of living?

Technological Advance The market system provides a strong incentive for technological advance. Better products and processes supplant inferior ones. An entrepreneur or firm that introduces a popular new product will gain revenue and economic profit at the expense of rivals. Technological advance also includes new and improved methods that reduce production or distribution costs. By passing part of its cost reduction to the consumer through a lower product price, a firm can increase sales and obtain economic profit at the expense of rival firms.

Moreover, the market system promotes the rapid spread of technological advance throughout an industry. Rival firms must follow the lead of the most innovative firm or else suffer immediate losses and eventual failure. In some cases, the result is **creative destruction**: The creation of new products and production methods completely destroys the market positions of firms that are wedded to existing products and older ways of doing business. Example: Compact discs demolished vinyl records in the 1980s, while online streaming displaced compact discs in the 2000s. In recent years, smartphones have subsumed many functions previously performed by stand-alone products, including wristwatches, compasses, printed maps, flashlights, video cameras, alarm clocks, GPS systems, document scanners, voice recorders, guitar tuners, newspapers, and books.

creative destruction The hypothesis that the creation of new products and production methods destroys the market power of firms committed to existing products and older ways of doing business.

Capital Accumulation Most technological advances require additional capital goods. The market system provides the resources necessary to produce additional capital goods through increased dollar votes for those goods. That is, the market system acknowledges dollar voting for capital goods as well as for consumer goods.

Who counts the dollar votes for capital goods? Answer: Entrepreneurs and business owners. They often use some of their profits to purchase capital goods. They do so because their additional capital may generate even greater profits in the future if the technological innovation that required the additional capital is successful.

▶ The output mix of the market system is determined by profits, which in turn depend heavily on consumer preferences. Economic profits cause industries to expand; losses cause industries to contract.

▶ Competition forces industries to use the least costly production methods.

▶ Competitive markets reallocate resources in response to changes in consumer tastes, technological advances, and changes in availability of resources.

▶ In a market economy, consumer income and product prices determine how output will be distributed.

▶ Competitive markets create incentives for technological advance and capital accumulation, both of which contribute to increases in standards of living.

The "Invisible Hand"

In his 1776 book *The Wealth of Nations*, Adam Smith noted that the operation of a market system creates a curious unity between private interests and social interests. Firms and resource suppliers, seeking to further their own self-interests and operating within the framework of a highly competitive market system, will simultaneously, as though guided by an "invisible hand," promote the public interest.

For example, we have seen that in a competitive environment, businesses seek to build new and improved products to increase profits. Those enhanced products increase society's well-being. Businesses also use the least costly combination of resources to produce a specific output because doing so is in their self-interest. But least-cost production is also clearly in the social interest because it "frees up" resources that can be used to produce other products or reduce the strain on the environment.

Firms and resource suppliers have their own interests in mind. But competition forces them to take other people's interests to heart. The invisible hand of competition ensures that when firms maximize their own profits and resource suppliers maximize their own incomes, they also help to maximize *society's* output and income.

Of the various virtues of the market system, three stand out:

- *Efficiency* The market system promotes the efficient use of resources by guiding them into the production of the goods and services most wanted by society. It also encourages the development and adoption of new and more efficient production techniques.

- *Incentives* The market system encourages skill acquisition, hard work, innovation, and entrepreneurship. Greater work skills and effort mean greater production and higher incomes, which usually translate into a higher standard of living. Successful innovations generate economic rewards. Lower-cost production raises profits while freeing up resources to be used elsewhere.

- *Freedom* The major noneconomic argument for the market system is its emphasis on personal freedom. Unlike central planning, the market system coordinates economic activity without coercion. The market system permits—indeed, it thrives on—freedom of enterprise and choice. Entrepreneurs and workers are free to further their own self-interest, subject to the rewards and penalties imposed by the market system itself.

Of course, no economic system, including the market system, is flawless. In Chapters 4 and 5, we discuss several well-known shortcomings of the market system and examine the government policies that try to remedy them.

The Demise of the Command Systems

Our discussion of how a market system answers the five fundamental questions provides insights into why the command systems of the Soviet Union, eastern Europe, and China (prior to its market reforms) failed. Those systems encountered two insurmountable problems.

The Coordination Problem The first difficulty was the **coordination problem.** The central planners had to coordinate the millions of individual decisions by consumers, resource suppliers, and businesses. Consider the setting up of a factory to produce tractors. The central planners had to

>> **LO2.4** Explain the operation of the "invisible hand."

invisible hand The tendency of *competition* to cause individuals and firms to unintentionally but quite effectively promote the interests of society even when each individual or firm is only attempting to pursue its own interests.

coordination problem The chronic failure of command economies to harmonize the economic activities of producers so as to efficiently satisfy consumer demands; caused by command economies eschewing economic coordination via markets, prices, and profits in favor of central planning.

establish a realistic annual production target, for example, 1,000 tractors. They then had to make available all the necessary inputs—labor, machinery, electric power, steel, tires, glass, paint, transportation—for the production and delivery of those tractors.

Because the outputs of many industries serve as inputs to other industries, the failure of any single industry to achieve its output target caused a chain reaction of repercussions. For example, if iron mines, for want of machinery or labor or transportation, did not supply the steel industry with the required inputs of iron ore, the steel mills were unable to fulfill the input needs of the many industries that depended on steel. Those steel-using industries (such as tractor, automobile, and transportation) were unable to fulfill their planned production goals. Eventually the chain reaction spread to all firms that used steel as an input and from there to other input buyers or final consumers.

The coordination problem became more difficult as the economies expanded. Products and production processes grew more sophisticated and the number of industries requiring planning increased. Planning techniques that worked for a simpler economy proved highly inadequate and inefficient for a more complicated economy. Bottlenecks and production stoppages became the norm, not the exception. In trying to cope, planners suppressed product variety, focusing on one or two products in each product category. What little got produced all looked the same.

A lack of a reliable success indicator added to the coordination problem in the Soviet Union before its demise and in China prior to its market reforms. We have seen that market economies rely on profit as a success indicator. Profit depends on consumer demand, production efficiency, and product quality. In contrast, the major success indicator for the command economies usually was a quantitative production target that the central planners assigned. Production costs, product quality, and product mix were secondary considerations. Managers and workers often sacrificed product quality and variety because they were being awarded bonuses for meeting quantitative, not qualitative, targets. If meeting production goals meant sloppy assembly work and little product variety, so be it.

It was also extremely difficult for planners to assign quantitative production targets without unintentionally producing distortions in output. If the plan specified a production target for producing nails in terms of *weight* (tons of nails), the enterprise made only large nails. But if it specified the target as a *quantity* (thousands of nails), the firm made only small nails, and lots of them!

incentive problem The difficulty common to command economies wherein the numerical production targets set by central planning boards cause managers to produce substandard or unwanted output.

The Incentive Problem   The command economies also faced an **incentive problem.** Central planners determined the output mix. When they misjudged how many automobiles, shoes, shirts, and chickens were wanted at the government-set prices, persistent shortages and surpluses of those products arose. But as long as the managers who oversaw the production of those goods were rewarded for meeting their assigned production goals, they had no incentive to adjust production in response to the shortages and surpluses. And there were no fluctuations in prices and profitability to signal that more or less of certain products was desired. Thus, many products were unavailable or in short supply, while other products were overproduced and sat for months or years in warehouses.

The Consider This story discusses the economic differences between North Korea and South Korea—many of them directly attributable to North Korea's nearly complete reliance on the command system and, thus, on dealing poorly with the coordination and incentive problems.

CONSIDER THIS . . .

Korea by Night

After the Second World War, the Korean peninsula was divided into North Korea and South Korea.

North Korea, under the influence of the Soviet Union, established a command economy that emphasized government ownership and central government planning. South Korea, protected by the United States, established a market economy based upon private ownership and the profit motive.

Today, South Korea is far more prosperous, with South Koreans enjoying an average annual income (adjusted for

Vladi333/Shutterstock

international differences in the cost of living) of $42,765 per year versus $1,700 in North Korea, or over 25 times higher. That differential is especially startling when you find out that North Korea was richer and more highly industrialized when the countries were separated in 1953.

South Korea's much greater prosperity shows up dramatically in the accompanying satellite photo of the Korean peninsula at night. The highly electrified South is a web of light while the North is as dark as the surrounding oceans save for its capital city, Pyongyang.

The Circular Flow Model

The dynamic market economy creates continuous, repetitive flows of goods and services, resources, and money. The **circular flow diagram,** shown in **Figure 2.2 (Key Graph),** illustrates those flows for a simplified economy in which there is no government. The figure groups the economy's decision makers into *businesses* and *households*. Additionally, we divide this economy's markets into the *resource market* and the *product market*.

Households

The blue rectangle on the right side of the circular flow diagram in Figure 2.2 represents **households,** defined as one or more persons occupying a housing unit. There are currently about 123 million households in the U.S. economy. Households buy the goods and services that businesses make available in the product market. Households obtain the income needed to buy those products by selling resources in the resource market.

All the resources in our no-government economy are ultimately owned or provided by households. For instance, the members of one household or another directly provide all of the labor and entrepreneurial ability in the economy. Households also own all of the land and all of the capital in the economy either directly, as personal property, or indirectly, as a consequence of owning all of the businesses in the economy (and thereby controlling all of the land and capital

>> **LO2.5** Describe the mechanics of the circular flow model.

circular flow diagram An illustration showing the flow of *resources* from *households* to *firms* and of products from firms to households. These flows are accompanied by reverse flows of *money* from firms to households and from households to firms.

households Economic entities (of one or more persons occupying a housing unit) that provide *resources* to the economy and use the *income* received to purchase *goods* and *services* that satisfy economic wants.

..Ill KEY GRAPH

FIGURE 2.2 **The circular flow diagram.**

Resources flow from households to businesses through the resource market, and products flow from businesses to households through the product market. Opposite these real flows are monetary flows. Households receive income from businesses (their costs) through the resource market, and businesses receive revenue from households (their expenditures) through the product market.

QUICK QUIZ FOR FIGURE 2.2

1. **The resource market is the place where:**
   a. households sell products and businesses buy products.
   b. businesses sell resources and households sell products.
   c. households sell resources and businesses buy resources (or the services of resources).
   d. businesses sell resources and households buy resources (or the services of resources).

2. **Which of the following would be determined in the product market?**
   a. manager's salary
   b. the price of equipment used in a bottling plant
   c. the price of 80 acres of farmland
   d. the price of a new pair of athletic shoes

3. **In this circular flow diagram:**
   a. money flows counterclockwise.
   b. resources flow counterclockwise.
   c. goods and services flow clockwise.
   d. households are on the selling side of the product market.

4. **In the circular flow diagram:**
   a. households spend income in the product market.
   b. firms sell resources to households.
   c. households receive income through the product market.
   d. households produce goods.

Answers: 1. c; 2. d; 3. b; 4. a

owned by businesses). Thus, all of the income in the economy—all wages, rents, interest, and profits—flows to households because they provide the economy's labor, land, capital, and entrepreneurial ability.

Businesses

businesses Economic entities (*firms*) that purchase resources and provide *goods* and *services* to the economy.

The blue rectangle on the left side of the circular flow diagram represents **businesses,** which are commercial establishments that attempt to earn profits for their owners by offering goods and services for sale.

Businesses sell goods and services in the product market in order to obtain revenue, and they incur costs in the resource market when they purchase the labor, land, capital, and entrepreneurial ability that they need to produce their goods and services.

There currently are about 30 million businesses in the United States, ranging from enormous corporations like Walmart, with 2020 sales of $559 billion and 2.2 million employees worldwide, to single-person sole proprietorships with sales of less than $100 per day.

Product Market

product market A market in which products are sold by *firms* and bought by *households*.

The red rectangle at the bottom of the diagram represents the **product market** in which households purchase the goods and services produced by businesses. Households use the income they receive from the sale of resources to buy goods and services. The money that they spend on goods and services flows to businesses as revenue.

Resource Market

resource market A market in which *households* sell and *firms* buy *resources* or the services of resources.

Finally, the red rectangle at the top of the circular flow diagram represents the **resource market** in which households sell resources to businesses. The households sell resources to generate income, and the businesses buy resources to produce goods and services. Productive resources flow from households to businesses, while money flows from businesses to households in the form of wages, rents, interest, and profits.

To summarize: The circular flow model depicts a complex web of economic activity in which businesses and households are both buyers and sellers. Businesses buy resources and sell products. Households buy products and sell resources. The counterclockwise flow of economic resources and finished products, which is illustrated by the red arrows in Figure 2.2, is paid for by the clockwise flow of money income and consumption expenditures illustrated by the blue arrows.

QUICK REVIEW
2.4

▸ Competition leads individuals and firms to promote the social interest, as if they were guided by a benevolent "invisible hand."

▸ Command systems fail economically because central planning cannot solve the coordination and incentive problems.

▸ The circular flow model illustrates how resources flow from households to businesses and how payments for those resources flow from businesses to households.

How the Market System Deals with Risk

>> LO2.6 Explain how the market system deals with risk.

Producing goods and services is risky. Input shortages can suddenly arise. Consumer preferences can quickly change. Natural disasters can destroy factories and cripple supply chains.

For an economic system to maximize its potential, it must develop methods for assessing and managing risk. The market system does so by confronting business owners with the financial consequences of their decisions. If they manage risks well, they may prosper. If they manage risks poorly, they may lose everything.

The Profit System

As explained in Chapter 1, entrepreneurial ability is the economic resource that organizes and directs the other three resources of land, labor, and capital toward productive uses. The owners of a firm may supply the entrepreneurial ability themselves, or they can hire professional managers to supply the necessary leadership and decision making. Either way, it falls to those acting as the firm's entrepreneurs to deal with risk.

The firm's managers are guided toward sensible decisions by the profit system. This system is actually a profit-and-loss system because entrepreneurs gain profits if they choose wisely but suffer losses if they choose poorly. Entrepreneurs therefore have a large financial incentive to avoid unnecessary risks and make prudent decisions.

Shielding Employees and Suppliers from Business Risk

Under the market system, only a firm's owners are subject to business risk and the possibility of losing money. In contrast, the firm's employees and suppliers are shielded from business risk because they are legally entitled to receive their contracted wages and payments on time and in full regardless of whether the firm is earning a profit or generating a loss.

Consider a new pizza parlor that is opening in a small town. Its investors put up $50,000 to get it going. They rent a storefront, lease ovens, purchase computers, and set some money aside as a reserve.

The firm then has to attract employees. To do so, it will offer wage contracts that promise to pay employees every two weeks without regard to whether the firm is making a profit or generating a loss. This guarantee shields the firm's employees from the risks of owning and operating the business. They will get paid even if the pizza parlor is losing money.

In the same way, the contracts that the firm signs with its suppliers and with anyone who loans the firm money (for instance, the local bank) will also specify that they will be paid on time and in full no matter how the firm is doing in terms of profitability.

Because everyone else is legally entitled to get paid before the firm's owners, the firm's owners are called **residual claimants.** That is, the owners are the legal recipients (claimants) of whatever profit or loss remains (is residual) after all other parties have been paid. The possibility of a profit after everyone else has been paid is the owner's compensation for bearing business risk.

Dealing with Losses So what happens if the firm starts losing money? The owners will take the financial hit. Suppose that the pizza parlor loses $1,500 during the month of October because it runs up $11,500 in costs but generates only $10,000 in revenue. In that situation, the investors' wealth will shrink by $1,500 as the firm is forced to dip into its reserve to cover the loss. If the firm continues to lose money in subsequent months and exhausts the reserve, the owners will then have to decide whether they want to close the shop or put in additional money in the hope that things will turn around.

But throughout all those months of losses, the suppliers and employees are safeguarded. Because they are paid on time and in full, they are shielded from the firm's business risks and whether it is generating a profit or a loss. However, they are not legally entitled to share in the profits if the firm ends up being profitable. That privilege is reserved under the market system for the firm's owners; it is their reward for bearing business risk.

The nearby Consider This story discusses how insurance subsidies affect risk management.

> **residual claimant** In a market system, the economic agent who receives (is claimant to) whatever profit or loss remains (is residual) at a firm after all other *input* providers have been paid. The residual is compensation for providing the economic input of *entrepreneurial ability* and flows to the firm's owners.

CONSIDER THIS . . .

Built on Sand

Insurance policies can help guide people toward better decisions by putting a price on risk. Consider fire insurance and its effect on building decisions. Anyone wanting to build a new home or business in a fire-prone area like Southern California will face substantially higher fire insurance costs than they would if they built in a drizzly locale like coastal Washington. Other things equal, Southern California will see less construction.

Those risk assessments go awry when the government subsidizes insurance premiums. Look at flood insurance. Millions of people who would have otherwise chosen to live

Robert J. Bennett/Pixtal/age fotostock

and work on higher ground live and work in floodplains because the federal government subsidizes flood insurance by about 50 percent.

If those people had been confronted with unsubsidized rates for flood insurance, they would have chosen to live and work on higher ground. But as things now stand, they will be flooded out repeatedly, with taxpayers picking up the tab for flood damages and reconstruction costs.

That's bad for both residents and taxpayers. But it's a predictable consequence of making the financial costs of risky behavior look artificially low.

Hasta La Vista, Venezuela

Venezuela, Once Prosperous, Starved. What Terminated Its Economy?

How can a modern, technologically sophisticated nation in possession of the world's largest oil reserves end up collapsing its economy so badly that there are no medicines in hospitals, toilet paper is unavailable, gasoline has to be rationed, and food gets so expensive that its citizens lost an average of 24 pounds of body weight in 2017?

The country in question is Venezuela, and all those problems began with the election of Hugo Chavez in 1998. He attained the presidency on a promise to alleviate poverty and ensure that everyone in Venezuela had a chance to participate in the country's prosperity, which included supersonic Concord flights to Paris, South America's best arts and entertainment scene, and a highly profitable oil industry that brought massive tax revenues to the government.

Several of Chavez's initial policy efforts were beneficial, including mass literacy programs and the construction of rural health clinics. Unfortunately, Chavez's early anti-poverty programs were just the start of a comprehensive campaign to totally transform Venezuela's economy and society.

As you know from this chapter, most economies are *mixed economies* in which the government sets broad rules but in which businesses have substantial autonomy over what to produce, how to produce it, and what to charge for it. That autonomy was slowly eliminated by Chavez and his successor, Nicolas Maduro, who both pursued an economic policy that they termed Bolivarian Socialism.

Industries were nationalized, meaning that they were taken over by the government without compensation to their owners. That included the oil industry, which pumped 3.4 million barrels per day when Chavez took over in 1998 but just 1.4 million barrels per day 20 years later.

Chavez and Maduro ruined the industry by putting "friends" in charge of the oil rigs. These cronies were thoroughly corrupt, directing into their own pockets the money needed for equipment repairs. The result was leaking pipelines, broken drills, and ever declining production.

The reduced production put a severe strain on the government's finances. By 2013, the government could no longer raise enough tax revenue to pay its bills. Instead of making the tough choices necessary to balance its budget, the government resorted to printing money to pay its bills.

Rapid money printing always and everywhere results in a *hyperinflation*, or a super-fast increase in the overall level of prices in the economy. Double the money supply and prices will double; triple the money supply and prices will triple; and so on.

Venezuela's inflation rate skyrocketed from 25 percent per year in 2012 to 2,600 percent per year in 2017. But oil production continued to fall and the government's deficit situation grew worse.

Maduro's solution? *Print even faster!* The result? Inflation accelerated to 1.3 *million* percent per year in 2018.

Román Camacho/SOPA Images/LightRocket/Getty Images

Maduro could not admit that his government's money printing was responsible for the hyperinflation. He blamed foreigners and rebels intent on overthrowing his government. To "fight" them, he imposed price controls on consumer goods.

Price controls are legal limits on how much sellers can charge for a product. For example, the government might make it illegal to charge more than $5 for a haircut. That *price ceiling* will be attractive to consumers, but it will quickly bankrupt producers because the prices that they have to pay for inputs like labor will keep increasing due to the hyperinflation. The cost of production soon blows past the legal selling price. The only avenues of escape are selling illegally at higher prices or going out of business.

With Maduro's troops imprisoning anybody who dared to sell at higher prices, many firms went bankrupt and closed permanently. As they did, shortages of every imaginable product arose. People began to starve and over 3 million Venezuelans fled to other countries.

So as you consider the pluses and minuses of the market economy and its limited level of government intervention, be sure to remember what became of a once prosperous country brought low by an incompetent, unresponsive, and corrupt government that tried to control every aspect of economic life.

Chavez and Maduro claimed to be saviors. But their socialist economic policies wrought nearly as much damage as the genocidal robots of the *Terminator* movies.

A few rays of hope began to shine by 2021, however, as Maduro decided to relax government control over some areas of the economy, thereby encouraging some brave businesspeople to start operating again. Whether this return to normalcy will continue remains to be seen, though. And unless things improve rapidly, we may have to continue to say *Hasta La Vista, Baby,* to Venezuela's once prosperous economy.

Benefits of Restricting Business Risk to Owners

Two major benefits arise from the market system's restriction of business risk to owners and investors.

Attracting Inputs Many people deeply dislike risk and would not be willing to participate in a business venture if they were exposed to the possibility of losing money. Many workers just want to do their jobs and get paid twice a month without having to worry about whether their employer is doing well or not. The same is true for most suppliers, whose only concern is receiving full and prompt payment for the inputs they supply to businesses.

For both groups, the concentration of business risk on owners is very welcome because they can supply their resources to a firm without worrying about the firm's profitability. That sense of security makes it much easier for firms to attract labor and other inputs, which in turn helps the economy innovate and grow.

Focusing Attention The profit system helps to achieve prudent risk management by focusing owners on the responsibility and the rewards for successfully managing risk. Owners can provide the risk-managing input of entrepreneurial ability themselves or hire it by paying a skilled manager. But either way, some individual's full-time job includes the specialized task of managing business risk.

QUICK REVIEW

2.5

▶ The market system incentivizes the prudent management of business risk by concentrating any profit or loss on a firm's owners and investors.

▶ The market system shields employees, suppliers, and lenders from business risks, but in exchange for that protection, they do not share any profit that might be earned.

▶ By focusing risk on owners and investors, the market system (a) creates an incentive for owners and investors to hire managerial and entrepreneurial specialists to prudently manage business risks and (b) encourages the participation of workers, suppliers, and lenders who dislike risk.

Summary

LO2.1 Define and explain laissez-faire capitalism, the command system, and the market system.
Laissez-faire capitalism is a hypothetical economic system in which government's role would be restricted to protecting private property and enforcing contracts. All real-world economic systems feature a larger role for government. Governments in command systems own nearly all property and resources and make nearly all decisions about what to produce, how to produce it, and who gets the output. Most countries today, including the United States, have market systems in which the government does play a large role, but in which most property and resources are privately owned and markets are the major force in determining what to produce, how to produce it, and who gets it.

LO2.2 List the main characteristics of the market system.
The market system is characterized by the private ownership of resources, including capital, and the freedom of individuals to engage in economic activities of their choice to advance their well-being. Self-interest is the driving force of such an economy, and competition functions as a regulatory or control mechanism.

In the market system, markets, prices, and profits organize and coordinate the many millions of individual economic decisions that occur daily.

Specialization, the use of advanced technology, and the extensive use of capital goods are common features of market systems. By functioning as a medium of exchange, money eliminates the problems of bartering and permits easy trade and greater specialization, both domestically and internationally.

LO2.3 Explain how the market system answers the five fundamental questions of what to produce, how to produce, who obtains the output, how to adjust to change, and how to promote technological progress.
Every economy faces five fundamental questions: (a) What goods and services will be produced? (b) How will the goods and services be produced? (c) Who will get the output? (d) How will the system accommodate change? (e) How will the system promote technological progress?

The market system produces products whose production and sale yield total revenue sufficient to cover total cost. It does not produce products for which total revenue continuously falls short of total cost. Competition forces firms to use the lowest-cost production techniques.

Economic profit (total revenue minus total cost) indicates that an industry is prosperous and promotes its expansion. Losses signify that an industry is not prosperous and hasten its contraction.

Consumer sovereignty means that both businesses and resource suppliers are subject to consumers' wants. Through their dollar votes, consumers decide on the composition of output.

The prices that a household receives for the resources it supplies to the economy determine that household's income. This income determines the household's claim on the economy's output.

By communicating changes in consumer tastes to entrepreneurs and resource suppliers, the market system prompts appropriate adjustments in the allocation of the economy's resources. The market system also encourages technological advance and capital accumulation, both of which raise a nation's standard of living.

LO2.4 Explain the operation of the "invisible hand."

Competition, the primary mechanism of control in the market economy, promotes a unity of self-interest and social interests. As if directed by an invisible hand, competition harnesses the self-interested motives of businesses and resource suppliers to further the social interest.

The command systems of the Soviet Union and pre-reform China met their demise because central planning could not solve the coordination problem and because the numerical targets given to managers created an incentive problem.

LO2.5 Describe the mechanics of the circular flow model.

The circular flow model illustrates the flows of resources and products from households to businesses and from businesses to households, along with the corresponding monetary flows. Businesses are on the buying side of the resource market and the selling side of the product market. Households are on the selling side of the resource market and the buying side of the product market.

LO2.6 Explain how the market system deals with risk.

By focusing business risks onto owners, the market system encourages the participation of workers and suppliers who dislike risk while at the same time creating a strong incentive for owners to manage business risks prudently.

Terms and Concepts

economic system	competition	invisible hand
laissez-faire capitalism	specialization	coordination problem
command system	division of labor	incentive problem
market system	medium of exchange	circular flow diagram
market	barter	households
private property	money	businesses
freedom of enterprise	consumer sovereignty	product market
freedom of choice	dollar votes	resource market
self-interest	creative destruction	residual claimant

Discussion Questions

McGraw Hill **connect**

1. Contrast how a market system and a command economy try to cope with economic scarcity. **LO2.1**
2. How does self-interest help achieve society's economic goals? Why is there such a wide variety of desired goods and services in a market system? In what way are entrepreneurs and businesses at the helm of the economy but commanded by consumers? **LO2.2**
3. Why are private property, and the protection of property rights, so critical to the success of the market system? How do property rights encourage cooperation? **LO2.2**
4. What are the advantages of using capital in the production process? What is meant by the term "division of labor"? What are the advantages of specialization in the use of human and material resources? Explain why exchange is the necessary consequence of specialization. **LO2.2**
5. What problem does barter entail? Indicate the economic significance of money as a medium of exchange. What is meant by the statement "We want money only to part with it"? **LO2.2**
6. Evaluate and explain the following statements: **LO2.2**
   a. The market system is a profit-and-loss system.
   b. Competition is the disciplinarian of the market economy.
7. Some large hardware stores, such as Home Depot, boast of carrying as many as 20,000 different products in each store. What motivated the producers of those individual products to make them and offer them for sale? How did the producers decide on the best combinations of resources to use? Who made those resources available, and why? Who decides whether these particular hardware products should continue to be produced and offered for sale? **LO2.3**
8. What is meant by the term "creative destruction"? How does the emergence of self-driving cars relate to this idea? **LO2.3**
9. In a sentence, describe the meaning of the phrase "invisible hand." **LO2.4**
10. In market economies, firms rarely worry about the availability of inputs to produce their products, whereas in command economies input availability is a constant concern. Why the difference? **LO2.4**
11. Distinguish between the resource market and the product market in the circular flow model. In what way are businesses and households both sellers and buyers in this model? What are the flows in the circular flow model? **LO2.5**
12. How does shielding employees and suppliers from business risk help to improve economic outcomes? Who is responsible for managing business risks in the market system? **LO2.6**
13. **LAST WORD** Why are price ceilings during a hyperinflation problematic? What generalizations do you draw from Venezuela's economic collapse? Would a Venezuelan-style economic collapse be less likely in the United States? Explain.

Review Questions

1. Decide whether each of the following descriptions most closely corresponds to being part of a command system, a market system, or a laissez-faire system. **LO2.1**
   a. A woman who wants to start a flower shop finds she cannot do so unless the central government has already decided to allow a flower shop in her area.
   b. Shops stock and sell the goods their customers want, but the government levies a sales tax on each transaction in order to fund elementary schools, public libraries, and welfare programs for the poor.
   c. The only taxes levied by the government are to pay for national defense, law enforcement, and a legal system designed to enforce contracts between private citizens.

2. Match each term with the correct definition. **LO2.2**
   private property
   freedom of enterprise
   mutually agreeable
   freedom of choice
   self-interest
   competition
   market
   a. An institution that brings buyers and sellers together
   b. The right of private persons and firms to obtain, control, employ, dispose of, and bequeath land, capital, and other property
   c. The presence in a market of independent buyers and sellers who compete with one another and who are free to enter and exit the market as each sees fit
   d. The freedom of firms to obtain economic resources, decide what products to produce with those resources, and sell those products in markets of their choice
   e. What each individual or firm believes is best for itself and seeks to obtain
   f. Economic transactions willingly undertaken by both the buyer and the seller because each feels that the transaction will make them better off
   g. The freedom of resource owners to dispose of their resources as they think best; of workers to enter any line of work for which they are qualified; and of consumers to spend their incomes in whatever way they feel is most appropriate

3. True or False: Money must be issued by a government for people to accept it. **LO2.2**

4. Assume that a business firm finds that its profit is greatest when it produces $40 worth of product A. Suppose also that each of the three techniques shown in the following table will produce the desired output. **LO2.3**
   a. With the resource prices shown, which technique will the firm choose? Why? Will production using that technique result in profit or loss? What will be the amount of that profit or loss? Will the industry expand or contract? When will that expansion or contraction end?
   b. Assume now that a new technique, technique 4, is developed. It combines 2 units of labor, 2 of land, 6 of capital, and 3 of entrepreneurial ability. With the resources priced as shown in the table, will the firm adopt the new technique? Explain.
   c. Suppose that an increase in the labor supply causes the price of labor to fall to $1.50 per unit, all other resource prices

remaining unchanged. Which technique will the producer now choose? Explain.
   d. "The market system causes the economy to conserve most in the use of resources that are particularly scarce in supply. Resources that are scarcest relative to the demand for them have the highest prices. As a result, producers use these resources as sparingly as is possible." Evaluate this statement. Does your answer to part *c*, above, bear out this contention? Explain.

Resource	Price per Unit of Resource	Resource Units Required		
		Technique 1	Technique 2	Technique 3
Labor	$3	5	2	3
Land	4	2	4	2
Capital	2	2	4	5
Entrepreneurial ability	2	4	2	4

5. Identify each of the following quotes as being associated with either the concept of the invisible hand or the concept of creative destruction. **LO2.4**
   a. "If you compare a list of today's most powerful and profitable companies with a similar list from 30 years ago, you will see lots of new entries."
   b. "Managers in the old Soviet Union often sacrificed product quality and variety because they were being awarded bonuses for quantitative, not qualitative, targets."
   c. "Each day, central planners in the old Soviet Union were tasked with setting 27 million prices—correctly."
   d. "It is not from the benevolence of the butcher, the brewer, or the baker that we expect our dinner, but from their regard to their own interest."

6. True or False: Households sell finished products to businesses. **LO2.6**

7. Aaliyah, Madison, Mia, and Maya have decided to pool their financial resources and business skills to open and run a new coffee shop. They will share any profits or losses that the business generates and will be personally responsible for making good on any debt that their business undertakes. Their business is a: **LO2.6**
   a. corporation.
   b. sole proprietorship.
   c. partnership.
   d. none of the above.

8. Ted and Fred are the owners of a gas station. They invested $150,000 each and pay an employee named Lawrence $35,000 per year. This year's revenues are $900,000, while costs are $940,000. Who is legally responsible for bearing the $40,000 loss? **LO2.6**
   a. Lawrence
   b. Ted
   c. Fred
   d. Ted and Fred
   e. Lawrence, Ted, and Fred

Problems

1. Table 2.1 contains information on three techniques for producing $15 worth of bar soap. Assume that we specified "$15 worth of bar soap" because soap costs $3 per bar and all three techniques produce 5 bars of soap ($15 = $3 per bar × 5 bars). So you know each technique produces 5 bars of soap. **LO2.3**

    a. What technique will you want to use if the price of a bar of soap falls to $2.75? Which technique will you use if the price of a bar of soap rises to $4? To $5?

    b. How many bars of soap will you want to produce if the price of a bar of soap falls to $2.00?

    c. Suppose that the price of soap is again $3 per bar but that the prices of all four resources are now $1 per unit. Which is now the least-profitable technique?

    d. If the resource prices return to their original levels (those shown in the table) but a new technique is invented that can produce 3 bars of soap (yes, 3 bars, not 5 bars!) using 1 unit of each of the four resources, will firms prefer the new technique? Why or why not?

2. Suppose Natasha currently makes $50,000 per year working as a manager at a cable TV company. She then develops two possible entrepreneurial business opportunities. In one, she will quit her job to start an organic soap company. In the other, she will try to develop an Internet-based competitor to the local cable company. For the soap-making opportunity, she anticipates annual revenue of $465,000. She estimates the costs for the necessary land, labor, and capital to be $395,000 per year. For the Internet opportunity, she anticipates costs for land, labor, and capital of $3,250,000 per year and revenues of $3,275,000 per year. (a) Should she quit her current job to become an entrepreneur? (b) If she does quit her current job, which opportunity would she pursue? **LO2.3**

3. With current technology, suppose a firm is producing 400 loaves of banana bread daily. Also assume that the least-cost combination of resources for producing those loaves is 5 units of labor, 7 units of land, 2 units of capital, and 1 unit of entrepreneurial ability, selling at prices of $40, $60, $60, and $20, respectively. If the firm can sell these 400 loaves at $2 per unit, what is its total revenue? Its total cost? Its profit or loss? Will it continue to produce banana bread? If this firm's situation is typical for the other makers of banana bread, will resources flow toward or away from this bakery good? **LO2.3**

4. Let's put dollar amounts on the flows in the circular flow diagram of Figure 2.2. **LO2.5**

    a. Suppose that businesses buy a total of $100 billion of the four resources (labor, land, capital, and entrepreneurial ability) from households. If households receive $60 billion in wages, $10 billion in rent, and $20 billion in interest, how much are households paid for providing entrepreneurial ability?

    b. If households spend $55 billion on goods and $45 billion on services, how much in revenues do businesses receive in the product market?

Avigator Fortuner/Shutterstock

Demand, Supply, and Market Equilibrium

>> LEARNING OBJECTIVES

LO3.1 Characterize and give examples of markets.

LO3.2 Describe *demand* and explain how it can change.

LO3.3 Describe *supply* and explain how it can change.

LO3.4 Explain how supply and demand interact to determine market equilibrium.

LO3.5 Explain how changes in supply and demand affect equilibrium prices and quantities.

LO3.6 Define government-set prices and explain how they can cause surpluses and shortages.

LO3.7 (Appendix) Use supply-and-demand analysis to analyze specific real-world situations.

The model of supply and demand is the economics profession's greatest contribution to human understanding. It explains the operation of the markets on which we depend for nearly everything that we eat, drink, and consume. It is also the economic model most often used to explain and analyze economic decision making. The model is so powerful and so widely used that to many people supply and demand *is* economics.

This chapter explains how the model works and how you can use it to predict the *prices* and *quantities* of goods and services bought and sold in markets.

Markets

Markets bring together buyers ("demanders") and sellers ("suppliers"). Everyday consumer markets include the corner gas station, Amazon.com, and the local bakery shop. The New York Stock Exchange and the Chicago Board of Trade are markets in which buyers and sellers from all over the world exchange bonds, stocks, and commodities. In labor markets, new college graduates "sell" and employers "buy" specific labor services. Ride-sharing apps like Uber and Lyft match people who want to buy rides with people who want to sell rides.

Some markets are local; others are national or international. Some are highly personal, involving face-to-face contact between demander and supplier; others are faceless, with buyer and seller never seeing or knowing each other.

To keep things simple, we will focus on markets in which large numbers of independently acting buyers and sellers come together to buy and sell standardized products. Markets with these characteristics are the economy's most highly competitive markets. They include the wheat market, the stock market, and the market for foreign currencies. All such markets involve demand,

>> **LO3.1** Characterize and give examples of markets.

supply, price, and quantity. As you will soon see, the price is "discovered" through the interacting decisions of buyers and sellers.

Demand

>> **LO3.2** Describe *demand* and explain how it can change.

demand A schedule or curve that shows the various amounts of a product that consumers are willing and able to purchase at each of a series of possible *prices* during a specified period of time.

demand schedule A table of numbers showing the amounts of a *good* or *service* buyers are willing and able to purchase at various *prices* over a specified period of time.

Demand is a schedule (table of numbers) or a curve that shows the various amounts of a product that consumers are willing and able to purchase at each of a series of possible prices during a specified period of time, *other things equal*. The table in Figure 3.1 is a hypothetical **demand schedule** for a *single consumer* purchasing gallons of gasoline.

The table reveals the relationship between the various prices of gasoline and the quantity (amount) of gasoline a particular consumer is willing and able to purchase at each price. We say "willing and able" because willingness alone is not effective in the market. You may be willing to buy an ultra-high-definition 4K television set, but if that willingness is not backed by the necessary dollars, it will not be reflected in the market. In the table in Figure 3.1, if the price of gasoline is $5 per gallon, our consumer is willing and able to buy 10 gallons per week; if the price is $4, the consumer is willing and able to buy 20 gallons per week; and so forth.

The table does not tell us which of the five possible prices will actually exist in the gasoline market. The price depends on the interaction between demand and supply. Demand is simply a statement of a buyer's plans, or intentions, with respect to purchasing a product.

To be meaningful, the quantities demanded at each price must relate to a specific period—a day, a week, a month. Saying "A consumer will buy 10 gallons of gas at $5 per gallon" is meaningless. Saying "A consumer will buy 10 gallons of gas *per week* at $5 per gallon" is meaningful. Unless a specific time period is stated, we do not know whether the demand for a product is large or small.

law of demand The principle that, other things equal, an increase in a product's *price* will reduce the quantity of it demanded, and conversely for a decrease in price.

Law of Demand

Other things equal, as price falls, the quantity demanded rises, and as price rises, the quantity demanded falls. In short, there is a *negative* or inverse relationship between price and quantity demanded. Economists call this inverse relationship the **law of demand.**

The other-things-equal assumption is critical here. Many factors other than the price of the product being considered affect the amount purchased. For example, the quantity of Nikes

FIGURE 3.1 An individual buyer's demand for gasoline.

Because price and quantity demanded are inversely related, an individual's demand schedule graphs as a downward sloping curve such as *D*. Other things equal, consumers will buy more of a product as its price declines and less of the product as its price rises. (Here and in later figures, *P* stands for price and *Q* stands for quantity demanded or supplied.)

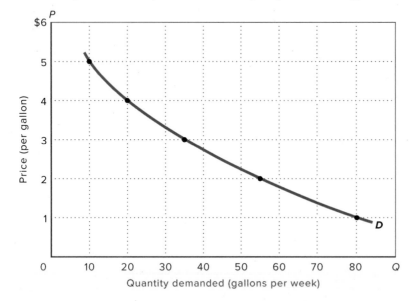

Demand for Gasoline	
Price per Gallon	Quantity (Amount) Demanded per Week
$5	10
4	20
3	35
2	55
1	80

purchased will depend not only on the price of Nikes but also on the prices of shoes produced by Adidas, Reebok, and New Balance. The law of demand in this case says that fewer Nikes will be purchased if the price of Nikes rises while the prices of Adidas, Reeboks, and New Balances remain constant. In short, if the *relative price* of Nikes rises, fewer Nikes will be bought. However, if the price of Nikes and the prices of all other competing shoes increase by some amount—say $5—consumers may buy more, fewer, or the same number of Nikes. To isolate the demand for Nikes, you have to hold other things equal.

Why is there an inverse relationship between price and quantity demanded? Let's look at three explanations, beginning with the simplest one:

- The law of demand is consistent with common sense. People ordinarily do buy more of a product at a low price than at a high price. Price is an obstacle that deters consumers. The higher that obstacle, the less of a product they will buy; the lower the price obstacle, the more they will buy. The fact that businesses conduct "clearance sales" to liquidate unsold items firmly supports the law of demand.

- In any specific time period, each buyer of a product will derive less satisfaction (or benefit, or utility) from each successive unit of the product consumed. The second Big Mac will yield less satisfaction than the first, and the third less than the second. That is, consumption is subject to **diminishing marginal utility.** And because successive units of a particular product yield less and less marginal utility, consumers will buy additional units only if the price of those units is progressively reduced.

- We can also explain the law of demand in terms of income and substitution effects. The **income effect** indicates that a lower price increases the purchasing power of a buyer's money income, enabling the buyer to purchase more of a product than before. A higher price has the opposite effect. The **substitution effect** suggests that buyers have an incentive to substitute a product whose price has fallen for other products whose prices have remained the same. The substitution occurs because the product whose price has fallen is now "a better deal" relative to the other products, whose prices remain unchanged.

For example, a decline in the price of chicken will increase the purchasing power of consumer incomes, enabling people to buy more chicken (the income effect). At a lower price, chicken is relatively more attractive and consumers tend to substitute it for pork, beef, and fish (the substitution effect). The income and substitution effects combine to make consumers able and willing to buy more of a product at a lower price than at a higher price.

The Demand Curve

The inverse relationship between price and quantity demanded for any product can be represented on a simple graph with quantity demanded on the horizontal axis and price on the vertical axis. The graph in Figure 3.1 plots the five price-quantity data points listed in the accompanying table and connects the points with a smooth curve, labeled *D*. This curve is called a **demand curve.** Its downward slope reflects the law of demand—people buy more of a product, service, or resource as its price falls, other things equal.

Market Demand

So far, we have concentrated on just one consumer. But competition requires more than one buyer in each market. By adding the quantities demanded by all consumers at each possible price, we can get from *individual* demand to *market* demand. If there are just three buyers in the market, as represented in the table in Figure 3.2, it is relatively easy to determine the total quantity demanded at each price. Figure 3.2 shows the graphical summing procedure: At each price we sum horizontally the quantities demanded by Joe, Jen, and Jay to obtain the total quantity demanded at that price. We then plot the price and the total quantity demanded as one point on the market demand curve. At the price of $3, for example, the three individual curves yield a total quantity demanded of 100 gallons (= 35 + 39 + 26).

diminishing marginal utility The principle that as a consumer increases the consumption of a *good* or *service*, the *marginal utility* obtained from each additional unit of the good or service decreases.

income effect A change in the quantity demanded of a product that results from the change in *real income* (*purchasing power*) caused by a change in the product's *price*.

substitution effect (1) A change in the quantity demanded of a *consumer good* that results from a change in its relative expensiveness caused by a change in the good's own *price.* (2) The reduction in the *quantity demanded* of the second of a pair of *substitute resources* that occurs when the price of the first resource falls and causes *firms* that employ both resources to switch to using more of the first resource (whose price has fallen) and less of the second resource (whose price has remained the same).

demand curve A curve that illustrates the *demand* for a product by showing how each possible *price* (on the *vertical axis*) is associated with a specific *quantity demanded* (on the *horizontal axis*).

FIGURE 3.2 Market demand for gasoline, three buyers.

The market demand curve D is the horizontal summation of the individual demand curves (D_1, D_2, and D_3) of all the consumers in the market. At the price of $3, for example, the three individual curves yield a total quantity demanded of 100 gallons (= 35 + 39 + 26).

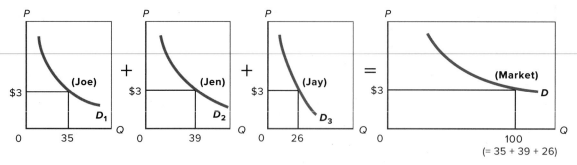

Market Demand for Gasoline, Three Buyers				
	Quantity Demanded			Total Quantity
Price per Gallon	Joe	Jen	Jay	Demanded per Week
$5	10 +	12 +	8 =	30
4	20 +	23 +	17 =	60
3	35 +	39 +	26 =	100
2	55 +	60 +	39 =	154
1	80 +	87 +	54 =	221

Competition, of course, ordinarily entails many more than three buyers of a product. For simplicity, we suppose that all the buyers in a market are willing and able to buy the same amounts at each possible price. Then we just multiply those amounts by the number of buyers to obtain the market demand. That is how we arrive at the demand schedule and demand curve D_1 in Figure 3.3 for a market of 200 gasoline buyers, each with the quantity demanded in the table in Figure 3.1.

FIGURE 3.3 Changes in the demand for gasoline.

A change in one or more of the determinants of demand causes a change in demand. An increase in demand is shown as a shift of the demand curve to the right, as from D_1 to D_2. A decrease in demand is shown as a shift of the demand curve to the left, as from D_1 to D_3. These changes in demand are to be distinguished from a change in quantity demanded, which is caused by a change in the price of the product, as shown by a movement from, say, point a to point b on fixed demand curve D_1.

Market Demand for Gasoline, 200 Buyers, (D_1)	
(1) Price per Gallon	(2) Total Quantity Demanded per Week
$5	2,000
4	4,000
3	7,000
2	11,000
1	16,000

In constructing a demand curve such as D_1 in Figure 3.3, economists assume that price is the most important influence on the amount of any product purchased. But other factors can and do affect purchases. These factors, called **determinants of demand,** are assumed to be constant when a demand curve like D_1 is drawn. When any of these determinants change, the demand curve will shift to the right or left. For this reason, determinants of demand are sometimes called *demand shifters.*

The basic determinants of demand are (1) consumers' tastes (preferences), (2) the number of buyers in the market, (3) consumers' incomes, (4) the prices of related goods, and (5) consumer expectations.

determinants of demand Factors other than *price* that determine the quantities demanded of a *good* or *service.* Also referred to as "demand shifters" because changes in the determinants of demand will cause the *demand curve* to shift either right or left.

Changes in Demand

A change in one or more of the determinants of demand will change the demand data (the demand schedule) in the table accompanying Figure 3.3 and therefore the location of the demand curve. A change in the demand schedule or, graphically, a shift in the demand curve, is called a *change in demand.*

If consumers collectively desire to buy more gasoline at each possible price than is reflected in column 2 in the table in Figure 3.3, that *increase in demand* shifts the demand curve to the right, say, from D_1 to D_2. Conversely, a *decrease in demand* occurs when consumers buy less gas at each possible price than is indicated in column 2. The leftward shift of the demand curve from D_1 to D_3 in Figure 3.3 shows that situation.

Now let's see how changes in each determinant affect demand.

Tastes A favorable change in consumer tastes (preferences) for a product—a change that makes the product more desirable—means that more of it will be demanded at each price. Demand will increase; the demand curve will shift rightward. An unfavorable change in consumer preferences will decrease demand, shifting the demand curve to the left.

New products may affect consumer tastes; for example, the introduction of Instagram and Snapchat greatly decreased the demand for Facebook among teens. Consumer concerns over obesity have increased the demand for broccoli, low-calorie beverages, and fresh fruit while decreasing the demand for beef, eggs, and whole milk. Over the past decade, the demand for vegan food and electric vehicles has increased rapidly, driven by a change in tastes.

Number of Buyers An increase in the number of buyers in a market is likely to increase demand; a decrease in the number of buyers will probably decrease demand.

The most obvious way that changes in the number of consumers can affect demand is by changing the number of potential consumers.

- The rising number of older persons in the United States, for example, has increased the demand for motor homes, medical care, and retirement communities.

- In contrast, out-migration from many small rural communities has reduced their populations and thus the demand for housing, home appliances, and auto repair in those towns.

A more subtle way in which changes in the number of buyers can affect demand is through network effects and congestion effects.

- A *network effect* happens when the value of a product increases as more people use it. This is true for things like cell phones and social apps. Having a cell phone or an Instagram account would not be of any value if you were the only person using a cell phone network or Instagram. There would be nobody to connect to! But the more people who join either of those networks, the more valuable they become and thus the greater the number of people who wish to use them. The result is an increase in demand and a rightward shift of the demand curve.

- A *congestion effect* happens when the value of a product decreases as more people use it. This is true, for instance, for driving on highways or streaming data on a wi-fi network that has limited bandwidth. The more people there are crowded onto a highway or trying to simultaneously stream data on a wi-fi network with finite capacity, the worse the user experience as congestion takes hold and things slow to a crawl. In these situations, quality declines, fewer people wish to use the product, and demand shifts to the left.

normal good A *good* or *service* whose consumption increases when *income* increases and falls when income decreases, other things equal.

inferior good A *good* or *service* whose consumption declines as *income* rises, other things equal.

substitute goods Products or *services* that can be used in place of each other. When the *price* of one falls, the *demand* for the other product falls; conversely, when the price of one product rises, the demand for the other product rises.

complementary goods Products and *services* that are used together. When the *price* of one falls, the demand for the other increases (and conversely).

Income For most products, a rise in income causes an increase in demand. Consumers typically buy more steaks, furniture, and electronic equipment as their incomes increase. Conversely, the demand for such products declines as their incomes fall. Products whose demand varies directly with money income are called *superior goods,* or **normal goods.**

Although most products are normal goods, there are some exceptions. As incomes increase beyond some point, the demand for used clothing, retread tires, and third-hand automobiles may decrease because the higher incomes enable consumers to buy new versions of those products. Similarly, rising incomes may cause the demand for charcoal grills to decline as wealthier consumers switch to gas grills. Goods whose demand varies inversely with money income are called **inferior goods.**

Prices of Related Goods A change in the price of a related good may either increase or decrease the demand for a product, depending on whether the related good is a substitute or a complement:

- A **substitute good** is one that can be used in place of another good.
- A **complementary good** is one that is used together with another good.

Substitutes Häagen-Dazs ice cream and Ben & Jerry's ice cream are substitute goods or, simply, *substitutes.* When two products are substitutes, an increase in the price of one will increase the demand for the other. Conversely, a decrease in the price of one will decrease the demand for the other. For example, when the price of Häagen-Dazs ice cream rises, consumers will buy less of it and increase their demand for Ben & Jerry's ice cream. The two brands are *substitutes in consumption.*

Complements Because complementary goods (or, simply, *complements*) are used together, they are typically demanded jointly. Examples include computers and software, smartphones and cellular service, and snowboards and lift tickets. If the price of a complement (for example, lettuce) goes up, the demand for the related good (salad dressing) will decline. Conversely, if the price of a complement (for example, tuition) falls, the demand for a related good (textbooks) will increase.

Unrelated Goods The vast majority of goods are not related to one another and are called *independent goods*. Examples are butter and golf balls, potatoes and automobiles, and bananas and wristwatches. A change in the price of one has little or no effect on the demand for the other.

Consumer Expectations Changes in consumer expectations may shift demand. A newly formed expectation of higher future prices may cause consumers to buy now in order to "beat" the anticipated price hike, thus increasing current demand. That is often what happens in "hot" real-estate markets. Buyers rush in because they think the price of homes will continue to escalate rapidly. Some buyers fear being "priced out of the market" and therefore not obtaining the home they desire. Other buyers—speculators—believe they will be able to sell the houses later at a higher price. Whatever their motivation, these expectation-driven buyers increase the current demand for houses.

Similarly, a change in expectations concerning future income may prompt consumers to change their current spending. For example, first-round NFL draft choices may splurge on new luxury cars in anticipation of lucrative professional football contracts. Or workers who become fearful of losing their jobs may reduce their demand for, say, vacation travel.

In summary, an *increase* in demand—the decision by consumers to buy larger quantities of a product at each possible price—may be caused by:

- A favorable change in consumer tastes.
- An increase in the number of buyers.
- Rising incomes if the product is a normal good.
- Falling incomes if the product is an inferior good.
- An increase in the price of a substitute good.
- A decrease in the price of a complementary good.
- A new consumer expectation that either prices or income will be higher in the future.

You should "reverse" these generalizations to explain a *decrease* in demand. Table 3.1 provides additional illustrations of the determinants of demand.

Determinant	Examples
Change in buyer tastes	Physical fitness rises in popularity, increasing the demand for jogging shoes and bicycles; smartphone use rises, reducing the demand for desktop and laptop computers; vegetarianism increases in popularity, raising the demand for non-meat "impossible" burgers.
Change in number of buyers	A decline in the birthrate reduces the demand for children's toys; an additional 600 million people on WhatsApp makes it a more attractive communications network; the migration of Californians to Colorado increases the demand for housing in Denver.
Change in income	A rise in incomes increases the demand for normal goods such as restaurant meals, sports tickets, and smartphones while reducing the demand for inferior goods such as turnips, bus passes, and cheap wine.
Change in the prices of related goods	A reduction in airfares reduces the demand for train transportation (substitute goods); a decline in the price of printers increases the demand for ink cartridges (complementary goods).
Change in consumer expectations	Inclement weather in South America creates an expectation of higher future coffee bean prices, thereby increasing today's demand for coffee beans. The expectation that other consumers will rush to buy toilet paper next week as a hurricane approaches causes many consumers to increase their purchases of toilet paper this week.

TABLE 3.1
Determinants of Demand: Factors That Shift the Demand Curve

Changes in Quantity Demanded

A *change in demand* must not be confused with a *change in quantity demanded*.

Recall that "demand" is a schedule or a curve. So a **change in demand** implies a change in the schedule and a corresponding shift of the curve.

A change in demand occurs when a consumer's state of mind about purchasing a product has changed in response to a change in one or more of the determinants of demand. Graphically, a change in demand is a shift of the demand curve to the right (an increase in demand) or to the left (a decrease in demand).

In contrast, a **change in quantity demanded** is a movement from one point to another point—from one price-quantity combination to another—along a fixed demand curve or schedule. The cause of such a change is an increase or decrease in the price of the product under consideration. In the table in Figure 3.3, for example, a decline in the price of gasoline from $5 to $4 will increase the quantity demanded from 2,000 to 4,000 gallons. Make sure you can identify the corresponding movement between those two points along fixed demand curve D_1 in Figure 3.3.

Let's review. In Figure 3.3 the shift of the demand curve D_1 to either D_2 or D_3 is a "change in demand." But the movement from point *a* to point *b* on curve D_1 represents a "change in quantity demanded." In this latter case, demand has not changed; it is the entire curve D_1, which remains fixed in place as we move from point *a* to point *b*.

change in demand A movement of an entire *demand curve* (or of the numerical entries in a demand schedule) such that the *quantity demanded* changes at every particular *price;* caused by a change in one or more of the *determinants of demand.*

change in quantity demanded A change in the *quantity demanded* along a fixed *demand curve* (or within a fixed demand schedule) as a result of a change in the *price* of the product.

Supply

Supply is a schedule or curve showing the various amounts of a product that producers are willing and able to make available for sale at each of a series of possible prices during a specific period, other things equal. The table in Figure 3.4 is a hypothetical **supply schedule** for a single supplier (producer) of gasoline. It shows the quantities of gasoline that are supplied at various prices, other things equal.

>> **LO3.3** Describe *supply* and explain how it can change.

FIGURE 3.4 An individual supplier's supply of gasoline.

Because price and quantity supplied are directly related, the supply curve for an individual supplier graphs as an upsloping curve. Other things equal, suppliers (producers) will offer more of a product for sale as its price rises and less of the product for sale as its price falls.

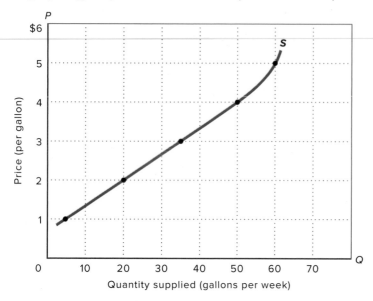

Supply of Gasoline	
Price per Gallon	Quantity (Amount) Supplied per Week
$5	60
4	50
3	35
2	20
1	5

Law of Supply

The table in Figure 3.4 shows that a positive or direct relationship prevails between price and quantity supplied. As price rises, the quantity supplied rises; as price falls, the quantity supplied falls. This relationship is called the **law of supply.** Other things equal, firms will produce and offer for sale more of their product at a high price than at a low price.

Price is an obstacle from the standpoint of the consumer, who is on the paying end. The higher the price, the less the consumer will buy. The supplier, though, is on the receiving end of the product's price. To a supplier, price represents *revenue,* which serves as an incentive to produce and sell a product. The higher the price, the greater this incentive and the greater the quantity supplied. This, again, is basically common sense.

Consider oil producers and refiners who are deciding how much gasoline to supply. As the price of gasoline rises, as shown in the table in Figure 3.4, they will find it profitable to increase production since the higher price will allow them to cover the higher costs associated with more rapid production, including having to drill deeper wells, having to hire additional workers, and having to pay for more shipping and distribution. The result is more gasoline as the price of gasoline rises.

Now consider manufacturers more generally. Beyond some quantity of production, manufacturers usually encounter increases in *marginal cost*—the added cost of producing one more unit of output. Certain productive resources—in particular, the firm's plant and machinery—cannot be expanded quickly, so the firm uses more of other resources, such as labor, to produce more output. But as labor becomes more abundant relative to the fixed plant and equipment, the additional workers have relatively less space and access to equipment. For example, the added workers may have to wait to gain access to machines. As a result, each added worker produces less added output, and the marginal cost of successive units of output rises accordingly. The firm will not produce the more costly units unless it receives a higher price for them. Again, price and quantity supplied are directly related; they increase together along a supply curve or schedule.

The Supply Curve

As with demand, it is convenient to represent individual supply graphically. In Figure 3.4, curve *S* is the **supply curve** that corresponds with the price-quantity data supplied in the accompanying table. The upward slope of the curve reflects the law of supply—producers offer more of a good, service, or resource for sale as its price rises.

supply A schedule or curve that shows the various amounts of a product that producers are willing and able to make available for sale at each of a series of possible *prices* during a specified period of time.

supply schedule A table of numbers showing the amounts of a *good* or *service* producers are willing and able to make available for sale at each of a series of possible *prices* during a specified period of time.

law of supply The principle that, other things equal, an increase in the *price* of a product will increase the quantity of it supplied, and conversely for a price decrease.

supply curve A curve that illustrates the *supply* for a product by showing how each possible *price* (on the *vertical axis*) is associated with a specific *quantity supplied* (on the *horizontal axis*).

FIGURE 3.5 **Changes in the supply of gasoline.**

A change in one or more of the determinants of supply causes a change in supply. An increase in supply is shown as a rightward shift of the supply curve, as from S_1 to S_2. A decrease in supply is depicted as a leftward shift of the curve, as from S_1 to S_3. In contrast, a change in the *quantity supplied* is caused by a change in the product's price and is shown by a movement from one point to another, as from *b* to *a* on fixed supply curve S_1.

Market Supply of Gasoline, 200 Producers, (S_1)	
(1) Price per Gallon	(2) Total Quantity Supplied per Week
$5	12,000
4	10,000
3	7,000
2	4,000
1	1,000

Market Supply

To derive market supply from individual supply, we sum the quantities supplied by each producer at each price. That is, we "horizontally add" the supply curves of the individual producers. The price–quantity data supplied in the table accompanying Figure 3.5 are for an assumed 200 identical producers in the market, each willing to supply gasoline according to the supply schedule shown in Figure 3.4. Curve S_1 in Figure 3.5 is a graph of the market supply data. Note that the values of the axes in Figure 3.5 are the same as those used in our graph of market demand (Figure 3.3). The only difference is that we change the label on the horizontal axis from "quantity demanded" to "quantity supplied."

Determinants of Supply

In constructing a supply curve, we assume that price is the most significant influence on the quantity supplied of any product. But other factors can and do affect supply. The supply curve is drawn on the assumption that these other factors do not change. If one of them does change, a *change in supply* will occur, and the entire supply curve will shift.

The basic **determinants of supply** are (1) resource prices, (2) technology, (3) taxes and subsidies, (4) prices of other goods, (5) producer expectations, and (6) the number of sellers in the market. A change in any one or more of these determinants of supply, or *supply shifters,* will shift the supply curve for a product either right or left. A shift to the *right,* as from S_1 to S_2 in Figure 3.5, signifies an *increase* in supply: Producers supply larger quantities of the product at each possible price. A shift to the *left,* as from S_1 to S_3, indicates a *decrease* in supply: Producers offer less output at each price.

determinants of supply
Factors other than *price* that determine the quantities supplied of a *good* or *service.* Also referred to as "supply shifters" because changes in the determinants of supply will cause the *supply curve* to shift either right or left.

Changes in Supply

Let's consider how changes in each of the determinants affect supply. The key idea is that costs are a major factor underlying supply curves; anything that affects costs usually shifts the supply curve.

Resource Prices The prices of the resources used in the production process help determine a firm's costs of production. Higher *resource* prices raise production costs and, assuming a particular product price, squeeze profits. That reduction in profits reduces firms' incentive to supply output at each product price. For example, an increase in the price of sand, crushed rock, or Portland cement will increase the cost of producing concrete and reduce its supply.

In contrast, lower *resource* prices reduce production costs and increase profits. So when resource prices fall, firms supply greater output at each product price. For example, a decrease in the price of iron ore will decrease the price of steel.

Technology   Improvements in technology (techniques of production) enable firms to produce units of output with fewer resources. Because resources are costly, using fewer of them lowers production costs and increases supply. Example: Technological advances in producing computer monitors have greatly reduced their cost. Thus, manufacturers now offer more monitors than previously at the various prices; the supply of monitors has increased.

Taxes and Subsidies   Businesses treat most taxes as costs. An increase in sales or property taxes will increase production costs and reduce supply. In contrast, subsidies are "taxes in reverse." If the government subsidizes the production of a good, the subsidy in effect lowers the producers' costs and increases supply.

Prices of Other Goods   Firms that produce a particular product, say soccer balls, can sometimes use their plant and equipment to produce alternative goods, say basketballs or volleyballs. If the prices of those other goods increase, soccer ball producers may switch production to those other goods in order to increase profits. This *substitution in production* would decrease the supply of soccer balls. Alternatively, when the prices of basketballs and volleyballs decline relative to the price of soccer balls, producers of those goods may decide to produce more soccer balls instead.

Producer Expectations   Changes in expectations about the future price of a product may affect the producer's current willingness to supply that product. Farmers anticipating a higher wheat price in the future might withhold some of their current wheat harvest from the market, thereby causing a decrease in the current supply of wheat. In contrast, in many manufacturing industries, the expectation that selling prices will increase in a few months may induce firms to add another shift of workers or to expand their production facilities, causing current supply to increase.

Number of Sellers   Other things equal, the larger the number of suppliers, the greater the market supply. As more firms enter an industry, the supply curve shifts to the right. Conversely, the smaller the number of firms in the industry, the less the market supply. As firms leave an industry, the supply curve shifts to the left. Example: Before Uber, Lyft, and other ride-sharing apps, cities restricted the number of taxi licenses, thereby restricting the number of drivers who could legally provide rides. When Uber and other ride-sharing services made their debut, millions of additional drivers and their cars became available worldwide, massively increasing the supply of rides.

Table 3.2 is a checklist of the determinants of supply, along with additional illustrations.

TABLE 3.2
Determinants of Supply: Factors That Shift the Supply Curve

Determinant	Examples
Change in resource prices	A decrease in the price of microchips increases the supply of computers; an increase in the price of crude oil reduces the supply of gasoline.
Change in technology	The development of lower-cost space-launch technology increases the supply of satellite broadband; improvements in artificial intelligence increase the supply of customer-service chatbots.
Changes in taxes or subsidies	An increase in the excise tax on cigarettes reduces the supply of cigarettes; a decline in subsidies to state universities reduces the supply of higher education; tax credits (subsidies) for child care increase the number of daycare centers; a tax on indoor tanning reduces the number of tanning salons.
Change in prices of other goods	An increase in the price of cucumbers decreases the supply of watermelons; an increase in the price of alcohol-based hand sanitizers causes a decrease in the supply of gin.
Change in producer expectations	An expectation of a substantial rise in future lumber prices decreases the supply of logs today; the belief that gasoline prices will fall next year increases the supply of oil this year.
Change in number of suppliers	An increase in the number of tattoo parlors increases the supply of tattoos; the formation of women's professional basketball leagues increases the supply of women's professional basketball games.

Changes in Quantity Supplied

The difference between a change in supply and a change in quantity supplied parallels the difference between a change in demand and a change in quantity demanded. Because supply is a schedule or curve, a **change in supply** means a change in the schedule and a shift of the curve. An increase in supply shifts the curve to the right; a decrease in supply shifts it to the left. The cause of a change in supply is a change in one or more of the determinants of supply.

In contrast, a **change in quantity supplied** is a movement from one point to another along a fixed supply curve. The cause of this movement is a change in the price of the specific product being considered.

Consider supply curve S_1 in Figure 3.5. A decline in the price of gasoline from \$4 to \$3 decreases the quantity of gasoline supplied per week from 10,000 to 7,000 gallons. This movement from point *b* to point *a* along S_1 is a change in quantity supplied, not a change in supply. Supply is the full schedule of prices and quantities shown, and this schedule does not change when the price of gasoline changes.

> **change in supply** A movement of an entire *supply curve* (or of the numerical entries in a schedule) such that the *quantity supplied* changes at every particular *price;* caused by a change in one or more of the *determinants of supply.*

> **change in quantity supplied** A change in the *quantity supplied* of a product along a fixed *supply curve* (or within a fixed supply schedule) as a result of a change in the product's *price.*

Market Equilibrium

With our understanding of demand and supply, we can now show how the decisions of buyers of gasoline and sellers of gasoline interact to determine the equilibrium price and quantity of gasoline. In the table in Figure 3.6, columns 1 and 2 repeat the market supply of gasoline (from the table in Figure 3.5), and columns 2 and 3 repeat the market demand for gasoline (from the table in Figure 3.3). We assume this is a competitive market so that neither buyers nor sellers can unilaterally influence the price.

> **\>\> LO3.4** Explain how supply and demand interact to determine market equilibrium.

Equilibrium Price and Quantity

The **equilibrium price** (or *market-clearing price*) is the price where the intentions of buyers and sellers match. It is the price where quantity demanded equals quantity supplied. The table in Figure 3.6 reveals that at \$3, *and only at that price,* the number of gallons of gasoline that sellers wish to sell (7,000) is identical to the number of gallons of gasoline that consumers want to buy (also 7,000). At \$3 and 7,000 gallons of gasoline, there is neither a shortage nor a surplus of gasoline. So 7,000 gallons of gasoline is the **equilibrium quantity:** the quantity at which the intentions of buyers and sellers match, so that the quantity demanded equals quantity supplied.

Graphically, the equilibrium price is indicated by the intersection of the supply curve and the demand curve in **Figure 3.6 (Key Graph).** (The horizontal axis now measures both quantity demanded and quantity supplied.) With neither a shortage nor a surplus at \$3 per gallon, the market is *in equilibrium,* meaning "in balance" or "at rest."

Competition among buyers and among sellers drives the price to the equilibrium price; once there, it will remain there unless it is subsequently disturbed by changes in demand or supply (shifts of the curves).

To better understand the equilibrium price, let's consider other prices.

- **At any above-equilibrium price, quantity supplied exceeds quantity demanded.** For example, at \$4, sellers will offer 10,000 gallons of gasoline, but buyers will purchase only 4,000. The \$4 price encourages sellers to offer lots of gasoline, but discourages many consumers from buying it. The result is a **surplus** (or *excess supply*) of 6,000 gallons that will go unsold.

- **Surpluses drive prices down.** Even if the \$4 price existed temporarily, it could not persist. Competition among the sellers would prompt them to lower the price to encourage buyers to take the surplus off their hands. As the price fell, the incentive for suppliers to produce

> **equilibrium price** The *price* in a competitive market at which the *quantity demanded* and the *quantity supplied* are equal, there is neither a shortage nor a surplus, and there is no tendency for price to rise or fall.

> **equilibrium quantity** (1) The quantity at which the intentions of buyers and sellers in a particular market match at a particular *price* such that the *quantity demanded* and the *quantity supplied* are equal; (2) the profit-maximizing output of a *firm.*

> **surplus** The amount by which the *quantity supplied* of a product exceeds the *quantity demanded* at a specific (above-equilibrium) *price.*

.‖‖ KEY GRAPH

FIGURE 3.6 Equilibrium price and quantity.

The intersection of the downsloping demand curve *D* and the upsloping supply curve *S* indicates the equilibrium price and quantity, here $3 and 7,000 gallons of gasoline. The shortages of gasoline at below-equilibrium prices (for example, 7,000 gallons at $2) push price up. The rising prices increase the quantity supplied and reduce the quantity demanded until equilibrium is achieved. The surpluses caused by above-equilibrium prices (for example, 6,000 gallons at $4) push price down. As price drops, the quantity demanded rises and the quantity supplied falls until equilibrium is established. At the equilibrium price and quantity, there are neither shortages nor surpluses of gasoline and, consequently, no pressure for prices to rise or fall.

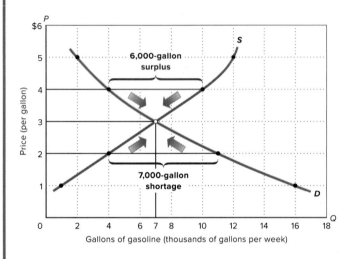

Market Supply of and Demand for Gasoline			
(1) Total Quantity Supplied per Week	(2) Price per Gallon	(3) Total Quantity Demanded per Week	(4) Surplus (+) or Shortage (−)*
12,000	$5	2,000	+10,000 ↓
10,000	4	4,000	+6,000 ↓
7,000	3	7,000	0
4,000	2	11,000	−7,000 ↑
1,000	1	16,000	−15,000 ↑

*Arrows indicate the effect on price.

QUICK QUIZ FOR FIGURE 3.6

1. **Demand curve *D* is downsloping because:**
   a. producers offer less of a product for sale as the price of the product falls.
   b. lower prices of a product create income and substitution effects that lead consumers to purchase more of it.
   c. the larger the number of buyers in a market, the lower the product price.
   d. price and quantity demanded are directly (positively) related.

2. **Supply curve *S*:**
   a. reflects an inverse (negative) relationship between price and quantity supplied.
   b. reflects a direct (positive) relationship between price and quantity supplied.

   c. depicts the collective behavior of buyers in this market.
   d. shows that producers will offer more of a product for sale at a low product price than at a high product price.

3. **At the $3 price:**
   a. quantity supplied exceeds quantity demanded.
   b. quantity demanded exceeds quantity supplied.
   c. the product is abundant and a surplus exists.
   d. there is no pressure on price to rise or fall.

4. **At price $5 in this market:**
   a. there will be a shortage of 10,000 units.
   b. there will be a surplus of 10,000 units.
   c. quantity demanded will be 12,000 units.
   d. quantity demanded will equal quantity supplied.

Answers: 1. b; 2. b; 3. d; 4. b.

---

gasoline would decline and consumers' incentive to buy gasoline would increase. As Figure 3.6 shows, the market will move to its equilibrium at $3.

- **At any below-equilibrium price, quantity demanded exceeds quantity supplied.** Consider a $2 price, for example. We see both from column 2 of the table and from the demand curve in Figure 3.6 that quantity demanded exceeds quantity supplied at that price. The result is a **shortage** (or *excess demand*) of 7,000 gallons of gasoline.

- **Shortages drive prices up.** The $2 price cannot persist because many consumers who want to buy gasoline at this price will not obtain it. They will express a willingness to pay more than $2 to get a gallon of gasoline and competition among these buyers will drive up the price, eventually to the $3 equilibrium level.

Unless disrupted by changes in supply or demand, the $3 equilibrium price of gasoline will prevail indefinitely.

shortage The amount by which the *quantity demanded* of a product exceeds the *quantity supplied* at a particular (below-equilibrium) *price*.

CONSIDER THIS . . .

Emergent Equilibria

Market equilibrium is a surprising phenomenon. Buyers' demand curves show a *negative* relationship between price and quantity, while sellers' supply curves show a *positive* relationship. Given that contradiction, you would never expect the interaction of demand and supply to lead to the perfectly synchronized outcome of quantity supplied exactly equaling quantity demanded.

But that is precisely what happens billions of times per day in markets all over the world. Market equilibrium and market rationing emerge spontaneously from the interactions of buyers and sellers who are simply pursuing their own interests and who are not in any way attempting to coordinate.

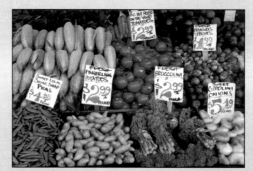
Lee Prince/Shutterstock

Adam Smith tried to explain this miraculous result as the work of an "invisible hand" that guided people's interactions toward a coordinated, socially beneficial outcome.

Nowadays, some economists classify market equilibrium as an "emergent property," or a behavior demonstrated by an entire system that is not found in any of its constituent parts. In the same way that a human brain as a whole is capable of consciousness but its individual neurons are not, so too markets synchronize the actions of individual buyers and sellers without any of them intending to harmonize their activities. Market equilibrium emerges, as if by magic, from a stew of uncoordinated individual intentions.

Rationing Function of Prices

The *rationing function of prices* refers to the ability of the forces of supply and demand to establish a price at which selling and buying decisions are consistent. In our example, the equilibrium price of $3 clears the market, leaving no burdensome surplus for sellers and no inconvenient shortage for buyers. And it is the combination of freely made individual decisions that sets this market-clearing price. In effect, the market outcome says that all buyers who are willing and able to pay $3 for a gallon of gasoline will obtain it; all buyers who cannot or will not pay $3 will go without gasoline. Similarly, all producers who are willing and able to offer gasoline for sale at $3 a gallon will sell it; all producers who cannot or will not sell for $3 per gallon will not sell their product.

Efficient Allocation

A competitive market not only rations goods to consumers but also allocates society's resources efficiently to the particular product. Competition among gasoline producers forces them to use the best technology and right mix of productive resources. If they didn't, their costs would be too high relative to the market price, and they would be unprofitable. The result is **productive efficiency:** the production of any particular good in the least costly way.

When society produces gasoline at the lowest achievable per-unit cost, it is expending the least-valued combination of resources to produce that product and therefore is making available more-valued resources to produce other desired goods. Suppose society has only $100 worth of resources available. If it can produce a gallon of gasoline for $3, then it will have $97 remaining to produce other goods. This situation is clearly better than producing the gasoline for $5 and having only $95 available for the alternative uses.

Competitive markets also produce **allocative efficiency:** the *particular mix* of goods and services most highly valued by society (minimum-cost production assumed). For example, society wants engineers with suitable backgrounds working on improving the gasoline supply and reducing its environmental impact, not helping to improve cupcake recipes. It wants diamonds to be used for jewelry, not crushed up and used as an additive to give concrete more sparkle. It wants streaming online music, not cassette players, compact discs, or phonographs. Moreover, society does not want to devote all its resources to gasoline, diamonds, and streaming music. It wants to assign resources to other uses, too, like medical research and professional sports leagues. Competitive markets make those assignments in an allocatively efficient manner.

productive efficiency The production of a *good* in the least costly way; occurs when production takes place at the output level at which per-unit production costs are minimized.

allocative efficiency The apportionment of resources among *firms* and industries to obtain the production of the products most wanted by society (consumers); the output of each product at which its *marginal cost* and *marginal benefit* are equal, and at which the sum of *consumer surplus* and *producer surplus* is maximized.

> ▶ In competitive markets, prices adjust to the equilibrium level at which quantity demanded equals quantity supplied.
>
> ▶ The equilibrium price and quantity are those indicated by the intersection of the supply and demand curves for any product or resource.

> ▶ The market equilibrium generates both productive efficiency (lowest cost production) as well as allocative efficiency (producing the right amount of the product relative to other products).

Changes in Supply, Demand, and Equilibrium

>> LO3.5 Explain how changes in supply and demand affect equilibrium prices and quantities.

What effects do changes in supply and demand have on equilibrium price and quantity?

Changes in Demand

Suppose that the supply of some good (for example, health care) is constant and demand increases, as shown in Figure 3.7a. As a result, the new intersection of the supply and demand curves is at higher values on both the price and the quantity axes. Clearly, an increase in demand raises both equilibrium price and equilibrium quantity. Conversely, a decrease in demand such as that shown in Figure 3.7b reduces both equilibrium price and equilibrium quantity. (The value of

FIGURE 3.7 **Changes in demand and supply and the effects on price and quantity.**

The increase in demand from D_1 to D_2 in (a) increases both equilibrium price and equilibrium quantity. The decrease in demand from D_3 to D_4 in (b) decreases both equilibrium price and equilibrium quantity. The increase in supply from S_1 to S_2 in (c) decreases equilibrium price and increases equilibrium quantity. The decline in supply from S_3 to S_4 in (d) increases equilibrium price and decreases equilibrium quantity. The boxes in the top right corners summarize the respective changes and outcomes. The upward arrows in the boxes signify increases in equilibrium price (*P*) and equilibrium quantity (*Q*); the downward arrows signify decreases in these items.

(a)
Increase in demand

(b)
Decrease in demand

(c)
Increase in supply

(d)
Decrease in supply

graphical analysis is now apparent: We need not fumble with columns of figures to determine the outcomes; we need only compare the new and the old points of intersection on the graph.)

Changes in Supply

What happens if the demand for some good (for example, automobiles) is constant but supply increases, as in Figure 3.7c? The new intersection of supply and demand is located at a lower equilibrium price but at a higher equilibrium quantity. An increase in supply reduces equilibrium price but increases equilibrium quantity. In contrast, if supply decreases, as in Figure 3.7d, equilibrium price rises while equilibrium quantity declines.

Complex Cases

When both supply and demand change, the final effect is a combination of the individual effects.

Supply Increase; Demand Decrease What effect will a supply increase and a demand decrease for some good (for example, apples) have on equilibrium price? Both changes decrease price, so the net result is a price drop greater than that resulting from either change alone.

What happens to equilibrium quantity? Here the effects of the changes in supply and demand are opposed: The increase in supply increases equilibrium quantity, but the decrease in demand reduces it. The direction of the change in equilibrium quantity depends on the relative sizes of the changes in supply and demand. If the increase in supply is larger than the decrease in demand, the equilibrium quantity will increase. But if the decrease in demand is greater than the increase in supply, the equilibrium quantity will decrease.

Supply Decrease; Demand Increase A decrease in supply and an increase in demand for some good (for example, gasoline) both increase price. Their combined effect is an increase in equilibrium price greater than that caused by either change separately. But their effect on the equilibrium quantity is indeterminate and depends on the relative sizes of the changes in supply and demand. If the decrease in supply is larger than the increase in demand, the equilibrium quantity will decrease. In contrast, if the increase in demand is greater than the decrease in supply, the equilibrium quantity will increase.

Supply Increase; Demand Increase What if supply and demand both increase for some good (for example, smartphones)? A supply increase drops equilibrium price, while a demand increase boosts it. If the increase in supply is greater than the increase in demand, the equilibrium price will fall. If the opposite holds, the equilibrium price will rise.

The effect on equilibrium quantity is certain: The increases in supply and demand both raise the equilibrium quantity. Therefore, the equilibrium quantity will increase by an amount greater than that caused by either change alone.

Supply Decrease; Demand Decrease What about decreases in both supply and demand for some good (for example, new homes)? If the decrease in supply is greater than the decrease in demand, equilibrium price will rise. If the reverse is true, equilibrium price will fall. Because the decreases in supply and demand each reduce equilibrium quantity, we can be sure that equilibrium quantity will fall.

Table 3.3 summarizes these four cases. To understand them fully, you should draw supply and demand diagrams for each case to confirm the effects listed in this table.

	Change in Supply	Change in Demand	Effect on Equilibrium Price	Effect on Equilibrium Quantity
1	Increase	Decrease	Decrease	Indeterminate
2	Decrease	Increase	Increase	Indeterminate
3	Increase	Increase	Indeterminate	Increase
4	Decrease	Decrease	Indeterminate	Decrease

TABLE 3.3
Effects of Changes in Both Supply and Demand

GLOBAL PERSPECTIVE 3.1

AVERAGE PRICE OF A LOAF OF WHITE BREAD, SELECTED NATIONS, 2020

The market equilibrium price of a 500 gram (1.1 pound) loaf of white bread differs substantially across countries, reflecting local differences in supply and demand, as well as government interventions like subsidies and price ceilings. Foreign prices were converted to U.S. dollars using current exchange rates.

Source: Numbeo, www.numbeo.com.

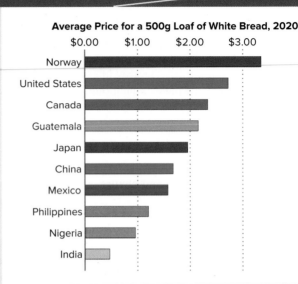

Average Price for a 500g Loaf of White Bread, 2020

Norway, United States, Canada, Guatemala, Japan, China, Mexico, Philippines, Nigeria, India

CONSIDER THIS . . .

Salsa and Coffee Beans

If you forget the other-things-equal assumption, you can encounter situations that *seem* to be in conflict with the laws of demand and supply. For example, suppose salsa manufacturers sell 1 million bottles of salsa at $4 a bottle in one year; 2 million bottles at $5 in the next year; and 3 million at $6 in the year thereafter. Price and quantity purchased vary directly, and these data seem to be at odds with the law of demand.

But there is no conflict here; the data do not refute the law of demand. The catch is that the law of demand's other-things-equal assumption has been violated over the three years in the example. Specifically, because of changing tastes and rising incomes, the demand for salsa has increased sharply, as in

Nancy R. Cohen/Photodisc/
Getty Images

Figure 3.7a. The result is higher prices *and* larger quantities purchased.

Another example: The price of coffee beans occasionally shoots upward at the same time that the quantity of coffee beans harvested declines. These events seemingly contradict the direct relationship between price and quantity denoted by supply. The catch again is that the other-things-equal assumption underlying the upsloping supply curve is violated. Poor coffee harvests decrease supply, as in Figure 3.7d, increasing the equilibrium price of coffee and reducing the equilibrium quantity.

The laws of demand and supply are not refuted by observations of price and quantity made over periods of time in which either demand or supply curves shift.

Special cases arise when a decrease in demand and a decrease in supply, or an increase in demand and an increase in supply, exactly cancel out. In both cases, the net effect on equilibrium price will be zero; price will not change.

Global Perspective 3.1 shows that the price of a standard loaf of white bread varies considerably from country to country, reflecting substantial differences in local demand and supply.

Application: Government-Set Prices

>>**LO3.6** Define government-set prices and explain how they can cause surpluses and shortages.

Prices in most markets are free to rise or fall to their equilibrium levels, no matter how high or low those levels might be. However, government sometimes concludes that supply and demand will produce prices that are unfairly high for buyers or unfairly low for sellers. So government may place legal limits on how high or low a price may go. Is that a good idea?

Price Ceilings on Gasoline

A **price ceiling** sets the maximum legal price a seller may charge for a product or service. A price at or below the ceiling is legal; a price above it is not. The rationale for establishing price ceilings (or *ceiling prices*) on specific products is that they purportedly enable consumers to obtain some "essential" good or service that they could not afford at the equilibrium price. Examples are rent controls and usury laws, which specify maximum "prices" for rent and interest rates, respectively.

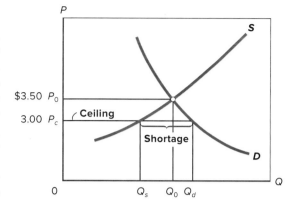

FIGURE 3.8
A price ceiling.

A price ceiling is a maximum legal price such as P_c. When the ceiling price is below the equilibrium price, a persistent product shortage results. Here that shortage is shown by the horizontal distance between Q_d and Q_s.

Graphical Analysis We can show the effects of price ceilings graphically. Suppose that rapidly rising world income boosts sales of automobiles and shifts the demand for gasoline to the right so that the market equilibrium price reaches $3.50 per gallon, shown as P_0 in Figure 3.8. The rapidly rising price of gasoline greatly burdens low- and moderate-income households, which pressure government to "do something." To keep gasoline prices down, the government imposes a ceiling price P_c of $3 per gallon. To affect the market, a price ceiling must be below the equilibrium price. A ceiling price of $4, for example, would have had no effect on the price of gasoline in the current situation.

What are the effects of this $3 ceiling price? The rationing ability of the free market is rendered ineffective. Because the ceiling price P_c is below the market-clearing price P_0, there is a lasting shortage of gasoline. The quantity of gasoline demanded at P_c is Q_d and the quantity supplied is only Q_s; a persistent shortage of amount $Q_d - Q_s$ occurs.

The price ceiling P_c prevents the usual market adjustment in which competition among buyers bids up price, inducing more production and rationing some buyers out of the market. That process would normally continue until the shortage disappeared at the equilibrium price and quantity, P_0 and Q_0.

By preventing these market adjustments from occurring, the price ceiling creates two related problems.

Rationing Problem How will the available supply Q_s be apportioned among buyers who want the greater amount Q_d? Should gasoline be distributed on a first-come, first-served basis—that is, to those willing and able to get in line the soonest or stay in line the longest? Or should gas stations decide how to distribute it? Because an unregulated shortage does not lead to an equitable distribution of gasoline, the government must establish some formal system for rationing it to consumers. One option is to issue ration coupons, which authorize bearers to purchase a fixed amount of gasoline per month. The rationing system might entail first the printing of coupons that permit the purchase of a certain amount of gasoline and then the equal distribution of the coupons so that every household receives the same number of coupons.

Black Markets Ration coupons will not prevent a second problem from arising. The demand curve in Figure 3.8 reveals that many buyers are willing to pay more than the ceiling price P_c. And, of course, it is more profitable for gas stations to sell at prices above the ceiling. Thus, despite the laws imposed by the price controls, *black markets* arise in which gasoline is illegally bought and sold at prices above the legal limits. Counterfeiting of ration coupons will also be a problem. And since the price of gasoline is now "set by the government," the government may face political pressure to set the price even lower.

Rent Controls

About 200 cities in the United States, including New York City, Boston, and San Francisco, have at one time or another enacted **rent controls:** maximum rents established by law (or, more recently, maximum rent increases for existing tenants). Such laws are intended to protect low-income families from escalating rents and to make housing more affordable to the poor.

What have been the actual economic effects? On the demand side, the below-equilibrium rents attract a larger number of renters. Some are locals seeking to move into their own apartments after

price ceiling A legally established maximum *price* for a *good,* or *service.* Normally set at a price below the *equilibrium price.*

rent control A law that sets a maximum price on the rents that a landlord can legally charge tenants for renting an apartment or a house.

sharing housing with friends or family. Others are outsiders attracted into the area by the artificially lower rents. But a large problem occurs on the supply side. Price controls make it less attractive for landlords to offer housing on the rental market. Many owners may decide to get out of the rental business altogether, opting either to sell their rental units or convert them to condominiums (which are generally exempt from rent-control laws). And for those owners who choose to continue renting out property, low rents make it unprofitable for them to repair or renovate their rental units. (Rent controls are one cause of the many abandoned apartment buildings found in larger cities.) Also, insurance companies, pension funds, and other potential new investors in housing will find it more profitable to invest in office buildings, shopping malls, or motels, where rents are not controlled.

In brief, rent controls distort market signals and thus resources are misallocated: Too few resources are allocated to rental housing and too many to alternative uses. Ironically, although rent controls are often legislated to lessen the effects of perceived housing shortages, controls in fact are a primary cause of such shortages. For that reason, most American cities that have ever had rent control laws have either abandoned them or are currently in the process of dismantling or weakening them.

Price Floors on Wheat

price floor A legally established minimum *price* for a *good,* or service. Normally set at a price above the *equilibrium price.*

A **price floor** is a minimum price fixed by the government. A price at or above the price floor is legal; a price below it is not. Price floors above equilibrium prices are usually invoked when society feels that the market system has not provided a sufficient income for certain groups of resource suppliers or producers. Supported prices for agricultural products and minimum wage laws are two examples of price (or wage) floors. Let's look at the former.

Suppose that many farmers have extremely low incomes when the price of wheat is at its equilibrium value of $2 per bushel. The government decides to help out by establishing a legal price floor (or *price support*) of $3 per bushel.

What will be the effects? At any price above the equilibrium price, quantity supplied will exceed quantity demanded—that is, there will be a persistent excess supply or surplus of the product. Farmers will be willing to produce and offer for sale more than private buyers are willing to purchase. Like a price ceiling, a price floor disrupts the rationing ability of the free market.

Graphical Analysis Figure 3.9 illustrates the effect of a price floor graphically. Suppose that S and D are the supply and demand curves for wheat. Equilibrium price and quantity are P_0 and Q_0, respectively. If the government imposes a price floor of P_f, farmers will produce Q_s but private buyers will purchase only Q_d. The surplus is the excess of Q_s over Q_d.

The government may cope with the surplus resulting from a price floor in two ways:

- It can restrict supply (for example, by instituting acreage allotments by which farmers agree to take a certain amount of land out of production) or increase demand (for example, by researching new uses for the product involved). These actions may reduce the difference between the equilibrium price and the price floor and thereby reduce the size of the surplus.

- If these efforts are not successful, then the government must purchase the surplus output at the $3 price (thereby subsidizing farmers) and store or otherwise dispose of it.

FIGURE 3.9
A price floor.

A price floor is a minimum legal price such as P_f. When the price floor is above the equilibrium price, a persistent product surplus results. Here that surplus is shown by the horizontal distance between Q_s and Q_d.

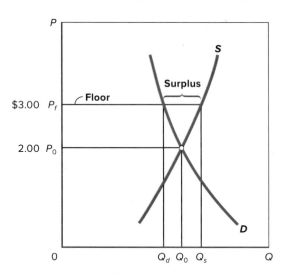

Additional Consequences Price floors such as P_f in Figure 3.9 not only disrupt prices' rationing ability but also distort resource allocation. Without the price floor, the $2 equilibrium price of wheat would cause financial losses and force high-cost wheat producers to plant other crops or abandon farming altogether. But the $3 price floor allows them to continue to grow wheat and remain farmers. So society devotes too many of its scarce resources to wheat production and too few to producing other, more valuable, goods and services. It fails to achieve allocative efficiency.

That's not all. Consumers of wheat-based products pay higher prices because

LAST WORD

Pandemic Prices

Dramatic Shifts in Supply and Demand Explain Much of the Economics of the COVID-19 Pandemic, Including Shortages of Consumer Goods and Vacillating Prices for Housing and Used Cars.

The COVID-19 pandemic that began in late 2019 became gravely serious in March 2020, when local and national governments began strict lockdowns that kept the large majority of workers and consumers at home except for occasional trips out for grocery shopping or crucial medical appointments. The strictest of the lockdowns ended in the United States within a few weeks, but the economic dislocations continued well into 2023 (when this edition went to print).

The most obvious economic effect of the pandemic, initially, was the empty store shelves caused by panic buying. Uncertain about how long the lockdowns might last, nervous consumers rushed to stores to stock up on items like toilet paper, hand sanitizer, and canned food that they feared would soon be in short supply. That massive increase in demand generated a self-fulfilling prophecy as stores could not restock quickly enough to keep up with the panic buying. Store managers were also reluctant to raise prices as demand increased, lest they be accused of price gouging. Thus, retail prices remained largely fixed (similar to a government-imposed price ceiling) as demand shifted massively rightward, with the result being huge shortages as quantity demanded far exceeded quantity supplied at the traditional, unchanged prices.

The supply and demand model also explains the brief crash in the stock market that was observed in the spring of 2020. Stocks are ownership shares in companies, and stocks derive their value from investors' expectations about how profitable companies will be in the future. When it became obvious that the pandemic would be severe, expectations about future profits fell, since it was assumed that the lockdowns and other anti-pandemic efforts would greatly hinder economic activity. As a result, the demand for stocks decreased precipitously, causing the equilibrium price of stocks to decline by nearly one-third. Fortunately, when it subsequently became clear that the pandemic would not be as awful as was initially feared, the demand for stocks rebounded and so did stock prices.

With both international and domestic travel heavily restricted around the world, hotel chains, rental car companies, and even individuals renting apartments on Airbnb experienced a dramatic decrease in the demand for their services. Things got so bad for rental car companies like Hertz and Avis that they began selling off their rental car fleets to try to generate enough cash to survive until the demand for rental cars rebounded. But when it did rebound, about a year later, the rental car companies were again caught by surprise, with their much reduced fleets being unable to keep up with renewed demand as consumers and businesspeople began traveling again in large numbers. The result of robust demand meeting limited supply was much higher rental car prices.

The decision of rental car companies to sell off their fleets in 2020 drove the price of used cars down nearly 20 percent that spring

F Armstrong Photography/Shutterstock

as the supply of used cars massively increased. But over the next 18 months, the price of used cars (as measured by the Manheim Index) nearly doubled because supply-chain disruptions caused a worldwide shortage of computer chips that in turn led to major carmakers like Honda and Ford being forced to dramatically decrease the production of new cars. Since new cars compete with used cars among car buyers, the reduced supply of new cars ended up increasing the demand for used cars, thereby causing their prices to soar. The reduced supply of new cars also drove up the price of new cars, but not nearly as dramatically since carmakers put pressure on new car dealers to resist price increases in order to avoid being accused of price gouging.

Working from home using Zoom and other digital tools became much more common during the pandemic, as many businesses sent workers home for the initial lockdowns and then kept them working remotely over the next two years as various virus mutations came and went. This newfound ability to work from home caused millions of formerly city-dwelling workers to temporarily and then in many cases permanently move to new locations, many of them suburban or rural. Their relocation increased the demand for housing in suburban and rural areas at the same time as their departure put downward pressure on housing prices in crowded urban areas.

The pandemic also witnessed widespread labor shortages due to unprecedentedly generous government unemployment benefits that delivered to tens of millions of workers a higher income than they would have earned if they had returned to work. Many of those workers chose to stay unemployed (so as to collect the high unemployment benefits) even when jobs were available. That decrease in labor supply drove up the equilibrium wage. But not all firms could afford to pay the higher equilibrium wage. The result was widespread labor shortages in industries such as transportation, hospitality, and child care services.

of the price floor. Taxpayers pay higher taxes to finance the government's purchase of the surplus. And the price floor may cause environmental damage by encouraging wheat farmers to bring hilly, erosion-prone "marginal land" into production.

With all price ceilings and price floors, good intentions lead to bad economic outcomes. Government-controlled prices cause shortages or surpluses, distort resource allocation, and produce negative side effects.

**QUICK REVIEW
3.4**

▶ An increase in demand increases equilibrium price and quantity; a decrease in demand decreases equilibrium price and quantity.

▶ An increase in supply reduces equilibrium price but increases equilibrium quantity; a decrease in supply increases equilibrium price but reduces equilibrium quantity.

▶ Over time, equilibrium price and quantity may change in directions that seem at odds with the laws of demand and supply because the other-things-equal assumption is violated.

▶ Government-controlled prices in the form of ceilings and floors stifle the rationing function of prices, distort resource allocations, and cause negative side effects.

Summary

LO3.1 Characterize and give examples of markets.

Markets bring buyers and sellers together. Some markets are local, others international. Some have physical locations, while others are online. In highly competitive markets, large numbers of buyers and sellers come together to buy and sell standardized products. All such markets involve demand, supply, price, and quantity, with price being "discovered" through the interacting decisions of buyers and sellers.

LO3.2 Describe *demand* and explain how it can change.

Demand is a schedule or curve representing buyers' willingness and ability to purchase a particular product at each of various prices in a specific period. The law of demand states that consumers will buy more of a product at a low price than at a high price. So, other things equal, the relationship between price and quantity demanded is negative or inverse; it graphs as a downward sloping curve.

Market demand curves are found by adding horizontally the demand curves of the many individual consumers in the market.

A change in demand is different from a change in quantity demanded.

A *change in demand* occurs when there is a change in one or more of the determinants of demand: consumer tastes; the number of buyers in the market; the money incomes of consumers; the prices of related goods; and consumer expectations. A change in demand will shift the market demand curve either right or left. A shift to the right is an increase in demand; a shift to the left is a decrease in demand.

A *change in quantity demanded* is a movement from one point to another point on a fixed demand curve caused by a change in a product's price, holding all other factors constant.

LO3.3 Describe *supply* and explain how it can change.

Supply is a schedule or curve showing the amounts of a product that producers are willing to offer in the market at each possible price during a specific period of time. The law of supply states that, other things equal, producers will offer more of a product at a high price than at a low price. Thus, the relationship between price and quantity supplied is positive or direct; it graphs as an upward sloping curve.

The market supply curve is the horizontal summation of the supply curves of the individual producers of the product.

A *change in supply* occurs when there is a change in one or more of the determinants of supply (resource prices, production techniques, taxes or subsidies, the prices of other goods, producer expectations, or the number of sellers in the market). A change in supply shifts a product's supply curve. A shift to the right is an increase in supply; a shift to the left is a decrease in supply.

In contrast, a change in the price of the product being considered causes a *change in the quantity supplied*, which is shown as a movement from one point to another point along a fixed supply curve.

LO3.4 Explain how supply and demand interact to determine market equilibrium.

The equilibrium price and quantity are established at the intersection of the supply and demand curves. The interaction of market demand and market supply adjusts the price to the point at which the quantities demanded and supplied are equal. This is the equilibrium price. The corresponding quantity is the equilibrium quantity.

The ability of market forces to synchronize selling and buying decisions to eliminate potential surpluses and shortages is known as the rationing function of prices. The equilibrium quantity in competitive markets reflects both productive efficiency (least-cost production) and allocative efficiency (producing the right amount of the product relative to other products).

LO3.5 Explain how changes in supply and demand affect equilibrium prices and quantities.

A change in either demand or supply changes the equilibrium price and quantity. Increases in demand raise both equilibrium price and equilibrium quantity; decreases in demand lower both equilibrium price and equilibrium quantity. Increases in supply lower equilibrium price and raise equilibrium quantity. Decreases in supply raise equilibrium price and lower equilibrium quantity.

Simultaneous changes in demand and supply affect equilibrium price and quantity in various ways, depending on their direction and relative magnitudes (see Table 3.3).

LO3.6 Define government-set prices and explain how they can cause surpluses and shortages.

A price ceiling is a maximum price set by government and is designed to help consumers. Effective price ceilings produce persistent product shortages, and if an equitable distribution of the product is sought, government must ration the product to consumers.

A price floor is a minimum price set by government and is designed to aid producers. Effective price floors lead to persistent product surpluses; the government must either purchase the product or eliminate the surplus by imposing restrictions on production or increasing private demand.

Legally fixed prices stifle the rationing function of prices and distort the allocation of resources.

Terms and Concepts

demand	substitute goods	change in quantity supplied
demand schedule	complementary goods	equilibrium price
law of demand	change in demand	equilibrium quantity
diminishing marginal utility	change in quantity demanded	surplus
income effect	supply	shortage
substitution effect	supply schedule	productive efficiency
demand curve	law of supply	allocative efficiency
determinants of demand	supply curve	price ceiling
normal good	determinants of supply	rent control
inferior good	change in supply	price floor

Discussion Questions

Mc Graw Hill connect

1. Explain the law of demand. Why does a demand curve slope downward? How is a market demand curve derived from individual demand curves? **LO3.2**
2. What are the determinants of demand? What happens to the demand curve when any of these determinants change? Distinguish between a change in demand and a movement along a fixed demand curve, noting the cause(s) of each. **LO3.2**
3. Suppose that Rhonda has a TikTok account. If all of her TikTok friends switch to Snapchat, in which direction will Rhonda's demand for TikTok shift? What will likely happen to Rhonda's demand for Snapchat? **LO3.2**
4. Explain the law of supply. Why does the supply curve slope upward? How is the market supply curve derived from the supply curves of individual producers? **LO3.3**
5. What are the determinants of supply? What happens to the supply curve when any of these determinants change? Distinguish between a change in supply and a change in the quantity supplied, noting the cause(s) of each. **LO3.3**
6. Between 2018 and 2021, an outbreak of African Swine Fever that spread to dozens of countries led to the slaughter of nearly one-quarter of all of the world's domesticated pigs. What impact would you expect that to have had on the supply of pig leather as well as on other pork byproducts such as drumheads, violin strings, and pig-bristle paint brushes? Explain. **LO3.5**
7. For each stock in the stock market, the number of shares sold daily equals the number of shares purchased. That is, the quantity of each firm's shares demanded equals the quantity supplied. Why, then, do the prices of stock shares change? **LO3.5**
8. What do economists mean when they say "Price floors and ceilings stifle the rationing function of prices and distort resource allocation"? **LO3.6**
9. **LAST WORD** What caused used car prices to fall near the start of the pandemic and then soar over the next two years? What government policy helped to generate labor shortages in several industries? Expectations about what in particular caused the stock market to crash near the start of the pandemic?

Review Questions

Mc Graw Hill connect

1. What effect will each of the following have on the demand for small cars such as the Mini Cooper and Fiat 500? **LO3.2**
   a. Small cars become more fashionable.
   b. The price of large cars rises (with the price of small cars remaining the same).
   c. Income declines and small cars are an inferior good.
   d. Consumers anticipate that the price of small cars will decrease substantially in the near future.
   e. The price of gasoline substantially drops.
2. True or False: A "change in quantity demanded" is a shift of the entire demand curve to the right or to the left. **LO3.2**
3. Yogi Berra was once asked about a popular New York restaurant. He said, "Nobody ever goes there anymore—it's too crowded." All joking aside, he was referring to: **LO3.2**
   a. a shortage.
   b. a network effect.
   c. a surplus.
   d. a congestion effect.

4. What effect will each of the following have on the supply of auto tires? **LO3.3**
   a. A technological advance in the methods of producing tires
   b. A decline in the number of firms in the tire industry
   c. An increase in the price of rubber used in the production of tires
   d. The expectation that the equilibrium price of auto tires will be lower in the future than it is now
   e. A decline in the price of the large tires used for semi trucks and earth-hauling rigs (with no change in the price of auto tires)
   f. The levying of a per-unit tax on each auto tire sold
   g. The granting of a 50-cent-per-unit subsidy for each auto tire produced

5. "In the corn market, demand often exceeds supply, and supply sometimes exceeds demand." "The price of corn rises and falls in response to changes in supply and demand." In which of these two statements are the terms "supply" and "demand" used correctly? Explain. **LO3.4**

6. Suppose that in the market for computer memory chips, the equilibrium price is $50 per chip. If the current price is $55 per chip, then there will be a(an) _____ of memory chips. **LO3.4**
   a. shortage
   b. surplus
   c. equilibrium quantity
   d. none of the above

7. Critically evaluate: "In comparing the two equilibrium positions in Figure 3.7b, I note that a smaller amount is actually demanded at a lower price. This observation refutes the law of demand." **LO3.5**

8. Label each of the following scenarios with the set of symbols that best indicates the price change and quantity change that occur in each scenario. In some scenarios, it may not be possible from the information given to determine the direction of a particular price change or a particular quantity change. We will symbolize those cases as, respectively, "P?" and "Q?" The four possible combinations of price and quantity changes are: **LO3.5**
   P↓Q?   P? Q↓
   P↑Q?   P? Q↑

   a. On a hot day, both the demand for lemonade and the supply of lemonade increase.
   b. On a cold day, both the demand for ice cream and the supply of ice cream decrease.
   c. When Hawaii's Mt. Kilauea erupts violently, tourists' demand for sightseeing flights increases, but the supply of pilots willing to provide these dangerous flights decreases.
   d. In a hot area of Arizona where a lot of electricity is generated with wind turbines, the demand for electricity falls on windy days as people switch off their air conditioners and enjoy the breeze. But at the same time, the amount of electricity supplied increases as the wind turbines spin faster.

9. Suppose the total demand for wheat and the total supply of wheat per month in the Kansas City grain market are as shown in the following table. Suppose that the government establishes a price ceiling of $3.70 for wheat. What might prompt the government to establish this price ceiling? Explain carefully the main effects. Demonstrate your answer graphically. Next, suppose that the government establishes a price floor of $4.60 for wheat. What will be the main effects of this price floor? Demonstrate your answer graphically. **LO3.6**

Thousands of Bushels Demanded	Price per Bushel	Thousands of Bushels Supplied
85	$3.40	72
80	3.70	73
75	4.00	75
70	4.30	77
65	4.60	79
60	4.90	81

10. A price ceiling will result in a shortage only if the ceiling price is _____ the equilibrium price. **LO3.6**
    a. less than
    b. equal to
    c. greater than

Problems

1. Suppose there are three buyers of candy in a market: Tex, Dex, and Rex. The market demand and the individual demands of Tex, Dex, and Rex are shown in the following table. **LO3.2**
   a. Fill in the missing values.
   b. Which buyer demands the least at a price of $5? The most at a price of $7?
   c. Which buyer's quantity demanded increases the most when the price decreases from $7 to $6?
   d. In which direction would the market demand curve shift if Tex withdrew from the market? What would happen to the market demand curve if Dex doubled his purchases at each possible price?
   e. Suppose that at a price of $6, the total quantity demanded increases from 19 to 38. Is this a "change in the quantity demanded" or a "change in demand"? Explain.

Price per Candy	Individual Quantities Demanded						Total Quantity Demanded
	Tex		Dex		Rex		
$8	3	+	1	+	0	=	____
7	8	+	2	+	____	=	12
6	____	+	3	+	4	=	19
5	17	+	____	+	6	=	27
4	23	+	5	+	8	=	____

2. The figure below shows the supply curve for tennis balls, S_1, for Drop Volley Tennis, a producer of tennis equipment. Use the figure and the table below to give your answers to the following questions. **LO3.3**

a. Use the figure to fill in the quantity supplied on supply curve S_1 for each price in the following table.

Price	S_1 Quantity Supplied	S_2 Quantity Supplied	Change in Quantity Supplied
$3	_____	4	_____
2	_____	2	_____
1	_____	0	_____

b. If production costs were to increase, the quantities supplied at each price would be as shown by the third column of the table ("S_2 Quantity Supplied"). Use those data to draw supply curve S_2 on the same graph as supply curve S_1.
c. In the fourth column of the table, enter the amount by which the quantity supplied at each price changes due to the increase in product costs. (Use positive numbers for increases and negative numbers for decreases.)
d. Did the increase in production costs cause a "decrease in supply" or a "decrease in quantity supplied"? Explain.

3. Refer to the following expanded table from review question 9. **LO3.4**
   a. What is the equilibrium price? At what price is there neither a shortage nor a surplus? Fill in the surplus-shortage column and use it to confirm your answers.
   b. Graph the demand for wheat and the supply of wheat. Be sure to label the axes of your graph correctly. Label equilibrium price P and equilibrium quantity Q.
   c. How big is the surplus or shortage at $3.40? At $4.90? How big a surplus or shortage results if the price is 60 cents higher than the equilibrium price? 30 cents lower than the equilibrium price?

Thousands of Bushels Demanded	Price per Bushel	Thousands of Bushels Supplied	Surplus (+) or Shortage (−)
85	$3.40	72	_____
80	3.70	73	_____
75	4.00	75	_____
70	4.30	77	_____
65	4.60	79	_____
60	4.90	81	_____

4. How will each of the following changes in demand and/or supply affect equilibrium price and equilibrium quantity in a competitive market? That is, do price and quantity rise, fall, or remain unchanged, or are the answers indeterminate because they depend on the magnitudes of the shifts? **LO3.5**
   a. Supply decreases and demand is constant.
   b. Demand decreases and supply is constant.
   c. Supply increases and demand is constant.
   d. Demand increases and supply increases.
   e. Demand increases and supply is constant.
   f. Supply increases and demand decreases.
   g. Demand increases and supply decreases.
   h. Demand decreases and supply decreases.

5. Use two market diagrams to explain how an increase in state subsidies to public colleges might affect tuition and enrollments in both public and private colleges. **LO3.5**

6. **ADVANCED ANALYSIS** Assume that demand for a commodity is represented by the equation $P = 10 - .2Q_d$ and supply by the equation $P = 2 + .2Q_s$, where Q_d and Q_s are quantity demanded and quantity supplied, respectively, and P is price. Using the equilibrium condition $Q_s = Q_d$, solve the equations to determine equilibrium price and equilibrium quantity. **LO3.5**

7. Suppose that the demand and supply schedules for rental apartments in the city of Gotham are as given in the following table. **LO3.6**

Monthly Rent	Apartments Demanded	Apartments Supplied
$2,500	10,000	15,000
2,000	12,500	12,500
1,500	15,000	10,000
1,000	17,500	7,500
500	20,000	5,000

a. What is the market equilibrium rental price per month and the market equilibrium number of apartments demanded and supplied?
b. If the local government can enforce a rent-control law that sets the maximum monthly rent at $1,500, will there be a surplus or a shortage? Of how many units? How many units will actually be rented each month?
c. Suppose that a new government is elected that wants to keep out the poor. It declares that the minimum rent that landlords can charge is $2,500 per month. If the government can enforce that price floor, will there be a surplus or a shortage? Of how many units? And how many units will actually be rented each month?
d. Suppose that the government wishes to decrease the market equilibrium monthly rent by increasing the supply of housing. Assuming that demand remains unchanged, how many additional units of housing would the government need to supply to get the market equilibrium rental price to fall to $1,500 per month? To $1,000 per month? To $500 per month?

Additional Examples of Supply and Demand

LO3.7 Use supply-and-demand analysis to analyze specific real-world situations.

Supply-and-demand analysis is a powerful tool for understanding equilibrium prices and quantities. The information provided in this chapter is fully sufficient for moving forward in the book, but you may find that additional examples of supply and demand are helpful. This appendix provides several concrete illustrations of changes in supply and demand.

Changes in Supply and Demand

As Figure 3.7 demonstrates, changes in supply and demand cause changes in equilibrium price, quantity, or both. The following applications illustrate this fact in several real-world markets. The simplest situations are those in which either supply changes while demand remains constant or demand changes while supply remains constant. Let's consider a simple case first, before looking at more complex applications.

Lettuce

Every now and then, extreme weather severely reduces the size of some crop. Suppose, for example, that a severe freeze destroys a sizable portion of the lettuce crop. This unfortunate situation implies a significant decline in supply, which we represent as a leftward shift of the supply curve from S_1 to S_2 in Figure 1. At each price, consumers desire as much lettuce as before, so the freeze does not affect the demand for lettuce. That is, demand curve D_1 does not shift.

What are the consequences of the reduced supply of lettuce? As Figure 1 shows, the leftward shift of the supply curve disrupts the previous equilibrium in the lettuce market and

drives the equilibrium price upward from P_1 to P_2. Consumers respond to that price hike by reducing the quantity of lettuce demanded from Q_1 to Q_2. Equilibrium is restored at P_2 and Q_2.

Consumers who are willing and able to pay price P_2 obtain lettuce; consumers unwilling or unable to pay that price do not. Some consumers continue to buy as much lettuce as before, even at the higher price. Others buy some lettuce but not as much as before, and still others opt out of the market completely.

The latter two groups use the money they would have spent on lettuce to obtain other products—carrots, for example. (Because of our other-things-equal assumption, the prices of other products have not changed.)

Pink Salmon

Now let's see what happens when both supply and demand change at the same time. Several decades ago, people who caught salmon earned as much as $1 for each pound of pink salmon—the type of salmon most commonly used for canning. In Figure 2 that price is represented as P_1, at the intersection of supply curve S_1 and demand curve D_1. The corresponding quantity of pink salmon is shown as Q_1 pounds.

As time passed, supply and demand changed in the market for pink salmon. On the supply side, improved technology in the form of larger, more efficient fishing boats greatly increased the catch and lowered the cost of obtaining it. Also, high profits at price P_1 encouraged many new fishers to enter the industry. As a result of these changes, the supply of pink salmon greatly increased and the supply curve shifted to the right, as from S_1 to S_2 in Figure 2.

FIGURE 1 **The market for lettuce.**
The decrease in the supply of lettuce, shown here by the shift from S_1 to S_2, increases the equilibrium price of lettuce from P_1 to P_2 and reduces the equilibrium quantity from Q_1 to Q_2.

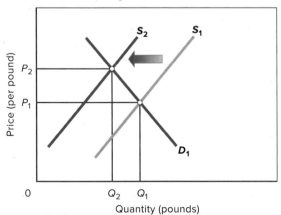

FIGURE 2 **The market for pink salmon.**
In the last several decades, the supply of pink salmon has increased and the demand for pink salmon has decreased. As a result, the price of pink salmon has declined, as from P_1 to P_2. Because supply has increased by more than demand has decreased, the equilibrium quantity of pink salmon has increased, as from Q_1 to Q_2.

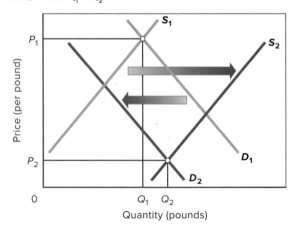

Over the same years, the demand for pink salmon declined, as represented by the leftward shift from D_1 to D_2 in Figure 2. That decrease was caused by increases in consumer income and reductions in the price of substitute products. As buyers' incomes rose, consumers shifted demand away from canned fish and toward higher-quality fresh or frozen fish, including more-valued chinook, sockeye, and coho salmon. Moreover, the emergence of fish farming, in which salmon are raised in ocean net pens, lowered the prices of these other species, thus reducing the demand for pink salmon.

The altered supply and demand reduced the price of pink salmon to as low as $0.10 per pound, as represented by the drop in price from P_1 to P_2 in Figure 2. Both the supply increase and the demand decrease helped reduce the equilibrium price. However, in this particular case, the equilibrium quantity of pink salmon increased, as represented by the move from Q_1 to Q_2. Both shifts reduced the equilibrium price, but equilibrium quantity increased because the increase in supply exceeded the decrease in demand.

Gasoline

The price of gasoline in the United States has increased rapidly several times during the past several years. For example, the average price of a gallon of gasoline rose from around $1.88 in April 2020 during the lowest point of the COVID-19 recession to $3.22 in July 2021. What caused this 71 percent increase in the price of gasoline? How would we graph this increase?

We begin in Figure 3 with the price of a gallon of gasoline at P_1, representing the $1.88 price. Simultaneous supply and demand factors disturbed this equilibrium. Supply uncertainties

FIGURE 3 The market for gasoline.

An increase in the demand for gasoline, as shown by the shift from D_1 to D_2, coupled with a decrease in supply, as shown by the shift from S_1 to S_2, boosts equilibrium price (here from P_1 to P_2). In this case, equilibrium quantity increases from Q_1 to Q_2 because the increase in demand outweighs the decrease in supply.

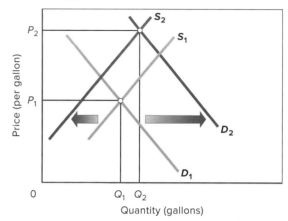

relating to Middle East politics and expanded demand for oil by fast-growing countries such as China pushed up the price of oil from just under $17 per barrel in April 2020 to a bit over $73 per barrel in July 2021. Oil is the main input for producing gasoline, so any sustained rise in its price boosts the per-unit cost of producing gasoline. Such increases in cost decrease the supply of gasoline, as represented by the leftward shift of the supply curve from S_1 to S_2 in Figure 3.

While the supply of gasoline declined between April 2020 and July 2021, the demand for gasoline increased, as depicted by the rightward shift of the demand curve from D_1 to D_2.

CONSIDER THIS . . .

Uber and Dynamic Pricing

The ride-sharing service known as Uber rose to prominence in 2013 by offering consumers an alternative to government-regulated taxi companies. Uber works via the Internet, matching people who need a ride with people who are willing to use their own vehicles to provide rides. Both parties can find each other easily and instantly via a smartphone app and Uber makes its money by taking a percentage of the fare.

Uber is innovative in many ways, including empowering anybody to become a paid driver, breaking up local taxi monopolies, and making it effortless to arrange a quick pickup. But Uber's most interesting feature is dynamic pricing, under which Uber sets equilibrium prices in real time, constantly adjusting fares so as to equalize quantity demanded and quality supplied. The result is extremely short waiting times for both riders and drivers as

SURGE PRICING ✕

Demand is off the charts! Rates have increased to get more Ubers on the road.

1.75x

TIMES THE NORMAL RATE

Uber Manila Tips

Uber will, for instance, set a substantially higher "surge price" in a given location if demand suddenly increases due to, say, a bunch of people leaving a concert all at once and wanting rides. The higher fare encourages more Uber drivers to converge on the area, thereby minimizing waiting times for both drivers and passengers.

The short wait times created by Uber's use of dynamic pricing stand in sharp contrast to taxi fares, which are fixed by law and therefore unable to adjust to ongoing changes in supply and demand. On days when demand is high relative to supply, taxi shortages arise. On days when demand is low relative to supply, drivers sit idle for long stretches of time. All of that inefficiency and inconvenience is eliminated by Uber's use of market equilibrium prices to equalize the quantity demanded of rides with the quantity supplied of rides.

Incomes in general were rising over this period because the U.S. economy was expanding out of the COVID-19 recession. Rising incomes increase the demand for all normal goods, including gasoline.

The combined decline in gasoline supply and increase in gasoline demand boosted the price of gasoline from $1.88 to $3.22, as represented by the rise from P_1 to P_2 in Figure 3. Because the demand increase outweighed the supply decrease, the equilibrium quantity expanded, from Q_1 to Q_2.

In other periods, the price of gasoline has *declined* as the demand for gasoline has increased. Test your understanding of the analysis by explaining how such a price decrease could occur.

Upward Sloping versus Vertical Supply Curves

As you already know, the typical good or service has an upward sloping supply curve because a higher market price causes producers to increase the quantity supplied. There are, however, some goods and services whose quantities supplied are fixed and totally unresponsive to changes in price. Examples include the amount of land in a given area, the number of seats in a stadium, and the limited part of the electromagnetic spectrum that is reserved for cellular telephone transmissions. These goods and services have vertical supply curves because the same fixed amount is available no matter what price is offered to suppliers.

Reactions to Demand Shifts

Markets react very differently to a shift in demand depending upon whether they have upward sloping or vertical supply curves.

Upward Sloping Supply Curves When a market has an upward sloping supply curve, any shift in demand will cause both the equilibrium price *and* the equilibrium quantity to adjust. As we saw in Figure 3.7(a), price and quantity both change.

Vertical Supply Curves When a market has a vertical supply curve, any shift in demand will cause only the equilibrium price to change; the equilibrium quantity remains the same because the quantity supplied is fixed and cannot adjust.

Consider Figure 4, in which the supply of land in San Francisco is fixed at quantity Q_0. If demand increases from D_1 to D_2, the movement from the initial equilibrium at point *a* to the final equilibrium at point *b* is accomplished solely by a rise in the equilibrium price from P_1 to P_2. Because the quantity of land is fixed, the increase in demand cannot cause any change in the equilibrium quantity supplied. The entire adjustment from the initial equilibrium to the final equilibrium has to come in the form of a higher equilibrium price.

This fact explains why real estate prices are so high in San Francisco and other major cities. With the quantity of land in fixed supply, any increase in the demand for land leads to an increase in the price of land.

FIGURE 4 **The market for land in San Francisco.**
Because the quantity of land in San Francisco is fixed at Q_0, the supply curve is vertical above Q_0 in order to indicate that the same quantity of land will be supplied no matter what the price is. As demand increases from D_1 to D_2, the equilibrium price rises from P_1 to P_2. Because the quantity of land is fixed at Q_0, the movement from equilibrium *a* to equilibrium *b* involves only a change in the equilibrium price; the equilibrium quantity remains at Q_0 due to land being in fixed supply.

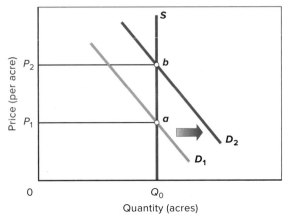

Preset Prices

In this chapter, we saw that an effective government-imposed price ceiling (legal maximum price) causes quantity demanded to exceed quantity supplied—a shortage. By contrast, an effective government-imposed price floor (legal minimum price) causes quantity supplied to exceed quantity demanded—a surplus.

We now want to establish that shortages and surpluses can occur in markets other than those in which government imposes price floors and ceilings. Such market imbalances happen when sellers set prices in advance of sales and those prices turn out to be below or above equilibrium prices. Consider the following two examples.

Olympic Figure Skating Finals

Tickets for the women's figure skating championship at the Olympics are among the world's "hottest tickets." The popularity of this event and the high incomes of buyers translate into tremendous ticket demand. The Olympic officials set the price for the tickets in advance. Invariably, the price, although high, is considerably below the equilibrium price that would equate quantity demanded and quantity supplied. A severe shortage of tickets therefore occurs in the *primary market*— that is, the market involving the official ticket office.

The shortage, in turn, creates a *secondary market* in which buyers bid for tickets held by initial purchasers rather than the original seller. Scalping tickets—selling them above the original ticket price—may be legal or illegal, depending on local laws.

Figure 5 shows how the shortage in the primary ticket market looks in terms of supply and demand analysis. Demand curve D represents the demand for tickets and supply curve S represents the supply of tickets. The supply curve is vertical because a fixed number of tickets are printed to match the

FIGURE 5 The market for tickets to the Olympic women's figure skating finals.

The demand curve D and supply curve S for the Olympic women's figure skating finals produce an equilibrium price that is above the P_1 price printed on the ticket. At price P_1 the quantity of tickets demanded, Q_2, greatly exceeds the quantity of tickets available, Q_1. The resulting shortage of ab (= Q_2 − Q_1) gives rise to a legal or illegal secondary market.

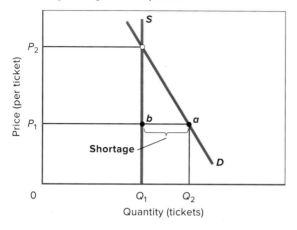

FIGURE 6 The market for tickets to the Olympic curling preliminaries.

The demand curve D and supply curve S for the Olympic curling preliminaries produce an equilibrium price below the P_1 price printed on the ticket. At price P_1 the quantity of tickets demanded is less than the quantity of tickets available. The resulting surplus of ba (= Q_1 − Q_2) means the event is not sold out.

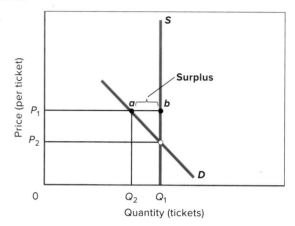

arena's capacity. At the printed ticket price of P_1, the quantity of tickets demanded, Q_2, exceeds the quantity supplied, Q_1. The result is a shortage of ab–the horizontal distance between Q_2 and Q_1 in the primary market.

Olympic Curling Preliminaries

Contrast the shortage of tickets for the women's figure skating finals at the Olympics to the surplus of tickets for one of the preliminary curling matches. For the uninitiated, curling is a sport in which participants slide a heavy round object called a "stone" down a lane painted on an ice rink toward a target while teammates called "sweepers" use brooms to alter the course of the stone.

Curling is a popular spectator sport in a few nations, including Canada, but it does not draw many fans in most countries. So the demand for tickets to most of the preliminary

curling events is not very strong. We demonstrate this weak demand as D in Figure 6. As in our previous example, the supply of tickets is fixed by the size of the arena and is shown as vertical line S.

We represent the printed ticket price as P_1 in Figure 6. In this case, the printed price is much higher than the equilibrium price of P_2. At the printed ticket price, quantity supplied is Q_1 and quantity demanded is Q_2. So a surplus of tickets of ba (= Q_1 − Q_2) occurs. No ticket scalping occurs and there are numerous empty seats. Only if the Olympic officials had priced the tickets at the lower price P_2 would the event have been a sellout. (Actually, Olympic officials try to adjust to demand realities for curling contests by holding them in smaller arenas and by charging less for tickets. Nevertheless, the stands are rarely full for the preliminary contests, which compete against final events in other winter Olympic sports.)

Appendix Summary

LO3.7 Use supply-and-demand analysis to analyze specific real-world situations.

A decrease in the supply of a product increases its equilibrium price and reduces its equilibrium quantity. In contrast, an increase in the demand for a product boosts both its equilibrium price and its equilibrium quantity.

Simultaneous changes in supply and demand affect equilibrium price and quantity in various ways, depending on the relative magnitudes of the changes in supply and demand. Equal increases in supply and demand, for example, leave equilibrium price unchanged.

Products (such as land) whose quantities supplied do not vary with price have vertical supply curves. For these products, any shift in demand will lead to a change in the equilibrium price but no change in the equilibrium quantity.

Sellers set prices of some items such as tickets in advance of the event. These items are sold in a primary market that involves the original sellers and buyers. If preset prices turn out to be below the equilibrium prices, shortages occur, and scalping in legal or illegal secondary markets arises. The prices in the secondary market then rise above the preset prices. In contrast, surpluses occur when the preset prices end up exceeding the equilibrium prices.

Appendix Discussion Questions

1. Why are shortages or surpluses more likely with preset prices (such as those on tickets) than with flexible prices (such as those on gasoline)? **LO3.7**
2. Most scalping laws make it illegal to sell—but not to buy—tickets at prices above those printed on the tickets. Assuming the existence of such laws, use supply-and-demand analysis to explain why the equilibrium ticket price in an illegal secondary market tends to be higher than in a legal secondary market. **LO3.7**
3. Go to the website of the Energy Information Administration, www.eia.gov, and follow the links to find the current retail price of gasoline. How does the current price of regular gasoline compare with the price a year ago? What must have happened to supply, demand, or both to explain the observed price change? **LO3.7**
4. Suppose the supply of apples sharply increases because of perfect weather conditions throughout the growing season. Assuming no

change in demand, explain the effect on the equilibrium price and quantity of apples. Explain why quantity demanded increases even though demand does not change. **LO3.7**
5. Assume the demand for lumber suddenly rises because of rapid growth in demand for new housing. Assume no change in supply. Why does the equilibrium price of lumber rise? What would happen if the price did not rise under the demand and supply circumstances described? **LO3.7**
6. Assume that both the supply of bottled water and the demand for bottled water rise during the summer but that supply increases more rapidly than demand. What can you conclude about the changes in equilibrium price and equilibrium quantity? **LO3.7**
7. When asked for investment advice, humorist Will Rogers joked that people should "[b]uy land. They ain't making any more of the stuff." Explain his advice in terms of the supply-and-demand model. **LO3.7**

Appendix Review Questions

1. Will the equilibrium price of orange juice increase or decrease in each of the following situations? **LO3.7**
   a. A medical study reporting that orange juice reduces cancer is released at the same time that a freak storm destroys half of the orange crop in Florida.
   b. The prices of all beverages except orange juice fall by half, while unexpectedly perfect weather in Florida results in an orange crop that is 20 percent larger than normal.
2. Consider the market for coffee beans. Suppose that the prices of all other caffeinated beverages go up 30 percent while at the same time a new fertilizer boosts production at coffee plantations dramatically. What is likely to happen to the equilibrium price and quantity of coffee beans? **LO3.7**
3. True or False. A price ceiling will result in a shortage only if the ceiling price is greater than the equilibrium price. **LO3.7**
4. Suppose that you are the economic advisor to a local government that has to deal with a politically embarrassing surplus that was caused by a price floor that the government recently imposed. Your first suggestion is to get rid of the price floor, but the politicians don't want to do that. Instead, they present you with the following list of options that they hope will get rid of

the surplus while keeping the price floor. Identify each one as either *could work* or *can't work*. **LO3.7**
   a. Restricting supply
   b. Decreasing demand
   c. Purchasing the surplus at the floor price
5. Suppose both the demand for olives and the supply of olives decline by equal amounts over some time period. Use graphical analysis to show the effect on equilibrium price and quantity. **LO3.7**
6. Governments can use subsidies to increase demand. For instance, a government can pay farmers to use organic fertilizers rather than traditional fertilizers. That subsidy increases the demand for organic fertilizer. Consider two industries, one in which supply is nearly vertical and the other in which supply is nearly horizontal. Assume that firms in both industries would prefer a higher market equilibrium price, which would mean higher profits. Which industry would probably spend more resources lobbying the government to increase the demand for its output? (Assume that both industries have similarly sloped demand curves.) **LO3.7**
   a. The industry with a nearly flat supply curve
   b. The industry with a nearly vertical supply curve

Appendix Problems

1. Demand and supply often shift in the retail market for gasoline. Below are two demand curves and two supply curves for gallons of gasoline in the month of May in a small town in Maine. Some of the data are missing. **LO3.7**

Price	Quantities Demanded		Quantities Supplied	
	D_1	D_2	S_1	S_2
$4.00	5,000	7,500	9,000	9,500
_____	6,000	8,000	8,000	9,000
2.00	_____	8,500	_____	8,500
_____	_____	9,000	5,000	_____

   a. Use the following facts to fill in the missing data in the table. If demand is D_1 and supply is S_1, the equilibrium quantity is 7,000 gallons per month. When demand is D_2 and supply is S_1, the equilibrium price is $3.00 per gallon. When demand is D_2 and supply is S_1, there is an excess demand of 4,000 gallons per month at a price of $1.00 per gallon. If demand is D_1 and supply is S_2, the equilibrium quantity is 8,000 gallons per month.
   b. Compare two equilibriums. In the first, demand is D_1 and supply is S_1. In the second, demand is D_1 and supply is S_2. By how much does the equilibrium quantity change? By how much does the equilibrium price change?

c. If supply falls from S_2 to S_1 while demand declines from D_2 to D_1, does the equilibrium price rise, fall, or stay the same? What happens if only supply falls? What happens if only demand falls?

d. Suppose that supply is fixed at S_1 and that demand starts at D_1. By how many gallons per month would demand have to increase at each price such that the equilibrium price per gallon would be $3.00? $4.00?

2. The following table shows two demand schedules for a given style of men's shoe—that is, how many pairs per month will be demanded at various prices at Stromnord, a men's clothing store.

Price	D_1 Quantity Demanded	D_2 Quantity Demanded
$75	53	13
70	60	15
65	68	18
60	77	22
55	87	27

Suppose that Stromnord has exactly 65 pairs of this style of shoe in inventory at the start of the month of July and will not receive any more pairs of this style until at least August 1. **LO3.7**

a. If demand is D_1, what is the lowest price that Stromnord can charge so that it will not run out of this model of shoe in the month of July? What if demand is D_2?

b. If the price of shoes is set at $75 for both July and August and demand will be D_2 in July and D_1 in August, how many pairs of shoes should Stromnord order if it wants to end the month of August with exactly zero pairs of shoes in its inventory? How many pairs of shoes should it order if the price is set at $55 for both months?

3. Use the following table to answer the questions that follow: **LO3.7**

a. If this table reflects the supply of and demand for tickets to a particular World Cup soccer game, what is the stadium capacity?

b. If the preset ticket price is $45, would we expect to see a secondary market for tickets? Why or why not? Would the price of a ticket in the secondary market be higher than, the same as, or lower than the price in the primary (original) market?

c. Suppose for some other World Cup game the quantity of tickets demanded is 20,000 lower at each ticket price than shown in the table. If the ticket price remains $45, would the event be a sellout?

Quantity Demanded, Thousands	Price	Quantity Supplied, Thousands
80	$25	60
75	35	60
70	45	60
65	55	60
60	65	60
55	75	60
50	85	60

CHAPTER

4

Market Failures Caused by Externalities and Asymmetric Information

>> LEARNING OBJECTIVES

LO4.1 Explain consumer surplus, producer surplus, and how properly functioning markets maximize total surplus and allocate resources optimally.

LO4.2 Explain how positive and negative externalities cause under- and overallocations of resources.

LO4.3 Explain why society is usually unwilling to pay the costs of completely eliminating negative externalities, such as air pollution.

LO4.4 Understand why asymmetric information may justify government intervention in some markets.

We begin this chapter by demonstrating how properly functioning markets allocate resources efficiently. We then explore *externalities* and *asymmetric information*, which are two major causes of *market failure*, or situations in which markets underproduce, overproduce, or fail to produce goods and services. When a market failure occurs, an economic role for government may arise, with interventions like pollution taxes helping to restore allocative and productive efficiency.

Efficiently Functioning Markets

>> **LO4.1** Explain consumer surplus, producer surplus, and how properly functioning markets maximize total surplus and allocate resources optimally.

In Chapter 3, we saw that competitive markets usually produce an assignment of resources that is "right" from an economic perspective. We now want to focus on the word "usually" and discuss exceptions. We must do so because robust competition involving many buyers and many sellers may not, by itself, be enough to guarantee that a market will allocate resources correctly. Under certain circumstances, markets may fail to deliver the highest possible amount of net benefits from the limited amount of resources available to society.

The best way to understand these instances of **market failure** is to first understand how properly functioning competitive markets achieve economic efficiency. We touched on this subject in Chapter 3, but we now want to expand and deepen that analysis.

Two conditions must hold for a competitive market to produce efficient outcomes:

- The market demand curve must reflect the full willingness to pay of every person receiving benefits from the product being sold in the market.

- The market supply curve must reflect all of the costs of production, including those that may fall onto persons not directly involved with the production of the product being sold in the market.

If these conditions hold, then the market will produce only units for which benefits are at least equal to costs. It will also maximize the **total surplus,** or social surplus, that is shared between consumers and producers. This is important because the *total surplus* measures the net benefits accruing to society from the conversion of scarce resource inputs into various forms of output. When the total surplus is maximized, society is getting as much benefit as possible from its limited supply of resources.

The fact that total surplus is shared between consumers and producers can be expressed in equation form as,

$$\text{Total Surplus} = \text{Consumer Surplus} + \text{Producer Surplus}$$

Let's now dig in more deeply with respect to what, exactly, economists mean by "consumer surplus" and "producer surplus."

Consumer Surplus

The share of the total surplus that is received by a consumer or consumers in a market is called **consumer surplus.** It is defined as the difference between the maximum price a consumer is (or consumers are) willing to pay for a product and the actual price that they do pay.

The maximum price that a person is willing to pay is equal to the marginal benefit that they receive, which in turn depends on the opportunity cost of that person's consumption alternatives. Suppose that Ted is offered the chance to purchase an apple. He would like to have it for free, but the maximum amount he is willing to pay depends on the alternative uses to which he can put his money. If his maximum willingness to pay for an apple is $1.25, then we know that he is willing to forgo up to—but not more than—$1.25 of other goods and services. Paying even one cent more would entail giving up too much of other goods and services. Paying even one cent more would exceed the marginal benefit that he would receive from purchasing and consuming the apple.

However, if Ted pays any market price less than $1.25, he will receive a consumer surplus equal to the difference between the $1.25 maximum price that he was willing to pay and the lower market price. For instance, if the market price is $0.50 per apple, Ted will receive a consumer surplus of $0.75 per apple (= $1.25 − $0.50). In nearly all markets, consumers individually and collectively gain more total utility or satisfaction in dollar terms from their purchases than the amount of their expenditures (= product price × quantity). This utility surplus arises because each consumer who buys the product pays only the market equilibrium price even though many were willing to pay *more* than the equilibrium price to obtain the product.

The concept of maximum willingness to pay also gives us another way to understand demand curves. You learned in previous chapters that demand curves are equivalent to MB (marginal benefit) curves. It is also the case that they are equivalent to maximum willingness to pay curves. Consider Table 4.1, where the first two columns show the maximum amounts that six consumers would each be willing to pay for a bag of oranges. Bashir, for instance, is willing to pay a maximum of $13, while Blessing is willing to pay a maximum of $8.

Notice that the maximum prices that these individuals are willing to pay represent points on a demand curve because the lower the market price, the more bags of oranges will be demanded. At a price of $12.50, for instance, Bashir will be the only person listed in the table who will purchase a bag. But at a price of $11.50, both Bashir and Barb will want to purchase a bag. And at a price of $10.50, Bashir, Barb, and Bill will each want to purchase a bag. The lower the price, the greater the total quantity demanded.

market failure The inability of a *market* to bring about the allocation of *resources* that best satisfies the wants of society; in particular, the overallocation or underallocation of resources to the production of a particular *good* or *service* because of *externalities* or *asymmetric information,* or because markets fail to provide desired *public goods.*

total surplus The sum of consumer surplus and producer surplus; a measure of social welfare; also known as social surplus.

consumer surplus The difference between the maximum *price* a consumer is (or consumers are) willing to pay for an additional unit of a product and its market price; the triangular area below the demand curve and above the market price.

TABLE 4.1
Consumer Surplus

(1) Person	(2) Maximum Price Willing to Pay (= MB)	(3) Actual Price (Equilibrium Price)	(4) Consumer Surplus
Bashir	$13	$8	$5 (= $13 − $8)
Barb	12	8	4 (= $12 − $8)
Bill	11	8	3 (= $11 − $8)
Beeja	10	8	2 (= $10 − $8)
Brent	9	8	1 (= $9 − $8)
Blessing	8	8	0 (= $8 − $8)

Lower prices also imply larger consumer surpluses. When the price is $12.50, Bashir gets only $0.50 in consumer surplus because his maximum willingness to pay of $13 is only $0.50 higher than the market price of $12.50. But if the market price falls to $8, then his consumer surplus would be $5(= $13 − $8). The third and fourth columns of Table 4.1 show how much consumer surplus each consumer will receive if the market price of a bag of oranges is $8. Only Blessing receives no consumer surplus because her maximum willingness to pay exactly matches the $8 equilibrium price.

Graphing Consumer Surplus It is easy to show on a graph both the individual consumer surplus received by each particular buyer in a market as well as the collective consumer surplus received by all the buyers in a market. Consider Figure 4.1, which shows the market equilibrium price $P_1 = $8 as well as the downward sloping demand curve D for bags of oranges.

Demand curve D includes not only the six consumers in Table 4.1 but also every other consumer of oranges in the market. The consumer surplus of each individual who is willing to buy at the $8 market price is simply the vertical distance from the horizontal line that marks the $8 market price up to that buyer's maximum willingness to pay. The collective consumer surplus obtained by all of our named and unnamed buyers is found by adding together each of their individual consumer surpluses.

To obtain the Q_1 bags of oranges represented in Figure 4.1, consumers are collectively *willing* to pay the total amount that is equal to the sum of the amounts represented by the green triangle and yellow rectangle, which both lie under the demand curve and to the left of Q_1. But consumers only *have* to pay the amount represented by the yellow rectangle (= $P_1 \times Q_1$). So the green triangle is the consumer surplus in this market. It is the sum of the vertical distances between the demand curve and the $8 equilibrium price at each quantity up to Q_1. Alternatively, it is the sum of the gaps between maximum willingness to pay and actual price, such as those we calculated in Table 4.1. Thus, consumer surplus can also be defined as the area that lies below the demand curve and above the price line that extends horizontally from P_1.

Consumer surplus and price are inversely (negatively) related. Given the demand curve, higher prices reduce consumer surplus; lower prices increase it. To test this generalization, draw in an equilibrium price above $8 in Figure 4.1 and observe the reduced size of the triangle representing consumer surplus. Next, draw in an equilibrium price below $8 and see that consumer surplus increases.

producer surplus The difference between the actual *price* a producer receives (or producers receive) and the minimum acceptable price; the triangular area above the *supply curve* and below the market price.

FIGURE 4.1
Consumer surplus.

Consumer surplus—shown as the green triangle—is the difference between the maximum prices consumers are willing to pay for a product and the lower equilibrium price, here assumed to be $8. For quantity Q_1, consumers are willing to pay the sum of the amounts represented by the green triangle and the yellow rectangle. Because they need to pay only the amount shown as the yellow rectangle, the green triangle shows consumer surplus.

Producer Surplus

Like consumers, producers also receive a share of the total surplus generated by a market equilibrium. This **producer surplus** is the difference between the actual price a producer receives (or producers receive) and the minimum price that a consumer would have to pay the producer to make a particular unit of output available.

TABLE 4.2
Producer Surplus

(1) Person	(2) Minimum Acceptable Price (= MC)	(3) Actual Price (Equilibrium Price)	(4) Producer Surplus
Chander	$3	$8	$5 (= $8 − $3)
Chaaya	4	8	4 (= $8 − $4)
Chuck	5	8	3 (= $8 − $5)
Chazen	6	8	2 (= $8 − $6)
Chuma	7	8	1 (= $8 − $7)
Chad	8	8	0 (= $8 − $8)

A producer's minimum acceptable price for a particular unit will equal the producer's marginal cost of producing that unit. That marginal cost will be the sum of the rent, wages, interest, and profit that the producer will need to pay in order to obtain the land, labor, capital, and entrepreneurship required to produce that unit. In this section, we are assuming that the marginal cost of producing a unit includes *all* of the costs of production, including those that may fall onto individuals not directly involved in production.

A producer's minimum acceptable price, which equals the marginal cost, can also be interpreted as the opportunity cost of bidding resources away from the production of other products. To see why, suppose that Leah is an apple grower. The resources necessary for her to produce one apple could be used to produce other things. To get them directed toward producing an apple, it is necessary to pay Leah what it will cost her to bid the necessary resources away from other entrepreneurs who would like to use them to produce other products. Leah would, naturally, like to get paid as much as possible to produce the apple for you. But her minimum acceptable price is the lowest price you could pay her such that she can just break even after bidding away resources from other uses.

The size of the producer surplus earned on any particular unit is the difference between the market price that the producer actually receives and the producer's minimum acceptable price. Consider Table 4.2, which shows the minimum acceptable prices of six different orange growers. With a market price of $8, Chander, for instance, has a producer surplus of $5, which is equal to the market price of $8 minus his minimum acceptable price of $3. Chad, by contrast, receives no producer surplus because his minimum acceptable price of $8 just equals the market equilibrium price of $8.

Chander's minimum acceptable price is lower than Chad's minimum acceptable price because Chander is a more efficient producer than Chad, by which we mean that Chander produces oranges using a less-costly combination of resources than Chad uses. The differences in efficiency between Chander and Chad are likely due to differences in the type and quality of resources available to them. Chander, for instance, may own land perfectly suited to growing oranges, while Chad has land in the desert that requires costly irrigation if it is to be used to grow oranges. Thus, Chad has a higher marginal cost of producing oranges.

The minimum acceptable prices that producers are willing to accept form points on a supply curve because the higher the price, the more bags of oranges will be supplied. At a price of $3.50, for instance, only Chander is willing to supply a bag of oranges. But at a price of $5.50, Chander, Chaaya, and Chuck are all willing to supply a bag of oranges.

Please note that in previous chapters you learned that supply curves are equivalent to MC (marginal cost curves). You now know that supply curves are also equivalent to minimum-acceptable-price curves since the minimum prices that producers are willing to accept are equal to their marginal costs of production.

Graphing Producer Surplus The supply curve in Figure 4.2 includes not only the six producers named in Table 4.2 but also every other producer of oranges in

FIGURE 4.2
Producer surplus.

Producer surplus—shown as the blue triangle—is the difference between the actual price producers receive for a product (here $8) and the lower minimum payments they are willing to accept. For quantity Q_1, producers receive the sum of the amounts represented by the blue triangle plus the yellow area. Because we would only need to pay them the amount shown by the yellow area to get them to produce Q_1, the blue triangle represents producer surplus.

the market. At the market price of $8 per bag, Q_1 bags are produced because only those producers whose minimum acceptable prices are less than $8 per bag will choose to produce oranges with their resources. Those lower acceptable prices for each of the units up to Q_1 are shown by the portion of the supply curve lying to the left of and below the assumed $8 market price.

The individual producer surplus of each seller is thus the vertical distance from the seller's minimum acceptable price on the supply curve up to the $8 market price. Their collective producer surplus is shown by the blue triangle in Figure 4.2. In that figure, producers collect revenues of $P_1 \times Q_1$, which is the sum of the blue triangle and the yellow area. But producers would only need to receive the yellow area in order to make them just willing to supply Q_1 bags of oranges. The sellers therefore receive a producer surplus shown by the blue triangle. That surplus is the sum of the vertical distances between the supply curve and the $8 equilibrium price at each of the quantities to the left of Q_1.

There is a direct (positive) relationship between equilibrium price and the amount of producer surplus. Given the supply curve, lower prices reduce producer surplus; higher prices increase it. If you pencil in a lower equilibrium price than $8, you will see that the producer surplus triangle gets smaller. If you pencil in an equilibrium price above $8, the size of the producer surplus triangle increases.

---

productive efficiency The production of a *good* in the least costly way; occurs when production takes place at the output level at which per-unit production costs are minimized.

allocative efficiency The apportionment of resources among *firms* and industries to obtain the production of the products most wanted by society (consumers); the output of each product at which its *marginal cost* and *marginal benefit* are equal, and at which the sum of *consumer surplus* and *producer surplus* is maximized.

FIGURE 4.3
Efficiency: maximum combined consumer and producer surplus.

At quantity Q_1 the combined amount of consumer surplus, shown as the green triangle, and producer surplus, shown as the blue triangle, is maximized. Efficiency occurs at Q_1 because maximum willingness to pay, indicated by the points on the demand curve, equals minimum acceptable price, shown by the points on the supply curve. All units prior to Q_1 generate net benefits because maximum willingness to pay exceeds minimum acceptable price for each of those units.

▶ Consumer surplus is the difference between the maximum price that a consumer is willing to pay for a product and the lower price actually paid.

▶ Producer surplus is the difference between the minimum price that a producer is willing to accept for a product and the higher price actually received.

▶ In a graph of demand and supply, consumer surplus is represented by the area below the demand curve and above the market price; producer surplus by the area above the supply curve and below the market price.

Total Surplus and Efficiency

In Figure 4.3 we bring together the demand and supply curves of Figures 4.1 and 4.2 to show the equilibrium price and quantity and the previously described regions of consumer and producer surplus. All markets that have downward sloping demand curves and upward sloping supply curves yield consumer and producer surplus.

Because we are assuming in Figure 4.3 that the demand curve reflects buyers' full willingness to pay and the supply curve reflects all of the costs facing sellers, the equilibrium quantity in Figure 4.3 reflects economic efficiency, which consists of productive efficiency (lowest-cost production) and allocative efficiency (directing scarce resources toward their highest-valued use).

- **Productive efficiency** is achieved because competition forces orange growers to use the best technologies and combinations of resources available. Doing so minimizes the per-unit cost of the output produced.

- **Allocative efficiency** is achieved because the correct quantity of oranges—Q_1—is produced relative to other goods and services. Scarce resources are allocated to orange production only as long as the marginal benefit of additional orange production exceeds the opportunity cost of redirecting resources away from the production of other products.

Three Equivalent Conditions for Allocative Efficiency There are three equally valid ways to understand why the market equilibrium quantity Q_1 is the correct (allocatively efficient) quantity of oranges.

Marginal Benefit = Marginal Cost Recall from Chapter 1 that the correct amount of society's scarce resources is efficiently allocated to a particular good or service when that product is produced at the output level at which MB = MC (see Figure 1.3). In this chapter, we have emphasized that demand curves are MB curves and supply curves are MC curves. In particular, the points on the demand curve in Figure 4.3 measure the marginal benefit of oranges at each level of output, while the points on the supply curve measure the marginal cost of oranges at each level of output. As a result, MB = MC where the demand and supply curves intersect—which means that the market equilibrium quantity Q_1 must be allocatively efficient.

Maximum Willingness to Pay = Minimum Acceptable Price The second way to understand why the market equilibrium quantity Q_1 is allocatively efficient is to take advantage of the fact that demand and supply curves can also be interpreted as, respectively, maximum-willingness-to-pay and minimum-acceptable-price curves.

In Figure 4.3, the maximum willingness to pay on the demand curve for each bag of oranges up to Q_1 exceeds the corresponding minimum acceptable price on the supply curve. So people gain more utility from producing and consuming those units than they would if they produced and consumed anything else that could be made with the resources that went into making those units.

Only at the equilibrium quantity Q_1—where the maximum willingness to pay exactly equals the minimum acceptable price—does society exhaust all opportunities to produce units for which marginal benefits exceed marginal costs (including opportunity costs). Producing Q_1 units therefore achieves allocative efficiency.

Total Surplus is Maximized The third way to understand why the market equilibrium quantity Q_1 is allocatively efficient relies on the fact that producing Q_1 units maximizes total surplus (= the combined area of consumer and producer surplus) in Figure 4.3. If any other amount were produced, the total surplus would be less than it is at Q_1 units, implying that either consumers or producers (or both!) will end up receiving a smaller amount of surplus than they do when exactly Q_1 units are produced. The market equilibrium quantity is, consequently, allocatively efficient because it represents the only allocation of resources to this product that will maximize the sum of consumer and producer surplus (= the full areas of the blue and green triangles in Figure 4.3).

Recap and Implications Let's briefly summarize what we have learned about the efficiency of the market equilibrium.

- When demand curves reflect buyers' full willingness to pay and when supply curves reflect all of the costs facing sellers, competitive markets produce equilibrium quantities that maximize the sum of consumer and producer surplus.

- Allocative efficiency occurs at the market equilibrium quantity, where three conditions exist simultaneously:

  1. MB = MC (see Figure 1.3).
  2. Maximum willingness to pay = minimum acceptable price.
  3. Total surplus (= sum of consumer and producer surplus) is at a maximum.

Economists are enamored of markets because properly functioning markets automatically achieve allocative efficiency. Other methods of allocating resources—such as government central planning—do exist. But because other methods cannot do any better than properly functioning markets—and in many cases, do much worse—economists usually prefer to see resources allocated through markets.

QUICK REVIEW

4.2

- When demand curves reflect buyers' full willingness to pay and supply curves reflect all of the costs facing sellers, the market equilibrium quantity will be both productively and allocatively efficient.

- Total surplus (= sum of consumer surplus and producer surplus) represents the net benefits (social surplus) received by members of society from the production and consumption of the market equilibrium quantity of output.

- At the equilibrium price and quantity in a competitive market, MB = MC, maximum willingness to pay equals minimum acceptable price, and total surplus is maximized. Each of these conditions implies allocative efficiency.

Externalities and Efficiency Losses

Figures 4.4a and 4.4b demonstrate that both underproduction and overproduction cause reductions in the size of the total surplus. These reductions are known as **efficiency losses,** or deadweight losses.

>> **LO4.2** Explain how positive and negative externalities cause under- and overallocations of resources.

FIGURE 4.4 Efficiency losses (or deadweight losses).

Quantity levels either less than or greater than the efficient quantity Q_1 create efficiency losses. (a) Triangle *dbe* shows the efficiency loss associated with underproduction at output Q_2. (b) Triangle *bfg* illustrates the efficiency loss associated with overproduction at output level Q_3.

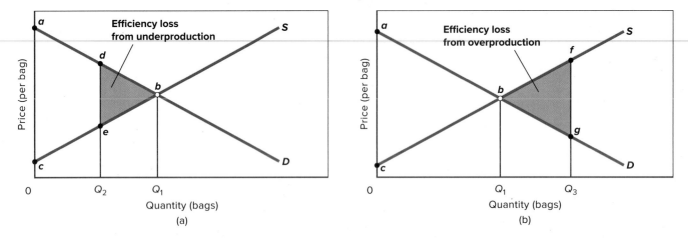

(a)   (b)

efficiency loss Reductions in combined consumer and producer surplus caused by an underallocation or over-allocation of resources to the production of a *good* or *service*. Also called *deadweight loss.*

deadweight loss A reduction in the total net benefit that society can obtain from its limited supply of resources. Caused by an underalloca-tion or overallocation of resources to the production of a particular *good* or *service*. Also called *efficiency loss.*

Deadweight Losses from Underproduction

First consider Figure 4.4a, which analyzes the case of underproduction by considering what hap-pens if output falls from the efficient level Q_1 to the smaller amount Q_2. When that happens, the sum of consumer and producer surplus, previously *abc,* falls to *adec.* Thus total surplus declines by the amount of the gray triangle to the left of Q_1. That triangle (*dbe*) represents an efficiency loss to buyers and sellers. And because buyers and sellers are members of society, it represents a **deadweight loss** to society as a whole.

For output levels from Q_2 to Q_1, consumers' maximum willingness to pay (as reflected by points on the demand curve) exceeds producers' minimum acceptable price (as reflected by points on the supply curve). By failing to produce these units for which a consumer is willing to pay more than a producer is willing to accept, society suffers a loss of net benefits. As a concrete example, consider a particular unit for which a consumer is willing to pay $10 and a producer is willing to accept $6. The $4 difference between those values is a net benefit that will not be realized if this unit is not produced. In addition, the resources that should have gone to producing this unit will go instead to producing other products that will generate a smaller net benefit.

Deadweight Losses from Overproduction

Next, consider the case of overproduction shown in Figure 4.4b, in which the number of oranges produced is Q_3 rather than the efficient level Q_1. In Figure 4.4b the total surplus declines by *bfg—* the gray triangle to the right of Q_1. This triangle subtracts from the total consumer and producer surplus of *abc* that would occur if the quantity had been Q_1. That is, for all units from 0 to Q_1, benefits exceed costs, so that those units generate the economic surplus shown by triangle *abc.* But the units from Q_1 to Q_3 are such that costs exceed benefits. Thus, they generate a loss of total surplus shown by triangle *bfg.* The total economic surplus for all units from 0 to Q_3 is therefore the economic surplus given by *abc* for the units from 0 to Q_1 *minus* the loss of surplus indicated by *bfg* for the units from Q_1 to Q_3.

Producing any unit beyond Q_1 generates an efficiency loss because consumers' willingness to pay for such units is less than producers' minimum acceptable price to produce such units. As a concrete example, note that producing an item for which the maximum willingness to pay is $7 and the minimum acceptable price is $10 subtracts $3 from society's net benefits. Such produc-tion is uneconomical and creates an efficiency loss (or deadweight loss) for society.

In summary: When demand reflects consumers' full willingness to pay and when supply reflects all costs, the market equilibrium quantity will automatically equal the allocatively efficient output level and there will be neither efficiency losses from underproduction nor effi-ciency losses from overproduction. But if for any reason more or less than the market equilib-rium quantity is produced, deadweight losses will result, either from underproduction or overproduction.

Externalities

An **externality** occurs when some of the costs or benefits of a good or service are passed onto or "spill over to" someone other than the immediate buyer or seller. These spillovers are called "externalities" because they accrue to some third party that is external to the market transaction.

Externalities can be positive or negative. An example of a negative externality is the cost of breathing polluted air; an example of a positive externality is the benefit of having everyone else inoculated against some disease. As you will see, both types of externality generate allocative inefficiency and deadweight losses.

Negative Externalities **Negative externalities** occur when producers or suppliers impose costs on third parties who are not directly involved in a market transaction. Consider the costs of breathing polluted air that are imposed on third parties living downwind of smoke-spewing factories. Because polluting firms do not take account of such costs, they oversupply the products they make, producing units for which total costs (including those that fall on third parties) exceed total benefits. The same is true when airlines fail to account for the costs that noisy jet engines impose on people living near airports.

Overproduction In terms of supply and demand, this failure to account for all costs—including the costs of negative externalities—shifts firms' supply curves to the right of (below) where they would be if firms properly accounted for all costs. This can be seen in **Figure 4.5a (Key Graph),** which illustrates how negative externalities affect the allocation of resources.

When producers shift some of their costs onto the community as external costs, producers' marginal costs are lower than they would be if they had to pay those costs themselves. Thus their supply curves do not include or "capture" all the costs legitimately associated with the production

externality A cost or benefit from production or consumption that accrues to someone other than the immediate buyers and sellers of the product being produced or consumed (see *negative externality* and *positive externality*).

negative externality A cost imposed without compensation on third parties by the production or consumption of sellers or buyers. Example: A manufacturer dumps toxic chemicals into a river, killing fish prized by sports fishers. Also known as an external cost or a spillover cost.

..ıl KEY GRAPH

FIGURE 4.5 **Negative and positive externalities.**

(a) With negative externalities borne by society, the producers' supply curve S is to the right of (below) the total-cost supply curve S_t. Consequently, the equilibrium output Q_e is greater than the optimal output Q_o, and the efficiency loss is *abc*.
(b) When positive externalities accrue to society, the market demand curve D is to the left of (below) the total-benefit demand curve D_t. As a result, the equilibrium output Q_e is less than the optimal output Q_o and the efficiency loss is *xyz*.

(a)
Negative externalities

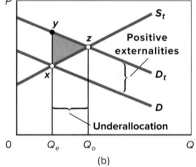

(b)
Positive externalities

QUICK QUIZ FOR FIGURE 4.5

1. In Figure 4.5a, the supply curve S_t lies to the left of (above) supply curve S because:
   a. marginal costs are rising faster for S_t than S.
   b. S reflects more efficient, lower-cost production methods.
   c. only S_t reflects the costs that fall on people other than buyers and sellers.
   d. only S_t reflects the law of increasing opportunity costs.

2. In Figure 4.5a, the market equilibrium will be located at:
   a. point *a*.
   b. point *b*.
   c. point *c*.
   d. Q_o.

3. In Figure 4.5b, there is an underallocation of resources to the production of this product because:
   a. low prices are depressing the quantity demanded.
   b. the vertical distance from point *x* to point *y* fails to reflect net benefits.
   c. demand curve D_t externalizes consumers' opportunity costs.
   d. equilibrium reflects the absence from the market of the consumers who benefit from this product without having to pay for it.

4. In Figure 4.5b, the market equilibrium price will be:
   a. less than the price at point *x*.
   b. equal to the vertical distance between D_t and D.
   c. less than the price at point *z*.
   d. equal to the price at point *y*.

Answers: 1. c; 2. c; 3. d; 4. c

of their products. A polluting producer's supply curve such as S in Figure 4.5a therefore understates the total cost of production. The polluter's supply curve S lies to the right of (below) the total-cost supply curve S_t, which includes the spillover costs. Through polluting and thus transferring costs to society, the firm enjoys lower production costs than it would if it had to pay for those negative externalities. By dumping those costs onto others, it produces more at each possible price than it would if it had to account for all costs. That is why supply curve S lies to the right of (below) supply curve S_t.

Efficiency Losses from Overproduction   The market outcome is shown in Figure 4.5a. Equilibrium output Q_e (which is determined by the intersection of supply curve S and demand curve D) is larger than the optimal output Q_o. Resources are overallocated to the production of this commodity; too many units of it are produced. In fact, there is a net loss to society for every unit from Q_o to Q_e. That net loss occurs because, for each of those units, the total MC to society (including the costs of the negative externality) exceeds the MB to society. You can see this clearly by noting that for all the units between Q_o and Q_e, the supply curve that accounts for all costs, S_t, lies above the demand curve D that accounts for benefits. Therefore, MC exceeds MB for those units.

The negative externality results in a deadweight efficiency loss represented by triangle *abc*. The resources that went into producing the units between Q_o and Q_e should have been used elsewhere in the economy to produce other things.

Positive Externalities   **Positive externalities** occur when people who are not directly involved in a market transaction receive benefits from the market transaction without having to pay for them. An example would be people living near Disneyland who enjoy the park's nightly fireworks display even though they did not purchase admission to the park. These people receive something beneficial (positive) despite being outside of (external to) the market transaction between Disneyland and its paying customers. These nonpaying beneficiaries are sometimes referred to as "free riders," after the scofflaws who ride public transportation without paying for a ticket.

Underproduction   When positive externalities are present, market demand curves fail to include the willingness to pay of the people who receive the positive externality. This failure to account for all benefits—including those received by people not directly involved in the market transaction—shifts market demand curves to the left of (below) where they would be if they included all benefits and total willingness to pay. In such cases, markets fail to produce all units for which benefits (including those that are received by third parties) exceed costs. As a result, products featuring positive externalities are underproduced.

Vaccinations are a good example of how positive externalities reduce demand. When John gets vaccinated against a disease, he benefits not only himself (because he can no longer contract the disease) but also everyone else around him (because they know that in the future he will never be able to infect them). These other people would presumably be willing to pay some positive amount of money for the benefits they receive when John is vaccinated. But there is no way to make them pay.

Thus, the market demand for vaccinations will include John's personal willingness to pay for the benefits that he personally receives from the vaccination, but it will fail to include the benefits that others receive. As a result, demand will be too low and vaccinations will be underproduced.

Efficiency Losses from Underproduction   Figure 4.5b shows the impact of positive externalities on resource allocation. When external benefits occur, the market demand curve D lies to the left of (below) the total-benefits demand curve, D_t. At any particular price, fewer units of output are demanded along D than along D_t. That's because D includes only the benefits received by people paying for the product, while D_t includes not only those paid-for benefits but also the external benefits received by free riders. D_t is the demand curve that would exist if everybody receiving benefits had to pay for them.

With D lying to the left of (below) D_t, the market equilibrium output Q_e (which is determined by the intersection of demand curve D and supply curve S_t) is less than the optimal output Q_o. The market fails to produce enough output and resources are underallocated to this product. The underproduction implies that society is missing out on a significant amount of potential net benefits. For every unit from Q_e to Q_o, the demand curve that accounts for all benefits, D_t, lies above the supply curve S that accounts for all costs—including the opportunity cost of producing other products with the resources that were used to produce these units. Because D_t includes all benefits while S includes all costs, we see that MB > MC for each of these units. We conclude that society

positive externality   A benefit obtained without compensation by third parties from the production or consumption of sellers or buyers. Example: A beekeeper benefits when a neighboring farmer plants clover. Also known as an *external benefit* or a spillover benefit.

should redeploy some of its resources away from the production of other items and toward the production of these units for which net benefits are positive.

In terms of our previous analysis, the positive externality results in a deadweight efficiency loss represented by triangle *xyz*. Shifting the demand curve from *D* to *D_t* eliminates that deadweight loss. The underallocation of resources to this product disappears as the market equilibrium shifts from *x* to *z*.

▶ Quantities less than or greater than the allocatively efficient level of output create efficiency losses, often called deadweight losses.

▶ An externality occurs when a benefit or cost of a market transaction falls on parties other than the immediate buyers and sellers interacting in the market.

▶ Negative externalities lead to overproduction and overallocation, while positive externalities lead to underproduction and underallocation.

Government Intervention

Government intervention may achieve economic efficiency when externalities affect large numbers of people or when community interests are at stake. Governments can counter the overproduction caused by negative externalities with direct controls or Pigovian taxes. And governments can counter the underproduction caused by positive externalities with subsidies or government provision.

Direct Controls The most direct way of reducing negative externalities arising from a certain activity is to pass legislation limiting that activity. Such **direct controls** force the offending firms to incur the actual costs of the offending activity. Historically, direct controls in the form of uniform emission standards—limits on allowable pollution—have dominated U.S. air pollution policy. Similarly, clean-water legislation limits the amount of heavy metals, detergents, and other pollutants that firms can discharge into rivers and bays. And toxic-waste laws dictate special procedures and dump sites for disposing of contaminated soil and solvents. Violating these laws means fines and, in some cases, imprisonment.

Direct controls raise the marginal cost of production because polluting firms must operate and maintain pollution-control equipment. Raising the marginal cost of production shifts the supply curve leftward (or upward). For example, in Figure 4.6b, the supply curve *S*, which does not reflect external costs, shifts leftward (upward) to the total-cost supply curve, *S_t*. The equilibrium price increases, equilibrium output falls from *Q_e* to the socially optimal amount *Q_o*, and the initial overallocation of resources shown in Figure 4.6a is corrected. Observe that the efficiency loss shown by triangle *abc* in Figure 4.6a disappears after the overallocation is corrected in Figure 4.6b.

Pigovian Taxes Another way to approach negative externalities is for government to levy taxes or charges on the related good. These targeted tax assessments are often called **Pigovian taxes** in honor of Arthur Pigou, the first economist to study externalities. Example: The U.S. government

direct controls Government policies that directly constrain activities that generate *negative externalities*. Examples include maximum emissions limits for factory smokestacks and laws mandating the proper disposal of toxic wastes.

Pigovian tax A *tax* or charge levied on the production of a product that generates *negative externalities*. If set correctly, the tax will precisely offset the overallocation (overproduction) generated by the negative externality.

FIGURE 4.6 Correcting for negative externalities.

(a) Negative externalities result in an overallocation of resources. (b) Government can correct this overallocation in two ways: (1) using direct controls, which would shift the supply curve from *S* to *S_t* and reduce equilibrium output from *Q_e* to *Q_o*, or (2) imposing a specific tax *T*, which would also shift the supply curve from *S* to *S_t*, eliminating the overallocation of resources and thus the efficiency loss.

(a)
Negative externalities

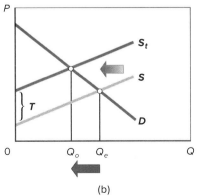

(b)
Correcting the overallocation
of resources via direct controls
or via a tax

CONSIDER THIS . . .

The Fable of the Bees

Economist Ronald Coase received the Nobel Prize for his so-called **Coase theorem,** which pointed out that private individuals could often use private bargaining to negotiate their own mutually agreeable solutions to externality problems without the need for government interventions like pollution taxes.

LilKar/Shutterstock

This is a very important insight because it means that we shouldn't automatically call for government intervention every time we see an externality problem. Consider the positive externalities that bees provide by pollinating farmers' crops. Should we assume that beekeeping will be underprovided unless the government intervenes with, for instance, subsidies to encourage more hives and hence more pollination?

As it turns out, no. Research has shown that farmers and beekeepers long ago used private bargaining to develop customs and payment systems that avoid free riding by farmers and encourage beekeepers to keep the optimal number of hives. Free riding is avoided by the custom that all farmers in an area simultaneously hire beekeepers to provide bees to pollinate their crops. And farmers always pay the beekeepers for their pollination services because if they didn't, then no beekeeper would ever work with them in the future—a situation that would lead to massively reduced crop yields due to a lack of pollination.

The "Fable of the Bees" is a good reminder that it is a fallacy to assume that the government must always get involved to remedy externalities. In many cases, the private sector can solve both positive and negative externality problems on its own.

Coase theorem The idea, first stated by economist Ronald Coase, that some *externalities* can be resolved through private negotiations among the affected parties.

has placed a tax on CFCs, which deplete the stratospheric ozone layer protecting Earth from excessive solar ultraviolet radiation. Facing this tax, manufacturers must decide whether to pay the tax or expend additional funds to purchase or develop substitute products. In either case, the tax raises the marginal cost of producing CFCs, shifting the supply curve for this product leftward (upward).

In Figure 4.6b, a tax equal to T per unit increases the firm's marginal cost, shifting the supply curve from S to S_t. The equilibrium price rises, and the equilibrium output declines from Q_e to the economically efficient level Q_o. The tax eliminates the initial overallocation of resources and the associated efficiency loss.

Many governments have imposed Pigovian pollution taxes on carbon dioxide (CO_2) in order to raise the marginal cost of burning fossil fuels and thereby offset the negative externalities imposed by carbon dioxide emissions. Global Perspective 4.1 shows the percentage of carbon-dioxide emissions that are taxed at a rate of $70 per ton or higher in each of ten countries.

GLOBAL PERSPECTIVE 4.1

PERCENTAGE OF CO_2 EMISSIONS TAXED, SELECTED NATIONS, 2018

Countries vary widely in the percentage of their total carbon dioxide (CO_2) emissions that they tax at a price of $70 per ton or higher. The percentages vary across countries due to both differences in the tax rate per ton and differences in which industries (agricultural, industrial, transportation, etc.) are subject to CO_2 taxes in each country.

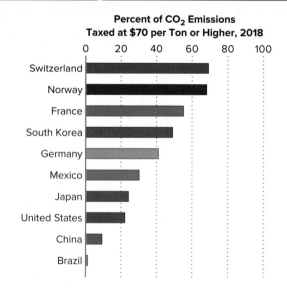

Percent of CO_2 Emissions
Taxed at $70 per Ton or Higher, 2018

Source: Effective Carbon Rates 2021, Organization for Economic Co-operation and Development (OECD), oecd.org.

FIGURE 4.7 Correcting for positive externalities.

(a) Positive externalities result in an underallocation of resources. (b) This underallocation can be corrected through a subsidy to consumers, which shifts market demand from D to D_t and increases output from Q_e to Q_o. (c) Alternatively, the underallocation can be eliminated by providing producers with a subsidy of U, which shifts their supply curve from S_t to S_t', increasing output from Q_e to Q_o and eliminating the underallocation, and thus the efficiency loss, shown in graph a.

(a)
Positive externalities

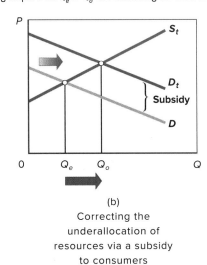

(b)
Correcting the
underallocation of
resources via a subsidy
to consumers

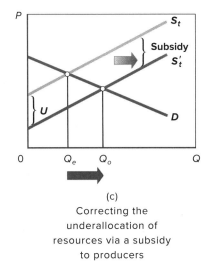

(c)
Correcting the
underallocation of
resources via a subsidy
to producers

Subsidies and Government Provision Where spillover benefits (positive externalities) are large and diffuse, government has three options for correcting the underallocation of resources:

- **Subsidies to buyers** Figure 4.7a replicates the supply-demand situation for positive externalities that you first encountered in Figure 4.5b. Government could correct the underallocation of resources to inoculations by subsidizing consumers of the product. It could give each new parent in the United States a discount coupon to be used for a series of inoculations for their child. The coupon would reduce the "price" to the mother by, say, 50 percent. As Figure 4.7b shows, this program would shift the demand curve for inoculations from too-low D to the appropriate D_t. The number of inoculations would rise from Q_e to the economically optimal Q_o, eliminating the underallocation of resources and the associated efficiency loss.

- **Subsidies to producers** A subsidy to producers is a tax in reverse. Taxes are payments *to* the government that increase producers' costs. Subsidies are payments *from* the government that decrease producers' costs. As Figure 4.7c shows, a subsidy of U per inoculation to physicians and medical clinics would reduce their marginal costs and shift their supply curve rightward (upward) from S_t to S_t'. The output of inoculations would increase from Q_e to the optimal level Q_o, correcting the underallocation of resources and the associated efficiency loss.

- **Government provision** Finally, where positive externalities are extremely large, the government may decide to provide the product for free to everyone. The U.S. government largely eradicated the crippling disease polio by administering free vaccines to all children. India ended smallpox by paying people in rural areas to come to public clinics to have their children vaccinated.

Table 4.3 lists several methods for correcting externalities, including those we have discussed thus far. The nearby Consider This box also relates how one of those methods—private bargaining—can help to correct for externalities privately, without government intervention.

TABLE 4.3
Methods for Dealing with Externalities

Problem	Resource Allocation Outcome	Ways to Correct
Negative externalities (spillover costs)	Overproduction of output and therefore overallocation of resources	1. Private bargaining 2. Liability rules and lawsuits 3. Taxes on producers 4. Direct controls 5. Markets for externality rights
Positive externalities (spillover benefits)	Underproduction of output and therefore underallocation of resources	1. Private bargaining 2. Subsidies to consumers 3. Subsidies to producers 4. Government provision

▶ Governments can attempt to counter the overproduction caused by negative externalities and the underproduction caused by positive externalities.

▶ Government policies for coping with the overallocation of resources, and therefore efficiency losses, caused by negative externalities include (a) private bargaining, (b) liability rules and lawsuits,

(c) direct controls, (d) Pigovian taxes, and (e) markets for externality rights.

▶ Government policies for correcting the underallocation of resources, and therefore efficiency losses, associated with positive externalities include (a) private bargaining, (b) subsidies to producers, (c) subsidies to consumers, and (d) government provision.

Society's Optimal Amount of Externality Reduction

>> **LO4.3** Explain why society is usually unwilling to pay the costs of completely eliminating negative externalities, such as air pollution.

Negative externalities such as pollution reduce the utility of those affected. These spillovers are not economic goods but rather economic "bads." If something is bad, shouldn't society eliminate it? Why should society allow firms to discharge *any* impure waste into public waterways or to emit *any* pollution whatsoever into the air?

Economists answer these questions by pointing out that reducing pollution and negative externalities is not free. There are costs as well as benefits to reducing pollution. As a result, the correct question to ask is not, "Do we pollute a lot or pollute zero?" That is an all-or-nothing question that ignores marginal costs and marginal benefits. Instead, the correct question is, "What is the optimal amount to clean up—that is, the amount that equalizes the marginal cost of cleaning up with the marginal benefit of a cleaner environment?"

If we ask that question, we see that reducing a negative externality has a "price." Society must decide how much of a reduction it wants to "buy." High costs may mean that totally eliminating pollution might not be desirable, even if it is technologically feasible. Because of the *law of increasing opportunity costs*, cleaning up the second 10 percent of pollutants from an industrial smokestack normally is more costly than cleaning up the first 10 percent. Eliminating the third 10 percent is more costly than cleaning up the second 10 percent, and so on. Therefore, cleaning up the last 10 percent of pollutants is the most costly reduction of all.

The marginal cost (MC) to the firm and hence to society—the opportunity cost of the extra resources used—rises as pollution is reduced more and more. At some point, MC may rise so high that it exceeds society's marginal benefit (MB) of further pollution reduction. Additional actions to reduce pollution will therefore lower society's well-being; total cost will rise more than total benefit.

MC, MB, and Optimal Abatement

optimal reduction of an externality The reduction of a *negative externality* such as pollution to the level at which the *marginal benefit* and *marginal cost* of reduction (abatement) are equal.

Figure 4.8 shows both the upward sloping marginal-cost curve MC for pollution abatement (reduction) as well as the downward sloping marginal-benefit curve MB for pollution abatement.

- MB slopes downward because of the *law of diminishing marginal utility:* The more pollution society reduces, the lower the utility (benefit) of the next unit of pollution reduction.

FIGURE 4.8 Society's optimal amount of pollution abatement.

The optimal amount of externality reduction—in this case, pollution abatement—occurs at Q_1, where society's marginal cost MC and marginal benefit MB of reducing the spillover are equal.

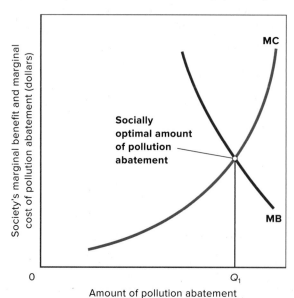

- MC slopes upward because of the *law of increasing opportunity costs:* the more pollution society reduces, the higher the cost of each additional unit of pollution reduction.

The **optimal reduction of an externality** occurs when society's marginal cost and marginal benefit of reducing that externality are equal (MC = MB). In Figure 4.8 the optimal amount of pollution abatement is Q_1 units. When MB exceeds MC, additional abatement moves society toward economic efficiency; the added benefit of cleaner air or water exceeds the benefit forgone of any alternative use of the required resources. When MC exceeds MB, additional abatement reduces economic efficiency; there would be greater benefits from using resources in some other way than to further reduce pollution.

In reality, it is difficult to measure the marginal costs and benefits of pollution control. Nevertheless, Figure 4.8 demonstrates that a positive level of pollution may be economically efficient. This efficiency occurs not because pollution is desirable but because beyond some level, further abatement may reduce society's net well-being. For example, it would cost the government billions of dollars to clean up every last piece of litter in America. Thus, it is better to tolerate some trash blowing around if the money saved by not trying to pick up every last piece will yield larger net benefits when spent elsewhere.

Shifts of the Abatement MB and MC Curves

The locations of the MC and MB curves in Figure 4.8 are not forever fixed. They can, and probably do, shift over time. For example, suppose that the technology of pollution-control equipment improved noticeably. We would expect the cost of pollution abatement to fall, society's MC curve to shift rightward, and the optimal level of abatement to rise. Or suppose that society decides that it wants cleaner air and water because of new information about the adverse health effects of pollution. The MB curve in Figure 4.8 will shift rightward, and the optimal level of pollution control would increase beyond Q_1. Test your understanding of these statements by drawing the new MC and MB curves in Figure 4.8.

Government's Role When Externalities Are Present

Correcting for market failures is neither easy nor straightforward. For starters, government officials must correctly identify both the existence and the cause of any particular market failure. That process may be difficult, time consuming, and costly. Then, even after a market failure is correctly identified and diagnosed, political pressures may hamper or block remedial action due to the fact that the main personal objective of many politicians is to get elected and stay elected. Only in some cases will voting to correct a market failure serve that purpose. In others, it may even be the case that political pressures incline politicians to vote for laws that make the market failure worse, not better.

Political pressures can, as a result, lead to overregulation in some cases, and underregulation in others. Some government taxes and subsidies are imposed not because their benefits exceed their costs but because their benefits accrue to firms located in states represented by powerful elected officials. Sometimes direct controls are imposed at the behest of large corporations who know that their smaller competitors will not be able to afford them. Policies to correct negative externalities can be blocked in the legislature by the entities that are producing the spillovers.

In short, the economic role of government, although critical to a well-functioning economy, is not always perfectly carried out. Economists use the term *government failure* to describe economically inefficient outcomes caused by shortcomings in the public sector. You can read more about government failure in the next chapter.

CONSIDER THIS . . .

Congestion Pricing

Driving is costly. The private costs include paying for gas and the opportunity cost of the time drivers spend in traffic getting to their destinations. But there are external costs, too.

If you are the only person driving down a highway, there is no way for you to impose a negative externality on other drivers. But if traffic is moderate or heavy, your entering a roadway imposes an additional amount of congestion on other drivers. That additional crowding slows traffic down, raising time and gasoline costs for you and everyone else. And the problem is mutual, because the presence of the other drivers imposes a negative congestion externality on you, too.

One solution is to charge people for using the roadway, as with toll roads and the paid express lanes now found in many major cities. The fees that are assessed raise the

Stefano Carnevali/Shutterstock

direct private cost of driving to you and other drivers. But that higher private cost will discourage some people from driving, especially at peak hours. If the tolls are set correctly, drivers will collectively save more in reduced congestion costs than they pay in tolling fees. In the case of highways that have paid express lanes running in parallel with free lanes, drivers will sort themselves according to their opportunity costs and their willingness and ability to pay. Those with low opportunity costs for time will prefer to endure heavier traffic in the free lanes even if they have the ability to pay for the express lanes. But those who have a high opportunity cost for time will prefer to pay for the express lanes whenever they can afford to do so.

▶ Negative-externality reduction comes at a cost, and the marginal cost of each additional reduction is higher than for the previous reduction.

▶ The optimal amount of negative-externality reduction occurs where society's marginal cost and

marginal benefit of reducing the externality are equal.

▶ Political pressures often cause governments to respond inefficiently when attempting to correct for market failures.

Asymmetric Information

>> **LO4.4** Understand why asymmetric information may justify government intervention in some markets.

asymmetric information A situation where one party to a market transaction has more information about a product or service than the other. The result may be an under- or overallocation of resources.

private information Facts known by one party to a market transaction but hidden from others; results in *asymmetric information*.

We have already discussed the two most prominent sources of market failure: negative and positive externalities. But there is also another, subtler, type of market failure that is caused by **asymmetric information,** or the situation that occurs when one party to a market transaction possesses **private information** that is not readily available to the other party at a low cost.

This asymmetry (inequality) of information makes it difficult to distinguish trustworthy sellers from untrustworthy sellers or trustworthy buyers from untrustworthy buyers. When information is asymmetric, society's scarce resources may be allocated inefficiently, thus implying that the government should intervene. The government may, for example, take steps to equalize the information available to market participants. Under rare circumstances, the government may even supply a good or service whose private sector production has been hobbled by asymmetric information.

When Sellers Possess Private Information

Situations in which sellers possess *private information* that is not available to buyers at a low cost can result in market failure and an underallocation of resources to the production of a good or service. Two examples of this information asymmetry will help you understand the problem.

Example: Gasoline Market Assume an absurd situation: Suppose there is no system of weights and measures established by law, no government inspection of gasoline pumps, and no law against false advertising. Each gas station can use whatever measure it chooses; it can define a gallon of gas as it pleases. A station can advertise that its gas is 87 octane, when in fact it is only 75. It can rig its pumps to indicate that it is providing more gas than the amount being delivered.

Obviously, the consumer's cost of obtaining reliable information under such chaotic conditions is exceptionally high, if not prohibitive. Customers or their representatives would have to buy samples of gas from various gas stations, have them tested for octane level, and test the accuracy of calibrations at the pump. And these activities would have to be repeated regularly, since a station owner could alter the product quality and the accuracy of the pump at will.

Because of the high cost of obtaining information about the seller, many consumers would opt out of this chaotic market. One tankful of a 50 percent mixture of gasoline and water would be enough to discourage most motorists from further driving. More realistically, the conditions in this market would encourage consumers to vote for political candidates who promise to provide a government solution. The oil companies and honest gasoline stations would most likely welcome government intervention. They would realize that accurate information, by enabling this market to work, would expand their total sales and profits.

The government has in fact intervened in the market for gasoline and other markets with similar potential information difficulties. It has established a system of weights and measures, employed inspectors to check the accuracy of gasoline pumps, and passed laws against fraudulent claims and misleading advertising. Clearly, these government activities have produced net benefits for society.

Example: Licensing of Surgeons Suppose that anyone can hang out a shingle and claim to be a surgeon, much as anyone can become a house painter. The market would eventually sort the true surgeons from the frauds. As people died from botched surgeries, lawsuits for malpractice would eventually identify and eliminate most of the medical impostors. And people needing surgery for themselves or their loved ones would seek out information about physician quality from newspaper reports, websites, or people who have undergone similar operations.

But this process of obtaining information will take considerable time and impose unacceptably high human and economic costs. There is a fundamental difference between getting an amateurish paint job on one's house and being on the receiving end of a heart surgery performed by a bogus physician. The marginal cost of obtaining information about sellers in the surgery market will be excessively high. That will make the risk of proceeding to surgery too high for many consumers. The result will be too few surgeries being performed and an underallocation of resources to surgery.

The government has remedied this market failure through a system of qualifying tests and licensing. The licensing provides consumers with inexpensive information about a service—surgery—that they only rarely purchase.

The government has pursued similar policies in several other areas of the economy that are afflicted by asymmetric information. For example, it approves new medicines, regulates the securities industry, and requires warnings on containers of potentially hazardous substances. It also requires warning labels on cigarette packages and disseminates information about communicable diseases. And it issues warnings about unsafe toys and inspects restaurants for health-related violations. Each of these efforts provides either increased certainty about product quality or sufficient warning about a risk that would otherwise remain obscure.

When Buyers Possess Private Information

Situations in which buyers possess *private information* not available to sellers at a low cost can also result in market failure and an underallocation of resources to the production of a good or service. The buyers may be consumers purchasing consumer goods or firms bidding for resources. In either case, the private information held by buyers may put them in a position to take advantage of the sellers. The sellers, knowing that this could be a problem, are naturally reluctant to interact with buyers. The result is reduced—or even zero—market activity.

Moral Hazard The **moral hazard problem** arises when a person behaves more recklessly after obtaining a contract that shifts the costs of bad outcomes onto another party, such as an insurance company or the government. Examples: A truck driver starts speeding and passing aggressively after obtaining auto insurance because he knows that if he wrecks, the insurance company will be stuck with the bill. Lenders start making loans to shady, high-risk firms after obtaining government loan guarantees because they know that the government will have to pay back the loans if the firms go bankrupt.

moral hazard problem The possibility that individuals or institutions will behave more recklessly after they obtain insurance or similar contracts that shift the financial burden of bad outcomes onto others. Example: A bank whose deposits are insured against losses may make riskier loans and investments.

You might hope that people would not manifest this behavior, but the financial temptation and the ethical dilemma (moral hazard) are too much for many people. They begin to take on more risks because they know that someone else will have to bear the consequences if anything goes wrong.

Private markets may underallocate resources to a good or service that is affected by the moral hazard problem because the sellers of the product will not be able to tell which specific buyers may be affected by moral hazard, the degree to which that moral hazard may lead them to engage in costly behavior, and whether such buyers are very common or few and far between. All that information about buyer behavior is private information held by the buyers, who of course know their own inclinations and can costlessly observe their own actions.

To see why this information asymmetry will tend to repel sellers, suppose a firm offers an insurance policy that pays a set amount of money per month to people who get divorced. Such insurance would spread the economic risk of divorce across thousands of people, thereby helping to protect spouses and children from the economic hardship that divorce often brings.

Unfortunately, the moral hazard problem reduces the likelihood that insurance companies can profitably provide this type of insurance. After purchasing divorce insurance, policyholders can look forward to fewer hardships should a divorce occur. But that reduction in future risk will cause some policyholders to fear divorce less. They will begin to take fewer steps to avert divorce and thereby raise the likelihood of getting divorced. For example, married couples would have less incentive to get along or to iron out marital difficulties if they obtain divorce insurance. At the extreme, some couples might be motivated to obtain a divorce, collect the insurance, and then continue to live together. Such insurance could even promote divorce, the very outcome that it is intended to protect against. The moral hazard problem would force the insurer to charge such a high premium that few policies would be bought.

If the insurer could identify in advance those people most prone to alter their behavior, the firm could exclude them from buying the insurance. But the firm's marginal cost of getting such information is too high compared with the marginal benefit. The result is a failed market.

Although divorce insurance will not be available, society recognizes the benefits of protecting people against the hardships of divorce. It has corrected for this underallocation of "hardship insurance" through child-support laws that dictate payments to the spouse who retains the children.

The moral hazard problem also arises in the following situations:

- Medical malpractice insurance may increase the amount of malpractice.
- Unemployment compensation may lead some workers to shirk.
- Guaranteed contracts for professional athletes may reduce the quality of their performance.

adverse selection problem
A problem arising when information known to one party to a contract or agreement is not known to the other party, causing the latter to incur major costs. Example: Individuals who have the poorest health are most likely to buy health insurance.

Adverse Selection   The **adverse selection problem** manifests itself in insurance markets whenever the people who are most likely to need insurance payouts are the people most likely to buy insurance. For example, those in poorest health will be the most likely to purchase health insurance. Or, at the extreme, a person planning to hire an arsonist to "torch" her failing business will have a much stronger incentive to buy fire insurance than a person not planning to incinerate her business.

The adverse selection problem tends to eliminate the unbiased pooling of low and high risks, which is the basis of profitable insurance. With the insurance pool dominated by high risks, premiums must shoot up. And as they do, people with low risks will decide not to buy insurance. The sorting (selection) of people purchasing insurance will become biased toward those with high risks and therefore disadvantageous (adverse) to the insurance company. Insurance rates must then be set so high that few people would want to (or be able to) buy such insurance.

In theory, one solution to the adverse selection problem would be for insurance companies to charge different rates to high-risk and low-risk customers. That is not possible in practice, however, because the information necessary to distinguish between high-risk and low-risk applicants is private information held by buyers. There is, consequently, virtually nothing that a private insurance company can do to prevent adverse selection when buyers hold tightly to their private information.

Governments, by contrast, do have a way of overcoming the adverse selection problem: they can require that every potential customer purchase insurance. That way the insurance pool will include both the low-risk customers as well as the high-risk customers, thereby eliminating the possibility of adverse selection. This is, for example, the strategy followed by the 48 states that require every licensed driver to purchase automobile insurance. It is also the strategy applied by the Social Security system in the United States, which provides insurance against poverty during old age. By mandating nearly universal participation, the people who are most likely to need the minimum benefits that Social Security provides are automatically participants in the program. So, too, are those not likely to need the benefits. With both groups participating at equal rates, adverse selection is averted.

Qualification

We should not leave you with the incorrect impression that every information asymmetry requires a government intervention. In many cases, households and businesses have invented ingenious methods that can overcome information asymmetries without the need for government involvement.

For example, many firms offer product warranties to overcome the lack of information about themselves and their products. Franchising also helps overcome this problem. When you visit a Wendy's or a Marriott, you know what you are going to get, as opposed to stopping at Slim's Hamburger Shop or the Triple Eight Motel.

Also, some private firms and organizations specialize in providing information to buyers and sellers. *Consumer Reports, Mobil Travel Guide,* and numerous Internet sites provide product information; labor unions collect and disseminate information about job safety; and credit bureaus provide information about credit histories and past bankruptcies to lending institutions and insurance companies. Brokers, bonding agencies, and intermediaries also provide information to clients.

However, economists agree that the private sector cannot remedy all information problems. In some situations, government intervention is desirable to promote an efficient allocation of society's scarce resources.

Visible Pollution, Hidden Costs

How Can Governments Reduce Air Pollution at the Lowest Possible Cost If Only the Polluters Themselves Know the Costs of Abatement?

Governments around the world are interested in reducing the emission of gases like carbon dioxide (CO_2) and methane that are released when fossil fuels are burned. Such gasses are believed to be prime drivers of *global warming* and *climate change,* but the costs of reducing the emissions of such gasses can vary widely depending on what policy a government chooses to pursue. An outright ban on burning fossil fuels, for instance, would be extremely costly as it would shut down tens of thousands of existing businesses, plunging their employees into unemployment.

Thus, governments have pursued less draconian methods of reducing air pollution. If implemented correctly, these alternatives, such as carbon taxes and emissions limits, can generate major reductions at a reasonable cost, thereby avoiding the severe economic dislocation that would come with a sudden outright ban on the burning of fossil fuels.

Sensible pollution-abatement policies account for marginal benefits and marginal costs. Society will want as much of an activity like burning gasoline to power ambulances as is associated with the allocatively efficient output level that takes into account all costs (including negative externalities) as well as all benefits. A draconian policy that bans gasoline would go too far; we need ambulances and are willing to tolerate some air pollution in order to transport sick and injured people rapidly and affordably to hospitals.

The trick for government, then, is to figure out how to achieve the allocatively efficient output level at the lowest possible cost. As you know from this chapter, that can be accomplished by figuring out the marginal cost of pollution abatement for each source of pollution and comparing it with the marginal benefit associated with mitigating that source of pollution. The government should then eliminate all of the polluting activities for which the marginal benefit of abatement exceeds the marginal cost of abatement.

That's a great strategy, but can the government implement it? The answer is yes, but the government needs to overcome an important obstacle. The costs of pollution abatement are not obvious. Would it, for instance, be less costly to eliminate 1 million tons per year of CO_2 emissions by shutting down a small factory in Memphis or by paying to retire highly inefficient older vehicles in Denver? To the extent those costs are known, they are often known to the emitters themselves, but not to the government.

The government therefore encounters an asymmetric information problem. How can it reduce pollution at the lowest cost when it is the polluters themselves that are the only ones likely to know what those costs are? One way is to compel the information. Mandatory vehicle smog checks are a good example. Ninety percent of auto emissions are generated by just 25 percent of vehicles, so it is worthwhile for governments to impose the inspection costs needed to identify the high emitters.

Nordroden/123RF

Tradeable emissions permits ("cap and trade") are another way to overcome the asymmetric information problem. These work by giving polluters a financial incentive to reveal their emission reduction costs and, better yet, follow through on emissions reductions. Suppose the U.S. government knows that the allocatively optimal amount of CO_2 emissions is 4 billion tons per year, but that 5 billion tons are currently being emitted. The government will cap the total amount of emissions by printing up and handing out to polluters only 4 billion tons' worth of tradable emissions permits. Each permit may be for, say, 1 ton of CO_2 emissions, and emitting that amount of CO_2 is legal only if you have a permit.

The government will have to hand out the permits without knowing whether they are going to the emitters that have the lowest costs of abatement. But that turns out not to matter if the government makes the permits tradeable, so that they can be bought and sold freely. An emissions-trading market will pop up and what you'll find is that the firms with the highest costs of emissions reduction will purchase permits away from the firms with the lowest costs of emission reduction.

The high-cost firms benefit because it is less expensive for them to buy permits to keep on polluting than it is to reduce their own pollution. And the low-cost firms benefit because they can make more money selling their permits than it will cost them to reduce their emissions (which they must do after they sell away their permits). Both sides win, the externality is reduced at the lowest cost, and society achieves the allocatively efficient level of pollution by setting up a market and allowing the invisible hand to work its magic.

Tradeable pollution permits have worked successfully in several regions for several different types of emissions. They are an economically sophisticated way of overcoming the asymmetric information problem in pollution abatement in order to reduce emissions at the lowest possible cost.

▶ Asymmetric information—which occurs when either buyers or sellers have private information that is not available to other market participants—can lead to mistrust that results in market failure and a misallocation of resources.

▶ The moral hazard problem is the tendency of one party to a contract or agreement to alter its behavior in ways that are costly to the other party; for example, a person who obtains insurance may intentionally incur additional risk.

▶ Adverse selection occurs in an insurance market when policies are purchased predominantly by buyers with higher risk profiles, thereby making the provision of insurance prohibitively expensive.

▶ While governments have in specific cases intervened to overcome market failures caused by asymmetric information, the private sector has in many other cases developed ingenious ways to solve asymmetric information problems.

Summary

LO4.1 Explain consumer surplus, producer surplus, and how properly functioning markets maximize total surplus and allocate resources optimally.

Consumer surplus is the difference between the maximum price that a consumer is willing to pay for a product and the lower price actually paid; producer surplus is the difference between the minimum price that a producer is willing to accept for a product and the higher price actually received.

Graphically, consumer surplus is represented by the triangle under the demand curve and above the actual price. Producer surplus is shown by the triangle above the supply curve and below the actual price.

The combined amount of producer and consumer surplus, or total surplus, is represented graphically by the triangle to the left of the intersection of the supply and demand curves that is below the demand curve and above the supply curve.

At the equilibrium price and quantity in a competitive market, marginal benefit equals marginal cost, maximum willingness to pay equals minimum acceptable price, and total surplus is maximized.

Output levels that are either less than or greater than the equilibrium output create efficiency losses, also called deadweight losses. These losses are reductions in total surplus. Underproduction creates efficiency losses because output is not being produced for which maximum willingness to pay exceeds minimum acceptable price. Overproduction creates efficiency losses because output is being produced for which minimum acceptable price exceeds maximum willingness to pay.

LO4.2 Explain how positive and negative externalities cause under- and overallocations of resources.

Externalities, or spillovers, are costs or benefits that accrue to someone other than the immediate buyer or seller. Such costs or benefits are not captured in market demand or supply curves and therefore cause the output of certain goods to vary from society's optimal output. Negative externalities (or spillover costs or external costs) result in an overallocation of resources to a particular product. Positive externalities (or spillover benefits or external benefits) result in an underallocation of resources to a particular product.

Direct controls and specifically targeted Pigovian taxes can improve resource allocation in situations where negative externalities affect many people and community resources. Both direct controls (for example, smokestack emission standards) and Pigovian taxes (for example, taxes on the production of toxic chemicals) increase production costs and hence product price. As product price rises, the externality, overallocation of resources, and efficiency loss are reduced because less output is produced.

Government can correct the underallocation of resources and efficiency losses either by subsidizing consumers (which increases market demand) or by subsidizing producers (which increases market supply). Such subsidies increase the equilibrium output, reducing or eliminating the positive externality, the underallocation of resources, and the efficiency loss.

The Coase theorem suggests that under the right circumstances private bargaining can solve externality problems. Thus, government intervention is not always needed to deal with externality problems.

LO4.3 Explain why society is usually unwilling to pay the costs of completely eliminating negative externalities, such as air pollution.

The socially optimal amount of externality abatement occurs where society's marginal cost and marginal benefit of reducing an externality are equal. With pollution, for example, the optimal amount of pollution abatement is likely to be less than a 100 percent reduction.

Market failures present government with opportunities to improve the allocation of resources and thereby enhance society's total well-being, but political pressures may make it difficult or impossible to implement an effective solution.

LO4.4 Understand why asymmetric information may justify government intervention in some markets.

Asymmetric information can cause a market to fail if the party with less information decides to withdraw from the market because it fears being exploited by the party with more information. If the party with less information reduces its participation in a market, the reduction in the size of the market may cause an underallocation of resources to the production of the product sold in the market.

The moral hazard problem is the tendency of one party to a contract or agreement to alter their behavior in ways that are costly to the other party. For example, a person who buys insurance may willingly incur added risk.

The adverse selection problem arises when one party to a contract or agreement has less information than the other party and incurs a cost because of that asymmetrical information. For example, an insurance company offering "no medical exam required" life insurance policies may attract customers who have life-threatening diseases.

Terms and Concepts

market failure	deadweight loss	optimal reduction of an externality
total surplus	externality	asymmetric information
consumer surplus	negative externality	private information
producer surplus	positive externality	moral hazard problem
productive efficiency	direct controls	adverse selection problem
allocative efficiency	Coase theorem	
efficiency loss	Pigovian tax	

Discussion Questions

1. Use the ideas of consumer surplus and producer surplus to explain why economists say competitive markets are efficient. Why are below- or above-equilibrium levels of output inefficient, according to these two ideas? **LO4.1**

2. What divergences arise between equilibrium output and efficient output when (a) negative externalities and (b) positive externalities are present? How might government correct these divergences? Cite an example (other than the text examples) of an external cost and an external benefit. **LO4.2**

3. Why are spillover costs and spillover benefits also called negative and positive externalities? Show graphically how a tax can correct for a negative externality and how a subsidy to producers can correct for a positive externality. How does a subsidy to consumers differ from a subsidy to producers in correcting a positive externality? **LO4.2**

4. An apple grower's orchard provides nectar to a neighbor's bees, while the beekeeper's bees help the apple grower by pollinating his apple blossoms. Use Figure 4.5b to explain why this situation of dual positive externalities might lead to an underallocation of resources to both apple growing and beekeeping. How might this underallocation get resolved via the means suggested by the Coase theorem? **LO4.2**

5. The LoJack car recovery system allows the police to track stolen cars. As a result, they not only recover 90 percent of LoJack-equipped cars that are stolen but also arrest many auto thieves and shut down many "chop shops" that rip apart stolen vehicles to get their parts. Thus, LoJack provides both private benefits and positive externalities. Should the government consider subsidizing LoJack purchases? **LO4.2**

6. Explain why zoning laws, which allow certain land uses only in specific locations, might be justified in dealing with negative externalities. Explain why in areas where buildings sit close together, tax breaks to property owners for installing extra fire-prevention equipment might be justified due to positive externalities. **LO4.2**

7. Because medical records are private, individuals applying for health insurance will know more about their own health conditions than will the insurance companies to which they are applying for coverage. Is this information asymmetry likely to increase or decrease the insurance premium? Why? **LO4.4**

8. Why is it in the interest of people purchasing new homes as well as the builders of new homes to have government building codes and building inspectors? **LO4.4**

9. Which of the following are moral hazard problems? Which are adverse selection problems? **LO4.4**
   a. A person with a terminal illness buys several life insurance policies through the mail.
   b. A person drives carelessly because she has automobile insurance.
   c. A person who intends to torch his warehouse takes out a large fire insurance policy.
   d. A professional athlete who has a guaranteed contract fails to stay in shape during the off season.
   e. A person who anticipates having a large family takes a job with a firm that offers exceptional child care benefits.

10. **LAST WORD** What information does a government need if it wants to attempt to reduce a widespread negative externality like air pollution? Who, typically, is actually in possession of that information? How do markets in tradeable emissions permits solve the asymmetric information problem affecting pollution abatement efforts?

Review Questions

1. Draw a supply and demand graph and identify the areas of consumer surplus and producer surplus. Given the demand curve, how will an increase in supply affect the amount of consumer surplus shown in your diagram? Explain. **LO4.1**

2. Assume that candle wax is traded in a perfectly competitive market in which the demand curve captures buyers' full willingness to pay while the supply curve reflects all production costs. For each of the following situations, indicate whether the total output should be increased, decreased, or kept the same in order to achieve allocative and productive efficiency. **LO4.1**
   a. Maximum willingness to pay exceeds minimum acceptable price.
   b. MC > MB.
   c. Total surplus is at a maximum.
   d. The current quantity produced exceeds the market equilibrium quantity.

3. Efficiency losses _____. **LO4.1**
   a. are not possible if suppliers are willing to produce and sell a product.
   b. can result only from underproduction.
   c. can result only from overproduction.
   d. none of the above.
4. Match each of the following characteristics or scenarios with either the term *negative externality* or the term *positive externality*. **LO4.2**
   a. Resources are overallocated.
   b. Xochitl installs a very nice front garden, raising the property values of all the other houses on her block.
   c. Market demand curves are too far to the left (too low).
   d. Resources are underallocated.
   e. Water pollution from a factory forces neighbors to buy water purifiers.
5. Use marginal cost–marginal benefit analysis to determine if the following statement is true or false: "The optimal amount

of pollution abatement for some substances, say, dirty water from storm drains, is very low; the optimal amount of abatement for other substances, say, cyanide poison, is close to 100 percent." **LO4.3**
6. People drive faster when they have auto insurance. This example illustrates: **LO4.4**
   a. adverse selection.
   b. asymmetric information.
   c. moral hazard.
7. Government inspectors who check on the quality of services provided by retailers and government requirements for licensing in various professions are both attempts to resolve: **LO4.4**
   a. the moral hazard problem.
   b. the asymmetric information problem.
8. True or False: A market may collapse and have relatively few transactions between buyers and sellers if buyers have more information than sellers. **LO4.4**

Problems

McGraw Hill connect

1. Refer to Table 4.1. If the six people listed in the table are the only consumers in the market, and the equilibrium price is $11 (not the $8 shown), how much consumer surplus will the market generate? **LO4.1**
2. Refer to Table 4.2. If the six people listed in the table are the only producers in the market, and the equilibrium price is $6 (not the $8 shown), how much producer surplus will the market generate? **LO4.1**
3. Look at Tables 4.1 and 4.2 together. What is the total surplus if Bashir buys a unit from Chander? If Barb buys a unit from Chaaya? If Bashir buys a unit from Chad? If you match up pairs of buyers and sellers so as to maximize the total surplus of all transactions, what is the largest total surplus that can be achieved? **LO4.1**
4. **ADVANCED ANALYSIS** Assume the following values for Figures 4.4a and 4.4b: $Q_1 = 20$ bags. $Q_2 = 15$ bags. $Q_3 = 27$ bags. The market equilibrium price is $45 per bag. The price at a is $85 per bag. The price at c is $5 per bag. The price at f is $59 per bag. The price at g is $31 per bag. Apply the formula for the area of a triangle (Area $= 1/2 \times$ Base $\times$ Height) to answer the following questions. **LO4.1**
   a. What is the dollar value of the total surplus ($=$ producer surplus $+$ consumer surplus) when the allocatively efficient output level is produced? What is the dollar value of the consumer surplus at that output level?
   b. What is the dollar value of the deadweight loss when output level Q_2 is produced? What is the total surplus when output level Q_2 is produced?
   c. What is the dollar value of the deadweight loss when output level Q_3 is produced? What is the dollar value of the total surplus when output level Q_3 is produced?
5. Refer to Tables 4.1 and 4.2, which show, respectively, the willingness to pay and the willingness to accept of buyers and sellers of bags of oranges. For the following questions, assume that the equilibrium price and quantity depend on the following changes in supply and demand. Also assume that the only

market participants are those listed by name in the two tables. **LO4.2**
   a. What are the equilibrium price and quantity for the data displayed in the two tables?
   b. Instead of bags of oranges, assume that the data in the two tables deal with a good (such as fireworks displays) that can be enjoyed by free riders who do not pay for it. If all the buyers in the two tables free ride, what quantity will private sellers supply?
   c. Assume that we are back to talking about bags of oranges (a private good), but the government has decided that tossed orange peels impose a negative externality on the public that must be rectified by imposing a $2-per-bag tax on sellers. What is the new equilibrium price and quantity? If the new equilibrium quantity is the optimal quantity, by how many bags were oranges overproduced before?
6. Consider a used-car market with asymmetric information. The owners of used cars know what their vehicles are worth but have no way of credibly demonstrating those values to potential buyers. Thus, potential buyers must always worry that the used car they are being offered may be a low-quality "lemon." **LO4.4**
   a. Suppose that there are equal numbers of good and bad used cars in the market. Good used cars are worth $13,000, and bad used cars are worth $5,000. What is the average value of a used car?
   b. By how much does the average value exceed the value of a bad used car? By how much does the value of a good used car exceed the average value?
   c. Would a potential seller of a good used car be willing to accept the average value as payment for the vehicle?
   d. If a buyer negotiates with a seller to purchase the seller's used car for a price equal to the average value, is the car more likely to be good or bad?
   e. Will the used-car market come to feature mostly—if not exclusively—lemons? Explain. How much will used cars end up costing if all the good cars are withdrawn from the market?

Public Goods, Public Choice, and Government Failure

>> LEARNING OBJECTIVES

LO5.1 Describe free riding and public goods, and illustrate why private firms cannot normally produce public goods.

LO5.2 Explain the difficulties of conveying economic preferences through majority voting.

LO5.3 Define government failure and explain its causes.

In the previous chapter, we discussed *externalities* and *asymmetric information*, two types of *market failure* that can cause markets to either overproduce or underproduce relative to the social optimum.

This chapter takes as its starting point *public goods*, which can be afflicted by a more extreme variety of market failure in which production drops all the way to zero. In these situations, government often steps forward to produce the missing public good. But that leads to an interesting economic problem: How much should the government provide? What quantity of a public good is allocatively efficient?

We also study why governments often fail to intervene in the economy in socially optimal ways. Causes include corruption, special interest lobbying, and the voting paradoxes that can make it nearly impossible for government officials to discern the "will of the people." Our study of these problems—collectively known as *government failure*—balances our analysis of *market failure*. Markets can go haywire, but so can government. Vigilance is warranted with respect to both.

Public Goods

Demand-side market failures arise when demand curves underreport how much consumers are willing and able to pay for a product. When that happens, demand curves shift left and equilibrium output is below the social optimum. That was the case with the positive externalities studied in the previous chapter.

The underreporting of demand reaches its most extreme form in the case of public goods. Markets may fail to produce *any* of a public good because its demand curve may reflect *none* of its potential consumers' willingness to pay. But to understand public goods, we first need to understand the characteristics that define private goods.

>> **LO5.1** Describe free riding and public goods, and illustrate why private firms cannot normally produce public goods.

demand-side market failures Underallocations of resources that occur when private demand curves understate consumers' full willingness to pay for a *good* or *service*.

private good A *good* or *service* that is individually consumed and that can be profitably provided by privately owned *firms* because they can exclude nonpayers from receiving the benefits.

rivalry The characteristic displayed by certain goods and services that consumption by one person precludes consumption by others.

excludability The characteristic displayed by those goods and services for which sellers are able to prevent nonbuyers from obtaining benefits.

public good A *good* or *service* that is characterized by *nonrivalry* and *nonexcludability*. These characteristics typically imply that no private *firm* can break even when attempting to provide such products. As a result, they are often provided by governments, who pay for them using general *tax* revenues.

nonrivalry The idea that one person's benefit from a certain *good* does not reduce the benefit available to others; a characteristic of a *public good*.

nonexcludability The inability to keep nonpayers (free riders) from obtaining benefits from a certain good; a characteristic of a *public good*.

free-rider problem The inability of potential providers of an economically desirable *good* or *service* to obtain payment from those who benefit, because of *nonexcludability*.

Characteristics of Private Goods

The vast majority of goods and services consumed by people on a daily basis are private goods produced by private, for-profit companies.

Private goods are distinguished by rivalry and excludability.

- **Rivalry** (in consumption) means that when one person consumes a product, it is not available for another person to consume. When Garcia purchases and drinks a bottle of mineral water, it is not available for Johnson to purchase and consume.
- **Excludability** means that sellers can prevent people who do not pay for a product from obtaining its benefits. Only people who are willing and able to pay the market price for bottles of water can obtain these drinks and the benefits they confer.

Excludability is the key feature when it comes to understanding why for-profit companies are happy to produce private goods for consumers. Indeed, it is only because private goods are excludable that private producers are willing to produce them. Excludability means that private producers can "put a fence around" private goods and require payment by consumers. That is crucial because if private firms were not able to charge customers for their products, they would not be able to cover their production costs and would soon go bankrupt.

Consumers fully express their personal demands for private goods in the market. If Garcia likes bottled mineral water, that fact will be known by her desire to purchase the product. Other things equal, the higher the price of bottled water, the fewer bottles she will buy. This is simply *individual* demand, as described in Chapter 3.

The *market* demand for a private good is the horizontal summation of the individual demand schedules (review Figure 3.2). Suppose just two consumers comprise the market for bottled water and the price is $1 per bottle. If Garcia will purchase 3 bottles and Johnson will buy 2, the market demand reflects consumers' demand for 5 bottles at the $1 price. Similar summations of quantities demanded at other prices will generate the market demand schedule and curve.

Suppose the equilibrium price of bottled water is $1. Garcia and Johnson will buy a total of 5 bottles, and the sellers will obtain total revenue of $5 (= $1 × 5). If the sellers' cost per bottle is $0.80, their total cost will be $4 (= $0.80 × 5). So sellers charging $1 per bottle will obtain $5 of total revenue, incur $4 of total cost, and earn $1 of profit on the 5 bottles sold.

Because firms can charge for private goods, they are able to "tap market demand." Consumers willing to pay the market price obtain the goods; nonpayers go without. A competitive market not only makes private goods available to consumers but also allocates society's resources efficiently to the particular product. There is neither underproduction nor overproduction of the product.

Public Goods Characteristics

Public goods are the opposite of private goods in terms of rivalry and excludability. In fact, public goods are distinguished by *non*rivalry and *non*excludability.

- **Nonrivalry** (in consumption) means that one person's consumption of a good does not preclude consumption of the good by others. Everyone can simultaneously obtain the benefit from a public good such as national defense, street lighting, or a global positioning system.
- **Nonexcludability** means there is no effective way of excluding individuals from the benefit of the good once it comes into existence. You cannot exclude someone from benefiting from national defense, street lighting, or a global positioning system.

These two characteristics create a **free-rider problem.** Once a producer has provided a public good, everyone, including nonpayers, can obtain the benefit.

Because most people do not voluntarily pay for something that they can obtain for free, most people become free riders. These free riders like the public good and would be willing to pay for it if producers could somehow force them to pay—but nonexcludability means that there is no way for producers to withhold the good from the free riders, whose willingness to pay is, consequently, not expressed in the market. From the producers' viewpoint, free riding reduces demand. The more free riding, the less demand. And if all consumers free ride, demand will collapse to zero.

The low or zero demand caused by free riding makes it virtually impossible for private firms to profitably provide public goods. With little or no demand, firms cannot effectively "tap market demand" for revenues and profits. As a result, they will not produce public goods. Society will

CONSIDER THIS . . .

Street Entertainers

Street entertainers are often found in tourist areas of major cities. These entertainers illuminate the concepts of free riders and public goods.

Most street entertainers have a hard time earning a living from their activities (unless event organizers pay them) because they have no way of excluding non-payers from the benefits of their entertainment. They essentially are providing public, not private, goods and must rely on voluntary payments.

The result is a significant free-rider problem. Only a few in the audience put money in the container or instrument case, and many who do so contribute only token amounts. The rest are free riders who obtain the benefits of the street entertainment and retain their money for purchases that they themselves initiate.

500px/Alamy Stock Photo

Street entertainers are acutely aware of the free-rider problem, and some have found creative ways to lessen it. For example, some entertainers involve the audience directly in the act. This usually creates a greater sense of audience willingness (or obligation) to contribute money at the end of the performance.

"Pay for performance" is another creative approach to lessening the free-rider problem. A good example is the street entertainer painted up to look like a statue. When people drop coins into the container, the "statue" makes a slight movement. The greater the contributions, the greater the movement. But these human "statues" still face a free-rider problem: Nonpayers also get to enjoy the acts.

therefore suffer efficiency losses because goods for which marginal benefits exceed marginal costs are not produced. Thus, if society wants a public good to be produced, it must turn to nonmarket provision by entities that do not have to worry about profitability.

One option is private philanthropy. But many public goods—such as national defense and universal public education—are too expensive for private philanthropy. So society often looks to government to provide public goods.

Those government-provided public goods will still be nonexcludable; so the government won't have any better luck preventing free riding. But the government doesn't have to worry about profitability because it can finance the provision of public goods through taxation. It can therefore provide public goods when private firms and philanthropic organizations can't.

Examples of public goods include national defense, outdoor fireworks displays, the light beams projected by lighthouses, public art displays, and public concerts. All of these goods or services show both nonrivalry and nonexcludability.

In a few special cases, private firms can provide public goods because the production costs of these public goods can be covered by the profits generated by closely related private goods. For instance, private companies can make a profit providing broadcast TV—which is a nonrival, non-excludable public good—because they control who gets to air TV commercials, which are rival and excludable private goods. The money that broadcasters make from selling airtime for ads allows them to turn a profit despite having to provide their main product, broadcast TV, for free.

For the large majority of public goods, however, private provision is unprofitable. As a result, they must be furnished, if at all, by either private philanthropy or the government. For many less expensive or less important public goods like fireworks displays or public art, society may feel comfortable relying on private philanthropy. But when it comes to public goods like national defense, people normally look to the government.

This leads to an important question: Once a government decides to produce a particular public good, how can it determine the optimal amount that it should provide? How can it avoid either underallocating or overallocating society's scarce resources to the production of the public good?

Optimal Quantity of a Public Good

If consumers need not reveal their true demand for a public good in the marketplace, how can society determine the optimal amount of that good? The answer is that the government must try to estimate the demand for the public good through surveys or public votes. It can then compare the marginal benefit (MB) of an added unit of the good against the government's marginal cost (MC) of providing it. Adhering to the MB = MC rule, government can provide the "right," or "efficient," amount of the public good.

▶ Private goods are characterized by rivalry (one person's consumption precludes anyone else's consumption) and excludability (nonpayers can be excluded from consumption).

▶ Public goods are characterized by nonrivalry (consumption by one person does not diminish anyone else's consumption) and nonexcludability (nonpayers cannot be excluded from consumption).

▶ The socially optimal amount of a public good is the amount at which the marginal cost and marginal benefit of the good are equal: MB = MC.

Demand for Public Goods

The demand for a public good is somewhat unusual. Suppose Garcia and Johnson are the only two people in the society, and their marginal willingness to pay for a public good, national defense, is as shown in Table 5.1. Economists might have discovered these schedules through a survey asking questions about how much each citizen is willing to pay for various types and amounts of public goods rather than go without them.

Notice that the schedules in Table 5.1 are price-quantity schedules, implying that they are demand schedules. Rather than depicting demand in the usual way—the quantity of a product someone is willing to buy at each possible price—these schedules show the price someone is willing to pay for an extra unit at each possible quantity. That is, Garcia is willing to pay $4 for the first unit of the public good, $3 for the second, $2 for the third, and so on.

Suppose the government produces 1 unit of this public good. Because of nonrivalry, Garcia's consumption of the good does not preclude Johnson from also consuming it, and vice versa. So both consume the good, and neither volunteers to pay for it. But from Table 5.1 we can find the amount these two people would be willing to pay, together, rather than do without this 1 unit of the good. Columns 1 and 2 show that Garcia would be willing to pay $4 for the first unit of the public good; columns 1 and 3 show that Johnson would be willing to pay $5 for it. So the two people are jointly willing to pay $9 (= $4 + $5) for this first unit.

For the second unit of the public good, the collective price they are willing to pay is $7 (= $3 from Garcia + $4 from Johnson); for the third unit they would pay $5 (= $2 + $3); and so on. By finding the collective willingness to pay for each additional unit (column 4), we can construct a schedule of the **collective demand for a public good** (= collective willingness-to-pay for the public good). Here we are *not* adding the quantities demanded at each possible price, as we do when we determine the market demand for a private good. Instead, we are adding the prices that people are willing to pay for the last unit of the public good at each possible quantity demanded.

Figure 5.1 shows the same adding procedure graphically, using the data from Table 5.1. Note that we sum Garcia's and Johnson's willingness-to-pay curves *vertically* to derive the collective willingness-to-pay curve (demand curve). The summing procedure is downward from the top graph to the middle graph to the bottom (total) graph. For example, the height of the collective demand curve D_c at 2 units of output in the bottom graph is $7, the sum of the amounts that Garcia and Johnson are each willing to pay for the second unit (= $3 + $4). Likewise, the height of the collective demand curve at 4 units of the public good is $3 (= $1 + $2).

Please note that each of these demand curves is not only a willingness-to-pay curve but also a marginal-benefit (MB) curve. Consequently, we can interpret the collective demand curve for a public good as capturing both the collective willingness to pay for each possible unit of a public good as well as the collective marginal benefit of each unit of the public good.

collective demand for a public good A schedule or a curve showing the collective willingness to pay of consumers for a public good. Can be found by vertically adding individual demand curves, which is equivalent to adding the respective maximum prices that individual consumers are willing to pay for the last unit of the public good at each possible quantity demanded.

TABLE 5.1 Demand for a Public Good, Two Individuals

(1) Quantity of Public Good	(2) Garcia's Willingness to Pay (Price)		(3) Johnson's Willingness to Pay (Price)		(4) Collective Willingness to Pay (Price)
1	$4	+	$5	=	$9
2	3	+	4	=	7
3	2	+	3	=	5
4	1	+	2	=	3
5	0	+	1	=	1

Comparing MB and MC

We can now determine the optimal quantity of the public good. The collective demand curve D_c in Figure 5.1c measures society's marginal benefit of each unit of this particular good. The supply curve S measures society's marginal cost of each unit. The optimal quantity of this public good occurs where marginal benefit equals marginal cost, or where the two curves intersect. In Figure 5.1c that point is 3 units of the public good, where the collective willingness to pay for the last (third) unit—the marginal benefit—just matches that unit's marginal cost ($5 = $5). As we saw in Chapter 1, equating marginal benefit and marginal cost efficiently allocates society's scarce resources.

Cost-Benefit Analysis

The above example suggests a practical means, called **cost-benefit analysis,** for deciding whether to provide a particular public good and how much of it to provide. Let's go through an extended example that applies cost-benefit analysis to an infrastructure project.

Concept Suppose the federal government is contemplating several different plans for a highway construction project. Because the economy's resources are limited, any decision to use more resources in the public sector will mean fewer resources for the private sector. There will be an opportunity cost, as well as a benefit. The cost is the loss of satisfaction resulting from the accompanying decline in the production of private goods; the benefit is the extra satisfaction resulting from the output of more public goods. Should the needed resources be shifted from the private to the public sector? The answer is yes if the benefit from the new highways exceeds the cost of having fewer private goods. The answer is no if the cost of the forgone private goods is greater than the benefit associated with the new highways.

Illustration Roads and highways can be run privately, as excludability is possible with toll booths. However, the U.S. federal highway system is almost entirely nonexclusive because anyone with a car can get on and off most federal highways without restriction. Federal highways therefore satisfy one characteristic of a public good, nonexcludability. Highways are also nonrival; unless a highway is already extremely crowded, one person's driving on the highway does not preclude another person's driving on the highway. Thus, the federal highway system is effectively a public good. We can now turn to two important questions: Should the federal government expand the federal highway system? If so, what is the proper size or scope for the overall project?

Table 5.2 lists four increasingly ambitious and increasingly costly highway improvement plans: widening existing two-lane highways; building new two-lane highways; building new four-lane highways; and building new six-lane highways. The extent to which government should undertake highway construction depends on the costs and benefits. The costs are largely the costs of constructing and maintaining the highways; the benefits are improved flows of people and goods throughout the country.

(a)
Garcia

(b)
Johnson

(c)
Collective demand and supply

FIGURE 5.1
The optimal amount of a public good.

Two people—Garcia and Johnson—are the only members of a hypothetical economy. (a) D_1 shows Garcia's willingness to pay for various quantities of a particular public good. (b) D_2 shows Johnson's willingness to pay for these same quantities of this public good. (c) The collective demand for this public good is shown by D_c and is found by summing vertically Garcia's and Johnson's individual willingness-to-pay curves. The supply S of the public good is upward sloping, reflecting rising marginal costs. The optimal amount of the public good is 3 units, determined by the intersection of D_c and S. At that output, marginal benefit (reflected in the collective demand curve D_c) equals marginal cost (reflected in the supply curve S).

cost-benefit analysis
A method for deciding whether or not to provide a public good that involves a comparison of the total cost of providing that public good with its collective benefit (measured by collective willingness to pay).

TABLE 5.2 Cost-Benefit Analysis for a National Highway Construction Project (in Billions)

(1) Plan	(2) Total Cost of Project	(3) Marginal Cost	(4) Total Benefit	(5) Marginal Benefit	(6) Net Benefit (4) − (2)
No new construction	$ 0		$ 0		$ 0
		$ 50		$200	
A: Widen existing highways	50		200		150
		90		150	
B: New 2-lane highways	140		350		210
		100		120	
C: New 4-lane highways	240		470		230
		380		110	
D: New 6-lane highways	620		580		−40

The table shows that total benefit (column 4) exceeds total cost (column 2) for plans A, B, and C, indicating that some highway construction is economically justifiable. We see this directly in column 6, where total costs (column 2) are subtracted from total benefits (column 4). Net benefits are positive for plans A, B, and C. Plan D is not economically justifiable because net benefits are negative.

But the question of optimal size or scope for this project remains. Comparing the marginal cost (the change in total cost) and the marginal benefit (the change in total benefit) relating to each plan determines the answer. The guideline is well known to you from previous discussions:

- Increase an activity, project, or output as long as the marginal benefit (column 5) exceeds the marginal cost (column 3).

- Stop the activity at, or as close as possible to, the point at which the marginal benefit equals the marginal cost.

- Do not undertake a plan for which marginal cost exceeds marginal benefit.

Applying those rules, we see that plans A, B, and C should all be undertaken because marginal benefit exceeds marginal cost for each of them. But the federal government should stop there because plan D's marginal cost ($380 billion) exceeds its marginal benefit ($110 billion). Plan D should not be undertaken. Also note that Plan C is closest to the theoretical optimum because its marginal benefit ($120 billion) still exceeds marginal cost ($100 billion) while coming closest to the MB = MC ideal.

marginal cost–marginal benefit rule As it applies to *cost-benefit analysis*, the tenet that a government project or program should be expanded to the point where the *marginal cost* and *marginal benefit* of additional expenditures are equal.

This **marginal cost–marginal benefit rule** tells us which plan provides the maximum excess of total benefits over total costs or, in other words, the plan that provides society with the maximum net benefit. You can confirm directly in column 6 that the maximum net benefit (= $230 billion) is associated with plan C.

Cost-benefit analysis shatters the myth that "economy in government" and "reduced government spending" are synonymous. "Economy" is concerned with using scarce resources efficiently. If the marginal cost of a proposed government program exceeds its marginal benefit, then the proposed public program should not be undertaken. But if the marginal benefit exceeds the marginal cost, then it would be uneconomical or "wasteful" not to spend on that government program. Economy in government does not mean minimization of public spending. It means allocating resources between the private and public sectors and among public goods to achieve maximum net benefit.

Quasi-Public Goods

quasi-public good A *good* or *service* to which *excludability* could apply but that has such a large *positive externality* that government sponsors its production to prevent an underallocation of resources.

Government provides many goods that fit the economist's definition of a public good. However, it also provides other goods and services that could be produced and delivered in such a way that exclusion would be possible. Such goods, called **quasi-public goods,** include education, streets and highways, police and fire protection, libraries and museums, preventive medicine, and sewage disposal. They could all be priced and provided by private firms through the market system. But because the benefits of these goods flow well beyond the benefit to individual buyers, the market system would underproduce these goods. Therefore, government often provides them to avoid the underallocation of resources that would otherwise occur if these goods with large positive externalities were produced solely by the private sector.

The Reallocation Process

How are resources reallocated from the production of private goods to the production of public and quasi-public goods? If the economy's resources are fully employed, government must free up resources from the production of private goods and make them available for producing public and quasi-public goods. It does so by reducing the private demand for resources. And it does that by levying taxes on households and businesses, taking some of their income out of the circular flow (see Figure 2.2). With lower incomes and hence less purchasing power, households and businesses must curtail their consumption and investment spending. As a result, the private demand for goods and services declines, as does the private demand for resources. So, by diverting purchasing power from private spenders to government, taxes remove resources from private use.

Government then spends the tax proceeds to provide public and quasi-public goods and services. Taxation releases resources from the production of private consumer goods (food, clothing, television sets) and private investment goods (wi-fi networks, software for flying taxis, distribution centers). Government shifts those resources to the production of public and quasi-public goods (post offices, submarines, parks), changing the composition of the economy's total output.

Public Choice Theory and Voting Paradoxes
Public Choice Theory

Market failures, such as public goods and externalities, impede economic efficiency and justify government intervention in the economy. But the government's response to market failures is not without its own problems and pitfalls. In fact, government may sometimes fail as badly or even worse than markets.

That is why it is important to study **public choice theory**—the economic analysis of government decision making, politics, and elections. We are going to find that the intricacies and limitations of democratic voting can make it impossible for government officials to determine the public will and thus what government actions they should take in order to ensure allocative efficiency in the economy.

Revealing Preferences through Majority Voting

Through some process, society must decide which public goods it wants and in what amounts. It also must determine the extent to which it wants government to intervene in private markets to correct externalities. Decisions must be made about the extent and type of business regulation, income redistribution, policies to mitigate *asymmetric information* problems, and so on. Furthermore, society must collect taxes for financing government. How should government apportion (divide) the total tax burden among the public?

Decisions such as these are made collectively in the United States through a democratic process that relies heavily on majority voting. Candidates for office offer alternative policy packages, and citizens elect people who they think will make the best decisions on their collective behalf. Voters "retire" officials who do not adequately represent their collective wishes. Also, at the state and local levels, citizens sometimes vote directly on public expenditures or new legislation.

Although the democratic process does a reasonably good job of revealing society's preferences, it is imperfect. Public choice theory demonstrates that majority voting can produce inefficiencies and inconsistencies.

Inefficient Voting Outcomes Society's well-being is enhanced when government provides a public good whose total benefit exceeds its total cost. Unfortunately, traditional one-person-one-vote majority voting does not always deliver that outcome.

>> **LO5.2** Explain the difficulties of conveying economic preferences through majority voting.

public choice theory The economic analysis of government decision making, politics, and elections.

FIGURE 5.2
Inefficient voting outcomes.

Majority voting can produce inefficient decisions. (a) Majority voting leads to rejection of a public good that would entail a greater total benefit than total cost. (b) Majority voting results in acceptance of a public good that has a higher total cost than total benefit.

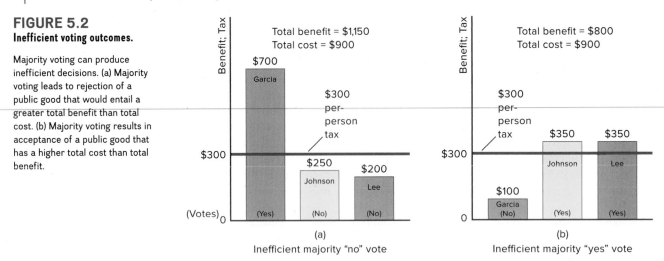

Illustration: Inefficient "No" Vote Assume that the government can provide a public good (say, national defense) at a total expense of $900. Also assume that the society is composed of only three individuals—Garcia, Johnson, and Lee—and that they will share the $900 tax expense equally, each being taxed $300 if the proposed public good is provided. And assume, as Figure 5.2a illustrates, that Garcia would receive $700 worth of benefits from having this public good; Johnson, $250; and Lee, $200.

What will be the result if a majority vote determines whether or not this public good is provided? Although people do not always vote strictly according to their own economic interest, it is likely Johnson and Lee will vote "no" because they will incur tax costs of $300 each while gaining benefits of only $250 and $200, respectively. Garcia will vote "yes." So the majority vote will defeat the proposal even though the total benefit of $1,150 (= $700 for Garcia + $250 for Johnson + $200 for Lee) exceeds the total cost of $900. Resources should be devoted to this good, but they will not be. Too little of this public good will be produced.

Illustration: Inefficient "Yes" Vote Now consider a situation in which the majority favors a public good even though its total cost exceeds its total benefit. Figure 5.2b shows the details. Again, Garcia, Johnson, and Lee will equally share the $900 cost of the public good; each will be taxed $300. But because Garcia's benefit now is only $100 from the public good, she will vote against it. Meanwhile, Johnson and Lee will benefit by $350 each. They will vote for the public good because the benefit ($350) exceeds their tax payments ($300). The majority vote will provide a public good costing $900 that produces total benefits of only $800 (= $100 for Garcia + $350 for Johnson + $350 for Lee). Society's resources will be inefficiently allocated to this public good. Too much of it will be produced.

Implications The point is that an inefficient outcome may occur as an overproduction or an underproduction of a specific public good, and therefore as an overallocation or underallocation of resources for that particular use. Earlier in this chapter, we saw that government can improve economic efficiency by providing public goods that the market system will not make available. Now we have extended that analysis to reveal that inefficient voting outcomes may cause a government to either underprovide or overprovide public goods.

In our examples, each person has only a single vote, no matter how much they might gain or lose from a public good. In the first example (inefficient "no" vote), Garcia would be willing to purchase a vote from either Johnson or Lee if buying votes were legal. That way, Garcia could be assured of obtaining the national defense she so highly values. But because buying votes is illegal, many people with strong preferences for certain public goods may have to go without them.

Because majority voting fails to incorporate the intensity of individual voters' preferences, it may produce economically inefficient outcomes.

Interest Groups and Logrolling Some, but not all, of the inefficiencies of majority voting get resolved through the political process. Two examples follow.

Interest Groups People who share strong preferences for a particular public good may band together into interest groups and use advertisements, mailings, and direct persuasion to convince others of the merits of the public good in question. Garcia might try to persuade Johnson and Lee that it is in their best interest to vote for national defense—that national defense is much more valuable to them than their respective $250 and $200 valuations. Such appeals are common in democratic politics. Sometimes they are successful; sometimes they are not.

Political Logrolling Perhaps surprisingly, **logrolling**—the trading of votes to secure desired outcomes—can also turn an inefficient outcome into an efficient one. In our first example (Figure 5.2a), suppose that Johnson has a strong preference for a different public good—for example, a new road—which Garcia and Lee do not think is worth the tax expense. The stage is set for Garcia and Johnson to trade votes to ensure provision of both national defense and the new road. That is, Garcia and Johnson would each vote "yes" on both measures. Garcia would get the national defense and Johnson would get the road. Without the logrolling, both public goods would have been rejected. This logrolling will add to society's well-being if, as was true for national defense, the road creates a greater overall benefit than cost.

But logrolling need not increase economic efficiency. Even if national defense and the road each cost more than the total benefit each produces, both might still be provided if there is vote trading. Garcia and Johnson might still engage in logrolling if each expects to secure a sufficient net gain from her or his favored public good, even though the gains would come at Lee's expense.

logrolling The trading of votes by legislators to secure favorable outcomes on decisions concerning the provision of *public goods* and *quasi-public goods*.

Paradox of Voting

Another difficulty with majority voting is the **paradox of voting,** a situation in which society may not be able to rank its preferences consistently through paired-choice majority voting.

Preferences Consider Table 5.3, in which we again assume a community of three voters: Garcia, Johnson, and Lee. Suppose the community has three alternative public goods from which to choose: national defense, a road, and a weather warning system. Each member of the community prefers the three alternatives in a certain order. For example, one person might prefer national defense to a road and a road to a weather warning system. We can attempt to determine the community's preferences through paired-choice majority voting. Specifically, a vote can be held between any two of the public goods, and the winner of that vote can then be matched against the third public good in another vote.

The three goods and the three voters' individual preferences are listed in the top part of Table 5.3. Garcia prefers national defense to the road and the road to the weather warning system. By implication, Garcia prefers national defense to the weather warning system. Johnson values the road more than the weather warning system and the warning system more than national defense. Lee's order of preference is weather warning system, national defense, and road.

Voting Outcomes The lower part of Table 5.3 shows the outcomes of three hypothetical elections decided through majority vote. In the first, national defense wins against the road because a majority of voters (Garcia and Lee) prefer national defense to the road. In the second election, to see whether this community wants a road or a weather warning system, a majority of voters (Garcia and Johnson) prefer the road.

paradox of voting A situation where paired-choice voting by majority rule fails to provide a consistent ranking of society's preferences for *public goods* or *public services*.

TABLE 5.3 Paradox of Voting

Public Good	Preferences		
	Garcia	Johnson	Lee
National defense	1st choice	3d choice	2d choice
Road	2d choice	1st choice	3d choice
Weather warning system	3d choice	2d choice	1st choice

Election	Voting Outcomes: Winner
1. National defense vs. road	National defense (preferred by Garcia and Lee)
2. Road vs. weather warning system	Road (preferred by Garcia and Johnson)
3. National defense vs. weather warning system	Weather warning system (preferred by Johnson and Lee)

We have determined that the majority of people in this community prefer national defense to a road and prefer a road to a weather warning system. It seems logical to conclude that the community prefers national defense to a weather warning system. But it does not!

To demonstrate this conclusion, we hold a direct election between national defense and the weather warning system. Row 3 shows that a majority of voters (Johnson and Lee) prefer the weather warning system to national defense. As listed in Table 5.3, then, the three paired-choice majority votes imply that this community is irrational: It seems to prefer national defense to a road and a road to a weather warning system, but it would rather have a weather warning system than national defense.

The problem is not irrational community preferences but rather a flawed procedure for determining those preferences. We see that the outcome from paired-choice majority voting may depend on the order in which the votes are taken. Different sequences can lead to different outcomes, many of which may fail to reflect the electorate's underlying preferences. As a consequence, government may find it difficult to provide the "correct" public goods by acting in accordance with majority voting.

Important note: This critique is not meant to suggest that majority voting has no place in making decisions about public goods or that it is among the least-good ways of making such decisions. Majority voting is, for instance, *much* more likely to reflect community preferences than decisions made by a dictator or an aristocracy. As British Prime Minister Winston Churchill astutely joked, "Democracy is the worst form of government—except for all the others."

Median-Voter Model

median-voter model The theory that under majority rule the median (middle) voter will be in the dominant position to determine the outcome of an election.

Another aspect of majority voting reveals further insights into real-world phenomena. The **median-voter model** suggests that, under majority rule and consistent voting preferences, the median voter will in a sense determine the outcomes of elections. The median voter is the person holding the middle position on an issue: Half the other voters have stronger preferences for a public good, amount of taxation, or degree of government regulation, while half have weaker or negative preferences. The extreme voters on each side of an issue prefer the median choice rather than the other extreme position, so the median voter's choice predominates.

Example Suppose that a society composed of Garcia, Johnson, and Lee has agreed that it needs a weather warning system but that there is disagreement about how expensive a system to set up.

To start the process of figuring out how expensive a system to build, each person independently submits a total dollar amount that they think should be spent on the warning system, assuming each will be taxed one-third of that amount. Two successive elections will then be needed to determine the size of the system. That's because each person can be expected to vote for their own proposal—so that no majority will occur if all the proposals are placed on the ballot at the same time. Thus, the group decides to hold two sequential paired-choice votes: They will first vote between two of the proposals and then match the winner of that vote against the remaining proposal.

The three proposals are as follows: Garcia desires a $400 system; Johnson wants an $800 system; Lee opts for a $300 system. Which proposal will win? The median-voter model suggests the winner will be the $400 proposal submitted by the median voter, Garcia. Half the other voters favor a more costly system; half favor a less costly system. To understand why the $400 system will be the outcome, let's conduct two sequential paired-choice votes.

1. First, suppose that the $400 proposal is matched against the $800 proposal. Garcia naturally votes for her $400 proposal, and Johnson votes for his own $800 proposal. Lee, who proposed the $300 expenditure for the warning system, votes for the $400 proposal because it is closer to her own proposal. So Garcia's $400 proposal is selected by a 2-to-1 majority vote.

2. Next, we match the $400 proposal against the $300 proposal. Again the $400 proposal wins. It gets a vote from Garcia and a vote from Johnson, who proposed the $800 expenditure and for that reason prefers a $400 expenditure to a $300 expenditure. Garcia, the median voter in this case, is in a sense the person who has decided the level of expenditure on the weather warning system.

Real-World Applicability Although our illustration is simple, it explains a great deal. We do note a tendency for public choices to match most closely the median view. Political candidates, for example, take one set of positions to win the nomination of their political parties; in so doing, they tend to appeal to the median voter within the party to get the nomination. They then shift their views more closely to the political center when they square off against opponents from the opposite political party. In effect, they redirect their appeal toward the median voter within the total population. They conduct polls and adjust their positions on issues accordingly.

Implications The median-voter model has two important implications:

- At any point in time, many people will be dissatisfied by the extent of government involvement in the economy. The size of government will largely be determined by the median preference, leaving many people desiring a much larger, or a much smaller, public sector.

- Some people may "vote with their feet" by moving into political jurisdictions where the median voter's preferences are closer to their own. They may move from the city to a suburb where the level of government services, and therefore taxes, is lower. Or they may move into an area known for its excellent, but expensive, school system. Some may move to other states; a few may even move to other countries.

Because our personal preferences for publicly provided goods and services are not static, the median preference shifts over time. Moreover, information about people's preferences is imperfect, leaving much room for politicians to misjudge the true median position. When they do, they may have a difficult time getting elected or reelected.

QUICK REVIEW
5.3

▶ Majority voting can produce voting outcomes that are inefficient; projects having greater total benefits than total costs may be defeated, and projects having greater total costs than total benefits may be approved.

▶ The paradox of voting occurs when voting by majority rule does not provide a consistent ranking of society's preferences for public goods and services.

▶ The median-voter model suggests that under majority rule and consistent voting preferences, the voter who has the middle preference will determine the outcome of an election.

Alternative Voting Mechanisms

Because majority voting can lead to inefficient voting outcomes, economists have proposed several alternative voting mechanisms. Instead of the traditional one-person-one-vote (1p1v) system in which each voter gets one vote and a simple majority wins, these alternative voting systems allow for people to cast multiple votes as a way of accounting for the strength of their respective preferences. By doing so, alternative voting mechanisms are more likely than 1p1v to avoid inefficient voting outcomes and thereby approve only those public goods for which total benefit exceeds total cost.

quadratic voting system
A majority voting system in which voters can express strength of preference by purchasing as many votes as they like at a price equal to the square of the number of votes purchased. Quadratic voting is more likely (but not guaranteed) to result in economically efficient decisions than traditional one-person-one-vote (1p1v) majority voting systems.

Quadratic Voting Quadratic voting is an alternative voting mechanism that leads to fewer inefficient voting outcomes than 1p1v. Under quadratic voting, the winning side of an election (Yes or No) is still determined by the "50 percent plus 1" majority voting rule that you are familiar with. But under a quadratic voting system, each voter can purchase and then cast as many votes as she desires. Naturally, voters with strong preferences will wish to buy more votes because the outcome matters more for them than for people with weak preferences. The question then becomes: how many votes will each voter want to purchase?

The answer, as you might have guessed, is that each voter will purchase votes up to the point where the marginal benefit from purchasing additional votes equals the marginal cost of purchasing additional votes. Under quadratic voting, the cost of purchasing votes is quadratic, meaning that it increases exponentially with the square of the number of votes purchased. If a voter desires

TABLE 5.4 Desired Number of Votes and their Cost under Quadratic Voting

Desired Number of Votes (v)	Cost to Purchase Desired Number of Votes (= v^2)
0	$ 0
1	1
2	4
3	9
4	16
5	25
6	36
7	49
8	64
9	81
10	100
11	121
12	144
13	169
14	196
15	225
16	256
17	289
18	324
19	361
20	400

to purchase v votes, the cost will be v^2 dollars. Table 5.4 shows this relationship for purchases of up to 20 votes. In the first row of the table, you can see that the cost to purchase zero votes is the square of zero, or $0 (= 0^2)$. The second row shows that the cost to purchase 1 vote is the square of 1, or $1 (= 1^2)$. The third row shows that the cost to purchase two votes is the square of 2, or $4 (= 2^2)$. Continuing down the table you can see that the cost of purchasing 12 votes is the square of 12, or $144 (= 12^2)$. The final row shows that the cost of purchasing 20 votes is $400 (= 20^2)$.

Note that the quadratic cost of purchasing votes implies that the marginal cost of vote buying is increasing with each additional vote purchased. As an example, the marginal cost of a fifth vote is $9 (= $25 cost of 5 votes minus $16 cost of 4 votes) while the marginal cost of a sixth vote is $11 (= $36 cost of 6 votes minus $25 cost of 5 votes).

Example As you saw in Figure 5.2a, ordinary 1p1v majority voting can fail because it cannot account for the strength of voters' preferences. As we went over before, Garcia stands to realize a large net benefit of $400 (= $700 personal benefit minus $300 cost of tax) if Yes passes. So she will vote Yes. Meanwhile, Johnson and Lee would realize modest net losses of, respectively, $50 and $75 if Yes were to pass. So they will both vote No. When all the votes are counted, we end up with an inefficient majority No vote (two against, one in favor) despite total benefit exceeding total cost by $250 (= $1,150 total benefit minus $900 total cost).

The vote goes the wrong way because 1p1v does not allow Garcia to express how strongly she favors a Yes vote and her potential gain of $400. Neither is there any way for 1p1v to capture the fact that Johnson and Lee are only mildly opposed, since they will lose only $50 and $75, respectively, if Yes wins. By contrast, quadratic voting *does* account for differences in strength of preference. By doing so, quadratic voting makes it more likely that projects with positive net benefits will be approved by voters.

To see that process in action, consider again the example in Figure 5.2a, but this time assume that we are going to conduct the election using a quadratic voting system. Garcia, Johnson, and Lee can purchase as many votes as they like. Let's first figure out how many each will purchase and then total up the votes in favor versus the votes against. We assume that each of them will rationally purchase votes up to the point where MB = MC.

- Garcia will want to purchase 20 votes and use them all to vote Yes. To see why she will purchase 20 votes, note that if the public good is approved, Garcia will personally gain $400 (= $700 benefit to Garcia minus $300 tax payment by Garcia). Thus, she will want to spend up to $400 buying votes. Looking at Table 5.4, we see that Garcia can purchase 20 votes for $400. So she will purchase 20 votes and vote Yes with each of them.

- Johnson will purchase 7 votes and use them all to vote No. To see why he will purchase 7 votes, note that if the public good is approved, Johnson will personally lose $50 (= $250 benefit to Johnson minus $300 tax payment by Johnson). Thus he would be willing to spend up to $50 buying votes so as to prevent that $50 loss. Looking at Table 5.4, we see that Johnson can purchase 7 votes for $49. So he will purchase 7 votes and vote No with each of them. (He would not purchase 8 votes because that would cost him $64, which would be a bigger loss of money than the $50 he would lose if the public good gets approved.)

- Lee will purchase 10 votes and use them all to vote No. To see why she will purchase 10 votes, note that if the public good is approved, Lee will personally lose $100 (= $200 benefit to Lee minus $300 tax payment by Lee). Thus she would be willing to spend up to $100 buying votes to prevent that $100 loss. Looking at Table 5.4, we see that Lee can purchase 10 votes for $100. So she will purchase 10 votes and vote No with each of them. (She would not purchase 11 votes because that would cost her $121, or more than the $100 she would lose if the public good got approved.)

Looking over the vote buying decision of Garcia, Johnson, and Lee, we see that there are 20 Yes votes (all from Garcia) against 17 No votes (7 from Johnson plus 10 from Lee). Thus, Yes will win by a vote of 20 to 17, and this public good with positive net benefits will be approved. So quadratic voting achieves the socially optimal outcome in this example, whereas traditional one-person-one-vote (1p1v) majority voting fails to do so.

Discussion This example is not unique. Economists have found that in many situations quadratic voting is more likely to yield economically efficient outcomes than the traditional 1p1v voting system. But no voting system is perfect and it is easy to construct examples in which quadratic voting and other alternative voting systems fail as badly as 1p1v in achieving the economically efficient outcome.

Another consideration that weighs against quadratic voting is the fact that we have a long tradition in our society of employing 1p1v majority voting. It is straightforward to explain and the public is used to it. 1p1v majority voting also allows for strength of preference to be expressed in other ways, including logrolling and lobbying (which are studied in the next section). So while quadratic voting has found some support among experts, it is not likely to displace traditional 1p1v majority voting any time soon!

One final point. In our example above, we had Garcia, Johnson, and Lee purchasing votes with cash. Such a system would obviously favor the wealthy and those with high incomes. Proponents of quadratic voting overcome this problem by handing out an equal number of pieces of "currency" to each voter. For instance, each voter might be given 1,000 "voice credits" as their budget for purchasing votes in several upcoming elections. Under quadratic voting, 1 vote in one of those elections would cost 1 voice credit, 2 votes would cost 4 voice credits, 3 votes would cost 9 voice credits, and so on. With each person endowed with an equal number of voice credits, we could utilize a voting system that accounts for strength of preference without having to worry about the rich outvoting the poor.

Mechanism Design Alternative voting mechanisms like quadratic voting are studied by economists interested in the field of **mechanism design.** In *economics* and *game theory,* a coordination mechanism, or simply a mechanism, is a procedure or set of rules for organizing how people interact to get something accomplished. The field of mechanism design studies how to set up the best procedures, or mechanisms, for any given situation—including auctions, on-line dating, and kidney donations.

The people who design mechanisms are called mechanism designers. With respect to democratic voting, their goal is to design a set of voting rules that will make the likelihood of inefficient votes as small as possible. But will the voting mechanism that works best for a small committee in Washington, D.C., be the same as for a statewide ballot measure in Texas? Probably not. So we need to be cautious about specific voting mechanisms like quadratic voting; they may work great in some contexts but fail miserably in others.

> **mechanism design** The part of *game theory* concerned with designing the rules of a *game* so as to maximize the likelihood of players reaching a socially optimal outcome.

▶ Quadratic voting systems account for strength of preference by allowing voters to purchase as many votes (v) as they like at a quadratically increasing price per vote (= v^2).

▶ To level the playing field, voters can be endowed with an equal number of voice credits that can be spent purchasing votes.

▶ Mechanism design studies the best sets of rules, or coordinating mechanisms, for organizing how people interact in particular situations, including voting, auctions, and on-line dating.

QUICK REVIEW
5.4

Government Failure

The term **government failure** refers to economically inefficient outcomes caused by shortcomings in the public sector. The *voting paradoxes* studied in the previous section were one source of government failure. They caused problems by making it difficult for government officials to discern voter preferences. Here, we deal with several other causes of government failure that all share an interesting common feature: they occur even when government officials know exactly what citizens want.

Representative Democracy and the Principal-Agent Problem

The U.S. system of representative democracy has the advantage of allowing us to elect full-time representatives who can specialize in understanding the pros and cons of different potential laws. But the system also suffers from principal-agent problems.

> **>> LO5.3** Define government failure and explain its causes.

> **government failure** Inefficiencies in resource allocation caused by problems in the operation of the *public sector* (government). Specific examples include the *principal-agent problem*, the *special-interest effect*, the *collective-action problem*, *rent seeking*, and *political corruption*.

principal-agent problem
(1) At a *firm*, a conflict of interest that occurs when agents (workers or managers) pursue their own objectives to the detriment of the principals' (stockholders') goals. (2) In *public choice theory*, a conflict of interest that arises when elected officials (who are the agents of the people) pursue policies that are in their own interests rather than policies that would be in the better interests of the public (the principals).

Principal-agent problems are conflicts that arise when tasks are delegated by one group of people (principals) to another group of people (agents). The conflicts arise because the agents' interests may not be the same as the principals' interests, in which case the agents may end up taking actions that are harmful to the principals for whom they work.

In the business world, principal-agent problems often arise when a company's managers (the agents) take actions that are not in the best interests of the company's shareholders (the principals). Examples include the managers spending huge amounts of company money on executive jets and lavish offices or holding meetings at expensive resorts. Those perks are very nice for managers, but extremely costly for shareholders. Yet managers may make many such decisions when they are free to pursue their own interests rather than those of the shareholders.

In a representative democracy, principal-agent problems often arise because politicians' goals, such as reelection, may be inconsistent with pursuing their constituents' best interests. Indeed, "sound economics" and "good politics" often differ. Sound economics calls for the public sector to pursue programs as long as marginal benefits exceed marginal costs. Good politics, however, suggests that politicians support programs and policies that maximize their chances of getting reelected. Economic inefficiency is the likely outcome.

special-interest effect Any political outcome in which a small group ("special interest") gains substantially at the expense of a much larger number of persons who each individually suffers a small loss.

Special-Interest Effect Efficient public decision making is often impaired by the **special-interest effect,** which occurs when a small group that shares a particular goal, or special interest, is able to get the government to grant them a personally advantageous program or policy even though doing so defies the will of the majority.

The small group of potential beneficiaries is usually well informed and highly vocal on the issue in question, and they court politicians by making campaign contributions and by hiring well-connected professional advocates known as "lobbyists" to aggressively press their case.

Normally, you would think that politicians would never vote for a policy that only a small group wants. Democracy, after all, favors the majority over the minority. But things go awry because benefits are concentrated but costs are diffuse. Because the special interest is small, any success it achieves will be highly concentrated and worth a lot to each member of the group. So members will lobby hard and be very vocal. By contrast, the cost of the program will be spread across hundreds of millions of taxpayers, so that individual taxpayers won't have much of a financial incentive to organize any resistance. Only one side will be heard and the special interest will likely get its way.

collective-action problem
The difficulty of getting a large group of voters to organize against a policy when the costs of that policy are widely dispersed (so that none of them individually has much of a personal incentive to take action).

Example: A $10 million subsidy to a group of six dronemakers would amount to less than 3 cents per person when spread out over the entire U.S. population. So the dronemakers will be happy to spend up to $10 million lobbying in favor of the subsidy while individual taxpayers won't have much of an incentive at all to tell their political representatives to vote no. The result? Politicians doing the bidding of a special-interest group rather than what would be allocatively efficient based on cost-benefit analysis.

See the Consider This story for a notorious example of the special-interest effect in action.

CONSIDER THIS . . .

Getting Fleeced

Each year the federal government provides millions of dollars in subsidized loans to Angora goat farmers in Texas, Arizona, and New Mexico. The federal government began the subsidy in the late 1940s to ensure a large supply of insulation for the jackets needed to keep pilots warm in the unheated military aircraft of that era.

The mohair subsidy should have ended in the 1950s when heated cabins became standard, but it survives because it costs taxpayers only a few cents each. This means

Hein Von Horsten/Gallo Images/Getty Images

that it would cost them more to organize and defeat the mohair subsidy than they would save by having the subsidy terminated.

As with other examples of the special-interest effect, the mohair subsidy is characterized by "concentrated benefits and diffuse costs." Concentrated benefits make proponents easy to organize, while diffuse costs make opponents difficult to organize. The outcome? A **collective-action problem** that explains why taxpayers are still getting fleeced, seven decades on.

Pork Barrel Politics The special-interest effect is evident in so-called *pork-barrel politics,* which are government projects that yield benefits mainly to a single political district and its political representative. In this case, the special-interest group comprises local constituents, while the larger group consists of relatively uninformed taxpayers scattered across a much larger geographic area. Politicians have a strong incentive to secure government projects ("pork") for their local constituents. Such projects win political favor because constituents value them highly. Meanwhile, the costs are borne mainly by taxpayers located elsewhere.

At the federal level, pork-barrel politics often consists of congressional members inserting specific provisions that authorize spending for local projects (that will benefit only local constituents) into comprehensive legislation (that is supposed to be about making laws for the entire country). Such narrow, specifically designated authorizations of expenditure are called **earmarks.** In 2021, legislation contained 285 earmarks totaling $16.8 billion. Although some of the earmarked projects deliver marginal benefits that exceed marginal costs, many others are questionable at best. These latter expenditures very likely reallocate some of society's scarce resources from higher-valued uses to lower-valued uses. "Vote for my special local project and I will vote for yours" becomes part of the overall strategy for securing "pork" and remaining elected.

Rent-Seeking Behavior The appeal to government for special benefits at someone else's expense is called **rent seeking.** The term "rent" in "rent seeking" is used loosely to refer to any payment in excess of the minimum amount that is needed to keep a resource employed in its current use. Those engaged in "rent seeking" attempt to use government influence to help them get paid more for providing a good or service than the *minimum* amount someone would have to pay them to provide that good or service.

Rent seeking goes beyond the usual profit seeking by which firms try to increase their profits by adjusting their output levels, improving their products, and incorporating cost-saving technologies. Rent seeking looks to obtain extra profit or income by influencing government policies. Corporations, trade associations, labor unions, and professional organizations employ vast resources to secure favorable government policies that result in rent—higher profit or income than would otherwise occur. The government is able to dispense such rent directly or indirectly through laws, rules, hiring, and purchases. Elected officials are willing to provide such rent because they want to be responsive to the key constituents who can help them remain in office.

Some examples of "rent-providing" legislation or policies are tariffs on foreign products that limit competition and raise prices to consumers, tax breaks that benefit specific corporations, government construction projects that create union jobs but cost more than the benefits they yield, occupational licensing that goes beyond what is needed to protect consumers, and large subsidies to farmers. None of these result in economic efficiency.

earmarks Narrow, specially designated spending authorizations placed in broad legislation by senators and representatives for the purpose of providing benefits to *firms* and organizations within their constituencies. Earmarked projects are exempt from competitive bidding and normal evaluation procedures.

rent-seeking behavior Attempts by individuals, firms, or unions to use political influence to receive payments in excess of the minimum amount they would normally be willing to accept to provide a particular good or service.

QUICK REVIEW
5.5

▶ Principal-agent problems are conflicts that occur when the agents who are supposed to be acting in the best interests of their principals instead take actions that help themselves but hurt their principals.

▶ Because larger groups are more difficult to organize and motivate than smaller groups, special interests can often obtain what they want politically even when what they want is opposed by a majority of voters.

▶ Rent seeking involves influencing government policies so that one can get paid more for providing a good or service than it costs to produce.

Limited and Bundled Choice

Economic theory points out that the political process forces citizens and their elected representatives to be less selective in choosing public goods and services than they are in choosing private goods and services.

In the marketplace, the citizen as a consumer can exactly satisfy personal preferences by buying certain goods and not buying others. However, in the public sector the citizen as a voter is confronted with, say, only two or three candidates for an office, each representing a different "bundle" of programs (public goods and services). None of these bundles of public goods is likely to fit exactly the preferences of any particular voter. Yet the voter must choose one of them. The candidate who comes closest to voter Smith's preference may endorse national health insurance, increases in Social Security benefits, subsidies to tobacco farmers, and tariffs on imported goods. Smith is likely to vote for that candidate even though Smith strongly opposes tobacco subsidies.

CONSIDER THIS . . .

Government, Scofflaw

An interesting example of government failure occurs when companies that are completely owned and operated by the government violate health and safety laws at higher rates than private companies.

A study of 1,000 hospitals, 3,000 power plants, and 4,200 water utilities found that public providers were substantially more likely than private companies to violate health and safety laws. Public hospitals and public power plants had 20 percent more high-priority violations of the Clean Air Act, while public water companies had 14 percent more health violations as well as 29 percent more monitoring violations of the Safe Drinking Water Act.

Jerry McBride/The Durango Herald/
Polaris/Newscom

One explanation is that public companies may have difficulty getting taxpayers and politicians to approve the funding that would be needed to improve their facilities by enough to comply with the law. But the law also appears to be applied much more leniently against public companies. As just one example, public power plants and public hospitals are 20 percent less likely to be fined when found to be in violation of the Clean Air Act. In addition, there is evidence that public violators are allowed to delay or avoid paying fines even when they are assessed. So they appear to be under substantially less pressure than private firms to comply with the law.

In other words, the voter must take the bad with the good. In the public sector, people are forced to "buy" goods and services they do not want. It is as if, in going to a sporting-goods store, you were forced to buy an unwanted pool cue to get a wanted pair of running shoes. This is a situation where resources are not being used efficiently to satisfy consumer wants. In this sense, the provision of public goods and services is inherently inefficient.

Congress is confronted with a similar limited-choice, bundled-goods problem. Appropriations legislation combines hundreds, even thousands, of spending items into a single bill. Many of these spending items may be completely unrelated to the main purpose of the legislation. Yet congressional representatives must vote on the entire package—yea or nay. Unlike consumers in the marketplace, they cannot be selective.

Bureaucracy and Inefficiency

Some economists contend that public agencies are generally less efficient than private businesses. The reason is not that lazy and incompetent workers somehow end up in the public sector while ambitious and capable people gravitate to the private sector. Rather, the market system creates incentives for internal efficiency that are absent from the public sector. Private enterprises have a clear goal—profit. Efficient management means lower costs and higher profit. The higher profit not only benefits the firm's owners but also enhances the promotion prospects of the firm's managers. Moreover, part of the managers' pay may be tied to profit via profit-sharing plans, bonuses, and stock options. There is no similar gain to government agencies and their managers—no counterpart to profit—to create a strong incentive to achieve efficiency.

The market system imposes a very obvious test of performance on private firms: the test of profit and loss. An efficient firm is profitable and therefore successful; it survives, prospers, and grows. An inefficient firm is unprofitable and unsuccessful; it declines and in time goes out of business. But there is no similar, clear-cut test for assessing the efficiency or inefficiency of public agencies. How can anyone determine whether a public hydroelectricity provider, a state university, a local fire department, or the Bureau of Indian Affairs is operating efficiently?

Furthermore, economists assert that government employees, together with the special-interest groups they serve, often gain sufficient political clout to block attempts to pare down or eliminate their agencies. Politicians who attempt to reduce the size of huge federal bureaucracies (such as those relating to agriculture, education, health, and national defense) incur sizable political risk because bureaucrats and special-interest groups will team up to defeat them.

Finally, critics point out that government bureaucrats tend to justify their continued employment by looking for and eventually finding new problems to solve. It is not surprising that social "problems," as defined by government, persist or even expand.

Inefficient Regulation and Intervention

Governments regulate many aspects of the market economy. Examples include health and safety regulations, environmental laws, banking supervision, and the imposition of wage and price controls. These interventions are designed to improve economic outcomes, but several forms of regulation and intervention have generated outcomes that are less beneficial than intended.

Regulatory Capture A government agency that is supposed to supervise a particular industry suffers from **regulatory capture** if its regulatory and monitoring activities come to be heavily influenced by the industry that it is supposed to be regulating.

Regulatory capture is often facilitated by the fact that nearly everyone who knows anything about the details of a regulated industry works in the industry. So when it comes time for the regulatory agency to find qualified people to help write intelligent regulations, it ends up hiring a lot of people from regulated firms. Those individuals bring their old opinions and sympathies with them when they become bureaucrats. As a result, many regulations end up favoring the interests of regulated firms.

Complaints about regulatory capture at the federal level have been voiced about the Food and Drug Administration's supervision of the pharmaceutical industry, the Securities and Exchange Commission's supervision of Wall Street financial firms, and the Bureau of Land Management's policies with respect to leasing federal lands for oil drilling, mining, and forestry.

regulatory capture The situation that occurs when a governmental *regulatory agency* ends up being controlled by the industry that it is supposed to be regulating.

Deregulation as an Alternative One potential solution to regulatory capture is for the government to engage in **deregulation** and intentionally remove most or even all of the regulations governing an industry.

Deregulation solves the problem of regulatory capture because there is no regulatory agency left to capture. But it works well in terms of economic efficiency only if the deregulated industry becomes competitive and is automatically guided toward allocative and productive efficiency by competitive forces and the invisible hand. If the deregulated industry instead tends toward monopoly or ends up generating substantial negative externalities, continued regulation might be the better option.

Proponents of deregulation often cite the deregulation of interstate trucking, railroads, and airlines in the 1970s and 1980s as an example of competition successfully replacing regulation. They do so because after regulation was removed, robust competition led to lower prices, increased output, and higher levels of productivity and efficiency.

But for government agencies tasked with environmental protection, human safety, and financial regulation, there is substantially less confidence as to whether competitive pressures might be able to replace regulation. Regulation may always be necessary. If so, the possibility of regulatory capture will have to be monitored closely because regulated firms will always have an incentive to capture their regulators.

deregulation The removal of most or even all of the government regulation and laws designed to supervise an industry. Sometimes undertaken to combat *regulatory capture*.

Corruption

Political corruption is the unlawful misdirection of governmental resources that occurs when government officials abuse their entrusted powers for personal gain. For instance, a police supervisor engages in political corruption if she accepts a bribe in exchange for illegally freeing a thief who had been lawfully arrested by another officer. Similarly, a government bureaucrat engages in political corruption if he refuses to issue a building permit to a homebuilder who is in full compliance with the law unless the homebuilder makes a "voluntary contribution" to the bureaucrat's favorite charity.

While relatively uncommon in the United States, political corruption is "business as usual" in many parts of the world. But it may be hard to tell in some cases if a particular activity is corrupt or not. For example, if a political candidate accepts campaign contributions from a special-interest group and then shows subsequent support for that group's legislative goals, has a subtle form of political corruption taken place? While there are strong opinions on both sides of the issue, it is often hard to tell in any particular case whether a special interest's campaign contribution amounts to a bribe. On the one hand, the special interest may indeed be trying to influence the politician's vote. On the other hand, the special interest may simply be trying to support and elect a person who already sees things their way.

political corruption The unlawful misdirection of government resources, or actions that occur when government officials abuse their entrusted powers for personal gain. (Also see *corruption*.)

Should Governments Subsidize Corporate Relocations?

Local and State Governments Spend an Estimated $45 Billion Each Year Trying to Tempt Established Businesses to Move to Their Locations. Is That a Good Deal?

In late 2017, Seattle-based Internet giant Amazon announced that it would be building a second headquarters, or HQ2. Its need for a second headquarters was not surprising; after two decades of relentless expansion, Amazon was well on its way to becoming the world's most valuable company and needed more office space to house its rapidly increasing managerial and executive staff.

But Amazon threw in an unexpected twist when it made the announcement. HQ2 would *not* be located in Amazon's home base of Seattle, where its first HQ was located. Amazon announced that it wanted to place its second headquarters elsewhere within the United States. It also announced that it wanted cities and states to apply for that opportunity and pitch Amazon on why it would be best for Amazon to put its HQ2 in their location. This application process set off a frenzy of subsidy offers, as local governments competed with each other to offer Amazon tax breaks, wage subsidies, free land, and a host of other taxpayer-paid inducements to get Amazon to build in their location.

Naturally, you could see why each local government might want HQ2 for its own. To begin with, Amazon announced that the project would bring with it 50,000 high paying jobs . The spending of those employees (average salary: $150,000) would greatly boost the economic prospects of established local businesses. The presence of HQ2 would also bring with it the chance to establish a local tech hub, attracting many Internet-economy startups to the area, thereby creating more jobs and even more opportunities for local residents.

Applications were submitted by 238 locales. Amazon looked them over before issuing yet another surprise. HQ2 would be split in two, with half being built in Queens, New York, and the other half being built in the Arlington, Virginia, area.

Now, you might think that those locations won the bidding war because of their generous offers. But New York and Arlington were the most natural locations for Amazon from the very start due to their proximity to major population centers and the airports and other distribution infrastructure that Amazon needs as the western hemisphere's largest Internet retailer. This made many people suspect that Amazon would have put HQ2 in NYC and Arlington no matter what. Thus, there would have been no need for either city to

SeaRick1/Shutterstock

give away billions in taxpayer subsidies; they would have gotten HQ2 anyways.

This situation is not unique. Research indicates that location subsidies are largely a waste of money. Seventy-five percent of businesses considering a new location end up going with their original first choice anyway. For those companies, the subsidies are just a nice unearned windfall.

For cities and governments, the subsidies represent a tremendous waste of taxpayer money. As just one example, the State of Virginia discovered that its film incentive program (to get Hollywood producers to shoot scenes in Virginia rather than elsewhere) returned only 20 cents to the Virginia economy for every $1 in subsidies given to movie producers. Many economists suspect that the economic returns to other location subsidy programs are just as bad if not worse.

So why do these deals persist? The answer appears to be politics. Politicians love to be seen at ribbon-cutting ceremonies, looking as though they, personally, are responsible for bringing new businesses, new jobs, and economic growth to their area. That's an illusion, of course, but one that serves the political goal of getting reelected. The subsidies are, consequently, an example of government failure induced by the principal-agent problem that exists between the voters who must pay for subsidies and the politicians whose main goal is staying in office.

The HQ2 episode had an unexpected ending. In early 2019, Amazon reversed its decision to build half of HQ2 in Queens after meeting with political resistance from a variety of local groups, including those concerned about location subsidies being a waste of money.

That said, the impression of impropriety lingers, and so laws have been passed in the United States limiting the amount of money that individuals can donate to specific candidates and making it illegal for certain groups to donate money directly to individual politicians (as distinct from directing funds toward supporting specific issues or advocacy groups—which is both legal and unrestricted). Proponents of these laws hope that the limitations strike a good balance—allowing individuals and groups to meaningfully support candidates they agree with but keeping contributions small enough that no one individual or group can singlehandedly donate enough money to sway a politician's vote.

Imperfect Institutions

It is possible to argue that the wide variety of criticisms of public-sector inefficiency discussed in this chapter are exaggerated and cynical. Perhaps they are. Nevertheless, they do tend to shatter the concept of a benevolent government that responds with precision and efficiency to its citizens' wants. The market system of the private sector is far from perfectly efficient, and government's economic function is mainly to correct that system's shortcomings. But the public sector is subject to deficiencies in fulfilling its economic function. "The relevant comparison is not between perfect markets and imperfect governments, nor between faulty markets and all-knowing, rational, benevolent governments, but between inevitably imperfect institutions."[1]

Because markets and governments are both imperfect, it is sometimes difficult to determine whether a particular activity can be performed more successfully in the private sector or in the public sector. It is easy to reach agreement on opposite extremes: National defense must lie with the public sector, while automobile production is best accomplished by the private sector. But what about health insurance? Fire protection? Housing? Education? It is hard to assess every good or service and to say absolutely that it should be assigned to either the public sector or the private sector. Evidence: All the goods and services just mentioned are provided in part by both private enterprises and public agencies.

▶ Unlike the private sector—where the profit motive helps to ensure efficiency and variety—government lacks a strong incentive to be efficient and typically offers only limited and bundled choices.

▶ Regulatory capture occurs when a regulated industry can control its government regulator

and get it to implement policies that favor the industry.

▶ Political corruption occurs when government officials abuse their powers for personal gain.

**QUICK REVIEW
5.6**

---

[1]Otto Eckstein, *Public Finance,* 3rd ed. (Englewood Cliffs, NJ: Prentice Hall, 1973), p. 17.

Summary

LO5.1 Describe free riding and public goods, and illustrate why private firms cannot normally produce public goods.

Private goods are characterized by rivalry (in consumption) and excludability. One person's purchase and consumption of a private good precludes others from also buying and consuming it. Producers can exclude nonpayers (free riders) from receiving the benefits. In contrast, public goods are characterized by nonrivalry (in consumption) and nonexcludability. Public goods are not profitable to private firms because nonpayers (free riders) can obtain and consume those goods without paying. Government can, however, provide desirable public goods, financing them through taxation.

The collective demand schedule for a particular public good is found by summing the prices that each individual is willing to pay for an additional unit. Graphically, that demand curve is found by summing vertically the individual demand curves for that good. The resulting total demand curve indicates the collective willingness to pay for (or marginal benefit of) any given amount of the public good.

The optimal quantity of a public good occurs where the society's willingness to pay for the last unit—the marginal benefit of the good—equals the marginal cost of the good.

LO5.2 Explain the difficulties of conveying economic preferences through majority voting.

Public choice theory suggests that government failures may result when majority voting fails to correctly indicate voter preferences.

Majority voting creates the possibility of (a) underallocations or overallocations of resources to particular public goods and (b) inconsistent voting outcomes that make it impossible for a democratic political system to definitively determine the will of the people.

The median-voter model predicts that, under majority rule, the person holding the middle position on an issue will determine the outcome of an election involving that issue.

Researchers have compared traditional 1-person-one-vote (1p1v) majority-voting systems with a variety of alternative voting systems, including quadratic voting. Quadratic voting is more likely than 1p1v to provide economically efficient outcomes because it accounts for the strength of voter preferences. Voters can purchase as many votes v as they like for a price equal to the number of votes squared v^2. Whichever side has the most votes wins.

Mechanism design is the branch of economics that studies how to design a set of rules, or coordinating mechanism, such that the people interacting in a given situation will be most likely to achieve economically efficient outcomes. Quadratic voting and 1p1v voting are two different coordinating mechanisms for collective decision making. In some situations, quadratic voting is more likely than 1p1v to achieve allocative efficiency.

LO5.3 Define government failure and explain its causes.

Politicians and other government officials may sometimes manifest a principal-agent problem, pursuing actions that serve their own interests (such as reelection) rather than those that would serve the public.

The special-interest effect implies that groups with shared goals can perpetuate unpopular policies as long as diffuse costs make opponents difficult to organize.

Rent seeking occurs whenever a special interest group attempts to get government policy altered in a way that would award the special interest with above-normal profits or compensation.

Economic theorists cite several reasons why government might be inefficient in providing public goods. (a) Citizens as voters face limited and bundled choices regarding candidates and public goods, whereas consumers in the private sector can be highly selective in their choices. (b) Government bureaucracies have less incentive to operate efficiently than do private businesses. (c) Regulated industries may sometimes capture their government regulatory agencies and mold government policies toward their own best interests.

Deregulation is one way to prevent industries from capturing their regulators. But deregulation works well in terms of economic efficiency only if the deregulated industry becomes competitive.

Neither governments nor markets are perfect economic institutions. Each has its own set of shortcomings, and citizens should be aware of where each is likely to fail and where each is likely to succeed.

Terms and Concepts

demand-side market failures	cost-benefit analysis	government failure
private good	marginal cost–marginal benefit rule	principal-agent problem
rivalry	quasi-public good	special-interest effect
excludability	public choice theory	collective-action problem
public good	logrolling	earmarks
nonrivalry	paradox of voting	rent seeking
nonexcludability	median-voter model	regulatory capture
free-rider problem	quadratic voting	deregulation
collective demand for a public good	mechanism design	political corruption

Discussion Questions

1. What are the two characteristics of public goods? Explain the significance of each for public provision as opposed to private provision. What is the free-rider problem as it relates to public goods? Is U.S. border patrol a public good or a private good? Why? What type of good is satellite TV? Explain. **LO5.1**

2. Explain how affirmative and negative majority votes can sometimes lead to inefficient allocations of resources to public goods. Use Figures 5.2a and 5.2b to show how society might be better off if Garcia were allowed to buy votes. **LO5.2**

3. "Majority voting ensures that government will produce only those public goods for which benefits exceed costs." Discuss. **LO5.2**

4. "The problem with our democratic institutions is that they don't correctly reflect the will of the people! If the people—rather than self-interested politicians or lobbyists—had control, we wouldn't have to worry about government taking actions that don't maximize allocative and productive efficiency." Critique. **LO5.2**

5. Does traditional one-person-one-vote (1p1v) majority voting allow voters to directly express differences in strengths of preference? Does quadratic voting do any better? Discuss the differences and then explain which system you prefer, and why. **LO5.2**

6. Jean-Baptiste Colbert was the Minister of Finance under King Louis XIV of France. He famously observed, "The art of taxation consists in so plucking the goose as to obtain the largest possible amount of feathers with the smallest possible amount of hissing." How does his comment relate to the special-interest effect? **LO5.3**

7. What is rent seeking, and how does it differ from the kinds of profit maximization and profit seeking that we discussed in previous chapters? Provide an actual or hypothetical example of rent seeking by firms in an industry, by a union, or by a professional association (for example, physicians, school teachers, or lawyers). Why do elected officials often accommodate rent-seeking behavior, particularly by special-interest groups located in their home states? **LO5.3**

8. How does the problem of limited and bundled choice in the public sector relate to economic efficiency? Why are public bureaucracies possibly less efficient than business firms? **LO5.3**

9. Explain: "Politicians would make more rational economic decisions if they weren't running for reelection every few years." **LO5.3**

10. Critique: "Thank goodness we have so many government regulatory agencies. They keep Big Business in check." **LO5.3**

11. **LAST WORD** What are the pluses and minuses of corporate location subsidies? Why do politicians like them so much? Would you be surprised to know that many of the 238 cities bidding for Amazon's HQ2 offered much larger location subsidies than did New York City and Alexandria, Virginia? Explain.

Review Questions

1. Draw a production possibilities curve with public goods on the vertical axis and private goods on the horizontal axis. Assuming the economy is initially operating on the curve, indicate how the production of public goods might be increased. How might the output of public goods be increased if the economy is initially operating at a point inside the curve? **LO5.1**

2. Use the distinction between the characteristics of private goods and public goods to determine whether the following should be produced through the market system or provided by government: (a) French fries, (b) airport screening, (c) court systems, (d) mail delivery, and (e) medical care. Explain your answers. **LO5.1**

3. We can apply voting paradoxes to the highway construction example of Table 5.2. Suppose there are only five people in a society, and each favors one of the five highway construction options listed in Table 5.2 ("No new construction" is one of the five options). Explain which of these highway options will be selected using a majority paired-choice vote. Will this option be the optimal size of the project from an economic perspective? LO5.2

4. True or False: The median-voter model explains why politicians so often stake out fringe positions that appeal only to a small segment of the electorate. LO5.2

5. In Figure 5.2b, we saw that traditional one-person-one-vote (1p1v) majority voting results in an inefficient majority Yes vote (two in favor, one opposed). Let's see whether the outcome is better under quadratic voting. LO5.2
   a. How much will Garcia be willing to spend on votes?
   b. How much each will Johnson and Lee be willing to spend on votes?
   c. How many votes will Garcia purchase? How many will Johnson and Lee each purchase?
   d. What is the total number of votes cast for No? For Yes?

e. Approval of this project requires a 50-percent-plus-1 majority. Will the project be approved?
f. Does quadratic voting lead to the economically efficient outcome here?

6. Suppose that total costs (TC) double for each project listed in Table 5.2. Which project(s) is (are) now economically viable? LO5.3
   a. Plan A only
   b. Plans C and D only
   c. Plans B and C
   d. Plans A and B only

7. Explain the paradox of voting through reference to the accompanying table, which shows the ranking of three public goods by voters Gbowee, Ebadi, and Yousafzai: LO5.3

	Rankings		
Public Good	Gbowee	Ebadi	Yousafzai
Courthouse	2nd choice	1st choice	3rd choice
School	3rd choice	2nd choice	1st choice
Park	1st choice	3rd choice	2nd choice

Problems

McGraw Hill connect

1. On the basis of the three individual demand schedules in the following table, and assuming these are the only three people in the society, determine (a) the market demand schedule on the assumption that the good is a private good and (b) the collective demand schedule on the assumption that the good is a public good. LO5.1

P	Q_d (D_1)	Q_d (D_2)	Q_d (D_3)
$8	0	1	0
7	0	2	0
6	0	3	1
5	1	4	2
4	2	5	3
3	3	6	4
2	4	7	5
1	5	8	6

2. Use your demand schedule for a public good, determined in problem 1, and the following supply schedule to ascertain the optimal quantity of this public good. LO5.1

P	Q_s
$19	10
16	8
13	6
10	4
7	2
4	1

3. Look back at Figures 5.2a and 5.2b, which show the costs and benefits to voters Garcia, Johnson, and Lee of two different public goods that the government will produce if a majority of voters support them. Suppose that Garcia, Johnson, and Lee have decided to have one single vote at which the funding for both of those public goods will be decided simultaneously. LO5.2

a. Given the $300 cost per person of each public good, what are Garcia's net benefits for each public good individually and for the two combined? Will she vote yes or no on the proposal to fund both projects simultaneously?
b. What are Lee's net benefits for each public good individually and for the two combined? Will she vote yes or no on the proposal to fund both projects simultaneously?
c. What are Johnson's net benefits for each public good individually and for the two combined? Will he vote yes or no on the proposal to fund both projects simultaneously—or will he be indifferent?
d. Who is the median voter here? Whom will the two other voters be attempting to persuade?

4. Political advertising is often directed at winning over so-called swing voters, whose votes might go either way. Suppose that two political parties—the Freedom Party and the Liberty Party—disagree on whether to build a new road. Polling shows that of 1,000 total voters, 450 are firmly for the new road and 450 are firmly against the new road. Thus, each party will try to win over a majority of the 100 remaining swing voters. LO5.2
   a. Suppose that each party spends $5,000 on untargeted TV, radio, and newspaper ads that are equally likely to reach any and all voters. How much per voter will be spent by both parties combined?
   b. Suppose that, instead, each party could direct all of its spending toward just the swing voters by using targeted social media ads. If all of the two parties' combined spending is targeted at just swing voters, how much will be spent per swing voter?
   c. Suppose that only the Freedom Party knows how to target voters using social media. How much per swing voter will it be spending? If at the same time the Liberty Party is still using only untargeted TV, radio, and newspaper ads, what portion of its total spending is likely to be reaching the 100 swing voters? How much per swing voter does that portion amount to?

d. Looking at your answers to part *c*, how much more per swing voter will the Freedom Party be spending than the Liberty Party? If spending per swing voter influences elections, which party is more likely to win?

5. Let's see whether quadratic voting can avoid the paradox of voting that arose in Table 5.3 when using 1p1v in a series of paired-choice majority votes. To reexamine this situation using quadratic voting, the following table presents the maximum willingness to pay of Garcia, Johnson, and Lee for each of the three public goods. Notice that each person's numbers for willingness to pay match her or his ordering of preferences (1st choice, 2nd choice, 3rd choice) presented in Table 5.3. Thus, Garcia is willing to spend more on her 1st choice of national defense ($400) than on her second choice of a road ($100) or her third choice of a weather warning system ($0). **LO5.2**

Public Good	Willingness to Pay		
	Garcia	Johnson	Lee
National defense	$400	$ 50	$150
Road	100	300	100
Weather warning system	0	150	250

a. Assume that voting will be done using a quadratic voting system and that Garcia, Johnson, and Lee are each given $500 that can only be spent on purchasing votes (i.e., any unspent money has to be returned). How many votes will Garcia purchase to support national defense? How many for the road? Place those values into the appropriate blanks in the table below and then do the same for the blanks for Johnson and Lee.

Public Good	Votes Purchased		
	Garcia	Johnson	Lee
National defense	_____	_____	12
Road	_____	17	_____
Weather warning system	0	_____	_____

b. Across all three voters, how many votes are there in favor of national defense? The road? The weather warning system?
c. If a paired-choice vote is taken of national defense versus the road, which one wins?
d. If a paired-choice vote is taken of the road versus the weather warning system, which one wins?
e. If a paired-choice vote is taken of national defense versus the weather warning system, which one wins?
f. Review your answers to parts *c, d,* and *e*. Has quadratic voting eliminated the paradox of voting that we found when using 1p1v?

6. Consider a specific example of the special-interest effect and the collective-action problem. In 2021, it was estimated that the total value of all corn-production subsidies in the United States was about $3 billion. The population of the United States was approximately 300 million people that year. **LO5.3**

a. On average, how much did corn subsidies cost per person in the United States in 2021? (Hint: A billion is a 1 followed by nine zeros. A million is a 1 followed by six zeros.)
b. If each person in the United States is willing to spend only $0.50 to support efforts to overturn the corn subsidy, and if antisubsidy advocates can only raise funds from 10 percent of the population, how much money will they be able to raise for their lobbying efforts?
c. If the recipients of corn subsidies donate just 1 percent of the total amount that they receive in subsidies, how much could they raise to support lobbying efforts to continue the corn subsidy?
d. By how many dollars does the amount raised by the recipients of the corn subsidy exceed the amount raised by the opponents of the corn subsidy?

7. Consider a corrupt provincial government in which each housing inspector examines two newly built structures each week. All the builders in the province are unethical and want to increase their profits by using substandard construction materials, but they can't do that unless they can bribe a housing inspector into approving a substandard building **LO5.3**

a. If bribes cost $1,000 each, how much will a housing inspector make each year in bribes? (Assume that inspectors work 52 weeks a year and get bribed for every house that they inspect.)
b. There is a provincial construction supervisor who gets to hire all of the housing inspectors. He himself is corrupt and expects his housing inspectors to share their bribes with him. Suppose that 20 inspectors work for him and that each passes along half the bribes collected from builders. How much will the construction supervisor collect each year?
c. Corrupt officials may have an incentive to reduce the provision of government services to help line their own pockets. Suppose that the provincial construction supervisor decides to cut the total number of housing inspectors from 20 to 10 in order to decrease the supply of new housing permits. This decrease in the supply of permits raises the equilibrium bribe from $1,000 to $2,500. How much per year will the construction supervisor now receive if he is still getting half of all the bribes collected by the 10 inspectors? How much more is the construction supervisor getting now than when he had 20 inspectors working in part *b*? Will he personally be happy with the reduction in government services?
d. What would happen if reducing the number of inspectors from 20 to 10 only increased the equilibrium bribe from $1,000 to $1,500? In this case, how much per year would the construction supervisor collect from his 10 inspectors? How much less is the construction supervisor getting than when he had 20 inspectors working in part *b*? In this case, will the construction supervisor be happy with the reduction in government services? Will he want to go back to using 20 inspectors?

Elasticity

>> **LEARNING OBJECTIVES**

LO6.1   Explain and calculate price elasticity of demand.

LO6.2   Explain the usefulness of the total-revenue test.

LO6.3   List the factors that affect price elasticity of demand.

LO6.4   Describe and apply price elasticity of supply.

LO6.5   Apply cross elasticity of demand and income elasticity of demand.

In this chapter we explain elasticity, an important concept that helps us answer such questions as: Why do the buyers of some products (for example, ocean cruises) respond to price increases by substantially reducing their purchases while the buyers of other products (say, gasoline) respond by cutting back their purchases only slightly? Why does the demand for some products (for example, books) rise a great deal when household income increases while the demand for other products (say, milk) rises just a little? In short, elasticity tells us the degree to which changes in prices and incomes affect supply and demand. Sometimes the responses are substantial, other times minimal or nonexistent.

Price Elasticity of Demand

According to the *law of demand*, other things equal, consumers will buy more of a product when its price declines and less when its price increases. But how much more or less will they buy? The amount varies from product to product and over different price ranges for the same product. It also may vary over time. For example, a firm contemplating a price hike wants to know how consumers will respond. If they remain highly loyal and continue to buy, the firm's revenue will rise. But if consumers defect en masse to other products, the firm's revenue will tumble.

Consumers' responsiveness (or sensitivity) to a price change is measured by a product's **price elasticity of demand.** For some products—for example, restaurant meals—consumers are highly responsive to price changes. That is, modest price changes cause very large changes in the quantity purchased. The demand for such products is *relatively elastic,* or simply *elastic.*

For other products—for example, toothpaste—consumers are much less sensitive to price changes. For those products, even substantial price changes cause only small changes in the amount purchased. The demand for such products is *relatively inelastic* or simply *inelastic.*

>> **LO6.1** Explain and calculate price elasticity of demand.

price elasticity of demand The ratio of the percentage change in *quantity demanded* of a product or *resource* to the percentage change in its *price;* a measure of the responsiveness of buyers to a change in the price of a product or resource.

The Price-Elasticity Coefficient and Formula

Economists measure the degree to which demand is price elastic (price sensitive) or inelastic (price insensitive) with the coefficient E_d, defined as

$$E_d = \frac{\text{percentage change in quantity demanded of product X}}{\text{percentage change in price of product X}}$$

The percentage changes in the equation are calculated by dividing the *change* in quantity demanded by the original quantity demanded and by dividing the *change* in price by the original price. So we can restate the formula as

$$E_d = \frac{\text{change in quantity demanded of X}}{\text{original quantity demanded of X}} \div \frac{\text{change in price of X}}{\text{original price of X}}$$

Using Averages An annoying problem arises in computing the price-elasticity coefficient. A price change from, say, $4 to $5 along a demand curve is a 25 percent (= $1/$4) increase, but the opposite price change from $5 to $4 along the same curve is a 20 percent (= $1/$5) decrease. Which percentage change in price should we use in the denominator to compute the price-elasticity coefficient? And when quantity changes, for example, from 10 to 20, there's a 100 percent (= 10/10) increase. But when quantity falls from 20 to 10 along the same demand curve, there's a 50 percent (=10/20) decrease. Should we use 100 percent or 50 percent in the numerator of the elasticity formula? Elasticity should be the same whether price rises or falls!

midpoint formula A method for calculating *price elasticity of demand* or *price elasticity of supply* that averages the starting and ending *prices* and quantities when computing percentages.

The simplest solution is to use the **midpoint formula** which simply averages the two prices and the two quantities. That is,

$$E_d = \frac{\text{change in quantity}}{\text{sum of quantities}/2} \div \frac{\text{change in price}}{\text{sum of prices}/2}$$

For the same $5–$4 price range, the midpoint formula yields $4.50 [= ($5 + $4)/2], and for the same 10–20 quantity range, the midpoint formula yields 15 units [= (10 + 20)/2]. The percentage change in price is now $1/$4.50, or about 22 percent, and the percentage change in quantity is $\frac{10}{15}$, or about 67 percent. So E_d is about 3. All the price-elasticity coefficients that follow are calculated using this midpoint formula, which eliminates the "up versus down" problem.

Using Percentages Why use percentages rather than absolute amounts in measuring consumer responsiveness? There are two reasons.

- First, if we use absolute changes, the choice of units will arbitrarily affect our impression of buyer responsiveness. To illustrate: If the price of a bag of popcorn at the local softball game decreases from $3 to $2, and consumers increase their purchases from 60 to 100 bags, it will seem that consumers are quite sensitive to price changes and therefore that demand is elastic: A price change of 1 unit has increased the amount demanded by 40 units. But if we change the monetary unit from dollars to pennies, we find that a price change of 100 units (pennies) causes a quantity change of 40 units, which may falsely lead us to believe that demand is inelastic. We avoid this problem by using percentage changes.

- Second, by using percentages, we can correctly compare consumer responsiveness to changes in the prices of different products. It makes little sense to compare the effects on quantity demanded of (1) a $1 increase in the price of a $10,000 used car with (2) a $1 increase in the price of a $1 soft drink. Here, the price of the used car increases by 0.01 percent while the price of the soft drink increases by 100 percent. We can more sensibly compare the consumer responsiveness to price increases by using the percentage increase in price for both.

Elimination of Minus Sign We know from the downward sloping demand curve that price and quantity demanded are inversely related. Thus, the price-elasticity coefficient of demand E_d will always be a negative number. For example, if price declines, then quantity demanded will increase. This means that the numerator in our formula will be positive and the denominator negative, yielding a negative E_d. For an increase in price, the numerator will be negative but the denominator positive, again yielding a negative E_d.

elastic demand Product or resource demand whose *price elasticity of demand* is greater than 1, so that any given percentage change in *price* leads to a larger percentage change in *quantity demanded*. As a result, quantity demanded is relatively sensitive to (elastic with respect to) price.

Economists usually ignore the minus sign and simply present the absolute value of the elasticity coefficient to avoid any ambiguity that might otherwise arise. You can easily confuse people by saying that an E_d of −4 is greater than an E_d of −2. We avoid this possible confusion when we say an E_d of 4 reveals greater elasticity than an E_d of 2. In what follows, we ignore the minus sign in the coefficient of price elasticity of demand and show only the absolute value.

Interpretations of E_d

We can interpret E_d, the coefficient of price elasticity of demand, as follows.

Elastic Demand Demand is **elastic** if a specific percentage change in price in the denominator results in a larger percentage change in quantity demanded in the numerator. In such cases, E_d will

FIGURE 6.1 Perfectly inelastic and elastic demands.

Demand curve D_1 in (a) represents perfectly inelastic demand ($E_d = 0$). A price increase will result in no change in quantity demanded. Demand curve D_2 in (b) represents perfectly elastic demand. A price increase will cause quantity demanded to decline from an infinite amount to zero ($E_d = \infty$).

(a)
Perfectly inelastic demand

(b)
Perfectly elastic demand

be greater than 1. Example: Suppose that a 2 percent decline in the price of cut flowers in the denominator results in a 4 percent increase in quantity demanded in the numerator. Then demand for cut flowers is elastic and

$$E_d = \frac{.04}{.02} = 2$$

Inelastic Demand If a specific percentage change in price produces a smaller percentage change in quantity demanded, demand is **inelastic.** In such cases, E_d will be less than 1. Example: Suppose that a 2 percent decline in the price of coffee in the denominator leads to only a 1 percent increase in quantity demanded in the numerator. That would imply that demand is inelastic and

$$E_d = \frac{.01}{.02} = .5$$

Unit Elasticity In some cases, a percentage change in price and the resulting percentage change in quantity demanded are the same. Example: Suppose that a 2 percent drop in the price of chocolate causes a 2 percent increase in quantity demanded. This case is termed **unit elasticity** because E_d is exactly 1, or unity. In this example,

$$E_d = \frac{.02}{.02} = 1$$

Extreme Cases When we say demand is "inelastic," we do not mean that consumers are completely unresponsive to a price change. In that extreme situation, where a price change results in no change in the quantity demanded, we say that demand is **perfectly inelastic.** The price-elasticity coefficient is zero because there is no response to a price change. Approximate examples include an acute diabetic's demand for insulin or an addict's demand for meth. A line parallel to the vertical axis, such as D_1 in Figure 6.1a, shows perfectly inelastic demand graphically.

Conversely, when we say demand is "elastic," we do not mean that consumers are completely responsive to a price change. In that extreme situation, where a small price reduction causes buyers to increase their purchases from zero to all they can obtain, the elasticity coefficient is infinite ($= \infty$) and we say that demand is **perfectly elastic.** A line parallel to the horizontal axis, such as D_2 in Figure 6.1b, shows perfectly elastic demand. You will see in Chapter 10 that perfectly elastic demand applies to firms that sell output in a purely competitive market.

inelastic demand Product or resource demand for which the *price elasticity of demand* is less than 1, so that any given percentage change in *price* leads to a smaller percentage change in *quantity demanded.* As a result, quantity demanded is relatively insensitive to (inelastic with respect to) price.

unit elasticity *Demand* or *supply* for which the *elasticity coefficient* is equal to 1; means that the percentage change in the *quantity demanded* or *quantity supplied* is equal to the percentage change in *price.*

perfectly inelastic demand Product or *resource* demand in which *price* can be of any amount at a particular quantity of the product or resource that is demanded; when the *quantity demanded* does not respond to a change in price; graphs as a vertical *demand curve.*

perfectly elastic demand Product or *resource* demand in which *quantity demanded* can be of any amount at a particular product or resource *price;* graphs as a horizontal *demand curve.*

▶ The price elasticity of demand coefficient E_d is the ratio of the percentage change in quantity demanded to the percentage change in price. The *averages* of the two prices and two quantities are used as the base references in calculating the percentage changes.

▶ When E_d is greater than 1, demand is elastic; when E_d is less than 1, demand is inelastic; when E_d is equal to 1, demand is of unit elasticity.

QUICK REVIEW

6.1

The Total-Revenue Test

>> **LO6.2** Explain the usefulness of the total-revenue test.

Firms want to know the effect of price changes on total revenue and thus on profits (= total revenue minus total cost).

Total revenue (TR) is the total amount the seller receives from the sale of a product in a particular time period; it is calculated by multiplying the product price (*P*) by the quantity sold (*Q*). In equation form:

$$TR = P \times Q$$

total revenue (TR) The total number of dollars received by a *firm* (or firms) from the sale of a product; equal to the total expenditures for the product produced by the firm (or firms); equal to the quantity sold (demanded) multiplied by the *price* at which it is sold.

Graphically, total revenue is represented by the $P \times Q$ rectangle lying below a point on a demand curve. At point *a* in Figure 6.2a, for example, price is $2 and quantity demanded is 10 units. So total revenue is $20 (= $2 \times 10), shown by the rectangle composed of the yellow and green areas under the demand curve. We know from basic geometry that we can find the area of a rectangle by multiplying the length of one side by the length of the other. Here, one side is "price" (with a length of $2 per unit) and the other is "quantity demanded" (with a length of 10 units).

Total revenue and the price elasticity of demand are related. In fact, the easiest way to determine whether demand is elastic or inelastic is to employ the **total-revenue test,** which assesses what happens to total revenue when price changes:

- If total revenue changes in the opposite direction from price, demand is elastic.
- If total revenue changes in the same direction as price, demand is inelastic.
- If total revenue does not change when price changes, demand is unit-elastic.

FIGURE 6.2

The total-revenue test for price elasticity.

(a) Price declines from $2 to $1, and total revenue increases from $20 to $40. So demand is elastic. The gain in revenue (blue area) exceeds the loss of revenue (yellow area). (b) Price declines from $4 to $1, and total revenue falls from $40 to $20. So, demand is inelastic. The gain in revenue (blue area) is less than the loss of revenue (yellow area). (c) Price declines from $3 to $1, and total revenue does not change. Demand is unit-elastic. The gain in revenue (blue area) equals the loss of revenue (yellow area).

(a)
Elastic

(b)
Inelastic

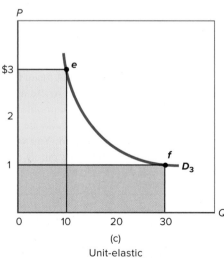

(c)
Unit-elastic

Elastic Demand

If demand is elastic, a decrease in price increases total revenue. Even though a lower price is received per unit, enough additional units are sold to more than make up for the lower price. For an example, look at demand curve D_1 in Figure 6.2a. At point a, total revenue is $20 (= 2×10). If the price declines from $2 to $1 (point b), the quantity demanded becomes 40 units and total revenue is $40 (= 1×40). As a result of the price decline, total revenue increases from $20 to $40. Total revenue has increased because the $1 price decline applies to 10 units, with a consequent revenue loss of $10 (the yellow area). But 30 more units are sold at $1 each, resulting in a revenue gain of $30 (the blue area). The overall result therefore is a net increase in total revenue of $20 (= $30 − $10).

The analysis is reversible: If demand is elastic, a price increase reduces total revenue. The revenue gained from a higher price per unit will be more than offset by the revenue lost from the lower quantity sold. E_d is greater than 1, and the percentage change in quantity demanded is greater than the percentage change in price.

Inelastic Demand

If demand is inelastic, a price decrease reduces total revenue. The increase in sales does not fully offset the decline in revenue per unit, and total revenue declines. Look at demand curve D_2 in Figure 6.2b. At point c on the curve, price is $4 and quantity demanded is 10. Thus total revenue is $40, shown by the combined yellow and green rectangle. If the price drops to $1 (point d), total revenue declines to $20. Total revenue has declined because the loss of revenue (the yellow area) from the lower unit price is larger than the gain in revenue (the blue area) from the accompanying increase in sales. Price has fallen, and total revenue has also declined.

Our analysis is again reversible: If demand is inelastic, a price increase will increase total revenue. So, other things equal, when price and total revenue move in the same direction, demand is inelastic. E_d is less than 1, and the percentage change in quantity demanded is less than the percentage change in price.

Unit Elasticity

In the case of unit elasticity, an increase or a decrease in price leaves total revenue unchanged. The loss in revenue from a lower unit price is exactly offset by the gain in revenue from the accompanying increase in sales. Conversely, the gain in revenue from a higher unit price is exactly offset by the revenue loss from the accompanying decline in the amount demanded.

Look at demand curve D_3 in Figure 6.2c. At the price of $3, 10 units will be sold, yielding total revenue of $30. At the lower $1 price, a total of 30 units will be sold, again resulting in $30 of total revenue. The $2 price reduction causes the revenue loss shown by the yellow area, but that loss is exactly offset by the revenue gain shown by the blue area. Total revenue does not change.

Other things equal, when price changes and total revenue remains constant, demand is unit-elastic (or unitary). E_d is 1, and the percentage change in quantity equals the percentage change in price.

Finally, note that unit elasticity implies the ultimate in reversibility. When demand is unit-elastic, both price increases and price decreases leave total revenue unchanged.

Price Elasticity along a Linear Demand Curve

Although the demand curves in Figure 6.2 nicely illustrate the total-revenue test for elasticity, it is important to understand that elasticity typically *varies* along any given demand curve. (The curve in Figure 6.2c is exceptional, with elasticity equal to 1 along the entire curve.)

Refer to Table 6.1 and Figure 6.3 which show how elasticity varies over different price ranges of the same demand schedule or curve. Plotting the hypothetical data for movie tickets shown in columns 1 and 2 of Table 6.1 yields demand curve D in Figure 6.3. That demand curve is linear. But column 3 of the table shows that the price elasticity coefficient declines as we move from higher prices to lower prices. For all downward sloping straight-line and most other demand curves, demand is more price elastic toward the upper left (here, the $5-$8 price range) than toward the lower right (here, the $4-$1 price range).

This is a consequence of the arithmetic properties of the elasticity measure. Specifically, in the upper-left segment of the demand curve, the percentage change in quantity is large because the original reference quantity is small. Similarly, the percentage change in price is small in that

total-revenue test A test to determine *elasticity of demand*. Demand is elastic if *total revenue* moves in the opposite direction from a *price* change; it is inelastic when it moves in the same direction as a price change; and it is of unitary elasticity when it does not change when price changes.

TABLE 6.1 Price Elasticity of Demand for Movie Tickets as Measured by the Elasticity Coefficient and the Total-Revenue Test

(1) Total Quantity of Tickets Demanded per Week, Thousands	(2) Price per Ticket	(3) Elasticity Coefficient (E_d)	(4) Total Revenue, (1) × (2)	(5) Total-Revenue Test
1	$8		$ 8,000	
		5.00		Elastic
2	7		14,000	Elastic
		2.60		
3	6		18,000	Elastic
		1.57		
4	5		20,000	Elastic
		1.00		
5	4		20,000	Unit-elastic
		0.64		
6	3		18,000	Inelastic
		0.38		
7	2		14,000	Inelastic
		0.20		
8	1		8,000	Inelastic

segment because the original reference price is large. The relatively large percentage change in quantity divided by the relatively small change in price yields a large E_d—an elastic demand.

The reverse holds true for the lower-right segment of the demand curve. Here, the percentage change in quantity is small because the original reference quantity is large; similarly, the percentage change in price is large because the original reference price is small. The relatively small percentage change in quantity divided by the relatively large percentage change in price results in a small E_d—an inelastic demand.

The demand curve in Figure 6.3a also illustrates that the slope of a demand curve—its flatness or steepness—is not a sound basis for judging elasticity. The catch is that slope is computed from absolute changes in price and quantity, while elasticity involves relative or percentage changes in price and quantity. The demand curve in Figure 6.3a is linear, which by definition means that the slope is constant throughout. But we have seen that the curve is elastic in its high-price ($8–$5) range and inelastic in its low-price ($4–$1) range. *So please do not confuse slope and elasticity. Slope can be constant even while elasticity varies significantly along the length of a curve.*

FIGURE 6.3 The relation between price elasticity of demand for movie tickets and total revenue.

(a) Demand curve *D* is based on Table 6.1 and is marked to show that the hypothetical weekly demand for movie tickets is elastic at higher price ranges and inelastic at lower price ranges. (b) The total-revenue curve TR is derived from demand curve *D*. When price falls and TR increases, demand is elastic; when price falls and TR is unchanged, demand is unit-elastic; and when price falls and TR declines, demand is inelastic.

(a)
Demand curve

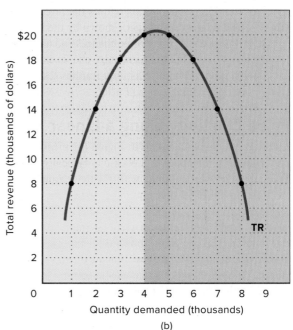

(b)
Total-revenue curve

TABLE 6.2 Price Elasticity of Demand: A Summary

Absolute Value of Elasticity Coefficient	Demand Is:	Description	Impact on Total Revenue of a:	
			Price Increase	Price Decrease
Greater than 1 ($E_d > 1$)	Elastic or relatively elastic	Quantity demanded changes by a larger percentage than does price	Total revenue decreases	Total revenue increases
Equal to 1 ($E_d = 1$)	Unit- or unitary elastic	Quantity demanded changes by the same percentage as does price	Total revenue is unchanged	Total revenue is unchanged
Less than 1 ($E_d < 1$)	Inelastic or relatively inelastic	Quantity demanded changes by a smaller percentage than does price	Total revenue increases	Total revenue decreases

Price Elasticity and the Total-Revenue Curve

Figure 6.3b plots the total revenue per week to the theater owner that corresponds to each price-quantity combination indicated along demand curve D in Figure 6.3a. The combination represented by point a yields total revenue of $8,000 (= $8 × 1,000 tickets). Figure 6.3b plots this $8,000 amount vertically at 1 unit (1,000 tickets) demanded. Similarly, the price–quantity-demanded combination represented by point b yields total revenue of $14,000 (= $7 × 2,000 tickets). This amount is graphed vertically at 2 units (2,000 tickets) demanded. The ultimate result of such graphing is total-revenue curve TR, which first slopes upward, then reaches a maximum, and finally turns downward.

Comparison of curves D and TR in Figure 6.3 sharply focuses the relationship between elasticity and total revenue. Lowering the ticket price in the elastic range of demand—for example, from $8 to $5—increases total revenue. Conversely, increasing the ticket price in that range reduces total revenue. In both cases, price and total revenue change in opposite directions, confirming that demand is elastic.

The $5–$4 price range of demand curve D reflects unit elasticity. When price either decreases from $5 to $4 or increases from $4 to $5, total revenue remains $20,000. In both cases, price has changed and total revenue has remained constant, confirming that demand is unit-elastic when we consider these particular price changes.

In the inelastic range of demand curve D, lowering the price—for example, from $4 to $1—decreases total revenue. Conversely, raising the price in the inelastic range boosts total revenue. In both cases, price and total revenue move in the same direction, confirming that demand is inelastic.

Table 6.2 summarizes the characteristics of price elasticity of demand.

Determinants of Price Elasticity of Demand

Price elasticity of demand varies by situation. However, the following generalizations are often helpful.

>> **LO6.3** List the factors that affect price elasticity of demand.

- **Substitutability** Generally, the more substitute goods that are available, the greater the price elasticity of demand. Various candy bar brands are generally substitutable for one another, making the demand for one brand of candy bar, say, Snickers, highly elastic. Toward the other extreme, the demand for tooth repair is quite inelastic because there simply are no close substitutes when that procedure is required.

  The elasticity of demand for a product depends on how narrowly the product is defined. Demand for Skechers sneakers is more elastic than the overall demand for shoes. Many other brands are readily substitutable for Skechers sneakers, but there are few, if any, good substitutes for shoes.

- **Proportion of income** Other things equal, the higher the price of a good relative to consumers' incomes, the greater the price elasticity of demand. A 10 percent increase in the price of low-priced pencils or chewing gum amounts to a few more pennies spent from a consumer's income, and quantity demanded will probably decline only slightly. Thus, price elasticity for low-priced items tends to be low. But a 10 percent increase in the price of relatively high-priced products like automobiles or houses means additional expenditures of perhaps $3,000 or $30,000, respectively. These price increases are significant fractions of most families' annual incomes, and quantities demanded will likely diminish significantly. The price elasticities for such items tend to be high.

TABLE 6.3 Selected Price Elasticities of Demand

Product or Service	Coefficient of Price Elasticity of Demand (E_d)	Product or Service	Coefficient of Price Elasticity of Demand (E_d)
Newspapers	.10	Milk	.63
Electricity (household)	.13	Household appliances	.63
Bread	.15	Liquor	.70
Major League Baseball tickets	.23	Movies	.87
Cigarettes	.25	Beer	.90
Telephone service	.26	Shoes	.91
Sugar	.30	Motor vehicles	1.14
Medical care	.31	Beef	1.27
Eggs	.32	China, glassware, tableware	1.54
Legal services	.37	Residential land	1.60
Automobile repair	.40	Restaurant meals	2.27
Clothing	.49	Lamb and mutton	2.65
Gasoline	.58	Fresh peas	2.83

Source: Compiled from numerous studies and sources reporting price elasticity of demand.

- *Luxuries versus necessities* In general, price elasticity of demand is higher for luxury goods than it is for necessities. Electricity is generally regarded as a necessity; it is difficult to get along without it. A price increase will not significantly reduce the amount of lighting and power used in a household. (Note electricity's very low price-elasticity coefficient in Table 6.3, which lists selected price elasticities of demand.) An extreme case: A person does not decline an operation for acute appendicitis because the physician's fee has just gone up.

    In contrast, vacation travel and jewelry are luxuries, which, by definition, can easily be forgone. If the prices of vacation travel and jewelry rise, consumers need not buy them and will suffer no great hardship without them.

    What about the demand for a common product like salt? It is highly inelastic on three counts: Few good substitutes are available; salt is a negligible item in the family budget; and it is a "necessity" rather than a luxury.

- *Time* Generally, product demand is more elastic over longer time periods. Consumers often need time to adjust to price changes. For example, when the price of a product rises, consumers need time to find and experiment with other products. Consumers may not immediately reduce their purchases very much when the price of beef rises by 10 percent, but in time they may shift to chicken, pork, or fish. A related consideration is product durability. Studies show that "short-run" demand for gasoline is more inelastic ($E_d = 0.26$) than is "long-run" demand ($E_d = 0.58$). In the short run, people are stuck with their present cars and trucks, but with rising gasoline prices they eventually replace them with smaller, more fuel-efficient gas-powered vehicles, or with gas-electric hybrids or fully electric cars. Some also switch to mass transit.

Applications of Price Elasticity of Demand

Price elasticity of demand has great practical significance, as the following examples show.

Large Crop Yields The demand for most farm products is highly inelastic; E_d is perhaps 0.20 or 0.25. As a result, increases in the supply of farm products arising from a good growing season or from increased productivity tend to depress both the prices of farm products and the total revenues (incomes) of farmers. For farmers as a group, the inelastic demand for their products means that large crop yields may be undesirable. For policymakers, it means that achieving the goal of higher total farm income requires that farm output be restricted.

Excise Taxes The government pays attention to elasticity of demand when it selects goods and services to tax. If the government levies a $1 excise tax on a product and 10,000 units are sold, tax revenue will be $10,000 (= $1 × 10,000 units sold). (An **excise tax** is a tax levied on the production of a specific product or on the quantity of the product purchased.) If the government raises

excise tax A tax levied on the production of a specific product or on the quantity of the product purchased.

the tax to $1.50, but the higher price that results reduces sales to 4,000 because of elastic demand, tax revenue will decline to $6,000 (= $1.50 × 4,000 units sold). Because a higher tax on a product with elastic demand will bring in less tax revenue, legislatures tend to tax products that have inelastic demand, such as liquor, gasoline, and cigarettes.

Decriminalization of Illegal Drugs In recent years, proposals to legalize drugs have been widely debated. Proponents contend that drugs should be treated like alcohol; they should be made legal for adults and regulated for purity. Legalization, they argue, will reduce drug trafficking significantly by taking the profit out of it. Because addicts' demand for drugs is highly inelastic, the amounts consumed at the lower prices would increase only modestly. Addicts' total expenditures for drugs like cocaine and heroin would decline, and so would the crime that finances those expenditures.

Opponents argue that the overall demand for illegal drugs is far more elastic than proponents think. In addition to addicts' inelastic demand, there is another market segment whose demand is relatively elastic. This segment consists of the "dabblers" who use hard drugs when their prices are low but who abstain or substitute (perhaps with alcohol) when drug prices are high. Thus, the lower prices associated with legalization would increase dabblers' consumption. Also, legalization might make drug use more socially acceptable, increasing overall demand.

Marijuana prices in the State of Washington fell by 77 percent in the three years after marijuana was legalized in 2014. Many economists predict that the legalization of cocaine and heroin could reduce street prices by up to 80 percent, as well. According to one important study, such price declines could increase the number of occasional users of heroin by 54 percent and the number of occasional users of cocaine by 33 percent. The total quantity of heroin demanded would rise by an estimated 100 percent, and the quantity of cocaine demanded would rise by 50 percent.[1] Moreover, many existing and first-time dabblers might become addicts. The overall result, say the opponents of legalization, would be higher social costs, including a possible increase in street crime.

The Consider This story examines the high price elasticities of demand for air travel that were revealed by a low-cost airline.

CONSIDER THIS . . .

The Southwest Effect

Southwest Airlines grew from three planes in 1967 to America's largest domestic airline by being committed to low prices and efficiency.

Since its inception, Southwest has also been committed to making air travel so inexpensive that people who could never afford to fly before finally can. That has led to the famous Southwest Effect, whereby ticket prices plunge after Southwest enters a new market and undercuts existing carriers. As just one example, the price of flying from Denver to Phoenix fell by 36.4 percent after Southwest began service out of Denver in 2006.

Chris Parypa/Essentials/rypson/iStockphoto

Those sharp price declines allow us to estimate price elasticity of demand, including for new passengers who could not afford to fly previously. When Southwest entered the market in three California cities, fares dropped by 50 percent while passenger traffic increased 200 percent, implying a highly elastic demand for air travel at those airports. And because "highly elastic demand" implies that "lower prices will increase total revenue," Southwest found those price declines very favorable indeed.

Its higher-cost rivals? Not so much. Nearly the entire increase in passenger traffic, revenue, and profits went to Southwest.

▶ When price changes, total revenue will change in the opposite direction if demand is price-elastic, in the same direction if demand is price-inelastic, and not at all if demand is unit-elastic.

▶ Demand is typically elastic in the high-price (low-quantity) range of the demand curve and inelastic in the low-price (high-quantity) range of the demand curve.

▶ Price elasticity of demand is greater (a) the larger the number of substitutes available; (b) the higher the price of a product relative to one's budget or income; (c) the greater the extent to which the product is a luxury; and (d) the longer the time period involved.

QUICK REVIEW
6.2

---

[1]Henry Saffer and Frank Chaloupka, "The Demand for Illicit Drugs," *Economic Inquiry,* July 1999, pp. 401–411.

Price Elasticity of Supply

>> **LO6.4** Describe and apply price elasticity of supply.

Price elasticity also applies to supply. If the quantity supplied by producers is relatively responsive to price changes, supply is elastic. If it is relatively insensitive to price changes, supply is inelastic.

We measure the price elasticity or inelasticity of supply with the coefficient E_s, defined almost like E_d except that we substitute "percentage change in quantity supplied" for "percentage change in quantity demanded" as follows:

$$E_s = \frac{\text{percentage change in quantity supplied of product X}}{\text{percentage change in price of product X}}$$

For reasons explained earlier, the averages, or midpoints, of the before and after quantities supplied and the before and after prices are used as reference points for the percentage changes. Suppose an increase in the price of a good from \$4 to \$6 increases the quantity supplied from 10 units to 14 units. The percentage change in price would be 2/5, or 40 percent, and the percentage change in quantity would be 4/12, or 33 percent. Consequently,

$$E_s = \frac{.33}{.40} = .83$$

In this case, supply is inelastic because the price-elasticity coefficient is less than 1. If E_s is greater than 1, supply is elastic. If it is equal to 1, supply is unit-elastic. E_s is never negative, because price and quantity supplied are directly related. Thus, there are no minus signs to drop (which we needed to do when calculating elasticity of demand).

price elasticity of supply
The ratio of the percentage change in *quantity supplied* of a product or *resource* to the percentage change in its *price;* a measure of the responsiveness of producers to a change in the price of a product or resource.

The degree of **price elasticity of supply** depends on how quickly and easily producers can shift resources between alternative uses. The more easily and rapidly producers can shift resources between alternative uses, the greater the price elasticity of supply. Take the case of Christmas trees. A firm's response to an increase in the price of trees depends on its ability to shift resources from the production of other products (whose prices we assume remain constant) to the production of trees. Shifting resources takes time: The more time available, the greater the "shiftability." So we can expect a greater response, and therefore greater elasticity of supply, the longer a firm has to adjust to a price change.

In analyzing the impact of time on elasticity, economists distinguish among the immediate market period, the short run, and the long run.

Price Elasticity of Supply: The Immediate Market Period

immediate market period
The length of time during which the producers of a product are unable to change the quantity supplied in response to a change in price and in which there is a *perfectly inelastic supply.*

The **immediate market period** is the length of time over which producers are unable to respond to a change in price with a change in quantity supplied. Suppose the owner of a small farm brings to market one truckload of tomatoes that is the entire season's output. The supply curve for the tomatoes is perfectly inelastic (vertical); the farmer will sell the truckload whether the price is high or low. Why? Because the farmer can offer only one truckload of tomatoes even if the price of tomatoes is much higher than anticipated. The farmer might like to offer more tomatoes for sale, but tomatoes cannot be produced overnight. The farmer needs another full growing season to respond to a higher-than-expected price. Similarly, because the product is perishable, the farmer cannot withhold it from the market. If the price is lower than anticipated, the farmer will still sell the entire truckload.

The farmer's costs of production will not enter into this decision to sell. Though the price of tomatoes may fall far short of production costs, the farmer will nevertheless sell everything he brought to market to avoid a total loss through spoilage. In the immediate market period, both the supply of tomatoes and the quantity of tomatoes supplied are fixed. The farmer offers only one truckload no matter how high or low the price.

Figure 6.4a shows the farmer's vertical supply curve during the immediate market period. Supply is perfectly inelastic because the farmer does not have time to respond to a change in demand, say, from D_1 to D_2. The resulting price increase from P_o to P_m simply determines which buyers get the fixed quantity supplied; it elicits no increase in output.

However, not all supply curves are perfectly inelastic immediately after a price change. If the product is not perishable and the price rises, producers may choose to increase quantity supplied by drawing down their inventories of unsold, stored goods. This will cause the market supply curve to attain some positive slope. For our tomato farmer, the immediate market period may be a full growing season; for producers of goods that can be inexpensively stored, there may be no immediate market period at all.

FIGURE 6.4 Time and the elasticity of supply.

The greater the amount of time producers have to adjust to a change in demand, here from D_1 to D_2, the greater will be their output response. (a) In the immediate market period, there is insufficient time to change output, and so supply is perfectly inelastic. (b) In the short run, plant capacity is fixed, but changing the intensity of its use can alter output; supply is therefore more elastic. (c) In the long run, all desired adjustments, including changes in plant capacity, can be made, and supply becomes still more elastic.

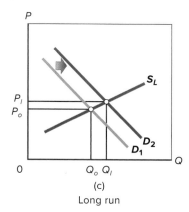

(a)	(b)	(c)
Immediate market period	Short run	Long run

Price Elasticity of Supply: The Short Run

The **short run** in microeconomics is a period of time too short to change plant capacity but long enough to use the fixed-sized plant more intensively or less intensively. In the short run, our farmer's plant (land and farm machinery) is fixed. But he does have time in the short run to cultivate tomatoes more intensively by applying more labor and more fertilizer and pesticides to the crop. The result is a somewhat greater output in response to increased demand; this greater output is reflected in a more elastic supply of tomatoes, as shown by the upward sloping S_s in Figure 6.4b. Note now that the increase in demand from D_1 to D_2 is met by an increase in quantity (from Q_o to Q_s), so there is a smaller price adjustment (from P_o to P_s) than would be the case in the immediate market period. The equilibrium price is therefore lower in the short run than in the immediate market period.

short run In *microeconomics*, a period of time in which producers are able to change the quantities of some but not all of the *resources* they employ; a period in which some resources (usually *plant*) are fixed and some are variable.

Price Elasticity of Supply: The Long Run

The **long run** in microeconomics is a time period long enough for firms to adjust their plant sizes and for new firms to enter (or existing firms to leave) the industry. In the "tomato industry," for example, our farmer has time to acquire additional land and buy more machinery and equipment. Furthermore, other farmers may, over time, be attracted to tomato farming by the increased demand and higher price. Such adjustments create a larger supply response, as represented by the more elastic supply curve S_l in Figure 6.4c. The outcome is a smaller price rise (P_o to P_l) and a larger output increase (Q_o to Q_l) in response to the increase in demand from D_1 to D_2.

There is no total-revenue test for elasticity of supply. Supply shows a positive or direct relationship between price and amount supplied; the supply curve slopes upward. Regardless of the degree of elasticity or inelasticity, price and total revenue always move together.

long run In *microeconomics*, a period of time long enough to enable producers of a product to change the quantities of all the resources they employ, so that all resources and costs are variable and no resources or costs are fixed.

Applications of Price Elasticity of Supply

Price elasticity of supply has widespread applicability, as the following examples show.

Antiques and Reproductions *Antiques Roadshow* is a popular PBS television program in which people bring antiques for appraisal by experts. Some people are pleased to learn that their old furniture or funky folk art is worth a large amount, say, $30,000 or more.

The high price of antiques results from strong demand and limited, highly inelastic supply. Because genuine antiques cannot be reproduced, their quantity supplied either does not rise or rises only slightly as price goes up. The higher price might prompt the discovery of a few more remaining originals and thus add to the quantity available for sale, but this quantity response is usually quite small. So the supply of antiques and other collectibles tends to be inelastic. For one-of-a-kind antiques, the supply is perfectly inelastic.

Factors such as increased population, higher income, and greater enthusiasm for collecting antiques have increased the demand for antiques over time. Because the supply of antiques is limited and inelastic, those increases in demand have greatly boosted the prices of antiques.

Contrast the inelastic supply of original antiques with the elastic supply of modern "made-to-look-old" reproductions. Such faux antiques are quite popular and widely available at furniture stores and knickknack shops. When the demand for reproductions increases, the firms making them simply boost production. Because the supply of reproductions is highly elastic, increased demand raises their prices only slightly.

Volatile Gold Prices The price of gold is quite volatile, sometimes shooting upward one period and plummeting downward the next. The main sources of these fluctuations are shifts in demand interacting with highly inelastic supply. Gold production is a costly and time-consuming process of exploration, mining, and refining. Moreover, the physical availability of gold is highly limited—all the gold ever mined would fit into a cube roughly 21 meters (69 feet) on each side. For both reasons, increases in gold prices do not elicit substantial increases in quantity supplied. In addition, gold mining is costly to shut down and existing gold bars are expensive to store. Price decreases therefore do not produce large drops in the quantity of gold supplied. In short, the supply of gold is inelastic.

The demand for gold is partly derived from the demand for its uses, such as for jewelry, dental fillings, and coins. But people also demand gold as a speculative financial investment. They increase their demand for gold when they fear economic turmoil that might undermine the value of currency and other types of investment. They reduce their demand when events settle down. Because of the inelastic supply of gold, even relatively small changes in demand produce relatively large changes in price.

Cross Elasticity and Income Elasticity of Demand

>> LO6.5 Apply cross elasticity of demand and income elasticity of demand.

As we've seen, price elasticities measure the responsiveness of the quantity demanded or supplied of a good to a change in price. The *consumption* of a good is also affected by price changes and, additionally, by income changes.

Cross Elasticity of Demand

cross elasticity of demand The ratio of the percentage change in *quantity demanded* of one good to the percentage change in the *price* of some other good. A positive coefficient indicates the two products are *substitute goods;* a negative coefficient indicates they are *complementary goods.*

The **cross elasticity of demand** measures the sensitivity of consumer purchases of one product (call it X) to a change in the price of some other product (call it Y). We calculate the coefficient of cross elasticity of demand E_{xy} as the percentage change in the consumption of X to the percentage change in the price of Y:

$$E_{xy} = \frac{\text{percentage change in quantity demanded of product X}}{\text{percentage change in price of product Y}}$$

Cross elasticity (also known as cross-price elasticity) allows us to quantify and more fully understand substitute and complementary goods, introduced in Chapter 3. The coefficient of cross elasticity of demand can be either positive or negative.

Substitute Goods If cross elasticity of demand is positive, meaning that sales of X move in the same direction as a change in the price of Y, then X and Y are substitute goods. An example is Evian water (X) and Dasani water (Y). An increase in the price of Evian causes consumers to buy more Dasani, resulting in a positive cross elasticity. The larger the positive cross-elasticity coefficient, the greater is the substitutability between the two products.

Complementary Goods When cross elasticity is negative, we know that X and Y "go together"; an increase in the price of one decreases the demand for the other. So the two are complementary goods. For example, a decrease in the price of smartphones will increase the number of smartphone cases that are purchased. The larger the negative cross-elasticity coefficient, the greater is the complementarity between the two goods.

Independent Goods A zero or near-zero cross elasticity suggests that the two products are unrelated or independent goods. An example is walnuts and wireless earbuds: We do not expect a change in the price of walnuts to have any effect on purchases of wireless earbuds, and vice versa.

Application The cross-elasticity coefficient is important to businesses and government. For example, suppose that the Coca-Cola Corporation is considering whether to lower the price of its Sprite

GLOBAL PERSPECTIVE 6.1

CROSS ELASTICITY OF DEMAND BETWEEN EDUCATION SPENDING AND INCREASES IN THE PRICE OF FOOD, SELECTED NATIONS

The amount by which education spending falls when food prices go up is higher in lower-income countries like Tanzania and Vietnam, where family budgets are tighter and any increase in food costs is more likely to mean cutbacks on education spending. The decline in education spending is noticeably smaller in high-income countries like Japan and the United States, where family budgets are less constrained.

Cross Elasticity of Demand Between Education Spending and Increases in the Price of Food

	−0.30	−0.20	−0.10	0
Tanzania				
Benin				
Vietnam				
Ecuador				
Zimbabwe				
Russia				
Argentina				
South Korea				
Japan				
United States				

Source: Economic Research Service, United States Department of Agriculture.

brand. Before making its decision, it wants to know about the price elasticity of demand for Sprite (will the price cut increase or decrease total revenue?), but it is also interested in knowing if the increased sales of Sprite will come at the expense of its Coke brand. How sensitive are the sales of Coke to a change in the price of Sprite? By how much will the increased sales of Sprite "cannibalize" the sales of Coke? A low cross elasticity would indicate that Coke and Sprite are weak substitutes for each other and that a lower price for Sprite will have little effect on Coke sales.

Government also uses the idea of cross elasticity of demand in assessing whether a proposed merger between two large firms will substantially reduce competition and therefore violate the antitrust laws. For example, the cross elasticity between Coke and Pepsi is high, making them strong substitutes. In addition, the Coca-Cola Corporation and its rival producer PepsiCo sell about 70 percent of all carbonated cola drinks consumed in the United States. Taken together, the high cross elasticities and the large market shares suggest that the government would likely block a merger between Coca-Cola Corporation and PepsiCo because the merger would substantially lessen competition. In contrast, the cross elasticity between cola and gasoline is low or zero. A merger between Coca-Cola Corporation and the Shell Oil Company would have a minimal effect on competition. So government would let that merger happen.

Global Perspective 6.1 presents, for several countries, the cross elasticity of demand that quantifies the responsiveness of household educational expenditures to a one-percent increase in the price of food. The poorer the country, the larger the decline in education spending.

Income Elasticity of Demand

Income elasticity of demand measures the degree to which consumers respond to a change in their incomes by buying more or less of a particular good. The coefficient of income elasticity of demand E_i is determined with the formula

$$E_i = \frac{\text{percentage change in quantity demanded}}{\text{percentage change in income}}$$

income elasticity of demand The ratio of the percentage change in the *quantity demanded* of a good to a percentage change in consumer *income;* measures the responsiveness of consumer purchases to income changes.

Normal Goods For most goods, the income-elasticity coefficient E_i is positive, meaning that more of those goods are demanded as incomes rise. Such goods are called normal or superior goods (see Chapter 3). But the value of E_i varies greatly among normal goods. For example, income elasticity of demand for automobiles is about +3.0, while income elasticity for most farm products is only about +0.2.

Inferior Goods A negative income-elasticity coefficient designates an inferior good. Cabbage, long-distance bus tickets, and used clothing are likely inferior goods. Consumers decrease their purchases of inferior goods as incomes rise.

TABLE 6.4 Cross and Income Elasticities of Demand

Value of Coefficient	Description	Type of Good(s)
Cross elasticity:		
Positive ($E_{wz} > 0$)	Quantity demanded of W changes in same direction as change in price of Z	Substitutes
Negative ($E_{xy} < 0$)	Quantity demanded of X changes in opposite direction from change in price of Y	Complements
Income elasticity:		
Positive ($E_i > 0$)	Quantity demanded of the product changes in same direction as change in income	Normal or superior
Negative ($E_i < 0$)	Quantity demanded of the product changes in opposite direction from change in income	Inferior

Insights Coefficients of income elasticity of demand provide insights into the economy. For example, when recessions (business downturns) occur and incomes fall, income elasticity of demand helps predict which products' demand will decline more rapidly.

Products with relatively high income-elasticity coefficients, such as automobiles ($E_i = +3.0$), housing ($E_i = +1.5$), and restaurant meals ($E_i = +1.4$), are generally hit hardest by recessions. Those with low or negative income-elasticity coefficients are much less affected. For example, food products prepared at home ($E_i = +0.2$) respond relatively little to income fluctuations. When incomes drop, purchases of food (and toothpaste and toilet paper) drop little compared to purchases of concert tickets, luxury vacations, and high-definition TVs. Products we view as essential tend to have lower income-elasticity coefficients than products we view as luxuries. When our incomes fall, we cannot easily eliminate or postpone the purchase of essential products.

Table 6.4 provides a convenient synopsis of the cross-elasticity and income-elasticity concepts.

Global Perspective 6.2 shows that the income elasticity of gasoline demand varies substantially across countries and is larger in lower-income countries.

GLOBAL PERSPECTIVE 6.2

INCOME ELASTICITY OF DEMAND FOR GASOLINE, SELECTED NATIONS

The income elasticity of gasoline demand varies widely across countries, with larger demand responses found in lower-income countries in which driving is a luxury for much of the population.

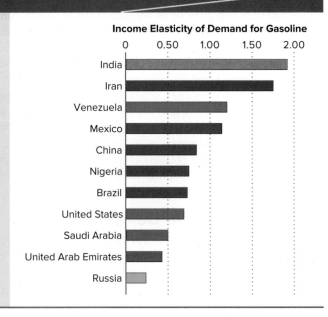

Income Elasticity of Demand for Gasoline

Source: U.S. Energy Information Administration.

QUICK REVIEW 6.3

▶ Price elasticity of supply measures the sensitivity of suppliers to changes in the price of a product. The price-elasticity-of-supply coefficient E_s is the ratio of the percentage change in quantity supplied to the percentage change in price. The elasticity of supply varies directly with the amount of time producers have to respond to the price change.

▶ The cross-elasticity-of-demand coefficient E_{xy} is computed as the percentage change in the quantity demanded of product X divided by the percentage change in the price of product Y. If the cross-elasticity coefficient is positive, the two products are substitutes; if negative, they are complements.

▶ The income-elasticity coefficient E_i is computed as the percentage change in quantity demanded divided by the percentage change in income. A positive coefficient indicates a normal or superior good. A negative coefficient implies an inferior good.

Elasticity and Pricing Power: Why Different Consumers Pay Different Prices

Firms and Nonprofit Institutions Often Recognize and Exploit Differences in Price Elasticity of Demand.

All the buyers of a product traded in a highly competitive market pay the same market price for the product, regardless of their individual price elasticities of demand. If the price rises, Jones may have an elastic demand and greatly reduce her purchases. Singh may have a unit-elastic demand and reduce his purchases less than Jones. Lopez may have an inelastic demand and hardly curtail her purchases at all. But all three consumers will pay the single higher price regardless of their respective demand elasticities.

In later chapters, we will find that not all sellers must passively accept a "one-for-all" price. Some firms have "market power" or "pricing power" that allows them to set their product prices in their best interests. For some goods and services, firms may find it advantageous to determine differences in price elasticity of demand and then charge different prices to different buyers.

It is extremely difficult to tailor prices for each customer on the basis of price elasticity of demand, but it is relatively easy to observe differences in group elasticities. Consider airline tickets. Business travelers generally have inelastic demand for air travel. Because their time is highly valuable, they do not see slower modes of transportation as realistic substitutes. Also, their employers pay for their tickets as part of their business expenses. In contrast, leisure travelers tend to have elastic demand. They have the option to drive rather than fly or to simply not travel at all. They also pay for their tickets out of their own pockets and thus are more sensitive to price.

Airlines recognize the difference between the groups in terms of price elasticity of demand and charge business travelers more than leisure travelers. To accomplish that, they have to dissuade business travelers from buying the less expensive round-trip tickets aimed at leisure travelers. One way to do this is by placing restrictions on the lower-priced tickets. For instance, airlines have at times made such tickets nonrefundable, required at least a two-week advance purchase, and required Saturday-night stays. These restrictions chase off most business travelers who engage in last-minute travel and want to be home for the weekend. As a result, a business traveler often pays hundreds of dollars more for a ticket than a leisure traveler on the same plane.

Discounts for children are another example of pricing based on group differences in price elasticity of demand. For many products, children have more elastic demands than adults because children have low budgets, often financed by their parents. Sellers recognize the elasticity difference and price accordingly. The barber spends as much time cutting a child's hair as an adult's but charges the child much less. A child takes up a full seat at the baseball game but pays a

Granger Wootz/Tetra images/Getty Images

lower price than an adult. A child snowboarder occupies the same space on a chairlift as an adult snowboarder but qualifies for a discounted lift ticket.

Finally, consider pricing by colleges and universities. Price elasticity of demand for higher education is greater for prospective students from low-income families than similar students from high-income families. This makes sense because tuition is a much larger proportion of household income for a low-income student or family than for a high-income student or family. Desiring a diverse student body, colleges charge different *net* prices (= tuition *minus* financial aid) to the two groups on the basis of price elasticity of demand. High-income students pay full tuition, unless they receive merit-based scholarships. Low-income students receive considerable financial aid in addition to merit-based scholarships and, in effect, pay a lower *net* price.

It is common for colleges to announce a large tuition increase and immediately cushion the news by emphasizing that they also are increasing financial aid. In effect, the college is increasing the tuition for students who have inelastic demand by the full amount and raising the *net* tuition of those with elastic demand by some lesser amount or not at all. Through this strategy, colleges boost revenue to cover rising costs while maintaining affordability for a wide range of students.

There are a number of other examples of dual or multiple pricing. All relate directly to price elasticity of demand. We will revisit this topic again in Chapter 11 when we analyze *price discrimination*—charging different prices to different customers for the same product.

Summary

LO6.1 Explain and calculate price elasticity of demand.

Price elasticity of demand measures consumer response to price changes. If consumers are relatively sensitive to price changes, demand is elastic. If they are relatively unresponsive to price changes, demand is inelastic.

The price-elasticity coefficient E_d measures the degree of elasticity or inelasticity of demand. The coefficient is found by the formula

$$E_d = \frac{\text{percentage change in quantity demanded of X}}{\text{percentage change in price of X}}$$

Economists use the averages of prices and quantities in determining percentage changes in price and quantity. If E_d is greater than 1, demand is elastic. If E_d is less than 1, demand is inelastic. Unit elasticity is a special case in which E_d equals 1.

Perfectly inelastic demand is graphed as a line parallel to the vertical axis; perfectly elastic demand is graphed as a line above and parallel to the horizontal axis.

Elasticity varies at different price ranges on a demand curve, tending to be elastic in the upper-left segment and inelastic in the lower-right segment. Elasticity cannot be judged by the steepness or flatness of a demand curve.

LO6.2 Explain the usefulness of the total-revenue test.

If total revenue changes in the opposite direction from prices, demand is elastic. If price and total revenue change in the same direction, demand is inelastic. Where demand is unit elastic, a change in price leaves total revenue unchanged.

LO6.3 List the factors that affect price elasticity of demand.

The number of available substitutes, how broadly or narrowly a product is defined, the size of an item's price relative to one's income, whether the product is a luxury or a necessity, and length of time it takes the market to adjust are all determinants of elasticity of demand.

LO6.4 Describe and apply price elasticity of supply.

The coefficient of price elasticity of supply is found by the formula

$$E_s = \frac{\text{percentage change in quantity supplied of X}}{\text{percentage change in price of X}}$$

The averages of the prices and quantities are used for computing percentage changes. Elasticity of supply depends on the ease of shifting resources between alternative uses, which varies directly with the time producers have to adjust to a price change.

LO6.5 Apply cross elasticity of demand and income elasticity of demand.

Cross elasticity of demand indicates how sensitive the purchase of one product is to changes in the price of another product. The coefficient of cross elasticity of demand is found by the formula

$$E_{xy} = \frac{\text{percentage change in quantity demanded of X}}{\text{percentage change in price of Y}}$$

Positive cross elasticity of demand identifies substitute goods; negative cross elasticity identifies complementary goods.

Income elasticity of demand indicates the responsiveness of consumer purchases to a change in income. The coefficient of income elasticity of demand is found by the formula

$$E_i = \frac{\text{percentage change in quantity demanded of X}}{\text{percentage change in income}}$$

The coefficient is positive for normal (superior) goods and negative for inferior goods.

Industries that sell products that have high income-elasticity-of-demand coefficients are particularly hard hit by recessions. Those with products that have low or negative income-elasticity-of-demand coefficients fare much better.

Terms and Concepts

price elasticity of demand	perfectly elastic demand	short run
midpoint formula	total revenue (TR)	long run
elastic demand	total-revenue test	cross elasticity of demand
inelastic demand	excise tax	income elasticity of demand
unit elasticity	price elasticity of supply	
perfectly inelastic demand	immediate market period	

Discussion Questions

Mc Graw Hill connect

1. Explain why the choice between 1, 2, 3, 4, 5, 6, 7, and 8 "units," or 1,000, 2,000, 3,000, 4,000, 5,000, 6,000, 7,000, and 8,000 movie tickets, makes no difference in determining elasticity in Table 6.1. **LO6.1**

2. What effect would a rule stating that university students must live in university dormitories have on the price elasticity of demand for dormitory space? How might this rule affect room rates? **LO6.1**

3. You were gifted a box of 50 thermos bottles with a unique logo that you do not need and you plan to sell them on eBay. You were initially thinking of asking for $20 per bottle, but then you found out that demand is elastic at $20. Should you lower your asking price? What if demand were inelastic at $20? **LO6.2**

4. The income elasticities of demand for movies, dental services, and clothing have been estimated to be +3.4, +1.0, and +0.5, respectively. Interpret these coefficients. What does a negative income-elasticity coefficient mean? **LO6.5**

5. Research has found that an increase in the price of beer would reduce the amount of marijuana consumed. Is cross elasticity of demand between the two products positive or negative? Are these products substitutes or complements? What might be the logic behind this relationship? **LO6.5**

6. **LAST WORD** What is the purpose of charging different prices to different groups of customers? Supplement the two broad examples in the Last Word with two additional examples of your own. (Hint: Think of price discounts based on group characteristics or time of purchase.)

Review Questions

1. Suppose that the total revenue received by a company selling basketballs is $600 when the price is set at $30 per basketball and $600 when the price is set at $20 per basketball. Without using the midpoint formula, can you tell whether demand is elastic, inelastic, or unit-elastic over this price range? **LO6.2**

2. How would the following changes in price affect total revenue? That is, would total revenue increase, decrease, or remain unchanged? **LO6.2**
   a. Price falls, and demand is inelastic.
   b. Price rises, and demand is elastic.
   c. Price rises, and supply is elastic.
   d. Price rises, and supply is inelastic.
   e. Price rises, and demand is inelastic.
   f. Price falls, and demand is elastic.
   g. Price falls, and demand is unit-elastic.

3. What are the major determinants of price elasticity of demand? Use those determinants and your own reasoning in judging whether demand for each of the following products is probably elastic or inelastic: (*a*) bottled water, (*b*) toothpaste, (*c*) Crest toothpaste, (*d*) ketchup, (*e*) diamond bracelets, (*f*) Microsoft's Windows operating system. **LO6.3**

4. In 2017, Leonardo da Vinci's painting *Salvador Mundi* sold for $450 million. Portray this sale in a demand and supply diagram and comment on the elasticity of supply. Comedian George Carlin once mused, "If a painting can be forged well enough to fool some experts, why is the original so valuable?" Provide an answer. **LO6.4**

5. Suppose the cross elasticity of demand for products A and B is +3.6 and for products C and D is −5.4. What can you conclude about how products A and B are related? Products C and D? **LO6.5**

Problems

1. Look at the demand curve in Figure 6.2a. Use the midpoint formula and points *a* and *b* to calculate the elasticity of demand for that range of the demand curve. Do the same for the demand curves in Figures 6.2b and 6.2c using, respectively, points *c* and *d* for Figure 6.2b and points *e* and *f* for Figure 6.2c. **LO6.1**

2. Investigate how demand elasticities are affected by increases in demand. Shift each of the demand curves in Figures 6.2a, 6.2b, and 6.2c to the right by 10 units. For example, point *a* in Figure 6.2a would shift rightward from location (10 units, $2) to (20 units, $2), while point *b* would shift rightward from location (40 units, $1) to (50 units, $1). After making these shifts, apply the midpoint formula to calculate the demand elasticities for the shifted points. Are they larger or smaller than the elasticities you calculated in problem 1 for the original points? In terms of the midpoint formula, what explains the change in elasticities? **LO6.1**

3. Graph the accompanying demand data, and then use the midpoint formula for E_d to determine price elasticity of demand for each of the four possible $1 price changes. What can you conclude about the relationship between the slope of a curve and its elasticity? Explain why demand is elastic in the northwest segment of the demand curve and inelastic in the southeast segment. **LO6.1**

Product Price	Quantity Demanded
$5	1
4	2
3	3
2	4
1	5

4. Calculate total-revenue data from the demand schedule in problem 3. Graph total revenue below your demand curve. Generalize about the relationship between price elasticity and total revenue. **LO6.2**

5. Danny "Dollar" dela Cruz is a neighborhood's 9-year-old entrepreneur. His most recent venture is selling homemade brownies that he bakes himself. At a price of $1.50 each, he sells 100. At a price of $1 each, he sells 300. Is demand elastic or inelastic over this price range? If demand had the same elasticity for a price decline from $1.00 to $0.50 as it does for the decline from $1.50 to $1, would cutting the price from $1.00 to $0.50 increase or decrease Danny's total revenue? **LO6.2**

6. What is the formula for measuring the price elasticity of supply? Suppose the price of apples goes up from $20 to $22 a box. In direct response, Goldsboro Farms supplies 1,200 boxes of apples instead of 1,000 boxes. Compute the coefficient of price elasticity (midpoint approach) for Goldsboro's supply. Is its supply elastic or inelastic? Explain. **LO6.4**

7. **ADVANCED ANALYSIS** Currently, at a price of $1 each, 100 popsicles are sold per day in the perpetually hot town of Rostin. Consider the elasticity of supply. In the short run, a price increase from $1 to $2 is unit-elastic ($E_d = 1.0$). How many popsicles will be sold each day in the short run if the price rises to $2 each? In the long run, a price increase from $1 to $2 has an elasticity of supply of 1.50. How many popsicles will be sold per day in the long run if the price rises to $2 each? (Hint: Apply the midpoint approach to the elasticity of supply.) **LO6.4**

8. Inbee likes to play golf. The number of times per year that she plays depends on the price of playing a round of golf, her

income, and the price of other types of entertainment—in particular, the price of going to a movie instead of playing golf. The three demand schedules in the following table show how many rounds of golf per year Inbee will demand at each price per round under three different scenarios. In scenario D_1, Inbee's income is $50,000 per year and movies cost $9 each. In scenario D_2, Inbee's income is also $50,000 per year, but the price of seeing a movie rises to $11. And in scenario D_3, Inbee's income goes up to $70,000 per year, while movies cost $11. **LO6.5**

| Price | Quantity Demanded | | |
	D_1	D_2	D_3
$50	15	10	15
35	25	15	30
20	40	20	50

a. Using the data under D_1 and D_2, calculate the cross elasticity of Inbee's demand for golf at all three prices. (To do so, apply the midpoint approach to the cross elasticity of demand.) Is the cross elasticity the same at all three prices? Are movies and golf substitute goods, complementary goods, or independent goods? Explain.

b. Using the data under D_2 and D_3, calculate the income elasticity of Inbee's demand for golf at all three prices. (To do so, apply the midpoint approach to the income elasticity of demand.) Is the income elasticity the same at all three prices? Is golf an inferior good? Explain.

Utility Maximization

>> LEARNING OBJECTIVES

LO7.1   Define and explain total utility, marginal utility, and the law of diminishing marginal utility.

LO7.2   Describe how rational consumers maximize utility.

LO7.3   Explain how to derive a demand curve by observing the outcomes of price changes.

LO7.4   Discuss how the utility-maximization model highlights the income and substitution effects of a price change.

LO7.5   Apply the theory of consumer behavior to real-world phenomena.

LO7.6   (Appendix) Understand budget lines, indifference curves, and utility maximization.

If you were to compare the shopping carts of any two consumers, you would observe striking differences. Why does Paula have potatoes, peaches, and Pepsi in her cart, while Sam has sugar, saltines, and 7-Up in his? Why didn't Paula also buy pasta and plums? Why weren't soup and spaghetti on Sam's grocery list?

Given a certain budget, how does a consumer decide which goods and services to buy? This chapter develops a model to answer this question.

Law of Diminishing Marginal Utility

The simplest theory of consumer behavior rests on the **law of diminishing marginal utility,** which states that added satisfaction declines as a consumer acquires additional units of a given product. Although consumer wants in general are insatiable, wants for particular items can be satisfied. In a specific span of time over which consumers' tastes remain unchanged, consumers can obtain as much of a particular good or service as they can afford. But the more of that product they obtain, the less they want more of it.

Consider durable goods. A consumer's desire for an automobile, if they don't own a car, may be very strong. But the desire for a second car is less intense; and for a third or fourth, weaker and weaker. Unless they are collectors, even the wealthiest families rarely have more than a half-dozen cars, although their incomes would allow them to purchase a whole fleet of vehicles.

Terminology

Recall that **utility** is want-satisfying power. The utility of a good or service is the satisfaction or pleasure one gets from consuming it. Keep in mind three characteristics of utility:

- "Utility" and "usefulness" are not synonymous. Paintings by Picasso may offer great utility to art connoisseurs but are useless functionally (other than for hiding a crack on a wall).

>> **LO7.1** Define and explain total utility, marginal utility, and the law of diminishing marginal utility.

law of diminishing marginal utility The principle that as a consumer increases the consumption of a *good* or *service,* the *marginal utility* obtained from each additional unit of the good or service decreases.

utility The want-satisfying power of a *good* or *service;* the satisfaction or pleasure a consumer obtains from the consumption of a good or service (or from the consumption of a collection of *goods* and *services*).

- Utility is subjective. The utility of a specific product may vary widely from person to person. A lifted pickup truck may have great utility to someone who drives off-road but little utility to someone unable or unwilling to climb into the rig. Eyeglasses have tremendous utility to someone with poor eyesight but no utility to a person with 20-20 vision.

- Utility is difficult to quantify. But for purposes of illustration, we assume that people can measure satisfaction with units called *utils* (units of utility). For example, a particular consumer may get 100 utils of satisfaction from a smoothie and 10 utils of satisfaction from a candy bar. These imaginary units of satisfaction are convenient for quantifying consumer behavior.

Total Utility and Marginal Utility

total utility The total amount of satisfaction derived from the consumption of a single product or a combination of products.

marginal utility The extra *utility* a consumer obtains from the consumption of 1 additional unit of a *good* or *service;* equal to the change in *total utility* divided by the change in the quantity consumed.

Total utility is the total amount of satisfaction or pleasure a person derives from consuming some specific quantity—for example, 10 units—of a good or service. **Marginal utility** is the *extra* satisfaction a consumer realizes from an additional unit of that product—for example, from the eleventh unit. Alternatively, marginal utility is the change in total utility that results from the consumption of 1 more unit of a product.

To be concrete, let's explore an example involving the consumption of tacos. **Figure 7.1 (Key Graph)** and the accompanying table demonstrate the relation between total utility and marginal utility in this situation. Column 2 of the table shows the total utility associated with each level of taco consumption, while Column 3 shows the marginal utility—the change in total utility—that results from the consumption of each additional taco.

The curves in the two associated figures reflect the data in the table. Starting at the origin in Figure 7.1a, observe that each of the first five units increases total utility (TU), but by a diminishing amount. Total utility reaches a maximum with the sixth taco and then declines.

So in Figure 7.1b marginal utility (MU) remains positive but diminishes through the first five tacos (because total utility increases at a declining rate). Marginal utility is zero for the sixth taco (because that taco doesn't change total utility). Marginal utility then becomes negative with the seventh taco and beyond (because total utility is falling). Figure 7.1b and table column 3 reveal that each successive taco yields less extra utility, meaning fewer utils, than the preceding taco. In other words, the table and graph illustrate the law of diminishing marginal utility.

Marginal Utility and Demand

The law of diminishing marginal utility explains why the demand curve for a given product slopes downward. If successive units of a good yield smaller and smaller amounts of marginal utility, then the consumer will buy additional units of a product only if its price falls. The consumer for whom Figure 7.1 is relevant may buy two tacos at a price of $1 each. But because he obtains less marginal utility from additional tacos, he will choose not to buy more at that price. He would rather spend additional dollars on products that provide more utility. Therefore, additional tacos, which have less utility, are not worth buying unless the price declines. (When marginal utility becomes negative, Taco Bell would have to pay you to consume another taco!) Thus, diminishing marginal utility supports the idea that price must decrease for quantity demanded to increase. In other words, consumers behave in ways that make demand curves slope downward.

QUICK REVIEW
7.1

▶ Utility is the benefit or satisfaction a person receives from consuming a good or a service.

▶ The law of diminishing marginal utility indicates that gains in satisfaction become smaller as successive units of a specific product are consumed.

▶ Diminishing marginal utility provides a simple rationale for the law of demand.

..ıll KEY GRAPH

FIGURE 7.1 Total and marginal utility.

Curves TU and MU are graphed from the data in the table. (a) As more of a product is consumed, total utility increases at a diminishing rate, reaches a maximum, and then declines. (b) Marginal utility, by definition, reflects the changes in total utility. Thus marginal utility diminishes with increased consumption, becomes zero when total utility is at a maximum, and is negative when total utility declines. As shown by the shaded rectangles in (a) and (b), marginal utility is the change in total utility associated with each additional taco. Or, alternatively, each new level of total utility is found by adding marginal utility to the preceding level of total utility.

(1) Tacos Consumed per Meal	(2) Total Utility, Utils	(3) Marginal Utility, Utils
0	0	
1	10	10
2	18	8
3	24	6
4	28	4
5	30	2
6	30	0
7	28	−2

(a)
Total utility

(b)
Marginal utility

QUICK QUIZ FOR FIGURE 7.1

1. **Marginal utility:**
   a. is the extra output a firm obtains when it adds another unit of labor.
   b. explains why product supply curves slope upward.
   c. typically rises as successive units of a good are consumed.
   d. is the extra satisfaction from the consumption of 1 more unit of some good or service.

2. **Marginal utility in Figure 7.1b is positive, but declining, when total utility in Figure 7.1a is positive and:**
   a. rising at an increasing rate.
   b. falling at an increasing rate.
   c. rising at a decreasing rate.
   d. falling at a decreasing rate.

3. **When marginal utility is zero in graph (b), total utility in graph (a) is:**
   a. also zero.
   b. neither rising nor falling.
   c. negative.
   d. rising, but at a declining rate.

4. **Suppose the person represented by these graphs experienced a diminished taste for tacos. As a result the:**
   a. TU curve would get steeper.
   b. MU curve would get flatter.
   c. TU and MU curves would shift downward.
   d. MU curve, but not the TU curve, would collapse to the horizontal axis.

Answers: 1. d; 2. c; 3. b; 4. c

Theory of Consumer Behavior

>> **LO7.2** Describe how rational consumers maximize utility.

In addition to explaining the law of demand, diminishing marginal utility explains how consumers allocate their incomes among the many goods and services available for purchase.

Consumer Choice and the Budget Constraint

For simplicity, we will make the following assumptions about consumers.

rational behavior Human behavior based on comparison of *marginal costs* and *marginal benefits;* behavior designed to maximize *total utility.* See *rational.*

- *Rational behavior* Consumers are rational. They try to use their income to derive the greatest amount of satisfaction, or utility, from it. Consumers want to get "the most for their money" or, technically speaking, "maximize their total utility." They engage in **rational behavior.**

- *Preferences* Each consumer has clear-cut preferences for certain goods and services that are available in the market. Buyers also have a good idea of how much marginal utility they get from successive units of the products they might purchase.

budget constraint The limit that the size of a consumer's income (and the *prices* that must be paid for *goods* and *services*) imposes on the ability of that consumer to obtain goods and services.

- *Budget constraint* At any point in time the consumer has a fixed, limited amount of income. Because each consumer supplies a finite amount of human and property resources to society, they earn only a limited income. Thus, every consumer faces a **budget constraint,** even those who earn millions of dollars a year. Of course, this budget limitation is more severe for a consumer with an average income than for a consumer with an extraordinarily high income.

- *Prices* Goods are scarce relative to the demand for them, so every good carries a price tag. We assume that the price of each good is unaffected by the amount purchased by any particular person. After all, each person's purchase is a tiny part of total demand. Also, because consumers have a limited number of dollars, they cannot buy everything they want. Consumers must compromise. When they do, each consumer will choose the most personally satisfying mix of goods and services that they can afford.

Utility-Maximizing Rule

Of all the different combinations of goods and services that a consumer can attain with their budget, which specific combination will yield the maximum utility or satisfaction? *To maximize satisfaction, consumers should allocate their income so that the last dollar spent on each product yields the same amount of extra (marginal) utility.* This is the **utility-maximizing rule.** When consumers have "balanced their margins" using this rule, they have achieved **consumer equilibrium** and have no incentive to alter their expenditure pattern. In fact, all else equal, any person who has achieved consumer equilibrium will be worse off—total utility would decline—if there is any alteration in the bundle of goods purchased.

utility-maximizing rule The principle that to obtain the greatest *total utility,* a consumer should allocate *money income* so that the last dollar spent on each *good* or *service* yields the same *marginal utility* (MU). For two goods X and Y, with prices P_x and P_y, total utility will be maximized by purchasing the amounts of X and Y such that $MU_x/P_x = MU_y/P_y$ for the last dollar spent on each good.

Numerical Example

An illustration will help explain the utility-maximizing rule. For simplicity, we limit our example to two products. Suppose consumer Holly is analyzing which combination of two products she should purchase with her fixed daily income of $10. These two products are apples and oranges.

Holly's preferences for apples and oranges and their prices are the basic data determining the combination that will maximize her satisfaction. Table 7.1 summarizes those data. Column 2a shows the amounts of marginal utility she derives from each successive unit of A (apples), and column 3a shows the same thing for product B (oranges). Both columns reflect the law of diminishing marginal utility, which, in this example, is assumed to begin with the second unit purchased.

consumer equilibrium In marginal utility theory, the combination of goods purchased that maximizes *total utility* by applying the *utility-maximizing rule.*

Marginal Utility per Dollar To see how the utility-maximizing rule works, we must think about the marginal-utility information in columns 2a and 3a on a per-dollar-spent basis. Holly's choices are influenced not only by the extra utility that successive apples will yield but also by how many dollars (and therefore how many oranges) she must give up to obtain additional apples.

The rational consumer must compare the extra utility from each product with its added cost (that is, its price). Switching examples for a moment, suppose that you prefer a pizza whose marginal utility is 36 utils to a burrito whose marginal utility is 24 utils. But if the pizza's price is $12 and the burrito costs only $6, you would choose the burrito rather than the pizza. Why? Because the marginal utility *per dollar spent* is 4 utils for the burrito (= 24 utils/$6) compared to only

TABLE 7.1 The Utility-Maximizing Combination of Apples and Oranges Obtainable with an Income of $10*

(1) Unit of Product	(2) Apple (Product A): Price = $1		(3) Orange (Product B): Price 5 = $2	
	(a) Marginal Utility, Utils	(b) Marginal Utility per Dollar (MU/Price)	(a) Marginal Utility, Utils	(b) Marginal Utility per Dollar (MU/Price)
First	10	10	24	12
Second	8	8	20	10
Third	7	7	18	9
Fourth	6	6	16	8
Fifth	5	5	12	6
Sixth	4	4	6	3
Seventh	3	3	4	2

*It is assumed in this table that the amount of marginal utility received from additional units of each of the two products is independent of the quantity of the other product. For example, the marginal-utility schedule for apples is independent of the number of oranges obtained by the consumer.

3 utils for the pizza (= 36 utils/$12). You could eat two burritos for $12 and, assuming that the marginal utility of the second burrito is 16 utils, your total utility would be 40 utils. Clearly, 40 units of satisfaction (= 24 utils + 16 utils) from two burritos are superior to 36 utils from the same $12 expenditure on one pizza.

Returning to our main example about apples and oranges in Table 7.1, notice that if we want to state the marginal utilities in that table on a per-dollar-spent basis, we must divide the marginal-utility data of columns 2a and 3a by the prices of apples and oranges—$1 and $2, respectively. The results are shown in columns 2b and 3b.

Decision-Making Process Table 7.1 shows Holly's preferences on a unit basis and a per-dollar basis. It also shows the price of apples and oranges. With $10 to spend, in what order should Holly allocate her dollars to apples and oranges to achieve the highest amount of utility? What specific combination of the two products will she possess after she spends her $10 optimally?

Concentrating on columns 2b and 3b in Table 7.1, we find that Holly should first spend $2 on the first orange because its marginal utility per dollar of 12 utils is higher than the first apple's 10 utils. Now Holly finds herself indifferent about whether to buy a second orange or the first apple because the marginal utility per dollar of both is 10 utils. So she buys both of them. Holly now has 1 apple and 2 oranges. Also, the last dollar she spent on each good yielded the same marginal utility per dollar (10). But this combination of apples and oranges does not represent the maximum amount of utility that Holly can obtain. Her total cost so far is only $5 [= (1 × $1) + (2 × $2)], so she has $5 remaining, which she can spend to achieve a higher level of total utility.

Examining columns 2b and 3b again, we find that Holly should spend the next $2 on a third orange because marginal utility per dollar for the third orange is 9 compared with 8 for the second apple. Now, with 1 apple and 3 oranges, she is again indifferent between a second apple and a fourth orange because both provide 8 utils per dollar. So Holly purchases 1 more of each. Now the last dollar spent on each product provides the same marginal utility per dollar (8), and Holly's income of $10 is exhausted.

The utility-maximizing combination of goods attainable by Holly is therefore 2 apples and 4 oranges. By summing marginal-utility information from columns 2a and 3a, we find that Holly is obtaining 18 (= 10 + 8) utils of satisfaction from the 2 apples and 78 (= 24 + 20 + 18 + 16) utils of satisfaction from the 4 oranges. Her $10, optimally spent, yields 96 (= 18 + 78) utils of satisfaction.

Table 7.2 summarizes our step-by-step process for maximizing Holly's utility. Note that we have implicitly assumed that Holly spends her entire income. She neither borrows nor saves. However, saving can be regarded as a "commodity" that yields utility and can be incorporated into our analysis.

Inferior Options Holly can obtain other combinations of apples and oranges with $10, but none will yield as much total utility as do 2 apples and 4 oranges. For example, she can obtain 4 apples and 3 oranges for $10. But this combination yields only 93 utils, clearly inferior to the 96 utils

TABLE 7.2 Sequence of Purchases to Achieve Consumer Equilibrium, Given the Data in Table 7.1

Choice Number	Potential Choices	Marginal Utility per Dollar	Purchase Decision	Income Remaining
1	First apple	10	First orange for $2	$8 = $10 − $2
	First orange	12		
2	First apple	10	First apple for $1 and second orange for $2	$5 = $8 − $3
	Second orange	10		
3	Second apple	8	Third orange for $2	$3 = $5 − $2
	Third orange	9		
4	Second apple	8	Second apple for $1 and fourth orange for $2	$0 = $3 − $3
	Fourth orange	8		

provided by 2 apples and 4 oranges. There are other combinations of apples and oranges (such as 4 apples and 5 oranges or 1 apple and 2 oranges) in which the marginal utility of the last dollar spent is the same for both goods. But all of those combinations either are unobtainable with Holly's limited income or do not exhaust her income (e.g., 1 apple and 2 oranges) and therefore do not yield the maximum utility attainable.

Algebraic Generalization

Economists generalize the utility-maximizing rule by saying that consumers maximize their satisfaction when they allocate their income so that the last dollar spent on product A, the last on product B, and so forth, yield equal amounts of marginal utility. The marginal utility per dollar spent on A is indicated by the MU of product A divided by the price of A (column 2b in Table 7.1), and the marginal utility per dollar spent on B is indicated by the MU of product B divided by the price of B (column 3b in Table 7.1). The utility-maximizing rule requires that these ratios be equal for the last dollar spent on A and the last dollar spent on B. Algebraically,

$$\frac{\text{MU of product A}}{\text{Price of A}} = \frac{\text{MU of product B}}{\text{Price of B}}$$

And, of course, the consumer must exhaust all available income. Table 7.1 shows us that the combination of 2 units of A (apples) and 4 of B (oranges) fulfills these conditions in that

$$\frac{8 \text{ utils}}{\$1} = \frac{16 \text{ utils}}{\$2}$$

and all of the consumer's $10 income is spent.

If the equation is not fulfilled, then some reallocation of the consumer's expenditures between A and B (from the low to the high marginal-utility-per-dollar product) will increase the consumer's total utility. For example, if the consumer spent $10 on 4 of A (apples) and 3 of B (oranges), we would find that

$$\frac{\text{MU of A of 6 utils}}{\text{Price of A of \$1}} < \frac{\text{MU of B of 18 utils}}{\text{Price of B of \$2}}$$

Here the last dollar spent on A provides only 6 utils of satisfaction, while the last dollar spent on B provides 9 (= 18/$2). Thus, the consumer can increase total satisfaction by purchasing more B and less A. As dollars are reallocated from A to B, the marginal utility per dollar of A will increase while the marginal utility per dollar of B will decrease. At some new combination of A and B, the two will be equal and consumer equilibrium will be achieved. Here that combination is 2 A (apples) and 4 B (oranges).

The nearby Consider This story discusses how a government effort to influence consumers' utility maximization decisions went awry.

CONSIDER THIS . . .

There's No Accounting for Taste

In 2015, the federal government started requiring restaurants to print calorie counts next to menu items. The regulation was intended to help consumers make healthful choices. In particular, it was assumed that if they could see how many calories each item contained, consumers would consume fewer total calories. They would opt for salads instead of milkshakes.

Letterberry/Shutterstock

But a funny thing happened when the new rules went into effect. Some people started consuming *more* calories. They did so because their preferences were not what policymakers expected. Instead of trying to maximize the amount of healthfulness per dollar of money spent, they instead chose to maximize the number of calories per dollar of money spent. Their preferences were such that when it came to maximizing utility, what they wanted was the maximum number of calories, not the maximum amount of health. So when the new regulations provided them with calorie counts, they went for milkshakes instead of salads and double cheeseburgers instead of chicken skewers.

The lesson? Know what people are trying to maximize before you attempt to alter their behavior.

▶ The theory of consumer behavior assumes that, with limited income and a set of product prices, consumers make rational choices on the basis of well-defined preferences.

▶ A consumer maximizes utility by allocating income so that the marginal utility per dollar spent is the same for the last dollar spent on every good purchased.

QUICK REVIEW
7.2

Utility Maximization and the Demand Curve

Once you understand the utility-maximizing rule, you can easily see why product price and quantity demanded are inversely related. Recall that the basic determinants of an individual's demand for a specific product are (1) preferences or tastes, (2) income, and (3) the prices of other goods. The utility data in Table 7.1 reflect our consumer's preferences. We continue to suppose that her money income is $10. And concentrating on the construction of an individual demand curve for oranges, we assume that the price of apples, now representing all "other goods," is still $1.

>> **LO7.3** Explain how to derive a demand curve by observing the outcomes of price changes.

Deriving the Demand Schedule and Curve

We can derive a single consumer's demand schedule for oranges by considering alternative prices at which oranges might be sold and then determining the quantity the consumer will purchase. We already know one such price-quantity combination from the utility-maximizing example: Given tastes, income, and the prices of other goods, Holly will purchase 4 oranges at $2.

Now let's assume the price of oranges falls to $1. The marginal-utility-per-dollar data of column 3b in Table 7.1 will double because the price of oranges has been halved; the new data for column 3b are (by coincidence) identical to the data in column 3a. The doubling of the MU per dollar for each successive orange means that the purchase of 2 apples and 4 oranges is no longer an equilibrium combination. By applying the same reasoning we used previously, we now find that Holly's utility-maximizing combination is 4 apples and 6 oranges. As Figure 7.2 shows, Holly will purchase 6 oranges when the price of

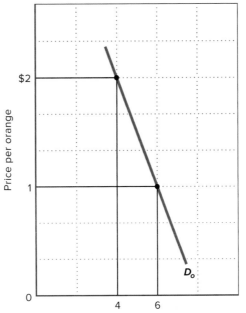

FIGURE 7.2
Deriving an individual demand curve.

The consumer represented by the data in the table maximizes utility by purchasing 4 oranges at a price of $2. The decline in the price of oranges to $1 disrupts the consumer's initial utility-maximizing equilibrium. The consumer restores equilibrium by purchasing 6 rather than 4 oranges. Thus, a simple price-quantity schedule emerges, which locates two points on a downsloping demand curve.

Price per Orange	Quantity Demanded
$2	4
1	6

oranges is $1. Using the data in this table, we can sketch the downward sloping demand curve for oranges, D_o, shown in Figure 7.2. This exercise, then, clearly links the utility-maximizing behavior of a consumer and that person's downward sloping demand curve for a particular product.

Income and Substitution Effects

>> **LO7.4** Discuss how the utility-maximization model highlights the income and substitution effects of a price change.

substitution effect (1) A change in the quantity demanded of a *consumer good* that results from a change in its relative expensiveness caused by a change in the good's own *price*. (2) The reduction in the *quantity demanded* of the second of a pair of *substitute resources* that occurs when the price of the first resource falls and causes *firms* that employ both resources to switch to using more of the first resource (whose price has fallen) and less of the second resource (whose price has remained the same).

income effect A change in the quantity demanded of a product that results from the change in *real income* (*purchasing power*) caused by a change in the product's *price*.

Recall from Chapter 3 that the **substitution effect** is the impact that a change in a product's price has on its expensiveness relative to other products and consequently on its quantity demanded. In contrast, the **income effect** is the impact that a change in a product's price has on a consumer's real income and consequently on the quantity demanded of that good. Both effects help explain why a demand curve such as that in Figure 7.2 slopes downward.

Let's first look at the substitution effect. Before the price of oranges declined, Holly was in equilibrium when purchasing 2 apples and 4 oranges because

$$\frac{\text{MU of apples of } 8}{\text{Price of apples of } \$1} = \frac{\text{MU of oranges of } 16}{\text{Price of oranges of } \$2}$$

But after the price of oranges declines from $2 to $1,

$$\frac{\text{MU of apples of } 8}{\text{Price of apples of } \$1} < \frac{\text{MU of oranges of } 16}{\text{Price of oranges of } \$1}$$

Clearly, the last dollar spent on oranges now yields greater utility (16 utils) than does the last dollar spent on apples (8 utils). Thus Holly will switch, or substitute, purchases away from apples and toward oranges so as to restore consumer equilibrium. This substitution effect contributes to the inverse relationship between price and quantity demanded: When the price of oranges declines, the substitution effect causes Holly to buy more oranges.

What about the income effect? The decline in the price of oranges from $2 to $1 increases Holly's real income. Before the price decline, she maximized her utility and achieved consumer equilibrium by purchasing 2 apples and 4 oranges. But at the lower $1 price for oranges, Holly would have to spend only $6 rather than $10 to buy that particular combination of goods. The lower price of oranges has freed up $4 that she can spend on buying more apples, more oranges, or more of both. How many more of each fruit she ends up buying will be determined by applying the utility-maximizing rule to the new situation. But it is quite likely that the increase in real income caused by the lower price of oranges will make Holly buy more oranges than before the price reduction. Any such increase in orange purchases is the income effect of the price reduction, and it, too, helps to explain why demand curves are downward sloping: When the price of oranges falls, the income effect causes Holly to buy more oranges.

QUICK REVIEW
7.3

▶ A downward sloping demand curve can be derived by changing the price of one product in the consumer-behavior model and noting the change in the utility-maximizing quantity of that product demanded.

▶ By providing insights on the substitution and income effects of a price decline, the utility-maximization model helps explain why demand curves slope downward.

Applications and Extensions

>> **LO7.5** Apply the theory of consumer behavior to real-world phenomena.

The theory of consumer behavior helps to explain many real-world phenomena.

iPads

Every so often a new product captures consumers' imaginations. One such product is Apple's iPad, which debuted in April 2010. Less than three years later, Apple sold its 100-millionth unit.

The swift ascendancy of the iPad resulted mainly from a leapfrog in technology. It was the first touchscreen tablet computer and became a hit because it was much better for the consumption of digital media—music, videos, and many games—than existing laptop or desktop computers. Those larger machines still held the advantage if a consumer wanted to create content or edit documents, but for consuming digital content the iPad was superior.

In the language of our analysis, Apple's introduction of the iPad severely disrupted consumer equilibrium. Consumers en masse concluded that iPads had a higher marginal-utility-to-price ratio (= MU/P) than the ratios for alternative products. They therefore shifted spending away from those other products and toward iPads as a way to increase total utility.

This example demonstrates a simple but important point: New products succeed by enhancing consumers' total utility. This "delivery of value" generates a revenue stream. If revenues exceed production costs, substantial profits can result—as they have for Apple.

The Diamond-Water Paradox

Early economists such as Adam Smith were puzzled by the fact that some "essential" goods had much lower prices than some "unimportant" goods. Why would water, essential to life, be priced below diamonds, which have much less usefulness? The paradox is resolved when we acknowledge that water is in great supply relative to demand and thus has a very low price per gallon. Diamonds, in contrast, are rare. Their supply is small relative to demand and, as a result, they have a very high price per carat.

Moreover, the marginal utility of the last unit of water consumed is very low. The reason follows from our utility-maximizing rule. Consumers (and producers) respond to the very low price of water by using a great deal of it—for generating electricity, irrigating crops, watering lawns, quenching thirst, and so on. Consumption is expanded until marginal utility, which declines as more water is consumed, equals its low price. In contrast, relatively few diamonds are purchased because of their high price, meaning that their marginal utility remains high. In equilibrium:

$$\frac{\text{MU of water (low)}}{\text{Price of water (low)}} = \frac{\text{MU of diamonds (high)}}{\text{Price of diamonds (high)}}$$

Although the marginal utility of the last unit of water consumed is low and the marginal utility of the last carat of diamond purchased is high, the total utility of water is very high and the total utility of diamonds quite low. The total utility derived from the consumption of water is large because of the enormous amounts of water consumed. Total utility is the sum of the marginal utilities of all gallons of water consumed, including trillions of gallons that have far higher marginal utilities than the last unit consumed. In contrast, the total utility derived from diamonds is low because their high price means that relatively few diamonds are bought. Thus the water-diamond "paradox" is solved: Water has much more total utility than diamonds even though the price of diamonds greatly exceeds the price of water. Their relative prices relate to marginal utility, not total utility.

Cash and Noncash Gifts

Marginal-utility analysis also helps us understand why people generally prefer cash gifts to noncash gifts costing the same amount. The reason is simply that the noncash gifts may not match the recipient's preferences and thus may not add as much to total utility as cash does. In other words, consumers know their own preferences better than the gift giver does, and the $100 cash gift provides more choices.

For example, Uncle Fred may have paid $30 for the snowboard goggles he gave you for the holidays, but you would pay only $15 for them. Thus, a $15, or 50 percent, value loss is involved. Multiplied by billions of gifts a year, the total potential loss of value is huge.

But some of that loss is prevented by the creative ways individuals handle the problem. For example, newlyweds set up gift registries to help match up their wants to the noncash gifts received. Also, people obtain cash refunds or exchanges for gifts so they can buy goods that provide more utility. And people have even been known to "recycle gifts" by giving them to someone else at a later time. All three actions support the proposition that individuals take actions to maximize their total utility.

There's a Tax for That

Taxes that Target Particular Products Change Consumer Behavior, Sometimes in Very Surprising Ways.

As you know from this chapter, economists model consumer decisions about how much to spend on various products as being the result of consumers maximizing the total utility that they can get from their limited budgets. The way consumers do that is by weighing the marginal utility per dollar that they can get from every unit of every product that they can afford to buy. The greater the marginal utility per dollar of any particular unit, the more likely it is to be purchased. Those units with the highest marginal utility per dollar will be purchased first, followed by those with successively less and less marginal utility per dollar, until the consumer's budget runs out.

The result, or consumer equilibrium, is a situation in which the last dollar spent on each product that is purchased yields the same marginal utility per dollar. Unless something changes with respect to the size of the consumer's budget or the prices of the various available products, the consumer will always spend their budget the same way, consistent with that particular consumer equilibrium.

Taxes, however, can upset a given consumer equilibrium by changing the prices that consumers have to pay for products. This is particularly true for *excise taxes*, like liquor taxes and tobacco taxes, that are targeted at particular products. A three pack per day smoker might cut down to just one pack per day if a steep tobacco tax (of, say, $10 per pack) is suddenly imposed by the local government. In terms of utility maximization, the marginal utility *per dollar* spent on each pack of cigarettes declines because the tax increases the number of dollars necessary to purchase each pack. Each pack still has the same marginal utility, but the amount of marginal utility *per dollar* declines because you have to spend more dollars (due to the tax) to purchase each pack.

Because excise taxes decrease the marginal utility per dollar of every unit consumed, consumers naturally shy away from such products, reallocating their spending toward other products whose marginal utilities per dollar have not changed. Excise taxes thus have the general effect of causing people to consume less of whatever particular product is being taxed. The consequences of that avoidance have often been surprising, as you can see from several famous examples related to home construction.

Bricked-Up Windows In 1696, the British government started imposing a Window Tax, which charged homeowners per window for however many windows their houses had.

The underlying idea behind the Window Tax was to tax the rich, since at that time only richer people could afford glass windows. The response to the tax, though, was not healthy. To reduce their tax bills, many existing homeowners bricked up their windows. And many new homes and apartment buildings were built with very few windows. By the time of the Industrial Revolution of the 19th century, the result was extremely poorly ventilated tenements for poor city workers who

Adisa/Shutterstock

consequently suffered from airborne diseases like tuberculosis at appalling rates.

Closetless Houses Back when the Spanish Empire controlled what is now the Desert Southwest of the United States, a property tax was imposed on the number of rooms that a house had, the idea being to tax the rich, since, at that time, only richer people could afford houses with multiple rooms. The response by homeowners was to build houses with as few rooms as possible, which, among other things, meant no closets. Thus, in New Mexico and Arizona today, you can find old homes with no closets.

Narrow Dutch Homes The Dutch city of Amsterdam was built around canals, so that nearly every structure in the city has a side that faces a canal. Another unique thing about Amsterdam is that the "canal houses" that face the local canals are extremely narrow, sometimes only 10 or 12 feet wide. That's because, traditionally, houses in Amsterdam were assessed a property tax based on how many feet of frontage each house had on the side of the house facing the local canal. Faced with that tax system, local homeowners responded by building homes that were narrow, deep, and tall, since a homeowner could build both deep and high without increasing their tax bill.

These architectural examples are a reminder that when a tax is imposed, the lower marginal utility per dollar that results will cause people to do their best to consume less of the product being taxed. In these examples, that means fewer windows, fewer rooms, and less frontage. But the principle is general. Whatever is being taxed will be demanded and consumed less as consumers rearrange their purchases to achieve a new consumer equilibrium.

Summary

LO7.1 Define and explain total utility, marginal utility, and the law of diminishing marginal utility.
The law of diminishing marginal utility states that beyond a certain quantity, additional units of a specific good will yield declining amounts of extra satisfaction.

LO7.2 Describe how rational consumers maximize utility.
The utility-maximization model assumes that the typical consumer is rational and acts on the basis of well-defined preferences. Because income is limited and goods have prices, consumers cannot purchase all the goods and services they want. Consumers therefore select the attainable combination of products that maximizes their utility or satisfaction.

A consumer's utility is maximized when income is allocated so that the last dollar spent on each product purchased yields the same amount of extra satisfaction. Algebraically, the utility-maximizing rule is fulfilled when

$$\frac{\text{MU of product A}}{\text{Price of A}} = \frac{\text{MU of product B}}{\text{Price of B}}$$

and the consumer's total income is spent.

LO7.3 Explain how to derive a demand curve by observing the outcomes of price changes.
The utility-maximizing rule and the demand curve are logically consistent. Because marginal utility declines, a lower price is needed to induce the consumer to buy more of a particular product.

LO7.4 Discuss how the utility-maximization model highlights the income and substitution effects of a price change.
The utility-maximization model illuminates the income and substitution effects of a price change. The income effect implies that a decline in the price of a product increases the consumer's real income and enables the consumer to buy more of that product with a fixed income. The substitution effect implies that a lower price makes a product relatively more attractive and therefore increases the consumer's willingness to substitute it for other products.

LO7.5 Apply the theory of consumer behavior to real-world phenomena.
The theory of consumer behavior can explain many real-world phenomena, including the rapid adoption of popular consumer goods like the iPad that feature disruptive technologies, the diamond-water paradox, and people's preference for cash gifts.

Terms and Concepts

law of diminishing marginal utility

utility

total utility

marginal utility

rational behavior

budget constraint

utility-maximizing rule

consumer equilibrium

substitution effect

income effect

Discussion Questions

1. Complete the following table and answer the questions below: **LO7.1**

Units Consumed	Total Utility	Marginal Utility
0	0	
1	10	10
2	—	8
3	25	—
4	30	—
5	—	3
6	34	—

  a. At which rate is total utility increasing: a constant rate, a decreasing rate, or an increasing rate? How do you know?

  b. "A rational consumer will purchase only 1 unit of the product represented by these data, because that amount maximizes marginal utility." Do you agree? Why or why not?

  c. "It is possible that a rational consumer will not purchase any units of the product represented by these data." Do you agree? Why or why not?

2. Mrs. Simpson buys loaves of bread and quarts of milk each week at prices of $2 and $1.60, respectively. At present, she is buying these products in amounts such that the marginal utilities from the last units purchased of the two products are 160 and 140 utils, respectively. Is she buying the utility-maximizing combination of bread and milk? If not, how should she reallocate her expenditures between the two goods? **LO7.2**

3. How can time be incorporated into the theory of consumer behavior? Explain the following comment: "Want to make millions of dollars? Invent a product that saves Americans lots of time." **LO7.2**

4. Explain: **LO7.2**
  a. Before economic growth, there were too few goods; after growth, there is too little time.
  b. It is irrational for an individual to take the time to be completely rational in economic decision making.
  c. Telling your spouse the name of the restaurant where you would like to eat for your birthday makes sense in terms of utility maximization.

5. In the last decade or so, there has been a dramatic expansion of small retail convenience stores (such as 7-Eleven, Kwik Trip, and Circle K), although their prices are generally much higher than prices in large supermarkets. What explains the success of the convenience stores? **LO7.2**

6. Many apartment-complex owners are installing water meters for each apartment and billing the occupants according to the amount of water they use. This system contrasts with the former procedure of having a central meter for the entire complex and dividing up the collective water expense as part of the rent. Where individual meters have been installed, water usage has declined 10 to 40 percent. Explain that drop in terms of price and marginal utility. **LO7.3**

7. Using the utility-maximization rule as your point of reference, explain the income and substitution effects of an increase in the price of product B, with no change in the price of product A. **LO7.4**

8. **ADVANCED ANALYSIS** A "mathematically fair bet" is one in which the amount won will on average equal the amount bet—for example, when a gambler bets $100 for a 10 percent chance to win $1,000 ($100 = 0.10 × $1,000). Assuming diminishing marginal utility of dollars, explain why this is not a fair bet in terms of utility. Why does a bet become less fair when the "house" takes a cut of each dollar bet? Is gambling irrational? **LO7.4**

9. Rank each of the following three gift possibilities in terms of how much utility they are likely to generate, and explain your reasoning: a store-specific gift card worth $15, a $15 item from that specific store, and $15 cash that can be spent anywhere. **LO7.5**

10. **LAST WORD** Why are houses in Amsterdam narrow rather than closetless? What unfortunate negative side effect resulted from the British Window Tax? How would current American homeowners likely react to a tax on south-facing rooftop solar panels?

Review Questions

1. True or False: The law of diminishing marginal utility predicts the consumption behavior of drug addicts quite well. **LO7.1**

2. Frank spends $75 on 10 magazines and 25 newspapers. The magazines cost $5 each and the newspapers cost $2.50 each. Suppose that his MU from the final magazine is 10 utils while his MU from the final newspaper is also 10 utils. According to the utility-maximizing rule, Frank should: **LO7.2**
   a. reallocate spending from magazines to newspapers.
   b. reallocate spending from newspapers to magazines.
   c. be satisfied because he is already maximizing his total utility.
   d. None of the above.

3. Demand curves slope downward because, other things equal, **LO7.3**
   a. an increase in a product's price lowers MU.
   b. a decrease in a product's price lowers MU.
   c. a decrease in a product's price raises MU per dollar and makes consumers wish to purchase more units.

   d. an increase in a product's price raises MU per dollar and makes consumers wish to purchase more units.

4. Jermaine spends his money on cucumbers and lettuce. If the price of cucumbers falls, the MU per dollar of cucumbers will _____ and Jermaine will _____ cucumbers for lettuce. **LO7.4**
   a. fall; substitute
   b. rise; substitute
   c. fall; supply
   d. rise; demand

5. Aaliyah spends her money on lemonade and iced tea. If the price of lemonade falls, it is as though her income _____. **LO7.4**
   a. increases
   b. decreases
   c. stays the same

Problems

1. Mylie's total utility from singing the same song over and over is 50 utils after one repetition, 90 utils after two repetitions, 70 utils after three repetitions, 20 utils after four repetitions, −50 utils after five repetitions, and −200 utils after six repetitions. Write down her marginal utility for each repetition. Once Mylie's total utility begins to decrease, does each additional singing of the song hurt more than the previous song or less than the previous song? **LO7.1**

2. John likes Coca-Cola. After consuming one Coke, John has a total utility of 10 utils. After two Cokes, he has a total utility of 25 utils. After three Cokes, he has a total utility of 50 utils. Does John show diminishing marginal utility for Coke, or does he show increasing marginal utility for Coke? Suppose that John has $3 in his pocket. If Cokes cost $1 each and John is willing to spend one of his dollars on purchasing a first can of Coke, would he spend his second dollar on a Coke, too? What about the third dollar? If John's marginal utility for Coke keeps on increasing no matter how many Cokes he drinks, would it be fair to say that he is addicted to Coke? **LO7.1**

3. Suppose that Omar's marginal utility for cups of coffee is constant at 1.5 utils per cup no matter how many cups he drinks. In contrast, his marginal utility per doughnut is 10 for the first doughnut he eats, 9 for the second, 8 for the third, and so on (that is, declining by 1 util per additional doughnut). In addition, suppose that coffee costs $1 per cup, doughnuts cost $1 each, and Omar has a budget that he can spend only on doughnuts, coffee, or both. How big would that budget have to be before he will spend a dollar buying a first cup of coffee? **LO7.2**

4. Columns 1 through 4 in the following table show the marginal utility, measured in utils, that Ricardo would get by purchasing various amounts of products A, B, C, and D. Column 5 shows the marginal utility Ricardo gets from saving. Assume that the prices of A, B, C, and D are, respectively, $18, $6, $4, and $24 and that Ricardo has an income of $106. **LO7.2**
   a. What quantities of A, B, C, and D will Ricardo purchase in maximizing his utility?
   b. How many dollars will Ricardo choose to save?
   c. Check your answers by substituting them into the algebraic statement of the utility-maximizing rule.

Column 1		Column 2		Column 3		Column 4		Column 5	
Units of A	MU	Units of B	MU	Units of C	MU	Units of D	MU	Number of Dollars Saved	MU
1	72	1	24	1	15	1	36	1	5
2	54	2	15	2	12	2	30	2	4
3	45	3	12	3	8	3	24	3	3
4	36	4	9	4	7	4	18	4	2
5	27	5	7	5	5	5	13	5	1
6	18	6	5	6	4	6	7	6	$\frac{1}{2}$
7	15	7	2	7	$3\frac{1}{2}$	7	4	7	$\frac{1}{4}$
8	12	8	1	8	3	8	2	8	$\frac{1}{8}$

5. You are choosing between two goods, X and Y, and your marginal utility from each is shown in the following table. If your income is $9 and the prices of X and Y are $2 and $1, respectively, what quantities of each will you purchase to maximize utility? What total utility will you realize? Assume that, other things remaining unchanged, the price of X falls to $1. What quantities of X and Y will you now purchase? Using the two prices and quantities for X, derive a demand schedule (a table showing prices and quantities demanded) for X. **LO7.3**

Units of X	MU$_x$	Units of Y	MU$_y$
1	10	1	8
2	8	2	7
3	6	3	6
4	4	4	5
5	3	5	4
6	2	6	3

6. **ADVANCED ANALYSIS** Let $MU_A = z = 10 - x$ and $MU_B = z = 21 - 2y$, where z is marginal utility per dollar measured in utils, x is the amount spent on product A, and y is the amount spent on product B. Assume that the consumer has $10 to spend on A and B—that is, $x + y = 10$. How is the $10 best allocated between A and B? How much utility will the marginal dollar yield? **LO7.3**

7. Suppose that with a budget of $100, Fatima spends $60 on sushi and $40 on bagels when sushi costs $2 per piece and bagels cost $2 per bagel. Then, after the price of bagels falls to $1 per bagel, she spends $50 on sushi and $50 on bagels. How many pieces of sushi and how many bagels did Fatima consume before the price change? At the new prices, how much money would it have cost Fatima to buy those same quantities (that is, the quantities that she consumed before the price change)? Given that it used to take Fatima's entire $100 to buy those quantities, how big is the income effect caused by the lower price of bagels? **LO7.4**

Indifference Curve Analysis

LO7.6 Understand budget lines, indifference curves, and utility maximization.

The utility-maximization rule requires individuals to measure and compare utility, much as a business measures and compares costs or revenues. Such *cardinal utility* is measured in units such as 1, 2, 3, and 4 and can be added, subtracted, multiplied, and divided, just like the cardinal numbers in mathematics. More importantly, cardinal utility allows precise quantification of the marginal utilities upon which the utility-maximizing rule depends. The marginal-utility theory of consumer demand rests, in fact, on the assumption that economists can measure cardinal utility. But in reality, measuring cardinal utility is highly difficult, at best. (For instance, can you state exactly how many utils you are getting from reading this appendix right now or how many utils you get from watching a sunset?)

To avoid this measurement problem, economists have developed an alternative explanation of consumer behavior and equilibrium that does not require cardinal measurement. In this more-advanced analysis, the consumer must simply *rank* various combinations of goods in terms of preference. For instance, Fatima can simply report that she *prefers* 4 units of A to 6 units of B without having to assign number values to each option. In the same way, she can tell us that 4 units of C makes her indifferent to 9 units of D. The model of consumer behavior that is based on such *ordinal utility* rankings is called *indifference curve analysis*. It has two main elements: budget lines and indifference curves.

The Budget Line: What Is Attainable

A **budget line** (or, more technically, a budget constraint) is a schedule or curve showing various combinations of two products a consumer can purchase with a specific income. If the price of product A is $1.50 and the price of product B is $1, a consumer could purchase all the combinations of A and B shown in the table in Figure 1 with $12 of income. At one extreme, the consumer might spend their income on 8 units of A and have nothing left to spend on B. Or, by giving up 2 units of A and thereby "freeing" $3, the consumer could have 6 units of A and 3 of B. And so on to the other extreme, at which the consumer could buy 12 units of B at $1 each, spending his entire income on B and spending nothing on A.

Figure 1 also shows the budget line graphically. Note that the graph is not restricted to whole units of A and B as is the table. Every point on the graph represents a possible combination of A and B, including fractional quantities. The slope of the graphed budget line measures the ratio of the price of B to the price of A. More precisely, the absolute value of the slope is $P_B/P_A = \$1.00/\$1.50 = \frac{2}{3}$. The slope is the mathematical way of saying that the consumer must forgo 2 units of A (measured on the vertical axis) to buy 3 units of B (measured on the horizontal axis). In moving down the budget or price line, the consumer must give up 2 units of A (at $1.50 each) to obtain 3 more units of B (at $1 each), yielding a slope of $\frac{2}{3}$.

Note that all combinations of A and B that lie on or inside the budget line are attainable with the consumer's $12 income. They can afford to buy not only the combinations of A and B that lie along the budget line but also those that lie below it. They could, for instance, afford to buy 2 units of A and 4 units of B, thereby using up only $7 (= $3 spent on 2 units of A at a price of $1.50 each + $4 spent on 4 units of B at a price of $1 each). That combination is clearly attainable because it would use up only half of the consumer's $12 budget. But to achieve maximum utility, the consumer will want to spend the full $12. The budget line shows all combinations that cost exactly the full $12.

FIGURE 1 A consumer's budget line.

The budget line shows all the combinations of any two products that someone can purchase, given the prices of the products and the person's money income.

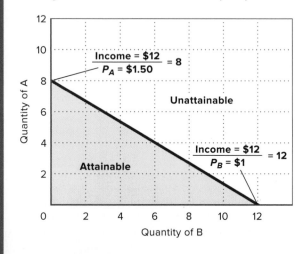

Units of A (Price = $1.50)	Units of B (Price = $1)	Total Expenditure
8	0	$12 (= $12 + $0)
6	3	$12 (= $9 + $3)
4	6	$12 (= $6 + $6)
2	9	$12 (= $3 + $9)
0	12	$12 (= $0 + $12)

budget line A line that shows the different combinations of two products a consumer can purchase with a specific money income, given the products' *prices*.

The budget line has two other significant characteristics:

- *Income changes* The location of the budget line varies with income. An increase in income shifts the budget line to the right; a decrease in money income shifts it to the left. To verify this, recalculate the table in Figure 1, assuming that money income is (a) $24 and (b) $6, and plot the new budget lines in Figure 1.
- *Price changes* A change in product prices also shifts the budget line. A decline in the prices of both products—the equivalent of an increase in real income—shifts the curve to the right. (You can verify this effect by recalculating the table in Figure 1 and replotting Figure 1 assuming that $P_A = \$0.75$ and $P_B = \$0.50$.) Conversely, an increase in the prices of A and B shifts the curve to the left. (Assume $P_A = \$3$ and $P_B = \$2$, and rework the table and Figure 1 to verify.)

Note what happens if P_B changes while P_A and income remain constant. If P_B drops from $1 to $0.50, the lower end of the budget line fans outward to the right. Conversely, if P_B increases from $1 to $1.50, the lower end of the line fans inward to the left. In both instances, the line remains "anchored" at 8 units on the vertical axis because P_A has not changed.

Indifference Curves: What Is Preferred

Budget lines reflect objective market data, specifically income and prices. They reveal combinations of products A and B that can be purchased, given current income and prices.

Indifference curves, in contrast, reflect "subjective" information about consumer preferences for A and B. An **indifference curve** shows all the combinations of two products A and B that will yield the same total satisfaction or total utility to a consumer. The table and graph in Figure 2 present a hypothetical indifference curve for products A and B. The consumer's subjective preferences are such that they will realize the same total utility from each combination of A and B shown in the table or on the curve. So the consumer will be indifferent to (will not care about) which combination is actually obtained.

Indifference curves have several important characteristics.

Indifference Curves Slope Downward

An indifference curve slopes downward because more of one product means less of the other if total utility is to remain unchanged. Suppose the consumer moves from one combination of A and B to another, say, from *j* to *k* in Figure 2. In doing so, the consumer obtains more of product B, increasing their total utility. But because total utility is the same everywhere on the curve, the consumer must give up some of the

FIGURE 2 A consumer's indifference curve.

Every point on indifference curve *I* represents some combination of products A and B, and all those combinations are equally satisfactory to the consumer. That is, each combination of A and B on the curve yields the same total utility.

Combination	Units of A	Units of B
j	12	2
k	6	4
l	4	6
m	3	8

other product, A. Thus "more of B" necessitates "less of A," and the quantities of A and B are inversely related. A curve that reflects inversely related variables is downward sloping.

Indifference Curves Are Convex to the Origin

The slope of a curve at a particular point is measured by drawing a straight line that is tangent to that point and then measuring the "rise over run" of the straight line (see the appendix to Chapter 1). If you drew such straight lines for several points on the curve in Figure 2, you would find that their slopes decline (in absolute terms) as you move down the curve. An indifference curve is therefore convex (bowed inward) to the origin of the graph. Its slope diminishes or becomes flatter as we move down the curve from *j* to *k* to *l*, and so on. Technically, the slope of an indifference curve at each point measures the **marginal rate of substitution (MRS)** which shows the rate at which the consumer must substitute one good for the other to remain equally satisfied. The diminishing slope of the indifference curve means that the willingness to substitute B for A diminishes as more of B is obtained.

---

indifference curve A curve showing the different combinations of two products that yield the same satisfaction or *utility* to a consumer.

marginal rate of substitution (MRS) The rate at which a consumer is willing to substitute one good for another (from a given combination of goods) and remain equally satisfied (have the same *total utility*); equal to the slope of a consumer's *indifference curve* at each point on the curve.

In a move from point *k* to point *l*, the consumer is willing to give up only 2 units of A to get 2 more units of B, so the MRS is $\frac{2}{2}$, or 1. Between *l* and *m*, the consumer is willing to give up only 1 unit of A in return for 2 more units of B, and the MRS falls to $\frac{1}{2}$.

In general, as the amount of B *increases,* the marginal utility of additional units of B *decreases.* Similarly, as the quantity of A *decreases,* its marginal utility *increases.* As Figure 2 shows in moving down the curve, the consumer will be willing to give up smaller and smaller amounts of A to offset acquiring each additional unit of B. The result is a curve with a diminishing slope, a curve that is convex to the origin. The MRS declines as one moves southeast along the indifference curve.

The Indifference Map

The single indifference curve of Figure 2 reflects some constant (but unspecified) level of total utility or satisfaction. It is possible and useful to sketch a whole series of indifference curves or an **indifference map,** as shown in Figure 3. Each curve reflects a different level of total utility and therefore never crosses another indifference curve. Specifically, each curve to the right of our original curve (labeled I_3 in Figure 3) reflects combinations of A and B that yield more utility than I_3. Each curve to the left of I_3 reflects less total utility than I_3. As we move out from the origin, each successive indifference curve represents a higher level of utility. To understand why, draw a 45-degree line northeast from the origin; note that its

points of intersection with successive curves entail larger amounts of both A and B and therefore higher levels of total utility.

Equilibrium at Tangency

Because the axes in Figures 1 and 3 are identical, we can superimpose a budget line on the consumer's indifference map, as Figure 4 shows. By definition, the budget line indicates all the combinations of A and B that the consumer can attain with their money income, given the prices of A and B. Of these attainable combinations, the consumer will prefer the combination that yields the greatest satisfaction or utility. Specifically, the utility-maximizing combination will be the combination lying on the highest attainable indifference curve. This point is called the consumer's **equilibrium position.**

In Figure 4 the consumer's equilibrium position is at point *X,* where the budget line is tangent to I_3. Point *Y* is not the equilibrium position because *Y* is on a lower indifference curve, I_2. By moving "down" the budget line—by shifting dollars from purchases of A to purchases of B—the consumer can attain an indifference curve farther from the origin and thereby increase the total utility derived from the same income. Point *Z* is not the equilibrium position for the same reason: Point *Z* is on a lower indifference curve, I_1. By moving "up" the budget line—by reallocating dollars from B to A—the consumer can move to the higher indifference curve I_3 and increase total utility.

---

indifference map A set of *indifference curves,* each representing a different level of *utility,* that together show the preferences of a consumer.

---

equilibrium position In the indifference curve model, the combination of two goods at which a consumer maximizes his or her *utility* (reaches the highest attainable *indifference curve*), given a limited amount to spend (a *budget constraint*).

FIGURE 3 An indifference map.

An indifference map is a set of indifference curves. Curves farther from the origin indicate higher levels of total utility. Thus any combination of products A and B represented by a point on I_4 has greater total utility than any combination of A and B represented by a point on I_3, I_2, or I_1.

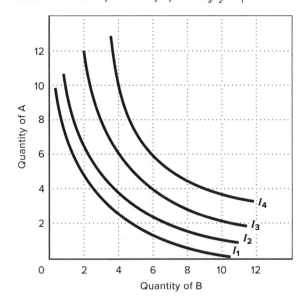

FIGURE 4 The consumer's equilibrium position.

The consumer's equilibrium position is represented by point *X,* where the black budget line is tangent to indifference curve I_3. The consumer buys 4 units of A at $1.50 per unit and 6 of B at $1 per unit with a $12 money income. Points *Z* and *Y* represent attainable combinations of A and B but yield less total utility, as is evidenced by the fact that they are on lower indifference curves. Point *W* would entail more utility than *X,* but it requires a greater income than the $12 represented by the budget line.

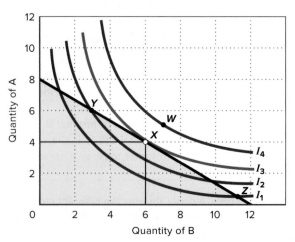

What can we say about point W on indifference curve I_4? Although W would yield a greater total utility than X, point W is beyond (outside) the budget line and hence is not attainable by the consumer. Point X represents the optimal attainable combination of products A and B. At the equilibrium position, X, the definition of tangency implies that the slope of the highest attainable indifference curve equals the slope of the budget line. Because the slope of the indifference curve reflects the MRS (marginal rate of substitution) and the slope of the budget line is P_B/P_A, the consumer's optimal or equilibrium position is the point where

$$\text{MRS} = \frac{P_B}{P_A}$$

Equivalency at Equilibrium

An important difference exists between the marginal-utility theory of consumer demand and the indifference curve theory of consumer demand. The marginal-utility theory assumes that utility is *numerically* measurable. The consumer needs that information to determine the utility-maximizing (equilibrium) position, which is defined by

$$\frac{\text{Marginal utility of A}}{\text{Price of A}} = \frac{\text{Marginal utility of B}}{\text{Price of B}}$$

The indifference curve approach imposes a less stringent requirement on the consumer, who needs only specify whether a particular combination of A and B will yield more than, less than, or the same amount of utility as some other combination of A and B. The consumer need only say, for example, that 6 of A and 7 of B will yield more (or less) satisfaction than 4 of A and 9 of B. Indifference curve theory does not require the consumer to specify *how much* more (or less) satisfaction will be realized.

That said, it is a remarkable mathematical fact that both models of consumer behavior will, in any given situation, point to exactly the same consumer equilibrium and, consequently, exactly the same demand behavior. This fact allows us to deduce an interesting property about marginal utilities that must also hold true in equilibrium. In indifference curve analysis, the MRS equals P_B/P_A at equilibrium; in the marginal-utility approach, the ratio of marginal utilities equals P_B/P_A. We therefore deduce that, at equilibrium, the MRS (in the marginal-utility approach) is equivalent to the ratio of the marginal utilities of the last purchased units of the two products (in the indifference-curve approach).

The Derivation of the Demand Curve

With a fixed price for A, an increase in the price of B will make the bottom of the budget line fan inward to the left. We can use that fact to derive a demand curve for product B. In Figure 5a we reproduce the part of Figure 4 that shows our initial consumer equilibrium at point X. The budget line determining this equilibrium position assumes that income is $12 and that $P_A = \$1.50$ and $P_B = \$1$. Let's see what happens to the equilibrium position when we increase P_B to $1.50 and hold both income and the price of A constant.

CONSIDER THIS . . .

Indifference Maps and Topographical Maps

The familiar topographical map may help you understand the idea of indifference curves and indifference maps. Each line on a topographical map represents a particular elevation above sea level, such as 500 feet. Similarly, an indifference curve represents a particular level of total utility. When you move from one point on a specific elevation line to another, the elevation remains the same. So it is with an indifference curve. A move from one position to another on the curve leaves total utility unchanged. Neither elevation lines nor indifference curves can intersect. If they did, the meaning of each line or curve would be violated. An elevation line is "an equal-elevation line"; an indifference curve is "an equal-total-utility curve."

Ryan McVay/Photodisc/Getty Images

Like the topographical map, an indifference map contains not just one line but a series of lines. That is, the topographical map may have elevation lines representing successively higher elevations of 100, 200, 300, 400, and 500 feet. Similarly, the indifference curves on the indifference map represent successively higher levels of total utility. The climber whose goal is to maximize elevation wants to get to the highest attainable elevation line; the consumer desiring to maximize total utility wants to get to the highest attainable indifference curve.

Finally, both topographical maps and indifference maps show only a few of the many such lines that could be drawn. The topographical map, for example, leaves out the elevation lines for 501 feet, 502, 503, and so on. The indifference map leaves out all the indifference curves that could be drawn between those that are displayed.

The result is shown in Figure 5a. The budget line fans to the left, yielding a new equilibrium point X' (where the inwardly fanned budget line is tangent to lower indifference curve I_2). At X' the consumer buys 3 units of B and 5 of A, compared with 4 of A and 6 of B at X. Our interest is in B, and we now have sufficient information to locate two points on the demand curve for B. At equilibrium point X the price of B is $1 and 6 units are purchased; at equilibrium point X' the price of B is $1.50 and 3 units are purchased.

Figure 5b shows these data graphically as points on the consumer's demand curve for B. Note that the horizontal axes of Figures 5a and 5b are identical; both measure the quantity demanded of B. We can therefore drop vertical reference lines from Figure 5a down to the horizontal axis of Figure 5b. On the vertical axis of Figure 5b we locate the two chosen prices of B. Knowing that these prices yield the relevant quantities demanded, we locate two points on the demand curve for B. By simple manipulation of the price of B in an indifference curve–budget line context, we have obtained a downward sloping demand curve for B. We have thus again derived the law of demand assuming other things equal, because only the price of B changed (the price of A and the consumer's income and tastes remained constant). But in this case, we have derived the demand curve without resorting to the assumption that consumers can measure utility in units called "utils." In this indifference curve approach, consumers simply compare combinations of products A and B and determine which combination they prefer, given their incomes and the prices of the two products.

FIGURE 5 Deriving the demand curve.
(a) When the price of product B is increased from $1 to $1.50, the equilibrium position moves from X to X', decreasing the quantity demanded of product B from 6 to 3 units. (b) The demand curve for product B is determined by plotting the $1–6-unit and the $1.50–3-unit price-quantity combinations for product B.

(a)
Two equilibrium positions

(b)
The demand curve for product B

Appendix Summary

LO7.6 Understand budget lines, indifference curves, and utility maximization.

The indifference curve approach to consumer behavior is based on the consumer's budget line and indifference curves.

The budget line shows all combinations of two products that the consumer can purchase, given product prices and income. A change in either product prices or income moves the budget line.

An indifference curve shows all combinations of two products that will yield the same total utility to a consumer. Indifference curves slope downward and are convex to the origin.

An indifference map consists of a number of indifference curves; the farther from the origin, the higher the total utility associated with a curve.

The consumer is in equilibrium (utility is maximized) at the point on the budget line that lies on the highest attainable indifference curve. At that point the budget line and indifference curve are tangent.

Changing the price of one product shifts the budget line and determines a new equilibrium point. A downward sloping demand curve can be graphed by plotting the price-quantity combinations associated with two or more equilibrium points.

Appendix Terms and Concepts

budget line

indifference curve

marginal rate of substitution (MRS)

indifference map

equilibrium position

Appendix Discussion Questions

1. What information is embodied in a budget line? What shifts occur in the budget line when income (*a*) increases or (*b*) decreases? What shifts occur in the budget line when the price of the product shown on the vertical axis (*c*) increases or (*d*) decreases? **LO7.6**
2. What information is contained in an indifference curve? Why are such curves (*a*) downward sloping and (*b*) convex to the origin? Why does total utility increase as the consumer moves to

indifference curves farther from the origin? Why can't indifference curves intersect? **LO7.6**
3. Using Figure 4, explain why the point of tangency of the budget line with an indifference curve is the consumer's equilibrium position. Explain why any point where the budget line intersects an indifference curve is not equilibrium. Explain: "The consumer is in equilibrium where MRS = P_B/P_A." **LO7.6**

Appendix Review Questions

1. Consider two bundles of coffee and chocolate and how Ted feels about them. The first bundle consists of two cups of coffee and two chocolate bars. The second bundle consists of one cup of coffee and three chocolate bars. If the first bundle gives Ted a total utility of 18 utils while the second bundle gives Ted a total utility of 19 utils, could the two bundles be on the same indifference curve? Why or why not? **LO7.6**
2. Xenia spends her money on flowers and cookies so as to maximize her total utility. The price of flowers and cookies is $2 each. At that price, Xenia buys three flowers and two cookies.

When the price of flowers decreases to $1, Xenia buys eight flowers and one cookie. Which of the following statements about Xenia's reaction to the price change is **not** true? **LO7.6**
a. Xenia's budget line shifted outward when the price of flowers fell.
b. Xenia moved to a higher indifference curve after the price of flowers fell.
c. Xenia's demand curve for flowers shifted to the right.
d. Xenia's attainable set was smaller before the price of flowers fell.

Appendix Problems

1. Assume that the data in the following table give an indifference curve for Mr. Chen. Graph this curve, putting A on the vertical axis and B on the horizontal axis. Assuming that the prices of A and B are $1.50 and $1, respectively, and that Mr. Chen has $24 to spend, add his budget line to your graph. What combination of A and B will Mr. Chen purchase? Does your answer meet the MRS = P_B/P_A rule for equilibrium? **LO7.6**

Units of A	Units of B
16	6
12	8
8	12
4	24

2. Explain graphically how indifference analysis can be used to derive a demand curve. **LO7.6**
3. **ADVANCED ANALYSIS** First, graphically illustrate a doubling of income without price changes in the indifference curve model. Next, on the same graph, show a situation in which the person whose indifference curves you are drawing buys considerably more of good B than good A after the income increase. What can you conclude about the relative coefficients of the income elasticity of demand for goods A and B (Chapter 6)? **LO7.6**

8

Behavioral Economics

>> LEARNING OBJECTIVES

LO8.1 Define behavioral economics and contrast it with neoclassical economics.

LO8.2 Discuss brain characteristics that affect human decision making.

LO8.3 Show how prospect theory helps to explain many consumer behaviors.

LO8.4 Describe how time inconsistency and myopia cause suboptimal long-run decisions.

LO8.5 Define and give examples of fairness and its effect on economic behavior.

neoclassical economics The dominant and conventional branch of economic theory that attempts to predict human behavior by building economic models based on simplifying assumptions about people's motives and capabilities. These include that people are fundamentally *rational;* motivated almost entirely by *self-interest;* good at math; and unaffected by *heuristics, time inconsistency,* and *self-control problems.*

Scientific theories are judged by the accuracy of their predictions. Conventional **neoclassical economics** makes many accurate predictions about human behavior, especially when it comes to financial incentives and how consumers and businesses respond to changing prices. However, several neoclassical predictions fail quite dramatically. These include predictions about how people deal with risk and uncertainty; choices that require willpower or commitment; and decisions that involve fairness, reciprocity, or trust.

Behavioral economics attempts to make better predictions about human behavior by combining insights from economics, psychology, and biology. This chapter introduces behavioral economics and the areas in which it has most dramatically increased our understanding of economic behavior.

Systematic Errors and the Origin of Behavioral Economics

>> **LO8.1** Define behavioral economics and contrast it with neoclassical economics.

We tend to think of ourselves as being very good at making decisions. While we may make a few mistakes here and there, we generally proceed through life with confidence, believing firmly that we will react sensibly and make good choices. Ultimately, we feel that our decisions are **rational,** meaning that they maximize our chances of achieving what we want.

Unfortunately, scientists have amassed overwhelming evidence to the contrary. People constantly make decision errors that reduce—rather than enhance—the likelihood of getting what they want. In addition, many errors are **systematic errors** that people tend to repeat over and over.

Behavioral economics developed as a field of study because neoclassical economics could not explain why people make systematic errors. The underlying problem is that neoclassical economics assumes that people are fundamentally rational. Under that assumption, people might make some initial mistakes when encountering a new situation, but as they gain experience, they should learn and adapt. As a result, decision errors should be rare and confined to novel situations.

When evidence began to pile up that even highly experienced people make systematic errors, neoclassical economists assumed that people were just ignorant of their best interests. They assumed that a little education would fix everything. But people often persisted in making the same error even after they were informed that their behavior went against their own interests.

As a result, several researchers realized that it was necessary to relax the assumption that people are fundamentally rational. By doing so, economists developed alternative theories that make more accurate predictions about human behavior. The collective results of those efforts are what we today call behavioral economics, which is based upon people's actual behavior—which can be irrational, prone to systematic errors, and difficult to modify.

Comparing Behavioral Economics with Neoclassical Economics

Behavioral economists argue that neoclassical economics makes a number of highly unrealistic assumptions about human capabilities and motivations, including:

- People have stable preferences that aren't affected by context.
- People are eager and accurate calculating machines.
- People are good planners who possess plenty of willpower.
- People are almost entirely selfish and self-interested.

Neoclassical economics made these simplifying assumptions for two main reasons. First, they render neoclassical models of human behavior both mathematically elegant and easy to solve. Second, they allow for very precise predictions about human behavior.

Unfortunately, precision is not the same thing as accuracy. As behavioral economist Richard Thaler has written, "Would you rather be elegant and precisely wrong—or messy and vaguely right?" Behavioral economists err on the side of being messy and vaguely right.

Table 8.1 summarizes how the two approaches differ in several areas.

Focusing on the Mental Processes Behind Decisions Behavioral economics puts significant emphasis on the mental processes driving behavior. By contrast, neoclassical economics focuses almost entirely on predicting behavior, without caring very much (or at all) about the underlying mental processes.

Neoclassical economics can focus on prediction because its assumption of rationality allows neoclassical economists to separate *what* people do from *how* they do it. That separation is possible because a perfectly rational person would always choose the rational course of action, the one

behavioral economics The branch of economic theory that combines insights from economics, psychology, and biology to make more accurate predictions about human behavior than conventional *neoclassical economics,* which is hampered by its core assumptions that people are fundamentally *rational* and almost entirely self-interested. Behavioral economics can explain *framing effects, anchoring, mental accounting,* the *endowment effect, status quo bias, time inconsistency,* and *loss aversion.*

rational Behaviors and decisions that maximize a person's chances of achieving their goals. See *rational behavior.*

systematic errors Suboptimal choices that (1) are not *rational* because they do not maximize a person's chances of achieving his or her goals and (2) occur routinely, repeatedly, and predictably.

TABLE 8.1 Major Differences between Behavioral Economics and Conventional Neoclassical Economics

Topic	Neoclassical Economics	Behavioral Economics
Rationality	People are fundamentally rational and will adjust their choices and behaviors to best achieve their goals. Consequently, they will not make systematic errors.	People are irrational and make many errors that reduce their chances of achieving their goals. Some errors are regularly repeated, systematic errors.
Stability of preferences	People's preferences are completely stable and unaffected by context.	People's preferences are unstable and often inconsistent because they depend on context (framing effects).
Capability for making mental calculations	People are eager and accurate calculators.	People are bad at math and avoid difficult computations if possible.
Ability to assess future options and possibilities	People are just as good at assessing future options as current options.	People place insufficient weight on future events and outcomes.
Strength of willpower	People have no trouble resisting temptation.	People lack sufficient willpower and often fall prey to temptation.
Degree of selfishness	People are almost entirely self-interested and self-centered.	People are often selfless and generous.
Fairness	People do not care about fairness and only treat others well if doing so will get them something they want.	Many people care deeply about fairness and will often help others even when doing so will yield no personal benefits.

that maximizes their chances of getting what they want. How that person happened to discover that rational course of action might be interesting—but that information is not necessary to predict a perfectly rational person's behavior. To predict their behavior you only need to figure out what a rational person would do; you then assume that, because they are rational, they will select the rational course of action. That may seem circular to you, but that line of reasoning—based on the assumption that people are perfectly rational and will always choose the rational option—allows neoclassical economists to ignore the underlying mental processes involved in decision making.

For behavioral economists, the fact that people are not perfectly rational suggests two important reasons for understanding the underlying mental processes that drive decisions:

- We can make better predictions about behavior.
- We can help people make better decisions.

Improving Outcomes by Improving Decision Making Neoclassical economics and behavioral economics differ on how to improve human welfare. Neoclassical economics focuses on giving people more options. That's because fully rational people can be trusted to select the best option from any set of options. As a result, the only way to make people even happier is to provide them with more options.

By contrast, the existence of irrationality leads behavioral economists to conclude that it may be possible to make people better off without providing additional options. In particular, improvements in utility and happiness may be possible simply by getting people to make better choices from the set of options already available to them.

Behavioral Economics and Neoclassical Economics as Complements We should not view behavioral economics and neoclassical economics as fundamentally opposed or mutually exclusive. Instead, many economists think of them as complementary approaches that can be used together to improve our understanding of human behavior.

As an example, consider how using the two approaches in tandem can help us better understand how customers behave at a local supermarket.

Neoclassical Economics at the Supermarket The major neoclassical contribution to our understanding of the customers' shopping behavior can be summarized by the phrase "incentives matter." In particular, customers care a great deal about prices. When prices go up, they buy less. When prices go down, they buy more.

Behavioral Economics at the Supermarket People tend to buy what they happen to see. This behavior, called impulse buying, contradicts the neoclassical assumption that consumers carefully calculate marginal utilities and compare prices before making purchases. However, impulse buying is a very common behavior that retailers often exploit.

For instance, nearly all supermarkets place staple products like milk and eggs against the back walls of their stores. This placement increases impulse buying by forcing customers to walk past hundreds of other items on the way to the milk and eggs. A few of those items will catch their eyes, and customers end up purchasing products that they had no intention of buying when they first entered the store.

Marketers also know that impulse purchases are highest for items that are stacked on shelves at eye level. Thus food manufacturers actively pay supermarkets for the privilege of having their brands stacked at eye level. In cereal aisles, the most expensive shelf space isn't at eye level for an adult, but a foot or two lower—at the eye level of a toddler sitting in a shopping cart or of a child walking with a parent. Because kids are even more prone to impulse buying than adults, cereal makers are willing to pay to have their products stacked at kid-friendly eye levels.

Our Efficient, Error-Prone Brains

>> **LO8.2** Discuss brain characteristics that affect human decision making.

The human brain is one of the most complex objects in the universe. One hundred billion neurons share 10,000 times as many connections. Working together, they allow you to observe your environment, think creatively, and interact with people and objects.

The brain, however, is rather error-prone. Its many weaknesses are most dramatically illustrated by visual illusions, such as the one in Figure 8.1. If you follow the instructions in that figure, you will quickly discover that your brain can't consistently tell what color an object is.

The brain devotes more neurons toward processing and interpreting visual information than any other activity. So, if the brain makes errors with visual processing, we should expect to find errors in everything else it does, too.

Heuristics Are Energy Savers

The brain's information-processing limitations are the result of evolutionary pressures. It was typically very difficult for our ancestors to get enough food to eat. Food matters because our brains are extremely energy intensive. In fact, while your brain accounts for just 5 percent of your body weight, it burns 20 percent of all the calories you go through each day. So back when our ancestors had to hunt, gather, and scavenge to survive, getting enough energy was a constant challenge.

In response, the brain evolved many low-energy mental shortcuts, or **heuristics.** Because they are shortcuts, heuristics are not the most accurate mental-processing options. But in a world where calories were hard to come by, a low-energy "good enough" heuristic was superior to a "perfect but costly" alternative.

Your brain's susceptibility to the visual-processing failure demonstrated in Figure 8.1 is the result of your brain using a host of error-prone heuristics. But think about the good trade-off you are getting. In everyday life, the visual-processing failure in Figure 8.1 hardly ever comes up. So, it would be a waste of resources to devote more brainpower to fixing the issue. In economic terms, there are diminishing returns to employing additional units of brainpower. Heuristics are used because the opportunity cost of perfection is too high.

Some Common Heuristics The following examples will help you understand how the brain employs heuristics.

Catching a Baseball with the Gaze Heuristic Consider the problem faced by a centerfielder in a baseball game when a ball is hit in his general direction. The mentally expensive way to catch the ball would be for the player to use the laws of physics to determine where the ball is heading so that he can run to that spot before the ball arrives.

What baseball players actually do is lock their eyes on the ball and then adjust their position on the field as necessary to keep the ball in front of them and at the same angle above the horizon as when they first locked their eyes on it. As long as they can run fast enough, this *gaze heuristic* always gets them to the correct place to make the catch. You don't need to learn physics to catch a baseball!

Riding a Bicycle with the Steering Heuristic There is a simple heuristic for staying upright as you ride a bicycle: If you begin to fall, steer in the direction you are falling. This *steering heuristic* works because turning in the direction of a fall generates a centrifugal force that can hold you up long enough for you to steady the bike. This heuristic is almost never articulated, but it is precisely what little kids subconsciously learn to do when they use training wheels.

Guesstimating Ranks with the Recognition Heuristic Which German city has the larger population, Munich or Stuttgart?

Even people who know nothing about Germany tend to get the right answer to this question. They correctly guess "Munich" by subconsciously employing the *recognition heuristic*, which assumes that if one option is more easily recognized, it is probably more important or more highly ranked.

The recognition heuristic isn't foolproof, but it tends to work because relatively important people and places are much more likely to be mentioned in the media. Thus, whichever option is easier to recognize will probably be larger or more important.

A lot of advertising is designed to trigger the recognition heuristic. Indeed, companies spend billions to ensure that consumers are familiar with their products because when it comes time to buy, consumers will be biased toward the products that seem the most familiar.

Are the two boxes really colored differently?

Lay a finger horizontally across the middle of the image to see for yourself.

FIGURE 8.1
A visual illusion.

The human brain uses a large number of heuristics (shortcuts) to process both visual and other types of information. Many of them utilize context to interpret specific bits of information. When that context changes (as it does here when you put your finger horizontally across the middle of the image), so does the brain's heuristic-filtered interpretation.

heuristics The brain's low-energy mental shortcuts for making decisions. They are "fast and frugal" and work well in most situations but in other situations result in *systematic errors*.

The Implications of Hardwired Heuristics As you study the rest of this chapter, remember that most heuristics appear to be hardwired into the brain, and, consequently, impossible to unlearn or avoid. That possibility has three important implications:

1. It may be very difficult for people to alter detrimental behaviors or routines even after you point out what they're doing wrong.

2. People may be easy prey for those who understand their hardwired tendencies.

3. If you want people to make a positive behavioral change, it may be helpful to put them in a situation where a heuristic will kick in and subconsciously lead them toward the desired outcome.

Brain Modularity

The human brain is modular. Specific areas deal with specific sensations, activities, and emotions—such as vision, breathing, and anger.

This modular structure is the result of millions of years of evolution, with the human brain evolving in stages from the much less complex brains of our distant, hominid ancestors. The oldest parts of the brain are located in the back of the head, where the spine enters the skull. The newest parts are up front, near the forehead.

The older parts control automatic activities like breathing and sweating as well as automatic emotional reactions such as fear and joy. The newer parts allow you to think creatively, imagine the future, and keep track of your social network. They are largely under conscious control.

System 1 and System 2 It is useful to think of the brain's decision-making systems as falling into two categories. System 1 uses a lot of heuristics in the older parts of your brain to produce quick, unconscious reactions. When you get a "gut instinct," System 1 is responsible. By contrast, System 2 uses the newer parts of your brain to undertake slow, deliberate, and conscious calculations of costs and benefits. When you find yourself "thinking things over," you are using System 2.

Conflicts sometimes arise between our unconscious System 1 intuitions and our conscious System 2 deliberations. For example, System 1 may urge you to eat an entire box of cookies as fast as possible, while System 2 admonishes you to stick to your diet and have only one cookie. That said, a large body of evidence suggests that most decisions are either fully or mostly the result of System 1 intuitions and heuristics. That matters because those unconscious mental processes suffer from a variety of cognitive biases.

cognitive biases Misperceptions or misunderstandings that cause *systematic errors*. Most result either (1) from *heuristics* that are prone to *systematic errors* or (2) because the brain is attempting to solve a type of problem (such as a calculus problem) for which it was not evolutionarily evolved and for which it has little innate capability.

Cognitive Biases **Cognitive biases** are the misperceptions or misunderstandings that cause systematic errors.

Cognitive biases are placed into two general categories. The first are mental-processing errors that result from faulty heuristics. As previously discussed, faulty heuristics are the result of evolution trading off accuracy for speed and efficiency.

The second category consists of mental-processing errors that result from our brains not having evolved capacities for dealing with modern problems and challenges, such as solving calculus problems or programming computers. Because our ancestors never encountered math, engineering, or statistics, our brains have a total absence of System 1 heuristics for dealing with those sorts of problems. In addition, our slower and more deliberative System 2 mental processes provide only limited assistance because they evolved to deal with other types of problems, such as determining whether it is better to go hunting in the morning or in the evening.

As a result, most people find recently developed mental challenges like math and physics to be very tiresome. In addition, the System 2 processes that we are recruiting to solve modern problems were designed for pre-modern situations and don't work particularly well when directed at many current situations.

Psychologists have identified scores of cognitive biases. Here are a few that are relevant to economics and decision making.

Confirmation Bias The term *confirmation bias* refers to the human tendency to pay attention only to information that agrees with one's preconceptions. Information that contradicts those preconceptions is either ignored completely or rationalized away. Confirmation bias allows bad decisions to continue long after an impartial weighing of the evidence would have put a stop to them. When you see someone persisting with a failed policy or incorrect opinion despite overwhelming evidence that they should try something else, confirmation bias is probably at work.

Self-Serving Bias The term *self-serving bias* refers to people's tendency to attribute their successes to personal effort or personal character traits while attributing any failures to factors beyond their control. Self-serving bias makes it difficult for people to learn from their mistakes because they incorrectly assume that anything that went wrong was beyond their control.

Overconfidence Effect The *overconfidence effect* refers to people's tendency to be overly confident about how likely their judgments and opinions are to be correct. As an example, people who rated their answers to a particular quiz as being "99 percent likely to be right" were in fact wrong more than 40 percent of the time. Such overconfidence can lead to bad decisions because people will tend to take actions without pausing to verify if their initial hunches are actually true.

Hindsight Bias People engage in *hindsight bias* when they retroactively believe that they were able to predict past events. For example, consider an election between two candidates named Terence and Philip. Before the election, many people will predict that Terence will lose. But after Terence ends up winning, many of those same people will convince themselves that they "knew all along" that Terence was going to win. This faulty "I-knew-it-all-along" perspective causes people to massively overestimate their predictive abilities.

Availability Heuristic The *availability heuristic* causes people to base their estimates about the likelihood of an event not on objective facts but on whether or not similar events come to mind quickly and are readily available in their memories. Because vivid, emotionally charged images come to mind more easily, people tend to think that dramatic events such as homicides, shark attacks, and lightning strikes are much more common than they really are. At the same time, they underestimate the likelihood of unmemorable events. You are five times more likely to die of stomach cancer than to be murdered, but most people rate the likelihood of being murdered as much higher.

The availability heuristic makes people spend too much of their time and effort attempting to protect themselves against dangers of low actual probability while neglecting to protect themselves against uncharismatic threats of substantially higher probability.

Planning Fallacy The *planning fallacy* is the tendency to massively underestimate the time needed to complete a task. Last-minute test cramming is a good example. If you see a student cramming for an exam, it's likely that they underestimated—by many hours!—how long they needed to prepare for the exam. The planning fallacy also helps to explain why construction projects, business initiatives, and government reform efforts all tend to extend beyond their planned schedules.

Framing Effects **Framing effects** occur when a change in context (frame) causes people to react differently to a particular piece of information or to an otherwise identical situation.

Figure 8.2 gives an example of a framing effect. The middle symbol is identical in both rows, but it is interpreted differently depending on whether it is surrounded by letters or numbers. When surrounded by letters in the top row, the brain tends to interpret the symbol as the letter B. When surrounded by numbers in the bottom row, the brain tends to interpret the symbol as the number 13.

Changes in context can also cause extraordinary changes in behavior. Experiments have shown that ordinary people are twice as likely to litter, steal, or trespass if experimenters tag an area with graffiti and scatter lots of trash around. By changing the area's appearance from neat and orderly to rundown and chaotic, experimenters got ordinary people to subconsciously choose to engage in more crime.

Framing effects can also cause consumers to change their purchases. At the local supermarket, apples command a higher price if

framing effects In *prospect theory*, changes in people's decision making caused by new information that alters the context, or "frame of reference," that they use to judge whether options are viewed as gains or losses relative to the *status quo*.

FIGURE 8.2
The letter illusion is the result of a framing effect.

In each row, the middle symbol is the same. When that symbol is surrounded by the letters A and C in the top row, our brains tend to register the symbol as the letter B. But when it is surrounded by the numbers 12 and 14 in the bottom row, our brains tend to register it as the number 13. What our brain "sees" is largely a matter of context (frame).

each one comes with a pretty sticker and meat sells faster if it is packaged in shiny plastic containers. At a high-end retailer, expensive packaging increases the perceived value of the merchandise. So does having a nice physical space in which to shop. Thus, high-end retailers spend a lot on architecture and displays.

▸ Behavioral economics differs from neoclassical economics because its models of decision making take into account the fact that heuristics and cognitive biases cause people to make systematic errors.

▸ To conserve energy, the brain relies on low-energy mental shortcuts, or heuristics, that will usually produce the correct decision or answer.

▸ Cognitive biases are systematic misperceptions or bad decisions that arise because (1) heuristics are error-prone in certain situations or (2) evolution did not prepare our brains to handle many modern tasks such as solving calculus problems.

Prospect Theory

>> LO8.3 Show how prospect theory helps to explain many consumer behaviors.

Neoclassical economics focuses much of its attention on consumer-choice situations in which people deal with "goods" rather than "bads." When deciding how to spend a budget, a consumer considers only items that bring positive marginal utility—that is, "good" things. She then uses the *utility-maximizing rule* to get as much utility as possible from her limited budget.

Unfortunately, life often forces us to deal with bad things, too. Our houses may burn down. A potential investment may go bad. The money we lend may not be repaid.

How people cope with negative possibilities is a central focus of behavioral economics. Three interesting facts summarize how people deal with goods and bads:

status quo The existing state of affairs; in *prospect theory*, the current situation from which gains and losses are calculated.

- People judge good things and bad things in relative terms, as gains and losses relative to their current situation (that is, the **status quo**).

- People experience both diminishing marginal utility for gains (meaning that each successive unit of gain feels good, but not as good as the previous unit) as well as diminishing marginal *disutility* for losses (meaning that each successive unit of loss hurts, but less painfully than the previous unit).

loss aversion In *prospect theory*, the property of most people's preferences that the pain generated by losses feels substantially more intense than the pleasure generated by gains.

- People experience **loss aversion,** meaning that for losses and gains near the status quo, losses are felt *much* more intensely than gains—in fact, about 2.5 times more intensely. Thus, for instance, the pain experienced by investors who lose one dollar from their status quo level of wealth will be about 2.5 times more intense than the pleasure they would have felt if they had gained one dollar relative to their status quo level of wealth.

prospect theory A *behavioral economics* theory of preferences having three main features: (1) people evaluate options on the basis of whether they generate gains or losses relative to the *status quo;* (2) gains are subject to *diminishing marginal utility*, while losses are subject to diminishing marginal disutility; and (3) people are prone to *loss aversion.*

These three facts form the basis of **prospect theory,** which sheds important light on how consumers plan for and deal with life's ups and downs and helps to explain why they often appear narrow-minded and fail to "see the big picture." To examine how powerful prospect theory is—and why its pioneer, Daniel Kahneman, was awarded the Nobel Prize in Economics— let's use some examples of consumer behaviors that are hard to explain without the insights provided by prospect theory.

Framing Effects and Advertising

Because people evaluate situations in terms of gains and losses, their decision making can be very sensitive to the mental frame that they use to determine whether a possible outcome should be viewed as a gain or as a loss. Think about the following two examples:

- Would you be happy with a salary of $100,000 per year? You might say yes. But what if your salary last year was $140,000? Are you still going to say yes? Now that you know you are taking a $40,000 pay cut, does that $100,000 salary seem as good as it did before?

- Suppose you have a part-time job. One day, your boss walks in and says that she is giving you a 10 percent raise. Would that please you? It probably would. Now, imagine that she also mentions that everyone else at your firm is getting a 15 percent raise. Will you be just as pleased? Or does your raise now seem like a loss compared to what everyone else is getting?

CONSIDER THIS . . .

Rising Consumption and the Hedonic Treadmill

For many sensations, people's brains are wired to notice changes rather than states. For example, your brain can sense acceleration—your change in speed—but not speed itself. As a result, standing still feels the same as moving at a constant 50 miles per hour. And if you accelerate from one constant speed to another—say, from 50 miles per hour to 70 miles per hour—you will feel the acceleration only while it's happening. Once you stabilize at the higher speed, you will feel like you are standing still again.

Consumption appears to work in much the same way. If you are used to a given level of consumption—say, $50,000 per year—then you will get a lot of enjoyment for a while if your consumption accelerates to $100,000 per year. But, as time passes, you will get used to that higher level of

Stewart Cohen/Stockbyte/ Getty Images

consumption, so that $100,000 per year seems ordinary and doesn't bring you any more pleasure than $50,000 per year used to bring you when it was your status quo.

Economist Richard Easterlin coined the term *hedonic treadmill* (pleasure treadmill) to describe this phenomenon. Just as a person walking on a real treadmill gets nowhere, people trying to make themselves permanently happier by consuming more also get nowhere because they end up getting used to any higher level of consumption. Indeed, except for the extremely poor, people across the income spectrum report similar levels of happiness and satisfaction with their lives. This has led several economists, including Robert Frank, to argue that we should all stop trying to consume more because doing so doesn't make us any happier in the long run. What do you think? Should we all step off of the hedonic treadmill?

Prospect theory accounts for the fact that people's preferences can change drastically depending on whether contextual information makes them define a situation as a gain or a loss. It is important to recognize these framing effects because they can be manipulated by advertisers, lawyers, and politicians. For instance, would an advertising agency be better off marketing a particular brand of hamburger as "20% fat" or as "80% lean"? Both phrases describe the same meat, but one frames the situation as a loss (20% fat) while the other frames it as a gain (80% lean).

Would you be more willing to take a particular medicine if you were told that 99.9 percent of the people who take it live or if you were told that 0.1 percent of the people who take it die? Continuing to live is a gain, whereas dying is a loss. Which frame sounds better to you?

Framing effects have major consequences for consumer behavior because any frame that alters whether consumers consider a situation to be a gain or a loss will affect their consumption decisions. The Consider This story examines how mental frames about consumption evolve as incomes increase.

Anchoring and Credit Card Bills

Before people can calculate their gains and losses, they must first define the status quo from which to measure those changes. But irrelevant information can unconsciously influence people's feelings about the status quo. Here's a striking example. Find a group of people and ask each person to write down the last two digits of their Social Security number. Then ask each person to write down their best estimate of the value of some object that you show them—say, a nice wireless keyboard. You will find that the people whose Social Security numbers end in higher numbers—say, 67 or 89—will give higher estimates of the keyboard's value than people whose Social Security numbers end in smaller numbers like 18 or 37. The overall effect can be huge. Among students in one MBA class at MIT, those with Social Security numbers ending between 80 and 99 gave an average estimate of $56 for a wireless keyboard, while their classmates whose Social Security numbers ended between 00 and 20 gave an average estimate of just $16.

Psychologists and behavioral economists call this phenomenon **anchoring** because people's estimates about the value of the keyboard are influenced, or "anchored," by the recently considered information about the last two digits of their Social Security numbers. Why irrelevant information can anchor subsequent valuations is not fully understood. But the anchoring effect is real and can lead people to unconsciously alter how they evaluate different options.

anchoring The tendency people have to unconsciously base, or "anchor," the valuation of an item they are currently thinking about on recently considered but logically irrelevant information.

Unfortunately, credit card companies have a good understanding of anchoring. They use anchoring to increase their profits by showing very small minimum-payment amounts on borrowers' monthly credit card statements. The companies could require larger minimum payments, but the minimum-payment numbers that they present are typically only about 2 percent of what a customer owes. This small amount acts as an anchor that causes people to unconsciously make smaller payments each month. Small payments can make a huge difference in how long it takes to pay off their bill and how much in total interest they end up paying. For customers who owe $1,000 on a credit card that charges the typical interest rate of 19 percent per year, it will take 22 years and $3,398.12 in total payments (including accumulated interest) to pay off the debt if they make only the minimum monthly payments. By showing such small minimum-payment amounts, credit card companies anchor many customers into the expensive habit of paying off their debts slowly rather than quickly.

Mental Accounting and Overpriced Warranties

The utility-maximizing rule (Chapter 7) assumes that people look at all of their potential consumption options simultaneously when trying to maximize their total utility. But Nobel laureate Richard Thaler famously noted that people sometimes look at consumption options in isolation, rather than simultaneously. Thaler coined the term **mental accounting** to describe this behavior because it seems that people arbitrarily put certain options into totally separate "mental accounts" that they consider without thinking about any options outside of those accounts.

mental accounting The tendency people have to create separate "mental boxes" (or "accounts") in which they deal with particular financial transactions in isolation, rather than dealing with them as part of an overall decision-making process that would consider how to best allocate their limited budgets across all possible options by using the *utility-maximizing rule*.

As an example of mental accounting, consider the extended warranties offered by retailers when customers purchase expensive products like big screen TVs. These warranties are very much overpriced given that the products they insure hardly ever break down. Personal financial experts universally tell people not to buy them. Yet many people do buy them because they engage in mental accounting. That is, they mentally label their purchase of the TV as an isolated, individual transaction, sticking it into a separate mental account that might have a title like "Purchase of New TV."

Viewing the purchase in isolation exaggerates the size of the potential loss that would come from a broken TV. Customers who view the transaction in isolation see the possibility of a $1,000 loss on their $1,000 purchase as a potential total loss—"Holy cow! I could lose 100 percent of my $1,000 outlay if this TV breaks!" By contrast, people who can see the big picture are able to compare the potential $1,000 loss with the much larger value of their entire future income stream, which for the average worker will be more than $1 million over their lifetime. By following that thought process, they realize that the potential loss of $1,000 is relatively minor—and thus not a good enough reason to purchase an expensive warranty for a product that is very unlikely to break down.

The Endowment Effect and Market Transactions

endowment effect The tendency people have to place higher valuations on items they possess (are endowed with) than on identical items that they do not possess; perhaps caused by *loss aversion*.

Prospect theory also offers an explanation for the **endowment effect,** which is the tendency that people have to put a higher valuation on anything that they already possess (are endowed with) than on identical items that they do not yet own but might purchase. For instance, if we show a person a new coffee mug and ask them to tell us the maximum amount that they would pay to buy it, they might say $10. But if we then give the mug to them so that they own it, and then we ask how much we would have to pay them to buy it back from them, they will very likely report a much higher value—say, $15.

The mug owner is not just bluffing or driving a hard bargain. Rather, the human brain appears to be wired to put a higher value on things we own than on things we don't. Economist John List has shown that this tendency can moderate if people have business experience buying things for resale. But without such experience, the endowment effect can be quite strong. When it is, it can make market transactions more difficult because sellers will demand higher prices for the items they are selling ("Hey, my mug is worth $15 to me!") than the values put on those items by potential buyers ("Dude, your mug is worth only $10 to me").

Several researchers have suggested that loss aversion may be responsible for the endowment effect. They argue that once a person possesses something, the thought of parting with it feels like a potential loss. As a result, the person will demand a lot of money as compensation for selling the item. Meanwhile, potential purchasers do not feel any sense of loss, so they end up assigning lower values to the same items.

PERCENTAGE OF POPULATION CONSENTING TO BE ORGAN DONORS

People tend to stick with whatever option is presented as the default option. Thus, the seven countries with high percentages consenting to be organ donors have organ-donation programs in which the default option is participation. By contrast, the four countries with low percentages consenting to be organ donors have organ-donation programs where the default option is *not* participating.

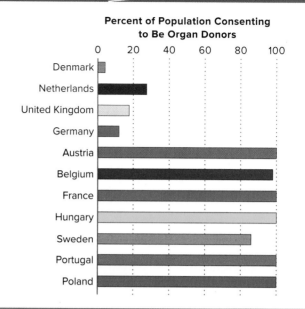

Percent of Population Consenting to Be Organ Donors

Source: Johnson, Eric, and Daniel Goldstein. "Defaults and Donation Decisions." *Transplantation* 78, no. 12 (December 27, 2004). Permission from Wolters Kluwer Health.

Status Quo Bias

Prospect theory also explains **status quo bias,** which is the tendency people have of favoring an option that is presented to them as the default (status quo) option. As an example, consider Global Perspective 8.1. It shows, for a set of European countries, the percentages of their respective populations that are enrolled in organ-donation programs.

As you can see, seven of the 11 countries have very high participation rates while the other four have low participation rates. You might suspect cultural differences at work, but that explanation doesn't make sense when you note that countries like Germany and Austria, which are culturally very similar, have widely different participation rates.

The explanation lies in the default option that people are given when they are asked whether they wish to participate. In the seven countries with high participation rates, the default option is participation, so those who don't want to participate must check off a box indicating that they don't want to participate. By contrast, in the four countries with low participation rates, the default option is *not* participating, so that those wishing to participate must explicitly check off a box indicating that they want to participate.

In all countries, nearly everyone chooses to do nothing. That is, they almost never check off the box that is the opposite of the default option. Consequently, they end up agreeing to the default option. Thus, the huge differences in participation rates among the 11 countries are driven almost entirely by the default option.

Prospect theory explains status quo bias as a combination of the endowment effect and loss aversion. When people are put into a novel situation, they have no preexisting preferences for any of the options. As a result, the way the options are framed becomes very important. If any option is presented as the default, people tend to treat it as an endowment that they wish to hold on to. They treat any other option as a prospect that could potentially cause a loss. Loss aversion then kicks in and causes most people to stick with the default option. The result is a bias toward the status quo.

Status quo bias can explain several consumer behaviors. Consider brand loyalty. If you have gotten used to eating Heinz ketchup, then status quo bias will make you reluctant to purchase any other brand of ketchup. Overcoming that feeling of potential loss is a difficult challenge for competing brands. Rivals seeking to challenge an established brand are often forced to resort to deep discounts or free samples to get consumers to even try their products.

status quo bias The tendency most people have when making choices to select any option that is presented as the default (*status quo*) option. Explainable by *prospect theory* and *loss aversion*.

Myopia and Time Inconsistency

>> **LO8.4** Describe how time inconsistency and myopia cause suboptimal long-run decisions.

Our ancient ancestors had little cause to spend much time worrying about anything that would happen in the distant future. Infectious diseases, predatory animals, and the constant threat of starvation made life extremely precarious. Consequently, they had to be almost entirely focused on the present and how to get through the next few weeks or months.

Today, however, people living in industrialized countries rarely die from infectious diseases, see predatory animals mostly on TV, and are under little threat of starvation. Living past 80 is now routine, and most of us will die of old age. As a result, long-run challenges like planning for retirement and saving for college are now common tasks that nearly everyone faces.

Unfortunately, our brains were designed for our ancestors' more immediate concerns. Thus, we often have difficulty with long-run planning and decisions that involve trade-offs between the present and the future. Two of the major stumbling blocks are myopia and time inconsistency.

Myopia

myopia Refers to the difficulty human beings have with conceptualizing the more distant future. Leads to decisions that overly favor present and near-term options at the expense of more distant future possibilities.

In biology, myopia, or nearsightedness, refers to a defect of the eye that makes distant objects appear fuzzy, out of focus, and hard to see. Economists use the word **myopia** to describe the human brain's difficulty in conceptualizing the future. Compared with the present, the future seems fuzzy, out of focus, and hard to see.

For example, our brains are very good at weighing current benefits against current costs in order to make immediate decisions. But our brains seem to stumble when it comes to conceptualizing either future costs or future benefits. As a result, we have difficulty evaluating possibilities that will occur more than a few weeks or months into the future.

As a result of myopia, people who are forced to choose between something that generates benefits quickly and something that won't yield benefits for a long time will typically favor the more immediate option.

Imagine that Terence has $1,000 that he can either spend on a vacation next month or save for his retirement in 30 years. Myopia will cause him great difficulty in imagining the additional spending power that he will be able to enjoy in 30 years if he saves the money. In contrast, it is very easy for him to imagine all the fun he could have next month if he goes on vacation. As a result, he will be strongly biased toward spending the money next month. With myopia obscuring the benefits of the long-term option, the short-term option seems much more attractive.

Myopia also makes it hard to stick with a diet or follow an exercise plan. Compared with the immediate and obvious pleasures of eating doughnuts or hanging out, the future benefits from eating better or exercising consistently are just too hazy in most people's minds to be very attractive. The nearby Consider This story discusses a green business model that works with, rather than against, people's myopia.

CONSIDER THIS . . .

A Bright Idea

In sunny areas, a solar panel can make up for the cost of its installation in just a few years by greatly reducing or even eliminating a household's electricity bill. After those years of payback are finished, there will be almost nothing but benefits because the solar panel will continue to provide free electricity at only modest maintenance costs. Consequently, nearly every household in sunny areas could rationally profit from installing solar panels.

Unfortunately, myopia discourages most people from wanting to reap the net benefits. Because people are myopic, they focus too strongly on the upfront costs of installing solar panels while at the same time discounting the long-run benefits from being able to generate their own electricity.

Federico Rostagno/Shutterstock

The result is major inefficiency as most homeowners end up forgoing solar panels.

Sunrun and other solar-panel installers have figured out a way to work with, rather than against, people's myopia. They do so by offering leasing and financing options that eliminate the need for consumers to pay for the upfront costs of installing a solar system. Instead, the installer pays for the upfront costs and then makes its money by splitting the resulting savings on monthly electricity bills with consumers.

This arrangement actually benefits from myopia because consumers get to focus on instant savings rather than initial costs. The same strategy can also be used to promote other investments that would normally be discouraged by myopia, such as installing energy-efficient furnaces, air conditioners, and appliances.

Time Inconsistency

Time inconsistency is the tendency to systematically misjudge in the present what you will want to do in the future. This misperception causes a disconnect between what you currently think you will want to do in the future and what you actually end up wanting to do when the future arrives. It is as though your present self does not understand what your future self will want.

Waking up early is a good example. At 8 p.m. on a Tuesday, you may really like the idea of waking up early the next morning so that you can exercise before starting the rest of your day. So you set your alarm 90 minutes earlier than you normally do. But when your alarm goes off the next morning, you throw the alarm across the room and go back to sleep. The switch in your preferences from the night before is the essence of time inconsistency. Your future self ends up disagreeing with your current self.

Self-Control Problems Time inconsistency is a major cause of **self-control problems.** To see why, imagine that before heading out to a restaurant with friends, you anticipate being perfectly content sticking to your favorite diet and, consequently, ordering only a single salad. But then, at the restaurant, you end up selecting more than just the one salad you originally planned to eat.

Because you were time inconsistent and didn't understand what your future self would want, you placed yourself in a situation where it was very difficult to stick to your diet. If you had been able to correctly predict what your future self would want, you might have decided to stay home rather than put yourself in temptation's way. Alternatively, you could have gone to the restaurant, but not before making your friends promise to prevent you from ordering dessert.

Time inconsistency makes it hard for many workers to save money. Before their paychecks arrive, they mistakenly assume that their future selves will want to save money as much as their current selves do. But once the money becomes available, their future selves end up wanting to spend everything and save nothing.

Fighting Self-Control Problems with Precommitments The key to fighting time inconsistency and self-control problems is to have a good understanding of what your future self is likely to want. You can then make **precommitments** to prevent your future self from doing much damage.

Automatic Payroll Deductions Precommitment strategies can help future selves save more money. Consider automatic payroll deductions. If a pilot named Blaire signs up for such a program, a fixed percentage of her income will be automatically deducted from each of her paychecks and deposited directly into her retirement savings account. Because that money never gets to her checking account, there is no way for Blaire's future self to fall prey to temptation and spend it. As the old saying goes, "Out of sight, out of mind."

Salary Smoothing School teachers and college professors often have the choice of having their annual salaries paid out over 9 larger monthly installments (to match the length of the school year) or 12 smaller monthly installments (to match the length of the calendar year). If we observe which option they actually choose, we find that the vast majority opt to have their salaries spread out over 12 months rather than 9 months.

They do so because they fear self-control problems. They are afraid that if they opt to be paid over 9 months, they won't have the self-control to save enough money during the 9-month period to last them through the three months of summer vacation when they aren't getting paid. To avoid that situation, they opt to spread out their salaries evenly over the entire calendar year. That precommitment ensures that their future selves are never given the chance to blow through all the money too quickly.

Early Withdrawal Penalties Sometimes, one cognitive bias can be used to offset another. Retirement accounts that have early-withdrawal penalties are a good example. They use loss aversion to offset time inconsistency and self-control problems.

In some cases, the penalties for early withdrawal are as high as 25 percent, meaning that if a saver wanted to withdraw $1,000 before reaching retirement, they would have to pay $250 (= 25 percent of $1,000) as a penalty. While that amount is substantial in itself, loss aversion makes it even more painful to contemplate. As a result, most people can't bring themselves to make an early withdrawal.

time inconsistency The human tendency to systematically misjudge at the present time what will actually end up being desired at a future time.

self-control problems Refers to the difficulty people have in sticking with earlier plans and avoiding suboptimal decisions when finally confronted with a particular decision-making situation. A manifestation of *time inconsistency* and potentially avoidable by using *precommitments*.

precommittments Actions taken ahead of time that make it difficult for the future self to avoid doing what the present self desires. See *time inconsistency* and *self-control problems*.

▸ Prospect theory models decision making by accounting for the fact that people's choices are affected by whether a possible outcome is perceived as a prospective gain or a prospective loss relative to the current status quo situation.

▸ Because our ancestors were focused on short-term survival, our brains suffer from myopia and are not good at dealing with decisions that involve the future.

▸ Precommitments can be used to compensate for time inconsistency and the self-control problems that arise when the future self doesn't want to do what the present self prefers.

Fairness and Self-Interest

>> **LO8.5** Define and give examples of fairness and its effect on economic behavior.

Neoclassical models assume that people are purely self-interested. They do so because "pure self-interest" seems like a good basis for predicting many economic behaviors, especially those happening in market situations where people are dealing mostly with strangers and are, consequently, unlikely to be particularly sentimental or charity-minded.

Adam Smith, the founder of modern economics, put this line of thinking into words. The most-quoted passage from *The Wealth of Nations* reads,

> It is not from the benevolence of the butcher, the brewer, or the baker that we expect our dinner, but from their regard to their own interest. We address ourselves not to their humanity but to their self-love, and never talk to them of our own necessities but of *their* advantages.

Smith, however, did not believe that people are *exclusively* focused on self-love and their own interests. He believed that we are also strongly motivated by charity, selflessness, and the desire to work for the common good. He expressed this view at length in his other influential book, *The Theory of Moral Sentiments*. The book's opening sentence reads:

> How selfish soever man may be supposed, there are evidently some principles in his nature which interest him in the fortune of others and render their happiness necessary to him though he derives nothing from it except the pleasure of seeing it.

Behavioral economists have discovered that this human propensity to care about others extends into every type of economic behavior. While self-interest is always present, most people care deeply about others. As a result, economic transactions are heavily influenced by moral and ethical factors.

Field Evidence for Fairness

Field evidence has helped behavioral economists identify the ethical and moral factors that appear to have the largest influence on economic behavior. Fairness is among the most important.

fairness A person's opinion as to whether a price, wage, or allocation is considered morally or ethically acceptable.

Fairness is a person's opinion as to whether a price, wage, or allocation is considered morally or ethically acceptable. Standards of fairness vary from person to person, and economists generally take no stand on what should be considered right or wrong. But fairness has been studied extensively because many common economic behaviors indicate that people care substantially about fairness and not just about maximizing what they can get for themselves.

Consider the following examples—none of which would be undertaken by a purely self-interested person.

- *Giving to Charity* Each year, U.S. charities receive over $300 billion of cash donations and 8 billion hours of free labor. These donations of time and money are inconsistent with the idea that people are interested only in themselves. In fact, many cash donations are anonymous, which suggests that many donors have extremely pure motives and are not donating just to make themselves look good.

- *Obeying the Law* In many countries, the large majority of citizens are law-abiding despite having many opportunities to break the law without getting caught. Similarly, the large majority of taxpayers complete their tax returns honestly despite having many opportunities to cut corners and hide income.

- *Purchasing "Fair-Trade" Products* Many consumers are willing to pay premium prices to purchase products that have been certified by the Fair Trade organization as having been produced by companies that meet high standards for workers' rights and environmental sustainability. These customers clearly care about more than just getting the lowest price.

Experimental Evidence for Fairness

Our understanding of fairness and how it affects economic transactions has been refined in recent decades by the results of experimental games specifically designed to test people's feelings about fairness.

The games' most important feature is that they are played for real money. If people were motivated only by self-interest, we would expect everyone playing the games to stick to selfish strategies that maximize their own winnings and to not care about what happens to anyone else.

As it turns out, however, most players actually demonstrate fairness and generosity when they play the games, often going out of their way to share with less-fortunate players even when they are under no compulsion to do so. That said, their kindness goes only so far. If other players are acting selfishly, the average person will withhold cooperation and may even retaliate.

The Dictator Game The strongest experimental evidence against the idea that people are interested only in what they can get for themselves comes from the **dictator game.**

The Rules In the game, two people interact anonymously. One of them is randomly designated as the "dictator." It is their job to split an amount of money determined (and funded) by the researcher running the game. A typical amount is $10.

The dictator can dictate whatever split he prefers. He can choose to keep all the money for himself. He can choose to give all the money to the other player. Or he can make some other split that sums to $10 (such as $8.67 for himself and $1.33 for the other person).

Because the game is fully anonymous, the dictator doesn't have to worry about retaliation by the other person. The dictator can get away with being as selfish as he wants.

How Players Behave What happens when people play the dictator game? After running the experiment many thousands of times in many different countries, experimenters have found that only one-third of dictators keep all of the money for themselves. The other two-thirds show substantial generosity, allocating an average of 42 percent of the money to the other player. In addition, 17 percent of all dictators split the money perfectly evenly, and a little over 5 percent of all dictators give the other player everything.

Implications for Fairness The way dictators behave suggests two important things about fairness.

First, the majority of people appear to be genuinely concerned about being fair to other people. They are willing to take less for themselves in order to ensure that the other player receives something, too. And they are willing to give substantially to the other player even though the game's guarantee of anonymity allows them to take everything for themselves without fear of retaliation.

Second, generosity varies widely. Between the third of dictators who keep everything for themselves and the 5 percent who give everything to the other person lies the large majority who allocate some but not all of the money to the other person. Within that group, every possible split of the money can be found. Thus behavioral economists believe that individuals vary widely in their beliefs about fairness. Some are perfectly selfish, others totally selfless. Most of us lie somewhere in between.

To better understand how those widely divergent beliefs affect behavior in more realistic situations, economists designed a slightly more complex game.

The Ultimatum Game Like the dictator game, the **ultimatum game** involves two players anonymously splitting an amount of money. But there is no longer a dictator who arbitrarily decides how the money is split. Instead, both players need to agree on any proposed split if it is to take place.

That difference in the rules ensures that the ultimatum game mirrors the many real-world situations in which a project or proposal must obtain the consent and support of all parties before it is undertaken. For example, consider a business transaction between a potential seller and a potential buyer. Even if there are substantial net benefits available to both parties, no transaction will take place unless the buyer and seller can agree on a price.

dictator game A mutually anonymous behavioral economics game in which one person ("the dictator") unilaterally determines how to split an amount of money with the second player.

ultimatum game A *behavioral economics* game in which a mutually anonymous pair of players interact to determine how an amount of money is to be split. The first player suggests a division. The second player either accepts that proposal (in which case the split is made accordingly) or rejects it (in which case neither player gets anything).

The Rules As with the dictator game, the researcher puts up an amount of money to be split. This pot of money represents the net benefits that a buyer and a seller can split if they can agree on a price. It also represents the net benefits that will be forgone if the two parties cannot reach an agreement.

At the start of the experiment, one of the players is randomly assigned to be "the proposer" while the other player is randomly assigned to be "the responder." The game begins with the proposer proposing a split. As in the dictator game, the proposed split can range anywhere from suggesting that all the money go to the proposer to suggesting that all the money go to the responder.

The responder examines the proposed split and decides whether to accept it or reject it. If she accepts it, the split is made and the researcher immediately pays both players their shares. If the responder rejects the proposed split, neither player gets anything. The game simply ends and both players go home without receiving any money at all—a situation similar to when a business negotiation fails and all the potential benefits are forgone.

How Players Behave When the ultimatum game is played, two behaviors stand out.

First, the splits proposed by proposers in the ultimatum game are much more equal on average than the splits imposed by dictators in the dictator game. Whereas one-third of dictators keep all the money for themselves in the dictator game, almost none of the proposers suggest allocating all the money to themselves in the ultimatum game.

This large difference in behavior arises because the people acting as proposers in the ultimatum game realize that suggesting a highly unequal split is almost certain to greatly offend a responder's sense of fairness and lead to a rejection. In addition, most proposers also seem to understand that even moderately unfair offers may offend responders. As a result, the large majority of proposers suggest either perfectly equal splits or splits that are only slightly biased in the proposer's favor (such as 55 percent going to the proposer).

The second behavior that stands out is the decisiveness and emotional intensity with which responders reject offers that they consider unfair. In fact, rejection decisions are typically not made in a cool and calculating fashion. Responders do not calmly weigh the costs and benefits of accepting an unfair offer. Rather, they become angry and reject as a way of retaliating against the proposer. Their rejections are not just negative responses; they are acts of vengeance designed to hurt the proposer by denying the proposer money.

The full extent to which unfair offers make responders angry can be gauged by looking at high-stakes versions of the ultimatum game in which proposers and responders attempt to split hundreds or even thousands of dollars. You might think that when such large amounts of money are on the line, responders would be willing to accept unfair splits. But what we actually see is responders continuing to reject splits that they consider to be unfair. Their preference for fair treatment is so strong that they will reject unfair offers even when doing so means giving up a lot of money.

Implications for Market Efficiency The willingness of proposers to make more generous offers when faced with the threat of rejection can be viewed as the simplest expression of the invisible hand.

As we discussed in Chapter 2, the invisible hand is a metaphor that captures the tendency of the market system to align private interests with social interests and get people behaving in ways that benefit not only themselves but other people, too.

In the ultimatum game, the threat of rejection helps to align private interests with social interests. It does so by motivating selfish people to make substantially more generous offers. The result is a higher level of cooperation and utility as offers get accepted and players split the net benefits.

A similar process can be seen in the real world with respect to consumer sovereignty. As discussed in Chapter 2, consumer sovereignty is the right of consumers to spend their incomes on the goods and services that they are most willing and able to buy. Crucially, that right includes the ability to reject any product that does not meet the consumer's expectations.

That right of rejection leads to substantial social benefits because it motivates producers to produce products that will be acceptable to consumers. Over time, those efforts lead to increased allocative and productive efficiency as better products get produced at lower cost.

Save More Tomorrow!

How a Little Behavioral Economics Has Helped Millions of People Save Much More for Retirement.

Because our ancestors had much shorter life spans, it made sense for them to focus their attention on immediate problems rather than long-term problems. Before modern medicines and secure food supplies, human life expectancy was only 25 or 30 years, on average. Under such circumstances, only those people whose brains were laser-focused on getting through the next few months or years were likely to survive. Anyone thinking dreamily about what they might be doing in 30 or 40 years was less likely to survive and reproduce.

We are, consequently, the descendants of human beings who were laser-focused on solving near-term problems. We have inherited from them the tendency to ignore long-term issues in favor of focusing on short-term problems. That means that our brains are poorly designed for many modern issues, such as retirement planning, that involve making good choices today so as to have good outcomes many years or even decades into the future.

One depressing consequence of our inherited "short-termism" is that the average American has very little money saved up and available for emergencies. The Federal Reserve's annual *Report on the Economic Well Being of U.S. Households* consistently finds that nearly 40 percent of U.S. households cannot pay a $400 emergency expense without having to go into debt. That's another way of saying that nearly 40 percent of Americans have less than $400 of savings that they can tap into during a crisis.

Governments have been aware for at least several generations of how hard it is for people to save money when left to their own devices. One response was the implementation of government programs that make saving for retirement mandatory. Germany pioneered the first compulsory retirement savings system in 1889 and the U.S. federal government established our Social Security system in 1935, during the depths of the Great Depression, at a time when less than half of elderly Americans had enough income to be self-supporting.

The money saved into the Social Security system derives from a tax on wages. In most cases, the tax is split evenly between workers and employers, with each contributing 6.2 percent of a worker's earnings into the system. Some of that combined 12.4 percent goes toward paying the retirement benefits of current retirees, while the remainder flows into a government-run savings account that accumulates money to pay for the retirement benefits of current workers when they eventually retire.

Gustavo Frazao/Shutterstock

A key point is that Social Security was only designed to prevent older Americans from falling into abject poverty; it was not designed to provide a generous income in old age. In 2021, the average retiree received only about $1,500 per month in Social Security benefits. By comparison, the federal poverty line for a single person that year was an income of about $1,100 per month. Thus, there is a strong need to try to get people to save on their own for retirement, above and beyond what they are required to save into the Social Security system.

The government has tried to make that easy, with a wide variety of "tax-advantaged" savings accounts—including Individual Retirement Accounts (IRAs) and 401(k)'s—that allow workers to save and invest without paying any income taxes. Unfortunately, many workers fail to enroll in such programs because, to take advantage of them, they usually need to fill out a form with their employer. That small hurdle—of requesting a form, filling it out, and submitting it—turns out to be a substantial barrier for most workers, even when they want to save more.

To overcome that problem, behavioral economists Richard Thaler and Shlomo Benartzi convinced employers to make enrollment in such programs automatic, so that it was no longer necessary to request and submit a form to enroll. They also set things up so that saving more didn't trigger a sense of loss aversion. In particular, workers committed to having a portion of *future* raises directed towards retirement savings. That way, they would never have to cut back on any current spending in order to make room for additional savings.

That combination, known as the Save More Tomorrow program, has been shown to nearly quadruple employee savings rates, from 3.5 percent of income to 13.9 percent of income. It works well because it does not fight our tendency to focus on immediate problems. And it has been used widely, helping an estimated 16 million Americans save more for retirement.

▶ Behavioral economists have found extensive evidence that people care substantially about fairness.

▶ The dictator and ultimatum games show how people interact anonymously to split pots of money. In the dictator game, one person has total control over the split. In the ultimatum game, both players must agree to the split.

▶ Player behavior in the dictator game indicates that many people will share with others even when anonymity allows them to be perfectly selfish and keep all the money for themselves.

▶ Player behavior in the ultimatum game shows that people put a very high value on being treated fairly; they would rather reject an unfair offer and get nothing than accept it and get something.

QUICK REVIEW

8.3

Summary

LO8.1 Define behavioral economics and contrast it with neoclassical economics.

Traditional, neoclassical economics assumes that people are fully rational decision makers who will always learn from their mistakes as they try to maximize utility in any given situation. That assumption makes it impossible to account for the fact that people make systematic errors in which they regularly and repeatedly engage in behaviors that reduce their likelihood of achieving what they want.

Behavioral economics attempts to explain systematic errors by combining insights from economics, psychology, and biology that show that the human brain is prone to information processing errors.

Behavioral economics complements traditional neoclassical economics. The major insight of neoclassical economics is that incentives matter for behavior. The major insight of behavioral economics is that the brain makes systematic errors that must also be taken into account if we wish to make more accurate models of human behavior.

LO8.2 Discuss brain characteristics that affect human decision making.

Our brains make systematic errors for two reasons. First, evolution did not prepare our brains for dealing with many modern problems, especially those having to do with math, physics, and statistics. Second, our brains make mistakes when dealing with long-standing challenges (like interpreting visual information) because caloric limitations forced our brains to adopt low-energy heuristics (shortcuts) for completing mental tasks.

Heuristics sacrifice accuracy for speed and low energy usage. In most cases, the lack of accuracy is not important because the resulting errors are relatively minor. However, in some cases, those errors can generate cognitive biases that substantially impede rational decision making. Examples include confirmation bias, the overconfidence effect, the availability heuristic, and framing effects.

LO8.3 Show how prospect theory helps to explain many consumer behaviors.

Prospect theory attempts to accurately describe how people deal with risk and uncertainty. It models a person's preferences about uncertain outcomes as being based on whether those outcomes will cause gains or losses relative to the current status quo to which the person has become accustomed.

Prospect theory also accounts for loss aversion and the fact that most people perceive the pain of losing a given amount of money as being about 2.5 times more intense than the pleasure they would receive from an equal-sized gain.

LO8.4 Describe how time inconsistency and myopia cause suboptimal long-run decisions.

Myopia refers to the difficulty that most people have in conceptualizing the future. It causes people to put insufficient weight on future outcomes when making decisions.

Time inconsistency refers to the difficulty that most people have in correctly predicting what their future selves will want. It causes self-control problems because people are not able to correctly anticipate the degree to which their future selves may fall prey to various temptations.

People sometimes use precommitments to help them overcome self-control problems. Precommitments are courses of action that would be very difficult for the future self to alter. They consequently force the future self to do what the present self desires.

LO8.5 Define and give examples of fairness and its effect on economic behavior.

Behavioral economists have found extensive evidence that people are *not* purely self-interested. Rather, they care substantially about fairness and are often willing to give up money and other possessions to benefit other people.

The field evidence for fairness includes donations to charity, law-abiding behavior, and the willingness of many consumers to pay premium prices for Fair Trade products.

The dictator and ultimatum games provide experimental evidence on fairness by showing how pairs of people interact to split a pot of money that is provided by the researcher. In the dictator game, one person has total control over the split. In the ultimatum game, both players must agree to the split.

The dictator game shows that many people will share with others even when anonymity allows them to be perfectly selfish and keep all the money for themselves. The ultimatum game shows that people put a very high value on being treated fairly. They would rather reject an unfair offer and get nothing than accept it and get something.

Terms and Concepts

neoclassical economics	status quo	myopia
behavioral economics	loss aversion	time inconsistency
rational	prospect theory	self-control problems
systematic errors	anchoring	precommitments
heuristics	mental accounting	fairness
cognitive biases	endowment effect	dictator game
framing effects	status quo bias	ultimatum game

Discussion Questions

McGraw Hill connect

1. Suppose that Joe enjoys and repeatedly does stupid things like getting heavily into debt and insulting police officers. Do these actions constitute systematic errors? If he gets what he wants each time, would economists consider his stupid actions to be errors? Explain. **LO8.1**

2. Why do behavioral economists consider it helpful to base a theory of economic behavior on the actual mental processes that people use to make decisions? Why do neoclassical economists not care about whether a theory incorporates those actual mental processes? **LO8.1**

3. Economist Gerd Gigerenzer characterizes heuristics as "fast and frugal" ways of reaching decisions. Are there any costs to heuristics being "fast and frugal"? Explain and give an example of how a fast and frugal method for doing something in everyday life comes at some costs in terms of other attributes forgone. **LO8.2**

4. "There's no such thing as bad publicity." Evaluate this statement in terms of the recognition heuristic. **LO8.2**

5. For each of the following cognitive biases, provide at least one example from your own life. **LO8.2**
   a. Confirmation bias
   b. Self-serving bias
   c. The overconfidence effect
   d. Hindsight bias
   e. The availability heuristic
   f. The planning fallacy
   g. Framing effects

6. Suppose that Amir is loss averse. In the morning, Amir's stockbroker calls to tell him that he has gained $1,000 on his stock portfolio. In the evening, his accountant calls to tell him that he owes an extra $1,000 in taxes. At the end of the day, does Amir feel emotionally neutral because the dollar value of the gain in his stock portfolio exactly offsets the amount of extra taxes he has to pay? Explain. **LO8.3**

7. You just accepted a campus job helping to raise money for your school's athletic program. You are told to draft a fund-raising letter. The bottom of the letter asks recipients to write down a donation amount. If you want to raise as much money as possible, which would be preferable: mentioning that your school is ranked third in the nation in sports or that your school is better than 99 percent of other schools at sports? Explain. **LO8.3**

8. In the early 1990s, New Jersey and Pennsylvania reformed their automobile insurance systems so that citizens could opt for either a less-expensive policy that does not allow people to sue if they get into accidents or a more-expensive policy that does allow people to sue if they get into accidents. In New Jersey, the default option was the less-expensive policy that did not allow suing. In Pennsylvania, the default option was the more-expensive policy that did allow suing. Given those options, which policy do you think most people in New Jersey ended up with? What about in Pennsylvania? Explain. **LO8.3**

9. Give an example from your own life of a situation where you or someone you know uses a precommitment to overcome a self-control problem. Describe why the precommitment is useful and what it compensates for. Do not cite any precommitment strategy that was mentioned in this chapter. **LO8.4**

10. What would a behavioral economist say about each of the following statements? **LO8.5**
    a. "Nobody is truly charitable—people donate money just to show off."
    b. "America has a ruthless capitalist system. Considerations of fairness are totally ignored."
    c. "Selfish people always get ahead. It's like nobody even notices!"

11. Do people playing the dictator game show only self-interested behavior? How much divergence do we see in the splits that dictators give to the other player? **LO8.5**

12. Evaluate the following statement. "We shouldn't generalize from what people do in the ultimatum game because $10 is a trivial amount of money. When larger amounts of money are on the line, people will act differently." **LO8.5**

13. **LAST WORD** Why are modern human brains so focused on the short run as opposed to the long run? How generous are Social Security benefits for seniors? And how does Save More Tomorrow avoid loss aversion?

Review Questions

1. Which of the following are systematic errors? **LO8.1**
   a. A colorblind person repeatedly runs red lights.
   b. An accountant makes occasional math errors that are sometimes on the high side and sometimes on the low side.
   c. Many people see faces in clouds.
   d. Miranda pays good money for a nice-looking apple that turns out to be rotten inside.
   e. Elvis always wants to save more but then spends his whole paycheck, month after month.

2. Identify each statement as being associated with neoclassical economics or behavioral economics. **LO8.1**
   a. People are eager and accurate calculators.
   b. People are often selfless and generous.
   c. People have no trouble resisting temptation.
   d. People place insufficient weight on future events and outcomes.
   e. People treat others well only if doing so will get them something they want.

3. Label each of the following behaviors with the correct bias or heuristic. **LO8.2**
   a. Your uncle says that he knew all along that the stock market was going to crash in 2020.
   b. When Fred does well at work, he credits his intelligence. When anything goes wrong, he blames his secretary.
   c. Ellen thinks that being struck dead by lightning is much more likely than dying from an accidental fall at home.
   d. The sales of a TV that is priced at $999 rise after another very similar TV priced at $1,300 is placed next to it at the store.
   e. The sales of a brand of toothpaste rise after new TV commercials announce that the brand "is preferred by 4 out of 5 dentists."

4. Erik wants to save more, but whenever a paycheck arrives, he ends up spending everything. One way to help him overcome this tendency would be to: **LO8.4**
   a. teach him about time inconsistency.
   b. tell him that self-control problems are common.
   c. have him engage in precommitments that will make it difficult for his future self to overspend.

5. Many proposers in the ultimatum game offer half to the responder with whom they are paired. This behavior could be motivated by (select all that might apply): **LO8.5**
   a. fear that a fair-minded responder might reject an unequal split.
   b. a desire to induce the responder to reject the offer.
   c. a strong sense of fairness in the proposers.
   d. unrestrained greed in the proposers.

Problems

1. One type of systematic error arises because people tend to think of benefits in percentage terms rather than in absolute dollar amounts. For example, Samir is willing to drive 20 minutes out of his way to save $4 on a grocery item that costs $10 at a local market. But he is unwilling to drive 20 minutes out of his way to save $10 on a laptop that costs $400 at a local store. In percentage terms, how big are the savings on the grocery item? On the laptop? In absolute terms, how big are the savings on the grocery item? On the laptop? If Samir is willing to sacrifice 20 minutes of his time to save $4 in one case, shouldn't he also be willing to sacrifice 20 minutes of his time to save $10 in the other situation? Explain. **LO8.2**

2. Anne is a bargain-minded shopper. Normally, her favorite toothpaste costs the same at both of her local supermarkets, but the stores are having competing sales this week. At one store, there is a bonus offer: Buy 2, get 1 free. At the other store, toothpaste is being sold at 40 percent off. Anne instantly opts for the first offer. Was that really the less-expensive choice? (Hint: Is "buy 2, get 1 free" the same as 50 percent off?) **LO8.2**

3. The coffee shop near the local college normally sells 10 ounces of roasted coffee beans for $10. But the shop sometimes puts the beans on sale. During some sales, it offers "33 percent more for free." Other weeks, it takes "33 percent off" the normal price. After reviewing the shop's sales data, the shop's manager finds that "33 percent more for free" sells a lot more coffee than "33 percent off." Are the store's customers making a systematic error? Which is actually the better deal? Explain. **LO8.2**

4. Angela owes $500 on a credit card and $2,000 on a student loan. The credit card has a 15 percent annual interest rate, and the student loan has a 7 percent annual interest rate. Her sense of loss aversion makes her more anxious about the larger loan. As a result, she plans to pay it off first—despite the fact that professional financial advisors almost always tell people to pay off their highest-interest-rate loans first. Suppose Angela has only $500 at the present time to help pay down her loans and that this $500 will be the only money she will have for making debt payments for at least the next year. If she uses the $500 to pay off the credit card, how much interest will accrue on the other loan over the coming year? On the other hand, if she uses the $500 to pay off part of the student loan, how much in combined interest will she owe over the next year on the remaining balances on the two loans? By how many dollars will she be better off if she uses the $500 to completely pay off the credit card rather than partly paying down the student loan? (Hint: If you owe X dollars at an annual interest rate of r percent, your annual interest payment will be X × r, where the interest rate r is expressed as a decimal.) **LO8.3**

5. **ADVANCED ANALYSIS** In the algebraic version of prospect theory, the variable x represents gains and losses. A positive value for x is a gain, a negative value for x is a loss, and a zero value for x represents remaining at the status quo. The so-called value function, v(x), has separate equations for translating gains and losses into, respectively, positive values (utility) and negative values (disutility). The gain or loss is typically measured in

dollars, and the resulting value (utility or disutility) is measured in utils. A typical person values gains ($x > 0$) using the function $v(x) = x^{0.88}$ and losses ($x < 0$) using the function $v(x) = -2.5*(-x)^{0.88}$. In addition, if the person stays at the status quo (where $x = 0$), then $v(x) = 0$. First use a scientific calculator (or a spreadsheet program) and the typical person's value functions for gains and losses to fill out the missing spaces in the following table. Then answer the questions that follow. **LO8.3**

Gain or Loss	Total Value of Gain or Loss	Marginal Value of Gain or Loss
−3	−6.57	———
−2	———	−2.10
−1	−2.50	−2.50
0	0.00	———
1	———	1.00
2	1.84	———
3	———	0.79

a. What is the total value of gaining $1? Of gaining $2?

b. What is the marginal value of going from $0 to gaining $1? Of going from gaining $1 to gaining $2? Does the typical person experience diminishing marginal utility from gains?

c. What is the marginal value of going from $0 to losing $1? Of going from losing $1 to losing $2? Does the typical person experience diminishing marginal disutility from losses?

d. Suppose that a person simultaneously gains $1 from one source and loses $1 from another source. What is the person's total utility after summing the values from these two events? Can a *combination* of events that leaves a person with the same wealth as they started with be perceived negatively? Does your answer shed light on status quo bias?

e. Suppose that an investor has one investment that gains $2 while another investment simultaneously loses $1. What is the person's total utility after summing the values from these two events? Will an investor need to have gains that are bigger than her losses just to feel as good as she would if she did not invest at all and simply remained at the status quo?

6. Ted has always had difficulty saving money, so on June 1, he enrolls in a Christmas savings program at his local bank and deposits $750. That money is totally locked away until December 1 so that Ted can be certain he will still have it once the holiday shopping season begins. Suppose that the annual interest rate is 10 percent on ordinary savings accounts (which allow depositors to withdraw their money at any time). How much interest is Ted giving up by precommitting his money into the Christmas savings account for six months instead of depositing it into an ordinary savings account? (Hint: If you invest X dollars at an annual interest rate of r percent, you will receive interest equal to X × r, where the interest rate r is expressed as a decimal.) **LO8.4**

Businesses and the Costs of Production

>> LEARNING OBJECTIVES

LO9.1   Explain why economic costs include both explicit and implicit costs.

LO9.2   Relate the law of diminishing returns to a firm's short-run production costs.

LO9.3   Distinguish between fixed and variable costs and among total, average, and marginal costs.

LO9.4   Use economies of scale to link a firm's size and its average costs in the long run.

LO9.5   Give business examples of short-run costs, economies of scale, and minimum efficient scale (MES).

Our attention now turns from consumer behavior to producer behavior. In market economies, a wide variety of businesses produce an even wider variety of goods and services. Each business requires economic resources to produce its products. In obtaining and using resources, a firm makes monetary payments to resource owners (for example, workers) and incurs opportunity costs when using resources it already owns (for example, entrepreneurial talent). Those payments and opportunity costs together make up the firm's *costs of production*, which we discuss in this chapter.

Economic Costs

Because resources are scarce, firms wanting a particular resource have to bid it away from other firms. For this reason, economists define an **economic cost** as the payment that must be made to obtain and retain the services of a resource. It is the income the firm must provide to resource suppliers to attract resources away from alternative uses.

This section explains how firms incorporate opportunity costs to calculate economic costs. If you need a refresher on opportunity costs, see Chapter 1.

Explicit and Implicit Costs

All resources have an opportunity cost. This is true both for the resources that a firm purchases from outsiders and for the resources that it already owns.

Consider a table-making firm that starts this month with $5,000 in cash. It also owns a small forest from which it gets the oak that it turns into tables.

Suppose that during the month the firm uses its entire $5,000 of cash to pay its workers. Clearly, the $5,000 purchase of labor comes at the opportunity cost of forgoing the best alternative uses of that money.

Less obvious is the opportunity cost of the oak that the firm grows. Suppose that one oak tree has a market value of $1,500, meaning that the table-making firm could sell it to outsiders for

>> **LO9.1** Explain why economic costs include both explicit and implicit costs.

economic cost A payment that must be made to obtain and retain the *services* of a *resource;* the income a *firm* must provide to a resource supplier to attract the resource away from an alternative use; equal to the quantity of other products that cannot be produced when resources are instead used to make a particular product.

$1,500. Using the oak to make tables therefore has an opportunity cost of $1,500. Choosing to convert one oak tree into tables means giving up the best alternatives that the firm could have purchased with $1,500.

Economists refer to these two types of economic costs as *explicit costs* and *implicit costs*:

explicit cost The monetary payment made by a *firm* to an outsider to obtain a *resource*.

- A firm's **explicit costs** are the monetary payments it makes to purchase resources from others. Because these costs involve an obvious cash transaction, they are called explicit costs. Explicit costs are *opportunity costs* because any amount of money that the firm uses to purchase a particular resource X is money that could have been used to purchase alternative resources. By purchasing X, the firm has to forego the best alternatives that could have been purchased with the same money.

implicit cost The monetary income a *firm* sacrifices when it uses a *resource* it owns rather than supplying the resource in the market; equal to what the resource could have earned in the best-paying alternative employment; includes a *normal profit*.

- A firm's **implicit costs** are the opportunity costs of using the resources that it already owns rather than selling those resources to outsiders for cash. Because these costs are present but not obvious, they are called implicit costs.

A firm's economic costs are the sum of its explicit costs and its implicit costs:

$$\text{Economic costs} = \text{Explicit costs} + \text{Implicit costs}$$

Accounting Profit and Normal Profit

Suppose that, after considering many potential business ventures, you decide to open a retail t-shirt shop. As explained in Chapter 2, you will be providing two different economic resources to your new enterprise: labor and entrepreneurial ability. Your labor includes the routine tasks that are necessary to run the business—things like answering customer e-mails, taking inventory, and sweeping the floor. Providing entrepreneurial ability includes the nonroutine tasks involved with organizing the business and directing its strategy—things like deciding on whether to include children's clothing in your product mix and how to brand your store.

Your first chance to provide entrepreneurial ability starts with the basic organizational structure of your business and its use of resources, including your labor input as an employee. You decide to work full time at your new business, so you quit your old job, which paid you $22,000 per year. You invest $20,000 of savings that has been earning $1,000 interest per year. You decide that your new firm will occupy a small retail space that you own and that you had previously rented out for $5,000 per year. Finally, you decide to hire one clerk, whom you will pay $18,000 per year.

After a year in business, you total up your accounts and find the following:

Total sales revenue		$120,000
Cost of t-shirts	$40,000	
Clerk's salary	18,000	
Utilities	5,000	
Total (explicit) costs		63,000
Accounting profit		57,000

accounting profit The *total revenue* of a *firm* less its *explicit costs*; the profit (or net income) that appears on accounting statements and that is reported to the government for tax purposes.

These numbers look very good. You are happy with your $57,000 **accounting profit,** the profit number that accountants calculate by subtracting total explicit costs from total sales revenue. This is the profit (or "net income") that appears on your accounting statement and that you report to the government for tax purposes.

But don't celebrate yet! Your $57,000 accounting profit overstates the economic success of your business because it ignores your implicit costs. Success is not defined as "total sales revenue that exceeds total explicit costs." Rather, the true measure of success is doing as well as you possibly can—that is, making more money in your new venture selling t-shirts than you could pursuing any other business venture.

To determine whether you are achieving that goal, you must take into account all of your opportunity costs—both your implicit costs as well as your explicit costs. To make these calculations, let's continue with our example.

By providing your own financial capital, retail space, and labor, you incurred three different implicit costs during the year: $1,000 of forgone interest, $5,000 of forgone rent, and $22,000 of forgone wages. There is also another implicit cost that you must account for: how much income you chose to forgo by applying your entrepreneurial abilities to your retail t-shirt venture rather than to other potential business ventures. But what dollar value should we place on the profits that you might have made if you had provided your entrepreneurial ability to another venture?

The answer is given by estimating a **normal profit,** the typical (or "normal") amount of accounting profit that you likely would have earned in other ventures. Let's assume that with your particular set of skills and talents, your entrepreneurial abilities would have yielded a normal profit of $5,000 in other potential ventures. Knowing that value, we can take all of your implicit costs into account and subtract them from your accounting profit:

Accounting profit		$57,000
Forgone interest	$ 1,000	
Forgone rent	5,000	
Forgone wages	22,000	
Forgone entrepreneurial income (normal profit)	5,000	
Total implicit costs		33,000
Economic profit		24,000

After subtracting your $33,000 of implicit costs from your accounting profit of $57,000, we are left with an economic profit of $24,000.

Economic Profit

Please distinguish clearly between accounting profit and economic profit. Accounting profit is the result of subtracting only explicit costs from revenue: *Accounting Profit = Revenue − Explicit Costs.* By contrast, **economic profit** accounts for all your economic costs—both explicit costs and implicit costs: *Economic Profit = Revenue − Explicit Costs − Implicit Costs.*

By subtracting *all* your economic costs from your revenue, you determine how your current business venture compares with your best alternative business venture. In our example, the fact that you are generating an economic profit of $24,000 means that you are making $24,000 more than you could expect to make in your best alternative business venture.

By contrast, suppose that your t-shirt business had done poorly, so that this year your firm generated an economic loss (a negative economic profit) of $8,000. In that case, you did $8,000 worse in your current venture than you could have done in your best alternative venture. As a result, you would wish to switch to that alternative and make yourself $8,000 better off.

From these examples, we see that there is an important behavioral threshold at $0 of economic profit. If a firm is breaking even (that is, earning exactly $0 of economic profit), then its entrepreneurs know they are doing exactly as well as they could expect to do in their best alternative business venture. They are earning enough to cover all their explicit and implicit costs, including the normal profit they could expect to earn in other business ventures. Thus, they have no incentive to change. By contrast, those achieving positive economic profits know they are doing better than they could in alternative ventures and will want to continue doing what they are doing or maybe even expand their business. Those with an economic loss know they can do better by switching to something else.

For these reasons, economists focus on economic profits rather than accounting profits. Simply put, economic profits allocate resources to their best use. Entrepreneurs running economic losses close their businesses, thereby liberating the land, labor, capital, and entrepreneurial ability that they had been using. These resources are freed up for use by firms that are generating positive economic profits or at least breaking even. Resources thus flow from producing goods and services with lower net benefits toward producing goods and services with higher net benefits. Allocative efficiency increases as profit signals lead firms to produce more of what consumers want the most.

Figure 9.1 summarizes the relationships among the various cost and profit concepts that we have just discussed. To test yourself, enter the cost numbers used in our example in the appropriate blocks.

normal profit The payment made by a *firm* to obtain and retain *entrepreneurial ability,* the minimum *income* that entrepreneurial ability must receive to induce *entrepreneurs* to provide their entrepreneurial ability to a firm; the level of *accounting profit* at which a firm generates an *economic profit* of zero after paying for entrepreneurial ability.

economic profit The return flowing to those who provide the economy with the *economic resource* of *entrepreneurial ability,* the *total revenue* of a *firm* less its *economic costs* (which include both *explicit costs* and *implicit costs*); also called "pure profit" and "above-normal profit."

FIGURE 9.1
Economic profit versus accounting profit.

Economic profit is equal to total revenue less economic costs. Economic costs are the sum of explicit and implicit costs and include a normal profit to the entrepreneur. Accounting profit is equal to total revenue less accounting (explicit) costs.

Short Run and Long Run

When the demand for a firm's product changes, the firm's profitability may depend on how quickly it can adjust its use of resources. It can easily and quickly adjust the quantities employed of hourly labor, raw materials, fuel, and power. It needs much more time to adjust its *plant capacity*—the size of the factory building, the amount of machinery and equipment, and other capital resources. In some heavy industries such as aircraft manufacturing, a firm may need several years to alter plant capacity. Because of these differences in adjustment time, economists find it useful to distinguish between two conceptual periods: the short run and the long run.

short run In *microeconomics*, a period of time in which producers are able to change the quantities of some but not all of the *resources* they employ; a period in which some resources (usually *plant*) are fixed and some are variable.

Short Run: Fixed Plant In microeconomics, the **short run** is a period too brief for a firm to alter its plant capacity, yet long enough to permit a change in the degree to which the plant's current capacity is used. The firm's plant capacity is fixed in the short run. However, the firm can vary its output by applying larger or smaller amounts of labor, materials, and other resources. That is, it can use its existing plant capacity more or less intensively in the short run.

long run In *microeconomics*, a period of time long enough to enable producers of a product to change the quantities of all the resources they employ, so that all resources and costs are variable and no resources or costs are fixed.

Long Run: Variable Plant In microeconomics, the **long run** is a period long enough for a firm to adjust the quantities of all the resources that it employs, including plant capacity. From the industry's viewpoint, the long run also includes enough time for existing firms to leave the industry or for new firms to enter the industry. While the short run is a "fixed-plant" period, the long run is a "variable-plant" period.

Illustrations If Boeing hires 100 extra workers for one of its commercial airline plants or adds an entire shift of workers, we are speaking of the short run. If it adds a new production facility and installs more equipment, we are referring to the long run. The first situation is a *short-run adjustment;* the second is a *long-run adjustment.*

The short run and the long run are conceptual periods rather than calendar time periods. In light-manufacturing industries, changes in plant capacity may be accomplished almost overnight. A small t-shirt manufacturer can increase its plant capacity in a matter of days by ordering and installing two or three new cutting tables and several extra sewing machines. But for heavy industry the long run is a different matter. Shell Oil may need several years to construct a new gasoline refinery.

QUICK REVIEW
9.1

▶ Explicit costs are money payments a firm makes to outside suppliers of resources; implicit costs are the opportunity costs associated with a firm's use of resources it already owns.

▶ Normal profit is the typical (normal) amount of accounting profit that an entrepreneur would likely earn in alternative business ventures; normal profit is the implicit cost of entrepreneurship.

▶ Accounting profit is total revenue minus explicit costs.

▶ Economic profit is total revenue minus explicit *and* implicit costs, including a normal profit.

▶ In the short run, a firm's plant capacity is fixed. In the long run, a firm can vary its plant size and firms can enter or leave the industry.

Short-Run Production Relationships

>> **LO9.2** Relate the law of diminishing returns to a firm's short-run production costs.

A firm's cost to produce a specific amount of output depends on both the prices and the quantities of the resources (inputs) needed to produce that output. Resource supply and demand determine resource prices. The technological aspects of production, specifically the relationships between inputs and output, determine the quantities of resources needed. Here we focus on the *labor*-output relationship, given a fixed plant capacity. But before examining that relationship, we need to define three terms:

total product (TP) The total output of a particular *good* or *service* produced by a *firm* (or a group of firms or the entire economy).

- **Total product (TP)** is the total quantity, or total output, of a particular good or service produced.
- **Marginal product (MP)** is the extra output or added product associated with adding one unit of a variable resource, in this case labor, to the production process.

$$\text{Marginal product} = \frac{\text{change in total product}}{\text{change in labor input}}$$

- **Average product (AP),** also called labor productivity, is output per unit of labor input.

$$\text{Average product} = \frac{\text{total product}}{\text{units of labor}}$$

In the short run, a firm can for a time increase its output by adding units of labor to its fixed plant. But by how much will output rise when it adds more labor? And why do we say "for a time"?

Law of Diminishing Returns

The answers are provided in general terms by the **law of diminishing returns.** This law assumes that technology is fixed and thus that production techniques do not change. Consequently, as successive units of a variable resource (say, labor) are added to a fixed resource (say, capital or land), beyond some point the extra (or marginal) product of each additional unit of the variable resource will decline. For example, if additional workers are hired to work with a constant amount of capital equipment, output will eventually rise by smaller and smaller amounts as more workers are added.

Rationale Suppose a farmer has a fixed resource—80 acres of land—planted in corn. If the farmer does not cultivate the corn fields (clear the weeds), the yield will be 40 bushels per acre. If she cultivates the land once, output may rise to 50 bushels per acre. A second cultivation may increase output to 57 bushels per acre, a third to 61, and a fourth to 63. Succeeding cultivations will add less and less to the land's yield. If this were not so, the world's needs for corn could be fulfilled by extremely intense cultivation of this single 80-acre plot of land. Indeed, if diminishing returns did not occur, the world could be fed out of a flowerpot.

The law of diminishing returns also holds true in nonagricultural industries. Consider a typical McDonald's restaurant, which houses a wide variety of specialized equipment for taking orders, processing payments, and making food. If the location hired just one or two workers, total output and productivity (output per worker) would be very low. Equipment would stand idle much of the time. In short, the restaurant would be understaffed, and production would be inefficient because there would be too much capital relative to the amount of labor.

The restaurant could eliminate those inefficiencies by hiring more workers. Then the equipment would be more fully used, and workers could specialize in doing a single job. As more workers are added, production will become more efficient, and the marginal product of each succeeding worker will rise.

But the rise will not continue indefinitely. Beyond a certain point, adding more workers will cause overcrowding. Workers will have to wait in line to use specific pieces of equipment, like the espresso machine or the vertical toaster. Total output will increase at a diminishing rate because, given the fixed size of the plant and equipment, each worker will have less capital equipment to work with as more labor is hired. The marginal product of additional workers will decline because there will be more labor in proportion to the fixed amount of capital. Eventually, adding more workers would cause so much congestion that marginal product would become negative and total product would decline. At the extreme, the addition of more and more labor would exhaust all the standing room, and total product would fall to zero.

The law of diminishing returns assumes that all units of labor are of equal quality. Each successive worker is presumed to have the same innate ability, motor coordination, education, and work experience. Marginal product ultimately diminishes, but not because successive workers are less skilled or less energetic. It declines because the firm is using more workers relative to the amount of plant and equipment available.

Tabular Example Table 9.1 illustrates the law of diminishing returns. Column 2 shows the total product, or total output, resulting from combining each level of a variable input (labor) in column 1 with a fixed amount of capital.

marginal product (MP) The additional output produced when 1 additional unit of a resource is employed (the quantity of all other resources employed remaining constant); equal to the change in *total product* divided by the change in the quantity of a resource employed.

average product (AP) The total output produced per unit of a *resource* employed; equal to *total product* divided by the quantity of the employed resource.

law of diminishing returns The principle that as successive increments of a variable *resource* are added to a fixed resource, the *marginal product* of the variable resource will eventually decrease.

(1) Units of the Variable Resource (Labor)	(2) Total Product (TP)	(3) Marginal Product (MP), Change in (2)/ Change in (1)		(4) Average Product (AP), (2)/(1)
0	0			—
1	10	10	Increasing	10.00
2	25	15	marginal	12.50
3	45	20	returns	15.00
4	60	15	Diminishing	15.00
5	70	10	marginal	14.00
6	75	5	returns	12.50
7	75	0	Negative	10.71
8	70	−5	marginal returns	8.75

TABLE 9.1
Total, Marginal, and Average Product: The Law of Diminishing Returns

Column 3 shows the marginal product (MP), the change in total product associated with each additional unit of labor. With no labor input, total product is zero; a plant with no workers will produce no output. The first three units of labor generate increasing marginal returns, with marginal products of 10, 15, and 20 units, respectively. Beginning with the fourth unit of labor, marginal product diminishes continuously, becoming zero with the seventh unit of labor and negative with the eighth.

Average product, or output per labor unit, is shown in column 4. It is calculated by dividing total product (column 2) by the number of labor units needed to produce it (column 1). At 5 units of labor, for example, AP is 14 (= 70/5).

Graphical Portrayal Figure 9.2 (Key Graph) shows the diminishing-returns data in Table 9.1 graphically and further clarifies the relationships among total, marginal, and average products.

Note first in Figure 9.2a that total product, TP, goes through three phases: It rises initially at an increasing rate; then it increases, but at a diminishing rate; finally, after reaching a maximum, it declines.

Marginal product—shown by the MP curve in Figure 9.2b—is the slope of the total-product curve. Marginal product measures the change in total product associated with each *additional* unit of labor. To make that clear graphically, we plot the marginal product for each additional unit of labor halfway between the related units of labor in Figure 9.2b.

The three phases of total product are also reflected in marginal product. Where total product is increasing at an increasing rate, marginal product is rising. Here, extra units of labor are adding larger and larger amounts to total product. Where total product is increasing but at a decreasing rate, marginal product is positive but falling. Each additional unit of labor adds less to total product than did the previous unit. When total product is at a maximum, marginal product is zero. When total product declines, marginal product becomes negative.

Average product, AP (Figure 9.2b), displays the same tendencies as marginal product. It increases, reaches a maximum, and then decreases as more and more units of labor are added to the fixed plant. But note the relationship between marginal product and average product: Where marginal product exceeds average product, average product rises. And where marginal product is less than average product, average product declines. Marginal product intersects average product where average product is at a maximum.

This relationship is a mathematical necessity. If you add a number to a total that is larger than the current average of that total, the average must rise. If you add a number to a total that is smaller than the current average of that total, the average must fall. You raise your average examination grade only when your score on an additional (marginal) examination is greater than the average of all your past scores. You lower your average when your grade on an additional exam is below your current average. In our production example, when the amount an extra worker adds to total product exceeds the average product of all workers currently employed, average product will rise. Conversely, when the amount an extra worker adds to total product is less than the current average product, average product will decrease.

The law of diminishing returns is embodied in the shapes of all three curves. But economists are most concerned with its effects on marginal product.

Short-Run Production Costs

>> **LO9.3** Distinguish between fixed and variable costs and among total, average, and marginal costs.

Production information such as that provided in Table 9.1 and Figures 9.2a and 9.2b must be coupled with resource prices to determine the total and per-unit costs of producing various levels of output. We know that in the short run, resources associated with the firm's plant are fixed. Other resources, however, are variable in the short run. As a result, short-run costs can be either fixed or variable.

Fixed, Variable, and Total Costs

Let's see what distinguishes fixed costs, variable costs, and total costs from one another.

fixed cost Any cost that in total does not change when the *firm* changes its output.

Fixed Costs **Fixed costs** do not vary with changes in output. Fixed costs are associated with the very existence of a firm's plant and therefore must be paid even if its output is zero. Rent payments, interest on a firm's debts, and insurance premiums are generally fixed costs; they do not change even if a firm produces more. In column 2 of Table 9.2 we assume that the firm's total fixed cost is $100. By definition, this fixed cost is incurred at all levels of output, including zero. The firm cannot avoid paying fixed costs in the short run.

.ıll KEY GRAPH

FIGURE 9.2 The law of diminishing returns.

(a) As a variable resource (labor) is added to fixed amounts of other resources (land or capital), the total product that results will eventually increase by diminishing amounts, reach a maximum, and then decline. (b) Marginal product is the change in total product associated with each new unit of labor. Average product is simply output per labor unit. Note that marginal product intersects average product at the maximum average product.

(a)
Total product

(b)
Marginal and average product

QUICK QUIZ FOR FIGURE 9.2

1. **Which of the following is an assumption underlying these figures?**
   a. Firms first hire "better" workers and then hire "poorer" workers.
   b. Capital and labor are both variable, but labor increases more rapidly than capital.
   c. Consumers will buy all the output (total product) produced.
   d. Workers are of equal quality.

2. **Marginal product is:**
   a. the change in total product divided by the change in the quantity of labor.
   b. total product divided by the quantity of labor.
   c. always positive.
   d. unrelated to total product.

3. **Marginal product in graph (b) is zero when:**
   a. average product in graph (b) stops rising.
   b. the slope of the marginal-product curve in graph (b) is zero.
   c. total product in graph (a) begins to rise at a diminishing rate.
   d. the slope of the total-product curve in graph (a) is zero.

4. **Average product in graph (b):**
   a. rises when it is less than marginal product.
   b. is the change in total product divided by the change in the quantity of labor.
   c. can never exceed marginal product.
   d. falls whenever total product in graph (a) rises at a diminishing rate.

Answers: 1. d; 2. a; 3. d; 4. a

Variable Costs Variable **costs** change with the level of output. They include payments for materials, fuel, power, transportation services, and most labor. In column 3 of Table 9.2 we find that total variable costs changes directly with output. But note that the increases in variable costs associated with additional one-unit increases in output are not equal. As production begins, variable costs will for a time increase by a decreasing amount; this is true through the fourth unit of output in Table 9.2. Beyond the fourth unit, however, variable costs rise by increasing amounts for each additional unit of output.

variable cost A cost that increases when the *firm* increases its output and decreases when the firm reduces its output.

TABLE 9.2 Total-, Average-, and Marginal-Cost Schedules for an Individual Firm in the Short Run

	Total-Cost Data			Average-Cost Data			Marginal Cost
(1) Total Product (Q)	**(2)** Total Fixed Cost (TFC)	**(3)** Total Variable Cost (TVC)	**(4)** Total Cost (TC) TC = TFC + TVC	**(5)** Average Fixed Cost (AFC) $AFC = \dfrac{TFC}{Q}$	**(6)** Average Variable Cost (AVC) $AVC = \dfrac{TVC}{Q}$	**(7)** Average Total Cost (ATC) $ATC = \dfrac{TC}{Q}$	**(8)** Marginal Cost (MC) $MC = \dfrac{\text{change in TC}}{\text{change in Q}}$
0	$100	$ 0	$ 100				
							$ 90
1	100	90	190	$100.00	$90.00	$190.00	
							80
2	100	170	270	50.00	85.00	135.00	
							70
3	100	240	340	33.33	80.00	113.33	
							60
4	100	300	400	25.00	75.00	100.00	
							70
5	100	370	470	20.00	74.00	94.00	
							80
6	100	450	550	16.67	75.00	91.67	
							90
7	100	540	640	14.29	77.14	91.43	
							110
8	100	650	750	12.50	81.25	93.75	
							130
9	100	780	880	11.11	86.67	97.78	
							150
10	100	930	1,030	10.00	93.00	103.00	

The reason lies in the shape of the marginal-product curve. At first, as in Figure 9.2b, marginal product is increasing, so smaller and smaller increases in the amounts of variable resources are needed to produce an additional unit of output. Hence, the variable cost of successive units of output decreases. But as diminishing returns are encountered, marginal product begins to decline, and larger and larger additional amounts of variable resources are needed to produce successive units of output. Total variable cost therefore increases by increasing amounts.

total cost The sum of *fixed cost* and *variable cost.*

Total Cost   Total cost is the sum of total fixed cost and total variable cost at each level of output:

$$TC = TFC + TVC$$

TC is shown in column 4 of Table 9.2. At zero units of output, total cost is equal to the firm's total fixed cost. Then for each unit of the 10 units of production, total cost increases by the same amount as total variable cost.

Figure 9.3 shows graphically the fixed-, variable-, and total-cost data given in Table 9.2. Observe that total variable cost, TVC, is measured vertically from the horizontal axis at each level of output. The amount of fixed cost, shown as TFC, is added vertically to the TVC curve to obtain the points on the total-cost curve TC.

The distinction between fixed and variable costs is significant to the business manager. Variable costs can be controlled or altered in the short run by changing production levels. Fixed costs are beyond the business manager's current control; they are incurred in the short run and must be paid regardless of output level.

FIGURE 9.3
Total cost is the sum of total fixed cost and total variable cost.

Total variable cost (TVC) changes with output. Total fixed cost (TFC) is independent of the level of output. The total cost (TC) at any output is the vertical sum of the total fixed cost and total variable cost at that output.

Per-Unit, or Average, Costs

Producers are certainly interested in their total costs, but they are equally concerned with per-unit, or average, costs. In particular, average-cost data are more meaningful for making comparisons with product price, which is always stated on a per-unit basis. Table 9.2 columns 5 to 7 show average fixed cost, average variable cost, and average total cost.

AFC Average fixed cost (AFC) for any output level is found by dividing total fixed cost (TFC) by that amount of output (Q). That is,

$$AFC = \frac{TFC}{Q}$$

Because the total fixed cost is, by definition, the same regardless of output, AFC must decline as output increases. As output rises, the total fixed cost is spread over a larger and larger output. When output is just 1 unit in Table 9.2, TFC and AFC are the same at $100. But at 2 units of output, the total fixed cost of $100 becomes $50 of AFC per unit; then it becomes $33.33 per unit as $100 is spread over 3 units, and $25 per unit when spread over 4 units. This process is sometimes called "spreading the overhead." Figure 9.4 shows that AFC graphs as a continuously declining curve as total output increases.

FIGURE 9.4
The average-cost curves.

AFC falls as a given amount of total fixed costs is apportioned over a larger and larger output. AVC initially falls because of increasing marginal returns but then rises because of diminishing marginal returns. Average total cost (ATC) is the vertical sum of average variable cost (AVC) and average fixed cost (AFC).

AVC Average variable cost (AVC) for any output level is calculated by dividing total variable cost (TVC) by that amount of output (Q):

$$AVC = \frac{TVC}{Q}$$

Due to increasing and then diminishing returns, AVC declines initially, reaches a minimum, and then increases again. A graph of AVC is a U-shaped or saucer-shaped curve, as Figure 9.4 shows.

Because total variable cost reflects the law of diminishing returns, so must AVC, which is derived from total variable cost. Because marginal returns increase initially, fewer and fewer additional variable resources are needed to produce each of the first four units of output. As a result, variable cost per unit declines. AVC hits a minimum with the fifth unit of output, and beyond that point AVC rises as diminishing returns require more and more variable resources to produce each additional unit of output.

That is, production is relatively inefficient—and therefore costly—at low levels of output. Because the firm's fixed plant is understaffed, average variable cost is relatively high. As output expands, however, greater specialization and better use of the firm's capital equipment yield more efficiency, and variable cost per unit of output declines. As still more variable resources are added, a point is reached where crowding causes diminishing returns to set in. Once diminishing returns start, each additional unit of input does not increase output by as much as preceding units did, which means that AVC eventually increases.

ATC Average total cost (ATC) for any output level Q is found by dividing total cost (TC) by that output (Q) or by adding AFC and AVC at that output:

$$ATC = \frac{TC}{Q} = \frac{TFC}{Q} + \frac{TVC}{Q} = AFC + AVC$$

Graphically, ATC can be found by adding vertically the AFC and AVC curves, as in Figure 9.4. Thus the vertical distance between the ATC and AVC curves measures AFC at any level of output.

Marginal Cost

One final and very crucial cost concept remains. **Marginal cost (MC)** is the extra, or additional, cost of producing one more unit of output. MC can be determined for each added unit of output by noting the change in total cost entailed by that unit's production:

$$MC = \frac{change\ in\ TC}{change\ in\ Q}$$

average fixed cost (AFC) A *firm's* total *fixed cost* divided by output (the quantity of product produced).

average variable cost (AVC) A firm's total *variable cost* divided by output (the quantity of product produced).

average total cost (ATC) A firm's *total cost* divided by output (the quantity of product produced); equal to *average fixed cost* plus *average variable cost*.

marginal cost (MC) The extra (additional) cost of producing 1 more unit of output; equal to the change in *total cost* divided by the change in output (and, in the short run, to the change in total *variable cost* divided by the change in output).

Calculations Table 9.2 allows us to calculate marginal cost easily. In column 4 of Table 9.2, production of the first unit of output increases total cost from $100 to $190. Therefore, the additional, or marginal, cost of that first unit is $90 (column 8). The marginal cost of the second unit is $80 (= $270 − $190); the MC of the third is $70 (= $340 − $270); and so forth. Column 9 shows the MC for each of the 10 units.

MC can also be calculated from the TVC column because the only difference between total cost and total variable cost is the constant amount of total fixed costs ($100). Thus, the change in total cost and the change in total variable cost associated with each additional unit of output are always the same.

Marginal Decisions The firm can control marginal costs directly and immediately. Specifically, MC designates all the cost incurred in producing the last unit of output. Thus, it also designates the cost that can be "saved" by not producing that last unit. Average-cost figures do not provide this information. For example, suppose the firm is undecided whether to produce 3 or 4 units of output. At 4 units, Table 9.2 indicates that ATC is $100. But the firm does not increase its total costs by $100 by producing the fourth unit, nor does it save $100 by not producing that unit. Rather, the change in costs associated with producing the 4th unit is just the $60 marginal cost, as column 8 in Table 9.2 reveals.

A firm's decisions regarding what output level to produce are typically marginal decisions—that is, decisions to produce a few more or a few less units. Marginal cost is the change in total cost that arises when one more or one fewer unit of output is produced.

The nearby Consider This story explains why firms should ignore *sunk costs* when making business decisions.

Graphical Portrayal Marginal cost is shown graphically in **Figure 9.5 (Key Graph)**. Marginal cost at first declines sharply, reaches a minimum, and then rises rather abruptly. The curve's shape reflects the fact that total variable cost and therefore total cost increase at first by decreasing amounts and then by increasing amounts (see columns 3 and 4, Table 9.2).

CONSIDER THIS . . .

Ignoring Sunk Costs

It is a deep-seated human tendency to drag past costs—so-called sunk costs—into marginal-benefit versus marginal-cost calculations. Doing so is known as the *sunk cost fallacy*.

As an example of this error, suppose a family that's on vacation stops at a roadside stand to buy some apples. After driving a bit, the family discovers that the apples are mushy and gross. Would it be logical for a family member to insist that everyone eat the apples "because we paid a premium price for them"?

Absolutely not. When you think through an upcoming decision like whether to eat the mushy fruit or not, you should consider only current and future costs, not past costs. Yes, the apples cost some money, but that money was spent in the past and the amount that was spent cannot be changed. As a result, that past amount remains the same no matter what you do today. In particular, it remains the same whether you decide to eat the apples or not. Thus, since that past spending is independent

Tom Grill/Photographer's Choice/
Getty Images

of the upcoming decision, it should be ignored when comparing the MB and MC of the upcoming decision and deciding what to do. Only costs and benefits that vary with the upcoming decision should be considered.

Let's apply this way of thinking to a business example. Suppose that a firm spends $1 million on R&D to bring out a new product, only to discover that the product sells very poorly. Should the firm continue to produce the product at a loss even when there is no realistic hope for future success? Obviously, it should not. In making this decision, the firm should realize that the amount it spent developing the product is irrelevant; it should stop production and cut its losses.

The emotional tendency that drives the sunk cost fallacy is the desire to "get one's money's worth" out of a past expenditure. But giving in to that emotion can lead to "throwing good money after bad." Instead, you should ignore all past costs and focus solely on those that depend on the decision at hand.

..ıl KEY GRAPH

FIGURE 9.5 The relationship of the marginal-cost curve to the average-total-cost and average-variable-cost curves.

The marginal-cost (MC) curve cuts through the average-total-cost (ATC) curve and the average-variable-cost (AVC) curve at their respective minimum points. When MC is below average total cost, ATC falls; when MC is above average total cost, ATC rises. Similarly, when MC is below average variable cost, AVC falls; when MC is above average variable cost, AVC rises.

QUICK QUIZ FOR FIGURE 9.5

1. **The marginal-cost curve first declines and then increases because of:**
   a. increasing, then diminishing, marginal utility.
   b. the decline in the gap between ATC and AVC as output expands.
   c. increasing, then diminishing, marginal returns.
   d. constant marginal revenue.

2. **The vertical distance between ATC and AVC measures:**
   a. marginal cost.
   b. total fixed cost.
   c. average fixed cost.
   d. economic profit per unit.

3. **ATC is:**
   a. AVC − AFC.
   b. MC + AVC.
   c. AFC + AVC.
   d. (AFC + AVC) + Q.

4. **When the marginal-cost curve lies:**
   a. above the ATC curve, ATC rises.
   b. above the AVC curve, ATC rises.
   c. below the AVC curve, total fixed cost increases.
   d. below the ATC curve, total fixed cost falls.

Answers: 1. c; 2. c; 3. c; 4. a

MC and Marginal Product The MC curve's shape is a consequence of the law of diminishing returns. Looking back at Table 9.1, we can see the relationship between marginal product and marginal cost. If all units of a variable resource (here labor) are hired at the same price, the marginal cost of each extra unit of output will fall as long as the marginal product of each additional worker is rising. Therefore, in Table 9.1, suppose that each worker can be hired for $10. Because the first worker's marginal product is 10 units of output, and hiring this worker increases the firm's costs by $10, the marginal cost of each of these 10 extra units of output is $1 (= $10/10 units). The second worker also increases costs by $10, but the marginal product is 15, so the marginal cost of each of these 15 extra units of output is $0.67 (= $10/15 units). Similarly, the MC of each of the 20 extra units of output contributed by the third worker is $.50 (= $10/20 units). To generalize, as long as marginal product is rising, marginal cost will fall.

With the fourth worker, diminishing returns set in and marginal cost begins to rise. For the fourth worker, marginal cost is $0.67 (= $10/15 units); for the fifth worker, MC is $1 ($10/10 units); for the sixth, MC is $2 (= $10/5 units); and so on.

If the price (cost) of the variable resource remains constant, increasing marginal returns will be reflected in a declining marginal cost, and diminishing marginal returns in a rising marginal cost. The MC curve is a mirror reflection of the marginal-product curve. As you can see in Figure 9.6, when marginal product is rising, marginal cost is necessarily falling. When marginal product is at its maximum, marginal cost is at its minimum. And when marginal product is falling, marginal cost is rising.

Relation of MC to AVC and ATC Figure 9.5 shows that the marginal-cost curve MC intersects both the AVC and the ATC curves at their respective minimum points. As noted earlier, this

FIGURE 9.6
The relationship between productivity curves and cost curves.

The marginal-cost (MC) curve and the average-variable-cost (AVC) curve in (b) are mirror images of the marginal-product (MP) and average-product (AP) curves in (a). Assuming that labor is the only variable input and that its price (the wage rate) is constant, then when MP is rising, MC is falling, and when MP is falling, MC is rising. Under the same assumptions, when AP is rising, AVC is falling, and when AP is falling, AVC is rising.

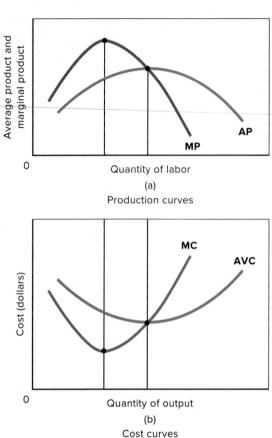

(a)
Production curves

(b)
Cost curves

marginal-average relationship is a mathematical necessity, which a simple illustration will reveal. Suppose an NBA basketball player has scored an average of 20 points a game over the first three games of the season. Now, whether his average rises or falls as a result of playing a fourth (marginal) game will depend on whether the additional points he scores in that game are fewer or more than his current 20-point average. If in the fourth game he scores fewer than 20 points, his average will fall. For example, if he scores 16 points in the fourth game, his total points will rise from 60 to 76 and his average will fall from 20 to 19 (= 76/4). Conversely, if in the fourth (marginal) game he scores more than 20 points, say, 24, his total will increase from 60 to 84 and his average will rise from 20 to 21 (= 84/4).

So it is with costs. When the additional amount (the marginal cost) added to total cost is less than the current average total cost, ATC will fall. Conversely, when the marginal cost exceeds ATC, ATC will rise. This means in Figure 9.5 that as long as MC lies below ATC, ATC will fall; and whenever MC lies above ATC, ATC will rise. Therefore, at the point of intersection where MC equals ATC, ATC has just ceased to fall but has not yet begun to rise. This, by definition, is the minimum point on the ATC curve. The marginal-cost curve intersects the average-total-cost curve at the ATC curve's minimum point.

Marginal cost can be defined as the addition either to total cost or to total variable cost resulting from one more unit of output; thus this same rationale explains why the MC curve also crosses the AVC curve at the AVC curve's minimum point. No such relationship exists between the MC curve and the average-fixed-cost curve because the two are not related; marginal cost includes only those costs that change with output, and fixed costs by definition are those that are independent of output.

Global Perspective 9.1 demonstrates that manufacturing costs vary substantially across countries. Germany's average manufacturing costs are a full 21 percent higher than those in the United States, while China's are 6 percent lower. But the United States and Germany are the world's second and fourth largest manufacturing countries, respectively, after first-place China. How is that possible given their much higher average production costs? *Specialization.* Higher cost producers can survive by specializing their manufacturing efforts on products with higher selling prices.

Shifts of the Cost Curves

Changes in either resource prices or technology will change costs and shift cost curves. If fixed costs double from $100 to $200, the AFC curve in Figure 9.5 will shift upward because, at each level of output, fixed costs are higher. The ATC curve will also move upward because AFC is a component of ATC. But the positions of the AVC and MC curves would be unaltered because their locations are based on the prices of variable rather than fixed resources. However, if the price (wage) of labor or some other variable input rises, AVC, ATC, and MC will rise, and those cost curves will all shift upward. The AFC curve will remain in place because fixed costs have not changed. And, of course, reductions in the prices of fixed or variable resources will reduce costs and shift the cost curves downward.

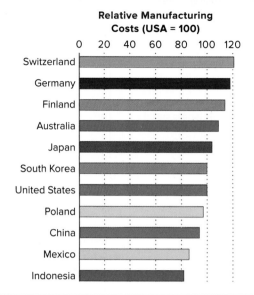

GLOBAL PERSPECTIVE 9.1

RELATIVE MANUFACTURING COSTS, SELECTED NATIONS

Total costs per unit of output vary substantially from country to country in the manufacturing sector, as you can see in this figure in which U.S. manufacturing costs are assigned an index value of 100 and average manufacturing costs in other countries are presented relative to that index value. Switzerland, for instance, has production costs that are on average about 20 percent higher than those found in the United States while Indonesia has production costs that are about 18 percent lower than those found in the United States.

Source: Boston Consulting Group.

The discovery of a more efficient technology will increase the productivity of all inputs. The cost figures in Table 9.2 would all be lower. To illustrate, if labor is the only variable input, if wages are $10 per hour, and if average product is 10 units, then AVC will be $1. But if a technological improvement increases the average product of labor to 20 units, then AVC will decline to $0.50. More generally, an upward shift in the productivity curves shown in Figure 9.6a means a downward shift in the cost curves shown in Figure 9.6b.

▶ According to the law of diminishing returns, beyond some point, output will increase by diminishing amounts as more units of a variable resource (labor) are added to a fixed resource (capital).

▶ In the short run, the total cost of any level of output is the sum of total fixed and total variable costs (TC = TFC + TVC).

▶ Average fixed, average variable, and average total costs are, respectively, the fixed, variable, and total costs per unit of output. Marginal cost is the extra cost of producing one more unit of output.

▶ Average fixed cost declines continuously as output increases. The AVC and ATC curves are U-shaped, reflecting increasing and then diminishing returns. The MC curve falls but then rises, intersecting both the AVC curve and the ATC curve at their respective minimum points.

QUICK REVIEW
9.2

Long-Run Production Costs

In the long run an industry and its individual firms can undertake all desired resource adjustments. That is, they can change the amount of all inputs used. The firm can alter its plant capacity; it can build a larger plant or revert to a smaller plant than that assumed in Table 9.2. The industry also can change its overall capacity; the long run allows sufficient time for new firms to enter or for existing firms to leave an industry.

We will discuss the impact of the entry and exit of firms to and from an industry in the next chapter; here we are concerned only with changes in plant capacity made by a single firm. Let's couch our analysis in terms of average total cost (ATC), making no distinction between fixed and variable costs because all resources, and therefore all costs, are variable in the long run.

>> **LO9.4** Use economies of scale to link a firm's size and its average costs in the long run.

Firm Size and Costs

Suppose a manufacturer with a single plant begins on a small scale and, as the result of successful operations, expands to successively larger plant sizes with larger output capacities. What happens to average total cost as this occurs? For a time, successively larger plants will reduce average total cost. However, eventually the building of a still larger plant will cause ATC to rise.

FIGURE 9.7
The long-run average-total-cost curve: five possible plant sizes.

The long-run average-total-cost curve is made up of segments of the short-run cost curves (ATC-1, ATC-2, etc.) of the various-size plants from which the firm might choose. Each point on the bumpy planning curve shows the lowest unit cost attainable for any output when the firm has had time to make all desired changes in its plant size.

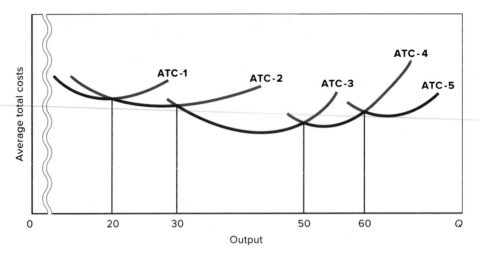

Figure 9.7 illustrates this situation for five possible plant sizes. ATC-1 is the short-run average-total-cost curve for the smallest of the five plants, and ATC-5, the curve for the largest. Constructing larger plants will lower the minimum average total costs through plant size 3. But then larger plants will mean higher minimum average total costs.

The Long-Run Cost Curve

The vertical lines perpendicular to the output axis in Figure 9.7 indicate the outputs at which the firm should change plant size to realize the lowest attainable average total costs of production. These are the outputs at which the per-unit costs for a larger plant drop below those for the current, smaller plant. For all outputs up to 20 units, the lowest average total costs are attainable with plant size 1. However, if the firm's volume of sales expands beyond 20 units but less than 30, it can achieve lower per-unit costs by constructing a larger plant, size 2. Although total cost will be higher at the expanded levels of production, the cost per unit of output will be less. For any output between 30 and 50 units, plant size 3 will yield the lowest average total costs. From 50 to 60 units of output, the firm must build the size-4 plant to achieve the lowest unit costs. Lowest average total costs for any output over 60 units require construction of the still larger plant, size 5.

Tracing these adjustments, we find that the long-run ATC curve for the enterprise is made up of segments of the short-run ATC curves for the various plant sizes that can be constructed. The long-run ATC curve shows the lowest average total cost at which *any output level* can be produced after the firm has had time to make all appropriate adjustments in its plant size. In Figure 9.7 the blue, bumpy curve is the firm's long-run ATC curve or, as it is often called, the firm's *planning curve.*

In most lines of production the choice of plant size is much wider than in our illustration. In many industries the number of possible plant sizes is virtually unlimited, and in time quite small changes in the volume of output will lead to changes in plant size. Graphically, this implies an unlimited number of short-run ATC curves, one for each output level, as suggested by **Figure 9.8 (Key Graph).** Then, rather than being made up of segments of short-run ATC curves as in Figure 9.7, the long-run ATC curve is made up of all the points of tangency of the unlimited number of short-run ATC curves from which the long-run ATC curve is derived. Therefore, the planning curve is smooth rather than bumpy. Each point on the planning curve tells us the minimum ATC of producing the corresponding level of output.

Economies and Diseconomies of Scale

We have assumed that, for a time, larger and larger plant sizes will lead to lower unit costs but that, beyond some point, successively larger plants will mean higher average total costs. That is, we have assumed the long-run ATC curve is U-shaped. But why should this be? It turns out that the U shape is caused by economies and diseconomies of large-scale production, as we explain in a moment. But before we do, please understand that the U shape of the long-run average-total-cost

..ıl KEY GRAPH

FIGURE 9.8 The long-run average-total-cost curve: unlimited number of plant sizes.

If the number of possible plant sizes is very large, the long-run average-total-cost curve approximates a smooth curve. Economies of scale, followed by diseconomies of scale, cause the curve to be U-shaped.

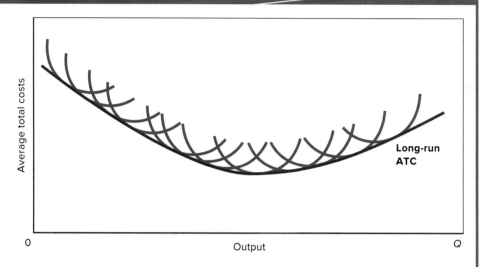

QUICK QUIZ FOR FIGURE 9.8

1. **The unlabeled red curves in this figure illustrate the:**
   a. long-run average-total-cost curves of various firms constituting the industry.
   b. short-run average-total-cost curves of various firms constituting the industry.
   c. short-run average-total-cost curves of various plant sizes available to a particular firm.
   d. short-run marginal-cost curves of various plant sizes available to a particular firm.

2. **The unlabeled red curves in this figure derive their shapes from:**
   a. decreasing, then increasing, short-run returns.
   b. increasing, then decreasing, short-run returns.
   c. economies, then diseconomies, of scale.
   d. diseconomies, then economies, of scale.

3. **The long-run ATC curve in this figure derives its shape from:**
   a. decreasing, then increasing, short-run returns.
   b. increasing, then decreasing, short-run returns.
   c. economies, then diseconomies, of scale.
   d. diseconomies, then economies, of scale.

4. **The long-run ATC curve is often called the firm's:**
   a. planning curve.
   b. capital-expansion path.
   c. total-product curve.
   d. production possibilities curve.

Answers: 1. c; 2. b; 3. c; 4. a

---

curve *cannot* be the result of rising resource prices or the law of diminishing returns. First, our discussion assumes that resource prices are constant. Second, the law of diminishing returns does not apply to production in the long run. This is true because the law of diminishing returns only deals with situations in which a productive resource or input is held constant. Under our definition of "long run," all resources and inputs are variable.

Economies of Scale **Economies of scale,** or economies of mass production, explain the downsloping part of the long-run ATC curve, as indicated in Figure 9.9, graphs (a), (b), and (c). As plant size increases, a number of factors will for a time lead to lower average costs of production.

Labor Specialization Increased specialization in the use of labor becomes more achievable as a plant increases in size. Hiring more workers means jobs can be divided and subdivided. Each worker may now have just one task to perform instead of five or six. Workers can work full time on the tasks for which they have special skills. By contrast, skilled machinists in a small plant may spend half their time performing unskilled tasks, leading to higher production costs.

Further, by working at fewer tasks, workers become even more proficient at those tasks. The jack-of-all-trades doing five or six jobs is not likely to be efficient in any of them. Concentrating on one task, the same worker may become highly efficient.

economies of scale The situation when a firm's *average total cost* of producing a product decreases in the *long run* as the firm increases the size of its *plant* (and, hence, its output).

FIGURE 9.9
Various possible long-run average-total-cost curves.

(a) Economies of scale are rather rapidly obtained as plant size rises, and diseconomies of scale are not encountered until a considerably large scale of output has been achieved. Thus, long-run average total cost is constant over a wide range of output. (b) Economies of scale are extensive, and diseconomies of scale occur only at very large outputs. Average total cost therefore declines over a broad range of output. (c) Economies of scale are exhausted quickly, followed immediately by diseconomies of scale. Minimum ATC thus occurs at a relatively low output.

(a)

(b)

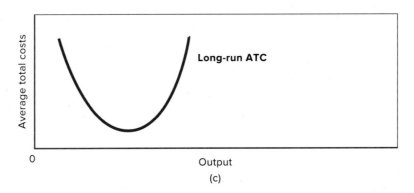

(c)

Finally, greater labor specialization eliminates the loss of time that occurs whenever a worker shifts from one task to another.

Managerial Specialization Large-scale production also means better use of, and greater specialization in, management. A supervisor who can handle 20 workers is underused in a small plant that employs only 10 people. The production staff could be doubled with no increase in supervisory costs.

Small firms cannot use management specialists to best advantage. For example, a marketing specialist working in a small plant may have to spend some of her time on functions outside of her area of expertise—for example, accounting, personnel, and finance. A larger scale of operations would allow her to supervise marketing full time, while other specialists perform other managerial functions. Greater productivity and efficiency, along with lower unit costs, would be the net result.

Efficient Capital Small firms often cannot afford the most efficient equipment. In many lines of production, such machinery is available only in very large and extremely expensive units. Furthermore, effective use of the equipment demands a high volume of production, and that again requires large-scale producers.

In the automobile industry the most efficient fabrication method employs robotics and elaborate assembly-line equipment. Effective use of this equipment demands an annual output of several hundred thousand automobiles. Only very large-scale producers can afford to purchase and use this equipment efficiently. The small-scale producer is faced with a dilemma. To fabricate automobiles using other equipment is inefficient and therefore more costly per unit. But so, too, is buying and underutilizing the equipment used by the large manufacturers. Because it cannot spread the high equipment cost over very many units of output, the small-scale producer will be stuck with high costs per unit of output.

Other Factors Many products entail design and development costs, as well as other "startup" costs, which must be incurred regardless of projected sales. These costs decline per unit as output is increased. Similarly, advertising costs decline per auto, per computer, per stereo system, and per box of detergent as more units are produced and sold. Also, the firm's production and marketing expertise usually rises as it produces and sells more output. This *learning by doing* is a further source of economies of scale.

All these factors contribute to lower average total costs for the firm that is able to expand its scale of operations. Where economies of scale are possible, an increase in all resources of, say, 10 percent will cause a more-than-proportionate increase in output of, say, 20 percent. The result will be a decline in ATC.

In many U.S. manufacturing industries, economies of scale have been of great significance. Firms that have expanded their scale of operations to obtain economies of mass production have survived and flourished. Those unable to expand have become relatively high-cost producers, doomed to struggle to survive.

Diseconomies of Scale In time the expansion of a firm may lead to diseconomies and therefore higher average total costs.

The main factor causing **diseconomies of scale** is the difficulty of efficiently controlling and coordinating a firm's operations as it becomes a large-scale producer. In a small plant a single key executive may make all the basic decisions for the plant's operation. Because of the firm's small size, the executive is close to the production line, understands the firm's operations, and can make efficient decisions because the small plant size requires only a relatively small amount of information to be examined and understood in order to optimize production.

This neat picture changes as a firm grows. One person cannot assemble, digest, and understand all the information essential to decision making on a large scale. Authority must be delegated to many vice presidents, second vice presidents, and so forth. This expansion of the management hierarchy leads to problems of communication and cooperation, bureaucratic red tape, and the possibility that decisions will not be coordinated. At the same time, each new manager must be paid a salary. Thus, declining efficiency in making and executing decisions goes hand-in-hand with rising average total costs as bureaucracy expands beyond a certain point.

Also, in massive production facilities workers may feel alienated from their employers and care little about working efficiently. Opportunities to shirk, by avoiding work in favor of on-the-job leisure, may be greater in large plants than in small ones. Countering worker alienation and shirking may require additional worker supervision, which increases costs.

Where diseconomies of scale are operative, an increase in all inputs of, say, 10 percent will cause a less-than-proportionate increase in output of, say, 5 percent. As a consequence, ATC will increase. The rising portion of the long-run cost curves in Figure 9.9 illustrates diseconomies of scale.

Constant Returns to Scale In some industries a rather wide range of output may exist between the output at which economies of scale end and the output at which diseconomies of scale begin. That is, there may be a range of **constant returns to scale** over which long-run average cost does not change. The $q_1 q_2$ output range of Figure 9.9a is an example. Here a given percentage increase in all inputs of, say, 10 percent will cause a proportionate 10 percent increase in output. Thus, in this range, ATC is constant.

Minimum Efficient Scale and Industry Structure

Economies and diseconomies of scale are an important determinant of an industry's structure. Here we introduce the concept of **minimum efficient scale (MES)**, which is the lowest level of

diseconomies of scale The situation when a firm's *average total cost* of producing a product increases in the *long run* as the firm increases the size of its *plant* (and, hence, its output).

constant returns to scale The situation when a firm's *average total cost* of producing a product remains unchanged in the *long run* as the firm varies the size of its *plant* (and, hence, its output).

minimum efficient scale (MES) The lowest level of output at which a *firm* can minimize long-run *average total cost*.

output at which a firm can minimize long-run average costs. In Figure 9.9a that level occurs at q_1 units of output. Because of the extended range of constant returns to scale, firms producing substantially greater outputs could also realize the minimum attainable long-run average costs. Specifically, firms within the q_1 to q_2 range would be equally efficient. So we would not be surprised to find an industry with such cost conditions to be populated by firms of quite different sizes. The apparel, food processing, furniture, advertising, snowboard, banking, and small-appliance industries are examples. With an extended range of constant returns to scale, relatively large and relatively small firms can coexist in an industry and be equally successful.

Compare this with Figure 9.9b, where economies of scale continue over a wide range of outputs and diseconomies of scale appear only at very high levels of output. This pattern of declining long-run average total cost occurs in the automobile, aluminum, steel, and other heavy industries. The same pattern holds in several of the new industries related to information technology, for example, computer microchips, operating system software, and social networking apps.

Given consumer demand, efficient production will be achieved with a few large-scale producers. Small firms cannot realize the minimum efficient scale and will not be able to compete. In the extreme, economies of scale might extend beyond the market's size, resulting in what is termed **natural monopoly,** a relatively rare market situation in which average total cost is minimized when only one firm produces the particular good or service.

Where economies of scale are few and diseconomies come into play quickly, the minimum efficient size occurs at a low level of output, as shown in Figure 9.9c. In such industries a particular level of consumer demand will support a large number of relatively small producers. Many retail trades and some types of farming fall into this category. So do certain kinds of light manufacturing such as the baking, clothing, and shoe industries. Fairly small firms are more efficient than larger-scale producers in such industries.

Our point here is that the shape of the long-run average-total-cost curve is determined by technology and the economies and diseconomies of scale that result. The shape of the long-run ATC curve, in turn, can be significant in determining whether an industry is populated by a relatively large number of small firms or is dominated by a few large producers, or lies somewhere in between.

But we must be cautious in our assessment because industry structure does not depend on cost conditions alone. Government policies, the geographic size of markets, managerial strategy and skill, and other factors, such as demand being influenced by *network effects,* must be considered in explaining the structure of a particular industry.

natural monopoly An *industry* in which *economies of scale* are so great that a single *firm* can produce the industry's product at a lower average total cost than would be possible if more than one firm produced the product.

QUICK REVIEW

9.3

▶ Most firms have U-shaped long-run average-total-cost curves, reflecting economies and then diseconomies of scale.

▶ Economies of scale are the consequence of greater specialization of labor and management, more efficient capital equipment, and the spreading of startup costs over more units of output.

▶ Diseconomies of scale are caused by the problems of coordination and communication that arise in large firms.

▶ Minimum efficient scale (MES) is the lowest level of output at which a firm's long-run average total cost is at a minimum.

Applications and Illustrations

>> **LO9.5** Give business examples of short-run costs, economies of scale, and minimum efficient scale (MES).

The business world offers many examples relating to short-run costs, economies of scale, and minimum efficient scale (MES). Here are just a few.

Rising Gasoline Prices

Changes in supply and demand often lead to rapid increases in the price of gasoline. Because gasoline powers the vast majority of all motor vehicles, including those used by businesses, increases in gasoline prices lead to increases in firms' short-run variable costs, marginal costs, and average total costs. In terms of our analysis, their AVC, MC, and ATC curves all shift upward.

The extent of these upward shifts depends upon the relative importance of gasoline as a variable input in a firm's production processes. Package-delivery companies like FedEx that use a lot of gasoline-powered vehicles will see substantial upward shifts while tech companies like YouTube and Microsoft that mainly deliver their products over the Internet may see only small upward shifts.

The Weber Metals Stamping Machine

In 2018, Weber Metals, a U.S. firm located in southern California, introduced a 140-foot-tall metal-stamping machine that is the size of small skyscraper and weighs as much as 50 locomotives. This $180 million machine—which presses raw sheets of aluminum and titanium into large aerospace components, such as wings and rocket tubes—enables airplane manufacturers and space-launch companies like Boeing and Northrup-Grumman to make crucial parts at lower costs as compared with older stamping presses.

This single giant machine can make tens of thousands of components per year. But to achieve the cost savings that are possible with this mega machine, the aerospace manufacturers that place orders with Weber Metals must have sufficient production to use all of that capacity. So only large firms with high output levels can use this cost-saving piece of equipment to achieve economies of scale.

Successful Startup Firms

The U.S. economy has greatly benefited over the past several decades from the explosive growth of scores of highly successful startup firms. These firms typically reduce their costs by moving from higher to lower points on their short-run cost curves and by downward and to-the-right shifts of their short-run cost curves via economies of scale. Startup firms that have achieved economies of scale include Intel (microchips), Starbucks (coffee), Microsoft (software), Instagram (social media), Amazon (online shopping), and Cisco Systems (Internet switching).

A major source of lower average total costs for rapidly growing firms is the ability to spread huge product development and advertising costs over a larger number of units of output. These firms also achieve economies of scale from learning by doing and through increased specialization of labor, management, and equipment. After starting up, such firms experience declining average total costs over the years or even decades that it takes them to eventually reach their MES.

Aircraft and Concrete Plants

Why are there only three plants in the United States (all operated by Boeing) that produce large commercial aircraft but thousands of plants (owned by hundreds of firms) that produce ready-mix concrete? The answer is that MES is radically different in the two industries. First, economies of scale are extensive in assembling large commercial aircraft, but only very modest in mixing concrete. Manufacturing airplanes is a complex process that requires huge facilities, thousands of workers, and very expensive, specialized machinery and software. Economies of scale extend to huge plant sizes. But mixing Portland cement, sand, gravel, and water to produce concrete requires only a handful of workers and relatively inexpensive equipment. Economies of scale are exhausted at a relatively small size.

The differing MESs also derive from vast differences in the size of geographic markets. The market for commercial airplanes is global, and aircraft manufacturers can deliver new airplanes anywhere in the world by flying them there. In contrast, the geographic market for a concrete plant is roughly the 50-mile radius within which the concrete can be delivered before it "sets up." So thousands of small concrete plants locate close to their customers in hundreds of small and large cities in the United States.

CHAPTER 8

LAST WORD

Living on a Cloud

Cloud Computing Has Allowed Even Small Firms to Enjoy the Benefits of Digital Economies of Scale.

The modern business world is highly computational as well as highly competitive. Massive computing power is required by major media firms like Netflix and Disney+ to stream video simultaneously to tens of millions of users. So, too, do major retail sites like eBay and Etsy require vast computing capacity to match buyers with sellers and keep track of payments, shipping details, and returns. And social media giants like Instagram, Facebook, and TikTok need enough computational power to facilitate literally billions of people interacting simultaneously all around the world.

Smaller businesses also need quite a bit of computing power for tasks as (relatively) simple as running payroll and keeping track of inventory. But until about 10 years ago, most businesses were forced to obtain the computing power that they needed by buying and operating their own computers. For such firms, the position and shape of their U-shaped average total cost curves were substantially affected by how much computing power they owned at any point in time and thus how quickly they would hit output levels associated with diseconomies of scale and rising ATC per unit of output produced.

Such firms could, at least in theory, buy more computers so as to increase the range of output over which they enjoyed economies of scale. But purchasing additional computers is a substantial fixed cost that will only improve a firm's profits if those additional fixed costs can be spread over many units of output. That reality makes purchasing additional computers risky for firms that have to deal with uncertainty with respect to how many units of output they are likely to be able to sell in the future.

Consider, for instance, a growing web-design startup. Should it buy more computers now in order to deal with a possibly much higher volume of sales in six months or a year? If it buys those computers and that higher volume *does* arrive, then the larger range of output over which it has economies of scale will help it to increase profits. But if it buys the computers and higher sales are *not* achieved, its profits will fall as the additional fixed costs associated with purchasing those additional computers will have to be borne despite there being no increase in sales.

A similar problem faces businesses that must cope with strong seasonal variations in sales. A company that specializes in customized wooden Christmas gifts will need a lot of computing power during the holiday shopping season but very little the rest of the year. It is thus not totally obvious whether it would make sense for it to purchase additional computers to handle the Christmas rush since those computers would stand idle the rest of the year.

The rise of "cloud computing" has solved these sorts of problems because businesses no longer have to bear the fixed costs of

pp76/iStock/Getty Images

purchasing additional computing power. They can, instead, outsource their computational needs to firms like Amazon Web Services (AWS) and Microsoft Azure that rent computing capacity, as needed, to other firms.

To do this, AWS, Azure, and other cloud computing companies purchase and maintain massive numbers of computers, hooking them all together in giant "server farms" that can offer instant, on-demand computational power for projects small and large.

From the perspective of the businesses contracting with AWS and its competitors, the computing power that they are renting seems to be "somewhere else" and almost magically delivered over the Internet, as if it existed on a giant magical cloud in cyberspace; hence the term "cloud computing."

Even more magical is the fact that the ability to rent computing capacity "as needed" implies that—as far as computing costs are concerned—the businesses renting computing capacity end up enjoying constant, or even diminishing, returns to scale just as long as the cost per computation charged by the cloud computing companies remains constant or declines (which it has, thanks to intense competition).

Even better, there are massive long-run economies of scale available to firms like AWS and Azure that own and operate the giant server farms that provide the computing power behind could computing. Thus, the more that ordinary businesses stop buying their own computers and instead rent computing power from "the cloud," the lower the cost of cloud computing as AWS, Azure, and their competitors increase the size of their server farms and thereby achieve the lower ATC per unit that comes with continually declining long-run ATC curves.

So, here's to cloud computing and its ability to let businesses large and small enjoy computational economies of scale!

Summary

LO9.1 Explain why economic costs include both explicit and implicit costs.

The economic cost of using a resource to produce a good or service is the value or worth of that resource in its best alternative use. Economic costs include explicit costs, which flow to resources owned and supplied by others, and implicit costs, which are the opportunity costs of using resources that are already owned. One implicit cost is a normal profit for the entrepreneur. Economic profit occurs when total revenue exceeds total costs (= explicit costs + implicit costs, including a normal profit).

In the short run, a firm's plant capacity is fixed. The firm can use its plant more or less intensively by adding or subtracting units of variable resources, but it does not have sufficient time in the short run to alter plant size.

LO9.2 Relate the law of diminishing returns to a firm's short-run production costs.

The law of diminishing returns describes what happens to output as a fixed plant is used more intensively. As successive units of a variable resource such as labor are added to a fixed plant, beyond some point the marginal product associated with each additional unit of a resource declines.

LO9.3 Distinguish between fixed and variable costs and among total, average, and marginal costs.

Costs can be classified as variable or fixed in the short run. Fixed costs are independent of the level of output; variable costs vary with output. The total cost of any output is the sum of fixed and variable costs at that output.

Average fixed, average variable, and average total costs are, respectively, fixed, variable, and total costs per unit of output. Average fixed cost declines continuously as output increases because a fixed sum is being spread over a larger and larger number of units of production. A graph of average variable cost is U-shaped, reflecting increasing returns followed by diminishing returns. Average total cost is the sum of average fixed and average variable costs; its graph is also U-shaped.

Marginal cost is the extra, or additional, cost of producing one more unit of output. It is the amount by which total cost and total variable cost change when one more unit of output is produced. Graphically, the MC curve intersects the ATC and AVC curves at their minimum points.

Lower resource prices shift cost curves downward, as does technological progress. Higher input prices shift cost curves upward.

LO9.4 Use economies of scale to link a firm's size and its average costs in the long run.

The long run is a period of time sufficiently long for a firm to vary the amounts of all resources used, including plant size. In the long run, all costs are variable. The long-run ATC, or planning, curve is composed of segments of short-run ATC curves, and it represents the various plant sizes a firm can construct in the long run.

The long-run ATC curve is generally U-shaped. Economies of scale are first encountered as a small firm expands. Greater specialization in the use of labor and management, use of the most efficient equipment, and the spreading of startup costs across more units of output all contribute to economies of scale. As the firm continues to grow, it will encounter diseconomies of scale stemming from the managerial complexities that accompany large-scale production. The output ranges over which economies and diseconomies of scale occur in an industry are often an important determinant of that industry's structure.

A firm's minimum efficient scale (MES) is the lowest level of output at which it can minimize its long-run average cost. In some industries, MES occurs at such low levels of output that numerous firms can populate the industry. In other industries, MES occurs at such high output levels that only a few firms can exist in the long run.

LO9.5 Give business examples of short-run costs, economies of scale, and minimum efficient scale (MES).

Rising gasoline prices increase (shift upward) the AVC, ATC, and MC cost curves of firms like FedEx that use gasoline as an input in their production processes.

Starbucks, Instagram, and many other successful startup firms reduced costs and shifted their cost curves down and to the right by spreading product-development and advertising costs over larger numbers of units and by exploiting the economies of scale that can be generated through learning by doing and increased specialization of labor, management, and equipment.

Terms and Concepts

economic cost	total product (TP)	average variable cost (AVC)
explicit cost	marginal product (MP)	average total cost (ATC)
implicit cost	average product (AP)	marginal cost (MC)
accounting profit	law of diminishing returns	economies of scale
normal profit	fixed cost	diseconomies of scale
economic profit	variable cost	constant returns to scale
short run	total cost	minimum efficient scale (MES)
long run	average fixed cost (AFC)	natural monopoly

Discussion Questions

McGraw Hill connect

1. Distinguish between explicit and implicit costs, giving examples of each. What are some explicit and implicit costs of attending college? **LO9.1**

2. Distinguish among accounting profit, economic profit, and normal profit. Which type of profit determines how entrepreneurs allocate resources among different business ventures? Explain. **LO9.1**

3. Complete the following table by calculating marginal product and average product.

Inputs of Labor	Total Product	Marginal Product	Average Product
0	0	___	
1	15	___	___
2	34	___	___
3	51	___	___
4	65	___	___
5	74	___	___
6	80	___	___
7	83	___	___
8	82		___

Plot the total, marginal, and average products and explain in detail the relationship between each pair of curves. Explain why marginal product first rises, then declines, and ultimately becomes negative. What bearing does the law of diminishing returns have on short-run costs? Be specific. "When marginal product is rising, marginal cost is falling. And when marginal product is diminishing, marginal cost is rising." Illustrate and explain graphically. **LO9.2**

4. Why can the distinction between fixed costs and variable costs be made in the short run? Classify the following as fixed or variable costs: advertising expenditures, fuel, interest on company-issued bonds, shipping charges, payments for raw materials, real estate taxes, executive salaries, insurance premiums, wage payments, sales taxes, and rental payments on leased office machinery. "There are no fixed costs in the long run; all costs are variable." Explain. **LO9.3**

5. List several fixed and variable costs associated with owning and operating an automobile. Suppose you are considering whether to drive your car or fly 1,000 miles to Florida for spring break. Which costs—fixed, variable, or both—would you take into account in making your decision? Would any implicit costs be relevant? Explain. **LO9.3**

6. Use the concepts of economies and diseconomies of scale to explain the shape of a firm's long-run ATC curve. What does "minimum efficient scale" mean? What bearing can the shape of the long-run ATC curve have on the structure of an industry? **LO9.4**

7. **LAST WORD** What sorts of business risks does the availability of cloud computing help to mitigate or eliminate? Do firms that "rent" cloud computing services benefit from the long-run economies of scale available to the firms that offer cloud computing services?

Review Questions

McGraw Hill connect

1. Linda sells 100 bottles of homemade ketchup for $10 each. The cost of the ingredients, the bottles, and the labels was $700. In addition, it took her 20 hours to make the ketchup, and to do so she took time off from a job that paid her $20 per hour. Linda's accounting profit is _____ while her economic profit is _____ . **LO9.1**
   a. $700; $400
   b. $300; $100
   c. $300; negative $100
   d. $1,000; negative $1,100

2. Which of the following are short-run adjustments, and which are long-run adjustments? **LO9.1**
   a. Wendy's builds a new restaurant.
   b. SpaceX hires 200 more production workers.
   c. A farmer increases the amount of fertilizer used on his corn crop.
   d. An Amazon distribution center adds a third shift of workers.

3. A firm has a total fixed cost of $60 and total variable costs as indicated in the table. Complete the table and check your calculations by referring to problem 4 at the end of Chapter 10. **LO9.3**
   a. Graph total fixed cost, total variable cost, and total cost. Explain how the law of diminishing returns influences the shapes of the variable-cost and total-cost curves.
   b. Graph AFC, AVC, ATC, and MC. Explain the derivation and shape of each of these four curves and their relationships to one another. Specifically, explain in nontechnical terms why the MC curve intersects both the AVC and the ATC curves at their minimum points.
   c. Explain how the location of each curve graphed in question 3b would be altered if (1) total fixed cost is $100 rather than $60 and (2) total variable cost is $10 less at each level of output.

Total Product	Total Fixed Cost	Total Variable Cost	Total Cost	Average Fixed Cost	Average Variable Cost	Average Total Cost	Marginal Cost
0	$ ___	$ 0	$ ___			$ ___	
1	___	45	___	$ ___	$ ___	___	$ ___
2	___	85	___	___	___	___	___
3	___	120	___	___	___	___	___
4	___	150	___	___	___	___	___
5	___	185	___	___	___	___	___
6	___	225	___	___	___	___	___
7	___	270	___	___	___	___	___
8	___	325	___	___	___	___	___
9	___	390	___	___	___	___	___
10	___	465	___	___	___	___	___

4. When seven workers are employed at the same time at a local McDonald's, the restaurant's average product is 10 Big Macs per worker per hour. If adding an additional worker causes the average product to fall to 9.5 Big Macs per worker per hour, then we know that the eighth worker's marginal product must be: **LO9.2**
   a. less than 10 Big Macs per hour.
   b. equal to 10 Big Macs per hour.
   c. more than 10 Big Macs per hour.
   d. a negative number.
5. Indicate how each of the following would shift the (1) MC curve, (2) AVC curve, (3) AFC curve, and (4) ATC curve of a manufacturing firm. In each case specify the direction of the shift. **LO9.3**
   a. A reduction in business property taxes
   b. An increase in the nominal wages of production workers
   c. A decrease in the price of electricity
   d. An increase in insurance rates on plant and equipment
   e. An increase in transportation costs

6. True or False. The U shape of the long-run ATC curve is the result of diminishing returns. **LO9.4**
7. Suppose a firm has only three possible plant-size options, represented by the ATC curves shown in the figure. What plant size will the firm choose in producing (*a*) 50, (*b*) 130, (*c*) 160, and (*d*) 250 units of output? Draw the firm's long-run average-cost curve on the diagram and describe this curve. **LO9.4**

Problems

_{Mc Graw Hill} **connect**

1. Gomez runs a small pottery firm. She hires one helper at $12,000 per year, pays annual rent of $5,000 for her shop, and spends $20,000 per year on materials. She has $40,000 of her own funds invested in equipment (pottery wheels, kilns, and so forth) that could earn her $4,000 per year if alternatively invested. She has been offered $15,000 per year to work as a potter for a competitor. She estimates her entrepreneurial talents are worth $3,000 per year. Total annual revenue from pottery sales is $72,000. Calculate the accounting profit and the economic profit for Gomez's pottery firm. **LO9.1**
2. Imagine you have some workers and some handheld computers that you can use to take inventory at a warehouse. There are diminishing returns to taking inventory. If one worker uses one computer, he can inventory 100 items per hour. Two workers sharing a computer can together inventory 150 items per hour. Three workers sharing a computer can together inventory 160 items per hour. And four or more workers sharing a computer can together inventory fewer than 160 items per hour. Computers cost $100 each and you must pay each worker $25 per hour. If you assign one worker per computer, what is the cost of inventorying a single item? What is the cost if you assign two workers per computer? Three? How many workers per computer should you assign if you wish to minimize the cost of inventorying a single item? **LO9.2**

3. Let's explore how rising costs helped to kill off most printed newspapers after the Internet became available in the mid-1990s. Imagine that you are a newspaper publisher in the year 2004. You are in the middle of a one-year factory rental contract that requires you to pay $500,000 per month, and you have contractual salary obligations of $1 million per month that you can't get out of. You also have a marginal printing cost of $0.25 per paper as well as a marginal delivery cost of $0.10 per paper. If sales fall by 20 percent from 1 million newspapers per month to 800,000 newspapers per month, what happens to the AFC per newspaper, the MC per newspaper, and the minimum amount that you must charge to break even? **LO9.3**
4. There are economies of scale in ranching, especially with regard to fencing land. Suppose that barbed-wire fencing costs $10,000 per mile to set up. How much would it cost to fence a single property whose area is one square mile if that property also happens to be perfectly square, with sides that are each one mile long? How much would it cost to fence exactly four such properties, which together would contain four square miles of area? Now consider how much it would cost to fence in four square miles of ranch land if, instead, it comes as a single large square that is two miles long on each side. Which is more costly—fencing in the four, one-square-mile properties or the single four-square-mile property? **LO9.4**

CHAPTER

10

Pure Competition

LO10.1 List the names and give the main characteristics of the four basic market models.

LO10.2 List the conditions required for purely competitive markets.

LO10.3 Explain how purely competitive firms maximize profits or minimize losses.

LO10.4 Relate why the marginal-cost curve and supply curve of competitive firms are identical.

LO10.5 Demonstrate how industry entry and exit produce economic efficiency.

LO10.6 Describe the differences between constant-cost, increasing-cost, and decreasing-cost industries.

LO10.7 Show how long-run competitive equilibrium generates economic efficiency.

LO10.8 Discuss creative destruction and the profit incentives for innovation.

market structure The characteristics of an *industry* that define the likely behavior and performance of its *firms*. The primary characteristics are the number of firms in the industry, whether they are selling a *differentiated product*, the ease of entry, and how much control firms have over output prices. The most commonly discussed market structures are *pure competition, monopolistic competition, oligopoly, pure monopoly,* and *monopsony*.

In Chapter 6, we examined the relationship between product demand and total revenue, and in Chapter 9 we discussed the costs of production. Now we want to connect revenues and costs to see how a business decides what price to charge and how much output to produce. But a firm's decisions concerning price and production depend greatly on the character of the industry in which it operates. There is no "average" or "typical" industry. At one extreme is a single producer that dominates the market; at the other extreme are industries in which thousands of firms each produce a tiny fraction of market supply. Between these extremes lie many other industries that differ in the number of firms and in the ways in which those firms interact.

Since we cannot examine each industry individually, we will focus on four basic *models* of **market structure.** These four models will help you understand how price and output are determined in the many product (output) markets in the economy. They will also help you evaluate the efficiency or inefficiency of those markets, as well as the public policies (such as antitrust laws) that are intended to promote efficient market outcomes.

Four Market Models

>> **LO10.1** List the names and give the main characteristics of the four basic market models.

Economists group industries into four distinct market structures based on the number of firms in the industry, whether those firms produce a standardized or differentiated product, how easy it is for firms to enter the industry, and how much control firms have over the price of their product.

These are the four models:

- **Pure, or perfect, competition** involves a very large number of firms producing a standardized product (for example, a product like cotton, for which each producer's output is virtually identical to every other producer's output). New firms can enter or exit the industry very easily. Firms must accept the market price.

TABLE 10.1 Characteristics of the Four Basic Market Models

Characteristic	Pure Competition	Monopolistic Competition	Oligopoly	Pure Monopoly
		Market Model		
Number of firms	A very large number	Many	Few	One
Type of product	Standardized	Differentiated	Standardized or differentiated	Unique; no close substitutes
Control over price	None	Some, but within rather narrow limits	Limited by mutual interdependence; considerable with collusion	Considerable
Conditions of entry	Very easy, no obstacles	Relatively easy	Significant obstacles	Blocked
Nonprice competition	None	Considerable emphasis on advertising, brand names, trademarks	Typically a great deal, particularly with product differentiation	Mostly public relations advertising
Examples	Financial markets, agricultural products, raw materials	Restaurants, gyms, gas stations, retail trade, dresses, shoes	Airlines, automobiles, wireless service providers, space travel, waste disposal	Local utilities, patented pharmaceuticals

- **Pure monopoly** is a market structure in which one firm (for example, a local electric utility) is the sole seller of a product or service. Because the entry of additional firms is blocked, one firm constitutes the entire industry. The monopoly firm produces a single unique product and has full control over that product's price.

- **Monopolistic competition** is characterized by a relatively large number of sellers producing differentiated products (clothing, furniture, books). Present in this model is widespread *nonprice competition,* a selling strategy in which firms try to distinguish their products on attributes like design and workmanship (an approach called *product differentiation*). Both entry into and exit from monopolistically competitive industries is quite easy. Monopolistically competitive firms possess some, but not much, control over selling prices.

- **Oligopoly** involves only a few sellers of a standardized or differentiated product, so each firm is affected by its rivals' decisions and must take those decisions into account in determining its own price and output.

Table 10.1 summarizes the characteristics of the four models. In discussing these market models, we occasionally distinguish the characteristics of pure competition from those of the three other market structures, which we collectively designate as **imperfect competition.**

Pure Competition: Characteristics and Occurrence

Although pure competition is relatively rare in the real world, this market model is highly relevant to several industries. Specifically, we can learn much about the markets for agricultural goods, oil and natural gas, basic metals, and securities like stocks and bonds by studying the pure-competition model. Also, pure competition is a meaningful starting point for any discussion of price and output determination. Moreover, the operation of a purely competitive economy provides a standard, or norm, for evaluating the efficiency of the real-world economy.

Let's look more closely at the characteristics of pure competition:

- *Very large numbers* A basic feature of pure competition is the presence of a large number of independently acting sellers, often offering their products in large national or international markets. Examples include the markets for farm commodities, the stock market, and the foreign exchange market.

- *Standardized product* Purely competitive firms produce a standardized (identical or homogeneous) product. As long as the price is the same, consumers are indifferent about which seller to buy the product from. Buyers view the products of firms B, C, and D as perfect substitutes for the product of firm A. Because purely competitive firms sell standardized products, they make no attempt to differentiate or brand their products and do not engage in other forms of nonprice competition.

pure, or perfect, competition A *market structure* in which a very large number of *firms* sells a *standardized product,* into which entry is very easy, in which the individual seller has no control over the product *price,* and in which there is no nonprice competition; a market characterized by a very large number of buyers and sellers.

pure monopoly A *market structure* in which one *firm* sells a unique product, into which entry is blocked, in which the single firm has considerable control over product *price,* and in which *nonprice competition* may or may not be found.

>> LO10.2 List the conditions required for purely competitive markets.

monopolistic competition A *market structure* in which many *firms* sell a *differentiated product,* entry is relatively easy, each firm has some control over its product *price,* and there is considerable *nonprice competition.*

oligopoly A *market structure* in which a few *firms* sell either a *standardized* or *differentiated product,* into which entry is difficult, in which the firm has limited control over product *price* because of *mutual interdependence* (except when there is collusion among firms), and in which there is typically *nonprice competition.*

imperfect competition All *market structures* except *pure competition;* includes *monopoly, monopolistic competition,* and *oligopoly.*

>> LO10.3 Explain how purely competitive firms maximize profits of minimize losses.

price taker A seller (or buyer) that is unable to affect the *price* at which a product or *resource* sells by changing the amount it sells (or buys).

average revenue Total revenue from the sale of a product divided by the quantity of the product sold (demanded); equal to the *price* at which the product is sold when all units of the product are sold at the same price.

total revenue (TR) The total number of dollars received by a *firm* (or firms) from the sale of a product; equal to the total expenditures for the product produced by the firm (or firms); equal to the quantity sold (demanded) multiplied by the *price* at which it is sold.

marginal revenue The change in *total revenue* that results from the sale of 1 additional unit of a *firm's* product; equal to the change in total revenue divided by the change in the quantity of the product sold.

- *"Price takers"* In a purely competitive market, individual firms do not exert control over product price. Each firm produces such a small fraction of total output that increasing or decreasing its output will not perceptibly influence total supply or, therefore, product price. In other words, the competitive firm is a **price taker**: It cannot change the market price; it can only adjust to it. Thus the individual competitive producer is at the mercy of the market. Charging a price higher than the market price would be futile. Consumers will not buy from firm A at $2.05 when its 9,999 competitors are selling an identical product at $2 per unit. Conversely, because firm A can sell as much as it chooses at $2 per unit, it has no reason to charge a lower price, say, $1.95. Doing that would shrink its profit.

- *Free entry and exit* New firms can freely enter and existing firms can freely leave purely competitive industries. No significant legal, technological, financial, or other obstacles prohibit new firms from selling their output in a competitive market.

Demand as Seen by a Purely Competitive Seller

Let's now examine demand from a purely competitive seller's viewpoint to see how it affects revenue. This seller might be a wheat farmer, a stockbroker, a contract clothing manufacturer, or some other pure competitor. Because each purely competitive firm offers only a negligible fraction of total market supply, it must accept the price determined by the market. It is a price taker, not a pricemaker.

Perfectly Elastic Demand

The demand schedule faced by the *individual firm* in a purely competitive industry is perfectly elastic (horizontal) at the market price, as Figure 10.1 shows. According to column 1 of the table in Figure 10.1, the market price is $131. The firm represented cannot obtain a higher price by restricting its output, nor does it need to lower its price to increase its sales volume. Columns 1 and 2 show that the firm can produce and sell as many or as few units as it likes at the market price of $131.

We are *not* saying that *market* demand is perfectly elastic in a competitive market. Rather, market demand graphs as a downward sloping curve. An entire industry (all firms producing a particular product) *can* affect price by changing industry output. For example, all firms, acting independently but simultaneously, can increase price by reducing output. But the *individual* competitive firm cannot do that because its output is such a small fraction of its industry's total output. For the individual competitive firm, the market price is therefore a fixed value at which it can sell as many or as few units as it cares to. Graphically, then, the individual competitive firm's demand curve plots as a horizontal line such as *D* in Figure 10.1.

Average, Total, and Marginal Revenue

The firm's demand schedule is also its average-revenue schedule. To say that all buyers must pay $131 per unit is to say that the revenue per unit, or **average revenue** received by the seller, is $131. Price and average revenue are the same thing for a purely competitive firm.

The **total revenue** for each sales level is found by multiplying price by the corresponding quantity the firm can sell. (Column 1 multiplied by column 2 in the table in Figure 10.1 yields column 3.) In this case, total revenue increases by a constant amount, $131, for each additional unit of sales. Each unit sold adds exactly its constant price—no more and no less—to total revenue.

When a firm is pondering a change in its output, it will consider how its total revenue will change. **Marginal revenue (MR)** is the change in total revenue (or the extra revenue) that results from selling one more unit of output. In column 3 of the table in Figure 10.1, total revenue is zero when zero units are sold. The first unit of output sold increases total revenue from zero to $131, so marginal revenue for that unit is $131. The second unit sold increases total revenue from $131 to $262, and marginal revenue is again $131. Note in column 4 that marginal revenue is a constant $131. *In pure competition, marginal revenue and price are equal.*

Figure 10.1 shows the purely competitive firm's TR, demand, MR, and AR curves. Total revenue (TR) is a straight line that slopes upward to the right. Its slope is constant because each extra unit of sales increases TR by $131. The demand curve (*D*) is horizontal, indicating perfect price elasticity. The MR curve coincides with the demand curve because the product price (and hence MR) is constant. The AR curve equals price and therefore also coincides with the demand curve.

FIGURE 10.1 A purely competitive firm's demand and revenue curves.

The demand curve (*D*) of a purely competitive firm is a horizontal line (perfectly elastic) because the firm can sell as much output as it wants at the market price (here, $131). Because each additional unit sold increases total revenue by the amount of the price, the firm's total-revenue (TR) curve is a straight upsloping line and its marginal-revenue (MR) curve coincides with the firm's demand curve. The average-revenue (AR) curve also coincides with the demand curve.

Firm's Demand Schedule		Firm's Revenue Data	
(1) Product Price (*P*) (Average Revenue)	(2) Quantity Demanded (*Q*)	(3) Total Revenue (TR), (1) × (2)	(4) Marginal Revenue (MR)
$131	0	$ 0	
131	1	131	$131
131	2	262	131
131	3	393	131
131	4	524	131
131	5	655	131
131	6	786	131
131	7	917	131
131	8	1,048	131
131	9	1,179	131
131	10	1,310	131

▶ In a purely competitive industry, a large number of firms produce a standardized product, and there are no significant barriers to entry.

▶ The demand experienced by a purely competitive firm is perfectly elastic—horizontal on a graph—at the market price.

▶ Marginal revenue and average revenue for a purely competitive firm coincide with the firm's demand curve; total revenue rises by the product price for each additional unit sold.

Profit Maximization in the Short Run: Total-Revenue–Total-Cost Approach

Because the purely competitive firm is a price taker, it cannot attempt to maximize its profit by raising or lowering the price it charges. With its price set by supply and demand in the overall market, the only variable that the firm can control is its output. Thus, the purely competitive firm attempts to maximize its economic profit (or minimize its economic loss) by adjusting its *output*.

In the short run, the firm has a fixed plant. Thus it can adjust its output only by changing the amount of variable resources (materials, labor) it uses. It adjusts those variable resources to achieve the output level that maximizes its profit or minimizes its loss.

There are two ways to determine the level of output at which a competitive firm will realize maximum profit or minimum loss. One method is to compare total revenue and total cost; the other is to compare marginal revenue and marginal cost. Both approaches apply to all firms, whether they are pure competitors, pure monopolists, monopolistic competitors, or oligopolists.[1]

We begin with the total-revenue–total-cost approach. Confronted with the market price of its product, the competitive producer will ask three questions: (1) Should we produce this product? (2) If so, in what amount? (3) What economic profit (or loss) will we realize?

Let's demonstrate how a pure competitor answers these questions, given the particular set of cost data in columns 1 to 4 of the table in Figure 10.2. These data reflect explicit and implicit costs, including a normal profit. Assuming that the market price is $131, we find the total revenue for each output level by multiplying output (total product) by price. Total-revenue data are in column 5. Then in column 6 we find the profit or loss at each output level by subtracting total cost, TC (column 4), from total revenue, TR (column 5).

Should the firm produce? Definitely. It can obtain a profit by doing so. How much should it produce? Nine units. Column 6 tells us that this is the output at which total economic profit is at a maximum. What economic profit (or loss) will it realize? It will achieve a $299 economic profit—the difference between total revenue ($1,179) and total cost ($880) at that output level.

Figure 10.2a compares total revenue and total cost graphically for this profit-maximizing case. Remember that the TR curve for a purely competitive firm is a straight line (Figure 10.1). Total cost increases with output because more production requires more resources. But the rate of increase in total cost varies with the firm's efficiency, which in turn varies with the number of variable inputs that are combined with the firm's current amount of capital (which is fixed in the short run). Stated differently, the cost data reflect the law of diminishing returns. From zero to four units of output, total cost increases at a decreasing rate as the firm temporarily experiences increasing returns. At higher levels of output, however, efficiency falls as crowding causes diminishing returns. Once that happens, the firm's total cost increases at an increasing rate because each additional unit of input yields less output than the previous unit.

break-even point An output at which a *firm* makes a *normal profit* (*total revenue = total cost*) but not an *economic profit*.

Total revenue and total cost are equal where the two curves in Figure 10.2a intersect (at roughly 2 units of output). Total revenue covers all costs (including a normal profit, which is included in the cost curve), but there is no economic profit. Economists call this output a **break-even point**: an output at which a firm makes a normal profit but not an economic profit. Another break-even point occurs where total cost catches up with total revenue, somewhere between 13 and 14 units of output in Figure 10.2a. Any output level between the two break-even points will yield an economic profit. The firm achieves maximum profit, however, where the vertical distance between the TR and TC curves is greatest. For our particular data, profit is maximized at 9 units of output, where profit is $299. That profit-maximizing level of output is easier to see in Figure 10.2b, where total profit is graphed for each level of output.

Profit Maximization in the Short Run: Marginal-Revenue–Marginal-Cost Approach

In the second approach, the firm compares the amounts that each *additional* unit of output will add to total revenue and to total cost. In other words, the firm compares the *marginal revenue* (MR) and the *marginal cost* (MC) of each successive unit of output, with the goal of either increasing the size of its profit (if it was already making a profit at the previous level of output) or decreasing the size of its loss (if it was already incurring a loss at the previous level of output).

Assuming that producing is preferable to shutting down, the firm should produce any unit of output whose marginal revenue exceeds its marginal cost because the firm will gain more in revenue from selling that unit than it will add to its costs by producing it. The firm will increase its

---

[1]To make sure you understand these two approaches, we will apply both of them to output determination under pure competition. But since we want to emphasize the marginal approach, we will limit our graphical application of the total-revenue approach to a situation where the firm maximizes profits. We will then use the marginal approach to examine three cases: profit maximization, loss minimization, and shutdown.

FIGURE 10.2 **Total-revenue–total-cost approach to profit maximization for a purely competitive firm.**

(a) The firm's profit is maximized at that output (9 units) where total revenue, TR, exceeds total cost, TC, by the maximum amount. (b) The vertical distance between TR and TC in (a) is plotted as a total-economic-profit curve. Maximum economic profit is $299 at 9 units of output.

				PRICE: $131	
(1) Total Product (Output) (Q)	(2) Total Fixed Cost (TFC)	(3) Total Variable Cost (TVC)	(4) Total Cost (TC)	(5) Total Revenue (TR)	(6) Profit (+) or Loss (−)
0	$100	$ 0	$ 100	$ 0	$−100
1	100	90	190	131	−59
2	100	170	270	262	−8
3	100	240	340	393	+53
4	100	300	400	524	+124
5	100	370	470	655	+185
6	100	450	550	786	+236
7	100	540	640	917	+277
8	100	650	750	1,048	+298
9	100	780	**880**	**1,179**	**+299**
10	100	930	1,030	1,310	+280

profit or decrease its loss. Conversely, if the marginal cost of a unit of output exceeds its marginal revenue, the firm should not produce that unit. Producing it would add more to costs than to revenue, and profit would decline or loss would increase.

In the initial stages of production, where output is relatively low, marginal revenue will usually (but not always) exceed marginal cost (MR > MC). So it is profitable to produce through this range of output. At later stages of production, where output is relatively high, rising marginal costs will exceed marginal revenue (MR < MC). Obviously, a profit-maximizing firm will want to avoid output levels in that range. Separating these two production ranges is a unique output level at which marginal revenue exactly equals marginal cost (MR = MC). This output level is the key to the output-determining rule: *As long as producing some positive amount of output is preferable to shutting down and producing nothing, the firm will maximize profit or minimize loss in the short run by producing the quantity of output at which marginal revenue equals marginal cost (MR = MC).* This profit-maximizing guide is known as the **MR = MC rule.**

Keep in mind these features of the MR = MC rule:

> **MR = MC rule** The principle that a *firm* will maximize its profit (or minimize its loss) by producing the output at which *marginal revenue* and *marginal cost* are equal, provided product *price* is equal to or greater than *average variable cost.*

- For most sets of MR and MC data, MR and MC will be precisely equal at a fractional level of output. In such instances, the firm should produce the last complete unit of output for which MR exceeds MC.

- The MR = MC rule applies only if producing is preferable to shutting down. If marginal revenue does not equal or exceed average variable cost, the firm will shut down rather than produce.

- The MR = MC rule is an accurate guide to profit maximization for all firms whether they are purely competitive, monopolistic, monopolistically competitive, or oligopolistic.

- The MR = MC rule can be restated as $P = MC$ when applied to a purely competitive firm. Because the demand schedule faced by a competitive seller is perfectly elastic (horizontal) at the going market price, product price P and marginal revenue MR are equal. So, under pure competition (and only under pure competition), we may substitute P for MR in the MR = MC rule. Doing so gives us $P = MC$. This version of the rule tells us that, when producing is preferable to shutting down, the competitive firm should produce the quantity of output at which price equals marginal cost ($P = MC$).

Now let's apply the MR = MC rule or, because we are considering pure competition, the $P = MC$ rule. It is crucial that you understand MR = MC analysis because it reappears in subsequent chapters.

Profit-Maximizing Case

The first five columns of the table in **Figure 10.3 (Key Graph)** include AFC, AVC, ATC, and MC data. We will compare the MC data of column 5 with price (which equals marginal revenue) for each unit of output. Suppose first that the market price, and therefore marginal revenue, is $131, as shown in column 6.

What is the profit-maximizing output? Every unit of output up to and including the ninth unit represents greater marginal revenue than marginal cost. Each of the first 9 units therefore adds to the firm's profit and should be produced. The tenth unit, however, should not be produced. It would add more to cost ($150) than to revenue ($131). So 9 units is the profit-maximizing output.

The economic profit realized by producing 9 units can be calculated by subtracting total cost from total revenue. Multiplying price ($131) by output (9), we find that total revenue is $1,179. From the ATC data in column 4, we see that ATC is $97.78 at 9 units of output. Multiplying $97.78 by 9 gives us total cost of $880 (rounded).[2] The difference of $299 (= $1,179 − $880) is the economic profit. Clearly, this firm will prefer to operate rather than shut down.

Perhaps an easier way to calculate the economic profit is to use this simple equation, in which A is average total cost:

$$\text{Profit} = (P - A) \times Q$$

So, by subtracting the average total cost ($97.78) from the product price ($131), we obtain a per-unit profit of $33.22. Multiplying that amount by 9 units of output, we determine that the profit is $299 (rounded). Take some time now to verify the numbers in column 7. You will find

---

[2]Most of the unit-cost data in the table are rounded figures. Therefore, economic profits calculated from them will typically vary by a few cents from the profits determined in the total-revenue–total-cost approach. Here, we simply ignore the few-cents differentials to make our answers consistent with the results of the total-revenue–total-cost approach.

..ıll KEY GRAPH

FIGURE 10.3 Short-run profit maximization for a purely competitive firm.

The MR = MC output level enables the purely competitive firm to maximize profits or to minimize losses. In this example, MR (= P in pure competition) and MC are equal at an output Q of 9 units. There, P exceeds the average total cost A = $97.78, so the firm realizes an economic profit of P − A per unit. The total economic profit is represented by the green rectangle and is 9 × (P − A).

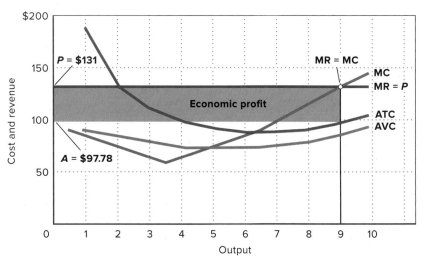

(1) Total Product (Output)	(2) Average Fixed Cost (AFC)	(3) Average Variable Cost (AVC)	(4) Average Total Cost (ATC)	(5) Marginal Cost (MC)	(6) Price = Marginal Revenue (MR)	(7) Total Economic Profit (+) or Loss (−)
0						$−100
1	$100.00	$90.00	$190.00	$ 90	$131	−59
2	50.00	85.00	135.00	80	131	−8
3	33.33	80.00	113.33	70	131	+53
4	25.00	75.00	100.00	60	131	+124
5	20.00	74.00	94.00	70	131	+185
6	16.67	75.00	91.67	80	131	+236
7	14.29	77.14	91.43	90	131	+277
8	12.50	81.25	93.75	110	131	+298
9	11.11	86.67	97.78	130	131	+299
10	10.00	93.00	103.00	150	131	+280

QUICK QUIZ FOR FIGURE 10.3

1. **Curve MR is horizontal because:**
   a. product price falls as output increases.
   b. the law of diminishing marginal utility is at work.
   c. the market demand for this product is perfectly elastic.
   d. the firm is a price taker.

2. **At a price of $131 and 7 units of output:**
   a. MR exceeds MC, and the firm should expand its output.
   b. total revenue is less than total cost.
   c. AVC exceeds ATC.
   d. the firm would earn only a normal profit.

3. **In maximizing profits at 9 units of output, this firm is adhering to which of the following decision rules?**
   a. Produce where MR exceeds MC by the greatest amount.
   b. Produce where P exceeds ATC by the greatest amount.
   c. Produce where total revenue exceeds total cost by the greatest amount.
   d. Produce where average fixed costs are zero.

4. **Suppose price declined from $131 to $100. This firm's:**
   a. marginal-cost curve would shift downward.
   b. economic profit would fall to zero.
   c. profit-maximizing output would decline.
   d. total cost would fall by more than its total revenue.

that any output other than that which adheres to the MR = MC rule will mean either profits below $299 or losses.

The graph in Figure 10.3 shows price (= MR) and marginal cost graphically. Price equals marginal cost at the profit-maximizing output of 9 units. There the per-unit economic profit is P − A, where P is the market price and A is the average total cost for an output of 9 units. The total economic profit is 9 × (P − A), shown by the green rectangular area.

Note that the firm wants to maximize its total profit, not its per-unit profit. Per-unit profit is greatest at 7 units of output, where price exceeds average total cost by $39.57 (= $131 − $91.43). But by producing only 7 units, the firm would be forgoing the production of 2 additional units of output that would contribute to total profit. The firm is happy to accept lower per-unit profits for additional units of output because they nonetheless add to total profit.

Loss-Minimizing Case

Now let's assume that the market price is $81 rather than $131. Should the firm still produce? If so, how much? And what will be the resulting profit or loss?

The first five columns of the table in Figure 10.4 are the same as the first five columns of the table in Figure 10.3. Column 6 shows the new price (equal to MR), $81. Comparing columns 5 and 6, we find that the first unit of output adds $90 to total cost but only $81 to total revenue. One might conclude: "Don't produce–close down!" But that conclusion would be hasty. Remember that in the very early stages of production, marginal product is low, making marginal cost unusually high. The price–marginal cost relationship improves with increased production. For units 2 through 6, price exceeds marginal cost. Each of these 5 units adds more to revenue than to cost, and as column 7 shows, they decrease the total loss. Together they more than compensate for the

FIGURE 10.4 **Short-run loss minimization for a purely competitive firm.**

If price *P* exceeds the minimum AVC (here, $74 at *Q* = 5) but is less than ATC, the MR = MC output (here, 6 units) will permit the firm to minimize its losses. In this instance the loss is *A* − *P* per unit, where *A* is the average total cost at 6 units of output. The total loss is shown by the red area and is equal to 6 × (*A* − *P*).

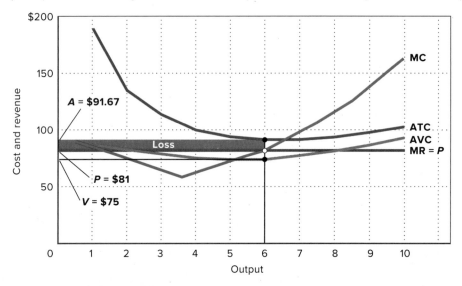

(1) Total Product (Output)	(2) Average Fixed Cost (AFC)	(3) Average Variable Cost (AVC)	(4) Average Total Cost (ATC)	(5) Marginal Cost (MC)	Loss-Minimizing Case		Shutdown Case	
					(6) $81 Price = Marginal Revenue (MR)	(7) Profit (+) or Loss (−), $81 Price	(8) $71 Price = Marginal Revenue (MR)	(9) Profit (+) or Loss (−), $71 Price
0						$−100		**$−100**
1	$100.00	$90.00	$190.00	$ 90	$81	−109	$71	−119
2	50.00	85.00	135.00	80	81	−108	71	−128
3	33.33	80.00	113.33	70	81	−97	71	−127
4	25.00	75.00	100.00	60	81	−76	71	−116
5	20.00	74.00	94.00	70	81	−65	71	−115
6	**16.67**	**75.00**	**91.67**	**80**	**81**	**−64**	71	−124
7	14.29	77.14	91.43	90	81	−73	71	−143
8	12.50	81.25	93.75	110	81	−102	71	−182
9	11.11	86.67	97.78	130	81	−151	71	−241
10	10.00	93.00	103.00	150	81	−220	71	−320

"loss" taken on the first unit. Beyond 6 units, however, MC exceeds MR (= P). The firm should therefore produce 6 units. In general, the profit-seeking producer should always compare marginal revenue (or price under pure competition) with the rising portion of the marginal-cost schedule or curve.

Will production be profitable? No, because at 6 units of output the average total cost of $91.67 exceeds the price of $81 by $10.67 per unit. If we multiply that amount by the 6 units of output, we find the firm's total loss is $64. Alternatively, comparing the total revenue of $486 (= 6 × $81) with the total cost of $550 (= 6 × $91.67), we see again that the firm's loss is $64.

Then why produce? Because this loss is less than the firm's $100 of fixed costs, which is the $100 loss the firm would incur in the short run by closing down. The firm receives enough revenue per unit ($81) to cover its average variable costs of $75 and also provide $6 per unit, or a total of $36, to apply against fixed costs. Therefore, the firm's loss is only $64 (= $100 − $36), not $100.

The graph in Figure 10.4 illustrates this loss-minimizing case. For every output level at which price P exceeds average variable cost AVC but is less than ATC, the firm can pay part, but not all, of its fixed costs by producing. The loss is minimized by producing the output at which MC = MR (here, 6 units). At that output, each unit contributes P − V to covering fixed cost, where V is the AVC at 6 units of output. The per-unit loss is A − P = $10.67, and the total loss is 6 × (A − P), or $64, as shown by the red area.

Shutdown Case

Suppose now that the market price is only $71. Should the firm produce? No, because at every output level the firm's average variable cost is greater than the price (compare columns 3 and 8 of the table in Figure 10.4). The smallest loss it can incur by producing is greater than the $100 fixed cost it would lose by shutting down (as shown by column 9). The best action is to shut down.

You can see this shutdown situation in Figure 10.5. Price comes closest to covering average variable costs at the MR (= P) = MC output of 5 units. But even here, price or revenue per unit would fall short of average variable cost by $3 (= $74 − $71). By producing at the MR (= P) = MC output level, the firm would lose its $100 worth of fixed cost plus $15 ($3 of variable cost on each of the 5 units), for a total loss of $115. This outcome compares unfavorably with the $100 fixed-cost loss the firm would incur by shutting down and producing no output. So it makes sense for the firm to shut down rather than produce at a $71 price—or at any price less than the minimum average variable cost of $74.

The shutdown case reminds us of the qualifier to our MR (= P) = MC rule. A competitive firm maximizes profit or minimizes loss in the short run by producing the output at which MR (= P) = MC, *provided that market price exceeds minimum average variable cost.*

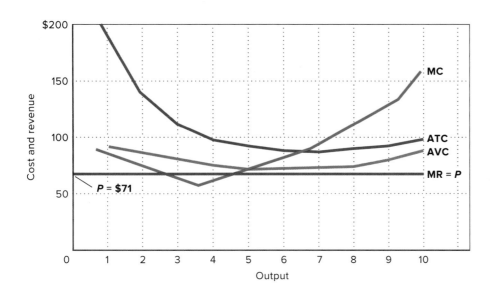

FIGURE 10.5
The short-run shutdown case for a purely competitive firm.

If price P falls below the minimum AVC (here, $74 at Q = 5), the competitive firm will minimize its losses in the short run by shutting down. There is no level of output at which the firm can produce and incur a loss smaller than its total fixed cost.

CONSIDER THIS . . .

The "Still There" Motel

Have you ever driven by a poorly maintained business facility and wondered why the owner does not either fix up the property or go out of business? The somewhat surprising reason is that it may be unprofitable to improve the facility yet profitable to continue to operate the business as it deteriorates. Seeing why will aid your understanding of the "stay open or shut down" decision facing firms experiencing declining demand.

Consider the story of the Still There Motel on Old Highway North, Anytown, USA. The owner built the motel on the basis of traffic patterns and competition existing several decades ago. But as interstate highways were built, the motel found itself located on a relatively untraveled stretch of road. Also, it faced severe competition from "chain" motels located much closer to the interstate highway.

As demand and revenue fell, Still There moved from profitability to loss ($P <$ ATC). But at first its room rates and annual revenue were sufficient to cover its total variable

LWA/Photodisc/Getty Images

costs and contribute some to the payment of fixed costs such as insurance and property taxes ($P >$ AVC). By staying open, Still There lost less than it would have if it had shut down. But since its total revenue did not cover its total costs (or $P <$ ATC), the owner realized that something must be done in the long run. The owner decided to lower total costs by reducing annual maintenance. In effect, the owner opted to allow the motel to deteriorate as a way of temporarily regaining profitability.

This renewed profitability of Still There cannot last because in time no further reduction of maintenance costs will be possible. The deterioration of the motel structure will produce even lower room rates, and therefore even less total revenue. The owner of Still There knows that sooner or later total revenue will again fall below total cost (or P will again fall below ATC), even with an annual maintenance expense of zero. When that occurs, the owner will close down the business, tear down the structure, and sell the vacant property. But in the meantime, the motel is still there—open, deteriorating, and profitable.

QUICK REVIEW
10.2

▶ A firm will choose to produce if it can at least break even and generate a normal profit.

▶ Profit is maximized, or loss minimized, at the output at which marginal revenue (or price in pure competition) equals marginal cost, provided

that price exceeds variable cost at that output level.

▶ If the market price is below the minimum average variable cost, the firm will minimize its losses by shutting down.

Marginal Cost and Short-Run Supply

>> **LO10.4** Relate why the marginal-cost curve and supply curve of competitive firms are identical.

In the preceding section we selected three different prices and asked what quantity the profit-seeking competitive firm, faced with certain costs, would choose to offer in the market at each price. This set of product prices and corresponding quantities supplied constitutes part of the supply schedule for the competitive firm.

Table 10.2 summarizes the supply-schedule data for those three prices ($131, $81, and $71) and four others. This table confirms the direct relationship between product price and quantity supplied. Note first that the firm will not produce at price $61 or $71 because both are less than the $74 minimum AVC. Then note that quantity supplied increases as price increases. Observe finally that economic profit is higher at higher prices.

TABLE 10.2 The Supply Schedule of a Competitive Firm Confronted with the Cost Data in the Table in Figure 10.3

Price	Quantity Supplied	Maximum Profit (+) or Minimum Loss (−)
$151	10	$+480
131	9	+299
111	8	+138
91	7	−3
81	6	−64
71	0	−100
61	0	−100

Generalized Depiction

Figure 10.6 (Key Graph) generalizes the MR = MC rule and the relationship between short-run production costs and the firm's supply behavior.

Figure 10.6 (Key Graph) displays ATC, AVC, and MC curves, along with several marginal-revenue lines drawn at possible market prices. Let's observe quantity supplied at each of these prices:

- Price P_1 is below the firm's minimum average variable cost, so at this price the firm won't operate at all. Quantity supplied will be zero, as it will be at all other prices below P_2.

..ıl KEY GRAPH

FIGURE 10.6 The $P = MC$ rule and the competitive firm's short-run supply curve.

Application of the $P = MC$ rule, as modified by the shutdown case, reveals that the (solid) segment of the firm's MC curve that lies above AVC is the firm's short-run supply curve. More specifically, at price P_1, $P = MC$ at point a, but the firm will produce no output because P_1 is less than minimum AVC. At price P_2 the firm will operate at point b, where it produces Q_2 units and incurs a loss equal to its total fixed cost. At P_3 it operates at point c, where output is Q_3 and the loss is less than total fixed cost. With the price of P_4, the firm operates at point d; in this case the firm earns a normal profit because at output Q_4 price equals ATC. At price P_5 the firm operates at point e and maximizes its economic profit by producing Q_5 units.

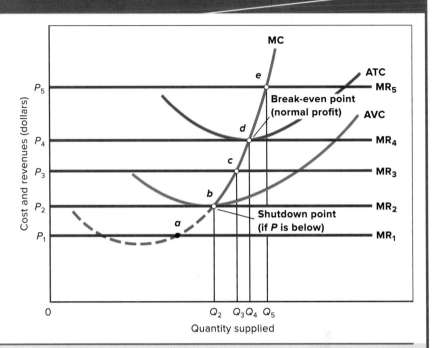

QUICK QUIZ FOR FIGURE 10.6

1. **Which of the following might increase product price from P_3 to P_5?**
   a. An improvement in production technology.
   b. A decline in the price of a substitute good.
   c. An increase in the price of a complementary good.
   d. Rising incomes if the product is a normal good.

2. **An increase in price from P_3 to P_5 would:**
   a. shift this firm's MC curve to the right.
   b. mean that MR$_5$ exceeds MC at Q_3 units, inducing the firm to expand output to Q_5.
   c. decrease this firm's average variable costs.
   d. enable this firm to obtain a normal, but not an economic, profit.

3. **At P_4:**
   a. this firm has no economic profit.
   b. this firm will earn only a normal profit and thus will shut down.
   c. MR$_4$ will be less than MC at the profit-maximizing output.
   d. the profit-maximizing output will be Q_5.

4. **Suppose P_4 is \$10, P_5 is \$15, Q_4 is 8 units, and Q_5 is 10 units. This firm's:**
   a. supply curve is elastic over the $Q_4 - Q_5$ range of output.
   b. supply curve is inelastic over the $Q_4 - Q_5$ range of output.
   c. total revenue will decline if price rises from P_4 to P_5.
   d. marginal-cost curve will shift downward if price falls from P_5 to P_4.

Answers: 1. d; 2. b; 3. a; 4. b

- Price P_2 is just equal to the minimum average variable cost. The firm will supply Q_2 units of output (where MR$_2$ = MC) and just cover its total variable cost. Its loss will equal its total fixed cost. (Actually, the firm will be indifferent as to shutting down or supplying Q_2 units of output, but we assume it produces.)

- At price P_3 the firm will supply Q_3 units of output to minimize its short-run losses. At any of the other prices between P_2 and P_4 the firm will also minimize its losses by producing and supplying the quantity at which MR $(= P) =$ MC. In this range, the firm will lose money by producing—but that loss will be less than what it would lose $(=$ the amount of its fixed costs) if it shut down production and produced and sold nothing.

- The firm will just break even at price P_4. There it will supply Q_4 units of output (where MR$_4$ = MC), earning a normal profit but not an economic profit. Total revenue will just cover total cost, including a normal profit, because the revenue per unit (MR$_4$ = P_4) and the average total cost per unit (ATC) are the same.

- At price P_5 the firm will realize an economic profit by producing and supplying Q_5 units of output. In fact, at any price above P_4 the firm will obtain economic profit by producing to the point where MR $(= P) =$ MC.

TABLE 10.3 Output Determination in Pure Competition in the Short Run

Question	Answer
Should this firm produce?	Yes, if price is equal to, or greater than, minimum average variable cost. This means that the firm is profitable or that its losses are less than its fixed cost.
What quantity should this firm produce?	Produce where MR (= P) = MC; there, profit is maximized (TR exceeds TC by a maximum amount) or loss is minimized.
Will production result in economic profit?	Yes, if price exceeds average total cost (so that TR exceeds TC). No, if average total cost exceeds price (so that TC exceeds TR).

Note that each of the MR (= P) = MC intersection points labeled *b, c, d,* and *e* in Figure 10.6 indicates a possible product price (on the vertical axis) and the corresponding quantity that the firm would supply at that price (on the horizontal axis). Thus, these points are on the upward sloping supply curve of the competitive firm. Note, too, that quantity supplied will be zero at any price below the minimum average variable cost (AVC). *We can conclude that the portion of the firm's marginal-cost curve lying above its average-variable-cost curve is its short-run supply curve.* In Figure 10.6, the solid segment of the marginal-cost curve MC is this firm's **short-run supply curve.** It tells us the amount of output the firm will supply at each price in a series of prices.

Table 10.3 summarizes the MR = MC approach to determining the competitive firm's profit-maximizing output level.

Changes in Supply

short-run supply curve A *supply curve* that shows the quantity of a product a *firm* in a purely competitive *industry* will offer to sell at various *prices* in the *short run;* the portion of the firm's short-run *marginal cost curve* that lies above its *average-variable-cost* curve.

Changes in such factors as the prices of variable inputs or in technology will alter costs and shift the MC or short-run supply curve to a new location. All else equal, for example, a wage increase will increase marginal cost and shift the supply curve in Figure 10.6 upward as viewed from the horizontal axis (leftward as viewed from the vertical axis). That is, supply would decrease. Similarly, technological progress that increases the productivity of labor will reduce marginal cost and shift the MC or supply curve downward as viewed from the horizontal axis (rightward as viewed from the vertical axis). This shift represents an increase in supply.

Firm and Industry: Equilibrium Price

We have established the competitive firm's short-run supply curve by applying the MR (= P) = MC rule. But which of the various possible prices will actually be the market equilibrium price?

We know that the market equilibrium price is the price at which the total quantity supplied of the product equals the total quantity demanded. So to determine the equilibrium price, we first need to obtain a total supply schedule and a total demand schedule. We find the total supply schedule by assuming a particular number of firms in the industry and supposing that each firm has the same individual supply schedule as the firm represented in Figure 10.6. Then we sum the quantities supplied at each price level to obtain the total (or market) supply schedule. Columns 1 and 3 in Table 10.4 repeat the supply schedule for the individual competitive firm, as derived in Table 10.2. Suppose 1,000 firms compete in this industry, all having the same total and unit costs as the single firm we discussed. We can calculate the market supply schedule (columns 2 and 3) by multiplying the quantity-supplied figures of the single firm (column 1) by 1,000.

Market Price and Profits To determine the equilibrium price and output, we must compare the total-supply data with total-demand data. Let's assume that total demand is shown in columns 3 and 4 in Table 10.4. By comparing the total quantity supplied and the total quantity demanded at the seven possible prices, we determine that the equilibrium price is $111 and the equilibrium quantity is 8,000 units for the industry—8 units for each of the 1,000 identical firms.

Will these conditions of market supply and demand make this industry profitable or unprofitable? Multiplying product price ($111) by output (8 units), we find that each firm's total revenue is $888. The total cost is $750, found in column 4 of the table in Figure 10.2. The $138 difference is each firm's economic profit. For the industry, total economic profit is $138,000. Therefore, this industry is profitable.

Another way of calculating economic profit is to determine per-unit profit by subtracting average total cost ($93.75) from product price ($111) and multiplying the difference (per-unit

TABLE 10.4 Firm and Market Supply and Market Demand

(1) Quantity Supplied, Single Firm	(2) Total Quantity Supplied, 1,000 Firms	(3) Product Price	(4) Total Quantity Demanded
10	10,000	$151	4,000
9	9,000	131	6,000
8	8,000	111	8,000
7	7,000	91	9,000
6	6,000	81	11,000
0	0	71	13,000
0	0	61	16,000

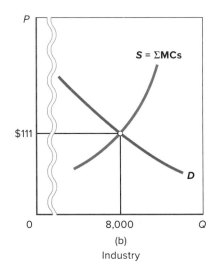

FIGURE 10.7
Short-run competitive equilibrium for (a) a firm and (b) the industry.

The horizontal sum of the 1,000 firms' individual supply curves (*s*) determines the industry supply curve (*S*). Given industry demand (*D*), the short-run equilibrium price and output for the industry are $111 and 8,000 units. Taking the equilibrium price as given, the individual firm establishes its profit-maximizing output at 8 units and, in this case, realizes the economic profit represented by the green area.

profit of $17.25) by the firm's equilibrium level of output (8). Again we obtain an economic profit of $138 per firm and $138,000 for the industry.

Figure 10.7 shows this analysis graphically. The individual supply curves of each of the 1,000 identical firms—one of which is shown as $s = $ MC in Figure 10.7a—are summed horizontally to get the total-supply curve $S = \Sigma$MC of Figure 10.7b.[3]

The point in Figure 10.7b where the total-demand curve *D* intersects the total-supply curve *S* yields the equilibrium price, $111, and equilibrium quantity (for the industry), 8,000 units. This equilibrium price is given and unalterable to the individual firm; that is, each firm's demand curve is perfectly elastic at the equilibrium price, as indicated by *d* in Figure 10.7a. Because the individual firm is a price taker, the marginal revenue curve coincides with the firms's demand curve *d*. This $111 price exceeds the average total cost at the firms's equilibrium MR = MC output of 8 units, so the firm earns an economic profit represented by the green area in Figure 10.7a.

Assuming no changes in costs or market demand, these diagrams reveal a genuine equilibrium in the short run. No shortages or surpluses occur in the market to cause price or total quantity to change. Nor can any firm in the industry increase its profit by altering its output. Note, too, that higher unit and marginal costs, on the one hand, or weaker market demand on the other, could change the situation so that Figure 10.7a resembles Figure 10.4 or Figure 10.5.

Firm versus Industry Figure 10.7 underscores a point made earlier: Product price is a given fact to the *individual* competitive firm, but the supply plans of all competitive producers *as a group* are a basic determinant of product price. That seems like an inconsistency until you realize that it is a prime example of the *fallacy of composition*. The **fallacy of composition** is a logical pitfall into which one stumbles when one assumes that what is true for an individual (or a part) is true for a group (or the whole). This assumption is not correct. *A statement that is valid for an individual or a part is not necessarily valid for the larger group or whole.* Here are three examples:

fallacy of composition The false notion that what is true for the individual (or part) is necessarily true for the group (or whole).

- It is true that atoms are not alive. But it is false to generalize from that fact and conclude that nothing made of atoms is alive. What is true for individual atoms is not necessarily true for groups of atoms like you and your best friend. Both you and your best friend are very much alive.

- You may leap to your feet to see an outstanding play at a football game. But if all the spectators leap to their feet at the same time, nobody—including you—will have a better view than when all remained seated. What is true for the individual spectator is not true for the audience as a whole.

- An individual stockholder can sell shares of, say, Google stock without affecting the price of the stock. The individual's sale will not noticeably reduce the share price because the sale is a negligible fraction of the total shares of Google being bought and sold. But if every Google shareholder decides to sell their shares on the same day, the market will be flooded with shares and the share price will fall precipitously.

---

[3]The Greek symbol Σ means "add up" or "sum together." So ΣMC means that we should horizontally sum together the MC curves of the individual firms.

If we keep the fallacy of composition in mind, we find that there is no inconsistency in Figure 10.7. Although one firm, supplying a negligible fraction of total supply, cannot affect price, the sum of the supply curves of all the firms in the industry constitutes the industry supply curve, and that curve does have an important bearing on price. The individual firms are *price takers*. Their collective supply is a *pricemaker*.

▶ A competitive firm's short-run supply curve is the portion of its marginal cost (MC) curve that lies above its average variable cost (AVC) curve.

▶ If price *P* is greater than minimum average variable cost, the firm will produce the amount of output where MR (= *P*) = MC in order to either maximize its profit (if price exceeds minimum ATC)

or minimize its loss (if price lies between minimum AVC and minimum ATC).

▶ Market supply in a competitive industry is the horizontal sum of the individual supply curves of all of the firms in the industry. The market equilibrium price is determined where the industry's market supply curve intersects the industry's market demand curve.

Profit Maximization in the Long Run

>> **LO10.5** Demonstrate how industry entry and exit produce economic efficiency.

Both the entry of firms into an industry and the exit of firms from an industry can take place only in the long run. In the short run, the industry is composed of a specific number of firms, each with a fixed plant size. Firms may shut down in the sense that they can produce zero units of output in the short run, but they do not have sufficient time to liquidate their assets and go out of business.

In the long run, by contrast, firms have sufficient time to either expand or contract their capacities. The number of firms in the industry may increase or decrease as new firms enter or existing firms leave.

The length of time constituting the long run varies substantially by industry, however, so do not think in terms of a specific number of years, months, or days. Instead, focus your attention on the incentives provided by profits and losses. The time horizons are far less important than the process by which profits and losses guide business managers toward the efficient use of resources.

Assumptions

To tell the long-run story, we need to return to our graphical analysis and examine profit maximization by pure competitors in the long run. Several assumptions will keep things simple:

- *Entry and exit only* The only long-run adjustment in our graphical analysis is caused by firms' entry or exit. Moreover, we ignore all short-run adjustments in order to concentrate on the effects of the long-run adjustments.

- *Identical costs* All firms in the industry have identical cost curves. This assumption lets us discuss an "average," or "representative," firm, knowing that all other firms in the industry are similarly affected by any long-run adjustments.

- *Constant-cost industry* The industry is a constant-cost industry. That is, the entry and exit of firms do not affect resource prices or, consequently, the individual firms' ATC curves.

The Goal of Our Analysis

The basic conclusion we seek to explain is this: After all long-run adjustments are completed in a purely competitive industry, product price will be exactly equal to, and production will occur at, each firm's minimum average total cost.

This conclusion follows from two basic facts: (1) Firms seek profits and shun losses, and (2) under pure competition, firms are free to enter and leave an industry. If market price initially exceeds minimum average total cost, the resulting economic profit will attract new firms to the industry. But this industry expansion will increase supply until price decreases to minimum average total cost. Conversely, if price is initially less than minimum average total cost, the resulting loss will cause firms to leave the industry. As they leave, total supply will decline, increasing the price to minimum average total cost.

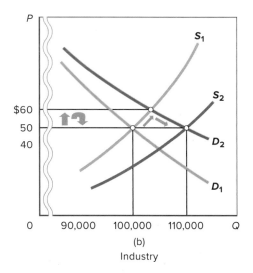

(a)
Single firm

(b)
Industry

FIGURE 10.8
Temporary profits and the reestablishment of long-run equilibrium in (a) a representative firm and (b) the industry.

A favorable shift in demand (D_1 to D_2) will upset the original industry equilibrium and produce economic profits. But those profits will entice new firms to enter the industry, increasing supply (S_1 to S_2) and lowering product price until economic profits are once again zero.

Long-Run Equilibrium

Consider the average firm in a purely competitive industry that is initially in long-run equilibrium. This firm is represented in Figure 10.8a. It is producing 100 units, the output level at which $MR = MC$ and price and minimum average total cost are equal at $50. Economic profit here is zero; the industry is in equilibrium or "at rest" because there is no tendency for firms to enter or to leave. The existing firms are earning normal profits, which means that their accounting profits are equal to the profits that the firms' owners can expect to receive on average in other industries. The $50 market price is determined in Figure 10.8b by market or industry demand D_1 and supply S_1. (S_1 is a short-run supply curve; we will develop the long-run industry supply curve in our discussion.) Remember that the firms' normal profits are considered an opportunity cost and, therefore, are included in the firms' cost curves.

As the two graphs show, equilibrium output in the industry is 100,000, and equilibrium output for the single firm is 100. If all firms in the industry are identical, there must be 1,000 firms ($= 100,000/100$).

Entry Eliminates Economic Profits　Let's upset the long-run equilibrium in Figure 10.8 and see what happens. Suppose a change in consumer tastes increases product demand from D_1 to D_2. Price will rise to $60, as determined at the intersection of D_2 and S_1, and the firm's marginal-revenue curve will shift upward to $60. This $60 price exceeds the firm's average total cost of $50 at output 100, creating an economic profit of $10 per unit. This economic profit will lure new firms into the industry. Some entrants will be newly created firms; others will shift from less prosperous industries.

As firms enter, the market supply of the product increases, pushing the product price below $60. Economic profits persist, and entry continues until short-run supply increases to S_2. Market price falls to $50, as does marginal revenue for each firm. Price and minimum average total cost are again equal at $50. The economic profits caused by the boost in demand have been eliminated, and the previous incentive for more firms to enter the industry has disappeared because the remaining firms are earning only a normal profit (zero economic profit). Entry ceases and a new long-run equilibrium is reached.

As Figures 10.8a and 10.8b show, total quantity supplied is now 110,000 units, and each firm is producing 100 units. Now 1,100 firms rather than the original 1,000 populate the industry. Economic profits have attracted 100 more firms.

Exit Eliminates Losses　Now let's consider a shift in the opposite direction. We begin in Figure 10.9b with curves S_1 and D_1 setting the same initial long-run equilibrium situation as in our previous analysis, including the $50 price.

Suppose consumer demand declines from D_1 to D_3. The market price and marginal revenue decrease to $40, making production unprofitable at the minimum ATC of $50. In time, the resulting economic losses will induce firms to leave the industry. Their owners will seek a normal profit elsewhere rather than accept the below-normal profits (losses) now confronting them. As this exodus of firms proceeds, industry supply decreases, pushing the price up from $40 toward $50.

FIGURE 10.9
Temporary losses and the reestablishment of long-run equilibrium in (a) a representative firm and (b) the industry.

An unfavorable shift in demand (D_1 to D_3) will upset the original industry equilibrium and produce losses. But those losses will cause firms to leave the industry, decreasing supply (S_1 to S_3) and increasing product price until all losses have disappeared.

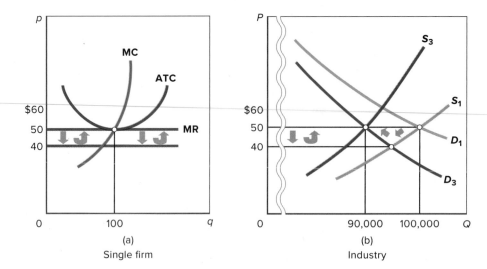

(a)
Single firm

(b)
Industry

Losses continue and more firms leave the industry until the supply curve shifts to S_3. Price is again $50, just equal to the minimum average total cost. Losses have been eliminated, and the remaining firms are earning only a normal profit (zero economic profit). Because this profit level is no better or worse than what entrepreneurs could expect to earn in other business ventures, there is no longer any incentive to exit the industry. Long-run equilibrium is restored.

In Figures 10.9a and 10.9b, total quantity supplied is now 90,000 units, and each firm is producing 100 units. Only 900 firms, not the original 1,000, populate the industry. Losses have forced 100 firms out.

You may have noticed that we have sidestepped the question of which firms will leave the industry when losses occur by assuming that all firms have identical cost curves. In the real world, of course, managerial talents differ. Even if resource prices and technology are the same for all firms, less skillfully managed firms tend to incur higher costs and therefore are the first to leave an industry when demand declines. Similarly, firms with less productive labor forces or higher transportation costs are likely candidates to quit an industry when demand decreases.

We have now reached an intermediate goal: Our analysis verifies that competition, reflected in the entry and exit of firms, eliminates economic profits or losses by adjusting price to equal minimum long-run average total cost. In addition, this competition forces individual firms to produce at the output level at which average total cost is minimized.

Long-Run Supply Curves

>> **LO10.6** Describe the differences between constant-cost, increasing-cost, and decreasing-cost industries.

Although our analysis has dealt with the long run, we have noted that the market supply curves in Figures 10.8b and 10.9b are short-run curves. What, then, is the character of the **long-run supply** of a competitive industry? Our analysis points us toward an answer. The crucial factor is the effect, if any, that changes in the number of firms in the industry will have on the costs of the individual firms in the industry.

Long-Run Supply for a Constant-Cost Industry

long-run supply A schedule or curve showing the prices at which a purely competitive industry will make various quantities of its product available in the *long run*.

constant-cost industry An *industry* in which the entry and exit of *firms* have no effect on the *prices* that firms in the industry must pay for resources and thus no effect on production costs.

Our analysis thus far has assumed that the industry under discussion is a **constant-cost industry** in which industry expansion or contraction does not affect resource prices and therefore production costs. Graphically, constant costs mean that firms' entry or exit does not shift individual firms' long-run ATC curves. This is the case when the industry's demand for resources is small in relation to the total demand for those resources. Its demand being relatively small, the industry can expand or contract without significantly affecting resource prices and costs.

What does the long-run supply curve of a constant-cost industry look like? The answer is contained in our previous analysis. There we saw that the entry and exit of firms changes industry output but always brings the product price back to its original level, where it is just equal to the constant minimum ATC. Specifically, we discovered in Figures 10.8 and 10.9 that the industry would supply 90,000, 100,000, or 110,000 units of output, all at a price of $50 per unit. In other words, the long-run supply curve of a constant-cost industry is perfectly elastic (horizontal).

This is demonstrated graphically in Figure 10.10, which uses data from Figures 10.8 and 10.9. Suppose industry demand is originally D_1, industry output is Q_1 (100,000 units), and product price is P_1 ($50). This situation, from Figure 10.8, is one of long-run equilibrium. We saw that when demand increases to D_2, upsetting this equilibrium, the resulting economic profits attract new firms. Because this is a constant-cost industry, entry continues and industry output expands until the price is driven back down to the level of the unchanged minimum ATC. This is at price P_2 ($50) and output Q_2 (110,000).

From Figure 10.9, we saw that a decline in market demand from D_1 to D_3 causes an exit of firms and ultimately restores equilibrium at price P_3 ($50) and output Q_3 (90,000 units). The points Z_1, Z_2, and Z_3 in Figure 10.10 represent these three price-quantity combinations. A line or curve connecting all such points shows the various price-quantity combinations that firms would produce if they had enough time to make all desired adjustments to changes in demand. This line or curve is the industry's long-run supply curve. In a constant-cost industry this curve (straight line) is horizontal, as in Figure 10.10, thus representing perfectly elastic supply.

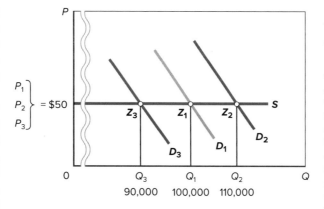

FIGURE 10.10
The long-run supply curve for a constant-cost industry.

In a constant-cost industry, the entry and exit of firms do not affect resource prices, or, therefore, unit costs. So an increase in demand (D_1 to D_2) raises industry output (Q_1 to Q_2) but not price ($50). Similarly, a decrease in demand (D_1 to D_3) reduces output (Q_1 to Q_3) but not price. Thus, the long-run industry supply curve (S) is horizontal through points Z_1, Z_2, and Z_3.

Long-Run Supply for an Increasing-Cost Industry

Constant-cost industries are a special case. Most industries are **increasing-cost industries,** in which firms' ATC curves shift upward as the industry expands and downward as the industry contracts. Usually, the entry of new firms will increase resource prices, particularly in industries using specialized resources whose long-run supplies do not readily increase in response to higher resource demand. Higher resource prices result in higher long-run average total costs for all firms in the industry. These higher costs shift each firm's long-run ATC curve upward.

Thus, when an increase in product demand results in economic profits and attracts new firms to an increasing-cost industry, a two-way squeeze works to eliminate those profits. As before, the entry of new firms increases market supply and lowers the market price. But now each firm's entire ATC curve also shifts upward. The overall result is a higher-than-original equilibrium price. The industry produces a larger output at a higher product price because the industry expansion has increased resource prices and the minimum average total cost.

Because more output will be supplied at a higher price, the long-run industry supply curve is upward sloping. Instead of supplying 90,000, 100,000, or 110,000 units at the same price of $50, an increasing-cost industry might supply 90,000 units at $45, 100,000 units at $50, and 110,000 units at $55. A higher price is required to induce more production because costs per unit of output increase as production rises.

Figure 10.11 nicely illustrates the situation. Original market demand is D_1 and industry price and output are P_1 ($50) and Q_1 (100,000 units), respectively, at equilibrium point Y_1. An increase in demand to D_2 upsets

increasing-cost industry
An *industry* in which expansion through the entry of new *firms* raises the *prices* that firms in the industry must pay for *resources* and therefore increases their production costs.

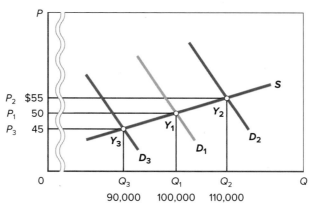

FIGURE 10.11
The long-run supply curve for an increasing-cost industry.

In an increasing-cost industry, the entry of new firms in response to an increase in demand (D_3 to D_1 to D_2) will bid up resource prices and thereby increase unit costs. As a result, an increased industry output (Q_3 to Q_1 to Q_2) will be forthcoming only at higher prices ($45 < $50 < $55). The long-run industry supply curve (S) therefore slopes upward through points Y_3, Y_1, and Y_2.

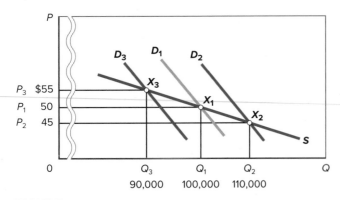

FIGURE 10.12 **The long-run supply curve for a decreasing-cost industry.**

In a decreasing-cost industry, the entry of new firms in response to an increase in demand (D_3 to D_1 to D_2) will lead to decreased input prices and, consequently, decreased unit costs. As a result, an increase in industry output (Q_3 to Q_1 to Q_2) will be accompanied by lower prices ($55 > $50 > $45). The long-run industry supply curve (S) therefore slopes downward through points X_3, X_1, and X_2.

decreasing-cost industry
An *industry* in which expansion through the entry of *firms* lowers the *prices* that firms in the industry must pay for resources and therefore decreases their production costs.

this equilibrium and leads to economic profits. New firms enter the industry, increasing both market supply and individual firms' production costs. A new price is established at point Y_2, where P_2 is $55 and Q_2 is 110,000 units.

Conversely, a decline in demand from D_1 to D_3 makes production unprofitable and causes firms to leave the industry. The resulting decline in resource prices reduces the minimum average total cost of production for firms that stay. A new equilibrium price is established at some level below the original price, say, at point Y_3, where P_3 is $45 and Q_3 is 90,000 units. Connecting these three equilibrium positions, we derive the upward sloping long-run supply curve S in Figure 10.11.

Long-Run Supply for a Decreasing-Cost Industry

In **decreasing-cost industries,** firms experience lower costs as their industry expands. The personal computer industry is an example. As demand for personal computers increased, new manufacturers entered the industry and greatly increased the resource demand for computer components (for example, memory chips, hard drives, monitors, and operating software). The expanded production of the components enabled the producers of those items to achieve substantial economies of scale. The decreased production costs of the components reduced their prices, which greatly lowered the computer manufacturers' average costs of production. The supply of personal computers increased by more than demand, and the price of personal computers declined.

Unfortunately, however, the industries that show decreasing costs when output expands also show increasing costs if output contracts. A good example is the American shoe-manufacturing industry as it contracted due to foreign competition. Back when the industry was doing well and there were many shoemaking firms, the cost of specialized technicians who repair shoe-making machinery could be spread across many firms. This was because the repairmen worked as independent contractors going from one firm's factory to another firm's factory on a daily basis as various pieces of equipment at different factories needed repairs. But as the demand for American footwear fell over time, there were fewer and fewer factories, so the cost of a repair technician had to be spread over fewer and fewer firms. Thus, costs per firm and per unit of output increased.

Figure 10.12 illustrates the situation. The original market demand is D_1 and industry price and output are P_1 ($50) and Q_1 (100,000 units), respectively, at equilibrium point X_1. An increase in demand to D_2 upsets this equilibrium and leads to economic profits. New firms enter the industry, increasing market supply but decreasing individual firms' production costs. A new price is established at point X_2, where P_2 is $45 and Q_2 is 110,000 units.

Conversely, a decline in demand from D_1 to D_3 makes production unprofitable and causes firms to leave the industry. The resulting increase in input prices increases the minimum average total cost of production for the remaining firms. A new equilibrium price is established at some level above the original price, say at point X_3, where P_3 is $55 and Q_3 is 90,000 units. Connecting these three equilibrium positions in Figure 10.12, we derive the downward sloping long-run supply curve S for this decreasing-cost industry.

QUICK REVIEW

10.4

▶ In pure competition, entrepreneurs remove resources from industries and firms that are generating economic losses and transfer them to industries and firms that are generating economic profits.

▶ In the long run, the entry of firms into an industry will compete away any economic profits, and the exit of firms will eliminate economic losses, so

price and minimum average total cost are equal. Entry and exit cease when the firms in the industry return to making a normal profit (zero economic profit).

▶ The long-run supply curves of constant-, increasing-, and decreasing-cost industries are horizontal, upward sloping, and downward sloping, respectively.

CONSIDER THIS . . .

Lithium Ion Batteries

Smartphones, electric cars, and pretty much any portable or mobile electronic device depend on lithium ion batteries, first popularized by Sony corporation in the early 1990s, to provide portable power.

The electrical needs of smartphones and laptops are small, though. And thus they don't require many lithium ion batteries. But when Tesla succeeded with the first popular electric vehicle in the 2010s, it also succeeded in massively increasing the demand for lithium ion batteries because the battery pack for a single Tesla automobile is about 16,000 times larger than the battery in a smartphone.

Fortunately for Tesla, though, electric vehicle manufacturing is a decreasing-cost industry, at least when it comes

University of College/Shutterstock

to the key component of lithium ion batteries. That is because there are substantial economies of scale in the production of lithium ion batteries. The fixed costs of manufacturing lithium ion batteries are high, so that when output scales up, the cost per unit falls dramatically. Thus, the more batteries are demanded by Tesla (and Apple, and Samsung, and Sony), the lower the cost per battery falls.

To hasten that decline, Tesla went so far as to set up its own battery-making "Gigafactories" that would spread fixed costs as widely as possible, to the benefit not only of itself but of consumers, who got to enjoy lower prices on electrical devices and vehicles as battery prices plunged.

Pure Competition and Efficiency

Figure 10.13 (Key Graph) demonstrates the efficiency characteristics of the individual firms (Figure 10.13a) and the market (Figure 10.13b) after long-run adjustments in pure competition. Assuming a constant- or increasing-cost industry, the final long-run equilibrium positions of all firms have the same basic efficiency characteristics. As Figure 10.13a shows, price (and marginal revenue) will settle where it is equal to minimum average total cost: P (and MR) = minimum ATC. Moreover, because the MC curve intersects the ATC curve at its minimum point, marginal cost and average total cost are equal: MC = minimum ATC. So in long-run equilibrium a triple equality occurs: P (and MR) = MC = minimum ATC. In long-run equilibrium, each firm produces at the output level Q_f that is associated with this triple equality.[4]

The triple equality tells us two important things about long-run equilibrium. First, although a competitive firm may realize economic profit or loss in the short run, it will earn only a normal profit by producing in accordance with the MR $(= P) = $ MC rule in the long run. Second, the triple equality also tells us that in long-run equilibrium, the profit-maximizing decision that leads each firm to produce the quantity at which $P = $ MC also implies that each firm will produce at the output level Q_f that is associated with the minimum point on each identical firm's ATC curve.

These conclusions are important because they suggest that pure competition leads to the most efficient possible use of society's resources. Indeed, subject only to qualifications relating to externalities and public goods, an idealized purely competitive market economy composed of constant- or increasing-cost industries will generate both productive efficiency and allocative efficiency. (Chapters 4 and 5 cover externalities and public goods.)

>> **LO10.7** Show how long-run competitive equilibrium generates economic efficiency.

Productive Efficiency: $P = $ Minimum ATC

Productive efficiency requires that goods be produced in the least costly way. In the long run, pure competition forces firms to produce at the minimum average total cost of production and to charge a price that is just consistent with that cost. Firms that do not use the best available (least-cost) production methods and combinations of inputs will not survive.

To see why, suppose that Figure 10.13 represents pure competition in the avocado industry. In the final equilibrium position shown in Figure 10.13a, suppose each firm in the industry is

productive efficiency The production of a *good* in the least costly way; occurs when production takes place at the output level at which per-unit production costs are minimized.

---

[4]This triple equality does not always hold for decreasing-cost industries in which individual firms produce a large fraction of the total market output. In such cases, MC may remain below ATC if average costs are decreasing. We will discuss this situation of "natural monopoly" in Chapter 12.

...ıll KEY GRAPH

FIGURE 10.13 **Long-run equilibrium: A competitive firm and market.**

(a) The equality of price (P), marginal cost (MC), and minimum average total cost (ATC) at output Q_f indicates that the firm is achieving productive efficiency and allocative efficiency. It is using the most efficient technology, charging the lowest price, and producing the greatest output consistent with its costs. It is receiving only a normal profit, which is incorporated into the ATC curve. The equality of price and marginal cost indicates that society allocated its scarce resources in accordance with consumer preferences. (b) In the purely competitive market, allocative efficiency occurs at the market equilibrium output Q_e. The sum of consumer surplus (green area) and producer surplus (blue area) is maximized.

(a) Single firm

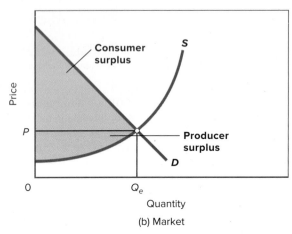

(b) Market

QUICK QUIZ FOR FIGURE 10.13

1. **We know the firm is a price taker because:**
   a. its MC curve slopes upward.
   b. its ATC curve is U-shaped.
   c. its MR curve is horizontal.
   d. MC and ATC are equal at the profit-maximizing output.

2. **At this firm's profit-maximizing output:**
   a. total revenue equals total cost.
   b. it is earning an economic profit.
   c. allocative, but not necessarily productive, efficiency is achieved.
   d. productive, but not necessarily allocative, efficiency is achieved.

3. **The equality of P, MC, and minimum ATC:**
   a. occurs only in constant-cost industries.
   b. encourages entry of new firms.
   c. means that the "right goods" are being produced in the "right ways."
   d. results in a zero accounting profit.

4. **When $P = MC = $ lowest ATC for individual firms, what we see in the market is that:**
   a. consumer surplus necessarily exceeds producer surplus.
   b. consumer surplus plus producer surplus is at a maximum.
   c. producer surplus necessarily exceeds consumer surplus.
   d. supply and demand are identical.

Answers: 1. c; 2. a; 3. c; 4. b

producing 100 units (say, truckloads) of avocados by using \$5,000 (equal to average total cost of \$50 × 100 units) worth of resources. If any firm produced that same amount of output at any higher total cost, say \$7,000, it would be wasting resources because all of the other firms in the industry produce that same amount of output using only \$5,000 of resources. Society would face a net loss of \$2,000 worth of alternative products. But this result cannot occur in pure competition; the high-cost firm would incur a loss of \$2,000, requiring it to either reduce its costs or go out of business.

Note, too, that consumers benefit from productive efficiency by paying the lowest product price possible under the prevailing technology and cost conditions. And the firm receives only a normal profit, which is part of its economic costs and thus incorporated in its ATC curve.

Allocative Efficiency: $P = MC$

Long-run equilibrium in pure competition guarantees productive efficiency, with output produced in the least-cost way. But productive efficiency by itself does not guarantee that anyone will want to buy the items that are being produced. For all we know, consumers might prefer to redirect the resources used to produce those items toward producing other products.

Fortunately, long-run equilibrium in pure competition also guarantees **allocative efficiency,** so we can be certain that society's scarce resources produce the goods and services that people most want to consume. Stated formally, allocative efficiency occurs when it is impossible to produce any net gains for society by altering the combination of goods and services that are produced from society's limited resources.

To understand how pure competition leads to allocative efficiency, recall the concept of opportunity cost while looking at Figure 10.13b, where Q_e total units are produced in equilibrium by the firms in a purely competitive industry. For every unit up to Q_e market demand curve D lies above market supply curve S. Recall the implications in terms of marginal benefits and marginal costs.

- For each unit of output on the horizontal axis, the point directly above it on demand curve D shows how many dollars' worth of other goods and services consumers are willing to give up to obtain that unit of output. Consequently, the demand curve shows the dollar value of the marginal benefit that consumers place on each unit.

- For each unit of output on the horizontal axis, the point directly above it on supply curve S shows how many dollars' worth of other products must be sacrificed in order to direct the underlying resources toward producing each unit of this product. Consequently, supply curve S shows the dollar value of each unit's marginal opportunity cost.

The fact that the demand curve lies above the supply curve for every unit up to Q_e means that marginal benefit exceeds marginal cost for every one of these units. Producing and consuming these units brings net benefits because consumers are willing to give up more of other goods to obtain these units than must be forgone to produce them. Furthermore, because the supply curve includes the opportunity cost of the other goods that must be given up when resources are directed to producing these units, we can be certain that consumers prefer to direct the necessary resources toward producing these units rather than anything else. In other words, allocative efficiency is achieved because redirecting the necessary resources toward producing anything else would make people less happy.

The fact that pure competition yields allocative efficiency can also be understood by looking at the situation facing each individual firm in long-run equilibrium. To see this, take the market equilibrium price P that is determined in Figure 10.13b and see how it affects the behavior of the individual firm shown in Figure 10.13a. This profit-maximizing firm takes P as fixed and produces Q_f units, the output level at which $P = $ MC.

By comparing the horizontal line at P with the upward sloping MC curve, it is clear that for every unit up to Q_f, the price at which each unit can be sold exceeds the marginal cost of producing it. That is equivalent to saying that these units are worth more to consumers than they cost to make. Why? Because consumers are willing to forgo P dollars' worth of other goods and services when they pay P dollars for these units, but at the same time the firm only has to use less than P dollars' worth of resources to produce them. Thus, if these units are produced and consumed, there are net benefits and society comes out ahead. And, as with our previous analysis, allocative efficiency also obtains because by spending their P dollars per unit on these units rather than anything else, consumers are indicating that they would rather have the necessary resources directed toward producing these units rather than anything else.

Maximum Consumer and Producer Surplus

We confirm the existence of allocative efficiency in Figure 10.13b, where we see that pure competition maximizes the sum of the total surplus to consumers and producers. Recall that **consumer surplus** is the difference between the maximum prices that consumers are willing to pay for a product (as shown by the demand curve) and the product's market price. In Figure 10.13b, consumer surplus is the green triangle, which is the sum of the vertical distances between the demand curve and equilibrium price. In contrast, **producer surplus** is the difference between the minimum prices that producers are willing to accept for a product (as shown by the supply curve) and the product's market price. Producer surplus is the sum of the vertical distances between the equilibrium price and the supply curve. Here producer surplus is the blue area.

At the equilibrium quantity Q_e, the combined amount of consumer surplus and producer surplus is maximized. Allocative efficiency occurs because, at Q_e, marginal benefit, reflected by points on the demand curve, equals marginal cost, reflected by points on the supply curve. Alternatively, consumers' maximum willingness to pay for unit Q_e equals the minimum acceptable price

allocative efficiency The apportionment of resources among *firms* and industries to obtain the production of the products most wanted by society (consumers); the output of each product at which its *marginal cost* and *marginal benefit* are equal, and at which the sum of *consumer surplus* and *producer surplus* is maximized.

consumer surplus The difference between the maximum *price* a consumer is (or consumers are) willing to pay for an additional unit of a product and its market price; the triangular area below the demand curve and above the market price.

producer surplus The difference between the actual *price* a producer receives (or producers receive) and the minimum acceptable price; the triangular area above the *supply curve* and below the market price.

of that unit to producers. At any output less than Q_e, the sum of consumer and producer surplus—the combined size of the green and blue area—would be less than that shown. At any output greater than Q_e, an efficiency loss (deadweight loss) would subtract from the combined consumer and producer surplus shown by the green and blue area.

After long-run adjustments, pure competition produces both productive and allocative efficiency. It yields a level of output at which $P =$ MC $=$ lowest ATC, marginal benefit $=$ marginal cost, maximum willingness to pay for the last unit $=$ minimum acceptable price for that unit, and combined consumer and producer surplus are maximized.

Dynamic Adjustments

Another attribute of purely competitive markets is their ability to restore efficiency when disrupted by changes in the economy. A change in consumer tastes, resource supplies, or technology will automatically set in motion the appropriate realignments of resources. For example, suppose that avocados become dramatically more popular. First, the demand for avocados will increase in the market, increasing the price of avocados. At current output, the price of avocados will exceed their marginal cost. At this point efficiency will be lost, but the higher price will create economic profits in the avocado industry and stimulate its expansion. The profitability of avocados will permit the industry to bid resources away from now-less-pressing uses, say, watermelons. Expansion of the industry will end only when the supply of avocados has expanded such that the price of avocados and their marginal cost are equal—that is, when allocative efficiency is restored.

Similarly, a change in the supply of a particular resource—for example, the field laborers who pick avocados—or in a production technique will upset an existing price–marginal-cost equality by either raising or lowering marginal cost. The resulting inequality of MC and P will cause producers, in either pursuing profit or avoiding loss, to reallocate resources until product supply is such that price once again equals marginal cost. In so doing, they will correct any inefficiency in the allocation of resources that the original change may have temporarily imposed on the economy.

"Invisible Hand" Revisited

The highly efficient allocation of resources that a purely competitive economy promotes comes about because businesses and resource suppliers seek to further their self-interest. For private goods with no externalities (Chapter 4), the "invisible hand" (Chapter 2) is at work. The competitive system not only maximizes profits for individual producers but also, at the same time, creates a pattern of resource allocation that maximizes consumer satisfaction. The invisible hand thus organizes the private interests of producers in a way that is fully in sync with society's interest in using scarce resources efficiently. Striving to obtain a profit produces highly desirable economic outcomes.

Technological Advance and Competition

>> **LO10.8** Discuss creative destruction and the profit incentives for innovation.

In explaining the model of pure competition, we assumed for simplicity that all the firms in an industry had the same cost curves. Competition, as a result, only involved entrepreneurs entering and exiting industries in response to changes in profits caused by changes in the market price. This form of competition is important, but it is just a game of copycat because firms entering an industry simply duplicate the production methods and cost curves of existing firms in order to duplicate their above-normal profits. In this type of competition, there is no dynamism and no innovation, just more of the same.

By contrast, the most dynamic and interesting parts of competition are the fights between firms over the creation of new production technologies and new products. As we explain in detail in Chapter 15, firms have a strong profit incentive to develop both improved ways of making existing products and totally new products. To put that incentive in context, recall one fact that you just learned about long-run equilibrium in perfect competition. When each firm in a purely competitive industry has the same productive technology and therefore the same cost structure for producing output, entry and exit assure that in the long run every firm will make exactly the same normal profit.

Entrepreneurs, of course, would like to earn more than a normal profit. As a result, they are constantly attempting two different strategies for increasing their profits. The first involves attempting to lower the production costs of existing products through better technology or improved business organization. Because pure competition implies that individual firms cannot affect the market price, anything that lowers an innovating firm's production costs will result in higher profits, since the innovating firm's revenues per unit (which are equal to the market price per unit) will stay the same while its costs per unit fall due to its improved production technology.

The second strategy for earning a rate of return greater than a normal profit is to try to develop a totally new product that is popular with consumers. If a firm is first-to-market with a popular new product, it will face no competition, as it is the only producer. As long as the product remains popular and the firm remains the only producer, it will be able to charge prices that are higher than production costs, thereby allowing it to earn above-normal profits. (We say much more about this in the next chapter, which covers pure monopoly.)

Notably, however, any advantages that innovative firms gain either by lowering the production costs of existing products or by introducing entirely new products will not normally persist. An innovative entrepreneur may put some of her current rivals out of business, but there are always other entrepreneurs with new ideas so that soon it may be *her* firm that is going out of business due to innovations made by others.

Creative Destruction

The innovations that firms achieve thanks to competition are considered by many economists to be the driving force behind economic growth and rising living standards. The transformative effects of competition are often referred to as **creative destruction** to capture the idea that the creation of new products and new production methods destroys the market positions of firms committed to existing products and old ways of doing business. In addition, just the *threat* that a rival may soon come out with a new technology or product can cause other firms to innovate and thereby replace or rectify their old ways of doing business. As argued decades ago by Harvard economist Joseph Schumpeter, the most important type of competition is

> competition from the new commodity, the new technology, the new source of supply, the new type of business organization—competition which commands a decisive cost or quality advantage and which strikes not at the margins of profits of the existing firms but at their foundation and their very lives. This kind of competition is . . . so . . . important that it becomes a matter of comparative indifference whether competition in the ordinary [short-run or long-run] sense functions more or less promptly. . . .
>
> . . . Competition of the kind we now have in mind acts not only when in being but also when it is merely an ever-present threat. It disciplines before it attacks. The businessman feels himself to be in a competitive situation even if he is alone in his field.[5]

creative destruction The hypothesis that the creation of new products and production methods destroys the market power of firms committed to existing products and older ways of doing business.

There are many examples of creative destruction. In the 1800s, wagons, ships, and barges were the only means of transporting freight until the railroads broke up their monopoly; the dominant market position of the railroads was, in turn, undermined by trucks and, later, by airplanes. Movies brought new competition to live theater, at one time the "only show in town." But movies were later challenged by broadcast television, which was then challenged by cable TV. Both are now challenged by Netflix, YouTube, and other video streaming services like Disney+. Cassettes replaced records before being supplanted in turn by compact discs. Then compact discs were done in by iPods and MP3 players, which in turn were done in by the ability of smartphones to play music—including music streamed (instead of purchased) via services like Spotify and Pandora. And online platforms like Amazon, eBay, and Etsy have stolen substantial business away from brick-and-mortar retailers.

The "creative" part of "creative destruction" leads to new products and lower-cost production methods that are of great benefit to society because they allow for a more efficient use of society's scarce resources. Keep in mind, however, that the "destruction" part of "creative destruction" can be hard on workers in the industries being displaced by new technologies. A delivery driver for Uber Eats or GrubHub may find her job displaced by drone delivery. And many jobs in malls and shopping centers have been eliminated due to consumers switching by the millions toward retail purchases made online at websites like Amazon.com, Walmart.com, and Target.com.

Normally, the process of creative destruction goes slowly enough that workers at firms being downsized can transition smoothly to jobs in firms that are expanding. But sometimes the change

---

[5]Joseph A. Schumpeter, Capitalism, *Socialism, and Democracy,* 3d. ed. (New York: Harper & Row, 1950), pp. 84–85.

The Pandemic Pause

When the COVID-19 Pandemic Hit, Millions of Businesses Were Faced with the Short-Run Shutdown Condition. How Did They React?

When pandemic lockdowns were first imposed by state and local governments during the spring of 2020, people were mostly stuck at home, unable to commute to workplaces and restricted from going out except for essential excursions, such as for grocery shopping or medical care. The severity of lockdown restrictions varied from place to place, but for many businesses the lockdowns meant a massive—if not total—decline in revenue.

The revenue recession continued for many industries even after the initial lockdowns were ended. For instance, running a restaurant in a downtown business district became extremely problematic in many cities because most white-collar firms were letting employees work remotely from home. Consequently, the number of people wanting to purchase meals—especially at lunchtime—from downtown restaurants fell precipitously. The same was true for rental cars and the demand for hotel rooms as tens of millions of people canceled vacation plans and former business travelers mostly stayed home since it became normal to replace in-person business meetings with video chats on Zoom or similar video-chat platforms.

Restaurants The initial lockdowns caused the number of seated indoor patrons at U.S. restaurants to fall literally 100% (to nothing) during the initial lockdowns in March and April 2020. Even after the lockdowns were lifted, average indoor seated patronage remained at least 50 percent below normal levels until about a year later.

Faced with such a massive decline in revenue, most restaurants ceased operations during the lockdowns, following the logic of the short-run shutdown condition, in which a firm that shuts down limits its losses to the size of its fixed costs. But when the lockdowns were lifted, many remained shuttered because the volume of patronage was not large enough to operate at a smaller loss than would occur if they kept the doors shut, the lights off, and the (variable cost) employees at home.

Short-run shutdowns can evolve into permanent shutdowns when businesses conditions do not revive quickly enough. And that's what happened to the nearly 80,000 U.S. restaurants—10 percent of the total number of restaurants—that closed permanently in 2020 due to the decline in business caused by the pandemic. Those that survived saw industrywide revenue fall by 27 percent despite heroic efforts to make up for the massive decline in indoor patronage with increased take-away, drive-through, and delivery sales. Restaurant managers also cut staff dramatically to try to weather the storm. By the end of the year, 3.1 million restaurant workers had lost their jobs, a 20 percent decline in employment from the start of 2020.

Hotels Hotels also suffered a massive downturn in patronage during the pandemic as both business and leisure travelers decided to stay home. Many hotels tried to economize on variable labor costs by cutting back on how often housekeeping serviced guest rooms and by

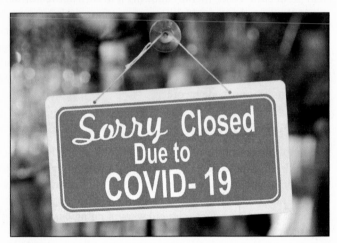

NNER/Shutterstock

eliminating perks like free breakfasts. But the decline in revenue was too steep and too long-lasting for many hotels to withstand. In tourism-dependent New York City, for instance, 20 percent of the city's 705 hotels went bankrupt and closed permanently during the first year of the pandemic.

It should be noted, however, that when the owners of a hotel close a property permanently, what comes next is typically a bankruptcy proceeding during which the bankrupt owners sell their hotel buildings to new owners who will then reopen the properties under a new name. Thus, while the businesses that owned the hotels at the start of the pandemic did shut down permanently in massive numbers as the result of the pandemic, it is not the case that all those hotel rooms will forever be lost to the world. Most will be back again as soon as the demand for hotel rooms normalizes and the new owners reopen the properties.

Rental Cars Meanwhile, over in the rental car industry, things would have been just as dire except for the fact that the giant rental car companies like Hertz and Avis had a hidden "savings account" that they could draw down to weather the storm. In particular, their massive fleets of rental cars were worth billions of dollars. Consequently, the big rental car companies began to sell off their car fleets to raise the cash necessary to cover their fixed costs during the downturn. They also laid off tens of thousands of workers since there were so few customers anyway. Thus, between selling off their rental cars and cutting back aggressively on labor costs, no major rental car company had to shut down permanently.[6]

---

[6]Hertz did file for bankruptcy in May 2020, but it stayed open throughout the pandemic and made enough money selling off cars that it was out of bankruptcy and profitable just a year later.

is too swift for all of them to find new jobs easily. And in other instances, such as a town with only one major employer—like a rural coal-mining town or a small town with a large auto factory—the loss of that one major employer can be devastating.

While the net effects of creative destruction are indisputably positive—including ongoing economic growth and rising living standards—creative destruction involves costs as well as benefits. And while the benefits are widespread, the costs tend to be borne almost entirely by the relatively few workers in declining industries who are not positioned to make easy transitions to new jobs.

▶ In purely competitive industries with free entry and exit of firms, each firm will end up with a zero economic profit, producing where $P =$ minimum ATC. The industry as a whole will produce the socially optimal level of output where $P =$ MC.

▶ When a purely competitive industry reaches long-run equilibrium, the market price P will equal MC and minimum ATC.

▶ Intense competition creates successful new businesses that displace incumbent firms and reallocate resources through a never-ending process termed creative destruction.

QUICK REVIEW
10.5

Summary

LO10.1 List the names and give the main characteristics of the four basic market models.

Economists group industries into four types of market structure: (a) pure competition, (b) pure monopoly, (c) monopolistic competition, and (d) oligopoly.

LO10.2 List the conditions required for purely competitive markets.

A purely competitive industry consists of a large number of independent firms producing a standardized product. Purely competitive firms are price takers. Firms can freely enter or exit a purely competitive industry.

LO10.3 Explain how purely competitive firms maximize profits or minimize losses.

In a competitive industry, no single firm can influence market price. The firm's demand curve is therefore perfectly elastic, and price equals marginal revenue.

A firm maximizes its short-run profit by producing the output at which total revenue exceeds total cost by the greatest amount.

Provided price exceeds minimum average variable cost, a competitive firm maximizes profit or minimizes loss in the short run by producing the output at which price or marginal revenue equals marginal cost.

If price is less than minimum average variable cost, a competitive firm minimizes its loss by shutting down. If price is greater than average variable cost but is less than average total cost, a competitive firm minimizes its loss by producing the $P =$ MC amount of output. If price exceeds average total cost, the firm maximizes its economic profit at the $P =$ MC amount of output.

LO10.4 Relate why the marginal-cost curve and supply curve of competitive firms are identical.

Applying the MR $(= P) =$ MC rule at various possible market prices leads to the conclusion that the segment of the firm's short-run marginal-cost curve that lies above the firm's average-variable-cost curve is its short-run supply curve.

The market supply curve of a perfectly competitive industry is the horizontal sum of the individual supply curves of the firms in that industry. The intersection of the market supply curve with the market demand curve determines the industry's equilibrium price and quantity.

LO10.5 Demonstrate how industry entry and exit produce economic efficiency.

In the short run, when plant and equipment are fixed, the firms in a purely competitive industry may earn profits or suffer losses. In the long run, when plant and equipment are adjustable, profits will attract new entrants, while losses will cause existing firms to leave the industry.

The entry or exit of firms will change industry supply. Entry or exit will continue until the market price determined by industry supply interacting with market demand generates a normal profit for firms in the industry. With firms earning a normal profit, there will be no incentive to either enter or exit the industry. This situation constitutes long-run equilibrium in a purely competitive industry.

Entry and exit help to improve resource allocation. Firms that exit an industry release their resources to be used more profitably in other industries. Firms that enter an industry bring with them resources that were less profitably used in other industries. Both processes increase allocative efficiency.

In the long run, the market price of a product will equal the minimum average total cost of production. At a higher price, economic profits will cause firms to enter the industry until those profits have been competed away. At a lower price, losses will force the exit of firms from the industry until the product price rises to equal average total cost.

LO10.6 Describe the differences between constant-cost, increasing-cost, and decreasing-cost industries.

The long-run supply curve is horizontal for a constant-cost industry, upward sloping for an increasing-cost industry, and downward sloping for a decreasing-cost industry.

LO10.7 Show how long-run competitive equilibrium generates an efficient allocation of resources.

The long-run equality of price and minimum average total cost means that competitive firms will use the most efficient known technology and charge the lowest price consistent with their production costs. That is, the purely competitive firms will achieve productive efficiency.

The long-run equality of price and marginal cost implies that resources will be allocated in accordance with consumer tastes. Allocative efficiency will occur. In the market, the combined amount of consumer surplus and producer surplus will be at a maximum.

The competitive price system will reallocate resources in response to changes in consumer tastes, in technology, or in resource supplies and will thereby maintain allocative efficiency over time.

LO10.8 Discuss creative destruction and the profit incentives for innovation.

Competition involves never-ending attempts by entrepreneurs and managers to earn above-normal profits by either creating new products or developing lower-cost production methods for existing products. These efforts cause creative destruction, the financial undoing of firms committed to existing products and old ways of doing business by new firms with new products and innovative ways of doing business.

Terms and Concepts

market structure	total revenue	increasing-cost industry
pure, or perfect, competition	marginal revenue	decreasing-cost industry
pure monopoly	break-even point	productive efficiency
monopolistic competition	MR = MC rule	allocative efficiency
oligopoly	short-run supply curve	consumer surplus
imperfect competition	fallacy of composition	producer surplus
price taker	long-run supply	creative destruction
average revenue	constant-cost industry	

Discussion Questions

1. Briefly state the basic characteristics of pure competition, pure monopoly, monopolistic competition, and oligopoly. Into which of these market classifications does each of the following most accurately fit? (*a*) a supermarket in your hometown; (*b*) the steel industry; (*c*) a Kansas wheat farm; (*d*) the commercial bank in which you have an account; (*e*) you cell phone service provider. In each case, justify your classification. **LO10.1**

2. Strictly speaking, pure competition is relatively rare. Then why do we study it? **LO10.2**

3. Explain how the market demand curve for a perfectly competitive industry can be downsloping while the demand curves for each of the firms in that perfectly competitive industry are horizontal. **LO10.3**

4. "Even if a firm is losing money, it may be better to stay in business in the short run." Is this statement ever true? If so, under what condition(s)? **LO10.3**

5. Consider a firm that has no fixed costs and that is currently losing money. Are there any situations in which it would want to stay open for business in the short run? If a firm has no fixed costs, is it sensible to speak of the firm's distinguishing between the short run and the long run? **LO10.3**

6. Why is the equality of marginal revenue and marginal cost essential for profit maximization in all market structures? Explain why price can be substituted for marginal revenue in the MR = MC rule when an industry is purely competitive. **LO10.3**

7. "The segment of a competitive firm's marginal-cost curve that lies above its AVC curve constitutes the firm's short-run supply curve." Explain using a graph and words. **LO10.4**

8. Explain how the long run differs from the short run in pure competition. **LO10.5**

9. Use the concept of opportunity costs to explain why profits encourage entry into purely competitive industries and how losses encourage exit from purely competitive industries. **LO10.5**

10. How do the entry and exit of firms in a purely competitive industry affect resource flows and long-run profits and losses? **LO10.7**

11. In long-run equilibrium, *P* = minimum ATC = MC. Of what significance for economic efficiency is the equality of *P* and minimum ATC? The equality of *P* and MC? Distinguish between productive efficiency and allocative efficiency in your answer. **LO10.7**

12. According to the basic model of pure competition, in the long run all firms in a purely competitive industry will earn normal profits. If all firms earn only a normal profit in the long run, why would any firms bother to develop new products or lower-cost production methods? Explain. **LO10.8**

13. "Ninety percent of new products fail within two years—so you shouldn't be so eager to innovate." Do you agree? Why or why not? **LO10.8**

14. **LAST WORD** How did hotels attempt to weather the decline in revenue caused by the COVID-19 pandemic? What option did rental car companies have that restaurants and hotels lacked in terms of raising funds to survive the downturn?

Review Questions

1. Suppose that the paper clip industry is perfectly competitive. Also assume that the market price for paper clips is 2 cents per paper clip. The demand curve faced by each firm in the industry is: **LO10.3**

   a. a horizontal line at 2 cents per paper clip.
   b. a vertical line at 2 cents per paper clip.
   c. the same as the market demand curve for paper clips.
   d. always higher than the firm's MC curve.

2. Use the following demand schedule to determine total revenue and marginal revenue for each possible level of sales: **LO10.3**

Product Price	Quantity Demanded	Total Revenue	Marginal Revenue
$2	0	$_____	$_____
2	1	_____	_____
2	2	_____	_____
2	3	_____	_____
2	4	_____	_____
2	5	_____	

a. What can you conclude about the structure of the industry in which this firm is operating? Explain.

b. Graph this firm's demand, TR, and MR curves.

c. Why do the demand and MR curves coincide?

d. "Marginal revenue is the change in total revenue associated with additional units of output." Explain verbally and graphically, using the data in the table.

3. A purely competitive firm whose goal is to maximize profit will choose to produce the amount of output at which: **LO10.3**
   a. TR and TC are equal.
   b. TR exceeds TC by as much as possible.
   c. TC exceeds TR by as much as possible.
   d. none of the above.

4. If it is possible for a perfectly competitive firm to do better financially by producing rather than shutting down, then it should produce the amount of output at which: **LO10.3**
   a. MR < MC.
   b. MR = MC.
   c. MR > MC.
   d. none of the above.

5. A perfectly competitive firm that makes car batteries has total fixed costs of $10,000 per month. The market price at which it can sell its output is $100 per battery. The firm's minimum AVC is $105 per battery. The firm is currently producing 500 batteries a month (the output level at which MR = MC). This firm is making a _____ and should _____ production. **LO10.3**
   a. profit; increase
   b. profit; shut down
   c. loss; increase
   d. loss; shut down

6. Consider a profit-maximizing firm in a competitive industry. For each of the following situations, indicate whether the firm should shut down production or produce where MR = MC. **LO10.4**
   a. P < minimum AVC.
   b. P > minimum ATC.
   c. Minimum AVC < P < minimum ATC.

7. When discussing pure competition, the term *long run* refers to a period of time long enough to allow: **LO10.5**
   a. firms already in an industry to either expand or contract their capacities.
   b. new firms to enter or existing firms to leave.
   c. both *a* and *b*.
   d. neither *a* or *b*.

8. Suppose that the pen-making industry is perfectly competitive. Also suppose that all current firms and any potential firms that might enter the industry have identical cost curves, with minimum ATC = $1.25 per pen. If the market equilibrium price of pens is currently $1.50, what would you expect the equilibrium price to be in the long run? **LO10.5**
   a. $0.25.
   b. $1.00.
   c. $1.25.
   d. $1.50.

9. Suppose that as the output of mobile phones increases, the cost of touch screens and other component parts decreases. If the mobile phone industry is purely competitive, we would expect the long-run supply curve for mobile phones to be: **LO10.6**
   a. upward sloping.
   b. downward sloping.
   c. horizontal.
   d. U-shaped.

10. Using diagrams for both the industry and a representative firm, illustrate competitive long-run equilibrium. Assuming constant costs, use these diagrams to show how (a) an increase and (b) a decrease in market demand will upset that long-run equilibrium. Trace graphically and describe verbally the adjustment processes by which long-run equilibrium is restored. Now rework your analysis for increasing- and decreasing-cost industries and compare the three long-run supply curves. **LO10.6**

11. Suppose that purely competitive firms producing cashews discover that P exceeds MC. Is their combined output of cashews too little, too much, or just right to achieve allocative efficiency? In the long run, what will happen to the supply of cashews and the price of cashews? Use a supply-and-demand diagram to show how that response will change the combined amount of consumer surplus and producer surplus in the market for cashews. **LO10.7**

Problems

Mc Graw Hill **connect**

1. A purely competitive firm finds that the market price for its product is $20. It has a fixed cost of $100 and a variable cost of $10 per unit for the first 50 units and then $25 per unit for all successive units. Does price exceed average variable cost for the first 50 units? For the first 100 units? What is the marginal cost per unit for the first 50 units? The marginal cost for units 51 and higher? For each of the first 50 units, does MR exceed MC? Is MR > MC for units 51 and higher? What output level will yield the largest possible profit for this purely competitive firm? (Hint: Draw a graph similar to Figure 10.2 using data for this firm.) **LO10.3**

2. A purely competitive wheat farmer can sell any wheat he grows for $10 per bushel. His five acres of land show diminishing returns because some are better suited for wheat production than others. The first acre can produce 1,000 bushels of wheat, the second acre 900, the third 800, and so on. Draw a table with multiple columns to help you answer the following questions: How many bushels will each of the farmer's five acres produce? How much revenue will each acre generate? What are the TR and MR for each acre? If the marginal cost of planting and harvesting an acre is $7,000 per acre for each of the five acres, how many acres should the farmer plant and harvest? **LO10.3**

3. Latoya runs a print shop that makes posters for large companies. It is a very competitive business. The market price is currently $1 per poster. She has fixed costs of $250. Her variable costs are $1,000 for the first thousand posters, $800 for the second thousand, and then $750 for each additional thousand posters. What is her AFC per poster (not per thousand!) if she prints 1,000 posters? 2,000? 10,000? What is her ATC per poster if she prints 1,000? 2,000? 10,000? If the market price fell to 70 cents per poster, would there be *any* output level at which Latoya would *not* shut down production immediately? LO10.3

4. Assume that the cost data in the following table are for a purely competitive producer: LO10.4

Total Product	Average Fixed Cost	Average Variable Cost	Average Total Cost	Marginal Cost
0				
1	$60.00	$45.00	$105.00	$45
2	30.00	42.50	72.50	40
3	20.00	40.00	60.00	35
4	15.00	37.50	52.50	30
5	12.00	37.00	49.00	35
6	10.00	37.50	47.50	40
7	8.57	38.57	47.14	45
8	7.50	40.63	48.13	55
9	6.67	43.33	50.00	65
10	6.00	46.50	52.50	75

a. At a product price of $56, will this firm produce in the short run? If it is preferable to produce, what will be the profit-maximizing or loss-minimizing output? What economic profit or loss will the firm realize per unit of output?

b. Answer the questions in part *a* assuming product price is $41.

c. Answer the questions in part *a* assuming product price is $32.

d. In the following table, complete the short-run supply schedule for the firm (columns 1 and 2) and indicate the profit or loss incurred at each output (column 3).

(1) Price	(2) Quantity Supplied, Single Firm	(3) Profit (+) or Loss (−)	(4) Quantity Supplied 1,500 Firms
$26	_____	$_____	_____
32	_____	_____	_____
38	_____	_____	_____
41	_____	_____	_____
46	_____	_____	_____
56	_____	_____	_____
66	_____	_____	_____

e. Now assume that there are 1,500 identical firms in this competitive industry. That is, there are 1,500 firms, each of which has the cost data shown in the table. Complete the industry supply schedule (column 4).

f. Suppose the market demand data for the product are as follows:

Price	Total Quantity Demanded
$26	17,000
32	15,000
38	13,500
41	12,000
46	10,500
56	9,500
66	8,000

What is the equilibrium price? What is the equilibrium output for the industry? For each firm? What will profit or loss be per unit? Per firm? Will this industry expand or contract in the long run?

5. The normal (accounting) profit in the economy is 5 percent. A firm in a purely competitive industry is earning $5.50 on every $50 invested by its founders. What is its percentage rate of return? Is the firm earning an economic profit? If so, how large? Will this industry see entry or exit? What will be the rate of return earned by firms in this industry once the industry reaches long-run equilibrium? LO10.5

6. A firm in a purely competitive industry is currently producing 1,000 units per day at a total cost of $450. If the firm produced 800 units per day, its total cost would be $300, and if it produced 500 units per day, its total cost would be $275. What are the firm's ATC per unit at these three levels of production? If every firm in this industry has the same cost structure, is the industry in long-run competitive equilibrium? From what you know about these firms' cost structures, what is the highest possible price per unit in long-run equilibrium? If that price ends up being the market price and if the normal rate of profit is 10 percent, then what will each firm's accounting profit per unit be? LO10.7

7. There are 300 purely competitive farms in the local dairy market. Of the 300 dairy farms, 298 have a cost structure that generates profits of $24 for every $300 invested. What is their percentage rate of return? The other two dairies have a cost structure that generates profits of $22 for every $200 invested. What is their percentage rate of return? Assuming that the normal rate of profit in the economy is 10 percent, will there be entry or exit? Will the change in the number of firms affect the two that earn $22 for every $200 invested? If so, how? What will be the rate of return earned by most firms in the industry in long-run equilibrium? If firms can copy each other's technology, what will be the rate of return eventually earned by all firms? LO10.7

CHAPTER 11

Pure Monopoly

>> LEARNING OBJECTIVES

LO11.1 List the characteristics of pure monopoly.

LO11.2 Explain the barriers to entry that shield pure monopolies from competition.

LO11.3 Explain how a pure monopolist sees demand.

LO11.4 Explain how a pure monopoly sets its profit-maximizing output and price.

LO11.5 Discuss the economic effects of monopoly.

LO11.6 Describe why a monopolist might charge different prices in different markets.

LO11.7 Discuss the various selling prices that a regulator might impose on a regulated monopoly.

We turn now from pure competition to pure monopoly, which is at the opposite end of the spectrum of industry structures listed in Table 10.1.

You deal with monopolies more often than you might think. When you purchase certain prescription drugs, you are buying monopolized products. When you turn on your lights, run your water faucet, subscribe to cable TV, or use the wi-fi on an airplane, you may be patronizing a monopoly, depending on your location.

What exactly is pure monopoly, and what conditions enable it to arise and survive? How does a pure monopolist determine its profit-maximizing price and output? Does a pure monopolist achieve the efficiency associated with pure competition? If not, what, if anything, should the government do about it? A simplified model of pure monopoly will help us answer these questions. It will be the first of three models of imperfect competition.

An Introduction to Pure Monopoly

Pure monopoly exists when a single firm is the sole producer of a product for which there are no close substitutes. A pure monopoly has these characteristics:

>> **LO11.1** List the characteristics of pure monopoly.

- *Single seller* In a pure, or absolute, monopoly, a single firm is the sole producer of a specific good or the sole supplier of a service; the firm and the industry are synonymous.

- *No close substitutes* A pure monopoly's product is unique in that there are no close substitutes. The consumer who chooses not to buy the monopolized product must do without it.

- *Pricemaker* The pure monopolist controls the total quantity supplied and thus has considerable control over price; it is a *pricemaker* (unlike a pure competitor, which has no such control and therefore is a *price taker*). The pure monopolist confronts the usual downward sloping product demand curve. It can change its product price by changing the quantity of the product it produces. The monopolist will use this power whenever it is advantageous to do so.

pure monopoly A *market structure* in which one *firm* sells a unique product, into which entry is blocked, in which the single firm has considerable control over product *price,* and in which *nonprice competition* may or may not be found.

- *Blocked entry* A pure monopolist has no immediate competitors because certain barriers keep potential competitors from entering the industry. Those barriers may be economic, technological, legal, or of some other type.

- *Nonprice competition* The product produced by a pure monopolist may be either standardized (as with natural gas and electricity) or differentiated (as with the Windows operating system or Frisbees). Monopolists that have standardized products engage mainly in public relations advertising, whereas those with differentiated products sometimes advertise their products' attributes.

Examples of Monopoly

Examples of *pure* monopoly are relatively rare, but there are many examples of less pure forms. In most cities, government-owned or government-regulated public utilities—natural gas and electric companies, the water company, and the cable TV company—are all monopolies or virtually so.

There are also many "near-monopolies" in which a single firm has the bulk of sales in a specific market. Intel, for example, produces 81 percent of the central microprocessors used in personal computers. Illumina produces 75 percent of the world's gene-sequencing machines. Google's smartphone operating system, Android, is installed on 87 percent of the world's cell phones.

Professional sports teams are, in a sense, monopolies because they are the sole suppliers of specific services in large geographic areas. With a few exceptions, a single major-league team in each sport serves each large American city. If you want to see a live Major League Baseball game in St. Louis or Seattle, you must patronize the Cardinals or the Mariners, respectively. Other geographic monopolies exist. For example, a small town may be served by only one airline or railroad. In a small, isolated community, the local barber shop, dry cleaner, or grocery store may approximate a monopoly.

Nonetheless, there is almost always some competition. Starlink's satellite broadband service is a substitute for terrestrial Internet connections and amateur softball is a substitute for professional baseball. The Linux operating system can substitute for Windows. But such substitutes are typically either more costly or in some way less appealing.

Barriers to Entry

>> **LO11.2** Explain the barriers to entry that shield pure monopolies from competition.

barrier to entry Anything that artificially prevents the entry of *firms* into an *industry*.

The factors that prohibit firms from entering an industry are called **barriers to entry.** In pure monopoly, strong barriers to entry effectively block all potential competition. Somewhat weaker barriers may permit oligopoly, a market structure dominated by a few firms. Still weaker barriers may permit the entry of a fairly large number of competing firms giving rise to monopolistic competition. And the absence of any effective entry barriers permits the entry of a very large number of firms, which provide the basis of pure competition. So barriers to entry are pertinent not only to the extreme case of pure monopoly but also to other market structures in which there are monopoly-like characteristics or monopoly-like behaviors.

We now discuss the five most prominent barriers to entry.

Economies of Scale

Modern technology in some industries is such that economies of scale—declining average total cost with added firm size—are extensive. In such cases, a firm's long-run average-cost schedule will decline over a wide range of output. Given market demand, only a few large firms or, in the extreme, only a single large firm can achieve low average total costs.

Figure 11.1 indicates economies of scale over a wide range of outputs. If total consumer demand is within that output range, then only a single producer can satisfy demand at least cost. Note, for example, that a monopolist can produce 200 units at a per-unit cost of $10 and a total cost of $2,000. If the industry has two firms and each produces 100 units, the unit cost is $15 and total cost rises to $3,000 (= 200 units × $15). A still more competitive situation with four firms each producing 50 units would boost unit and total cost to $20 and $4,000, respectively. Conclusion: When long-run ATC is declining, only a single producer, a monopolist, can produce any particular amount of output at the lowest total cost per unit.

FIGURE 11.1
Economies of scale: the natural monopoly case.

A declining long-run average-total-cost curve over a wide range of output quantities indicates extensive economies of scale. A single monopoly firm can produce, say, 200 units of output at lower cost ($10 each) than could two or more firms that had a combined output of 200 units.

If a pure monopoly exists in such an industry, economies of scale will serve as an entry barrier and will protect the monopolist from competition. New firms that try to enter the industry as small-scale producers cannot realize the cost economies of the monopolist. They will be undercut and forced out of business by the monopolist, which can sell at a much lower price and still make a profit because of its lower per-unit cost associated with its economies of scale. A new firm might try to start out big, that is, to enter the industry as a large-scale producer so as to achieve the necessary economies of scale. But the massive expense of the plant facilities along with customer loyalty to the existing product would make the entry highly risky. Therefore, the new and untried enterprise would find it difficult to secure financing for its venture. In most cases the risks and financial obstacles to "starting big" are prohibitive. This explains why efforts to enter such industries as computer operating software, commercial aircraft, and household laundry equipment are so rare.

A monopoly firm is referred to as a **natural monopoly** if the market demand curve intersects the long-run ATC curve at any point where average total costs are declining. If a natural monopoly were to set its price where market demand intersects long-run ATC, its price would be lower than if the industry were more competitive. But it will probably set a higher price. As with any monopolist, a natural monopolist may, instead, set its price far above ATC and obtain substantial economic profit. In that event, the lowest-unit-cost advantage of a natural monopolist would accrue to the monopolist as profit and not as lower prices to consumers. That is why the government regulates some natural monopolies, specifying the price they may charge. We will say more about that later.

natural monopoly An *industry* in which *economies of scale* are so great that a single *firm* can produce the industry's product at a lower average total cost than would be possible if more than one firm produced the product.

Network Effects

As explained in Chapter 3, **network effects** are present when the value of a product increases as more people use it. Social networking apps are a standard example. If you were the only person using Snapchat, that app would be pretty much useless to you since there would be nobody to interact with. But as more and more people join, there are more and more people to interact with. Thus, the value of the network to any individual user scales with the number of people using the network. The greater the number of people using a network, the greater your own demand for it will be, all other things equal.

Network effects help to determine an industry's tendency toward monopoly. If people are attracted to Snapchat because it has a billion users, they will likely be quite uninterested in a rival that has only 200 users, since any time spent on that smaller app is likely to be time spent nearly alone, with very little content and very few interactions. The implication is that industries that are subject to network effects will generally tend toward monopoly as customers pile into whichever networks already have the most users, thereby leaving smaller networks to wither and die.

Network effects also serve as powerful barriers to entry because startups with only a few users will have extreme difficulty competing with established firms like Instagram and TikTok that have billions of users. If the major source of value to potential customers is how

network effects Increases in the value of a product to each user, including existing users, as the total number of users rises.

many people are already on a network, then a new network with few users is pretty much worthless.

An additional implication of network effects is that they offer a *first-mover advantage*, in that the first firms to enter an industry with network effects are likely to end up with substantial monopoly power because if they are able to pick up a few customers early on, network effects will cause more and more people to follow, thereby guaranteeing the first firm, or firms, massive market share. As the saying goes, "The early bird gets the worm."

Legal Barriers to Entry: Patents and Licenses

Government also creates legal barriers to entry by awarding patents and licenses.

Patents A *patent* is the exclusive right of an inventor to use, or to allow another to use, their invention. Patents and patent laws aim to protect the inventor from rivals who would use the invention without having shared in the effort and expense of developing it. At the same time, patents provide the inventor with a monopoly position for the life of the patent. The world's nations have agreed on a uniform patent length of 20 years from the time of application. Patents have figured prominently in the growth of modern-day giants such as Apple, Pfizer, Intel, SpaceX, Amazon, and DuPont.

Research and development (R&D) is what leads to most patentable inventions and products. Firms that gain monopoly power through their own research or by purchasing the patents of others can use patents to strengthen their market position. The profit from one patent can finance the research required to develop new patentable products. In the pharmaceutical industry, patents on prescription drugs have produced large monopoly profits that have helped finance the discovery of new patentable medicines. So monopoly power achieved through patents may well be self-sustaining, even though patents eventually expire and generic drugs then compete with the original brand.

Licenses Government may also limit entry into an industry or occupation through *licensing*. At the national level, the Federal Communications Commission licenses only so many radio and television stations in each geographic area. In a few instances, the government licenses *itself* to provide some product and thereby create a public monopoly. For example, in 17 states only state-owned retail outlets can sell liquor. Similarly, many states have "licensed" themselves to run lotteries.

Ownership or Control of Essential Resources

A monopolist can use private property as an obstacle to potential rivals. For example, a firm that owns or controls a resource essential to the production process can prohibit the entry of rival firms. At one time the International Nickel Company of Canada (now called Vale Canada Limited) controlled 90 percent of the world's known nickel reserves. And it is very difficult for new sports leagues to be created because existing professional sports leagues have contracts with the best players and have long-term leases on the major stadiums and arenas.

Pricing and Other Strategic Barriers to Entry

Even if a firm is not protected from entry by, say, extensive economies of scale or ownership of essential resources, entry may effectively be blocked by the way the monopolist responds to attempts by rivals to enter the industry. Confronted with a new entrant, the monopolist may "create an entry barrier" by slashing its price, stepping up its advertising, or taking other strategic actions to make it difficult for the entrant to succeed.

Some examples of entry deterrence: In 2015 American Express was found guilty of an unlawful restraint of trade because it prohibited any merchant who had signed up to accept American Express credit cards from promoting rival credit cards—such as Visa or MasterCard—to their customers. As another example, in 2021 Endo Pharmaceuticals was found guilty of bribing generic drugmaker Impax Laboratories more than $112 million to not produce a generic rival for Endo's lucrative painkiller Opana ER.

Monopoly Demand

Now that we have explained the sources of monopoly, we want to build a model of pure monopoly so that we can analyze monopoly price and output decisions. Let's start with three assumptions:

- Patents, economies of scale, network effects, or resource ownership secures the firm's monopoly.
- No unit of government regulates the firm.
- The firm is a single-price monopolist; it charges the same price for all units of output.

>> LO11.3 Explain how a pure monopolist sees demand.

The crucial difference between a pure monopolist and a purely competitive seller lies on the demand side of the market. The purely competitive seller faces a perfectly elastic demand curve at the price determined by market supply and demand. The pure competitor is a price taker that can sell as much or as little as it wants at the going market price. Each additional unit sold adds the amount of the constant product price to the firm's total revenue. Therefore, marginal revenue for the competitive seller is constant and equal to product price. (Refer to the table and graph in Figure 10.1 for price, marginal-revenue, and total-revenue relationships for the purely competitive firm.)

The demand curve for the monopolist (and for any imperfectly competitive seller) is quite different from that of the pure competitor. Because the pure monopolist *is* the industry, its demand curve *is* the market demand curve. And because market demand is not perfectly elastic, the monopolist's demand curve is downward sloping. Columns 1 and 2 in Table 11.1 illustrate this concept. Note that quantity demanded increases as price decreases.

In Figure 10.7, we drew separate demand curves for the purely competitive industry and for a single firm in such an industry. But only a single demand curve is needed in pure monopoly because the firm and the industry are one and the same. We have graphed part of the monopolist's demand data in Table 11.1 as demand curve *D* in Figure 11.2. This is the monopolist's demand curve *and* the market demand curve.

The downward slope of the monopolist's demand curve has three important implications.

Marginal Revenue Is Less Than Price

With a fixed downward sloping demand curve, the pure monopolist can increase sales only by charging a lower price. Consequently, marginal revenue–the change in total revenue associated with a one-unit change in output–is less than price (average revenue) for every unit of output except the first. Why? The lower price of the extra unit of output also applies to all prior units of output. The monopolist could have sold these prior units at a higher price if it had not produced and sold the extra output. Each additional unit of output sold increases total revenue by an amount equal to its own price less the sum of the price cuts that apply to all prior units of output.

TABLE 11.1 Revenue and Cost Data of a Pure Monopolist

	Revenue Data				Cost Data			
(1) Quantity of Output	(2) Price (Average Revenue)	(3) Total Revenue, (1) × (2)	(4) Marginal Revenue		(5) Average Total Cost	(6) Total Cost, (1) × (5)	(7) Marginal Cost	(8) Profit [+] or Loss [−]
0	$172	$ 0				$ 100		$−100
			$162				$ 90	
1	162	162			$190.00	190		−28
			142				80	
2	152	304			135.00	270		+34
			122				70	
3	142	426			113.33	340		+86
			102				60	
4	132	528			100.00	400		+128
			82				70	
5	122	610			94.00	470		+140
			62				80	
6	112	672			91.67	550		+122
			42				90	
7	102	714			91.43	640		+74
			22				110	
8	92	736			93.75	750		−14
			2				130	
9	82	738			97.78	880		−142
			−18				150	
10	72	720			103.00	1030		−310

FIGURE 11.2

Price and marginal revenue in pure monopoly.

A pure monopolist, or any other imperfect competitor with a downward sloping demand curve such as *D*, must set a lower price in order to sell more output. Here, by charging $132 rather than $142, the monopolist sells an extra unit (the fourth unit) and gains $132 from that sale. But from this gain must be subtracted $30, which reflects the $10 less the monopolist charged for each of the first 3 units. Thus, the marginal revenue of the fourth unit is $102 (= $132 − $30), considerably less than its $132 price.

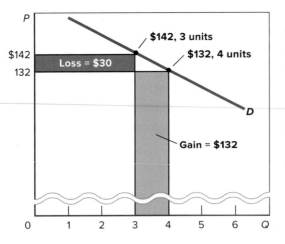

Figure 11.2 confirms this point. There, we have highlighted two price-quantity combinations from the monopolist's demand curve. The monopolist can sell 1 more unit at $132 than it can at $142 and in that way obtain $132 (the blue area) of extra revenue. But to sell that fourth unit for $132, the monopolist must also sell the first 3 units at $132 rather than $142. The $10 reduction in revenue on 3 units results in a $30 revenue loss (the red area). Thus, the net difference in total revenue from selling a fourth unit is $102: the $132 gain from the fourth unit minus the $30 forgone on the first 3 units. This net gain (marginal revenue) of $102 from the fourth unit is clearly less than the $132 price of the fourth unit.

As column 4 in Table 11.1 shows, marginal revenue is always less than the corresponding product price in column 2, except for the first unit of output. Because marginal revenue is the change in total revenue associated with each additional unit of output, the declining amounts of marginal revenue in column 4 mean that total revenue increases at a diminishing rate (as column 3 shows).

Figure 11.3 shows the relationship between the monopolist's MR curve and TR curve. To create this figure, we extended the demand and revenue data of columns 1 through 4 in Table 11.1, assuming that each successive $10 price cut elicits 1 additional unit of sales. That is, the monopolist can sell 11 units at $62, 12 units at $52, and so on.

FIGURE 11.3

Demand, marginal revenue, and total revenue for a pure monopolist.

(a) Because it must lower price on all units sold in order to increase its sales, an imperfectly competitive firm's marginal-revenue curve (MR) lies below its downward sloping demand curve (*D*). The elastic and inelastic regions of demand are highlighted. (b) Total revenue (TR) increases at a decreasing rate, reaches a maximum, and then declines. Note that in the elastic region, TR is increasing and hence MR is positive. When TR reaches its maximum, MR is zero. In the inelastic region of demand, TR is declining, so MR is negative.

(a)
Demand and marginal-revenue curves

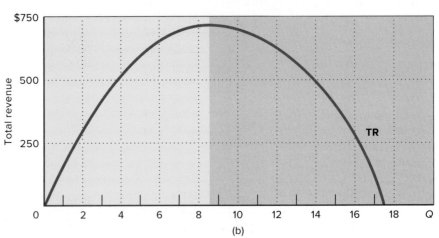

(b)
Total-revenue curve

Note that the monopolist's MR curve lies below the demand curve, indicating that marginal revenue is less than price at every output quantity but the very first unit. Observe also the relationship between total revenue (shown in the lower graph) and marginal revenue (shown in the top graph). Because marginal revenue is the change in total revenue, marginal revenue is positive while total revenue is increasing. When total revenue reaches its maximum, marginal revenue is zero. When total revenue is diminishing, marginal revenue is negative.

The Monopolist Is a Pricemaker

All imperfect competitors, whether pure monopolists, oligopolists, or monopolistic competitors, face downward sloping demand curves. As a result, any change in quantity produced causes a movement along their respective demand curves and a change in the price they can charge. Firms with downward sloping demand curves are thus *pricemakers*. By controlling output, they can "make the price." From columns 1 and 2 in Table 11.1 we find that the monopolist can charge a price of $72 if it produces and offers 10 units for sale, a price of $82 if it produces and offers 9 units for sale, and so forth.

The Monopolist Sets Prices in the Elastic Region of Demand

Recall from Chapter 6 that when demand is elastic, a decline in price will increase total revenue. When demand is inelastic, a decline in price will reduce total revenue. Beginning at the top of demand curve D in Figure 11.3a, observe that as the price declines from $172 to approximately $82, total revenue increases (and marginal revenue therefore is positive). Demand is therefore elastic in this price range. For prices below $82, total revenue decreases (marginal revenue is negative), indicating inelastic demand.

Please note that a monopolist will never choose a price-quantity combination where price reductions cause total revenue to decrease (marginal revenue to be negative). As a matter of fact, *the profit-maximizing monopolist will always want to avoid the inelastic segment of its demand curve in favor of some price-quantity combination in the elastic region.*

The monopolist's desire to avoid the inelastic segment of the demand curve follows from the monopolist's desire to maximize profit. If the monopolist were to increase output and force its way into the inelastic region of the demand curve, the monopolist would have to lower the selling price. But in the inelastic region, a lower price means less total revenue. That is problematic because increased output always means increased total cost. Thus, increasing output to get into the inelastic region of the demand curve implies lower total revenue accompanied by higher total cost—a combination that would reduce the monopolist's profit.

To avoid that, the monopolist will reject the inelastic segment of the demand curve in favor of the elastic segment where lowering the price increases total revenue. Within that segment of the demand curve, the monopolist will follow the normal procedure for profit maximization and set MR = MC to decide how much to produce.

QUICK REVIEW
11.1

▶ A pure monopolist is the sole supplier of a product or service for which there are no close substitutes.

▶ A monopoly survives because of entry barriers such as economies of scale, network effects, patents and licenses, the ownership of essential resources, and strategic actions to exclude rivals.

▶ The monopolist's demand curve is downward sloping, and its MR curve lies below its demand curve.

▶ The downward sloping demand curve means that the monopolist is a pricemaker.

▶ To maximize profit, the monopolist operates in the elastic region of demand.

Output and Price Determination

At what specific price-quantity combination will a profit-maximizing monopolist choose to operate? To answer this question, we must add production costs to our analysis.

>> **LO11.4** Explain how a pure monopoly sets its profit-maximizing output and price.

Cost Data

On the cost side, we will assume that although the firm is a monopolist in the product market, it hires resources competitively and employs the same technology and, therefore, has the same cost structure as the purely competitive firm that we studied in Chapter 10. By using the same cost data that we developed in Chapter 9 and applied to competitive firms in Chapter 10, we will be able to compare the output decisions of a pure monopoly with those of a pure competitor. This will help us demonstrate that the price and output decisions of a pure monopolist are not the result of having a different set of costs relative to pure competitors. Columns 5 through 7 in Table 11.1 restate the pertinent cost data from Table 9.2.

MR = MC Rule

A monopolist seeking to maximize total profit will use the same rationale as a profit-seeking firm in a competitive industry. If producing is preferable to shutting down, it will produce the output at which marginal revenue equals marginal cost (MR = MC).

A comparison of columns 4 and 7 in Table 11.1 indicates that the profit-maximizing output is 5 units because the fifth unit is the last unit of output whose marginal revenue exceeds its marginal cost. What price will the monopolist charge? The demand schedule shown as columns 1 and 2 in Table 11.1 indicates there is only one price at which 5 units can be sold: $122.

Figure 11.4 (Key Graph) graphs the demand, MR, ATC, and MC data of Table 11.1. The profit-maximizing output occurs at 5 units of output (Q_m), where the MR and MC curves intersect. There, MR = MC.

..ıll KEY GRAPH

FIGURE 11.4 Profit maximization by a pure monopolist.

The pure monopolist maximizes profit by producing at the MR = MC output, here Q_m = 5 units. Then, as seen from the demand curve, it will charge price P_m = $122. Average total cost will be A = $94, meaning that per-unit profit is $P_m - A$ and total profit is $5 \times (P_m - A)$. Total economic profit is thus represented by the green rectangle.

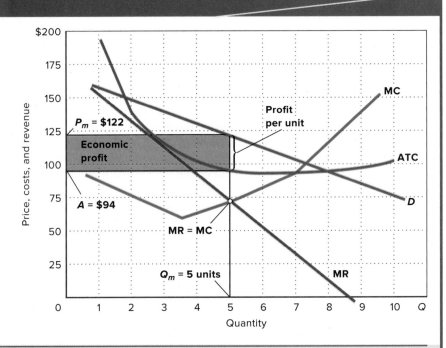

QUICK QUIZ FOR FIGURE 11.4

1. The MR curve lies below the demand curve in this figure because the:
   a. demand curve is linear (a straight line).
   b. demand curve is highly inelastic throughout its full length.
   c. demand curve is highly elastic throughout its full length.
   d. gain in revenue from an extra unit of output is less than the price charged for that unit of output.

2. The area labeled "Economic profit" can be found by multiplying the difference between P and ATC by quantity. It also can be found by:
   a. dividing profit per unit by quantity.
   b. subtracting total cost from total revenue.
   c. multiplying the coefficient of demand elasticity by quantity.
   d. multiplying the difference between P and MC by quantity.

3. This pure monopolist:
   a. charges the highest price that it could achieve.
   b. earns only a normal profit in the long run.
   c. restricts output to create an insurmountable entry barrier.
   d. restricts output to increase its price and total economic profit.

4. At this monopolist's profit-maximizing output:
   a. price equals marginal revenue.
   b. price equals marginal cost.
   c. price exceeds marginal cost.
   d. profit per unit is maximized.

Answers: 1. d; 2. b; 3. d; 4. c

TABLE 11.2 Steps for Graphically Determining the Profit-Maximizing Output, Profit-Maximizing Price, and Economic Profit (if Any) in Pure Monopoly

Step 1.	Determine the profit-maximizing output by finding where MR = MC.
Step 2.	Determine the profit-maximizing price by extending a vertical line upward from the output determined in step 1 to the pure monopolist's demand curve.
Step 3.	Determine the pure monopolist's economic profit using one of two methods:
	Method 1. Find profit per unit by subtracting the average total cost of the profit-maximizing output from the profit-maximizing price. Then multiply the difference by the profit-maximizing output to determine economic profit (if any).
	Method 2. Find total cost by multiplying the average total cost of the profit-maximizing output by that output. Find total revenue by multiplying the profit-maximizing output by the profit-maximizing price. Then subtract total cost from total revenue to determine economic profit (if any).

To find the price the monopolist will charge, we extend a vertical line from Q_m up to the demand curve D. The unique price P_m at which Q_m units can be sold is $122. So the monopolist sets the quantity at the profit-maximizing level Q_m while charging the profit-maximizing price of $122 that is associated with Q_m on the demand curve. With the price set at $122, customers will demand Q_m units of output. Thus, at a price of $122, quantity demanded will exactly equal the quantity that the monopoly wishes to supply to maximize its own profit.

Columns 2 and 5 in Table 11.1 show that at 5 units of output, the product price ($122) exceeds the average total cost ($94). The monopolist thus obtains an economic profit of $28 per unit, and the total economic profit is $140 (= 5 units × $28). In Figure 11.4, per-unit profit is $P_m - A$, where A is the average total cost of producing Q_m units. Total economic profit—the green rectangle—is found by multiplying this per-unit profit by the profit-maximizing output Q_m.

Another way to determine the profit-maximizing output is by comparing total revenue and total cost at each possible level of production and choosing the output with the greatest positive difference. Use columns 3 and 6 in Table 11.1 to verify that 5 units is the profit-maximizing output. An accurate graphing of total revenue and total cost against output will also show the greatest difference (the maximum profit) at 5 units of output. Table 11.2 is a step-by-step summary of the process for determining the profit-maximizing output, profit-maximizing price, and economic profit in pure monopoly.

No Monopoly Supply Curve

Recall that MR equals P in pure competition and that the supply curve of a purely competitive firm is determined by applying the MR ($= P$) = MC profit-maximizing rule. At any specific market-determined price, the purely competitive seller will maximize profit by supplying the quantity at which MC is equal to that price. When the market price increases or decreases, the competitive firm adjusts its output. Each market price is thus associated with a specific output, and all such price-output pairs define the supply curve. This supply curve turns out to be the portion of the firm's MC curve that lies above the AVC curve (see Figure 10.6).

At first glance we might suspect that the pure monopolist's MC is also its supply curve. But, in fact, *the pure monopolist has no supply curve.* There is no unique relationship between price and quantity supplied for a monopolist. Like the competitive firm, the monopolist equates marginal revenue and marginal cost to determine output, but for the monopolist marginal revenue is less than price. Because the monopolist does not equate marginal cost to price, it is possible for different demand conditions to bring about different prices for the same output. To understand why, refer to Figure 11.4 and pencil in a new, steeper MR curve that intersects the MC curve at the same point as the present MR curve. Then draw in a new demand curve that is roughly consistent with your new MR curve. With the new curves, the same MR = MC output of 5 units now means a higher profit-maximizing price. Conclusion: There is no single, unique price associated with each output level Q_m, and so there is no supply curve for the pure monopolist.

Misconceptions Concerning Monopoly Pricing

Our analysis exposes two fallacies concerning monopoly behavior.

Not Highest Price Because a monopolist can manipulate output and price, people often believe it will charge the highest price possible. That is incorrect. There are many prices above P_m in Figure 11.4,

FIGURE 11.5
The loss-minimizing position of a pure monopolist.

If demand *D* is weak and costs are high, the pure monopolist may be unable to make a profit. Because *Pm* exceeds *V*, the average variable cost at the MR = MC output Q_m, the monopolist will minimize losses in the short run by producing at that output. The loss per unit is $A - P_m$, and the total loss is indicated by the red rectangle.

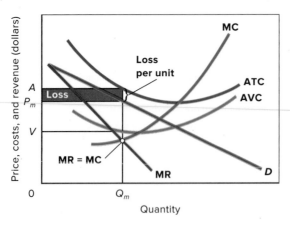

but the monopolist shuns them because they yield a smaller-than-maximum total profit. The monopolist seeks maximum total profit, not maximum price.

Total, Not Unit, Profit The monopolist seeks maximum *total* profit, not maximum *unit* profit. In Figure 11.4 a careful comparison of the vertical distance between ATC and price at various possible outputs indicates that per-unit profit is greater at a point slightly to the left of the profit-maximizing output Q_m. We see the same result in Table 11.1, where the per-unit profit at 4 units of output is \$32 (= \$132 − \$100) compared with \$28 (= \$122 − \$94) at the profit-maximizing output of 5 units. Here the monopolist accepts a lower-than-maximum per-unit profit because additional sales more than compensate for the lower unit profit. A monopolist would rather sell 5 units at a profit of \$28 per unit (for a total profit of \$140) than 4 units at a profit of \$32 per unit (for a total profit of only \$128).

Possibility of Losses by Monopolist

The likelihood of economic profit is greater for a pure monopolist than for a pure competitor. In the long run, the pure competitor is destined to have only a normal profit, whereas barriers to entry mean that any economic profit realized by the monopolist can persist. In pure monopoly, there are no new entrants to increase supply, drive down price, and eliminate economic profit.

But pure monopoly does not guarantee profit. The monopolist is not immune from changes in tastes that reduce the demand for its product. Nor is it immune from upward-shifting cost curves caused by escalating resource prices. If the demand and cost situation faced by the monopolist is far less favorable than that in Figure 11.4, the monopolist will incur losses in the short run. Consider the monopoly enterprise shown in Figure 11.5. Despite its dominance in the market (as, say, a seller of home sewing machines), it suffers a loss, as shown, because of weak demand and relatively high costs. Yet it continues to operate for the time being because its total loss is less than its fixed cost. More precisely, at output Q_m, the monopolist's price P_m exceeds its average variable cost *V*. Its loss per unit is $A - P_m$, and the total loss is shown by the red rectangle.

Like the pure competitor, the monopolist will not persist in operating at a loss. Faced with continuing losses, in the long run the firm's owners will move their resources to alternative industries that offer better profit opportunities. A monopolist such as the one depicted in Figure 11.5 must obtain a minimum normal profit in the long run or it will go out of business.

The nearby Consider This story discusses the curious case of government-auctioned monopolies. Note that the people bidding to become monopolists must believe that the monopolies that they are bidding on are going to be profitable.

CONSIDER THIS . . .

Salt Monopolies

Starting in the 1300s, the French government claimed for itself a monopoly over the sale of salt, which was a valuable commodity at the time, especially in inland areas away from the ocean. But as the centuries passed, the French monarchy found it convenient and profitable to auction off the monopoly right to sell salt.

Vincent Ting/Moment Open/Getty Images

The contract would be for a fixed number of years and the winner of the auction would attempt to make more money selling salt as monopolist than they paid to win the

auction. The government liked that it got paid a large lump sum in advance. It was also freed of the costs of hiring tens of thousands of government tax collectors; collection costs fell entirely on the auction winner.

How high would bids go? That depended on profit estimates. If a bidder thought he could make a monopoly profit of 5,000 livres selling salt, he would be willing to bid up to 5,000 livres to become the monopolist. The most aggressive bidders were the people who thought they could squeeze out the largest profit.

Economic Effects of Monopoly

Let's now evaluate pure monopoly from the standpoint of society as a whole. Our reference for this evaluation will be the outcome of long-run efficiency in a purely competitive market, identified by the triple equality $P = MC = $ minimum ATC.

>> **LO11.5** Discuss the economic effects of monopoly.

Price, Output, and Efficiency

Figure 11.6 (Key Graph) graphically contrasts the price, output, and efficiency outcomes of pure monopoly and a purely competitive *industry*. The $S = MC$ curve in Figure 11.6a reminds us that the market supply curve S for a purely competitive industry is the horizontal sum of the MC curves of all the firms in the industry. Suppose there are 1,000 such firms. Comparing their combined supply curve S with market demand D, we see that the purely competitive price and output are P_c and Q_c.

..ıl KEY GRAPH

FIGURE 11.6 **Inefficiency of pure monopoly relative to a purely competitive industry.**

(a) In a purely competitive industry, entry and exit of firms ensure that price (P_c) equals marginal cost (MC) and that the minimum average-total-cost output (Q_c) is produced. Both productive efficiency ($P = $ minimum ATC) and allocative efficiency ($P = $ MC) are obtained. (b) In pure monopoly, the MR curve lies below the demand curve. The monopolist maximizes profit at output Q_m, where MR = MC, and charges price P_m. Thus, output is lower (Q_m rather than Q_c) and price is higher (P_m rather than P_c) than they would be in a purely competitive industry. Monopoly is inefficient, since output is less than that required for achieving minimum ATC (here, at Q_c) and because the monopolist's price exceeds MC. Monopoly creates an efficiency loss (here, of triangle *abc*). There is also a transfer of income from consumers to the monopoly (here, of rectangle P_cP_mbd).

(a)
Purely competitive industry

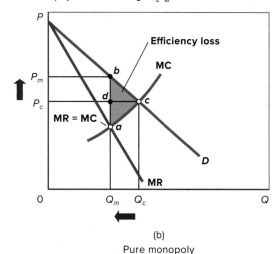

(b)
Pure monopoly

QUICK QUIZ FOR FIGURE 11.6

1. **The MR curve for a pure competitor is:**
   a. steeper than the MR curve for a monopoly.
   b. steeper than the demand curve for a monopoly.
   c. vertical.
   d. horizontal.

2. **The deadweight loss sustained by the monopoly is caused by:**
   a. the marginal revenue of each additional unit being less than the average revenue of all previous units.
   b. failure to maximize profit.
   c. the deadweight loss given by triangle *abc*.
   d. the reduction in consumer surplus given by triangle *dbc*.

3. **The perfectly competitive industry suffers no deadweight loss because:**
   a. Q_c always equals P_c when $P = $ MC = minimum ATC.
   b. every unit of output for which MB > MC is being produced.
   c. this product is a public good.
   d. MC > P_c for all units beyond Q_c.

4. **The profit-maximizing monopolist will charge customers:**
   a. the highest possible price per unit.
   b. the lowest possible price per unit.
   c. the price that minimizes ATC.
   d. the highest price per unit that it can charge at output level Q_m such that it will sell exactly Q_m units at that price.

Answers: 1.d; 2. a; 3. b; 4. d

Recall that this price-output combination results in both productive efficiency and allocative efficiency. *Productive efficiency* is achieved because free entry and exit force firms to operate where ATC is at a minimum. The sum of the minimum-ATC outputs of the 1,000 pure competitors is the industry output, Q_c. Product price is at the lowest level consistent with minimum average total cost. The *allocative efficiency* of pure competition results because production occurs up to the output at which price (the measure of a product's value or marginal benefit to society) equals marginal cost (the worth of the alternative products forgone by society in producing any given commodity). In short: $P = MC = \text{minimum ATC}$.

Now let's suppose that this industry becomes a pure monopoly (Figure 11.6b) as a result of one firm acquiring all its competitors. We also assume that no changes in costs or market demand result from this dramatic change in the industry structure. One thousand competing firms have become a single pure monopolist.

The competitive market supply curve S has become the monopolist's MC curve, the summation of the individual MC curves of its many branch plants. (Because the monopolist does not have a supply curve, we have removed the S label.) The important change, however, is on the demand side. From the viewpoint of each of the 1,000 individual competitive firms, demand was perfectly elastic, and marginal revenue was therefore equal to the market equilibrium price P_c. Thus, each competitive firm equated its marginal revenue of P_c dollars per unit with its individual marginal cost curve to maximize profits. But market demand and individual demand are the same to the pure monopolist. The firm is the industry, and thus the monopolist sees the downward sloping demand curve D shown in Figure 11.6b.

For the monopolist, marginal revenue is less than price, and graphically the MR curve lies below demand curve D. In using the MR = MC rule, the monopolist selects output Q_m and price P_m. The monopolist finds it profitable to sell a smaller output at a higher price than do the competitive producers.

Monopoly yields neither productive nor allocative efficiency. Note that the monopolist's output Q_m is less than Q_c, the output at which average total cost is lowest. In addition, the monopoly price P_m is higher than the competitive price P_c that we know in long-run equilibrium in pure competition equals minimum average total cost. Thus, the monopoly price exceeds minimum average total cost, which means that the monopoly will not be productively efficient.

The monopolist's underproduction also implies allocative inefficiency. At the monopoly output level Q_m, the monopoly price P_m that consumers are willing to pay exceeds the marginal cost of production. Consumers therefore value additional units of this product more highly than they do the alternative products that could be produced from the resources that are necessary to make more units of the monopolist's product. But the monopolist will not produce those additional units because doing so would reduce its profit, which is maximized at Q_m.

Also note that for every unit between Q_m and Q_c, marginal benefit exceeds marginal cost because the demand curve lies above the supply curve. By choosing not to produce these units, the monopolist reduces allocative efficiency because the resources that should have been used to make these units will be redirected instead toward producing items that bring lower net benefits to society. The total dollar value of this efficiency loss (or *deadweight loss*) is equal to the area of the gray triangle labeled *abc* in Figure 11.6b.

Income Transfer

In general, a monopoly transfers income from consumers to the owners of the monopoly. The owners receive the income as revenue. Because a monopoly has market power, it can charge a higher price than would a purely competitive firm with the same costs. So the monopoly in effect levies a "private tax" on consumers. This private tax can often generate substantial economic profits that can persist because entry to the industry is blocked.

Cost Complications

Given identical costs, a purely monopolistic industry will charge a higher price, produce a smaller output, and allocate economic resources less efficiently than a purely competitive industry. These inferior results are rooted in the entry barriers characterizing monopoly.

But we must recognize that costs may not be the same for purely competitive and monopolistic producers. The unit cost incurred by a monopolist may be either larger or smaller than that incurred by a purely competitive firm. Costs may differ for four reasons: (1) economies of scale, (2) a factor called "X-inefficiency," (3) the need for monopoly-preserving expenditures, and (4) the "very long run" perspective, which allows for technological advance.

Economies of Scale Where economies of scale are extensive, market demand may not be sufficient to support a large number of competing firms, each producing at minimum efficient scale. In such cases, an industry of one or two firms would have a lower average total cost than would the same industry made up of numerous competitive firms. At the extreme, only a single firm—a natural monopoly—might be able to achieve the lowest long-run average total cost.

Some firms relating to information technologies—for example, computer software, Internet service, and wireless communications—have displayed extensive economies of scale. As these firms have grown, their long-run average total costs have declined because of greater use of specialized inputs, the spreading of product development costs, and learning by doing.

Simultaneous consumption and *network effects* have also reduced costs by helping to drive economies of scale.

- A product's ability to satisfy a large number of consumers at the same time is called **simultaneous consumption** (or *nonrivalrous consumption*). Lenovo needs to produce a laptop for each customer, but Microsoft needs to produce its Windows program only once. Then, at very low marginal cost, Microsoft delivers its program over the Internet to millions of consumers. Music producers and video gamemakers have similarly low marginal costs when delivering their products to additional customers. Because their marginal costs are so low, their average total cost of output declines as more customers are added and the fixed costs of product development are spread over more and more users.

- As we discussed earlier in this chapter, *network effects* are present if a product's value to each user, including existing users, increases as the total number of users rises. Such network effects may drive a market toward monopoly because consumers tend to choose standard products that everyone else is using. The focused demand for these products permits their producers to grow rapidly and thus achieve economies of scale. Smaller firms get acquired or go out of business.

Even if natural monopoly develops, the monopolist is unlikely to pass cost reductions along to consumers as price reductions. So, with perhaps a handful of exceptions, economies of scale do not change the general conclusion that monopoly industries are inefficient relative to competitive industries.

X-Inefficiency In constructing all the average-total-cost curves used in this book, we have assumed that the firm uses the most efficient existing technology. This assumption is natural because firms cannot maximize profits unless they are minimizing costs. **X-inefficiency** occurs when a firm produces output at a higher cost than is necessary to produce it.

Why does X-inefficiency occur? Managers may have goals, such as expanding their power, avoiding business risk, or giving jobs to incompetent relatives, that conflict with cost minimization. X-inefficiency may also arise when a firm's workers are poorly motivated or ineffectively supervised. And a firm may simply become lethargic, relying on rules of thumb in decision making rather than careful calculations of costs and revenues.

For our purposes the relevant question is whether monopolistic firms tend more toward X-inefficiency than competitive producers do. Presumably they do. Firms in competitive industries are continually under pressure from rivals, forcing them to be internally efficient to survive. But monopolists are sheltered from such competitive forces by entry barriers. That lack of pressure may lead to X-inefficiency.

Rent-Seeking Expenditures **Rent-seeking behavior** is any activity designed to obtain a transfer of income or wealth to a particular firm or resource supplier at someone else's, or even society's, expense. We have seen that a monopolist can obtain an economic profit even in the long run. Therefore, it is no surprise that a firm may go to great expense to acquire or maintain a monopoly granted by government through legislation or an exclusive license. Such rent-seeking expenditures add nothing to the firm's output, but they clearly increase its costs. Taken alone, rent seeking implies that monopoly involves even higher costs and even less efficiency than suggested in Figure 11.6b.

---

simultaneous consumption The same-time derivation of *utility* from some product by a large number of consumers.

X-inefficiency The production of output, whatever its level, at a higher average (and total) cost than is necessary for producing that level of output.

rent-seeking behavior Attempts by individuals, firms, or unions to use political influence to receive payments in excess of the minimum amount they would normally be willing to accept to provide a particular good or service.

Technological Advance In the very long run, firms can reduce their costs through the discovery and implementation of new technology. If monopolists are more likely than competitive producers to develop more efficient production techniques over time, then the inefficiency of monopoly might be overstated.

In general, economists believe that a pure monopolist will not be technologically progressive. Although its economic profit provides ample means to finance research and development, it has little incentive to implement new techniques or introduce new products. The absence of competitors means there is no external pressure for technological advance. Because of its sheltered market position, the pure monopolist can afford to be complacent and lethargic. There simply is no major penalty for not being innovative.

One caveat: Research and technological advance may be one of the monopolist's barriers to entry. Thus, the monopolist may continue to seek technological advance to avoid falling prey to new rivals. In this case, technological advance is essential to maintaining the monopoly.

Assessment and Policy Options

Fortunately, monopoly is not widespread in the United States. Barriers to entry are seldom completely successful. Although research and technological advance may strengthen a monopoly's market position, technology may also undermine monopoly power. Over time, the creation of new technologies may destroy monopoly positions. For example, the development of courier delivery, fax machines, and e-mail has eroded the monopoly power of the U.S. Postal Service. Similarly, cable television monopolies are now challenged by satellite TV and by Internet streaming services such as Netflix and Disney+.

Patents eventually expire; and even before they do, the development of new and distinct substitutable products often circumvents existing patent advantages. New sources of monopolized resources sometimes are found, and competition from foreign firms may emerge. (See Global Perspective 11.1.) If a monopoly is sufficiently fearful of future competition from new products, it may keep its prices relatively low so as to discourage rivals from developing such products. In that case, consumers may pay nearly competitive prices.

So what, if anything, should government do about monopoly? Economists agree that government needs to examine monopoly on a case-by-case basis. Three general policy options are available:

- If the monopoly is achieved and sustained through anticompetitive actions, creates substantial economic inefficiency, and appears to be long-lasting, the government can file charges against the monopoly under the antitrust laws. If the firm is found guilty of monopoly abuse, the government can expressly prohibit it from engaging in certain business activities or can break the monopoly into two or more competing firms. An example of the breakup approach was the dissolution of Standard Oil into several competing firms in 1911.

 GLOBAL PERSPECTIVE 11.1

COMPETITION FROM FOREIGN MULTINATIONAL CORPORATIONS

Competition from foreign multinational corporations diminishes the market power of firms in the United States. Here are just a few of the hundreds of foreign multinational corporations that compete strongly with U.S. firms in certain American markets.

Company (Country)	Main Products
Bayer (Germany)	chemicals
Volkswagen (Germany)	automobiles
Michelin (France)	tires
Lenovo (China)	electronics
Nestlé (Switzerland)	food products
Trafigura Group (Singapore)	commodities trading
Panasonic (Japan)	electronics
Petrobras (Brazil)	gasoline
Royal Dutch Shell (Netherlands)	gasoline
Samsung (South Korea)	electronics
Toyota (Japan)	automobiles

Source: Fortune Global 500. Fortune Media IP Limited, 2021.

- If the monopoly is a natural monopoly, society can allow it to continue to expand. If no competition emerges from new products, government may then decide to regulate its prices and operations.

- If the monopoly appears to be unsustainable because of emerging new technology, society can simply choose to ignore it. In such cases, society simply lets the process of creative destruction (discussed in Chapter 10) do its work.

QUICK REVIEW
11.2

▶ The monopolist maximizes profit (or minimizes loss) at the output where MR = MC and charges the price that corresponds to that output on its demand curve.

▶ The monopolist has no supply curve because any of several prices can be associated with a specific quantity of output supplied.

▶ Assuming identical costs, a monopolist will be less efficient than a purely competitive industry because it will fail to produce units of output for which marginal benefits exceed marginal costs.

▶ The inefficiencies of monopoly may be offset or lessened by economies of scale and, less likely, by technological progress, but they may be intensified by the presence of X-inefficiency and rent-seeking expenditures.

Price Discrimination

We have assumed that the monopolist charges a single price to all buyers. But under certain conditions the monopolist can increase its profit by charging different prices to different buyers. In so doing, the monopolist is engaging in **price discrimination,** the practice of selling a specific product at more than one price when the price differences are not justifiable by cost differences. Price discrimination can take three forms:

- Charging each customer in a single market the maximum price they are willing to pay.

- Charging each customer one price for the first set of units purchased and a lower price for subsequent units purchased.

- Charging some customers one price and other customers another price.

>> **LO11.6** Describe why a monopolist might charge different prices in different markets.

price discrimination The selling of a product to different buyers at different *prices* when the price differences are not justified by differences in cost.

Conditions

Price discrimination is possible when the following conditions are met:

- *Monopoly power* The seller must be a monopolist or, at least, must possess some degree of monopoly power—that is, some ability to control output and price.

- *Market segregation* At relatively low cost to itself, the seller must be able to segregate buyers into distinct classes, each with a different willingness or ability to pay for the product. This separation of buyers is usually based on different price elasticities of demand.

- *No resale* The original purchaser cannot resell the product or service. This condition suggests that service industries, such as the transportation industry or the industries for legal and medical services, where resale is impossible, are good candidates for price discrimination.

Examples of Price Discrimination

Price discrimination is common in the U.S. economy. For example, airlines charge high fares to business travelers, whose demand for travel is inelastic, and they offer lower, highly restricted, nonrefundable fares to attract vacationers and others whose demands are more elastic.

Movie theaters and golf courses vary their charges on the basis of time (for example, higher rates on evenings and weekends) and age (for example, lower rates for children and senior discounts). Railroads vary the rate charged per ton-mile of freight according to the market value of the product being shipped. The shipper of 10 tons of television sets or refrigerators pays more than the shipper of 10 tons of gravel.

Discount coupons, redeemable at purchase, are a form of price discrimination. They enable firms to give price discounts to their most price-sensitive customers who have elastic demand.

Less price-sensitive consumers who have less elastic demand are not as likely to take the time to clip and redeem coupons. The firm thus makes a larger profit than if it had used a single-price, no-coupon strategy.

Finally, price discrimination often occurs in international trade. A Russian aluminum producer, for example, might sell aluminum for less in the United States than in Russia. In the United States, this seller faces an elastic demand because several substitute suppliers are available. But in Russia, where the manufacturer dominates the market and trade barriers impede imports, consumers have fewer choices and thus demand is less elastic.

Graphical Analysis

Figure 11.7 demonstrates graphically the most frequently seen form of price discrimination—charging different prices to different classes of buyers. The two side-by-side graphs represent a single pure monopolist selling its product, say, software, in two segregated parts of the market. Figure 11.7a illustrates demand for software by small-business customers; Figure 11.7b shows the demand for software by students. Student versions of the software are identical to the versions sold to businesses but are available (1 per person) only to customers with a student ID. Presumably, students have lower ability to pay for the software and are charged a discounted price.

The demand curve D_b in the graph on the left indicates a relatively inelastic demand for the product by business customers. The demand curve D_s in the right-hand graph reflects students' more elastic demand. The marginal revenue curves (MR_b and MR_s) lie below their respective demand curves, reflecting the demand–marginal revenue relationship.

For visual clarity we have assumed that average total cost (ATC) is constant. Therefore, marginal cost (MC) equals average total cost (ATC) at all quantities of output. These costs are the same for both versions of the software and therefore appear as the identical straight lines labeled "MC = ATC."

What price will the pure monopolist charge to each set of customers? Using the MR = MC rule for profit maximization, the firm will offer Q_b units of the software for sale to small businesses. It can sell that profit-maximizing output by charging price P_b. Again using the MR = MC rule, the monopolist will offer Q_s units of software to students. To sell those Q_s units, the firm will charge students the lower price P_s.

Price discrimination increases profit. The numbers (not shown) behind the curves in Figure 11.7 would clearly reveal that the sum of the two green profit rectangles exceeds the single profit

FIGURE 11.7
Price discrimination applied to different groups of buyers.

The price-discriminating monopolist represented here maximizes its total profit by dividing the market into two segments based on differences in elasticity of demand. It then produces and sells the MR = MC output in each market segment. (For visual clarity, average total cost, ATC, is assumed to be constant. Therefore, MC equals ATC at all output levels.) (a) The price-discriminating monopolist charges a high price (here P_b) to small-business customers because they have a relatively inelastic demand curve for the product. (b) The firm charges a low price (here P_s) to students because their demand curve is relatively elastic. The firm's total profit from using price discrimination (here, the sum of the two green rectangles) exceeds the profit (not shown) that would have occurred if the monopolist had charged the same price to all customers.

(a) Small businesses

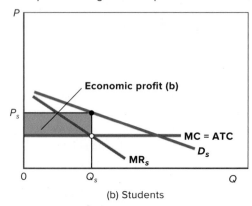

(b) Students

rectangle the firm would obtain from a single monopoly price. How do consumers fare? In this case, students clearly benefit by paying a lower price than they would if the firm charged a single monopoly price; however, the price discrimination results in a higher price for business customers. Therefore, compared to the single-price situation, students buy more of the software and small businesses buy less. Such price discrimination is widespread in the economy and is illegal only when it is part of a firm's strategy to lessen or eliminate competition. We discuss illegal price discrimination in Chapter 21, which covers antitrust policy.

Regulated Monopoly

Natural monopolies traditionally have been subject to *rate regulation* (price regulation), although the recent trend has been to deregulate wherever competition seems possible. For example, natural gas distribution, wireless communications, and long-distance electricity transmission have been, to one degree or another, deregulated. And regulators in some states are beginning to allow new entrants to compete with existing local telephone and electricity providers. Nevertheless, state and local regulatory commissions still regulate the prices that most local natural gas distributors, regional telephone companies, and local electricity suppliers can charge. These locally regulated monopolies are commonly called *public utilities*.

>> **LO11.7** Discuss the various selling prices that a regulator might impose on a regulated monopoly.

Let's consider the regulation of a local natural monopoly. Our example is a single firm that is the only seller of natural gas in the town of Springfield. **Figure 11.8 (Key Graph)** shows the firm's demand and the long-run cost curves. Due to extensive economies of scale, the demand curve cuts the natural monopolist's long-run ATC curve at a point where that curve is still falling. It would be inefficient to have several firms in this industry because each would produce a much smaller

..ıl KEY GRAPH

FIGURE 11.8 Rate regulation of a natural monopoly.

The socially optimal price P_r, found where D and MC intersect, will result in an efficient allocation of resources but may entail losses to the monopoly. The fair-return price P_f will allow the monopolist to break even but will not fully correct the underallocation of resources.

QUICK QUIZ FOR FIGURE 11.8

1. **The unregulated monopoly will underproduce output by:**
   a. Q_m units.
   b. $Q_r - Q_m$ units.
   c. overmaximizing its profit.
   d. $Q_f - Q_m$ units.

2. **From the viewpoint of the monopolist, the fair-return price and the socially optimum price both:**
   a. make marginal revenue per unit constant.
   b. make marginal revenue per unit equal to average revenue per unit.
   c. make the MR curve horizontal.
   d. all of the above.

3. **Which price generates a negative profit for this monopoly?**
   a. P_m
   b. the fair-return price
   c. the socially optimal price
   d. none of the above

4. **For this monopoly, a regulator who sets the regulated price at P_r per unit will need to take steps to deal with:**
   a. a substantial deadweight loss.
   b. the monopoly wanting to shut down.
   c. the monopoly wanting to expand production.
   d. an overallocation of resources at output level Q_r.

output, operating well to the left on the long-run ATC curve. In short, each firm's lowest average total cost would be substantially higher than that of a single firm. Therefore, efficient, lowest-cost production requires a single seller.

We know by application of the MR = MC rule that Q_m and P_m are the profit-maximizing output and price that an unregulated monopolist would choose. Because price exceeds average total cost at output Q_m, the monopolist enjoys a substantial economic profit. Furthermore, price exceeds marginal cost, indicating an underallocation of resources to this product or service. Can government regulation bring about better results from society's point of view?

Socially Optimal Price: P = MC

One sensible goal for regulators is to get the monopoly to produce the allocatively efficient output level. For the monopolist in Figure 11.8, this output level is Q_r, determined by the intersection of the demand curve D and the MC curve. Q_r is the allocatively efficient output level; for each unit of output up to Q_r, the demand curve lies above the MC curve, indicating that marginal benefit exceeds marginal cost for all of these units.

How can the regulatory commission motivate the monopoly to produce this output level? The trick is to set the regulated price P_r at a level such that the monopoly will be led by its profit-maximizing rule to voluntarily produce the allocatively efficient level of output. Because the monopoly will receive the regulated price P_r for all units that it sells, P_r becomes the monopoly's marginal revenue per unit. Thus, the monopoly's MR curve becomes the horizontal line moving rightward from price P_r on the vertical axis.

The monopoly will at this point follow its usual rule for maximizing profits or minimizing losses: It will produce where marginal revenue equals marginal cost. As a result, the monopoly will produce where the horizontal MR ($= P_r$) line intersects the MC curve at point r. That is, the monopoly will end up producing the socially optimal output Q_r not because it is socially minded but because Q_r happens to be the output that either maximizes profits or minimizes losses when regulators force the firm to sell all units at the regulated price P_r.

socially optimal price The *price* of a product that results in the most efficient allocation of an economy's *resources* and that is equal to the *marginal cost* of the product.

The regulated price P_r that achieves allocative efficiency is called the **socially optimal price**. Because it is determined by the intersection of the MC curve and the demand curve, the socially optimal price is often summarized by the equation $P = MC$.

Fair-Return Price: P = ATC

The socially optimal price suffers from a potentially fatal problem. P_r may be so low that average total costs are not covered, as is the case in Figure 11.8. In such situations, forcing the socially optimal price on the regulated monopoly will result in short-run losses and long-run exit. In our example, Springfield will be left without a gas company and its citizens without gas.

How can we rectify this problem? One option is to provide a public subsidy to cover the loss that the socially optimal price would entail. Another possibility is to condone price discrimination, allow the monopoly to charge some customers prices above P_r, and hope that the additional revenue that the monopoly gains from price discrimination is enough so that it can break even, with a zero economic profit.

In practice, regulatory commissions in the United States have often pursued a third option in which regulators set a regulated price that is high enough for monopolists to break even and continue in operation. This price is called a **fair-return price** because of a Supreme Court ruling requiring regulatory agencies to allow regulated utility owners to enjoy a "fair return" on their investments. In practice, a fair return is equal to a normal profit.

fair-return price For *natural monopolies* subject to rate (*price*) regulation, the price that would allow the regulated monopoly to earn a *normal profit*; a price equal to *average total cost*.

The regulator determines the fair-return price P_f at the point where the ATC curve intersects the demand curve at point f. Setting the regulated price at this level will cause the monopoly to produce Q_f units while guaranteeing that it will break even and not wish to exit the industry. To see why the monopoly will voluntarily produce Q_f units, note that the monopoly will receive P_f dollars for each unit it sells. Therefore, its marginal revenue per unit becomes P_f dollars so that the horizontal line moving rightward from P_f on the vertical axis becomes the regulated monopoly's MR curve. Because this horizontal MR curve is always higher than the monopoly's MC curve, marginal revenue will exceed marginal cost for every possible level of output up to Q_f units. Thus, the monopoly should be willing to supply whatever quantity of output is demanded by consumers at the regulated price P_f. That quantity is, of course, given by the demand curve. At price P_f, consumers will demand exactly Q_f units. Thus, by setting the regulated price per unit at P_f, the regulator gets the monopoly to voluntarily supply exactly Q_f units.

Even better, the regulator also guarantees that the monopoly firm will earn exactly a normal profit. In Figure 11.8, note that the rectangle $0afb$ is equal to both the monopoly's total cost and its total revenue. Its economic profit is therefore equal to zero, implying that it must be earning a normal accounting profit.

One final point about allocative efficiency: By choosing the fair-return price P_f, the regulator leads the monopoly to produce Q_f units. This amount of output is less than the socially optimal quantity Q_r, but it is more than the Q_m units that the monopolist would produce if left unregulated. So, although fair-return pricing does not lead to full allocative efficiency, it is still an improvement on what the monopoly would do if left to its own devices.

Dilemma of Regulation

Comparing the results of the socially optimal price ($P = MC$) and the fair-return price ($P = ATC$) suggests a policy dilemma, sometimes termed the **dilemma of regulation.** When its price is set to achieve the most efficient allocation of resources ($P = MC$), the regulated monopoly is likely to suffer losses. The firm's survival would presumably depend on permanent public subsidies taken from general tax revenues. On the other hand, although a fair-return price ($P = ATC$) allows the monopolist to cover costs, it only partially resolves the underallocation of resources that the unregulated monopoly price would foster. Despite this dilemma, regulation can improve on the results of monopoly from the social point of view. Price regulation (even at the fair-return price) can simultaneously reduce price, increase output, and reduce the economic profit of monopolies.

That said, we need to provide an important caution: Fair-price regulation of monopoly looks simple in theory but is amazingly complex in practice. In the actual economy, rate regulation is accompanied by large, expensive rate-setting bureaucracies and maze-like sets of procedures. Also, rate decisions require extensive public input via letters and public hearings. Rate decisions are subject to lengthy legal challenges. Further, because regulatory commissions must set prices sufficiently above costs to create fair returns, regulated monopolists have little incentive to minimize average total costs. When these costs creep up, the regulatory commissions must set higher prices. Regulated firms therefore are noted for higher-than-competitive wages, more managers and staff than necessary, nicer-than-typical office buildings, and other forms of X-inefficiency. These inefficiencies help explain the trend of federal, state, and local governments abandoning price regulation where the possibility of competition looks promising.

dilemma of regulation The trade-off faced by a *regulatory agency* in setting the maximum legal *price* a monopolist may charge: The *socially optimal price* is below *average total cost* (and either bankrupts the *firm* or requires that it be subsidized), while the higher, *fair-return price* does not produce *allocative efficiency*.

▶ Price discrimination occurs when a firm sells a product at different prices that are not based on cost differences.

▶ The conditions necessary for price discrimination are (a) monopoly power, (b) the ability to segregate buyers on the basis of demand elasticities, and (c) buyers' inability to resell the product.

▶ Compared with setting a single price for all customers, a monopoly utilizing perfect price discrimination will generate greater profit and greater output. Many consumers pay higher prices, but others pay prices below the single price.

▶ Monopoly price can be reduced and output increased through government regulation.

▶ The socially optimal price ($P = MC$) achieves allocative efficiency but may result in losses; the fair-return price ($P = ATC$) yields a normal profit but fails to achieve allocative efficiency.

QUICK REVIEW
11.3

The Silicon Bottleneck

The COVID-19 Pandemic Revealed a Lack of Spare Capacity in the Natural Monopoly Computer Chip Industry.

During the first year of the COVID-19 pandemic, the economy saw shortages of consumer goods that require computer chips—products like video game consoles, smartphones, and new cars. When reporters investigated, they discovered that those shortages were due to the makers of those products being unable to get their hands on enough of the right sorts of computer chips.

You can't make an iPhone without a cutting-edge computer chip. And cars and trucks require several dozen less powerful chips to control everything from anti-lock braking to Bluetooth connections. So when consumer-goods makers like Apple and Ford couldn't get enough of the chips they needed, they had to slow or halt production.

But why weren't chipmakers able to keep up with demand? What had gone wrong such that for the first time ever major automakers had to halt production on some models due to a lack of chips?

The story begins several decades earlier, when manufacturing firms decided to employ "just in time delivery" of inputs to factories as a way of saving money. Instead of keeping a substantial inventory of inputs like computer chips available at a factory site at all times in case there were delivery delays, manufacturers got comfortable with the idea that a computer-controlled global supply chain could deliver inputs just before they would be needed for the assembly of finished products.

Around the same time—starting in the late 1980s—the computer chip industry started to rearrange its production processes to take advantage of the efficiencies that could be gained from specialization and economies of scale. Firms like IBM that previously both designed and manufactured computer chips began to focus only on the design of chips while sending their blueprints out to other firms that specialized in the manufacture of chips.

That outsourcing has allowed for the rise of incredibly efficient chip-making firms like Taiwan Semiconductor that take advantage of economies of scale by setting up giant plants that can each make hundreds of thousands or even millions of chips each year from various blueprints sent in by the companies that specialize in chip design. With new chip-making factories costing upwards of $12 billion each, there are huge opportunities for economies of scale just as long as each of those factories can be kept busy running at full capacity 24 hours per day so as to spread their enormous fixed cost over as many units of output as possible.

At the start of the COVID-19 pandemic in March 2020, when lockdowns were first being imposed, there was a huge amount of uncertainty about the economy and whether there would be a major recession. Many consumer-goods makers like Ford and Apple assumed that a major recession was about to happen, which implied that consumers would be buying much less from them over the

Stockbakery/Shutterstock

coming year. Based on that forecast, those firms cut back on their orders of inputs, including computer chips.

But then a big surprise happened. The recession was the shortest on record, lasting just two months. As soon as the lockdowns were lifted, the economy began to grow again.

That meant that companies like Ford and Apple that had canceled chip orders at the start of the pandemic suddenly wanted lots of chips again. Unfortunately for them, though, they couldn't just buy more chips. That's because when they canceled their orders at the start of the pandemic, they lost their place in line at the chip-making factories. They could order more chips again, but those orders were now at the back of the line. It would be months if not years before they would get all the chips they wanted.

That lack of spare capacity has prompted two major responses. First, many manufacturing firms are backing away from just-in-time input deliveries and beginning to once again maintain substantial stocks of raw materials and other inputs, including computer chips, at their factories.

Second, there is now a wave of new construction going on in the chip-making industry, with dozens of new chip-making factories set to be finished in the next four or five years. Each of them will have to be run at full capacity, with waiting lists, in order to take advantage of their natural-monopoly economies of scale. But the increased overall capacity that they will collectively provide should shorten the length of computer-chip waiting lists across the entire industry. So when a consumer-goods manufacturer has to put in an unexpected order and go to the end of the line, they will hopefully get their chips in days or weeks rather than in months or years.

Summary

LO11.1 List the characteristics of pure monopoly.
A pure monopolist is the sole producer of a commodity for which there are no close substitutes.

LO11.2 Explain the barriers to entry that shield pure monopolies from competition.
The existence of pure monopoly and other imperfectly competitive market structures is explained by barriers to entry in the form of (*a*) economies of scale, (*b*) network effects, (*c*) patents and licenses, (*d*) ownership or control of essential resources, and (*e*) pricing and other strategic behavior.

LO11.3 Explain how a pure monopolist sees demand.
The pure monopolist's market situation differs from that of a competitive firm in that the monopolist's demand curve is downward sloping, causing the MR curve to lie below the demand curve.

As with all other types of imperfect competitors, the pure monopolist is a pricemaker whose choice of quantity will determine the price per unit that it receives.

The pure monopolist will always choose to produce a quantity that lies on the elastic region of its demand curve. By doing so, any increase in its output will increase total revenue, whereas if it produced in the inelastic portion of its demand curve, any increase in its output would reduce total revenue.

LO11.4 Explain how a pure monopoly sets its profit-maximizing output and price.
Like the competitive seller, the pure monopolist will maximize profit by equating marginal revenue and marginal cost. The monopolist does not, however, have a supply curve (= a predictable positive relationship between quantity produced and price) because its profit-maximizing quantity (that at which MR = MC) can be associated with any number of different prices depending upon the location of the demand curve.

Barriers to entry may permit a monopolist to enjoy economic profit even in the long run. However, (*a*) the monopolist does not charge the highest price possible, (*b*) the price that yields maximum total profit to the monopolist rarely coincides with the price that yields maximum per-unit profit, and (*c*) high costs and weak demand may prevent the monopolist from realizing any profit at all.

LO11.5 Discuss the economic effects of monopoly.
With the same costs, the pure monopolist will find it profitable to restrict output and charge a higher price than would sellers in a purely competitive industry. This restriction of output causes resources to be misallocated because price exceeds marginal cost in monopolized markets. Monopoly creates an efficiency loss (deadweight loss) for society.

A monopoly transfers income from consumers to itself by charging a higher price than would a purely competitive firm with the same costs. The monopoly in effect levies a "private tax" on consumers and, if demand is strong enough, will obtain substantial economic profits.

Monopolists and competitive producers may not face the same costs. On the one hand, economies of scale may reduce the per-unit production costs available to monopolists but not to competitors. Also, pure monopoly may be more likely than pure competition to reduce costs via technological advance because of the monopolist's ability to realize economic profit, which can be used to finance research.

On the other hand, X-inefficiency—the failure to produce with the least costly combination of inputs—is more common among monopolists than among competitive firms. Also, monopolists may make costly expenditures to maintain monopoly privileges that are conferred by government. Finally, the blocked entry of rival firms weakens the monopolist's incentive to be technologically progressive.

LO11.6 Describe why a monopolist might charge different prices in different markets.
A monopolist can increase its profit by practicing price discrimination, provided (*a*) it can segregate buyers on the basis of elasticities of demand and (*b*) its product or service cannot be readily transferred between the segregated groups of buyers.

LO11.7 Discuss the various selling prices that a regulator might impose on a regulated monopoly.
Price regulation can be used to eliminate wholly or partially the monopolist's tendency to underallocate resources and to earn economic profits. The socially optimal price is determined where the demand and MC curves intersect; the fair-return price is determined where the demand and ATC curves intersect.

Terms and Concepts

pure monopoly	simultaneous consumption	socially optimal price
barriers to entry	X-inefficiency	fair-return price
natural monopoly	rent-seeking behavior	dilemma of regulation
network effects	price discrimination	

Discussion Questions

1. "No firm is completely sheltered from rivals; all firms compete for consumer dollars. Therefore, pure monopoly does not exist." Do you agree? Explain. How might you use the concept of cross elasticity of demand to judge whether monopoly exists? **LO11.1**

2. Discuss the major barriers to entry into an industry. Explain how each barrier can foster monopoly. Which barriers, if any, do you feel give rise to monopoly that is socially justifiable? **LO11.2**

3. How does the demand curve faced by a purely monopolistic seller differ from that confronting a purely competitive firm? Why does

it differ? Of what significance is the difference? Why is the pure monopolist's demand curve not perfectly inelastic? **LO11.3**

4. Assume that a pure monopolist and a purely competitive firm have the same unit costs. Contrast the two with respect to (*a*) price, (*b*) output, (*c*) profits, (*d*) allocation of resources, and (*e*) impact on income transfers. Because both monopolists and competitive firms follow the MC = MR rule in maximizing profits, how do you account for the different results? Why might the costs of a purely competitive firm and those of a monopolist be different? What are the implications of such a cost difference? **LO11.5**

5. Critically evaluate and explain each statement: **LO11.5**
   a. Because they can control product price, monopolists can guarantee profitable production by simply charging the highest price consumers will pay.
   b. The pure monopolist seeks the output that will yield the greatest per-unit profit.
   c. An excess of price over marginal cost is the market's way of signaling the need for more production of a good.
   d. The more profitable a firm, the greater its monopoly power.
   e. The monopolist has a pricing policy; the competitive producer does not.
   f. With respect to resource allocation, the interests of the seller and of society coincide in a purely competitive market but conflict in a monopolized market.

6. Assume a monopolistic publisher has agreed to pay an author 10 percent of the total revenue from the sales of a book. Will the author and the publisher want to charge the same price for the book? Explain. **LO11.5**

7. U.S. pharmaceutical companies charge different prices for prescription drugs to buyers in different nations, depending on elasticity of demand and government-imposed price ceilings. Explain why these companies, for profit reasons, oppose laws allowing re-importation of drugs to the United States. **LO11.6**

8. Explain verbally and graphically how price (rate) regulation may improve the performance of monopolies. In your answer, distinguish between (*a*) socially optimal (marginal-cost) pricing and (*b*) fair-return (average-total-cost) pricing. What is the "dilemma of regulation"? **LO11.7**

9. It has been proposed that natural monopolists should be allowed to determine their profit-maximizing outputs and prices, and then government should tax their profits away and distribute them to consumers in proportion to their purchases from the monopoly. Is this proposal as socially desirable as requiring monopolists to equate price with marginal cost or average total cost? Explain. **LO11.7**

10. **LAST WORD** What are the benefits and risks associated with just-in-time delivery of inputs to factories? Why do computer chip factories run continuously rather than maintaining some spare capacity? What is the underlying economic concept that explains why 80 percent of the world's most advanced computer chips are produced by a single firm, Taiwan Semiconductor, rather than by many small firms?

Review Questions

1. Which of the following could explain why a firm is a monopoly? Select one or more answers from the choices shown. **LO11.2**
   a. Patents
   b. Economies of scale
   c. Inelastic demand
   d. Government licenses
   e. Downward sloping market demand
   f. The absence of network effects

2. The MR curve of a perfectly competitive firm is horizontal. The MR curve of a monopoly firm is: **LO11.3**
   a. horizontal, too.
   b. upward sloping.
   c. downward sloping.
   d. it depends.

3. Use the following demand schedule to calculate total revenue and marginal revenue at each quantity. Plot the demand, TR, and MR curves, and explain the relationships between them. Explain why the marginal revenue of the fourth unit of output is $3.50, even though its price is $5. Use Chapter 6's total-revenue test for price elasticity to designate the elastic and inelastic segments of your graphed demand curve. What generalization can you make about the relationship between marginal revenue and elasticity of demand? Suppose the marginal cost of successive units of output is zero. What output would the profit-seeking firm produce? Finally, use your analysis to explain why a monopolist will never produce in the inelastic region of demand. **LO11.3**

Price (*P*)	Quantity Demanded (*Q*)	Price (*P*)	Quantity Demanded (*Q*)
$7.00	0	$4.50	5
6.50	1	4.00	6
6.00	2	3.50	7
5.50	3	3.00	8
5.00	4	2.50	9

4. How often do *perfectly competitive* firms engage in price discrimination? **LO11.6**
   a. Never
   b. Rarely
   c. Often
   d. Always

5. Suppose that a monopoly firm can segregate its buyers into two different groups to which it can charge two different prices. To maximize profit, the monopoly should charge a higher price to the group that has: **LO11.6**
   a. the higher elasticity of demand.
   b. the lower elasticity of demand.
   c. richer members.

6. The socially optimal price (*P* = MC) is socially optimal because: **LO11.7**
   a. it reduces the monopolist's profit.
   b. it yields a normal profit.
   c. it minimizes ATC.
   d. it achieves allocative efficiency.

7. The main problem with imposing the socially optimal price ($P = MC$) on a monopoly is that the socially optimal price: **LO11.7**
   a. may be so low that the regulated monopoly can't break even.

b. may cause the regulated monopoly to engage in price discrimination.

c. may be higher than the monopoly price.

Problems

1. Connections are valuable and Metcalf's Law tells us that the value, V, of a network is approximately equal to the square of the number, n, of people or objects connected to the network. That is, $V = n^2$. Apply Metcalf's law to the following situation: Santiago is choosing between two local dating apps, one which has 5 users and the other which has 50 users. What is the value of the smaller network? Of the larger network? How many times bigger is the value of the larger network than the value of the smaller network? Which app will Santiago probably choose? Aside from anything else that might distinguish the two apps, does the larger network size of the more popular dating app constitute a barrier to entry? **LO11.2**

2. Suppose a pure monopolist faces the following demand schedule and the same cost data as the competitive producer discussed in problem 4 at the end of Chapter 10. Calculate the missing TR and MR amounts, and determine the profit-maximizing price and profit-maximizing output for this monopolist. What is the monopolist's profit? Verify your answer graphically and by comparing total revenue and total cost. **LO11.4**

Price	Quantity Demanded	Total Revenue	Marginal Revenue
$115	0	$_____	
100	1	_____	$_____
83	2	_____	_____
71	3	_____	_____
63	4	_____	_____
55	5	_____	_____
48	6	_____	_____
42	7	_____	_____
37	8	_____	_____
33	9	_____	_____
29	10	_____	_____

3. Suppose that a price-discriminating monopolist has segregated its market into two groups of buyers. The first group is described by the demand and revenue data that you developed for problem 1. The demand and revenue data for the second group of buyers are shown in the following table. Assume that MC is $13 in both markets and MC = ATC at all output levels. What price will the firm charge in each market? Based solely on these two prices, which market has the higher price elasticity of demand? What will be this monopolist's total economic profit? **LO11.6**

Price	Quantity Demanded	Total Revenue	Marginal Revenue
$71	0	$ 0	
63	1	63	$63
55	2	110	47
48	3	144	34
42	4	168	24
37	5	185	17
33	6	198	13
29	7	203	5

4. Assume that the most efficient production technology available for making vitamin pills has the cost structure given in the following table. Note that output is measured as the number of bottles of vitamins produced per day and that costs include a normal profit. **LO11.6**

Output	TC	MC
25,000	$100,000	$0.50
50,000	150,000	1.00
75,000	187,500	2.50
100,000	275,500	3.00

a. What is ATC per unit for each level of output listed in the table?

b. Are there economies of scale in production? (Answer yes or no.)

c. Suppose that the market price for a bottle of vitamins is $2.50. At that price the total market quantity demanded is 75,000,000 bottles. How many firms will be in this industry?

d. Suppose that, instead, the market quantity demanded at a price of $2.50 is only 75,000. How many firms will be in this industry?

e. Review your answers to parts *b, c,* and *d.* Does the level of demand determine this industry's market structure?

5. A new production technology for making vitamins is invented by a college professor who decides not to patent it. Thus, it is available for anybody to copy and use. The TC per bottle for production up to 100,000 bottles per day is given in the following table. **LO11.6**

Output	TC
25,000	$50,000
50,000	70,000
75,000	75,000
100,000	80,000

a. What is ATC for each level of output listed in the table?

b. Suppose that for each 25,000-bottle-per-day increase in production above 100,000 bottles per day, TC increases by $5,000 (so that, for instance, 125,000 bottles per day would generate total costs of $85,000, and 150,000 bottles per day would generate total costs of $90,000). Are there economies of scale at all output levels?

c. Suppose that the price of a bottle of vitamins is $1.33. At that price, the total quantity demanded by consumers is 75,000,000 bottles. How many firms will be in this industry?

d. Suppose that, instead, the market quantity demanded at a price of $1.33 is only 75,000. How many firms will be in this industry?

e. Review your answers to parts *b, c,* and *d*. Does the level of demand determine this industry's market structure?

f. Compare your answer to part *d* of this problem with your answer to part *d* of problem 4. Do both production technologies show constant returns to scale?

6. Suppose you have been tasked with regulating a single monopoly firm that sells 50-pound bags of concrete. The firm has fixed costs of $10 million per year and a variable cost of $1 per bag no matter how many bags are produced. **LO11.7**

a. If this firm keeps increasing its output level, will ATC per bag ever increase? Are there economies of scale at all output levels?

b. If you wished to regulate this monopoly by charging the socially optimal price, what price would you charge? At that price, what will be the size of the firm's profit or loss? Will the firm want to exit the industry?

c. You find out that if you set the price at $2 per bag, consumers will demand 10 million bags. How big will the firm's profit or loss be at that price?

d. If consumers instead demanded 20 million bags at a price of $2 per bag, how big would the firm's profit or loss be?

e. Suppose that demand is perfectly inelastic at 20 million bags, so that consumers demand 20 million bags no matter what the price is. What price should you charge if you want the firm to earn only a fair rate of return? Assume as always that TC includes a normal profit.

Monopolistic Competition

>> LEARNING OBJECTIVES

LO12.1 List the characteristics of monopolistic competition.

LO12.2 Explain why monopolistic competitors earn only a normal profit in the long run.

LO12.3 Explain why monopolistic competition delivers neither productive nor allocative efficiency.

LO12.4 Explain why product differentiation helps to compensate for economic inefficiency.

In the United States, most industries fall somewhere between the two poles of pure competition and pure monopoly. First, most real-world industries have fewer than the large number of producers required for pure competition but more than the single producer that defines pure monopoly. In addition, most firms offer differentiated products and have some discretion over their prices. As a result, competition often occurs on the basis of a wide variety of product attributes, including not only price but also quality, location, service, and advertising. Finally, entry into most real-world industries ranges from easy to very difficult but is rarely completely blocked as it is in the case of certain monopolies (such as those with patents or copyrights).

In this chapter, you will discover that *monopolistic competition* mixes a small amount of monopoly power with a large amount of competition. In the next chapter, you will see how *oligopoly* blends a large amount of monopoly power with considerable rivalry among existing firms. (You should quickly review Table 10.1 at this point.)

Monopolistic Competition

Monopolistic competition is characterized by (1) a relatively large number of sellers; (2) differentiated products (often promoted by heavy advertising); and (3) easy entry to, and exit from, the industry. The first and third characteristics provide the "competitive" aspect of monopolistic competition; the second characteristic provides the "monopolistic" aspect. In general, however, monopolistically competitive industries are much more competitive than they are monopolistic.

Relatively Large Number of Sellers

Monopolistic competition is characterized by a fairly large number of firms, say, 25, 35, or 70, not by the hundreds or thousands of firms in pure competition. Consequently, monopolistic competition involves:

- **Small market shares** Each firm has a comparatively small percentage of the total market and consequently has limited control over market price.

>> **LO12.1** List the characteristics of monopolistic competition.

monopolistic competition
A *market structure* in which many *firms* sell a *differentiated product*, entry is relatively easy, each firm has some control over its product *price*, and there is considerable *nonprice competition*.

- *No collusion* The presence of a relatively large number of firms ensures that *collusion* (coordination) by a group of firms to restrict output and set prices is unlikely.
- *Independent action* There is no interdependence among firms; each can determine its own pricing policy without considering rival firms' possible reactions. A single firm may realize a modest increase in sales by cutting its price, but that action's effect on competitors' sales will be nearly imperceptible and will probably trigger no response.

Differentiated Products

product differentiation A strategy in which one *firm*'s product is distinguished from competing products by means of its design, related *services*, quality, location, or other attributes (except *price*).

Unlike pure competition, in which there is a standardized product, monopolistic competition features **product differentiation.** Monopolistically competitive firms produce variations of a particular product. Their products have slightly different physical characteristics, offer varying degrees of customer service, provide varying amounts of locational convenience, or proclaim special qualities, real or imagined.

Product Attributes Product differentiation may entail physical or qualitative differences in the products. Real differences in functional features, materials, design, and workmanship are vital aspects of product differentiation. Personal computers, for example, differ in terms of storage capacity, speed, and quality of graphic displays. Most cities have a variety of retail stores selling clothes that differ greatly in styling, materials, and quality. Similarly, one pizzeria may feature thin-crust Neapolitan-style pizza, while another may tout its thick-crust Chicago-style pizza.

Service Service and the conditions surrounding the sale of a product are forms of product differentiation too. One shoe store may stress its clerks' fashion knowledge and helpfulness. A competitor may leave trying on shoes and carrying them to the register to its customers but offer lower prices. A store's prestige appeal, the firm's reputation for servicing or exchanging its products, and the credit it makes available are all service aspects of product differentiation.

Location Products may also be differentiated through the location and accessibility of the stores that sell them. Small convenience stores manage to compete with large supermarkets, even though these mini-marts sell fewer products and charge higher prices. They compete mainly on the basis of location—being close to customers and situated on busy streets. A motel's proximity to an interstate highway gives it a locational advantage that may allow it to charge a higher room rate than other motels in less convenient locations.

Brand Names and Packaging Product differentiation may also be created through the use of brand names and trademarks, packaging, and celebrity endorsements. Most aspirin tablets are very much alike, but many headache sufferers believe that one brand—for example, Bayer, Anacin, or Bufferin—is superior and worth a higher price than a generic substitute. A celebrity's name associated with watches, perfume, or athletic shoes may enhance those products' appeal for some buyers. Packaging that touts "natural spring" bottled water may attract additional customers.

Some Control over Price Monopolistic competitors have some control over their product prices because of product differentiation. If consumers prefer the products of specific sellers, then within limits they will pay more to satisfy their preferences. Sellers and buyers are not linked randomly, as in a purely competitive market. Nonetheless, the monopolistic competitor's control over price is quite limited because there are numerous potential substitutes for its product.

Easy Entry and Exit

Entry into monopolistically competitive industries is relatively easy. Because monopolistic competitors are typically small firms, both absolutely and relatively, economies of scale are few and capital requirements are low. However, financial barriers may result from the need to develop and advertise a product that differs from rivals' products. Some firms have trade secrets relating to their products or hold trademarks on their brand names, making it difficult and costly for other firms to imitate them.

Exit from monopolistically competitive industries is relatively easy. Nothing prevents an unprofitable monopolistic competitor from holding a going-out-of-business sale and shutting down.

Advertising

The expense and effort involved in product differentiation would be wasted if consumers were not aware of product differences. Thus, monopolistic competitors advertise their products, often heavily. The goal of product differentiation and advertising—so-called **nonprice competition**—is to make price less of a factor in consumer purchases and to make real or perceived product differences a greater factor. If advertising is successful, a firm's demand curve will shift to the right *and* become steeper, implying that demand will become less elastic at every possible price. That reduced elasticity, if achieved, will give the firm greater **pricing power** because less elastic demand implies that any price increase initiated by the monopolistically competitive firm will cause a smaller decrease in sales, all other things equal.

Please also keep in mind that advertising is not free. It is a variable cost that shifts AVC and ATC curves to the left (upward). Thus, when a monopolistically competitive firm decides to advertise, it is hoping that it will achieve a rightward shift and steepening of its demand curve large enough so as to more than make up for the fact that its cost curves are going to have to shift left (upward) to account for the cost of its advertising expenditures. If the change in demand allows the firm to increase revenue by enough to pay for its advertising expenditures, then the firm's profit will increase and the advertising campaign will be counted as a success. But if demand doesn't move at all or doesn't move enough, profit will decrease and the advertising campaign will be ruled a failure.

nonprice competition Competition based on distinguishing one's product by means of *product differentiation* and then *advertising* the distinguished product to consumers.

pricing power The ability of a firm to raise *price* without substantially reducing *quantity demanded*; increases as *demand* becomes increasingly *inelastic*.

Monopolistically Competitive Industries

Table 12.1 lists several manufacturing industries that approximate monopolistic competition. Economists measure the degree of industry concentration—the extent to which the largest firms account for the bulk of the industry's output—to identify monopolistically competitive (versus oligopolistic) industries. Two such measures are the four-firm concentration ratio and the Herfindahl index, listed in columns 2 and 3 of the table.

A **four-firm concentration ratio,** expressed as a percentage, is the ratio of the output (sales) of the four largest firms in an industry relative to total industry sales.

four-firm concentration ratio The percentage of total *industry* sales accounted for by the top four *firms* in an industry.

$$\text{Four-firm concentration ratio} = \frac{\text{Output of four largest firms}}{\text{Total output in the industry}}$$

Four-firm concentration ratios are very low in purely competitive industries in which there are hundreds or thousands of firms, each with a tiny market share. In contrast, four-firm ratios are high in oligopoly and pure monopoly. Industries in which the largest four firms account for 40 percent

TABLE 12.1 Percentage of Output Produced by Firms in Selected Low-Concentration U.S. Manufacturing Industries

(1) Industry	(2) Percentage of Industry Output* Produced by the Four Largest Firms	(3) Herfindahl Index for the Top 50 Firms	(1) Industry	(2) Percentage of Industry Output* Produced by the Four Largest Firms	(3) Herfindahl Index for the Top 50 Firms
Jewelry	32	550	Ready-mix concrete	14	89
Plastic pipe	31	303	Sawmills	14	93
Plastic bags	28	320	Textile bags	13	93
Asphalt paving	25	230	Wood pallets	12	55
Bolts, nuts, and rivets	23	198	Stone products	12	56
Women's dresses	22	236	Textile machinery	10	58
Wood trusses	21	158	Metal stamping	10	52
Curtains and draperies	20	172	Signs	9	36
Metal windows and doors	17	143	Sheet metal work	8	29
Quick printing	17	108	Retail bakeries	5	12

*As measured by the value of shipments. Data are for 2012.[1]

Source: U.S. Census Bureau, Census of Manufacturers, 2012.

---

[1]The U.S. Census Bureau's *Census of Manufacturers* is conducted every five years but data from the 2017 census were not available in time for this edition due to delays caused by the COVID-19 pandemic.

or more of the market are generally considered to be oligopolies. If the largest four firms account for less than 40 percent, they are likely to be monopolistically competitive. The four-firm concentration ratios in Table 12.1 range from 5 percent to 32 percent.

Concentration ratios such as those in Table 12.1 are helpful in categorizing industries but must be used cautiously because the market shares (percentage of total sales) are national in scope, whereas competition in many industries is often local. Thus, some industries with low national concentration ratios are in fact substantially concentrated in local markets.

Herfindahl index A measure of the concentration and competitiveness of an *industry;* calculated as the sum of the squared percentage market shares of the individual *firms* in the industry.

Column 3 of Table 12.1 lists the **Herfindahl index,** which is the sum of the squared percentage market shares of all firms in the industry. In equation form:

$$\text{Herfindahl index} = (\%S_1)^2 + (\%S_2)^2 + (\%S_3)^2 + \cdots + (\%S_n)^2$$

where $\%S_1$ is the percentage market share of firm 1, $\%S_2$ is the percentage market share of firm 2, and so on for each of the n total firms in the industry. By squaring the percentage market shares of all firms in the industry, the Herfindahl index purposely gives much greater weight to larger, and thus more powerful, firms than to smaller ones. For a purely competitive industry, the index would approach zero because each firm's market share is extremely small. In the case of a single-firm industry, the index will be at its maximum of 10,000 ($= 100^2$), indicating an industry with complete monopoly power.

Overall, the lower the Herfindahl index, the greater is the likelihood that an industry is monopolistically competitive rather than oligopolistic. Note that the index values in Table 12.1 (computed for the top 50 firms in the industry) are decidedly closer to the bottom limit of the Herfindahl index—0—than to its top limit—10,000.

The numbers in Table 12.1 are for manufacturing industries. In addition, many providers of professional services such as medical care, legal assistance, real estate sales, and basic bookkeeping are monopolistic competitors. Many retail establishments in metropolitan areas are monopolistically competitive, too, including grocery stores, gasoline stations, hair salons, dry cleaners, clothing stores, and restaurants.

Global Perspective 12.1 presents the number of restaurants per 100,000 residents found in various cities around the world. Our study of monopolistic competition will demonstrate that the economic profits earned by restaurant owners are mostly likely zero in each of these cities, despite the large differences in restaurant density. Free entry guarantees that profits will be driven to zero even in cities where dining out is extremely popular.

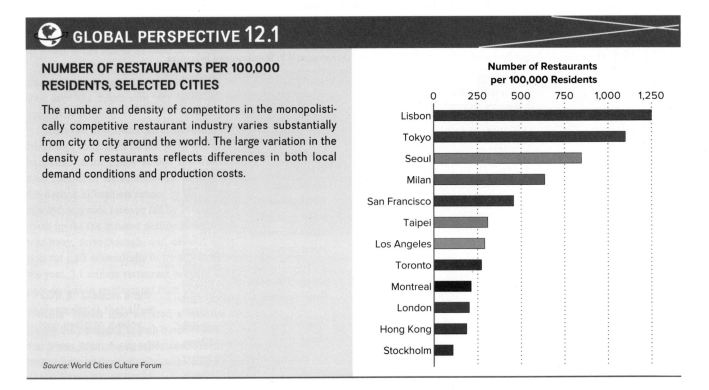

GLOBAL PERSPECTIVE 12.1

NUMBER OF RESTAURANTS PER 100,000 RESIDENTS, SELECTED CITIES

The number and density of competitors in the monopolistically competitive restaurant industry varies substantially from city to city around the world. The large variation in the density of restaurants reflects differences in both local demand conditions and production costs.

Source: World Cities Culture Forum

Price and Output in Monopolistic Competition

How does a monopolistic competitor decide on its price and output? To explain, we initially assume that each firm is producing a specific differentiated product and engaging in a particular amount of advertising.

>> **LO12.2** Explain why monopolistic competitors earn only a normal profit in the long run.

The Firm's Demand Curve

Our explanation is based on **Figure 12.1 (Key Graph),** which shows that the demand curve faced by a monopolistically competitive seller is highly, but not perfectly, elastic. This feature distinguishes monopolistic competition from pure monopoly and pure competition. The monopolistic competitor's demand is more elastic than the demand faced by a pure monopolist because the monopolistically competitive seller competes with many other firms producing close substitutes. The pure monopolist has no rivals at all. Yet, for two reasons, the monopolistic competitor's demand is not perfectly elastic like that of the pure competitor. First, the monopolistic competitor has fewer rivals; second, its products are differentiated, so they are not perfect substitutes.

The price elasticity of demand faced by the monopolistically competitive firm depends on the number of rivals and the degree of product differentiation. The more rivals and the weaker the product differentiation, the greater the price elasticity of each seller's demand—that is, the closer monopolistic competition will be to pure competition.

The Short Run: Profit or Loss

In the short run, monopolistically competitive firms maximize profit or minimize loss using exactly the same strategy as pure competitors and monopolists: They produce the level of output at which marginal revenue equals marginal cost (MR = MC). Thus, the monopolistically competitive firm in Figure 12.1a produces output Q_1, where MR = MC. As shown by demand curve D_1, it then charges price P_1. It realizes an economic profit, shown by the green area $[= (P_1 - A_1) \times Q_1]$.

But with less favorable demand or costs, the firm may incur a loss in the short run. We see this possibility in Figure 12.1b, where the firm's best strategy is to minimize its loss. It does so by producing output Q_2 (where MR = MC) and, as determined by demand curve D_2, by charging price P_2. Because price P_2 is less than average total cost A_2, the firm incurs a per-unit loss of $A_2 - P_2$ and a total loss represented as the red area $[= (A_2 - P_2) \times Q_2]$.

The Long Run: Only a Normal Profit

In the long run, firms will enter a profitable monopolistically competitive industry and leave an unprofitable one. Therefore a monopolistic competitor will earn only a normal profit in the long run or, in other words, will only break even. (Remember that the cost curves include both explicit and implicit costs, including a normal profit.)

Profits: Firms Enter In the case of short-run profit (Figure 12.1a), economic profits attract new rivals because entry to the industry is relatively easy. As new firms enter, the demand curve faced by the typical firm shifts to the left (falls) because each firm has a smaller share of total demand and now faces a larger number of close-substitute products. This decline in the firm's demand reduces its economic profit. When entry of new firms has reduced demand to the extent that the demand curve is tangent to the average-total-cost curve at the profit-maximizing output, the firm is just making a normal profit. This situation is graphed in Figure 12.1c, where demand is D_3 and the firm's long-run equilibrium output is Q_3. Any greater or lesser output will entail an average total cost that exceeds product price P_3, meaning a loss for the firm. At the tangency point between the demand curve and ATC, total revenue equals total costs. With the economic profit gone, there is no further incentive for additional firms to enter.

...ıll KEY GRAPH

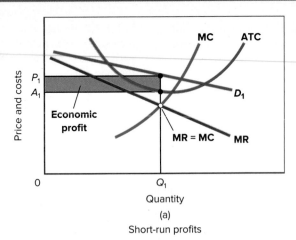

(a)
Short-run profits

FIGURE 12.1 A monopolistically competitive firm: short run and long run.

The monopolistic competitor maximizes profit or minimizes loss by producing the output at which MR = MC. The economic profit shown in (a) will induce new firms to enter, eventually eliminating economic profit. The loss shown in (b) will cause an exit of firms until normal profit is restored. After such entry and exit, the price will settle in (c) to where it just equals average total cost at the MR = MC output. At this price P_3 and output Q_3, the monopolistic competitor earns only a normal profit, and the industry is in long-run equilibrium.

(b)
Short-run losses

(c)
Long-run equilibrium

QUICK QUIZ FOR FIGURE 12.1

1. **Price exceeds MC in:**
   a. graph (a) only.
   b. graph (b) only.
   c. graphs (a) and (b) only.
   d. graphs (a), (b), and (c).

2. **Price exceeds ATC in:**
   a. graph (a) only.
   b. graph (b) only.
   c. graphs (a) and (b) only.
   d. graphs (a), (b), and (c).

3. **The firm represented by Figure 12.1c is:**
   a. making a normal profit.
   b. incurring a loss.

c. producing at the same level of output as a purely competitive firm.
   d. producing a standardized product.

4. **Which of the following pairs are both "competition-like elements" in monopolistic competition?**
   a. Price exceeds MR; standardized product.
   b. Entry is relatively easy; only a normal profit in the long run.
   c. Price equals MC at the profit-maximizing output; economic profits are likely in the long run.
   d. A firm's demand curve is downward sloping; differentiated products.

Answers: 1. d; 2. a; 3. a; 4. b

Losses: Firms Leave When the industry suffers short-run losses, as in Figure 12.1b, some firms will exit in the long run. Faced with fewer substitute products and an expanded share of total demand, the surviving firms will see their demand curves shift to the right (rise), as to D_3 in Figure 12.1c. Their losses will disappear and give way to normal profits.

Complications A representative firm in the monopolistic competition model earns only a normal profit in the long run. That outcome may not always occur, however, in the real world.

- Some firms may achieve sufficient product differentiation such that other firms cannot duplicate them, even over time. One hotel in a major city may have the best location relative to business and tourist activities. Or a firm may have developed a well-known brand name that gives it a slight but long-lasting advantage over imitators. Such firms may have sufficient monopoly power to realize modest economic profits even in the long run.

- Entry to some industries populated by small firms is not as free in reality as it is in theory. Because of product differentiation, financial barriers to entry are likely to be greater than they would be with a standardized product. The result is some monopoly power, with small economic profits even in the long run.

▶ Monopolistic competition involves a relatively large number of firms operating in a noncollusive way and producing differentiated products with easy industry entry and exit.

▶ In the short run, a monopolistic competitor will maximize profit or minimize loss by producing the level of output at which marginal revenue equals marginal cost.

▶ In the long run, easy entry and exit of firms cause monopolistic competitors to earn only a normal profit.

Monopolistic Competition and Efficiency

Economic efficiency requires each firm to produce the amount of output at which $P = MC =$ minimum ATC. The equality of price and minimum average total cost yields *productive efficiency*. The good is being produced in the least costly way, and the price is just sufficient to cover average total cost, including a normal profit. The equality of price and marginal cost yields *allocative efficiency*. The right amount of output is being produced, and thus the right amount of scarce resources is devoted to this specific use.

How efficient is monopolistic competition, as measured against this triple equality? Do monopolistically competitive firms produce the efficient output level associated with $P = MC =$ minimum ATC?

>> **LO12.3** Explain why monopolistic competition delivers neither productive nor allocative efficiency.

Neither Productive nor Allocative Efficiency

In monopolistic competition, neither productive nor allocative efficiency occurs in long-run equilibrium. In Figure 12.2, note that the profit-maximizing price P_3 slightly exceeds the lowest average total cost, A_4. In producing the profit-maximizing output Q_3, the firm's average total cost therefore is slightly higher than optimal from society's perspective—productive efficiency is not achieved. Also note that the profit-maximizing price P_3 exceeds marginal cost (here M_3), meaning that monopolistic competition causes an underallocation of resources. To measure the size of this inefficiency, note that the allocatively optimal amount of output is determined by point c, where demand curve D intersects the MC curve. So for all units between Q_3 and the level of output associated with point c, marginal benefits exceed marginal costs. Consequently, by producing only Q_3 units, this monopolistic competitor creates an efficiency (deadweight) loss equal in size to area acd. The total efficiency loss for the industry as a whole is the sum of the individual efficiency losses generated by each firm in the industry.

Excess Capacity

In monopolistic competition, the gap between the minimum-ATC output and the profit-maximizing output identifies **excess capacity:** plant and equipment that are underused because firms are producing less than the minimum-ATC output. This gap is shown as the distance between Q_4 and Q_3 in Figure 12.2. Note in the figure that the minimum ATC is at point b. If each

excess capacity *Plant* resources that are underused when imperfectly competitive *firms* produce less output than that associated with achieving minimum *average total cost.*

FIGURE 12.2
The inefficiency of monopolistic competition.

In long-run equilibrium a monopolistic competitor achieves neither productive nor allocative efficiency. Productive efficiency is not realized because production occurs where the average total cost A_3 exceeds the minimum average total cost A_4. Allocative efficiency is not achieved because the product price P_3 exceeds the marginal cost M_3. The results are an underallocation of resources as well as an efficiency loss and excess production capacity at every firm in the industry. This firm's efficiency loss is area *acd* and its excess production capacity is $Q_4 - Q_3$.

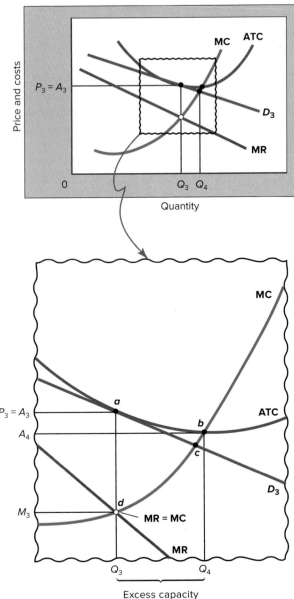

monopolistic competitor could profitably produce at this point on its ATC curve, the lower average total cost would enable a lower price than P_3. More importantly, if each firm produced at b rather than at a, fewer firms would be needed to produce the industry output. But because monopolistically competitive firms produce at a in long-run equilibrium, monopolistically competitive industries are overpopulated with firms, each operating below its optimal (lowest-ATC) capacity. For example, in most cities, an abundance of small motels and restaurants operate well below half capacity.

Product Variety

The situation portrayed in Figures 12.1c and 12.2 is not very satisfying to monopolistic competitors, because it foretells only a normal profit. But the profit-realizing firm of Figure 12.1a need not stand by and watch new competitors eliminate its profit by imitating its product, matching its customer service, and copying its advertising. Each firm has a product that is distinguishable in some way from other producers' products. By developing or improving its product, a monopolistic competitor may be able to postpone, at least for a while, the outcome of Figure 12.1c.

Although product differentiation and advertising add to the firm's costs, they can also increase the demand for its product. If demand increases by more than enough to compensate for the added costs, the firm will improve its profit position. As Figure 12.2 suggests, the firm has little or no prospect of increasing profit by cutting its price. So why not engage in nonprice competition?

Benefits of Product Variety

The product variety and product improvement that accompany the drive to maintain economic profit in monopolistic competition are a benefit for society. That benefit may offset the cost of the inefficiency associated with monopolistic competition. Consumers have a wide diversity of tastes: Some like regular fries, others like curly fries; some like contemporary furniture, others like traditional furniture. If a product is differentiated, then at any time the consumer can choose from a wide range of types, styles, and brands. Compared with pure competition, this variety provides an advantage to the consumer. The range of choice is widened, and producers more fully meet the wide variation in consumer tastes.

The product improvement promoted by monopolistic competition further differentiates products and expands choices.

>> **LO12.4** Explain why product differentiation helps to compensate for economic inefficiency.

And a successful product improvement by one firm obligates rivals to imitate or improve on that firm's temporary market advantage or else lose business. So society benefits from better products.

In fact, product differentiation creates a trade-off between consumer choice and productive efficiency. The stronger the product differentiation, the greater the excess capacity and, therefore, the greater the productive inefficiency. But the greater the product differentiation, the more likely it is that the firms will satisfy the great diversity of consumer tastes. The greater the excess-capacity problem, the wider the range of consumer choice.

Higher Wages, More McRestaurants

In the Monopolistically Competitive Restaurant Market, Higher Wages Favor Big Chain Restaurants over Small "Mom and Pop" Operations.

Restaurants are monopolistic competitors. Because each one has a unique location, it has some monopoly power. Additional bits of monopoly power are generated by product differentiation. Restaurants can differ on menu items, decor, speed of service, price, drive-through convenience, and a wide variety of additional characteristics.

Restaurants also differ in their production methods. Compare a McDonald's hamburger restaurant with a small "mom and pop" hamburger stand. The McDonald's will have a huge amount of specialized equipment. There will be special machines for frying, microwaving, making milkshakes, dispensing beverages into cups automatically, and of course cooking the hamburgers.

There will also in many cases be digital touchscreen computers for taking walk-up orders, wireless headsets for taking drive-through orders, and a fully computerized register system for keeping track of cash, credit, and debit transactions. And there will be a dining area that is often tastefully decorated at substantial expense. All these things imply that a McDonald's restaurant is capital intensive. It uses a large amount of capital equipment to produce and serve a hamburger.

By contrast, a small mom-and-pop hamburger stand will typically have only the bare minimum in terms of cooking equipment—a grill, a fryer, an unautomated beverage dispenser, and a refrigerator. Seating will be plain. The decor will be inexpensive and probably out of style. The mom-and-pop hamburger stand will use relatively little capital to produce and serve a hamburger.

In a monopolistically competitive restaurant market, equilibrium can often include both highly capitalized chain stores like McDonald's as well as lightly capitalized mom-and-pop operations. As long as both types of hamburger restaurant can make zero economic profits, each type will have representatives in the local restaurant market.

Economists have recently discovered, however, that wage increases can tilt the local restaurant market in favor of highly capitalized chain stores. In particular, increases in the minimum wage tend to reduce the proportion of mom-and-pop restaurants.

This happens because increases in the minimum wage have a relatively small impact on the cost curves of highly capitalized chain restaurants. While it is true that a highly capitalized McDonald's *does* hire minimum wage workers, the fact that it uses so much capital to produce hamburgers means that a large

Sorbis/Shutterstock

fraction of its costs derives from machinery and equipment. So when the minimum wage goes up, only a relatively minor part of its production costs go up.

By contrast, mom-and-pop restaurants use relatively little capital combined with lots of labor. So when the minimum wage is increased, the cost curves of mom-and-pop stores shift upward by more than the cost curves of highly capitalized chain restaurants. In both cases, economic profits will turn negative—but they will become much more negative at the mom-and-pop restaurants, which are heavily reliant on labor.

The result is a greater tendency on the part of mom-and-pop restaurants to exit the industry. Both types of restaurant will see exits. But when a new equilibrium is eventually reestablished, there will be a higher proportion of highly capitalized chain restaurants and a lower proportion of labor-intensive mom-and-pop restaurants.

Higher minimum wages are often promoted as a way to help low-wage workers. But they generate an unintended consequence in the monopolistically competitive restaurant market, where they favor big chain stores over small local operations. Voters and politicians may want to consider this when debating an increase in the minimum wage.

The nearby Consider This story relates a famous TV commercial from the 1980s that took a jab at competitors for not offering consumers the variety that they craved.

Further Complexity

Finally, the ability to engage in nonprice competition makes the market situation of a monopolistic competitor more complex than Figure 12.1 indicates. That figure assumes a given (unchanging)

CONSIDER THIS . . .

The Spice of Life

The Wendy's hamburger chain debuted a humorous TV commercial in 1987. The commercial depicted a Soviet communist fashion show. A woman walks down the runway in a drab grey factory uniform. The emcee shouts out, "Day wear!" Then she marches down the runway again in the same uniform but holding a flashlight. The emcee shouts out, "Evening wear!" She then marches out in the same uniform again but holding an inflatable beach ball. "Swimwear!"

Communist central planners didn't care about product differentiation. They typically made one design of a given

Chuck Nacke/Alamy Stock Photo

product to be able to mass produce it at the lowest possible cost. The result was a society of painful sameness.

The Wendy's TV commercial hammered home a single idea—that we should embrace the fact that the food produced by Wendy's was different from that produced by its main rivals, McDonald's and Burger King. Unlike the communist central planning of the old Soviet Union, the free-market system of the United States allows for huge amounts of product differentiation. If "variety is the spice of life," American capitalism is extremely well seasoned.

Source: Wendy's, "Soviet Fashion Show," 1987.

product and a given level of advertising expenditures. But we know that, in practice, product attributes and advertising are not fixed. The monopolistically competitive firm juggles three factors—price, product, and advertising—in seeking maximum profit. It must determine what variety of product, selling at what price, and supplemented by what level of advertising will result in the greatest profit. This complex situation is not easily expressed in a simple economic model. At best, we can say that each possible combination of price, product, and advertising poses a different demand and cost (production cost plus advertising cost) situation for the firm and that one combination will yield maximum profit. In practice, this optimal combination cannot be readily forecast but must be found by trial and error.

QUICK REVIEW

12.2

▶ A monopolistic competitor's long-run equilibrium output is such that price exceeds the minimum average total cost (implying that consumers do not get the product at the lowest price attainable) and price exceeds marginal cost (indicating that resources are underallocated to the product).

▶ The efficiency loss (or deadweight loss) associated with monopolistic competition is greatly muted by the benefits consumers receive from product variety.

Summary

LO12.1 List the characteristics of monopolistic competition.

The distinguishing features of monopolistic competition are (*a*) enough firms in the industry to ensure that each firm has only limited control over price, mutual interdependence is absent, and collusion is nearly impossible; (*b*) products are characterized by real or perceived differences so that economic rivalry entails both price and nonprice competition; and (*c*) entry to the industry is relatively easy. Many aspects of retailing, and some manufacturing industries in which economies of scale are few, approximate monopolistic competition.

Successful advertising shifts a monopolistically competitive firm's demand curve to the right and increases its slope, thereby giving the firm increased pricing power.

LO12.2 Explain why monopolistic competitors earn only a normal profit in the long run.

Monopolistically competitive firms may earn economic profits or incur economic losses in the short run. The easy entry and exit of firms result in only normal profits in the long run.

LO12.3 Explain why monopolistic competition delivers neither productive nor allocative efficiency.

The long-run equilibrium position of the monopolistically competitive producer is less efficient than that of the pure competitor. Under monopolistic competition, price exceeds marginal cost, indicating an underallocation of resources to the product. Price also exceeds minimum average total cost, indicating that consumers do not get the product at the lowest price that cost conditions might allow.

LO12.4 Explain why product differentiation helps to compensate for economic inefficiency.

Nonprice competition allows monopolistically competitive firms to offset the long-run tendency for economic profit to fall to zero. Through product differentiation, product development, and advertising, a firm may strive to increase the demand for its product more than enough to cover the added cost of such nonprice competition. Consumers benefit from the wide diversity of product choice that monopolistic competition provides.

Terms and Concepts

monopolistic competition

product differentiation

nonprice competition

pricing power

four-firm concentration ratio

Herfindahl index

excess capacity

Discussion Questions

1. How does monopolistic competition differ from pure competition? From pure monopoly? Explain fully what product differentiation may involve. Explain how the entry of firms into its industry affects the demand curve facing a monopolistic competitor and its economic profit. **LO12.1**

2. Suppose that a monopolistically competitive firm pays for an ad campaign that backfires, causing many consumers to dislike the firm's product. In which direction does demand shift, right or left? What happens to the slope and to the elasticity of demand? What happens to the firm's pricing power? **LO12.1**

3. Compare the elasticity of a monopolistic competitor's demand with that of a pure competitor and a pure monopolist. Assuming identical long-run costs, compare graphically the prices and outputs in the long run under pure competition and under monopolistic competition. Contrast the two market structures in terms of productive and allocative efficiency. Explain: "Monopolistically competitive industries are populated by too many firms, each of which produces too little." **LO12.2**

4. "Monopolistic competition is monopolistic up to the point at which consumers become willing to buy close substitute products and competitive beyond that point." Explain. **LO12.2**

5. "Competition in quality and service may be just as effective as price competition in giving buyers more for their money." Do you agree? Why or why not? Explain why monopolistically competitive firms frequently prefer nonprice competition to price competition. **LO12.2**

6. Critically evaluate and explain: **LO12.3**
   a. In monopolistically competitive industries, economic profits are competed away in the long run. Hence, there is no valid reason to criticize these industries' performance and efficiency.
   b. In the long run, monopolistic competition leads to a monopolistic price but not to monopolistic profits.

7. **LAST WORD** What would you expect to happen to the proportion of big chain restaurants relative to mom-and-pop restaurants in a town that lowers its minimum wage? Will the proportion change due to exits or due to entrances? Which type of restaurant will see more in the way of exits or entrances? Why?

Review Questions

1. A monopolistically competitive firm gets a massive amount of free advertising when a government agency gives it an award and millions of people mention the award to each other on social media. Which of the following is most likely to happen? **LO12.1**
   a. Demand becomes less elastic and pricing power decreases
   b. Demand becomes more elastic and pricing power decreases
   c. Demand becomes more elastic and pricing power increases
   d. Demand becomes less elastic and pricing power increases

2. There are 10 firms in an industry, and each firm has a market share of 10 percent. What is the industry's Herfindahl index? **LO12.1**

3. In the small town of Geneva, five firms make watches. The firms' respective output levels are 30 watches per year, 20 watches per year, 20 watches per year, 20 watches per year, and 10 watches per year. What is the four-firm concentration ratio for the town's watch-making industry? **LO12.1**

4. Which of the following best describes the efficiency of monopolistically competitive firms? **LO12.3**
   a. Allocatively efficient but productively inefficient
   b. Allocatively inefficient but productively efficient
   c. Both allocatively efficient and productively efficient
   d. Neither allocatively efficient nor productively efficient

Problems

1. Suppose that a small town has seven burger shops whose respective shares of the local hamburger market are (as percentages of all hamburgers sold): 23 percent, 22 percent, 18 percent, 12 percent, 11 percent, 8 percent, and 6 percent. What is the four-firm concentration ratio of the hamburger industry in this town? What is the Herfindahl index for the hamburger industry in this town? If the top three sellers combine to form a single firm, what would happen to the four-firm concentration ratio and to the Herfindahl index? **LO12.1**

2. Suppose that the most popular car dealer in your area sells 10 percent of all vehicles. If all other car dealers sell either the same number of vehicles or fewer, what is the largest value that the Herfindahl index could possibly take for car dealers in your area? In that same situation, what would the four-firm concentration ratio be? **LO12.1**

3. Suppose that a monopolistically competitive restaurant is currently serving 230 meals per day (the output where MR = MC). At that output level, ATC per meal is $10 and consumers are willing to pay $12 per meal. What is this firm's profit or loss? Will there be entry or exit? Will this restaurant's demand curve shift left or right? In long-run equilibrium, suppose that this restaurant charges $11 per meal for 180 meals and that the marginal cost of the 180th meal is $8. What is the firm's profit? Suppose that the allocatively efficient output level in long-run equilibrium is 200 meals. Is this firm's deadweight loss greater than or less than $60? Explain. **LO12.3**

CHAPTER

13

Oligopoly and Strategic Behavior

>> **LEARNING OBJECTIVES**

LO13.1 Describe the characteristics of oligopoly.

LO13.2 Discuss how game theory relates to oligopoly.

LO13.3 Explain the three main models of oligopoly pricing and output.

LO13.4 Contrast the potential positive and negative effects of advertising.

LO13.5 Discuss the efficiency of oligopoly.

LO13.6 Use additional game-theory terminology and demonstrate how to find a Nash equilibrium.

In the United States, most industries fall between the two poles of pure competition and pure monopoly. That is, most real-world industries have fewer than the large number of producers required for pure competition but more than the single producer that defines pure monopoly. In addition, most firms have differentiated (rather than standardized) products as well as some discretion over the prices they charge. Finally, entry to most real-world industries ranges from easy to very difficult but is rarely completely blocked.

While the monopolistic competition model (Chapter 12) mixes a small amount of monopoly power with a large amount of competition, the oligopoly model covered in this chapter blends a large amount of monopoly power with both considerable rivalry among existing firms and the threat of increased future competition. (You should quickly review Table 10.1 at this point.)

>> **LO13.1** Describe the characteristics of oligopoly.

oligopoly A *market structure* in which a few *firms* sell either a *standardized* or *differentiated product*, into which entry is difficult, in which the firm has limited control over product *price* because of *mutual interdependence* (except when there is collusion among firms), and in which there is typically *nonprice competition*.

Oligopoly

An **oligopoly** is a market dominated by a few large producers of a homogeneous or differentiated product. Because of their "fewness," oligopolists have considerable control over their prices, but each must consider the possible reaction of rivals to its own pricing, output, and advertising decisions.

A Few Large Producers

The phrase "a few large producers" is necessarily vague because oligopoly covers much ground. Oligopoly encompasses the online advertising industry, in which three huge firms—Google, Facebook, and Amazon—dominate the national market, and the situation in which four or five much smaller auto-parts stores enjoy roughly equal shares of the market in a medium-size town. Generally, however, terms such as "Big Three," "Big Four," and "Big Six" refer to an oligopolistic industry.

Homogeneous or Differentiated Products

An oligopoly may be either a **homogeneous oligopoly** or a **differentiated oligopoly,** depending on whether the firms in the oligopoly produce standardized (homogeneous) or differentiated products. Many industrial products (steel, zinc, copper, lead, cement) are standardized. In contrast, many consumer goods industries (automobiles, household appliances, electronics equipment, breakfast cereals, and many sporting goods) are differentiated oligopolies. These differentiated oligopolies typically engage in considerable nonprice competition supported by heavy advertising.

Control over Price, but Mutual Interdependence

Because oligopolistic industries have only a few firms, each firm is a "pricemaker"; like the monopolist, it can set its price and output levels to maximize its profit. But unlike the monopolist, which has no rivals, the oligopolist must consider how its rivals will react to any change in its price, output, product characteristics, or advertising. Oligopoly is thus characterized by *strategic behavior* and *mutual interdependence*. By **strategic behavior,** we mean self-interested behavior that takes into account the reactions of others. Firms develop and implement price, quality, location, service, and advertising strategies to grow their business and expand their profits. But because rivals are few, there is **mutual interdependence,** in which each firm's profit depends not just on its own price and sales strategies but also on those of the other firms in its highly concentrated industry. Therefore, oligopolistic firms base their decisions on how they think their rivals will react. Examples: In deciding whether to increase the price of its cosmetics, L'Oreal will try to predict the response of the other major producers, such as Clinique. In deciding on its advertising strategy, Burger King will consider how McDonald's might react.

Entry Barriers

The same barriers to entry that create pure monopoly also contribute to the creation of oligopoly. Economies of scale are important entry barriers in the aircraft, rubber, and copper industries. In those industries, three or four firms might each have sufficient sales to achieve economies of scale, but new firms would have such a small market share that they could not do so. They would then be high-cost producers, and as such they could not survive. A closely related barrier is the large expenditure for capital—the cost of obtaining necessary plant and equipment—required for entering certain industries. The jet engine, automobile, commercial aircraft, and petroleum-refining industries are all characterized by very high capital requirements.

The ownership and control of raw materials help explain why oligopoly exists in many mining industries, including gold, silver, and copper. Patents have served as entry barriers in the computer, chemicals, and pharmaceutical industries. Oligopolists can also prevent the entry of new competitors through preemptive and retaliatory pricing and advertising strategies.

Finally, social networking apps and other Internet businesses are also very often subject to *network effects* that make it hard for startups and other small rivals to compete with dominant firms like Facebook or Twitter that already have hundreds of millions or even billions of users. Other things equal, why would a person looking to interact with lots of people join a social network with only 50 people when she could join one that already has 3 billion? The same is true for someone wanting to sell goods on the Internet. Other things equal, they will want to sell their products on dominant online marketplaces like eBay, Amazon, and Etsy that are already popular with billions of buyers. The result is oligopoly maintained by network effects.

Mergers

Some oligopolies have emerged mainly through the growth of the dominant firms in a given industry (examples: breakfast cereals, chewing gum, candy bars). For other industries, mergers have been the route to oligopoly (examples: steel, airlines, banking, and entertainment). The merging, or combining, of two or more competing firms may substantially increase their market share, which in turn may help the new firm achieve greater economies of scale.

Another motive underlying the "urge to merge" is the desire for monopoly power. The larger firm that results from a merger has greater control over market supply and thus the price of its product. Also, because it is a larger buyer of inputs, it may be able to demand and obtain lower prices (costs) on its production inputs.

homogeneous oligopoly An *oligopoly* in which *firms* produce a *standardized product.*

differentiated oligopoly An *oligopoly* in which *firms* produce a *differentiated product.*

strategic behavior Self-interested economic actions that take into account the expected reactions of others.

mutual interdependence A situation in which a change in *price* strategy (or in some other strategy) by one *firm* will affect the sales and profits of another firm (or other firms). Any firm that makes such a change can expect its rivals to react to the change.

TABLE 13.1 Percentage of Output Produced by Firms in Selected High-Concentration U.S. Manufacturing Industries

(1) Industry	(2) Percentage of Industry Output* Produced by the Four Largest Firms	(3) Herfindahl Index for the Top 50 Firms	(1) Industry	(2) Percentage of Industry Output* Produced by the Four Largest Firms	(3) Herfindahl Index for the Top 50 Firms
Household laundry equipment	100	ND†	Primary aluminum	74	2,089
			Tires	73	1,531
Household refrigerators and freezers	93	ND	Bottled water	71	1,564
Cigarettes	88	2,897	Gasoline pumps	70	1,611
Beer	88	3,561	Bar soaps	70	2,250
Glass containers	86	ND	Burial caskets	69	1,699
Phosphate fertilizers	85	3,152	Printer toner cartridges	67	1,449
Small-arms ammunition	84	2,848	Alcohol distilleries	65	1,394
Electric light bulbs	84	3,395	Turbines and generators	61	1,263
Aircraft	80	3,287	Motor vehicles	60	1,178
Breakfast cereals	79	2,333	Primary copper	50	879
Aerosol cans	75	1,667			

*As measured by the value of shipments. Data are for 2012.[1]

†ND = not disclosed.

Source: U.S. Census Bureau, Census of Manufacturers, 2012.

Oligopolistic Industries

In Chapter 13, we listed the four-firm concentration ratio—the percentage of total industry sales accounted for by the four largest firms—for a number of monopolistically competitive industries (see Table 12.1). Column 2 of Table 13.1 shows the four-firm concentration ratios for 22 oligopolistic industries. For example, the four largest U.S. producers of aircraft make 80 percent of all aircraft produced in the United States.

When the largest four firms in an industry control 40 percent or more of the market (as in Table 13.1), that industry is considered oligopolistic. Using this benchmark, about one-half of all U.S. manufacturing industries are oligopolies.

Although concentration ratios help identify oligopoly, they have four shortcomings.

Localized Markets We have already noted that concentration ratios apply to the nation as a whole, whereas the markets for some products are highly localized because of high transportation costs. Local oligopolies can exist even though national concentration ratios are low.

interindustry competition The competition for sales between the products of one *industry* and the products of another industry.

Interindustry Competition Concentration ratios are based on somewhat arbitrary definitions of industries. In some cases, they disguise significant **interindustry competition**—competition between two products associated with different industries. The high concentration ratio for the primary aluminum industry shown in Table 13.1 understates the competition in that industry because aluminum competes with copper in many applications (for example, in the market for long-distance power lines).

import competition The competition that domestic *firms* encounter from the products and *services* of foreign producers.

World Trade The data in Table 13.1 only take account of output produced in the United States and may overstate concentration because they do not account for the **import competition** of foreign suppliers. The truck and auto tire industry is a good example. Although Table 13.1 shows that four U.S. firms produce 73 percent of the domestic output of tires, it ignores the fact that a very large portion of the truck and auto tires bought in the United States are imports. Many of the world's largest corporations are foreign, and many of them do business in the United States.

Dominant Firms The four-firm concentration ratio does not reveal the extent to which one or two firms dominate an industry. Suppose that in industry X one firm produces the entire industry

[1]The U.S. Census Bureau's *Census of Manufacturers* is conducted every five years but data from the 2017 census were not released in time for this edition due to delays caused by the COVID-19 pandemic.

output. In a second industry, Y, four firms compete, each with 25 percent of the market. The concentration ratio is 100 percent for both these industries. But industry X is a pure monopoly, while industry Y is an oligopoly that may be experiencing significant economic rivalry. Most economists would agree that monopoly power (or market power) is substantially greater in industry X than in industry Y, a fact disguised by their identical 100 percent concentration ratios.

The Herfindahl index addresses this problem. Recall that this index is the sum of the squared percentage market shares of all firms in the industry. In equation form:

$$\text{Herfindahl index} = (\%S_1)^2 + (\%S_2)^2 + (\%S_3)^2 + \cdots + (\%S_n)^2$$

where $\%S_1$ is the percentage market share of firm 1, $\%S_2$ is the percentage market share of firm 2, and so on for each firm in the industry. Also remember that by squaring the percentage market shares of all the firms in the industry, the Herfindahl index gives much greater weight to larger, and thus more powerful, firms than to smaller ones. In the case of the single-firm industry X, the index would be at its maximum of 100^2, or 10,000, indicating an industry with complete monopoly power. For our hypothetical four-firm industry Y, the index would be $25^2 + 25^2 + 25^2 + 25^2$, or 2,500, indicating much less market power.

The larger the Herfindahl index, the greater the market power within an industry. Note in Table 13.1 that the four-firm concentration ratios for the gasoline pumps industry and the bar soaps industry are identical at 70 percent. But the Herfindahl index of 2,250 for the bar soaps industry suggests greater market power than the 1,611 index for the gasoline pumps industry. Also, contrast the much larger Herfindahl indexes in Table 13.1 with those for the low-concentration manufacturing industries presented in Table 12.1.

Oligopoly Behavior: A Game-Theory Overview

Oligopoly pricing behavior has the characteristics of certain games of strategy such as poker, chess, and bridge. In these strategic games, the outcome depends not only on what one player does, but on what the opponent does. The best strategy for one player will depend on the opponent's strategy, and vice versa. Players (and oligopolists) must take into account not only what they themselves wish to accomplish but their rivals' actions and expected reactions as well.

The study of how people behave in strategic situations is called **game theory.** A classic example of game theory is the **prisoner's dilemma** game, in which two people—let's call them Betty and Al— have committed a diamond heist and are detained by the police as prime suspects. Unbeknownst to the two, the evidence against them is weak, so the police hope to convict the criminals by getting one or both of them to confess to the crime. The police place Betty and Al in separate holding cells and offer each of them the same deal: "If you confess that you and your partner stole the diamonds, you will receive a short prison sentence. But if you keep silent while your partner confesses, you will go to jail for many years while your partner walks away with only a short sentence."

The prisoners face the same dilemma. Each may be inclined to remain silent and hope that their partner will, too. But the offer made by the police means that it will be in the other person's better interest to confess so that they can be sure of a short sentence. What happens? Fearful that the other person will confess, both confess, even though both would have been better off saying nothing.

The "confess-confess" outcome of the prisoner's dilemma is conceptually identical to the "low price–low price" outcome of the game shown in Figure 13.1, which assumes that a *duopoly*, or two-firm oligopoly, is producing athletic shoes. Each of the two firms—let's call them RareAir and Uptown—has a choice of two pricing strategies: price high or price low. Each firm's profit will depend on the strategy it chooses *and* the strategy its rival chooses.

There are four possible combinations of strategies for the two firms, as shown by the lettered cells in Figure 13.1. For example, cell C represents a low-price strategy for Uptown along with a high-price strategy for RareAir. Figure 13.1 is called a *payoff matrix* because each cell shows the payoff (profit) to each firm that will result from each combination of strategies. Within each cell, RareAir's payoff has a blue background while Uptown's payoff has a yellow background. As Cell C shows, if Uptown adopts a low-price strategy and RareAir a high-price strategy, then Uptown will earn $15 million (yellow portion) and RareAir will earn $6 million (blue portion). Similarly, cell A shows that if both firms pursue a high-price strategy, RareAir and Uptown will each profit by $12 million.

>> **LO13.2** Discuss how game theory relates to oligopoly.

game theory The study of how people behave in strategic situations in which individuals must take into account not only their own possible actions but also the possible reactions of others. Originally developed to analyze the best ways to play games like poker and chess.

prisoner's dilemma A famous *game* analyzed in *game theory* in which two players who could have reached a mutually beneficial outcome through cooperation will instead end up at a mutually inferior outcome as they pursue their own respective interests (instead of cooperating). Helps to explain why collusion can be difficult for *oligopoly* firms to achieve or maintain.

FIGURE 13.1
Profit payoff (in millions) for a two-firm oligopoly.

Each firm has two possible pricing strategies. RareAir's strategies are shown in the top margin, and Uptown's in the left margin. Each lettered cell of this four-cell payoff matrix represents one combination of a RareAir strategy and an Uptown strategy and shows the profit that combination would earn for each. Assuming no collusion, the outcome of this game is Cell D, with both parties using low-price strategies and both parties earning $8 million of profits.

Mutual Interdependence Revisited

The data in Figure 13.1 are hypothetical, but their relationships are typical of real situations. Recall that oligopolistic firms can increase their profits, and influence their rivals' profits, by changing their pricing strategies. Each firm's profit depends on its own pricing strategy and that of its rivals. This mutual interdependence is the most obvious aspect of Figure 13.1. If Uptown adopts a high-price strategy, its profit will be $12 million provided that RareAir also employs a high-price strategy (cell A). But if RareAir uses a low-price strategy against Uptown's high-price strategy (cell B), RareAir will increase its market share and boost its profit from $12 million to $15 million. RareAir's higher profit will come at the expense of Uptown, whose profit will fall from $12 million to $6 million. Consequently, Uptown's high-price strategy is a good strategy only if RareAir *also* employs a high-price strategy. Thus, we see that neither firm has independent control of its profitability. Its profit outcome is mutually interdependent with the actions taken by its rival.

Collusion

collusion Cooperation or conspiracy in which *firms* act together (collude) to fix *prices,* divide a market, or otherwise restrict competition. Most collusion is illegal.

Figure 13.1 also implies that oligopolists can benefit from **collusion**—that is, cooperation with rivals. To see the benefits of collusion, note that the best outcome for both firms is cell A, where each would obtain a profit of $12 million. But that is possible only if both firms can successfully collude and commit to having both of them pursue the high-price strategy. Without collusion, the profit incentives of this prisoner's dilemma situation will cause both firms to end up in cell D, with each firm making only $8 million per year.

To see why the mutually beneficial equilibrium at cell A will break down without collusion, note that, starting from cell A, both RareAir and Uptown can see from the payouts in Figure 13.1 that each of them could increase its own profit by switching to a low price strategy. For RareAir, switching from the high-price strategy to the low-price strategy would move the game to cell B. If that were to happen, RareAir's profit would increase from $12 million (cell A) to a substantially higher—and therefore quite tempting—$15 million (cell B). If there is no collusion to keep RareAir from switching strategies, RareAir will "follow the money" and switch from the high-price strategy to the low-price strategy.

But will Uptown want to keep on pursuing the high-price strategy that is necessary (in conjunction with RareAir's new low-price strategy) to keep the game at cell B? The answer is no, because at cell B Uptown faces a huge profit incentive of its own to switch strategies, namely the $8 million it can receive in cell D by "going low" rather than the $6 million it would receive in cell B by "staying high." Given that there is no collusion to restrict the player's actions, Uptown will follow its profit incentive and also switch to a low-price strategy. The net result is that, absent collusion, both firms will pursue a low-price strategy and end up at cell D.

How can oligopolists avoid the low-profit outcome of cell D? By colluding, rather than setting prices competitively or independently. In our example, the two firms could agree to establish and maintain a high-price policy, in which case each firm's profit would increase from $8 million (cell D) to $12 million (cell A).

Note that what is good for colluding oligopolists is bad for consumers. The higher prices charged by successfully colluding oligopolists translate into higher costs borne by consumers. There are also deadweight efficiency losses because the colluding oligopolists must restrict output to below the allocatively efficient level in order to maintain high prices. By contrast, when oligopolists do not collude, their profit motives will typically lead them to select mutually "competitive" low-price strategies in which output is higher and efficiency is improved. This low-price outcome is clearly beneficial to consumers but not to the oligopolists, whose profits decrease.

Incentive to Cheat

The payoff matrix also explains why an oligopolist will be strongly tempted to cheat on any collusive agreement that may be negotiated among the firms in the industry. Suppose Uptown and RareAir come to an agreement in which they each promise to maintain a high-price policy, so that both firms can earn $12 million in profit (cell A). But as we just went over, both firms will be *strongly* tempted to cheat on this collusive pricing agreement because either firm can increase its profit to $15 million by lowering its price. That implies that the collusive agreement will be "unstable" because it contradicts each firm's profit motive. Both firms will probably cheat, and the game will settle back to cell D, with each firm using the low-price strategy. The lesson? Collusion agreements are often fragile, so that we mostly see oligopoly industries in which there is a substantial amount of low-price, competitive behavior.

▶ An oligopoly is composed of relatively few firms producing either homogeneous or differentiated products; these firms are mutually interdependent.

▶ Barriers to entry in oligopoly include scale economies, control of patents or strategic resources, the ability to engage in retaliatory pricing, and network effects. Oligopolies may result from internal growth of firms, mergers, or both.

▶ Game theory reveals that (a) oligopolies are mutually interdependent, (b) collusion enhances oligopoly profits, and (c) there is a temptation for oligopolists to cheat on a collusive agreement.

QUICK REVIEW

13.1

Three Oligopoly Models

To gain further insight into oligopolistic pricing and output behavior, we will examine three distinct pricing models: (1) the kinked-demand curve, (2) collusive pricing, and (3) price leadership.

Why not a single model, as in our discussions of the other market structures? There are two reasons:

>> **LO13.3** Explain the three main models of oligopoly pricing and output.

- *Diversity of oligopolies* Oligopoly encompasses a greater range and diversity of market situations than do other market structures. It includes the *tight* oligopoly, in which two or three firms dominate an entire market, and the *loose* oligopoly, in which six or seven firms share, say, 70 or 80 percent of a market while a "competitive fringe" of firms shares the remainder. It includes both differentiated and standardized products. It includes cases in which firms act in collusion and those in which they act independently. It embodies situations in which barriers to entry are very strong and situations in which they are not quite so strong. In short, the diversity of oligopoly does not allow us to explain all oligopolistic behaviors with a single market model.

- *Complications of interdependence* The mutual interdependence of oligopolistic firms complicates matters significantly. Because firms cannot predict the reactions of their rivals with certainty, they cannot predict their own demand or marginal-revenue data with certainty, either. Without such data, firms cannot determine their profit-maximizing price and output, even in theory, as we will see.

Despite these analytical difficulties, two interrelated characteristics of oligopolistic pricing have been observed. First, if the macroeconomy is generally stable, oligopolistic prices are typically inflexible (or "rigid" or "sticky"). Prices change less frequently under oligopoly than under pure competition, monopolistic competition, and, in some instances, pure monopoly. Second, when oligopolistic prices do change, firms are likely to change their prices together, suggesting that there is a tendency to act in concert, or collusively, in setting and changing prices (as we mentioned in the preceding section). The diversity of oligopolies and the presence of mutual interdependence are reflected in the models that follow.

Kinked-Demand Theory: Noncollusive Oligopoly

Imagine an oligopolistic industry made up of three hypothetical firms (Arch, King, and Dave's), each having about one-third of the total market for a differentiated product. Assume that the firms are "independent," meaning that they do not engage in collusive price practices. Assume, too, that the going price for Arch's product is P_0 and its current sales are Q_0, as shown in **Figure 13.2a (Key Graph)**.

..ıl KEY GRAPH

FIGURE 13.2 The kinked-demand curve.

(a) The slope of a noncollusive oligopolist's demand and marginal-revenue curves depends on whether its rivals match (straight lines D_1 and MR_1) or ignore (straight lines D_2 and MR_2) any price changes that it may initiate from the current price P_0. (b) In all likelihood an oligopolist's rivals will ignore a price increase but follow a price cut. This causes the oligopolist's demand curve to be kinked ($D_2\,eD_1$) and the marginal-revenue curve to have a vertical break, or gap (fg). Because any shift in marginal costs between MC_1 and MC_2 will intersect the vertical (dashed) segment of the marginal-revenue curve, no change in either price P_0 or output Q_0 will result from such a shift.

(a)

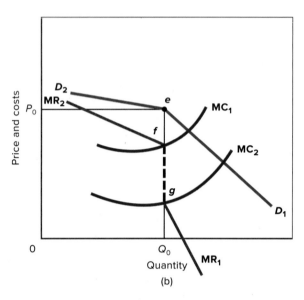

(b)

QUICK QUIZ FOR FIGURE 13.2

1. Suppose Q_0 in this figure represents annual sales of 5 million units for this firm. The other two firms in this three-firm industry sell 3 million and 2 million units, respectively. The Herfindahl index for this industry is:
   a. 100 percent.
   b. 400.
   c. 10.
   d. 3,800.

2. The D_2e segment of the demand curve D_2eD_1 in graph (b) implies that:
   a. this firm's total revenue will fall if it increases its price above P_0.
   b. other firms will match a price increase above P_0.
   c. the firm's relevant marginal-revenue curve will be MR_1 for price increases above P_0.
   d. the product in this industry is necessarily standardized.

3. By matching a price cut, this firm's rivals can:
   a. increase their market shares.
   b. increase their marginal revenues.
   c. maintain their market shares.
   d. lower their total costs.

4. A shift of the marginal-cost curve from MC_2 to MC_1 in graph (b) would:
   a. increase the "going price" above P_0.
   b. leave price at P_0 but reduce this firm's total profit.
   c. leave price at P_0 but reduce this firm's total revenue.
   d. make this firm's demand curve more elastic.

Answers: 1. d; 2. a; 3. c; 4. b

Now the question is, "What does the firm's demand curve look like?" Mutual interdependence and the uncertainty about rivals' reactions make this question hard to answer. The location and shape of an oligopolist's demand curve depend on how the firm's rivals will react to a price change introduced by Arch. There are two plausible assumptions about the reactions of Arch's rivals:

- *Match price changes* One possibility is that King and Dave's will exactly match any price change initiated by Arch. In this case, Arch's demand and marginal-revenue curves will look like the straight lines labeled D_1 and MR_1 in Figure 13.2a. Why are they so steep? Reason: If Arch cuts its price, its sales will increase only modestly because its two rivals will also cut their prices to prevent Arch from gaining an advantage over them. The small increase in sales that Arch (and its two rivals) will realize is at the expense of other industries; Arch will gain no sales from King and Dave's. In a similar fashion, if Arch raises its price, its sales will fall only modestly because King and Dave's will match its price increase. The industry will lose sales to other industries, but Arch will lose no customers to King and Dave's.

- *Ignore price changes* The other possibility is that King and Dave's will ignore any price change by Arch. In this case, the demand and marginal-revenue curves faced by Arch will resemble the straight lines D_2 and MR_2 in Figure 13.2a. Demand in this case is considerably more elastic than it was under the previous assumption. The reasons are clear: If Arch lowers its price and its rivals do not, Arch will gain sales significantly at the expense of its two rivals because it will be underselling them. Conversely, if Arch raises its price and its rivals do not, Arch will lose many customers to King and Dave's, which will be underselling it. Because of product differentiation, however, Arch's sales will not fall to zero when it raises its price; some of Arch's customers will pay the higher price because they have a strong preference for Arch's product. Nevertheless, Arch's demand curve will be much more elastic when its rivals ignore price changes than when they match them.

A Combined Strategy Now, which is the most logical assumption for Arch to make about how its rivals will react to any price change it might initiate? The answer is, "It depends on the direction of the price change." Common sense and observation of oligopolistic industries suggest that a firm's rivals will match price declines below P_0 as they act to prevent the price cutter from taking their customers. But they will ignore price increases above P_0 because the rivals of the price-increasing firm stand to gain the business lost by the price booster. In other words, the dark-green left-hand segment of the "rivals ignore" demand curve D_2 in Figure 13.2a seems relevant for price increases, and the dark-green right-hand segment of the "rivals match" demand curve D_1 seems relevant for price cuts. It is therefore reasonable to assume that the noncollusive oligopolist faces the **kinked-demand curve** $D_2 e D_1$, as shown in Figure 13.2b. Demand is highly elastic above the going price P_0 but much less elastic or even inelastic below that price.

Note also that if rivals match a price cut but ignore an increase, the marginal-revenue curve of the oligopolist will also have an odd shape. It, too, will be made up of two segments: the dark gray left-hand part of marginal-revenue curve MR_2 in Figure 13.2a and the dark gray right-hand part of marginal-revenue curve MR_1. Because of the sharp difference in elasticity of demand above and below the going price, there is a gap, or what we can simply treat as a vertical segment, in the marginal-revenue curve. We show this gap as the dashed segment in the combined marginal-revenue curve $MR_2 fg MR_1$ in Figure 13.2b.

kinked-demand curve A *demand curve* that has a flatter slope above the current *price* than below the current price. Applies to a *noncollusive oligopoly* firm if its rivals will match any price decrease but ignore any price increase.

Price Inflexibility This analysis helps explain why prices are generally stable in noncollusive oligopolistic industries. There are both demand and cost reasons.

On the demand side, the kinked-demand curve gives each oligopolist reason to believe that any change in price will be for the worse. If it raises its price, many of its customers will desert it. If it lowers its price, its sales at best will increase very modestly since rivals will match the lower price. Even if a price cut increases the oligopolist's total revenue somewhat, its costs may increase by a greater amount, depending on demand elasticity. For instance, if its demand is inelastic to the right of Q_0, as it may well be, then the firm's profit will surely fall. A price decrease in the inelastic region lowers the firm's total revenue, and the production of a larger output increases its total costs.

On the cost side, the broken marginal-revenue curve suggests that even if an oligopolist's costs change substantially, the firm may have no reason to change its price. In particular, every possible position of the marginal-cost curve between MC_1 and MC_2 in Figure 13.2b will result in the firm's deciding on exactly the same price and output. For all those positions, MR equals MC at output Q_0; at that output, it will charge price P_0.

This may seem strange, but the intuition is straightforward. Shifts of the marginal-cost curve up and down *between* the positions of MC_1 and MC_2 are not enough to overcome the firm's reluctance to change its price. Larger changes are required:

- The firm's marginal cost curve would have to shift to a position higher than MC_1 for the profit-maximizing (MR = MC) intersection between marginal cost and marginal revenue to call for a price higher than P_0. That is, marginal costs would have to shift up *a lot* for the firm to want to deal with the potential reductions in revenue caused by rivals leaving their prices unchanged in response to the firm's price increase.

- Similarly, the firm's marginal cost curve would have to shift to a position lower than MC_2 for the profit-maximizing ($MR = MC$) intersection between marginal cost and marginal revenue to indicate a profit-maximizing price lower than P_0. That is, marginal costs would have to shift down *a lot* for the firm to want to deal with the potential reductions in revenue caused by rivals matching a price reduction.

Criticisms of the Model The kinked-demand analysis of Figure 13.2 has two shortcomings. First, it does not explain how the firm's selling price got to P_0 in the first place. It only helps to explain why oligopolists tend to stick with an existing price. Consequently, the kinked-demand curve explains price inflexibility but not price itself.

Second, when the macroeconomy is unstable, oligopoly prices are not as rigid as the kinked-demand theory implies. During inflationary periods, many oligopolists have raised their prices often and substantially. And during downturns (recessions), some oligopolists have cut prices. In some instances these price reductions have set off a **price war**: successive and continuous rounds of price cuts by rivals as each firm attempts to maintain its market share.

Cartels and Other Collusion

Collusion occurs whenever the firms in an industry reach an agreement to fix prices, divide up the market, or otherwise restrict competition among themselves. By controlling price through collusion, oligopolists may be able to reduce uncertainty, increase profits, and perhaps even prohibit the entry of new rivals.

Price and Output Assume once again that there are three hypothetical oligopolistic firms (Gypsum, Sheetrock, and GSR) producing, in this instance, gypsum drywall panels for finishing interior walls. All three firms produce a homogeneous product and have identical cost curves. Each firm's demand curve is indeterminate unless we know how its rivals will react to any price change. Therefore, we suppose each firm assumes that its two rivals will match either a price cut or a price increase. In other words, each firm has a demand curve like the straight line D_1 in Figure 13.2a. And since they have identical cost data, and the same demand and thus marginal-revenue data, we can say that Figure 13.3 represents the position of each of our three oligopolistic firms.

What price and output combination should, say, Gypsum select? If Gypsum were a pure monopolist, the answer would be clear: Establish output at Q_0, where marginal revenue equals marginal cost, charge the corresponding price P_0, and enjoy the maximum profit attainable. However, Gypsum does have two rivals selling identical products, and if Gypsum's assumption that its rivals will match its price of P_0 proves to be incorrect, the consequences could be disastrous for Gypsum. Specifically, if Sheetrock and GSR actually charge prices below P_0, then Gypsum's demand curve D will shift sharply to the left as its potential customers turn to its rivals, which are now selling the same product at a lower price. Of course, Gypsum can retaliate by cutting its price too, but this will move all three firms down their demand curves, lowering their profits. It may even drive them to a point where average total cost exceeds price and losses are incurred.

So the question becomes, "Will Sheetrock and GSR want to charge a price below P_0?" Under our assumptions, and recognizing that Gypsum has little choice except to match any price they may set below P_0, the answer is no. Faced with the same demand and cost circumstances, Sheetrock and GSR will find it in their interest to produce Q_0 and charge P_0. This is a curious situation; each firm finds it most profitable to charge the same price, P_0, but only if

price war Successive, competitive, and continued decreases in the *prices* charged by *firms* in an oligopolistic *industry*. At each stage of the price war, one *firm* lowers its price below its rivals' price, hoping to increase its sales and revenues at its rivals' expense. The war ends when the price decreases cease.

FIGURE 13.3
Collusion and the tendency toward joint-profit maximization.

If oligopolistic firms face identical or highly similar demand and cost conditions, they may collude to limit their joint output and to set a single, common price. Thus each firm acts as if it were a pure monopolist, setting output at Q_0 and charging price P_0. This price and output combination maximizes each oligopolist's profit (green area) and thus the combined or joint profit of the colluding firms.

GLOBAL PERSPECTIVE 13.1

THE 13 OPEC NATIONS, AVERAGE DAILY OIL PRODUCTION, 2020

In 2020, the 13 OPEC nations—Algeria, Angola, Equatorial Guinea, Gabon, Iran, Iraq, Kuwait, Libya, Nigeria, the Republic of the Congo, Saudi Arabia, the United Arab Emirates, and Venezuela—produced about 32 percent of the world's oil. By comparison, the three largest non-OPEC oil-producing nations—the United States, Russia, and Canada—produced about 37 percent of the world's oil that year.

The average daily outputs of the OPEC nations ranged from 11,039,000 barrels per day in Saudi Arabia to just 161,000 barrels per day in Equatorial Guinea. By comparison, the average daily output of world's leading oil producer, the United States, was 16,467,000 barrels per day in 2020.

Source: BP Statistical Review of World Energy, BP p.l.c., 2021.

OPEC Country	Barrels of Oil
Saudi Arabia	11,039,000
Iraq	4,114,000
United Arab Emirates	3,657,000
Iran	3,084,000
Kuwait	2,686,000
Nigeria	1,798,000
Algeria	1,332,000
Angola	1,324,000
Venezuela	540,000
Libya	390,000
Republic of the Congo	307,000
Gabon	207,000
Equatorial Guinea	161,000

its rivals actually do so! How can the three firms ensure the price P_0 and quantity Q_0 solution in which each is keenly interested? How can they avoid the less profitable outcomes associated with either higher or lower prices?

The answer is evident: They can collude. They can get together, talk it over, and agree to charge the same price, P_0, and thereby enjoy the maximum profit available $[= (P_0 - A_0) \times Q_0$ units]. In addition to reducing the possibility of price wars, this will give each firm the maximum profit. (But it will also subject them to antitrust prosecution if they are caught!) For society, the result will be the same as would occur if the industry were a pure monopoly composed of three identical plants.

Overt Collusion: The OPEC Cartel Collusion may assume a variety of forms. The most comprehensive form of collusion is the **cartel,** a group of producers that typically creates a formal written agreement specifying how much each member will produce and charge. Output must be controlled—the market must be divided up—in order to maintain the agreed-upon price. The collusion is overt, or open to view.

cartel A formal agreement among *firms* (or countries) in an *industry* to set the *price* of a product and establish the outputs of the individual firms (or countries) or to divide the market for the product geographically.

Undoubtedly the most significant international cartel is the Organization of Petroleum Exporting Countries (OPEC), comprising 13 oil-producing nations (see Global Perspective 13.1). OPEC produces about 32 percent of the world's oil.

OPEC has in some cases been able to drastically alter oil prices by increasing or decreasing supply. In 1973, for instance, it caused the price of oil to almost quadruple by getting its members to restrict output. In the late 1990s it caused oil prices to rise from $11 per barrel to $34 per barrel over a 15-month period.

As a testimony to its continuing influence, U.S. President Joe Biden asked OPEC in the fall of 2021 to increase its output to help lower world energy prices after the price of oil had increased from around $40 per barrel to around $80 per barrel over the previous year as the world economy recovered from the COVID-19 pandemic.

Covert Collusion: Examples Cartels are illegal in the United States, and hence any collusion that exists is covert or secret. Yet we find numerous examples of cartels in operation, as shown by evidence from antitrust (antimonopoly) cases. In 2015, Apple had to pay ebook customers $450 million after it was convicted of colluding with book publishers including HarperCollins, Penguin Group, and Simon & Schuster to rig the price of ebooks sold on Apple devices. In 2019, carmakers BMW and Volkswagen were fined for colluding to delay the rollout of clean emissions technology. In 2021, international financial firms Credit Suisse, Bank of America, and Crédit Agricole were fined for rigging bond trades at the expense of their clients.

In many other instances, collusion is much subtler. Unwritten, informal understandings (historically called "gentlemen's agreements") are frequently made at cocktail parties, on golf courses, through phone calls, or at trade association meetings. In such agreements, executives reach verbal or even tacit (unspoken) understandings on product price, leaving market shares to be decided by nonprice competition. Although these agreements, too, violate antitrust laws—and can result in severe personal and corporate penalties—the elusive nature of informal understandings makes them more difficult to detect.

Obstacles to Collusion   Normally, cartels and similar collusive arrangements are difficult to establish and maintain. There are several barriers to collusion:

Demand and Cost Differences   When oligopolists face different costs and demand curves, it is difficult for them to agree on a price. This is particularly the case in industries where products are differentiated and change frequently. Even with highly standardized products, firms usually have somewhat different market shares and operate with differing degrees of productive efficiency. Thus it is unlikely that even homogeneous oligopolists would have the same demand and cost curves.

In either case, differences in costs and demand mean that the profit-maximizing price will differ among firms; no single price will be readily acceptable to all, as we assumed was true in Figure 13.3. So price collusion depends on compromises and concessions that are not always easy to obtain and hence act as an obstacle to collusion.

Number of Firms   Other things equal, the larger the number of firms, the more difficult it is to create a cartel or some other form of price collusion. Agreement on price by three or four producers that control an entire market may be relatively easy to accomplish. But such agreement is more difficult to achieve where there are, say, 10 firms, each with roughly 10 percent of the market, or where the Big Three have 70 percent of the market while a competitive fringe of 8 or 10 smaller firms battles for the remainder.

Cheating   As the *prisoner's dilemma* game makes clear, collusive oligopolists are tempted to engage in secret price cutting to increase sales and profit. The difficulty with such cheating is that buyers who are paying a high price for a product may become aware of the lower-priced sales and demand similar treatment. Or buyers receiving a price concession from one producer may use the concession as a wedge to get even larger price concessions from a rival producer. Buyers' attempts to play producers against one another may precipitate price wars among the producers. Although secret price concessions are potentially profitable, they threaten collusive oligopolies over time. Collusion is more likely to succeed when cheating is easy to detect and punish. Then the conspirators are less likely to cheat on the price agreement.

Recession   Long-lasting recession usually serves as an enemy of collusion because slumping markets increase average total cost. In technical terms, as the oligopolists' demand and marginal-revenue curves shift to the left in Figure 13.3 in response to a recession, each firm moves leftward and upward to a higher operating point on its average-total-cost curve. Firms find they have substantial excess production capacity, sales are down, unit costs are up, and profits are being squeezed. Under such conditions, businesses may feel they can avoid serious profit reductions (or even losses) by cutting price and thus gaining sales at the expense of rivals.

Potential Entry   The greater prices and profits that result from collusion may attract new entrants, including foreign firms. Since that would increase market supply and reduce prices and profits, successful collusion requires that colluding oligopolists block the entry of new producers.

Legal Obstacles: Antitrust Law   U.S. antitrust laws prohibit cartels and price-fixing collusion. So less obvious means of price control have evolved in the United States.

Price Leadership Model

price leadership   An informal method that *firms* in an *oligopoly* may employ to set the *price* of their product: One firm (the leader) is the first to announce a change in price, and the other firms (the followers) soon announce identical or similar changes.

Price leadership entails a type of implicit understanding by which oligopolists can coordinate prices without engaging in outright collusion involving formal agreements and secret meetings. Rather, a practice evolves whereby the "dominant firm"—usually the largest or most efficient in the industry—initiates price changes and all other firms more or less automatically follow the leader. Many industries, including farm machinery, cement, copper, newsprint, glass containers, steel, beer, fertilizer, cigarettes, and tin, are practicing, or have in the recent past practiced, price leadership.

Leadership Tactics An examination of price leadership in a variety of industries suggests that the price leader is likely to observe the following tactics.

Infrequent Price Changes Because price changes always carry the risk that rivals will not follow the lead, price adjustments are made only infrequently. The price leader does not respond to minuscule day-to-day changes in costs and demand. Price is changed only when cost and demand conditions have been altered significantly and on an industrywide basis as the result of, for example, industrywide wage increases, an increase in excise taxes, or an increase in the price of some basic input such as energy. In the automobile industry, price adjustments traditionally have been made when new models are introduced each fall.

Communications The price leader often communicates impending price adjustments to the industry through speeches by major executives, trade publication interviews, or press releases. By publicizing "the need to raise prices," the price leader seeks agreement among its competitors regarding the actual increase.

Limit Pricing The price leader does not always choose the price that maximizes short-run profits for the industry because the industry may want to discourage new firms from entering. If the cost advantages (economies of scale) of existing firms are a major barrier to entry, new entrants could surmount that barrier if the price leader and the other firms set product price high enough. New firms that are relatively inefficient because of their small size might survive and grow if the industry sets price very high. So, in order to discourage new competitors and to maintain the current oligopolistic structure of the industry, the price leader may keep price below the short-run profit-maximizing level. The strategy of establishing a price that blocks the entry of new firms is called *limit pricing.*

Breakdowns in Price Leadership: Price Wars Price leadership in oligopoly occasionally breaks down, at least temporarily, and sometimes results in a price war. In October 2009, for example, with the Christmas shopping season just getting under way, Walmart cut its price on 10 highly anticipated new books to just $10 each. Within hours, Amazon matched the price cut. Walmart then retaliated by cutting its price for the books to just $9 each. Amazon matched that reduction—at which point Walmart went to $8.99! Then, out of nowhere, Target jumped in at $8.98, a price that Amazon and Walmart immediately matched. And that is where the price finally came to rest—at a level so low that each company was losing money on each book it sold!

In 2014, a price war broke out between Amazon, Microsoft, and Google in the "cloud computing" market in which those Internet titans rent computing power and data storage to other businesses. Google started the price war by dropping its fees by 23 percent on many services. Amazon retaliated by cutting prices 34 percent. Then Google retaliated by dropping prices another 19 percent before Microsoft came in and matched its rivals' price declines. The tit for tat continued into the next year. By the time the dust had settled, cloud computing prices had fallen by up to 85 percent, depending on the specific service.

Most price wars eventually run their course. After a period of low or negative profits, they again yield price leadership to one of the industry's leading firms. That firm then begins to raise prices, and the other firms willingly follow suit.

► In the kinked-demand theory of oligopoly, price is relatively inflexible because a firm contemplating a price change assumes that its rivals will follow a price cut and ignore a price increase.

► Cartels agree on production limits and set a common price to maximize the joint profit of their members as if each were a subsidiary of a single pure monopoly.

► Collusion among oligopolists is difficult because of (a) demand and cost differences among sellers,

(b) the complexity of output coordination among producers, (c) the potential for cheating, (d) a tendency for agreements to break down during recessions, (e) the potential entry of new firms, and (f) antitrust laws.

► Price leadership involves an informal understanding among oligopolists to match any price change initiated by a designated firm (often the industry's dominant firm).

QUICK REVIEW
13.2

Oligopoly and Advertising

>> **LO13.4** Contrast the potential positive and negative effects of advertising.

We have noted that oligopolists would rather not compete on the basis of price and may go so far as to become involved in price collusion. That aversion to price competition results in a situation in which each firm's share of the total market is typically determined through product development and advertising, for two reasons:

- Product development and advertising campaigns are less easily duplicated than price cuts. A firm's rivals can quickly and easily match price cuts to cancel any potential gain in sales derived from that strategy. In contrast, product improvements and successful advertising can produce more permanent gains in market share because they cannot be duplicated as quickly and completely as price reductions.

- Oligopolists have sufficient financial resources to engage in product development and advertising. For most oligopolists, the economic profits earned in the past can help finance current advertising and product development.

Product development (or, more broadly, "research and development") is the subject of Chapter 15, so we will confine our present discussion to advertising. In 2021, firms spent an estimated $243 billion on advertising in the United States and $613 billion worldwide. Table 13.2 lists the 10 leading U.S. advertisers.

Advertising may affect prices, competition, and efficiency both positively and negatively, depending on the circumstances. We focus here on advertising by oligopolists, but the analysis is equally applicable to advertising by monopolistic competitors.

Positive Effects of Advertising

To make rational (efficient) decisions, consumers need information about product characteristics and prices. Media advertising may be a low-cost means of providing that information to consumers. Suppose you are in the market for a high-quality camera. If there were no advertising describing and promoting high-quality cameras, you would have to spend several days visiting physical stores or many hours scouring the Internet to determine the availability, prices, and features of various brands. This search would entail both direct costs (gasoline, parking fees) and indirect costs (the value of your time). By providing information about the available options, advertising reduces these direct and indirect costs.

By providing information about various competing goods, advertising also reduces monopoly power. In fact, advertising is frequently used to introduce new products designed to compete with existing brands. Could electric car pioneer Tesla have so strongly challenged traditional (internal combustion) auto producers without advertising? Could Uber and Lyft have sliced market share away from traditional taxi and limousine services without advertising? And the same question must be posed for payment apps like Venmo and Zelle, which would not have been able to make significant inroads against older electronic payment methods like Visa and Mastercard without the help of advertising.

Viewed this way, advertising is an efficiency-enhancing activity. It is a relatively inexpensive means of providing useful information to consumers and thus lowering their search costs. By enhancing competition, advertising results in greater economic efficiency. By facilitating the introduction of new products, advertising speeds up technological progress. By increasing sales and output, advertising can reduce long-run average total cost by helping firms obtain economies of scale.

TABLE 13.2 The Largest U.S. Advertisers

Company	Advertising Spending, Billions of $
Amazon	$6.9
Comcast	6.1
AT&T	5.5
Proctor & Gamble	4.3
Disney	3.2
Alphabet (Google)	3.1
Verizon	3.1
Charter Communications	3.0
American Express	3.0
General Motors	3.0

Source: "Ad Age Marketing Fact Pack 2021," *Ad Age.*

Potential Negative Effects of Advertising

Not all the effects of advertising are positive, of course. Much advertising is designed simply to manipulate or persuade consumers—that is, to alter their preferences in favor of the advertiser's product. A television commercial indicating that a

🌐 GLOBAL PERSPECTIVE 13.2

THE WORLD'S TOP 10 BRAND NAMES, 2021

Here are the world's top 10 brands, based on four criteria: the brand's market share within its category, the brand's worldwide appeal across age groups and nationalities, the loyalty of customers to the brand, and the ability of the brand to "stretch" to products beyond the original product.

World's Top 10 Brands

Apple
Amazon
Microsoft
Google
Samsung
Coca-Cola
Toyota
Mercedes-Benz
McDonald's
Disney

Source: "Best Global Brands 2021," *Interbrand,* 2021.

popular personality drinks a particular soft drink—and therefore that you should too—conveys little or no information about price or quality. In addition, advertising is sometimes based on misleading and extravagant claims that confuse consumers rather than enlighten them. Indeed, advertising sometimes persuades consumers to pay high prices for much-acclaimed but inferior products, forgoing better but unadvertised products selling at lower prices. Example: *Consumer Reports* has found that heavily advertised premium motor oils provide no better engine performance or longevity than do cheaper brands.

Firms often establish substantial brand-name loyalty and thus achieve monopoly power via their advertising (see Global Perspective 13.2). As a consequence, they are able to increase their sales, expand their market shares, and enjoy greater profits. Larger profits permit still more advertising and further enlargement of the firm's market share and profit. In time, consumers may lose the advantages of competitive markets and face the disadvantages of monopolized markets. Moreover, new entrants to the industry need to incur large advertising costs to establish their products in the marketplace; thus, advertising costs may be a barrier to entry.

Advertising can also be self-canceling. The advertising campaign of one fast-food hamburger chain may be offset by equally costly campaigns waged by rivals, so that each firm's demand remains unchanged. Few, if any, extra burgers will be purchased, and each firm's market share will stay the same. But because of all the advertising, every firm will experience higher costs. That, in turn, will either reduce profits, or, if there is successful price leadership, cause their product prices to rise.

When advertising either leads to increased monopoly power or is self-canceling, economic inefficiency results.

Oligopoly and Efficiency

Overall, is oligopoly an efficient market structure from society's standpoint? How do the oligopolist's price and output decisions measure up to the triple equality $P = MC = $ minimum ATC that occurs in pure competition?

>> **LO13.5** Discuss the efficiency of oligopoly.

Based on evidence that many oligopolists sustain sizable economic profits year after year, many economists believe that the outcome of some oligopolistic markets is approximately as shown in Figure 13.3. In that case, the oligopolist's production occurs where price exceeds marginal cost and average total cost. Moreover, production is below the output at which average total cost is minimized. In this view, neither productive efficiency ($P = $ minimum ATC) nor allocative efficiency ($P = MC$) is likely to occur under oligopoly.

A few observers assert that oligopoly is actually less desirable than pure monopoly because government usually regulates pure monopoly in the United States to guard against abuses of monopoly power. Informal collusion among oligopolists may yield price and output results similar to those under pure monopoly yet give the outward appearance of competition involving independent firms.

We should note, however, three qualifications to this view:

- *Increased foreign competition* In recent decades foreign competition has increased rivalry in a number of oligopolistic industries—steel, automobiles, video games, electric shavers, outboard motors, and even social media apps (TikTok is Chinese). This has helped to break down such cozy arrangements as price leadership and to stimulate much more competitive pricing.

- *Limit pricing* Recall that some oligopolists purposely keep prices below the short-run profit-maximizing level in order to bolster entry barriers. Thus consumers and society may get some of the benefits of competition—prices closer to marginal cost and minimum average total cost—even without the competition that free entry would provide.

- *Technological advance* Over time, oligopolistic industries may foster more rapid product development and greater improvement of production techniques than purely competitive industries would. Oligopolists have large economic profits from which they can fund expensive research and development (R&D). Moreover, barriers to entry may give oligopolists some assurance that they will reap the rewards of successful R&D. Thus, the short-run economic inefficiencies created by oligopolists may be partly or wholly offset by the oligopolists' contributions to better products, lower prices, and lower costs over time.

QUICK REVIEW
13.3

- Oligopolists emphasize nonprice competition because (a) advertising and product variations are harder to match than price changes and (b) oligopolists frequently have ample resources to fund nonprice competition.

- Advertising can help reduce monopoly power by presenting consumers with useful information about existing products and by helping to introduce new products.

- Advertising can hurt consumers and competition by promoting monopoly power and creating entry barriers.

Game Theory and Strategic Behavior

>> **LO13.6** Use additional game-theory terminology and demonstrate how to find a Nash equilibrium.

We have seen that game theory is helpful in explaining mutual interdependence and strategic behavior by oligopolists. This section provides additional oligopoly-based applications of game theory.

A One-Time Game: Strategies and Equilibrium

Consider Figure 13.4, which lists strategies and outcomes for two fictitious producers of computer memory chips called DRAMs (Dynamic Random Access Memory circuits). Chipco is the single producer of these chips in the United States and Dramco is the only producer in China. Each firm has two alternative strategies: (1) an international strategy, in which it competes directly against the other firm in both countries, and (2) a national strategy, in which it sells only in its home country.

The game and payoff matrix shown in Figure 13.4 is a **one-time game** because the firms select their optimal strategies in a single time period without regard to possible interactions in subsequent time periods. The game is also a **simultaneous game** because the firms choose their strategies at the same time; and it is a **positive-sum game,** a game in which the sum of the two firms' outcomes (here, profits) is positive. In contrast, the net gain in a **zero-sum game** is zero because one firm's gain must equal the other firm's loss, and the net gain in a **negative-sum game** is negative because the loser's loss exceeds the winner's gain. Positive-sum games correspond to "win-win" situations; zero-sum games to "I win-you lose" situations. In some positive-sum games, both firms may have positive outcomes. That is the case in Figure 13.4.

To determine optimal strategies, Chipco and Dramco examine their respective

FIGURE 13.4
A one-time game.

In this single-period, positive-sum game, Chipco's international strategy is its dominant strategy—the alternative that is superior to any other strategy regardless of whatever Dramco does. Similarly, Dramco's international strategy is also its dominant strategy. With both firms choosing international strategies, the outcome of the game is cell A, where each firm receives an $11 million profit. Cell A is a Nash equilibrium because neither firm will independently want to move away from it given the other firm's strategy.

payouts in the payout matrix. The payout values are given in millions of dollars, with Chipco's payouts listed in the yellow portions of each cell and Dramco's payouts printed in the blue portions of each cell. These payoffs indicate that both firms have a **dominant strategy**—an option that is better than any alternative option *regardless of what the other firm does*. To see why, notice that an International strategy would give Chipco a higher profit than a National strategy—regardless of whether Dramco chooses an International or a National strategy for itself. We verify this in two steps.

- First, suppose that Dramco pursues an International strategy. In that case, will it be better for Chipco to play an International strategy or a National strategy? Chipco's payoffs for those two options are given in the left column, in the yellow triangles within cells A and C. The better option is for Chipco to select International, since that would yield $11 million while the National option would only generate $5 million. So Chipco's better option if Dramco chooses an International strategy is to also select an International strategy.

- But what if Dramco instead plays a National strategy? Will it still be better for Chipco itself to play an International strategy? The answer is yes, which you can see by comparing Chipco's payouts in the right column, in cells B and D. The yellow triangles tell the tale. Chipco should opt for an International strategy because Chipco's $20 million payout for playing an International strategy exceeds the $17 million that it would get if it played a National strategy. Thus, Chipco's better option is the International strategy when Dramco is playing the National strategy.

Since the International strategy is Chipco's better option no matter which strategy Dramco selects, we know that International is Chipco's dominant strategy; it is the option that Chipco will want to select no matter what Dramco does.

Using similar logic, Dramco also concludes that the International option is its own dominant strategy. So, both firms will want to play International no matter what the other firm does. That implies that cell A, where both firms are playing their dominant strategy, will be a **Nash equilibrium**—an outcome of a strategic game from which neither rival wants to deviate. (The name comes from John Nash, the Nobel Prize-winning mathematician who discovered it.) At the Nash equilibrium, both rivals see their current strategy as optimal *no matter what the other firm does*. The Nash equilibrium is the only outcome in Figure 13.4 that, once achieved, is stable. It will be the default situation for these competitors unless they can figure out a way to collude successfully.

Credible and Empty Threats

In looking for optimal strategies, Chipco and Dramco both note that they could increase their profit from $11 million to $17 million if they could agree to jointly pursue national strategies (cell D) instead of independently pursuing international strategies (cell A). Presumably the national strategies would leave the firms as pure monopolists in their domestic economies, with each able to set higher prices and obtain greater profits as a result. But if this territorial agreement were put in place, both firms would have an incentive to cheat on the agreement by secretly selling DRAMs in the other country. That would temporarily move the game to either cell B or cell C. Once discovered, however, such cheating would undermine the territorial agreement and return the game to the Nash equilibrium (cell A).

Now let's add a new twist—a credible threat—to the game shown in Figure 13.4. A **credible threat** is a statement of coercion (a threat!) that is believable by the other firm. Suppose that Chipco is the lower-cost producer of DRAMs because of its superior technology. Also, suppose that Chipco approaches Dramco saying that Chipco intends to use its national strategy and expects Dramco to do the same. If Dramco decides against the national strategy, or agrees to the national strategy and then later cheats on the agreement, Chipco will immediately drop its price to an ultra-low level equal to its average total cost (ATC). Both firms know that Chipco's ATC price is below Dramco's ATC. Although Chipco will see its economic profit fall to zero, Dramco will suffer an economic loss and possibly go out of business.

If Chipco's threat is credible, the two firms represented in Figure 13.4 will abandon the Nash equilibrium (cell A) to deploy their national strategies and achieve highly profitable cell D. In game theory, credible threats such as this can help establish and maintain collusive agreements. A strong "enforcer" can help prevent cheating and maintain the group discipline needed for cartels, price-fixing conspiracies, and territorial understandings to successfully generate high profits.

one-time game A strategic interaction (*game*) between two or more parties (players) that all parties know will take place only once.

simultaneous game A strategic interaction (*game*) between two or more parties (players) in which every player moves (makes a decision) at the same time.

positive-sum game A strategic interaction (game) between two or more parties (players) in which the winners' gains exceed the losers' losses so that the gains and losses sum to something positive.

zero-sum game A strategic interaction (game) between two or more parties (players) in which the winners' gains exactly offset the losers' losses so that the gains and losses sum to zero.

negative-sum game A strategic interaction (game) between two or more parties (players) in which the winners' gains are less than the losers' losses so that the gains and losses sum to a negative number.

dominant strategy In a strategic interaction (*game*) between two or more players, a course of action (strategy) that a player will wish to undertake no matter what the other players choose to do.

Nash equilibrium The situation that occurs in some *simultaneous games* wherein every player is playing his or her *dominant strategy* at the same time and thus no player has any reason to change behavior.

credible threat In a *sequential game* with two players, a statement made by Player 1 that truthfully (credibly) threatens a penalizing action against Player 2 if Player 2 does something that Player 1 does not want Player 2 to do. Opposite of *empty threat*.

But credible threats are difficult to achieve in the actual economy. For example, Dramco might rightly wonder why Chipco had not previously driven it out of business through an ultra-low price strategy. Is Chipco fearful of the U.S. antitrust authorities?

If Dramco does not wish to participate in the proposed scheme, it might counter Chipco's threat with its own: Forget that you ever talked to us or we will take this illegal "offer" to the U.S. Justice Department. Dramco can make this threat because strict laws are in place against attempts to restrain trade through price-fixing and territorial agreements.

empty threat In a *sequential game* with two players, a noncredible (bluffing) statement made by Player 1 that threatens a penalizing action against Player 2 if Player 2 does something that Player 1 does not want Player 2 to do. Opposite of *credible threat*.

So Dramco may view Chipco's threat as simply an **empty threat**—a statement of coercion that is not believable by the threatened firm. If so, the Nash equilibrium will prevail, with both firms pursuing an international strategy.

Repeated Games and Reciprocity Strategies

The Chipco-Dramco game was a one-time game, but many strategic situations are repeated by the same oligopolists over and over again. For example, Coca-Cola and Pepsi are mutually interdependent on pricing, advertising, and product development year after year, decade after decade. The same is true for Boeing and Airbus, Walmart and Target, Uber and Lyft, Mastercard and Visa, Nike and Adidas, and numerous other dominant pairs.

repeated game A strategic interaction (*game*) between two or more parties (players) that all parties know will take place repeatedly.

In a **repeated game**—a game that recurs more than once—the optimal strategy may be to cooperate and restrain oneself from competing as hard as possible so long as the other firm reciprocates by also not competing as hard as possible.[1] To see how this works, consider two hypothetical producers of soft drinks: 2Cool and ThirstQ. If ThirstQ competes hard with 2Cool in today's situation in which 2Cool would like ThirstQ to take things easy, 2Cool will most likely retaliate against ThirstQ in any subsequent situation where the circumstances are reversed. In contrast, if ThirstQ cooperates with 2Cool in game 1, ThirstQ can expect 2Cool to reciprocate in game 2 of their repeated interaction. Both firms know full well the negative long-run consequences of ever refusing to cooperate. So the cooperation continues, not only in game 2, but in games 3, 4, 5, and beyond.

Figure 13.5 shows two side-by-side payoff matrixes for the two games. In Figure 13.5a, 2Cool and ThirstQ face a situation in which 2Cool is introducing a new cola called Cool Cola and has

FIGURE 13.5 A repeated game with reciprocity.

(a) In the first payoff matrix, 2Cool introduces its new Cool Cola with a large promotional advertising budget, but its rival ThirstQ maintains its normal advertising budget even though it could counter 2Cool with a large advertising budget of its own and drive the outcome from cell B to cell A. ThirstQ forgoes this $2 million of extra profit because it knows that it will soon be introducing its own new product (Quench It). (b) In the second payoff matrix, ThirstQ introduces Quench It with a large promotional advertising budget. Cool2 reciprocates ThirstQ's earlier accommodation by not matching ThirstQ's promotional advertising budget and instead allowing the outcome of the repeated game to be cell C. The profit of both 2Cool and ThirstQ therefore is larger over the two periods than if each firm had aggressively countered each other's single-period strategy.

(a) 2Cool introduces Cool Cola

(b) ThirstQ introduces Quench It

[1] We are assuming either an infinitely repeated game or a game of unknown time horizon. Games with a known ending date undermine reciprocity strategies.

two advertising options: a high promotional budget to introduce the new product and a normal advertising budget. ThirstQ has the same two options: a high promotional budget to try to counter 2Cool's product introduction and a normal advertising budget.

The analysis is now familiar to you. The dominant strategies for both firms in game 1 (Figure 13.5a) are their large promotional advertising budgets and the Nash equilibrium is cell A. Both firms could do better at cell D if each agreed to use normal advertising budgets. But 2Cool could do better still. It could achieve the $16 million of profit in cell B, but only if ThirstQ holds its advertising budget to its normal level during the introduction of Cool Cola.

ThirstQ might voluntarily do just that! It knows that game 2 (Figure 13.5b) is forthcoming in which it will be introducing its own new product, Quench It. By leaving its advertising budget at its normal level during 2Cool's introduction of Cool Cola, and thereby sacrificing profit of $2 million (= $10 million in cell A − $8 million in cell B), ThirstQ can expect 2Cool to reciprocate in the subsequent game in which ThirstQ introduces Quench It.

Without formally colluding—and risking antitrust penalties—game 1 ends at cell B and repeated game 2 ends at cell C. With reciprocity, 2Cool's total profit of $26 million (= $16 million in game 1 + $10 million in game 2) exceeds the $21 million (= $10 million + $11 million) it would have earned without the reciprocity. ThirstQ similarly benefits. To check your understanding, confirm this fact using the numbers in the two matrixes.

First-Mover Advantages and Preemption of Entry

The games we have highlighted thus far have been games in which the two firms simultaneously select their optimal strategies. But in some actual economic circumstances, firms apply strategies sequentially: One firm moves first and commits to a strategy to which a rival firm must subsequently respond. In such a **sequential game,** the final outcome may depend critically upon which firm moves first since the first mover may have the opportunity to establish an equilibrium that works in its favor.

Consider Figure 13.6, which identifies a game in which two large retailers—let's call them Big Box and Huge Box—are each considering building a large retail store in a small rural city. As indicated in the figure, each firm has two strategies: Build or Don't Build. The payoff matrix reflects the fact that the city is not large enough to support two big box retailers profitably. If both retailers simultaneously build, the outcome will be cell A and each firm will lose $5 million. If neither firm builds, the outcome will be cell D with both firms securing zero profit. If only Big Box builds, the outcome will be cell C and Big Box will profit handsomely at $12 million. If Huge Box builds, but Big Box stays out, the outcome will be cell B and Huge Box will secure the $12 million profit.

The equilibrium outcome of this sequential game depends on which firm moves first. Either cell B or Cell C could be the final outcome. Which one is achieved depends on which firm builds first. If Big Box builds first, then a comparison of Huge Box's payoffs in the yellow triangles in cells A and C shows that Huge Box's best response would be Don't Build. Thus, the outcome of the game when Big Box moves first is cell C. By contrast, if Huge Box moves first, then Big Box will compare its payoffs in the blue triangles in cells A and B and thereby determine that it would be better off choosing Don't Build. So the outcome of the game when Huge Box moves first is cell B.

As we have just gone over, the payoff matrix in Figure 13.6 clearly reveals that whoever builds first will preempt the other retailer from entering the market because the other retailer will always choose Don't Build. Thus, an extremely large **first-mover advantage** exists in this particular game.

But which firm will actually build first? That depends on which firm is better positioned financially and strategically. Suppose that a well-thought-out strategy and adequate financing leave Big Box better prepared than Huge Box to

sequential game A strategic interaction (*game*) between two or more parties (players) in which each party moves (makes a decision) in a predetermined order (sequence).

first-mover advantage In *game theory,* the benefit obtained by the party that moves first in a *sequential game.* A situation that occurs in a *sequential game* if the player who gets to move first has an advantage in terms of final outcomes over the player(s) who move subsequently.

FIGURE 13.6
A first-mover advantage and the preemption of entry.

In this game in which strategies are pursued sequentially, the firm that moves first can take advantage of the particular situation represented in which only a single firm can exist profitably in some geographical market. Here, we suppose that Big Box moves first with its "Build" strategy to achieve the $12 million profit outcome in cell C. Huge Box then will find that it will lose money if it also builds because that will result in a $5 million loss, as shown in cell A.

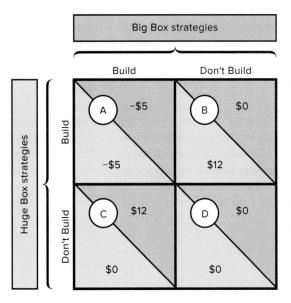

LAST WORD

The Rewards of Oligopoly Are . . . Sky Miles?

Nonprice Competition Between the Oligopoly Credit Card Issuers Generates Billions in Benefits for a Surprising Group.

The credit card industry in the United States is a highly concentrated oligopoly, with the top four card-issuing banks—Citigroup, JP Morgan Chase, American Express, and Capital One—accounting for 54 percent of all credit card lending in the United States.

There's a common misconception that companies like Visa and Mastercard lend money. But that's not true. Visa and Mastercard are in a different industry, electronic payments processing, and they get paid to maintain the computer networks that transfer payments information worldwide. The banks that issue credit cards work with the payments networks run by companies like Visa and Mastercard so that their credit cards will be accepted by any merchant who is enrolled with one of those payments networks. Thus, you might, for instance, see an ad for *Chase Visa* cards, meaning that JP Morgan Chase, the bank, is the lender for any money borrowed by consumers who use one of those cards and that those cards will be accepted by any merchant signed up with the Visa payments network.

An important twist pertains to the grace period that card-issuing banks offer cardholders. Suppose that the month of May arrives and you have a credit card. Each purchase that you make using your card generates a payment to the relevant merchant. The bank pays the merchant by lending you the money to pay them. But interest does not start accruing on that loan immediately. The bank will send you a credit card statement for the month of May and then give you a grace period (of typically 21 to 25 days) to pay off all the money you borrowed that month.

If you pay your outstanding balance by the due date, no interest will accrue. But if you fail to pay the balance by the due date, interest will begin to accumulate, typically at an interest rate of 18 or 19 percent per year.

It is that high interest rate on unpaid balances that card-issuing banks want; it's how they make their money as lenders. And it is consequently in each bank's own interest to try to get as many consumers as possible to use its own credit cards rather than those issued by its competitors.

If the credit card industry were purely competitive, then card-issuing banks would have to compete on the interest rates that they charge on unpaid balances. But as with many highly concentrated oligopoly industries, the credit card industry displays a reluctance by the firms in the industry to compete aggressively against each other on price (the interest rate on unpaid balances being the "price" paid by cardholders to borrow money). To do so would be to risk price wars that could destroy their oligopoly profits.

So, instead, the firms in oligopoly industries prefer to engage in nonprice competition in which they attempt to fight over the limited supply of customers by offering those consumers alternative reasons

Robert Goebel/Alamy Stock Photo

to select their respective products. By doing so, the firms in the industry can compete intensely for market share without having to worry about ending up in a situation in which prices have fallen to the competitive level at which it is no longer possible to earn positive economic profits.

Depending on the industry, nonprice competition may include advertising that builds brand loyalty, paying people to leave positive reviews online, and constantly supplying upgrades or new features that attract consumer interest. In the oligopoly credit card industry, however, nonprice competition largely takes the form of offering consumers different types of rewards programs, such as frequent flyer miles that can be redeemed for air travel or cashback programs that "refund" a small percentage of purchases to cardholders.

But where does the money come from to pay for all those rewards? From the cardholders who fail to pay their balances each month. Part of the interest that they pay goes to fund the rewards programs—which means that there is a huge transfer of wealth each year from the people who are paying interest on credit card loans each month to the people who pay off their balances each month. So if you want to come out ahead when using a credit card, pay off your balance each month. That way the people making interest payments will also be paying for your travel, cash-back, and other credit card rewards!

Also note that the more that the card issuers have to spend on rewards to win customers, the lower their profits. So also enjoy the fact that, other things equal, the more card issuers pay out in rewards, the smaller their above-competitive oligopoly profits.

move quickly to build a large retail store in this city. By exploiting its first-mover advantage, Big Box drives the outcome to cell C and preempts Huge Box's entry into this market. Big Box gets a $12 million profit while Huge Box gets nothing.

Brick and Mortar Examples Many retail businesses that rely on physical ("brick and mortar") stores have used variations of the first-mover strategy to a greater or lesser extent to preempt major rivals, or at least greatly slow their entry. Examples include Walmart, Home Depot, Costco, Walgreens, Starbucks, and many more. The strategy, however, is highly risky because it requires the commitment of huge amounts of investment funds to saturate the market and preclude entry by other firms. Also, to be the first mover in places that are being transformed from rural land into urban areas, firms may need to build their stores many months prior to the time when the area in question becomes developed enough to provide the store with significant business. That may mean losses until the market grows sufficiently for profitability. Some firms such as Walmart have become huge, profitable international enterprises by using a first-mover strategy. Other firms, such as Krispy Kreme Donuts, have lost millions of dollars because their extremely rapid expansion turned out to be unprofitable in many of their outlets because the expected customers never materialized.

Digital Examples Internet startups that are looking for funding from investors often back their pitch for money with an argument that combines network effects and first-mover advantages. These firms begin by asserting that their new online product or app will be subject to *network effects*, such that the more users they can get early on, the more users they will be likely to get later on because future users will be attracted by the fact that there are already so many existing users.

These startups then argue that unless they get off to a rapid (and well funded!) start, some other rival firm will get ahead of them in terms of attracting lots of early users. If that were to happen, they argue, the network effects present for this type of product would lead to that rival firm's eventual dominance. Thus, they claim, the only way to win the battle against potential rivals is to obtain a first mover advantage by getting lots of early funding to pay for the advertising necessary to gain lots of early adopters who will then, via network effects, attract more and more users until the startup comes to dominate its product category.

It is for a similar reason that most apps that are subject to network effects are free to users right from the beginning. By being free, they hope to attract lots of early adopters and thus, perhaps, speed the app toward a very large market share. To make up for giving their products away for free, the apps figure out other ways to make money, such as by selling ads.

QUICK REVIEW 13.4

▶ Positive-sum, zero-sum, and negative-sum games have combined payoffs across all players that sum to, respectively, something positive, zero, and something negative. Positive-sum games correspond to "win-win" situations, while zero-sum games correspond to "I win-you lose" situations.

▶ A dominant strategy for a firm in a two-firm game is a strategy that leads to better outcomes for the firm no matter what the other firm does.

▶ A Nash equilibrium occurs when both firms are simultaneously playing dominant strategies, so that neither firm has any incentive to alter its behavior.

▶ Reciprocity can improve outcomes in repeated games and there may be first-mover advantages in sequential games.

Summary

LO13.1 Describe the characteristics of oligopoly.
Oligopolistic industries are characterized by the presence of a few large producers, each having a significant fraction of the market. Firms thus situated engage in strategic behavior and are mutually interdependent: The behavior of any one firm directly affects, and is affected by, the actions of rivals. Products may be either virtually uniform or significantly differentiated. Various barriers to entry, including economies of scale and network effects, underlie and maintain oligopoly.

High four-firm concentration ratios are an indication of oligopoly (monopoly) power. By giving more weight to larger firms, the Herfindahl index is designed to measure market dominance in an industry.

LO13.2 Discuss how game theory relates to oligopoly.
Game theory (*a*) shows the interdependence of oligopolists' pricing policies, (*b*) reveals oligopolists' tendency to collude, and (*c*) explains oligopolists' temptation to cheat on collusive arrangements.

LO13.3 Explain the three main models of oligopoly pricing and output.

A kinked-demand curve may confront noncollusive oligopoly firms. This curve and the accompanying MR curve help explain the price rigidity that often characterizes oligopoly.

Collusion between oligopoly firms can lead to higher profits. But demand and cost differences, a larger number of firms, cheating through secret price concessions, recessions, new market entrants, and antitrust laws are all obstacles to collusive oligopoly.

Price leadership is an informal means of collusion whereby one firm, usually the largest or most efficient, initiates price changes and the other firms in the industry follow the leader.

LO13.4 Contrast the potential positive and negative effects of advertising.

Market shares in oligopolistic industries are usually determined on the basis of product development and advertising. Oligopolists emphasize nonprice competition because (*a*) advertising and product variations are less easy for rivals to match and (*b*) oligopolists frequently have ample resources to finance nonprice competition.

Advertising may affect prices, competition, and efficiency either positively or negatively. Positives: Advertising can provide consumers with low-cost information about competing products, help introduce new competing products into concentrated industries, and generally reduce monopoly power and its inefficiencies. Negatives: Advertising can promote monopoly power via persuasion and the creation of entry barriers. Moreover, it can be self-canceling when rivals engage in advertising; then it boosts costs and creates inefficiency while accomplishing little else.

LO13.5 Discuss the efficiency of oligopoly.

Oligopolistic markets generate neither productive nor allocative efficiency, but oligopoly may be superior to pure competition in promoting research and development and technological progress. Table 10.1 provides a concise summary of the characteristics of monopolistic competition and oligopoly as they compare to those of pure competition and pure monopoly.

LO13.6 Use additional game-theory terminology and demonstrate how to find a Nash equilibrium.

Games can be either one-time games or repeated games. Decisions in games may be made either simultaneously or sequentially. Positive-sum games allow for "win-win" opportunities, whereas zero-sum games feature "I win–you lose" outcomes.

A firm has a dominant strategy if that strategy is the firm's best option no matter what the other firm does. A Nash equilibrium occurs when both firms are pursuing a dominant strategy. Attempts by firms to rig games to achieve some other outcome are difficult to accomplish and maintain, although credible threats can sometimes work. In contrast, empty threats accomplish nothing and leave the outcome at the Nash equilibrium.

Reciprocity can improve outcomes for firms participating in repeated games.

In sequential games with first-mover advantages, the firm that moves first can preempt the other firm, making it unprofitable for the other firm to match the choice made by the first mover. Several real-world firms, including Walmart, have used first-mover advantages to saturate local markets and preempt entry by rivals. Internet firms have also employed first-mover advantages, especially in digital industries that are subject to network effects.

Terms and Concepts

oligopoly	collusion	negative-sum game
homogeneous oligopoly	kinked-demand curve	dominant strategy
differentiated oligopoly	price war	Nash equilibrium
strategic behavior	cartel	credible threat
mutual interdependence	price leadership	empty threat
interindustry competition	one-time game	repeated game
import competition	simultaneous game	sequential game
game theory	positive-sum game	first-mover advantage
prisoner's dilemma	zero-sum game	

Discussion Questions

Mc Graw Hill **connect**

1. Why do oligopolies exist? List five or six oligopolists whose products you own or regularly purchase. What distinguishes oligopoly from monopolistic competition? **LO13.1**
2. What is the meaning of a four-firm concentration ratio of 60 percent? 90 percent? **LO13.1**
3. Explain the general meaning of the profit payoff matrix below for oligopolists X and Y. All profit figures are in thousands. **LO13.2**

   a. Use the payoff matrix to explain the mutual interdependence that characterizes oligopolistic industries.
   b. Assuming no collusion between X and Y, what is the likely pricing outcome?
   c. In view of your answer to part *b*, explain why price collusion is mutually profitable. Why might the firms be tempted to cheat on the collusive agreement?

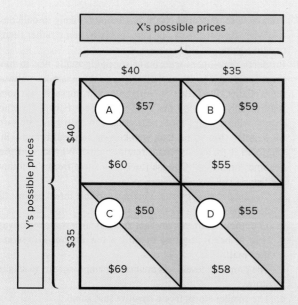

4. What assumptions about a rival's response to price changes underlie the kinked-demand curve for oligopolists? Why is there a gap in the oligopolist's marginal-revenue curve? How does the kinked-demand curve explain price rigidity in oligopoly? **LO13.3**

5. Why might price collusion occur in oligopolistic industries? Assess the economic desirability of collusive pricing. What are the main obstacles to collusion? Speculate as to why price leadership is legal in the United States, whereas price-fixing is not. **LO13.3**

6. Why is there so much advertising in monopolistic competition and oligopoly? How does such advertising help consumers and promote efficiency? How does advertising promote inefficiency? **LO13.4**

7. **ADVANCED ANALYSIS** Construct a strategic form payoff matrix involving two firms and their decisions on high versus low advertising budgets and the effects of each on profits. Show a circumstance in which both firms select high advertising budgets even though both would be more profitable with low advertising budgets. Why won't they unilaterally cut their advertising budgets? **LO13.4**

8. Is the game shown in Figure 13.1 a zero-sum game, or is it a positive-sum game? How can you tell? Are there dominant strategies in this game? If so, what are they? Which cell represents a Nash equilibrium and why? Explain why it is so difficult for Uptown and RareAir to achieve and maintain a more favorable cell than the Nash equilibrium in this single-period pricing game. **LO13.6**

9. Refer to the payoff matrix in discussion question 3. First, assume this is a one-time game. Explain how the $60/$57 outcome might be achieved through a credible threat. Next, assume this is a repeated game (rather than a one-time game) and that the interaction between the two firms occurs indefinitely. Why might collusion with a credible threat not be necessary to achieve the $60/$57 outcome? **LO13.6**

10. Refer to the following payoff matrix. **LO13.6**

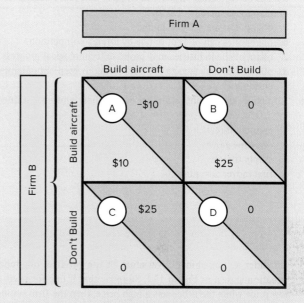

Assuming this is a sequential game with no collusion, what is the outcome if Firm A moves first to build a new type of commercial aircraft? Explain why first-mover strategies in the real world are only as good as the profit projections on which they are based. How could a supposed "win" from moving first turn out to be a big loss, while the "loss" of being preempted turns out to be a blessing in disguise?

11. How do network effects give Internet firms a boost with respect to first mover advantages? When network effects are at play for an Internet firm, how does an increase in the number of people using its product shift its demand curve, all other things equal? **LO13.6**

12. **LAST WORD** what is it about the credit card industry that allows its firms to not have to compete on price (the interest rate)? Who ultimately pays for credit card rewards? How do rewards payments affect industry profits?

Review Questions

connect

1. Which of the following apply to oligopoly industries? Select one or more answers from the choices shown. **LO13.1**
   a. A few large producers
   b. Many small producers
   c. Strategic behavior
   d. Price taking

2. Facepalm, Instarant, and Snaphat are rival firms in an oligopoly industry. If kinked-demand theory applies to these three firms, Facepalm's demand curve will be: **LO13.3**
   a. more elastic above the current price than below it.
   b. less elastic above the current price than below it.
   c. of equal elasticity both above and below the current price.
   d. none of the above.

3. Consider an oligopoly industry whose firms have identical demand and cost conditions. If the firms decide to collude, then they will want to collectively produce the amount of output that would be produced by: **LO13.3**
   a. a monopolistic competitor.
   b. a pure competitor.
   c. a pure monopolist.
   d. none of the above.

4. In an oligopoly, each firm's share of the total market is typically determined by: **LO13.4**
   a. scarcity and competition.
   b. kinked-demand curves and payoff matrices.
   c. homogeneous products and import competition.
   d. product development and advertising.

5. Some analysts consider oligopolies to be potentially less efficient than monopoly firms because at least monopoly firms tend to be regulated. Arguments in favor of a more benign view of oligopolies include: **LO13.5**
   a. oligopolies are self-regulating.
   b. oligopolies can be kept in line by foreign competition.
   c. oligopolistic industries may promote technological progress.
   d. oligopolies may engage in limit pricing to keep out potential entrants.

6. Collusive agreements can be established and maintained by: **LO13.6**
   a. credible threats.
   b. one-time games.
   c. empty threats.
   d. first-mover advantage.

7. True or false: Potential rivals may be more likely to collude if they view themselves as playing a repeated game rather than a one-time game. **LO13.6**

8. Property developers who build shopping malls like to have them "anchored" with outlets of one or more famous national retail chains, like Target or Nordstrom. Having such "anchors" is obviously good for the mall developers because anchor stores bring a lot of foot traffic that can help generate sales for smaller stores that lack well-known national brands. But what's in it for the national retail chains? Why should they become "anchors"? Choose the best answer from the following list. **LO13.6**
   a. The anchor stores want to make a credible threat against the developer.
   b. The anchor stores may feel there is a first-mover advantage to becoming one of only a few anchor stores at a new mall.
   c. The property developers are making empty threats to smaller stores.
   d. The smaller stores face a negative-sum game.

Problems

McGraw Hill **connect**

1. Consider a "punishment" variation of the two-firm oligopoly situation shown in Figure 13.1. Suppose that if one firm sets a low price while the other sets a high price, then the firm setting the high price can fine the firm setting the low price. Suppose that whenever a fine is imposed, X dollars are taken from the low-price firm and given to the high-price firm. What is the smallest amount that the fine X can be such that both firms will always want to set the high price? **LO13.6**

2. Consider whether the promises and threats made toward each other by duopolists and oligopolists are always credible (believable). Look back at Figure 13.1. Imagine that the two firms will play this game twice in sequence and that each firm publicly proclaims the following policy: Each says that if both it and the other firm choose the high price in the first game, then it will also choose the high price in the second game (as a reward to the other firm for cooperating in the first game). **LO13.6**
   a. As a first step toward thinking about whether this policy is credible, consider the situation facing both firms in the second game. If each firm bases its decision on what to do in the second game entirely on the payouts facing the firms in the second game, which strategy will each firm choose in the second game?

   b. Now move backward in time one step. Imagine that it is the start of the first game and each firm must decide what to do during the first game. Given your answer to part a, is the publicly stated policy credible? (Hint: No matter what happens in the first game, what will both firms do in the second game?)
   c. Given your answers to parts a and b, what strategy will each firm choose in the first game?

3. **ADVANCED ANALYSIS** Suppose you are playing a game in which you and one other person each pick a number between 1 and 100, with the person closest to some randomly selected number between 1 and 100 winning the jackpot. (Ask your instructor to fund the jackpot.) Your opponent picks first. What number do you expect her to choose? Why? What number would you then pick? Why are the two numbers so close? How might this example relate to why Home Depot and Lowes, Walgreens and Rite Aid, McDonald's and Burger King, and other major pairs of rivals locate so close to each other in many well-defined geographical markets that are large enough for both firms to be profitable? **LO13.6**

CHAPTER 14

Internet Oligopoly: Networks and Platforms

>> LEARNING OBJECTIVES

LO14.1 Describe how economies of scale help to explain both the high concentration of Internet industries and why so many digital products are provided to consumers at a price of zero.

LO14.2 Define network effects and explain their relationship to industry concentration among Internet firms.

LO14.3 Explain digital platforms and how they determine their pricing structure.

LO14.4 Summarize the debate regarding government regulation of Internet firms.

In the early 1990s, when the public Internet was just getting started, seven of the top 10 positions in the Fortune 500 list of the largest corporations in the United States were filled by major automakers (Ford, General Motors, and Chrysler) or major oil companies (Exxon, Mobil, Chevron, and Texaco). In comparison, as of early 2022, seven of the world's 10 most valuable corporations were Internet firms, including Apple, Microsoft, Amazon, Alphabet (the parent company of Google), and Meta (the parent company of Facebook).

Those changes reflect how fundamentally the Internet's ability to connect people and information has transformed not only *what* is being produced but also *how* it's being produced. Gone is an economy focused on producing physical objects using heat and combustion. Arrived is an economy focused on digital services powered by green energy.

One constant, though, is the prominence of highly concentrated oligopoly industries. This chapter explores why the digital economy continues to be dominated by large oligopoly firms while at the same time displaying an entirely new economic phenomenon: giant companies that give away their main products for free.

Zero-MC Digital Services and Internet Economies of Scale

You may have noticed that prominent software, search, and social media companies—such as Microsoft, Google, and Facebook—dominate their respective sectors of the **Internet.** While none of these digital firms is a *pure monopolist,* each is a highly dominant *oligopolist* that controls most of the market in its core area of expertise. Microsoft, for instance, controls 87 percent of the worldwide market for desktop and laptop operating-system software with its Windows product while Google processes 93 percent of all Internet searches outside of China.

>> **LO14.1** Describe how economies of scale help to explain both the high concentration of Internet industries and why so many digital products are provided to consumers at a price of zero.

GLOBAL PERSPECTIVE 14.1

PERCENTAGE OF POPULATION WITH INTERNET ACCESS, SELECTED NATIONS, 2021

In 2021, two-thirds of the world's 7.9 billion people regularly accessed the Internet, many of them via mobile devices. The Internet penetration rates of individual countries varied widely, however, ranging from nearly 95 percent in Germany to just 0.1 percent in North Korea, where the government restricts both internal and external communication.

In looking at these figures, bear in mind that a 1 percent change in Internet penetration implies a much larger number of people in a highly populous country like India (population: 1.4 billion) than in a less highly populated country like Germany (population: 84 million). As an exercise, you may want to calculate how many people a 1 percent increase in Brazil (population: 214 million) would imply.

Source: www.internetworldstats.com.

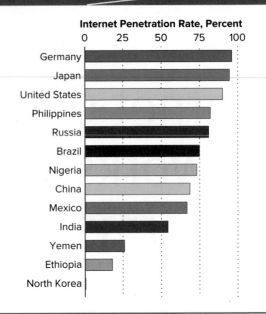

Internet Penetration Rate, Percent

Internet The world-wide *network* of interconnected computers that can communicate and share data; also known as the world wide web, or www.

Each of these dominant products has its own set of rivals, however. For example, Apple's iOS operating system competes against Microsoft's Windows operating system, and Microsoft's Bing search engine competes against Alphabet's Google search engine. But those rival products are not serious threats despite being backed by massively powerful firms that are constantly trying to replace the leading products with their own.

These facts lead to two key questions:

- Why are so many sectors of the Internet so heavily dominated by leading products?
- How do those leading products maintain their dominance despite well-funded, technologically sophisticated rivals?

Economists believe that the answers to these questions can be found by examining (1) the *economies of scale* present in the cost structures of many Internet businesses, and (2) the *network effects* that may arise when people use a compatible product or service. Together, economies of scale and network effects can drive digital products to dominant positions that can be very difficult for rivals to contest. They also explain why so many Internet services are free to users—a crucial fact that propels the high Internet usage rates that we see even in poorer nations, as summarized in Global Perspective 14.1.

Economies of Scale among Internet Businesses

Many prominent Internet industries—such as search and social media—have a tendency toward *natural monopoly,* the situation in which *economies of scale* are so strong that a single firm can produce an industry's entire output at a lower cost per unit than would be possible if several firms together produced that same amount of output. This tendency toward natural monopoly among Internet firms is the result of high *fixed costs* for product development coupled with extremely low *marginal costs* for extending service to additional users. As a result, Internet firms enjoy major economies of scale because their average total cost *per user* declines as additional people use their products.

High Fixed Costs The products produced by digital firms involve large costs that must be incurred *before* those products are offered to the public. Nobody wants to play a half-finished video game or shop on a website that crashes every three minutes. Nor does anyone want to stream an incomplete music track or a half-finished movie. Digital products must be complete and functional before they're used. Thus, the costs of developing digital products are fixed costs *with respect to the number of eventual users* because they have to be incurred whether a digital product ends up having no users, fifty users, or a billion users.

High fixed costs also apply to software maintenance and upgrades, and even to advertising costs. For example, Twitter may spend $150 million developing a new feature or $60 million on a massive online ad campaign, but there is no guarantee that those activities will attract any new users. They may even repel some current users. In short, Twitter's business model is dominated by fixed costs that are independent of the number of people using its service.

Low Marginal Costs A digital firm's marginal cost of onboarding and providing service to an additional user is extremely low for three reasons:

- Digital businesses are built on software, and software does not degrade or depreciate once it is built out. You can run the same code over and over again—forever!—without hurting it or having to pay for maintenance.

- The only marginal cost associated with running a piece of computer code one additional time is a very small amount of electricity that costs practically nothing thanks to the low cost of electricity in the modern world.

- The marginal cost of transferring data across the Internet is practically zero thanks to massive previous investments in data transfer capacity (bandwidth) in the form of fiber-optic cable, satellite relays, cell phone towers, and so on.

By contrast, the marginal cost of providing output or service in a traditional, nondigital business is typically quite high. Building an additional Ford automobile, for example, requires plenty of tangible physical inputs, such as steel, computer chips, and plastic. It also requires substantial amounts of human labor despite the mechanization of factories. And then the finished car still needs to be transported from factory to showroom on trucks, trains, and transport ships. The marginal cost of tangible products is thus quite high relative to the zero or near-zero marginal cost of digital products.

As an example of the extremely low marginal cost of providing a digital service, consider TikTok. Because it already owns massive server capacity and because it has already paid for the current version of its software, its marginal cost of servicing one more user is practically zero, or $MC = 0$. But TikTok *did* have to pay for all of that server capacity and for building out the current version of its software. Those high fixed costs in conjunction with its $MC = 0$ for servicing additional users imply that the ATC and MC curves for TikTok and similar Internet firms will tend to look like those in Figure 14.1.

Graphically, the key consequence of high fixed costs combined with zero or near-zero marginal costs is that the ATC curve starts at a high level when the quantity of users is low and declines rapidly as the quantity of users increases. Thus, ATC starts high on the left side of Figure 14.1, where the number of users is low, before falling rapidly as the quantity of users increases.

We can generalize by saying that if all or nearly all of a digital product's costs are fixed costs, then ATC will decline continuously as the number of users increases and those fixed costs are spread over more and more users. Another way to understand what is happening is to think back to our study of cost curves in Chapter 9. Recall that as long as MC is less than ATC, ATC must fall. That implies that if MC is zero—as it is in Figure 14.1—then ATC will decline continuously toward zero as the number of users increases. Thus, there will be economies of scale no matter how large the user base becomes.

Pricing, Profits, and Elasticity

You might think that having ATC declining steadily toward zero would be a good thing for a seller because it would seem to imply that the seller will have an easy time making a profit. After all, the profit of an Internet firm is simply the difference between the price per user that the firm charges and its ATC per user. With ATC falling steadily toward zero, it would seem that, by simply attracting enough users, an

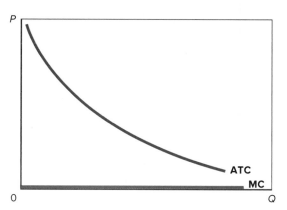

FIGURE 14.1
The MC and ATC curves for Internet companies with high fixed costs but zero marginal costs.

Many online businesses have large fixed costs for product development coupled with very low marginal costs (MC = 0) for providing service to additional users. Hence, ATC declines continuously as large fixed costs are spread over a larger and larger quantity (Q) of users.

FIGURE 14.2
Flat (elastic) and steep (inelastic) demand curves.

Many Internet businesses face highly elastic demand curves like D_1. If they raise their selling price above $P = 0$, they will lose a large quantity (Q) of users. However, Internet firms whose products are subject to network effects may enjoy steeper and less elastic demand curves like D_2. If they raise their selling price above $P = 0$, they will lose relatively few users.

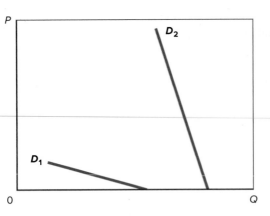

Internet firm could always get its ATC to fall below whatever price it charges, thereby guaranteeing itself a profit.

Sadly, things aren't nearly that easy. A profit will be achieved only if the firm can manage to do two things simultaneously. First, it must gain enough users so that ATC per user falls to a low level. Second, it must get all of those users to pay a price that exceeds ATC per user. For instance, an online newspaper may need to have 10,000 subscribers before the ATC of publishing the newspaper falls below $2.99 per user per month. But if the newspaper tries to charge $3.00 per user per month in order to make a small profit, will all of its subscribers stick around?

For many Internet businesses, the answer is no. The problem is that while the number of users may be very high when the product is given away for free ($P = 0$), the demand curve for most Internet products is quite flat, implying that demand is highly elastic at any positive price, as with demand curve D_1 in Figure 14.2. Consequently, any attempt to raise the selling price much higher than zero will cause the producer to lose many or even most of its users and thus any hope of spreading its large fixed costs over a large number of users.

However, not every Internet business faces this problem to the same extent. Internet firms that enjoy *network effects* may have steeper demand curves that imply relatively *in*elastic demand at any positive price, as with demand curve D_2 in Figure 14.2. Thus, if they raise their prices above zero, fewer users will quit. But even network effects are no guarantee that a digital firm will have substantial pricing power, and there are many popular Internet services for which demand appears to be highly elastic. Examples include Internet search services (Google, Bing, Yahoo), information reference sites (*Wikipedia, Dictionary.com*), and news and current-events sites (*The New York Times, The Wall Street Journal*).

The question thus arises: If Internet firms with highly elastic demand can't rely on being able to raise their prices above zero to cover their costs and at least break even, then how can they survive? Several different strategies have been developed, including selling advertising, selling data, and engaging in price discrimination. Some firms use two or more of these strategies simultaneously.

Selling Advertising   One strategy for covering the high fixed costs of product development without charging prices that might chase away users is selling advertising within an Internet product. Google, for example, sells targeted advertisements that are tailored to a user's search requests. Advertisers pay Google handsomely for targeted ads, and the revenue that Google makes from selling targeted ads more than covers the cost of providing search results for free to the billions of people who use Google's search engine.

Selling Data   Many Internet businesses make money by selling data about their users to other Internet businesses. For example, if you are on a website looking at engagement rings, then you are probably planning to get married relatively soon. That information can then be sold to companies offering wedding-related services so that they can target you with their ads.

Price Discrimination   Internet firms use various forms of price discrimination to cover their costs without chasing away a lot of users. Recall from Chapter 11 that *price discrimination* involves charging different prices to different groups of users based on differences in *price elasticity of demand*. The key to successful price discrimination is getting users to voluntarily self-select into different groups whose members are willing to pay different amounts for the same or very similar products. The following online pricing strategies involve price discrimination.

freemium pricing A pricing strategy in which an Internet business offers its core product for free but charges users for upgrades and special features that some users may be willing to pay for.

- **Freemium pricing** involves giving away a basic product for free and then charging users to unlock a set of additional features. This strategy is useful for maintaining a large network of users (those who are satisfied with the free version) while bringing in revenue from those who are willing to pay for the additional features. As an example, consider HootSuite, an app that helps users manage social media accounts on several platforms at the same time. Under its original pricing model, its service was free if you used it to manage your social media on three or fewer platforms, but you paid a monthly fee if you wanted to manage your social media on four or more platforms. HootSuite's free version helped to attract and retain users who had a high price elasticity (sensitivity), and its premium version allowed the company to obtain revenue from those with a lower price elasticity.

- **In-app purchases** are a variation on freemium pricing that is popular with video game developers, among others. Under this pricing model, video games are given away for free but revenue is obtained from the sale of digital items that enhance or extend game play. Fortnite is a good example. Playing Fortnite is free, but players can pay for items such as special equipment and weapons to outfit the digital characters that they control in the game. By making the basic game free, Fortnite has built a massive user base, retaining even those players who have an extremely high price elasticity of demand.

- **Subtractive versioning** occurs when users have the option to pay to remove something from the free version of a product. The most common example is the removal of advertising. Consider regular YouTube versus YouTube Premium. Regular YouTube is free, but it comes with ads. In contrast, users who are willing to pay a monthly fee for YouTube Premium can enjoy all of YouTube's audio and video content without ads. This tiered pricing model allows YouTube to retain users who have a high price elasticity while generating revenue from those who dislike advertising strongly and are willing to pay to avoid it.

in-app purchases A pricing strategy in which an internet business (that may or may not give away its core product for free) charges users of its application software ("app") for items that enhance the user experience within the application.

subtractive versioning A pricing strategy in which an internet business offers customers the option of paying to remove an annoying feature (such as advertising) from its base offering.

Zero MC Pricing and Competition

A key consequence of (1) economies of scale, (2) zero marginal costs, and (3) highly elastic demand is that Internet firms face substantial pressure to keep prices low or zero whenever they face any competition. This is especially true for Internet firms that offer similar products. There are hundreds of different smartphone apps for playing chess, fighting zombies, or doing yoga. Each firm tries to deliver a slightly different experience, but in the eyes of many consumers, their products are largely interchangeable. As a result, the competitive equilibrium involves each firm keeping the price of its basic product low or zero so that it will not lose users to competitors. The firms then attempt to generate revenue in other ways, such as by selling ads.

However, not all Internet firms have a lot of competitors. As noted earlier in this chapter, Internet behemoths like Google and Facebook are oligopolists that dominate their respective sectors of the Internet. That dominance might seem to provide them with enough market power to charge a price well above zero. As we will see, however, the large majority of Internet oligopolists don't use their market power to charge high prices for their main products. Instead, they usually opt to provide their main products for free and then rely on advertising or other alternative revenue streams to generate income. The reason they do that has to do with network effects, as we explain in the next section.

▶ Digital firms often have a low or zero marginal cost (MC) for providing services to additional users, resulting in economies of scale that may generate natural monopoly.

▶ Digital firms often face highly elastic demand. As a result, they set low or zero prices for their main products so as not to lose customers to rival firms.

▶ Internet businesses that give away their main products for free generate revenue by alternative means, including selling advertising, selling data, and engaging in price discrimination.

QUICK REVIEW
14.1

Network Effects

In economics, a **network** is a group of people or objects that are connected to each other by a service or piece of infrastructure that facilitates flows of goods, services, or information. Examples of the services or pieces of infrastructure that connect networks include roads, water pipes, waterways, 5G cellular networks, Amazon.com, WhatsApp, computer operating systems, wi-fi, social media apps, video game platforms, and the Internet itself.

A **network effect** is said to occur when the value of a network depends on the number of users connected to it. Network effects can be either positive or negative.

- **Positive network effects,** or positive network externalities, are present when a network's value to each user *increases* as more people join the network. Consider dating apps. The more people who join a particular dating site, the more chance each user has to find someone compatible. The larger the number of users, the more valuable the site becomes to each user. The same is true for review sites like Yelp. The more people who write restaurant reviews on Yelp, the more valuable Yelp becomes to each user.

>> LO14.2 Define network effects and explain their relationship to industry concentration among Internet firms.

network In *economics*, a group of people or objects that are connected to each other by a *service* or piece of *infrastructure* that facilitates flows of *goods*, services, or information.

network effect The phenomenon whereby the value of a *network* depends on the size of the network (number of users).

positive network effect The phenomenon observed when the value of a *network* increases as the size of the network (number of users) increases. Also called a positive network *externality*.

negative network effect The phenomenon observed when the value of a *network* decreases as the size of a network (number of users) increases. Also referred to as a negative network *externality*.

network congestion A *negative network effect* that occurs when a network's capacity limits are approached or exceeded and the quality of the network's services declines as a result.

network pollution A *negative network effect* that occurs on social networks when the presence of too many connected users degrades the average quality of the information that users obtain from the network.

tipping point The size of a *network* beyond which further network growth becomes self-sustaining (due to the network's sheer size creating large enough *positive network effects* to attract additional users, whose participation further increases the size of the network's positive network effects, thereby attracting even more users, and so on).

- **Negative network effects,** or negative network externalities, occur when a network's value to each user *decreases* as more people join the network. One source of negative network effects is **network congestion,** which happens when too many people attempt to use a network at the same time. As one example, think of how the download speeds of wi-fi networks slow dramatically if too many users try to stream data simultaneously. *Network pollution* is another type of negative network effect. Most commonly observed on social networks, **network pollution** occurs when the presence of too many users degrades the average quality of the information that users obtain from the network. If, for instance, too many people are connected to you on Facebook, your Facebook "news feed" may end up becoming highly polluted by irrelevant or undesired content from people you barely know. Other things equal, the larger the number of people who are connected to you on Facebook, the more likely your news feed is to be polluted.

As discussed in Chapter 3, network effects are *determinants of demand* (demand shifters).

- Positive network effects make a good or service more desirable, thereby increasing demand and shifting the demand curve to the right, all other things equal.

- Negative network effects make a product less desirable, thereby decreasing demand and shifting the demand curve to the left, all other things equal.

Also note that positive and negative network effects may exist at the same time. To give a nondigital example, consider going to big college party. In some respects, the greater the number of people in attendance, the more fun it gets, as there are more and more people for you to meet and mingle with. But if the party is indoors and more and more people show up, the room gets hot, food starts to run out, there's no room to dance, and you have to shout to be heard. Your personal demand for staying at the party will increase or decrease depending on how you weigh the pluses and minuses of the positive and negative network effects that occur as more and more people join the party.

Network Effects and Market Power

Positive network effects are important because they can generate monopoly power for any firm that develops a popular network that has many users. As an example, consider the first telephone networks, which were built in the United States in the late 1800s after Alexander Graham Bell patented the telephone in 1876.

When the first phone networks got started, only a handful of early adopters were connected within any particular network. As a result, there weren't many people to call, and most of them didn't even know each other. The networks were small, and so the value of being connected by a phone network to other people was also small.

As the size of telephone networks grew over the ensuing decades, their benefit to each user also grew as there were more and more people to call, including friends and coworkers. Entrepreneurial businesses also started adding phone lines to make entirely new services available, such as phoning in an order for a food delivery or calling a stockbroker to purchase shares in the Bell Telephone Company.

As telephones became increasingly common, the value of being a telephone user grew larger and larger. Eventually the United States reached a **tipping point** in terms of network size: Nonusers who had not previously seen enough benefit in getting a phone and joining a network found that the value of having a phone had grown large enough to convince them to join, too. In joining the network, each new user further increased the size and value of the network, thereby incentivizing even more nonusers to join. A snowball effect ensued in which previous network growth caused subsequent network growth, with nearly every American eventually getting a phone and joining a telephone network.

Competing Networks When networks compete against one another, the presence of positive network effects implies that the network that can attract the largest number of users will become the most valuable network to both current and potential users, all other things equal. Consider Facebook. It is the world's largest social networking site, with around 3 billion regular users. Facebook has many rivals, but if one of your main goals is to connect with as many people as possible, then you will have an incentive to join Facebook rather than any other social network because those rival social networks have fewer users and thus generate smaller positive network effects.

The advantage that Facebook's 3 billion users give it in terms of positive network effects implies that Facebook is somewhat insulated from competition in the social networking industry. While

TABLE 14.1 Social Networks with 500 Million or More Monthly Active Users, 2021

(1) Rank	(2) Network	(3) Owner	(4) Home Country	(5) Year Launched	(6) Monthly Active Users
1	Facebook	Meta	United States	2004	2.8 billion
2	YouTube	Alphabet	United States	2005	2.2 billion
3	WhatsApp	Meta	United States	2009	2.0 billion
4	Messenger	Meta	United States	2011	1.4 billion
5	Instagram	Meta	United States	2010	1.3 billion
6	WeChat	Tencent	China	2011	1.2 billion
7	TikTok	Bytedance	China	2016	740 million
8	Douyin	Bytedance	China	2016	600 million
9	QQ	Tencent	China	1999	600 million
10	Telegram	Telegram	United Arab Emirates	2013	570 million
11	Snapchat	Snap	United States	2011	520 million
12	Weibo	Sina	China	2009	530 million
13	Qzone	Tencent	China	2005	520 million

Source: Various corporate financial statements.

definitely not a single-firm monopoly, Facebook is the dominant firm in an oligopoly industry in which its only substantial rivals are firms that have targeted specific social networking niches—such as business networking in the case of LinkedIn—or have developed substantially different product experiences—such as Snapchat, which automatically erases posts, or Instagram and TikTok, which focus on allowing users to quickly share and rapidly comment on (Like!) single photos or short videos.

Table 14.1 lists the 13 online social networks that had 500 million or more monthly active users in 2021. Several, including Facebook Messenger, WhatsApp, and WeChat, can be categorized as more or less "pure" messaging services. Others, such as TikTok, YouTube, and Snapchat, are built more around the sharing of video or picture content. This diversity in terms of user experience reflects these platforms' ability to compete for users on the basis of *product differentiation* rather than merely on the basis of network size. If network size were the only thing that mattered, then all of the various networks' users would migrate to Facebook because it has the largest network and thus offers the largest number of possible connections. But billions of people have accounts on multiple social networks, largely because they appreciate the differences between the various networks in terms of interface design, featured content, page layout, and the demographics and interests of other users.

This behavior generalizes beyond social networking. The users of many different types of digital products often have accounts on multiple competing networks, a behavior known as **multi-homing** or multi-tenanting. Their willingness to use multiple networks is a competitive restriction that implies that digitial firms cannot rely on positive network effects alone to attract new users or to keep existing users actively engaged.

multi-homing The phenomenon that occurs when consumers use one or more competing Internet products simultaneously. Also called *multi-tenanting.*

The Exponential Scaling of Network Effects

The ability of positive network effects to shield Internet firms from rivals is supercharged by the fact that the strength of a network effect grows exponentially as additional users join a network. Figure 14.3 illustrates this point. When a network contains only 2 users, there is only 1 possible connection that can generate benefits, as shown in Figure 14.3a. But if there are 4 users, as in Figure 14.3b, there are 6 possible connections. And if there are 8 users, as in Figure 14.3c, there are 28 possible connections.

There is a simple mathematical formula that captures how quickly the number of connections in a network grows as the number of users increases. For any number of users n, there will be exactly $n(n - 1)/2$ connections. If you plug in some additional values for n, you will notice that the number of potential connections grows much faster than the number of users. As a result, the size of the network effect grows much faster than the number of users even if not every connection is actually used. Thus, if Facebook has twice as many users as a rival social network, the relative value of Facebook's network will not simply be twice as large. Instead, it will be many times larger, so long as Facebook can limit or prevent negative network effects such as network congestion and network pollution.

FIGURE 14.3 The number of connections in a network grows exponentially faster than the number of people or objects connected to the network.

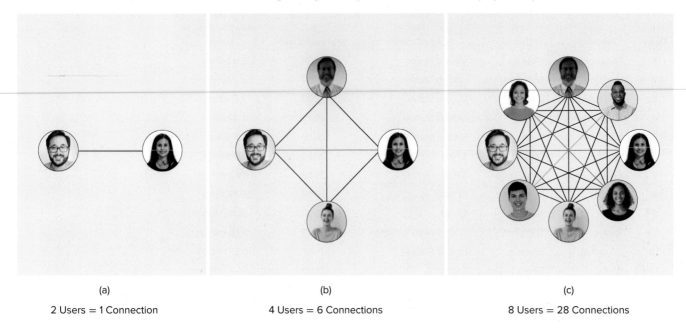

(a)

2 Users = 1 Connection

(b)

4 Users = 6 Connections

(c)

8 Users = 28 Connections

Photo credits: Eight users, clockwise from top (See panel (c)): (1) Jill Braaten/McGraw Hill Education; (2) fizkes/Shutterstock; (3) Juan Monino/Getty Images; (4) Krakenimages.com/Shutterstock; (5) WAYHOME studio/Shutterstock; (6) Dmitrii Rusev/EyeEm/Getty Images; (7) Pressmaster/Shutterstock; (8) pathdoc/Shutterstock

Facebook has worked hard to avoid negative network effects. It has done so by rapidly increasing its computing power so as to avoid network congestion and by using algorithms and privacy settings to mitigate the network pollution that would otherwise cause people's news feeds to be dominated by junk that they do not want to see. By taking these steps, Facebook has ensured that its users enjoy the positive network effects of being connected to the world's largest social network without having to endure very much in the way of network pollution or network congestion. The result is a situation in which Facebook's large size and attention to user experience give it a substantial competitive advantage over its smaller rivals.

Technological Lock-In

Network effects can have such a strong anticompetitive effect that inefficient or expensive products and technologies that involve a network can become "locked in" by the unwillingness of the network's users to switch to different products or technologies even when those alternatives work better or cost less. This phenomenon is known as **technological lock-in.**

technological lock-in The unwillingness of users to switch to a better product or technology because so many people are already using an older technology that enjoys *positive network effects.*

network switching cost The cost that a user will have to incur in order to switch from one *network* product to a competing *network* product.

Microsoft Office versus Google Workspace The Microsoft Office suite of business productivity apps provides a good example of technological lock-in. Microsoft Office has several high-quality competitors, including Google Workspace. Google Workspace is arguably just as good as Microsoft Office, and Google Workspace is free for most users, whereas Microsoft charges almost everyone for Office. So why does Microsoft Office have more users, especially among larger businesses?

The answer has to do with **network switching costs,** which are the costs that consumers must undertake if they are going to transition from one network to another. With respect to the costs involved with switching from Microsoft Office to Google Workspace, please note that Microsoft started selling its Office suite of business productivity apps in the 1980s and had a virtual monopoly on those types of software by the time Google launched its alternatives in 2006. That meant that anyone interested in switching from Office to Workspace had to consider whether doing so would be easy or not.

To understand why many people saw—and continue to see—that transition as cost-prohibitive, consider a law office that has been using Microsoft Office for many years. The first thing to note is that the law office will not want any of its employees to suddenly and independently switch to Google Workspace because doing so will make it much more difficult for all of the firm's employees to quickly and easily share documents, spreadsheets, and presentation slides. Thus, there will be intense pressure for everyone at the firm to stick with Microsoft Office unless everyone switches at the same time. But switching at the same time would be hard to organize, especially when one

CONSIDER THIS . . .

Making It Hard to Say Goodbye

Digital firms don't like it when users switch to rival products or decide to multi-home and use multiple related products. To discourage these actions, digital firms often make it annoying for consumers to use competing products.

For instance, Apple Music, Spotify, and Pandora do not allow you to transfer your playlists to rival streaming services. Various e-mail services, including Microsoft Outlook, use proprietary archiving systems so that you cannot download all of your old e-mails from one service and open them up on another. And social networks, including Facebook, do not provide their users with an easy way to export their photos and files to rival social networking apps.

These intentional frictions are a form of competition, but not all competition favors consumers, and these examples of "throwing sand in the gears" are prime examples of competitive behavior that hurts, rather than helps, consumers.

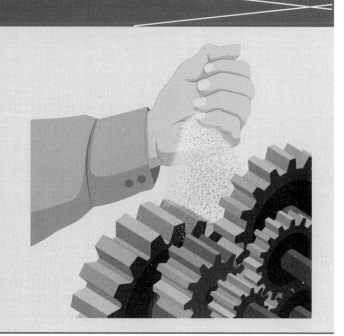

considers the firms' clients, who are unlikely to want to switch from Office to Workspace just because the law firm wants to switch. Alienating clients is a quick way to go bankrupt, and so the law firm will choose to stick with Microsoft Office.

Because millions of businesses have come to the same conclusion about switching, nearly 40 times as many businesses currently pay Microsoft for Office as pay Google for Workspace (the business versions of which are not free). However, the situation is quite different with individual users, who only rarely have to worry about organizing coordinated, simultaneous switches from one set of apps to the other. Among individual users, Workspace is far more popular than Office. Specifically, Google Workplace had 2.6 billion total users worldwide in 2020, or over twice as many as compared with the 1.2 billion people who used Microsoft Office that year.

But do note that while Workspace has grown to have over twice as many total users as Office, it is also true that Microsoft can still make billions of dollars per year by charging software licensing fees to individuals and businesses whose network switching costs are high enough to discourage them from switching from Office to Workspace.

The nearby Consider This feature discusses a related issue: artificial network switching costs that digital firms impose in order to discourage users from switching to rival products.

▶ Positive (negative) network effects occur when an increase in the size of a network increases (decreases) the value of the network to current and potential users.

▶ Positive network effects generate a tendency toward market power and monopoly because the

largest network will, other things equal, attract more users than smaller rival networks.

▶ The market power of large networks is constrained by product differentiation and multi-homing.

**QUICK REVIEW
14.2**

Digital Platforms

Amazon.com, Monster.com, and Xbox gaming consoles may not seem to have much in common, but they all serve as **digital platforms** that facilitate interactions between two or more distinct but interdependent groups of users.

- Amazon.com has two distinct sets of users: buyers and sellers.

- Monster.com links three distinct sets of users: people looking for jobs, employers wishing to hire, and advertisers looking to reach members of both groups.

- Xbox has two distinct sets of users: the gamers who play video games on the Xbox and the game developers whose video games are played on the Xbox.

>> LO14.3 Explain digital platforms and how they determine their pricing structure.

digital platform An *Internet* website or software application (app) that facilitates interactions between two or more distinct but interdependent sets of users.

TABLE 14.2 The 10 Largest Online Market Platforms by Gross Merchandise Volume, 2020

(1) Company	(2) Home Country	(3) Gross Merchandise Volume, billions
Taobao	China	$509
Tmall	China	480
Amazon Marketplace	United States	300
JD.com	China	392
Pinduoduo	China	256
Shopify	United States	120
eBay	United States	100
Walmart Marketplace	United States	92
Rakuten	Japan	41
Tokopedia	Indonesia	32

Source: Various corporate annual reports.

Other examples of digital platforms include Uber and Lyft, which allow ride-providers and ride-seekers to interact; Facebook, Twitter, and Instagram, which allow individuals to interact with one another and with advertisers; the Visa and Mastercard networks, which allow consumers and merchants to interact to complete payments; YouTube, Spotify, and Vimeo, which allow media consumers to interact with media creators and advertisers; and search engines Google, Bing, and Baidu, which facilitate interactions between advertisers and people seeking search results.

Several of the most popular digital platforms are online market platforms that allow buyers and sellers to complete transactions over the Internet. Table 14.2 lists the 10 largest online market platforms and the dollar value of the transactions that took place on each of them in 2020. Together, these market platforms facilitated about $2.3 trillion of transactions in 2020, or about 54 percent of the roughly $4.2 trillion of retail transactions that took place over the Internet that year.

Balancing User Engagement Against the Need to Charge Fees

The value of digital platforms comes from connecting different groups of people with each other. For example, gamers will not want to use a platform like Sony's PlayStation video game console unless game developers are making games for that platform. And game development studios will not want to develop games for the PlayStation platform unless there are gamers eager to play those games on PlayStation consoles. Thus, it is in Sony's financial interest to maximize both the number of gamers using PlayStation consoles and the number of developers making games for PlayStation consoles. The dream scenario for Sony is for both groups to be very large so that (1) gamers love the PlayStation platform because they end up with many different games to play and (2) game developers love the PlayStation platform because there are millions of gamers to sell their products to.

The general takeaway is that a digital platform will have an incentive to maximize the size of each of the groups using its platform, so that the sheer size of each group will increase the value of being on the platform to the members of the other groups using the platform. However, it is often difficult or impossible to maximize the size of all the groups at once. In particular, a platform has to figure out a way to make money in order to cover its costs and, ideally, make a profit. That necessity implies having to charge fees or prices to one or more of the groups using the platform, which means that the platform must act prudently because any group that is charged a fee will tend to use the platform less, which in turn will make the platform less attractive for the other groups using the platform.

As a concrete example, suppose that Sony decides to charge gamers a fee. That fee will discourage at least some gamers from buying PlayStation consoles, which in turn will make game developers less eager to invest money in making games for the PlayStation because there will be fewer PlayStation users to sell their products to. Thus, Sony has an interesting economic problem. It has to charge fees or prices to a least one of the groups, but it also has to take into account not only the reaction of the groups being charged but also the reactions of all the other groups using the platform.

Please note that this economic problem is not specific to Sony, the PlayStation, or video game platforms. Rather, it is a challenge that faces *all* digital platforms. Thus, in the next section, we use a totally different platform—TikTok—to demonstrate how platforms think about pricing and profit maximization when they know that they must consider how the fees or prices charged to one user group may affect the behavior of other user groups.

Platform Profit Maximization

TikTok offers its social networking platform for free to users; it makes its money by charging fees to advertisers. Indeed, "free for users but costly for advertisers" has been TikTok's pricing strategy since it got started in 2016. If it wanted to, though, TikTok could change things up and start charging its social networking users a monthly fee.

Example: Raising the Price for One Group of Users Figure 14.4a illustrates the consequences that would result from TikTok's decision to begin charging its social networking users a positive amount of money, thereby increasing the price of using TikTok from 0 to P_1 on the vertical axis. This price increase reduces the number of social networking users from Q_0 to Q_1, which we can think of as an upward movement along demand curve D from point c to point d. Associated with this upward movement is the fact that the revenue (= price per user times number of users) that TikTok collects from its users increases from zero dollars before the price increase (= \$0 per user times Q_0 users) to an amount equal to the area of the blue rectangle $0\,P_1 dQ_1$ after the price increase (= P_1 per user times Q_1 users).

The increased revenue that TikTok gets from its social networking users might look like pure gain, but TikTok needs to take into account the fact that the decline in the number of social networking users from Q_0 to Q_1 in Figure 14.4a will affect the behavior of another group that uses TikTok's platform—advertisers. Specifically, advertisers will be less willing to advertise on TikTok once they find out that the number of people who will be looking at their ads will be falling from Q_0 to Q_1. That decrease in advertisers' willingness to pay shows up in Figure 14.4b as a leftward shift in the demand for TikTok ads. Because TikTok gets to decide how many ads are displayed to viewers

FIGURE 14.4 **A digital platform's attempt to increase revenue from one group of users causes revenue to fall by even more among a different group of users.**

Consider a social networking platform that has two distinct groups of users from whom it can try to obtain revenue: social networking users and advertisers. In (a), the platform raises the price it charges social networking users from 0 to P_1, causing the number of social networking users to fall from Q_0 to Q_1 and the revenue collected from social networking users to rise from zero (= \$0 per user times Q_0 users) to the area of rectangle $0P_1 dQ_1$, shown in blue. In (b), the decline in the number of social networking users on the platform reduces the demand for advertisements placed on the platform from D_0 to D_1, causing the equilibrium price of advertisements to fall from P_0^A to P_1^A and the amount of advertising revenue to decrease by an amount equal to the area of rectangle $P_1^A P_0^A\ ef$, shown in yellow. Because the area of rectangle $0P_1 dQ_1$ that is shown in blue in (a) is less than the area of rectangle $P_1^A P_0^A\ ef$ that is shown in yellow in (b), the platform's total combined revenue across both groups of users declines.

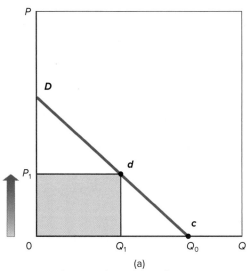

(a)
Increase in social media revenue
due to increase in price of social media

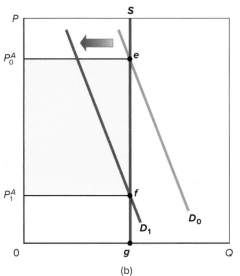

(b)
Decrease in advertising revenue
due to lower demand for ads

each day regardless of the price that it charges for ads, the supply curve for ads, S, is vertical in Figure 14.4b. Thus, when the demand for ads shifts left from D_0 to D_1, the equilibrium price of TikTok ads falls from P_0^A to P_1^A.

Note that when the demand for ads shifts left, the amount of TikTok's advertising revenue also declines, from the area of rectangle $0P_0^A eg$ to the area of rectangle $0P_1^A fg$. The dollar amount of the decline in advertising revenue is therefore equal to the difference between the areas of those two rectangles, or the area of the yellow rectangle, $P_1^A P_0^A ef$.

We can determine whether TikTok's decision to raise the price that it charges its social networking users from 0 to P_1 increased its overall profit by comparing the size of the blue revenue-gain rectangle in Figure 14.4a with the size of the yellow revenue-loss rectangle in Figure 14.4b. Because the area of the blue revenue-gain rectangle $0P_1 dQ_1$ in Figure 14.4a is less than the area of the yellow revenue-loss rectangle $P_1^A P_0^A ef$ in Figure 14.4b, it is immediately obvious that TikTok reduced its overall revenue by raising the price of social networking from 0 to P_1.

This decline in overall revenue also implies a decline in TikTok's overall profit. Why? TikTok is operating a digital business that has extremely low marginal costs for adding or subtracting users. Thus, we can think of TikTok's costs as not changing at all while it experiences the overall revenue decline illustrated in Figures 14.4a and 14.4b. The result is a lower profit for TikTok because overall revenue declines while costs stay the same.

To summarize: TikTok's new policy increased the amount of revenue that it received from its social networking users but prompted an even larger decline in advertising revenue. Thus, TikTok would have been better off sticking to its former policy of not charging its social networking users anything.

Two general points derive from our analysis of Figure 14.4.

- *A platform cannot look at each group of users in isolation.* Instead, the platform has to take into account the complicated reactions and interactions that exist across the distinct groups using its platform. Only then can it create the pricing policy that maximizes its overall profit.

- *After analyzing its situation, a platform may have a strong financial incentive to set a price of zero for one or more of the groups using its platform.* This incentive explains why consumers enjoy free social media apps (Instagram, Snapchat, Facebook), free news and information sites (*Wikipedia,* The Weather Channel), free business productivity apps (Google Workspace), and free e-mail, messaging, and video chat applications (WeChat, WhatsApp, Hotmail, Zoom). In each case, a platform has decided that the way to maximize profit is to offer its main product to consumers at a price of zero.

The Sizes of Elasticities and Other Responses Matter When looking at Figure 14.4, we should keep one other thing in mind. The *sizes* of both groups' responses to TikTok's decision to start charging its users a fee matter quite a bit. To see why, suppose that in Figure 14.4a the demand curve D had been steeper and thus more inelastic at every possible price. In that case, the decline in the number of users would have been smaller when TikTok raised the price from 0 to P_1. That smaller decline in the number of TikTok users would then have resulted in a smaller leftward shift in the demand for ads in Figure 14.4b, which in turn would have resulted in a smaller decline in TikTok's ad revenue.

If both groups' responses to the price increase had been smaller (due to a lower price elasticity of demand on the part of TikTok's social networking users and a smaller leftward shift in demand by advertisers), then TikTok might have been able to increase, rather than decrease, its overall profit by raising the price from 0 to P_1.

That ambiguity is important to notice because it implies that the profit-maximization problem faced by digital platforms is both complex and opaque. In actual practice, firms will not know ahead of time how strongly each group on a platform will react to any given change in prices or fees. As a result, accurate predictions are probably not possible. Thus pricing strategy is, to a significant extent, a matter of trial and error for many digital platforms, which may be reluctant, consequently, to deviate from whatever pricing system they are currently using.

Direct and Indirect Network Effects

Because platforms facilitate the interaction of two or more groups of users—such as the buyers, sellers, and advertisers on eBay—they allow for a richer set of network effects as compared with stand-alone networks that have only one group of users. In particular, when two or more networks are connected by a platform, we may observe *direct network effects* as well as *indirect network effects*.

A **direct network effect** occurs when an increase in the size of a network connected to a digital platform causes either benefits or harm to the members of that same network regardless of anything that may be going on within other networks connected to the platform. Thus, for instance, the presence of more buyers on eBay may generate a positive network effect among eBay's network of buyers because more buyers will result in more product reviews being written, which will help buyers avoid bad sellers. Under that scenario, the increase in the number of buyers has a direct effect on the value of being a member of the network of buyers regardless of any changes taking place in any other network using the platform.

By contrast, an **indirect network effect** occurs when an increase in the size of a given network connected to a digital platform causes a benefit or harm to the members of that network by affecting the value of another network that is connected to the same platform. For example, an increase in the number of buyers on eBay will make eBay a better place for sellers to sell (because, other things equal, a greater number of buyers implies greater demand and, consequently, higher prices). That improvement in selling conditions will very likely attract more sellers to eBay. But more sellers means increased competition among sellers and, consequently, lower prices for buyers. Thus, an increase in the number of buyers *indirectly* improves the value of being part of eBay's network of buyers by causing changes in one of the other networks on the eBay platform (in this example, an increase in the number of sellers).

As Figure 14.5 shows, Internet firms vary in the degree to which they are subject to direct or indirect network effects. This variation is partly due to the fact that not every Internet firm is a platform and partly due to the fact that every platform is unique, with varying degrees of direct and indirect network effects.

Network effects—both direct and indirect—are arguably the most important characteristics of the Internet economy. By one estimate, 70 percent of the profits earned by major Internet firms are the result of the market power that they possess due to network effects. In the next section, we discuss whether—and to what degree—government regulation of Internet industries may improve economic outcomes.

direct network effect A *network effect* that involves only a single network of users connected to a *digital platform*. Compare with *indirect network effect*.

indirect network effect A *network effect* involving two or more *networks* connected by a *digital platform*, in which a change in the number of users within one network causes changes felt by the users of a different network which in turn boomerang back to the original network of users to affect the value of their network. Compare with *direct network effect*.

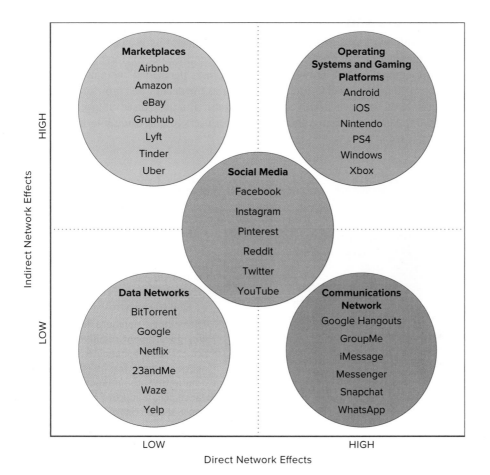

FIGURE 14.5
Prominent Internet firms grouped by direct and indirect network effects.

Operating systems and game platforms (top right) are high in both indirect and direct network effects, while communications networks (bottom right) are high in direct network effects but low in indirect network effects. Marketplaces (top left), social media (center), and data networks (bottom left) have different combinations of exposure to direct and indirect network effects.

Source: Niskanen Center.

▶ Digital platforms facilitate interactions between two or more networks of users, such as buyers and sellers (Etsy, Amazon Marketplace) or ride seekers and ride providers (Lyft, Uber).

▶ To maximize profit, a digital platform must take into account how the price it sets for one user group may affect the behavior of other user groups.

▶ The profit-maximizing pricing strategy for a digital platform often involves setting a price of zero for the members of one group while charging above-zero prices to the members of other groups.

Regulating the Digital Economy

>> **LO14.4** Summarize the debate regarding government regulation of Internet firms.

Many Internet industries are dominated by just a handful of companies, which suggests that governments should be concerned about monopoly power and should regulate those industries so as to promote competition and reduce efficiency losses. On the other hand, the large majority of the most popular Internet products are priced at zero, which suggests not only that no monopoly power is being exercised but also that consumers are receiving a huge amount of consumer surplus, as is discussed in the nearby Consider This feature.

In addition, many Internet firms appear to be more than happy to offer their main products for free to as many users as care to sign up for them—a fact that argues strongly against there being any *efficiency losses* from underproduction because such losses occur only when a firm with monopoly power restricts output to drive up price. With no such restrictions occurring, we should not have to worry about output being less than the socially optimal amount at which MB = MC.

These contradictory facts—of high market concentration on the one hand and unlimited output provided at $P = 0$ to consumers on the other—have left both economists and government regulators debating whether and in what ways Internet businesses should be regulated. The overall tendency has been to concentrate on business-to-business issues rather than on consumer issues. After all, with consumers getting so many products and services for free, there seems to be little reason for regulators to step in to protect them. By contrast, the leading digital products and platforms may be exploiting their market power to hurt their competitors. The latter possibility has drawn the most attention from regulators.

The Microsoft and Google Cases

In 2000, Microsoft was found guilty of using the dominance of its Windows operating system in the personal computer market to give its own web browser, Internet Explorer, a significant market advantage over competing web browsers. Microsoft had "persuaded" computer manufacturers such as Dell and Compaq to install Internet Explorer as the default web browser on their computers. That put rival browsers such as Netscape Navigator at a huge disadvantage because, to gain users, they had to persuade existing Internet Explorer users to quit using Internet Explorer after they had gotten used to it.

CONSIDER THIS ...

Digital Consumer Surplus

Economists have estimated the consumer surplus generated by various Internet products. The numbers are massive.

- Americans value *Wikipedia* as worth $150 per year on average to each of them, which implies a total consumer surplus of $50 billion per year across the entire U.S. population.
- Facebook is on average worth $576 per year to the average Facebook user in the United States, implying a total consumer surplus across all 260 million regular U.S. Facebook users of about $149 billion per year.

William Potter/Shutterstock

- Internet search is valued even more highly, with the average American claiming that they would pay up to $17,000 per year for search services, which implies a consumer surplus of $5.6 trillion across all Americans.

These huge numbers help to explain why government regulators have been reluctant to prosecute Internet businesses simply for being large or for dominating their sectors. Breaking Facebook up, for instance, might improve competition in social networking—but only at the cost of vastly reducing the consumer surplus that happy Facebook users receive as members of the world's largest social network.

More recently, Google has been found guilty of abusing its dominance in Internet search services, search advertising, and smartphone operating systems to favor some of its other products. Specifically, European Union antitrust (antimonopoly) regulators declared Google guilty on three separate counts: using its dominance in Internet search services to favor its own online marketplace, using its dominance in search advertising to coerce advertisers into not placing ads on rival ad networks, and using the dominant position of its Android operating system for smartphones to favor various Google services and apps over similar products offered by rivals.

Today, government regulators continue to examine Internet firms for various forms of anticompetitive behavior, most of it related to firms using their dominant positions in one area (such as operating systems or search) to coerce other business into favoring related products or services produced by the same firm. Other areas of concern include: major Internet firms using their deep pockets to buy up potential rivals (as Facebook did when it acquired Instagram in 2012); engaging in price fixing; and coercing retailers into selling their products on only one market platform rather than on several.

Winner-Take-All versus Contestable Industries

When economists began examining the economics of the then-new Internet in the 1990s, there was substantial concern that economies of scale and positive network effects would lead to **winner-take-all industries** in which a single monopoly firm would come to dominate its industry and enjoy an almost *uncontestable* control over that industry such that any potential rivals would be destined to go bankrupt. Once established, economists suggested, these unassailable monopolies would start charging high monopoly prices even if they had previously given their products away for free.

With nearly three decades of hindsight, those fears appear to have been largely unfounded. $P = 0$ pricing continues to be the norm for the most popular Internet products despite the existence of dominant firms. And while economies of scale and network effects do create substantial market power, the typical outcome is multi-firm oligopoly rather than single-firm monopoly.

In addition, even highly concentrated Internet industries such as social networking appear to be **contestable industries,** meaning that upstart firms are able to grow their user bases and gain market share even when dominant incumbent firms already enjoy economies of scale and positive network effects. Indeed, even Facebook (founded 2004) was once an upstart against MySpace and Friendster, the leading social networks of the early 2000s. The more recent ability of Instagram (started 2010), Snapchat (started 2011), and TikTok (started 2016) to compete against Facebook also argues in favor of most Internet industries being contestable industries in which the sheer size of the leading firm's user network is not an insurmountable barrier to competition.

The contestability of social networking and other Internet industries appears in large measure to be the result of two phenomena that we have already discussed:

- *Product differentiation.* TikTok and Snapchat, for example, offer a very different social networking experience than Facebook does. This product differentiation gives them the opportunity to contest the social networking market despite Facebook's substantially larger user base.

- *Multi-homing.* The users of a particular digital product typically have the opportunity to use one or more competing products *at the same time.* People are free, for instance, to employ several different e-mail or social networking apps simultaneously. That ability to "multi-home" makes for substantial contestability even when a leading product has a large number of users.

Dealing with Concentration

One problem that product differentiation and multi-homing do not solve is that of takeovers and mergers. As already noted, Facebook (a social network) purchased Instagram (a rival social network) in 2012. These types of acquisitions are obviously a problem in terms of limiting competition and increasing industry concentration. But as noted previously, regulators may not step in because if both services are still offered for free to consumers and if consumers can multi-home between them, then it's not clear that such mergers harm consumers to any significant degree.

Breaking Up Is Hard to Do An important related issue is whether government interventions to break up dominant digital firms into multiple competing businesses will be able to reduce industry concentration in the long run. To understand the problem, note that if an industry has strong

winner-take-all industries
Industries in which factors such as *economies of scale* and *positive network effects* might be expected to lead to *pure monopoly.*

contestable industries
Industries in which even dominant firms have to worry about competition because new entrants and existing competitors are able to compete successfully for market share and users.

The App Store Payments War

Apple Insisted on Being the Sole Payments Processor for Its App Store. Epic Games Cried Monopoly, Sued, and Won.

Apple, the computer company, is also a digital platform. In fact, its products and services constitute several digital platforms. Its Apple Music store, for instance, connects music listeners with music creators. Its Apple Podcasts service connects podcast listeners with podcast producers. And its Apple App Store connects the users of its iPhones, iPads, and desktop and laptop computers with app developers whose software products run on Apple devices.

Since the 1990s, an important part of Apple's business strategy has been to treat its platforms as "walled gardens" rather than as part of the "open web." Apple closely vets the content that can be viewed, listened to, or played on its various platforms. Thus, for example, the only way that a video game studio can sell an iPhone app is to first get approval from Apple.

Apple then goes one step further, requiring that any approved iPhone app be sold only through the Apple App Store. This requirement matters because Apple takes a commission of between 15 and 30 percent of all purchases made on the App Store. Thus, if an app sells for $10, Apple will receive between $1.50 and $3.00, depending on the app. Apple also takes similar percentages of any payments made to unlock premium features or to improve the experience of an app, such as buying a powerful weapon for a video game character.

However, Apple has never charged any fees or commissions on the retail sales that are facilitated by apps downloaded from the App Store. Thus, if you use the Amazon app on an iPhone to purchase tennis shoes from Amazon.com, all the money that you pay for those shoes will go to Amazon.

In 2020, the App Store facilitated $643 billion of billings and sales worldwide. Ninety percent of that amount was for transactions (such as buying shoes on Amazon.com) on which Apple took no commissions whatsoever. It was only on the remaining 10 percent of transactions that involved consumers purchasing apps or purchasing enhanced functionality for apps that Apple took its 15 to 30 percent commission.

Armed with that background information, Epic Games, the maker of the popular Fortnite video game, sued Apple in federal court in 2020, alleging that Apple's walled-garden strategy for the App Store constituted an illegal monopoly.

Epic Games filed the lawsuit after Fortnite was booted off the App Store for including an unauthorized payment system that enabled Fortnite players to make in-app purchases without having to use Apple's in-app payments system.

In suing Apple, Epic Games complained that app developers should be able to "steer" users to outside payment processors when charging them for in-app purchases.

The Federal judge who heard the case, Yvonne Gonzalez Rodgers, sided with Epic Games and ruled that "Apple's conduct in enforcing anti-steering restrictions is anticompetitive."

FellowNeko/Shutterstock

Apple quickly appealed the ruling to try to get it overturned. But if the ruling is upheld on appeal, app developers like Epic Games will be able to begin charging users for in-app purchases using alternative payment methods, such as PayPal, Zelle, or Venmo.

Lawmakers in other countries appeared to agree with Judge Gonzalez Rodgers over the issue of in-app payments. Within a month of her ruling in 2021, legislators in the United States, South Korea, and the European Union were all working on laws that would explicitly prohibit firms that control app stores from requiring that all in-app purchases be made using their own payment-processing systems.

Such laws would presumably reduce the fee rates that app makers have to pay for payments processing. Instead of having to pay Apple a 15 to 30 percent commission on any in-app purchases, app makers might have to pay only, say, 3 percent, which is what Visa and Mastercard typically charge for credit card purchases. That in turn would probably save app users billions of dollars, because competitive pressures would probably compel app makers to pass at least some of those cost savings on to app users in the form of lower prices for in-app purchases.

Apple would lose out because it would no longer be able to obtain the high profits associated with being a monopoly payments processor. But as long as Apple can make enough of a profit to want to continue operating its App Store, the world should continue to benefit from the $643 billion in commerce that Apple facilitates within its various walled gardens each year.

positive network effects, then it will have a long-run tendency to become highly concentrated, all other things equal. Thus, any attempt to break up the leading firms in that sort of highly concentrated industry into multiple smaller competitors will probably be futile in the long run because the positive network effects present in the industry will tend to reconcentrate the industry as time passes. The leading firms might not be the same as before, but overall industry concentration might hardly budge at all in the long run.

Focusing on Specific Practices Because breaking up digital firms that have positive network externalities may not promote competition in the long run, government regulators have fewer options than they have when regulating nondigital industries, in which such breakups have historically proven to be highly effective in permanently reducing industry concentration. Given this constraint, regulators have focused not on breaking up digital firms but, instead, on regulating specific anticompetitive practices. This chapter's Last Word discusses one recent example involving digital payments.

QUICK REVIEW 14.4

▶ Internet industries are more competitive and contestable than was expected when the Internet was new, thanks to the product differentiation and multi-homing that reduce the market power generated by positive network effects.

▶ Many digital products are provided for free to as many users as wish to consume them, indicating that the firms that produce them are not restricting output or raising prices above marginal cost the way that traditional, nondigital oligopolies and monopolies usually do when they achieve market power.

▶ Because consumers are receiving many Internet products for free and thus appear not to be harmed directly by the market power of leading Internet firms, government antitrust regulators have focused their attention on business-to-business issues and how leading Internet firms may be abusing their dominance in one area, such as Internet search, to reduce competition in other areas, such as Internet advertising.

Summary

LO14.1 Describe how economies of scale help to explain both the high concentration of Internet industries and why so many digital products are provided to consumers at a price of zero.

Many online businesses have high fixed costs for developing their products but low marginal costs for delivering those products to additional users. The result is rapidly falling average total cost curves accompanied by horizontal MC curves at or near MC = 0.

Many Internet businesses also confront highly elastic demand, which makes it difficult for them to raise the prices of their core products above zero without losing many or most of their users. Thus Internet firms have a strong financial incentive to set the prices of their core products at zero while developing alternative revenue strategies, such as charging for advertising, selling data about their customers, and engaging in various forms of price discrimination, such as freemium pricing, in-app purchases, and subtractive versioning.

LO14.2 Define network effects and explain their relationship to industry concentration among Internet firms.

A network is a group of people or objects that are connected by a service or piece of infrastructure that facilitates flows of goods, services, or information. A network effect occurs when the value of a network depends on the number of people or objects that are connected by the network. A positive (negative) network effect is present when having more (fewer) people or objects connected increases (decreases) the value of the network.

When positive network effects are present, an increase in the number of users connected to a network may cause the value of the network to rise high enough that many nonusers decide to join the network. When this tipping point is reached, the largest network in an industry will have substantial market power because its sheer size will make it the most attractive network for users to join, all other things equal.

But all other things need not be equal because consumers appreciate variety and may thus be attracted to smaller networks that offer product differentiation. The market power of large networks may also be undercut by multi-homing, or participation in more than one competing network.

Because the value of a network grows exponentially as the number of users increases, technological lock-in may occur around inferior products unless network switching costs are low.

LO14.3 Explain digital platforms and how they determine their pricing structure.

Digital platforms facilitate interactions between two or more distinct but interdependent groups of users, such as gamers and game developers (PlayStation), search-engine users and advertisers (Google), and ride-seekers and ride-providers (Uber).

To maximize its overall profit, a digital platform has to consider the complicated ways in which the price that it charges one user group may affect the demand and willingness to pay of other user groups. In many cases, the best option for a digital platform is to set a price of zero for one user group in order to maximize the revenue that it collects from other user groups.

LO14.4 Summarize the debate regarding government regulation of Internet firms.

The most popular digital products (such as search and social media) are provided for free to as many users as wish to consume them, which implies that the Internet firms that produce those products are *not* restricting output or raising prices above marginal cost the way that traditional, nondigital oligopolies and monopolies do when they achieve market power. As a result, government regulators have not felt any pressing need to restrict the market power of Internet firms in order to protect consumers. However, regulators have expressed substantial concern with respect to dominant Internet firms using their market power to take advantage of, or harm, other businesses.

Internet industries are more competitive and more contestable than was expected when the Internet was new. The fear that most Internet industries would devolve into winner-take-all monopolies proved not to be accurate because factors such as product differentiation and multi-homing have helped to prevent leading firms that enjoy strong positive network effects from becoming pure monopolies.

Terms and Concepts

Internet	negative network effect	digital platform
freemium pricing	network congestion	direct network effect
in-app purchases	network pollution	indirect network effect
subtractive versioning	tipping point	winner-take-all industries
network	multi-homing	contestable industries
network effect	technological lock-in	
positive network effect	network switching cost	

Discussion Questions

1. Why do the cost structures of many Internet businesses cause them to have continuously declining average total cost curves? **LO14.1**
2. "Because Internet companies have ATCs that fall toward zero as the number of users increases, the only thing they have to do to make a profit is attract a lot of users." Respond to this assertion and explain your reasoning. **LO14.1**
3. How does selling advertising to raise revenue solve the challenge that Internet firms have with highly elastic demand curves for their main products? **LO14.1**
4. Compare making cars to making video game software. Does making each additional car require a substantial amount of marginal and variable costs? What costs are involved in making each additional copy of a piece of software that has already been on the market for several months? In which case are fixed costs going to be a larger part of total costs? In which case will ATC have a greater tendency to decline as output increases? **LO14.1**
5. Define the term *network effect* and give at least one example not found in the textbook of a network effect that exists on the Internet or that affects an Internet business. Also give at least one non-textbook example of a network effect that occurs offline, in real life. In both cases, explain how the network effects of your examples vary with the number of users. **LO14.2**
6. What is a positive network effect, and how can positive network effects generate monopoly power? **LO14.2**
7. A social network grows rapidly at first, causing positive network effects that, other things equal, shift demand to the right. But then negative network effects rapidly increase, pushing demand to the left, other things equal. Could the two effects cancel each other out? Could the network, as a result, reach an equilibrium number of users, all other things equal? Explain your reasoning. **LO14.2**
8. What is network pollution and how does it relate to the fact that certain dating sites and restaurant review sites try to use information about users' current location to show them only dating profiles and restaurant reviews of, respectively, people and restaurants that are located nearby? (Hint: What would happen to the value of such a recommendation network if its users were instead shown profiles or reviews from any distance away?) **LO14.2**
9. What are network switching costs and how do they relate to the possibility of technological lock-in? **LO14.2**
10. What is a digital platform, and why might giving away its main product for free help a digital platform to maximize its overall profit? **LO14.3**
11. Microsoft and Sony compete in the market for video game consoles (Xbox versus PlayStation). Why do these firms subsidize the prices of their respective video game consoles to the point of selling each console at a loss? Why do they give developers (for free) the programming tools necessary to make video games on their respective platforms? **LO14.3**
12. Why did many early analysts expect the Internet to become dominated by winner-take-all industries? What factors have made Internet industries more contestable than originally expected? **LO14.4**
13. **LAST WORD** Why is Apple's insistence on processing in-app payments anticompetitive? What are the potential benefits of allowing alternative payment systems?

Review Questions

1. Which of the following are pricing strategies that Internet firms use to overcome highly elastic demand and the difficulty of raising their prices above zero? *Select all that apply.* **LO14.1**
   a. In-app purchases
   b. Zero-MC pricing
   c. Price discrimination
   d. Network effects
   e. Economies of scale

2. If _____ equals zero, then _____ will fall continuously as long as fixed costs exceed zero. **LO14.1**
   a. ATC; economies of scale
   b. ATC; MC
   c. economies of scale; MC
   d. MC; ATC
   e. *P*; economies of scale

3. Internet businesses often have: **LO14.1**
   a. large variable costs and zero marginal costs.
   b. large fixed costs and zero marginal costs.
   c. large variable costs and large fixed costs.
   d. large variable costs and zero fixed costs.
4. While the marginal cost of distributing a product like software over the Internet may be close to zero, the ATC per unit may be high due to: **LO14.1**
   a. fixed costs being distributed over many users.
   b. fixed costs being distributed over only a small number of users.
   c. free advertising.
   d. in-app purchases.
5. The ability to spread the large development costs of complicated software projects over millions of users helps to generate _____. *Choose the best answer.* **LO14.1**
   a. economies of scale
   b. network effects
   c. duplication errors
   d. natural monopolies
   e. pure competition
6. A rural cell phone network that crashes when 200,000 people show up for a pop-up concert is an example of: **LO14.2**
   a. network pollution.
   b. network congestion.
   c. economies of scale.
   d. MC = 0.
7. Congress has passed a law that prohibits unsolicited telemarketing calls to cell phones. This law is intended to reduce _____. *Choose the best answer.* **LO14.2**
   a. monopoly power
   b. positive network effects
   c. network pollution
   d. network congestion
   e. tipping points
8. An online industry with hundreds of millions of potential users consists of multiple firms that run networks that, unfortunately, subject users to substantial negative network effects after any of the networks gets more than a few thousand users. Such an industry would most likely be populated by _____. *Choose the best answer.* **LO14.2**
   a. many small firms
   b. one monopoly firm

   c. a few oligopoly firms
   d. foreign firms
9. Which of the following can help to offset the market power that can be generated by positive network effects? *Select all that apply.* **LO14.2**
   a. Oligopoly power
   b. Product differentiation
   c. Monopoly power
   d. Multi-homing
   e. Pure competition
10. When only 10 percent of your friends were on Snapchat, you didn't see much point in joining. But when the percentage rose to 40, you changed your mind. Here, 40 percent is an example of: **LO14.2**
    a. network switching costs.
    b. technological lock-in.
    c. negative network externalities.
    d. a tipping point.
11. Which of the following firms could most easily switch all of its employees over from Microsoft Office to Google Workspace, assuming that all of the firms are equally interested in doing so? **LO14.2**
    a. A firm with 78,324 employees
    b. A firm with 742,027 employees
    c. A firm with 72 employees
    d. A firm with 7 employees
12. An increase in the number of developers making apps for the Android mobile platform causes more smartphone users to use Android phones, which increases the demand for Android apps. This is an example of: **LO14.3**
    a. a congestion effect.
    b. a direct network effect.
    c. consumer surplus.
    d. an indirect network effect.
13. Governments that are considering regulations on digital businesses are often confronted with high _____ on the one hand and low _____ on the other. **LO14.4**
    a. product prices; industry concentration
    b. industry concentration; multi-homing
    c. multi-homing; product differentiation
    d. industry concentration; product prices
    e. multi-homing; industry concentration

Problems

1. Moore's Law states that the maximum speed at which computer chips can process information doubles approximately every 2 years. If that relationship continues to hold true in the future, how much faster will computer chips be in 12 years? (Hint: You may want to think of this problem in terms of exponential notation, such as 2^x.) **LO14.1**
2. *The New York Times* newspaper uses a metered subscription model in which anyone can look at up to 20 articles per month for free online but then must pay for a monthly subscription to read additional articles. In 2020, *The New York Times* had 130 million unique online readers per month but only 5 million digital subscribers. What percentage of *The New York Times'* online readership is a subscriber? What does this suggest about the elasticity of demand for the newspaper's product? **LO14.1**

3. Suppose that Instagram has a fixed cost of $1,200,000,000 and a variable cost that is constant at $0.02 per user. (Hint: In what follows, remember that a million is a 1 followed by six zeros and that a billion is a 1 followed by nine zeros. Also recall that ATC = AFC + AVC and that MC is the marginal change in ATC when you add an additional user.) **LO14.1**
   a. What is Instagram's marginal cost per user?
   b. What is Instagram's ATC for 1,000 users?
   c. What is Instagram's ATC for 1 million users?
   d. What is Instagram's ATC for 1 billion users?
   e. If Instagram has 1 billion users, how much revenue per user would it have to collect in order to break even?
4. The nearby game theory payoff matrix illustrates the competitive situation between two rival online e-mail providers, Zmail

and Gotmail. Each of these firms has two pricing strategies ($P = 0$ or $P > 0$) to choose from, and their respective payoffs depend not only on the pricing strategy that each of them sets for its own product but also on its competitor's pricing strategy. (Before attempting this problem, you may want to review the sections on game theory in the previous chapter.) **LO14.1**

a. Does Zmail have a dominant strategy (that is, one that Zmail will always want to follow no matter what pricing strategy Gotmail chooses)? If so, what is it?

b. Does Gotmail have a dominant strategy (that is, one that Gotmail will always want to follow no matter what pricing strategy Zmail chooses)? If so, what is it?

c. Does the game have a Nash equilibrium (that is, an outcome from which neither firm will want to deviate because each is playing its own dominant strategy)? If so, what cell is the outcome of that Nash equilibrium?

d. Based on your answers to parts *a*, *b*, and *c*, what price will each firm choose?

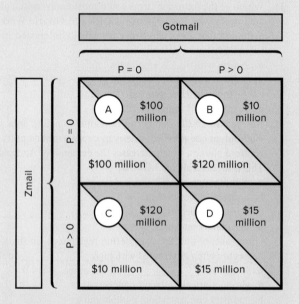

5. Metcalf's Law states that the value V of a network is "proportional" to the square of the number, n, of network users. Thus, $V = n^2$. Using that formula, what is the value of a network of 2 nodes? Of 3 nodes? By how much does the value of a network increase when it goes from having 2 nodes to 3 nodes? Now calculate the value of a network of 8 nodes and then the value of a network of 9 nodes. By how much does the value of a network increase when it increases from 8 nodes to 9 nodes? Is the marginal value of an additional node constant, or does it increase as the number of nodes increases? Explain. **LO14.2**

6. Consider the nearby payoff matrix, which shows the situation facing two friends, Jared and Amanda, as they each ponder what type of video game platform to purchase for their respective apartments. Their choices are Xbox and PlayStation, and each of them enjoys not only playing games by themselves but also playing them with each other over the Internet. However, the

games on the two platforms are typically proprietary, meaning that if Jared and Amanda get different platforms, they may not be able to play games with each other over the Internet. Answer the following questions based on the payoffs in the payoff matrix. (Before attempting this problem, you may want to review the sections on game theory in the previous chapter.) **LO14.3**

a. If Jared has already selected an Xbox, would it be better for Amanda to select an Xbox or a PlayStation?

b. If Jared has already selected a PlayStation, would it be better for Amanda to select an Xbox or a PlayStation?

c. Now suppose that Amanda chooses first and decides to get an Xbox. Would it be better for Jared to select an Xbox or a PlayStation?

d. Suppose that Amanda again chooses first but decides to go with a PlayStation. Would it be better for Jared to select an Xbox or a PlayStation?

e. Looking at your answers to parts *a* through *d*, are both Jared and Amanda better off if they decide on the same platform?

f. Assuming that both Jared and Amanda choose the same platform, which platform would make both of them better off?

g. Suppose that Jared and Amanda have both already selected an Xbox. If it will cost them $250 each to switch to the PlayStation platform, would it be worth their while to do so? (Hint: Think through each person's decision individually before answering the question.)

h. Again suppose that Jared and Amanda have both already selected an Xbox. If it will cost them $350 each to switch to the PlayStation platform, would it be worth their while to do so? (Hint: Think through each person's decision individually before answering the question.)

i. Looking at your answers to parts *g* and *h*, does the size of the network switching cost affect whether or not there is technological lock-in around the Xbox platform that both players initially selected?

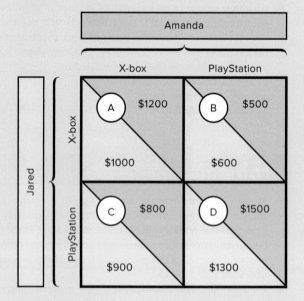

CHAPTER 15

Technology, R&D, and Efficiency

>> LEARNING OBJECTIVES

LO15.1 Differentiate among invention, innovation, and technological diffusion.

LO15.2 Explain how entrepreneurs and other innovators further technological advance.

LO15.3 Summarize how a firm determines its optimal amount of research and development (R&D).

LO15.4 Discuss how technological change can increase profits by raising revenues or lowering costs.

LO15.5 Explain why firms benefit from their innovation even though rivals have an incentive to imitate it.

LO15.6 Discuss the role of market structure in promoting technological advance.

LO15.7 Show how technological advance enhances productive and allocative efficiency.

technological advance (1) An improvement in the quality of existing products, the invention of entirely new products, or the creation of new or better ways of producing or distributing products. (2) Any improvement in the methods by which resources are combined such that the same quantity of inputs can be made to yield a combination of outputs that is preferred to any combination of outputs that was previously possible.

- "Just Do It." In 1968 two entrepreneurs from Oregon developed a lightweight sport shoe and formed a new company called Nike, incorporating a "swoosh" logo (designed by a graduate student for $35). Today, Nike sells $45 billion worth of goods annually.
- "Save money, live better." Expanding from a single store in 1962 to about 7,000 stores worldwide today, Walmart's annual revenue ($560 billion) exceeds that of General Motors and Amazon combined.

Nike and Walmart owe much of their success to **technological advance,** broadly defined as new and better goods, services, or ways of producing or distributing them. Nike pioneered innovative new products, and Walmart developed creative ways to manage inventories and distribute goods. The pursuit of technological advance is a major competitive activity among firms. In this chapter, we examine the microeconomics of that activity.

Invention, Innovation, and Diffusion

In economics, technological advance occurs over a theoretical time period called the *very long run,* which can be as short as a few months or as long as many years. Compare the concept of the very long run with the two shorter-duration time concepts that we've developed. In the *short run,* technology and plant and equipment are fixed. In the *long run,* technology is constant, but firms can change their plant sizes and are free to enter or exit industries. The **very long run** is a period in which technology can change and in which firms can develop and offer entirely new products.

>> **LO15.1** Differentiate among invention, innovation, and technological diffusion.

very long run In microeconomics, a period of time long enough that *technology* can change and *firms* can introduce new products.

In Chapter 1 we saw that technological advance shifts an economy's production possibilities curve outward, enabling the economy to obtain more goods and services. Technological advance is a three-step process of invention, innovation, and diffusion.

Invention

invention The conception of a new product or process combined with the first proof that it will work.

The basis of technological advance is **invention:** the conception of a new product or process combined with the first proof that it will work. Invention is a process of imagination, ingenious thinking, and experimentation. The result of the process is called *an* invention. The prototypes (basic working models) of the telephone, the automobile, and the microchip were inventions.

patent An exclusive right given to inventors to produce and sell a new product or machine for 20 years from the time of patent application.

Invention usually is based on scientific knowledge and is the product of individuals, working either on their own or as members of corporate or government research and development (R&D) teams. Governments encourage invention by providing the inventor with a **patent,** an exclusive right to sell any new and useful process, machine, or product for a set period of time. In 2020, the top five firms in terms of securing the most U.S. patents were IBM (9,130), Samsung (6,415), Canon (3,225), Microsoft (2,905), and Intel (2,867). These numbers do not reveal the quality of the patents; some patents are much more significant than others. Patents have a worldwide duration of 20 years from the time of application for the patent.

Innovation

innovation The first commercially successful introduction of a new product, use of a new method of production, or creation of a new form of business organization.

Innovation draws directly on invention. While invention is the discovery and first proof of workability, **innovation** is the first successful commercial introduction of a new product, the first use of a new method, or the creation of a new form of business enterprise. There are two types of innovation. **Product innovation** refers to new and improved products or services. **Process innovation** refers to new and improved methods of production or distribution.

product innovation The development and sale of a new or improved product (or service).

Unlike inventions, innovations cannot be patented. Nevertheless, innovation is a major factor in competition, because it sometimes enables a firm to leapfrog competitors by rendering their products or processes obsolete. For example, personal computers coupled with word-processing software pushed some major typewriter manufacturers into obscurity. More recently, innovations in online retailing and delivery by Amazon and other firms have threatened the existence of traditional "brick-and-mortar" retailers.

process innovation The development and use of new or improved production or distribution methods.

But innovation need not weaken or destroy existing firms. Aware that new products and processes may threaten their survival, existing firms have a powerful incentive to engage continuously in their own R&D. Innovative products and processes often enable such firms to maintain or increase their profits. The introduction of disposable contact lenses by Johnson & Johnson and iPhones by Apple are good examples.

Global Perspective 15.1 shows that the fraction of national income (GDP) that is directed toward R&D spending varies substantially across nations.

🌐 GLOBAL PERSPECTIVE 15.1

TOTAL R&D EXPENDITURES AS A PERCENTAGE OF GDP, SELECTED NATIONS

Relative R&D spending varies among leading industrial nations. From a microeconomic perspective, R&D helps promote economic efficiency; from a macroeconomic perspective, R&D helps promote economic growth.

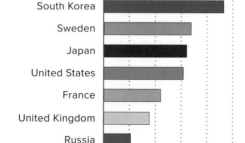

Total R&D Expenditures as a Percentage of GDP, Selected Nations

Source: Main Science and Technology Indicators, Organization for Economic Cooperation and Development (OECD), 2021.

Diffusion

Diffusion is the spread of an innovation to other products or processes through imitation or copying. To take advantage of new profit opportunities or to slow the erosion of profit, new and existing firms emulate the successful innovations of others. Alamo greatly increased its auto rentals by offering customers unlimited mileage, and Hertz, Avis, Budget, and others eventually followed. Tesla introduced the first commercially viable all-electric car, which prompted other automakers like Nissan, Chevrolet, and BMW to offer their own fully electric vehicles in short order. Early successful cholesterol-reducing drugs (statins) such as Bristol-Myers Squibb's Pravachol were soon followed by chemically distinct but similar statins such as Merck's Zocor and Pfizer's Lipitor. Early video game consoles such as those by Atari eventually gave rise to more popular consoles by Nintendo (Switch), Sony (PlayStation), and Microsoft (Xbox).

In each of these cases, other firms incorporated the new innovation into their own businesses and products through imitation, modification, and extension. The original innovation thus became commonplace and mainly of historical interest.

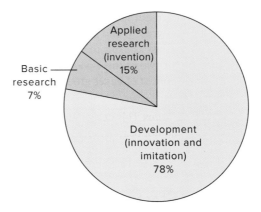

FIGURE 15.1
The composition of business R&D outlays in the United States, 2019.

Firms channel the bulk of their R&D spending to innovation and imitation because both have direct commercial value; less to applied research, that is, invention; and a relatively small amount to basic scientific research.

Source: "National Patterns of R&D Resources," National Science Foundation.

diffusion The spread of an *innovation* through its widespread imitation.

R&D Expenditures

As related to *businesses*, the term "research and development" is used loosely to include direct efforts toward invention, innovation, and diffusion. However, *government* also engages in R&D, particularly R&D focused on national defense. In 2019 *total* U.S. R&D expenditures (business *plus* government *plus* higher education) were $656 billion, or about 3.1 percent of GDP.

U.S. businesses spent nearly $486 billion on R&D in 2019. Figure 15.1 shows how these R&D expenditures were allocated. U.S. firms collectively channeled 78 percent of their R&D expenditures to "development" (innovation and imitation, the route to diffusion). They spent another 15 percent on applied research, or on pursuing invention. For reasons we will discuss later, only 7 percent of business R&D expenditures went for basic research, the search for general scientific principles. Of course, industries, and firms within industries, vary greatly in their emphasis on these three processes.

Modern View of Technological Advance

For decades, most economists regarded technological advance as a random *external* force to which the economy adjusted. In other words, they believed that the development of new technologies was rooted in the independent advance of science, which is largely external to the market system.

Most contemporary economists support a different view. They see capitalism itself as the driving force behind technological advance. Invention, innovation, and diffusion occur in response to incentives within the economy, meaning that technological advance is *internal* to capitalism. Specifically, technological advance arises from intense rivalry among individuals and firms that motivates them to seek and exploit new profit opportunities or to expand existing opportunities. That rivalry occurs both among existing firms and between existing firms and newly created firms. Moreover, many advances in "pure" scientific knowledge are motivated, at least in part, by the prospect of commercial applicability and eventual profit. In the modern view, entrepreneurs and other innovators are at the heart of technological advance.

Role of Entrepreneurs and Other Innovators

It is helpful to distinguish between "entrepreneurs" and "other innovators":

- **Entrepreneurs** Recall that an entrepreneur is an initiator, innovator, and risk bearer. Their entrepreneurial ability is the productive resource that combines the other productive resources of land, labor, and capital in new and unique ways to produce new goods and services. In the past a single individual—for example, Andrew Carnegie in steel or Levi Strauss in blue

>> **LO15.2** Explain how entrepreneurs and other innovators further technological advance.

entrepreneurs Individuals who provide *entrepreneurial ability* to *firms* by setting strategy, advancing innovations, and bearing the financial risk if their firms do poorly.

jeans—carried out the entrepreneurial role. Air conditioning, the ballpoint pen, cellophane, insulin, xerography, and the helicopter all have an individualistic heritage. Today, entrepreneurship is just as likely to be carried out by entrepreneurial teams. These teams may include only two or three people working as their own bosses on some new product idea, or they may consist of larger groups of entrepreneurs who have pooled their financial resources.

- *Other innovators* This designation includes other key people involved in the pursuit of innovation who do not bear personal financial risk. Among them are key executives, scientists, and other salaried employees engaged in commercial R&D activities. (They are sometimes called *intrapreneurs* because they provide the spirit of entrepreneurship within existing firms.)

Forming Startups

startups Newly formed firms that are attempting to pioneer a new product or production method.

Entrepreneurs often form small new companies called **startups** that focus on creating and introducing a new product or employing a new production or distribution technique. Two twenty-somethings named Steve Jobs and Steve Wozniak formed a startup in the mid-1970s after months of tinkering on a prototype personal computer that they had built in a garage during their free time. When neither of their employers—respectively, Hewlett-Packard and Atari, the developer of Pong (the first video game)—was interested in funding the development of their new computer, they founded their own computer company: Apple. Other examples of successful startups are Starbucks, Amazon, Google, and Amgen, a biotechnology firm specializing in new medical treatments.

Innovating within Existing Firms

Innovators also work within existing corporations, large and small. Such innovators are salaried workers, although many firms' compensation systems provide them with substantial bonuses or profit shares. Examples of firms known for their skillful internal innovators are 3M Corporation (the U.S. developer of Scotch tape, Post-it notes, and Thinsulate insulation) and SpaceX (the first commercially successful private space launch company). R&D work in major corporations has produced significant technological improvements in such products as television sets, smartphones, home appliances, and automobiles.

Some large firms, aware that excessive bureaucracy can stifle creative thinking and technological advance, have divested some of their R&D and manufacturing divisions to form new, more flexible, innovative firms. Two significant examples of "spin-off firms" are Internet payments processor PayPal, which was spun off by eBay, and Yum! Brands, which operates restaurant chains Taco Bell, KFC, and Pizza Hut. It was spun off by Pepsi.

Anticipating the Future

In 1949 a writer for *Popular Mechanics* magazine boldly predicted, "Computers in the future may weigh no more than 1.5 tons." Today's notebook computers weigh less than 3 pounds, while an iPhone weighs under 4 ounces.

Anticipating the future is difficult, but that is what innovators try to do. Those with strong anticipatory ability and determination have a knack for introducing new and improved products or services at just the right time.

The rewards for success are both monetary and nonmonetary. Product innovation and development are creative endeavors, with such intangible rewards as personal satisfaction. Also, many people simply enjoy participating in the competitive "contest." Of course, the winners can reap huge monetary rewards in the form of economic profits, stock appreciation, or large bonuses. Extreme examples include Microsoft founder Bill Gates, whose net worth in 2021 was $124 billion, and Facebook founder Mark Zuckerberg, whose net worth reached $97 billion in 2021.

Past successes often give entrepreneurs and innovative firms access to resources needed to create further innovations that anticipate consumer wants. The market tends to entrust the production of goods and services to businesses that have consistently succeeded in satisfying (or creating) consumer wants. The market does not care whether the winning entrepreneurs and innovative firms are American, Brazilian, Japanese, German, or South African. The scope of entrepreneurship and innovation is global.

FIGURE 15.3 **The expected-rate-of-return schedule and curve.**

As they relate to R&D, a firm's expected-rate-of-return schedule (the table) and curve (the graph) show the firm's expected gain in profit, as a percentage of R&D spending, for each level of R&D spending. Curve *r* slopes downward because the firm assesses its potential R&D projects in descending order of expected rates of return.

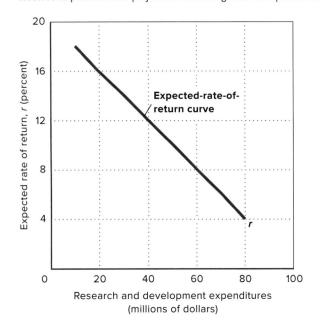

R&D, Millions	Expected Rate of Return, %
$10	18
20	16
30	14
40	12
50	10
60	8
70	6
80	4

MedTech can use this same method to estimate the expected rates of return for R&D expenditures of $2 million, $3 million, $4 million, and so on. Suppose those marginal rates of return are those indicated in the table in Figure 15.3, where they are also graphed as the **expected-rate-of-return curve,** which shows the marginal benefit of each dollar of expenditure on R&D. The curve slopes downward because of diminishing returns to R&D expenditures. A firm will direct its initial R&D expenditures to the highest expected-rate-of-return activities and then use additional funding for activities with successively lower expected rates of return. That is, the firm will experience lower and lower expected rates of return as it expands its R&D spending.

expected-rate-of-return curve As it relates to research and development (*R&D*), a curve showing the anticipated gain in *profit*, as a percentage of R&D expenditure, from an additional dollar spent on R&D.

Optimal R&D Expenditures

Figure 15.4 combines the interest-rate cost-of-funds curve (Figure 15.2) and the expected-rate-of-return curve (Figure 15.3). The curves intersect at MedTech's **optimal amount of R&D,** which is $60 million. This amount can also be determined from the table in Figure 15.4 as the amount of funding for which the expected rate of return and the interest cost of borrowing are equal (here, 8 percent).

As Figure 15.4 shows, at $60 million of R&D expenditures, the marginal benefit and marginal cost of the last dollar spent on R&D are equal. MedTech should undertake all R&D expenditures up to $60 million because those outlays yield a higher marginal benefit or expected rate of return, *r*, than the 8 percent marginal cost or interest-rate cost of borrowing, *i*. But it should not undertake R&D expenditures beyond $60 million; for these outlays, *r* (marginal benefit) is less than *i* (marginal cost). Only at $60 million does *r = i*, telling us that MedTech will spend $60 million on R&D.

Our analysis reinforces three important points:

optimal amount of R&D The level of *R&D* at which the *marginal benefit* and *marginal cost* of R&D expenditures are equal.

- *Optimal versus affordable R&D* Figure 15.4 shows that R&D expenditures make sense to a firm only as long as the expected return from the outlay equals or exceeds the cost of obtaining the funds needed to finance it. Many R&D expenditures may be affordable but not worthwhile because their marginal benefit is likely to be less than their marginal cost.

- *Expected, not guaranteed, returns* The outcomes from R&D are expected, not guaranteed. Therefore, some R&D decisions may be more like an informed gamble than a typical business decision. For every successful outcome, there are scores of costly disappointments. Some famous examples are Ford's Edsel automobile, New Coke by Coca-Cola, and Samsung's Galaxy Note 7 smartphone, which was prone to catching on fire. Samsung lost $17 billion.

FIGURE 15.4 A firm's optimal level of R&D expenditures.

The firm's optimal level of R&D expenditures ($60 million) occurs where its expected rate of return equals the interest-rate cost of funds, as shown in both the table and the graph. At $60 million of R&D spending, the firm has taken advantage of all R&D opportunities for which the expected rate of return, r, exceeds or equals the 8 percent interest cost of borrowing, i.

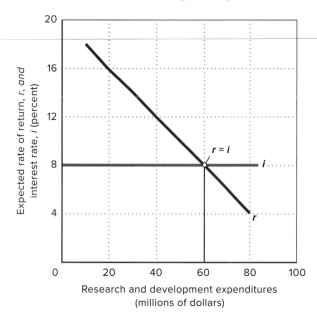

Expected Rate of Return, %	R&D, Millions	Interest-Rate Cost-of-Funds, %
18	$10	8
16	20	8
14	30	8
12	40	8
10	50	8
8	60	8
6	70	8
4	80	8

- *Adjustments* Firms adjust their R&D expenditures when expected rates of return on various projects change (when curves such as r in Figure 15.4 shift). The U.S. war on terrorism, for example, increased the expected rate of return on R&D for improved security devices used at airports, train stations, harbors, and other public places. It also increased the expected return on new methods of detecting and responding to potential bioterrorism. The revised realities prompted many firms to increase their R&D expenditures for these purposes.

Increased Profit via Innovation

>> **LO15.4** Discuss how technological change can increase profits by raising revenues or lowering costs.

How can technological change increase a firm's profit? Although the answer may seem obvious—by increasing revenue or reducing production costs—insights can be gained by exploring these two possibilities in some detail.

Increased Revenue via Product Innovation

Firms in the United States and abroad have profitably introduced hundreds of new products in the past few decades. Examples include artificial meat, cordless drills, snowboards, smartphones, ride-sharing apps, and electric cars. All these items reflect technological advance in the form of product innovation.

How do such new products gain consumer acceptance? As you know from Chapter 7, to maximize their satisfaction, consumers purchase products that have the highest marginal utility per dollar. They determine which products to buy by comparing the ratios of MU/price for the various goods. They first select the unit of the good with the highest MU/price ratio, then the one with the next highest, and so on, until their incomes are used up.

The first five columns of Table 15.1 repeat some of the information in Table 7.1. Before the introduction of new product C, the consumer maximized her total utility from $10 of income by buying 2 units of A at $1 per unit and 4 units of B at $2 per unit. Her total budget of $10 was thus fully expended, with $2 spent on A and $8 on B. As shown in columns 2b and 3b, the marginal utility per dollar spent on the last unit of each product was 8 (= 8/$1 = 16/$2). The total utility, derived from columns 2a and 3a, was 96 utils (= 10 + 8 from the first 2 units of A plus 24 + 20 + 18 + 16 from the first 4 units of B).

TABLE 15.1 Utility Maximization with the Introduction of a New Product (Income = $10)*

(1) Unit of Product	(2) Product A: Price = $1		(3) Product B: Price = $2		(4) New Product C: Price = $4	
	(a) Marginal Utility, Utils	(b) Marginal Utility per Dollar (MU/Price)	(a) Marginal Utility, Utils	(b) Marginal Utility per Dollar (MU/Price)	(a) Marginal Utility, Utils	(b) Marginal Utility per Dollar (MU/Price)
First	10	10	24	12	52	13
Second	8	8	20	10	48	12
Third	7	7	18	9	44	11
Fourth	6	6	16	8	36	9
Fifth	5	5	12	6	32	8

*It is assumed in this table that the amount of marginal utility received from additional units of each of the three products is independent of the quantity purchased of the other products. For example, the marginal-utility schedule for product C is independent of the amount of A and B purchased by the consumer.

Now suppose an innovative firm offers new product C (columns 4a and 4b in Table 15.1), priced at $4 per unit. Note that the first unit of C has a higher marginal utility per dollar (13) than any unit of A or B and that the second unit of C and the first unit of B have equal MU/price ratios of 12. To maximize satisfaction, the consumer now buys 2 units of C at $4 per unit, 1 unit of B at $2 per unit, and zero units of A. Our consumer has spent all of her $10 income ($8 on C and $2 on B), and the MU/price ratios of the last units of B and C are equal at 12. As determined via columns 3a and 4a, the consumer's total utility is now 124 utils (= 24 from the first unit of B plus 52 + 48 from the first 2 units of C).

Total utility has increased by 28 utils (= 124 utils − 96 utils), and that is why the consumer purchased product C. Consumers will buy a new product only if it increases the total utility they obtain from their limited incomes.

From the innovating firm's perspective, these "dollar votes" represent new product demand that yields increased revenue.

Other related points:

- *Importance of price* Consumer acceptance of a new product depends on both its marginal utility and its price. (Confirm that the consumer represented in Table 15.1 will buy zero units of new product C if its price is $8 rather than $4.) To be successful, a new product must not only deliver utility to consumers but also do so at an acceptable price.

- *Product improvements* Most product innovation consists of incremental improvements to existing products rather than radical inventions. Examples include more fuel-efficient automobile engines, new varieties of pizza, more flavorful bubble gum, "rock shocks" for mountain bikes, and clothing made of wrinkle-free fabrics.

Reduced Costs via Process Innovation

The introduction of better methods of producing products—process innovation—is also a path toward enhanced profit and a positive return on R&D expenditures. Suppose a manufacturing firm replaces old equipment with more productive equipment embodying a technological advance. As a result, it can now produce more units of output at each level of resource usage. That implies higher profits because the firm can sell more units and make more revenue from the same amount of inputs. The productivity increase can also be understood as a downward shift of the firm's ATC curve, since the cost to produce any given unit will decline. Given a fixed product price, lower ATC per unit translates into higher profits.

Example: Computer-based inventory control systems, such as those pioneered by Walmart, enabled innovators to reduce the number of people needed to keep track of inventories. The new systems also enabled firms to keep goods arriving "just in time," reducing the cost of storing inventories. The consequence? Significant increases in sales per worker, declines in average total cost, and increased profit.

Imitation and R&D Incentives

>> **LO15.5** Explain why firms benefit from their innovation even though rivals have an incentive to imitate it.

imitation problem The potential for a *firm's* rivals to produce a close variation of (imitate) a firm's new product or process, greatly reducing the originator's profit from *R&D* and *innovation.*

fast-second strategy An approach by a dominant *firm* in which it allows other firms in its *industry* to bear the risk of innovation and then quickly becomes the second firm to offer any successful new product or adopt any improved production process.

Our analysis of product and process innovation explains how technological advance enhances a firm's profit. But it also hints at a potential **imitation problem:** A firm's rivals may be able to imitate its new product or process, greatly reducing the originator's profit from its R&D effort. For example, in the 1980s, U.S. auto firms took apart Japanese Honda Accords, piece by piece, to discover the secrets of their high quality. This reverse engineering—which ironically was perfected earlier by the Japanese—helped the U.S. firms incorporate innovative features into their own cars. This type of imitation is perfectly legitimate and fully anticipated; it is often the main path to widespread diffusion of an innovation.

In fact, a dominant firm that is making large profits from its existing products may let smaller firms in the industry incur the high costs of product innovation while it closely monitors their successes and failures. The dominant firm then moves quickly to imitate any successful new product; its goal is to become the second firm to embrace the innovation. In using this **fast-second strategy,** the dominant firm counts on its own product-improvement abilities, marketing prowess, or economies of scale to prevail.

Examples abound: Royal Crown introduced the first diet cola, but Diet Coke and Diet Pepsi dominate diet-cola sales today. Meister Brau introduced the first low-calorie beer, but Miller popularized the product with its Miller Lite. Books.com became the first online bookseller in the early 1990s, but it was Amazon that perfected the online bookstore business on the way to becoming America's largest general-purpose Internet retailer.

Benefits of Being First

Imitation and the fast-second strategy raise an important question: What incentive does any firm have to bear the expenses and risks of innovation if competitors can imitate its new or improved product? Why not let others bear the costs and take the risks of product development and then just imitate the successful innovations? There are several legal protections for, and potential advantages to, those who take the lead.

Patents Some technological breakthroughs can be patented. Once patented, they cannot be legally imitated for two decades from the time of patent application. The purpose of patents is to reduce imitation and its negative effect on the incentive for engaging in R&D. In 2021, for instance, a jury in Texas found computer chipmaker Intel guilty of infringing on two patents owned by another company. The $2.18 billion that Intel was ordered to pay serves as a reminder that the courts take patent infringement very seriously.

There are hundreds of other examples of long-run profits based on U.S. patents; they involve products from prescription drugs to pop-top cans to self-driving cars. As Global Perspective 15.2, shows, foreign citizens and firms hold many U.S. patents.

 GLOBAL PERSPECTIVE 15.2

DISTRIBUTION OF U.S. PATENTS, BY FOREIGN NATION

Foreign citizens, corporations, and governments hold 48 percent of U.S. patents. The top 10 foreign countries in terms of U.S. patent holdings since 1963 are listed below, with the number of U.S. patents (through 2020) in parentheses.

Top 10 Foreign Countries

Japan (1,332,692)
Germany (457,473)
South Korea (280,360)
Taiwan (225,060)
United Kingdom (180,368)
France (176,686)
Canada (162,098)
China (138,522)
Italy (79,520)
Switzerland (72,595)

Source: U.S. Patent and Trademark Office.

Copyrights and Trademarks *Copyrights* protect publishers of books, computer software, movies, videos, and musical compositions from having their works copied. *Trademarks* give the original innovators of products the exclusive right to use a particular product name ("M&Ms," "Barbie" dolls, "Wheaties"). By reducing the problem of direct copying, these legal protections increase the incentive for product innovation. Recent international trade agreements have strengthened worldwide copyright and trademark laws.

Brand-Name Recognition Along with trademark protection, brand-name recognition may give the original innovator a major marketing advantage for years or even decades. Consumers often identify a new product with the firm that first introduced and popularized it in the mass market. Examples include Kleenex tissues, Johnson & Johnson's Band-Aids, Gatorade sports drink, and Kellogg's Corn Flakes.

Trade Secrets and Learning by Doing Some innovations involve trade secrets, without which competitors cannot imitate the product or process. For example, Coca-Cola has successfully kept its formula for Coke a secret from potential rivals. Also, a firm's head start with a new product often allows it to achieve substantial cost reductions through *learning by doing*. The innovator's lower production cost may allow for continued profit even after imitators have entered the market.

Time Lags Time lags between innovation and diffusion often lead to a substantial economic profit. It takes time for an imitator to imitate. It must learn the properties of a new innovation, design a substitute product, gear up a factory for production, and conduct a marketing campaign. Various entry barriers, such as high initial costs, economies of scale, and price-cutting, may extend the time lag between innovation and imitation. In practice, it may take years or even decades before rival firms can successfully imitate a profitable new product and cut into the innovator's market share. In the meantime, the innovator continues to profit. The nearby Consider This story gives a humorous historical example of an entrepreneur using misdirection to prevent competitors from easily copying his innovation.

Profitable Buyouts

A final advantage of being first arises from the possibility of a buyout (outright purchase) of the innovating firm by a larger firm. Here, the innovative entrepreneurs take their rewards immediately, as cash or as shares in the purchasing firm, rather than waiting for uncertain long-run profits.

Examples: Once the popularity of cellular communications became evident, AT&T bought out McCaw Communications, an early leader in this new technology. When Minnetonka's Softsoap became a huge success, it sold its product to Colgate-Palmolive. More recently, the established

CONSIDER THIS . . .

Trade Secrets

Trade secrets have long played an important role in maintaining returns from research and development (R&D). Long before Coca-Cola's secret formula or Colonel Sanders' secret herbs and spices, legend has it that the Roman citizen Erasmo (c. A.D. 130) had a secret ingredient for violin strings.* As the demand for his new product grew, he falsely identified his strings as *catgut,* when they were actually made of sheep intestines. Why the deception? At the time, it was considered to be extremely bad luck to kill a cat. By identifying

Don Farrall/Photodisc/Getty Images

his strings as catgut, he hoped that nobody would imitate his product and reduce his monopoly profit. Moreover, his product name would help him preserve his valuable trade secret.

*We found this anecdote in Dennis W. Carleton and Jeffrey Perloff, *Modern Industrial Organization,* 2d ed. (New York: HarperCollins, 1994), p. 139. Their source, in turn, was L. M. Boyd, *San Francisco Chronicle,* October 27, 1984, p. 35.

FIGURE 15.5
The growth of business R&D expenditures in the United States, 1995–2019.

Inflation-adjusted R&D expenditures by firms are substantial and growing, suggesting that R&D continues to be profitable for firms, even in the face of possible imitation. All figures are in constant, inflation-adjusted, 2012, U.S. dollars.

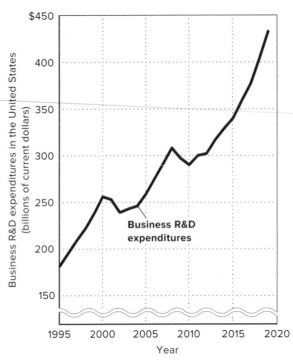

Source: National Science Foundation.

software giant Microsoft bought out social networking pioneer LinkedIn and the dominant firm in ride-sharing, Uber, bought out home-delivery pioneer Postmates. Such buyouts are legal under current antitrust laws as long as they do not substantially lessen competition in the affected industry.

In short, despite the imitation problem, significant protections and advantages enable most innovating firms to profit from their R&D efforts, as implied by the continuing high levels of R&D spending by firms year after year. As Figure 15.5 shows, business R&D spending in the United States not only remains substantial but has grown over the past quarter-century. These high levels of spending simply would not continue if imitation consistently and severely depressed rates of return on R&D expenditures.

QUICK REVIEW

15.2

▶ A firm's optimal R&D expenditure is the amount at which the expected rate of return (marginal benefit) from the R&D expenditure just equals the interest-rate cost of borrowing (marginal cost) required to finance it.

▶ Product innovation can entice consumers to substitute a new product for existing products to increase their total utility, thereby increasing the innovating firm's revenue and profit.

▶ Process innovation can lower a firm's production costs and increase its profit by increasing total product and decreasing average total cost.

▶ A firm faces reduced profitability from R&D if competitors can successfully imitate its new product or process. Nevertheless, there are significant potential protections and benefits to being first, including patents, copyrights, and trademarks; brand-name recognition; trade secrets; cost reductions from learning by doing; and major time lags between innovation and imitation.

Role of Market Structure

>> **LO15.6** Discuss the role of market structure in promoting technological advance.

Is some particular market structure or firm size best suited to technological progress? For example, is a highly competitive industry consisting of thousands of relatively small firms likely to produce more technological progress than a monopoly? Or is perhaps an intermediate market structure like oligopoly or monopolistic competition more likely to produce rapid technological progress?

Inverted-U Theory of R&D

inverted-U theory The idea that, other things equal, *R&D* expenditures as a percentage of sales rise with *industry* concentration, reach a peak at a *four-firm concentration ratio* of about 50 percent, and then fall as the ratio further increases.

Some experts on technological progress have postulated the **inverted-U theory** of R&D, which deals with the relationship between market structure and technological advance. This theory is illustrated in Figure 15.6, which relates R&D spending as a percentage of a firm's sales (vertical axis) to the industry's *four-firm concentration ratio* (horizontal axis) that we introduced in Chapter 12. The inverted-U shape of the curve suggests that R&D effort is at best weak in very-low-concentration industries (pure competition) and very-high-concentration industries (pure monopoly). Starting from the lowest concentrations, R&D spending as a percentage of sales rises with concentration until a concentration ratio of 50 percent or so is reached, meaning that the four largest firms account for about one-half the total industry output. Beyond that, relative R&D spending decreases as concentration rises.

The logic of the inverted-U theory follows from a basic understanding of the different market structures. Firms in industries with very low concentration ratios are mainly competitive firms. They are small, and their size makes it difficult for them to finance R&D. Moreover, entry to these industries is easy, making it difficult to sustain economic profit from innovations that are not supported by patents. As a result, firms in these industries spend little on R&D

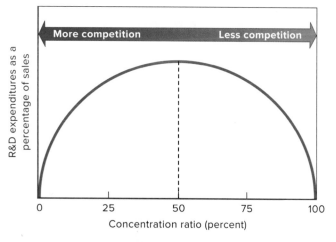

FIGURE 15.6
The inverted-U theory of R&D expenditures.

The inverted-U theory suggests that R&D expenditures as a percentage of sales rise with industry concentration until the four-firm concentration ratio reaches about 50 percent. Further increases in industry concentration are associated with lower relative R&D expenditures.

relative to their sales. At the other end (far right) of the curve, where concentration is exceptionally high, monopoly profit is already high, and innovation will not add much more profit. Furthermore, innovation typically requires costly retooling of very large factories, which will cut into whatever additional profit is realized. As a result, the expected rate of return from R&D is quite low in monopoly, as are expenditures for R&D relative to sales. Finally, the lack of rivals makes the monopolist quite complacent about R&D.

The optimal industry structure for R&D is one in which expected returns on R&D spending are high and funds to finance it are readily available and inexpensive. Those factors seem to occur in industries where a few firms are absolutely and relatively large but where the concentration ratio is not so high as to prohibit vigorous competition by smaller rivals. Rivalry among the larger oligopolistic firms and competition between the larger and the smaller firms then provide a strong incentive for R&D. The inverted-U theory of R&D, as represented by Figure 15.6, also points toward this "loose" oligopoly as the optimal structure for R&D spending.

Market Structure and Technological Advance: The Evidence

Various industry studies and cross-industry studies collectively support the inverted-U theory of R&D. Other things equal, the optimal market structure for technological advance seems to be an industry in which there is a mix of large oligopolistic firms (a 40 to 60 percent four-firm concentration ratio), with several highly innovative smaller firms.

But our "other-things-equal" qualification is important here. Whether or not a particular industry is highly technical may well be a more important determinant of R&D than its structure. While some concentrated industries (electronics, aircraft, and petroleum) devote large quantities of resources to R&D and are very innovative, others (cigarettes, aluminum, gypsum products) are not. The level of R&D spending within an industry seems to depend as much on its technical character and "technological opportunities" as on its market structure. There simply may be more opportunities to innovate in the computer and pharmaceutical industries, for example, than in the brick-making and coal-mining industries.

Conclusion: The inverted-U curve shown in Figure 15.6 is a useful depiction of the general relationship between R&D spending and market structure, other things equal.

Technological Advance and Efficiency

Technological advance contributes significantly to economic efficiency. New and better processes and products enable society to produce more output, as well as a higher-valued mix of output.

>> **LO15.7** Show how technological advance enhances productive and allocative efficiency.

Productive Efficiency

Technological advance as embodied in process innovation improves *productive efficiency* by increasing the productivity of inputs and by reducing average total costs. In other words, it enables society to produce the same amount of a particular good or service while using fewer resources, thereby freeing the unused resources to produce other goods and services. If society desires more of the now less expensive good, process innovation enables it to have that greater

Patent Medicine

Pharmaceutical Companies Have Gamed the Patent System to Extend their Monopoly Profits Well Past the Normal 20-Year Expiration Date.

The United States of America became the first country to establish a patent system when, in 1787, the Delegates to the Constitutional Convention in Philadelphia gave Congress the legal right "To promote the progress of science and the useful arts, by securing for limited times to authors and inventors the exclusive right to their respective writings and discoveries."

The oldest delegate at the Convention was 81-year-old Benjamin Franklin, known around the world for his many inventions and scientific discoveries, including bifocals, swim fins, the odometer, mapping the Gulf Stream, proving that lightning was electricity, and explaining that electricity flows from positive to negative.

Franklin led the charge, so to speak, on giving Congress the legal right to establish a patent system. But he also made sure that the system would only give inventors a *temporary* right to benefit financially from their creations.

On the one hand, a patent system should provide inventors with a monopoly over products derived from their inventions so that inventors will have a strong financial incentive to bear the research and development (R&D) costs necessary to come up with innovative solutions to old problems.

On the other hand, the monopolies created by patents should be temporary, rather than permanent, because indefinite patent protection would almost certainly create monopoly businesses that would be too strong for subsequent new inventions to compete against.

Congress eventually decided to make patents last for 20 years, so that inventors would have 20 years of monopoly protection to benefit financially from their inventions. After that, their inventions would become part of the public domain, meaning that anyone would be free to make use of their inventions for any legal purpose, including to produce copycat products that would compete against the original monopoly products created during the 20 years of patent protection.

This system worked very well with respect to the development of innovative new medicines until quite recently. Major drug companies were willing to spend over $1 billion per drug to bring new drugs to market, anticipating that with 20 years of patent protection, they would have plenty of time to try to make back their investments.

It was true, of course, that not every patented drug would be a hit with consumers and doctors, but drug companies could expect enough of their newly patented drugs to be financially successful so as to make it worth their while to stay in the drug-development business and spend the funds necessary to invent and patent a continual stream of new medicines whose monopoly protections would generate new revenue streams after the 20-year monopolies on older drugs ran out.

Over the past two decades, however, it has become routine practice for drug companies to game the patent system so as to effectively extend the monopoly over a patented drug beyond the 20-year mark. To show you how the process works, let's discuss a fictional drug

lenetstan/Shutterstock

called Expensivir that has been very successful financially for its patent holder, SketchoMeds.

About five years before Sketcho's patent on Expensivir is set to expire, Sketcho will begin patenting everything from how Expensivir is manufactured to what kind of capsule or syringe is used to deliver the drug. By doing so, Sketcho will guarantee that even after the original patent on Expensivir's chemical formula expires, Sketcho will still be the only company legally allowed to sell Expensivir because any other firm that would like to produce and sell the same chemical would end up violating one or more of the more recently obtained patents.

By building this sort of "legal fortress" around Expensivir, SketchoMeds will be able to extend the effective life of its monopoly over the manufacture and sale of Expensivir well past the 20-year limit intended by Congress.

The result is something that Ben Franklin would never have condoned—overlapping patents that effectively grant permanent monopolies to companies that should be inventing new products rather than continuing to get paid for old inventions. This state of affairs actually impedes the *creative destruction* that is believed by most economists to be essential for innovation and invention and reduces the ability of a market economy to raise living standards and improve the quality of life.

As if to confirm those fears, the same drug companies that pioneered the creation of legal fortresses around drugs whose patents were set to expire also began to rapidly ratchet up the prices of those drugs, sometimes by several hundred percent in a single year. Sadly, there was little evidence that any of that massive increase in revenue went into R&D. Consistent with the *inverted-U theory of R&D*, these nearly impervious monopolists invested very little of their monopoly revenue into new research and development.

quantity without sacrificing other goods. Viewed either way, process innovation enhances productive efficiency: It reduces society's per-unit cost of whatever mix of goods and services it chooses. It is thus an important means of shifting an economy's production possibilities curve rightward.

Allocative Efficiency

Technological advance as embodied in *product* (or service) innovation enhances allocative efficiency by giving society a more preferred mix of goods and services. Recall that consumers buy a new product rather than an old product only when buying the new one increases the total utility obtained from their limited incomes. Obviously, then, a popular new product—and the new mix of products it implies—creates a higher level of total utility for society.

In terms of markets, the demand for the new product rises, and the demand for the old product declines. The high economic profit engendered by the new product attracts resources away from less valued uses and to the production of the new product. In theory, such shifting of resources continues until the price of the new product equals its marginal cost.

There is a caveat here, however. Innovation (either product or process) can create monopoly power through patents or first-mover advantages. When new monopoly power results from an innovation, society may lose part of the improved efficiency it otherwise would have gained from that innovation. Why? The profit-maximizing monopolist restricts output to keep its product price above marginal cost. For example, Microsoft's innovative Windows product has resulted in dominance in the market for operating systems for personal computers. Microsoft's substantial monopoly power permits it to charge prices that are well above both marginal cost and minimum average total cost.

▶ Evidence generally supports the inverted-U theory of R&D, which holds that a firm's R&D spending as a percentage of its sales rises with its industry four-firm concentration ratio, reaches a peak at a 50 percent concentration ratio, and then declines as concentration increases further.

▶ Technological advance generally enhances both productive and allocative efficiency, but patents and the advantages of being first with an innovation may increase monopoly power in some situations.

QUICK REVIEW

15.3

Summary

LO15.1 Differentiate among invention, innovation, and technological diffusion.

Technological advance is evidenced by new and improved goods, services, and production or distribution processes. In economic models, technological advance occurs only in the *very long run*.

Invention is the discovery of a product or process through the use of imagination, ingenuity, and experimentation. Innovation is the first successful commercial introduction of a new product, the first use of a new method, or the creation of a new form of business enterprise. Diffusion is the spread of an earlier innovation among competing firms. Firms channel a majority of their R&D expenditures to innovation and imitation, rather than basic scientific research or invention.

Historically, most economists viewed technological advance as a random, external force to which the economy adjusted. Most contemporary economists see technological advance as occurring in response to profit incentives within the economy and thus as an integral part of capitalism.

LO15.2 Explain how entrepreneurs and other innovators further technological advance.

Entrepreneurs and other innovators try to anticipate the future. They play a central role in technological advance by initiating changes in

products and processes. Entrepreneurs often form startup firms that focus on creating and introducing new products. Sometimes, innovators work in the R&D labs of major corporations. Entrepreneurs and innovative firms often rely heavily on the basic research done by university and government scientists.

LO15.3 Summarize how a firm determines its optimal amount of research and development (R&D).

A firm's optimal amount of R&D spending occurs where its expected return (marginal benefit) from R&D equals its interest-rate cost of funds (marginal cost) to finance R&D. Entrepreneurs and firms use several sources to finance R&D, including (*a*) bank loans, (*b*) bonds, (*c*) venture capital (funds given in return for a share of the profits if the business succeeds), (*d*) undistributed corporate profits (retained earnings), and (*e*) personal savings.

LO15.4 Discuss how technological change can increase profits by raising revenues or lowering costs.

Process innovation can lower a firm's production costs by improving its internal production techniques. Such improvement increases the firm's total output from any given set of inputs, thereby lowering its average total cost and increasing its profit. The added profit provides a positive rate of return on the R&D spending that produced the process innovation.

LO15.5 Explain why firms benefit from their innovation even though rivals have an incentive to imitate it.

Product innovation succeeds when it provides consumers with a higher marginal utility per dollar spent than do existing products. The new product enables consumers to obtain greater total utility from a given income. From the firm's perspective, product innovation increases net revenue sufficiently to yield a positive rate of return on the R&D spending that produced the innovation.

Imitation poses a potential problem for innovators because it threatens their returns on R&D expenditures. Some dominant firms use a fast-second strategy, letting smaller firms initiate new products and then quickly imitating the successes. Nevertheless, there are significant legal protections and potential benefits for firms that take the lead with R&D and innovation, including (*a*) patent protection, (*b*) copyrights and trademarks, (*c*) lasting brand-name recognition, (*d*) benefits from trade secrets and learning by doing, (*e*) high

economic profits during the time lag between a product's introduction and its imitation, and (*f*) the possibility of lucrative buyout offers from larger firms.

LO15.6 Discuss the role of market structure in promoting technological advance.

The inverted-U theory of R&D holds that a firm's R&D spending as a percentage of its sales rises with its industry four-firm concentration ratio, reaches a peak at about a 50 percent concentration ratio, and then declines as concentration increases further. Empirical evidence is not clear-cut but lends general support to this theory. For any specific industry, however, the available technological opportunities may count more than market structure in determining R&D spending and innovation.

LO15.7 Show how technological advance enhances productive and allocative efficiency.

In general, technological advance enhances both productive and allocative efficiency. But in some situations, patents and the advantages of being first with an innovation can increase monopoly power.

Terms and Concepts

technological advance	process innovation	optimal amount of R&D
very long run	diffusion	imitation problem
invention	startups	fast-second strategy
patent	venture capital	inverted-U theory of R&D
innovation	interest-rate cost-of-funds curve	
product innovation	expected-rate-of-return curve	

Discussion Questions

McGraw Hill connect

1. What is technological advance, broadly defined? How does technological advance enter into the definition of the *very long run*? Which of the following are examples of technological advance, and which are not: an improved production process; entry of a firm into a profitable purely competitive industry; the imitation of a new production process by another firm; an increase in a firm's advertising expenditures? **LO15.1**

2. Contrast the older and the modern views of technological advance as they relate to the economy. What is the role of entrepreneurs and other innovators in technological advance? How does research by universities and government affect innovators and technological advance? Why do you think some university researchers are becoming more like entrepreneurs and less like "pure scientists"? **LO15.2**

3. Consider the effect that corporate profit taxes have on investing. Look back at Figure 15.4. Suppose that the *r* line is the rate of return a firm earns before taxes. If corporate profit taxes are imposed, the firm's after-tax returns will be lower (and the higher the tax rate, the lower the after-tax returns). If the firm's decisions about R&D spending are based on comparing after-tax returns with the interest-rate cost of funds, how will increased taxes on corporate profits affect R&D spending? How, if at all, does this effect modify your views on corporate profit taxes? Discuss. **LO15.3**

4. Answer the following lettered questions on the basis of the information in this table: **LO15.3**

Amount of R&D, $ Millions	Expected Rate of Return on R&D, %
$10	16
20	14
30	12
40	10
50	8
60	6

   a. If the interest-rate cost of funds is 8 percent, what is this firm's optimal amount of R&D spending?
   b. Explain why $20 million of R&D spending is not optimal.
   c. Why isn't $60 million optimal either?

5. Explain: "The success of a new product depends not only on its marginal utility but also on its price." **LO15.4**

6. Learning how to use software takes time. So, after customers have learned to use a particular software package, it is easier to sell them software upgrades than to convince them to switch to new software. What implications does this conclusion have for

expected rates of return on R&D spending for software firms developing upgrades versus firms developing imitative products? **LO15.5**

7. Why might a firm making a large economic profit from its existing product employ a fast-second strategy? What risks does it run in pursuing this strategy? What incentives does a firm have to engage in R&D when rivals can imitate its new product? **LO15.5**

8. Do you think the overall level of R&D would increase or decrease over the next 20 to 30 years if the lengths of new patents were extended from 20 years to, say, "forever"? What would happen if the duration were reduced from 20 years to, say, 3 years? **LO15.5**

9. Make a case that neither pure competition nor pure monopoly is conducive to a great deal of R&D spending and innovation.

Why might oligopoly be more favorable to R&D spending and innovation than either pure competition or pure monopoly? What is the inverted-U theory of R&D, and how does it relate to your answers to these questions? **LO15.6**

10. **LAST WORD** What balance of incentives was Congress attempting to get right when it chose 20 years as the length of time that a patent would last? How have drug companies managed to extend the monopoly on selling a particular drug past the 20-year duration of the patent on that drug? If drug companies can maintain highly lucrative monopolies on existing drugs indefinitely, do they have much of an incentive to invest in R&D to invent new drugs that might not even sell well?

Review Questions

1. Listed below are several possible actions by firms. Write "INV" beside those that reflect invention, "INN" beside those that reflect innovation, and "DIF" beside those that reflect diffusion. **LO15.1**
   a. An auto manufacturer adds full self-driving as a standard feature in its luxury cars to keep pace with a rival firm whose luxury cars already have this feature.
   b. A video game production company pioneers the first fully immersive 3D metaverse music video channel.
   c. A firm develops and patents a working model of a self-erasing whiteboard for classrooms.
   d. A light-bulb firm is the first to produce and market super-efficient laser-based lighting.
   e. A rival toymaker introduces a new Stacie doll to compete with Mattel's Barbie doll.

2. A firm is considering three possible one-year investments, which we will name X, Y, and Z.
   • Investment X will cost $10 million now and return $11 million next year, for a net gain of $1 million.
   • Investment Y will cost $100 million now and return $105 million next year, for a net gain of $5 million.
   • Investment Z will cost $1 million now and return $1.2 million next year, for a net gain of $200,000.
   The firm currently has $150 million of cash on hand that it can loan out at 15 percent interest. Which of the three possible investments should it undertake? **LO15.3**
   a. X only
   b. Y only
   c. Z only
   d. X and Y

   e. X and Z
   f. X, Y, and Z

3. An additional unit of Old Product X will bring Cindy an MU of 15 utils, an additional unit of New Product Y will bring Cindy an MU of 30 utils, and an additional unit of New Product Z will bring Cindy an MU of 40 utils. If a unit of Old Product X costs $10, a unit of New Product Y costs $30, and a unit of New Product Z costs $20, which product will Cindy prefer to spend her money on? **LO15.4**
   a. Old Product X
   b. New Product Y
   c. New Product Z
   d. More information is required.

4. The inverted-U theory suggests that R&D expenditures as a percentage of sales _____ with industry concentration after the four-firm concentration ratio exceeds about 50 percent. **LO15.6**
   a. rise
   b. fall
   c. fluctuate
   d. flat-line

5. Which statement about market structure and innovation is true? **LO15.7**
   a. Innovation helps only dominant firms.
   b. Innovation keeps new firms from ever catching up with leading firms.
   c. Innovation often leads to productive and allocative efficiency.
   d. Innovation always leads to entrenched monopoly power.

Problems

1. Suppose a firm expects that a $20 million expenditure on R&D in the current year will result in a new product that can be sold next year. Selling that product next year will increase the firm's revenue next year by $30 million and its costs next year by $29 million. **LO15.3**
   a. What is the expected rate of return on this R&D expenditure?

   b. Suppose the firm can get a bank loan at 6 percent interest to finance its $20 million R&D project. Will the firm undertake the project?
   c. Now suppose the interest-rate cost of borrowing falls to 4 percent because the firm decides to use its retained earnings to finance the R&D. Will this lower interest rate change the firm's R&D decision?

d. Now suppose that the firm has savings of $20 million—enough money to fund the R&D expenditure without borrowing. If the firm has the chance to invest this money either in the R&D project or in government bonds that pay 3.5 percent per year, which option should it choose?

e. What option should the company choose if the government bonds pay 6.5 percent per year rather than 3.5 percent per year?

2. **ADVANCED ANALYSIS** A firm faces the following costs: total cost of capital = $1,000; price paid for labor = $12 per labor unit; and price paid for raw materials = $4 per raw-material unit. **LO15.4**

   a. Suppose the firm can produce 5,000 units of output this year by combining its fixed capital with 100 units of labor and 450 units of raw materials. What are the total cost and average total cost of producing the 5,000 units of output?

   b. Now assume the firm improves its production process so that it can produce 6,000 units of output this year by combining its fixed capital with 100 units of labor and 450 units of raw materials. What are the total cost and average total cost of producing the 6,000 units of output?

   c. If units of output can always be sold for $1 each, then by how much does the firm's profit increase after it improves its production process?

   d. Suppose that implementing the improved production process would require a one-time-only cost of $1,100. If the firm considers only this year's profit, would the firm implement the improved production process? What if the firm considers its profit not just this year but in future years as well?

Roschetzky Photography/Shutterstock

The Demand for Resources

>> **LEARNING OBJECTIVES**

LO16.1 Explain the significance of resource pricing.

LO16.2 Relate the marginal revenue productivity of a resource to a firm's demand for that resource.

LO16.3 List the factors that increase or decrease resource demand.

LO16.4 Discuss the determinants of elasticity of resource demand.

LO16.5 Determine how a competitive firm selects its optimal combination of resources.

LO16.6 Explain the marginal productivity theory of income distribution.

When you finish your education, you will probably look for a new job. But why would someone want to hire you? The answer, of course, is that you have a lot to offer! Employers have a strong demand for educated, productive workers like you.

We need to learn more about the demand for labor and other resources. So we now turn from the pricing and production of *goods and services* to the pricing and employment of *resources*. Although firms come in various sizes and operate under substantially different market conditions, each has a demand for productive resources. Firms obtain needed resources from households—the direct or indirect owners of land, labor, capital, and entrepreneurial resources. So, in terms of the circular flow model (Figure 2.2), we shift our attention from the bottom loop of the diagram (where businesses supply products that households demand) to the top loop (where businesses demand resources that households supply).

This chapter looks at the *demand* for economic resources. Although the discussion is couched in terms of labor, the principles developed also apply to land, capital, and entrepreneurial ability. In Chapter 17, we will combine resource (labor) demand with labor supply to analyze wage rates. In Chapter 18, we will use resource demand and resource supply to examine the prices of, and returns to, other productive resources. Issues relating to the use of natural resources are the subject of Chapter 19.

Significance of Resource Pricing

Studying resource pricing is important for several reasons:

- *Money-income determination* Resource prices are a major factor in determining households' incomes. Firms' expenditures to acquire economic resources flow as wage, rent, interest, and profit incomes to the households that supply those resources.

>> **LO16.1** Explain the significance of resource pricing.

- *Cost minimization* To the firm, resource prices are costs. And to obtain the greatest profit, the firm must produce the profit-maximizing output with the most efficient (least costly) combination of resources. Resource prices play the main role in determining the quantities of land, labor, capital, and entrepreneurial ability that firms will combine in producing each good or service (see Table 2.1).

- *Resource allocation* Just as product prices allocate finished goods and services to consumers, resource prices allocate resources among industries and firms. In a dynamic economy, where technology and product demand often change, the efficient allocation of resources over time calls for the continuing shift of resources from one use to another. Resource pricing is a major factor in those shifts.

- *Policy issues* Many policy issues surround the resource market. Examples: To what extent should government redistribute income through taxes and transfers? Should government increase the legal minimum wage? Should government encourage or restrict labor unions? The facts and debates relating to these policy questions are grounded in resource pricing.

Marginal Productivity Theory of Resource Demand

>> **LO16.2** Relate the marginal revenue productivity of a resource to a firm's demand for that resource.

In discussing resource demand, we assume that a firm sells its output in a purely competitive product market and hires a certain resource in a purely competitive resource market. In a competitive *product market*, the firm is a "price taker" and can sell as little or as much output as it chooses at the market price. Because the firm is selling such a negligible fraction of total output, its output decisions exert no influence on product price. Similarly, the firm is a "price taker" (or "wage taker") in the competitive *resource market*. It purchases such a negligible fraction of the total supply of the resource that its buying (or hiring) decisions do not influence the resource price.

Resource Demand as a Derived Demand

derived demand The demand for a resource that depends on the demand for the products it helps to produce.

Resource demand is the starting point for any discussion of resource prices. Resource demand is a schedule or a curve showing the amounts of a resource that buyers are willing and able to purchase at various prices over some period of time. Resource demand is a **derived demand**, which means that the demand for a resource is derived from the demand for the products that the resource helps to produce. This is true because resources usually do not directly satisfy customer wants. Rather, they do so indirectly through their use in producing goods and services. Almost nobody wants to consume an acre of land, a John Deere tractor, or a farmer's labor services, but millions of households do want to consume the food that these resources help produce. Similarly, the demand for airplanes generates a demand for assemblers, and the demands for such services as income-tax preparation, haircuts, and child care create derived demands for accountants, barbers, and child care workers.

Marginal Revenue Product

Because resource demand is derived from product demand, the strength of the demand for any resource will depend on two factors:

- The resource's productivity in helping to create a good or service.
- The market value or price of the good or service it helps to produce.

marginal product (MP) The additional output produced when 1 additional unit of a resource is employed (the quantity of all other resources employed remaining constant); equal to the change in *total product* divided by the change in the quantity of a resource employed.

Other things equal, a resource that is highly productive in turning out a highly valued commodity will be in great demand. A relatively unproductive resource that is capable of producing only a minimally valued commodity will be in little demand. And no demand whatsoever will exist for a resource that is phenomenally efficient in producing something that no one wants to buy.

Productivity Table 16.1 shows the roles of resource productivity and product price in determining resource demand. Here we assume that a firm adds a single variable resource, labor, to its fixed plant. Columns 1 and 2 give the number of units of the resource applied to production and the resulting total product (output). Column 3 provides the **marginal product (MP),** or additional output, resulting from using each additional unit of labor. Columns 1 through 3 remind us that the law of diminishing returns applies here, causing the marginal product of labor to fall beyond some

TABLE 16.1 The Demand for Labor: Pure Competition in the Sale of the Product

(1) Units of Resource	(2) Total Product (Output)	(3) Marginal Product (MP)	(4) Product Price	(5) Total Revenue, (2) × (4)	(6) Marginal Revenue Product (MRP) (4) − (2)
0	0		$2	$ 0	
		7			$14
1	7		2	14	
		6			12
2	13		2	26	
		5			10
3	18		2	36	
		4			8
4	22		2	44	
		3			6
5	25		2	50	
		2			4
6	27		2	54	
		1			2
7	28		2	56	

point. For simplicity, we assume that these diminishing marginal returns—these declines in marginal product—begin with the first worker hired.

Product Price The derived demand for a resource depends also on the price of the product it produces. Column 4 in Table 16.1 adds this price information. Product price is constant, in this case at $2, because the product market is competitive. The firm is a price taker and cannot therefore sell at any price higher than $2 per unit.

Multiplying column 2 by column 4 provides the total-revenue data of column 5. From these total-revenue data we can compute **marginal revenue product (MRP)**—the change in total revenue resulting from the use of each additional unit of a resource (labor, in this case). In equation form,

$$\text{Marginal revenue product} = \frac{\text{Change in total revenue}}{\text{Unit change in resource quantity}}$$

The MRPs are listed in column 6 in Table 16.1.

Rule for Employing Resources: MRP = MRC

The MRP schedule, shown as columns 1 and 6 in Table 16.1, is the firm's demand schedule for labor. To understand why, you must first know the rule that guides a profit-seeking firm in hiring any resource: *To maximize profit, a firm should hire additional units of a specific resource as long as each successive unit adds more to the firm's total revenue than it adds to the firm's total cost.*

Economists use special terms to designate what each additional unit of labor (or other variable resource) adds to total cost and what it adds to total revenue. We have seen that MRP measures how much each successive unit of a resource adds to total revenue. The amount that each additional unit of a resource adds to the firm's total (resource) cost is called its **marginal resource cost (MRC).** In equation form,

$$\text{Marginal resource cost} = \frac{\text{change in total (resource) cost}}{\text{unit change in resource quantity}}$$

So we can restate our rule for hiring resources as follows: *It will be profitable for a firm to hire additional units of a resource up to the point at which that resource's MRP is equal to its MRC.* For example, as the rule applies to labor, if the number of workers a firm is currently hiring is such that the last worker's MRP exceeds their MRC, the firm can profit by hiring more workers. But if the number being hired is such that the last worker's MRC exceeds his or her MRP, the firm is hiring workers who are not "paying their way," and it can increase its profit by discharging some workers. You may recognize that this **MRP = MRC rule** is similar to the MR = MC profit-maximizing rule employed in our discussion of price and output determination. The rationale of the two rules is the same, but the point of reference is now *inputs* of a resource, not *outputs* of a product.

MRP as Resource Demand Schedule

Let's continue to focus on labor, knowing that the analysis also applies to other resources. In a purely competitive labor market, market supply and market demand establish the wage rate.

marginal revenue product (MRP) The change in a firm's *total revenue* when it employs 1 additional unit of a *resource* (the quantity of all other resources employed remaining constant); equal to the change in *total revenue* divided by the change in the quantity of the resource employed.

marginal resource cost (MRC) The amount by which the total cost of employing a *resource* increases when a *firm* employs 1 additional unit of the resource (the quantity of all other resources employed remaining constant); equal to the change in the *total cost* of the resource divided by the change in the quantity of the resource employed.

MRP = MRC rule The principle that to maximize profit (or minimize losses), a *firm* should employ the quantity of a resource at which its *marginal revenue product* (MRP) is equal to its *marginal resource cost* (MRC), the latter being the wage rate in a purely competitive labor market.

FIGURE 16.1
The purely competitive seller's demand for a resource.

The MRP curve is the resource demand curve; each of its points relates a particular resource price (= MRP when profit is maximized) with a corresponding quantity of the resource demanded. Under pure competition, product price is constant; therefore, the downward slope of the $D = MRP$ curve is due solely to the decline in the resource's marginal product (law of diminishing marginal returns).

Because each firm hires such a small fraction of market supply, it cannot influence the market wage rate; it is a wage taker, not a wagemaker. Thus, for each additional unit of labor hired, each firm's total resource cost increases by exactly the amount of the constant market wage rate. More specifically, the MRC of labor exactly equals the market wage rate. Thus, resource "price" (the market wage rate) equals resource "cost" (marginal resource cost) for a firm that hires a resource in a competitive labor market. As a result, the MRP = MRC rule tells us that, in pure competition, the firm will hire workers up to the point at which the market *wage rate* (its MRC) equals its MRP.

In terms of the data in columns 1 and 6 of Table 16.1, if the market wage rate is, say, $13.95, the firm will hire only one worker; only the first worker results in an increase in profits. To see why, note that for the first worker, MRP (= $14) exceeds MRC (= $13.95). Thus, hiring the first worker is profitable. For each successive worker, however, MRC (= $13.95) exceeds MRP (= $12 or less), indicating that it will not be profitable to hire any of those workers. If the wage rate is $11.95, by the same reasoning we discover that the firm will hire both the first and second workers. Similarly, if the wage rate is $9.95, three workers will be hired. And so forth. Here is the key generalization: The MRP schedule constitutes the firm's demand for labor because each point on this schedule (or curve) indicates the number of workers the firm would hire at each possible wage rate.

In Figure 16.1, we show the $D = MRP$ curve based on the data in Table 16.1.[1] The competitive firm's resource demand curve identifies an inverse relationship between the wage rate and the quantity of labor demanded, other things equal. The curve slopes downward because of diminishing marginal returns.

Resource Demand under Imperfect Product Market Competition

Resource demand (here, labor demand) is more complex when the firm is selling its product in an imperfectly competitive market, one in which the firm is a pricemaker. That is because imperfect competitors (pure monopolists, oligopolists, and monopolistic competitors) face downsloping product demand curves. As a result, whenever an imperfect competitor's product demand curve is fixed in place, the only way to increase sales is by setting a lower price (and thereby moving down along the fixed demand curve).

The productivity data in Table 16.1 are retained in columns 1 to 3 in Table 16.2. But here in Table 16.2 we show in column 4 that product price must be lowered to sell the marginal product of each successive worker. The MRP of the purely competitive seller of Table 16.1 falls for only one reason: Marginal product diminishes. But the MRP of the imperfectly competitive seller of Table 16.2 falls for two reasons: Marginal product diminishes *and* product price falls as output increases.

We emphasize that the lower price accompanying each increase in output (total product) applies not only to the marginal product of each successive worker but also to all prior output units that otherwise could have been sold at a higher price. Observe that the marginal product of the second worker is 6 units of output. These 6 units can be sold for $2.40 each, or, as a group, for $14.40. But $14.40 is not the MRP of the second worker. To sell these 6 units, the firm must take a 20-cent price cut on the 7 units produced by the first worker—units that otherwise could have been sold for $2.60 each. Thus, the MRP of the second worker is only $13[= $14.40 − (7 × 20 cents)], as shown.

---

[1]Note that we plot the points in Figure 16.1 halfway between succeeding numbers of resource units because MRP is associated with the addition of 1 more unit. Thus in Figure 16.1, for example, we plot the MRP of the second unit ($12) not at 1 or 2 but at 1.5 (which is halfway between 1 and 2). This "smoothing" enables us to sketch a continuously downsloping curve rather than one that moves downward in discrete steps (like a staircase) as each new unit of labor is hired.

TABLE 16.2 The Demand for Labor: Imperfect Competition in the Sale of the Product

(1) Units of Resource	(2) Total Product (Output)	(3) Marginal Product (MP)	(4) Product Price	(5) Total Revenue, (2) × (4)	(6) Marginal Revenue Product (MRP)
0	0		$2.80	$ 0	
		7			$18.20
1	7		2.60	18.20	
		6			13.00
2	13		2.40	31.20	
		5			8.40
3	18		2.20	39.60	
		4			4.40
4	22		2.00	44.00	
		3			2.25
5	25		1.85	46.25	
		2			1.00
6	27		1.75	47.25	
		1			−1.05
7	28		1.65	46.20	

Similarly, the third worker adds 5 units to total product, and these units are worth $2.20 each, or $11 total. But to sell these 5 units, the firm must take a 20-cent price cut on the 13 units produced by the first two workers. So the third worker's MRP is only $8.40[= $11 − (13 × 20 cents)]. The numbers in column 6 reflect such calculations.

In Figure 16.2 we graph the MRP data from Table 16.2 and label it "D = MRP (imperfect competition)." The broken-line resource demand curve, in contrast, is that of the purely competitive seller represented in Figure 16.1. A comparison of the two curves demonstrates that, other things equal, the resource demand curve of an imperfectly competitive seller is less elastic than that of a purely competitive seller. Consider the effects of an identical percentage decline in the wage rate (resource price) from $11 to $6 in Figure 16.2. Comparison of the two curves reveals that the imperfectly competitive seller (solid curve) does not expand the quantity of labor it employs by as large a percentage as does the purely competitive seller (broken curve).

It is not surprising that the imperfectly competitive producer is less responsive to resource price cuts than the purely competitive producer. When resource prices fall, MC per unit declines for both imperfectly competitive firms as well as purely competitive firms. Because both types of firms maximize profits by producing where MR = MC, the decline in MC will cause both types of firms to produce more. But the effect will be muted for imperfectly competitive firms because their downsloping demand curves cause them to also face downsloping MR curves—so that for each additional unit sold, MR declines. By contrast, MR is constant (and equal to the market equilibrium price P) for competitive firms, so that they do not have to worry about MR per unit falling as they produce more units. As a result, competitive firms increase production by a larger amount than imperfectly competitive firms whenever resource prices fall.

Market Demand for a Resource

The total, or market, demand curve for a specific resource shows the various total amounts of the resource that firms will purchase or hire at various resource prices, other things equal. Recall that the total, or market, demand curve for a *product* is found by summing horizontally the demand curves of all individual buyers in the market. The market demand curve for a particular *resource* is derived in essentially the same way—by summing horizontally the individual demand or MRP curves for all firms hiring that resource.

FIGURE 16.2
The imperfectly competitive seller's demand curve for a resource.

An imperfectly competitive seller's resource demand curve D (solid) slopes downward because both marginal product and product price fall as resource employment and output rise. This downward slope is greater than that for a purely competitive seller (dashed resource demand curve) because the pure competitor can sell the added output at a constant price.

GLOBAL PERSPECTIVE 16.1

TOP OIL IMPORTING AREAS, 2020

On average, 42.3 million barrels per day of oil were imported into various countries and areas during 2020. China's average daily importation of 11.2 million barrels thus constituted about 26 percent of all crude oil imports worldwide during 2020. European imports represented about 22 percent, U.S. imports about 14 percent, and Indian imports about 10 percent of overall world imports of crude oil that year.

Source: "Statistical Review of World Energy 2021," BP.

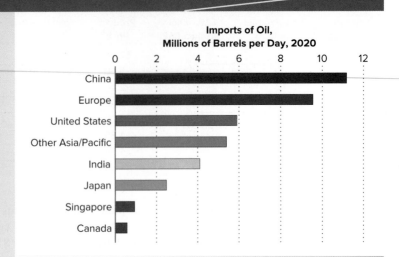

Imports of Oil, Millions of Barrels per Day, 2020

Global Perspective 16.1 shows the average volume of oil imported into selected countries and areas during 2020. These locations' respective demands for imported oil form part of the horizontally summed worldwide demand curve for oil that helps to determine the market price of oil.

QUICK REVIEW

16.1

▶ To maximize profit, a firm will purchase or hire a resource in an amount at which the resource's marginal revenue product equals its marginal resource cost (MRP = MRC).

▶ Application of the MRP = MRC rule to a firm's MRP curve demonstrates that the MRP curve is the firm's resource demand curve. In a purely competitive resource market, resource price (the wage rate) equals MRC.

▶ The resource demand curve of a purely competitive seller is downward sloping solely because the marginal product of the resource diminishes.

▶ The resource demand curve of an imperfectly competitive seller is downward sloping because marginal product diminishes *and* product price falls as output is increased.

▶ The market demand for a product is the horizontal sum of the demand curves of all the buyers in the market.

Determinants of Resource Demand

>> **LO16.3** List the factors that increase or decrease resource demand.

What will alter the demand for a resource? That is, what will shift the resource demand curve? The fact that resource demand is derived from *product demand* and depends on *resource productivity* suggests two resource demand shifters. Also, our analysis of how changes in the prices of other products can shift a product's demand curve (Chapter 3) suggests a third factor: changes in the *prices of other resources*.

Changes in Product Demand

Other things equal, an increase in the demand for a product will increase the demand for a resource used in its production, whereas a decrease in product demand will decrease the demand for that resource.

Let's see how this works. Recall that a change in the demand for a product will change its price. In Table 16.1, let's assume that an increase in product demand boosts product price from $2 to $3. You should calculate the new resource demand schedule (columns 1 and 6) that would result and plot it in Figure 16.1 to verify that the new resource demand curve lies to the right of the old demand curve. Similarly, a decline in the product demand (and price) will shift the resource demand curve to the left. This effect—resource demand changing along with product demand—demonstrates that resource demand is derived from product demand.

CONSIDER THIS . . .

Superstars

In what economist Robert Frank calls "winner-take-all markets," a few highly talented performers have huge earnings relative to the average performers in the market. Because consumers and firms seek out "top" performers, small differences in talent or popularity get magnified into huge differences in pay.

Erik Pendzich/Alamy Stock Photo

In these markets, consumer spending gets channeled toward a few performers. The media then "hypes" these individuals, which further increases the public's awareness of their talents. Many more consumers then buy the stars' products. Although it is not easy to stay on top, several superstars emerge.

The high earnings of superstars result from the high revenues they generate from their work. Consider Kylie Jenner. If she sold only a few thousand dollars of cosmetics each year and attracted only a few hundred followers on Instagram, the revenue she would produce—her marginal revenue product—would be quite modest. So, too, would be her earnings.

But she is in fact the most followed woman on Instagram and the owner of a fashion and cosmetics business that generates hundreds of millions of dollars per year in revenue. Her status as social media influencer is extraordinary and she sells millions of units of cosmetics per year. Her extraordinarily high net earnings derive, as a result, from her extraordinarily high MRP.

So it is for the other superstars in the "winner-take-all markets." Influenced by the media, but coerced by no one, consumers direct their spending toward a select few. The resulting strong demand for these stars' services reflects their high MRP. And because top talent (by definition) is very limited, superstars receive amazingly high earnings.

Example: Assuming no offsetting change in supply, a decrease in the demand for new houses will drive down house prices. Those lower prices will decrease the MRP of construction workers, and therefore the demand for construction workers will fall. The resource demand curve in Figure 16.1 will shift to the left.

The Consider This story discusses why superstars earn such high incomes. As you might expect, it has something to do with their MRPs.

Changes in Productivity

Other things equal, an increase in the productivity of a resource will increase the demand for the resource, and a decrease in productivity will reduce the demand for the resource. Thus, if we doubled the MP data of column 3 in Table 16.1, the MRP data of column 6 would also double, indicating a rightward shift of the resource demand curve.

The productivity of any resource may be altered over the long run in several ways:

- *Quantities of other resources* The marginal productivity of any resource will vary with the quantities of the other resources used with it. The greater the amount of capital and land resources used with, say, labor, the greater will be labor's marginal productivity and, thus, labor demand.

- *Technological advance* Technological improvements that increase the quality of other resources, such as capital, have the same effect on other resources. For example, the better the *quality* of capital, the greater the productivity of labor used with it. Dockworkers employed with a specific amount of real capital in the form of unloading cranes are more productive than dockworkers with the same amount of real capital embodied in older conveyor-belt systems.

- *Quality of the variable resource* Improvements in the quality of the variable resource, such as labor, will increase its marginal productivity and therefore its demand. In effect, there will be a new demand curve for a different, more skilled, kind of labor.

All these considerations help explain why the average level of (real) wages is higher in industrially advanced nations (for example, the United States, Germany, and Japan) than in developing nations (for example, Nicaragua, Ethiopia, and Cambodia). Workers in industrially advanced nations are generally healthier, better educated, and better trained than are workers in developing countries. Also, in most industries they work with a larger and more efficient stock of capital goods and more abundant natural resources. The resulting increased productivity creates a strong demand for labor. On the supply side of the market, labor is scarcer relative to capital in industrially advanced nations than in most developing nations. A strong demand and a relatively scarce supply of labor result in high wage rates in the industrially advanced nations.

Changes in the Prices of Other Resources

Changes in the prices of other resources may change the demand for a specific resource. For example, a change in the price of capital may change the demand for labor. The direction of the change in labor demand depends on whether labor and capital are substitutes or complements in production.

substitution effect (1) A change in the quantity demanded of a *consumer good* that results from a change in its relative expensiveness caused by a change in the good's own *price*. (2) The reduction in the *quantity demanded* of the second of a pair of *substitute resources* that occurs when the price of the first resource falls and causes *firms* that employ both resources to switch to using more of the first resource (whose price has fallen) and less of the second resource (whose price has remained the same).

output effect The possibility that when the *price* of the first of a pair of *substitute resources* falls, the *quantity demanded* of both resources will rise because the reduction in the price of the first resource so greatly reduces production costs that the volume of output created with the two resources increases by so much that the quantity demanded of the second resource increases even after accounting for the *substitution effect*. (See the second definition listed in the entry for *substitution effect*.)

Substitute Resources Suppose the technology in a certain production process is such that labor and capital are substitutable. A firm can produce some specific amount of output using a relatively small amount of labor and a relatively large amount of capital, or vice versa. Now assume that the price of machinery (capital) falls. The effect on the demand for labor will be the net result of two opposed effects: the substitution effect and the output effect.

- *Substitution effect* The decline in the price of machinery prompts the firm to substitute machinery for labor. This substitution allows the firm to produce its output at lower cost. So, at the fixed wage rate, smaller quantities of labor are now employed. This **substitution effect** decreases the demand for labor. More generally, the substitution effect indicates that a firm will purchase more of an input whose relative price has declined. Conversely, it will use less of an input whose relative price has increased.

- *Output effect* Because the price of machinery has fallen, the costs of producing various outputs must also decline. With lower costs, the firm finds it profitable to produce and sell a greater output. The greater output increases the demand for all resources, including labor. Thus, this **output effect** increases the demand for labor. More generally, the output effect means that the firm will purchase more of one particular input when the price of the other input falls. It will purchase less of that particular input when the price of the other input rises.

- *Net effect* The substitution and output effects are both present when the price of an input changes, but they work in opposite directions. For a decline in the price of capital, the substitution effect decreases the demand for labor, while the output effect increases it. The net change in labor demand depends on the relative sizes of the two effects: If the substitution effect outweighs the output effect, a decrease in the price of capital decreases the demand for labor. If the output effect exceeds the substitution effect, a decrease in the price of capital increases the demand for labor.

Complementary Resources Recall from Chapter 3 that certain products, such as computers and software, are complementary goods; they "go together" and are jointly demanded. Resources may also be complementary; an increase in the quantity of one resource used in the production process requires an increase in the amount used of the other resource, and vice versa. Suppose a small design firm does computer-assisted design (CAD) with a relatively expensive personal computer as its basic piece of capital equipment. Each computer requires exactly one design engineer to operate it; the machine is not automated—it will not run itself—and a second engineer would have nothing to do.

Now assume that a technological advance in the production of these computers substantially reduces their price. There can be no substitution effect because labor and capital must be used in *fixed proportions*, one person for one machine. Capital cannot be substituted for labor. But there is an output effect. Other things equal, the reduction in the price of capital goods means lower production costs. Producing a larger output will therefore be profitable. In producing more output, the firm will use both more capital and more labor. When labor and capital are complementary, a decline in the price of capital increases the demand for labor through the output effect.

Table 16.3 summarizes the effects of an *increase* in the price of capital on the demand for labor.

Now that we have discussed the determinants of labor demand, let's again review their effects. Stated in terms of the labor resource, the demand for labor will increase (the labor demand curve will shift rightward) when:

- The demand for (and therefore the price of) the product produced by that labor *increases*.

- The productivity (MP) of labor *increases*.

- The price of a substitute input *decreases,* provided the output effect exceeds the substitution effect.

- The price of a substitute input *increases,* provided the substitution effect exceeds the output effect.

- The price of a complementary input *decreases*.

Be sure that you can "reverse" these effects to explain a *decrease* in labor demand.

TABLE 16.3 The Effect of an Increase in the Price of Capital on the Demand for Labor, D_L

| (1) Relationship of Inputs | (2) Increase in the Price of Capital | | |
	(a) Substitution Effect	(b) Output Effect	(c) Combined Effect
Substitutes in production	Labor substituted for capital	Production costs up, output down, and less of both capital and labor used	D_L increases if the substitution effect exceeds the output effect; D_L decreases if the output effect exceeds the substitution effect
Complements in production	No substitution of labor for capital	Production costs up, output down, and less of both capital and labor used	D_L decreases (because only the output effect applies)

Table 16.4 provides several illustrations of the determinants of labor demand, listed by the categories we have discussed.

Occupational Employment Trends

Changes in labor demand affect wage rates and employment in specific occupations. Increases in labor demand for certain occupational groups result in increases in their employment; decreases in labor demand result in decreases in their employment. Let's first look at occupations for which labor demand is growing and then examine occupations for which it is declining.

The Fastest-Growing Occupations Table 16.5 lists the 10 fastest-growing U.S. occupations for 2020 to 2030, as measured by percentage changes and projected by the Bureau of Labor Statistics. Service occupations dominate the list. In general, the demand for service workers in the United States is rapidly outpacing the demand for manufacturing, construction, and mining workers.

Of the 10 fastest-growing occupations in percentage terms, two—nurse practitioners, and exercise trainers and group fitness instructors—are related to health and fitness. The rising demand for these occupations is derived from the growing demand for health services, which is caused by several factors, including the aging of the population and the desire on the part of consumers to stay fit so as to avoid costly medical bills. Meanwhile, the presence of wind turbine service technicians and solar photovoltaic installers on this top 10 list demonstrates the robust movement toward green energy that is currently being undertaken by both U.S. power companies and U.S. electricity consumers.

The Most Rapidly Declining Occupations Table 16.6 lists the 10 U.S. occupations with the greatest projected job loss (in percentage terms) between 2020 and 2030. Several of these occupations owe their declines mainly to labor-saving technological change. For example, automated or computerized equipment has greatly reduced the need for parking enforcement workers and telephone operators.

TABLE 16.4 Determinants of Labor Demand: Factors That Shift the Labor Demand Curve

Determinant	Examples
Change in product demand	Gambling increases in popularity, increasing the demand for workers at casinos.
	Consumers decrease their demand for leather coats, decreasing the demand for tanners.
	The federal government increases spending on homeland security, increasing the demand for security personnel.
Change in productivity	An increase in the skill levels of physicians increases the demand for their services.
	Computer-assisted graphic design increases the productivity of, and demand for, graphic artists.
Change in the price of another resource	An increase in the price of electricity increases the cost of producing aluminum and reduces the demand for aluminum workers.
	The price of security equipment used by businesses to protect against illegal entry falls, decreasing the demand for night guards.
	The price of cell-phone equipment decreases, reducing the cost of cell-phone service; this in turn increases the demand for cell-phone assemblers.
	Health-insurance premiums rise, and firms substitute part-time workers who are not covered by insurance for full-time workers who are.

TABLE 16.5 The 10 Fastest-Growing U.S. Occupations in Percentage Terms, 2020–2030

Occupation	Employment, Thousands of Jobs		Percentage Increase*
	2020	2030	
Motion picture projectionists	1.7	2.9	70.5
Wind turbine service technicians	6.9	11.7	68.2
Ushers, lobby attendants, and ticket takers	81.5	131.9	61.8
Nurse practitioners	220.3	335.2	52.2
Solar photovoltaic installers	11.8	17.9	52.1
Cooks, restaurant	1,153.2	1,716.7	48.9
Agents and business managers of artists, performers, and athletes	18.7	27.3	46.3
Costume attendants	5.4	7.7	44.3
Exercise trainers and group fitness instructors	309.8	431.4	39.3
Modelmakers, wood	1.0	1.3	38.6

*Percentages and employment numbers may not reconcile due to rounding.

Source: Table 1.3: Fastest Growing Occupations, 2020 and Projected 2030, Bureau of Labor Statistics, 2021.

TABLE 16.6 The 10 Most Rapidly Declining U.S. Occupations in Percentage Terms, 2020–2030

Occupation	Employment, Thousands of Jobs		Percentage Decrease*
	2020	2030	
Word processors and typists	45.2	28.9	36.0
Parking enforcement workers	7.9	5.1	35.0
Nuclear power reactor operators	5.3	3.6	32.9
Cutters and trimmers, hand	8.1	5.7	29.7
Telephone operators	4.8	3.6	25.4
Watch and clock repairers	2.8	2.1	24.9
Door-to-door sales workers, news and street vendors, and related workers	54.0	41.0	24.1
Switchboard operators, including answering service	59.9	46.3	22.7
Data entry keyers	158.4	122.8	22.5
Shoe machine operators and tenders	5.0	3.9	21.6

*Percentages and employment numbers may not reconcile due to rounding.

Source: Table 1.5: Fastest Declining Occupations, 2020 and Projected 2030, Bureau of Labor Statistics, 2021.

QUICK REVIEW 16.2

▶ A resource demand curve will shift because of changes in product demand, changes in the productivity of the resource, and changes in the prices of other inputs.

▶ If resources A and B are substitutable, a decline in the price of A will decrease the demand for B provided the substitution effect exceeds the output effect. But if the output effect exceeds the substitution effect, the demand for B will increase.

▶ If resources C and D are complements, a decline in the price of C will increase the demand for D.

Elasticity of Resource Demand

>> **LO16.4** Discuss the determinants of elasticity of resource demand.

The employment changes just discussed have resulted from shifts in resource demand curves. Such changes in demand must be distinguished from changes in the quantity of a resource demanded, which are caused by a change in the price of the specific resource. Such changes are caused not by a shift of the demand curve but, rather, by a movement from one point to another on a fixed resource demand curve. For example, in Figure 16.1 we note that an increase in the wage rate from $5 to $7 will reduce the quantity of labor demanded from 5 to 4 units. This is a change in the *quantity of labor demanded* as distinct from a *change in the demand for labor*.

The sensitivity of resource quantity to changes in resource prices along a fixed resource demand curve is measured by the **elasticity of resource demand**. In coefficient form,

$$E_{rd} = \frac{\text{Percentage change in resource quantity demanded}}{\text{Percentage change in resource price}}$$

When E_{rd} is greater than 1, resource demand is elastic; when E_{rd} is less than 1, resource demand is inelastic; and when E_{rd} equals 1, resource demand is unit-elastic. What determines the elasticity of resource demand? Several factors are at work.

Ease of Resource Substitutability The degree to which resources are substitutable is a fundamental determinant of elasticity. The greater the substitutability of other resources, the more elastic is the demand for a particular resource. For example, the high degree to which computerized voice-recognition systems are substitutable for human beings implies that the demand for customer service representatives at call centers is quite elastic. In contrast, good substitutes for physicians are rare, so demand for them is less elastic or even inelastic. If a furniture manufacturer finds that several types of wood are equally satisfactory in making coffee tables, a rise in the price of any one type of wood may cause a sharp drop in the amount demanded as the producer substitutes some other type of wood. At the other extreme, there may be no reasonable substitutes. Bauxite is absolutely essential in the production of aluminum ingots. Thus, the demand for bauxite by aluminum producers is inelastic.

Time can play a role in the ease of input substitution. For example, a firm's truck drivers may obtain a substantial wage increase with little or no immediate decline in employment. But over time, as the firm's trucks wear out and are replaced, that wage increase may motivate the company to purchase larger trucks or even self-driving trucks so as to deliver the same total output with fewer drivers.

Elasticity of Product Demand Because the demand for labor is a derived demand, the elasticity of the demand for labor's output will influence the elasticity of the demand for labor. Other things equal, the greater the price elasticity of product demand, the greater the elasticity of resource demand. For example, suppose that the wage rate falls. The result is a decline in the cost of producing the product and a drop in the product's price. If the elasticity of product demand is great, the resulting increase in the quantity of the product demanded will be large and thus necessitate a large increase in the quantity of labor demanded, which implies an elastic demand for labor. But if the demand for the product is inelastic, the increase in the amount of the product demanded will be small, implying that the increase in the quantity of labor demanded will also be small. In such cases, the demand for labor will be inelastic.

Ratio of Resource Cost to Total Cost The larger the proportion of total production costs accounted for by a resource, the greater the elasticity of demand for that resource. In the extreme, if labor cost is the only production cost, then a 20 percent increase in wage rates will shift all the firm's cost curves upward by 20 percent. If product demand is elastic, this substantial increase in costs will cause a relatively large decline in sales and a sharp decline in the amount of labor demanded. Thus, labor demand is highly elastic. But if labor accounts for only 50 percent of production cost, then a 20 percent increase in wage rates will increase costs by only 10 percent. With the same elasticity of product demand, the result will be a relatively small decline in sales and therefore in the amount of labor demanded. In this case, the demand for labor is much less elastic.

> **elasticity of resource demand** A measure of the responsiveness of *firms* to a change in the *price* of a particular *resource* they employ or use; the percentage change in the quantity demanded of the *resource* divided by the percentage change in its *price*.

► Elasticity of resource demand measures the extent to which producers change the quantity of a resource they hire when its price changes.

► For any particular resource, the elasticity of resource demand will be less the greater the difficulty of substituting other resources, the smaller the elasticity of product demand, and the smaller the proportion of total cost accounted for by the resource.

QUICK REVIEW
16.3

Optimal Combination of Resources*

>> **LO16.5** Determine how a competitive firm selects its optimal combination of resources.

So far, we have focused on one variable input, labor. But in the long run firms can vary the amounts of all the resources they use. That's why we need to consider what combination of resources a firm will choose when *all* its inputs are variable. While our analysis is based on two resources, labor and capital, it can be extended to any number of inputs.

We will consider two related questions:

- What combination of resources will minimize costs at a specific level of output?
- What combination of resources will maximize profit?

The Least-Cost Rule

least-cost combination of resources The quantity of each resource that a *firm* must employ in order to produce a particular output at the lowest total cost; the combination at which the ratio of the *marginal product* of a resource to its *marginal resource cost* (to its *price* if the resource is employed in a competitive market) is the same for the last dollar spent on each of the resources employed.

A firm produces a specific amount of output with the **least-cost combination of resources** when the last dollar spent on each resource yields the same marginal product. That is, the cost to produce any particular quantity of output is minimized when the ratio of MP to price is equal for all resources.

To see how this rule minimizes costs, consider firms that are competitive buyers in resource markets. Because each firm is too small to affect resource prices, each firm's marginal resource costs will equal market resource prices, and each firm will be able to hire as many units as it would like of any and all resources. Thus, if there are just two resources, labor and capital, a competitive firm will minimize its total cost of producing a specific quantity of output when their respective ratios of MP to price are equal:

$$\frac{\text{Marginal product of labor (MP}_L)}{\text{Price of labor } (P_L)} = \frac{\text{Marginal product of capital (MP}_C)}{\text{Price of capital } (P_C)} \tag{1}$$

Throughout, we refer to the marginal products of labor and capital as MP_L and MP_C, respectively. We symbolize the price of labor by P_L and the price of capital by P_C.

A concrete example will show why fulfilling the condition in equation 1 leads to least-cost production. Assume that the price of both capital and labor is $1 per unit but that Siam Soups currently employs them in such amounts that the marginal product of labor is 10 and the marginal product of capital is 5. A comparison of the MP to price ratios for these values reveals that,

$$\frac{MP_L = 10}{P_L = \$1} > \frac{MP_C = 5}{P_C = \$1}$$

Since we have an inequality here—rather than the equality that equation 1 tells us is necessary for cost minimization—Siam is clearly not minimizing costs with the amounts of capital and labor that it is currently employing.

Suppose Siam spends $1 less on capital and shifts that dollar to labor. It loses the 5 units of output produced by the last dollar's worth of capital, but it gains 10 units of output from the extra dollar's worth of labor. Net output increases by 5 (= 10 − 5) units for the same total cost. More shifting of dollars from capital to labor will push the firm *down* along its MP curve for labor and *up* along its MP curve for capital, increasing output and moving the firm toward a position of equilibrium where equation 1 is fulfilled. At that equilibrium position, the MP per dollar for the last unit of both labor and capital might be, for example, 7. And Siam will be producing a greater output for the same (original) cost.

Whenever the same total-resource cost can result in a greater total output, the cost per unit—and therefore the total cost of any specific level of output—can be reduced. Being able to produce a *larger* output for a *specific* total cost is the same as being able to produce a *specific* output for a *smaller* total cost.

The cost of producing any specific level of output can be reduced as long as equation 1 does not hold. But when dollars have been shifted between capital and labor to the point where equation 1 holds, no additional changes in the use of capital or labor will reduce costs further. Siam will be producing that output using the least-cost combination of capital and labor.

---

*Note to Instructors: We consider this section to be optional. If desired, it can be skipped without loss of continuity. It can also be deferred until after the discussion of wage determination in the next chapter.

All the long-run cost curves developed in Chapter 9 and used thereafter assume that the least-cost combination of inputs has been realized at each level of output. Any firm that combines resources in violation of the least-cost rule of equation 1 would have a higher-than-necessary average total cost at each level of output.

The producer's least-cost rule is analogous to the consumer's utility-maximizing rule described in Chapter 7. In achieving the utility-maximizing combination of goods, the consumer considers both his or her preferences as reflected in diminishing-marginal-utility data and the prices of the various products. Similarly, in achieving the cost-minimizing combination of resources, the producer considers both the marginal-product data and the prices (costs) of the various resources.

The Profit-Maximizing Rule

Minimizing cost is not sufficient for maximizing profit. A firm can produce any level of output in the least costly way by applying equation 1. But only one unique level of output maximizes profit. As you know from Chapter 10 this unique profit-maximizing output level occurs when the firm produces the quantity of output at which marginal revenue equals marginal cost ($MR = MC$). Near the beginning of this current chapter we determined that this profit-maximizing condition requires that firms purchase and use the quantity of each resource at which $MRP = MRC$ for that resource.

In a purely competitive resource market, the marginal resource cost (MRC) is equal to the resource price P. Thus, for any competitive resource market, we have as our profit-maximizing equation

$$MRP \text{ (resource)} = P \text{ (resource)}$$

This condition must hold for every variable resource, and in the long run all resources are variable. In competitive markets, a firm will therefore achieve its **profit-maximizing combination of resources** when each resource is employed to the point at which its marginal revenue product equals its resource price. For two resources, labor and capital, we need both

$$MRP_L = P_L \qquad \text{and} \qquad MRP_C = P_C$$

We can combine these conditions by dividing both sides of each equation by their respective prices and equating the results to get

$$\frac{MRP_L}{P_L} = \frac{MRP_C}{P_C} = 1 \qquad (2)$$

Equation 2 must hold if a firm is to maximize its profit. Please note carefully that in equation 2, it is not sufficient that the MRPs of the two resources be *proportionate* to their prices; the MRPs must be *equal* to their respective prices and the ratios therefore equal to 1. For example, if $MRP_L = \$15$, $P_L = \$5$, $MRP_C = \$9$, and $P_C = \$3$, then the ratios of MRP to resource price are equal to each other (at $3 = \$15/\$5 = \$9/\$3$) *but not equal to 1*. So Siam will not be maximizing profit. It is underemploying both capital and labor even though the ratios of MRP to resource price are identical for both resources. The firm can expand its profit by hiring additional amounts of both capital and labor until it moves down its downward sloping MRP_L and MRP_C curves to the points at which $MRP_L = \$5$ and $MRP_C = \$3$. The ratios will then be 5/5 and 3/3 and equal to 1.

The profit-maximizing condition found in equation 2 implies the cost-minimizing condition of equation 1. That is, if a firm is maximizing profit according to equation 2, then it must be using the least-cost combination of inputs to do so. However, the converse is not true: A firm operating at least cost according to equation 1 may not be operating at the output level that will maximize its profit. That can happen because the least-cost condition in equation 1 only specifies how any given level of output can be produced in the least-cost way. It does not guarantee that the firm will be producing at the specific and unique output level that will maximize profit. To identify that specific and unique output level, you need to apply equation 2.

Numerical Illustration

A numerical illustration will help you understand the least-cost rule (equation 1) and the profit-maximizing rule (equation 2). In columns 2, 3, 2′, and 3′ in Table 16.7 we show the total products and marginal products for various amounts of labor and capital that are assumed to be the only inputs Siam needs in producing its soup. Both inputs are subject to diminishing returns.

profit-maximizing combination of resources The quantity of each *resource a firm* must employ to maximize its *profit* or minimize its loss; the combination of resource inputs at which the *marginal revenue product* of each resource is equal to its *marginal resource cost* (to its *price* if the resource is employed in a competitive market).

TABLE 16.7 Data for Finding the Least-Cost and Profit-Maximizing Combination of Labor and Capital, Siam Soups*

Labor (Price = $8)					Capital (Price = $12)				
(1) Quantity	(2) Total Product (Output)	(3) Marginal Product	(4) Total Revenue	(5) Marginal Revenue Product	(1') Quantity	(2') Total Product (Output)	(3') Marginal Product	(4') Total Revenue	(5') Marginal Revenue Product
0	0		$ 0		0	0		$ 0	
		12		$24			13		$26
1	12		24		1	13		26	
		10		20			9		18
2	22		44		2	22		44	
		6		12			6		12
3	28		56		3	28		56	
		5		10			4		8
4	33		66		4	32		64	
		4		8			3		6
5	37		74		5	35		70	
		3		6			2		4
6	40		80		6	37		74	
		2		4			4		2
7	42		84		7	38		76	

*To simplify, it is assumed in this table that the productivity of each resource is independent of the quantity of the other. For example, the total and marginal products of labor are assumed not to vary with the quantity of capital employed.

We also assume in Table 16.7 that labor and capital are supplied in competitive resource markets at $8 and $12, respectively, and that Siam's soup sells competitively at $2 per unit. For both labor and capital we can determine the total revenue associated with each input level by multiplying total product by the $2 product price. These data are shown in columns 4 and 4'. They enable us to calculate the marginal revenue product of each successive input of labor and capital, as shown in columns 5 and 5', respectively.

Producing at Least Cost What is the least-cost combination of labor and capital for Siam to use in producing, say, 50 units of output? The answer, which we can obtain by trial and error, is that the least-cost way of producing 50 units of output is for Siam to employ 3 units of labor and 2 units of capital. Columns 2 and 2' indicate that this combination of labor and capital does, indeed, result in the required 50 (= 28 + 22) units of output. Now, note from columns 3 and 3' that hiring 3 units of labor gives us $MP_L/P_L = \frac{6}{8} = \frac{3}{4}$ and hiring 2 units of capital gives us $MP_C/P_C = \frac{9}{12} = \frac{3}{4}$. So equation 1 is fulfilled and Siam should be producing 50 units at the lowest possible cost.

Can we use the numbers in Table 16.7 to verify that production costs are in fact minimized? Yes. Begin by noting that the total cost of employing 3 units of labor and 2 of capital is $48 [= (3 × $8) + (2 × $12)]. Other combinations of labor and capital will also yield 50 units of output, but at a higher cost than $48. For example, 5 units of labor and 1 unit of capital will produce 50 (= 37 + 13) units, but total cost is higher, at $52 [= (5 × $8) + (1 × $12)]. This comes as no surprise because 5 units of labor and 1 unit of capital violate the least-cost rule— $MP_L/P_L = \frac{4}{8}$, $MP_C/P_C = \frac{13}{12}$. Only the combination (3 units of labor and 2 units of capital) that minimizes total cost will satisfy equation 1. All other combinations capable of producing 50 units of output violate the cost-minimizing rule of equation 1, and therefore cost more than $48 to produce.

Maximizing Profit We have seen that equation 1 will tell Siam the cost-minimizing amounts of capital and labor that it must employ to produce 50 units at the lowest cost. But will 50 units of output maximize Siam's profit? No, because the profit-maximizing equalities of equation 2 are not satisfied when the firm employs 3 units of labor and 2 units of capital. To maximize profit, each input should be employed until its price equals its marginal revenue product. But for 3 units of labor, labor's MRP in column 5 is $12 while its price is only $8. This means the firm could increase its profit by hiring more labor. Similarly, for 2 units of capital, we see in column 5' that capital's MRP is $18 and its price is only $12. This indicates that more capital should also be employed. By producing only 50 units of output (even though they are produced at least cost), labor and capital are being used in less-than-profit-maximizing amounts.

The firm needs to expand its employment of both labor and capital if it wants to increase profit. Increasing both of those inputs will increase output. But up to what point should Siam utilize more labor and more capital to produce more output?

To find Siam's profit-maximizing output level, we need to find the amounts of labor and capital that will satisfy equation 2. Table 16.7 shows that equation 2 is fulfilled when Siam employs 5 units of labor and 3 units of capital. That is the profit-maximizing combination of inputs at which the MRPs of labor and capital are equal to their prices *and* the ratios of their MRPs to price are both equal to 1.[2] The firm's total cost will be $76, made up of $40 (= 5 × $8) of labor and $36 (= 3 × $12) of capital. Total revenue will be $130, found either by multiplying the total output of 65 (= 37 + 28) by the $2 product price or by summing the total revenues attributable to labor ($74) and to capital ($56). The difference between total revenue and total cost in this instance is $54 (= $130 − $76). Experiment with other combinations of labor and capital to demonstrate that they yield an economic profit of less than $54.

Note that the profit-maximizing combination of 5 units of labor and 3 units of capital is also a least-cost combination for this particular level of output. Using these resource amounts satisfies the least-cost requirement of equation 1 in that $MP_L/P_L = \frac{4}{8} = \frac{1}{2}$ and $MP_C/P_C = \frac{6}{12} = \frac{1}{2}$. So, again, let us emphasize that profit maximization implies cost minimization, but not the other way around. There is a least-cost way to produce any given amount of output, but only one unique level of output that will maximize profit. Equation 1 identifies the least-cost way to produce any given level of output. Equation 2 identifies the profit-maximizing level of output.

▶ Any specific level of output will be produced with the least-costly combination of variable resources when each input's marginal product per dollar is the same (least-cost rule).

▶ A firm is employing the profit-maximizing combination of resources when each resource is used to the point where its marginal revenue product equals its price (profit-maximizing rule).

▶ The least-cost rule identifies the least-costly combination of resources to produce any given level of output, but not the unique profit-maximizing output level or the amount of resources needed to produce the profit-maximizing output level. That level and the associated amount of resources needed to produce it are identified by the profit-maximizing rule.

Marginal Productivity Theory of Income Distribution

Our discussion of resource pricing is the cornerstone of the controversial view that fairness and economic justice are one of the outcomes of a competitive capitalist economy. In effect, workers receive income payments (wages) equal to the marginal contributions they make to their employers' outputs and revenues. In other words, workers are paid according to the value of the labor services that they contribute to production. Similarly, owners of the other resources receive income based on the value of the resources they supply in the production process.

In this **marginal productivity theory of income distribution,** income is distributed according to a person's contribution to society's output. So, if you are willing to accept the proposition "To each according to the value of what they create," income payments based on marginal revenue product provide a fair and equitable distribution of society's income.

This conclusion sounds reasonable, but you need to be aware of serious criticisms of this theory of income distribution:

- *Inequality* Critics argue that the distribution of income resulting from payment according to marginal productivity may be highly unequal because productive resources are very unequally distributed in the first place. Aside from their differences in mental and physical attributes, individuals encounter substantially different opportunities to enhance their productivity through education and training and the use of more and better equipment. Some people may not be able to participate in production at all because of mental or physical disabilities, and they would obtain no income under a system of distribution based solely on marginal productivity. Ownership of property resources is also highly unequal. Many owners of land and capital resources obtain their property by inheritance rather than through their own productive effort. Hence, income from inherited property conflicts with the "To each according to the value of what they create" idea. Critics say that these inequalities call for progressive taxation and government spending programs aimed at creating a more equitable income distribution.

>> **LO16.6** Explain the marginal productivity theory of income distribution.

marginal productivity theory of income distribution The hypothesis that the *wage* rate paid to *labor* will tend to equal the *marginal revenue product* of labor.

---

[2]Because we are dealing with discrete (nonfractional) units of the two outputs here, the use of 4 units of labor and 2 units of capital is equally profitable. The fifth unit of labor's MRP and its price (cost) are equal at $8, so that the fifth labor unit neither adds to nor subtracts from the firm's profit; similarly, the third unit of capital has no effect on profit.

Labor and Capital: Substitutes or Complements?

Automatic Teller Machines (ATMs) Have Complemented Some Types of Labor While Substituting for Other Types of Labor.

As you have learned from this chapter, a firm achieves its least-cost combination of inputs when the last dollar it spends on each input makes the same contribution to total output. This raises an interesting real-world question: What happens when technological advance makes available a new, highly productive capital good for which MP/P is greater than it is for other inputs, say, a particular type of labor?

The answer is that the least-cost mix of resources abruptly changes, and the firm responds accordingly. If the new capital is a substitute for a particular type of labor, the firm will replace that particular type of labor with the new capital (substitution effect). But if the new capital complements a particular type of labor, the firm will add additional amounts of that type of labor (output effect).

Consider bank tellers. One of their core functions, before ATMs became common in the 1980s, was to handle deposits and withdrawals of cash. Bank tellers had several other tasks that they needed to handle, but one particular type of labor

Picturenet/Blend Images/Getty Images

they supplied was handling cash transactions. The task of handling cash transactions can, however, be equally well-managed by ATMs—but at one-quarter the cost. Naturally, banks responded to that cost advantage by installing more ATMs.

That might make you think that ATMs displaced tellers because it would seem natural in this scenario that ATMs were a substitute for bank tellers. But the data tells a different story! The number of human bank tellers actually *increased* over time as the number of ATMs soared. In 1985, there were 60,000 ATMs and 485,000 bank tellers. In 2015, there were 425,000 ATMs and 526,000 bank tellers. This means that over that entire time period, ATM machines must have been a complement to the labor provided by bank tellers.

The process was not instantaneous. Eighty thousand bank teller jobs were indeed lost during the 1990s because bank managers at first *did* think of ATMs and bank tellers as substitutes. But by the early 2000s, bank managers realized that the cost savings offered by ATMs had given them the chance to operate in new ways that would actually require more tellers rather than fewer tellers.

Before ATMs, the average branch needed 20 employees. After ATMs, the average branch needed only 13 employees. That major increase in efficiency gave banks the chance to compete against one another by opening more branches—and more branches meant having to hire more human tellers. Thus, the efficiencies generated by having ATMs handle cash transactions at one-fourth the cost caused the demand for bank tellers to increase.

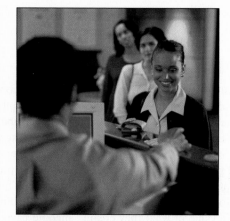

Keith Brofsky/Photodisc/Getty Images

In addition, the banks also realized that bank tellers could be trained in more complex tasks like selling financial products and helping to issue home mortgages. Once banks figured out these new ways to employ tellers, ATMs turned from a substitute for bank teller labor into a complement for bank teller labor. By freeing human beings from having to handle cash transactions, ATMs acted as a complement for other types of human labor, such as selling financial products.

We can generalize from the history of ATMs. Capital is, overall, a complement to, rather than a substitute for, human labor. Certain types of human labor *are* substituted away as new technologies arrive, but humans end up being complemented by capital as they perform other tasks. Some types of work will disappear and the government may need to help displaced workers train for new jobs. But the newly deployed capital will end up increasing wages because it will, as a complement, increase the overall demand for human labor.

- *Market imperfections* The marginal productivity theory of income distribution rests on the assumption that markets are competitive. However, not all labor markets are competitive. In some labor markets, employers exert their wage-setting power to pay less-than-competitive wages. And some workers, through labor unions, professional associations, and occupational licensing laws, wield wage-setting power in selling their services. Even the process of collective bargaining over wages suggests a power struggle over the division of income. In wage setting through negotiations, market forces—and income shares based on marginal productivity—may get partially pushed into the background. In addition, discrimination in the labor market can distort earnings patterns. In short, because of real-world market imperfections, wage rates and other resource prices are not always based solely on contributions to output.

▸ The marginal productivity theory of income distribution holds that resources are paid according to people's marginal contributions to output.

▸ Critics point out that incomes based on marginal productivity may be highly unfair given differences in people's life histories, access to education and training, and whether they were lucky enough to inherit land or capital.

▸ Incomes may differ from marginal productivity due to factors like discrimination, union labor contracts, and occupational licensing rules.

QUICK REVIEW
16.5

Summary

LO16.1 Explain the significance of resource pricing.
Resource prices help determine money incomes while simultaneously rationing scarce resources to various industries and firms.

LO16.2 Relate the marginal revenue productivity of a resource to a firm's demand for that resource.
The demand for a resource depends on its productivity and on the market value (price) of the good it is used to produce.

Marginal revenue product (MRP) is the extra revenue that a firm obtains when it employs 1 more unit of a resource. A firm's demand curve for a resource is identical to the firm's MRP curve for that resource because the firm equates resource price and MRP in determining its profit-maximizing level of resource employment. More specifically, each point on the MRP (= resource demand) curve indicates how many resource units the firm will hire at a specific resource price. Because the marginal product of additional units declines in accordance with the law of diminishing returns, the firm's resource demand (= MRP) curve slopes downward.

The resource demand curve of an imperfectly competitive seller is less elastic than that of a perfectly competitive seller.

The market demand curve for a resource is derived by summing horizontally the demand curves of all the firms hiring that resource.

LO16.3 List the factors that increase or decrease resource demand.
The demand curve for a resource will shift as the result of (a) a change in the demand for, and therefore the price of, the product the resource is producing; (b) changes in the resource's productivity; and (c) changes in the prices of other resources.

If resources A and B are substitutable for each other, a decline in the price of A will decrease the demand for B provided the substitution effect is greater than the output effect. But if the output effect *exceeds* the substitution effect, a decline in the price of A will increase the demand for B.

If resources C and D are complementary, there is only an output effect; a change in the price of C will change the demand for D in the opposite direction.

LO16.4 Discuss the determinants of elasticity of resource demand.
The elasticity of demand for a resource measures the responsiveness of producers to a change in the resource's price. The coefficient of the elasticity of resource demand is

$$E_{rd} = \frac{\text{Percentage change in resource quantity demanded}}{\text{Percentage change in resource price}}$$

When E_{rd} is greater than 1, resource demand is elastic; when E_{rd} is less than 1, resource demand is inelastic; and when E_{rd} equals 1, resource demand is unit-elastic.

The elasticity of demand for a resource will be greater (a) the greater the ease of substituting other resources for labor, (b) the greater the elasticity of demand for the product, and (c) the larger the proportion of total production costs attributable to the resource.

LO16.5 Determine how a competitive firm selects its optimal combination of resources.
Any specific level of output will be produced with the least costly combination of variable resources when the marginal product per dollar's worth of each input is the same—that is, when

$$\frac{\text{MP of labor}}{\text{Price of labor}} = \frac{\text{MP of capital}}{\text{Price of capital}}$$

A firm is employing the profit-maximizing combination of resources when each resource is used to the point where its marginal revenue product equals its price. In terms of labor and capital, that occurs when the MRP of labor equals the price of labor and the MRP of capital equals the price of capital—that is, when

$$\frac{\text{MP of labor}}{\text{Price of labor}} = \frac{\text{MP of capital}}{\text{Price of capital}} = 1$$

LO16.6 Explain the marginal productivity theory of income distribution.
The marginal productivity theory of income distribution holds that resources are paid according to people's marginal contributions to output. Critics say that such an income distribution is too unequal and that real-world market imperfections result in pay above and below marginal contributions to output.

Terms and Concepts

derived demand	MRP = MRC rule	least-cost combination of resources
marginal product (MP)	substitution effect	profit-maximizing combination of resources
marginal revenue product (MRP)	output effect	marginal productivity theory of income distribution
marginal resource cost (MRC)	elasticity of resource demand	

Discussion Questions

1. What is the significance of resource pricing? Explain how the factors determining resource demand differ from those determining product demand. Explain the meaning and significance of the fact that the demand for a resource is a derived demand. Why do resource demand curves slope downward? **LO16.1**

2. In 2021, Zillow, an online real estate marketplace, announced that it would reduce employment by 2,000 workers. What does this decision reveal about how Zillow viewed its marginal revenue product (MRP) and marginal resource cost (MRC)? Why didn't Zillow reduce employment by more than 2,000 workers or by fewer than 2,000 workers? **LO16.3**

3. What factors determine the elasticity of resource demand? What effect will each of the following have on the elasticity or the location of the demand for resource C, which is being used to produce commodity X? Where there is any uncertainty as to the outcome, specify the causes of that uncertainty. **LO16.4**
   a. An increase in the demand for product X.
   b. An increase in the price of substitute resource D.
   c. An increase in the number of resources substitutable for C in producing X.
   d. A technological improvement in the capital equipment with which resource C is combined.
   e. A fall in the price of complementary resource E.
   f. A decline in the elasticity of demand for product X due to a decline in the competitiveness of product market X.

4. In each of the following four cases, MRP_L and MRP_C refer to the marginal revenue products of labor and capital, respectively, and P_L and P_C refer to their prices. Indicate whether each of the following is consistent with maximum profits for the firm. If not, state which resource(s) should be used in larger amounts and which resource(s) should be used in smaller amounts. **LO16.5**
   a. $MRP_L = \$8$; $P_L = \$4$; $MRP_C = \$8$; $P_C = \$4$.
   b. $MRP_L = \$10$; $P_L = \$12$; $MRP_C = \$14$; $P_C = \$9$.
   c. $MRP_L = \$6$; $P_L = \$6$; $MRP_C = \$12$; $P_C = \$12$.
   d. $MRP_L = \$22$; $P_L = \$26$; $MRP_C = \$16$; $P_C = \$19$.

5. Florida citrus growers say that crackdowns on illegal immigration are increasing the market wage rates necessary to get their oranges picked. Some are turning to $100,000 to $300,000 mechanical harvesters known as "trunk, shake, and catch" pickers, which vigorously shake oranges from the trees. If widely adopted, what will be the effect on the demand for human orange pickers? What does that effect imply about the relative strengths of the substitution and output effects? **LO16.5**

6. **LAST WORD** To save money, some fast-food chains now have their customers place their orders at computer kiosks. Will the kiosks necessarily reduce the total number of workers employed in the fast-food industry?

Review Questions

1. Pooja is a baker and runs a large cupcake shop. She has already hired 11 employees and is thinking of hiring a 12th. Pooja estimates that a 12th worker would cost her $100 per day in wages and benefits while increasing her total revenue from $2,600 per day to $2,750 per day. Should Pooja hire a 12th worker? Explain. **LO16.2**

2. Complete the following labor demand table for a firm that is hiring labor competitively and selling its product in a competitive market. **LO16.2**

Units of Labor	Total Product	Marginal Product	Product Price	Total Revenue	Marginal Revenue Product
0	0	_____	$2	$_____	
1	17	_____	2	_____	$_____
2	31	_____	2	_____	_____
3	43	_____	2	_____	_____
4	53	_____	2	_____	_____
5	60	_____	2	_____	_____
6	65	_____	2	_____	_____

a. How many workers will the firm hire if the market wage rate is $27.95? $19.95? Explain why the firm will not hire a larger or smaller number of units of labor at each of these wage rates.
b. Show this firm's labor demand curve in schedule form and graphically.
c. Now again determine the firm's demand curve for labor, assuming that it is selling in an imperfectly competitive market and that, although it can sell 17 units at $2.20 per unit, it must lower product price by 5 cents in order to sell the marginal product of each successive labor unit. Compare this demand curve with that derived in part b. Which curve is more elastic? Explain.

3. Alice runs a shoemaking factory that uses both labor and capital to make shoes. Which of the following would shift the factory's demand for capital? You can select one or more correct answers from the choices shown. **LO16.3**
   a. Many consumers decide to walk barefoot all the time.
   b. New shoemaking machines are twice as efficient as older machines.
   c. The wages that the factory has to pay its workers rise due to an economywide labor shortage.

4. FreshLeaf is a commercial saladmaker that produces "salad in a bag" that is sold at many local supermarkets. Its customers like lettuce but don't care so much what type of lettuce is included in each bag of salad. Therefore, would you expect FreshLeaf's demand for iceberg lettuce to be elastic, inelastic, unit-elastic, or some combination of these elasticities? **LO16.4**

5. Suppose the productivity of capital and labor are as shown in the table. The output of these resources sells in a purely competitive market for $1 per unit. Both capital and labor are hired under purely competitive conditions at $3 and $1, respectively. **LO16.5**
   a. What is the least-cost combination of labor and capital the firm should employ in producing 80 units of output? Explain.
   b. What is the profit-maximizing combination of labor and capital the firm should use? Explain. What is the resulting level of output? What is the economic profit? Is this the least costly way of producing the profit-maximizing output?

6. A software company in Silicon Valley uses programmers (labor) and computers (capital) to produce apps for mobile devices. The firm estimates that when it comes to labor, MP_L = 5 apps per month while P_L = $1,000 per month. And when it comes to

Units of Capital	MP of Capital	Units of Labor	MP of Labor
0		0	
	24		11
1		1	
	21		9
2		2	
	18		8
3		3	
	15		7
4		4	
	9		6
5		5	
	6		4
6		6	
	3		1
7		7	
	1		$\frac{1}{2}$
8		8	

capital, MP_C = 8 apps per month while P_C = $1,000 per month. If the company wants to maximize its profits, it should: **LO16.5**
a. increase labor while decreasing capital.
b. decrease labor while increasing capital.
c. keep the current amounts of capital and labor just as they are.
d. none of the above.

Problems

1. A delivery company is considering adding another vehicle to its delivery fleet; each vehicle is rented for $100 per day. Assume that the additional vehicle would be capable of delivering 1,500 packages per day and that each package that is delivered brings in 10 cents in revenue. Also assume that adding the delivery vehicle would not affect any other costs. **LO16.2**
   a. What is the MRP? What is the MRC? Should the firm add this delivery vehicle?
   b. Now suppose that the cost of renting a vehicle doubles to $200 per day. What are the MRP and MRC? Should the firm add a delivery vehicle under these circumstances?
   c. Next suppose that the cost of renting a vehicle falls back down to $100 per day but, due to extremely congested freeways, an additional vehicle would only be able to deliver 750 packages per day. What are the MRP and MRC in this situation? Would adding a vehicle under these circumstances increase the firm's profits?

2. Suppose that marginal product tripled while product price fell by one-half in Table 16.1. What would be the new MRP values in Table 16.1? What would be the net impact on the location of the resource demand curve in Figure 16.1? **LO16.2**

3. Suppose that a monopoly firm finds that its MR is $50 for the first unit sold each day, $49 for the second unit sold each day, $48 for the third unit sold each day, and so on. Further suppose that the first worker hired produces 5 units per day, the second 4 units per day, the third 3 units per day, and so on. **LO16.3**
   a. What is the firm's MRP for each of the first five workers?
   b. Suppose that the monopolist is subjected to rate regulation and the regulator stipulates that it must charge exactly $40 per unit for all units sold. At that price, what is the firm's MRP for each of the first five workers?

c. If the daily wage paid to workers is $170 per day, how many workers will the unregulated monopoly demand? How many will the regulated monopoly demand? Looking at those figures, will the regulated or the unregulated monopoly demand more workers at that wage?
d. If the daily wage paid to workers falls to $77 per day, how many workers will the unregulated monopoly demand? How many will the regulated monopoly demand? Looking at those figures, will the regulated or the unregulated monopoly demand more workers at that wage?
e. Comparing your answers to parts c and d, does regulating a monopoly's output price *always* increase its demand for resources?

4. Consider a small landscaping company run by Mr. Viemeister. He is considering increasing his firm's capacity. If he adds one more worker, the firm's total monthly revenue will increase from $50,000 to $58,000. If he adds one more tractor, monthly revenue will increase from $50,000 to $62,000. Each additional worker costs $4,000 per month, while an additional tractor would also cost $4,000 per month. **LO16.5**
   a. What is the marginal product of labor? The marginal product of capital?
   b. What is the ratio of the marginal product of labor to the price of labor (MP_L/P_L)? What is the ratio of the marginal product of capital to the price of capital (MP_C/P_C)?
   c. Is the firm using the least-costly combination of inputs?
   d. Does adding an additional worker or adding an additional tractor yield a larger increase in total revenue for each dollar spent?

CHAPTER

17

Wage Determination

>> **LEARNING OBJECTIVES**

LO17.1 Explain why labor productivity tracks real hourly compensation so closely over time.

LO17.2 Show how wage rates and employment levels are determined in competitive labor markets.

LO17.3 Demonstrate how monopsony can reduce wages below competitive levels.

LO17.4 Discuss how unions increase wage rates.

LO17.5 Explain why wages and employment are determined by collective bargaining in a situation of bilateral monopoly.

LO17.6 Discuss how minimum wage laws affect labor markets.

LO17.7 List the major causes of wage differentials.

LO17.8 Identify the types, benefits, and costs of pay-for-performance plans.

LO17.9 (Appendix) Describe U.S. union membership, collective bargaining, and the economic effects of unions.

Roughly 155 million Americans go to work each day. We work at an amazing variety of jobs and receive considerable differences in pay. What determines our hourly wage or annual salary? Why is the salary for a topflight major-league baseball player $30 million or more a year, but the average pay for a schoolteacher around $60,000 per year? Why are starting salaries for college graduates who major in engineering and accounting so much higher than those for graduates majoring in English and Sociology?

Having explored the major factors that underlie labor demand, we now bring *labor supply* into our analysis to answer these questions. Generally speaking, labor supply and labor demand interact to determine hourly wage rates and annual salaries. Collectively, those wages and salaries make up about 70 percent of all income paid to U.S. resource suppliers.

Labor, Wages, and Earnings

>> **LO17.1** Explain why labor productivity tracks real hourly compensation so closely over time.

Economists use the term *labor* broadly to apply to (1) blue- and white-collar workers of all varieties; (2) professional people such as lawyers, physicians, dentists, and teachers; and (3) owners of small businesses, including barbers, plumbers, and retailers who provide labor as they operate their own businesses.

Wages are the price that employers pay for labor. Wages take the form of not only direct money payments such as hourly pay, annual salaries, bonuses, commissions, and royalties, but also fringe benefits such as paid vacations, health insurance, and pensions. Unless stated

🌐 GLOBAL PERSPECTIVE 17.1

HOURLY WAGES OF PRODUCTION WORKERS, SELECTED NATIONS

Wage differences are pronounced worldwide even after using the purchasing power parity (PPP) method to adjust for international differences in the cost of living. The data shown here indicate that after adjusting for differences in the cost of living, hourly compensation in the United States is not as high as in some European nations but is substantially higher than in many other developed and developing nations.

Source: Author calculations based on data from the Conference Board, the Organization for Economic Cooperation and Development, and the World Bank.

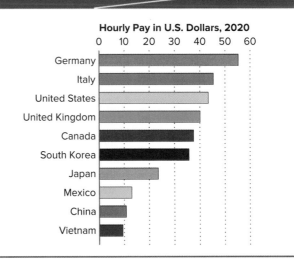

Hourly Pay in U.S. Dollars, 2020

otherwise, we use the term *wages* to mean all such payments and benefits converted to an hourly basis. Doing so reminds us that the **wage,** or wage rate, is the price paid per unit of labor services for one hour of work.

We also distinguish between nominal wages and real wages. A **nominal wage** is the amount of money received per hour, day, or year. A **real wage** is the quantity of goods and services a worker can obtain with nominal wages. Real wages reveal the "purchasing power" of nominal wages.

Your real wage depends on your nominal wage and the prices of the goods and services you purchase. Suppose you receive a 5 percent increase in your nominal wage, but at the same time the price level increases by 3 percent. Then your real wage has increased by 2 percent (= 5 percent − 3 percent). Unless otherwise indicated, we assume that the overall price level remains constant. In other words, we discuss only *real* wages.

> **wage** The *price* paid for the use or *services* of *labor* per unit of time (per hour, per day, and so on).
>
> **nominal wage** The amount of *money* received by a worker per unit of time (hour, day, etc.); money wage.
>
> **real wage** The amount of *goods* and *services* a worker can purchase with his or her *nominal wage;* the *purchasing power* of the *nominal wage.*

General Level of Wages

Wages differ among nations, regions, occupations, and individuals. Wage rates are much higher in the United States than in China or India. They are slightly higher in the north and east of the United States than in the south. One physician may earn twice as much as another physician for the same number of hours of work. Average wages also differ by gender, race, and ethnic background.

The general, or average, level of wages includes a wide range of different wage rates. It includes the wages of bakers, barbers, brick masons, and brain surgeons. By averaging such wages, we can more easily compare wages among regions and among nations.

As Global Perspective 17.1 suggests, the general level of real wages in the United States is relatively high, but not the highest in the world.

The simplest explanation for the high real wages in the United States and other industrially advanced economies (hereafter referred to simply as advanced economies) is that the demand for labor in those nations is relatively large compared to the supply of labor.

Role of Productivity

The demand for labor, or for any other resource, depends on its productivity. In general, the greater the productivity of labor, the greater is the demand for it. And if the total supply of labor is fixed, then the stronger the demand for labor, the higher is the average level of real wages. The demand for labor in the United States and other advanced economies is large because labor in those countries is highly productive. There are several reasons for that high productivity:

- *Plentiful capital* Workers in the advanced economies use large amounts of physical capital (equipment and nonresidential structures). In the United States in 2020, $255,870 of physical capital was available, on average, for each worker.

- *Access to abundant natural resources* In advanced economies, natural resources tend to be abundant compared to the size of the labor force. Some of those resources are available domestically and others are imported from abroad. The United States, for example, is richly endowed with arable land, mineral resources, and energy sources.

- *Advanced technology* Not only do workers in advanced economies have more capital equipment to work with, but that equipment is technologically superior to the equipment available to the vast majority of workers worldwide. Moreover, work methods in the advanced economies steadily improve through scientific study and research.

- *Labor quality* The education and training received by workers in advanced economies are generally superior to those received by workers in developing nations. Thus, workers in advanced economies tend to be more efficient than many of their counterparts in less economically developed economies.

- *Other factors* Less obvious factors also may explain the high productivity in advanced economies. In the United States, for example, these factors include (*a*) the efficiency and flexibility of management; (*b*) a business, social, and political environment that emphasizes production and productivity; (*c*) the vast size of the domestic market, which enables firms to engage in mass production; and (*d*) the increased specialization of production enabled by free-trade agreements with other nations.

Real Wages and Productivity

Figure 17.1 shows the close long-run relationship in the United States between output per hour of work and real hourly compensation (= wages and salaries + employers' contributions to social insurance and private benefit plans). Because every bit of real output in the economy flows to resource suppliers, real income and real output are two ways of viewing the same thing. Consequently, real income (compensation) per worker can increase only at about the same rate as output per worker. When workers produce more real output per hour, more real income is available to them for each hour worked.

In the actual economy, however, suppliers of land, capital, and entrepreneurial talent also share in the income from production. Real wages therefore do not always rise in lockstep with gains in

FIGURE 17.1
Output per hour and real hourly compensation in the United States, 1970–2020.

Over long time periods, output per hour of work and real hourly compensation are closely related.

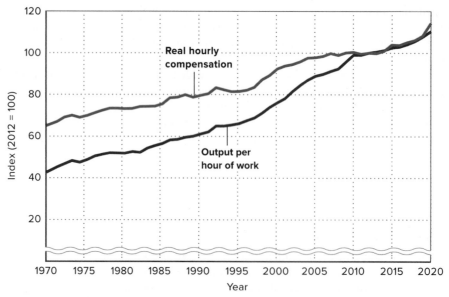

Source: Bureau of Labor Statistics.

productivity over short time spans. But over long periods, productivity and real wages tend to rise together.

Long-Run Trend of Real Wages

Basic supply-and-demand analysis helps explain the long-term trend of real-wage growth in the United States. The nation's labor force has grown significantly over the decades. But as a result of the productivity-increasing factors we described, increases in

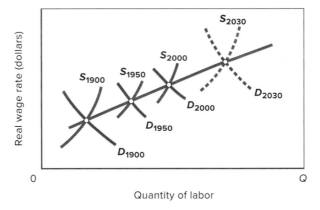

FIGURE 17.2
The long-run trend of real wages in the United States.

The productivity of U.S. labor has increased substantially over the long run, causing the demand for labor *D* to shift rightward (that is, to increase) more rapidly than increases in the supply of labor *S*. The result has been ongoing increases in real wages.

labor demand have outstripped increases in labor supply. Figure 17.2 shows several such increases in labor supply and labor demand. The result has been a long-run, or secular, increase in wage rates and employment. For example, real hourly compensation in the United States has roughly doubled since 1960. Over that same period, employment has increased by nearly 100 million workers, from 54 million workers in 1960 to about 150 million today.

A Purely Competitive Labor Market

Average wage levels disguise the great variation of wage rates among occupations and within occupations. What determines the wage rate paid for a specific type of labor? Demand-and-supply analysis again is revealing. Let's begin by examining labor demand and labor supply in a **purely competitive labor market.** In this type of market:

- Numerous firms compete with one another in hiring a specific type of labor.
- Each of many qualified workers with identical skills supplies that type of labor.
- Individual firms and individual workers are "wage takers" because neither can exert any control over the market wage rate.

>> **LO17.2** Show how wage rates and employment levels are determined in competitive labor markets.

purely competitive labor market A *resource market* in which many *firms* compete with one another in hiring a specific kind of *labor,* numerous equally qualified workers supply that labor, and no one controls the market *wage rate.*

Market Demand for Labor

Suppose 200 firms demand a particular type of labor, say, carpenters. These firms need not be in the same industry; industries are defined according to the products they produce and not the resources they employ. Thus, firms producing wood-framed furniture, wood windows and doors, and houses and apartment buildings will demand carpenters. To find the total, or market, labor demand curve for a particular labor service, we sum horizontally the labor demand curves (the marginal revenue product curves) of the individual firms, as indicated in **Figure 17.3 (Key Graph).** The horizontal summing of the 200 labor demand curves like *d* in Figure 17.3b yields the market labor demand curve *D* in Figure 17.3a.

Market Supply of Labor

On the supply side of a purely competitive labor market, we assume that no union is present and that workers individually compete for available jobs. The supply curve for each type of labor slopes upward, indicating that employers as a group must pay higher wage rates to obtain more workers. They must do so to bid workers away from other industries, occupations, and localities. Within limits, workers have alternative job opportunities. For example, they may work in other industries in the same locality, they may work in their present occupations in different cities or states, or they may work in other occupations.

Firms that want to hire these workers (here, carpenters) must pay higher wage rates to attract them away from alternative job opportunities. They must also pay higher wages to induce people who are not currently in the labor force—who are perhaps doing household activities or enjoying leisure—to seek employment. In short, assuming that wages are constant in other labor markets, higher wages in a particular labor market entice more workers to offer their labor

..ıl KEY GRAPH

FIGURE 17.3 **Labor supply and labor demand in (a) a purely competitive labor market and (b) a single competitive firm.**

In a purely competitive labor market (a), market labor supply S and market labor demand D determine the equilibrium wage rate W_c and the equilibrium number of workers Q_c. Each individual competitive firm (b) takes this competitive wage W_c as given. Thus, the individual firm's labor supply curve $s = $ MRC is perfectly elastic at the going wage W_c. Its labor demand curve, d, is its MRP curve (here labeled mrp). The firm maximizes its profit by hiring workers up to where MRP = MRC. Area $0abc$ represents both the firm's total revenue and its total cost. The green area is its total wage cost; the blue area is its nonlabor costs, including a normal profit—that is, the firm's payments to the suppliers of land, capital, and entrepreneurship.

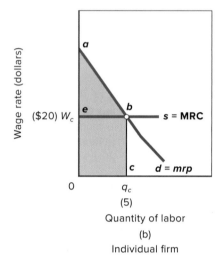

(a)
Labor market

(b)
Individual firm

QUICK QUIZ FOR FIGURE 17.3

1. **The supply-of-labor curve S slopes upward in graph (a) because:**
   a. the law of diminishing marginal utility applies.
   b. the law of diminishing returns applies.
   c. workers can afford to "buy" more leisure when the wage rate increases.
   d. higher wages are needed to attract workers away from other labor markets, household activities, and leisure.

2. **This firm's labor demand curve d in graph (b) slopes downward because:**
   a. the law of diminishing marginal utility applies.
   b. the law of diminishing returns applies.
   c. the firm must lower its price to sell additional units of its product.
   d. the firm is a competitive employer, not a monopsonist.

3. **In employing five workers, the firm represented in graph (b):**
   a. has a total wage cost of $6,000.
   b. is adhering to the general principle of undertaking all actions for which the marginal benefit exceeds the marginal cost.
   c. uses less labor than would be ideal from society's perspective.
   d. experiences increasing marginal returns.

4. **A rightward shift of the labor supply curve in graph (a) would shift curve:**
   a. $d = mrp$ leftward in graph (b).
   b. $d = mrp$ rightward in graph (b).
   c. $s = $ MRC upward in graph (b).
   d. $s = $ MRC downward in graph (b).

Answers: 1. d; 2. b; 3. b; 4. d

services in that market. This fact is expressed graphically by the upward sloping market labor supply curve S in Figure 17.3a.

Labor Market Equilibrium

The intersection of the market labor demand curve and the market labor supply curve determines the equilibrium wage rate and level of employment in a purely competitive labor market. In Figure 17.3a the equilibrium wage rate is W_c ($20) and the number of workers hired is Q_c (1,000). To the individual firm the market wage rate W_c is given. Each of the many firms employs such a small fraction of the total available supply of this type of labor that no single firm can influence the wage rate. As shown by the horizontal line s in Figure 17.3b, the labor supply faced by an individual firm is perfectly elastic. It can hire as many or as few workers as it wants to at the market wage rate.

Each individual firm will maximize its profit (or minimize its loss) by hiring this type of labor up to the point at which marginal revenue product equals marginal resource cost. This is merely an application of the MRP = MRC rule we developed in Chapter 16.

As Table 17.1 indicates, when an individual competitive firm faces the market price for a resource, the marginal cost of that resource (MRC) is constant and is equal to the market price for each and every unit that the competitive firm may choose to purchase. Note that MRC is constant at $20 and matches the $20 wage rate. Each additional worker hired adds precisely their own wage rate ($20 in this case) to the firm's total resource cost. Thus the firm in a purely competitive labor market maximizes its profit by hiring workers up to the point at which its wage rate equals MRP. In Figure 17.3b this firm will hire q_c(5) workers, paying each worker the market wage rate W_c($20). The other 199 firms (not shown) that are hiring workers in this labor market will also each employ 5 workers and pay $20 per hour.

To determine a firm's total revenue from employing a particular number of labor units, we sum the MRPs of those units. For example, if a firm employs 3 labor units with marginal revenue products of $25 $24, and $23, respectively, then the firm's total revenue is $72 (= $25 + $24 + $23). In Figure 17.3b, total revenue is represented by area $0abc$ under the MRP curve to the left of q_c.

What area represents the firm's total cost, including a normal profit? Answer: For q_c units, the same area—$0abc$. The green rectangle represents the firm's total wage cost ($0q_c \times 0W_c$). The blue triangle (total revenue minus total wage cost) represents the firm's nonlabor costs—its explicit and implicit payments to land, capital, and entrepreneurship. Thus, in this case, total cost (wages plus other income payments) equals total revenue. This firm and others like it are earning only a normal profit. Thus Figure 17.3b represents a long-run equilibrium for a firm that is selling its product in a purely competitive product market and hiring its labor in a purely competitive labor market. (The nearby Consider This story discusses how equilibrium wages are distributed between fringe benefits and take-home pay.)

TABLE 17.1
The Supply of Labor: Pure Competition in the Hire of Labor

(1) Units of Labor	(2) Wage Rate	(3) Total Labor Cost	(4) Marginal Resource (Labor) Cost
0	$20	$ 0	
1	20	20	$20
2	20	40	20
3	20	60	20
4	20	80	20
5	20	100	20
6	20	120	20

CONSIDER THIS . . .

Fringe Benefits vs. Take-Home Pay

Figure 17.2 shows that total compensation has risen significantly over the past several decades. Not shown in that figure, however, is the fact that the amount of take-home pay received by middle-class American workers has increased by much less. One contributing factor has been the rise of fringe benefits.

To see why fringe benefits matter, recall that throughout this chapter we have defined the wage as the total price that employers pay to obtain labor and compensate workers for providing it. Under our definition, wages are the sum of take-home pay (such as hourly pay and annual salaries) and fringe benefits (such as paid vacations, health insurance, and pensions).

So now consider an equilibrium wage, such as W_c in Figure 17.3. If workers want higher fringe benefits, they can

Numbeos/E+/Getty Images

have them—but only if take-home pay falls by an equal amount. With the equilibrium wage fixed by supply and demand, the only way workers can get more fringe benefits is by accepting lower take-home pay.

This is an important point to understand because in recent decades, workers have received an increasing fraction of their total compensation in the form of fringe benefits—especially health insurance. Those fringe benefits are costly and in a competitive labor market, each $1 increase in fringe benefits means $1 less for paychecks.

That trade-off helps to explain why take-home pay has increased by less than total compensation in recent decades. With a rising fraction of total compensation flowing toward fringe benefits, the increase in take-home pay was much less than the overall increase in total compensation.

Monopsony Model

>> **LO17.3** Demonstrate how monopsony can reduce wages below competitive levels.

monopsony A *market structure* in which there is only a single buyer of a good, *service,* or *resource.*

In a purely competitive labor market, each employer hires too small an amount of labor to influence the wage rate. Each firm can hire as little or as much labor as it needs, but only at the market wage rate, as reflected in its horizontal labor supply curve. The situation is quite different when the labor market is a **monopsony,** in which there is only a single buyer. A labor market monopsony has the following characteristics:

- There is only a single buyer of a particular type of labor.

- The workers providing this type of labor have few employment options other than working for the monopsony because they are either geographically immobile or because finding alternative employment would mean having to acquire new skills.

- The firm is a "wage maker" because the wage rate it must pay varies directly with the number of workers it employs.

There are various degrees of monopsony power. In *pure* monopsony, such power is at its maximum because only a single employer hires labor in the labor market. The best real-world examples are the labor markets in some towns that depend almost entirely on one major firm. For example, a Colorado ski resort, a Wisconsin paper mill, or an Alaskan fish processor may provide most of the employment in its geographically isolated locale.

In other cases, three or four firms may each hire a large portion of the labor supply in a certain market and therefore have some monopsony power. Moreover, if they tacitly or openly act in concert in hiring labor, they greatly enhance their monopsony power.

Upward Sloping Labor Supply to Firm

When a firm hires most of the available supply of a certain type of labor, its decision to employ more or fewer workers affects those workers' wage rate. Specifically, if a firm is large in relation to the size of the labor market, it will have to pay a higher wage rate to attract labor away from other employment or from leisure. Suppose that there is only one employer of a particular type of labor in a certain geographic area. In this pure monopsony situation, the labor supply curve for the *firm* and the total labor supply curve for the *labor market* are identical. This labor supply curve—represented by curve S in Figure 17.4—slopes upward because the monopsonist must pay higher wage rates if it wants to attract and hire additional workers. This same curve is also the monopsonist's average-cost-of-labor curve. Each point on curve S indicates the wage rate (cost) per worker that must be paid to attract the corresponding number of workers. The larger the number of workers, the higher the wage rate.

MRC Higher than the Wage Rate

When a monopsonist pays a higher wage to attract an additional worker, it must pay that higher wage not only to the additional worker, but also to all the workers it currently employs at a lower wage. If it does not, labor morale will deteriorate, and the employer will be plagued with labor unrest. Paying a uniform wage to all workers means that the cost of an extra worker—the marginal resource (labor) cost (MRC)—is the sum of that additional worker's wage rate and the amount necessary to bring the wage rate of all current workers up to the new wage level.

Table 17.2 illustrates this point. One worker can be hired at a wage rate of $16. But hiring a second worker forces the firm to pay a higher wage rate of $17. The marginal resource (labor) cost of the second worker is $18—the $17 paid to the second worker plus a $1 raise for the first worker. From another viewpoint, total labor cost is now $34 (= 2 × $17), up from $16 (= 1 × $16). So the MRC of the second worker is $18 (= 34 − $16), not just the $17 wage rate paid to that second worker. Similarly, the marginal labor cost of the third worker is $20—the $18 that must be

FIGURE 17.4
The wage rate and level of employment in a monopsonistic labor market.

In a monopsonistic labor market the employer's marginal resource (labor) cost curve (MRC) lies above the labor supply curve S. Equating MRC with MRP at point b, the monopsonist hires Q_m workers (compared with Q_c under competition). As indicated by point c on S, it pays only wage rate W_m (compared with the competitive wage W_c).

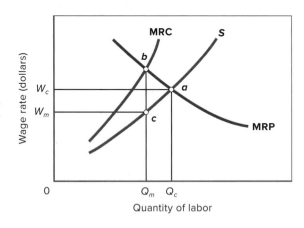

paid to attract that third worker from alternative employment plus $1 raises, from $17 to $18, for the first two workers.

Here is the key point: Because the monopsonist is the only employer in the labor market, its marginal resource (labor) cost exceeds the wage rate. Graphically, the monopsonist's MRC curve lies above the average-cost-of-labor curve, or labor supply curve *S*, as Figure 17.4 clearly shows.

TABLE 17.2
The Supply of Labor: Monopsony in the Hiring of Labor

(1) Units of Labor	(2) Wage Rate	(3) Total Labor Cost	(4) Marginal Resource (Labor) Cost
0	$15	$ 0	
1	16	16	$16
2	17	34	18
3	18	54	20
4	19	76	22
5	20	100	24
6	21	126	26

Equilibrium Wage and Employment

How many units of labor will the monopsonist hire, and what wage rate will it pay? To maximize profit, the monopsonist will employ the quantity of labor Q_m in Figure 17.4, because at that quantity MRC and MRP are equal (point *b*). The monopsonist next determines how much it must pay to attract these Q_m workers. From the supply curve *S*, specifically point *c*, it sees that it must pay wage rate W_m. Clearly, it need not pay a wage equal to MRP; it can attract and hire exactly the number of workers it wants (Q_m) with wage rate W_m. And that is the wage that it will pay.

Contrast these results with those that would prevail in a competitive labor market. With competition in the hiring of labor, the level of employment would be greater (at Q_c) and the wage rate would be higher (at W_c). Other things equal, the monopsonist maximizes its profit by hiring a smaller number of workers and thereby paying a less-than-competitive wage rate. Society obtains a smaller output, and workers receive a wage rate that is less by *bc* than their marginal revenue product. Just as a monopolistic seller finds it profitable to restrict product output to realize an above-competitive price for its goods, the monopsonistic employer finds it profitable to restrict employment in order to reduce wage rates below competitive wage rates.

Examples of Monopsony Power

Monopsonistic labor markets are uncommon in the United States. In most labor markets, several potential employers compete for most workers, particularly for workers who are occupationally and geographically mobile. Also, where monopsony labor market outcomes might have otherwise occurred, unions have often sprung up to counteract that power by forcing firms to negotiate wages. Nevertheless, economists have found some evidence of monopsony power in the markets for nurses, professional athletes, and public school teachers.

In the case of nurses, the major employers in most locales are a relatively small number of hospitals. Further, nurses' highly specialized skills are not readily transferable to other occupations. Other things equal, the smaller the number of hospitals in a town or city (that is, the greater the degree of monopsony), the lower the beginning salaries of nurses.

Professional sports leagues also provide a good example of monopsony, particularly regarding the pay of first-year players. The National Football League, the National Basketball Association, and Major League Baseball assign first-year players to teams through "player drafts." That device prohibits other teams from competing for a player's services, at least for several years, until the player becomes a "free agent." In this way, each league exercises monopsony power, which results in lower salaries than would occur under competitive conditions.

▶ Real wages have increased over time in the United States because labor demand has increased relative to labor supply.

▶ Over the long term, real wages per worker have increased at approximately the same rate as worker productivity.

▶ The competitive employer is a wage taker and employs workers at the point where the wage rate (= MRC) equals MRP.

▶ The labor supply curve to a monopsonist slopes upward, causing MRC to exceed the wage rate for each worker. Other things equal, the monopsonist hiring where MRC = MRP will employ fewer workers and pay a lower wage rate than would a purely competitive employer.

QUICK REVIEW
17.1

Three Union Models

>> **LO17.4** Discuss how unions increase wage rates.

Thus far we have assumed that workers compete with one another in selling their labor services. But in some labor markets, workers unionize and sell their labor services collectively.

When a union is formed in an otherwise competitive labor market, it usually bargains with a relatively large number of employers. It has many goals, the most important of which is to raise wage rates. It can pursue that objective in several ways.

Demand-Enhancement Model

From the union's viewpoint, increasing the demand for union labor is highly desirable. As Figure 17.5 shows, an increase in the demand for union labor will create a higher union wage along with more jobs.

Unions can increase the demand for their labor by increasing the demand for the goods or services they help produce. Political lobbying is the main tool for increasing the demand for union-produced goods or services. For example, construction unions have lobbied for new highways, mass-transit systems, and stadium projects. Teachers' unions and associations have pushed for increased public spending on education. U.S. steel unions and forest-product workers have lobbied for tariffs and quotas on foreign imports of steel and lumber. Such trade restrictions shift the demand for labor away from foreign countries and toward unionized U.S. labor.

Unions can also increase the demand for union labor by altering the price of other inputs. For example, although union members are generally paid significantly more than the minimum wage, unions have strongly supported increases in the minimum wage. The purpose may be to raise the price of low-wage, nonunion labor, which in some cases is substitutable for union labor. A higher minimum wage for nonunion workers will discourage employers from substituting such workers for union workers and thereby bolster the demand for union members.

Unions have sometimes sought to increase the demand for their labor by supporting policies that will reduce or hold down the price of a complementary resource. For example, unions in industries that represent workers who transport fruits and vegetables may support legislation that allows low-wage agricultural workers from other countries to temporarily work in the United States. Where union labor and another resource are complementary, a price decrease for the other resource will increase the demand for union labor through the output effect (see Chapter 16).

exclusive unionism The policy, pursued by many *craft unions*, in which a *union* first gets employers to agree to hire only union workers and then excludes many workers from joining the union so as to restrict the supply of labor and drive up wages. Compare with *inclusive unionism*. The policies typically employed by a *craft union*.

Exclusive or Craft Union Model

Unions can also boost wage rates by reducing the supply of labor, and over the years organized labor has favored policies to do just that. For example, labor unions have supported legislation that has (1) restricted permanent immigration, (2) reduced child labor, (3) encouraged compulsory retirement, and (4) enforced a shorter workweek.

Moreover, certain types of unions have adopted techniques to restrict the number of workers who can join their union. This is especially true of *craft unions*, whose members possess a particular skill, such as carpenters, masons, and plumbers. Craft unions have sometimes forced employers to agree to hire only union members, thereby gaining virtually complete control of the labor supply. Then, by following restrictive membership policies—for example, long apprenticeships, very high initiation fees, and limits on the number of new members admitted—they have artificially restricted labor supply. As Figure 17.6 indicates, such practices result in higher wage rates and constitute what is called **exclusive unionism.** By excluding workers from unions and therefore from the labor supply, craft unions succeed in elevating wage rates.

This craft union model applies to many professional organizations, such as the American Medical Association, the National Education Association, and the American Bar Association.

FIGURE 17.5
Unions and demand enhancement.

When unions can increase the demand for union labor (say, from D_1 to D_2), they can realize higher wage rates (W_c to W_u) and more jobs (Q_c to Q_u).

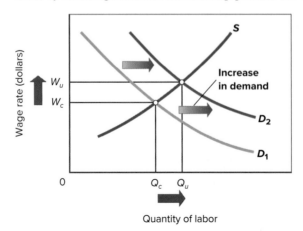

These groups often seek to enact laws requiring **occupational licensing.** These laws mandate that some occupational group (for example, physicians, lawyers, plumbers, cosmetologists, pest controllers) can practice their trade only if they meet certain requirements. Those requirements might include level of education, amount of work experience, the passing of an examination, and personal characteristics ("the practitioner must be of good moral character"). Members of the licensed occupation typically dominate the licensing board that administers such laws. The result is self-regulation, which often leads to policies that serve to restrict entry to the occupation and reduce labor supply.

The expressed purpose of licensing is to protect consumers from incompetent practitioners—surely a worthy goal. But such licensing results in above-competitive wages and earnings for those in the licensed occupation (Figure 17.6). Moreover, licensing requirements often include a residency requirement, which inhibits the interstate movement of qualified workers. Some 1,100 occupations are now licensed in the United States. This chapter's Last Word gives examples of licensing requirements that restrict the employment prospects of lower-income workers.

FIGURE 17.6
Exclusive or craft unionism.

By reducing the supply of labor (say, from S_1 to S_2) through the use of restrictive membership policies, exclusive unions achieve higher wage rates (W_c to W_u). However, restriction of the labor supply also reduces the number of workers employed (Q_c to Q_u).

occupational licensing The laws of state or local governments that require that a worker satisfy certain specified requirements and obtain a license from a licensing board before engaging in a particular occupation.

Inclusive or Industrial Union Model

Instead of trying to limit their membership, however, most unions seek to organize all available workers. This is especially true of the *industrial unions,* such as those of the automobile workers and steelworkers. Such unions seek as members all available unskilled, semiskilled, and skilled workers in an industry. It makes sense for a union to be exclusive when its members are skilled craftworkers for whom the employer has few substitutes. But it does not make sense for a union to be exclusive when trying to organize unskilled and semiskilled workers. To break a strike, employers could then easily substitute unskilled or semiskilled nonunion workers for the unskilled or semiskilled union workers.

By contrast, an industrial union that includes virtually all available workers in its membership can put firms under great pressure to agree to its wage demands. Because of its legal right to strike, such a union can threaten to deprive firms of their entire labor supply. And an actual strike can do just that. Further, with virtually all available workers in the union, it will be difficult in the short run for new nonunion firms to emerge and thereby undermine what the union is demanding from existing firms.

Figure 17.7 illustrates such **inclusive unionism.** Initially, the competitive equilibrium wage rate is W_c and the level of employment is Q_c. Now suppose an industrial union is formed that demands a higher, above-equilibrium wage rate of, say, W_u. That wage rate W_u would create a perfectly elastic labor supply over the range *ae* in Figure 17.7. If firms wanted to hire any workers in this range, they would have to pay the union-imposed wage rate. If they decide against meeting this wage demand, the union will call a strike. If firms decide it is better to pay the higher wage rate than to suffer a strike, they will cut back on employment from Q_c to Q_u.

By agreeing to the union's wage demand, individual employers become wage takers at the union wage rate W_u. Because labor supply is perfectly elastic over range *ae,* the marginal resource (labor) cost is equal to the wage rate W_u

inclusive unionism The policy, pursued by *industrial unions,* in which a *union* attempts to include every worker in a given *industry* so as to be able to restrict the entire industry's labor supply and thereby raise wages. Compare with *exclusive unionism.*

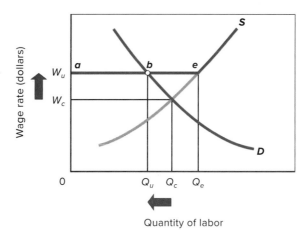

FIGURE 17.7
Inclusive or industrial unionism.

By organizing virtually all available workers in order to control the supply of labor, inclusive industrial unions may impose a wage rate, such as W_u, which is above the competitive wage rate W_c. In effect, this changes the labor supply curve from S to aeS. At wage rate W_u, employers will cut employment from Q_c to Q_u.

over this range. The Q_u level of employment is the result of employers' equating this MRC (now equal to the union wage rate) with MRP, according to the profit-maximizing rule.

Note from point e on labor supply curve S that Q_e workers desire employment at wage W_u. But as indicated by point b on labor demand curve D, only Q_u workers are employed. The result is a surplus of labor of $Q_e - Q_u$ (also shown by distance be). In a purely competitive labor market without the union, the effect of a surplus of unemployed workers would be lower wages. Specifically, the wage rate would fall to the equilibrium level W_c where the quantity of labor supplied equals the quantity of labor demanded (each Q_c). But this drop in wages does not happen because workers are acting collectively through their union. Individual workers cannot offer to work for less than W_u, nor can employers pay less than that.

Wage Increases and Job Loss

Have U.S. unions been successful in raising the wages of their members? Evidence suggests that union members on average achieve a 15 percent wage advantage over nonunion workers. But when unions are successful in raising wages, their efforts also have another major effect.

As Figures 17.6 and 17.7 suggest, the wage-raising actions achieved by unions reduce employment in unionized firms. Simply put, a union's success in achieving above-equilibrium wage rates tends to be accompanied by a decline in the number of workers employed. That result acts as a restraining influence on union wage demands. A union cannot expect to maintain solidarity within its ranks if it seeks a wage rate so high that 20 to 30 percent of its members lose their jobs.

Bilateral Monopoly Model

>> LO17.5 Explain why wages and employment are determined by collective bargaining in a situation of bilateral monopoly.

bilateral monopoly A market in which there is a single seller (*monopoly*) and a single buyer (*monopsony*).

Suppose a strong industrial union is formed in a monopsonist labor market rather than a competitive labor market, thereby creating a combination of the monopsony model and the inclusive unionism model. Economists call the result **bilateral monopoly** because in its pure form there is a single seller and a single buyer. The union is a monopolistic "seller" of labor that controls labor supply and can influence wage rates, but it faces a monopsonistic "buyer" of labor that can also affect wages by altering the amount of labor that it employs. This is not an uncommon case, particularly in less pure forms in which a single union confronts two, three, or four large employers. Examples: steel, automobiles, construction equipment, professional sports, and commercial aircraft.

Indeterminate Outcome of Bilateral Monopoly

We show this situation in Figure 17.8, where Figure 17.7 is superimposed onto Figure 17.4. The monopsonistic employer will seek the below-competitive-equilibrium wage rate W_m, and the union will press for some above-competitive-equilibrium wage rate such as W_u. Which will be the outcome? We cannot say with certainty. The outcome is "logically indeterminate" because the bilateral monopoly model does not explain what will happen at the bargaining table. We can expect the wage outcome to lie somewhere between W_m and W_u. Beyond that, about all we can say is that the party with the greater bargaining power and the more effective bargaining strategy will probably get a wage closer to the one it seeks.

FIGURE 17.8
Bilateral monopoly in the labor market.

A monopsonist seeks to hire Q_m workers (where MRC = MRP) and pay wage rate W_m corresponding to quantity Q_m on labor supply curve S. The inclusive union it faces seeks the above-equilibrium wage rate W_u. The actual outcome cannot be predicted by economic theory. It will result from bargaining between the two parties.

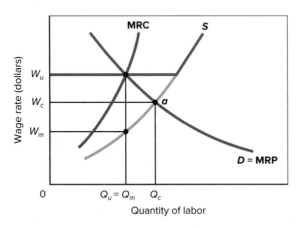

Desirability of Bilateral Monopoly

The wage and employment outcomes in this situation might be more economically desirable than the term "bilateral monopoly" implies. The monopoly on one side of the market might in effect cancel out the monopoly on the other side, yielding competitive or near-competitive results. If either the union or management prevailed in this market—that is, if the actual wage rate were either

W_u or W_m—employment would be restricted to Q_m (where MRP = MRC), which is below the competitive level.

But now suppose the monopoly power of the union roughly offsets the monopsony power of management, and the union and management agree on wage rate W_c, which is the competitive wage. Once management accepts this wage rate, its incentive to restrict employment disappears; no longer can it depress wage rates by restricting employment. Instead, management hires at the most profitable resource quantity, Q_c workers, which is the quantity of labor at which the bargained wage rate W_c (which is now the firm's MRC) is equal to the MRP. Thus, with monopoly on both sides of the labor market, the resulting wage rate and level of employment may be closer to competitive levels than would be the case if monopoly existed on only one side of the market.

▶ In the demand-enhancement union model, a union increases the wage rate by increasing labor demand through actions that increase product demand or alter the prices of related inputs.

▶ In the exclusive (craft) union model, a union increases wage rates by artificially restricting labor supply, through, say, long apprenticeships or occupational licensing.

▶ In the inclusive (industrial) union model, a union raises the wage rate by gaining control over a firm's labor supply and threatening to withhold labor via a strike unless a negotiated wage is obtained.

▶ Bilateral monopoly occurs in a labor market where a monopsonist bargains with an inclusive, or industrial, union. Wage and employment outcomes are determined by collective bargaining in this situation.

The Minimum-Wage Controversy

Since the passage of the Fair Labor Standards Act in 1938, the United States has had a federal **minimum wage.** That wage has ranged between 30 and 50 percent of the average wage paid to manufacturing workers and was most recently raised to $7.25 in July 2009. Numerous states, however, have minimum wages that are higher than the federal minimum wage. For example, in 2022 the minimum wage in the state of California was $15 an hour. The purpose of the minimum wage is to provide a "wage floor" that will help less-skilled workers earn enough income to escape poverty.

>> LO17.6 Discuss how minimum wage laws affect labor markets.

minimum wage The lowest *wage* that employers may legally pay for an hour of work.

Case against the Minimum Wage

Critics, reasoning in terms of Figure 17.7, contend that an above-equilibrium minimum wage (say, W_u) will simply cause employers to hire fewer workers. Downward sloping labor-demand curves are a reality. The higher labor costs may even force some firms out of business. Then some of the poor, low-wage workers whom the minimum wage was designed to help will find themselves out of work. Critics point out that workers who are *unemployed* and desperate to find a job at a minimum wage of $7.25 per hour are clearly worse off than they would be if *employed* at a market wage rate of, say, $6.50 per hour.

A second criticism is that the minimum wage is "poorly targeted" to reduce household poverty. Critics note that much of the benefit of the minimum wage accrues to workers, including many teenagers, who do not live in impoverished households.

Case for the Minimum Wage

Advocates of the minimum wage say that critics analyze its impact in an unrealistic context. They argue that it is not right to assume that all labor markets are competitive or that wages will always reach the competitive level in the absence of a minimum wage (as in Figure 17.7). Rather, they contend that much of the low-pay labor market is not competitive. Thus, they believe that the monoposony labor market of Figure 17.4 is a better model for these markets. There, the minimum wage can increase wage rates without causing significant unemployment. That is possible because a higher minimum wage may produce even more jobs by eliminating the motive that monopsonistic firms have for restricting employment. For example, a minimum-wage floor of W_c in Figure 17.4 would change the firm's labor supply curve to $W_c a$ and prompt the firm to increase its employment from Q_m workers to Q_c workers.

Proponents also contend that additional benefits may arise even when a labor market is competitive. For instance, the higher wage rate might prompt firms to find more productive tasks for low-paid workers, thereby raising their productivity. Alternatively, the minimum wage may reduce *labor turnover* (the rate at which workers voluntarily quit). With fewer low-productivity trainees, the *average* productivity of the firm's workers would rise. In either case, the alleged negative employment effects of the minimum wage might not occur.

Evidence and Conclusions

Which view is correct? There is no clear answer. All economists agree that firms will not hire workers who cost more per hour than the value of their hourly output. So there is some minimum wage sufficiently high that it would severely reduce employment. Consider $50 an hour, as an absurd example. Because the majority of U.S. workers earned over $25 per hour in 2021, a minimum wage of $50 per hour would render the majority of U.S. workers unemployable because their employers would have to pay a wage that far exceeds their workers' marginal revenue products.

However, a minimum wage will cause unemployment only in labor markets where the minimum wage is higher than the equilibrium wage. Because the current minimum wage of $7.25 per hour is much lower than the average hourly wage of about $25.77 in 2021, any unemployment caused by the $7.25 per hour minimum wage is likely to fall on low-skilled workers who earn low wages due to their low productivity. These workers are mostly teenagers, adults who did not complete high school, and immigrants with low levels of education. Many also lack proficiency with the English language. For these groups, recent research suggests that a 10 percent increase in the minimum wage will cause a 1 to 3 percent decline in employment. However, estimates vary from study to study, and significant controversy remains.

The overall effect of the minimum wage is thus uncertain. On the one hand, the employment and unemployment effects of the minimum wage do not appear to be as great as many critics fear. On the other hand, because a large part of its effect is dissipated on nonpoverty families, the minimum wage is not as strong an antipoverty tool as many supporters contend.

Voting patterns and surveys make it clear, however, that the minimum wage has strong political support. Perhaps these patterns stem from two perceptions: (1) More workers are believed to be helped than hurt by the minimum wage, and (2) the minimum wage provides some assurance that employers are not taking undue advantage of vulnerable, low-skilled workers.

Wage Differentials

>> **LO17.7** List the major causes of wage differentials.

wage differential The difference between the *wage* received by one worker or group of workers and that received by another worker or group of workers.

Hourly wage rates and annual salaries differ greatly across occupations. Table 17.3 lists average annual salaries for a number of occupations to illustrate occupational **wage differentials.** For example, anesthesiologists on average earn ten times as much as retail salespersons. In addition, there are large wage differentials within some of the occupations listed. For example, although average wages for retail salespersons are relatively low, some top salespersons selling on commission make several times the average wage listed for their occupation.

What explains these wage differentials? Once again, the forces of demand and supply are revealing. As Figure 17.9 shows, wage differentials can arise on either the supply or the demand side of labor markets. Figures 17.9a and 17.9b represent labor markets for two occupational groups that have identical *labor supply curves*. Labor market (a) has a relatively high equilibrium wage (W_a) because labor demand is very strong. In labor market (b), the equilibrium wage is relatively low (W_b) because labor demand is weak. Clearly, the wage differential between occupations (a) and (b) results solely from differences in the magnitude of labor demand.

Contrast these situations with Figures 17.9c and 17.9d, where the *labor demand* curves are identical. In labor market (c), the equilibrium wage is relatively high (W_c) because labor supply is low. In labor market (d), labor supply is highly abundant, so the equilibrium wage (W_d) is relatively low. The wage differential between (c) and (d) results solely from the differences in the size of labor supply.

Although Figure 17.9 provides a good starting point for understanding wage differentials, we need to know *why* demand and supply conditions differ in various labor markets. There are several reasons.

Marginal Revenue Productivity

The strength of labor demand—how far rightward the labor demand curve is located—differs greatly among occupations due to differences in how much various occupational groups contribute to their respective employers' revenue. This revenue contribution, in turn, depends on the workers' productivity and the strength of the demand for the products they are helping to produce. Where labor is highly

TABLE 17.3 Average Annual Wages in Selected Occupations, 2020

Occupation	Average Annual Wages
1. Anesthesiologists	$271,440
2. Petroleum engineers	154,330
3. Financial managers	151,510
4. Law professors	134,760
5. Pharmacists	125,460
6. Civil engineers	95,440
7. Registered nurses	80,010
8. Dental hygienists	78,050
9. Police officers	67,290
10. Electricians	61,500
11. Carpenters	54,200
12. Travel agents	46,650
13. Barbers	38,050
14. Janitors	31,410
15. Retail salespersons	30,940
16. Child care workers	26,790
17. Fast food cooks	24,300

Source: Occupational Employment and Wages, U.S. Bureau of Labor Statistics, May 2020.

(a)

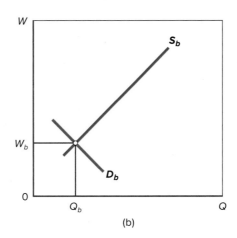

(b)

FIGURE 17.9
Labor demand, labor supply, and wage differentials.

Wage differentials in labor markets can be caused by differences in either supply or demand conditions. Because the labor supply curves S_a and S_b are identical in the labor markets depicted in graphs (a) and (b), differences in demand are the sole cause of the $W_a - W_b$ wage differential. And because the labor demand curves D_c and D_d are identical in (c) and (d), the $W_c - W_d$ wage differential results solely from differences in labor supply.

(c)

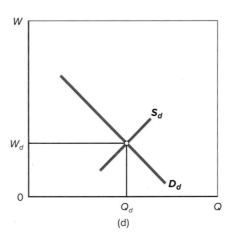

(d)

productive and product demand is strong, labor demand also is strong and, other things equal, pay is high. Top professional athletes, for example, are highly productive at producing sports entertainment, for which millions of people are willing to pay billions of dollars over the course of a season. Because the **marginal revenue productivity** of these players is so high, they are in very high demand by sports teams. This high demand leads to their extremely high salaries (as in Figure 17.9a). In contrast, most workers generate much more modest revenue for their employers. The result is much lower demand for their labor and, consequently, much lower wages (as in Figure 17.9b).

Noncompeting Groups

On the supply side of the labor market, workers differ in their mental and physical capacities and in their education and training. At any given time the labor force is made up of many **noncompeting groups** of workers, each representing several occupations for which the members of a particular group qualify. In some groups qualified workers are relatively few, whereas in others they are plentiful.

Ability At any time, only a few workers have the skills or physical attributes to be hired as brain surgeons, concert violinists, top fashion models, research chemists, or professional athletes. Because the supply of these particular types of labor is very small in relation to labor demand, their wages are high (as in Figure 17.9c). The members of these and similar groups do not compete with one another or with other skilled or semiskilled workers. The violinist does not compete with the surgeon, nor does the surgeon compete with the violinist or the fashion model.

Education and Training Another source of wage differentials is differing amounts of **human capital**, which is the personal stock of knowledge, know-how, and skills that enables a person to be productive and thus to earn income. Like expenditures on machinery and equipment, productivity-enhancing expenditures on education or training are investments. In both cases, people incur *present costs* with the intention that those expenditures will lead to greater *future earnings*.

The left side of Figure 17.10 indicates that workers who have made greater investments in education achieve higher incomes while the right side demonstrates that they also enjoy lower *unemployment rates*. These two positive consequences of obtaining more education are the result of two underlying factors: (1) There are fewer highly educated workers, so their supply is limited relative to less-educated workers, and (2) more-educated workers tend to be more productive and thus in greater demand.

Another positive consequence of obtaining more education is that better-educated workers see their earnings rise more rapidly over their careers than those of less-educated workers. Why? Employers provide more on-the-job training to the better-educated workers, boosting their marginal revenue productivity and therefore their earnings.

Although education yields higher incomes, it carries substantial costs. A college education involves not only direct costs (tuition, fees, books) but also indirect or opportunity costs (forgone earnings). Does the higher pay received by better-educated workers compensate for these costs? The answer is yes. Rates of return are estimated at 10 to 13 percent for investments in secondary education and 8 to 12 percent for investments in college education. Overall, each year of schooling raises a worker's wage by about 8 percent.

The nearby Consider This story gives a famous artist's perspective on the returns to human capital.

marginal revenue product (MRP) The change in a firm's total *revenue* when it employs 1 additional unit of a *resource* (the quantity of all other resources employed remaining constant); equal to the change in *total revenue* divided by the change in the quantity of the resource employed.

noncompeting groups Collections of workers who do not compete with each other for employment because the skill and training of the workers in one group are substantially different from those of the workers in other groups.

human capital The knowledge and skills that make a person productive.

FIGURE 17.10
Education levels, weekly earnings, and unemployment rate.

Weekly earnings are higher, and employment rates lower, for more educated workers.

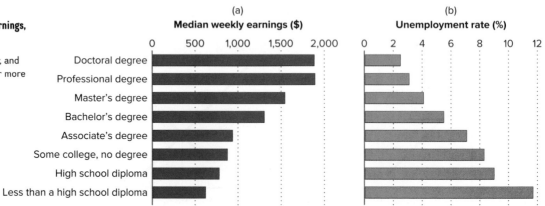

Source: U.S. Bureau of Labor Statistics, 2020.

CONSIDER THIS . . .

My Entire Life

Human capital is the accumulation of prior investments in education, training, and experience that increase productivity and earnings. It is the stock of knowledge, know-how, and skills that enables individuals to be productive and thus earn income. A valuable stock of human capital, together with a strong demand for one's services, can add up to a large capacity to earn income. For some people, high earnings have little to do with actual hours of work and much to do

Ralph Gatti/AFP/Getty Images

with their tremendous skill, which reflects their accumulated stock of human capital.

The point is demonstrated in the following story: It is said that a tourist once spotted the famous Spanish artist Pablo Picasso (1881–1973) in a Paris café. The tourist asked Picasso if he would do a sketch of his wife for pay. Picasso sketched the wife in a matter of minutes and said, "That will be 10,000 francs [roughly $2,000]." Hearing the high price, the tourist became irritated, saying, "But that took you only a few minutes."

"No," replied Picasso, "it took me my entire life!"

Compensating Differences

In virtually all locales, construction laborers receive much higher wages than salesclerks. These wage differentials are called **compensating wage differences** because they must be paid to compensate for nonmonetary differences in various jobs.

The construction job involves dirty hands, a sore back, possible accidents, and irregular employment, both seasonally and during recessions (economywide economic slowdowns). The retail sales job means clean clothing, pleasant air-conditioned surroundings, and little fear of injury. Other things equal, it is easy to see why workers would rather process a credit-card payment than pick up a shovel. Thus the amount of labor supplied to construction firms (as in Figure 17.9c) is smaller than that supplied to retail shops (as in Figure 17.9d).

Compensating differences spring up throughout the economy. Other things equal, jobs having high risk of injury or death pay more than comparable, safer jobs. Jobs lacking employer-paid health insurance, pensions, and vacation time pay more than comparable jobs that provide these benefits. Jobs with more flexible hours pay less than jobs with rigid work-hour requirements. Jobs with greater risk of unemployment pay more than comparable jobs with little unemployment risk. Entry-level jobs in occupations that provide very poor prospects for pay advancement pay more than entry-level jobs that have clearly defined "job ladders."

compensating wage differences Differences in the wages received by workers in different jobs to compensate for the nonmonetary differences between the jobs.

Market Imperfections

Differences in marginal revenue productivity, amounts of human capital, and nonmonetary aspects of jobs explain most wage differentials. But some persistent differentials result from market imperfections that impede workers from moving from lower-paying jobs to higher-paying jobs.

Lack of Job Information Workers may simply be unaware of job opportunities and wage rates in other geographic areas and in other jobs for which they qualify. Consequently, the flow of qualified labor from lower-paying to higher-paying jobs—and thus the adjustments in labor supply—may not be sufficient to equalize wages within occupations.

Geographic Immobility Workers take root geographically. Many are reluctant to move to new places. Doing so would involve leaving friends, relatives, and associates. It would mean forcing children to change schools, having to sell homes, and incurring the costs and inconveniences of adjusting to a new job and a new community. As Adam Smith noted over two centuries ago, "A [person] is of all sorts of luggage the most difficult to be transported." Workers' reluctance or inability to move enables geographic wage differentials within the same occupation to persist.

Unions and Government Restraints Wage differentials may be reinforced by artificial restrictions imposed by unions and government. We have noted that craft unions typically restrict membership. After all, if carpenters and bricklayers become too plentiful, the wages they can command will decline. Thus the low-paid nonunion carpenter of Brush, Colorado, may be willing to move to Chicago in the pursuit of higher wages. But her chances of succeeding in the big city are slim. She may be unable to get a union card, and no card means no job. Similarly, an optometrist or lawyer qualified to practice in one state may not meet other states' licensing requirements. Other artificial barriers involve pension plans, health insurance benefits, and seniority rights that might be jeopardized by moving from one job to another.

Discrimination Despite legislation to the contrary, discrimination sometimes results in lower wages being paid to women and racial minorities than to white men doing very similar or even identical work. Also, women and minorities may be crowded into certain low-paying occupations, driving down wages in those occupations. If this *occupational segregation* keeps qualified women and minorities from taking higher-paying jobs, then differences in pay will persist. We study labor-market discrimination in depth in Chapter 23.

Pay for Performance

>> **LO17.8** Identify the types, benefits, and costs of pay-for-performance plans.

The models of wage determination in this chapter assume that worker pay is always a standard amount for each hour's work, for example, $15 per hour. But pay schemes are often much more complex. For instance, many workers receive annual salaries rather than hourly pay. And workers receive differing amounts of fringe benefits (health insurance, paid vacations, paid sick-leave days, pension contributions, and so on). Finally, some pay plans are designed to elicit a desired level of performance from workers. This last aspect of pay plans requires further elaboration.

The Principal-Agent Problem

principal-agent problem (1) At a *firm*, a conflict of interest that occurs when agents (workers or managers) pursue their own objectives to the detriment of the principals' (stockholders') goals. (2) In *public choice theory*, a conflict of interest that arises when elected officials (who are the agents of the people) pursue policies that are in their own interests rather than policies that would be in the better interests of the public (the principals).

The **principal-agent problem** (see Chapter 5) extends to all paid employees. Firms hire workers because the firms need workers to produce the goods and services the firms sell in trying to turn a profit. Workers are the firms' agents; they are hired to advance the firms' goals. The principals are the firms; they hire the worker agents to advance those goals. Firms and workers have one interest in common: They both want the firm to survive and thrive, which will ensure profit for the firm and continued employment and wages for the workers.

But the interests of firms and workers are not identical. As a result, a principal-agent problem arises. Workers may shirk on the job, thereby providing less than the agreed-upon effort. They may increase their leisure during paid work hours, without forfeiting income. The night security guard in a warehouse may leave work early or spend time reading a novel rather than making the assigned rounds. A salaried manager may spend time gaming online rather than attending to company business.

Firms (principals) have a profit incentive to reduce or eliminate shirking. One option is to monitor workers, but monitoring is difficult and costly. Hiring another worker to supervise or monitor the security guard might double the cost of maintaining a secure warehouse. Another way of resolving a principal-agent problem is an **incentive pay plan** that ties worker compensation more closely to worker output or performance. Incentive pay schemes include piece rates; commissions and royalties; bonuses, stock options, and profit sharing; and efficiency wages.

incentive pay plan A compensation structure that ties worker pay directly to performance. Such plans include piece rates, bonuses, *stock options*, commissions, and *profit-sharing plans*.

Piece Rates *Piece rates* are compensation paid according to the units of output a worker produces. If a principal pays fruit pickers by the bushel or truck drivers by the mile, it need not be concerned with shirking or with monitoring costs.

Commissions and Royalties Unlike piece rates, commissions and royalties tie compensation to the value of sales. Employees who sell products or services—including real estate agents, insurance agents, stockbrokers, and retail salespersons—commonly receive *commissions* equal to a percentage of the monetary value of their sales. Recording artists and authors receive *royalties*, computed as a percentage of sales revenues from their works. These types of compensation link the financial interests of the salespeople, artists, and authors to the firm's profit interest.

Bonuses, Stock Options, and Profit Sharing *Bonuses* are payments above one's annual salary that are based on some factor such as the performance of the individual worker, a group of workers, or the firm itself. A professional baseball player may receive a bonus based on a high batting average, the number of home runs hit, or the number of runs batted in. A business manager may receive a bonus based on his unit's profitability. *Stock options* allow workers to buy shares of their employer's stock at a fixed, lower price when the stock price rises. Stock options are part of the

LAST WORD

Occupational Licensing

Many Industries Impose Licensing Requirements as a Way of Restricting Competition.

Occupational licensing laws operate at the state and local level. They were originally created to protect the public from harm by ensuring that the members of licensed professions met high standards for training and expertise. This makes perfect sense for physicians and emergency medical technicians (EMTs), who are literally responsible for people's lives. But various business groups whose activities pose little or no threat to anyone have managed to get their industries covered by licensing requirements as a way of limiting competition and driving up prices.

Consider interior design. You have probably put up a poster, painted a wall, or rearranged your furniture at least a few times in your life. These acts of interior design probably didn't strike you as requiring any particular training or being in any way a threat to the public. But the National Associa-tion of Interior Designers dis-agrees. They have spent decades lobbying state governments to impose occupational licensing requirements on interior design-ers. And they have succeeded in Florida, Maryland, and Nevada.

In those states, anyone who wishes to work as an interior designer has to complete six years of training and internships before they can even apply for a license. Those six years plus the cost of all that training limits the supply of interior designers and thereby raises the wages of the few who do obtain a license. Those few naturally lobby to maintain the licensing requirement.

The six years of training that are required to obtain an interior-design license in those three states stand in stark contrast to the average of just 33 days that are required across all 50 states to obtain a license to work as an Emer-gency Medical Technician, or EMT. The EMT licensing requirements are much less onerous because EMTs have not organized themselves politically the way interior designers have. So the EMT licensing requirements reflect only what is actually required for competence. There has been no attempt to artificially increase the EMT require-ments in order to reduce the supply of EMTs and thereby artificially increase EMT wages.

There are dozens of examples of industries where occupational licensing is not obviously needed to protect the public or in which

licensing requirements have been made artificially excessive to drive up wages. Thirty-six states "protect" the public by requiring make-up artists to spend an average of seven months earning a license. Forty-six states "safeguard" gym-goers by requiring personal trainers to take an average of four years of classes and internships. And three states "defend" the public by requiring eight months of classes and training to obtain a license to install home entertainment systems.

These examples of unnecessary or excessive licensing might be funny except for the burden they place on consumers and workers. Not only do consumers have to pay higher prices because of reduced supply, they also enjoy fewer choices because they cannot legally hire an unlicensed provider even if that person is perfectly capable of doing the job well. Even worse, unnecessary licensing requirements substantially limit job opportuni-ties for low-income workers. Instead of being able to start working as soon as any honestly needed training is completed, they are forced to go through months or even years of costly artificial requirements whose only purpose is to limit competi-tion for those who already have licenses.

These barriers to employ-ment have grown more burden-some and pervasive in recent decades. Whereas only about 1 in 20 jobs required an occupa-tional license in the 1950s, nearly 1 in 3 do today. And of the 1,100 or so occupations that require a license at either the federal or state level, over 100 are for lower-wage jobs in fields such as cosmetology, child care, floristry, barbering, bus driving, bartending, tree trim-ming, hair braiding, massage therapy, and travel agency. Thus, unnecessary occupational licensing presents a major impediment to millions of poorer people hoping to set up their own businesses or switch careers. If they live in a state that requires licensing, they will have to pay fees, take classes, endure internships, and pass tests to obtain jobs that many consumers would be happy to pay them to do without a license. Unfortunately, that state of affairs is likely to continue indefinitely due to the power of the *special-interest effect* under which a small group of insiders can impose large costs on outsiders.

compensation packages of top corporate officials, as well as many workers in high-tech firms. *Profit-sharing plans* allocate a percentage of a firm's profit to its employees.

Efficiency Wages The rationale behind *efficiency wages* is that employers will enjoy greater effort from their workers by paying them above-equilibrium wage rates. Glance back at Figure 17.3, which shows a competitive labor market in which the equilibrium wage rate is $10. What happens if an employer decides to pay an above-equilibrium wage of $12 per hour? Rather than putting the firm at a cost disadvantage compared with rival firms paying only $10, the higher wage might improve worker effort and productivity so that unit labor costs actually fall. For example, if each worker produces 10 units of output per hour at the $12 wage rate compared with only 6 units at the $10 wage rate, unit labor costs for the high-wage firm will be only $1.20 (= $12/10) compared to $1.67 (= $10/6) for firms paying the equilibrium wage.

An above-equilibrium wage may enhance worker efficiency in several ways. It enables the firm to attract higher-quality workers. It lifts worker morale. And it lowers turnover, resulting in a more experienced workforce, greater worker productivity, and lower recruitment and training costs. Because the opportunity cost of losing a higher-wage job is greater, workers are more likely to put forth their best efforts with less supervision and monitoring. In fact, efficiency wage payments have proven effective for many employers.

QUICK REVIEW

17.3

▶ Proponents of the minimum wage argue that it assists the working poor and counters monopsony power where it may exist; critics say that it is poorly targeted to reduce poverty and that it reduces employment.

▶ Wage differentials are attributable in general to the forces of supply and demand, influenced by differences in workers' marginal revenue productivity, education, and skills and by nonmonetary differences in jobs. Several labor market imperfections also play a role.

▶ As it applies to labor, the principal-agent problem is one of workers pursuing their own interests to the detriment of the employer's profit objective.

▶ Pay-for-performance plans (piece rates, commissions, royalties, bonuses, stock options, profit sharing, and efficiency wages) are designed to improve worker productivity by overcoming the principal-agent problem.

Summary

LO17.1 Explain why labor productivity tracks real hourly compensation so closely over time.

The term "labor" encompasses all people who work for pay. The wage rate is the price paid per unit of time for labor. The nominal wage rate is the amount of money received per unit of time; the real wage rate is the purchasing power of the nominal wage.

The long-run growth of real hourly compensation—the average real wage—roughly matches that of productivity, with both increasing over the long run.

Global comparisons suggest that real wages in the United States are relatively high, but not the highest, internationally. High real wages in advanced industrial countries stem largely from high labor productivity.

LO17.2 Show how wage rates and employment levels are determined in competitive labor markets.

Specific wage rates depend on the structure of the particular labor market. In a competitive labor market, the equilibrium wage rate and level of employment are determined at the intersection of the labor supply curve and labor demand curve. For the individual firm, the market wage rate establishes a horizontal labor supply curve, meaning that the wage rate equals the firm's constant marginal resource cost. The firm hires workers to the point where its MRP equals its MRC.

LO17.3 Demonstrate how monopsony can reduce wages below competitive levels.

Under monopsony, the marginal resource cost curve lies above the resource supply curve because the monopsonist must bid up the wage rate to hire extra workers and must pay that higher wage rate to all workers. The monopsonist hires fewer workers than are hired under competitive conditions, pays less-than-competitive wage rates (has lower labor costs), and thus obtains greater profit.

LO17.4 Discuss how unions increase wage rates.

A union may raise competitive wage rates by (*a*) increasing the derived demand for labor, (*b*) restricting the supply of labor through exclusive unionism, or (*c*) directly enforcing an above-equilibrium wage rate through inclusive unionism. On average, unionized workers earn wage rates 15 percent higher than those of comparable nonunion workers.

LO17.5 Explain why wages and employment are determined by collective bargaining in a situation of bilateral monopoly.

In many industries, the labor market takes the form of bilateral monopoly, in which a strong union "sells" labor to a monopsonistic employer. The wage-rate outcome of this labor market model depends on union and employer bargaining power.

LO17.6 Discuss how minimum wage laws affect labor markets.

Economists disagree about the desirability of the minimum wage as an antipoverty mechanism. While it causes unemployment for some low-income workers, it raises the incomes of those who retain their jobs.

LO17.7 List the major causes of wage differentials.

Wage differentials are largely explainable in terms of (*a*) marginal revenue productivity of various groups of workers; (*b*) noncompeting groups arising from differences in the capacities and education of

different groups of workers; (*c*) compensating wage differences that must be paid to offset nonmonetary differences in jobs; and (*d*) market imperfections in the form of lack of job information, geographic immobility, union and government restraints, and discrimination.

LO17.8 Identify the types, benefits, and costs of pay-for-performance plans.

The principal-agent problem arises when workers provide less-than-expected effort. Firms may combat this problem by monitoring workers or by creating incentive pay schemes that link worker compensation to performance.

Terms and Concepts

wage

nominal wage

real wage

purely competitive labor market

monopsony

exclusive unionism

occupational licensing

inclusive unionism

bilateral monopoly

minimum wage

wage differential

marginal revenue productivity

noncompeting groups

human capital

compensating wage differences

principal-agent problem

incentive pay plan

Discussion Questions

1. Explain why the general level of wages is high in the United States and other industrially advanced countries. What is the single most important factor underlying the long-run increase in average real-wage rates in the United States? **LO17.1**
2. Why is a firm in a purely competitive labor market a wage taker? What would happen if it decided to pay less than the going market wage rate? **LO17.2**
3. Describe wage determination in a labor market in which workers are unorganized and many firms actively compete for the services of labor. Show this situation graphically, using W_1 to indicate the equilibrium wage rate and Q_1 to show the number of workers hired by the firms as a group. Show the labor supply curve of the individual firm, and compare it with that of the total market. Why the differences? In the diagram representing the firm, identify total revenue, total wage cost, and revenue available for the payment of nonlabor resources. **LO17.2**
4. Suppose the formerly competing firms in question 3 form an employers' association that hires labor as a monopsonist would. Describe verbally the effect on wage rates and employment. Adjust the graph you drew for question 3, showing the monopsonistic wage rate and employment level as W_2 and Q_2, respectively. Using this monopsony model, explain why hospital administrators sometimes complain about a "shortage" of nurses. How might such a shortage be corrected? **LO17.3**

5. Assume a monopsonistic employer is paying a wage rate of W_m and hiring Q_m workers, as indicated in Figure 17.8. Now suppose an industrial union is formed that forces the employer to accept a wage rate of W_c. Explain verbally and graphically why in this instance the higher wage rate will be accompanied by an increase in the number of workers hired. **LO17.5**
6. Have you ever worked for the minimum wage? If so, for how long? Would you favor increasing the minimum wage by a dollar? By two dollars? By five dollars? Explain your reasoning. **LO17.6**
7. "Many of the lowest-paid people in society—for example, short-order cooks—also have relatively poor working conditions. Hence, the notion of compensating wage differentials is disproved." Do you agree? Explain. **LO17.7**
8. What is meant by investment in human capital? Use this concept to explain (*a*) wage differentials and (*b*) the long-run rise of real-wage rates in the United States. **LO17.7**
9. What is the principal-agent problem? Have you ever worked in a setting where this problem has arisen? If so, do you think increased monitoring would have eliminated the problem? Why don't firms simply hire more supervisors to eliminate shirking? **LO17.8**
10. **LAST WORD** Speculate as to why we see unnecessary occupational licensing only in some industries but not in others. Consider who gets the costs, who enjoys the benefits, and how hard it would be to organize opposition to unnecessary licensing in various industries.

Review Questions

1. Brenda owns a construction company that employs bricklayers and other skilled tradespeople. Her firm's MRP for bricklayers is $22.25 per hour for each of the first seven bricklayers, $18.50 for an eighth bricklayer, and $17.75 for a ninth bricklayer. Given that she is a price taker when hiring bricklayers, how many bricklayers will she hire if the market equilibrium wage for bricklayers is $18.00 per hour? **LO17.2**

2. Because a perfectly competitive employer's MRC curve is _____, it will hire _____ workers than would a monopsony employer with the same MRP curve. **LO17.3**
   a. upsloping; more
   b. upsloping; fewer
   c. flat; more
   d. flat; fewer
   e. downsloping; more
   f. downsloping; fewer

3. True or False: When a labor market consists of a single monopsony buyer of labor interacting with a single monopoly seller of labor (such as a trade union), the resulting quantity of labor that is hired will always be inefficiently low. **LO17.5**

4. The market equilibrium wage is currently $12 per hour among hairdressers. At that wage, 17,323 hairdressers are currently employed in the state. The state legislature then sets a minimum wage of $11.50 per hour for hairdressers. If there are no changes to either the demand or supply for hairdressers when that minimum wage is imposed, the number of hairdressers employed in the state will be: **LO17.6**
   a. fewer than 17,323.
   b. still 17,323.
   c. more than 17,323.
   d. This is a bilateral monopoly so you can't tell.

5. On average, 50-year-old workers are paid several times more than workers in their teens and twenties. Which of the following is the most likely explanation for that huge difference in average earnings? **LO17.7**
   a. Older workers have more human capital and higher MRPs.
   b. Employers engage in widespread discrimination against younger workers.
   c. Young people lack information about the existence of the high-paying jobs occupied by older workers.
   d. Older workers receive compensating differences because they do jobs that are more risky than the jobs done by younger workers.

6. Manny owns a local fast-food franchise. Angel runs it for him. In this situation, Manny is the _____ and Angel is the _____. **LO17.8**
   a. free rider; entrepreneur
   b. agent; principal
   c. principal; agent
   d. producer; consumer

7. A principal is worried that her agent may not do what she wants. As a solution, she should consider: **LO17.8**
   a. commissions.
   b. bonuses.
   c. profit sharing.
   d. all of the above.

Problems

Mc Graw Hill **connect**

1. Firms compensate workers with "benefits" in addition to wages and salaries. The most prominent benefit offered by many firms is health insurance. Suppose that in 2010, workers at one steel plant were paid $20 per hour and in addition received health benefits at the rate of $4 per hour. Also suppose that by 2020 workers at that plant were paid $21 per hour but received $9 in health insurance benefits. **LO17.1**
   a. By what percentage did total compensation (wages plus benefits) change at this plant from 2010 to 2020? What was the approximate average annual percentage change in total compensation?
   b. By what percentage did wages change at this plant from 2010 to 2020? What was the approximate average annual percentage change in wages?
   c. If workers value a dollar of health benefits as much as they value a dollar of wages, by what total percentage will they feel that their incomes have risen over this time period? What if they consider only wages when calculating their incomes?
   d. Is it possible for workers to feel as though their wages are stagnating even if total compensation is rising? Explain.

2. Complete the following labor supply table for a firm hiring labor competitively: **LO17.2**

Units of Labor	Wage Rate	Total Labor Cost	Marginal Resource (Labor) Cost
0	$14	$ _____	$ _____
1	14	_____	_____
2	14	_____	_____
3	14	_____	_____
4	14	_____	_____
5	14	_____	_____
6	14	_____	

   a. Show graphically this firm's labor supply and marginal resource (labor) cost curves. Are the curves the same or different? If they are different, which one is higher?
   b. Plot the labor demand data of review question 2 in Chapter 16 on the graph used in part *a* above. What are the equilibrium wage rate and level of employment?

3. Assume a firm is a monopsonist that can hire its first worker for $6 but must increase the wage rate by $3 to attract each successive worker (so that the second worker must be paid $9, the third $12, and so on). **LO17.3**

   a. Draw the firm's labor supply and marginal resource cost curves. Are the curves the same or different? If they are different, which one is higher?

   b. On the same graph, plot the labor demand data of review question 2 in Chapter 16. What are the equilibrium wage rate and level of employment?

   c. Compare these answers with those you found in problem 2 above. By how much does the monopsonist reduce wages below the competitive wage? By how much does the monopsonist reduce employment below the competitive level?

4. Suppose that low-skilled workers employed in clearing woodland can each clear one acre per month if each is equipped with a shovel, a machete, and a chainsaw. Clearing one acre brings in $1,000 in revenue. Each worker's equipment costs the worker's employer $150 per month to rent and each worker toils 40 hours per week for four weeks each month. **LO17.5**

   a. What is the marginal revenue product of hiring one low-skilled worker to clear woodland for one month?

   b. How much revenue per hour does each worker bring in?

   c. If the minimum wage is $11.20, will the revenue per hour in part b exceed the minimum wage? If so, by how much per hour?

   d. Now consider the employer's total costs, which include the equipment costs as well as a normal profit of $50 per acre. If the firm pays workers the minimum wage of $11.20 per hour, what will be the firm's economic profit or loss per acre?

   e. At what value would the minimum wage have to be set so that the firm makes zero economic profit from employing an additional low-skilled worker to clear woodland?

5. Suppose that a car dealership wishes to see if efficiency wages will help improve its salespeople's productivity. Currently, each salesperson sells an average of one car per day while being paid $20 per hour for an eight-hour day. **LO17.8**

   a. What is the current labor cost per car sold?

   b. Suppose that when the dealer raises the price of labor to $30 per hour the average number of cars sold by a salesperson increases to two per day. What is now the labor cost per car sold? By how much is it higher or lower than it was before? Has the efficiency of labor expenditures by the firm (cars sold per dollar of wages paid to salespeople) increased or decreased?

   c. Suppose that if the wage is raised a second time to $40 per hour, the number of cars sold rises to an average of 2.5 per day. What is now the labor cost per car sold?

   d. If the firm's goal is to maximize the efficiency of its labor expenditures, which of the three hourly salary rates should it use: $20 per hour, $30 per hour, or $40 per hour?

   e. By contrast, which salary maximizes the productivity of the car dealer's workers (cars sold per worker per day)?

Labor Unions and Their Impacts

LO17.9 Describe U.S. union membership, collective bargaining, and the economic effects of unions.

Unions can increase wage rates by augmenting the demand for labor (Figure 17.5) or by restricting or controlling the supply of labor (Figures 17.6 and 17.7). This appendix provides some additional information about U.S. unions, collective bargaining, and union impacts.

Union Membership

In 2021, the Bureau of Labor Statistics estimated that 14.0 million U.S. workers—10.3 percent of employed wage and salary workers—belonged to unions. A further 1.8 million workers who were not dues-paying union members were estimated to work in jobs whose wages and working conditions were covered by union contracts.

In 2021, the **American Federation of Labor and the Congress of Industrial Organizations (AFL-CIO)** claimed to represent about 12.5 million workers across its 57 unions. Examples of AFL-CIO unions are the United Autoworkers, Communications Workers, and United Steelworkers. Another 3 million or so members were claimed by the **Strategic Organizing Center** (formerly Change to Win), a loosely federated group of seven unions that includes the Service Employees International

Union (SEIU) and the Teamsters. There are also dozens of **independent unions** that are not affiliated with either federation.

The likelihood that any particular worker will be a union member depends mainly on occupation and on the industry in which the worker is employed. As Figure 1a shows, the **unionization rate**—the percentage of workers unionized—is high in government, transportation, telecommunications, construction, and manufacturing. The unionization rate is very low in finance, agriculture, and retail trade. Figure 1b shows that unionism also varies greatly by occupation. Protective service workers (fire and police), teachers, production workers, transportation services employees, and social workers have high unionization rates; sales workers, food workers, and managers have very low rates.

Because disproportionately more men than women work in the industries and occupations with high unionization rates, men are more likely to be union members than women. Specifically, 10.6 percent of male wage and salary workers belong to unions compared with 9.9 percent of women. For the same reason, African Americans have higher unionization rates than whites: 11.5 percent compared with 10.3 percent. The unionization rate for Asians is 7.7 percent; Hispanics, 9.0 percent.

FIGURE 1 Union membership as a percentage of employed wage and salary workers, selected industries and occupations, 2021.

In percentage terms, union membership varies greatly by (a) industry and (b) occupation.

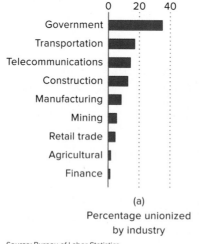

(a) Percentage unionized by industry

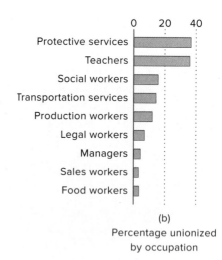

(b) Percentage unionized by occupation

Source: Bureau of Labor Statistics.

AFL-CIO An acronym for the American Federation of Labor–Congress of Industrial Organizations; the largest federation of *labor unions* in the United States.

Strategic Organizing Center (SOC) A loose federation of American unions that includes the Service Workers and Teamsters unions; the second largest union federation after the *AFL-CIO*.

independent unions U.S. unions that are not affiliated with the *AFL-CIO* or *Strategic Organizing Center*.

unionization rate The percentage of a particular population of workers that belongs to *labor unions;* alternatively, the percentage of a population of workers that is represented by one union or another in *collective bargaining*.

Unionism in the United States is largely an urban phenomenon. Seven heavily urbanized, heavily industrialized states (New York, California, Pennsylvania, Illinois, Ohio, Washington, and Michigan) account for approximately half of all union members. Just two states—California and New York—account for 30 percent of all union members. By comparison, those two states account for about 17 percent of all employees nationwide.

The Decline of Unionism

Since the mid-1950s, union membership has not kept pace with the growth of the labor force. While 25 percent of employed wage and salary workers belonged to unions in the mid-1950s, today only 10.8 percent are union members. Over recent years, even the absolute number of union members has declined significantly. More than 22 million workers were unionized in 1980 but only 14.0 million in 2021.

Some of the major reasons for the decline of U.S. unionism involve structural changes in the economy. Employment has shifted away from manufactured goods (where unions have been stronger) and toward services (where unions have been weaker). Consumer demand has shifted toward foreign manufactured goods and away from goods produced by union labor in the United States. Industry has shifted from the northeast and midwest, where unionism is a way of life in many cities, to hard-to-organize areas of the south and southwest.

Also, management has greatly intensified its opposition to unions and has increasingly engaged in aggressive collective bargaining, including the use of strikebreakers. Within unionized firms, employers have substituted machinery for workers, subcontracted work to nonunion suppliers, and shifted the production of components to low-wage nations. At the same time, nonunion firms have greatly improved their wage, fringe benefits, and working conditions, thus reducing the demand for unionism.

Collective Bargaining

Despite the overall decline of unionism, **collective bargaining** (the negotiation of labor contracts) remains an important feature of labor-management relations in several U.S. industries. The goal of collective bargaining is to establish a "work agreement" between a firm and a union.

Collective bargaining agreements (contracts) typically cover several topics.

Union Status

Union status is the degree of security and control afforded to a union, as a collective entity, by the work agreement.

In an **open shop,** an employer may hire either union or nonunion workers. Those who are nonunion are not obligated to join the union or to pay union dues; they may continue on their jobs indefinitely as nonunion workers. Nevertheless, the wages, hours, and working conditions set forth in the work agreement apply to the nonunion workers as well as to the union workers.

By contrast, in a **closed shop,** every worker must be (or must become) a member of the union before being hired. Under federal labor law, such shops are illegal in industries other than transportation and construction.

A **union shop** permits the employer to hire nonunion workers. But these workers must join the union within a specified period, say 30 days, or relinquish their jobs.

An **agency shop** allows nonunion workers but requires nonunion workers to either pay "agency fees" (which are like union dues but assessed only on nonunion workers in a unionized workplace) or donate an equivalent amount to charity. Union and agency shops are legal in the private sector except in the 28 states that expressly prohibit them through so-called **right-to-work laws.** As for the public sector, the U.S. Supreme Court ruled in 2018 in the *Janus* case that "state and public sector unions may no longer extract agency fees from nonconsenting employees." The decision also made public sector union membership opt-in rather than opt-out. As a result, government workplaces are now effectively open shops even where unions exist to represent government employees in collective bargaining agreements.

Managerial Prerogatives

Most work agreements contain clauses outlining certain decisions that are reserved solely for management. These managerial prerogatives usually cover such matters as the size and location of plants, the products to be manufactured, and the types of equipment and materials to be used in production and in production scheduling.

Wages and Hours

The focal point of almost all bargaining agreements is wages (including fringe benefits) and hours. Both labor and management press for the advantage in wage bargaining. The arguments that unions use most frequently in demanding wage boosts are (1) "what others are getting"; (2) the employer's

---

collective bargaining The negotiation of labor contracts between *labor unions* and *firms* or government entities.

open shop A place of employment in which the employer may hire nonunion workers and in which the workers need not become members of a *labor union.*

closed shop A place of employment where only workers who are already members of a labor union may be hired.

union shop A place of employment where the employer may hire either *labor union* members or nonmembers but where nonmembers must become members within a specified period of time or lose their jobs.

agency shop A place of employment where the employer may hire either *labor union* members or nonmembers but where those employees who do not join the union must either pay union dues or donate an equivalent amount of money to a charity.

right-to-work law A state law that makes it illegal to require that a worker join a *labor union* in order to retain his or her job; laws that make *union shops* and *agency shops* illegal.

ability to pay, based on its profitability; (3) increases in the cost of living; and (4) increases in labor productivity.

Hours of work, voluntary versus mandatory overtime, holiday and vacation provisions, profit sharing, health plans, and pension benefits are other contract issues that must be addressed in the bargaining process.

Seniority and Job Protection

Unions stress length of service, or *seniority*, as the basis for worker promotion and layoff. They want the worker with the longest continuous service to have the first chance at relevant promotions, to be the last one laid off, and to be the first one recalled from layoff.

In recent years, unions have become increasingly sensitive to losing jobs to nonunion subcontractors and to overseas workers. Unions sometimes seek limits on the firm's ability to subcontract out work or to relocate production facilities overseas.

Grievance Procedures

Even the most detailed and comprehensive work agreement cannot spell out all the specific issues and problems that might occur. For example, suppose a particular worker gets reassigned to a less pleasant job. Was this reassignment for legitimate business reasons or, as the person suspects, because of a personality conflict with a particular manager? Labor contracts contain grievance procedures to resolve such matters.

The Bargaining Process

The date for the beginning of collective bargaining on a new contract is usually specified in the existing contract and is typically 60 days before the current contract expires.

The union normally takes the initiative, presenting its demands in the form of specific wage, fringe-benefit, and other adjustments to the present union-management contract. The firm then makes a counteroffer. It is not unusual for the original union demand and the firm's first offer to be far apart, not only because of the parties' conflicting goals but also because starting far apart leaves plenty of room for compromise and counteroffers during negotiations.

Hanging over the negotiations is the contract deadline, which occurs the moment the present contract expires. At that time there is a possibility of a **strike**—a work stoppage by the union. But there is also the possibility that at the deadline the firm may engage in a **lockout,** in which it forbids the

workers to return to work until a new contract is signed. In this setting of uncertainty prior to the deadline, both parties feel pressure to find mutually acceptable terms.

Although bluster and bickering often occur in collective bargaining, labor and management usually display a remarkable capacity for compromise and agreement. They typically reach a compromise that is written into a new contract. Nevertheless, strikes and lockouts occasionally do occur. When they happen, workers lose income and firms lose profit. To stem their losses, both parties usually look for and eventually find ways to settle the labor dispute and get the workers back to work.

Bargaining, strikes, and lockouts occur within a framework of federal labor law, specifically the **National Labor Relations Act (NLRA).** This act was first passed as the Wagner Act of 1935 and later amended by the Taft-Hartley Act of 1947 and the Landrum-Griffin Act of 1959. The act sets forth the *dos and don'ts* of union and management labor practices. For example, while union members can picket in front of a firm's business, they cannot block access to the business by customers, co-workers, or strikebreakers hired by the firm. Firms cannot refuse to meet and talk with the union's designated representatives.

Either unions or management can file charges of unfair labor practices under the labor law. The **National Labor Relations Board (NLRB)** has the authority to investigate such charges and to issue cease-and-desist orders in the event of a violation. The NLRB also conducts the elections that decide which specific union, if any, a group of workers might want to represent them in collective bargaining.

Economic Effects of Unions

Overall, union members earn about a 15 percent wage premium (wage advantage). The effects of unions on output and efficiency, however, are more complicated.

Featherbedding and Work Rules

Some unions diminish output and efficiency by engaging in "make-work" or "featherbedding" practices and resisting the introduction of output-increasing machinery and equipment. These productivity-reducing practices often arise in periods of technological change.

---

strike The withholding of *labor* services by an organized group of workers (a *labor union*).

lockout A negotiating tactic in which a *firm* forbids its unionized workers to return to work until a new *collective bargaining* agreement is signed; a means of imposing costs (lost wages) on union workers.

National Labor Relations Act (NLRA) The basic labor-relations law in the United States. Defines the legal rights of unions and management and identifies unfair union and management labor practices; established the *National Labor Relations Board*. Often referred to as the Wagner Act, after the legislation's sponsor, New York Senator Robert F. Wagner.

National Labor Relations Board (NLRB) The board established by the *National Labor Relations Act* of 1935 to investigate unfair labor practices, issue *cease-and-desist orders,* and conduct elections among employees to determine if they wish to be represented by a *labor union*.

More generally, unions may reduce efficiency by establishing work rules and practices that impede putting the most productive workers in particular jobs. Under seniority rules, for example, workers may be promoted for their employment tenure rather than for their ability to perform the available job with the greatest efficiency. Also, unions may restrict the kinds of tasks that particular workers may perform. For example, contract provisions may prohibit sheet-metal workers or bricklayers from doing the simple carpentry work often associated with their jobs. Observance of such rules means, in this instance, that firms will be forced to hire unneeded and underused carpenters.

Finally, critics of unions contend that union contracts often chip away at managerial prerogatives to establish work schedules, determine production targets, introduce new technology, and make other decisions contributing to productive efficiency.

Output Losses from Strikes

Unions can also use strikes to impair efficiency and reduce output. If union and management reach an impasse during contract negotiations, a strike may result, and the firm's production may cease for the strike's duration. The firm will forgo sales and profit; workers will sacrifice income; and the economy might lose output. U.S. strike activity, however, has dwindled in the past few decades. In 2020, there were 8 major work stoppages—strikes or lockouts involving 1,000 or more employees. The amount of work time lost to the 2020 stoppages was less than 0.01 percent of the total work time provided by employees that year.

But the amount of work time lost is an imprecise indicator of strikes' potential economic costs. These costs may be greater than expected if strikes disrupt production in nonstruck firms that either supply inputs to struck firms or buy products from them. Example: An extended strike in the auto industry might reduce output and cause layoffs in firms producing, for instance, glass, tires, paints, and fabrics used in producing cars. It also may reduce sales and cause layoffs in auto dealerships.

On the other hand, the costs of strikes may be less than expected if nonstruck firms increase their output to offset the loss of production by struck firms. While the output of General Motors declines when its workers strike, auto buyers may shift their demand to Ford, Toyota, or Kia, which will respond by increasing their employment and output. Therefore, although GM and its employees are hurt by a strike, society as a whole may experience little or no decline in employment, real output, and income.

Efficiency Losses from Labor Misallocation

A third and more subtle way that unions might reduce efficiency and output is through the union wage advantage itself. Unions are as subject to supply and demand as anyone else. The only way they can succeed in raising wages is by restricting the supply of labor utilized by unionized firms (so that the demand and supply for labor intersect at the union wage rate).

That implies that some workers who would have otherwise worked at those firms (if they were not unionized) have to find jobs at nonunion firms. That movement of workers to the nonunion sector depresses wages at nonunion firms. It also implies that the total output produced in the economy will decrease because workers are not flowing naturally to the firms where their marginal revenue product (MRP) is highest.

To understand why, notice that as the displaced workers increase the supply of labor in the nonunion sector, they will drive down the marginal product of labor in that sector. Diminishing returns cannot be avoided: as workers migrate to the nonunion sector, the marginal product of labor in that sector *will* decline. So the economy's total output will fall because workers are being displaced from jobs where they would have had higher marginal products to jobs where they have lower marginal products.

Attempts to estimate the efficiency loss associated with union wage gains, however, suggest that the amount of output lost every year is very small: perhaps 0.2 to 0.4 percent (or one-fifth of 1 percent to two-fifths of 1 percent) of U.S. GDP. In 2020 this cost would have amounted to somewhere between $41 billion to $82 billion.

Offsetting Factors

Some long-run consequences of unionization may enhance productivity and reduce the efficiency loss from unions. One such impact is lower worker turnover within unionized firms. Compared with the rates at nonunion firms, the quit rates (resignation rates) for union workers are 31 to 65 percent lower, depending on the industry.

The union wage premium may reduce worker turnover by increasing the desirability of the union job relative to alternative employment. In economic terms, the higher opportunity cost of quitting reduces the frequency of quitting. Unions also may reduce turnover by using collective communication—the **voice mechanism**—to correct job dissatisfactions that otherwise would be "resolved" by workers quitting and taking other jobs—the **exit mechanism.** It might be risky for individual workers to express their dissatisfaction to employers because employers might retaliate by firing them as "troublemakers." But a union can provide workers with a collective voice to communicate problems and grievances to management and to press for satisfactory resolutions.

A lower quit rate may give a firm a more experienced, more productive workforce. Over time, that might offset a part of the higher costs and reduced profitability associated with the union premium. Also, having fewer resignations might reduce the firm's recruitment, screening, and hiring costs. Additionally, reduced turnover may encourage

voice mechanism Communication by workers through their *union* to resolve grievances with an employer.

exit mechanism The method of resolving workplace dissatisfaction by quitting one's job and searching for another.

employers to invest more in the training (and therefore the productivity) of their workers. If a worker quits or "exits" at the end of, say, a year's training, the employer will get no return from providing that training. Lower turnover increases the likelihood that the employer will receive a

return on the training it provides, thereby increasing its willingness to upgrade the skills of its workforce. All these factors may increase the long-run productivity of the unionized labor force and therefore reduce the efficiency loss caused by the union wage premium.

Appendix Summary

LO17.9 Describe U.S. union membership, collective bargaining, and the economic effects of unions.
Union membership has declined as a percentage of the labor force and in absolute numbers in recent decades. Some of the key causes are structural changes such as the shift from manufacturing employment to service employment. Other causes include improved wages and working conditions in nonunion firms and increased managerial opposition to unions.

Collective bargaining determines the terms of union work agreements, which typically cover (*a*) union status and managerial

prerogatives; (*b*) wages, hours, and working conditions; (*c*) control over job opportunities; and (*d*) grievance procedures. The bargaining process is governed by the National Labor Relations Act.

Union wages are on average about 15 percent higher than nonunion wages in comparable jobs. Restrictive union work rules, output losses from strikes, and labor misallocation from the union wage advantage are ways that unions may reduce efficiency, output, and productivity. The efficiency losses from unions may be partially offset in the long run by union productivity advances deriving from reduced labor turnover.

Appendix Terms and Concepts

American Federation of Labor and the Congress of Industrial Organizations (AFL-CIO)

Strategic Organizing Center

independent unions

unionization rate

collective bargaining

open shop

closed shop

union shop

agency shop

right-to-work laws

strike

lockout

National Labor Relations Act (NLRA)

National Labor Relations Board (NLRB)

voice mechanism

exit mechanism

Appendix Discussion Questions

1. Which industries and occupations have the highest rates of unionization? Which have the lowest? Speculate on the reasons for such large differences. **LO17.9**
2. What percentage of wage and salary workers are union members? Is this percentage higher, or is it lower, than in previous decades? Which of the factors explaining the trend do you think is most dominant? **LO17.9**
3. Explain how featherbedding and other restrictive work practices can reduce labor productivity. Why might strikes reduce the economy's output less than the loss of production by the struck firms? **LO17.9**

4. What is the estimated size of the union wage advantage? How might this advantage diminish the efficiency with which labor resources are allocated in the economy? Normally, labor resources of equal potential productivity flow from low-wage employment to high-wage employment. Why does that not happen to close the union wage advantage? **LO17.9**
5. Contrast the voice mechanism and the exit mechanism for communicating dissatisfaction. In what two ways do labor unions reduce labor turnover? How might such reductions increase productivity? **LO17.9**

Appendix Review Questions

1. True or false: In the United States, unions have been gaining in membership and power for several decades. **LO17.9**
2. Suppose that you are president of a newly established local union about to bargain with an employer for the first time. List the basic areas you want covered in the work agreement. Why might you begin with a larger wage demand than you actually are willing to accept? What is the logic of a union threatening an

employer with a strike during the collective bargaining process? Of an employer threatening the union with a lockout? What is the role of the deadline in encouraging agreement in collective bargaining? **LO17.9**
3. True or false. "To the extent that they succeed in their goals, unions only ever reduce productivity and efficiency." **LO17.9**

Appendix Problems

1. Suppose that a delivery company currently uses one employee per vehicle to deliver packages. Each driver delivers 50 packages per day, and the firm charges $20 per package for delivery. **LO17.9**
   a. What is the MRP per driver per day?
   b. Now suppose that a union forces the company to place a supervisor in each vehicle at a cost of $300 per supervisor per day. The presence of the supervisor causes the number of packages delivered per vehicle per day to rise to 60 packages per day. What is the MRP per supervisor per day? By how much per vehicle per day do firm profits fall after supervisors are introduced?
   c. How many packages per day would each vehicle have to deliver in order to maintain the firm's profit per vehicle after supervisors are introduced?
   d. Suppose that the number of packages delivered per day cannot be increased beyond 60 packages per day but that the price per delivery might potentially be raised. What price would the firm have to charge for each delivery in order to maintain the firm's profit per vehicle after supervisors are introduced?

2. Suppose that a car factory initially hires 1,500 workers at $30 per hour and that each worker works 40 hours per week. Then the factory unionizes, and the new union demands that wages be raised by 10 percent. The firm accedes to that request in collective bargaining negotiations but then decides to cut the factory's labor force by 20 percent due to the higher labor costs. **LO17.9**
   a. What is the new union wage? How many workers does the factory employ after the agreement goes into effect?
   b. How much in total did the factory's workers receive in wage payments each week before the agreement? How much do the factory's remaining workers receive in wage payments each week after the agreement?
   c. Suppose that the workers who lose their jobs as a result of the agreement end up unemployed. By how much do the total wages received each week by the initial 1,500 workers (both those who continue to be employed at the factory and those who lose their jobs) change from before the agreement to after the agreement?
   d. If the workers who lose their jobs as a result of the agreement end up making $15 per hour at jobs where they work 40 hours per week, by how much do the total wages received each week by the initial 1,500 workers change from before the agreement to after the agreement?

CHAPTER 1

Rent, Interest, and Profit

>> LEARNING OBJECTIVES

LO18.1 Explain economic rent and how it is determined.

LO18.2 Define interest and explain why interest rates vary.

LO18.3 Explain the loanable funds theory of interest rates.

LO18.4 Relate interest rates to the time-value of money.

LO18.5 Explain the role of interest rates in allocating capital, modulating R&D spending, and determining the economy's total output.

LO18.6 Explain why economic profits occur and how profits and losses allocate resources.

LO18.7 List the share of U.S. earnings received by each of the factors of production.

In Chapter 17, we focused on the wages and salaries that firms pay to obtain labor. Here we focus on the rent, interest, and profit that firms pay to obtain, respectively, land, capital, and entrepreneurship. Our analysis will provide answers to numerous practical questions, including:

How do *land prices* and *land rents* get established, and why do they differ from property to property? For example, why do 20 acres of land in the middle of the Nevada desert sell for $5,000 while 20 acres along The Strip in Las Vegas command $500 million?

What determines *interest rates* and causes them to change? For instance, why were interest rates on 3-month bank certificates of deposit 2.69 percent in December 2018 but only 0.35 percent in December 2021? How does interest compound over time, and how does that compounding relate to the so-called present value and future value of a particular sum of money?

What are the sources of *profits* and *losses,* and why do they vary? For example, why did JC Penny spend 2021 shutting down nearly 200 stores after going bankrupt while its super-successful rival, Walmart, enjoyed a $40 billion profit?

>> **LO18.1** Explain economic rent and how it is determined.

economic rent Any payment to a resource provider or seller of output in excess of the *economic cost* (opportunity cost) of providing that resource or output.

Economic Rent

To most people, "rent" means the money paid for the use of an apartment, house, or room in a residence hall. Economists use "rent" in a much narrower sense. **Economic rent** is any payment in excess of the *economic cost* (opportunity cost) needed to bring a resource into production or to obtain output from a producer. When the owner of a factor of production or the seller of output receives a payment in excess of the opportunity cost of producing that factor or output, the excess is economic rent.

Economic profit is a form of economic rent that you are already familiar with. Economic profit is an economic rent because it is the amount of profit in excess of the normal rate of profit that reflects the actual opportunity cost of entrepreneurship.

The most famous example of economic rent, however, is the money received by landowners for allowing others to use their land. Since land is a free gift of nature and has no production cost, it also has no opportunity cost. That implies that any amount of money received by landowners (from, for example, tenant farmers) is an economic rent, since the payment they receive is entirely in excess of the opportunity cost of providing land (which is zero since it has no production cost).

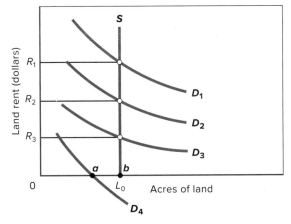

FIGURE 18.1
The determination of land rent.

Because the supply S of land (and other natural resources) is perfectly inelastic, demand is the sole active determinant of land rent. An increase in demand from D_2 to D_1 or a decrease in demand from D_2 to D_3 will cause a considerable change in rent: from R_2 to R_1 in the first instance and from R_2 to R_3 in the second. But the amount of land supplied will remain at L_0. If demand is very weak (D_4) relative to supply, land will be a "free good," commanding no rent.

Let's examine this idea and some of its implications through supply-and-demand analysis. We first assume that all land has a single use, for example, growing wheat. We assume, too, that all land is of the same grade or quality, meaning that each arable (tillable) acre of land is as productive as every other acre. And we suppose that land is rented or leased in a competitive market in which many producers are demanding land and many landowners are offering land in the market.

In Figure 18.1, curve S represents the supply of arable land available in the economy as a whole, and curve D_2 represents producers' demand for use of that land. As with all economic resources, the demand for land is a derived demand, meaning that the demand for land is derived from the demand for the products that land helps to produce. Demand curves such as D_2 reflect the marginal revenue product ($MRP = MP \times P$) of land. The curve slopes downward because of diminishing returns (MP declines) and because, for producers as a group, additional units of land result in greater output and thus lower output prices (P is less).

Perfectly Inelastic Supply

The unique feature of our analysis is on the supply side. For all practical purposes, the supply of land is perfectly inelastic (in both the short run and the long run), as reflected in supply curve S. Land has no production cost; it is a free and nonreproducible gift of nature. The economy has only so much land, and that's that. Of course, within limits any parcel of land can be made more usable by clearing, drainage, and irrigation. But these are capital improvements and not changes in the amount of land itself. Moreover, increases in the usability of land affect only a small fraction of the total amount of land and do not change the basic fact that land is fixed in supply.

Equilibrium Rent and Changes in Demand

Because the supply of land is fixed, demand is the only active determinant of land rent. And what determines the demand for land? The factors we discussed in Chapter 16: the price of the products produced on the land, the productivity of land, and the prices of the other resources that are combined with land.

If demand is D_2, as we have suggested, the equilibrium rent will be R_2. The quantity of land L_0 that producers wish to rent will equal the quantity of land available (also L_0). But if the demand for land in Figure 18.1 increases from D_2 to D_1, land rent will rise from R_2 to R_1. On the other hand, if the demand for land declines from D_2 to D_3, land rent will fall from R_2 to R_3. Finally, if the demand for land is only D_4, land rent would be zero. In this situation, land would be a free good—a good for which demand is so weak relative to supply that an excess supply of it occurs even if the market price is zero. In Figure 18.1, we show this excess supply as distance $b - a$ at rent of zero. Land was essentially a free good in the free-land era of U.S. history.

The ideas underlying Figure 18.1 help answer one of our chapter-opening questions. Land prices and rents are so high along the Las Vegas Strip because of the tremendous demand for that land, which is capable of producing exceptionally high revenue from gambling, lodging, and entertainment. In contrast, the demand for isolated land in the middle of the Nevada desert is highly limited because very little revenue can be generated from its use. (It is an entirely different matter, of course, if a precious metal can be mined from isolated desert land, which is true of some lonely parcels in the Silver State.)

Productivity Differences and Rent Differences

So far we have assumed that all land is equally productive. That assumption is unrealistic because land varies widely in terms of productivity. For example, differences in rainfall, soil quality, and other factors make land in Kansas excellently suited to wheat production. The sagebrush plains of Wyoming are much less well suited to growing wheat, and the Arizona desert is practically useless for growing wheat. Such productivity differences are reflected in resource demands and economic rents. Competitive bidding by producers will establish a high rent for highly productive Kansas land. Less productive Wyoming land will command a much lower rent, and Arizona desert land may command no rent at all.

Look again at Figure 18.1. As before, assume that land can be used only for wheat production. But this time assume that there are four different plots of land. Each plot is the same size L_0 but differs in productivity so that different marginal revenue products emerge when each plot of land is combined with identical amounts of labor, capital, and entrepreneurial talent.

These differences in marginal revenue products lead to four different demand curves: D_1, D_2, D_3, and D_4. D_1 is the highest demand curve because plot 1 has the highest productivity. D_4 is the lowest demand curve because plot 4 has the lowest productivity. When combined with supply curve S, the different demand curves yield different equilibrium rents: R_1, R_2, R_3, and R_4. The differences in rents mirror the differences in productivity.

Location itself can affect productivity and rent. Other things equal, renters will pay more for a unit of land that is strategically located with respect to materials, transportation, labor, and customers than they will for a unit of land whose location is remote from these things. One example is the enormously high land prices near major ski resorts.

Land Rent: A Surplus Payment

The perfectly inelastic supply of land must be contrasted with the relatively elastic supply of nonland resources. Consider capital, which includes apartment buildings, fiber optic networks, and machinery. When the prices of these and other capital goods rise, entrepreneurs respond by increasing the production of capital goods. Conversely, a decline in the prices of capital goods results in reduced production of capital goods. Thus, the supply curves of nonland resources normally slope upward, so that the prices paid for such resources provide an **incentive function**. A high price provides an incentive to offer more of the resource, whereas a low price prompts resource suppliers to offer less.

In contrast, rent serves no incentive function because the total area of land in a nation will always stay exactly the same no matter what land prices are. As a result, economists consider land rents to be *surplus payments* that are not necessary to ensure that land is made available for economic use. From this perspective, the sum of all the land rents paid across a nation constitutes a giant surplus payment because it has no effect on the total supply of land in the nation. Similarly, the individual land rents paid on particular plots of land are also surplus payments because they likewise have no effect on the sizes of those individual plots.

Land Ownership: Fairness versus Allocative Efficiency

If land is a gift of nature, costs nothing to produce, and would be available even without rental payments, why should rent be paid to those who just happen to be landowners? Socialists have long argued that all land rents are unearned incomes because the act of owning land and renting it out to others produces nothing of value in and of itself. They believe that land should be nationalized (owned by the state) so that the government can use the rents to further the well-being of the entire population.

Opponents of land nationalization argue that private land ownership allows the *invisible hand* to work its magic in terms of allocating scarce land resources to their best possible uses. In a nation where land is privately owned and rents are charged, individuals and firms must consider opportunity costs when deciding whether to secure the use of a particular piece of land. In other words, they have an incentive to allocate each piece of land to its highest-value use. In general, renters will allocate land to uses that generate enough revenue to both pay the rent and cover all other costs, including a normal profit.

Private land ownership also aids economic growth and development because as consumer tastes change and as new technologies are developed, the best uses for particular pieces of land can change. These changing opportunity costs are reflected in land rents, whose changing values help to reallocate land from lower-value uses to higher-value uses as the economy evolves.

incentive function The inducement that an increase in the price of a commodity gives to sellers to make more of it available (and conversely for a decrease in *price*), and the inducement that an increase in price offers to buyers to purchase smaller quantities (and conversely for a decrease in price).

Those who are willing and able to pay the market rent get to use the land, while those who are unwilling or unable to pay the market rent do not.

▶ Economic rent is the price paid for the use of land and other natural resources whose supply is fixed (perfectly inelastic).

▶ Differences in land rents arise from differences in land productivity and location.

▶ Rent is socially useful because it puts an opportunity cost on land parcels, thereby helping to allocate each parcel of land to its best possible use.

Interest

Interest is the price paid for the use of money. It is the amount of money that a borrower must pay a lender for the use of the lender's money over some period of time. For example, a borrower might be required to pay $100 of interest for the use of $1,000 for one year.

>> LO18.2 Define interest and explain why interest rates vary.

Because borrowers pay for loans of money with money, interest is often stated as a percentage of the amount of money borrowed. Thus we say that interest is "12 percent annually" rather than "$120 per year per $1,000." Equivalently, we say that "the interest rate is 12 percent."

Money Is Not a Resource

When considering why borrowers are willing to pay interest to borrow money, it is important to remember that money is not itself an economic resource. Whether money comes in the form of paper currency, checking accounts, or cryptocurrencies like Bitcoin and Ether, you cannot directly produce any goods and services with it.

Thus, borrowers do not value money for its own sake. Rather, they value money because of what it can purchase. Individuals and households are willing to pay interest to borrow for consumption spending because they would rather consume certain goods and services sooner rather than later. Businesses are willing to pay interest because they can use the money that they borrow to expand their businesses and increase their profits. For example, borrowed money can be used to fund the acquisition of capital goods such as computers, machinery, and warehouses. Borrowed money can also be used to fund research and development (R&D) expenditures in the hopes of developing inventions or other intellectual property that may generate future profits.

Interest Rates and Interest Income

The interest rate on money loans determines the **interest income** earned by households for providing capital to firms. Firms have the choice of either leasing capital from households or purchasing their own capital. Because businesses have this option, households cannot charge more for the use of their capital than what businesses would have to pay in interest payments to borrow money to purchase their own capital.

interest income The *income* received by the owners of *capital* for supplying capital to *businesses*.

As an example, consider a custom t-shirt shop that needs a $10,000 embroidering machine to expand production. If the owners of the shop can borrow the money to buy such a machine at an interest rate of 8 percent per year, then anyone wishing to lease them an identical machine could charge them no more than $800 per year for it (because the shop has the option of paying $800 interest per year to borrow $10,000 at an 8 percent interest rate and using that money to purchase an identical machine).

Range of Interest Rates

For convenience, economists often speak in terms of a single interest rate. However, there are many different interest rates in the economy. Table 18.1 lists several interest rates often referred to in the media. On December 21, 2021, these rates ranged from 0.08 to 17.13 percent. What explains these differences?

- *Risk* Loans to different borrowers for different purposes carry varying degrees of risk. The greater the chance that a borrower will not repay the loan, the higher the interest rate the lender will charge to compensate for that risk.

- *Maturity* The time length of a loan, or its maturity (when it needs to be paid back), also affects the interest rate. Other things equal, longer-term loans usually command higher interest rates than shorter-term loans. Longer-term loans must offer higher interest rates to compensate lenders for having to forgo alternative opportunities for longer periods of time.

TABLE 18.1 Selected Interest Rates, December 21, 2021

Type of Interest Rate	Annual Percentage
30-year Treasury Bond rate (interest rate on federal government securities used to finance the public debt)	1.89%
3-month Treasury Bill rate (interest rate on federal government securities used to finance the public debt)	0.08
Prime interest rate (interest rate used as a reference point for a wide range of bank loans)	3.25
30-year mortgage rate (fixed-interest rate on loans for houses)	3.23
4-year automobile loan rate (interest rate for new autos by automobile finance companies)	3.42
Tax-exempt state and municipal bond rate (interest rate paid on low-risk bonds issued by a state or local government)	4.24
Federal funds effective rate (interest rate on overnight loans between banks)	0.08
Consumer credit card rate (interest rate charged for credit card purchases)	17.13

Source: Selected Interest Rates (Daily)-H.15, Board of Governors of the Federal Reserve System, 2021.

- *Loan size* If two loans have equal maturity and risk, the interest rate on the smaller of the two loans usually will be higher. The administrative costs of issuing a large loan and a small loan are about the same in dollars, but the cost is greater *as a percentage* of the smaller loan.
- *Taxability* Interest on certain state and municipal bonds is exempt from the federal income tax. Because lenders are interested in their after-tax interest rate, the bonds issued by state and local governments can attract lenders even though they pay lower before-tax interest rates than other bonds of similar maturity and risk.

Pure Rate of Interest

pure rate of interest The hypothetical *interest rate* that is completely *risk*-free and only compensates investors for their willingness to patiently forgo alternative consumption and investment opportunities until their money is repaid.

When economists talk of "the" interest rate, they typically have in mind the **pure rate of interest.** This is the hypothetical interest rate that would serve purely and solely to compensate lenders for their willingness to patiently forgo alternative consumption and investment opportunities until their money is repaid.

The pure rate of interest is best approximated by the interest rates of long-term, virtually risk-less securities, such as the 30-year Treasury Bond issued by the U.S. federal government. Because such bonds involve minimal risk and negligible administrative costs, their interest rate can be thought of as compensating purely and solely for the use of money over an extended period of time. In December 2021, the pure rate of interest in the United States was 1.89 percent.

Loanable Funds Theory of Interest Rates

>> LO18.3 Explain the loanable funds theory of interest rates.

loanable funds theory of interest The concept that the supply of and demand for *loanable funds* determine the equilibrium rate of *interest.*

The **loanable funds theory of interest** explains the interest rate on any particular type of loan in terms of the supply of and demand for *funds available for lending* in the loanable funds market for that particular type of loan. As Figure 18.2 shows, the equilibrium interest rate (here, 8 percent) on a particular type of loan is the rate at which the quantities of loanable funds supplied and demanded are equal for that type of loan.

To gain a deeper understanding of the loanable funds theory of interest, let's focus on a simplified lending market. First, assume that, for a particular type of loan, households or consumers are the sole suppliers of loanable funds, while businesses are the sole demanders of loanable funds. Also assume that lending occurs directly between households and businesses so that there are no financial institutions acting as intermediaries.

Supply of Loanable Funds

The supply of loanable funds in our simplified lending market is represented by curve *S* in Figure 18.2. Its upward slope indicates that households will make available a larger quantity of funds at high interest rates than at low interest rates. Most people prefer to use their incomes to purchase goods and services *today,* rather than delay purchases to sometime in the *future.* For people to delay consumption and increase their saving, they must be "bribed" or compensated by an interest payment. The larger the amount of that payment, the greater the deferral of household consumption and thus the greater the amount of money made available for loans.

Demand for Loanable Funds

Businesses borrow loanable funds primarily to add to their stocks of capital goods, such as new plants or warehouses, machinery, and equipment. Assume that a firm wants to buy a machine that will increase output and sales such that the firm's total revenue will rise by $110 for the year. Also assume that the machine costs $100 and has a useful life of just one year. Comparing the $10 (= $110 increase in total revenue minus $100 cost of machine) earned with the $100 cost of the machine, we find that the expected rate of return on this investment is 10 percent (= $10 / $100) for the one year.

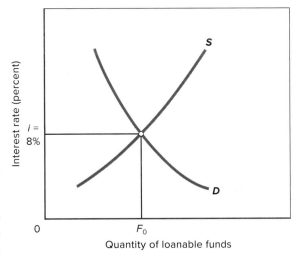

FIGURE 18.2
A loanable funds market.

The upsloping supply curve S for loanable funds in a specific lending market reflects the idea that at higher interest rates, households will defer more of their present consumption (save more), making more funds available for lending. The downsloping demand curve D for loanable funds in such a market indicates that businesses will borrow more at lower interest rates than at higher interest rates. At the equilibrium interest rate (here, 8 percent), the quantities of loanable funds lent and borrowed are equal (here, F_0 each).

To determine whether the investment would be profitable and whether it should be made, the firm must compare the interest rate—the price of loanable funds—with the 10 percent expected rate of return. If funds can be borrowed at some rate less than the rate of return (say, at 8 percent, as in Figure 18.2), then the investment is profitable and should be made. But if funds can be borrowed only at an interest rate above the 10 percent rate of return (say, at 14 percent), the investment is unprofitable and should not be made.

Why does the demand for loanable funds slope downward, as in Figure 18.2? At higher interest rates, fewer investment projects will be profitable and therefore a smaller quantity of loanable funds will be demanded. At lower interest rates, more investment projects will be profitable and therefore more loanable funds will be demanded.

Extending the Model

There is a loanable funds market for nearly every type of loan in the economy. The best known are the markets for corporate and government bonds. But there are also loanable funds markets for student loans, home mortgages, and car loans. Each type of loan ends up with its own equilibrium interest rate determined by the demand and supply for loanable funds in its particular market.

We now extend the simple loanable funds model to better capture the diversity of lending markets.

Financial Institutions Households rarely directly lend their savings to the businesses that are borrowing funds for investment. Instead, they place their savings in banks (and other financial institutions). The banks pay interest to savers in order to attract loanable funds. In turn, the banks lend those funds to businesses. Businesses borrow the funds from the banks, paying them interest for the use of the money. Financial institutions profit by charging borrowers higher interest rates than the interest rates they pay savers. Both interest rates, however, are based on the supply of and demand for loanable funds in their respective markets.

Changes in Supply Anything that causes households to be thriftier will prompt them to save more at each interest rate, shifting the supply curve rightward. For example, if interest earned on savings is suddenly exempted from taxation, we would expect the supply of loanable funds to increase and the equilibrium interest rate to decrease.

Conversely, a decline in thriftiness would shift the supply-of-loanable-funds curve leftward and increase the equilibrium interest rate. For example: If the government expanded social insurance to cover the costs of hospitalization, prescription drugs, and retirement living more fully, households' incentive to save might diminish.

Changes in Demand On the demand side, anything that increases the rate of return on potential investments will increase the demand for loanable funds. Let's return to our earlier example, where a firm will receive additional revenue of $110 by purchasing a $100 machine and, therefore, will realize a 10 percent return on investment.

What factors might increase or decrease the rate of return? Suppose a technological advance raises the productivity of the machine such that the firm's total revenue increases by $120 rather than $110. The rate of return will then be 20 percent, not 10 percent. Before the technological advance, the firm would have demanded zero loanable funds at an interest rate of 14 percent. But now it will demand $100 of loanable funds at that interest rate, which means that the demand curve for loanable funds has shifted to the right.

Similarly, an increase in consumer demand for the firm's product will increase the price of its product. So even though the machine's productivity is unchanged, its potential revenue will rise from $110 to perhaps $120, increasing the firm's rate of return from 10 percent to 20 percent. Again the firm will be willing to borrow more than previously at our presumed 8 or 14 percent interest rate, implying that the demand curve for loanable funds has shifted rightward. This shift in demand increases the equilibrium interest rate.

Conversely, a decline in productivity or in the price of the firm's product will shift the demand curve for loanable funds leftward, reducing the equilibrium interest rate.

Other Participants Participation in many loanable funds markets may go well beyond our simplification of households as suppliers of funds and businesses as demanders of funds. For example, while households are suppliers of loanable funds, many also demand such funds. Households borrow to finance expensive purchases such as houses, automobiles, furniture, and household appliances. Governments also are on the demand side of a loanable funds market when they borrow to finance budget deficits. And businesses that have revenues in excess of their current expenditures may offer to lend some of those revenues in various loanable funds markets. Thus, like households, businesses operate on both the supply and the demand sides of various loanable funds markets.

Finally, in addition to gathering and making available the savings of households, banks and other financial institutions also increase funds through the lending process and decrease funds when the money that is used to pay off loans is retained by the banks rather than being lent out again to other borrowers. The Federal Reserve (the nation's central bank) controls the amount of this bank activity and thus influences a wide variety of interest rates.

This fact helps answer one of our chapter-opening questions: Why did the interest rate on 3-month certificates of deposit in the United States fall from 2.69 percent in December 2018 to only 0.35 percent in December 2021? The answer is that the COVID-19 recession (economic downturn) of 2020 induced two important responses: (1) The demand for loanable funds temporarily declined as businesses reduced their purchases of capital goods at the start of the pandemic; and (2) the Federal Reserve, fighting recession and sluggish recovery, took monetary actions that greatly increased the supply of loanable funds.

Time-Value of Money

>> LO18.4 Relate interest rates to the time-value of money.

Interest is central to understanding the **time-value of money**—the idea that a specific amount of money is more valuable to a person the sooner it is obtained. To see where money's time-value comes from, suppose that you could choose between being paid $1,000 today or $1,000 in a year. The fact that $1,000 received today can be invested at interest and grow into more than $1,000 in a year implies that it is better to receive $1,000 today than $1,000 in a year. By how much is it better? It is better by the amount of interest that can be gained over the course of the year. The higher the interest rate, the greater the time-value of money.

time-value of money The idea that a specific amount of *money* is more valuable to a person the sooner it is received because the money can be placed in a financial account or *investment* and earn *compound interest* over time; the *opportunity cost* of receiving a sum of money later rather than earlier.

The fact that money can be invested to earn interest also implies that:

- A given amount of money today can be thought of as being equivalent to a larger amount of money in the future.

- A given amount of money in the future can be thought of as being equivalent to a smaller amount of money today.

We explore these ideas next.

Compound Interest

compound interest *Interest* that is paid both on an original sum of money and on interest that has already been paid on that sum.

Compound interest is the total interest that accumulates over time on money that is held in an interest-bearing account as new interest is earned on previous interest that was not withdrawn. Table 18.2 helps to explain compound interest, as well as the related ideas of future value and

TABLE 18.2 Compound Interest, Future Value, and Present Value, 10 Percent Interest Rate

(1) Beginning Period Value	(2) Computation	(3) Total Interest	(4) End Period Value
$1,000 (Year 1)	$1,000 × 1.10 = $1,100	$100	$1,100 (= $1,000 + $100)
$1,100 (Year 2)	$1,100 × 1.10 = $1,210	$210 (= $100 + $110)	$1,210 (= $1,000 + $210)
$1,210 (Year 3)	$1,210 × 1.10 = $1,331	$331 (= $100 + $110 + $121)	$1,331 (= $1,000 + $331)

present value. Suppose that at the start of Year 1, Max places $1,000 in an interest-bearing account that pays 10 percent interest. He intends to let the *principal* (the initial deposit) and interest compound for 3 years. The first entry of each row shows the amount of the money in the account at the start of the year. The second entry in each row shows the computation as to how that amount grows during the year, given a particular interest rate. We find that growth by multiplying the dollar amount at the beginning of each year by $1 + i$, where i is the interest rate expressed as a decimal.

In year 1, the 10 percent interest rate increases the money in the account from $1,000 to $1,100 (= $1,000 × 1.10). So, as shown in Column 3, total interest earned is $100. Column 4 simply lists the $1,100 again but reinforces that this amount consists of the original principal plus the total interest. Similarly, in year 2, the $1,100 now in the account grows to $1,210 (= $1,100 × 1.10) because $110 of new interest accrues on the $1,100. At the end of year 2, the principal remains $1,000, but the total interest is $210, and the total amount in the account is $1,210. Interest in year 3 is $121, and total interest rises to $331. After this $331 of total interest is added to the $1,000 principal, the accumulation is $1,331. As Column 3 shows, compound interest builds and builds over time.

Future Value and Present Value

Now note from Table 18.2 that we can look at the time-value of money in two distinct ways. **Future value** is the amount to which some current amount of money will grow as interest compounds over time. In our table, the future value (FV) of $1,000 today at 10 percent interest is $1,331 three years from now. Future value is always forward-looking.

But we can just as easily look backward from the end value of $1,331 and ask how much that amount is worth today, given the 10 percent interest rate. **Present value** is today's value of some amount of money to be received in the future. In terms of the table, the present value (PV) of $1,331 is $1,000. Here, FV is "discounted" by three years at 10 percent to remove the $331 of compounded interest and therefore to obtain PV. (If you are interested in the mathematics, see the text in the footnote.)[1]

With any positive interest rate (and assuming no inflation), a person would prefer to receive $1,000 today rather than $1,000 in the future. The higher the interest rate, the greater is the *future value* of a specific amount of money today. To confirm, substitute a 20 percent interest rate for the 10 percent rate in Table 18.2 and rework the analysis. The analysis presented in the table can be extended to any number of years.

The time-value of money is an important concept. For example, it helps explain the optimal timing of natural resource extraction (Chapter 19). It is also critical to the entire field of financial economics (Chapter 37). In our present chapter, our goal is to simply stress that *money has time value because of the potential for compound interest.*

Role of Interest Rates

As noted earlier in this chapter, interest rates on money loans determine the *interest income* earned by the owners of capital goods, who are paid interest income to compensate them for providing capital to firms. This fact implies that interest rates are the critical prices determining both the *level* and *composition* of new investments in capital goods as well as the amount of research and development (R&D) spending in the economy.

future value The amount to which some current amount of *money* will grow if *interest* earned on the amount is left to compound over time. (*See compound interest.*)

present value Today's value of some amount of *money* that is to be received at a particular future date.

>> **LO18.5** Explain the role of interest rates in allocating capital, modulating R&D spending, and determining the economy's total output.

---

[1]The mathematics is as follows:

$$FV = PV(1 + i)^t \quad \text{and} \quad PV = \frac{FV}{(1 + i)^t}$$

where i is the interest rate and t is time, here the number of years of compounding.

Interest and Total Output

Lower equilibrium interest rates encourage businesses to borrow more for investment, other things equal. As a result, total spending in the economy rises, and if the economy has unused resources, so does total output. Conversely, higher equilibrium interest rates discourage businesses from borrowing for investment, thereby reducing investment and total spending. Such a decrease in spending may be desirable if an economy is experiencing inflation.

Interest and the Allocation of Capital

Prices are rationing devices. And interest rates are prices. Thus, when it comes to allocating capital in the economy, the interest rates charged on investment loans ration the available supply of loanable investment funds to investment projects that have expected rates of return at or above the interest rate cost of the borrowed funds.

Suppose that the computer industry expects to earn a return of 12 percent on the money it invests in physical capital and it can secure the required funds at an interest rate of 8 percent. It will therefore borrow and expand its physical capital. However, if the expected rate of return on additional capital in the steel industry is only 6 percent, that industry will find it unprofitable to expand its capital at 8 percent interest. The interest rate allocates money, and ultimately physical capital, to the industries in which it will be most productive and therefore most profitable. Such an allocation of capital goods benefits society.

But the interest rate does not perfectly ration capital to its most productive uses. Large oligopolistic borrowers may be better able than competitive borrowers to pass interest costs on to consumers because they can change prices by controlling output. Also, the size, prestige, and monopsony power of large corporations may help them obtain funds on more favorable terms than can smaller firms, even when the smaller firms have similar rates of profitability.

Interest and R&D Spending

In Chapter 15, we noted that the decision on how much to spend on R&D depends on the cost of borrowing funds and the expected rate of return. Other things equal, the lower the interest rate and thus the lower the cost of borrowing funds for R&D, the greater is the amount of R&D spending that is potentially profitable. Low interest rates encourage R&D spending; high interest rates discourage it.

Also, the interest rate allocates R&D funds to firms and industries for which the expected rate of return on R&D is the greatest. Ace Microcircuits may have an expected rate of return of 16 percent on an R&D project, while Glow Paints has only a 2 percent expected rate of return on an R&D project. With the interest rate at 8 percent, loanable funds will flow to Ace, not to Glow. Society will benefit by allocating R&D spending to projects that have high enough expected rates of return to justify using scarce resources for R&D rather than for other purposes.

Nominal and Real Interest Rates

nominal interest rate The *interest rate* expressed in terms of annual amounts currently charged for *interest* and not adjusted for *inflation*.

real interest rate The *interest rate* expressed in dollars of constant value (adjusted for *inflation*) and equal to the *nominal interest rate* less the expected rate of *inflation*.

Our discussion so far has assumed that there is no inflation. If inflation exists, we must distinguish between nominal and real interest rates, just as we distinguished between nominal and real wages in Chapter 17. The **nominal interest rate** is the interest rate expressed in dollars of current value. The **real interest rate** is the interest rate expressed in purchasing power—dollars of inflation-adjusted value.

Example: Suppose the nominal interest rate and the rate of inflation are both 10 percent. If you borrow $100, you must pay back $110 a year from now. However, because of 10 percent inflation, each of these 110 dollars will be worth 10 percent less. Thus, the real value or purchasing power of your $110 at the end of the year is only $100. In inflation-adjusted dollars, you are borrowing $100 and at year's end you are paying back $100. While the nominal interest rate is 10 percent, the real interest rate is zero. We determine the real interest rate by subtracting the 10 percent inflation rate from the 10 percent nominal interest rate. The real interest rate, not the nominal rate, affects investment and R&D decisions.

For a comparison of nominal interest rates on bank loans in selected countries, see Global Perspective 18.1. Note that some countries had negative nominal interest rates in 2020, meaning that savers would get back less than the amount they invested. Those negative nominal interest rates were the result of deliberate central bank monetary policies intended to get people to consume more. The central banks in those countries were hoping that consumers would save less and consume due to savings earning a negative rate of return.

SHORT-TERM NOMINAL INTEREST RATES, SELECTED NATIONS

These data show the short-term nominal interest rates (percentage rates on 3-month loans) in various countries in 2020. Because these are nominal rates, much of the variation reflects differences in rates of inflation. But differences in central bank monetary policies and default risk also influence the variation.

Source: Organisation for Economic Co-operation and Development (OECD).

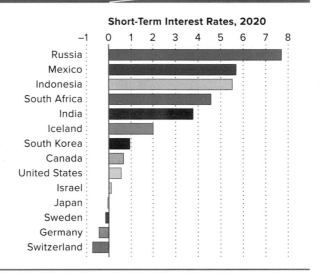

Short-Term Interest Rates, 2020

Country
Russia
Mexico
Indonesia
South Africa
India
Iceland
South Korea
Canada
United States
Israel
Japan
Sweden
Germany
Switzerland

▶ Interest is the price paid for the use of money and determines the interest income earned by households for providing capital to firms.

▶ The range of interest rates is influenced by risk, maturity, loan size, and taxability.

▶ In the loanable funds model, the equilibrium interest rate is determined by the demand for and supply of loanable funds.

▶ The time-value of money is the idea that $1 can be converted into more than $1 of future value through compound interest and therefore that $1 received in the future has less than $1 of present value.

▶ Interest rates on investment loans affect the total level of investment and therefore the levels of total spending and total output; they also allocate money and real capital to specific industries and firms. Interest rates also affect the level and composition of R&D spending.

Economic Profit

Recall from previous chapters that economists define profit narrowly. **Economic, or pure, profit** is what remains after all costs—both explicit and implicit costs, including a normal profit—have been subtracted from a firm's total revenue. Economic profit may be either positive or negative (a loss).

Entrepreneurship and Profit

Economic profit motivates individuals to provide the economic resource known as entrepreneurship. For illustration, let's suppose that two entrepreneurs establish a startup company called Upside and that they are the only owners. They do not incorporate or borrow. Instead, they use their own funds to finance the firm.

As discussed in previous chapters, the resource that these entrepreneurs provide is clearly *not* labor. Typical workers simply complete assigned tasks and engage in routine activities. For their labor inputs, they are compensated with wages and salaries.

Entrepreneurs, by contrast, make nonroutine decisions that involve substantial financial risk. Among other things, they (1) decide their firm's strategy for combining land, labor, and capital to produce a good or service; (2) decide whether and how to develop new products and new production processes; and (3) personally bear the financial risks associated with the success or failure of their firm.

With regard to those financial risks, it is crucial to understand that a firm's entrepreneurs are its *residual claimants*, meaning that they only receive whatever residual revenue—if any—remains after all the other factors of production have been paid. As residual claimants, the entrepreneurs at Upside receive whatever accounting profit or accounting loss the firm generates. Thus, the two entrepreneurs bear the financial risks of running the firm. If Upside loses money, the entrepreneurs lose money.

>> **LO18.6** Explain why economic profits occur and how profits and losses allocate resources.

economic, or pure, profit The return flowing to those who provide the economy with the *economic resource* of *entrepreneurial ability;* the *total revenue* of a *firm* less its *economic costs* (which include both *explicit costs* and *implicit costs*); also called "above-normal profit."

Insurable and Uninsurable Risks

insurable risk An eventuality for which both the frequency and magnitude of potential losses can be estimated with considerable accuracy. Insurance companies are willing to sell insurance against such risks.

uninsurable risk An eventuality for which the frequency or magnitude of potential losses is unpredictable or unknowable. Insurance companies are not willing to sell insurance against such risks.

As residual claimants, entrepreneurs face two types of financial risks. **Insurable risks** are risks for which it is possible to buy insurance from an insurance company. **Uninsurable risks** are risks for which it is not possible to buy insurance from an insurance company.

Individuals and firms who purchase insurance policies (contracts) from an insurance company are called *policyholders*. In exchange for an annual premium (fee), the policyholders obtain the insurance company's guarantee to reimburse them for any financial losses caused by any of the risks covered under the insurance contract. To be able to keep that promise, the insurance company must be able to collect enough in premiums from its policyholders in the present to fully reimburse those who suffer losses in the future. Insurers insure only risks whose frequencies of occurrence can be predicted with relative accuracy, such as fire, flood, theft, accident, and death. Risks whose frequencies of occurrence cannot be predicted accurately are uninsurable.

Sources of Uninsurable Risks

Uninsurable risks fall into four main categories:

- *Changes in the general economic environment* An economywide downturn in business (a recession) can lead to greatly reduced demand, sales, and revenues, and thus to business losses. An otherwise prosperous firm may experience substantial losses through no fault of its own.

- *Changes in the structure of the economy* Consumer tastes, technology, resource availability, and prices change unpredictably in the real world, bringing changes in production costs and revenues. For example, an airline earning an economic profit one year may sustain substantial losses the next year after the price of jet fuel skyrockets.

- *Changes in government policy* A newly instituted regulation, the removal of a tariff (tax on imports), or a change in national defense policy may significantly alter the costs and revenues of the affected industry and firms.

- *New products or production methods pioneered by rivals* Any firm can suddenly find itself losing sales and revenue to popular new products sold by rivals. Similarly, a firm may find itself having to sell its product at a loss if rival firms cut their prices after figuring out a lower-cost way to make the same product.

Profit as Compensation for Bearing Uninsurable Risks

Economists consider entrepreneurship as its own economic resource—separate from land, labor, and capital—because it is not possible to run a business without someone who is willing to undertake and live with uninsurable risks. Entrepreneurs are rewarded with profit precisely to compensate them for taking on the uninsurable risks of running a business. Indeed, their willingness to bear those uninsurable risks means that the providers of the firm's other inputs (land, labor, and capital) can almost completely ignore those risks.

Again consider our startup company, Upside, and suppose that its two entrepreneurs used $100,000 of their own money to fund the firm. If revenues ever run below costs, the entrepreneurs will use that pile of money to cover the losses and make sure that the firm's workers and other resource suppliers get paid on time and in full. The resource suppliers are shielded from the losses because the entrepreneurs have taken it on themselves to bear the firm's uninsurable financial risks. In such situations, no bill is sent to the workers or other resource suppliers asking them to help make up the firm's losses. The entrepreneurs, who took on the firm's uninsurable risks, are "on the hook."

Thus, entrepreneurship boils down to a simple bargain: In exchange for making sure that everyone else gets paid if things go wrong, the entrepreneur gets to receive the firm's profits if things go right.

Sources of Economic Profit

There are three main ways in which entrepreneurs can generate economic profits (that is, accounting profits that exceed normal profits):

- *Create popular new products* If an entrepreneur can develop a popular new product at a sufficiently low cost, his or her firm will generate economic profits until competitors bring out competing products.

CONSIDER THIS . . .

Profit and Efficiency

Entrepreneurs focus on a single number: profit. That might make you think that entrepreneurs will end up neglecting the other aspects of their business. But a wonderful thing about the market system is that the only way for a firm to maximize profit is by paying close attention to *every* aspect of its operations.

This is true because entrepreneurs have to make many simultaneous decisions about how to spend their firm's limited budgets. Should they allocate a little more money to research and development? Should they reduce spending on advertising?

FatCamera/E+/Getty Images

How about allocating more money for bonuses?

The only way to give one activity more resources is to give another activity fewer resources. If an entrepreneur wishes to maximize her firm's overall profit, she will have to get all of these marginal decisions right, and simultaneously. She will also have to find the correct allocation of the firm's limited resources across all possible tasks so that MB = MC for each budget item. So while profit is just a single number, focusing on profit forces entrepreneurs to be efficient in every aspect of their firm's operations.

- *Reduce production costs below rivals' costs* Entrepreneurs who implement more efficient production methods for existing products can generate economic profits until competitors match or exceed their efficiency gains.

- *Create and maintain a profitable monopoly* Entrepreneurs who possess a monopoly for their products may be able to generate economic rents by restricting their outputs and raising their prices. Such economic profits may persist if entry to the industry is blocked. But remember from Chapter 12 that a monopoly does not guarantee a profit. If demand is weak relative to production costs, monopolies can and will go bankrupt.

By reallocating resources toward the production of popular new products that consumers prefer to old products, entrepreneurs improve allocative efficiency. By reducing production costs, they improve productive efficiency. Thus, with the important exception of monopoly, the entrepreneur's pursuit of profit clearly benefits society. The Consider This story illustrates how profit prompts competitive entrepreneurs to pay attention to the wide variety of factors that affect allocative and productive efficiency.

Entrepreneurs, Profits, and Corporate Stockholders

In the actual economy, economic profits are distributed widely beyond the entrepreneurs who start and guide businesses because the corporation form of business enterprise has allowed millions of individuals who are not entrepreneurs to purchase ownership shares in corporations and thereby share in the risks and rewards of ownership.

Some of these people participate in the for-profit economy by purchasing the stock of individual firms or by investing in mutual funds, which in turn buy corporate stock. Millions of additional people share in corporations' profits through the financial investments of their pension and retirement funds. But at their core, all of the profits that are shared with these direct and indirect corporate shareholders are made possible by the activities of entrepreneurs. For instance, without Bill Gates and Paul Allen, there would have been no Microsoft Corporation—and, consequently, no Microsoft profits (dividends) to distribute to the millions of owners of Microsoft stock.

In short, economic profit is the main energizer of the capitalistic economy. It influences both the level of economic output and the allocation of resources among alternative uses. The expectation of economic profit motivates firms to innovate. Innovation stimulates new investment, thereby increasing total output and employment.

Profit also helps allocate resources among alternative lines of production, distribution, and sales. Entrepreneurs seek profit and shun losses. The occurrence of continuing profits in a firm or industry is a signal that society wants that particular firm or industry to expand. It attracts resources from firms and industries that are not profitable. In contrast, continuing losses penalize firms or industries that fail to adjust their productive efforts to match consumer wants. Such losses signal society's desire for the afflicted entities to contract.

So, in terms of our final chapter-opening question, Walmart garnered large profits because it was delivering a mix of products many consumers wanted at exceptionally low prices. These profits signaled that society wanted more of its scarce resources allocated to Walmart stores. JC Penny, by contrast, was not delivering products equivalent in value to the costs of the resources used to provide them—so the firm suffered heavy and sustained losses. The losses and JC Penny's bankruptcy signaled that society would benefit from a reallocation of all or part of those resources to other uses.

QUICK REVIEW

18.3

▶ Pure, or economic, profit is what remains after all explicit and implicit costs (including a normal profit) are subtracted from a firm's total revenue.

▶ As residual claimants, entrepreneurs receive accounting profit. They earn economic profit if their accounting profit exceeds the normal profit they could earn as entrepreneurs elsewhere.

▶ Economic profit has three sources: the bearing of uninsurable risk, the uncertainty of innovation, and monopoly power.

▶ The corporate structure of business enables millions of individuals to share in the risks and rewards of enterprise.

▶ Profit and profit expectations affect the levels of investment, total spending, and domestic output; profit and loss also allocate resources among alternative uses.

Income Shares

>> **LO18.7** List the share of U.S. earnings received by each of the factors of production.

Our discussion would not be complete without a brief examination of how U.S. income is distributed among wages, rent, interest, and profit.

Figure 18.3 shows how the income generated in the United States in 2020 was distributed among the five "functional" income categories tracked by the U.S. government. These five categories do not match up perfectly with the economic definitions of wages, rent, interest, and profit. The biggest difference is "proprietors' income," which is the income received by doctors, lawyers, small-business owners, farmers, and the owners of other unincorporated enterprises. In terms of our four economic categories, proprietors' income is a combination of wages and profit. The wages compensate for labor, while the profits compensate for entrepreneurship. The economists who have looked into this combination believe that the large majority of proprietors' income is implicitly composed of wages and salaries rather than profit. That is, the large majority of proprietors' income is compensation for labor rather than compensation for entrepreneurship.

Taking that fact into account, note the dominant role of labor income in the U.S. economy. Even with labor income narrowly defined as wages and salaries, labor receives 69 percent of all income earned by Americans in a typical year. But if we add in proprietors' income because most of it is believed to be a payment for labor, then labor's share of national income rises to 79 percent, a percentage that has been remarkably stable since at least 1900. That leaves 21 percent for "capitalists" in the form of rent, interest, and profit. Ironically, income from capital is a relatively small share of the U.S. economy, though we call it a capitalist system.

FIGURE 18.3
The functional distribution of U.S. income, 2020.

Sixty-nine percent of U.S. income is received as wages and salaries. Income to property owners—corporate profit, interest, and rents—accounts for about 21 percent of total income. The dollar amounts are in billions of dollars.

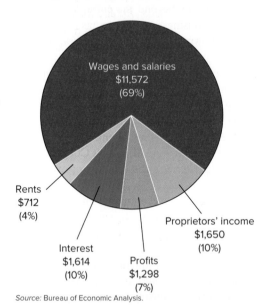

Wages and salaries
$11,572
(69%)

Rents
$712
(4%)

Interest
$1,614
(10%)

Profits
$1,298
(7%)

Proprietors' income
$1,650
(10%)

Source: Bureau of Economic Analysis.

Determining the Price of Credit

A Variety of Lending Practices May Cause the Effective Interest Rate to Be Quite Different from What It Appears to Be.

Borrowing and lending—receiving and granting credit—are a way of life. Individuals receive credit when they negotiate a mortgage loan and when they use their credit cards. Individuals make loans when they open a savings account in a commercial bank or buy a government bond.

It is sometimes difficult to determine exactly how much interest we pay and receive when we borrow and lend. Let's suppose that you borrow $10,000 that you agree to repay plus $1,000 of interest at the end of one year. In this instance, the interest rate is 10 percent per year. To determine the interest rate i, we compare the interest paid with the amount borrowed:

$$i = \frac{\$1,000}{\$10,000} = 10\%$$

But in some cases a lender—say, a bank—will discount the interest payment from the loan amount at the time the loan is made. Thus, instead of giving the borrower $10,000, the bank discounts the $1,000 interest payment in advance, giving the borrower only $9,000. This increases the interest rate:

$$i = \frac{\$1,000}{\$9,000} = 11\%$$

While the absolute amount of interest paid is the same, in the second case the borrower has only $9,000 available for the year.

An even more subtle point is that, to simplify their calculations, many financial institutions assume a 360-day year (twelve 30-day months). This means the borrower has the use of the lender's funds for 5 days less than the normal year. This use of a "short year" also increases the actual interest rate paid by the borrower.

The interest rate paid may change dramatically if a loan is repaid in installments. Suppose a bank lends you $10,000 and charges interest in the amount of $1,000 to be paid at the end of the year. But the loan contract requires that you repay the $10,000 loan in 12 equal monthly installments. As a result, the average amount of the loan outstanding during the year is only $5,000. Therefore:

$$i = \frac{\$1,000}{\$5,000} = 20\%$$

Here interest is paid on the total amount of the loan ($10,000) rather than on the outstanding balance (which averages $5,000 for the year), making for a much higher interest rate.

Another factor that influences the effective interest rate is whether or not interest is compounded. Suppose you deposit $10,000 in a savings account that pays a 10 percent interest rate compounded semiannually. In other words, interest is paid twice a year. At the end of the first 6 months, $500 of interest (10 percent of $10,000 for half a year) is added to your account. At the end of the year, interest is calculated on $10,500 so that the second interest payment is $525 (10 percent of $10,500 for half a year). Thus:

$$i = \frac{\$1,025}{\$10,000} = 10.25\%$$

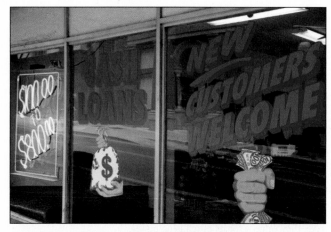

JoeFox Liverpool/Radharc Images/Alamy Stock Photo

This 10.25 percent return means that a bank offering a 10 percent interest rate compounded semiannually would pay more interest to its customers than a competitor offering a simple (noncompounded) rate of, say, 10.2 percent.

Two pieces of legislation have attempted to clarify interest charges and payments. The Truth in Lending Act of 1968 requires that lenders state the costs and terms of consumer credit in concise and uniform language, in particular, as an annual percentage rate (APR). More recently, the Truth in Savings Act of 1991 requires that all advertisements of deposit accounts by banks and other financial institutions disclose all fees connected with such accounts as well as the interest rates and APRs on each account. Nevertheless, some "payday" check-cashing firms that lend money to people in return for postdated personal checks have been found to receive interest payments on one- and two-week loans that are equivalent to APRs of hundreds of percent per year. These interest rates have prompted calls for state legislators to protect consumers from "predatory lenders."

More recently, many banks have established fee-based "bounce (overdraft) protection" for checking accounts. The bank agrees to pay each overdraft for a flat fee of around $35. These fees are essentially interest on a loan for the amount of the overdraft. When the overdraft amount is small, the annual interest on the loan can easily exceed 1,000 percent.

Similarly, late-payment fees on credit card accounts can boost the actual interest rate paid on credit card balances to extremely high levels. Furthermore, low "teaser" rates designed to attract new customers often contain "fine print" that raises the interest rate to 16 percent, or even 28 percent, if a payment on the account is late. Also, low initial rates on some variable rate mortgages eventually "reset" to higher rates, greatly increasing the monthly payments that are due. "Let the borrower (or depositor) beware" remains a fitting motto in the world of credit.

Summary

LO18.1 Explain economic rent and how it is determined.

Economic rent is a payment to a resource or output provider that exceeds the economic cost (opportunity cost) of providing that resource or output. Economic rent is a surplus payment because it exceeds the opportunity cost of provision.

Differences in land rent result from differences in demand, often stemming from differences in the fertility and climate features of the land or differences in location.

Because the supply of land is fixed by nature, rent is a surplus payment that is socially unnecessary from the viewpoint of causing land to be supplied.

Although land rent is a surplus payment rather than a cost to the economy as a whole, individuals and firms correctly regard land rents as costs. The payment of land rents by individuals and firms is socially useful because it puts an opportunity cost on the use of land and provides the incentive to put each piece of land to its best possible use.

LO18.2 Define interest and explain why interest rates vary.

Interest is the price paid for the use of money. Because money is not itself an economic resource, people do not value money for its own sake; they value it for its purchasing power.

The interest rate on money loans determines the interest income earned by households for providing capital to firms.

Interest rates vary because loans differ as to risk, maturity, amount, and taxability.

The pure rate of interest is the hypothetical interest rate that would serve purely and solely to compensate lenders for their willingness to patiently forgo alternative consumption and investment opportunities until their money is repaid. The pure rate is best approximated by the interest rate on long-term, virtually riskless, 20-year U.S. Treasury bonds.

LO18.3 Explain the loanable funds theory of interest rates.

In the loanable funds theory of interest rates, the equilibrium interest rate in a loan market is determined by the demand for and supply of loanable funds in that market. Other things equal, an increase in the supply of loanable funds reduces the equilibrium interest rate, whereas a decrease in supply increases the interest rate. Similarly, an increase in the demand for loanable funds raises the equilibrium interest rate, whereas a decrease in demand reduces it.

LO18.4 Relate interest rates to the time-value of money.

The time-value of money is the idea that $1 today has more value than $1 in the future because the $1 today can be placed in an interest-bearing account and earn compound interest over time. Future value is the amount to which a current amount of money will grow through interest compounding. Present value is the current value of some money payment to be received in the future.

LO18.5 Explain the role of interest rates in allocating capital, modulating R&D spending, and determining the economy's total output.

The equilibrium interest rate influences the level of investment and helps ration financial and physical capital to specific firms and industries. This rate also influences the size and composition of R&D spending. The real interest rate, not the nominal rate, is critical to investment and R&D decisions.

LO18.6 Explain why economic profits occur and how profits and losses allocate resources.

As residual claimants, entrepreneurs receive a firm's accounting profits (total revenue minus explicit costs) in exchange for assuming the uninsurable risks associated with running a business. Entrepreneurs can earn an economic profit (total revenue minus both explicit and implicit costs, including a normal profit) if their firm's accounting profit exceeds the normal profit that their entrepreneurship could on average earn in other business ventures.

The corporate form of business organization has allowed the millions who own corporate stock to share in the financial risks and economic profits engendered by entrepreneurship. Profits are the key energizer of business firms within the capitalist system. Profit expectations influence innovation and investment activities and therefore the economy's levels of employment and economic growth. The basic function of profits and losses, however, is to allocate resources in accord with consumers' preferences.

LO18.7 List the share of U.S. earnings received by each of the factors of production.

The largest share of all income earned by Americans—69 percent—goes to labor, a share narrowly defined as "wages and salaries." When labor's share is more broadly defined to include "proprietors' income," it rises to 79 percent of national income, leaving about 21 percent for rent, interest, and profit payments to the providers of land, capital, and entrepreneurship.

Terms and Concepts

economic rent	time-value of money	real interest rate
incentive function	compound interest	economic, or pure, profit
interest income	future value	insurable risks
pure rate of interest	present value	uninsurable risks
loanable funds theory of interest	nominal interest rate	

Discussion Questions

1. How does the economist's use of the term "rent" differ from everyday usage? Explain: "Though rent need not be paid by society to make land available, rental payments are useful in guiding land into the most productive uses." **LO18.1**

2. Explain why economic rent is a surplus payment when viewed by the economy as a whole but a cost of production from the standpoint of individual firms and industries. Explain: "Land rent performs no 'incentive function' for the overall economy." **LO18.1**

3. If money is not an economic resource, why is interest paid and received for its use? What considerations account for the fact that interest rates differ greatly on various types of loans? Use those considerations to explain the relative sizes of the interest rates on the following: **LO18.2**
   a. A 10-year $1,000 government bond.
   b. A $20 pawnshop loan.
   c. A 30-year mortgage loan on a $225,000 house.
   d. A 24-month $18,000 commercial bank loan to finance the purchase of an automobile.
   e. A 60-day $100 loan from a personal finance company.

4. Why does the supply of loanable funds slope upward? Why does the demand for loanable funds slope downward? Explain the equilibrium interest rate. List some factors that might cause it to change. **LO18.3**

5. Here is the deal: You can pay your college tuition at the beginning of the academic year or the same amount at the end of the academic year. You either already have the money in an interest-bearing account or will have to borrow it. Deal, or no deal? Explain your financial reasoning. Relate your answer to the time-value of money, present value, and future value. **LO18.4**

6. What are the major economic functions of the interest rate? How might the fact that many businesses finance their investment activities internally affect the efficiency with which the interest rate performs its functions? **LO18.5**

7. Distinguish between nominal and real interest rates. Which is more relevant in making investment and R&D decisions? If the nominal interest rate is 12 percent and the inflation rate is 8 percent, what is the real rate of interest? **LO18.5**

8. How do the concepts of accounting profit and economic profit differ? Why is economic profit smaller than accounting profit? What are the three basic sources of economic profit? Classify each of the following according to those sources: **LO18.6**
   a. A firm's profit from developing and patenting a new medication that greatly reduces cholesterol and thus diminishes the likelihood of heart disease and stroke.
   b. A restaurant's profit that results from the completion of a new highway past its door.
   c. The profit received by a firm due to an unanticipated change in consumer tastes.

9. Why is the distinction between insurable and uninsurable risks significant for the theory of profit? Carefully evaluate: "All economic profit can be traced to either uncertainty or the desire to avoid it." What are the major functions of economic profit? **LO18.6**

10. What is the combined rent, interest, and profit share of the income earned by Americans in a typical year if proprietors' income is included within the labor (wage) share? **LO18.7**

11. **LAST WORD** Assume that you borrow $5,000, and you pay back the $5,000 plus $250 in interest at the end of the year. Assuming no inflation, what is the real interest rate? What will the interest rate be if the $250 of interest had been discounted at the time the loan was made? What would the interest rate be if you are required to repay the loan in 12 equal monthly installments?

Review Questions

1. When using a supply-and-demand model to illustrate how land rents are set, economists typically draw the supply curve as a vertical line because: **LO18.1**
   a. the supply of land is fixed.
   b. the supply of land is perfectly inelastic.
   c. the quantity supplied of land does not increase when rents go up.
   d. all of the above.

2. In the 1980s land prices in Japan surged upward in a "speculative bubble." Land prices then fell for 11 straight years between 1990 and 2001. What can we safely assume happened to land rent in Japan over those 11 years? Use graphical analysis to illustrate your answer. **LO18.1**

3. Fanwei puts $1,000 in a savings account that pays 3 percent per year. What is the future value of her money one year from now? **LO18.4**
   a. $970
   b. $1,000
   c. $1,003
   d. $1,030

4. As shown in Table 18.2, $1,000 invested at 10 percent compound interest will grow into $1,331 after three years. What is the present value of $2,662 in three years if it is discounted back to the present at a 10 percent compound interest rate? (Hint: $2,662 is twice as much as $1,331.) **LO18.4**

5. Entrepreneurs are the residual claimants at their respective firms, which means that they: **LO18.6**
   a. get paid only if there is any money left over after all the other factors of production have been paid.
   b. must bear the financial risks of running their firms.
   c. receive whatever accounting profits or losses their firms generate.
   d. all of the above.

6. True or False: As a capitalist economy, the vast majority of U.S. national income flows to the owners of capital. **LO18.7**

Problems

1. Suppose that you own a 10-acre plot of land that you would like to rent out to wheat farmers. For them, bringing in a harvest involves $30 per acre for seed, $80 per acre for fertilizer, and $70 per acre for equipment rentals and labor. With these inputs, the land will yield 40 bushels of wheat per acre. If the price at which wheat can be sold is $5 per bushel and if farmers want to earn a normal profit of $10 per acre, what is the most that any farmer would pay to rent your 10 acres? What price would the farmer pay to rent your 10 acres if the price of wheat rises to $6 per bushel? **LO18.1**

2. Suppose that the demand for loanable funds for car loans in the Milwaukee area is $10 million per month at an interest rate of 10 percent per year, $11 million at an interest rate of 9 percent per year, $12 million at an interest rate of 8 percent per year, and so on. If the supply of loanable funds is fixed at $15 million, what will be the equilibrium interest rate? **LO18.3**

3. **ADVANCED ANALYSIS** To fund its wars against Napoleon, the British government sold consol bonds. These bonds were called "perpetuities" because they would pay £3 every year in perpetuity (forever). If a citizen could purchase a consol for £25, what would the consol's annual interest rate be? What if the price were £50? £100? Bonds are known as "fixed-income" securities because the future payments that they will make to investors are fixed by the bond agreement in advance. Do the interest rates of bonds and other investments that offer fixed future payments vary positively or inversely with their current prices? Explain. **LO18.4**

4. Suppose that the interest rate is 4 percent. What is the future value of $100 four years from now? How much of the future value is total interest? By how much would total interest be greater at a 6 percent interest rate than at a 4 percent interest rate? **LO18.4**

5. You are currently a worker earning $60,000 per year but are considering becoming an entrepreneur. You will not switch unless you earn an accounting profit that is on average at least as great as your current salary. You look into opening a small grocery store. Suppose that the store has annual costs of $150,000 for labor, $40,000 for rent, and $30,000 for equipment. There is a one-half probability that revenues will be $200,000 and a one-half probability that revenues will be $400,000. **LO18.6**

   a. In the low-revenue situation, what will your accounting profit or loss be? What will your accounting profit or loss be in the high-revenue situation?

   b. *On average*, how much do you expect your revenue to be? Your accounting profit? Your economic profit? Will you quit your job and try your hand at being an entrepreneur? Explain.

   c. Suppose the government imposes a 25 percent tax on accounting profits. This tax is levied only if a firm is earning positive accounting profits. What will your after-tax accounting profit be in the low-revenue case? In the high-revenue case? What will your *average* after-tax accounting profit be? What will be your *average* after-tax economic profit? Will you now want to quit your job and try your hand at being an entrepreneur? Explain.

   d. Other things equal, does the imposition of the 25 percent profit tax increase or decrease the supply of entrepreneurship in the economy?

Environmental Economics

>> LEARNING OBJECTIVES

LO19.1 Explain why falling birthrates make running out of natural resources unlikely.

LO19.2 Describe why using a mix of energy sources is efficient.

LO19.3 Discuss why running out of oil would not mean running out of energy.

LO19.4 Show how the profit motive can encourage resource conservation.

LO19.5 Explain how property rights can prevent deforestation and species extinction.

To produce goods and services, society must use natural resources. Some natural resources, such as solar energy, forests, and fish, are renewable. Others including oil and coal are in fixed supply and can be used only once. This chapter explores two issues in relation to our supplies of resources and energy. The first is whether we are likely to run out of resources in the future. The second is how to best manage our resources so that we can maximize the benefits that we receive from them now and in the future.

Resource Supplies: Doom or Boom?

Since the beginning of the Industrial Revolution in the late eighteenth century, an unprecedented increase in both population and living standards has taken place. The world's population has increased from 1 billion people in 1800 to about 8 billion today, and the average person living in the United States enjoys a standard of living at least 12 times higher than that of the average American in 1800. Human beings are now consuming vastly more resources than before the Industrial Revolution both in absolute terms and in per capita terms. This fact has led many observers to wonder if our current economic system and its high living standards are sustainable. In particular, will the limited supply of natural resources be sufficient to maintain or increase our standard of living in coming decades?

To answer this question, we must look at both resource demand *and* resource supply. We begin by examining human population growth because larger populations imply a greater demand for resources, all other things equal.

>> **LO19.1** Explain why falling birthrates make running out of natural resources unlikely.

Population Growth

We can trace the debate over the sustainability of resources back to 1798, when Thomas Malthus, an Anglican minister in England, published *An Essay on the Principle of Population*. Malthus argued that human living standards could only temporarily rise above subsistence levels because any temporary increase in living standards would cause people to have more children and thereby increase the population. With so many more people to feed, per capita living standards would be driven back down to subsistence levels.

🌐 GLOBAL PERSPECTIVE 19.1

TOTAL FERTILITY RATES FOR THE 12 MOST POPULOUS COUNTRIES, 2020

The total fertility rate—or average number of births per biological female per lifetime—varies substantially for the 12 most populous countries in the world. China, with a population of just over 1.4 billion, has a total fertility rate of 1.3, which is well below the long-run replacement level of 2.1 births per biological female per lifetime necessary to keep a human population constant over time. By contrast, Nigeria, with 206 million people, and Ethiopia, with 115 million people, had total fertility rates of more than four births per biological female per lifetime in 2020.

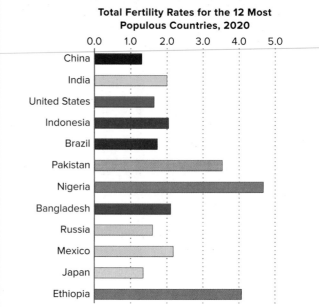

Total Fertility Rates for the 12 Most Populous Countries, 2020

Source: Various national statistical agencies; and *CIA World Factbook,* Central Intelligence Agency, 2021.

Falling Birthrates Fortunately for society, higher living standards have not produced higher birthrates. In fact, the opposite has happened. Higher living standards are associated with lower birthrates. Birthrates are falling rapidly throughout the world, and the majority of the world's population now lives in countries with birthrates that are lower than the **replacement rate** necessary to keep their respective populations stable over time.

Global Perspective 19.1 lists the total fertility rates for the 12 most populous countries, which together house two-thirds of the world's population. The **total fertility rate** is the average number of children that biological females are anticipated to have during their lifetimes. Taking into account infant and child mortality, a total fertility rate of about 2.1 births per biological female is necessary to keep the population constant, because 2.1 children equals 2 children to replace each of the biological parents plus 0.1 extra child who can be expected to die or become infertile before becoming old enough to reproduce.

As Global Perspective 19.1 shows, total fertility rates in the majority of the dozen countries that represent two-thirds of the world's population are at or below the replacement rate already. And total fertility rates are falling rapidly in the rest, heading for below-replacement levels. The overall effect is that world population growth is slowing and expected to turn negative sometime this century.

In the countries that have been experiencing below-replacement fertility for many decades, populations are already declining and are projected to fall rapidly over the next few decades as the number of elderly people dying each year exceeds the number of babies being born each year. Over 50 countries expect to see their populations decline by 2050, including Japan by over 18 million (a 15 percent decrease), Russia by 11 million (an 8 percent decrease), and Latvia by 430,000 (a 22 percent decrease).

Overall, a survey of top **demographers** (scientists who study human populations) found that on average, they thought that the world's population would peak at about 9.5 billion people around the year 2075 before beginning to fall. The decline may be rapid. If the worldwide total fertility rate declines to one birth per woman per lifetime, then each generation will be only half as large as the previous generation. Even a rate of 1.3 births per woman per lifetime would reduce a country's population by half in just under 45 years.

The Demographic Transition The world's population increased so rapidly from 1800 to the present day because higher living standards bring with them much lower death rates. Before modernization happens, death rates are typically so high that women have to give birth to more than six children per lifetime just to ensure that, on average, two will survive to adulthood. But once living

replacement rate The *total fertility rate* necessary to offset deaths in a country and thereby keep the size of its population constant (without relying on immigration). For most countries, a total fertility rate of about 2.1 births per woman per lifetime.

total fertility rate The average number of children per lifetime birthed by a nation's women.

demographers Scientists who study the characteristics of human populations.

standards begin to rise and modern medical care becomes available, childhood death rates plummet, and nearly all children survive to adulthood. The result is a temporary population explosion because parents—initially unaware that a revolutionary change in death rates has taken place—for a while keep on having six or more children. The result is one or two generations of very rapid population growth until parents adjust to the new situation and reduce the number of children they choose to have. The **demographic transition** is this three-step shift from (1) the traditional situation of both high birth and high death rates through (2) a transition period of high birthrates and low death rates and then to (3) the final situation of simultaneously low birth and low death rates.

The overall world population is still increasing because many populous countries—for instance, Nigeria, Egypt, and the Philippines—began modernizing only relatively recently. They are still in the transition phase where death rates have fallen but birthrates are still relatively high. Nevertheless, birthrates are falling rapidly nearly everywhere, and the end of rapid population growth is at hand. Furthermore, because the fertility rate tends to fall below the replacement rate as countries modernize, we can also expect total world population to begin declining. This is a critical fact to keep in mind when considering whether we are likely to face a resource crisis: Other things constant, fewer people imply less resource demand.

What explains today's lower fertility rates? Possible candidates include changing attitudes toward religion, the much wider career opportunities available to women in modern economies, and the expense of raising children in modern societies. Indeed, children have been transformed from economic assets that could be put to work at an early age in agricultural societies into economic liabilities that are very costly to raise in modern societies where child labor is illegal and where children must attend school until adulthood.

demographic transition
The massive decline in birthrates that occurs once a developing country achieves higher standards of living because the perceived marginal cost of additional children begins to exceed the perceived marginal benefit.

Resource Consumption per Person

In his 1968 book *The Population Bomb*, Paul Ehrlich of Stanford University made the Malthusian prediction that the Earth's population would soon outstrip resources. He predicted that, "in the 1970s and 1980s, hundreds of millions of people will starve to death in spite of any crash programs embarked upon now."[1] Contrary to this prediction, no such famines materialized then, and none appear likely today.

Falling Resource Prices What prevented the famines that Ehrlich predicted? First, the population growth rate slowed dramatically as living standards around the world rose and the demographic transition kicked in. Second, the long-run evidence indicates that the supply of productive resources available to be made into goods and services has been increasing faster than the demand for those resources for at least 150 years. Figure 19.1 tracks *The Economist* magazine's commodity price index for the years 1850 to 2021. The index currently contains 25 important commodities including aluminum, copper, corn, rice, wheat, coffee, rubber, sugar, and soybeans. In earlier days, it included commodities such as candle wax, silk, and indigo, which were important at the time. The index adjusts for inflation so that we can see how the real cost of commodities has evolved over time, and it is standardized so that the real price of commodities during the years 1845–1850 has an index value of 100.

Source: *The Economist.*

FIGURE 19.1
The Economist **magazine's commodity price index, 1850–2021.**

The Economist magazine's commodity price index attempts to keep track of the prices of the commodities most common in international trade. It is adjusted for inflation and scaled so that commodity prices in the years 1845–1850 are set to an index value of 100. The figure shows that real commodity prices are volatile (vary considerably from year to year) but are now over 50 percent lower than they were in the mid-nineteenth century. This implies that commodity supplies have increased faster than commodity demands.

---

[1] Paul R. Ehrlich, *The Population Bomb* (Ballantine Books, 1971).

CONSIDER THIS . . .

I'll Betcha

After Paul Ehrlich wrote *The Population Bomb* and predicted skyrocketing resource prices and widespread famines in the 1970s and 1980s, he met friendly but firm opposition from economist Julian Simon, who was an optimist about humanity's future, believing that entrepreneurship and human ingenuity would increase resource supplies faster than resource demand would rise. There would be no famines, he argued, and, moreover, resource prices would fall because supply increases would outpace demand increases.

Mike Flippo/123RF

To put Ehrlich to the test, Simon challenged him to a wager in 1980, and $20,000 was at stake. If resource prices rose by 1990, Ehrlich would get the money. If resource prices fell by 1990, Simon would win. In addition, Simon allowed Ehrlich to choose the resources they were going to monitor for the bet. Ehrlich chose copper, tin, chromium, nickel, and tungsten.

The prices of all five fell during the 1980s and there were no widespread famines, either. Simon pocketed the $20,000 and converted many people into optimists about resource constraints.

Figure 19.1 shows that a dramatic long-run decline in real commodity prices has occurred. With the 2021 value of the index at about 56, the real cost of buying commodities today is over 40 percent lower than it was in 1850. These lower prices mean that commodity supplies have increased faster than commodity demands. The only way that commodity prices could have fallen so much in the face of increasing demand is if the supply curve for commodities shifted to the right faster than the demand curve for commodities shifted to the right. (This trend caused Paul Ehrlich to lose a famous bet against economist Julian Simon, as discussed in the nearby Consider This.)

But what of the future? Will supply continue to outpace demand? Prospects are hopeful. First, the rapid and continuing decline in birthrates means that the huge population increases of the nineteenth and twentieth centuries are not likely to continue in the future. Indeed, the population declines that have already begun in many countries will reduce the demand for goods and services in the future. Second, resource consumption per person (as distinct from goods and services consumption per person) also has either leveled off or declined over recent decades in the richest countries, which currently consume the largest fraction of the world's resources.

Consumption Trends for Water, Energy, and Materials The leveling off or decline of per capita resource consumption in industrially advanced countries like the United States can be observed in Figures 19.2 and 19.3, which show, respectively, how much water and energy have been consumed on a daily or annual basis in both total and per capita terms over the last few decades in the United States.

FIGURE 19.2
Total and per capita water consumption in the United States, 1950–2015.

Total water consumption in the United States fell by 25 percent between 1980 and 2015 after reaching a peak of 430 billion gallons per day in 1980. Per capita water consumption peaked in 1975 at 1,941 gallons per person per day before falling by 49 percent, to only 991 gallons per person per day in 2015. (These data are reported every 5 years. The 2020 data were not available at the time of publication, but they may be available when you read this. If interested, check the U.S. Geological Survey website.)

Source: U.S. Geological Survey.

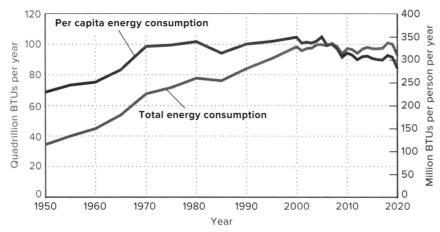

Source: U. S. Energy Information Administration

FIGURE 19.3
Total and per capita energy consumption in the United States, 1950–2020.

Per capita energy consumption in the United States peaked at 360.0 million British thermal units (BTUs) per person per day in 1979. It fell dramatically during the early 1980s recession and then rose again until 1999, after which it has been mostly falling, down to a value of 305.8 million BTUs per person per day in 2019. Total energy consumption between 1950 and 2000 nearly tripled, increasing from 34.6 quadrillion BTUs in 1950 to 98.1 quadrillion BTUs in 2000. Since 2000, total energy usage has been approximately steady at around 100 quadrillion BTUs per year, except for a sharp downturn in 2020 caused by the COVID-19 pandemic.

The red lines in each figure show total use while the blue lines trace per capita use. To accommodate both sets of data, the units measuring total use are on the vertical scales on the *left* side of each figure while the units measuring per capita use are on the vertical scales on the *right* side of each figure.

The blue line in Figure 19.2 shows that per capita water use in the United States peaked in 1975 at 1,941 gallons per person per day. It then fell by 49 percent to just 991 gallons per person per day in 2015.

The blue line in Figure 19.3 shows annual per capita energy use from all sources, including fossil fuels, solar electricity, and wind power. Annual per capita energy consumption peaked at 360.0 million British thermal units per person in 1979 before falling sharply during the early 1980s recession, gradually rising through the late 1990s and then holding steady at around 300 million **British thermal units** (BTUs) per person per year through 2019. The average then fell precipitously to 281.9 million BTUs per person per year in 2020 due to the economic downturn that occurred during the first year of the COVID-19 pandemic.

Setting aside the data for 2020, it is important to note that the 17 percent decline in per capita energy usage between 1979 and 2019 was especially remarkable given that the U.S. economy's per capita output of goods and services increased by 93 percent over the same period. That of course implies that we are producing much more output per capita using substantially less energy per capita. The decline in per capita energy usage has also more than compensated for U.S. population growth in recent decades, so that total energy usage in the U.S. economy (red line in Figure 19.3) has held roughly constant at or under 100 quadrillion BTUs per year since the year 2000.

British thermal unit (BTU) The amount of energy required to raise the temperature of 1 pound of water by 1 degree Fahrenheit.

The Likely Long-Run Decline in Resources Demand We have already provided evidence that the world's population is likely to decline after mid-century. Figures 19.2 and19.3 show that per capita consumption levels are also likely to either level off or decline. Together, these two facts suggest that the total demand for resources is likely to reach a peak in the relatively near future before falling over time as populations decline. Our mix of energy sources is also getting "greener," with an increasingly large fraction of energy consumption being provided by alternative energy sources like wind and solar rather than by fossil fuels.

That said, resource demand is likely to increase substantially for the next few decades as large parts of the world modernize and begin to consume as much per capita as the citizens of rich countries do today. For instance, per capita energy use in the United States in 2019 was 305.8 million BTUs per person. If every person in the world were to use that much energy, total annual energy demand would be 2,346 quadrillion BTUs, or about four times the 2019 world production of 611 quadrillion BTUs. One of the world's great economic challenges over the coming decades will be to supply the resources that will be demanded as living standards in low-income countries rise to those typical of high-income countries. But because population growth rates are slowing and because per capita resource use in rich countries has leveled off, we can now foresee a maximum total demand for resources even if living standards all over the world rise to rich-country levels. Given the ongoing improvements in technology and productivity that characterize modern economies and that allow us to produce increasingly more from any given set of inputs, it seems unlikely that we will encounter a situation where the total demand for resources exhausts their overall supply.

▶ Commodity prices have been falling for more than a century, indicating that resource supply has increased faster than resource demand.

▶ Because total fertility rates are low and falling, population growth for the world will turn negative and thereby reduce the number of people demanding resources.

▶ Resource consumption per person has also been falling in the United States and other rich countries.

▶ Significant increases in resource demands are likely over the next few decades, however, as living standards in poorer countries rise toward those in richer countries.

Energy Economics

>> **LO19.2** Describe why using a mix of energy sources is efficient.

Energy economics studies how people deal with energy scarcity. The analysis involves both supply and demand. In terms of energy supply, people are interested in finding and exploiting low-cost energy sources. But because energy is only one input into a production process, the best energy source in a given situation is, paradoxically, often rather expensive—yet still the best choice when other costs are taken into account. The economy therefore develops and exploits both costly and less costly energy sources, ranging from renewables to fossil fuels to nuclear power.

Energy Efficiency Is Increasing

In terms of demand, the most interesting fact is that per capita energy use has leveled off or declined in recent years in developed countries, as we previously illustrated for the United States in Figure 19.3. This fact implies that the world economy has become increasingly efficient at using energy to produce goods and services. Between 1990 and 2019, for example, Americans were able to make and consume 56 percent more goods and services per person despite using about 10 percent less energy per person. This increase in energy efficiency has been part of a long historical trend. Whereas 1 million BTUs of energy yielded $63.09 worth of goods and services in the United States in 1950, the same amount of energy yielded $190.74 worth of goods and services in 2019 (using constant year 2012 dollars to account for inflation).

Keep this huge increase in energy efficiency in mind when considering the likely magnitude of future energy demand. Because better technology means that more output can be produced with the same amount of energy input, rising living standards in the future will not necessarily depend on using more energy. Living standards can be raised without increasing energy inputs.

Efficient Electricity Use

We just noted that the United States and other developed economies have grown increasingly efficient at energy use. An interesting fact about energy efficiency, though, is that it often involves using a *mix* of energy inputs, some of which are much more expensive than others. The best way to see why this is true is to examine electric power generation.

The Challenge: Highly Variable Demand A typical electric company has to serve tens of thousands of homes and businesses and is expected to deliver an uninterrupted supply of electricity 24 hours a day, 7 days a week. The difficulty of this task is compounded by the massive changes in energy demand that occur over the course of a day. Demand is extremely low at night when people are sleeping, begins to rise rapidly in the morning as people wake up and turn on their lights, rises even more when they are at work, falls a bit as they commute home, rises back up a bit in the evening when they turn on their televisions, and finally collapses as they turn out their lights and go to sleep.

Electric companies have to deal with this large daily variation in the demand for electricity. In doing so, they are forced to confront an interesting problem: The power plants that have the lowest variable (operating) costs also have the highest fixed costs in terms of plant construction. For instance, large coal-burning electricity plants can produce energy at a variable cost of about 4 cents per kilowatt hour. But they can do so only if they are built large enough to exploit economies of scale and if they then operate at full capacity. To understand this problem, imagine that such a plant has a maximum generating capacity of 20 megawatts per hour but that its customers' peak afternoon demand for electricity is 25 megawatts per hour. One solution would be to build two 20-megawatt gas-fired plants. But that would be very wasteful because one would be operating at full capacity (and hence minimum cost), while the other would be producing only 5 megawatts of its 20-megawatt capacity. Given that such plants cost hundreds of millions of dollars to build, building a second plant would be highly inefficient.

The Solution: Mixing Generation Technologies Electric companies use a mix of different types of generation technology to accommodate daily variations in the demand for electricity. This strategy turns out to be optimal because even though some electricity generation plants have very high operating costs, they have low fixed costs (that is, they are relatively inexpensive to build). Thus, the power company in our example might build one large coal-fired plant to generate 20 of the required 25 megawatts of energy at 4 cents per kilowatt-hour, but it would then build a small 5-megawatt natural gas generator to supply the rest. Such plants produce electricity at the much higher cost of 15 cents per kilowatt hour, but they are relatively inexpensive to build. This solution saves the electric company from building a second very expensive coal-fired plant that would wastefully operate well below its full capacity.

The result of mixing energy-generating technologies is that the United States currently generates electricity from a variety of energy sources. As you can see in Figure 19.4, 59 percent is generated by coal and natural gas plants. The rest comes from nuclear power and a variety of renewable energy sources including hydropower, wind, and solar.

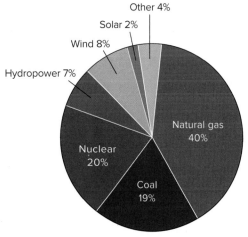

FIGURE 19.4
Sources of U.S. electricity generation, 2020.

Fifty-nine percent of U.S. electricity was generated by coal or natural gas plants in 2020. Another 20 percent came from nuclear plants, while hydropower, wind, and solar combined for 17 percent of the total.

Source: U. S. Energy Information Administration

Running Out of Energy?

Some observers worry that we may soon run out of the energy needed to power our economy. Their fears are based largely on the possibility that the world may run out of oil sometime this century. However, there is no likelihood of running out of energy. If anything, running out of oil would not mean running out of energy—just running out of what has for many decades been the cheapest source of energy *for transportation*. Fortunately for us, several alternative energy sources are quickly becoming less expensive.

>> **LO19.3** Discuss why running out of oil would not mean running out of energy.

Plunging Photovoltaic Prices

The main driver of this trend is falling solar electricity prices. Economies of scale in the production of crystalline silicon photovoltaic cells have allowed their cost per watt of electricity generated to fall since the late 1970s by about 10 percent per year—or by over 99 percent, cumulatively. In sunny locations, solar electricity is now the cheapest way to generate electricity, at least during the day. That cost advantage has widespread implications because the cost per mile of driving an electric vehicle has now fallen to only half as much as gasoline- or diesel-powered vehicles. As solar-electricity costs continue to fall, economic actors will have a strong financial incentive to switch away from gas- and diesel-powered vehicles toward electric vehicles. The switch won't happen instantly, though, because the purchase price of electric vehicles is still higher than the purchase price of gasoline and diesel vehicles. But electric vehicle prices are falling relative to those of internal combustion vehicles and so a full switch to electric vehicles over the next few decades seems likely.

Limitations on Solar Electricity Production

There is a bottleneck, however. Look back at Figure 19.4 and notice that solar accounts for only 2 percent of the electricity generated in the United States each year. This reflects several factors. First, it has only been in recent years that solar electricity prices have become competitive. Until the 2010s, there was no financial advantage to installing solar panels except in special cases where high costs could be tolerated or where there were no other practical alternatives (as with satellites). Second, at current prices, solar panels only perform well in terms of costs in sunny areas and southern latitudes (which enjoy more hours of sunlight each day). Thus, the "fraction of the map" where solar currently makes economic sense is limited. Third, solar has an intermittency problem. Solar panels can't generate electricity at night.

CONSIDER THIS . . .

Storage Wars

Many governments have subsidized wind turbines and solar energy projects to generate zero-emissions electricity. The amount of electricity that can be generated by these alternative methods can be massive relative to demand. On a gusty day, domestic wind turbines can provide over 100 percent of Denmark's electricity.

Unfortunately, wind turbines supply nothing on windless days and solar works only when the sun is up.

Coal and gas plants can modulate their output to fill in for the fluctuations in wind and solar, but another strategy for maximizing the potential of wind and solar generation is

Henglein and Steets/Cultura/Getty Images

to develop low-cost storage technologies so that electricity can be stored up on windy days for use on windless days and during the daytime for nighttime use.

Potential storage technologies include super-efficient lithium-ion batteries like those used in cell phones, supercapacitors that can discharge huge volumes of electricity very rapidly, and using flywheels to store energy. Wind and solar will reach their full potential when the marginal cost of energy storage falls below the marginal cost of using coal and gas to fill in for the fluctuations in wind and solar electricity generation. When that point is reached, unsubsidized market pressures can be expected to displace coal and gas in favor of wind and solar.

This problem of intermittency (not being constant) is shared with wind-powered electricity generation, which only works when the wind is blowing. It means that electric utilities cannot rely on solar or wind alone for powering their grids. They must still invest in large amounts of coal, natural gas, and nuclear generation capabilities because those sources can generate electricity both day and night and without regard to whether or not the wind is blowing or the sun shining.

This continuing need for nonrenewable electric power is a perplexing problem for utilities. If daytime lasted 24 hours per day and the wind always blew, utilities would consider ditching all their older plants for solar and wind. But as things now stand, they have to invest in both the older, higher-cost generating technologies *as well as* the newer, lower-cost green technologies.

One solution to the intermittency problem would be the creation of large amounts of low-cost electricity storage. If low-cost electricity storage were widely available, then we could store solar electricity generated during the day for use at night, and wind energy generated when it's gusty for use when the air is still. Unfortunately, as discussed in the nearby Consider This story, electric storage technologies are not yet up to the task. But as costs fall and storage capacities expand, utilities will probably start ditching traditional generation technologies in favor of low-cost solar and wind.

Multiple Oil Substitutes

Look at Table 19.1, which lists the oil prices at which other energy sources become economically viable. For instance, biodiesel, a type of diesel fuel made from decomposed plant wastes, is so expensive to produce that it becomes economically viable (that is, less costly to produce than oil) only if oil costs $110 or more per barrel. In contrast, ethanol made from corn in the United States costs less to produce and is an economically viable alternative to oil even if the price of oil is only $80 per barrel. (For comparison, note that the price of oil was $75 per barrel in early 2022, but had ranged as high as $103 per barrel and as low as $16 per barrel over the previous 10 years.)

Table 19.1 makes a key point: Even if we run out of oil, alternatives would quickly become available. At a price of $40 per barrel of oil, vast reserves of energy derived from tar sands, the conversion of natural gas and coal to liquid petroleum, and even ethanol derived from cheap Brazilian sugar cane become economically viable alternatives. At $50 per barrel, shale oil becomes a viable alternative. At $80 per barrel, corn-based ethanol becomes viable. And at $110 per barrel, so does biodiesel.

These "alternative" prices can be thought of as a giant supply curve for energy, with rising oil prices leading to increased energy production. Thus, even if the supply of oil begins to dry up and oil prices consequently rise, other energy supplies will quickly be brought online to fill the energy gap created by the decline in the amount of oil available. Also, the alternative prices listed in Table 19.1 are *current* alternative prices. As technologies improve, the costs of producing these oil

TABLE 19.1 Oil Prices at Which Alternative Energy Sources Become Economically Viable

Oil Price per Barrel at Which Alternative Fuel Becomes Economically Viable	Alternative Fuel
$110	Biodiesel
80	U.S. corn-based ethanol*
50	Shale oil
40	Tar sands; Brazilian sugar-cane-based ethanol; gas to liquids†; coal to liquids‡
20	Conventional oil

*Excludes tax credits.
†Gas to liquid is economically viable at $40 if natural gas price is $2.50 or less per million BTUs.
‡Coal to liquid is economically viable at $40 if coal price is $15 per ton or less.

alternatives are likely to fall. And as they are adopted more widely, the demand for oil will decline, thus making it highly unlikely that we will run out of oil any time soon.

Fracking and Falling Oil Extraction Costs An additional recent development also makes it unlikely that we will run out of oil any time soon. New drilling technologies like hydraulic fracturing have dramatically increased the amount of below-ground oil that can be extracted at a profit. Many older oil fields that had been abandoned because it would have been too costly with older technology to extract their oil are now profitable again with these new technologies, which involve techniques such as injecting superheated steam into oil fields to push out the remaining oil.

Hydraulic fracturing (or, informally, fracking) has vastly increased U.S. oil production, which rose from 5 million barrels per day in 2008 to nearly 11 million barrels per day in 2018, catapulting the United States into first place as the world's largest oil producer. The increase in output was so large that it more than eliminated the decades-long U.S. trade deficit in petroleum. For the first time since the first part of the twentieth century, the United States is now a net exporter of oil. One should keep these facts in mind whenever anyone claims that we will be running out of oil any time soon.

Environmental Impacts Finally, we need to acknowledge that energy sources differ not only in their prices and production costs but also in the negative externalities they may generate. Recall from Chapter 4 that negative externalities are costs—such as those associated with air pollution—that are imposed on third parties and are therefore not reflected in production costs or market prices. These negative externalities need to be accounted for if you want to eliminate the deadweight efficiency losses that they impose.

Some energy sources like solar and wind are very "green," creating almost zero pollution or other externalities. Traditional energy sources like oil and coal are more problematic. For example, burning coal generates substantial particulate and carbon dioxide emissions that may contribute to health problems as well as global warming. For this reason, many governments have instituted carbon taxes, tradable pollution credits, and tradable emissions permits. Each of them forces producers that utilize fossil fuels to pay for the costs that their activities impose on third parties. This increase in production costs eliminates the deadweight efficiency loss by reducing output levels down to the socially optimal level at which MB = MC.

These taxes and permit costs can have a dramatic effect on the prices that consumers pay for various types of fuel and, thus, on which types of fuel they are most likely to demand. Consider biodiesel. Table 19.1 indicates that the cost of producing biodiesel is so high that it only becomes competitive with oil if the price of oil is $110 per barrel or higher. But that $110 alternative price ignores the market value of the tradable pollution credits that the U.S. Environmental Protection Agency awards to biofuel producers for reducing carbon emissions. Taking those credits into account, biofuel becomes competitive with oil at just $55 dollars per barrel. The vast majority of consumers won't know that an emissions trading permit system even exists. They will only see that the price of biodiesel looks much lower. But that lower price will provide them with a stronger incentive to switch from oil to biodiesel any time the price of oil rises above $55 per barrel.

A caveat is needed here. Cleanliness is mostly a matter of cost. Coal, for instance, can be made almost as clean as solar if one is willing to pay for smokestack scrubbers to clean soot from emissions and underground storage facilities to sequester carbon dioxide away from the atmosphere. At sufficiently high energy prices, clean methods of producing energy are not confined to wind, solar, and other "green" energy sources. Indeed, the U.S. government now mandates that all new coal-burning electricity plants invest in both scrubbers and sequestration. But as solar and wind prices continue to fall, the high cost of scrubbers and sequestration facilities will loom larger in utilities' decision making. Why would they want to continue with technologies that have high clean-up costs when they can save all those costs by switching to wind or solar? It is not surprising that between 2010 and 2020 the amount of electricity generated at coal-burning electricity plants in the United States fell by nearly 60 percent while the number of coal mines operating in the United States also fell by nearly 60 percent. Over that same period, the fraction of U.S. electricity produced by coal-fired plants fell from nearly 44 percent in 2010 down to the 19 percent listed in Figure 19.4 for the year 2020. Utilities are paying attention to the cost of alternatives, and coal is being phased out all over the country.

QUICK REVIEW
19.2

▸ Energy efficiency has consistently improved so that more output can be produced for every unit of energy used by the economy.

▸ After taking into account differences in fixed construction costs, utility companies have found it efficient to use a variety of energy sources (coal, natural gas, nuclear) to deal with the large daily variations in energy demand.

▸ The intermittency of solar and wind electricity generation means that power companies still

need to build traditional power plants even though the cost of solar and wind generation is now lower in some places than that of coal, natural gas, and nuclear.

▸ We are unlikely to run out of oil because new extraction technologies have vastly increased the supply of extractable oil and because many oil alternatives like ethanol will become economically viable if oil prices rise.

Natural Resource Economics

>> **LO19.4** Show how the profit motive can encourage resource conservation.

net benefits The total benefits of some activity or policy less the total costs of that activity or policy.

A major focus of natural resource economics is to design policies for extracting or harvesting a natural resource that will maximize the **net benefits** of extraction *over time*. The net benefits are simply the total dollar value of all benefits minus the total dollar value of all costs, including future costs and benefits as well as current costs and benefits. A project's net benefit must take into account the fact that present and future decisions about how fast to extract or harvest a resource typically cannot be made independently. Other things equal, taking more today means having less in the future, and having more in the future means taking less today.

Renewables vs. Nonrenewables

In determining net benefits, it is important to understand the large differences between renewable natural resources and nonrenewable natural resources.

renewable natural resources Things such as forests, water in reservoirs, and wildlife that are capable of growing back or building back up (renewing themselves) if they are harvested at moderate rates.

nonrenewable natural resource Things such as oil, natural gas, and metals, that are either in actual fixed supply or that renew so slowly as to be in virtual fixed supply when viewed from a human time perspective.

- **Renewable natural resources** are capable of growing back, or renewing themselves, if they are harvested at moderate rates. Solar energy, forests, wildlife, the atmosphere, and the oceans are renewable natural resources either because they will continue providing their benefits no matter what we do (as is the case with solar energy) or because, if we manage them well, we can continue to enjoy their benefits in perpetuity (as is the case with the atmosphere, the oceans, rainforests, and aquifers).
- **Nonrenewable natural resources** either are in actual fixed supply or are renewed so slowly as to be in virtual fixed supply when viewed from a human time perspective. Nonrenewable resources include oil, coal, and metals found in the earth's crust. By conserving nonrenewable resources in the present, we are able to use more of them in the future.

Optimal Resource Management

The key to optimally managing both renewable and nonrenewable resources over time is designing incentives that prompt decision makers to consider not only current net benefits but also future net benefits. Once these incentives are in place, decision makers can weigh the costs and benefits of present use against the costs and benefits of future use to determine the optimal allocation of a resource between present and future. The key concept used in weighing these alternatives is *present value*.

Using Present Values to Evaluate Future Possibilities

Suppose that a highly impoverished country has just discovered that it possesses a small oil field. Should the country pump this oil today when it can make a profit of $50 per barrel, or should it wait 5 years to pump the oil if it believes that 5 years from now, it will be able to make a profit of $60 per barrel due to lower production costs?

Answering this question requires consideration of the time-value of money, which was discussed at length in Chapter 18. For the question at hand, we need to compare $60 worth of money in 5 years with $50 worth of money today. Economists make this comparison by converting the future quantity of money (in this case $60) into a present-day equivalent measured in present-day money. By using this conversion, they can compare the two quantities of money using the same unit of measurement: present-day dollars.

Understanding Present Values How do we calculate the present-day equivalent, or **present value,** of any future sum of money (in this case, $60 in 5 years)? The intuition is simple. Suppose that the current market interest rate is 5 percent per year. How much money would a person have to save and invest today at 5 percent interest to end up with exactly $60 in 5 years? The correct answer turns out to be $47.01. That is, if $47.01 is invested at an interest rate of 5 percent per year, it will grow into precisely $60 in 5 years. Stated slightly differently, $47.01 today is the equivalent of $60 in 5 years because it is possible to transform $47.01 today into $60 in 5 years by investing it at the market interest rate of 5 percent.

Now let's return to our example of the oil field. If the country pumps its oil today, it will get $50 per barrel worth of present-day dollars. But if it pumps its oil in 5 years and gets $60 per barrel at that time, it will get only $47.01 per barrel worth of present-day dollars because the present value of $60 in 5 years is precisely $47.01 today. By measuring both possibilities in present-day dollars, the better choice of action becomes obvious: The country should pump its oil today, because $50 worth of present-day money is obviously greater than $47.01 worth of present-day money.

present value Today's value of some amount of *money* that is to be received at a particular future date.

Allocating Resources over Time By enabling decision makers to compare the costs and benefits of present use with the costs and benefits of future use, present-value calculations help to ensure that a resource will be used at whatever point in time it is most valuable.

This conclusion is especially important when it comes to conservation because there is always a temptation to use up a resource as fast as possible rather than conserving some or all of it for future use. By putting a present-day dollar value on the net benefits to be gained by conservation and future use, present-value calculations allow for a financial incentive that can help to ensure that resources will be conserved for future use whenever doing so will generate higher net benefits than using them in the present. When future net benefits are properly accounted for, resource use tends to be conservative and sustainable; when they are ignored, environmental devastation tends to take place, as we discuss below.

Nonrenewable Resources

Nonrenewable resources such as oil, coal, and metals must be mined or pumped from the ground before they can be used. Oil and mining companies attempt to make a profit from extracting and selling them. But because extraction is costly and because future selling prices are uncertain, profits are not guaranteed. Therefore, these companies must plan their operations carefully if they hope to realize a profit.

The "User Cost" of Present Use It usually takes many years to completely pump out a commercial oil field or dig out a mine. That long duration implies that an extraction company's goal of "maximizing profits" actually involves choosing an extraction strategy that maximizes a *stream* of profits—potential profits today as well as potential profits in the future. There is, of course, a trade-off. If the company extracts more today, its revenues will be larger today because it will have more product to sell today. On the other hand, more extraction today means that less of the resource will be available for future extraction.

Consequently, future revenues will be smaller because future extraction will necessarily be reduced. Indeed, every bit of a resource that is extracted and sold today comes at the opportunity cost of not being able to be extracted and sold in the future. Natural resource economists refer to this opportunity cost as the **user cost** of extraction because the user of a resource always faces the opportunity cost of reduced future extraction if she opts to extract in the present.

user cost The *opportunity cost* of extracting and selling a *nonrenewable natural resource* today rather than waiting to extract and sell the resource in the future; the *present value* of the decline in future revenue that will occur because a nonrenewable natural resource is extracted and sold today rather than being extracted and sold in the future.

FIGURE 19.5
Choosing the optimal extraction level.

A firm that takes account only of current extraction costs, *EC*, will produce Q_0 units of output in the current period—that is, all units for which the market price *P* exceeds extraction costs, *EC*. If it also takes account of user cost, *UC*, and the fact that current output reduces future output and profits, it will produce only Q_1 units of output—that is, only those units for which the current price exceeds the sum of extraction costs and user cost.

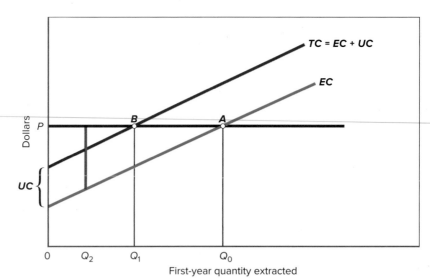

extraction cost All costs associated with extracting a natural resource and readying it for sale.

Present Use versus Future Use The concept of user cost is helpful in showing how a resource-extraction firm will choose to behave in terms of how much it will extract in the present as opposed to the future. To give a simple example, consider the case of Black Rock, a coal-mining company whose mine will have to shut down in two years, when the company's lease expires. Because the mine will close in two years, the mine's production can be thought of as taking place either during the current year or next year. Black Rock wants to determine how much to mine this year so that it can maximize its stream of profits over both years.

Extraction When Considering Only Extraction Costs To see how Black Rock's managers might think about the problem, look at Figure 19.5, which depicts the situation facing the company during the first year. Begin by noticing *P*, the market price at which Black Rock can sell each and every ton of coal that it extracts. The firm's managers obviously want to consider this price when deciding how much output to produce.

Next, consider the company's production costs, which we will call **extraction costs**, or *EC*. The extraction costs include all costs associated with running the mine, digging out the coal, and preparing the coal for sale. Notice that the *EC* curve in Figure 19.5 is upward sloping to reflect the fact that the company's marginal extraction costs increase the more the company extracts. Why? Faster extraction involves renting or buying more equipment and either hiring more workers or paying overtime to existing workers. Rapid extraction is costly, and the *EC* curve slopes upward to reflect this fact.

Next, consider how much output the firm's managers will choose to produce if they fail to take user cost into account. If the firm's managers ignore user cost, then they will choose to extract and sell Q_0 tons of coal (shown where the horizontal *P* line crosses the upward sloping *EC* line at point *A*). They will do this because for each and every ton of coal extracted up to Q_0, the market price at which it can be sold exceeds its marginal extraction cost—making each of those tons of coal profitable to produce. Stated a little differently, the company is applying the MR $(= P) =$ MC rule of profit maximization that we discussed in Chapter 10—but doing so *without* accounting for the opportunity cost of current extraction.

Extraction When Also Considering User Cost The previous analysis considers only potential first-year profits. But none of the Q_0 tons of coal that our previous analysis indicated should be mined in the first year actually *have* to be mined in the first year. Each and every ton could be left in the ground and mined during the second year. Black Rock's managers need to ask whether the company's total stream of profits will increase if it leaves some or all of those tons of coal in the ground this year and instead mines and sells them next year.

They can answer this question by taking account of user cost. Specifically, the company's managers can put a dollar amount on how much future profits are reduced by current extraction and then take that dollar amount into account when determining the optimal amount to extract this year. Look again at Figure 19.5. There, each ton of coal that is extracted this year has a user cost of *UC* dollars per ton that is equal to the present value of the firm's profits if the firm delays the extraction and sale of each ton of coal until the second year. Taking user cost into account results in a total cost curve, or TC, that is exactly UC dollars higher than the extraction cost curve (EC) at every extraction level. This parallel upward shift reflects the fact that once the company takes user cost into account, its total costs must equal the sum of extraction costs and user cost. That is, $TC = EC + UC$.

If the firm's managers take user cost into account, they will choose to produce less output this year. In fact, they will choose to extract only Q_1 units of coal this year (shown where the horizontal P line crosses the upward sloping TC line at point B). They will produce exactly this much coal because for each and every ton of coal that is extracted up to Q_1, the market price at which it can be sold exceeds its total cost—including not only the current extraction cost but also the cost of forgone future profits, UC. The company is still applying the MR ($= P$) = MC rule, but now it is doing so while accounting for the opportunity cost of current extraction.

Why Delay Is More Profitable for Some Units For every ton of coal up to Q_1, it is more profitable for Black Rock to extract during the first year than during the second year. To understand why, let's look again at Figure 19.5 and examine one particular ton of coal, Q_2, that lies between zero units produced and Q_1 units produced. The profit that the firm can get by extracting that particular ton this year is equal to the difference between its extraction cost and the market price. In terms of the figure, this first-year profit equals the length of the vertical red line that runs between the point on the EC curve above output level Q_2 and the horizontal P line.

Notice that the red line is longer than the vertical distance between the EC curve and the TC curve. Thus, the first-year profit is greater than the present value of the second-year profit because the vertical distance between the EC curve and the TC curve is equal to UC, which is by definition the present value of the profit that the company would get if it delayed producing unit Q_2 until the second year. Therefore, if the firm wants to maximize its profit, it should mine that particular ton of coal, Q_2, during the first year rather than during the second year.

The same is not true for the tons of coal between output levels Q_1 and Q_0. For these tons of coal, the first-year profit—which, as before, equals the vertical distance between the EC curve and the horizontal P line—is less than UC, the present value of the second-year profit that can be obtained by delaying production until the second year. Consequently, the company should delay the extraction of these units until the second year.

Incomplete Property Rights Lead to Excessive Present Use

We just demonstrated that profit-maximizing extraction companies are very happy to decrease current extraction if they can benefit financially from doing so. In particular, they are willing to reduce current extraction if they have the ability to profit from the future extraction and sale of their product. Indeed, this type of financial situation gives them the incentive to conserve any and all resources that would be more profitably extracted in the future.

This pleasant result breaks down completely if weak or uncertain property rights do not allow extraction companies to profit by conserving resources for future use. For instance, look back at Figure 19.5 and consider how much Black Rock would produce if it were suddenly told that its lease would expire at the end of this year rather than at the end of next year. This would be the equivalent of having a user cost equal to zero because there would be no way for the company to profit in the future by reducing current extraction. The firm will take into account only current extraction costs, EC. The result will be that it will extract and sell Q_0 tons of coal, more than the Q_1 tons that it would have extracted if it were able to stay in business for the second year and thereby profit from conservation.

Application: Conflict Minerals

Resources tend to be extracted much too quickly if there is no way to profit from conservation. That certainly is the case with so-called **conflict minerals,** which are minerals like gold, tungsten, tantalum, and tin that are mined by civil-war combatants in several war zones around the world to provide the hard currency that they need to finance their military activities. Most of these wars are, however, very unpredictable, so that control of the mines is tenuous, slipping from one army to another depending on the tide of war.

This fluidity has destroyed any incentive to conserve these resources. Because nobody can be sure of controlling a mine for more than a few months, extraction rates are always extremely high.

This behavior is wasteful because once the war finally ends and money is needed to rebuild the country, whichever side wins will find precious little left in the way of conflict minerals to help pay

conflict minerals Minerals (especially gold, tin, tantalum, and tungsten) that are minded and sold by combatants in war zones in Africa as a way to help finance their military activities.

for reconstruction. The incentives created by the uncertainty of war see to it that extraction takes place at far too rapid a pace, making no allowance for the possibility that future extraction would be better than present extraction.

▶ Because nonrenewable resources are finite, it is very important to allocate their limited supply efficiently between present and future uses.

▶ If resource-extraction companies can benefit from both present and future extraction, they will limit current extraction to only those units that are more profitable to extract in the present than in

the future. As a result, resources are conserved for future use.

▶ If resource users have no way of benefiting from the conservation of a resource, they will use too much of it in the present and not save enough of it for future use, even if future use would be more beneficial than present use.

Renewable Resources

>> **LO19.5** Explain how property rights can prevent deforestation and species extinction.

You have just learned that, under the right circumstances, extraction companies will have a strong profit incentive to conserve *nonrenewable* resources like oil and coal for future use. A similar incentive can also hold true for companies and individuals dealing with *renewable* resources like forests and wildlife. If property rights are structured properly, decision makers will have an incentive to manage a renewable resource on a sustainable basis, harvesting it slowly enough that the resource can always replenish itself.

Elephant Preservation

If a renewable wildlife resource is harvested too fast, it can go extinct. This was the situation facing elephants in Africa during the 1970s and 1980s when elephant populations in most parts of Africa declined drastically due to the illegal poaching of elephants for their ivory tusks. It was the case, however, that elephant populations in a few countries expanded considerably. The difference resulted from the fact that in certain countries like Botswana and Zimbabwe, property rights over elephants were given to local villagers, thereby giving them a strong financial incentive to preserve their local elephant populations. In particular, local villagers were allowed to keep the money that could be earned by taking foreign tourists on safari to see the elephants in their area as well as the money that could be made by selling hunting rights to foreign sports hunters. This gave them a strong incentive to prevent poaching, and villagers quickly organized very effective patrols to protect and conserve their local elephant populations.

By contrast, elephants belonged to the government in other countries, meaning that locals had no personal stake in the long-term survival of their local elephant populations since any elephant tourism money flowed to the government. This created the perverse incentive that the only way for a local person to benefit financially from an elephant was by killing it to poach its ivory. Indeed, most of the poaching in these countries was done by local people who had no way to benefit from the long-term survival of their local elephant populations. As with nonrenewable resources, the inability to benefit from conservation and future use causes people to increase their present use of renewable resources like elephant populations, sometimes catastrophically.

Forest Management

Forests provide many benefits, including wildlife habitat, erosion prevention, oxygen production, recreation, and, of course, wood. In 2020, just over 10 billion acres (4 billion hectares), or about 31 percent of the world's land area, was forested. By comparison, about 766 million acres (310 million hectares), or about 34 percent of the United States' land area, was forested.

The Importance of Property Rights Global Perspective 19.2 shows that the rate of reforestation or deforestation varies dramatically by country. What explains these large differences? For the most part, differences in property rights.

In some locations, including the United States and western Europe, forests are either private property or strictly regulated government property, so that ownership is clear and it is possible for owners to prevent others from chopping down their trees. Clear ownership promotes conservation because owners know that they can benefit in the future from reductions in current harvesting rates. By contrast, deforestation is proceeding rapidly in countries where property rights over forests are poorly enforced or nonexistent, so that nobody has a personal financial incentive to conserve today in order to have more tomorrow.

GLOBAL PERSPECTIVE 19.2

PERCENTAGE CHANGE IN THE AMOUNT OF LAND COVERED BY FORESTS, 2010–2020

The percentage change in the amount of land covered by forests varies greatly by nation. These differences in deforestation and reforestation rates are largely driven by differences in property rights.

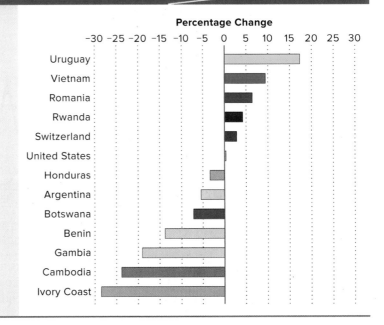

Source: Food and Agriculture Organization of the United Nations.

To understand why, consider the situation facing competing loggers if nobody owns the logging rights to a given forest. In that situation, whoever chops down the forest first will be able to reap economic benefits because anybody can establish a property right to a tree by chopping it down and bringing it to market. In this situation, everybody has an incentive to chop down as many trees as quickly as possible, before anyone else can. Nobody has an incentive to preserve trees for future use because—without enforceable property rights—person A has no way to prevent person B from chopping down the trees that person A would like to preserve.

To reduce or eliminate nonsustainable logging, governments and international agencies have been taking increasingly strong steps to define and enforce property rights over forests. In the United States and western Europe, where strong property rights over forests have been established, virtually all wood production is generated by commercially run forestry companies. These companies buy large tracts of land on which they plant and harvest trees. Whenever a harvest takes place and the trees in a given area are chopped down, seedlings are planted to replace the felled trees, thereby replenishing the stock of trees. These companies are deeply concerned about the long-term sustainability of their operations, and many plant trees with the expectation that more than a century may pass before they are harvested.

It must be emphasized that forestry companies in countries with strong property rights *replant* after they harvest a forest. They do this because they know that they can benefit from the seedlings' eventual harvest, even if that is 50 or 100 years in the future. In countries where property rights are not secure, nobody has an incentive to replant after cutting down a forest because there is no way to prevent someone else from stealing the harvest.

fishery A stock of fish or other marine animal that is composed of a distinct group, for example, New England cod, Pacific tuna, or Alaskan crab.

Optimal Fisheries Management

A **fishery** is a stock of fish or other marine animal that can be thought of as a logically distinct group. A fishery is typically identified by location and species— for example, Newfoundland cod, Pacific tuna, or Alaskan crab. Table 19.2 lists the top 10 U.S. fisheries in terms of how much their respective catches were worth in 2018. For comparison, note that the total dollar value of all the commercial fish and seafood caught in 2018 was $5.4 billion.

TABLE 19.2

Top 10 U.S. Fisheries in Dollar Terms, 2018

Fishery	Market Value of Catch
American Lobster	$630,000,000
Pacific salmon	599,000,000
Sea scallop	532,000,000
Shrimp	510,000,000
Alaskan pollock	451,000,000
Blue crab	196,000,000
Menhaden	161,000,000
Tuna	149,000,000
Sablefish	111,000,000
Pacific halibut	87,000,000

Source: Fisheries Economics of the United States, 2018, National Oceanic and Atmospheric Administration.

FIGURE 19.6
The collapse of two fisheries, 1973–2004.

This figure shows how many metric tons of Atlantic tuna and Maine red hake were caught by U.S. fishing boats each year from 1973 to 2004. Overfishing has caused the populations of both species to collapse, Maine red hake very abruptly, Atlantic tuna more slowly.

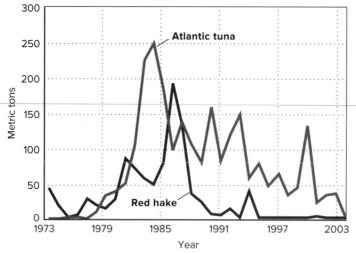

Source: National Oceanic and Atmospheric Administration.

The key difficulty with fishery management is that the only way for a person to establish property rights over a fish swimming in the open ocean is to catch it and kill it. As long as the fish is alive and swimming in the open ocean, it belongs to nobody. But as soon as it is caught, it belongs to the person who caught it. This property rights system means that the only way to benefit economically from a fish is to catch it and thereby turn it into a private good.

This creates an incentive for fishers to be very aggressive and try to outfish each other, since the only way for them to benefit from a particular fish is to catch it before someone else does. The calamitous result of this perverse incentive has been tremendous overfishing, which has caused many fisheries to collapse and which threatens many others with collapse as well.

Two examples of fishery collapse are presented in Figure 19.6, which shows the number of metric tons per year of Maine red hake and Atlantic tuna that were caught between 1973 and 2004 by U.S. fishers. A **fishery collapse** happens when a fishery's population is sent into a rapid decline because fish are being harvested faster than they can reproduce. The speed of the decline depends on how much faster harvesting is than reproduction. In the case of Maine red hake, the decline was very abrupt, with the annual catch falling from 190.3 million metric tons in 1986 down to only 4.1 million tons five years later. After making a minor resurgence in 1994, the fishery then totally collapsed, so that the catch was less than 1 ton per year for most of the following decade despite the best efforts of fishers to catch more. The collapse of the Atlantic tuna fishery was more gradual because the ratio of harvest to reproduction was not as extreme as it was for Maine red hake. But even when harvesting exceeds reproduction by only a small amount in a given year, the population declines. And if that pattern holds for many years, the population will be forced into collapse. This was the case for Atlantic tuna. Its annual catch collapsed more gradually, from a peak of 248.9 million metric tons in 1984 down to only 4.1 million metric tons in 2004.

fishery collapse A rapid decline in a *fishery*'s population because its fish are being harvested faster than they can reproduce.

Overfishing and fishery collapse are now extremely common, so much so that worldwide stocks of large predatory fish like tuna, halibut, swordfish, and cod are believed to be 90 percent smaller than they were just 50 years ago. In addition, Table 19.3 shows that just 7 percent of the world's fisheries are estimated to be underfished. Of the remainder, 34 percent are categorized as overfished, while 60 percent are believed to be fished up to, but not beyond, their maximum sustainable levels.

Policies to Limit Catch Sizes

Governments have tried several different policies to limit the number of fish that are caught each year. These policies attempt to lower annual catch sizes down to sustainable levels, where the size of the catch does not exceed a fishery's ability to regenerate. Unfortunately, many of these policies not only fail to reduce catch sizes but also create perverse incentives that raise fishing costs because they do not stop the fishing free-for-all in which each fisher tries to catch as many fish as possible as fast as possible before anyone else can get to them.

TABLE 19.3
Status of the World's Fisheries

Status	Percentage
Underfished	6
Maximally sustainably fished	60
Overfished	34

Source: The State of the World Fisheries and Aquaculture 2020, Food and Agriculture Organization of the United Nations.

Shortening the Length of Fishing Seasons

Governments have in some cases attempted to reduce catch sizes by limiting the number of

CONSIDER THIS . . .

The Tragedy of the Commons

In an article titled "The Tragedy of the Commons," ecologist Garret Hardin explained the crucial role that individual property rights play in resource preservation.

Hardin discussed the public plots of grazing land that were set aside in many villages in medieval Europe. These plots were called commons, after the fact that they were held in common and could be used by anyone. They were a form of welfare designed to help poor people graze and feed animals even if they couldn't afford any land of their own.

Hardin pointed out that this welfare system often failed due to a lack of individual property rights. In particular, the commons were overrun, overgrazed, and turned into barren

Stockbyte/Digital Vision/Getty Images

patches of dirt because they were "first come, first served." The fact that anybody could use the commons meant that nobody had an individual incentive to try to preserve an existing patch of grass. That was because any grass that one person chose to preserve would just end up being eaten by somebody else's animals. So if a person saw any uneaten grass, his best strategy was to let his animals devour it before somebody else's animals did.

As soon as Hardin published his article, people realized that similar **tragedy of the commons** situations were prone to occur wherever individual property rights were lacking. Consider overfishing and deforestation. They both occur because a lack of individual property rights means that each user is incentivized to take as much as possible, as quickly as possible, before anyone else can get to the resource.

---

days per year that a certain species can be caught. The duration of the legal crabbing season in Alaska was once cut down from several months to just 4 days, for example. Unfortunately, this policy failed to reduce catch sizes because crabbers compensated for the short legal crabbing season by buying massive boats that could harvest in 4 days the same amount of crab that they had previously needed months to gather.

Fishers bought the new, massive boats because while the new policy limited the number of days over which crabbers were allowed to compete, it did not lessen their incentive to try to catch as many crabs as possible before anyone else could get to them. Indeed, the massive new boats were a sort of arms race, with each fisher trying to buy a bigger, faster boat than his competitors in order to capture more crabs than them during the limited 4-day season. The result, however, was a stalemate because if everybody is buying bigger, faster boats, then nobody gains an advantage. Consequently, the policy actually made the situation worse. Not only did it fail to reduce catch size, it also drove up fishing costs. This was an especially pernicious result because the policy had been designed to help fishers by preserving the resource upon which their livelihoods depended.

Limiting the Number of Boats Another failed policy attempted to limit catch size by limiting the number of fishing boats allowed to fish in a specific area. This policy failed because fishers compensated for the limit on the number of boats by operating bigger boats. That is, many small boats that could each catch only a few tons of fish were replaced by a few large boats that could each catch many tons of fish. Once again, catch sizes did not fall.

Limiting the Total Catch A policy that does work to reduce catch size goes by the acronym **TAC,** which stands for **total allowable catch.** Under this system, biologists set the TAC for a given fishery at the level of its sustainable harvesting rate, for instance, 100,000 tons per year. Fishers can then fish until a total of 100,000 tons have been brought to shore. At that point, fishing is halted for the year.

This policy has the benefit of actually limiting the size of the catch to sustainable levels. But it still encourages an arms race among the fishers because each fisher wants to try to catch as many fish as possible before the TAC limit is reached. The result is that even under a TAC, fishing costs rise because fishers buy bigger, faster boats as each one tries to fulfill as much of the overall TAC catch limit as possible.

Assigning Individual Transferable Quotas The catch-limiting system that economists prefer not only limits the total catch size but also eliminates the fishing-boat arms race that drives up costs. The system is based on the issuance of **individual transferable quotas,** or **ITQs,** which are individual catch-size limits that specify that the holder of an ITQ has the right to harvest a given quantity of a particular species during a given period of time, for instance, 1,000 tons of Alaskan king crab during the year 2017.

tragedy of the commons
The tendency for commonly owned *natural resources* to be overused, neglected, or degraded because their common ownership gives nobody an incentive to maintain or improve them.

total allowable catch (TAC)
The overall limit set by a government or a fisheries commission on the total number of fish or tonnage of fish that fishers collectively can harvest during some particular time period. Used to set the fishing limits for *individual transferable quotas (ITQs)*.

individual transferable quotas (ITQs) Limits (quotas) set by a government or a fisheries commission on the total number or total weight of a species that an individual fisher can harvest during some particular time period; fishers can sell (transfer) the right to use all or part of their respective individual quotas to other fishers.

Is Economic Growth Bad for the Environment?

Measures of Environmental Quality Are Higher in Richer Countries.

Many people are deeply concerned that environmental degradation is an inevitable consequence of economic growth. Their concern is lent credence by sensational media events like oil and chemical spills and by the indisputable fact that modern chemistry and industry have created and released into the environment many toxic chemicals that human beings did not even know how to make a couple of centuries ago.

Economists, however, tend to be rather positive about economic growth and its consequences for the environment. They are positive because significant evidence indicates that richer societies spend much more money on keeping their respective environments healthy than do less wealthy societies. Viewed from this perspective, economic growth and rising living standards are good for the environment because as societies get richer, they tend to spend more on things like reducing emissions from smokestacks, preventing the dumping of toxic chemicals, and insisting that sewage be purified before its water is returned to the environment. They also tend to institute better protections for sensitive ecosystems and engage in greater amounts of habitat preservation for endangered species.

But are these increasing expenditures on environmentally beneficial goods and services enough to overcome the massive increases in environmental harm that seem likely to accompany the enormous amounts of production and consumption in which rich societies engage? The empirical record suggests that the answer is yes. The best evidence for this is given by the accompanying figure, in which

Dudarev Mikhail/Shutterstock

each of 171 countries is represented by a point that indicates both its GDP per capita (measured on the horizontal axis using a logarithmic scale) and its year 2020 score on the Environmental Performance Index, or EPI.

GDP per capita stands for Gross Domestic Product per capita, and is a measure of a country's average income per person. For instance, GDP per capita in the United States in 2020 was $63,414, meaning that if you took the dollar value of all the goods and services

The individual catch sizes of all the ITQs that are issued for a given fishery during a specific year add up to the fishery's overall TAC for the year so that they put a sustainable limit on the overall catch size. This preserves the fishery from overexploitation. But the fact that the ITQ quotas are *individual* also eliminates the need for an arms race. Because each fisher knows that they can take as long as they want to catch their individual quota, they do not need a superexpensive, technologically sophisticated boat that is capable of hauling in massive amounts of fish in only a few days in order to beat their competitors to the punch. Instead, they can use smaller, slower boats since they know that they can fish slowly—perhaps year round if it suits them.

Efficiency Gains This move toward smaller boats and more leisurely fishing greatly reduces fishing costs. But ITQs also offer another cost-saving benefit because they encourage all of the fishing to be done by the lowest-cost, most-efficient fishing vessels. This is true because ITQs are *tradable* fishing quotas, meaning that they can be sold and thereby traded to other fishers. As we will explain, market pressures will cause them to be sold to the fishers who can catch fish most efficiently, at the lowest possible cost.

To see how this works, imagine a situation in which the market price of tuna is $10 per ton but in which a fisherman named Sven can barely make a profit because his old, slow boat is so expensive that it costs him $9 per ton to catch tuna. At that cost, if he does his own fishing and uses his ITQ quota of 1,000 tons himself, he will make a profit of only $1,000 (= $1 per ton × 1,000 tons). At the same time, one of his neighbors, Leilani, has just bought a new, super-efficient ship that can harvest fish at the very low cost of $6 per ton. This difference in fishing costs means that Sven and Leilani will both find it advantageous to negotiate the sale of Sven's ITQ to Leilani. Sven, for his

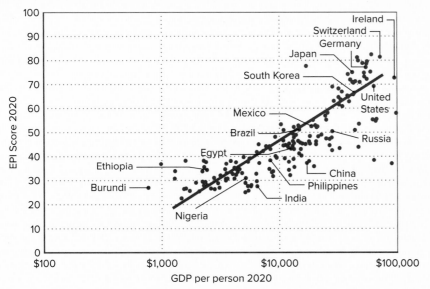

EPI Score 2020

GDP per person 2020

Source: Yale University.

When EPI scores are combined with measures of GDP per person in the figure, a clear pattern emerges: Richer countries have higher EPI scores. In fact, the relationship between the two variables is so strong that 70 percent of the differences between countries in terms of EPI scores are explained by their differences in GDP per person. The figure is therefore clear confirmation not only that economic growth can go together with a healthy environment, but that economic growth actually promotes a healthy environment by making people rich enough to pay for pollution-reduction technologies that people living in poorer countries cannot afford.

Looking to the future, many economists are hopeful that economic growth and rising living standards will pay for the invention and implementation of new technologies that could make for an even cleaner environment. If the current pattern continues to hold, increased standards of living will lead to better environmental outcomes.

produced and consumed in the United States that year and divided it by the U.S. population, the average amount per person was $63,414.

The EPI Index, by contrast, compares countries based on how well they are doing in terms of 32 environmental indicators, including atmospheric carbon emissions, measures of air and water quality, the degree of wilderness protection, energy efficiency, and measures of whether a country's fisheries and forests are being overexploited. Out of a maximum possible EPI score of 100, Denmark received the highest score of 82.5. The United States was ranked 24th with a score of 69.3 while the lowest-ranked country, Liberia, received a score of 22.6.

Note: The horizontal axis within the graph is measured using a logarithmic scale, so that each successive horizontal unit represents a 10-fold increase in GDP per person. This is useful because it happens to be the case that the relationship between EPI and GDP per person is such that a 10-fold increase in GDP per person is associated with an increase in EPI of about 20 points. Graphing the data using a logarithmic scale makes this relationship obvious.

Source: The PPP-adjusted per capita GDP data are from the World Bank while the EPI data are from the Yale Center for Environmental Law and Policy, epi.yale.edu.

part, would be happy to accept any price higher than $1,000 since $1,000 is the most that he can make if he uses the ITQ himself. Suppose that they agree on a price of $2 per ton, or $2,000 total. In such a case, both are better off. Sven is happy because he gets $2,000 rather than the $1,000 that he would have earned if he had done his own fishing. And Leilani is happy because she is about to make a tidy profit. The 1,000 tons of tuna that she can catch with Sven's ITQ will bring $10,000 in revenues when they are sold at $10 per ton, while her cost of bringing in that catch will be only $8,000 (= $6,000 in fishing costs at $6 per ton plus the $2,000 that she paid Sven for the right to use his 1,000-ton ITQ).

Social Benefits Notice, though, that society also benefits. If Sven had used his ITQ himself, he would have run up fishing costs of $9,000 while harvesting the 1,000 tons of tuna. But because the permit was sold to Leilani, only $6,000 in fishing costs will be incurred. The tradable nature of ITQs promotes overall economic efficiency by creating an incentive structure that tends to move production toward the producers who have the lowest production costs. That frees up resources for other uses, thereby improving both allocative and productive efficiency in the economy.

It remains to be seen, however, if ITQs and other catch-reduction policies will be enough to save the world's deep-sea fisheries. Since current international law allows countries to enforce ITQs and other conservation measures only within 200 miles of their shores, most of the world's oceans are a fishing free-for-all. Unless better incentive structures are put in place to limit catch sizes in international waters, economic theory suggests that open-ocean fisheries will continue to decline as fishers compete to catch as many fish as possible as fast as possible before anyone else can get to them.

Support for Aquaculture The main goal of fisheries management programs has been to prevent fisheries collapse by providing the incentives (or disincentives!) necessary to support the sustainable harvesting of renewable marine resources. But a side effect of reducing harvesting rates is higher prices for fish and other seafood, since reducing harvesting rates down to sustainable levels represents a decrease in supply relative to the higher, unsustainable rates of harvesting that would take place without ITQs, TACs, and so on.

aquaculture The cultivation of aquatic animals and plants for food.

That increase in the price of fish and seafood has helped the world's **aquaculture** industry to flourish because higher prices are received not only by fishers who catch wild seafood but also by aquacultural "fish farmers" who raise fish and other seafood in cages or pens, many of those enclosures floating at sea or in rivers or lakes. Without the higher prices for fish and seafood resulting from reduced harvests of wild-caught marine life, the majority of aquacultural businesses might not have been viable over the past few decades. But thanks in large measure to the higher prices promoted by sustainable harvesting practices for wild-caught marine life, aquaculture has grown rapidly, from producing just 5 percent of the world's total supply of seafood products in 1960 to over half by 2013. If current growth rates continue, around two-thirds of the world's supply of seafood will be harvested from fish farms rather than from wild sources by the early 2030s.

Aquaculture is not without its problems, which have included the overuse of antibiotics in certain locations and the pollution of wild aquatic habitats in others, especially when fish and other marine animals are raised in pens or cages in high concentration. But to the extent that aquaculture can be conducted sustainably and in an ecologically responsible fashion, each additional ton of fish that is farmed will, other things equal, substitute for a ton of wild-caught equivalents and thus promote the slower and more sustainable harvesting of wild fisheries. In addition, if the productive efficiencies of fish farms continue to improve, it may well become possible that the cost of producing farmed seafood ends up being so much less than the cost of fishing for wild fish that the wild-fishing industry may become unprofitable and gradually disappear so that virtually all commercially available fish will come from fish farms and other aquacultural operations.

QUICK REVIEW
19.4

▶ When property rights are absent, renewable resources tend to be depleted quickly because users have no way of benefiting from conservation.

▶ Governments that establish and enforce property rights over renewable resources encourage conservation by allowing users to benefit financially from future harvesting as well as present harvesting.

▶ Total allowable catch limits (TACs) combined with individual transferable quotas (ITQs) promote the preservation and efficient harvesting of fisheries. The TACs preserve fisheries by capping total harvest sizes. The ITQs promote efficiency by providing financial incentives that encourage all fishing to be done by the most efficient fishers.

Summary

LO19.1 Explain why falling birthrates make running out of natural resources unlikely.
Resource use per person has either fallen or leveled off during the past several decades in industrially advanced economies. This fact, combined with rapidly slowing population growth, implies that the total demand for resources is likely to reach a peak in the next 50 years before falling over time as human populations decline.

LO19.2 Describe why using a mix of energy sources is efficient.
Differences in fixed costs mean that society uses a wide variety of energy sources despite some of these energy sources costing much more than others. For instance, coal-fired electric generating plants use low-cost coal, but they are extremely expensive to build and are therefore used only in situations where very large generating capacities are required. By contrast, when smaller amounts of electricity are required, it often makes more sense to employ other generating technologies such as natural gas even though they use more expensive fuel.

LO19.3 Discuss why running out of oil would not mean running out of energy.
We are not running out of energy. Even if we run out of oil, there are plenty of other energy sources, including solar electricity, wind power, biodiesel, and nuclear energy. In addition, the demand for oil is set to fall rapidly because electric vehicles now cost half as much to fuel as gasoline- or diesel-powered vehicles. By massively increasing the supply of extractable oil, hydraulic fracking and other recent oil extraction technologies have also made it highly unlikely that we will run out of oil in our lifetimes.

LO19.4 Show how the profit motive can encourage resource conservation.
Renewable natural resources like forests and fisheries as well as nonrenewable natural resources like oil and coal tend to be overused in the present unless institutions provide resource harvesters with a way to benefit from conservation. Governments can ensure this benefit by strictly defining and enforcing property rights so that users know that if they conserve a resource today, they will be able to use it or sell it in the future.

LO19.5 Explain how property rights can prevent deforestation and species extinction.

Encouraging conservation is especially difficult in the open ocean, where it is impossible to define or enforce property rights over fish because, by international law, nobody owns the open ocean and so anyone can fish there. This lack of property rights leads to severe overfishing and the likelihood of fishery collapse.

Closer to shore, however, governments can define property rights within their sovereign waters and impose limits on fishing. The best system involves combining total allowable catch (TAC) limits for a given fishery with individual transferable quotas (ITQs) for individual fishers.

Terms and Concepts

replacement rate	renewable natural resources	fishery
total fertility rate	nonrenewable natural resources	fishery collapse
demographers	present value	tragedy of the commons
demographic transition	user cost	total allowable catch (TAC)
British thermal unit (BTU)	extraction cost	individual transferable quotas (ITQs)
net benefits	conflict minerals	aquaculture

Discussion Questions

1. Describe Thomas Malthus's theory of human reproduction. Does it make sense for some species—say, bacteria or rabbits? What makes humans different? **LO19.1**
2. Demographers have been surprised that total fertility rates have fallen below 2.0, especially because most people in most countries tell pollsters that they would like to have at least two children. Can you think of any possible economic factors that may be motivating biological women in so many countries to average fewer than two children per lifetime? What social or political changes may play a role? **LO19.1**
3. Resource consumption per person in the United States is either flat or falling, depending on the resource. Yet living standards are rising because of technological improvements that allow more output to be produced for every unit of input used in production. What does this fact say about the likelihood of society running out of resources? Could we possibly maintain or improve our living standards even if the population were expected to rise in the future rather than fall? Explain. **LO19.1**
4. A community has a nighttime energy demand of 50 megawatts but a peak daytime demand of 75 megawatts. It has the chance to build a 90-megawatt coal-fired plant that could easily supply all of its energy needs even at peak daytime demand. Should it proceed, or might there be lower-cost options? Explain. **LO19.2**
5. Suppose that you hear two people arguing about energy. One says that we are running out of energy. The other counters that we are running out of cheap energy. Explain which person is correct and why. **LO19.3**
6. Recall the model of nonrenewable resource extraction presented in Figure 19.5. Suppose that a technological breakthrough means that extraction costs will fall in the future (but not in the present). What effect will this breakthrough have on future profits and, therefore, on current user cost? Will current extraction increase or decrease? Compare this situation to one in which future extraction costs remain unchanged but current extraction costs fall. In the latter situation, does current extraction increase or decrease? Does the firm's behavior make sense in both situations? That is, does its response to the changes in production

costs in each case maximize the firm's stream of profits over time? Explain. **LO19.4**
7. If the current market price rises, does current extraction increase or decrease? What happens if the future market price rises? Do these changes in current extraction help to ensure that the resource is extracted and used when it is most valuable? Explain. **LO19.4**
8. **ADVANCED ANALYSIS** Suppose that a government wants to reduce its economy's dependence on coal and decides as a result to tax coal-mining companies $1 per ton for every ton of coal that they mine. Assuming that coal-mining companies treat this tax as an increase in extraction costs this year, what effect will the tax have on current extraction in the model used in Figure 19.5? Now, think one step ahead. Suppose that the tax will be in place forever, so that it will also affect extraction costs in the future. Will the tax increase or decrease user cost? Does this effect increase or decrease the change in current extraction caused by the shift of the *EC* curve? Given your finding, should environmental taxes be temporary? Explain. **LO19.4**
9. **ADVANCED ANALYSIS** User cost is equal to the present value of future profits in the model presented in Figure 19.5. Will the optimal quantity to mine in the present year increase or decrease if the market rate of interest rises? Explain. Does your result make intuitive sense? (Hint: If interest rates are up, would you want to have more or less money right now to invest at the market interest rate?) **LO19.4**
10. Various cultures have come up with their own methods to limit catch size and prevent fishery collapse. In old Hawaii, certain fishing grounds near shore could be used only by certain individuals. And among lobstermen in Maine today, strict territorial rights are handed out so that only certain people can harvest lobsters in certain waters. Discuss specifically how these systems provide incentives for conservation. Then think about the enforcement of these property rights. Do you think similar systems could be successfully enforced for deep-sea fishing, far off shore? Explain. **LO19.5**
11. Aquaculture is the growing of fish, shrimp, and other seafood in enclosed cages or ponds. The cages and ponds not only keep the seafood from swimming away but also provide aquaculturists

with strong property rights over their animals. Does this system provide a good incentive for low-cost production as compared with fishing in the open seas where there are few or no property rights? **LO19.5**

12. **LAST WORD** The figure in the Last Word section shows that a 10-fold increase in a country's GDP per person is associated, on average, with a 20- to 30-point increase in EPI. However, GDP per person was $63,414 in the United States in 2020 but just $28,377 in Greece; yet Greece had an EPI score of 69.1 that was almost as high as the United States' EPI score of 69.3. So is getting rich absolutely necessary to achieving a clean environment? Discuss.

Review Questions

1. The long-run downward trend in commodity prices is consistent with the idea that: **LO19.1**
   a. we are quickly running out of resources.
   b. resource demands have been increasing faster than resource supplies.
   c. birthrates will soon increase due to the falling cost of living.
   d. resource supplies have increased faster than resource demands.

2. It would cost the town of Irondale $50 million to build a gas-powered generator that could produce a maximum of 5 megawatts of electricity at 15 cents per hour. Another alternative is for Irondale to build a $100 million coal-fired generator that could produce a maximum of 15 megawatts of electricity at 5 cents per hour. Irondale should: **LO19.2**
   a. build the coal-fired generator because its hourly operating costs are so much lower.
   b. build the gas-powered generator because it is less expensive to build.
   c. build the coal-fired generator because, while it would cost twice as much to build, it would produce three times as much electricity.
   d. obtain more information before deciding what to do.

3. After mining 9,273 tons of coal, Blue Sky Mining's managers note that the marginal cost of mining the next ton of coal would be $40 per ton. They also calculate that the user cost of mining that next ton of coal would be $35. If the market price of coal is $72, should Blue Sky mine an additional ton of coal? **LO19.4**
   a. Yes.
   b. No.
   c. More information is needed.

4. Good methods for helping to protect natural resources include (select all that apply): **LO19.5**
   a. establishing property rights and giving them to local users.
   b. encouraging first-come, first-served harvesting.
   c. teaching people to consider user cost.
   d. having the government set up and enforce ITQs.

5. Ingvar and Olaf are the only two fishermen in their area. Each has been assigned an ITQ that allows him to catch 20 tons of salmon. Ingvar's MC of catching salmon is $6 per ton while Olaf's MC of catching salmon is $7 per ton. If the price of salmon is $10 per ton, then to maximize efficiency, the two fishers should trade ITQs until Ingvar is in charge of catching _____ tons while Olaf catches _____ tons. **LO19.5**
   a. 20; 20
   b. 30; 10
   c. 40; 0
   d. 0; 40

Problems

1. Suppose that the current (first) generation consists of 1 million people, half of whom are biological women. If the total fertility rate is 1.3 and the only way people die is of old age, how big will the fourth generation (the great-grandchildren) be? How much smaller (in percentage terms) is each generation than the previous generation? How much smaller (in percentage terms) is the fourth generation than the first generation? Are you surprised by how quickly the population declines? **LO19.1**

2. A coal-fired power plant can produce electricity at a variable cost of 4 cents per kilowatt-hour when running at its full capacity of 30 megawatts per hour, 16 cents per kilowatt-hour when running at 20 megawatts per hour, and 24 cents per kilowatt-hour when running at 10 megawatts per hour. A gas-fired power plant can produce electricity at a variable cost of 12 cents per kilowatt-hour at any capacity from 1 megawatt per hour to its full capacity of 5 megawatts per hour. The cost of constructing a coal-fired plant is $50 million, but it costs only $10 million to build a gas-fired plant. **LO19.2**
   a. Consider a city that has a peak afternoon demand of 80 megawatts of electricity. If it wants all plants to operate at full capacity, what combination of coal-fired plants and gas-fired plants would minimize construction costs?

   b. How much will the city spend on building that combination of plants?
   c. What will be the average cost per kilowatt-hour if you average over all 80 megawatts that are produced by that combination of plants? (Hint: A kilowatt is one thousand watts, and a megawatt is one million watts.)
   d. What would be the average cost per kilowatt-hour if the city had instead built three coal-fired plants?

3. Suppose that Sea Shell Oil Company (SS) is pumping oil at a field off the coast of Nigeria. At this site, it has an extraction cost of $30 per barrel for the first 10 million barrels it pumps each year and then $60 per barrel for all subsequent barrels that it pumps each year, up to the site's maximum capacity of 90 million barrels per year. **LO19.4**
   a. Suppose the user cost is $50 per barrel for all barrels and the current market price for oil is $90 per barrel. How many barrels will SS pump this year? What is the total accounting profit on the total amount of oil it pumps? What is the total economic profit on those barrels of oil?
   b. What will happen if the current market price for oil rises to $120 per barrel, while the user cost remains at $50 per barrel? How many barrels will SS pump, and what will be its accounting profit and its economic profit?

c. If the current market price remains at $120 per barrel but the user cost rises to $95 per barrel, how many barrels will SS pump this year? What will be its accounting profit and its economic profit?

4. Eric and Kyle are fishermen with different equipment and, as a result, different costs for catching fish. Eric's costs for catching fish are $1,000 per ton for the first 5 tons and then $2,500 per ton for any additional tons. Kyle can harvest fish at a cost of $3,000 for the first 15 tons and then $1,400 for any additional tons. **LO19.5**

   a. If society wants 30 tons of fish and for some reason will allow only one of the two fishers to do all the fishing, which one should society choose if it wants to minimize the cost of catching those 30 tons of fish? How much will the total cost of catching the fish be? What will be the average cost per ton for the 30 tons?

   b. If society wants 30 tons of fish and wants them for the least cost regardless of who catches them, how much should Eric and Kyle each catch? How much will the total cost of catching 30 tons be? What will be the average cost per ton for the 30 tons?

   c. Suppose that Eric and Kyle can both sell whatever amount of fish they catch for $3,000 per ton. Also suppose that Eric is initially given ITQs for 30 tons of fish, while Kyle is given ITQs for zero tons of fish. Suppose that Kyle is willing to pay Eric $550 per ton for as many tons of ITQs as Eric is willing to sell to Kyle. How much profit would Eric make if he used all the ITQs himself? What is the profit situation if Eric sells 25 tons' worth of his ITQs to Kyle while using the other 5 tons of ITQs to fish for himself?

   d. What price per ton can Kyle offer to pay Eric for his 25 tons of ITQs such that Eric will make exactly as much money from that deal (in which he sells 25 tons' worth of ITQs to Kyle while using the rest to fish for himself) as he would by using all 30 tons of ITQs for himself?

CHAPTER
20

Public Finance: Expenditures and Taxes

>> LEARNING OBJECTIVES

LO20.1 Use a circular flow diagram to illustrate how the government's revenue and expenditure decisions affect resource allocation.

LO20.2 Identify the main categories of government spending and the main sources of government revenue.

LO20.3 List the main categories of federal revenue and spending, and describe the difference between marginal and average tax rates.

LO20.4 List the main categories of state and local revenue and spending.

LO20.5 Discuss the magnitude and distribution across job categories of government employment.

LO20.6 Summarize the different philosophies regarding the distribution of a nation's tax burden.

LO20.7 Explain the principles relating to tax shifting, tax incidence, and the efficiency losses caused by taxes.

LO20.8 Discuss the probable incidence of U.S. taxes.

The U.S. economy relies heavily on the private sector (households and businesses) and the market system to decide what gets produced, how it gets produced, and who gets the output. But the private sector is not the only entity in the decision process. The public sector (federal, state, and local government) also affects these economic decisions.

Government influences what gets produced and how it gets produced through laws that regulate the activities of private firms and also by directly producing certain goods and services, such as national defense and education. As discussed in Chapter 5, many of these government-produced goods and services are *public goods* that the private sector has trouble producing because of free-rider problems. Also, government influences who receives society's output of goods and services through various taxes and through welfare and income-transfer payments that redistribute income from the rich to the poor.

Government-provided goods, services, and transfer payments are funded by taxes, borrowing, and proprietary income—the income that governments receive from running government-owned enterprises such as hospitals, utilities, toll roads, and lotteries.

Public finance is the subdiscipline of economics that studies the various ways in which governments raise and spend money. In this chapter, we view the economy through the lens of public finance. Our main goal is to understand how taxes and income transfers not only pay for government-produced goods and services but also affect the distribution of income.

Government and the Circular Flow

In Figure 20.1, we add government to the circular flow model introduced in Figure 2.2. Here flows (1) through (4) are the same as the corresponding flows in that figure. Flows (1) and (2) show business expenditures for the resources provided by households. These expenditures are costs to businesses but represent wage, rent, interest, and profit income to households. Flows (3) and (4) show household expenditures for the goods and services produced by businesses.

Now consider what happens when we add government. Flows (5) through (8) show government purchases in both product and resource markets. Flows (5) and (6) represent government purchases of such products as paper, computers, and military hardware from private businesses. Flows (7) and (8) represent government purchases of resources. The federal government employs and pays salaries to members of Congress, the armed forces, meat inspectors, and so on. State and local governments hire and pay teachers, bus drivers, and police. The federal government might also lease or purchase land to expand a military base, and a city might buy land on which to build a new elementary school.

Governments rely on three revenue sources to pay for those goods and services: taxes, borrowing, and the proprietary income generated by government-run or government-sponsored businesses like public utilities and state lotteries. These revenues flowing from households and businesses to government are included in flows (11) and (12), which are labeled as "net taxes" for two reasons. First, the vast majority of the money raised by these three revenue sources comes from taxes. Second, the labels refer to *net* taxes to indicate that these flows include not only taxes paid by individuals and firms *to* the government but also "taxes in reverse," that is, transfer payments *from* the government that are given to households and businesses. Thus, flow (11) entails subsidies to farmers, shipbuilders, and airlines as well as income, sales, and excise (product) taxes paid by businesses to government. Most business subsidies are "concealed" in the form of low-interest loans, loan guarantees, tax concessions, or public facilities provided at prices below their cost. Similarly, flow (12) includes not only taxes collected by government from households (personal income taxes, payroll taxes) but also transfer payments made by government to households. These include welfare payments and Social Security benefits.

>> **LO20.1** Use a circular flow diagram to illustrate how the government's revenue and expenditure decisions affect resource allocation.

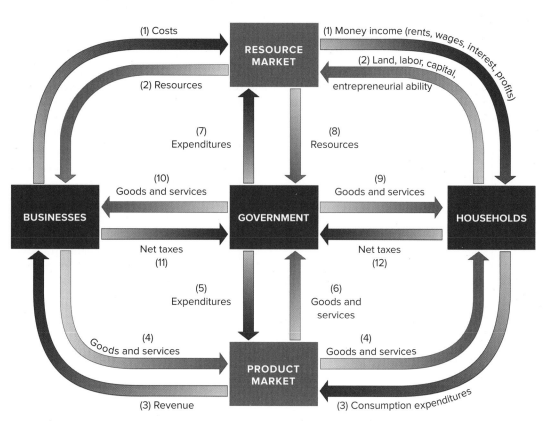

FIGURE 20.1
Government within the circular flow diagram.

Government buys products from the product market and employs resources from the resource market to provide goods and services to households and businesses. Government finances its expenditures through the net taxes (taxes minus transfer payments) it receives from households and businesses.

Government Finance

>> **LO20.2** Identify the main categories of government spending and the main sources of government revenue.

How large is the U.S. public sector? What are the main expenditure categories of federal, state, and local governments? How are these expenditures financed?

Government Purchases and Transfers

Government expenditures fall into two categories: government expenditures to purchase goods and services, and transfer payments made to individuals and businesses. They differ dramatically in terms of whether they exhaust (use up or absorb) resources.

government purchases (G) Expenditures by government for *goods* and *services* that government consumes in providing public services as well as expenditures for publicly owned capital that has a long lifetime; the expenditures of all governments in the economy for those *final goods* and final *services*.

transfer payment A payment of *money* (or *goods* and *services*) by a government to a *household* or *firm* for which the payer receives no *good* or *service* directly in return.

- **Government purchases** are *exhaustive*. The products purchased directly absorb (require the use of) resources and are part of domestic output. For example, the purchase of a missile absorbs the labor of physicists and engineers along with steel, explosives, and many other inputs.
- **Transfer payments** are *nonexhaustive*. They do not directly absorb resources or create output. Social Security benefits, welfare payments, veterans' benefits, and unemployment compensation are examples of transfer payments. Their recipients make no current contribution to domestic output in return for them.

Federal, state, and local governments spent $8,934 billion (roughly $8.9 trillion) in 2020. Of that total, government purchases were $3,078 billion while government transfers (including interest payments on government debt as well as federal and local subsidies granted on an emergency basis to businesses to help them through the COVID-19 pandemic) totaled $5,856 billion. Figure 20.2 shows these amounts as percentages of U.S. domestic output for 2020 and compares them to the similar percentages for 1970 and 2019.

The Pandemic Spending Spike

The year 2020 was very unusual for government spending because the COVID-19 pandemic struck that year, with lockdowns beginning nationwide starting in March. While state and local governments also acted to support individuals and businesses, the federal government led the charge, spending lavishly on extended and augmented unemployment benefits and on various government programs that lent or granted funds to businesses so that they could continue paying their employees even if those businesses had to slow or halt operations. Those bailout efforts on the part of the federal government led to the highest levels of government spending since the Second World War, when the entire economy was mobilized to defeat Germany, Japan, and Italy.

The extremely high levels of government spending in 2020 are made obvious in Figure 20.2 if you compare them with the normal, pre-pandemic level of spending for 2019. In addition, you can get a good sense of the pre-pandemic long-run trends affecting government spending in the United States by comparing Figure 20.2's data for 1970 and 2019. A comparison of those two years reveals that prior to the pandemic, the long-run trend had been one of government purchases as a percentage of output falling and government transfers as a percentage of output rising. The transfer payments then skyrocketed in 2020 as the federal government responded to the pandemic.

FIGURE 20.2
Government purchases, transfers, and total spending as percentages of U.S. output, 1970, 2019, and 2020.

By comparing the vertical bars for 1970 and 2019, you can see that with respect to normal (nonpandemic) years, government purchases have declined as a percentage of U.S. output since 1970 while government transfer payments have risen. By comparing the vertical bars for 2019 and 2020, you can see that transfer payments and total government spending skyrocketed to abnormally high levels in 2020 as federal, state, and local governments dispensed funds generously to help workers and businesses threatened by the COVID-19 pandemic.

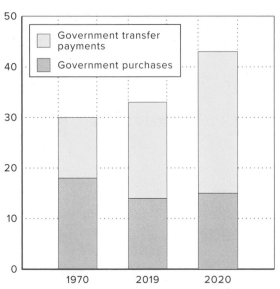

Source: Bureau of Economic Analysis.

Government Revenues

As noted earlier, the funds used to pay for government purchases and transfers come from three sources: taxes, proprietary income, and borrowing.

Taxes and Proprietary Income Across all levels of government, taxes revenues are nearly thirty times larger than proprietary income, with taxes being levied on everything from airline and theater tickets to cell phone plans, business profits, personal income, and particular imported

GLOBAL PERSPECTIVE 20.1

TOTAL TAX REVENUE AS A PERCENTAGE OF TOTAL OUTPUT, SELECTED NATIONS, 2020*

A nation's "tax burden" is its tax revenue from all levels of government as a percentage of its total output (GDP). Among the world's industrialized nations, the United States has a very moderate tax burden.

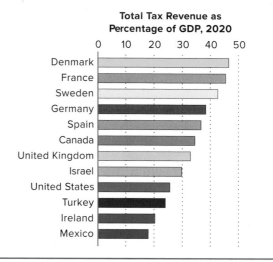

Total Tax Revenue as Percentage of GDP, 2020

Nation
Denmark
France
Sweden
Germany
Spain
Canada
United Kingdom
Israel
United States
Turkey
Ireland
Mexico

*Includes government nontax revenue from fees, charges, fines, and sales of government property.

Source: Organisation for Economic Co-operation and Development (OECD).

products. The cumulative effect of so many taxes is substantial, with about 29 percent of all income in the United States going to pay taxes.

In the United States, the so-called Tax Freedom Day falls each year on the day in April that lies 29 percent of the way between January 1st and December 31st. On that day the average American worker has earned enough (from the start of the year) to pay an equal share of the taxes required to finance U.S. government spending for the year. Tax Freedom Day arrives even later in several other countries, as can be inferred from the data in Global Perspective 20.1.

Borrowing and Deficits Borrowing allows a government to spend more in a given time period than it collects in tax revenues and proprietary income during that period. During an economic downturn, a government can use borrowed funds to maintain high levels of spending on goods, services, and transfer payments even if tax revenues and proprietary income are falling due to the slowing economy.

Any money borrowed by a government, however, is money that cannot be put to other uses. During an economic downturn, this opportunity cost is likely to be small because any funds that the government does not borrow are likely to sit idle and unused by other parties due to the lack of economic activity during the downturn. But if the government borrows when the economy is doing well, many economists worry that the opportunity cost may be high. In particular, the government's borrowing may "crowd out" private-sector investment. As an example, a billion dollars borrowed and spent by the federal government on roads is a billion dollars that was not lent to private companies to fund the expansion of factories or the development of new technologies.

Government spending that is financed by borrowing is often called deficit spending because a government's budget is said to be "in deficit" if the government's spending in a given time period exceeds the money that it collects from taxes and proprietary income during that period. The federal deficit ballooned during the COVID-19 pandemic because the federal government borrowed the funds needed to pay for the economic stimulus programs that helped to limit the economic damage caused by the pandemic.

▶ A circular flow diagram shows how the government affects the allocation of resources in the economy through its revenue and expenditure decisions.

▶ The funds used to pay for government purchases and transfers come from taxes, income, and borrowing.

▶ The ability to borrow allows a government to maintain a high level of spending during an economic downturn even if taxes and income are falling.

QUICK REVIEW

20.1

>> **LO20.3** List the main categories of federal revenue and spending, and describe the difference between marginal and average tax rates.

Federal Finance

Now let's look separately at the federal, state, and local units of U.S. government and compare their expenditures and taxes. Figure 20.3 offers summary statistics for the federal government for 2020.

FIGURE 20.3
Federal expenditures and tax revenues, 2020.

Federal expenditures are dominated by spending on pensions and income security, health, and national defense. At the same time, fully 85 percent of federal tax revenue is derived from just two sources: the personal income tax (47 percent) and payroll taxes (38 percent). The $3,130 billion difference between expenditures and revenues in 2020 reflects massive pandemic-relief spending.

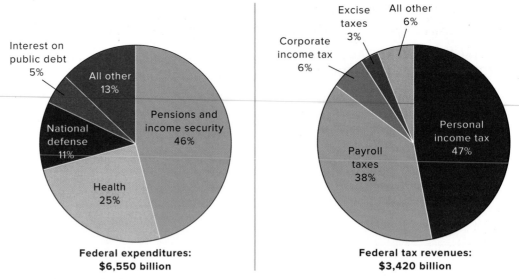

Federal expenditures:
$6,550 billion

Federal tax revenues:
$3,420 billion

Source: U.S. Department of the Treasury.

When examining Figure 20.3, please note that 2020 was the year that the COVID-19 pandemic began, thereby prompting massive emergency increases in federal spending to augment and extend unemployment benefits and to give emergency grants to businesses so that they could continue paying employees even if the firms had to slow down or even stop production in order to comply with lockdowns and other public health efforts. The increase in federal spending was so large that the annual federal budget deficit ballooned from just under $1 trillion in 2019 to a bit more than $3.1 trillion in 2020.

Federal Expenditures

Four areas of federal spending stand out: (1) pensions and income security, (2) national defense, (3) health, and (4) interest on the public debt.

The *pensions and income security* category—which includes the many income-maintenance programs for the aged, persons with disabilities, the unemployed, and families with no breadwinner—usually makes up about 36 percent of federal spending in a given year. But its share swelled to the 46 percent indicated in Figure 20.3 due to the various emergency relief programs that went into effect in 2020 in response to the COVID-19 pandemic.

With the massive size of those relief programs causing the *pensions and income security* category to swell to a value well above its normal size, the other categories had to shrink to values less than normal. Thus, *national defense*, which normally accounts for around 14 percent of all federal spending, represented only 11 percent in 2020; the share of federal spending devoted to paying *interest on the public debt* was only 5 percent in 2020 versus the previous year's value of around 8 percent; and the *health* category—which reflects the cost of government health programs for the retired (Medicare) and those with low incomes (Medicaid)—represented 25 percent of federal spending in 2020, down from a more typical value of around 28 percent.

Federal Tax Revenues

The revenue side of Figure 20.3 shows that the personal income tax, payroll taxes, and the corporate income tax are the largest revenue sources, accounting respectively for 47, 38, and 6 cents of each tax dollar collected in 2020. Since tax revenues for 2020 ended up being relatively unaffected by the COVID-19 pandemic, the percentage shares of the various categories on the revenue side of Figure 20.3 were in fact essentially unchanged relative to what they are in a normal, nonpandemic year.

personal income tax A *tax* levied on the taxable income of individuals, *households*, and unincorporated *firms*.

Personal Income Tax The **personal income tax** is the kingpin of the federal tax system and merits special comment. This tax is levied on *taxable income*—that is, on the incomes of households and unincorporated businesses after certain deductions (business expenses, charitable contributions, home-mortgage interest payments, certain state and local taxes, and the individual or family deduction) are taken into account.

TABLE 20.1 Federal Personal Income Tax Rates, 2022*

(1) Total Taxable Income	(2) Marginal Tax Rate,%	(3) Total Tax on Highest Income In Bracket	(4) Average Tax Rate on Highest Income in Bracket,% (3) ÷ (1)
$0–$20,550	10	$ 2,055	10
$20,551–$83,550	12	9,615	12
$83,551–$178,150	22	30,427	17
$178,151–$340,100	24	69,295	20
$340,101–$431,900	32	98,671	23
$431,901–$647,850	35	174,254	27
$647,850 and above	37		

*For a married couple filing a joint return.

The federal personal income tax is a *progressive tax*, meaning that people with higher incomes pay a larger percentage of their incomes as taxes than do people with lower incomes. The progressivity is achieved by applying higher tax rates to successive layers (or "brackets") of income.

Columns 1 and 2 in Table 20.1 show the mechanics of the income tax for a married couple filing a joint return in 2022. Note that a 10 percent tax rate applies to all taxable income up to $20,550 and a 12 percent rate applies to additional income up to $83,550. The rates on additional layers of income then go up to 22, 24, 32, 35, and 37 percent.

The income ranges to which each rate applies are referred to as *tax brackets* because the lowest and highest dollar values in each range "bracket" (or set apart) that range of income. Thus, you may hear people say things like, "a 10 percent income tax rate applies to the lowest tax bracket, which runs from $0 to $20,550," or, "for married couples filing jointly, the $83,551 to $178,150 tax bracket is taxed at a 22 percent rate."

The tax rate that applies to the income within a given bracket is referred to as that bracket's **marginal tax rate** because it applies to every additional (marginal) dollar within that bracket. Thus, if a couple's taxable income is $90,000, they will pay the marginal rate of 10 percent on each dollar from $0 to $20,550, 12 percent on each dollar from $20,551 to $83,550, and 22 percent on each dollar from $83,551 to $90,000. You should confirm that their total income tax is $11,034.

The marginal tax rates in column 2 overstate the personal income tax bite because the rising rates in that column apply only to the income within each successive bracket. To get a better idea of the couple's actual tax burden, we must consider the **average tax rate,** which is the total amount of income tax paid by the couple divided by their total taxable income. The couple in our previous example is said to be in the 22 percent tax bracket because they pay a marginal tax rate of 22 percent on the final (highest) dollar of their taxable income. But their *average* tax rate is only 12.3 percent (= $11,034/$90,000).

As we will discuss in more detail shortly, a tax whose average rate rises as income increases is said to be a progressive tax because it claims both a progressively larger absolute amount of income as well as a progressively larger proportion of income as income rises. Thus, we can say that the federal personal income tax is progressive.

Payroll Taxes Social Security contributions are **payroll taxes**—taxes based on wages and salaries—used to finance two compulsory federal programs for retired workers: Social Security (an income-enhancement program for people over age 65) and Medicare (which pays for medical services for people over age 65). Employers and employees pay these taxes equally. In 2022, employees and employers each paid 7.65 percent on the first $147,000 of an employee's annual earnings and 1.45 percent on all additional earnings.

Corporate Income Tax The federal government also taxes corporate income. The **corporate income tax** is levied on a corporation's profit, or "net income," which is the difference between the firm's total revenue and its total expenses. For almost all corporations, the tax rate is 21 percent.

marginal tax rate The *tax* rate paid on an additional dollar of *income*.

average tax rate Total tax paid divided by total *taxable income* or some other base (such as total income) against which to compare the amount of tax paid. Expressed as a percentage.

payroll tax A *tax* levied on employers of labor equal to a percentage of all or part of the *wages* and salaries paid by them and on employees equal to a percentage of all or part of the wages and salaries received by them.

corporate income tax A tax levied on the net income (accounting profit) of corporations.

sales tax A *tax* levied on the cost (at retail) of a broad group of products.

excise tax A tax levied on the production of a specific product or on the quantity of the product purchased.

Excise Taxes Taxes on commodities or on purchases take the form of **sales** and **excise taxes.** The two differ primarily in terms of coverage. Sales taxes fall on a wide range of products, whereas excises are levied individually on a small, select list of commodities, including airline tickets and cigarettes. Sales taxes are calculated as a percentage of the price paid for a product, whereas excise taxes are levied on a per-unit basis—for example, $2 per pack of cigarettes or $0.50 per gallon of gasoline.

As Figure 20.3 suggests, the federal government collects various excise taxes (on the sale of such commodities as alcohol, tobacco, and gasoline) but does not levy a general sales tax. However, sales taxes are the primary revenue source of most state governments.

State and Local Finance

>> **LO20.4** List the main categories of state and local revenue and spending.

State and local governments have different mixes of revenues and expenditures than the federal government has.

State Finances

Figure 20.4 shows that sales and excise taxes are the primary source of tax revenue for state governments. These taxes account for about 46 percent of all their tax revenue. State personal income tax rates, which are much lower than the federal rates, are the second most important source of state tax revenue. They bring in about 38 percent of total state tax revenue. Corporate income taxes and license fees account for most of the remainder of state tax revenue.

Public welfare expenditures account for about 38 percent of all state spending. State expenditures on education are next in relative weight, at about 37 percent of the total. States also spend heavily on hospitals and health (8 percent), highway maintenance and construction (8 percent), and public safety (4 percent). That leaves about 5 percent of all state spending for a variety of other purposes.

These tax and expenditure percentages combine data from all the states, so they reveal little about the finances of individual states. States vary significantly in the taxes levied. For example, although personal income taxes are a major source of revenue for all state governments combined, nine states do not levy a personal income tax. Also, there are great variations in the sizes of tax revenues and disbursements among the states, both in the aggregate and as percentages of personal income.

Forty-five states augment their tax revenues with state-run lotteries to help close the gap between their tax receipts and expenditures. Individual states also receive large intergovernmental grants from the federal government. In fact, about 27 percent of their total revenue comes from the federal government. States also take in revenue from miscellaneous sources such as state-owned utilities and liquor stores.

property tax A *tax* on the value of property (*capital, land, stocks* and *bonds,* and other *assets*) owned by *firms* and *households.*

Local Finances

The local levels of government include counties, municipalities, school districts, cities, and towns. Figure 20.5 shows that local governments obtain about 72 percent of their tax revenue from **property taxes.** Sales and excise taxes contribute about 18 percent of all local government tax revenue.

FIGURE 20.4
State expenditures and tax revenues, 2019.

State governments focus their spending on education and welfare. Their primary source of tax revenue is sales and excise taxes. The deficit between state expenditures and state tax revenues is filled by proprietary income and intergovernmental grants from the federal government. The state expenditures numbers here include state grants to local governments.

State expenditures:
$1,919 billion

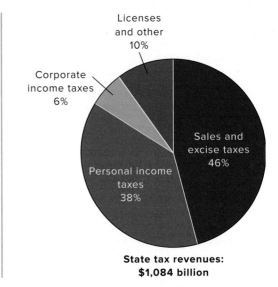

State tax revenues:
$1,084 billion

Source: U.S. Census Bureau.

FIGURE 20.5 **Local expenditures and tax revenues, 2019.**

The expenditures of local governments go largely to education, while a large majority of local tax collections are obtained via property taxes. The large deficit between local expenditures and local tax revenues is filled by proprietary income and federal and state intergovernmental grants.

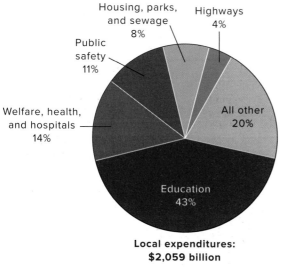

Housing, parks, and sewage 8%
Highways 4%
Public safety 11%
Welfare, health, and hospitals 14%
All other 20%
Education 43%

Local expenditures:
$2,059 billion

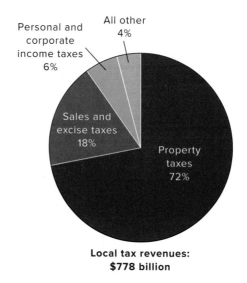

Personal and corporate income taxes 6%
All other 4%
Sales and excise taxes 18%
Property taxes 72%

Local tax revenues:
$778 billion

Source: U.S. Census Bureau.

About 43 percent of local government expenditures go to education. Welfare, health, and hospitals (14 percent); public safety (11 percent); housing, parks, and sewerage (8 percent); and streets and highways (4 percent) are also major spending categories.

The tax revenues of local government cover less than one-half of their expenditures. The bulk of the remaining revenue comes from intergovernmental grants from federal and state governments. Also, local governments receive considerable amounts of proprietary income, including from state lotteries, which are discussed in the Consider This story nearby.

CONSIDER THIS . . .

State Lotteries: A Good Bet?

State lotteries generated about $94.9 billion in revenue in 2021. Of that amount, approximately $57 billion went to prizes and $11.9 billion went to administrative costs. That left $26 billion that could be spent by the states as they saw fit.

Though nowadays common, state lotteries are still controversial. Critics argue that (1) it is morally wrong for states to sponsor gambling; (2) lotteries generate compulsive gamblers who impoverish themselves and their families; (3) low-income families spend a larger portion of their incomes on lotteries than do high-income families; (4) as a cash business, lotteries attract criminals and other undesirables; and (5) lotteries send the message that luck and fate—rather than education, hard work, and saving—are the route to wealth.

Defenders contend that (1) lotteries are preferable to taxes because they are voluntary rather than compulsory; (2) they are a relatively painless way to finance government services such as education, medical care, and welfare; and

Mark Steinmetz/Amanita Pictures/McGraw Hill

(3) lotteries compete with illegal gambling and are thus socially beneficial in curtailing organized crime.

As a further point for debate, also note that state lotteries are monopolies, with states banning competing private lotteries. The resulting lack of competition allows many states to restrict prizes to only about half the money wagered. These payout rates are substantially lower than the 80–95 percent payout rates typically found in private betting operations such as casinos.

Thus, while lotteries are indeed voluntary, they are overpriced and underprovided relative to what would happen if there were a free market in lotteries. But, then again, a free market in lotteries would eliminate monopoly profits for state lotteries and possibly add government costs for regulation and oversight. Consequently, the alternative of allowing a free market in lottery tickets and then taxing the firms selling lottery tickets would probably net very little additional revenue to support state spending programs.

FIGURE 20.6   Job functions of state and local employees, and federal employees, 2020.

A majority of state and local workers are employed in education. Federal employment is dominated by the postal service and national defense, which together employ just over half of federal employees.

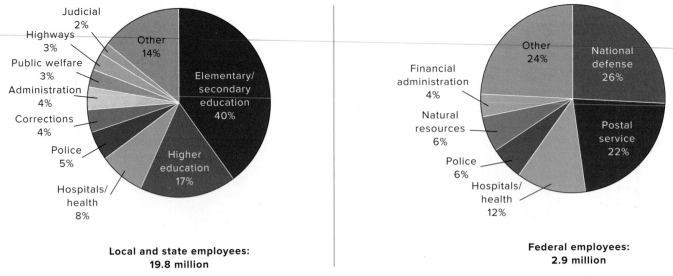

**Local and state employees:
19.8 million**

**Federal employees:
2.9 million**

Source: U.S. Census Bureau.

Local, State, and Federal Employment

>> **LO20.5** Discuss the magnitude and distribution across job categories of government employment.

In 2020, U.S. governments (local, state, and federal) employed about 21.7 million workers, or about 14 percent of the U.S. labor force. Figure 20.6 shows the percentages of government employees assigned to different tasks at both the federal level and the state and local level.

As Figure 20.6 makes clear, the types of jobs done by government workers depend on the level of government. Nearly 60 percent of state and local government employment is focused on education. The next largest sector is hospitals and health care, which accounts for about 8 percent of state and local government employment. Police and corrections make up another 9 percent. Smaller categories like highways, public welfare, and judicial together make up less than 8 percent of state and local employment. The "other" category includes workers in parks and recreation, firefighting, transit, and libraries.

Almost half of federal government jobs are in national defense or the postal service. A further 12 percent of federal government jobs are in hospitals or health care. The natural resources, police, and financial administration categories each account for between 4 and 6 percent of federal employment. The "other" category at the federal level is composed of workers in justice and law, corrections, air transportation, and social insurance administration.

**QUICK REVIEW
20.2**

▶ Income security and national defense are the main categories of federal spending. Personal income, payroll, and corporate income taxes are the primary sources of federal revenue.

▶ States rely on sales and excise taxes for revenue; their spending is largely for education and public welfare.

▶ Education is the main expenditure for local governments, most of whose revenue comes from property taxes.

▶ State and local employment is dominated by education, while federal employment is dominated by national defense and the postal service.

Apportioning the Tax Burden

>> **LO20.6** Summarize the different philosophies regarding the distribution of a nation's tax burden.

Taxes are the major source of funding for the goods and services provided by government and the wages and salaries paid to government workers. Without taxes, there would be no public schools, no national defense, no public highways, no courts, no police, and no other government-provided public and quasi-public goods. As Supreme Court Justice Oliver Wendell Holmes said, "Taxes are the price we pay for civilization."

But taxes are controversial. To begin with, many people would prefer to obtain government goods and services without paying for them. Many argue that certain taxes cause more harm than good, either by discouraging beneficial economic activity or by unfairly reducing the income flowing to workers and investors. And millions more chafe at the huge variety of taxes that governments levy, including income taxes, Social Security taxes, Medicare taxes, property taxes, sales taxes, liquor taxes, cigarette taxes, cell phone taxes, hotel taxes, gasoline taxes, profit taxes, and estate taxes. For these and other reasons, people are intently focused on the overall level of taxes, the amount they must personally pay, and the idea of tax fairness (which is often defined in terms of their own circumstances).

The public's attention to taxes has spurred public-finance economists to research the size, distribution, and impact of taxes on society—the so-called *tax burden*. Their investigations reveal with reasonable clarity both the size of the tax burden as well as how it is apportioned across the income distribution. Whether you yourself consider their findings to be good news or bad news, however, depends significantly on your opinion about the fairest way to allocate taxes and the tax burden. So before turning to their findings, let's first discuss the major philosophical viewpoints regarding taxation.

Benefits Received versus Ability to Pay

Two basic philosophies coexist regarding how the tax burden should be apportioned.

Benefits-Received Principle The **benefits-received principle** asserts that households should purchase government goods and services in the same way they buy other commodities. That is, those who benefit most from government-supplied goods or services should pay the taxes necessary to finance them. A few public goods are now financed on this basis. For example, money collected as gasoline taxes is typically used to finance highway construction and repairs. Thus people who benefit from good roads pay the cost of those roads. Difficulties immediately arise, however, when we consider widespread application of the benefits-received principle:

> **benefits-received principle** The idea that those who receive the benefits of *goods* and *services* provided by government should pay the taxes required to finance them.

- How will the government determine the benefits that individual households and businesses receive from national defense, education, the court system, and police and fire protection? Recall from Chapter 5 that public goods are characterized by nonrivalry and nonexcludability. Thus, benefits from public goods are widespread and diffuse. Even in the seemingly straightforward case of highway financing, it is difficult to measure benefits. Good roads benefit owners of cars in different degrees. But others also benefit. For example, businesses benefit because good roads bring them workers and customers.

- The benefits-received principle cannot logically be applied to income redistribution programs. It would be absurd to ask low-income families to pay the taxes needed to finance their welfare payments. It would also be self-defeating to tax only unemployed workers to finance the unemployment benefits they receive.

Ability-to-Pay Principle The **ability-to-pay principle** asserts that the tax burden should be apportioned according to taxpayers' income and wealth. In practice, this principle means that individuals and businesses with larger incomes should pay more taxes in both absolute and relative terms than those with smaller incomes.

> **ability-to-pay principle** The idea that those who have greater *income* (or *wealth*) should pay a greater proportion of it as taxes than those who have less income (or wealth).

In justifying the ability-to-pay principle, proponents contend that each additional dollar of income received by a household yields a smaller amount of satisfaction or marginal utility when it is spent. Because consumers act rationally, the first dollars of income received in any time period will be spent on high-urgency goods that yield the greatest marginal utility. Successive dollars of income will be spent on less urgently needed goods and finally for trivial goods and services. Thus a dollar taken through taxes from a person whose income is only a few dollars represents a greater utility sacrifice than a dollar taken through taxes from a rich person who has many dollars. To balance the sacrifices that taxes impose on people of different incomes, the tax burden should fall mostly or entirely on those with higher incomes.

Application problems arise here, too. Although we might agree that the household earning $100,000 per year has a greater ability to pay taxes than a household receiving $10,000, we don't know exactly how much more ability to pay the first family has. Should the wealthier family pay the *same* percentage of its larger income, and hence a larger absolute amount, as taxes? Or should it be made to pay a *larger* percentage of its income as taxes? And how much larger should that percentage be? Who is to decide?

There is no scientific way of making utility comparisons among individuals and thus of measuring someone's relative ability to pay taxes. In practice, the solution hinges on guesswork, the tax views of the political party in power, expediency, and how urgently the government needs revenue.

Progressive, Proportional, and Regressive Taxes

Any discussion of taxation leads ultimately to the question of tax rates. Taxes are classified as progressive, proportional, or regressive, depending on the relationship between average tax rates and taxpayer incomes. We focus on incomes because all taxes—whether on income, a product, a building, or a parcel of land—are ultimately paid out of someone's income.

progressive tax At the individual level, a *tax* whose *average tax rate* increases as the taxpayer's *income* increases. At the national level, a *tax* for which the *average tax rate* (= tax revenue/*GDP*) rises with *GDP*.

regressive tax At the individual level, a *tax* whose *average tax rate* decreases as the taxpayer's *income* increases. At the national level, a *tax* for which the *average tax rate* (= tax revenue/*GDP*) falls as *GDP* rises.

proportional tax At the individual level, a *tax* whose *average tax rate* remains constant as the taxpayer's *income* increases or decreases. At the national level, a *tax* for which the *average tax rate* (= tax revenue/*GDP*) remains constant as *GDP* rises or falls.

- A tax is **progressive** if its average rate increases as income increases. Such a tax claims not only a larger absolute (dollar) amount but also a larger percentage of income as income increases.

- A tax is **regressive** if its average rate declines as income increases. Such a tax takes a smaller proportion of income as income increases. A regressive tax may or may not take a larger absolute amount of income as income increases. (You may want to develop an example to substantiate this fact.)

- A tax is **proportional** if its average rate *remains the same* regardless of the size of income. Proportional income taxes are often called *flat taxes* or *flat-rate taxes* because their average rates do not vary with (are flat with respect to) income levels.

We can illustrate these ideas with the personal income tax. Suppose tax rates are such that a household pays 10 percent of its income in taxes regardless of the size of its income. This income tax is *proportional*. Now suppose that a household with an annual taxable income of less than $10,000 pays 5 percent in income taxes; a household with an income of $10,000 to $20,000 pays 10 percent; a household with a $20,000 to $30,000 income pays 15 percent; and so forth. This income tax is *progressive*. Finally, suppose the rate declines as taxable income rises: You pay 15 percent if you earn less than $10,000; 10 percent if you earn $10,000 to $20,000; 5 percent if you earn $20,000 to $30,000; and so forth. This income tax is *regressive*.

In general, progressive taxes are those that fall relatively more heavily on people with high incomes; regressive taxes are those that fall relatively more heavily on the poor.

Let's examine the progressivity, or regressivity, of several taxes.

Personal Income Tax As noted earlier, the federal personal income tax is progressive, with marginal tax rates ranging from 10 to 37 percent in 2019. Rules that allow deductions for interest on home mortgages and property taxes tend to make the tax less progressive than these marginal rates suggest. Nevertheless, average tax rates rise with income.

Sales Taxes At first thought, a general sales tax with, for example, a 5 percent rate would seem to be proportional. But in fact it is regressive with respect to income. A larger portion of a low-income person's income is exposed to the tax than is the case for a high-income person. Example: "Low-income" Smith has an income of $15,000 and spends it all. "High-income" Jones has an income of $300,000 but spends only $200,000 and saves the rest. Assuming a 5 percent sales tax applies to all expenditures, we find that Smith pays $750 (5 percent of $15,000) in sales taxes and Jones pays $10,000 (5 percent of $200,000). But Smith pays $750/$15,000, or 5 percent of income as sales taxes while Jones pays $10,000/$300,000, or 3.3 percent of income as sales taxes. General sales taxes are, consequently, regressive rather than proportional.

Corporate Income Tax The federal corporate income tax is essentially a proportional tax with a flat 21 percent tax rate. In the short run, the corporate owners (shareholders) bear the tax through lower dividends and share values. In the long run, workers may bear some of the tax since it reduces the return on investment and therefore slows capital accumulation. It also causes corporations to relocate to other countries that have lower tax rates. With less capital per worker, U.S. labor productivity may decline and wages may fall. To the extent this happens, the corporate income tax may be somewhat regressive.

Payroll Taxes   Payroll taxes are levied upon wages and salaries by certain states as well as by the federal government. The federal payroll tax is known as the FICA tax after the Federal Insurance Contributions Act, which mandated one payroll tax to fund the Social Security program and another to fund the Medicare program.

Both taxes are split equally between employer and employee. Thus, the 12.4 percent Social Security tax is split in half, with 6.2 percent paid by employees and an additional 6.2 percent paid by employers. In the same way, the 2.9 percent Medicare tax is also split in half, with 1.45 percent paid by employees and 1.45 percent paid by employers.

Crucially, however, only the Medicare tax applies to all wage and salary income without limit. The Social Security tax, by contrast, is "capped," meaning that it applies only up to a certain limit, or cap. In 2022, the cap was $147,000.

Overall, the FICA tax is regressive. To see why, consider a person with $147,000 in wage income. He would pay $11,245.50, or 7.65 percent (= 6.2 percent + 1.45 percent) of his wages in FICA taxes. By contrast, someone with twice that income, or $294,000, would pay $13,377.00 (= $11,245.50 on the first $147,000 + $2,131.50 on the second $147,000), which is only 4.6 percent of his wage income. Thus the average FICA tax falls as income rises, which means the FICA tax is regressive.

But payroll taxes are even more regressive than suggested by this example because they only apply to wage and salary income. People earning high incomes tend to derive a higher percentage of their total incomes from nonwage sources like rents and dividends than do people who have incomes below the $147,000 cap on which Social Security taxes are paid. Thus, if our individual with the $294,000 of wage income also received $294,000 of nonwage income, his $13,377.00 of FICA tax would be only 2.3 percent of his total income of $588,000.

Property Taxes   Most economists conclude that property taxes on buildings are regressive for the same reasons as are sales taxes. First, property owners add the tax to the rents that they charge tenants. Second, property taxes, as a percentage of income, are higher for low-income families than for high-income families because the poor must spend a larger proportion of their incomes for housing.

Tax Incidence and Efficiency Loss

Determining whether a particular tax is progressive, proportional, or regressive is complicated because those on whom taxes are levied do not always pay the taxes themselves. That is, some or all of the tax burden may be passed on to others. We therefore need an understanding of **tax incidence,** the degree to which a tax falls on a particular person or group. The tools of elasticity of supply and demand will help. Let's focus on a hypothetical excise tax levied on wine producers. Do the producers really pay this tax, or is some fraction of the tax shifted to wine consumers?

Elasticity and Tax Incidence

In Figure 20.7, S and D represent the pretax market for a certain domestic wine. The no-tax equilibrium price and quantity are $8 per bottle and 15 million bottles. Suppose that government levies an excise tax of $2 per bottle at the winery. Who will actually pay this tax?

Division of Burden   Because the government imposes the tax on the sellers (suppliers), we can view the tax as an addition to the marginal cost of the product. Now sellers must get $2 more for each bottle to receive the same per-unit profit they were

>> **LO20.7** Explain the principles relating to tax shifting, tax incidence, and the efficiency losses caused by taxes.

tax incidence   The degree to which a *tax* falls on a particular person or group.

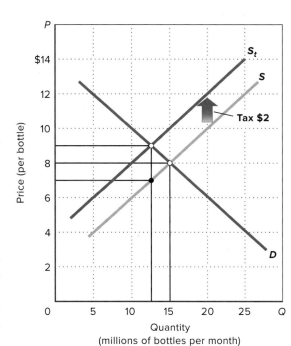

FIGURE 20.7
The incidence of an excise tax.

An excise tax of a specified amount (here, $2 per unit) shifts the supply curve upward by the amount of the tax per unit: the vertical distance between S and S_t. This results in a higher price (here, $9) to consumers and a lower after-tax price (here, $7) to producers. Thus, consumers and producers share the burden of the tax in some proportion (here, equally at $1 per unit).

getting before the tax. While sellers are willing to offer, for example, 5 million bottles of untaxed wine at $4 per bottle, they must now receive $6 per bottle (= $4 + $2 tax) to supply 5 million bottles. The tax shifts the supply curve upward (leftward) as shown in Figure 20.7, where S_t is the after-tax supply curve.

The after-tax equilibrium price is $9 per bottle, whereas the before-tax equilibrium price was $8. So, in this case, consumers pay half the $2 tax as a higher price; producers pay the other half in the form of lower after-tax per-unit revenue. That is, after remitting the $2 tax per unit to government, producers receive $7 per bottle, or $1 less than the $8 before-tax price. So, in this case, consumers and producers share the burden of the tax equally: Half of the $2 per bottle tax is shifted to consumers in the form of a higher price, and half is paid by producers.

Note also that the equilibrium quantity declines because of the tax levy and the higher price that it imposes on consumers. In Figure 20.7 the equilibrium quantity declines from 15 million bottles to 12.5 million bottles per month.

Elasticities If the elasticities of demand and supply are different from those shown in Figure 20.7, the incidence of tax will also differ. Two generalizations are relevant.

Variations in Demand Elasticity Given a Fixed Supply Curve First, given a specific supply schedule or curve, the more inelastic the demand for the product, the larger is the portion of the tax shifted to consumers. To verify this conclusion, sketch graphically the extreme cases in which demand is perfectly elastic and perfectly inelastic. In the first case, the incidence of the tax is entirely on sellers; in the second, the tax is shifted entirely to consumers.

Figure 20.8 contrasts the more usual cases where demand is either relatively elastic or relatively inelastic in the relevant price range. With elastic demand (Figure 20.8a), a small portion of the tax ($P_2 - P_1$) is shifted to consumers, and producers bear most of the tax ($P_1 - P_3$). With inelastic demand (Figure 20.8b), most of the tax ($P_5 - P_4$) is shifted to consumers, and producers pay only a small amount ($P_4 - P_6$). In both graphs, the per-unit tax is represented by the vertical distance between S_t and S.

Note also that the decline in equilibrium quantity (from Q_1 to Q_2 in Figure 20.8a and from Q_4 to Q_5 in Figure 20.8b) is smaller when demand is more inelastic. This is the basis of our previous applications of the elasticity concept to taxation in earlier chapters: Revenue-seeking legislatures place heavy excise taxes on liquor, cigarettes, automobile tires, cellular service, and other products whose demand is thought to be inelastic. Since demand for these products is relatively inelastic, the tax does not reduce sales by much, so the tax revenue stays high.

Variations in Supply Elasticity Given a Fixed Demand Curve Second, given a specific demand schedule or curve, the more inelastic the supply, the larger is the portion of the tax borne by producers. When supply is elastic (Figure 20.9a), consumers bear most of the tax ($P_2 - P_1$) while producers bear only a small portion ($P_1 - P_3$). But where supply is inelastic (Figure 20.9b), the reverse is true: The major portion of the tax ($P_4 - P_6$) falls on sellers, and a relatively small amount ($P_5 - P_4$) is shifted to buyers. The equilibrium quantity also declines less with an inelastic supply than it does with an elastic supply.

FIGURE 20.8
Demand elasticity and the incidence of an excise tax.

(a) If demand is elastic in the relevant price range, price rises modestly (P_1 to P_2) when an excise tax is levied. Hence, the producers bear most of the tax burden. (b) If demand is inelastic, the price increases substantially (P_4 to P_5) and most of the tax is borne by consumers.

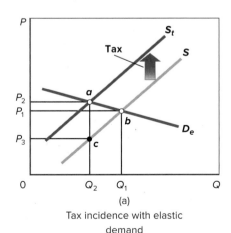

(a)
Tax incidence with elastic demand

(b)
Tax incidence with inelastic demand

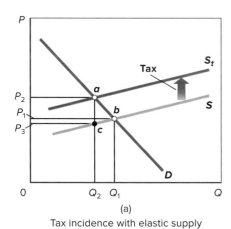

(a)
Tax incidence with elastic supply

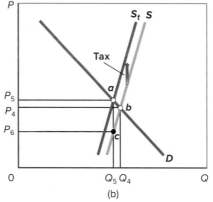

(b)
Tax incidence with inelastic supply

FIGURE 20.9
Supply elasticity and the incidence of an excise tax.

(a) If supply is elastic, an excise tax results in a large price increase (P_1 to P_2) and the tax is therefore paid mainly by consumers. (b) If supply is inelastic, the price rise is small (P_4 to P_5) and sellers bear most of the tax.

Gold is an example of a product with an inelastic supply and therefore one where the burden of an excise tax (such as an extraction tax) would mainly fall on producers. In contrast, because the supply of baseballs is relatively elastic, producers would pass on to consumers much of an excise tax on baseballs.

Efficiency Loss of a Tax

We just observed that producers and consumers typically each bear part of an excise tax levied on producers. Let's now look more closely at the overall economic effect of an excise tax. Consider **Figure 20.10 (Key Graph),** which is identical to Figure 20.7 but contains the additional detail we need for our discussion. As with Figure 20.7, we are discussing a wine market in which the government imposes an excise tax of $2 per bottle.

Tax Revenues   The $2 excise tax on wine increases its market price from $8 to $9 per bottle and reduces the equilibrium quantity from 15 million bottles to 12.5 million. Government tax revenue is $25 million (= $2 × 12.5 million bottles), shown as the rectangle *efac* in Figure 20.10. The elasticities of supply and demand in this case are such that consumers and producers each pay half this total amount, or $12.5 million (= $1 × 12.5 million bottles). The government uses this $25 million of tax revenue to provide public goods and services; so this transfer of dollars from consumers and producers to government involves no loss of well-being to society.

Efficiency Loss   The $2 tax on wine does more than require consumers and producers to pay $25 million of taxes; it also reduces the equilibrium amount of wine produced and consumed by 2.5 million bottles. The fact that consumers and producers demanded and supplied 2.5 million more bottles of wine before the tax means that those 2.5 million bottles provided benefits in excess of their production costs.

Segment *ab* of demand curve *D* in Figure 20.10 indicates the willingness to pay—the marginal benefit—associated with each of the 2.5 million bottles consumed before (but not after) the tax. Segment *cb* of supply curve *S* reflects the marginal cost associated with producing those bottles. For all but the very last one of these 2.5 million bottles, the marginal benefit (shown by a point on *ab*) exceeds the marginal cost (shown by a point on *cb*). Not producing these 2.5 million bottles of wine reduces well-being by an amount represented by the triangle *abc*. The area of this triangle identifies the **efficiency loss of the tax** (also called the *deadweight loss of the tax*). This loss is society's sacrifice of net benefit because the tax reduces production and consumption of the product below their levels of economic efficiency, where marginal benefit and marginal cost are equal. Here, the efficiency loss is $2.5 million, which you should confirm by using the formula for the area of a triangle (= 1/2 × base × height). Hint: treat the line segment running from point *a* to point *c* as the base of the triangle.

efficiency loss of a tax The loss of *net benefits* to society because a tax reduces the production and consumption of a taxed good below the level of *allocative efficiency*. Also called the *deadweight loss* of the tax.

Role of Elasticities   Most taxes create some degree of efficiency loss, but just how much depends on the supply and demand elasticities. Glancing back at Figure 20.8, we see that the efficiency loss area *abc* is greater in Figure 20.8a, where demand is relatively elastic, than in

..ıl KEY GRAPH

FIGURE 20.10 Efficiency loss (or deadweight loss) of an excise tax paid by producers.

The levy of a $2 tax per bottle of wine increases the price per bottle from $8 to $9 and reduces the equilibrium quantity from 15 million to 12.5 million. The efficiency loss of the tax arises from the 2.5 million decline in output; the amount of that loss is shown as deadweight loss triangle *abc*. Tax revenue to the government is $25 million (area *efac*). Here, that tax revenue is split evenly between producers and consumers. In general, the split depends on the elasticities of the demand and supply curves.

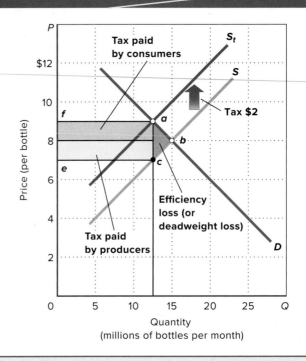

QUICK QUIZ FOR FIGURE 20.10

1. **From the perspective of suppliers, the $2 per bottle excise tax:**
   a. increases the quantity demanded, all other things equal.
   b. ensures that MR exceeds the equilibrium price after the tax is imposed.
   c. increases marginal costs.
   d. decreases average costs.

2. **After the tax is imposed, the producers in this industry will retain:**
   a. $9 per bottle for themselves.
   b. $8 per bottle for themselves.
   c. $7 per bottle for themselves.
   d. $0 per bottle for themselves.

3. **Remembering that the formula for the area of a triangle is $\frac{1}{2}$ times base times height, we see that the dollar value of the deadweight loss is equal to:**
   a. $1 million.
   b. $2.5 million.
   c. $5 million.
   d. $10 million.

4. **If the government doubles the excise tax, the deadweight loss will:**
   a. remain unchanged.
   b. double.
   c. triple.
   d. quadruple.

Answers: 1. c; 2. c; 3. b; 4. d

Figure 20.8b, where demand is relatively inelastic. Similarly, area *abc* is greater in Figure 20.9a than in Figure 20.9b, indicating a larger efficiency loss where supply is more elastic. Other things equal, the greater the elasticities of supply and demand, the greater the efficiency loss of a particular tax.

Two taxes yielding equal revenues do not necessarily impose equal costs on society. The government must keep this fact in mind in designing a tax system to finance beneficial public goods and services. In general, it should minimize the efficiency loss of the tax system in raising any specific dollar amount of tax revenue.

Qualifications We must acknowledge, however, that other tax goals may be as important as, or even more important than, minimizing efficiency losses from taxes. Here are two examples:

- ***Redistributive goals*** Government may wish to impose progressive taxes as a way to redistribute income. The 10 percent excise tax the federal government placed on selected luxuries in 1990 was an example. Because the demand for luxuries is elastic, substantial efficiency losses from this tax were to be expected. However, Congress apparently concluded that the benefits from the redistribution effects of the tax would exceed the efficiency losses.

Ironically, in 1993 Congress repealed the luxury taxes on personal airplanes and yachts, mainly because the taxes had reduced quantity demanded so much that widespread layoffs of workers were occurring in those industries. But the 10 percent tax on luxury automobiles remained in place until it expired in 2003.

- *Reducing negative externalities* Our analysis of the efficiency loss of a tax assumes no negative externalities arising from either the production or consumption of the product in question. Where such spillover costs occur, an excise tax on producers might actually improve allocative efficiency by reducing output and thus lessening the negative externality. For example, the $2 excise tax on wine in our example might be part of a broader set of excise taxes on alcoholic beverages. The government may have concluded that the consumption of these beverages produces certain negative externalities. Therefore, it might have purposely levied this $2 tax to shift the market supply curve in Figure 20.10 to increase the price of wine, decrease alcohol consumption, and reduce the amount of resources devoted to wine.

Excise taxes that are intended to reduce the production and consumption of products with negative externalities are sometimes referred to as *sin taxes*. This name captures the idea that governments are motivated to impose these taxes to discourage activities that are perceived to be harmful or sinful. Excise taxes on cigarettes and alcohol in particular are commonly referred to as sin taxes.

▶ The benefits-received principle of taxation asserts that those who benefit from government services should pay the taxes needed to finance them. The ability-to-pay principle asserts that taxes should be apportioned by income and wealth.

▶ A tax is (a) progressive if the average amount taxed away increases with income, (b) regressive if the average amount taxed away decreases with income, and (c) proportional if the average amount taxed away remains constant as income increases.

▶ Given fixed demand, more elastic supply shifts tax burdens to consumers; given fixed supply, more elastic demand shifts tax burdens to producers.

▶ Taxes imposed in markets raise the market equilibrium price, reduce the market equilibrium output, and normally generate efficiency losses.

Probable Incidence of U.S. Taxes

Let's look now at the probable incidence of each of the major sources of tax revenue in the United States.

>> **LO20.8** Discuss the probable incidence of U.S. taxes.

Personal Income Tax and Inheritance Tax

The incidence of the personal income tax generally is on the individual because there is little chance for shifting it. For every dollar paid in income tax, individuals have one less dollar in their pocketbooks. The same ordinarily holds true for inheritance taxes.

Payroll Taxes

As discussed earlier, employees and employers in 2022 each paid 7.65 percent in FICA taxes on a worker's annual earnings up to the 2019 Social Security cap of $147,000 and then 1.45 percent on any additional earnings. Workers bear the full burden of their half of the Social Security and Medicare payroll taxes. As is true for the income tax, they cannot shift the payroll taxes that they pay to anyone else.

But what about the other half of the FICA tax that is levied on employers? Who pays that? The consensus view is that part of the employers' half of the FICA tax gets shifted to workers in the form of lower before-tax wages. By making it more costly to hire workers, the payroll tax reduces the demand for labor relative to supply. The result is lower market wages that employers pay workers. In a sense, employers "collect" some of their portion of the payroll tax from their workers.

Corporate Income Tax

In the short run, the incidence of the corporate income tax falls on the company's stockholders (owners), who bear the burden of the tax through lower dividends or smaller amounts of retained corporate earnings. Why? A firm currently charging the profit-maximizing price and producing the profit-maximizing output (determined by where MR = MC) will have no reason to change product price, output, or wages when a corporate income tax is imposed. The price and output combination yielding the greatest profit before the tax will still yield the greatest profit after the tax (since the tax affects neither MR nor MC). So, the company's stockholders will not be able to shift the tax to consumers or workers.

As previously indicated, the situation may be different in the long run. Workers in general may bear a significant part of the corporate income tax in the form of lower wage growth. Because it reduces the return on investment, the corporate income tax may slow the accumulation of capital (plant and equipment). It also may prompt some U.S. firms to relocate abroad in countries that have lower corporate tax rates. In either case, the tax may slow the growth of U.S. labor productivity, which depends on American workers having access to more and better equipment. We know from Figure 17.1 that the growth of labor productivity is the main reason labor demand grows over time. If the corporate income tax reduces the growth of labor productivity, then labor demand and wages may rise less rapidly. In this indirect way—and over long periods of time—workers may bear part of the corporate income tax.

Sales and Excise Taxes

A *sales tax* is a general excise tax levied on a full range of consumer goods and services, whereas a *specific excise tax* is levied only on a particular product. Sales taxes are usually transparent to consumers because they are applied at the retail level and appear on the receipts that retail customers receive. By contrast, excise taxes are often "hidden" in the price of a product since they are usually assessed at the producer or wholesaler level. But regardless of whether they are hidden or clearly visible, both sales taxes and specific excise taxes are often shifted partly or largely to consumers as higher equilibrium product prices (as in Figures 20.7, 20.8, and 20.9).

The burden of sales taxes and excise taxes may get shifted to different extents, however. Because a sales tax covers a much wider range of products than an excise tax, there is little chance for consumers to avoid the price boosts that sales taxes entail. They cannot reallocate their expenditures to untaxed, lower-priced products. Therefore, sales taxes tend to be shifted in their entirety from producers to consumers.

Excise taxes, however, fall on a select list of goods. Therefore, the possibility of consumers turning to substitute goods and services is greater. An excise tax on theater tickets that does not apply to other types of entertainment might be difficult to pass on to consumers via price increases. Why? The answer is provided in Figure 20.8a, where demand is elastic. A price boost to cover the excise tax on theater tickets might cause consumers to substitute alternative types of entertainment. The higher price would reduce sales so much that a seller would be better off to bear all, or a large portion of, the excise tax.

With some products, modest price increases to cover taxes may have a smaller effect on sales. The excise taxes on gasoline, cigarettes, and alcohol provide examples. Here consumers have few good substitute products to which they can turn as prices rise. For these goods, sellers are better able to shift nearly all the excise tax to consumers. Example: Cigarette prices have gone up nearly in lockstep with substantial increases in cigarette excise taxes over the past few decades.

Property Taxes

Many property taxes are borne by the property owner because there is no other party to whom they can be shifted. This is typically true for taxes on land, personal property, and owner-occupied residences. Even when land is sold, the property tax is not likely to be shifted. The buyer will understand that future taxes will have to be paid on it, and this expected taxation will be reflected in the price the buyer is willing to offer for the land.

Taxes on rented and business property are a different story. Taxes on rented property can be, and usually are, shifted wholly or partly from the owner to the tenant by the process of boosting the rent. Business property taxes are treated as a business cost and are taken into account in establishing product price; hence such taxes are ordinarily shifted to the firm's customers.

Table 20.2 summarizes the probable incidence of various types of taxes.

TABLE 20.2 The Probable Incidence of Taxes

Type of Tax	Probable Incidence
Personal income tax	The household or individual on which it is levied.
Payroll taxes	Workers pay the full tax levied on their earnings and part of the tax levied on their employers.
Corporate income tax	In the short run, the full tax falls on business owners, including corporate shareholders. In the long run, some of the tax may be borne by workers through lower wages.
Sales tax	Consumers who buy the taxed products.
Specific excise taxes	Consumers, producers, or both, depending on elasticities of demand and supply.
Property taxes	Owners in the case of land and owner-occupied residences; tenants in the case of rented property; consumers in the case of business property.

The U.S. Tax Structure

Is the overall U.S. tax structure—federal, state, and local taxes combined—progressive, proportional, or regressive? The question is difficult to answer. But most economists who study taxes conclude the following:

- *The federal tax system is progressive.* Overall, higher-income groups pay larger percentages of their income as federal taxes than do lower-income groups. Although federal payroll taxes and excise taxes are regressive, the federal income tax is sufficiently progressive to make the overall federal tax system progressive. About 45 percent of federal income tax filers owe no tax at all. In fact, because of fully refundable tax credits designed to reduce poverty and promote work, millions of households receive tax rebates even though their income tax bill is zero. Most of the federal income tax is paid by higher-income taxpayers. In 2018 (the latest year for which data have been compiled), the top 1 percent of income-tax filers paid 38.8 percent of the federal income tax, while the top 5 percent paid 59.4 percent. The overall progressivity of the federal tax system can be confirmed by comparing effective (average) tax rates, which are found by dividing the total of federal income, payroll, and excise taxes paid at various income levels by the total incomes earned by the people at those various income levels. In 2017, the 20 percent of the households with the lowest income paid an effective tax rate of zero percent. The 20 percent of households with the highest income paid a 24.4 percent rate. The top 1 percent paid a 30.2 percent rate.

- *The state and local tax structures are largely regressive.* As a percentage of income, property taxes and sales taxes fall as income rises. Also, state income taxes are generally less progressive than the federal income tax.

- *The overall U.S. tax system is progressive.* Higher-income people carry a substantially larger tax burden, as a percentage of their income, than do lower-income people.

- *The overall U.S. tax system is more progressive than that of other rich countries.* A study by the Organization for Economic Cooperation and Development (OECD) concluded that the U.S. tax system is the most progressive among OECD nations and therefore more progressive than those of Canada, Japan, France, Sweden, Germany, Korea, Australia, the United Kingdom, and dozens of other rich industrialized nations.

▶ Some taxes are borne by those taxed while other taxes are shifted to someone else.

▶ The personal income tax and the corporate income tax (in the short run) are borne by those taxed.

▶ Sales taxes are shifted to consumers; the employer share of the payroll tax is partly shifted to workers;

excise taxes may be shifted to consumers; and property taxes on rental properties are shifted to tenants.

▶ The federal tax structure is progressive. The state and local tax structures are regressive. The overall U.S. tax structure is progressive.

QUICK REVIEW

20.4

Taxation and Spending: Redistribution versus Recycling

Many Think of Taxes as the Best Way to Level the Income Distribution, but the Real Action Is in Government Expenditures.

Modern governments face substantial political pressure to ensure a fair distribution of society's economic output. In many people's minds, this boils down to taxing the rich more than the poor, which is why there is such a focus on whether particular taxes are progressive or regressive.

But taxing the rich cannot by itself ensure redistribution from the rich to the poor. One other thing is needed: The taxes taken from the rich have to flow to the poor, either as goods and services provided by the government or as cash transfer payments that the poor can use to purchase goods and services for themselves and their families.

Until recently, however, economists had only patchy data about whether our government's taxation and spending policies actually redistributed income from the rich to the poor. The problem was that the U.S. government only publishes statistics on whether the rich are being taxed more than the poor. It does not publish statistics on who receives most of its spending.

Two economists from the nonpartisan Tax Foundation took it upon themselves to calculate those statistics. By combining data on government spending with household questionnaire responses in which people report what goods and services they consume, economists Gerald Prante and Scott A. Hodge generated credible estimates of whether the government transfers significant amounts of income and spending power from the rich to the poor.*

PhotoDisc/Getty Images

As it turns out, the government *does* transfer an enormous amount of income from those with high incomes to those with low incomes. Not only do people with high incomes pay a much larger fraction of their incomes in taxes, it is also the case that the majority

---

*Gerald Prante and Scott A. Hodge, "The Distribution of Tax and Spending Policies in the United States," Tax Foundation Special Report No. 211, November 2013.

Summary

LO20.1 Use a circular flow diagram to illustrate how the government's revenue and expenditure decisions affect resource allocation.
In the circular flow diagram, the government interacts with households and businesses through resource markets and product markets. The funds used to pay for government purchases and transfers come from taxes, proprietary income, and borrowing.

LO20.2 Identify the main categories of government spending and the main sources of government revenue.
Government purchases exhaust (use up or absorb) resources; transfer payments do not.

Government purchases declined from about 18 percent of U.S. output in 1970 to 14 percent in 2019, the last year before the COVID-19 pandemic. By contrast, transfer payments over that

period grew from 12 percent of national output to 19 percent. Then, in 2020, the advent of the pandemic caused government transfer spending to increase massively, to 28 percent of national output, causing overall government spending to balloon to 43 percent of national output, the highest level seen since the Second World War.

The ability to borrow allows governments to maintain high spending during economic downturns, such as the 2020 recession (economic downturn) that was caused by the coronavirus.

LO20.3 List the main categories of federal revenue and spending, and describe the difference between marginal and average tax rates.
The main categories of federal spending are pensions and income security, national defense, health, and interest on the public debt.

of that money gets transferred to those with low incomes because government spending is indeed concentrated on programs that are used more by the poor than by the rich. These include welfare, subsidized health care, public education, and jobs programs. The poor also benefit from government-provided public goods that are available to everyone on an equal basis—things like public roads, clean drinking water, national defense, and so on.

The size and impact of the income transfers from rich to poor are most clearly understood by looking at the nearby figure, which groups the 133 million households living in the United States in 2012 into fifths (quintiles) on the basis of household income. The quintiles are labeled Bottom 20%, Second 20%, Third 20%, Fourth 20%, and Top 20%. The yellow and blue bars above each quintile show,

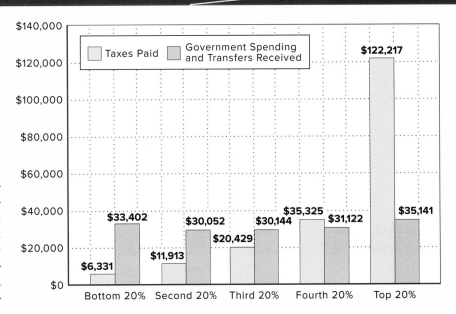

respectively, how much in taxes its members paid on average and how much in government spending they received on average during 2012.

The first thing to notice is how much more money the poor received in government spending than they paid in taxes that year. A comparison of the yellow and blue bars for the bottom quintile reveals that the poorest households received $27,071 (= $33,402 in government spending − $6,331 in taxes) more in government spending than they paid in taxes in 2012. By contrast, households in the top 20 percent of the income distribution paid $87,076 more in taxes than they received in government spending that year.

This $87,076 per-household excess paid by households in the top quintile plus the $4,203 per-household excess paid by the households in the second-highest quintile provided the money that allowed the members of the lower three quintiles to receive more in government spending than they paid in taxes. In total, the transfers from the top two quintiles to the bottom three quintiles amounted to more than

$1 trillion in 2012, or about 10 percent of all income earned by households that year.

Prante and Hodge also found that the average tax rates paid by the five quintiles (on their total incomes, including government spending received) were, respectively, 14.7 percent for the bottom quintile, 19.5 percent for the second quintile, 23.5 percent for the third quintile, 26.9 percent for the fourth quintile, and 35.2 percent for the top quintile. Thus, the overall tax system is highly progressive (due to the federal income tax) despite many individual taxes being quite regressive.

But more significantly, the spending made possible by taxing the rich more than the poor disproportionately flows back to the poor rather than being recycled to the rich. In fact, households in the top quintile receive back only 29 cents in government spending for each dollar they pay in taxes—which means that the remaining 71 cents are channeled to poorer households.

Federal revenues come primarily from personal income taxes, payroll taxes, and corporate income taxes.

The tax rate that applies to any particular range of income is that range's marginal tax rate. The average tax rate is the total amount of taxes paid on a taxpayer's taxable income divided by the amount of taxable income.

LO20.4 List the main categories of state and local revenue and spending.

States derive their revenue primarily from sales and excise taxes and personal income taxes; major state expenditures go to education, public welfare, health and hospitals, and highways. Local communities derive most of their revenue from property taxes; education is their most important expenditure. State and local tax revenues are supplemented by sizable revenue grants from the federal government.

LO20.5 Discuss the magnitude and distribution across job categories of government employment.

Slightly over half of state and local government employees work in education. Just over half of federal government employees work either for the postal service or in national defense.

LO20.6 Summarize the different philosophies regarding the distribution of a nation's tax burden.

The benefits-received principle of taxation states that those who receive the benefits of goods and services provided by government should pay the taxes required to finance them. The ability-to-pay principle states that those who have greater income should be taxed more, absolutely and relatively, than those who have less income.

A tax is proportional if its average rate remains the same regardless of income. A tax is progressive (regressive) if its average rate increases (decreases) as income increases.

LO20.7 Explain the principles relating to tax shifting, tax incidence, and the efficiency losses caused by taxes.

Excise taxes affect supply and therefore equilibrium price and quantity. The more inelastic the demand for a product, the greater is the portion of an excise tax that is borne by consumers. The greater the inelasticity of supply, the larger is the portion of the tax that is borne by the seller.

Taxation involves the loss of some output whose marginal benefit exceeds its marginal cost. The more elastic the supply and demand curves, the greater is the efficiency loss (or deadweight loss) resulting from a particular tax.

LO20.8 Discuss the probable incidence of U.S. taxes.

The federal personal income tax is progressive. General sales, excise, payroll, and property taxes are regressive. The overall U.S. tax system is progressive.

Some taxes are borne by those taxed; other taxes are shifted to someone else. The income tax, the payroll tax levied on workers, and the corporate income tax (in the short run) are borne by those taxed. In contrast, sales taxes are shifted to consumers, part of the payroll tax levied on employers is shifted to workers, and, in the long run, part of the corporate income tax is shifted to workers. Specific excise taxes may or may not be shifted to consumers, depending on the elasticities of demand and supply. Property taxes on owner-occupied property are borne by the owner; those on rental property are borne by tenants.

Terms and Concepts

government purchases	corporate income tax	progressive tax
transfer payments	sales tax	regressive tax
personal income tax	excise tax	proportional tax
marginal tax rate	property tax	tax incidence
average tax rate	benefits-received principle	efficiency loss of a tax
payroll tax	ability-to-pay principle	

Discussion Questions

1. Use a circular flow diagram to show how the allocation of resources and the distribution of income are affected by each of the following government actions. **LO20.1**
   a. The construction of a new high school.
   b. A 2-percentage-point reduction of the corporate income tax.
   c. An expansion of preschool programs for disadvantaged children.
   d. The levying of an excise tax on polluters.
2. What do economists mean when they say government purchases are "exhaustive" expenditures whereas government transfer payments are "nonexhaustive" expenditures? Cite an example of a government purchase and a government transfer payment. **LO20.2**
3. What are the main categories of government spending? What are the main categories of government revenue? **LO20.2**
4. What is the most important source of revenue and the major type of expenditure at the federal level? **LO20.3**
5. For state and local governments, what are the three most important sources of revenue and types of expenditure? **LO20.4**
6. How do the top two categories of federal employment differ from the top two categories of local and state employment? **LO20.5**
7. Distinguish between the benefits-received and the ability-to-pay principles of taxation. Which philosophy is more evident in our present tax structure? Justify your answer. To which principle of taxation do you subscribe? Why? **LO20.6**
8. What is meant by a progressive tax? A regressive tax? A proportional tax? Comment on the progressivity or regressivity of each of the following taxes, indicating in each case where you think the tax incidence lies: (*a*) the federal personal income tax, (*b*) a 4 percent state general sales tax, (*c*) a federal excise tax on

automobile tires, (*d*) a municipal property tax on real estate, (*e*) the federal corporate income tax, (*f*) the portion of the payroll tax levied on employers. **LO20.6**
9. What is the tax incidence of an excise tax when demand is highly inelastic? Highly elastic? What effect does the elasticity of supply have on the incidence of an excise tax? What is the efficiency loss of a tax, and how does it relate to elasticity of demand and supply? **LO20.7**
10. Given the inelasticity of cigarette demand, discuss an excise tax on cigarettes in terms of efficiency loss and tax incidence. **LO20.7**
11. **ADVANCED ANALYSIS** Suppose the equation for the demand curve for some product X is $P = 8 - 0.6Q$ and the supply curve is $P = 2 + 0.4Q$. What are the equilibrium price and quantity? Now suppose an excise tax is imposed on X such that the new supply equation is $P = 4 + 0.4Q$. How much tax revenue will this excise tax yield the government? Graph the curves, and label the area of the graph that represents the tax collection "TC" and the area that represents the efficiency loss of the tax "EL." Briefly explain why area EL is the efficiency loss of the tax but TC is not. **LO20.7**
12. Is it possible for a country with a regressive tax system to have a tax-spending system that transfers resources from the rich to the poor? **LO20.8**
13. **LAST WORD** Does a progressive tax system by itself guarantee that resources will be redistributed from the rich to the poor? Explain. Is the *tax* system in the United States progressive, regressive, or proportional? Does the *tax-spending* system in the United States redistribute resources from higher-income earners to lower-income earners? Explain.

Review Questions

1. The city of Joslyn has three sources of revenue: borrowing, proprietary income from running the local electric power utility, and taxes. Last year, its total revenue was $150 million. If it received $10 million from running the electric power utility and borrowed $40 million, how much did it collect in taxes? **LO20.2**
   a. $140 million
   b. $110 million
   c. $100 million
   d. Nothing

2. Suppose George made $20,000 last year and that he lives in the country of Harmony. The way Harmony levies income taxes, all citizens must pay 10 percent in taxes on their first $10,000 in earnings and then 50 percent in taxes on anything else they might earn. Given that George earned $20,000 last year, his marginal tax rate on the last dollar he earns will be _____, and his average tax rate for his entire income will be _____. **LO20.3**
   a. 50 percent; 50 percent
   b. 50 percent; less than 50 percent
   c. 10 percent; 50 percent
   d. 10 percent; less than 50 percent

3. The nation of Upstandia uses kroner for money, and its tax code is such that a person making 100,000 kroner per year pays 40,000 kroner per year in income taxes; a person making 200,000 kroner per year pays 70,000 kroner per year in income taxes; and a person making 300,000 kroner per year pays 90,000 kroner per year in income taxes. Upstandia's income tax system is: **LO20.6**
   a. progressive.
   b. regressive.
   c. proportional.

4. Identify whether each of the following taxes is progressive or regressive. **LO20.6**
   a. Personal income tax
   b. Sales taxes
   c. Payroll taxes
   d. Property taxes

5. The efficiency loss of imposing an excise tax is due to: **LO20.7**
   a. paying a higher price per unit.
   b. producing and consuming fewer units.

6. True or False: The incidence of property taxes that are levied on rented houses and apartments is high—meaning that those property taxes are paid almost entirely by the landlords. **LO20.8**

Problems

1. Suppose a tax is such that an individual with an income of $10,000 pays $2,000 of tax, a person with an income of $20,000 pays $3,000 of tax, a person with an income of $30,000 pays $4,000 of tax, and so forth. What is each person's average tax rate? Is this tax regressive, proportional, or progressive? **LO20.7**

2. Suppose in Fiscalville there is no tax on the first $10,000 of income, but there is a 20 percent tax on earnings between $10,000 and $20,000 and a 30 percent tax on income between $20,000 and $30,000. Any income above $30,000 is taxed at 40 percent. If your income is $50,000, how much will you pay in taxes? Determine your marginal and average tax rates. Is Fiscalville's income tax progressive? Explain. **LO20.7**

3. For tax purposes, "gross income" is all the money a person receives in a given year from any and all sources. But income taxes are levied on "taxable income" rather than gross income. The difference between the two is the result of many exemptions and deductions. To see how they work, suppose you made $60,000 last year in wages, earned $10,000 from investments, and received a $5,000 gift from your grandmother. Also assume that you are a single parent with one small (4-year-old) child living with you. **LO20.7**
   a. What is your gross income?
   b. Gifts of up to $16,000 per year from any person are not counted as taxable income. Given that exemption, what is your taxable income?

   c. Next, assume you paid $700 in interest on your student loans last year, put $2,000 into a health savings account (HSA), and deposited $4,000 into an individual retirement account (IRA). These expenditures are all *tax exempt*, meaning that any money spent on them reduces taxable income dollar-for-dollar. Knowing that fact, now what is your taxable income?
   d. Next, you can either take the so-called *standard deduction* or apply for itemized deductions (which involve a lot of tedious paperwork). You opt for the standard deduction that allows you as head of your household to exempt another $19,400 from your taxable income. Taking that deduction into account, what is your taxable income?
   e. Apply the tax rates shown in Table 20.1 to your taxable income. How much federal income tax will you owe? What marginal tax rate applies to your last dollar of taxable income?
   f. As the parent of a young dependent child, you qualify for the government's $3,600-per-child "tax credit" for children aged 5 and under. (For older children, the credit is a little less.) Like all tax credits, this $3,600 credit "pays" for $3,600 of the tax you owe. Given this credit, how much money will you have to pay in taxes? Using that actual amount, what is your average tax rate relative to your taxable income? What is your average tax rate relative to your gross income?

CHAPTER

21

Antitrust Policy and Regulation

>> **LEARNING OBJECTIVES**

LO21.1 Explain the core elements of the major antitrust laws in the United States.

LO21.2 Describe the key issues relating to the interpretation and application of antitrust laws.

LO21.3 Identify and explain the difficulties related to regulating the prices charged by natural monopolies.

LO21.4 Discuss social regulation, its benefits and costs, and its optimal level.

antitrust policy The use of the *antitrust laws* to promote *competition* and *economic efficiency*.

industrial regulation The older and more traditional type of business or commercial regulation in which government is concerned with the *prices* charged and the *services* provided to the public in specific *industries*. Differs from *social regulation*.

In this chapter, we look at three sets of government policies toward business.

Antitrust policy consists of laws and government actions designed to prevent monopoly and promote competition. **Industrial regulation** pertains to government regulation of firms' prices (or "rates") within selected industries. **Social regulation** is government regulation of the conditions under which goods are produced, the physical characteristics of the goods that are produced, and the impact of production and consumption on society.

The Antitrust Laws

>> **LO21.1** Explain the core elements of the major antitrust laws in the United States.

Antitrust policy has three main goals: preventing monopolization, promoting competition, and achieving allocative efficiency. Although virtually all economists agree that these are meritorious goals, opinions are sharply divided about the appropriateness and effectiveness of U.S. antitrust policy.

Historical Background

Just after the U.S. Civil War (1861–1865), local markets widened into national markets because of improved transportation, mechanized production methods, and sophisticated corporate structures. In the 1870s and 1880s, dominant firms formed in several industries, including petroleum, meatpacking, railroads, sugar, lead, coal, whiskey, and tobacco. Some of these oligopolists, near-monopolists, or monopolists were known as trusts—businesses that assign control to a single group of decision makers ("trustees"). Because these trusts "monopolized" industries, the word "trust" became synonymous with "monopoly" in common usage. The public, government, and historians began to define a business monopoly as a large-scale dominant seller, even though that seller was not always a sole seller as specified in the model of pure monopoly.

social regulation Regulation in which government is concerned with the conditions under which *goods* and *services* are produced, their physical characteristics, and the impact of their production on society. Differs from *industrial regulation*.

These dominant firms often used questionable tactics in consolidating their industries, charging high prices to customers and extracting price concessions from resource suppliers. Farmers and owners of small businesses were particularly vulnerable to the large corporate monopolies and were among the first to oppose them. Consumers, labor unions, and economists were not far behind in their opposition.

Recall the main economic case against monopoly from Chapter 12: A monopolist maximizes profit by producing the output level at which marginal revenue (rather than price) equals marginal cost. At this MR = MC point, an underallocation of resources to the monopolized product occurs, and the economy suffers an efficiency loss. The higher price charged by the monopolist also transfers income from consumers to the monopolist. This transfer causes significant resentment, and angry consumers then demand that elected officials "do something about the situation."

Responding to that pressure, government officials in the late 1800s and early 1900s instituted two alternative means of control as substitutes for, or supplements to, market forces:

- *Regulatory agencies* In the few markets that give rise to a *natural monopoly*, the government established public regulatory agencies to control the firm's economic behavior.
- *Antitrust laws* In most other markets, government control took the form of antitrust (antimonopoly) legislation designed to inhibit or prevent the growth of monopoly.

Four pieces of federal legislation, as refined and extended by various amendments, constitute the basic law relating to monopoly structure and conduct.

Sherman Act of 1890

The public resentment of trusts that emerged in the 1870s and 1880s culminated in the **Sherman Act** of 1890. This cornerstone of antitrust legislation is surprisingly brief and, at first glance, directly to the point. The core of the act resides in two provisions:

- *Section 1* "Every contract, combination in the form of a trust or otherwise, or conspiracy, in restraint of trade or commerce among the several States, or with foreign nations is declared to be illegal."
- *Section 2* "Every person who shall monopolize, or attempt to monopolize, or combine or conspire with any person or persons, to monopolize any part of the trade or commerce among the several states, or with foreign nations, shall be deemed guilty of a felony" (as later amended from "misdemeanor").

The Sherman Act thus outlawed *restraints of trade* (for example, collusive price-fixing and dividing up markets) and *monopolization*. Today, the U.S. Department of Justice, the Federal Trade Commission, injured private parties, or state attorneys general can file antitrust suits against alleged violators of the act. The courts can issue injunctions to prohibit anticompetitive practices. They can also break up monopolists into competing firms. Courts can fine and imprison violators. Parties injured by illegal combinations and conspiracies can sue the perpetrators for *treble damages*— that is, three times the amount of the monetary injury done to them.

The Sherman Act seemed to provide a sound foundation for positive government action against business monopolies. However, early court interpretations limited the scope of the act and created legal ambiguities. It became clear that a more explicit statement of the government's antitrust sentiments was needed.

Clayton Act of 1914

The **Clayton Act** of 1914 elaborated on the Sherman Act. Four sections were designed to strengthen and make explicit the intent of the Sherman Act:

- Section 2 outlaws *price discrimination* when such discrimination is not justified on the basis of cost differences and when it reduces competition.
- Section 3 prohibits **tying contracts,** in which a producer requires that a buyer purchase another (or other) of its products as a condition for obtaining a desired product.
- Section 7 prohibits the acquisition of stocks of competing corporations when the outcome would be less competition.
- Section 8 prohibits the formation of **interlocking directorates**—situations where a director of one firm is also a board member of a competing firm—in large corporations where the effect would be reduced competition.

regulatory agency An agency, commission, or board established by the federal government or a state government to control the *prices* charged and the *services* offered by a *natural monopoly* or *public utility*.

antitrust laws Legislation (including the *Sherman Act* and *Clayton Act*) that prohibits anticompetitive business activities such as *price fixing,* bid rigging, monopolization, and *tying contracts.*

Sherman Act The federal antitrust law of 1890 that makes *monopoly* and conspiracies to restrain trade criminal offenses.

Clayton Act The federal antitrust law of 1914 that strengthened the *Sherman Act* by making it illegal for *firms* to engage in certain specified practices including *tying contracts, interlocking directorates,* and certain forms of *price discrimination.*

tying contract A requirement imposed by a seller that a buyer purchase another (or other) of its products as a condition for buying a desired product; a practice forbidden by the *Clayton Act.*

interlocking directorate A situation where one or more members of the board of directors of a *corporation* are also on the board of directors of a competing corporation; illegal under the *Clayton Act.*

The Clayton Act sought to outlaw the techniques that firms might use to develop monopoly power and, in that sense, was a preventive measure. Whereas Section 2 of the Sherman Act focused on breaking up monopolies that already existed, Section 7 of the Clayton Act tries to get ahead of the problem by prohibiting anticompetitive mergers that are likely to generate monopolies.

Federal Trade Commission Act of 1914

Federal Trade Commission Act The federal law of 1914 that established the *Federal Trade Commission*.

cease-and-desist order An order from a court or government agency to a corporation or individual to stop engaging in a specified practice.

Wheeler-Lea Act The federal law of 1938 that amended the *Federal Trade Commission Act* by prohibiting unfair and deceptive acts or practices of commerce (such as false and misleading advertising and the misrepresentation of products).

The **Federal Trade Commission Act** created the five-member Federal Trade Commission (FTC), which has joint federal responsibility with the U.S. Justice Department for enforcing the antitrust laws. The act gave the FTC the power to investigate unfair competitive practices on its own initiative or at the request of injured firms. It can hold public hearings on such complaints and, if necessary, issue **cease-and-desist orders** in cases where it discovers "unfair methods of competition in commerce."

The **Wheeler-Lea Act** of 1938 amended the Federal Trade Commission Act to give the FTC the additional responsibility of policing "deceptive acts or practices in commerce." In so doing, the FTC tries to protect the public against false or misleading advertising and product misrepresentation. Thus, the Federal Trade Commission Act, as modified by the Wheeler-Lea Act, (1) established the FTC as an independent antitrust agency and (2) made unfair and deceptive sales practices illegal.

The FTC is highly active in enforcing the deceptive advertising statutes. In 2016, for example, the FTC fined German automaker Volkswagen $10 billion for ads that falsely claimed that Volkswagen vehicles generated low emissions. As another example, two United States Senators asked the FTC, in the summer of 2021, to investigate whether automaker Tesla's description of its cars as having "full self-driving" capabilities constituted illegal advertising after Tesla executives admitted publicly that the vehicles were not, in fact, fully self-driving yet.

Celler-Kefauver Act of 1950

Celler-Kefauver Act The federal law of 1950 that amended the *Clayton Act* by prohibiting the acquisition of the assets of one *firm* by another firm when the effect would be less competition.

The **Celler-Kefauver Act** amended the Clayton Act, Section 7, which prohibits a firm from merging with a competing firm (and thereby lessening competition) by acquiring its stock. However, firms could evade Section 7 by acquiring the physical assets (plant and equipment) of competing firms without formally merging. The Celler-Kefauver Act closed that loophole by prohibiting one firm from obtaining another firm's physical assets when the effect would be reduced competition. Section 7 of the Clayton Act now prohibits all anticompetitive mergers.

Antitrust Policy: Issues and Impacts

>> **LO21.2** Describe the key issues relating to the interpretation and application of antitrust laws.

The courts have been inconsistent in interpreting the antitrust laws. At times, they have applied them vigorously, adhering closely to the laws' spirit and objectives. At other times, their interpretations have rendered certain laws nearly powerless. The federal government, too, has varied considerably in its aggressiveness in enforcing the antitrust laws. Some administrations have made tough antitrust enforcement a high priority. Other administrations have taken a more laissez-faire approach, initiating few antitrust actions or even scaling back the budgets of the enforcement agencies.

Issues of Interpretation

In interpreting the antitrust laws, the courts have struggled with two questions: (1) Should the focus of antitrust policy be on monopoly behavior or on monopoly structure? (2) How broadly should markets be defined in antitrust cases?

Standard Oil case A 1911 antitrust case in which Standard Oil was found guilty of violating the *Sherman Act* by illegally monopolizing the petroleum *industry*. As a remedy the company was divided into several competing *firms*.

Monopoly Behavior versus Monopoly Structure A comparison of three landmark Supreme Court decisions reveals two distinct interpretations of Section 2 of the Sherman Act as it relates to monopoly behavior and structure.

In the 1911 **Standard Oil case,** the Supreme Court found Standard Oil guilty of monopolizing the petroleum industry through a series of abusive and anticompetitive actions. The Court's remedy was to divide Standard Oil into several competing firms. But the Standard Oil case left open an important question: Is every monopoly in violation of Section 2 of the Sherman Act or just those created or maintained by anticompetitive actions?

The Supreme Court's answer to that question was the legal doctrine known as the **rule of reason.** It states that not every monopoly is illegal. Only monopolies that "unreasonably" restrain trade violate Section 2 of the Sherman Act and are subject to antitrust action. Size alone is not an offense.

The rule of reason was applied in the 1920 **U.S. Steel case,** with the Supreme Court deciding that U.S. Steel was innocent of "monopolizing" because it had not resorted to illegal acts against competitors in obtaining and then maintaining its monopoly power. Unlike Standard Oil, which was a so-called "bad trust," U.S. Steel was a "good trust" and therefore not in violation of the law.

In the **Alcoa case** of 1945, the courts touched off a 20-year turnabout. They held that, even though a firm's behavior might be legal, the mere possession of monopoly power (Alcoa held 90 percent of the aluminum ingot market) violated the antitrust laws. Thus Alcoa was found guilty of violating the Sherman Act.

Over the past several decades, the courts have returned to the rule of reason first established in the 1920 U.S. Steel case. For instance, the government has made no attempt to break up Intel's near monopoly in the sale of personal-computer microprocessors. The government apparently believes that Intel has served society well and has engaged in no anticompetitive practices. In the case of Intel and other large companies, a dominant market share may be the result of superior technology, superior products, economies of scale, or any combination of these factors—none of which are necessarily anticompetitive.

Defining the Relevant Market Courts often decide whether or not market power exists by considering the share of the market held by the dominant firm. They have roughly adhered to a "90-60-30 rule" in defining monopoly: If a firm has a 90 percent market share, it is definitely a monopolist. If it has a 60 percent market share, it probably is a monopolist. If it has a 30 percent market share, it clearly is not a monopolist. The market share depends on how the market is defined. If the market is defined broadly to include a wide range of somewhat similar products, the firm's market share will appear small. If the market is defined narrowly to exclude such products, the market share will seem large. The Supreme Court has the final say on how broadly to define relevant markets, but the Supreme Court has not always been consistent.

In the Alcoa case, the Court used a narrow definition of the relevant market: the aluminum ingot market. But in the **DuPont cellophane case** of 1956, the Court defined the market very broadly. The government contended that DuPont, along with a licensee, controlled 100 percent of the cellophane market. But the Court accepted DuPont's contention that the relevant market included all "flexible packaging materials"—waxed paper, aluminum foil, and so forth, in addition to cellophane. Despite DuPont's monopoly in the "cellophane market," it controlled only 20 percent of the market for "flexible wrapping materials." Thus, the Court ruled, DuPont was not a monopoly.

Issues of Enforcement

The degree of federal antitrust enforcement makes a difference in the overall degree of antitrust action in the economy. It is true that individual firms can sue other firms under the antitrust laws, but major antitrust suits often last years and are highly expensive. Injured parties therefore often look to the federal government to initiate and litigate such cases. Once the federal government makes a conviction, the injured parties simply sue the violator to obtain treble damages. Thus a lack of federal antitrust action usually means diminished legal action by firms.

Why might one presidential administration enforce the antitrust laws more strictly than another? The main reason is differences in political philosophies.

The *active antitrust perspective* holds that competition is insufficient in some circumstances to achieve allocative efficiency and ensure fairness to consumers and competing firms. Firms occasionally use illegal tactics against competitors to dominate markets. For example, competitors collude to fix prices or merge to enhance their monopoly power. Thus, active, strict enforcement of the antitrust laws is needed to stop illegal business practices, prevent anticompetitive mergers, and remedy monopoly. In this view, the antitrust authorities need to act much like the officials in a football game. They must observe the players, spot infractions, and enforce the rules.

In contrast, the *laissez-faire perspective* holds that antitrust intervention is largely unnecessary, particularly as it relates to monopoly. In this view, competition is a long-run dynamic process in which firms battle against one another for market dominance. In some markets, a firm successfully monopolizes the market, usually because of its innovativeness or business skill. In exploiting its monopoly power to raise prices, these firms create profit incentives and profit opportunities for

rule of reason The rule stated and applied in the *U.S. Steel case* that only combinations and contracts unreasonably restraining trade are subject to actions under the antitrust laws and that size and possession of *monopoly* power are not by themselves illegal. Compare with *per se violation.*

U.S. Steel case The antitrust action brought by the federal government against the U.S. Steel Corporation in which the courts ruled (in 1920) that only unreasonable restraints of trade were illegal and that size and the possession of monopoly power were not by themselves violations of the *antitrust laws.*

Alcoa case A 1945 case in which the courts ruled that the possession of monopoly power, no matter how reasonably that power had been used, was a violation of the antitrust laws; temporarily overturned the *rule of reason* applied in the *U.S. Steel case.*

DuPont cellophane case The antitrust case brought against DuPont in which the U.S. Supreme Court ruled (in 1956) that while DuPont had a monopoly in the narrowly defined market for cellophane, it did not monopolize the more broadly defined market for flexible packaging materials. It was thus not guilty of violating the *Sherman Act.*

other entrepreneurs and firms to develop alternative technologies and new products to better serve consumers. Therefore, the argument goes, government should not try to break up a monopoly. Rather, it should stand aside and allow the long-run competitive process to work.

Effectiveness of Antitrust Laws

Have the antitrust laws been effective? Although this question is difficult to answer, we can observe how the laws have been applied to monopoly, mergers, price-fixing, price discrimination, and tying contracts.

Monopoly Citing the rule of reason, the government has generally been lenient in applying antitrust laws to monopolies that have developed naturally. Generally, the federal government will sue a firm only if it has a very high market share and there is evidence of abusive conduct in achieving, maintaining, or extending its market dominance.

Even if the federal government wins the antitrust lawsuit, there is still the matter of *remedy*: What actions should the court order to correct the anticompetitive practices in question?

Remedies fall into two main categories.

- A **structural remedy** seeks to change the structure of an offending business so that once the new structure is put in place, profit incentives will encourage competition and thus there will be little need to monitor the new situation as it will be unlikely to revert toward monopoly. The most famous example of a structural remedy was the court-ordered breakup of Standard Oil into dozens of smaller companies that, once established, had a strong profit incentive to compete against each other.

- A **behavioral remedy** seeks to modify the future conduct of the guilty party, such as by requiring a firm found guilty of illegal price discrimination to start charging the same price to all customers, or a firm found guilty of imposing tying contracts to allow items to be purchased separately. The main drawback of behavioral remedies is that they are likely to require ongoing supervision because, in most cases, the behavioral remedy will not have altered the underlying profit incentives that led to the illegal behavior in the first place.

The issue of which type of remedy to apply arose in two landmark technology cases. The first was the **AT&T case,** in which the government charged the American Telephone and Telegraph company (AT&T) with violating the Sherman Act by engaging in anticompetitive practices designed to maintain its domestic telephone monopoly. As part of an out-of-court settlement between the government and AT&T, in 1982 AT&T agreed to divest itself of its 22 regional telephone-operating companies.

The second case was the **Microsoft case** in which computer software maker Microsoft was found guilty of violating the Sherman Act by taking several unlawful actions designed to maintain its monopoly of operating systems for personal computers. A lower court ordered that Microsoft be split into two competing firms. A court of appeals upheld the lower-court finding of abusive monopoly but rescinded the breakup of Microsoft. Instead of a structural remedy, the eventual outcome was a behavioral remedy in which Microsoft was prohibited from engaging in a set of specific anticompetitive business practices.

Mergers The government's treatment of mergers varies with the type of merger and its effect on competition.

Merger Types There are three basic types of mergers, as represented in Figure 21.1. This figure shows two stages of production (the input stage and the output, or final-product, stage) for two distinct final-goods industries (autos and blue jeans). Each rectangle (A, B, C, . . . , X, Y, Z) represents a particular firm.

A **horizontal merger** occurs between two competitors that sell similar products in the same geographic market. In Figure 21.1, this type of merger is shown as a combination of glass producers T and U. Real-world examples of such mergers include Heinz purchasing Kraft, Charter Communications acquiring Time Warner Cable, and Walt Disney purchasing 21st Century Fox.

A **vertical merger** occurs between firms at different stages of the production process. In Figure 21.1, the merger between firm Z, a producer of denim fabric, and firm F, a producer of blue

---

structural remedy A directive imposed by a regulator on an offending monopoly firm that seeks to resolve the firm's illegal monopoly behavior by changing the structure of the offending business, for instance by breaking it up into multiple competing firms.

behavioral remedy A directive imposed by a regulator on an offending *monopoly* firm that seeks to resolve the firm's illegal monopoly behavior by requiring different actions be taken by the firm in the future, such as not engaging in price fixing or refraining from using tying contracts.

AT&T case A major antitrust case decided in 1984 that broke up the American Telephone and Telegraph company (AT&T), which had run a domestic telephone monopoly across the entire United States for many decades, into 22 regional telephone operating companies.

Microsoft case A 2002 antitrust case in which Microsoft was found guilty of violating the *Sherman Act* by engaging in a series of unlawful activities designed to maintain its *monopoly* in operating systems for personal computers; as a remedy the company was prohibited from engaging in a set of specific anticompetitive business practices.

horizontal merger The merger into a single *firm* of two firms producing the same product and selling it in the same geographic market.

vertical merger The merger of one or more *firms* engaged in different stages of the production of a particular *final good*.

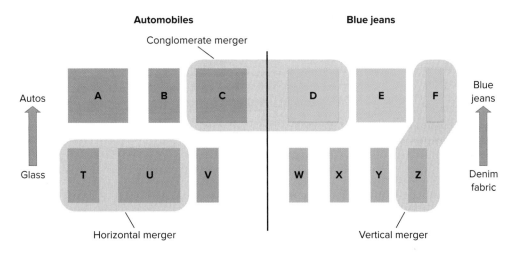

FIGURE 21.1
Types of mergers.

Horizontal mergers (T + U) bring together firms selling the same product in the same geographic market; vertical mergers (F + Z) connect firms having a buyer-seller relationship; and conglomerate mergers (C + D) join firms in different industries or firms operating in different geographic areas.

jeans, is a vertical merger. Vertical mergers are mergers between firms that have buyer-seller relationships. Real-world examples of such mergers are PepsiCo's mergers with Pizza Hut, Taco Bell, and Kentucky Fried Chicken. PepsiCo supplies soft drinks to each of these fast-food outlets. (PepsiCo later spun off these entities into a separate company now called Yum! Brands.)

A **conglomerate merger** is any merger that is not horizontal or vertical; in general, it is the combination of firms in different industries or firms operating in different geographic areas. Conglomerate mergers can extend the line of products sold, extend the territory in which products are sold, or combine totally unrelated companies. In Figure 21.1, the merger between firm C, an auto manufacturer, and firm D, a blue jeans producer, is a conglomerate merger. Real-world examples of conglomerate mergers include the merger between Amazon (e-commerce) and the Whole Foods Markets (supermarkets) and the merger between Microsoft (software) and LinkedIn (social networking).

Merger Guidelines: The Herfindahl Index The federal government has established very loose merger guidelines based on the Herfindahl index. Recall from Chapter 13 that this measure of concentration is the sum of the squared percentage market shares of the firms in an industry. An industry of only four firms, each with a 25 percent market share, has a Herfindahl index of 2,500 ($= 25^2 + 25^2 + 25^2 + 25^2$). In pure competition, where each firm's market share is minuscule, the index approaches 0 ($= 0^2 + 0^2 + \ldots + 0^2$). In pure monopoly, the index for that single firm is 10,000 ($= 100^2$).

The U.S. government uses Section 7 of the Clayton Act to block horizontal mergers that will substantially lessen competition. It is likely to challenge a horizontal merger if the post-merger Herfindahl index would be above 1,800 and if the merger has substantially increased the index (added 100 or more points). However, other factors, such as economies of scale, the degree of foreign competition, and the ease of entry of new firms, are also considered. Furthermore, horizontal mergers are usually allowed if one of the merging firms is suffering major and continuing losses.

Recently, the federal government successfully challenged horizontal mergers between Snyder's of Hanover and Utz Quality Foods, makers of pretzels; Polypore and Microporous, battery-parts makers; and DraftKings and Fantasy Duel, providers of online fantasy sports contests.

Most vertical mergers escape antitrust prosecution because they do not substantially lessen competition in either of the two markets. However, the FTC sued in 2017 to prevent AT&T, which owns many cable TV systems, from merging with Time Warner, which provides a large amount of the content shown on cable TV systems through its ownership of CNN, HBO, DC Comics, and Warner Brothers. It was the first FTC litigation against a vertical merger in almost 40 years. The FTC argued in court that if the merger proceeded, the combined company might deny Time Warner content to non-AT&T cable networks. The case was decided in favor of AT&T in 2018, with a federal judge allowing the merger to proceed.

Conglomerate mergers are generally permitted. If an auto manufacturer acquires a blue jeans producer, no antitrust action is likely because neither firm increases its own market share as a result. Thus the Herfindahl index remains unchanged in each industry.

conglomerate merger The merger of two *firms* operating in separate industries or separate geographic areas so that neither firm is a supplier, customer, or competitor of the other; any merger that is neither a *horizontal merger* nor a *vertical merger*.

GLOBAL PERSPECTIVE 21.1

NUMBER OF MERGERS, SELECTED COUNTRIES, 2020

The number of corporate mergers varies substantially from country to country, with the United States by itself accounting for about 30 percent of all merger activity worldwide.

Number of Mergers, 2020

Country	
United States	
China	
United Kingdom	
France	
Australia	
Japan	
Germany	
India	
South Korea	
Russia	
Singapore	
Mexico	

(Scale: 0, 5,000, 10,000, 15,000, 20,000)

Source: Institute for Mergers, Acquisitions and Alliances (IMAA).

Global Perspective 21.1 shows the number of corporate mergers (some friendly, others by acquisition) that took place in 2020 in various countries.

per se violations Collusive actions, such as attempts by *firms* to fix *prices* or divide a market, that are violations of the *antitrust laws,* even if the actions themselves are unsuccessful.

Price-Fixing Price-fixing investigations and court actions are common. Evidence of price-fixing, even by small firms, will bring antitrust action, as will other collusive activities such as scheming to rig bids on government contracts or dividing up sales in a market. In antitrust law, these activities are known as **per se violations;** they are "in and of themselves" illegal, and therefore they are not subject to the rule of reason. To gain a conviction, the government or other party making the charge need show only that there was a conspiracy to fix prices, rig bids, or divide up markets, not that the conspiracy succeeded or caused serious damage to other parties. (See the nearby Consider This story.)

Price Discrimination Price discrimination is a common business practice that rarely reduces competition and therefore is rarely challenged by government. The exception occurs when a firm engages in price discrimination as part of a strategy to block entry or drive out competitors.

CONSIDER THIS . . .

Of Sea Fish and eBooks (and Other Things in Common)

Examples of price-fixing are numerous. Here are just a few:

- In 2013, Apple was convicted along with five publishers—Harper Collins, Penguin, Simon & Schuster, Hachette, and Macmillan—of horizontal price-fixing in the market for ebooks to be sold on Apple's iBook store. Apple was ordered to pay $450 million in reparations to those harmed by the scheme, which raised prices 20 percent in Apple's online bookstore.
- In 2016, the French equivalent of the FTC fined thirteen consumer goods companies—including U.S. firms

Charles Brutlag/Shutterstock

Colgate-Palmolive, Sara Lee, Gillette, and Procter and Gamble—$1.1 billion for fixing the prices of personal hygiene products.

- In 2018, tuna oligopolists StarKist and Bumble Bee pled guilty to price fixing and faced fines of $100 million and $25 million, respectively.
- In 2018, six Korean firms—including Hyundai Steel and Dongkuk Steel—were fined $106 million by the FTC for colluding to fix the price of construction rebar in the United States.
- In 2021, Pilgrim's Pride pled guilty to price fixing and paid a $107 million fine for conspiring with several other major chicken producers to fix the wholesale price of chicken.

Tying Contracts The federal government strictly enforces the prohibition of tying contracts, particularly by dominant firms. For example, it stopped movie distributors from forcing theaters to buy the projection rights to a full package of films as a condition of showing a blockbuster movie. Also, it stopped two large distributors of medical products (Cardinal Health and O&M Distribution) from charging customers a premium on their entire product lines if the customers refused to purchase sutures exclusively from them rather than from a rival firm.

Conclusions What can we conclude about the overall effectiveness of antitrust laws? Antitrust policy has not been very effective in restricting the rise of or in breaking up monopolies or oligopolies resulting from firms' legally undertaken internal expansions. The antitrust laws have been used more effectively against predatory or abusive monopoly, but their effectiveness has been diminished by the slow legal process and the long lag between the filing of charges and the implementation of remedies. In contrast, antitrust policy has been effective in prosecuting price-fixing and tying contracts, as can be seen by the examples given in the Consider This story.

Most economists conclude that, overall, U.S. antitrust policy has been moderately effective in achieving its goal of promoting competition and efficiency. Much of the success of antitrust policy arises from its deterrent effect on price-fixing and anticompetitive mergers.

▶ The Sherman Act of 1890 outlaws restraints of trade and monopolization. The Clayton Act of 1914 as amended by the Celler-Kefauver Act of 1950 outlaws price discrimination (when anticompetitive), tying contracts, anticompetitive mergers, and interlocking directorates.

▶ The Federal Trade Commission Act of 1914 as bolstered by the Wheeler-Lea Act of 1938 created the Federal Trade Commission (FTC) and gave it authority to investigate unfair methods of competition and deceptive acts or practices in commerce.

▶ Currently, the courts judge monopoly using a "rule of reason," first established in the U.S. Steel case

of 1920. Under this rule, only monopolists that achieve or maintain their status abusively are in violation of the Sherman Act.

▶ The degree of enforcement of antitrust laws depends on the general antitrust philosophy of each U.S. presidential administration.

▶ Government treats existing monopoly relatively leniently, as long as it is not abusive; blocks most horizontal mergers between dominant, profitable firms in highly concentrated industries; and vigorously prosecutes price-fixing and tying contracts.

Industrial Regulation

Antitrust policy assumes that society will benefit if a monopoly is prevented from evolving or if it is dissolved where it already exists. We now turn to a special situation in which there is a good economic reason for an industry to be organized monopolistically.

Natural Monopoly

A **natural monopoly** exists when economies of scale are so extensive that a single firm can supply the entire market at a lower average total cost than could a number of competing firms. Clear-cut circumstances of natural monopoly are relatively rare, but such conditions exist for many public utilities, such as local electricity, water, and natural gas providers. Where natural monopoly occurs, competition is uneconomical. If the market were divided among many producers, economies of scale would not be achieved, and unit costs and prices would be higher than necessary.

There are two possible alternatives for promoting better economic outcomes where natural monopoly exists:

- *Public ownership* or some approximation of it has been established in a few instances. Examples include the Postal Service, the Tennessee Valley Authority, and Amtrak at the national level and mass transit, water supply systems, and garbage collection at the local level.

- *Public regulation,* sometimes called *industrial regulation*, has been the preferred option in the United States. In this type of regulation, government commissions engage in rate regulation, setting the prices (or "rates") charged by regulated natural monopolists such that they earn no more than a "fair" rate of return on their capital assets.

>> **LO21.3** Identify and explain the difficulties related to regulating the prices charged by natural monopolies.

natural monopoly An *industry* in which *economies of scale* are so great that a single *firm* can produce the industry's product at a lower average total cost than would be possible if more than one firm produced the product.

TABLE 21.1 The Main Regulatory Commissions Providing Industrial Regulation

Commission (Year Established)	Jurisdiction
Federal Energy Regulatory Commission (1930)*	Electricity, gas, gas pipelines, oil pipelines, water-power sites
Federal Communications Commission (1934)	Telephones, television, cable television, radio, telegraph, CB radios, ham operators
State public utility commissions (various years)	Electricity, gas, telephones

*Originally called the Federal Power Commission; renamed in 1977.

public interest theory of regulation The presumption that the purpose of the regulation of an *industry* is to protect the public (consumers) from abuse of the power possessed by *natural monopolies*.

Table 21.1 lists the two major federal regulatory commissions and their jurisdictions. It also notes that all 50 states have commissions that regulate the intrastate activities and "utility rates" of local natural monopolies.

The economic objective of industrial regulation is embodied in the **public interest theory of regulation,** which holds that industrial regulation is necessary to prevent a natural monopoly from charging monopoly prices and harming consumers and society. The goal of such regulation is to garner for society at least some of the cost reductions associated with natural monopoly while avoiding the restrictions of output and high prices associated with unregulated monopoly. If competition is inappropriate or impractical, society should allow or even encourage a monopoly but regulate its prices. Regulation should then be structured so that ratepayers benefit from the natural monopolists' lower per-unit costs.

In practice, regulators engaging in rate of return regulation seek to establish rates that will cover production costs and yield a "fair" return to the enterprise. The goal is to set price equal to average total cost so that the regulated firm receives a normal profit.

Problems with Industrial Regulation

There is considerable disagreement on the effectiveness of industrial regulation. Let's examine two criticisms.

Costs and Inefficiency An unregulated firm has a strong incentive to reduce its costs at each level of output because lower costs mean a higher profit. The regulatory commission that is applying rate of return regulation will, however, always adjust the regulated rate so as to confine the regulated firm to a normal profit, or a "fair return," on the value of its assets. That means that if a regulated firm figures out a way to lower its operating costs, the rising profit generated by those lower costs will lead the regulatory commission to lower the firm's prices in order to reduce its profit down to the level that is considered fair. The regulated firm therefore has little or no incentive to reduce its operating costs since it will at most benefit from a higher rate of profit only briefly before the regulatory commission lowers the prices that the firm can charge customers.

In addition, because the regulatory commission must allow the regulated firm a fair rate of return, the regulated monopolist actually has an incentive to be inefficient, since any inefficiently high production costs that cause profits to temporarily fall below the fair rate of return will automatically cause the regulatory commission to allow the firm to charge higher prices so that the firm can once again receive a normal rate of return. Consequently, a regulated firm may reason that it might as well have high salaries for its workers and opulent working conditions for management, because the "return" is the same in percentage terms whether costs are minimized or not. So, although a natural monopoly reduces costs through economies of scale, industrial regulation fosters considerable X-inefficiency (see Chapter 11). Because competition is absent, the potential cost savings from natural monopoly may never materialize.

Perpetuating Monopoly Industrial regulation sometimes perpetuates monopoly long after the conditions of natural monopoly have ended. How?

Technological change often creates the potential for competition in some or even all portions of the regulated industry. Examples: Trucks began competing with railroads; satellite television began competing with cable television; and cell phones began competing with landlines.

But spurred by the firms they regulate, commissions often protect the regulated firms from new competition by either blocking entry or by regulating competitors. Industrial regulation therefore may perpetuate a monopoly that is no longer a natural monopoly and would otherwise erode. Ordinary monopoly, protected by government, may supplant natural monopoly. If so, the regulated prices may exceed those that would occur with competition. The beneficiaries of outdated regulation are the regulated firms and their employees. The losers are consumers and potential entrants.

Example: Until the mid-1990s, long-distance telephone companies (such as AT&T) and cable-television providers (such as Time Warner) were prohibited from offering local telephone services in competition with regulated local and regional telephone companies. But the very fact that AT&T, Time Warner, and other firms wanted to compete with regulated monopolies calls into question whether those local providers were in fact natural monopolies, rather than government-protected ordinary monopolies.

Deregulation

Beginning in the 1970s, evidence of inefficiency in regulated industries and the contention that the government was regulating potentially competitive industries contributed to a wave of deregulation. Since then, Congress and many state legislatures have passed legislation that has deregulated in varying degrees the airline, trucking, banking, railroad, natural gas, television, and electricity industries. Deregulation has also occurred in the telecommunications industry, where antitrust authorities dismantled the regulated national telephone monopoly known as the Bell System (AT&T). Deregulation in the 1970s and 1980s was one of the most extensive experiments in economic policy to take place during the last hundred years.

The overwhelming consensus among economists is that deregulation has produced large net benefits for consumers and society. Most of the gains from deregulation have occurred in three industries: airlines, railroads, and trucking. Airfares (adjusted for inflation) declined by about one-third, and airline safety has continued to improve. Trucking and railroad freight rates (again, adjusted for inflation) dropped by about one-half.

Significant efficiency gains were also realized in long-distance telecommunications, and there have been slight efficiency gains in cable television, stock brokerage services, and the natural gas industry. Moreover, deregulation has unleashed a wave of technological advances that resulted in new and improved products and services, including cell phones, fiber-optic cable, microwave communication systems, and the Internet.

The most recent and perhaps controversial industry to be deregulated is electricity. Deregulation is relatively advanced at the wholesale level, where firms can buy and sell electricity at market prices. They are also free to build generating facilities and sell electricity to local electricity providers at unregulated prices. In addition, several states have deregulated retail prices and encouraged households and businesses to choose among available electricity suppliers. This competition has generally lowered electricity rates for consumers and enhanced allocative efficiency.

▶ Natural monopoly occurs where economies of scale are so extensive that only a single firm can produce the product at minimum average total cost.

▶ The public interest theory of regulation says that government must regulate natural monopolies to prevent abuses arising from monopoly power. Regulated firms, however, have less incentive than competitive firms to reduce costs. That is, regulated firms tend to be X-inefficient.

▶ The legal cartel theory of regulation suggests that some firms seek government regulation to reduce price competition and ensure stable profits.

▶ Deregulation initiated by government in the past several decades has yielded large annual efficiency gains for society.

Social Regulation

Industrial regulation has focused on the regulation of prices (or rates) in natural monopolies. But in the early 1960s a new type of regulation began to emerge. **Social regulation** is government regulation that is concerned with the conditions under which goods and services are produced, the impact of production on society, and the physical qualities of the goods themselves.

The federal government carries out most social regulation, although states also play a role. Table 21.2 lists the main federal regulatory commissions engaged in social regulation.

Distinguishing Features

Social regulation differs from industrial regulation in several ways.

First, social regulation applies to far more firms than industrial regulation does. Social regulation is often applied "across the board" to all industries and directly affects more producers than

>> **LO21.4** Discuss social regulation, its benefits and costs, and its optimal level.

social regulation Regulation in which government is concerned with the conditions under which *goods* and *services* are produced, their physical characteristics, and the impact of their production on society. Differs from *industrial regulation*.

TABLE 21.2 The Main Federal Regulatory Commissions Providing Social Regulation

Commission (Year Established)	Jurisdiction
Food and Drug Administration (1906)	Safety and effectiveness of food, drugs, and cosmetics
Equal Employment Opportunity Commission (1964)	Hiring, promotion, and discharge of workers
Occupational Safety and Health Administration (1971)	Industrial health and safety
Environmental Protection Agency (1972)	Air, water, and noise pollution
Consumer Product Safety Commission (1972)	Safety of consumer products
Consumer Financial Protection Bureau (2011)	Fairness and transparency in lending and other financial services

industrial regulation does. For instance, while the industrial regulation of the Federal Energy Regulatory Commission (FERC) applies to a relatively small number of energy production firms, the rules and regulations issued by the Occupational Safety and Health Administration (OSHA) apply to firms in all industries.

Second, social regulation intrudes into the day-to-day production process to a greater extent than industrial regulation. While industrial regulation focuses on rates, costs, and profits, social regulation often dictates the design of products, the conditions of employment, and the nature of the production process. For example, the Consumer Product Safety Commission (CPSC) regulates the design of potentially unsafe products, the Environmental Protection Agency (EPA) regulates the amount of pollution allowed during production, and the Consumer Financial Protection Bureau acts to ensure fairness and transparency in financial services like banking and lending.

Social regulation expanded rapidly during the same period in which industrial regulation waned. Between 1970 and 1980, the U.S. federal government created 20 new social regulatory agencies. More recently, Congress has established new social regulations to be enforced by existing regulatory agencies. For example, the Equal Employment Opportunity Commission, which is responsible for enforcing laws against workplace discrimination on the basis of race, gender, age, or religion, now also enforces the Americans with Disabilities Act. Under this social regulation, firms must provide reasonable accommodations for qualified workers and job applicants with disabilities. Also, sellers must provide reasonable access for customers with disabilities.

The Optimal Level of Social Regulation

While economists agree on the need for social regulation, they disagree on whether or not the current level of such regulation is optimal. Recall that an activity should be expanded as long as its marginal benefit (MB) exceeds its marginal cost (MC). If the MB of social regulation exceeds its MC, then there is too little social regulation. But if MC exceeds MB, there is too much. Unfortunately, the marginal costs and benefits of social regulation are not always easy to measure. Thus ideology about the proper size and role of government often drives the debate over social regulation as much as, or perhaps more than, economic cost-benefit analysis.

In Support of Social Regulation Proponents of social regulation say that it has achieved notable successes and has greatly enhanced society's overall well-being. They point out that the problems that social regulation confronts are serious and substantial. According to the National Safety Council, about 5,000 workers die annually in job-related accidents and around 1.2 million workers suffer injuries that force them to miss a day or more of work. Air pollution continues to cloud major U.S. cities, imposing large costs in terms of reduced property values and increased health care expenses. Numerous children and adults die each year because of poorly designed or manufactured products (for example, car tires) or tainted food (for example, E. coli in beef). Discrimination against some ethnic and racial groups, persons with disabilities, and older workers reduces their earnings and imposes heavy costs on society.

Proponents of social regulation acknowledge that social regulation is costly. But they correctly point out that a high "price" for something does not necessarily mean that it should not be purchased. They say that the appropriate economic test is whether the benefits of social regulation exceed the costs. The public often underestimates the benefits because they are more difficult to measure than costs and often become apparent only after some time has passed (for example, the benefits of reducing carbon dioxide emissions).

Proponents of social regulation point to its many specific benefits. For example, it is estimated that highway fatalities would be 40 percent greater annually in the absence of automobile safety features mandated through regulation. Compliance with child safety-seat and seat-belt laws has significantly reduced the auto fatality rate for small children. The national air quality standards set by law clearly link cleaner air, other things equal, with increases in home values. Affirmative action regulations have increased the labor demand for racial and ethnic minorities and women. The use of childproof lids has resulted in a 90 percent decline in child deaths caused by accidental swallowing of poisonous substances.

Criticisms of Social Regulation Critics contend that, in many instances, social regulation has been expanded to the point where the marginal costs exceed the marginal benefits. They believe that society will obtain net benefits by cutting back on irritating social regulation. They note that many social regulation laws are poorly written, with difficult-to-understand regulatory objectives and standards. As a result, regulators pursue goals well beyond the original intent of the legislation. Businesses complain that regulators often press for additional improvements, unmindful of costs.

Also, decisions must often be made and rules formed on the basis of inadequate information. For example, Consumer Product Safety Commission officials may make decisions about certain ingredients in products on the basis of limited laboratory experiments that suggest that those ingredients might cause cancer. Such laws, say critics, lead to excessive regulation of business.

Moreover, critics argue that social regulations produce many unintended and costly side effects. For instance, the federal gas mileage standard for automobiles has been blamed for an estimated 2,000 to 3,900 traffic deaths a year because auto manufacturers have reduced the weight of vehicles to meet the higher miles-per-gallon standards. Other things equal, drivers of lighter cars have a higher fatality rate than drivers of heavier vehicles.

Finally, opponents of social regulation say that the regulatory agencies may attract over-zealous workers who are hostile toward the market system and believe too fervently in regulation. For example, some staff members of government agencies may see large corporations as "bad guys" who regularly cause pollution, provide inadequate safety for workers, deceive their customers, and generally abuse their power. Such biases can lead to seemingly never-ending calls for still more regulation, rather than objective assessments of the costs and benefits of new regulation.

Two Reminders

The debate over the proper amount of social regulation will surely continue. By helping determine costs and benefits, economic analysis can lead to more informed discussions and to better decisions. In this regard, economic analysis provides two pertinent reminders.

There Is No Free Lunch Fervent supporters of social regulation need to remember that "there is no free lunch." Social regulation can produce higher prices, stifle innovation, and reduce competition.

Social regulation raises product prices in two ways. It does so directly because companies normally pass compliance costs on to consumers, and it does so indirectly by reducing labor productivity. Resources invested in making workplaces accessible are not, for example, available for investment in new machinery designed to increase output per worker. Where the wage rate is fixed, a drop in labor productivity increases the marginal and average total costs of production. In effect, the supply curve for the product shifts leftward, causing the price of the product to rise.

Social regulation may have a negative impact on the rate of innovation. Technological advance may be stifled by, say, the fear that a new plant will not meet EPA guidelines or that a new medicine will require years of testing before being approved by the Food and Drug Administration (FDA).

Social regulation may weaken competition because it usually places a relatively greater burden on small firms than on large firms. The costs of complying with social regulation are, in effect, fixed costs. Because smaller firms produce less output over which to distribute those costs, their compliance costs per unit of output put them at a competitive disadvantage. Social regulation is more likely to force smaller firms out of business, thus contributing to the increased concentration of industry.

Finally, social regulation may prompt some U.S. firms to move their operations to countries in which the rules are not as burdensome and therefore production costs are lower.

LAST WORD

Antitrust Online

The Internet Has Presented Antitrust Authorities with Both Old and New Causes for Concern.

The Airline Tariff Publishing case was the first important example of how digital communication platforms could be used by businesses to engage in price-fixing. In the late 1980s, U.S. airlines began to post both current and future prices for airline tickets on a centralized computer system known as the Airline Tariff Publishing Company. The system was set up so that travel agents could comparison shop for their clients. But the airlines used the system's ability to list the start dates and end dates for ticket purchases as a way of colluding.

As an example, suppose that American Airlines and Delta Airlines had both been charging $200 for a one-way ticket between New York and Chicago. American could then post a higher price of $250 for the route with the stipulation that nobody could start buying tickets at that price until the next month. Delta could then respond by also saying that it would start selling tickets at the higher price next month. In that way, the two airlines could tacitly coordinate their price setting ahead of time so as to collude on a major price increase.

The antitrust authorities at the U.S. Department of Justice stopped this practice in 1994 by getting the airlines to agree to the behavioral remedy that any fare changes would have to become immediately available to consumers. Airlines could no longer use suggested future prices as a way of signaling each other about how to collude.

The monopoly power gained during the 1990s and early 2000s by online giants such as Microsoft and Google has also led to business practices that have raised the ire of antitrust authorities. Microsoft, for example, was fined $2.7 billion after being convicted in 2000 of using the near-monopoly (95 percent market share) dominance of its Windows operating system software to coerce computer makers into favoring Microsoft's Internet Explorer web browser over rival browsers such as Netscape Navigator.

More recently, European Union antitrust officials fined Google $5 billion for using the dominance of its smartphone operating system, Android, to coerce smartphone manufacturers into installing Google search bars and Google mobile apps over search bars and mobile apps produced by other companies.

The Internet has also spawned a new and unprecedented threat to competition—collusion by pieces of software that use pricing algorithms (automatically applied rules for setting prices) to constantly

Grzegorz Knec/Alamy Stock Photo

adjust a company's online prices in response to seeing what rival firms are charging for similar products. The problem for regulators is that the pricing algorithms of different firms can end up interacting in ways that collusively raise prices for consumers. This is especially true for pieces of software that use artificial intelligence to learn how to achieve particular goals. Two such pieces of software could each be programmed to try to maximize profits and, as they interacted with each other, "realize" that the best way to do so is by coordinating rather than competing.

That possibility is especially challenging because, given the way antitrust laws are currently written, firms can be prosecuted for collusion only if they make an anticompetitive "agreement" with each other. If the algorithms come to collude on their own, there is no such agreement to prosecute. In fact, the behavior of the two pieces of software could just as easily be interpreted as independent parallel conduct rather than coordination since the algorithms never communicate with each other directly. And, in addition, should asking a piece of software to try to figure out how to maximize profits be illegal just by itself?

These issues are still very much up in the air but being faced squarely by U.S. regulators, who made their first prosecution against the collusive use of algorithmic pricing software in 2015 and who established the Office of Technology Research and Investigation as part of the Federal Trade Commission's Bureau of Consumer Protection that same year.

Less Government Is Not Always Better Than More On the opposite side of the issue, opponents of social regulation need to remember that less government is not always better than more government. While the market system is a powerful engine for producing goods and services and generating income, it has flaws and can camouflage abuses. Through appropriate amounts of social regulation, government can increase economic efficiency and thus society's well-being. Ironically, by "taking the rough edges off of capitalism," social regulation may be a strong pro-capitalism force. Properly conceived and executed, social regulation helps maintain political support for the market system. Such support might quickly wane should there be a steady drumbeat of reports of unsafe workplaces, unsafe products, discriminatory hiring, deceived loan customers, and the like. Social regulation helps the market system deliver not only goods and services but also a "good society."

▶ Social regulation is concerned with the production, consumption, and physical characteristics of goods.

▶ Defenders of social regulation point to the benefits arising from policies that keep dangerous products from the marketplace, reduce workplace injuries and deaths, contribute to clean air and water, and reduce employment discrimination.

▶ Critics of social regulation say uneconomical policy goals, inadequate information, unintended side effects, and overzealous enforcement personnel create excessive regulation, for which regulatory costs exceed regulatory benefits.

**QUICK REVIEW
21.3**

Summary

LO21.1 Explain the core elements of the major antitrust laws in the United States.

The cornerstones of U.S. antitrust policy are the Sherman Act of 1890 and the Clayton Act of 1914. The Sherman Act specifies that "every contract, combination . . . or conspiracy in the restraint of interstate trade . . . is . . . illegal" and that any person who monopolizes or attempts to monopolize interstate trade is guilty of a felony.

If a company is found guilty of violating the antimonopoly provisions of the Sherman Act, the government can either break up the monopoly into competing firms (a structural remedy) or prohibit it from engaging in specific anticompetitive business practices (a behavioral remedy).

The Clayton Act bolsters and makes more explicit the provisions of the Sherman Act. It declares that price discrimination, tying contracts, intercorporate stock acquisitions, and interlocking directorates are illegal when they reduce competition.

The Federal Trade Commission Act of 1914 created the Federal Trade Commission to investigate antitrust violations and to prevent the use of "unfair methods of competition." The FTC Act was amended by the Wheeler-Lea Act of 1938 to outlaw false and deceptive advertising. Empowered by cease-and-desist orders, the FTC serves as a watchdog agency over unfair, deceptive, or false claims made by firms about their own products or their competitors' products.

The Celler-Kefauver Act of 1950 amended the Clayton Act of 1914 to prohibit one firm from acquiring the assets of another firm when doing so will substantially reduce competition.

LO21.2 Describe the key issues relating to the interpretation and application of antitrust laws.

The key issues in applying antitrust laws include (a) determining whether an industry should be judged by its structure or by its behavior, (b) defining the scope and size of the dominant firm's market, and (c) deciding how strictly to enforce the antitrust laws.

The courts treat price-fixing among competitors as a *per se violation*, meaning that the conduct is illegal whether or not the conspiracy causes harm. In contrast, antitrust enforcement uses a *rule of reason* to assess monopoly. Only monopolies that unreasonably (abusively) achieve or maintain their status violate the law. Antitrust officials are more likely to challenge price-fixing, tying contracts, and horizontal mergers than to try to break up existing monopolies.

LO21.3 Identify and explain the difficulties related to regulating the prices charged by natural monopolies.

The objective of industrial regulation is to protect the public from the market power of natural monopolies by regulating prices and quality of service.

Critics of industrial regulation contend that it can lead to inefficiency and rising costs. Legislation passed in the late 1970s and the 1980s has brought about varying degrees of deregulation in the airline, trucking, banking, railroad, and television broadcasting industries.

Studies indicate that deregulation of airlines, railroads, trucking, and telecommunications has produced sizable annual gains to society through lower prices, lower costs, and increased output.

LO21.4 Discuss social regulation, its benefits and costs, and its optimal level.

Social regulation is concerned with the production, consumption, and physical characteristics of goods. Whereas industrial regulation is on the wane, social regulation continues to expand. The optimal amount of social regulation occurs where MB = MC.

People who support social regulation point to its numerous successes and assert that it has greatly enhanced society's well-being. Critics of social regulation contend that businesses are excessively regulated to the point where marginal costs exceed marginal benefits. They also say that social regulation often produces unintended and costly side effects.

Terms and Concepts

antitrust policy	cease-and-desist order	AT&T case
industrial regulation	Wheeler-Lea Act	Microsoft case
social regulation	Celler-Kefauver Act	horizontal merger
regulatory agency	Standard Oil case	vertical merger
antitrust laws	rule of reason	conglomerate merger
Sherman Act	U.S. Steel case	per se violations
Clayton Act	Alcoa case	natural monopoly
tying contracts	DuPont cellophane case	public interest theory of regulation
interlocking directorates	structural remedy	social regulation
Federal Trade Commission Act	behavioral remedy	

Discussion Questions

Mc Graw Hill connect

1. Both antitrust policy and industrial regulation deal with monopoly. What distinguishes the two approaches? How does government decide to use one form of remedy rather than the other? **LO21.1, LO21.3**

2. Describe the major provisions of the Sherman and Clayton Acts. What government entities are responsible for enforcing those laws? Are firms permitted to initiate antitrust suits against other firms? **LO21.1**

3. Contrast the outcomes of the Standard Oil and U.S. Steel cases. What was the main antitrust issue in the DuPont cellophane case? In what major way do the Microsoft and Standard Oil cases differ? **LO21.2**

4. Why might one administration interpret and enforce the antitrust laws more strictly than another? How might a change of administrations affect a major monopoly case in progress? **LO21.2**

5. Suppose a proposed merger of firms will simultaneously lessen competition and reduce unit costs through economies of scale. Do you think such a merger should be allowed? Explain. **LO21.2**

6. In the 1980s, PepsiCo Inc., which then had 28 percent of the soft-drink market, proposed to acquire the Seven-Up Company. Shortly thereafter, the Coca-Cola Company, with 39 percent of the market, indicated it wanted to acquire the Dr Pepper Company. Seven-Up and Dr Pepper each controlled about 7 percent of the market. In your judgment, was the government's decision to block these mergers appropriate? Why or why not? **LO21.2**

7. Why might a firm charged with violating the Clayton Act, Section 7, try arguing that the products sold by the merged firms are in separate markets? Why might a firm charged with violating Section 2 of the Sherman Act try convincing the court that none of its behavior in achieving and maintaining its monopoly was illegal? **LO21.2**

8. "The social desirability of any particular firm should be judged not on the basis of its market share but on the basis of its conduct and performance." Make a counterargument, referring to the monopoly model. **LO21.2**

9. What types of industries, if any, should be subjected to industrial regulation? What specific problems does industrial regulation entail? **LO21.3**

10. In view of the problems involved in regulating natural monopolies, compare socially optimal (marginal-cost) pricing and fair-return pricing by referring again to Figure 11.8. Assuming that a government subsidy might cover any loss resulting from marginal-cost pricing, which pricing policy would you favor? Why? What problems might such a subsidy entail? **LO21.3**

11. How does social regulation differ from industrial regulation? What benefits and costs are associated with social regulation? **LO21.4**

12. Use economic analysis to explain why the optimal amount of product safety may be less than the amount that would totally eliminate the risk of accidents and deaths. Use automobiles as an example. **LO21.4**

13. **LAST WORD** On what basis were the airlines found guilty of violating antitrust laws in the Airline Tariff Publishing case? What was the remedy? By contrast, why might it be hard to prosecute algorithmic collusion, which also uses prices posted electronically?

Review Questions

Mc Graw Hill connect

1. True or False: Under the "rule of reason" established by the Supreme Court in the U.S. Steel case, a monopoly seller should be found guilty of violating antitrust laws even if it is charging low prices to consumers and acting the same way a competitive firm would act. **LO21.2**

2. How would you expect antitrust authorities to react to: **LO21.2**
   a. a proposed merger of Ford and General Motors.
   b. evidence of secret meetings by contractors to rig bids for highway construction projects.
   c. a proposed merger of a large shoe manufacturer and a chain of retail shoe stores.
   d. a proposed merger of a small life-insurance company and a regional candy manufacturer.
   e. an automobile rental firm that charges higher rates for last-minute rentals than for rentals reserved weeks in advance.

3. When confronted with a natural monopoly that restricts output and charges monopoly prices, the two methods that governments have for promoting better outcomes are: **LO21.3**
   a. public ownership and public regulation.
   b. sole proprietorships and public goods.
   c. antitrust law and horizontal mergers.
   d. creative destruction and laissez-faire.

4. True or False: Economists believe that social regulation is an exception to the MB = MC rule because social regulation should in every case extend as far as possible in order to ensure safe products, less pollution, and improved working conditions. **LO21.4**

Problems

1. Suppose that there are only three types of fruit sold in the United States. Annual sales are 1 million tons of blueberries, 5 million tons of strawberries, and 10 million tons of bananas. Suppose that of those total amounts, the Sunny Valley Fruit Company sells 900,000 tons of blueberries, 900,000 tons of strawberries, and 7.9 million tons of bananas. **LO21.2**
   a. What is Sunny Valley's market share in blueberries? If a court applies the 90-60-30 rule when considering just the blueberry market, would it rule that Sunny Valley is a monopoly?
   b. What is Sunny Valley's market share in all types of berries? Would the court rule Sunny Valley to be a monopolist in that market?
   c. What is Sunny Valley's market share in the market for all types of fruit, and would the court consider Sunny Valley to be a monopolist?

2. Carrot Computers and its competitors purchase touch screens for their tablet computers from several suppliers. The six makers of touch screens have market shares of, respectively, 19 percent, 18 percent, 14 percent, 16 percent, 20 percent, and 13 percent. **LO21.2**
   a. What is the Herfindahl index for the touch screen manufacturing industry?
   b. By how much would a proposed merger between the two smallest touch screen makers increase the Herfindahl index? Is the government likely to challenge that proposed merger?
   c. If Carrot Computers horizontally merges with its competitor Blueberry Handhelds, by how much would the Herfindahl index change for the touch screen industry?

CHAPTER

22

Agriculture: Economics and Policy

>> LEARNING OBJECTIVES

LO22.1 Explain why agricultural prices and farm income are unstable.

LO22.2 Discuss the huge employment exodus from agriculture.

LO22.3 Explain the rationale for farm subsidies and price supports.

LO22.4 Summarize criticism of the agricultural price-support system.

LO22.5 List the main elements of existing federal farm policy.

Agriculture is one of the largest industries in the United States. Major segments of agriculture provide real-world examples of pure competition, while also illustrating the effects of government policies that interfere with supply and demand.

This chapter examines the circumstances in the agriculture industry that have resulted in government intervention, the types and outcomes of government intervention, and recent major changes in farm policy. These policies affect the majority of the food you consume. So pay attention: If you eat, these policies affect *you*.

Economics of Agriculture

>> **LO22.1** Explain why agricultural prices and farm income are unstable.

farm commodities Agricultural products such as grains, milk, cattle, fruits, and vegetables that are usually sold to processors, who use the products as inputs in creating *food products*.

food products Processed *farm commodities* sold through grocery stores and restaurants. Examples: bread, meat, fish, chicken, pork, lettuce, peanut butter, and breakfast cereal.

Although economists refer to *the* agriculture industry, this segment of the economy is extremely diverse. Agriculture encompasses cattle ranches, fruit orchards, dairies, poultry plants, pig farms, feedlots, indoor hydroponic vegetable farms, and much more. Some farm commodities (for example, soybeans and corn) are produced by thousands of individual farmers. Other farm commodities (such as poultry) are produced by just a handful of large firms. Some farm products (for example, wheat, milk, and sugar) are heavily subsidized through federal government programs; other farm products (such as fruits, nuts, and potatoes) receive much less government support.

Moreover, agriculture includes both farm products, or **farm commodities** (for example, wheat, soybeans, cattle, and rice), and **food products** (items sold through restaurants or grocery stores). Generally, the number of competing firms in the market diminishes as farm products are refined into commercial food products. Although thousands of ranches and farms raise cattle, four firms (Tyson, JBS, Cargill, and Smithfield) account for about 80 percent of red meat produced at cattle slaughtering/meat packing plants. And thousands of farms grow tomatoes, but only three companies (Heinz, Del-Monte, and Hunt) make the bulk of the ketchup sold in the United States. In this chapter, we focus on farm commodities (or farm products) and the farms and ranches that produce them. Farm commodities usually are sold in highly competitive markets, whereas food products tend to be sold in markets characterized by monopolistic competition or oligopoly.

Partly because of large government subsidies, farming remains a generally profitable industry. U.S. consumers allocate about 9 percent of their spending to food, and farmers and ranchers receive about $400 billion of cash revenue annually from sales of crops and livestock. Over the years, however, U.S. farmers have experienced severely fluctuating prices and periodically low incomes. Further, they have had to adjust to the reality that agriculture is a declining industry. The farm share of GDP has declined from about 7 percent in 1950 to less than 1 percent today.

The Short Run: Price and Income Instability

Price and income instability in agriculture results from (1) an inelastic demand for agricultural products, (2) fluctuations in farm output, and (3) shifts of the demand curve for farm products.

Inelastic Demand for Agricultural Products In industrially advanced economies, the price elasticity of demand for agricultural products is low. For agricultural products in the aggregate, the elasticity coefficient is between 0.20 and 0.25, suggesting that the prices of farm products would have to fall by 40 to 50 percent for consumers to increase their purchases by a mere 10 percent. Consumers apparently put a low value on additional farm output compared with the value they put on additional units of alternative goods. Why?

Recall that the basic determinant of demand elasticity is substitutability. When the price of one product falls, consumers tend to substitute that product for other products whose prices have not fallen. But in relatively wealthy societies, this substitution effect is very modest for food. Although people may eat more, they do not switch from three meals a day to, say, five or six meals a day in response to a decline in the relative prices of farm products. Real biological factors constrain an individual's capacity to substitute food for other products.

The inelasticity of agricultural demand is also related to diminishing marginal utility. In a high-income economy, the population is generally well fed and well clothed; it is relatively saturated with the food and fiber of agriculture. Additional farm products therefore are subject to rapidly diminishing marginal utility. Thus, very large price cuts are needed to induce small increases in food and fiber consumption.

Fluctuations in Output Farm output tends to fluctuate from year to year, mainly because farmers have limited control over their output. Floods, droughts, unexpected frost, insect damage, and similar disasters can mean poor crops, while an excellent growing season means bumper crops (unusually large outputs). Such natural occurrences are beyond farmers' control, but they exert an important influence on output.

Curve D in Figure 22.1 illustrates the inelastic demand for agricultural products. Combining that inelastic demand with the instability of farm production, we can see why agricultural prices and incomes are unstable. Even if the market demand for farm products remains fixed at D, its price inelasticity will magnify small changes in output into relatively large changes in agricultural prices and income. For example, suppose that a "normal" crop of Q_n results in a "normal" price of P_n and a "normal" farm income represented by the yellow rectangle. A bumper crop or a poor crop will cause large deviations from these normal prices and incomes because of the inelasticity of demand at that output level.

If a good growing season occurs, the resulting large crop of Q_b will reduce farm income to that of area $0P_bbQ_b$. When demand is inelastic, an increase in the quantity sold is accompanied by a more-than-proportionate decline in price. Thus, total revenue (that is, total farm income) will decline disproportionately.

Similarly, a small crop caused by, say, drought will boost total farm income to that represented by area $0P_ppQ_p$. A decline in output will cause more-than-proportionate increases in price and income when demand is

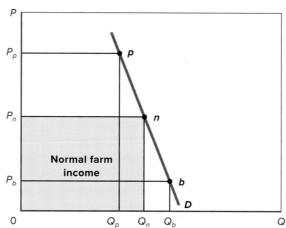

FIGURE 22.1
The effects of changes in farm output on agricultural prices and income.

Because of the inelasticity of demand for farm products, a relatively small change in farm output (from Q_n to Q_p or Q_b) will cause a relatively large change in agricultural prices (from P_n to P_p or P_b). Farm income will change from the yellow area to the larger $0P_ppQ_p$ area or to the smaller $0P_bbQ_b$ area.

FIGURE 22.2
The effect of a demand shift on agricultural prices and income.

Because of the highly inelastic demand for farm products, a small shift in demand (from D_1 to D_2) for farm products can drastically alter agricultural prices (P_1 to P_2) and farm income (area $0P_1aQ_n$ to area $0P_2bQ_n$), given a fixed level of production Q_n.

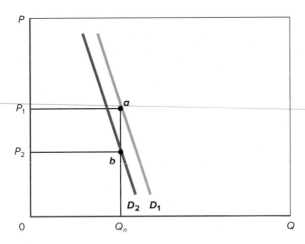

inelastic. Ironically, for farmers as a group, a poor crop may be a blessing and a bumper crop a hardship.

Conclusion: With a stable market demand for farm products, the inelasticity of demand turns relatively small changes in output into relatively larger changes in agricultural prices and income.

Fluctuations in Demand The third factor explaining the short-run instability of farm income results from shifts in the demand curve for agricultural products. Suppose that farm output is stabilized at the "normal" level of Q_n in Figure 22.2. Now, because of the inelasticity of the demand for farm products, short-run changes in the demand for those products will cause markedly different prices and incomes to be associated with this fixed level of output.

A slight decline in demand from D_1 to D_2 will reduce farm income from area $0P_1aQ_n$ to $0P_2bQ_n$. That analysis reveals that when demand is inelastic, a small decline in demand gives farmers significantly less income for the same amount of farm output. Conversely, a slight increase in demand—as from D_2 to D_1—provides a sizable increase in farm income for the same volume of output. Again, large price and income changes occur because demand is inelastic. The implication is that even moderately fluctuating demand will cause large changes in farm income.

But why is agricultural demand unstable? The major source of demand volatility in U.S. agriculture springs from its dependence on world markets. Indeed, about 35 percent of U.S. farm output is exported each year. But the prices that those exports command are highly unstable due to changes in weather and crop production in other countries. Better crops abroad mean less foreign demand for U.S. farm products. Similarly, cyclical fluctuations in incomes in Europe or Southeast Asia, for example, may shift the demand for U.S. farm products. Changes in foreign economic policies may also change demand. For instance, if the nations of western Europe decide to provide their farmers with greater protection from foreign competition, U.S. farmers will have less access to those markets, and demand for U.S. farm exports will fall.

International politics add to demand instability. Changing political relations between the United States and China, and between the United States and Russia, have boosted exports to those countries in some periods and reduced them in others. Changes in the international value of the dollar may also be critical. A lower value of the dollar increases the demand for U.S. farm products (which become cheaper to foreigners), whereas a higher value of the dollar diminishes foreign demand for U.S. farm products.

The Long Run: A Declining Industry

>> **LO22.2** Discuss the huge employment exodus from agriculture.

Two dynamic characteristics of agricultural markets explain "the farm problem," or why agriculture is a declining industry:

- Over time, the supply of farm products has increased rapidly because of technological progress.

- The demand for farm products has increased slowly because it is inelastic with respect to income and because it is largely limited by population growth, which has not been rapid in the United States.

Technology and Supply Increases

A rapid rate of technological advance has significantly increased the supply of agricultural products. This technological progress has many roots: the mechanization of farms, improved land-management techniques, soil conservation, irrigation, development of hybrid crops, availability of improved fertilizers and insecticides, polymer-coated seeds, and improvements in the breeding and care of livestock. The amount of capital used per farmworker increased by a factor of 15 between

1930 and 1980, permitting a fivefold increase in the amount of land cultivated per farmer. The simplest measure of these advances is the U.S. Agriculture Department's index of farm output per unit of farm labor. In 1950 a single unit of farm labor could produce 10 units of farm output. This amount increased to 30 in 1970, 42 in 1980, 64 in 1990, 84 in 2000, 106 in 2010, and 118 in 2017 (the most recent year for which data is available). Over the last half-century, productivity in agriculture has advanced twice as fast as productivity in the nonfarm economy.

Most of the technological advances in agriculture are not initiated by farmers. Rather, they are the result of government-sponsored programs of research and education and the initiative of the suppliers of farm inputs. Land-grant colleges, experiment stations, county agents of the Agricultural Extension Service, educational pamphlets issued by the U.S. Department of Agriculture (USDA), and the research departments of farm machinery, pesticide, and fertilizer producers have been the primary sources of technological advance in U.S. agriculture.

Recently, technological advance has been fueled by the incorporation of advanced information technologies into farming. Drones and in-ground sensors give farmers instant access to information about soil conditions and estimated crop yields. The Internet provides farm-product prices, available land for purchase or lease, and much more. Also, farmers now have sophisticated business software to help track and manage their operations.

Lagging Demand

Increases in the demand for agricultural products have failed to keep pace with increases in supply. The reason lies in the two major determinants of agricultural demand: income and population.

In developing countries, consumers must devote most of their meager incomes to agricultural products—food and clothing—to sustain themselves. But as income expands beyond the subsistence level and the problem of hunger diminishes, consumers increase their outlays on food at ever-declining rates. Once consumers' stomachs are filled, they turn to the amenities of life that manufacturing and services, not agriculture, provide. Economic growth in the United States has boosted average per capita income far beyond the subsistence level. As a result, increases in the incomes of U.S. consumers now produce less-than-proportionate increases in spending on farm products. Estimates indicate that a 10 percent increase in real per capita after-tax income produces about a 1 percent increase in consumption of farm products. That means a coefficient of income elasticity of 0.1 ($= 0.01/0.10$). So as the incomes of Americans rise, the demand for farm products increases far less rapidly than the demand for goods and services in general.

The second reason for lagging demand relates to population growth. Once a certain income level is reached, a consumer's intake of food and fiber becomes relatively fixed. Thus, subsequent increases in demand depend directly on growth in the number of consumers. In most advanced nations, including the United States, the demand for farm products increases at a rate roughly equal to the rate of population growth. Because U.S. population growth has not been rapid, the increase in U.S. demand for farm products has not kept pace with the rapid growth of farm output.

Graphical Portrayal

The combination of an inelastic and slowly increasing demand for agricultural products with a rapidly increasing supply puts strong downward pressure on agricultural prices and income. Figure 22.3 shows a large increase in agricultural supply accompanied by a very modest increase in demand. Because of the inelasticity of demand, those shifts result in a sharp decline in agricultural prices, accompanied by a relatively small increase in output. As a result, farm income declines. On the graph, we see that farm income before the increases in demand and supply (measured by the rectangle $0P_1aQ_1$)

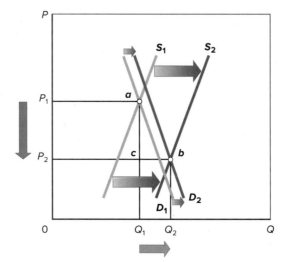

FIGURE 22.3
The long-run decline of agricultural prices and farm income.

In the long run, increases in the demand for U.S. farm products (from D_1 to D_2) have not kept pace with the increases in supply (from S_1 to S_2) resulting from technological advances. Because agricultural demand is inelastic, these shifts have tended to depress agricultural prices (from P_1 to P_2) and reduce farm income (from $0P_1aQ_1$ to $0P_2bQ_2$) while increasing output only modestly (from Q_1 to Q_2).

TABLE 22.1
U.S. Farm Employment and
Number of Farms, 1950–2020

	Farm Employment*		Number of Farms, Thousands
Year	In Millions of People	As Percentage of Total Employment	
1950	9.3	15.8	5,388
1960	6.2	9.4	3,962
1970	4.0	5.0	2,954
1980	3.5	3.5	2,440
1990	2.5	2.1	2,146
2000	2.2	1.6	2,172
2010	2.2	1.2	2,200
2020	2.6	1.4	2,020

*Includes self-employed farmers, unpaid farmworkers, and hired farmworkers.

Source: U.S. Department of Agriculture.

exceeds farm income after those increases ($0P_2bQ_2$). Because farm products have inelastic demand, an increase in supply relative to demand creates persistent downward pressure on farm income.

Consequences

The real-world consequences of the demand and supply changes over time are those predicted by the pure-competition model. Supply and demand conditions have increased the minimum efficient scale (MES) in agriculture and reduced crop prices. Farms that are too small to realize productivity gains and take advantage of economies of scale have discovered that their average total costs exceed the (declining) prices for their crops. Thus they can no longer operate profitably. In the long run, financial losses in agriculture have triggered a massive exit of workers to other sectors of the economy, as Table 22.1 shows. They have also caused a major consolidation of smaller farms into larger ones. A person farming, say, 240 acres of corn three decades ago is today likely to be farming two or three times that number of acres. Large corporate firms, collectively called **agribusiness,** have emerged in some areas of farming such as potatoes, beef, fruits, vegetables, and poultry. Today, there are 2 million farms in the United States compared to about 4 million in 1960, and farm labor constitutes about 1.4 percent of the U.S. labor force compared to 9.4 percent in 1960.

agribusiness The portion of the agricultural and food product industries that is dominated by large corporations.

Global Perspective 22.1 compares how the percentage of the labor force that is engaged in agriculture varies across countries. The percentage is highest in developing countries, reflecting the fact that their less technologically advanced economies do not yet provide sufficient numbers

---

GLOBAL PERSPECTIVE 22.1

AVERAGE PERCENTAGE OF LABOR FORCE IN AGRICULTURE, SELECTED NATIONS

High-income nations devote a much smaller percentage of their labor forces to agriculture than do low-income nations. Because their workforces are so heavily committed to producing the food and fiber needed for their populations, low-income nations have relatively less labor available to produce housing, schools, autos, and the other goods and services that contribute to a high standard of living.

Source: The World Bank Group.

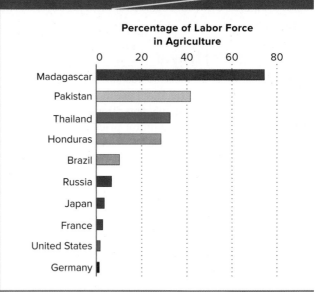

Percentage of Labor Force in Agriculture

of manufacturing and service jobs to allow the large majority of their citizens to move away from farm employment. But the trend everywhere is toward reduced agricultural employment and increased urbanization. In 2007, for the first time in world history, most people lived in urban areas rather than rural areas. The percentage of urban dwellers rose to 56 percent worldwide in 2020, and by the year 2050 it is expected that about 70 percent of the world's population will live in cities and towns. As the urban-dwelling percentage continues to rise, the share of labor employed in agriculture will continue to shrink.

Farm-Household Income

Traditionally, the income of farm households was well below that of nonfarm households. But that imbalance reversed in the early 1990s. In 2017, farm-household incomes averaged $113,495, or about 27 percent higher than the $89,632 received on average by all U.S. households. Outmigration, consolidation, rising farm productivity, and significant government subsidies have boosted farm income *per farm household*.

It needs to be noted, however, that the members of farm households that operate smaller farms have increasingly taken jobs in nearby towns and cities. On average, only about 20 percent of the income earned by farm households derives from farming activities. That average is, however, pulled down by the many rural households that operate small "residential farms." For households operating "commercial farms"—that is, farms that have annual sales of $350,000 or more—about 74 percent of their average income of $225,264 in 2017 was derived from farming. Although agriculture is a declining industry, the 10 percent of farm households operating commercial farms in the United States are doing remarkably well, at least as a group.

It is also useful to understand how concentrated agricultural production is across U.S. farms. Slightly more than half of U.S. farms sell less than $10,000 per year in agricultural products while only about 12 percent sell more than $250,000 per year. That high concentration is why such a large fraction of the average farm household's income derives from jobs in nearby towns and cities. Farming is just a sideline for most of the households that engage in agriculture.

▶ Agricultural prices and incomes are volatile in the short run because an inelastic demand converts small changes in farm output and demand into relatively large changes in prices and income.

▶ Technological progress has generated large increases in the supply of farm products over time.

▶ Increases in demand for farm products have been modest in the United States because demand is inelastic with respect to income and because population growth has been modest.

▶ The combination of large increases in supply and small increases in demand has made U.S. agriculture a declining industry (as measured by the value of agricultural output as a percentage of GDP).

Economics of Farm Policy

The federal government has subsidized agriculture since the 1930s with a "farm program" that includes (1) support for agricultural prices, income, and output; (2) soil and water conservation; (3) agricultural research; (4) farm credit; (5) crop insurance; and (6) subsidized sale of farm products in world markets. Between 2010 and 2018, American farmers received an average of about $16 billion of government subsidies each year.

>> **LO22.3** Explain the rationale for farm subsidies and price supports.

We will focus on the farm program's main elements: government policies designed to prop up prices and income.

Rationale for Farm Subsidies

Several arguments have been made to justify farm subsidies over the decades:

• Although farm products are necessities of life, many farmers have relatively low incomes, so the government should help them receive higher prices and incomes.

• The "family farm" is a fundamental U.S. institution and should be nurtured as a way of life.

• Farmers are subject to extraordinary hazards—floods, droughts, and insects—that most other industries do not face. Without government help, farmers cannot fully insure themselves against these disasters.

• Although many farmers face purely competitive markets for their outputs, they buy inputs of fertilizer, farm machinery, and gasoline from industries that have considerable market power. Whereas those resource-supplying industries are able to control their prices, farmers are at the mercy of the market in selling their output. Agriculture therefore warrants public aid to offset the disadvantageous market-power imbalances.

Background: The Parity Concept

parity concept The idea that year after year the sale of a specific output of a farm product should enable a farmer to purchase a constant amount of nonagricultural *goods* and *services*.

The Agricultural Adjustment Act of 1933 established the **parity concept** as a cornerstone of agricultural policy. Parity says that, year after year, for a fixed output of farm products, a farmer should be able to acquire a specific total amount of other goods and services. A particular real output should always result in the same real income: "If a farmer could take a bushel of corn to town in 1912 and sell it for enough money to buy a shirt, he should be able to sell a bushel of corn today and buy a shirt." In nominal terms, the parity concept suggests that the relationship between the prices received by farmers for their output and the prices they must pay for goods and services should remain constant. Thus, if the price of shirts tripled over some time period, then the price of corn should have tripled too. Such a situation is said to represent 100 percent of parity.

parity ratio The ratio of the *price* received by farmers from the sale of an agricultural commodity to the prices of other goods paid by them; usually expressed as a percentage; used as a rationale for *price supports*.

The **parity ratio** is the ratio of prices received to prices paid, expressed as a percentage:

$$\text{Parity ratio} = \frac{\text{Prices received by farmers}}{\text{Prices paid by farmers}}$$

Why farmers benefit from having 100 percent of parity is obvious. By 2018 nominal prices paid by farmers had increased about 30-fold since 1910–1914, whereas nominal prices received by farmers had increased only about 10-fold. In 2018 the parity ratio stood at 0.33 (or 33 percent), indicating that prices received in 2018 could buy only 33 percent of prices received in the 1910–1914 period. So a farm policy that enforced 100 percent of parity would generate substantially higher prices for farmers.

Economics of Price Supports

price supports The term used to refer to *price floors* applied to *farm commodities*; the minimum *price* that the government allows farmers to receive for farm commodities like wheat or corn.

The concept of parity provides the rationale for government *price floors* on farm products. In agriculture, those minimum prices are called **price supports**. We have shown that, in the long run, the market prices received by farmers have not kept up with the prices paid by them. One way to achieve parity, or some percentage thereof, is to have the government establish above-equilibrium price supports for farm products. This policy was the primary element of the farm program from its inception in the 1930s until major reforms in the mid-1990s.

Many different price-support programs have been tried, but they have all tended to have similar effects, some of which are subtle and negative. Suppose in Figure 22.4 that the equilibrium price is P_e and the price support is P_s. The major effects are as follows.

FIGURE 22.4
Price supports, agricultural surpluses, and transfers to farmers.

The market demand *D* and supply *S* of a farm product yield equilibrium price P_e and quantity Q_e. An above-equilibrium price support P_s results in consumption of quantity Q_c, production of quantity Q_s, and a surplus of quantity $Q_s - Q_c$. The yellow rectangle represents a transfer of money from taxpayers to farmers. Triangle *bac* within the yellow rectangle shows the efficiency loss (or a deadweight loss) to society.

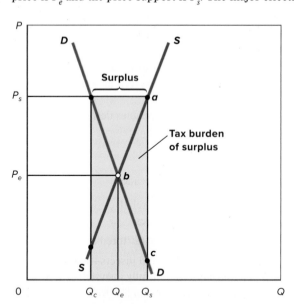

Surplus Output The most obvious result is a product surplus. Consumers are willing to purchase only Q_c units at the supported price, while farmers supply Q_s units. What happens to the $Q_s - Q_c$ surplus that results? The government must buy it to make the above-equilibrium price support effective.

Gain to Farmers Farmers benefit from price supports. In Figure 22.4, gross farm revenue rises from the free-market level represented by area $0P_ebQ_e$ to the larger, supported level shown by area $0P_saQ_s$.

Loss to Consumers Consumers lose; they pay a higher price (P_s rather than P_e) and consume less (Q_c rather than Q_e) of the product. In some instances, differences between the market price and the supported price are substantial. For example, the U.S.-supported price of a pound of sugar is about 60 percent higher than the world market price, and a quart of fluid milk costs consumers about twice as much as it would without government programs. Moreover, the burden of higher food prices falls disproportionately on the poor because they spend a larger part of their incomes on food.

Efficiency Losses Society loses because price supports create allocative inefficiency by encouraging an overallocation of resources to agriculture. A price floor (P_s) attracts more resources to the agricultural sector than would the free-market price (P_e). Viewed through the pure-competition model, the market supply curve in Figure 22.4 represents the marginal costs of all farmers producing this product at the various output levels. An efficient allocation of resources occurs at point b, where the market price P_e is equal to marginal cost. The output Q_e reflects that efficient allocation of resources.

In contrast, the output Q_s associated with the price support P_s represents an overallocation of resources. For all units of output between Q_e and Q_s, marginal cost (measured on curve S) exceeds the price people are willing to pay for those units (measured on curve D). Thus, for those units, marginal cost exceeds marginal benefit, implying an efficiency loss (or a deadweight loss) of area bac.

Other Social Losses Society loses in other ways. Taxpayers pay higher taxes to finance the government's purchase of the surplus. This added tax burden is equal to the surplus output $Q_s - Q_c$ multiplied by its price P_s, as shown by the yellow area in Figure 22.4. In addition, the mere collection of taxes imposes an efficiency loss, and the cost of storing surplus farm output adds to this tax burden.

Government's intervention in agriculture also entails administrative costs. Thousands of government workers are needed to administer U.S. price supports and other farm programs.

Finally, the *rent-seeking behavior* involved—the pursuit of political support to maintain price supports—is costly and socially wasteful. Farm groups spend considerable sums to sustain political support for price floors and other income-enhancement programs.

Environmental Costs Price supports encourage additional production. Although some of that extra output may come from the use of additional land, much of it comes from heavier use of fertilizer and pesticides that may pollute the environment. Research shows a positive relationship between the level of price-support subsidies and the use of agrochemicals.

Farm policy also may cause environmental problems in less obvious ways. Farmers benefit from price supports only when they use their land consistently for a specific crop such as corn or wheat. They therefore have a disincentive to practice crop rotation, which is a nonchemical technique for controlling pests. Farm policy thus encourages the substitution of chemicals for other forms of pest control.

In addition, price supports for farm products increase the demand for land. The land that farmers bring into farm production is often environmentally sensitive "marginal" land, such as steeply sloped, erosion-prone land or wetlands that provide wildlife habitat. Similarly, price supports result in the use of more water for irrigation, and the resulting runoff may contribute to soil erosion.

International Costs In reality, the costs of farm price supports go beyond those indicated by Figure 22.4. Price supports generate economic distortions that cross national boundaries. For example, the high prices caused by price supports make the U.S. agricultural market attractive to foreign producers. But inflows of foreign agricultural products would increase supplies in the United States, aggravating the problem of U.S. surpluses. To prevent that from happening, the United States is likely to impose import barriers in the form of tariffs or quotas. Those barriers tend to restrict the output of more-efficient foreign producers while encouraging more output from less-efficient U.S. producers. The result is a less-efficient use of world agricultural resources.

Similarly, as the United States and other industrially advanced countries with similar agricultural programs dump surplus farm products on world markets, the prices of such products decrease. Developing countries are often heavily dependent on world commodity markets for their incomes. So they are particularly hurt when their export earnings are reduced. So, for example, U.S. subsidies for rice production have imposed significant costs on Thailand, a major rice exporter. Similarly, U.S. cotton programs have adversely affected Egypt and Mexico.

Reduction of Surpluses

Figure 22.4 suggests that programs designed to reduce market supply (shift S leftward) or increase market demand (shift D rightward) would help boost the market price toward the supported price P_s. Further, such programs would reduce or eliminate farm surpluses. The U.S. government has tried both supply and demand approaches to reduce or eliminate surpluses.

acreage allotments A pre-1996 government program that limited the total number of acres to be used in producing (reduced amounts of) various food and fiber products and allocated these acres among individual farmers. These farmers had to limit their plantings to the allotted number of acres to obtain *price supports* for their crops.

Restricting Supply Until recently, public policy focused mainly on restricting farm output. In particular, **acreage allotments** accompanied price supports. In return for guaranteed prices for their crops, farmers agreed to limit the number of acres they planted in that crop. The U.S. Department of Agriculture first set the price support and then estimated the amount of the product consumers would buy at the supported price. It then translated that amount into the total number of planted acres necessary to provide it. The total acreage was apportioned among states, counties, and ultimately individual farmers.

These supply-restricting programs were only partially successful. They did not eliminate surpluses, mainly because acreage reduction did not result in a proportionate decline in production. Some farmers retired their worst land and kept their best land in production. They also cultivated their tilled acres more intensively. Superior seed, more and better fertilizer and insecticides, and improved farm equipment enhanced output per acre. And nonparticipating farmers expanded their planted acreage in anticipation of overall higher prices. Nevertheless, the net effect of acreage allotment undoubtedly was a reduction of farm surpluses and their associated costs to taxpayers.

Bolstering Demand Government has tried several ways to increase the demand for U.S. agricultural products. For example, both government and private industry have spent large sums on research to create new uses for agricultural goods. The production of "gasohol," which is a blend of gasoline and alcohol (ethanol) made mainly from corn, is one such successful attempt to increase the demand for farm output. (See the Consider This story for a fuller discussion of ethanol.)

Recent attempts to promote "biodiesel," a fuel made from soybean oil and other natural vegetable oils, also fit the demand-enhancement approach.

In a similar vein, the federal government has created a variety of programs to stimulate the consumption of various farm products. For example, the objective of the food-stamp program (whose official name is Supplemental Nutrition Assistance Program, or SNAP) is not only to reduce hunger but also to bolster the demand for food. Similarly, the Food for Peace program has enabled developing countries to buy U.S. surplus farm products with their own currencies rather than U.S. dollars.

CONSIDER THIS . . .

Putting Corn in Your Gas Tank

The U.S. federal government's promotion of greater production and use of corn-based ethanol serves both as a good example of an attempt by government to bolster the demand for U.S. farm products and as an example of how price changes can ripple through the economy and produce myriad secondary effects. Gasoline producers blend ethanol (an alcohol-like substance) with conventional gasoline refined from oil. The government's rationale for promoting ethanol is to reduce U.S. dependency on foreign oil, but the strongest proponents are from states in the Corn Belt.

The ethanol program has several facets, including tariffs on imported ethanol, subsidies to oil refineries that buy domestically produced ethanol, and mandates to industry to increase its use of alternative fuels. The rising demand for ethanol that resulted contributed to tripling of the inflation-adjusted price of a bushel of corn between 2005 and 2012.

But numerous secondary effects from the increased price of corn also occurred. Farmers shifted production

Fluxfoto/E+/Getty Images

toward corn and away from soybeans, sorghum, and other crops. The decreases in the supply of these other crops raised their prices, too. Also, because corn is used as a major feedstock, the prices of beef, pork, and chicken rose.

The ethanol subsidies had other secondary effects. The prices of seed, fertilizer, and farmland all increased. Because corn is a water-intensive crop, its expanded production resulted in faster withdrawals of irrigation water from underground aquifers. The refining of ethanol also depleted ground water or removed it from rivers. Moreover, the increased use of fertilizer in corn production increased the runoff of nitrogen from fertilizer into streams and rivers, causing environmental damage.

The price effects of ethanol subsidies, however, may moderate as farmers shift additional land to corn, increasing its supply and reducing its price. Nevertheless, the multiple impacts of public policy illustrate an important economic maxim: In the economy, it is difficult to do just *one* thing.

The federal government spends millions of dollars each year to advertise and promote global sales of U.S. farm products. Furthermore, U.S. negotiators have pressed hard in international trade negotiations to persuade foreign nations to reduce trade barriers to the importing of farm products.

Net Effect of Supply Restrictions and Demand Enhancements During the era of price supports that lasted from the 1930s through the 1990s, the government's supply-restricting and demand-increasing efforts boosted agricultural prices and reduced surplus production, but they did not eliminate the sizable surpluses. This suggested that major reforms might be useful.

The major reforms arrived in the mid-1990s. They were made possible because the political climate in the United States had changed with respect to agriculture. Among other things, the population of farming regions relative to cities had declined precipitously, so that farming regions had substantially less political power in the 1990s than in the 1930s. Today, urban congressional representatives constitute a 10-to-1 majority over their rural colleagues. The United States also had an increasingly difficult time defending its domestic farm-subsidy programs while simultaneously attempting to lead a decades-long push for international free trade. To lessen the charges of hypocrisy, reform was needed.

QUICK REVIEW
22.2

▶ The parity concept suggests that farmers should obtain a constant ratio of the prices they receive for their farm products and the prices they pay for goods and services in general.

▶ Price supports are government-imposed price floors (minimum prices) on selected farm products.

▶ Price supports cause surplus production (which the government must buy and store, or otherwise

dispose of), raise farm income, increase food prices to consumers, and overallocate resources to agriculture.

▶ Domestic price supports encourage nations to erect trade barriers against imported farm products and to dump surplus farm products on world markets.

Criticisms and Politics

It became apparent by the 1990s that price-support programs were not working well, and major criticisms of farm subsidies emerged.

>> **LO22.4** Summarize criticism of the agricultural price-support system.

Criticisms of the Parity Concept

Economists uniformly rejected the parity concept. They found no economic logic in the proposition that if a bushel of wheat could buy a shirt in 1900, it should still be able to buy a shirt a century later. The relative values of goods and services are established by supply and demand, and those relative values change over time as technology changes, resource prices change, tastes change, and substitute resources and new products emerge. A fully equipped personal computer, monitor, and printer cost as much as a cheap new automobile in 1985. That was not true just a decade later because the price of computer equipment had dropped so dramatically. Based on the parity concept, one could argue that price supports and subsidies were justified for computer manufacturers!

Criticisms of the Price-Support System

Criticisms of the price-support system were equally severe.

Symptoms, Not Causes The price-support strategy in agriculture treated the symptoms, not the causes, of the farm problem. The root cause of the long-run farm problem was misallocation of resources between agriculture and the rest of the economy. Historically, the problem had been one of too many farmers. But the price and income supports encouraged people to stay in farming rather than move to nonfarm occupations. That is, the price-support program slowed the reallocation of resources necessary to resolve the long-run farm problem.

Misguided Subsidies Because price supports were on a per-bushel basis, subsidies benefited the farmers who needed them the least. If the goal of farm policy was to raise low farm incomes, it followed that any federal program should have been aimed at farmers with the lowest incomes. But the poor, low-output farmer did not produce and sell enough in the market to get much aid from price supports. Instead, the large, prosperous farmer reaped the benefits because of sizable output.

A related point concerns land values. By making crops more valuable, price supports made the land itself more valuable. That was helpful to farmers who owned the land they farmed but not to farmers who rented land. Farmers rented about 40 percent of their farmland, mostly from well-to-do nonfarm landlords. Thus, price supports became a subsidy to people who were not actively engaged in farming.

Policy Contradictions Farm policy often led to contradictions. Whereas government-funded agricultural research was aimed at increasing farm productivity and the supply of farm products, acreage-allotment programs required farmers to take land out of production in order to reduce supply. Price supports for crops meant increased feed costs for ranchers and farmers and high consumer prices for animal products. Tobacco farmers were subsidized even though tobacco consumption was causing serious health problems. The U.S. sugar program raised prices for domestic producers by imposing import quotas that conflicted with free-trade policies. Conservation programs called for setting aside land for wildlife habitat, while price supports provided incentives to bring such acreage into production.

All these criticisms helped spawn policy reform. Nevertheless, nearly all these criticisms are as valid for current farm policy as they were for the price-support program.

Recent Farm Policies

>> **LO22.5** List the main elements of existing federal farm policy.

By the mid-1990s, there was a common feeling among economists and political leaders that the goals and techniques of farm policy needed to be reexamined and revised. Moreover, crop prices were relatively high at the time, and Congress wanted to reduce large federal budget deficits.

Freedom to Farm Act of 1996

Freedom to Farm Act A law passed in 1996 that revamped 60 years of U.S. farm policy by ending *price supports* and *acreage allotments* for wheat, corn, barley, oats, sorghum, rye, cotton, and rice.

In 1996, Congress radically revamped 60 years of U.S. farm policy by passing the **Freedom to Farm Act.** The law ended price supports and acreage allotments for wheat, corn, barley, oats, sorghum, rye, cotton, and rice. Farmers were allowed to respond to changing crop prices by planting as much or as little of these crops as they chose. Also, they were free to plant crops of their choice. If the price of oats increased, farmers could plant more oats and less barley. Markets, not government programs, were to determine the kinds and amounts of crops grown.

To ease the transition away from price supports, the Freedom to Farm Act granted declining annual "transition payments" through 2002. Based on the production levels that had previously been imposed on farmers under the price-support system, $37 billion of transition payments were scheduled through 2002.

This ambitious plan to wean American agriculture from subsidies unraveled in 1998 and 1999, when sharply reduced export demand and strong crop production in the United States depressed the prices of many farm products. Congress responded by supplementing the previously scheduled transition payments with large "emergency aid" payments to farmers. Agricultural subsidies for 1999–2002 averaged $20 billion annually—a higher subsidy than before the passage of the Freedom to Farm Act.

The Food, Conservation, and Energy Act of 2008

direct payments Cash subsidies paid to farmers based on past production levels; a permanent transfer payment unaffected by current crop *prices* and current production.

Since 2002, U.S. agricultural policy has substantially retreated from the free-market intent of the Freedom to Farm Act of 1996. The three subsidy programs introduced by the Food, Conservation, and Energy Act of 2008 continued the "freedom to plant" approach and provided revenue guarantees for farmers. But one of them transformed what were supposed to be temporary "transition payments" into "direct payments" that farmers could obtain year after year, without any time limit. These revenue guarantees kicked in automatically whenever crop prices (or total revenues) fell below target levels.

countercyclical payments (CCPs) Cash *subsidies* paid to farmers when market *prices* for certain crops drop below targeted prices. Payments are based on previous production and are received regardless of the current crop grown.

Direct Payments The **direct payments** under the 2008 law were fixed for each crop based on a farmer's *historical* pattern of production. They were unaffected by current crop prices or current production, so that farmers who had planted a particular crop five years ago might receive direct payments for that particular crop today even if they no longer grew that crop. In addition, these direct payments did not decline from year to year. They were a permanent transfer payment from the federal government (general taxpayers) to farmers. The payments ranged from 2.4 cents per bushel of oats up to 54 cents per bushel of wheat.

Countercyclical Payments This component of 2008 farm policy tied a separate set of subsidies to the difference between the market prices of specified farm products and a target price set for each crop. Like direct payments, these **countercyclical payments (CCPs)** were based on previous crops grown, and farmers received them regardless of the current crop planted. For example, the target price for corn in the years 2008–2012 was $2.63 per bushel. If the price of corn stayed at or above $2.63, farmers would receive no CCP. But if the price fell below $2.63, the farmer who had previously grown corn would receive a CCP payment to close the price gap even if they currently grew no corn. The CCP system returned price supports to a prominent role in farm policy, but it based those supports on past crops grown, not current crops planted.

Marketing Loans The 2008 law contained a **marketing loan program** under which farmers could receive a loan (on a per-unit-of-output basis) from a government lender. If the crop price at harvest was higher than the price specified in the loan (the loan price), a farmer had to repay the loan, with interest. If the crop price was lower than the loan price, a farmer could forfeit the harvested crop to the lender and be free of the loan. In this second case, the farmer received what amounted to a subsidy because the value of the loan that was paid back by forfeiting the harvested crop exceeded the revenue from the sale of that crop in the market.

The Agricultural Act of 2014

The **Agricultural Act of 2014** ended direct payments and countercyclical payments because it was politically difficult to justify paying farmers for crops they didn't grow.

The 2014 Act also established the dairy margin protection program, which makes payments if the price of milk falls too low or the cost of feed rises too high. The idea is to shield dairy producers' per-unit margin (= revenue per unit minus cost per unit).

The marketing loan program was continued as a way for farmers to reduce the risk of price and revenue variability. To help farmers further reduce risk, the Act created two new **crop insurance** programs:

- Under **price loss coverage,** farmers who pay the insurance premium are guaranteed an insurance payment if the price of their crop falls below a specified value, such as $3.50 per bushel of wheat.

- By contrast, **agricultural risk coverage** depends on the total revenue generated by all of the farmers in a given county who plant the same crop in a given year. The program makes insurance payments to participating farmers if the total revenue collectively received by all the farmers planting the crop in the county falls below a specific value, such as $150 million for corn producers in Kossuth County, Iowa.

Under the 2014 Act, farmers interested in these new crop insurance programs had to make a one-time decision (binding for the rest of their lives) about which program they wanted to use.

The Agricultural Act of 2018

The **Agricultural Act of 2018** made some minor changes to the 2014 Act. Price loss coverage and agricultural risk coverage, in particular, were continued with the only novelty being that farmers could now select which program they wanted to use each year. The dairy margin protection program also persisted as did various land conservation programs, including the Conservation Reserve Program discussed in this chapter's Last Word.

marketing loan program A federal farm subsidy under which certain farmers can receive a loan (on a per-unit-of-output basis) to plant a crop and then, depending on the harvest *price* of the crop, either pay back the loan with interest or keep the loan proceeds while forfeiting their harvested crop to the lender.

The Agricultural Act of 2014 The agricultural law enacted in the United States in 2014 that eliminated *direct payments* and *countercyclical payments* in favor of two types of *crop insurance—price loss coverage* and *agricultural risk coverage.*

crop insurance Insurance that farmers can purchase that will pay out if crop selling prices or crop revenues fall below predetermined values.

price loss coverage A form of crop insurance that pays participating farmers if the market price of their output falls below a predetermined value.

agricultural risk coverage A form of crop insurance that pays out if the total revenue generated by all the farmers planting a given crop in a given county falls below a predetermined value.

Agricultural Act of 2018 The 2018 act that made minor changes to programs and policies of the Agricultural Act of 2014.

Seeing the Forest for the Subsidies

Struggling to Eliminate a Glut of Farm Products, the Government Created a Glut of Lumber.

The federal government began heavily intervening in agriculture during the 1930s in an attempt to bolster farm incomes. Price supports were common, and they generated surplus output—gluts—of many farm products.

A surplus, of course, is a situation where the quantity supplied exceeds the quantity demanded at the current price. There are two ways to eliminate a surplus without affecting the price. One way is to increase demand. The other is to decrease supply. Starting with the Farm Bill of 1985, Congress enacted a new program designed to reduce the supply of farm products by converting farmland into forestland. As a bonus, the program was also expected to improve soil conservation by reducing agricultural runoff.

The program was called the Conservation Reserve Program. When the program started in 1986, it paid farmers $30 to $50 per acre for up to 15 years for farmland that was converted into forests by planting seedlings. This subsidy prompted farmers across the country to get into commercial forestry. They planted seedlings that when full-grown would be felled for lumber, electrical poles, and paper pulp.

In a broad sense, participants were still farming. But instead of planting annual crops like corn and wheat, they were now planting a crop that would take about 30 years to reach full maturity and become harvestable wood. In the meantime, they could pocket many years of subsidy payments. Between the subsidies and what they expected to receive for the wood, farmers anticipated that they would do quite well financially.

Unfortunately, the program worked too well. Since the program's inception, over 22 million acres (nearly as much territory as is occupied by the state of Indiana!) have been converted to commercial forestry as a result of the Conservation Reserve Program and other similar federal programs. The result has been a huge decline in the price of wood as a mountain of mature trees began to come onto the market in the mid-2010s. By 2018, the price of saw timber (the quality of wood that can be used for making lumber) had fallen to a 50-year low. The demand for wood was up—but the supply was *way* up. The result was plummeting prices for nearly every type of wood. The value of pine trees "on the stump," for example, fell from $45 per ton in 1987 to just $14 per ton in 2019.

The Conservation Reserve Program has handed out over $49.7 billion since its inception in 1986 and currently pays farmers $82 per acre for any farmland they convert to forestry. The glut of trees and the associated collapse in the price of wood has, however, defeated the original purpose of the program—which was to help bolster farm

1Apix/Alamy Stock Photo

incomes. Except for a temporary spike in prices caused by the COVID-19 pandemic, the prices of lumber, telephone poles, and pulp have fallen so low that, in retrospect, the farmers who converted farmland into woodland would probably have made more money continuing to farm agricultural crops than they are going to make harvesting the trees that they were subsidized into producing.

The Department of Agriculture has attempted to scale back the program by reducing the annual payments to a level where a property owner would be indifferent financially between planting trees to be harvested in 30 years or leasing acreage to farmers who want to produce annual crops like corn and wheat. But these lower subsidy payments also defeat the original purpose of the program, which was to raise farm incomes. If rural property owners can make just as much money renting to farmers as they can converting farmland into woodland, their incomes are not being improved by the program.

This may make you ask why such an expensive program can persist if its intended recipients are not being helped. The answer is that other industries besides farming benefit greatly from the program. Sawmills get cheap logs. Electrical utilities get cheap electrical poles. The construction industry gets cheap lumber. And paper mills get cheap pulp. Those industries lobby hard in Washington, D.C., for the continuation of the program, which looks set to endure indefinitely thanks to their efforts.

Summary

LO22.1 Explain why agricultural prices and farm income are unstable.

In the short run, the highly inelastic demand for farm products transforms small changes in output and small shifts in demand into large changes in prices and income.

LO22.2 Discuss the huge employment exodus from agriculture.

Over the long run, technological advance, together with a highly inelastic and relatively slow-growing demand for agricultural output, has made agriculture a declining industry in the United States and dictated that resources exit the industry.

LO22.3 Explain the rationale for farm subsidies and price supports.

Historically, farm policy has been based on the parity concept, which suggests that the relationship between prices received and paid by farmers should be constant over time.

The use of price floors or price supports has a number of economic effects: It (*a*) causes surplus production, (*b*) increases farmers' incomes, (*c*) causes higher consumer prices for farm products, (*d*) creates an overallocation of resources to agriculture, (*e*) obliges society to pay higher taxes to finance the purchase and storage of surplus output, (*f*) increases pollution because of the greater use of agrochemicals and vulnerable land, and (*g*) forces other nations to bear the costs associated with import barriers and depressed world agricultural prices.

With only limited success, the federal government has pursued programs to reduce agricultural supply and increase agricultural demand as a way to reduce the surpluses associated with price supports.

LO22.4 Summarize criticism of the agricultural price-support system.

Economists have criticized U.S. farm policy for (*a*) confusing symptoms (low farm incomes) with causes (excess capacity), (*b*) providing the largest subsidies to high-income farmers, and (*c*) creating contradictions among specific farm programs.

LO22.5 List the main elements of existing federal farm policy.

Based on free-market principles, the Freedom to Farm Act of 1996 ended price supports and acreage allotments for wheat, corn, barley, oats, sorghum, rye, cotton, and rice. To replace them, the law enacted declining annual transition payments through the year 2002, with those transition payments not being tied to crop prices or to the specific crop that a farmer was currently producing.

Beginning in 2002, the federal government retreated from the free-market principles of the Freedom to Farm Act. The Food, Conservation, and Energy Act of 2008, for instance, provided farmers with direct payments (based on previous crops planted), countercyclical payments (based on the differences between market prices and targeted prices), and marketing loans (based on a specified crop price and an option to either pay back the loan or forfeit the crop to the government lender).

The Agricultural Act of 2014 preserved marketing loans but ended direct payments and countercyclical payments in favor of two types of crop insurance. Price loss coverage pays participating farmers if the market price of their crop falls below a predetermined value. Agricultural risk coverage pays out if the total revenue generated by a given crop in a given county falls below a preselected value.

Terms and Concepts

farm commodities	acreage allotments	crop insurance
food products	Freedom to Farm Act	price loss coverage
agribusiness	direct payments	agricultural risk coverage
parity concept	countercyclical payments (CCPs)	Agricultural Act of 2018
parity ratio	marketing loan program	
price supports	Agricultural Act of 2014	

Discussion Questions

1. Carefully evaluate: "The supply and demand for agricultural products are such that small changes in agricultural supply result in drastic changes in prices. However, large changes in agricultural prices have modest effects on agricultural output." (Hint: A brief review of the distinction between *supply* and *quantity supplied* may be helpful.) Do exports increase or reduce the instability of demand for farm products? Explain. **LO22.1**

2. What relationship, if any, can you detect between the facts that farmers' fixed costs of production are large and the supply of most agricultural products is generally inelastic? Be specific in your answer. **LO22.1**

3. Explain how each of the following contributes to the farm problem: **LO22.1, LO22.2**
   a. The inelasticity of demand for farm products.
   b. The rapid technological progress in farming.
   c. The modest long-run growth in demand for farm commodities.
   d. The volatility of export demand.

4. The key to efficient resource allocation is shifting resources from low-productivity to high-productivity uses. In view of the high and expanding physical productivity of agricultural resources, explain why many economists want to divert additional resources away from farming in order to achieve allocative efficiency. **LO22.2**

5. Explain and evaluate: "Industry complains of the higher taxes it must pay to finance subsidies to agriculture. Yet the trend of agricultural prices has been downward, while industrial prices have been moving upward, suggesting that on balance agriculture is actually subsidizing industry." **LO22.3**

6. "Because consumers as a group must ultimately pay the total income received by farmers, it makes no real difference whether the income is paid through free farm markets or through price supports supplemented by subsidies financed out of tax revenue." Do you agree? Why or why not? **LO22.3**

7. If in a given year the indexes of prices received and paid by farmers were 120 and 165, respectively, what would the parity ratio be? Explain the meaning of that ratio. **LO22.3**

8. Explain the economic effects of price supports. Explicitly include environmental and global impacts in your answer. On what grounds do economists contend that price supports cause a misallocation of resources? **LO22.3**

9. Do you agree with each of the following statements? Explain why or why not. **LO22.3, LO22.4**

   a. The problem with U.S. agriculture is that there are too many farmers. That is not the fault of farmers but the fault of government programs.

   b. The federal government ought to buy up all U.S. farm surpluses and give them away to developing nations.

   c. All industries would like government price supports if they could get them; agriculture has obtained price supports only because of its strong political clout.

10. What are the effects of farm subsidies such as those of the United States and the European Union on (a) domestic agricultural prices, (b) world agricultural prices, and (c) the international allocation of agricultural resources? **LO22.3**

11. What was the major intent of the Freedom to Farm Act of 1996? Do you agree with the intent? Why or why not? Did the law succeed in reducing overall farm subsidies? Why or why not? **LO22.5**

12. Distinguish between price loss coverage and agricultural risk coverage. How do they help reduce the volatility of farm income? In what way do farm subsidies perpetuate the long-standing problem of too many resources in agriculture? **LO22.5**

13. **LAST WORD** What groups benefit and what groups have lost from the U.S. Conservation Reserve Program? Are the intended beneficiaries of the program actually doing better as a result of the program? Explain.

Review Questions   connect

1. Suppose that the demand for olive oil is highly inelastic. Also suppose that the supply of olive oil is fixed for the year. If the demand for olive oil suddenly increases because of a shortage of corn oil, you would expect _____ in the price of olive oil. **LO22.2**

   a. a large increase
   b. a small increase
   c. a large decrease
   d. a small decrease
   e. no change

2. Use supply and demand curves to depict equilibrium price and output in a competitive market for some farm product. Then show how an above-equilibrium price floor (price support) would cause a surplus in this market. Demonstrate in your graph how government could reduce the surplus through a policy that (a) changes supply or (b) changes demand. Identify each of the following actual government policies as primarily affecting the supply of or the demand for a particular farm product: acreage allotments, the food-stamp program, the Food for Peace program, a government buyout of dairy herds, and export promotion. **LO22.3**

3. Suppose that the government has been supporting the price of corn. Its free-market price is $2.50 per bushel, but the

government has been setting a support price of $3.50 per bushel. Which of the following programs might the government use in an effort to reduce the size of the corn surplus? (Select one or more answers from the choices shown.) **LO22.3**

   a. Decrease the support price.
   b. Institute an acreage allotment program.
   c. Decrease demand by taxing purchases of corn.
   d. Raise the support price.

4. The majority of farm subsidies flow toward _____. **LO22.4**

   a. poor, small-scale farmers
   b. rich, large-scale farmers
   c. government employees
   d. grain wholesalers

5. Which of the following are elements of current U.S. farm policy? Select all that apply. **LO22.5**

   a. Farmers are free to choose how much to plant of any particular crop.
   b. Direct payments.
   c. Price supports.
   d. Countercyclical payments.

Problems   connect

1. Suppose that corn currently costs $4 per bushel and wheat currently costs $3 per bushel. Also assume that the price elasticity of corn is 0.10, while the price elasticity of wheat is 0.15. For the following questions about elasticities, simply use the percentage changes that are provided rather than attempting to calculate those percentage changes yourself using the midpoint formula found in Chapter 6. **LO22.1**

   a. If the price of corn falls by 25 percent to $3 per bushel, by what percentage will the quantity demanded of corn increase? What will happen if the price of corn falls by 50 percent to $2 per bushel?

   b. To what value would the price of wheat have to fall to induce consumers to increase their purchases of wheat by 5 percent?

c. If the government imposes a $0.40 per bushel tax on corn so that the price of corn rises by 10 percent to $4.40 per bushel, by what percentage will the quantity demanded of corn decrease? If the initial quantity demanded is 10 billion bushels per year, by how many bushels will the quantity demanded decrease in response to this tax?

2. Suppose that both wheat and corn have an income elasticity of 0.1. **LO22.1**

   a. If the average income in the economy increases by 2 percent each year, by what percentage does the quantity demanded of wheat increase each year, holding all other factors constant? Holding all other factors constant, if 10 billion bushels are demanded this year, by how many bushels will the quantity demanded increase next year if incomes rise by 2 percent?

   b. Given that average personal income doubles in the United States about every 30 years, by about what percentage does the quantity demanded of corn increase every 30 years, holding all other factors constant?

3. Suppose that 10 workers were required in 2020 to produce 40,000 bushels of wheat on a 1,000-acre farm. **LO22.2**

   a. What is the average output per acre? Per worker?

   b. If in 2030 only 8 workers produce 44,000 bushels of wheat on that same 1,000-acre farm, what is the average output per acre? Per worker?

   c. By what percentage does productivity (output per worker) increase over those 10 years? Over those 10 years, what is the average annual percentage increase in productivity?

4. In 2019, it was estimated that the total value of all corn-production subsidies in the United States was about $2.7 billion. The population of the United States was approximately 328 million people that year. On average, how much did corn subsidies cost per person in the United States in 2019? (Hint: A billion is a 1 followed by nine zeros. A million is a 1 followed by six zeros.) **LO22.3**

CHAPTER

23

Income Inequality, Poverty, and Discrimination

>> LEARNING OBJECTIVES

LO23.1 Explain how income inequality is measured and described.

LO23.2 Discuss the extent and sources of income inequality.

LO23.3 Demonstrate how U.S. income inequality has changed since 1985.

LO23.4 Debate the economic arguments for and against income inequality.

LO23.5 Relate poverty to age, gender, and ethnicity.

LO23.6 Identify the major components of the U.S. income-maintenance system.

LO23.7 Discuss labor market discrimination.

Wide income disparity in the United States is easy to find. In 2020, social media star and cosmetics entrepreneur Kylie Jenner earned $590 million while author/director/producer Tyler Perry earned almost $100 million. In contrast, the salary of the president of the United States is $400,000 per year, and the typical schoolteacher earns about $60,000 per year. A full-time minimum-wage worker at a fast-food restaurant makes about $15,000 annually. Cash welfare payments (TANF) to a single mother with two children average just under $6,000 per year.

In 2020 about 37.2 million Americans—or 11.4 percent of the population—lived in poverty. An estimated 580,000 were homeless on any given night. What are the sources of income inequality? Is income inequality rising or falling? Is the United States making progress against poverty? These are some of the questions we answer in this chapter.

Facts about Income Inequality

>> **LO23.1** Explain how income inequality is measured and described.

Income comparisons are often made at the household level, rather than at the individual level, because many people's consumption depends not upon their own income but on that of their household. Such is the case, for instance, with minors who are too young to work and nonemployed adults who depend on the earnings of other adults in their household.

In 2020, U.S. household income was among the highest in the world, with an average value of $97,026 (= the sum of all the household income in the United States divided by the number of households) and a median value of $67,521 (= the income of the household that lies precisely in the middle of the household income distribution, with half of households making less each year and half of households making more each year). But those statistics tell us nothing about income inequality. To learn about income inequality, we must examine how income is distributed across households.

Distribution by Income Category

One way to measure **income inequality** is to look at the percentages of households in a series of income categories. Table 23.1 shows that 18.1 percent of all households had annual before-tax incomes of less than $25,000 in 2020, while 18.3 percent had annual incomes of $150,000 or more. These data suggest a wide dispersion of household income and considerable inequality of income in the United States.

(1) Personal Income Category	(2) Percentage of All Households in This Category
Under $15,000	9.4
$15,000–$24,999	8.7
$25,000–$34,999	8.1
$35,000–$49,999	11.6
$50,000–$74,999	16.5
$75,000–$99,999	12.2
$100,000–$149,999	15.3
$150,000–$199,999	8.0
$200,000 and above	10.3
Total	100.0

Note: Figures may not sum to exactly 100.0 percent due to rounding.

Source: Income and Poverty in the United States: 2020, U.S. Census Bureau.

TABLE 23.1
The Distribution of U.S. Income by Households, 2020

income inequality The unequal distribution of an economy's total *income* among *households* or families.

Distribution by Quintiles (Fifths)

We can also measure income inequality by dividing the total number of individuals, households, or families (two or more persons related by birth, marriage, or adoption) into five numerically equal groups, or *quintiles*, and examining the percentage of total personal (before-tax) income received by each quintile. We graph the relevant numbers for families in **Figure 23.1 (Key Graph)**, which also provides the upper income limit for each quintile. Any amount of income greater than that listed in each row of column 3 places a household into the next-higher quintile.

The Lorenz Curve and Gini Ratio

We can display the quintile distribution of personal income with a **Lorenz curve.** In Figure 23.1, we plot the cumulative percentage of households on the horizontal axis and their percentage of income on the vertical axis. The diagonal line 0e represents a *perfectly equal distribution of income* because each point along that line indicates that a particular percentage of households receive that same percentage of income. That is, points on the diagonal line show values where the percentage of households and percentage of income are the same: for example, 20 percent of all households receiving 20 percent of total income, 40 percent receiving 40 percent, 60 percent receiving 60 percent, and so on.

By plotting the quintile data from the table in Figure 23.1, we obtain the Lorenz curve for 2020. The bottom 20 percent of all households received 3.0 percent of the income, as shown by point *a*; the bottom 40 percent received 11.1 percent (= 3.0 + 8.1), as shown by point *b*; and so forth. The blue area between the diagonal line and the Lorenz curve indicates the degree of income inequality; the larger the blue area, the larger the inequality. For instance, if the actual income distribution were perfectly equal, the Lorenz curve and the diagonal would coincide and the blue area would disappear. But if the Lorenz curve sagged well below the diagonal, the blue area would be large, indicating a substantial amount of income inequality. In general, the farther the Lorenz curve sags below the diagonal, the larger is the blue area and the higher is the degree of income inequality.

The income inequality described by the Lorenz curve can be transformed into a **Gini ratio**—a numerical measure of the overall dispersion of income:

$$\text{Gini ratio} = \frac{\text{Area between Lorenz curve and diagonal}}{\text{Total area below the diagonal}}$$

$$= \frac{A \text{ (blue area)}}{A + B \text{ (blue + green area)}}$$

Lorenz curve A curve showing the distribution of income in an economy. The cumulated percentage of families (income receivers) is measured along the horizontal axis and the cumulated percentage of income is measured along the vertical axis.

Gini ratio A numerical measure of the overall dispersion of income among *households*, families, or individuals; found graphically by dividing the area between the diagonal line and the *Lorenz curve* by the entire area below the diagonal line.

..ıll KEY GRAPH

FIGURE 23.1 The Lorenz curve and Gini ratio.

The Lorenz curve is a convenient way to show the degree of income inequality (here, household income by quintile in 2020). The area between the diagonal (the line of perfect equality) and the Lorenz curve represents the degree of inequality in the distribution of total income. This inequality is measured numerically by the Gini ratio—area A (shown in blue) divided by area $A + B$ (the blue + green area). The Gini ratio can vary from zero (perfect equality) to one (perfect inequality). The Gini ratio for the distribution shown is 0.489.

(1) Quintile (2020)	(2) Percentage of Total Income	(3) Upper Income Limit
Lowest 20 percent	3.0	$ 27,026
Second 20 percent	8.1	52,179
Third 20 percent	14.0	85,076
Fourth 20 percent	22.6	141,110
Highest 20 percent	<u>52.2</u>	No limit
Total	100.0	

Source: Historical Income Tables: Households, Tables H-1 and H-2; and *Selected Characteristics of Households by Total Money Income,* Table HINC-01, United States Census.

Source: Bureau of Labor Statistics.

QUICK QUIZ FOR FIGURE 23.1

1. In Figure 23.1, if the blue area (between the Lorenz curve and the diagonal) is equal to 60 and the green area (below the Lorenz curve) is equal to 140, then the Gini ratio will be:
   a. approximately 0.43.
   b. exactly 0.30.
   c. approximately 0.60.
   d. exactly 0.70.

2. If the Gini ratio for household income is 0.29 in Sweden and 0.44 in the United States, then the income distribution is:
   a. less equal in the United States.
   b. less equal in Sweden.
   c. more equal in the United States.
   d. equally unequal in both countries.

3. If the Lorenz curve shown in Figure 23.1 sagged lower, income inequality would:
   a. decrease
   b. increase.
   c. double.
   d. remain unchanged.

4. If the Lorenz curve shown in Figure 23.1 sagged less, the amount of income going to the bottom 60 percent of the population would:
   a. increase.
   b. decrease.
   c. fall by almost half.
   d. more than triple.

Answers: 1. b; 2. a; 3. b; 4. a

The Gini ratio is 0.489 for the income distribution shown in Figure 23.1. Lower Gini ratios denote less inequality; higher ratios indicate more inequality. The Gini coefficient for complete income equality is zero and for complete inequality (where all households but one have zero income) is 1. So the higher the Gini coefficient, the more unequal the distribution of income.

Because Gini ratios are numerical, they are easier to use than Lorenz curves for comparing the income distributions of different ethnic groups and countries. For example, in 2020 the Gini ratio of U.S. household income for Hispanics was 0.460; for whites, 0.480; for Asians, 0.476; and for African Americans, 0.515.[1] In 2019, national Gini ratios ranged from a low of 0.242 in Slovenia to a high of 0.620 in South Africa. Examples within this range include Denmark, 0.287; Italy, 0.359; Mexico, 0.368; and Brazil, 0.539.[2]

---

[1]U.S. Census Bureau, *Historical Income Tables,* specifically "HINC-01, Selected Characteristics of Households by Total Money Income."

[2]*CIA World Factbook,* 2022, www.cia.gov.

Income Mobility: The Time Dimension

The income data we have examined so far have a major limitation: The income accounting period of one year is too short to be very meaningful. Because the Census Bureau data portray the income distribution in only a single year, they may conceal a more equal distribution over a few years, a decade, or even a lifetime. If Brad earns $1,000 in year 1 and $100,000 in year 2, while Jenny earns $100,000 in year 1 and only $1,000 in year 2, does society have income inequality? The answer depends on the period of measurement. A Gini coefficient calculated using annual data would indicate great income inequality between Brad and Jenny, but there would be complete equality if the Gini coefficient were calculated based on their respective cumulative incomes over the two-year period.

This point is important because evidence suggests considerable "churning around" in the income distribution over time. The movement of individuals or households from one income quintile to another over time is called **income mobility.** For most income receivers, income starts at a relatively low level during youth, reaches a peak during middle age, and then declines. Thus, if all people were to receive exactly the same income stream over their lifetimes, considerable income inequality would still exist in any specific year because of age differences. In any single year, the young and the old would receive low incomes while the middle-aged would receive high incomes.

If we change from a "snapshot" view of income distribution in a single year to a "time exposure" portraying incomes over much longer periods, we find considerable movement of income receivers among income classes.

income mobility The extent to which *income* receivers move from one part of the income distribution to another over some period of time.

- Looking at the top of the income distribution, 70 percent of the U.S. population will enjoy at least one year between ages 25 and 60 (the so-called "prime working years") in which their income places them in the top 20 percent of income earners. Similarly, 53 percent will spend at least one year in the top 10 percent of income earners, 36 percent will enjoy at least one year in the top 5 percent, and 11 percent of Americans will enjoy at least one year in the top 1 percent of income earners.[3]

- Looking at the bottom of the income distribution, 62 percent of the U.S. population will experience at least one year between ages 25 and 60 in which their income places them in the bottom 20 percent of incomes. And 42 percent will endure at least one year in which their income is in the bottom 10 percent.[4]

- Duration also matters. Between ages 25 and 60, 15 percent of the U.S. population will encounter five or more consecutive years in which their incomes place them in the top 20 percent of income earners while 6 percent will endure five or more consecutive years in which their incomes are in the bottom 10 percent.[5]

These facts about individual and family income mobility over time are significant; for many people, "low income" and "high income" are not permanent conditions. Also, the longer the time period considered, the more equal the distribution of income becomes.

Effect of Government Redistribution

The income data in Table 23.1 and Figure 23.1 include wages, salaries, dividends, and interest. They also include all cash transfer payments such as Social Security, unemployment compensation benefits, and welfare assistance to needy families. The data are before-tax data and therefore do not take into account the effects of personal income and payroll (Social Security) taxes that are levied directly on income receivers. Nor do they include in-kind or **noncash transfers,** which provide specific goods or services rather than cash. Noncash transfers include Medicare, Medicaid, housing subsidies, subsidized school lunches, and food stamps. Such transfers are "income-like," because they enable recipients to "purchase" goods and services.

One economic function of government is to redistribute income, if society so desires. Figure 23.2 and its table reveal that the U.S. government significantly redistributes income from higher- to

noncash transfer A *government transfer payment* in the form of *goods* and *services* rather than *money*, for example, food stamps, housing assistance, and job training; also called *in-kind transfers.*

---

[3]T. A. Hirschl and M. R. Rank, "The Life Course Dynamics of Affluence," 2015. PLoS ONE 10(1): e0116370. https://doi.org/10.1371/journal.pone.0116370

[4]M. R. Rank and T. A. Hirschl, "The Likelihood of Experiencing Relative Poverty over the Life Course," 2015. PLoS ONE 10(7): e0133513. https://doi.org/10.1371/journal.pone.0133513

[5]Ibid.

FIGURE 23.2 The impact of taxes and transfers on U.S. income inequality.

The distribution of household income is significantly more equal after taxes and transfers are taken into account than before. Transfers account for most of the lessening of inequality and provide most of the income received by the lowest quintile of households.

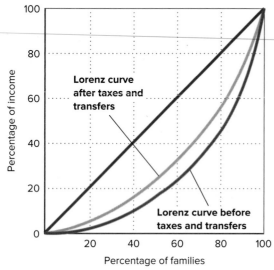

Quintile	Percentage of Total Income Received, 2018	
	(1) Before Taxes and Transfers	(2) After Taxes and Transfers
Lowest 20 percent	3.8	7.5
Second 20 percent	8.6	10.7
Third 20 percent	13.4	14.4
Fourth 20 percent	20.2	20.0
Highest 20 percent	56.0	47.4

Source: *Distribution of Household Income 2018*, Congressional Budget Office.

Source: Congressional Budget Office.

lower-income households. For example, households in the lowest quintile (fifth) would have received only 3.8 percent of total income if there had been no redistribution. *With* redistribution, they received 7.5 percent, about twice as much.

In fact, nearly all the reduction in U.S. income inequality is attributable to transfer payments. Together with job opportunities, transfer payments have been the most important means of alleviating poverty in the United States. (See the Chapter 20 Last Word for more on this topic.)

QUICK REVIEW 23.1

▶ Data reveal considerable income inequality in the United States; in 2020 the richest fifth of all households received 52.2 percent of before-tax income, and the poorest fifth received 3.0 percent.

▶ The Lorenz curve depicts income inequality graphically by comparing percentages of total families and percentages of total income. The Gini ratio is a number between zero (perfect equality) and 1 (perfect inequality) that measures the overall dispersion of income.

▶ The distribution of income is less unequal over longer time periods.

▶ Government taxes and transfers significantly reduce income inequality by redistributing income from higher-income groups to lower-income groups; the bulk of this redistribution results from transfer payments.

Causes of Income Inequality

>> **LO23.2** Discuss the extent and sources of income inequality.

There are several causes of income inequality in the United States. In general, the market system is permissive of a high degree of income inequality because it rewards individuals based on the contributions that they make, or the resources that they own, in producing society's output.

More specifically, the factors that contribute to income inequality are the following.

Ability

People have different mental and physical abilities. Some have inherited exceptional mental qualities that are essential to such high-paying occupations as medicine, corporate leadership, and law. Others are blessed with the physical capacity and coordination to become highly paid professional athletes. A rare few have the talent to become exceptionally great artists or musicians. The intelligence and skills of most people fall somewhere in between.

Education and Training

Ability alone rarely produces high income; people must develop and refine their capabilities through education and training. Individuals differ significantly in the amount of education and training they obtain and thus in their capacity to earn income. Such differences may be a matter of choice: Nguyen enters the labor force after graduating from high school, while Nyberg takes a job only after earning a college degree. Other differences may be involuntary: Nguyen and her parents may be unable to finance a college education.

People also receive varying degrees of on-the-job training, which contributes to income inequality. Some workers learn valuable new skills each year on the job and therefore experience significant income growth over time. Others receive little or no on-the-job training and earn no more at age 50 than they did at age 30. Moreover, firms tend to select for advanced on-the-job training the workers who have the most formal education. That added training magnifies the education-based income differences between less-educated and better-educated individuals.

Discrimination

Discrimination in education, hiring, training, and promotion undoubtedly causes some income inequality. If discrimination confines certain racial, ethnic, or gender groups to lower-pay occupations, the supply of labor in those occupations will increase relative to demand, and hourly wages and income in those lower-pay jobs will decline. Conversely, labor supply will be artificially reduced in the higher-pay occupations populated by "preferred" workers, raising their wage rates and income. In this way, discrimination can add to income inequality. In fact, economists cannot account for all racial, ethnic, and gender differences in work earnings on the basis of differences in years of education, quality of education, occupations, and annual hours of work. Many economists attribute the unexplained residual to discrimination.

Economists, however, do not see discrimination by race, gender, and ethnicity as a *dominant* factor explaining income inequality. The income distributions *within* racial or ethnic groups that historically have been targets of discrimination—for example, African Americans—are similar to the income distributions for whites. Other factors besides discrimination are obviously at work, too.

Preferences and Risks

Incomes also differ because of different preferences for market work relative to leisure, market work relative to work in the household, and types of occupations. People who choose to stay home with children, work part-time, or retire early usually have less income than those who make the opposite choices. Those who are willing to take arduous, unpleasant jobs (for example, underground mining or heavy construction), to work long hours with great intensity, or to "moonlight" tend to earn more.

Individuals also differ in their willingness to assume risk. We refer here not only to the race-car driver or the professional boxer but also to the entrepreneur. Although many entrepreneurs fail, many of those who develop successful new products or services realize very substantial incomes, thus contributing to income inequality.

Unequal Distribution of Wealth

Income is a *flow;* it represents a stream of wage and salary earnings, along with rent, interest, and profits, as depicted in Chapter 2's circular flow diagram. In contrast, wealth is a *stock,* reflecting at a particular moment the financial and real assets an individual has accumulated over time. A retired person may have very little income and yet own a home, mutual fund shares, and a pension plan that add up to considerable wealth. A new college graduate may be earning a substantial income as an accountant, middle manager, or engineer but has yet to accumulate significant wealth.

The ownership of wealth in the United States is more unequal than the distribution of income. This inequality of wealth leads to inequality in rent, interest, and dividends, which in turn contributes to income inequality. Those who own more machinery, real estate, farmland, stocks, and bonds and who have more money in savings accounts obviously receive greater income than people with less or no wealth.

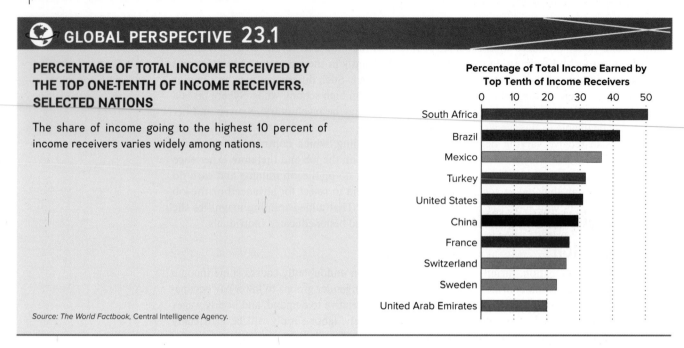

GLOBAL PERSPECTIVE 23.1

PERCENTAGE OF TOTAL INCOME RECEIVED BY THE TOP ONE-TENTH OF INCOME RECEIVERS, SELECTED NATIONS

The share of income going to the highest 10 percent of income receivers varies widely among nations.

Source: The World Factbook, Central Intelligence Agency.

Market Power

The ability to "rig the market" in one's own favor also contributes to income inequality. For example, in *resource* markets, certain unions and professional groups have adopted policies that limit the supply of their services, thereby boosting the incomes of those "on the inside." Also, legislation that requires occupational licensing for, say, doctors, dentists, and lawyers can bestow market power that favors the licensed groups. In *product* markets, "rigging the market" means gaining or enhancing monopoly power, which results in greater profit and thus greater income to the firms' owners.

Luck, Connections, and Misfortune

Other forces also play a role in producing income inequality. Luck and "being in the right place at the right time" have helped individuals stumble into fortunes. Discovering oil on a ranch, owning land along a proposed freeway interchange, and hiring the right press agent have accounted for some high incomes. Personal contacts and political connections are other potential routes to attaining high income.

In contrast, economic misfortunes such as prolonged illness, serious accident, the death of the family breadwinner, or unemployment may plunge a family into the low range of income. The burden of such misfortune is borne very unevenly by the population and thus contributes to income inequality.

Income inequality of the magnitude we have described is not exclusively an American phenomenon. Global Perspective 23.1 compares income inequality (here by individuals, not by households) in the United States with that in several other nations. Income inequality tends to be greatest in African and South and Central American nations, where land and capital resources are highly concentrated in the hands of a relatively small number of wealthy families.

Income Inequality over Time

>> **LO23.3** Demonstrate how U.S. income inequality has changed since 1985.

Economic growth has consistently raised incomes in the United States: In *absolute* dollar amounts, the entire distribution of income has been moving upward. But incomes may move up in *absolute* terms while leaving the *relative* distribution of income less equal, more equal, or unchanged. Table 23.2 shows how the distribution of household income has changed since 1985. This income is "before tax" and includes cash transfers but not noncash transfers.

Rising Income Inequality since 1985

It is clear from Table 23.2 that the distribution of income by quintiles has become more unequal since 1985. In 2020 the lowest 20 percent of households received 3.0 percent of total before-tax

TABLE 23.2 Percentage of Total Before-Tax Income Received by Each One-Fifth, and by the Top 5 Percent, of Households, Selected Years

Quintile	1985	1990	1995	2000	2005	2010	2015	2020
Lowest 20 percent	4.0	3.7	3.6	3.4	3.4	3.3	3.1	3.0
Second 20 percent	9.7	9.1	8.9	8.6	8.6	8.5	8.2	8.1
Third 20 percent	16.3	15.2	14.8	14.6	14.6	14.6	14.3	14.0
Fourth 20 percent	24.0	23.3	23.0	23.0	23.0	23.4	23.2	22.6
Highest 20 percent	46.6	48.7	50.4	49.8	50.4	50.3	51.1	52.2
Total	100.0	100.0	100.0	100.0	100.0	100.0	100.0	100.0
Top 5 percent	17.0	18.6	21.0	22.1	22.2	22.3	22.1	23.0

Note: Numbers may not add to 100.00 percent due to rounding.

Source: Historical Income Tables: Households, Table H-2, United States Census.

income, compared with 4.0 percent in 1985. Meanwhile, the income share received by the highest 20 percent rose from 46.6 in 1985 to 52.2 percent in 2020. The percentage of income received by the top 5 percent of households also rose significantly over the 1985–2020 period.

Causes of Growing Inequality

Economists suggest several major explanations for the increase in U.S. income inequality over the past several decades.

Greater Demand for Highly Skilled Workers Perhaps the most significant contributor to the growing income inequality has been an increasing demand for workers who are highly skilled and well-educated. Moreover, several industries requiring highly skilled workers have either recently emerged or expanded greatly, such as the computer software, business consulting, biotechnology, health care, and space exploration industries. Because highly skilled workers remain relatively scarce, their wages have been bid up. Consequently, the wage differences between them and less-skilled workers have increased.

The rising demand for skill has also shown up in rapidly rising pay for chief executive officers (CEOs), sizable increases in income from stock options, substantial increases in income for professional athletes and entertainers, and huge fortunes for successful entrepreneurs. This growth of "superstar" pay has also contributed to rising income inequality.

Demographic Changes The entrance of large numbers of less-experienced and less-skilled "baby boomers" into the labor force during the 1970s and 1980s may have contributed to greater income inequality in those two decades. Because younger workers tend to earn less income than older workers, their growing numbers contributed to income inequality. There has also been a growing tendency for those with high earnings potential to marry each other, thus increasing household income among the highest income quintiles. Finally, the number of households headed by single or divorced women has increased greatly. That trend has increased income inequality because such households lack a second major wage earner and also because the poverty rate for female-headed households is very high.

International Trade, Immigration, and Decline in Unionism Other factors are probably at work as well. Stronger international competition from imports has reduced the demand for and employment of less-skilled (but highly paid) workers in the automobile and steel industries. The decline in such jobs has reduced the average wage for less-skilled workers. It also has swelled the ranks of workers in already low-paying industries, placing further downward pressure on wages there.

Similarly, the transfer of jobs to lower-wage workers in developing countries has exerted downward wage pressure on less-skilled workers in the United States. Also, an upsurge in the immigration of unskilled workers has increased the number of low-income households in the United States. Finally, the decline in unionism in the United States has undoubtedly contributed to wage inequality, because unions tend to equalize pay within firms and industries.

Two cautions: First, when we note growing income inequality, we are not saying that the "rich are getting richer and the poor are getting poorer" in terms of absolute income. Both the rich and the poor are experiencing rises in real incomes. Rather, while incomes have risen in all quintiles, income growth has been fastest in the top quintile. Second, increased income inequality is not solely a U.S. phenomenon. The recent rise of inequality has also occurred in several other industrially advanced nations.

The Lorenz curve can be used to contrast the distribution of income at different points in time. If we plotted Table 23.2's data as Lorenz curves, we would find that the curves shifted farther away from the diagonal between 1980 and 2015. The Gini ratio rose from 0.419 in 1985 to 0.489 in 2020.

Equality versus Efficiency

>> LO23.4 Debate the economic arguments for and against income inequality.

The main policy issue concerning income inequality is how much is necessary and justified. While there is no general agreement on the justifiable amount, we can gain insight by exploring the cases for and against greater equality.

The Case for Equality: Maximizing Total Utility

The basic argument for an equal distribution of income holds that income equality maximizes total consumer satisfaction (utility) from any particular level of output and income. The rationale for this argument is shown in Figure 23.3, in which we assume that the money incomes of two individuals, Anderson and Brooks, are subject to diminishing marginal utility. In any time period, income receivers spend the first dollars received on the products they value most—products whose marginal utility is high. As their most pressing wants become satisfied, consumers then spend additional dollars of income on less-important, lower-marginal-utility goods. The identical diminishing-marginal-utility-from-income curves (MU_A and MU_B in the figure) reflect the assumption that Anderson and Brooks have the same capacity to derive utility from income.

Suppose that there is $10,000 worth of income (output) to be distributed between Anderson and Brooks. According to proponents of income equality, the optimal distribution is an equal distribution, which causes the marginal utility of the last dollar spent to be the same for both persons.

Now assume that the $10,000 of income initially is distributed unequally, with Anderson getting $2,500 and Brooks $7,500. The marginal utility, a, from the last dollar received by Anderson is high, and the marginal utility, b, from Brooks's last dollar of income is low. If a single dollar of

FIGURE 23.3 **The utility-maximizing distribution of income.**

With identical marginal-utility-of-income curves MU_A and MU_B, Anderson and Brooks will maximize their combined utility when any amount of income (say, $10,000) is equally distributed. If income is unequally distributed (say, $2,500 to Anderson and $7,500 to Brooks), the marginal utility derived from the last dollar will be greater for Anderson than for Brooks, and a redistribution of income toward equality will result in a net increase in total utility. The utility gained by equalizing income at $5,000 each, shown by the blue area below curve MU_A in panel (a), exceeds the utility lost, indicated by the red area below curve MU_B in (b).

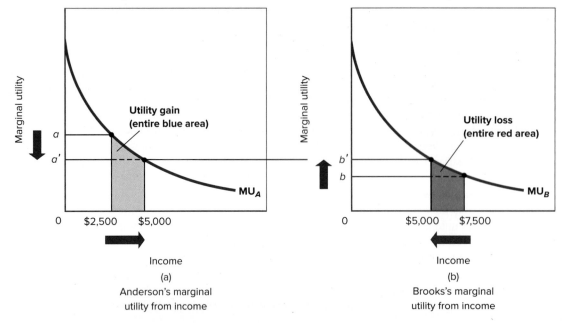

income is shifted from Brooks to Anderson—that is, toward greater equality—then Anderson's utility increases by a and Brooks's utility decreases by b. The combined utility then increases by a minus b (Anderson's large gain minus Brooks's small loss). The transfer of a second dollar from Brooks to Anderson again increases their combined utility, this time by a slightly smaller amount. Continued transfer of dollars from Brooks to Anderson increases their combined utility until the income is evenly distributed and both receive $5,000. At that time their marginal utilities from the last dollar of income are equal (at a' and b'), and any further income redistribution beyond the $2,500 already transferred would begin to create inequality and decrease their combined utility.

The area under the MU curve and to the left of the individual's particular income level represents the total utility of that income. Therefore, as a result of the $2,500 transfer, Anderson has gained utility represented by the blue area below curve MU_A, and Brooks has lost utility represented by the red area below curve MU_B. The blue area is obviously greater than the red area, so income equality yields greater combined total utility than income inequality does.

The Case for Inequality: Incentives and Efficiency

Although the logic of the argument for equality might seem solid, critics of income equality say that income equality is both unfair and unwise. They argue that income inequality largely reflects rewards to individuals for supplying their talents and resources to the economy. They conclude that it is not fair to take some of Brooks's income and give it to Anderson. Further, critics note that proponents of income equality falsely assume that there is some fixed amount of output produced and therefore income to be distributed. These critics argue that the way in which income is distributed partly determines the amount of output or income that is produced and is available for distribution.

Refer again to Figure 23.3 and assume that Anderson earns $2,500 while Brooks earns $7,500. In moving toward equality, society (the government) must tax away some of Brooks's income and transfer it to Anderson. This tax and transfer process diminishes the income rewards of high-income Brooks and raises the income rewards of low-income Anderson; in so doing, it reduces the incentives of both to earn high incomes. Why should high-income Brooks work hard, save and invest, or undertake entrepreneurial risks when taxation will reduce the rewards from such activities? And why should low-income Anderson be motivated to increase his income through market activities when the government stands ready to transfer income to him? Taxes reduce the rewards from increased productive effort; redistribution through transfers is a reward for diminished effort.

In the extreme, imagine a situation in which the government levies a 100 percent tax on income and distributes the tax revenue equally to its citizenry. Why would anyone work at all? Why would anyone assume business risk? Or why would anyone save (forgo current consumption) in order to invest? The economic incentives to "get ahead" will have been removed, greatly reducing society's total production and income.

The Equality-Efficiency Trade-off

At the essence of the income equality-inequality debate is a fundamental trade-off between equality and efficiency. In this **equality-efficiency trade-off,** greater income equality (achieved through redistribution of income) comes at the opportunity cost of reduced production and income. And greater production and income (through reduced redistribution) comes at the expense of less equality of income. The trade-off obligates society to choose how much redistribution it wants, in view of the costs. If society decides it wants to redistribute income, it needs to determine methods that minimize the adverse effects on fairness, incentives, productivity, and economic efficiency.

equality-efficiency trade-off The decrease in *economic efficiency* that may accompany a decrease in *income inequality;* the presumption that some income inequality is required to achieve economic efficiency.

The Economics of Poverty

>> **LO23.5** Relate poverty to age, gender, and ethnicity.

We now turn from the broader issue of income distribution to the more specific issue of very low income, or poverty. A society with a high degree of income inequality can have a high, moderate, or low amount of poverty. But what exactly is poverty?

Definition of Poverty

Poverty is a condition in which a person or a family does not have the means to satisfy basic needs for food, clothing, shelter, and transportation. The means include currently earned income, transfer payments, past savings, and property owned. The basic needs have many determinants, including family size and the health and age of its members.

poverty rate The percentage of the population with incomes below the official poverty income levels that are established by the federal government.

The federal government has established minimum income thresholds below which a person or a family is "in poverty." In 2020 an unattached individual receiving less than $12,760 per year in monetary income was said to be living in poverty. For a family of four, the poverty line was $26,200. For a family of six, it was $35,160. Based on these thresholds, in 2020 about 37.2 million Americans lived in poverty. In 2020, the **poverty rate**—the percentage of the population living in poverty—was 11.4 percent.

Incidence of Poverty

The low-income population is heterogeneous: They can be found in all parts of the nation; they are of all races and ethnicities, rural and urban, young and old. But as Figure 23.4 indicates, poverty is far from randomly distributed. For example, the poverty rate for African Americans and Hispanics is above the national average, while the rates for whites and Asians are below the average.

Figure 23.4 shows that female-headed households (no husband present), African Americans, foreign-born noncitizens, Hispanics, and children under 18 years of age have very high incidences of poverty. Marriage and full-time, year-round work are associated with low poverty rates, and, because of the Social Security system, the incidence of poverty among the elderly is less than that for the population as a whole.

The high poverty rate for children is especially disturbing because poverty tends to breed poverty. Poor children are at greater risk for a range of long-term problems, including poor health and inadequate education, crime, drug use, and teenage pregnancy. Many of today's impoverished children will reach adulthood unhealthy and illiterate and unable to earn above-poverty incomes.

As many as half of people in poverty are poor for only one or two years before climbing out of poverty. But poverty is much more long-lasting among some groups than among others. In particular, African American and Hispanic families, families headed by women, persons with little education and few labor market skills, and people who are dysfunctional because of drug use, alcoholism, or mental

FIGURE 23.4
Poverty rates among selected population groups, 2020.

Poverty is disproportionately borne by African Americans, Hispanics, children, foreign-born residents who are not citizens, and families headed by women. People who are employed full-time, have a college degree, or are married tend to have low poverty rates.

Source: Income and Poverty in the United States: 2020, Tables B-1 and B-6, U.S. Census Bureau.

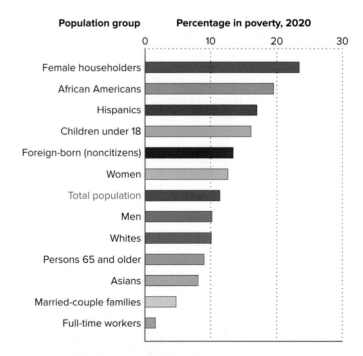

illness are more likely than others to remain in poverty. Also, long-lasting poverty is heavily present in depressed areas of cities, parts of the Deep South, and some Native American reservations.

Measurement Issues

Poverty data should be interpreted cautiously. The official income thresholds for defining poverty are necessarily arbitrary and therefore may inadequately measure the true extent of poverty in the United States.

Some observers say that the high cost of living in major metropolitan areas means that the official poverty thresholds exclude millions of families whose income is slightly above the poverty level but clearly inadequate to meet basic needs for food, housing, and medical care. These observers use city-by-city studies on "minimal income needs" to argue that poverty in the United States is much more widespread than officially measured and reported.

In contrast, some economists point out that using only income to measure poverty understates the standard of living of many of the people who are officially poor. When individual, household, or family *consumption* is considered rather than family *income*, some of the poverty in the United States disappears. Some low-income families maintain their consumption by drawing down past savings, borrowing against future income, or selling homes. Moreover, many poor families receive substantial noncash benefits such as food stamps and rent subsidies that boost their living standards. Such "in-kind" benefits are not counted as income in determining a family's official poverty status. One study found that if in-kind benefits were counted as a form of income, poverty rates would tend to be about 20 percent lower.

The U.S. Income-Maintenance System

Helping those who have a very low income is a widely accepted goal of public policy. A wide array of antipoverty programs, including education and training programs, subsidized employment, minimum-wage laws, and antidiscrimination policies, are designed to increase the earnings of the poor. In addition, a number of income-maintenance programs have been devised to reduce poverty; the most important are listed in Table 23.3. These programs involve large expenditures and have numerous beneficiaries.

>> **LO23.6** Identify the major components of the U.S. income-maintenance system.

TABLE 23.3 Characteristics of Major Income-Maintenance Programs

Program	Basis of Eligibility	Source of Funds	Form of Aid	Expenditures,* Billions	Beneficiaries, Millions
Social Insurance Programs					
Social Security	Age, disability, or death of parent or spouse; lifetime work earnings	Federal payroll tax on employers and employees	Cash	$1,096	65
Medicare	Age or disability	Federal payroll tax on employers and employees	Subsidized health insurance	$830	62
Unemployment compensation	Unemployment	State and federal payroll taxes on employers	Cash	$537	46
Public Assistance Programs					
Supplemental Security Income (SSI)	Age or disability; income	Federal revenues	Cash	$56	8
Temporary Assistance for Needy Families (TANF)	Certain families with children; income	Federal-state-local revenues	Cash and services	$17	3
Supplemental Nutrition Assistance Program (SNAP)	Income	Federal revenues	Cash via EBT cards	$79	40
Medicaid	Persons eligible for TANF or SSI and medically indigent	Federal-state-local revenues	Subsidized medical services	$671	73
Earned-income tax credit (EITC)	Low-wage working families	Federal revenues	Refundable tax credit, cash	$62	25

*Expenditures by federal, state, and local governments; excludes administrative expenses.

Source: Social Security Administration, *Annual Statistical Supplement, 2021*; Centers for Medicare and Medicaid Services; U.S. Department of Agriculture; Internal Revenue Service, www.irs.gov/taxstats; Bureau of Economic Analysis, and other government sources. Latest data.

entitlement programs
Government programs such as *social insurance, Medicare,* and *Medicaid* that guarantee (entitle) particular levels of transfer payments or noncash benefits to all who fit the programs' criteria.

social insurance programs
Programs that replace the earnings lost when people retire or are temporarily unemployed, that are financed by payroll *taxes,* and that are viewed as earned rights (rather than charity).

Social Security The social insurance program in the United States financed by federal *payroll taxes* on employers and employees and designed to replace a portion of the earnings lost when workers become disabled, retire, or die.

Medicare A federal program that provides for (1) compulsory hospital insurance for senior citizens, (2) low-cost voluntary insurance to help older Americans pay physicians' fees, and (3) subsidized insurance to buy prescription drugs. Financed by *payroll taxes.*

unemployment insurance
The social insurance program that in the United States is financed by state *payroll taxes* on employers and makes *income* available to workers who become unemployed and are unable to find jobs.

public assistance programs
Government programs that pay benefits to those who are unable to earn *income* (because of permanent disabilities or because they have very low income and dependent children); financed by general *tax* revenues and viewed as public charity (rather than earned rights).

The U.S. income-maintenance system consists of two kinds of programs: (1) social insurance and (2) public assistance, or "welfare." Both are known as **entitlement programs** because all eligible persons are legally entitled to receive the benefits set forth in the programs without having to do anything in return.

Social Insurance Programs

Social insurance programs partially replace earnings that have been lost due to retirement, disability, or temporary unemployment; they also provide health insurance for the elderly. The main social insurance programs are Social Security, unemployment compensation, and Medicare. Benefits are viewed as earned rights and do not carry the stigma of public charity. These programs are financed primarily out of federal payroll taxes. In these programs, the entire population shares the risk of an individual's losing income because of retirement, unemployment, disability, or illness. Workers (and employers) pay a tax on their wages into a government fund while they are working. The workers are then entitled to benefits when they retire or when a specified misfortune occurs.

Social Security and Medicare The major social insurance program is **Social Security.** This federal pension program replaces part of the earnings lost when workers retire or become disabled. This gigantic program ($1,096 billion in 2020) is financed by compulsory payroll taxes levied on both employers and employees. The retirement age at which a worker can collect full benefits was originally 65 years of age, but is being gradually increased to age 67. Currently, workers may retire at age 66 years and 2 months and receive full retirement benefits or retire early at age 62 with reduced benefits. When a worker dies, benefits accrue to his or her family survivors. Special provisions provide benefits for disabled workers.

Social Security covers over 90 percent of the workforce; some 65 million people receive Social Security benefits, with benefits for retirees averaging about $1,503 per month. In 2022, those benefits were financed with a combined Social Security and Medicare payroll tax of 15.3 percent, with both the worker and the employer paying 7.65 percent on their first $147,000 of earnings. The 7.65 percent tax comprises 6.2 percent for Social Security and 1.45 percent for Medicare. Self-employed workers pay a tax of 15.3 percent.

Medicare provides health insurance benefits to those 65 or older and people who are disabled. It is financed by payroll taxes on employers and employees. This 2.9 percent tax is paid on all work income, not just on the first $147,000. Medicare also makes available supplementary low-cost insurance programs that help pay for doctor visits and prescription drugs. In 2020, some 62 million people received $830 billion worth of Medicare benefits.

The number of retirees drawing Social Security and Medicare benefits is rapidly rising relative to the number of workers paying payroll taxes. As a result, Social Security and Medicare face serious long-term funding problems. These fiscal imbalances have spawned calls to reform the programs.

Unemployment Compensation All 50 states offer **unemployment insurance,** a federal–state social insurance program that makes income available to workers who are unemployed. This insurance is financed by a relatively small payroll tax, paid by employers, which varies by state and by the size of the firm's payroll. Any insured worker who becomes unemployed can, after a short waiting period, become eligible for benefit payments. The program covers almost all wage and salary workers. The size of payments and the number of weeks that are made available vary considerably from state to state.

In normal times, benefits approximate 33 percent of a worker's wages up to a certain maximum payment. Thus, benefits averaged about $378 weekly in 2019, the last year before the COVID-19 pandemic hit. But when the pandemic struck and millions of workers could not work due to lockdowns, Congress voted an additional $600 per week and also extended the period of eligibility from the normal 29 weeks to 53 weeks. Thus, while unemployed workers received $28 billion in unemployment insurance payments in 2019, they received $537 billion—or nearly 20 times more—in 2020. And whereas in a typical year only about 5 million workers collect unemployment benefits, around 46 million people claimed benefits during 2020.

Public Assistance Programs

Public assistance programs (welfare) provide benefits to people who are unable to earn income because of permanent disabling conditions or who have no or very low income and also have dependent children. These programs are financed out of general tax revenues and are regarded as public charity. They include "means tests" that require individuals and families to demonstrate low incomes in order to qualify for aid. The federal government finances about two-thirds of the welfare program expenditures, and states pay for the rest.

Many needy persons who do not qualify for social insurance programs are assisted through the federal government's **Supplemental Security Income (SSI)** program. This is a federal program (financed by general tax revenues) that provides a uniform nationwide minimum income for the elderly, blind, and disabled who are unable to work and who do not qualify for Social Security aid. In 2020 the average monthly payment was $783 for individuals and $1,175 for couples with both people eligible. More than half the states provide additional income supplements to the aged, blind, and disabled.

The **Supplemental Nutrition Assistance Program (SNAP)** was formerly known as the food-stamp program. SNAP is a federal program (financed through general tax revenues) that provides eligible low-income persons with funds that they can use to buy food. It is designed to provide all low-income Americans with a nutritionally adequate diet. Under the program, eligible households receive monthly deposits of spendable electronic money on debit cards known as Electronic Benefit Transfer (EBT) cards. The amount deposited onto a family's EBT card varies inversely with the family's earned income; the poorer the family, the more they receive.

Temporary Assistance for Needy Families (TANF) is the basic welfare program for low-income families in the United States. The program is financed through general federal tax revenues and consists of lump-sum payments of federal money to states to operate their own welfare and work programs. These lump-sum payments are called TANF funds, and in 2020 about 2.6 million people (including children) received $17 billion of TANF assistance, collectively.

In 1996 TANF replaced the six-decade-old Aid for Families with Dependent Children (AFDC) program. Unlike that welfare program, TANF established work requirements and placed limits on the length of time a family can receive welfare payments. Specifically, the TANF program:

- Set a lifetime limit of 5 years on receiving TANF benefits and requires able-bodied adults to work after receiving assistance for 2 years.

- Ended food-stamp eligibility for able-bodied persons aged 18 to 50 (with no dependent children) who are not working or engaged in job-training programs.

- Tightened the definition of "disabled children" as it applies for eligibility of low-income families for Supplemental Security Income (SSI) assistance.

- Established a 5-year waiting period on public assistance for new legal immigrants who have not become citizens.

Since 1996, the number of TANF recipients has fallen steadily, from 12.3 million people in 1996 down to just 2.6 million in 2020. That decline has been attributed by proponents of TANF as proof that it helped people transition from welfare into work and thus reduced overall rates of poverty. But many are not convinced, and point to the fact that if one looks at welfare rolls more broadly, including not only TANF but also SSI and SNAP, the number of welfare recipients has increased over time, from 16.0 percent of the U.S. population in 1996 to 20.3 percent in 2018. Thus, the substantial decline in the number of TANF recipients should not, they argue, be taken as proof that the underlying "welfare to work" logic behind TANF was actually a success.

Medicaid is a federal program (financed by general tax revenues) that provides medical benefits to people covered by the SSI and TANF (basic welfare) programs.

The **earned-income tax credit (EITC)** is a federal wage subsidy provided to low-income wage earners to supplement their families' incomes and encourage work. It is available for low-income working families, with or without children, and is delivered in the form of an income-tax credit. The credit reduces the federal income taxes that such families owe or provides them with cash payments if the credit exceeds their tax liabilities. One purpose of the credit is to offset Social Security taxes paid by low-wage earners and thus keep the federal government from "taxing families into poverty." But the EITC can exceed the amount of Social Security taxes, in some cases by as much as $2 per hour for the lowest-paid workers with families. Under the program, many people owe no income tax and receive direct checks from the federal government once a year. According to the Internal Revenue Service, 25 million taxpayers received $62 billion in payments from the EITC in 2020.

Supplemental Security Income (SSI) A federally financed and administered program that provides a uniform nationwide minimum *income* for the aged, blind, and disabled who do not qualify for benefits under *Social Security* in the United States.

Supplemental Nutrition Assistance Program (SNAP) A government program that provides food money to low-income recipients by depositing electronic money onto *Electronic Benefit Transfer (EBT) cards.* Formerly known as the food-stamp program.

Temporary Assistance for Needy Families (TANF) A state-administered and partly federally funded program in the United States that provides financial aid to poor families; the basic welfare program for low-income families in the United States; contains time limits and work requirements.

Medicaid A federal program that helps finance the medical expenses of individuals covered by the *Supplemental Security Income (SSI)* and *Temporary Assistance for Needy Families (TANF)* programs.

earned-income tax credit (EITC) A refundable federal *tax credit* for low-income working people designed to reduce poverty and encourage labor-force participation.

Several other welfare programs are not listed in Table 23.3. Some provide help in the form of noncash transfers. Head Start provides education, nutrition, and social services to economically disadvantaged 3- and 4-year-olds. Housing assistance in the form of rent subsidies and funds for construction is available to low-income families. Pell grants provide assistance to undergraduate students from low-income families. Low-income home energy assistance provides help with home heating bills. Other programs—such as veteran's assistance and black lung benefits—provide cash assistance to those eligible.

Economic Analysis of Discrimination

>> **LO23.7** Discuss labor market discrimination.

Although the majority of Americans who are in the lowest income quintile or in poverty are white, African Americans and Hispanics are in those two categories disproportionally to their total populations. For that reason, the percentages of all African Americans and Hispanics receiving public assistance from the TANF, SSI, and food stamp programs are also well above the average for the entire population. This fact raises the question of what role, if any, discrimination plays in reducing wages for some and increasing wages for others.

Discrimination is the practice of according people inferior treatment (for example, in hiring, occupational access, education and training, promotion, wages, or working conditions) on the basis of some factor such as race, gender, or ethnicity. People who practice discrimination are said to exhibit a *prejudice* or a *bias* against the groups they discriminate against.

Prejudice reflects complex, multifaceted, and deeply ingrained beliefs and attitudes. Thus, economics can contribute some insights into discrimination but no detailed explanations. With this caution in mind, let's look into the economics of discrimination.

discrimination The practice of according individuals or groups inferior treatment in hiring, occupational access, education and training, promotion, wage rates, or working conditions even though they have the same abilities, education, skills, and work experience as other workers.

Taste-for-Discrimination Model

taste-for-discrimination model A theory that views discrimination as a preference for which an employer is willing to pay.

The **taste-for-discrimination model** examines prejudice by using the emotion-free language of demand theory. It views discrimination as resulting from a preference or taste for which the discriminator is willing to pay. The model assumes that, for whatever reason, prejudiced people experience a subjective or psychic cost—a disutility—whenever they must interact with those they are biased against. Consequently, they are willing to pay a certain "price" to avoid interactions with the nonpreferred group. The size of this price depends directly on the degree of prejudice.

The taste-for-discrimination model is general; it can be applied to race, gender, age, and religion. Our discussion focuses on employer discrimination, in which employers discriminate against nonpreferred workers. For concreteness, we will look at a white employer discriminating against African American workers.

Discrimination Coefficient A prejudiced white employer behaves as if employing African American workers would add a cost. The amount of this cost—this disutility—is reflected in a **discrimination coefficient,** d, measured in monetary units. Because the employer is not prejudiced against whites, the cost of employing a white worker is the white wage rate, W_w. However, the employer's perceived "cost" of employing an African American worker is the African American worker's wage rate, W_{aa}, *plus* the cost d involved in the employer's prejudice, or $W_{aa} + d$.

discrimination coefficient A measure of the cost or disutility of prejudice; the monetary amount an employer is willing to pay to hire a preferred worker rather than a nonpreferred worker of the same ability.

The prejudiced white employer will have no preference between African American and white workers when the total cost per worker is the same—that is, when $W_w = W_{aa} + d$. Suppose the market wage rate for whites is $10 and the monetary value of the disutility the employer attaches to hiring African Americans is $2 (that is, $d = 2). This employer will be indifferent between hiring African Americans and whites only when the African American wage rate is $8, because at this wage the perceived cost of hiring either a white or an African American worker is $10:

$$\$10 \text{ white wage} = \$8 \text{ African-American wage} + \$2 \text{ discrimination coefficient}$$

It follows that our prejudiced white employer will hire African Americans only if their wage rate is sufficiently below that of whites. By "sufficiently" we mean at least the amount of the discrimination coefficient.

The greater a white employer's taste for discrimination as reflected in the value of d, the larger the difference between white wages and the lower wages at which African Americans will be hired. A "color-blind" employer whose d is $0 will hire equally productive African Americans and whites impartially if their wages are the same. A blatantly prejudiced white employer whose d is infinity would refuse to hire African Americans even if the African American wage is zero.

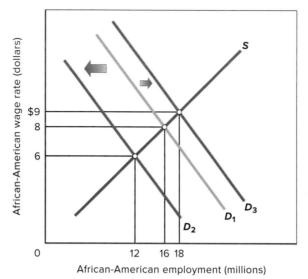

FIGURE 23.5
The African American wage and employment level in the taste-for-discrimination model.

An increase in prejudice by white employers as reflected in higher discrimination coefficients would decrease the demand for African American workers, here from D_1 to D_2, and reduce the African American wage rate and level of African American employment. Not shown, this drop in the African American wage rate would lower the African American–white wage ratio. In contrast, if prejudice were reduced such that discrimination coefficients of employers declined, the demand for African American labor would increase, as from D_1 to D_3, boosting the African American wage rate and level of employment. The higher African American wage rate would increase the African American–white wage ratio.

Most prejudiced white employers will not refuse to hire African Americans under *all* conditions. They will, in fact, *prefer* to hire African Americans if the actual white-black wage difference in the market exceeds the value of d. In our example, if whites can be hired at $10 and equally productive African Americans at only $7.50, the biased white employer will hire African Americans. That employer is willing to pay a wage difference of up to $2 per hour for whites to satisfy his or her bias, but not more. At the $2.50 actual difference, the employer will hire African Americans.

Conversely, if whites can be hired at $10 and African Americans at $8.50, only whites will be hired. Again, the biased employer is willing to pay a wage difference of up to $2 for whites; a $1.50 actual difference means that hiring whites is a "bargain" for this employer.

Prejudice and the Market African American–White Wage Ratio For a particular supply of African American workers, the actual African American-white wage ratio–the ratio determined in the labor market–will depend on the collective prejudice of white employers. To see why, consider Figure 23.5, which shows a labor market for African American workers. Initially, suppose the relevant labor demand curve is D_1, so the equilibrium African American wage is $8 and the equilibrium level of African American employment is 16 million. If we assume that the white wage (not shown) is $10, then the initial African American-white wage ratio is 0.8 (= $8/$10).

Now assume that prejudice against African American workers increases–that is, the collective d of white employers rises. An increase in d means an increase in the perceived cost of African American labor at each African American wage rate, and that higher cost reduces the demand for African American labor, say from D_1 to D_2. The African American wage rate falls from $8 to $6, and the level of African American employment declines from 16 million to 12 million. The increase in white employer prejudice reduces the African American wage rate and thus the actual African American-white wage ratio. If the white wage rate remains at $10, the new African American-white ratio is 0.6 (= $6/$10).

Conversely, suppose social attitudes change such that white employers become less biased and their discrimination coefficient as a group declines. The perceived cost of African American labor decreases at each African American wage rate, so the demand for African American labor increases, as from D_1 to D_3. In this case, the African American wage rate rises to $9, and employment of African American workers increases to 18 million. If the white wage remains at $10, the new African American-white wage ratio is 0.9 (= $9/$10).

Competition and Discrimination The taste-for-discrimination model suggests that competition will reduce discrimination in the very long run, as follows: The actual African American-white wage difference for equally productive workers–say, $2–allows nondiscriminators to hire African Americans for less than whites. Firms that hire African American workers will therefore have lower actual wage costs per unit of output and lower average total costs than will the firms that discriminate. These lower costs will allow nondiscriminators to underprice discriminating competitors, eventually driving them out of the market.

However, critics of the taste-for-discrimination model say that it overlooks entry barriers to new firms. They also point out that progress in eliminating racial discrimination has been slow. Discrimination based on race has persisted in the United States and other market economies for decades. To explain why, economists have proposed alternative models.

Statistical Discrimination

statistical discrimination
The practice of judging an individual on the basis of the average characteristics of the group to which he or she belongs rather than on his or her own personal characteristics.

A second theory of discrimination centers on the concept of **statistical discrimination,** in which people are judged on the basis of the average characteristics of the group to which they belong, rather than on their own personal characteristics or productivity. For example, insurance rates for teenage males are higher than those for teenage females. The difference is based on factual evidence indicating that, on average, young males are more likely than young females to be in accidents. But many young men are actually less accident-prone than the average young woman, and those men are discriminated against by having to pay higher insurance rates. The theory of statistical discrimination suggests that discriminatory outcomes are possible even where there is no prejudice.

Labor Market Example How does statistical discrimination show itself in labor markets? Employers with job openings want to hire the most productive workers available. They have their personnel department collect information concerning each job applicant, including age, education, and prior work experience. They may supplement that information with pre-employment tests, which they feel are helpful indicators of potential job performance. But collecting detailed information about job applicants is very expensive, and predicting job performance on the basis of limited data is difficult.

Example: Suppose an employer who plans to invest heavily in training a worker knows that on average women are less likely to be career-oriented than men, more likely to quit work in order to care for young children, and more likely to refuse geographic transfers. Thus, on average, the return on the employer's investment in training is likely to be less for a woman than for a man. All else equal, when choosing between two job applicants, one a woman and the other a man, this employer is likely to hire the man.

Note what is happening here. Average characteristics for a *group* are being applied to *individual* members of that group. The employer is falsely assuming that *each and every* woman worker has the same employment tendencies as the *average* woman. Such stereotyping means that numerous women who are career-oriented, who do not plan on quitting work in order to care for young children, and who are flexible as to geographic transfers will be discriminated against.

Profitable, Undesirable, but Not Malicious The firm that practices statistical discrimination is not being malicious in its hiring behavior (although it may be violating antidiscrimination laws). The decisions it makes will be rational and profitable because *on average* its hiring decisions are likely to be correct. Nevertheless, many people suffer because of statistical discrimination. And because it is profitable, statistical discrimination tends to persist.

Occupational Segregation: The Crowding Model

occupational segregation
The crowding of women or minorities into less desirable, lower-paying occupations.

The practice of **occupational segregation**—the crowding of women, African Americans, and certain ethnic groups into less desirable, lower-paying occupations—is still apparent in the U.S. economy. Statistics indicate that women are disproportionately concentrated in occupations such as teaching, nursing, and secretarial and clerical jobs. African Americans and Hispanics are crowded into low-paying jobs such as laundry workers, cleaners and household aides, hospital orderlies, and agricultural workers.

Let's look at a model of occupational segregation, using women and men as an example.

The Model The character and income consequences of occupational discrimination are revealed through a labor supply and demand model. We make the following assumptions:

- The labor force is equally divided between men and women workers. Let's say there are 6 million male and 6 million female workers.
- The economy comprises three occupations, X, Y, and Z, with identical labor demand curves, as shown in Figure 23.6.
- Men and women have the same labor-force characteristics; each of the three occupations could be filled equally well by men or by women.

FIGURE 23.6 The economics of occupational segregation.

(a) Because 1 million women are excluded from occupation X, the wage rate for men in that occupation is *M* rather than *B*. (b) Because another 1 million women are excluded from occupation Y, the wage for men in occupation Y is also *M* rather than *B*. (c) Because the 2 million women excluded from occupations X and Y are crowded into occupation Z, the wage rate for women there is *W* rather *B*. The elimination of discrimination will create flows of 1 million women to occupation X and 1 million women to occupation Y. The wage rate will equalize at *B* in all three occupations and the nation's output will rise by the sum of the two blue areas minus the single green area.

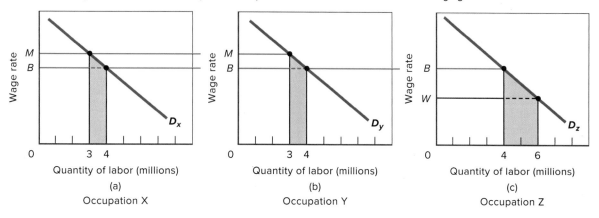

Effects of Crowding Suppose that, as a consequence of discrimination, the 6 million women are excluded from occupations X and Y and crowded into occupation Z, where they earn wage *W*. Assume that the men distribute themselves equally among occupations X and Y, meaning that 3 million male workers are in each occupation and have a common wage of *M*.

Because women are crowded into occupation Z, labor supply (not shown) is larger, and their wage rate *W* is much lower than *M*. Because of the discrimination, this equilibrium situation will persist as long as the crowding occurs. The occupational barrier means women cannot move into occupations X and Y in pursuit of a higher wage.

The result is a loss of output for society. To see why, recall that labor demand reflects labor's marginal revenue product, which is labor's contribution to domestic output. Thus, the blue areas for occupations X and Y in Figure 23.6 show the decrease in domestic output—the market value of the marginal output—caused by subtracting 1 million women from each of these occupations. Similarly, the green area for occupation Z shows the increase in domestic output caused by moving 2 million women into occupation Z. Although society would gain the added output represented by the green area in occupation Z, it would lose the output represented by the sum of the two blue areas in occupations X and Y. That output loss exceeds the output gain, producing a net output loss for society.

Eliminating Occupational Segregation Now assume that through legislation or sweeping changes in social attitudes, discrimination disappears. Women, attracted by higher wage rates, shift from occupation Z to X and Y; 1 million women move into X and another 1 million move into Y. Now there are 4 million workers in Z, and occupational segregation is eliminated. At that point there are 4 million workers in each occupation, and wage rates in all three occupations are equal, here at *B*. That wage equality eliminates the incentive for further reallocations of labor.

The new, nondiscriminatory equilibrium clearly benefits women, who now receive higher wages. It hurts men, who now receive lower wages. Women were initially harmed and men benefited through discrimination; removing discrimination corrects that situation.

Society also gains. The elimination of occupational segregation reverses the net output loss just discussed. Adding 1 million women to each of occupations X and Y in Figure 23.6 increases domestic output by the sum of the two blue areas. The decrease in domestic output caused by losing 2 million women from occupation Z is shown by the green area. The sum of the two increases in domestic output in X and Y exceeds the decrease in domestic output in Z. With the end of the discrimination, 2 million women workers have moved from occupation Z, where their contribution to domestic output (their MRP) is low, to higher-paying occupations X and Y, where their contribution to domestic output is high. Thus society gains a more efficient allocation of resources from the removal of occupational discrimination.

Examples: The easing of occupational barriers has led to a surge of women gaining advanced degrees in high-paying professions. For instance, the percentage of doctoral degrees—including law

Debating Universal Basic Income

The COVID-19 Pandemic Provided Some New Evidence in the Debate over Whether Governments Should Guarantee Minimum Monthly Incomes.

The idea of a universal basic income, or UBI, is not new. President Nixon wanted to implement one back in the late 1960s but could not muster the votes in Congress. UBI has become a hot topic again over the past decade. Specific plans vary, but the basic idea is simple: the government would guarantee a minimum monthly income to every citizen, with the money arriving by automatic deposits into recipients' bank accounts.

Advocates assert a wide variety of benefits, including a reduction in poverty, a reduction in income inequality, and a reduction in the amount of anxiety and stress caused by money problems. Some advocates go a step further and urge not only guaranteed monthly payments but replacing most or all of our existing government welfare and income maintenance programs with UBI. They argue that it would be much less costly for the government to administer a single monthly UBI payment than it is to administer the large and sometimes confusing array of payment and reimbursement systems that we currently use to deliver welfare and public assistance.

Detractors have cited high costs, unfairness, and unintended consequences as reasons for opposition. With respect to costs, they point out that sending every American a check for $1,000 each month would cost $3.96 trillion, or almost as much as the federal government currently collects each year in taxes. Based on those costs, they argue that voters would not accept the massive tax increases that would be necessary to fund UBI.

Opponents also contend that it would be unfair to send everyone a UBI check. Most people are employed. Over 60 percent of Americans own homes. Why should financially secure people get a government welfare check each month?

Finally, opponents of UBI insist that giving everybody a guaranteed $1,000 per month would reduce the incentive to work. Many people, they assert, would either work fewer hours or not work at all. Thus, they say, UBI would encourage laziness and freeloading off the people that continue to work and pay taxes.

The evidence that we have with respect to UBI is limited. Several intentionally designed scientific trials are under way in a dozen countries. None of them gives money to better-off people. Instead, benefits are being targeted at people with financial need, such as low-income mothers and poor rural villagers. The results will give evidence about whether UBI works and, if so, under what circumstances and for what sorts of beneficiaries.

By contrast, the COVID-19 pandemic provided an unintentional experiment relevant to the specific question of whether a universal basic income could reduce the incentive to work. That experiment arose because the enhanced unemployment benefits that Congress approved as part of its COVID response were universally available for over a year to every American worker who lost a job during the

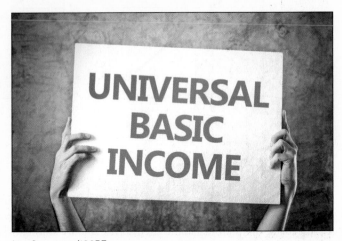

Igor Stevanovic/123RF

pandemic and were set up such that they would keep on paying for as long as an unemployed worker chose to stay unemployed rather than go back to work.

In addition, those benefits were large, exceeding what 68 percent of eligible workers could make each week if they were working. Thus, we had a chance to see what tens of millions of workers would do if their decision was to remain unemployed and collect around $2,700 per month in unemployment benefits or go back to work and make less than $2,700 per month. The experiment was made even more stark by the fact that after the first few months of the pandemic, labor shortages arose and jobs were easy to get—meaning that for the vast majority of people receiving unemployment benefits, unemployment was voluntary.

As you might not be surprised to find out, millions of people preferred to receive $2,700 per month without having to work than the lesser amounts they would have earned if they had gone back to work.

That fact is relevant to the UBI debate because it indicates that—at high enough levels—a monthly UBI payment *would* discourage work. But most advocates of UBI have not suggested such high levels and it's not clear from the evidence currently available whether UBI would have much of a deterrent effect on work if the guaranteed monthly amounts were substantially *less* than what people could make by working.

The intentionally designed scientific experiments that are under way will help provide more nuance. But even if the experiments indicate that there are net benefits in at least in certain cases, there will still be a large political fight over how much, for whom, and how to pay for it. A similar political fight doomed President Nixon's attempt at UBI fifty years ago.

degrees and medical degrees—earned by women in the United States has exceeded 50 percent since 2008. Across all graduate programs, women outnumbered men by a ratio of 148-to-100 in 2020. Women have also earned the majority of bachelor's degrees in the United States every year since 1982, and in 2020 earned 57 percent of all bachelor's degrees awarded in the United States.

Cost to Society as Well as to Individuals

It is obvious from all three models of discrimination that discrimination by characteristics such as race, ethnicity, gender, or age imposes costs on those who are discriminated against. They have lower wages, less access to jobs, or both. Preferred workers in turn benefit from discrimination through less job competition, greater job access, and higher wages. But discrimination does more than simply transfer earnings from some people to others, thus contributing to income inequality and increasing poverty. Where it exists, discrimination also diminishes the economy's total output and income. In that regard, discrimination acts much like any other artificial barrier to free competition. By arbitrarily blocking qualified individuals from high-productivity (and thus high-wage) jobs, discrimination keeps those discriminated against from providing their maximum contribution to society's total output and total income. In terms of production possibilities analysis, discrimination locates society inside the production possibilities curve that would be available to it if there were no discrimination. Discrimination redistributes a diminished amount of total income.

▶ Discrimination occurs when workers who have the same abilities, education, training, and experience as other workers receive inferior treatment with respect to hiring, occupational access, promotion, or wages.

▶ The taste-for-discrimination model sees discrimination as representing a preference or "taste" for which the discriminator is willing to pay.

▶ The theory of statistical discrimination says that employers often wrongly judge individuals on the basis of average group characteristics rather than on personal characteristics, thus harming those discriminated against.

▶ The crowding model of discrimination suggests that when women and minorities are systematically excluded from high-paying occupations and crowded into low-paying ones, their wages and society's domestic output are reduced.

QUICK REVIEW
23.4

Summary

LO23.1 Explain how income inequality is measured and described.

The distribution of income in the United States reflects considerable inequality. The richest 20 percent of households receive 52.2 percent of total income, while the poorest 20 percent receive 3.0 percent.

The Lorenz curve shows the percentage of total income received by each percentage of households. The extent of the gap between the Lorenz curve and a line of total equality illustrates the degree of income inequality.

The Gini ratio measures the overall dispersion of the income distribution. The Gini ratio ranges from zero to 1, with higher ratios signifying more income inequality.

LO23.2 Discuss the extent and sources of income inequality.

Recognizing that the positions of individual families in the income distribution change over time and incorporating the effects of noncash transfers and taxes would reveal less income inequality than do standard annual census data. Government transfers (cash and noncash) greatly lessen the degree of income inequality; taxes also reduce inequality, but not nearly as much as transfers.

Causes of income inequality include differences in abilities, in education and training, and in job tastes, along with discrimination, inequality in the distribution of wealth, and an unequal distribution of market power.

LO23.3 Demonstrate how U.S. income inequality has changed since 1985.

Census data show that income inequality has increased since 1980. The major cause of the recent increases in income inequality is a rising demand for highly skilled workers, which has boosted their earnings significantly.

LO23.4 Debate the economic arguments for and against income inequality.

The basic argument for income equality holds that it maximizes consumer satisfaction (total utility) from a particular level of total income. The main argument for income inequality holds that it provides the incentives to work, invest, and assume risk and is necessary for the production of output, which, in turn, creates income that is then available for distribution.

LO23.5 Relate poverty to age, gender, and ethnicity.

Current statistics reveal that 11.4 percent of the U.S. population lives in poverty. Poverty rates are particularly high for female-headed families, young children, African Americans, and Hispanics.

LO23.6 Identify the major components of the U.S. income-maintenance system.

In the United States, the government's income-maintenance program currently consists of social insurance programs (Social Security,

Medicare, and unemployment compensation) and public assistance programs (SSI, TANF, SNAP/food stamps, Medicaid, and the earned-income tax credit).

LO23.7 Discuss labor market discrimination.

Discrimination in the labor market occurs when women or minorities having the same abilities, education, training, and experience as men or white workers are given inferior treatment with respect to hiring, occupational choice, education and training, promotion, and wages.

In the taste-for-discrimination model, some white employers have a preference for discrimination, measured by a discrimination coefficient d. Prejudiced white employers will hire African American workers only if their wages are at least d dollars below those of whites. Declines in the discrimination coefficients of white employers will increase the demand for African American workers, raising the African American wage rate and the ratio of African American wages to white wages. Competition may eliminate discrimination in the long run.

Statistical discrimination occurs when employers base employment decisions about *individuals* on the average characteristics of *groups* of workers, which can lead to discrimination against individuals even in the absence of prejudice.

The crowding model of occupational segregation indicates how white men gain higher earnings at the expense of women and certain minorities who are confined to a limited number of occupations. The model shows that discrimination also causes a net loss of domestic output.

Terms and Concepts

income inequality

Lorenz curve

Gini ratio

income mobility

noncash transfers

equality-efficiency trade-off

poverty rate

entitlement programs

social insurance programs

Social Security

Medicare

unemployment insurance

public assistance programs

Supplemental Security Income (SSI)

Supplemental Nutrition Assistance Program (SNAP)

Temporary Assistance for Needy Families (TANF)

Medicaid

earned-income tax credit (EITC)

discrimination

taste-for-discrimination model

discrimination coefficient

statistical discrimination

occupational segregation

Discussion Questions

1. Use quintiles to briefly summarize the degree of income inequality in the United States. How and to what extent does government reduce income inequality? **LO23.1**
2. Assume that Amir, Beth, Carol, David, and Ed receive incomes of $500, $250, $125, $75, and $50, respectively. Construct and interpret a Lorenz curve for this five-person economy. What percentage of total income is received by the richest quintile and by the poorest quintile? **LO23.1**
3. How does the Gini ratio relate to the Lorenz curve? Why can't the Gini ratio exceed 1? What is implied about the direction of income inequality if the Gini ratio declines from 0.42 to 0.35? How would one show that change of inequality in the Lorenz diagram? **LO23.1**
4. Why is the lifetime distribution of income more equal than the distribution in any specific year? **LO23.1**
5. Briefly discuss the major causes of income inequality. With respect to income inequality, is there any difference between inheriting property and inheriting a high IQ? Explain. **LO23.2**
6. What factors have contributed to increased income inequality since 1985? **LO23.3**
7. Should a nation's income be distributed to its members according to their contributions to the production of that total income or according to the members' needs? Should society attempt to equalize income or economic opportunities? Are the issues of equity and equality in the distribution of income synonymous? To what degree, if any, is income inequality equitable? **LO23.4**
8. Do you agree or disagree? Explain your reasoning: "There need be no trade-off between equality and efficiency. An 'efficient'

economy that yields an income distribution that many regard as unfair may cause those with meager incomes to become discouraged and stop trying. So efficiency may be undermined. A fairer distribution of rewards may generate a higher average productive effort on the part of the population, thereby enhancing efficiency. If people think they are playing a fair economic game and this belief causes them to try harder, an economy with an equitable income distribution may be efficient as well."[6] **LO23.4**
9. Comment on or explain: **LO23.4**
   a. Endowing everyone with equal income will make for very unequal enjoyment and satisfaction.
   b. Equality is a "superior good"; the richer we become, the more of it we can afford.
   c. The mob goes in search of bread, and the means it employs is generally to wreck the bakeries.
   d. Some freedoms may be more important in the long run than freedom from want on the part of every individual.
   e. Capitalism and democracy are really a most improbable mixture. Maybe that is why they need each other—to put some rationality into equality and some humanity into efficiency.
   f. The incentives created by the attempt to bring about a more equal distribution of income are in conflict with the incentives needed to generate increased income.
10. How could the poverty rate fall while the number of people in poverty rises? Which group in each of the following pairs has

---

[6]Paraphrased from Andrew Schotter, *Free Market Economics* (New York: St. Martin's Press, 1985), pp. 30–31.

the higher poverty rate: (*a*) children or people age 65 or over? (*b*) African Americans or foreign-born noncitizens? (*c*) Asians or Hispanics? **LO23.5**

11. What are the essential differences between social insurance and public assistance programs? Why is Medicare a social insurance program, whereas Medicaid is a public assistance program? Why is the earned-income tax credit considered to be a public assistance program? **LO23.6**

12. The labor demand and supply data in the following table relate to a single occupation. Use them to answer the questions that follow. Base your answers on the taste-for-discrimination model. **LO23.7**

Quantity of Hispanic Labor Demanded, Thousands	Hispanic Wage Rate	Quantity of Hispanic Labor Supplied, Thousands
24	$16	52
30	14	44
35	12	35
42	10	28
48	8	20

a. Plot the labor demand and supply curves for Hispanic workers in this occupation.

b. What are the equilibrium Hispanic wage rate and quantity of Hispanic employment?

c. Suppose the white wage rate in this occupation is $16. What is the Hispanic-to-white wage ratio?

d. Suppose a particular employer has a discrimination coefficient *d* of $5 per hour. Will that employer hire Hispanic or white workers at the Hispanic-to-white wage ratio indicated in part *c*? Explain.

e. Suppose employers as a group become less prejudiced against Hispanics and demand 14 more units of Hispanic labor at each Hispanic wage rate in the table. What are the new equilibrium Hispanic wage rate and level of Hispanic employment? Does the Hispanic-to-white wage ratio rise or fall? Explain.

f. Suppose Hispanics as a group increase their labor services in that occupation, collectively offering 14 more units of labor at each Hispanic wage rate. Disregarding the changes indicated in part *e*, what are the new equilibrium Hispanic wage rate and level of Hispanic employment? Does the Hispanic-to-white wage ratio rise, or does it fall?

13. Statistical discrimination implies that discrimination can persist indefinitely, while the taste-for-discrimination model suggests that competition might reduce discrimination in the long run. Explain the difference. **LO23.7**

14. Use a demand-and-supply model to explain the impact of occupational segregation or "crowding" on the relative wage rates and earnings of men and women. Who gains and who loses from the elimination of occupational segregation? Is there a net gain or a net loss to society? Explain. **LO23.7**

15. **LAST WORD** What are the main arguments for and against UBI? What was the reaction of millions of U.S. workers during the pandemic to being offered the chance to make more in unemployment benefits than they could working? What is your personal opinion on the probable effects of UBI?

Review Questions

1. Suppose that the United States has a Gini ratio of 0.41 while Sweden has a Gini ratio of 0.31. Which country has a more equal distribution of income? Explain. **LO23.1**
   a. The United States.
   b. Sweden.
   c. They are actually equal.

2. Some part of income inequality is likely to be the result of discrimination. But other factors responsible for inequality include (select as many as apply): **LO23.2**
   a. differences in abilities and talents.
   b. differences in education and training.
   c. different preferences for work versus leisure.
   d. different preferences for low-paying but safe jobs relative to high-paying but dangerous jobs.

3. Suppose that a society contains only two members, a lawyer named Monique and a handyman named James. Five years ago, Monique made $100,000 while James made $50,000. This year, Monique will make $300,000 while James will make $100,000. Which of the following statements about this society's income distribution are true? **LO23.2**
   *Select **one or more** answers from the choices shown.*
   a. In absolute dollar amounts, the entire distribution of income has been moving upward.
   b. In absolute dollar amounts, the entire distribution of income has been stagnant.
   c. The relative distribution of income has become more equal.

d. The relative distribution of income has become less equal.
   e. The relative distribution of income has remained constant.
   f. The rich are getting richer while the poor are getting poorer.
   g. The rich are getting richer faster than the poor are getting richer.

4. Suppose that the last dollar that Victoria receives as income brings her a marginal utility of 10 utils while the last dollar that Fredrick receives as income brings him a marginal utility of 15 utils. If our goal is to maximize the combined total utility of Victoria and Fredrick, we should: **LO23.4**
   a. redistribute income from Victoria to Fredrick.
   b. redistribute income from Fredrick to Victoria.
   c. not engage in any redistribution because the current situation already maximizes total utility.
   d. none of the above.

5. True or false: If women are crowded into elementary education and away from fire fighting, wages in fire fighting will tend to be lower than if women weren't crowded into elementary education. **LO23.7**

6. In the taste-for-discrimination model, an increase in employer prejudice against African American workers would cause the discrimination coefficient to _____ and the demand curve for African American labor to shift _____. **LO23.7**
   a. decrease; right
   b. decrease; left
   c. increase; right
   d. increase; left

Problems

1. In 2021, *Forbes* magazine listed Jeff Bezos, the founder of Amazon, as the richest person in the United States. His personal wealth was estimated to be $177 billion. Given that there were about 333 million people living in the United States that year, how much could each person have received if Bezos's wealth had been divided equally among the population of the United States? (Hint: A billion is a 1 followed by 9 zeros while a million is a 1 followed by six zeros.) **LO23.1**

2. Imagine an economy with only two people. Lakshmi earns $20,000 per year, while Roger earns $80,000 per year. As shown in the following figure, the Lorenz curve for this two-person economy consists of two line segments. The first runs from the origin to point *a*, while the second runs from point *a* to point *b*. **LO23.1**

   a. Calculate the Gini ratio for this two-person economy using the geometric formulas for the area of a triangle (= ½ × base × height) and the area of a rectangle (= base × height). (Hint: The area under the line segment from point *a* to point *b* can be thought of as the sum of the area of a particular triangle and the area of a particular rectangle.)

   b. What would the Gini ratio be if the government taxed $20,000 away from Roger and gave it to Lakshmi? (Hint: The figure will change.)

   c. Start again with Lakshmi earning $20,000 per year and Roger earning $80,000 per year. What would the Gini ratio be if both their incomes doubled? How much has the Gini ratio changed from before the doubling in incomes to after the doubling in incomes?

3. In 2018, many unskilled workers in the United States earned the federal minimum wage of $7.25 per hour. By contrast, average earnings in 2018 were about $27 per hour, and certain highly skilled professionals, such as doctors and lawyers, earned $100 or more per hour. **LO23.6**

   a. If we assume that wage differences are caused solely by differences in productivity, how many times more productive was the average worker than a worker being paid the federal minimum wage? How many times more productive was a $100-per-hour lawyer compared to a worker earning minimum wage?

   b. Assume that there are 20 minimum-wage workers in the economy for each $100-per-hour lawyer. Also assume that both lawyers and minimum-wage workers work the same number of hours per week. If everyone works 40 hours per week, how much does a $100-per-hour lawyer earn in a week? How much does a minimum-wage worker earn in a week?

   c. Suppose that the government pairs each $100-per-hour lawyer with 20 nearby minimum-wage workers. If the government taxes 25 percent of each lawyer's income each week and distributes it equally among the 20 minimum-wage workers with whom each lawyer is paired, how much money will each of those minimum-wage workers receive each week? If we divide by the number of hours worked each week, how much does each minimum-wage worker's weekly transfer amount to on an hourly basis?

   d. Suppose the government taxes each lawyer 100 percent before dividing the money equally among the 20 minimum-wage workers with whom each lawyer is paired. How much per week will each minimum-wage worker receive? And how much is that on an hourly basis?

4. The desire to maximize profits can work against racial and other types of discrimination. To see why, consider two equally productive accountants named Ted and Jared. Ted is African American, and Jared is white. Both can complete 10 audits per month. **LO23.7**

   a. Suppose that for any accounting firm that hires either Ted or Jared, all the other costs of performing an audit (besides paying either Ted or Jared) come to $1,000 per audit. If the going rate that must be paid to hire an accountant is $7,000 per month, how much will it cost an accounting firm to produce one audit if it hires either Ted or Jared to do the work?

   b. If the market price that accounting firms charge their clients for an audit is $1,800, what would the accounting profit per audit be for a firm that hired either Ted or Jared? What is the profit rate as a percentage?

   c. Suppose that firm *A* dislikes hiring African American accountants, while firm *B* is happy to hire them. So Ted ends up working at firm *B* rather than firm *A*. If Ted works 11 months per year, how many audits will he complete for firm *B* each year? How much in accounting profits will firm *B* earn each year from those audits?

   d. Because firm *A* passed on hiring Ted because he is African American, firm *A* is forgoing the profits it could have earned if it had hired Ted. If the firm is willing to forgo up to $5,000 per year in profit to avoid hiring African American people, by how many dollars will firm *A* regret its decision not to hire Ted?

Health Care

>> LEARNING OBJECTIVES

LO24.1 Describe the health care industry in the United States.

LO24.2 Discuss the economic implications of rising health care costs.

LO24.3 Discuss the problem of limited access to health care.

LO24.4 List the demand and supply factors that explain rising health care costs.

LO24.5 Describe cost-containment strategies for health care.

LO24.6 Summarize the goals of the Affordable Care Act.

On March 23, 2010, President Barack Obama signed the **Affordable Care Act (ACA),** a wide-ranging law that proponents claimed would lower health care costs while increasing access to quality health care for millions of low-income Americans.

The legislation was designed to address a wide set of concerns relating to the provision, delivery, and cost of health care. These included the high and rapidly rising cost of health insurance for those who did have health insurance, the fact that tens of millions of Americans at any given moment were without health insurance, and the inability of many people with preexisting conditions to obtain health insurance.

The controversial law gave the federal government sweeping new powers to promote universal health insurance coverage and to regulate insurance policies. Because health care spending was 17.9 percent of GDP in 2010, the law effectively put the federal government in control of nearly one-fifth of the U.S. economy. This chapter applies microeconomic analysis to help explain the origin of the problems that the law was designed to address as well as the heated debate over whether the policies prescribed by the law are likely to achieve their goals.

Affordable Care Act (ACA)
A major health care law passed by the federal government in 2010. Major provisions include an individual health insurance mandate, a ban on insurers refusing to accept patients with preexisting conditions, and federal (rather than state) regulation of health insurance policies.

The Health Care Industry

Because the boundaries of the health care industry are not precise, defining the industry is difficult. In general, it includes services provided in hospitals, nursing homes, laboratories, and physicians' and dentists' offices. It also includes prescription and nonprescription drugs, artificial limbs, and eyeglasses. However, many goods and services that may affect health are not included, such as low-carb foods, vitamins, and gym memberships.

>> **LO24.1** Describe the health care industry in the United States.

Health care is one of the largest U.S. industries, employing about 20 million people, including about 939,000 practicing physicians, or 286 doctors per 100,000 of population. The United States has about 6,090 hospitals containing nearly 920,000 beds. Americans make nearly 1 billion visits to office-based physicians each year.

The U.S. Emphasis on Private Health Insurance

Many provisions of the Affordable Care Act focus on health insurance because a high proportion of U.S. health care spending is provided through employer-provided private health insurance. By

national health insurance
A program in which a nation's government provides a basic package of health care to all citizens at no direct charge or at a low cost-sharing level. Financing is out of general *tax* revenues.

contrast, many countries, including Canada, provide **national health insurance** in which the government uses tax revenues to provide basic health care to every resident at either no charge or at low cost-sharing levels. In such countries, relatively few people bother to buy private health insurance—and then only to cover services that the national health insurance system does not pay for.

The uniquely U.S. emphasis on employer-paid private health insurance is a relatively recent phenomenon. It began during the Second World War in response to price and wage controls that the federal government imposed to prevent inflation. The wage controls were problematic for the private companies charged with building the tanks, planes, and boats needed to win the war. These firms needed to expand output rapidly and knew that doing so would be possible only if they could attract workers away from other industries. Several manufacturers stumbled on the strategy of offering free health insurance as a way of attracting workers. Unable to raise wages, the companies recruited the workers they needed by offering health insurance as a fringe benefit paid for by the employer.

After the war, price and wage controls were lifted. Nevertheless, more and more companies began to offer "free" health insurance to their employees. They did so because a provision in the federal tax law makes it cheaper for companies to purchase insurance for their employees than it would be for employees to purchase insurance on their own. By 2007, nearly 88 percent of people with private health insurance received it as a benefit provided by their employer rather than by purchasing it themselves directly from an insurance company.

The prominence of employer-provided health insurance in the United States has had several important consequences. First, health care paid for via health insurance can create perverse incentives for overuse that, in turn, lead to higher prices. Second, health care reform efforts have tended to focus on regulating the private health insurance system with which most people are familiar rather than replacing it with something radically different, such as national health insurance.

Basic Insurance Terminology

Please note that whether health insurance is provided by an employer, by the government, or paid for by an individual directly, the basic vocabulary of insurance stays the same. A *premium* is a monthly fee paid into an insurance system by an individual on their own behalf or by a sponsor (an employer or the government) on the individual's behalf. The premium goes into a common pool of money that will be used to help pay for the future health care expenses of the people who are enrolled in the insurance system and for whom premiums are being paid.

Very few insurance systems promise to pay for all future health care expenses. Each system is bound by a legal contract called an *insurance policy* which lists exactly what it will and will not pay for in the future and how those costs are going to be split between the insurance system and the individuals enrolled in, or "covered by," that system. The amounts that must be paid for by covered individuals are referred to as *out-of-pocket costs* or *cost sharing* because they must be paid for by the covered individuals out of their own funds rather than by the insurance system.

deductible The dollar sum of (for example, health care) costs that an insured individual must pay before the insurer begins to pay.

There are three types of out-of-pocket costs: deductibles, copayments, and coinsurance. A **deductible** is the cumulative amount that an insured person must pay for by themselves during a given calendar year before the insurance system starts to pay for covered services. With a $2,000 annual deductible, for example, the individual would have to pay for the first $2,000 of covered services during a given year before the insurance system would begin to cover any costs in excess of $2,000.

copayment A fixed amount (such as $25 per office visit) that the insured individual must pay even after the annual deductible has been passed.

Most insurance policies require some form of cost sharing even after the annual deductible has been reached. A **copayment** is a fixed amount (such as $25 per office visit) that the individual must pay for a covered health care service even after the annual deductible has been passed. **Coinsurance** is the requirement that the insured person pay for a fixed percentage (such as 20 percent) of the costs of certain covered services even after the annual deductible has been passed.

coinsurance The percentage of (say, health care) costs that an insured individual pays while the insurer pays the remainder.

Many insurance policies require both copayments and coinsurance while also putting a maximum annual cap (limit) on the cumulative dollar amount of copayments and coinsurance that an insured individual must pay during a given year.

Twin Problems: Costs and Access

In recent decades, the U.S. health care system has suffered from two highly publicized problems:

- The cost of health care has risen rapidly in response to higher prices and an increase in the quantity of services provided. (Spending on health care, or total "health care costs," involves both "prices" and "quantities.") The price of medical care has traditionally increased faster than the overall price level in nearly all periods. Over the period 2017–2020, medical care prices rose by an average of 4.0 percent per year. In contrast, overall prices for all consumer goods increased by an average of about 1.9 percent annually for those four years. Health care spending (price × quantity) grew by 4.3 percent in 2017, 4.6 percent in 2018, 4.3 percent in 2019, and 9.7 percent in 2020 (the first year of the COVID-19 pandemic). It is projected to grow at an annual rate of 5.4 percent over the next 10 years, far faster than inflation.

- In 2021, some 31 million Americans, or about 9.3 percent of the population, had neither public nor private health insurance, and, as a result, had significantly reduced access to health care services.

Efforts to reform health care have focused on controlling costs and making it accessible to everyone. These two goals are related, because high and rising prices make health care services unaffordable to a significant portion of the U.S. population. In fact, a dual system of health care may be evolving in the United States. Those with insurance or other financial means receive excellent medical treatment, but many people, because of their inability to pay, often fail to seek out even basic treatment. Free county hospitals and private charity hospitals do provide services to those without insurance, but the quality of care can be considerably lower than that available to people who have insurance.

High and Rising Health Care Costs

We need to examine several aspects of health care costs and high health care spending.

Health Care Spending Health care spending in the United States is high and rising in both absolute terms and as a percentage of domestic output.

Total Spending on Health Care Figure 24.1a gives an overview of the major types of U.S. health care spending ($4.1 trillion in 2020). It shows that 31 cents of each health care dollar goes to hospitals, while 20 cents goes to physicians, and 12 cents is spent on dental, vision, and other miscellaneous health care services.

Figure 24.1b shows the sources of funds for health care spending. Sixty-nine percent of health care spending is financed by insurance. Public insurance (Medicaid, Medicare, and insurance for

FIGURE 24.1
Health care expenditures and finance.

Total U.S. health care expenditures are extremely large ($4.1 trillion in 2020). (a) Most health care expenditures are for hospitals and the services of physicians and other skilled professionals. (b) Public and private insurance pays for 69 percent of health care expenditures.

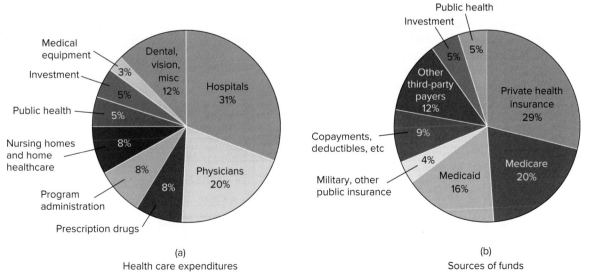

(a)
Health care expenditures

(b)
Sources of funds

Source: National Health Expenditure Data: Historical, Centers for Medicare and Medicaid Services.
Note: Numbers may not sum to 100 percent due to rounding.

FIGURE 24.2
U.S. health care expenditures as a percentage of GDP.

U.S. health care spending as a percentage of GDP has greatly increased since 1960.

Source: National Health Expenditure Data: Historical, Centers for Medicare & Medicaid Services

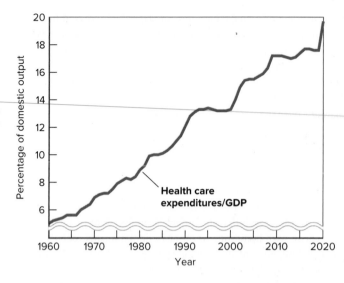

veterans, current military personnel, and government employees) is the source of 40 cents of each dollar spent. Private insurance accounts for 29 cents. Thus public and private insurance provide 69 cents of each dollar spent. Of the remaining 31 cents, 9 cents comes directly out of the patient's pocket. It is paid mainly as *deductibles, copayments,* or *coinsurance.* For a review of Medicare and Medicaid, see Chapter 23.

Percentage of GDP Figure 24.2 shows how U.S. health care spending has been increasing as a percentage of GDP. Health care spending absorbed 5.0 percent of GDP in 1960 but rose to 17.6 percent of GDP in the 2019 before spiking to 19.7 percent of GDP in 2020 due to the Covid-19 pandemic.

International Comparisons Global Perspective 24.1 reveals that among the industrialized nations, health care spending as a percentage of GDP (= gross domestic product, or national income) is highest in the United States. It is reasonable to assume that health care spending varies positively with output and incomes, but that fact doesn't account for the higher U.S. health expenditures as a percentage of GDP. Later in this chapter we explain why the United States is "in a league of its own" regarding the proportion of national income devoted to health care.

Quality of Care: Are We Healthier?

Comparing the quality of health care from country to country is difficult. Yet there is general agreement that medical care in the United States is among the best in the world. Average life expectancy in the United States has increased by about 8 years since 1970, and U.S. physicians

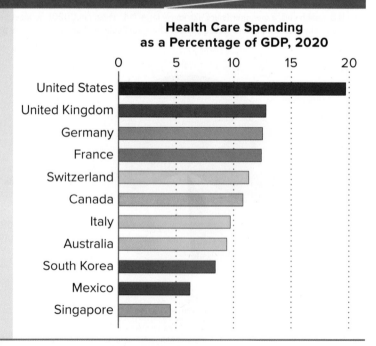

GLOBAL PERSPECTIVE 24.1

HEALTH CARE SPENDING AS A PERCENTAGE OF GDP, SELECTED NATIONS

The United States tops the chart when it comes to health care expenditures as a percentage of national income (GDP). In the United States, nearly 20 percent of national income was spent on health-care in 2020, compared to 13 percent or less in other developed nations.

Source: The World Bank, the Organization for Economic Co-operation and Development, and Center for Medicare and Medicaid Services.

and hospitals employ the most advanced medical equipment and technologies. Also, more than half the world's medical research is done in the United States. As a result, the incidence of disease has been declining and the quality of treatment has been improving. Polio has been virtually eliminated, ulcers are successfully treated without surgery, angioplasty and coronary bypass surgery greatly benefit those with heart disease, sophisticated body scanners are increasingly available diagnostic tools, and organ transplants and prosthetic joint replacements are almost routine.

However, the United States still faces many health challenges. Despite new screening and treatment technologies, the breast cancer mortality rate has shown only gradual improvement. Virtually forgotten diseases like tuberculosis and the measles have reappeared. And widespread obesity has caused the incidence of diabetes to soar. More generally, some experts say that high levels of health care spending have not produced significantly better health and well-being. U.S. health care expenditures are the highest in the world absolutely, as a proportion of GDP, and on a per capita basis. Yet many nations have lower rates of maternal and infant mortality and longer life expectancies.

Economic Implications of Rising Costs

The most visible economic effects of rising health care costs are higher health insurance premiums to employers and higher out-of-pocket costs to workers. But rising health care costs have other economic effects as well.

>> **LO24.2** Discuss the economic implications of rising health care costs.

Reduced Access to Care

Higher health care costs and insurance premiums reduce access to health care. Some employers reduce or eliminate health insurance as part of their pay packages, and some uninsured workers go without private health insurance. Consequently, the number of uninsured grows.

Labor Market Effects

Surging health care costs have three main effects on labor markets:

- *Slower wage growth* First, gains in workers' total compensation (wages plus fringe benefits, including health insurance paid for by employers) generally match gains in productivity. When health care costs (and thus insurance prices) rise more rapidly than productivity, firms wanting to maintain the existing level of health care benefits for their workers must reduce the growth of the wage portion of the total compensation package. Thus, in the long run, workers bear the burden of rising health care costs in the form of slower-growing wages.

- *Use of part-time and temporary workers* The high cost of employer-provided health insurance has led some employers to restructure their workforces. Full-time workers with health insurance benefits are employed in smaller numbers, and uninsured part-time or temporary workers are employed in greater numbers. Similarly, an employer with a generous but expensive health care plan might reduce its health insurance expense by firing its insured lower-wage workers—janitors, gardeners, and cafeteria staff—and replacing them with workers employed by outside independent contractors that provide little or no health insurance for their employees.

- *Outsourcing (and offshoring)* Burdened by rising health insurance costs, some firms find it profitable to shift part of their production to outside suppliers. This outsourcing may lower labor costs when the outside suppliers provide fewer medical benefits to their workers. Offshoring (international outsourcing) has shifted jobs to developing economies such as Mexico, India, and China. Although labor productivity in these countries is considerably lower than that in the United States, lower wages and fewer employer-provided medical benefits may be sufficient to make offshoring profitable.

Personal Bankruptcies

Large medical bills are a major cause of personal bankruptcy. Medical bills are often the last to be paid because there is nothing to repossess, shut off, or foreclose. Even individuals who pay all bills in a timely fashion can find themselves in tremendous financial difficulty when they face large, uninsured medical bills for major operations (such as open-heart surgery) and expensive medical procedures (such as cancer treatment).

Impact on Government Budgets

The budgets of federal, state, and local governments are negatively affected by soaring and sometimes unpredictable health care expenditures. In the past two decades, spending for health care through Medicare and Medicaid has been by far the fastest-growing segment of the federal budget. To pay for these rising expenditures, the government must either raise taxes, increase borrowing, or reduce the portion of the budget used for national defense, education, environmental programs, scientific research, and other spending categories.

The states are also finding it difficult to cover their share of the Medicaid bill. Most of them have been forced to raise their tax rates and search for new sources of revenue, and many of them have reduced spending on nonhealth programs such as infrastructure maintenance, welfare, and education. Local governments face similar budget strains in trying to finance public health services, hospitals, and clinics.

Too Much Spending?

Increased spending on computers or houses would be a sign of prosperity, not a cause for alarm, because society is obtaining more of each. What is different about increased spending on health care? Maybe nothing, say some economists. William Nordhaus of Yale, for example, estimated that the economic value of increases in longevity over the last 100 years nearly equals the total value of the additional GDP produced during that period. According to Kevin Murphy and Robert Topel, economists at the University of Chicago, reduced mortality from heart disease alone contributes $1.5 trillion of benefits a year in the United States. That amount nearly equals Canada's entire annual GDP.

While all economists agree that improved health care has greatly contributed to society's GDP and well-being, many economists think that health care expenditures in the United States are inefficiently large. The production of health care requires scarce resources such as capital in the form of hospitals and diagnostic equipment and the highly skilled labor of physicians, technicians, and nurses. The total output of health care in the United States may be so large that health care, at the margin, is worth less than the alternative goods and services these resources could produce. The United States therefore may be consuming health care beyond the MB = MC point that defines allocative efficiency.

Limited Access

>> **LO24.3** Discuss the problem of limited access to health care.

Even though the United States may overallocate resources to health care, not all Americans obtain the health care they need. Government surveys indicate that in 2021 about 31 million Americans, or roughly 9 percent of the population, had no health insurance for the entire year. As health care costs (and therefore health care insurance premiums) continue to rise, the number of uninsured could grow.

Who are the medically uninsured? As incomes rise, so does the probability of being insured. So it is no surprise that the uninsured are concentrated among those with low incomes and little wealth. Medicaid is designed to provide health care for the poor who are on welfare. But many poor people work at low or minimum-wage jobs without health care benefits, earning "too much" to qualify for Medicaid yet not enough to afford private health insurance. About half of the uninsured have a family head who works full time. Many single-parent families, African Americans, and Hispanics are uninsured simply because they are more likely to be poor.

Curiously, those with excellent health and those with the poorest health also tend to be uninsured. Many young people with excellent health simply choose not to buy health insurance. The chronically ill find it very difficult and too costly to obtain insurance. Because private health insurance is most frequently obtained through an employer, the unemployed are also likely to lack insurance. Meanwhile, among the employed, those working at smaller firms are also less likely to have health insurance because smaller firms tend to be less able to afford health insurance for their employees.

Low-wage workers are also less likely to be insured. Earlier we noted that, in the long run, employers pass on the increasing expense of health insurance to workers as lower wages. This option is not available to employers who are paying the minimum wage. Thus, as health care insurance premiums rise, employers cut or eliminate this benefit from the compensation package for their minimum- and low-wage workers.

Although many of the uninsured forgo health care, some do not. A few are able to pay for it out of pocket. Others may wait until their illness reaches a critical stage and then go to a hospital for admittance or to be treated in the emergency room. This form of treatment is more costly than if the patient had insurance and therefore had been treated earlier by a physician. It is estimated that hospitals provide about $42 billion of uncompensated ("free") health care per year. The hospitals then try to shift these costs to those who have insurance or who can pay out of pocket.

QUICK REVIEW

24.1

▶ Private, employer-funded health insurance plays a much larger role in the delivery of health care in the United States than it does in other countries.

▶ Health care spending in the United States has been increasing absolutely and as a percentage of gross domestic output.

▶ Rising health care costs have caused (a) more people to find health insurance unaffordable; (b) adverse labor market effects, including slower real-wage growth and increased use of part-time and temporary workers; and (c) restriction of non-health spending by governments.

▶ Rising health care spending may reflect an overallocation of resources to the health care industry.

▶ Approximately 9 percent of all Americans have no health insurance and, hence, inferior access to quality health care.

Why the Rapid Rise in Costs?

The rising prices, quantities, and costs of health care services are the result of the demand for health care increasing much more rapidly than supply. We will examine the underlying reasons in some detail. But first it will be helpful to understand certain characteristics of the health care market.

>> **LO24.4** List the demand and supply factors that explain rising health care costs.

Peculiarities of the Health Care Market

We know that purely competitive markets can achieve both allocative and productive efficiency: The most desired products are produced in the least costly way. We also know that many imperfectly competitive markets, perhaps aided by regulation or the threat of antitrust action, provide outcomes generally accepted as efficient. What, then, are the special features of the health care market that have contributed to rising prices and escalating costs?

- *Ethical and equity considerations* Ethical questions inevitably intervene in markets when decisions involve the quality of life, or literally life or death. In general, society regards health care as an "entitlement" or a "right" and is reluctant to ration it solely by price and income.

- *Asymmetric information* Health care buyers typically have little or no understanding of complex diagnostic and treatment procedures, but the physicians, who are the health care sellers of those procedures, possess detailed information. In this unusual situation, the doctor (supplier) as the agent of the patient (consumer) tells the patient what health care services to consume.

- *Positive externalities* The medical care market often generates positive externalities (spillover benefits). For example, an immunization against polio, smallpox, or measles benefits the immediate purchaser, but it also benefits society by reducing the risk that other members of society will be infected with a highly contagious disease. Similarly, a healthy labor force is more productive, contributing to society's general prosperity and well-being.

- *Third-party payments: insurance* Because three-quarters of all health care expenses are paid through public or private insurance, health care consumers pay much lower out-of-pocket "prices" than they would otherwise. Those lower prices result in "excess" consumption of health care services.

The Increasing Demand for Health Care

With these four features in mind, let's consider some factors that have increased the demand for health care over time.

Rising Incomes: The Role of Elasticities Because health care is a normal good, increases in domestic income have increased the demand for health care. Several studies of industrially advanced countries suggest that the income elasticity coefficient for health care is about 1. In other words, per capita health care spending rises approximately in proportion to increases in per capita income. For example, a 3 percent increase in income will generate a 3 percent increase in health care expenditures. Some evidence suggests that income elasticity may be higher in the United States, perhaps as high as 1.5.

Estimates of the price elasticity of demand for health care imply that it is quite inelastic, with this coefficient being as low as 0.2. Thus, the quantity of health care consumed declines relatively little as price increases. For example, a 10 percent increase in price will reduce the quantity demanded by only 2 percent. An important consequence is that total health care spending increases as the price of health care rises.

The relative insensitivity of health care spending to price changes results from four factors. First, people consider health care a necessity, not a luxury. Few, if any, good substitutes exist for medical care. Second, medical treatment is often provided in an emergency situation in which price considerations are secondary or irrelevant. Third, most consumers prefer a long-term relationship with their doctors and therefore do not "shop around" when health care prices rise. Fourth, most patients have insurance and are therefore not directly affected by the price of health care. If insured patients pay, for example, only 20 percent of their health care expenses, they are less concerned with price increases or price differences between hospitals and between doctors than they would be if they paid 100 percent.

An Aging Population The U.S. population is aging. People 65 years of age and older constituted approximately 9 percent of the population in 1960 but 17 percent in 2020. Projections for the year 2035 indicate 21 percent of the population will be 65 or over by that year.

This aging of the population affects the demand for health care because older people encounter more frequent and more prolonged spells of illness. Specifically, those 65 and older consume about three and one-half times as much health care as those between 19 and 64. People over 84 consume almost two and one-half times as much health care as those in the 65-to-69 age group. Health care expenditures are often extraordinarily high in the last year of one's life.

In 2011, the oldest of the 76 million members of the baby boom generation born between 1946 and 1964 began turning 65. As a result, we can expect a substantial surge in the demand for health care.

Unhealthy Lifestyles Substance abuse helps drive up health care costs. The abuse of alcohol, tobacco, and illicit drugs damages health and is therefore an important component of the demand for health care services. Alcohol is a major cause of injury-producing traffic accidents and liver disease. Tobacco use markedly increases the probability of cancer, heart disease, bronchitis, and emphysema. Illicit drugs are a major contributor to violent crime, health problems in infants, and the spread of AIDS. In addition, illicit-drug users make hundreds of thousands of costly visits to hospital emergency rooms each year. And overeating and lack of exercise contribute to heart disease, diabetes, and many other ailments. One study estimated that obesity-related medical conditions may account for 21 percent of all U.S. medical spending.

The Role of Doctors Physicians may increase the demand for health care in several ways.

Supplier-Induced Demand As we mentioned before, doctors have much more information about medical services than patients, who are not likely to be well informed about diagnostic tests such as magnetic resonance imaging or medical procedures such as joint replacements. Because of this asymmetric information (informational imbalance), a principal-agent problem emerges: The supplier, not the demander, decides what types and amounts of health care are to be consumed. This situation creates a possibility of "supplier-induced demand."

fee for service In the health care *industry*, payment to physicians for each visit made or procedure performed.

This possibility increases when doctors are paid on a **fee-for-service** basis, that is, paid separately for each service they perform. In that case, doctors have an incentive to suggest more health care services than are absolutely necessary (just as an auto repair shop has an incentive to recommend the replacement of parts that are worn but still working).

More surgery is performed in the United States, where many doctors are paid a fee for each operation, than in foreign countries, where doctors are often paid fixed salaries unrelated to the number of operations they perform. Furthermore, doctors who own X-ray or ultrasound machines do four times as many tests as doctors who refer their patients to radiologists. More generally, studies suggest that up to one-third of common medical tests and procedures are either inappropriate or of questionable value.

CONSIDER THIS . . .

Why Do Hospitals Sometimes Charge $25 for an Aspirin?

To save taxpayers money, Medicare and Medicaid set their payment rates for medical services above marginal cost but below average total cost. Doing so gives health care providers an incentive to provide services to Medicare and Medicaid patients because MR > MC. But it also means that government health insurance programs are not reimbursing the full cost of treating Medicare and Medicaid patients. In particular, the programs are not picking up their share of the fixed costs associated with providing health care.

As an example, consider an elderly person who uses Medicare. If he gets into a car accident and is taken to the local emergency room, the hospital will run up a wide variety of marginal costs, including ambulance charges, X-rays, medications, and the time of the nurses and doctors who help him. But the hospital also has a wide variety of fixed costs including rent, utility bills, computer

Oleg/Alamy Stock Photo

networks, and lots of hideously expensive medical equipment.

These costs have to be borne by somebody. So when Medicare and Medicaid fail to pay their full share of the fixed costs, other patients must pick up the slack. The result has been for hospitals to transfer as much as possible of the fixed costs onto patients with private health insurance. The hospitals overbill private insurance companies so as to make up for the fixed costs that the government refuses to pay.

That is why you will hear stories about hospitals charging patients with private insurance $25 for a single aspirin or $100 for a newborn baby's first pair of diapers. They are making up for the fact that hospitals around the country lost over $100.4 billion in 2020 because Medicare and Medicaid on average only reimbursed hospitals about 90 percent of the total cost of providing medical services to Medicare and Medicaid patients.

The seller's control over consumption decisions has another result: It eliminates much of the power buyers might otherwise have in controlling the growth of health care prices and spending. (The nearby Consider This story discusses a related factor that limits the ability of patients to help to control hospital charges.)

Defensive Medicine "Become a doctor and support a lawyer," says a bumper sticker. The number of medical malpractice lawsuits admittedly is high. To a medical doctor, each patient represents not only a person in need but also a possible malpractice suit. As a result, physicians tend to practice **defensive medicine.** They recommend more tests and procedures than are warranted medically or economically to protect themselves against the possibility of malpractice suits that might allege that "the doctor should have done more."

defensive medicine The recommendation by physicians of more tests and procedures than are warranted medically or economically as a way of protecting themselves against later malpractice suits.

Medical Ethics Medical ethics may drive up the demand for health care in two ways. First, doctors are legally and ethically committed to using "standard of care" (i.e., best-practice) techniques in serving their patients. This commitment often means using costly medical procedures that may benefit patients only slightly.

Second, public values seem to support the idea that human life should be sustained as long as possible. This moral imperative makes it difficult to confront the notion that health care is provided with scarce resources and therefore must be rationed like any other good. Can society afford to provide $5,000-per-day intensive care to a comatose patient unlikely to be restored to reasonable health? Public priorities seem to indicate that such care should be provided, and those values again increase the demand for health care.

Role of Health Insurance

Individuals and families face potentially devastating monetary losses from a variety of hazards. Your house may burn down, you may be in an auto accident, or you may suffer a serious illness. An insurance program protects you against the huge monetary losses that can result from such hazards. Insurance is a means of paying a relatively small known cost (the monthly premium) in exchange for obtaining protection against uncertain but potentially much larger costs. However, health insurance alters incentives in ways that can contribute to rising costs and the overconsumption of health care.

The Moral Hazard Problem The *moral hazard problem* refers to the tendency of one party to an agreement to alter her or his behavior in a way that is costly to the other party. Health insurance can change behavior in two ways. First, some insured people may be less careful about their health, taking fewer steps to prevent accident or illness. Second, insured individuals have greater incentives to use more health care than they would if they did not have insurance. Let's consider both aspects of moral hazard.

Less Prevention Health insurance may increase the demand for health care by encouraging behaviors that require more health care. Although most people with health care insurance are probably as careful about their health as are those without insurance, some may be more inclined to smoke, avoid exercise, and eat unhealthful foods, knowing they have insurance. Similarly, some individuals may take up ski jumping or rodeo bull riding if they have insurance covering the costs of orthopedic surgeons.

Overconsumption Insured people go to doctors more often and request more diagnostic tests and more complex treatments than they would if they were uninsured because, with health insurance, the price or opportunity cost of consuming health care is minimal. For example, many individuals with private insurance pay a fixed monthly premium for coverage. Beyond that, aside from any out-of-pocket costs, which are often quite modest, their health care looks "free." This situation differs from most markets, in which the price to the consumer reflects the full opportunity cost of each unit of the good or service.

Also, the availability of health insurance removes a consumer's budget constraint (spending limitation) when they decide to consume health care. Recall from Chapter 7 that budget constraints limit the purchases of most products. But insured patients face minimal or no out-of-pocket expenditures at the time they purchase health care. Because affordability is not a concern, health care may be overconsumed.

tax subsidy A grant in the form of reduced *taxes* through favorable *tax* treatment. For example, employer-paid health insurance is exempt from federal *income taxes* and *payroll taxes*.

Government Tax Subsidy Federal tax policy toward employer-financed health insurance works as a **tax subsidy** that strengthens the demand for health care services. Specifically, employees do not pay federal income or payroll tax on the value of the health insurance they receive as an employee benefit. Employees thus request and receive more of their total compensation as non-taxed health care benefits and less in taxed wages and salaries.

The government rationale for this tax treatment is that positive spillover benefits are associated with a healthy, productive workforce. So it is appropriate to encourage health insurance for workers. The tax break does enable more of the population to have health insurance, but it also contributes to greater consumption of health care. Combined with other factors, the tax break may result in an overconsumption of health care.

One estimate suggests that this tax subsidy costs the federal government $120 billion per year in forgone tax revenue and boosts private health insurance spending by about one-third. Nationwide, total U.S. health care spending may be 10 to 20 percent higher than otherwise because of the subsidy.

Graphical Portrayal A simple demand and supply model illustrates the effect of health insurance on the health care market. Figure 24.3a depicts a competitive market for health care services. Curve D shows the demand for health care services if all consumers are uninsured, and S represents the supply of health care. At market price P_a the equilibrium quantity of health care is Q_a.

Recall from our discussion of competitive markets that output Q_a results in allocative efficiency, which means there is no better alternative use for the resources allocated to producing that amount of health care. But allocative efficiency occurs only when consumers pay the full market price for a product, as is assumed in Figure 24.3a. What happens when we introduce health insurance that covers, say, two-thirds of all health care costs? In Figure 24.3b, with private or public health insurance in place, consumers increase their demand for health care, as from D to D_i. At each possible price they desire more health care than before because insurance will pick up a large part of the bill. Given the supply curve of health care S, this increase in demand raises the price of health care to P_b. But with the insurance, consumers pay only one-third of the new higher price. This new price is less than the price without the insurance because the new price is only $P_c (= \frac{1}{3} P_b)$ —rather than the previous price P_a. So consumers increase their consumption of health care from Q_a to Q_c.

The added consumption (and production) of health care is inefficient. Between Q_a and Q_c each unit's marginal cost to society (measured on curve S) exceeds its marginal benefit (measured on the

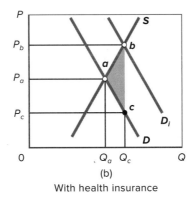

(a) Without health insurance

(b) With health insurance

FIGURE 24.3
Insurance and the overallocation of resources to health care.

(a) Without health insurance, the optimal amount of health care consumed is Q_a, where the marginal benefit and marginal cost of health care are equal. (b) The availability of private and public insurance increases the demand for health care, as from D to D_i, and reduces the price to the consumer from P_a to P_c (here, equal to one-third of the full price P_b). This lower after-insurance price results in overconsumption (Q_c rather than Q_a). Area *abc* represents the efficiency loss (or deadweight loss) from the overallocation of resources to health care.

before-insurance demand curve D). Each unit of health care between Q_a and Q_c is an overallocation of resources to health care. Area *abc* shows the efficiency loss (or *deadweight loss*) that results.

Rationing to Control Costs By reducing the marginal costs facing patients, both private health insurance and government health insurance drive up prices. But then why does the United States, with its emphasis on private health insurance, spend so much more on health care than countries such as the United Kingdom and Canada that provide national health insurance? If both types of insurance promote higher prices, why do we see higher health care spending in the United States than in those other countries?

One contributing factor is the fact that countries with national health insurance use various nonprice mechanisms to ration care. These mechanisms restrict the quantity of health care services supplied and, consequently, the amount of money spent providing health care.

Committees of medical and budgetary experts do some of the nonprice rationing. In the United Kingdom, for instance, the National Institute for Health and Care Excellence has set a general limit of £30,000 (approximately $40,000) on the cost of extending life for a year. Applying this rule to a specific situation, if an anticancer treatment would cost more than £30,000 to extend a cancer patient's life for a year, the United Kingdom's national health service would not pay for it. This cost rule keeps a lid on expenditures.

Waiting is another nonprice mechanism that rations care in countries with national health insurance. In the Canadian system, patients often have to wait weeks, months, or even years for certain diagnostic procedures and surgeries. These wait times are the result of the Canadian government's effort to control expenditures by restricting hospitals' capital spending. For example, there are only one-fourth as many magnetic resonance imaging (MRI) machines per million people in Canada as in the United States. The result is a substantial waiting list for MRI scans in Canada.

By contrast, private health insurers in the United States have not had to obey national committees that set spending limits. Nor have they had to answer to government budget officials attempting to control expenditures by restricting capital spending. Instead, private health insurers have faced a very different regulatory system that has tended to increase rather than decrease spending.

Requiring insurance companies to cover more people or treat more conditions is politically popular, while requiring them to cut coverage to save money is politically unpopular. Thus, there is constant political pressure for state insurance regulators to pass new regulations requiring insurance companies to spend more rather than less. States have incrementally imposed various rules expanding the number of conditions that insurers must cover as well as the amounts that insurers must spend on patient care. Insurance companies have responded by raising insurance premiums.

Many economists view this regulatory system as one of the factors that has contributed to the United States spending more of its GDP on health care than any other nation on earth. While regulators in other countries have sought ways to deny care and reduce costs, state regulators in the United States have tended to mandate that insurance companies expand treatment and incur additional costs.

As we discuss later in this chapter, the Affordable Care Act created federal health insurance regulators. Part of the controversy related to the law is whether the new federal regulators might eventually be tasked with denying care in the ways that European regulators do.

Supply Factors in Rising Health Care Prices

Supply factors have also played a role in rising health care prices. Specifically, the supply of health care services has increased, but more slowly than demand. A combination of factors has produced this relatively slow growth of supply.

Supply of Physicians The supply of physicians in the United States has increased over the years; in 1975 there were 169 physicians per 100,000 people; by 2019 there were 286. But this increase in supply has not kept up with the increase in the demand for physicians' services. As a result, physicians' fees and incomes have increased more rapidly than average prices and incomes for the economy as a whole.

Conventional wisdom has been that physician groups (for example, the American Medical Association) have purposely kept admissions to medical schools, and therefore the supply of doctors, artificially low. But that explanation is too simplistic. A rapidly rising cost of medical education seems to be the main cause of the relatively slow growth of doctor supply. Medical training requires 4 years of college, 4 years of medical school, an internship, and perhaps 3 or 4 years of training in a medical specialty. The opportunity cost of this education has increased because the salaries of similarly capable people have soared in other professions. The direct expenses have also increased, largely due to the increasingly sophisticated levels of medical care and therefore of medical training.

High and rising education and training costs have necessitated high and rising doctors' fees to ensure an adequate return on this investment in human capital. Physicians' incomes are indeed high, averaging in 2020 from about $243,000 for family care physicians up to $526,000 for plastic surgeons. But the costs of obtaining the skills necessary to become a physician are also very high. Data show that while doctors have high rates of return on their educational expenses, those returns are below the returns for the holders of master's of business administration degrees.

Slow Productivity Growth Productivity growth in an industry tends to reduce costs and increase supply. In the health care industry, productivity growth has been modest. One reason is that health care is a service, and it is generally more difficult to increase productivity for services than for goods. It is not easy, for example, to mechanize haircuts or child care. The same is true for physicians, nurses, and home care providers.

In addition, patients rarely shop for the lowest prices when seeking medical care. In fact, a patient may feel uncomfortable about being operated on by a physician who charges the lowest price. Moreover, if insurance pays for the surgery, there is no reason to consider price at all. The point is that unusual features of the market for health care limit competitive pricing and thus reduce incentives to achieve cost saving via advances in productivity.

Changes in Medical Technology Some technological advances in medicine have lowered costs. For example, the development of vaccines for polio, smallpox, and measles has greatly reduced health care expenditures for the treatment of those diseases. Reduced lengths of stays in hospitals have lowered the costs of medical care, too.

But many medical technologies developed since the Second World War have significantly increased the cost of medical care either by increasing prices or by making procedures available to a greater number of people. For example, because they give more accurate information, advanced body scanners costing up to $1,000 per scan are often used in place of X-rays that cost less than $100 per scan. Desiring to offer the highest quality of service, hospitals want to use the very latest equipment and procedures. These newer, more expensive treatments are believed to be more effective than older treatments. But doctors and hospital administrators both realize that the equipment's high fixed cost means that it must be used extensively if they are to reduce the average cost per patient and thereby recoup the cost of the equipment at relatively low ("fair return") charges per procedure.

Finally, consider new prescription medications. Pharmaceutical companies have developed very expensive drugs that often replace less expensive ones. Although these remarkable new medications greatly improve health care, they also contribute to rising health care costs.

The historical willingness of private and public insurance to pay for new treatments without regard to price and number of patients has contributed to the incentive to develop and use new technologies. Insurers, in effect, have encouraged research into and development of health care technologies, regardless of their cost. Recently, when insurance companies resisted paying for new expensive treatments such as bone marrow transplants, public outcries led them to change their minds. So expanding insurance coverage leads to the widespread use of new, often more expensive, medical technologies—which in turn leads to a demand for a wider definition of what should be covered by insurance.

QUICK REVIEW 24.2

▶ Characteristics of the health care market are (a) the widespread view of health care as a "right," (b) asymmetric information between consumers and suppliers, (c) the presence of positive externalities, and (d) payment mostly by insurance.

▶ The demand for health care has increased for many reasons, including rising incomes, an aging population, unhealthy lifestyles, the role of doctors as advisers to patients, the practice of defensive medicine, and a fee-for-service payment system via health insurance.

▶ Countries with national health insurance systems contain costs by denying care for certain procedures and by limiting capital expenditures.

▶ The supply of health care has grown slowly, primarily because of (a) relatively slow productivity growth in the health care industry, (b) rising costs of medical education and training, and (c) greater use of very-high-cost health care technologies.

Cost Containment: Altering Incentives

The Affordable Care Act is the latest in a long series of attempts to control the growth of health care costs, prices, and spending. Many of these efforts have tried to reduce the incentives to overconsume health care.

>> **LO24.5** Describe cost-containment strategies for health care.

Deductibles and Copayments

Insurance companies have reacted to rising health care costs by imposing sizable deductibles and copayments on those they insure. Instead of covering all of an insured's medical costs, a policy might now specify that the insured pay the first $250 or $500 of each year's health care costs (the deductible) and 15 or 20 percent of all additional costs (the copayment). The deductible and copayment are intended to alleviate the overuse problem by creating a direct payment and therefore an opportunity cost for the health care consumer. The deductible has the added advantage of reducing insurance companies' administrative costs.

Health Savings Accounts

A federal law enacted in 2003 established **health savings accounts (HSAs),** into which employees and their employers can make tax-free contributions on behalf of the employees. The employees own their accounts and can use them to pay for insurance deductibles and copays as well as a wide variety of medical services and products.

HSAs were designed to encourage individuals to save for health care expenses while also injecting an element of competition into health care delivery. Because HSAs are private property, HSA holders will presumably assess marginal costs and marginal benefits when choosing how much and what type of health care to obtain. They will also have a strong incentive to inquire about and compare prices.

health savings accounts (HSAs) Tax-free savings accounts into which people with high-deductible health insurance plans can place funds each year. Accumulated funds can be used to pay out-of-pocket medical expenses such as *deductibles* and *copayments.* Unused funds accumulate from year to year and can be used after retirement to supplement *Medicare.*

Managed Care

Managed-care organizations (or systems) are those in which medical services are controlled or coordinated by insurance companies or health care organizations to reduce health care expenditures. In 2020, 62 percent of all U.S. workers received health care through such "managed care" organizations. These organizations are of two main types.

- **Preferred provider organizations (PPOs)** require that hospitals and physicians accept discounted prices for their services as a condition for being included in an insurance plan. The policyholder receives a list of participating hospitals and doctors and is given, say, 80 to 100 percent reimbursement of health care costs when treated by PPO physicians and hospitals. If a patient chooses a doctor or hospital outside the PPO, the insurance company reimburses only 60 to 70 percent. In return for being included as a PPO provider, doctors and hospitals agree to rates set by the insurance company for each service. Because these fees are less than those usually charged, PPOs reduce health insurance premiums and health care expenditures.

preferred provider organization (PPO) An arrangement in which doctors and hospitals agree to provide health care to insured individuals at rates negotiated with an insurer.

health maintenance organizations (HMOs) Health care providers that contract with employers, insurance companies, labor unions, or government units to provide health care for their workers or others who are insured.

- **Health maintenance organizations (HMOs)** provide health care services to a specific group of enrollees in exchange for a set annual fee per enrollee. HMOs employ their own physicians and contract for specialized services with outside providers and hospitals. They then contract with firms or government units to provide medical care for their workers, who thereby become HMO members. Because HMOs have fixed annual revenue, they may lose money if they provide "too much" care. So they have an incentive to hold down costs. They also have an incentive to provide preventive care in order to reduce the potentially far larger expense of corrective care.

Both PPOs and HMOs are managed-care organizations because medical use and spending are "managed" by closely monitoring physicians' and hospitals' behavior. The purpose of close monitoring is to eliminate unnecessary tests and treatments. Doctors in managed-care organizations might not order an MRI scan or an ultrasound test or suggest surgery because their work is monitored and because they may have a fixed budget. In contrast, an independent fee-for-service physician facing little or no oversight may have a financial incentive to order the test or do the surgery. Doctors and hospitals in a managed-care organization often share in an "incentive pool" of funds when they meet their cost-control goals.

The advantages of managed-care plans are that they provide health care at lower prices than traditional insurance and emphasize preventive medicine. The disadvantages are that the patient usually is restricted to physicians employed by or under contract with the managed-care plan. Also, some say that the focus on reducing costs has gone too far, resulting in denial of highly expensive, but effective, treatment. This "too far" criticism is mainly leveled at HMOs, which have the strongest incentive to cut costs.

Medicare and DRG

In 1983 the federal government altered the way it pays for the hospital services received by Medicare patients. Rather than automatically paying all costs related to a patient's treatment and length of hospital stay, Medicare authorizes payments based on a **diagnosis-related group (DRG) system.** Under DRG, a hospital receives a fixed payment for treating each patient. That payment is an amount associated with the diagnosis—one of several hundred carefully detailed diagnostic categories—that best characterizes the patient's condition and needs.

diagnosis-related group (DRG) system Payments to doctors and hospitals under *Medicare* based on which of hundreds of carefully detailed diagnostic categories best characterize each patient's condition and needs.

DRG payments obviously give hospitals the incentive to restrict the amount of resources used in treating patients. It is no surprise that under DRG the length of hospital stays has fallen sharply, and more patients are treated on an outpatient basis. Critics, however, argue that the DRG system has diminished health care quality.

Limits on Malpractice Awards

Thirty states have enacted caps (of typically between $250,000 and $500,000) on the "pain and suffering" awards that can be made when a patient wins a medical malpractice lawsuit against a physician or hospital. Those who support malpractice caps say that patients should receive full compensation for economic losses but not be made wealthy through huge jury awards. They contend that capping the awards will reduce medical malpractice premiums and therefore lower health care costs. Opponents of caps counter that large "pain and suffering" awards deter medical malpractice and improve the overall quality of the health care system. Opponents also point out that malpractice awards are a negligible percentage of total health care costs.

**QUICK REVIEW
24.3**

- ▶ Policymakers have pursued several strategies when attempting to contain health care spending and prices.

- ▶ Insurance deductibles and copayments confront consumers with opportunity costs; managed-care

organizations attempt to restrict their members' use of health services; the diagnosis-related group (DRG) system caps the amount Medicare will spend on any procedure; and health savings accounts (HSAs) confront individuals with the marginal cost of routine health care expenses.

The Affordable Care Act

>> **LO24.6** Summarize the goals of the Affordable Care Act.

The primary goal of the Affordable Care Act of 2010 (sometimes referred to as "Obamacare") was not cost containment but rather the extension of health insurance coverage to every American. In truth, covering every single citizen would have been possible only if the United States had moved to a national health insurance system similar to that used in Canada. Such a move would have been impossible politically, however, because opinion polls indicated that 75 percent of Americans with employer-provided health insurance rated their coverage as good or very good.

Thus, President Obama and like-minded members of Congress did not pursue the creation of a national health insurance system. Rather, they moved to extend and expand the existing system in which nearly all Americans receive their health care through either employer-provided health insurance or government-provided health insurance (Medicaid and Medicare). In promoting the ACA, the president reassured audiences by telling them, "If you like your health care plan, you can keep it."

Major Provisions

The authors of the ACA understood that extending insurance coverage to millions of previously uninsured people would be costly. As with any group of people enrolled in a health insurance program, many would eventually become sick and need costly treatments. This problem was exacerbated by the fact that many of those without insurance were known to suffer from extremely costly medical conditions. These "preexisting medical conditions" meant that the people so afflicted were often without insurance coverage precisely because private insurance companies (which have to either break even or go bankrupt) considered them to be too expensive to insure. Thus, if those with costly preexisting conditions were to be covered, significant new revenue sources would have to be found.

The ACA aimed to help private insurance companies obtain the needed revenue from two main sources: a personal mandate to buy insurance and an assortment of new taxes. We will discuss each as we go over the ACA's major provisions.

Preexisting Conditions, Caps, and Drops The ACA made it illegal for insurance companies to deny coverage to anyone on the basis of a preexisting medical condition. This ban led to the enrollment of millions of individuals with costly health conditions.

The ACA also increased the amount of money that insurance companies had to pay out by prohibiting them from imposing annual or lifetime expenditure caps.

To prevent insurance companies from dropping policyholders just because they developed a costly illness, the ACA also made fraud the only legal reason that an insurance company could drop a policyholder. Because this provision forced insurance companies to keep very sick people enrolled, it also entailed significant cost increases for insurance companies.

Employer Mandate The ACA has an **employer mandate** (requirement) that every firm with 50 or more full-time employees must either purchase health insurance for their full-time employees or pay a fine of $2,000 per employee. This provision is intended to compel the extension of employer-paid health insurance to as many workers as possible so that private employers, rather than the government, will bear as much of the cost of extending insurance coverage to the uninsured as possible. Firms with fewer than 50 full-time employees are exempt from the employer mandate because the high cost of health insurance might bankrupt many smaller firms.

To date, many large employers have reacted to the employer mandate by limiting workers to only part-time work since part-time workers are not covered by the employer mandate. These employees thus ended up without insurance—and with lower earnings, too.

Personal Mandate The ACA also contained a **personal mandate** (requirement) that individuals had to purchase health insurance for themselves and their dependents unless they were already covered by either government insurance or employer-provided insurance. Anyone refusing would be fined the larger of either $695 per uninsured family member or 2.5 percent of family income.

The personal mandate was repealed as part of a large tax reform bill that was signed into law in 2018. But you should understand that the point of the personal mandate was to force higher-income healthy people (especially healthy young workers) to buy health insurance so that their insurance premiums could help pay for the high health care bills of those with costly preexisting conditions as well as the subsidies needed to make health insurance affordable for those with lower incomes.

Covering Those in Financial Need In the years before the ACA was passed, millions of lower-income Americans lacked private health insurance. The ACA attempted to cover those with lower incomes in three ways. First, the employer mandate was designed to force larger employers to

employer mandate The requirement under the *Patient Protection and Affordable Care Act* (*PPACA*) of 2010 that firms with 50 or more employees pay for insurance policies for their employees or face a fine of $2,000 per employee per year. Firms with fewer than 50 employees are exempt.

personal mandate The requirement under the *Patient Protection and Affordable Care Act* (*PPACA*) of 2010 that all U.S. citizens and legal residents purchase health insurance unless they are already covered by employer-sponsored health insurance or government-sponsored health insurance (*Medicaid* or *Medicare*).

provide health insurance for all of their full-time employees, including the poorer ones. Second, the law expanded the Medicaid system to cover anyone whose income was less than 133 percent of the poverty level. Third, the ACA subsidized the purchase price of health insurance for those who had to buy their own health insurance to comply with the individual mandate. These individual subsidies extended into the upper half of the income distribution because health insurance was so expensive that the personal mandate would have been financially ruinous for even middle-income workers if it had not been accompanied by subsidies. However, the subsidies got progressively less generous as incomes rose, so that those earning three to four times the poverty level had pay about 10 percent of their incomes to buy health insurance.

Insurance Exchanges Under the ACA, individuals in each state could shop for health insurance policies at government-managed insurance markets that were called **insurance exchanges.** It was hoped that the exchanges would reduce the growth of health care spending by fostering competition among insurance companies, but the exchanges have fared badly because the ACA required health insurance rates to be the same for all applicants in a given state. That was problematic because older adults run up far more health care costs than younger people. So there is an implicit wealth transfer from younger people to older people when both are being charged the same rate for health insurance.

As you might imagine, many younger people declined to participate since on average they were going to be paying more in premiums than they were likely to receive in benefits. By contrast, older people were eager to join because they would on average receive more in benefits than they paid in premiums.

Those two tendencies collapsed the insurance exchanges in over 20 states because there weren't enough healthy young people overpaying for health insurance to compensate for the high costs run up by the older people who were underpaying.

Other Provisions The 2,400-page ACA contains hundreds of additional provisions. Some of the more publicized include:

- Mandating that the adult children of parents with employer-provided health insurance remain covered by their parents' insurance through age 26.
- Making it illegal for insurance companies to charge copayments or apply deductibles to annual checkups or preventive care.
- Requiring insurers to spend at least 80 percent of the money they receive in premiums on either health care or improving health care.

Taxes To help pay for the extension of health insurance to millions of previously uninsured people, the ACA imposed several new taxes. These included:

- A 0.9 percentage point increase in the Medicare payroll tax for individuals earning more than $200,000 per year and for married couples earning more than $250,000 per year.
- A 3.8 percentage point increase in the capital gains tax for individuals earning more than $200,000 per year and for married couples earning more than $250,000 per year.
- A 40 percent tax payable by employers on any employer-provided insurance policy whose premium exceeds $10,200 per year for individual coverage or $27,500 per year for family coverage.
- A 2.9 percent excise tax applied to everything sold by medical device manufacturers.
- A 10 percent tax levied on indoor tanning.

Objections and Alternatives

The ACA was strongly opposed and passed Congress without a single approving vote in either chamber of Congress from members of the minority (Republican) party. The legislation also failed to achieve majority support in public opinion polls conducted on the eve of the legislation's passage.

Some critics worried that federal control over the pricing and content of insurance policies would lead to greater inefficiencies in health care by adding additional layers of bureaucracy. Others objected because they felt that the ACA might be the first step toward the creation of a national health insurance system in which nonprice rationing might become necessary to hold down

insurance exchanges
Government-regulated markets for health insurance in which individuals seeking to purchase health insurance to comply with the *personal mandate* of the *Patient Protection and Affordable Care Act* (*PPACA*) of 2010 will be able to comparison shop among insurance policies approved by regulators. Each state will have its own exchange.

Singapore's Efficient and Effective Health Care System

How Does Singapore Deliver Some of the Best Health Care in the World while Spending 73 Percent Less per Person than the United States?

In every health quality category monitored by the World Health Organization, the small island nation of Singapore is either number one in the world or near the top of the list. Among other achievements, Singapore has the world's lowest rate of infant mortality and the world's fourth-highest life expectancy.

One might expect that achieving these exceptional outcomes would be extremely expensive. But Singapore is also number one in another category. It spends less per person on health care than any other developed nation. In 2019 the United States spent 17.6 percent of its GDP on health care. Singapore spent just 4.8 percent.

How does Singapore deliver world-class health care while spending less than any other developed nation? The answer is a unique combination of government mandates to encourage competition, high out-of-pocket costs for consumers, and laws requiring people to save for future health expenditures.

Competition is encouraged by requiring hospitals to post prices for each of their services. Armed with this information, patients can shop around for the best deal. The government also publishes the track record of each hospital on each service so that consumers can make informed decisions about quality as well as price. With consumers choosing on the basis of cost and quality, local hospitals compete to reduce costs and improve quality.

Singapore also insists upon high out-of-pocket costs to avoid the overconsumption and high prices that result when insurance policies pick up most of the price for medical procedures. Indeed, out-of-pocket spending represents about 92 percent of all nongovernment health care spending in Singapore, compared to about 10 percent in the United States.

Having to pay for most medical spending out of pocket, however, means that Singapore's citizens are faced with having to pay for most of their health care themselves. How can this be done without bankrupting the average citizen? The answer is mandatory health savings accounts.

Singapore's citizens are required to save about 7 percent of their incomes into "MediSave" accounts. MediSave deposits are private property, so people have an incentive to spend the money in their accounts wisely. In addition, the citizens of Singapore also know that they won't be left helpless if the money in their MediSave accounts runs out. The government subsidizes the health care of those who have exhausted their MediSave accounts as well as the health care of the poor and others who have not been able to accumulate much money in their MediSave accounts.

Could elements of Singapore's system help to hold down medical costs in the United States? Two cases suggest that the answer is yes.

First, consider the health care plan offered by Whole Foods Markets to its employees. The company deposits $1,800 per year into a "personal wellness account" for each of its full-time employees. It simultaneously pays for a high-deductible health insurance plan that

Comstock/Stockbyte/Getty Images

will pick up 100 percent of all medical expenses exceeding $2,500 in a given year. This combination implies that employees are *at most* on the hook for $700 a year—that is, for the difference between the $1,800 in their personal wellness accounts and the $2,500 deductible on their health insurance policy (above which, all medical expenses are covered).

Because both the money in the personal wellness account as well as the $700 that employees might have to spend before reaching the $2,500 deductible are personal property, Whole Foods Markets has effectively created a system in which all medical spending up to $2,500 is an out-of-pocket expense. This forces employees to examine the opportunity cost of any potential medical expenditure. The result is less spending.

A similar plan offered to employees of the State of Indiana puts $2,750 per year into a health savings account and then provides an insurance policy that covers 80 percent of any medical expenses between $2,750 and $8,000 and 100 percent of any expenses above $8,000. The Indiana plan's design means that any state employee volunteering for the plan must pay 100 percent of all spending up to $2,750 from their health savings accounts. As with Singapore's system and Whole Foods' system, this encourages prudence. The result has been a 35 percent decline in total health care spending for those who volunteered for the plan versus state employees who opted to stick with the state's traditional PPO option. In addition, an independent audit showed that participants in the new plan were not cutting corners by skimping on preventive care like annual mammogram screenings for cancer. Thus, the savings appear to be permanent and sustainable.

The program is also popular, with positive personal recommendations causing voluntary participation to rise from 2 percent of state employees in the program's first year to 70 percent of state employees in the program's second year.

expenditures. Yet others pointed to financial projections indicating that the revenue sources legislated by the ACA would not be nearly sufficient to cover future health care expenses, especially over the longer run.

An additional concern was whether the ACA would reduce the growth rate of health care expenditures and thereby fulfill President Obama's promise that the law would "bend the cost curve down." Many economists worried that the large subsidies provided by the law would raise prices and increase consumption (as in Figure 24.3). With even middle-class individuals and families eligible for significant government subsidies, inefficient health care spending might increase significantly.

As an alternative, some opponents of the ACA pointed to the health care system in Singapore and recent experiments with the health insurance offered to employees of the State of Indiana. Both systems reduce wasteful expenditures by increasing the percentage of health care spending that comes directly out of consumers' pockets, thereby forcing them to consider opportunity costs and weigh marginal benefits against marginal costs. (See this chapter's Last Word feature for more.)

In evaluating the pros and cons of the ACA, one thing seems clear. It will not be the last word on health care reform in the United States. Indeed, the economic challenges related to health care will only get stronger. The combination of an aging population and advances in medical technology seems to be on a collision course with the reality of economic scarcity. Individuals and society will face increasingly difficult choices about how much health care to consume and how to pay for it. They must also deal with the fact that 31 million Americans remained uninsured in 2020 despite universal coverage being the primary goal of the ACA.

QUICK REVIEW

24.4

▶ The Affordable Care Act (ACA) was an attempt to extend either private or public health insurance coverage to all U.S. citizens and legal residents.

▶ The ACA included (1) a *personal mandate* that required individuals to purchase insurance coverage for themselves and their dependents if they were not already covered by employer or government health insurance as well as (2) an *employer mandate* that required all firms with more than 50 full-time employees to either offer health insurance coverage to their full-time employees or pay large fines.

▶ The ACA also bans insurance companies from denying coverage on the basis of preexisting conditions; includes various subsidies so that the personal mandate will not bankrupt those with low and middle incomes; provides for the creation of state insurance exchanges, where individuals can comparison shop for government-approved health insurance policies; and imposes various taxes to help pay for the increased expenditures that will be required to extend insurance coverage to the previously uninsured.

Summary

LO24.1 Describe the health care industry in the United States.

The U.S. health care industry comprises 20 million workers (including about 939,000 practicing physicians) and 6,090 hospitals.

Unlike nations with publicly funded systems of national health insurance, the United States delivers a large fraction of its health care through private, employer-provided health insurance.

U.S. health care spending is very high both in absolute and per capita levels relative to other industrialized countries.

LO24.2 Discuss the economic implications of rising health care costs.

Rising health care costs and prices have (*a*) reduced access to the health care system, (*b*) contributed to slower real wage growth and expanded the employment of part-time and temporary workers, and (*c*) caused governments to restrict spending on nonhealth programs and to raise taxes.

The core of the health care problem is an alleged overallocation of resources to the health care industry.

LO24.3 Discuss the problem of limited access to health care.

About 31 million Americans, or 9 percent of the population, did not have health insurance in 2020. The uninsured were concentrated among people with low incomes and wealth, the chronically ill, the unemployed, the young, those employed by small firms, and low-wage workers.

LO24.4 List the demand and supply factors that explain rising health care costs.

Special characteristics of the health care market include (*a*) the belief that health care is a "right," (*b*) an imbalance of information between consumers and suppliers, (*c*) the presence of positive externalities, and (*d*) the payment of most health care expenses by private or public insurance.

While rising incomes, an aging population, and substance abuse have all contributed to an increasing demand for health care, the role of doctors is also significant. Because of asymmetric information, physicians influence the demand for their own services. The fee-for-service payment system, combined with defensive medicine to protect against malpractice suits, also increases the demand for health care.

The moral hazard problem arising from health insurance takes two forms: (*a*) people may be less careful about their health, and (*b*) there is an incentive to overconsume health care.

The exemption of employer-paid health insurance from the federal income tax subsidizes health care. The subsidy increases demand, leading to higher prices and a likely overallocation of resources to health care.

Countries with systems of national health insurance also increase demand by subsidizing health care. Facing limited budgets, those countries engage in nonprice rationing to restrict health care expenditures. Rationing mechanisms include waiting lists, committees that set standards for denial of service, and restrictions on capital spending.

Because private insurance does not involve government expenditures, the state regulators charged with regulating private insurance companies in the United States focus more on expanding politically popular benefits than on restricting costs.

Slow productivity growth in the health care industry and, more important, cost-increasing advances in health care technology have restricted the expansion of the supply of medical care and have boosted prices.

LO24.5 Describe cost-containment strategies for health care.

Strategies that have attempted to contain health care prices and spending include (*a*) insurance deductibles and copayments to confront consumers with opportunity costs, (*b*) health savings accounts (HSAs) that make individuals balance marginal benefits with marginal costs, (*c*) managed-care organizations—preferred provider organizations (PPOs) and health maintenance organizations (HMOs)—that attempt to restrict their members' use of health services, (*d*) the diagnosis-related group (DRG) system that caps the amount Medicare will spend on any patient, and (*e*) limits on malpractice awards.

LO24.6 Summarize the goals of the Affordable Care Act.

The Affordable Care Act (ACA) of 2010 was an attempt to extend either private or public (Medicare and Medicaid) insurance coverage to all U.S. citizens and legal residents.

The ACA required firms with 50 or more full-time employees to provide their workers with health insurance. The ACA also included a personal mandate (subsequently reversed) that required citizens and legal residents to purchase insurance coverage for themselves and their dependents if they did not already have health insurance coverage through an employer or the government.

The ACA bans insurance companies from denying coverage on the basis of preexisting conditions, includes various subsidies so that the personal mandate will not bankrupt those with constrained financial resources, and imposes various taxes to help pay for extending insurance coverage to the previously uninsured.

Terms and Concepts

Affordable Care Act (ACA)	fee for service	health maintenance organizations (HMOs)
national health insurance	defensive medicine	diagnosis-related group (DRG) system
deductibles	tax subsidy	employer mandate
copayments	health savings accounts (HSAs)	personal mandate
coinsurance	preferred provider organizations (PPOs)	insurance exchanges

Discussion Questions

McGraw Hill connect

1. Why would increased spending as a percentage of GDP on, say, household appliances or education in a particular economy be regarded as economically desirable? Why, then, is there so much concern about rising expenditures as a percentage of GDP on health care? **LO24.1**
2. What are the "twin problems" of the health care industry as viewed by society? How are they related? **LO24.1**
3. What are the implications of rapidly rising health care prices and spending for (*a*) the growth of real wage rates, (*b*) government budgets, and (*c*) offshoring of U.S. jobs? Explain. **LO24.2**
4. What are the main groups without health insurance? **LO24.3**
5. List the special characteristics of the U.S. health care market and specify the problems created by each. **LO24.4**
6. What are the estimated income and price elasticities of demand for health care? How does each relate to rising health care costs? **LO24.4**
7. Briefly discuss the demand and supply factors that contribute to rising health care costs. Specify how (*a*) asymmetric information,

(*b*) fee-for-service payments, (*c*) defensive medicine, and (*d*) medical ethics might increase health care costs? **LO24.4**
8. How do advances in medical technology and health insurance interact to drive up the cost of medical care? **LO24.4**
9. Using the concepts in Chapter 7's discussion of consumer behavior, explain how health insurance results in an overallocation of resources to the health care industry. Use a demand and supply diagram to specify the resulting efficiency loss. **LO24.4**
10. How is the moral hazard problem relevant to the health care market? **LO24.4**
11. What is the rationale for exempting a firm's contribution to its workers' health insurance from taxation as worker income? What is the impact of this exemption on allocative efficiency in the health care industry? **LO24.4**
12. What are (*a*) preferred provider organizations and (*b*) health maintenance organizations? In your answer, explain how each is designed to alleviate the overconsumption of health care. **LO24.5**
13. What are health savings accounts (HSAs)? How might they reduce the overconsumption of health care resulting from

traditional insurance? How might they introduce an element of price competition into the health care system? **LO24.5**

14. Why is the ACA's attempt to extend insurance coverage to all Americans so costly? How does the ACA attempt to obtain the funds needed to extend insurance coverage to all Americans? **LO24.6**

15. How does the ACA attempt to ensure affordable health insurance for low-income Americans? **LO24.6**

16. **LAST WORD** What are the three major cost-reducing features of the Singapore health care system? Which one do you think has the largest effect on holding down the price of medical care in Singapore? What element of the Singapore system is shared by the State of Indiana system? What elements are missing? How difficult do you think it would be to implement those missing elements in the United States? Explain.

Review Questions

1. Which of the following best describes the United States' level of health care spending as compared to that of other nations? **LO24.1**
   a. The lowest of all nations
   b. A bit lower than average
   c. Average
   d. A bit higher than average
   e. The highest of all nations

2. Which of the following make(s) a person *less* likely to have health insurance? (Select one or more answers from the choices shown.) **LO24.3**
   a. Working for a larger firm
   b. Being a low-wage worker
   c. Being employed
   d. Having excellent health
   e. Being chronically ill

3. A patient named Jen visits Dr. Jan. Dr. Jan is nearly certain that Jen has only a cold. But because Dr. Jan is afraid of malpractice lawsuits, she orders an extensive battery of tests just to make sure that Jen can never claim—if she turns out to have something more severe—that Dr. Jan shirked her duties as a medical professional. Dr. Jan's behavior is an example of: **LO24.4**
   a. asymmetric information.
   b. fee for service.
   c. defensive medicine.
   d. positive externalities.

4. All MegaCorp employees who stay on the job for more than three years are rewarded with a 10 percent pay increase and

coverage under a private health insurance plan that MegaCorp pays for. Tai just passed three years as a MegaCorp employee and reacts to having health insurance by taking up several dangerous sports because now she knows that the insurance plan will pay for any injuries that she may sustain. This change in Tai's behavior is an example of: **LO24.4**
   a. defensive medicine.
   b. asymmetric information.
   c. the moral hazard problem.
   d. the personal mandate.

5. By increasing demand, health insurance creates: **LO24.4**
   a. a deadweight loss related to overconsumption.
   b. a deadweight loss related to underconsumption.
   c. neither of the above.

6. Raúl will consume any health care service just as long as its MB exceeds the money he must pay out of pocket. His insurance policy has a zero deductible and a 10 percent copay, so Raúl only has to pay 10 percent of the price charged for any medical procedure. Which of the following procedures will Raúl choose to consume? **LO24.5**
   a. An $800 eye exam that has an MB of $100 to Raúl
   b. A $90 hearing test that has an MB of $5 to Raúl
   c. A $35,000 knee surgery that has an MB of $3,000 to Raúl
   d. A $10,000 baldness treatment that has an MB of $16,000 to Raúl

7. True or False: Under the ACA as originally passed, Americans were free to decide for themselves whether or not they should have health insurance coverage. **LO24.6**

Problems

1. Suppose that the price elasticity for hip replacement surgeries is 0.2. Further suppose that hip replacement surgeries are originally not covered by health insurance and that at a price of $50,000 each, 10,000 such surgeries are demanded each year. **LO24.2**
   a. Suppose that health insurance begins to cover hip replacement surgeries and that everyone interested in getting a hip replacement has health insurance. If insurance covers 50 percent of the cost of the surgery, by what percentage would you expect the quantity demanded of hip replacements to increase? What if insurance covered 90 percent of the price? (Hint: Do not bother to calculate the percentage changes using the midpoint formula given in Chapter 6. If insurance covers 50 percent of the bill, just assume that the price paid by consumers falls 50 percent.)
   b. Suppose that with insurance companies covering 90 percent of the price, the increase in demand leads to a jump in the

price per hip surgery, from $50,000 to $100,000. How much will each insured patient now pay for a hip replacement surgery? Compared to the original situation, where hip replacements cost $50,000 each but people had no insurance to help subsidize the cost, will the quantity demanded increase or decrease? By how much?

2. The federal tax code allows businesses but not individuals to deduct the cost of health insurance premiums from their taxable income. Consider a company named HeadBook that could either spend $5,000 on an insurance policy for an employee named Vanessa or increase her annual salary by $5,000 instead. **LO24.4**
   a. As far as the tax code is concerned, HeadBook will increase its expenses by $5,000 in either case. If HeadBook pays for the policy, it incurs a $5,000 health care expense. If it raises Vanessa's salary by $5,000, it incurs $5,000 of salary

expense. If HeadBook is profitable and pays corporate profit taxes at a marginal 35 percent rate, by how much will Head-Book's tax liability be reduced in either case?

b. Suppose that Vanessa pays personal income tax at a marginal 20 percent rate. If HeadBook increases her salary by $5,000, how much of that increase will she have after paying taxes on that raise? If Vanessa can devote what remains after paying taxes on the $5,000 only to purchasing health insurance, how much will she be able to spend on health insurance for herself?

c. If HeadBook spends the $5,000 on a health insurance policy for Vanessa instead of giving it to her as a raise, how many more dollars will HeadBook be able to spend on Vanessa's health insurance than if she had to purchase it herself after being given a $5,000 raise and paying taxes on that raise?

d. Would Vanessa prefer to have the raise or to have HeadBook purchase insurance for her? Would HeadBook have any profit motive for denying Vanessa her preference?

e. Suppose the government changes the tax law so that individuals can now deduct the cost of health insurance from their personal incomes. If Vanessa gets the $5,000 raise and then spends all of it on health insurance, how much will her tax liability change? How much will she be able to spend on health insurance? Will she now have a preference for Head-Book to buy insurance on her behalf?

3. Preventive care is not always cost-effective. Suppose that it costs $100 per person to administer a screening exam for a particular disease. Also suppose that if the screening exam finds the disease, the early detection given by the exam will avert $1,000 of costly future treatment. **LO24.4**

a. Imagine giving the screening test to 100 people. How much will it cost to administer those 100 tests? Imagine a case in which 15 percent of those receiving the screening exam test positive. How much in future costly treatments will be averted? How much is saved by setting up a screening system?

b. Imagine that everything is the same as in part *a* except that now only 5 percent of those receiving the screening exam test positive. In this case, how much in future costly treatments will be averted? How much is lost by setting up a screening system?

CHAPTER

25

Immigration

>> LEARNING OBJECTIVES

LO25.1 Describe the extent of immigration into the United States.

LO25.2 Discuss why economists view economic immigration as increasing the market value of human capital.

LO25.3 Explain how immigration affects average wages, resource allocation, domestic output, and group income.

LO25.4 Describe unauthorized immigration's effects on employment, wages, and state and local budgets.

economic immigrants International migrants who have moved from one country to another to obtain economic gains such as better employment opportunities.

The population of the United States is composed largely of immigrants and their descendants, yet immigration has long been a matter of heated controversy. Some immigration issues are political, social, and legal; others are economic. Our focus will be on economic issues and **economic immigrants**—international migrants motivated by economic gain. How many such immigrants come to the United States each year? What economic impact do immigrants make? How should the United States handle unauthorized immigration?

Number of Immigrants

>> **LO25.1** Describe the extent of immigration into the United States.

legal immigrant A person who lawfully enters a country for the purpose of residing there.

unauthorized immigrants People who have entered a country unlawfully to reside there; also called undocumented workers, unauthorized workers, and illegal aliens.

H1-B provision A provision of the U.S. immigration law that allows the annual entry of 65,000 high-skilled workers in "specialty occupations" such as science, R&D, and computer programming to work legally and continuously in the United States for six years.

U.S. immigration consists of **legal immigrants**—immigrants who have permission to reside and work in the United States—and **unauthorized immigrants**—immigrants who arrive illegally or who enter legally on temporary visas but then fail to leave as stipulated. Legal immigrants include *permanent legal residents* ("green card" recipients) who have the right to stay in the country indefinitely and temporary legal immigrants, whose visas allow them to stay until a specific date. Unauthorized immigrants are alternatively called undocumented workers, undocumented immigrants, or illegal aliens.

Legal Immigrants

Figure 25.1 shows the annual levels of legal immigration into the United States since 1980. The spike in legal immigration from 1989 to 1991 resulted from an amnesty program through which many formerly unauthorized immigrants became legal residents. Between 2008 and 2019, legal immigration averaged 1.1 million persons per year. This number is higher than for earlier decades because beginning in 1990 the federal government increased the annual immigration quota from 500,000 to 700,000.

Augmenting quota immigrants in some years are thousands of legal immigrants who are refugees (people who flee their country for safety) or who enter the United States under special provisions of immigration law. As an example of the latter, the current **H1-B provision** of the immigration law allows 65,000 high-skilled workers in "specialty occupations" to enter and work continuously in the United States for six years. These high-skilled occupations include high-tech workers, scientists, and professors.

A total of 1,031,765 people became permanent legal residents of the United States in 2019. About 54 percent of them were women and 46 percent were men.

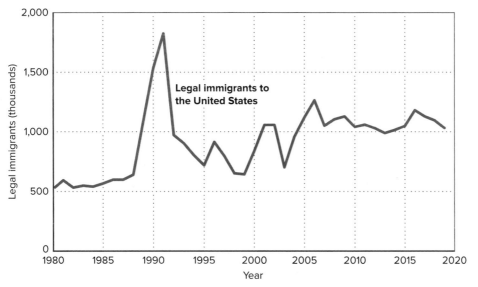

Source: Office of Immigration Statistics, U.S. Department of Homeland Security.

FIGURE 25.1

Legal immigration to the United States, 1980–2019.

Legal immigration grew slowly between 1980 and 1988 and then spiked from 1989 to 1991 when previously unauthorized immigrants gained legal status as permanent residents under the terms of an amnesty program. Since that spike, legal immigration has remained relatively high, partly because the annual legal immigration quota was raised from 500,000 to 700,000. Within the totals are thousands of refugees, grantees of political asylum, and entrants under special provisions of the immigration law.

Of these, about 69 percent were family-sponsored, as can be seen in Figure 25.2. That is, they were sponsored by parents, children, siblings, or other qualified relatives of legal permanent U.S. residents. Another 14 percent were admitted based on employment-based preferences. Most of these immigrants were sponsored by employers. Refugees, "diversity immigrants," and others accounted for the remaining 17 percent. The 50,000 quota for diversity immigrants is filled with qualified immigrants from countries with low rates of immigration to the United States. Because applications by diversity immigrants exceed the 50,000 quota, the slots are filled through an annual lottery.

Although the percentage varies somewhat each year, current U.S. immigration law is heavily weighted toward family reunification. This weighting is much heavier than that in Canada, which gives considerably stronger preference to immigrants with high levels of education and work skills. Of course, immigration by family ties and immigration by employment preferences are not necessarily mutually exclusive since a portion of the immigrants admitted through family ties are highly educated and skilled.

Table 25.1 shows the 10 leading countries of origin of U.S. legal permanent immigrants in 2019. Mexico topped the list. China, India, and the Dominican Republic were also heavy contributors to U.S. immigration in 2019. In recent years immigration has comprised about one-third of the total growth of the U.S. population and one-half the growth of the U.S. labor force.

FIGURE 25.2 **Legal immigration by major category of admission, 2019.**

The large bulk of legal U.S. immigrants obtain their legal status via family ties to American residents.

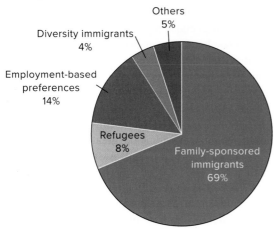

Source: Office of Immigration Statistics, U.S. Department of Homeland Security.

TABLE 25.1 U.S. Legal Immigrants by Top 10 Countries of Origin, 2019

Total	1,031,765
1. Mexico	153,502
2. China	60,029
3. India	51,139
4. Dominican Republic	49,815
5. Philippines	43,478
6. Cuba	39,580
7. Vietnam	38,944
8. El Salvador	24,326
9. Jamaica	21,337
10. Brazil	19,607

Source: 2019 Yearbook of Immigration Statistics, Office of Immigration Statistics, Department of Homeland Security.

Unauthorized Immigrants

Our figures and tables do not include unauthorized immigrants. The U.S. Census estimates the number of unauthorized immigrants living in the United States through a residual approach. It finds the current total number of *all* immigrants through census surveys and then subtracts the sum of the past annual inflows of *legal* immigrants. The residuals are large. In fact, the net annual inflow of unauthorized immigrants averaged about 250,000 per year from 2000 to 2009, with over 60 percent arriving from Mexico and Central America. The net flow reversed (and became a net *out*flow) during the 2007–2008 recession. That net outflow was modest (at about 10,000 persons per year) and continued until 2014, when net inflows resumed. The net inflow in 2015 was 500,000 persons, with smaller net inflows or even outflows through 2018 (the most recent year for which data was available).

While some unauthorized immigrants do move back and forth across the U.S.–Mexican border, in 2018 about 11.4 million unauthorized immigrants were residing continuously in the United States. Increasingly, unauthorized immigrants are continuous residents, not temporary workers who follow the agricultural harvest (as was typical several decades ago). An estimated 47 percent of the 11.4 million unauthorized immigrants originally came from Mexico, with many others arriving from nations spanning the globe. Unauthorized Mexican immigrants who work continuously in the United States work mainly outside of agriculture and, on average, have higher educational levels than Mexicans who do not migrate to the United States.

The Decision to Migrate

>> **LO25.2** Discuss why economists view economic immigration as increasing the market value of human capital.

People immigrate into the United States (emigrate from their home countries) legally or illegally:

- To take advantage of superior economic opportunities.
- To escape political or religious oppression.
- To reunite with family members or other loved ones, usually prior immigrants, who are already in the United States.

Why do some workers uproot their lives to move to the United States? Why do other workers stay put?

Earnings Opportunities

The main driver of economic immigration is the opportunity to improve the immigrant's earnings and therefore standard of living. The chief attractor for economic immigrants is the availability of higher pay in the United States. In particular, immigrants can earn much higher wages in the United States than they earn doing identical or nearly identical jobs in their home countries. Stated in economic terms, immigrants reap larger financial rewards from their stocks of human capital when working in the United States rather than in their home countries.

human capital The knowledge and skills that make a person productive.

Recall that **human capital** is the stock of knowledge, know-how, and skills that enables a person to be productive, and thus to earn income. Other things equal, a greater stock of human capital (for example, more education or better training) results in greater personal productivity and earnings. But whatever someone's stock of education and skill, the value of that human capital depends critically on its capacity to earn income. That is where economic migration comes in. By securing higher earnings, migrants can increase—often quickly and dramatically—the value of their human capital.

Other things equal, wage differences between nations strengthen the incentive to migrate and therefore increase the flow of immigrants toward the country providing the greater wage opportunities. Today, major "magnet countries" that attract a lot of immigrants include Australia, Switzerland, the United States, and several Western European nations. Global Perspective 25.1 shows the percentage of labor forces composed of foreign-born workers in selected nations in 2019, the latest year for which data are available. Along with earnings opportunities, significant differences in educational opportunities, health care availability, and public pensions and welfare benefits play a role in international migration decisions.

🌐 **GLOBAL PERSPECTIVE 25.1**

IMMIGRANTS AS A PERCENTAGE OF THE LABOR FORCE, SELECTED ADVANCED INDUSTRIAL COUNTRIES

Immigrants make up relatively large percentages of the labor forces in several advanced industrial countries, including Australia, Austria, and the United States, but not in other countries such as Finland.

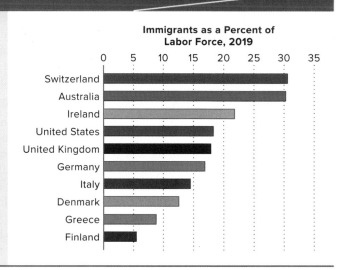

Immigrants as a Percent of Labor Force, 2019

Source: Organization for Economic Co-operation and Development.

Moving Costs

Immigration can be viewed as an investment decision. As with other investments, current sacrifices are necessary to achieve future benefits. In moving from one nation to another, workers incur personal costs. Some of these costs are explicit, out-of-pocket costs such as paying application fees (for example, $1,200 for a green card) and a number of moving expenses. For immigrants who enter the country illegally, a major explicit cost may be a payment to an expediter—a "coyote"—who charges as much as $10,000 to smuggle someone into the United States and transport them to a major city such as Chicago, New York, Houston, or Los Angeles. Other costs of migrating are implicit. They are opportunity costs such as the income given up while the worker is moving and looking for a job in the new country. Other costs are incurred in leaving family and friends and adapting to a new culture, language, and climate. For immigrants who enter the country illegally, there is the additional potential cost of being caught, jailed, and deported.

The prospective immigrant must estimate and weigh all such costs against the expected benefits of the higher earnings in the new country. A person who estimates that the stream of future earnings exceeds the explicit and implicit costs of moving will migrate; a person who sees those costs as exceeding the future stream of earnings will stay put.[1]

Factors Affecting Costs and Benefits

Earnings differences provide the major incentive to migrate, but many nonwage factors also affect a potential immigrant's cost-benefit analysis. Let's examine two key factors.

Distance Other things equal, greater distance reduces the likelihood of migration. Transportation costs rise with distance. In addition, migration to more distant countries is often seen as riskier because information about job market conditions in distant countries is usually less certain than information about job market conditions in nearby countries (although the Internet has greatly reduced this difference in recent years). Finally, the farther the move, the greater the possible costs of returning home to visit with friends and family. A short trip back across a border by automobile is one thing; an airline flight to a different continent, quite another.

The majority of international migrants move to countries relatively close to their home countries. Most Mexican migrants move to the United States. The majority of Eastern European migrants move to Western Europe. Close proximity reduces the cost of the move relative to anticipated benefits.

---

[1]As with other investment decisions, the decision to move internationally requires a comparison of the *present value* of the stream of additional earnings and the *present value* of the costs of moving. Present value considerations (discussed in Chapters 18 and 19) complicate the decision to migrate but do not alter the basic analytic framework: people immigrate when the benefits exceed the costs.

beaten paths Migration routes taken previously by family, relatives, friends, and other migrants.

Some migrants, of course, do move to faraway lands. They often follow **beaten paths**—routes taken previously by family, relatives, and friends. They also tend to cluster, at least for a while, in cities and neighborhoods populated by former and current immigrants of the same nationality or ethnic group. For example, thousands of Russian immigrants have located in the Brighton Beach neighborhood of Brooklyn, New York. Many South Asian immigrants have located in San Francisco. Earlier immigrants ease the transition for later immigrants by providing job information, employment contacts, temporary living quarters, language help, and cultural continuity.

Age Younger workers are much more likely to migrate than older workers. Age affects both benefits and costs in the calculation to move or stay put. Particularly relevant is the fact that younger migrants have more years to recoup their costs of moving. Spread over decades, the higher wage in the new country builds to a large accumulation of additional earnings relative to earnings if the person had not moved. In contrast, older people are closer to retirement and therefore may conclude that moving to another country simply is not worth the effort. Their added earnings over their remaining work years simply will not be sufficient to cover the costs of the disruption and move.

Younger migrants also tend to have lower moving costs than older workers. For example, they typically have accumulated fewer personal possessions to transport. Younger workers generally have fewer roots and ties to the local community and so may find it easier to adapt to new customs and cultures. This greater flexibility reduces the perceived costs of moving and increases the likelihood that the younger person will move.

Younger workers are also more likely to be single or, if married, less likely to have children. The potential costs of migrating multiply rapidly when spouses and children are present. Finding affordable housing large enough for families and enrolling children in new schools complicate the potential move.

Other Factors Several other factors may affect the decision to migrate to the United States. Studies show that immigrants who lack English language skills do not, in general, fare as well in the U.S. workforce as immigrants who speak English. For some highly skilled immigrants, lower tax rates or opportunities to set up businesses in the United States may be the draw. Also, some immigrants to the United States may be willing to endure low or even negative personal returns on immigration simply so that their children have greater economic opportunities than at home.

QUICK REVIEW
25.1

▶ An average of 1.1 million legal immigrants entered the United States each year between 2008 and 2019.

▶ In 2019 Mexico was the greatest single contributor (15 percent) to U.S. legal immigration. Hundreds of thousands of additional legal immigrants arrived from China, the Philippines, India, and many other nations.

▶ Economists view economic migration as a personal investment; a worker will move internationally when the expected gain in earnings exceeds the explicit and implicit costs of moving.

▶ Other things equal, the greater the migration distance and the older the prospective migrant, the less likely the person is to move.

Economic Effects of Immigration

>> **LO25.3** Explain how immigration affects average wages, resource allocation, domestic output, and group income.

Immigration affects U.S. wage rates, efficiency, output, and group income. Like international trade, migration produces large economic benefits but also creates short-term winners and losers. The wage-rate and division-of-income aspects of immigration are two main sources of controversy.

Personal Gains

The fact that economic immigration to the United States is sizable and continuous affirms that, in general, the economic benefit of immigration to immigrants exceeds its cost. In economic terms, the inflows of legal and unauthorized immigration indicate that this investment has a positive return for immigrants. Studies confirm that the returns to immigrating to the United States are, on average, quite substantial. This conclusion should not be a surprise. For example, the real wages earned by recent Mexican male migrants to the United States are as much as six times higher than those earned by similarly educated men in Mexico.

Nevertheless, not all economic immigrants to the United States succeed. Migration decisions are based on expected benefits and are made under circumstances of uncertainty and imperfect information. High average rates of return do not guarantee that all migrants will benefit. In some cases, the expected gain from immigration does not materialize. The anticipated job is not found in the new country, the living costs are higher than anticipated, the anticipated raises and promotions do not happen, or the psychological costs of being away from family and friends are greater than expected. Major **backflows**—return migration to the home country—therefore occur in most international migration patterns, including those between the United States and other countries.

Although this return migration may be costly to those involved, it increases the availability of information about the United States to other potential migrants. These people are then able to better assess the benefits and costs of their own potential moves.

Also, the skills that migrants possess are not always perfectly transferable between employers in different countries because of occupational licensing requirements, specific training, or language differences. This lack of **skill transferability** may mean that migrants earn less than similarly employed native-born workers in the United States. This result is common for immigrants who lack English-language skills.

However, a great deal of economic migration is characterized by **self-selection.** Because migrants choose to move while others with similar skills do not, it is possible that those who move possess greater motivation for personal economic gain and greater willingness to sacrifice current consumption for higher levels of later consumption. These migrants may therefore overcome the problem of imperfect skill transferability and eventually outdo domestic-born workers in wage and salary advancement. This outcome is common among highly skilled immigrants such as scientists, engineers, physicians, and entrepreneurs.

backflows The return of workers to the countries from which they originally emigrated.

skill transferability The ease with which people can shift their work talents from one job, region, or country to another job, region, or country.

self-selection As it relates to international migration, the idea that those who choose to move to a new country tend to have greater motivation for economic gain or greater willingness to sacrifice current consumption for future consumption than those with similar skills who choose to remain at home.

Impacts on Wage Rates, Efficiency, and Output

Although the personal outcomes of immigration are relatively straightforward and easy to understand, the broader economic outcomes are more complicated. A simple economic model of migration will help us sort through key cause-effect relationships and identify broader economic outcomes. In Figure 25.3a, D_u is the demand for labor in the United States; in Figure 25.3b, D_m is the demand for labor in Mexico. The demand for labor presumably is greater in the United States because it has more capital, advanced technology, and better infrastructure that enhance the productivity of labor. (Recall from Chapter 16 that the strength of labor demand is based on the marginal revenue productivity of labor.) Conversely, labor demand in Mexico is weaker because machinery and equipment are less abundant relative to labor, technology is less advanced, and infrastructure is less developed. We also assume that the before-migration labor forces of the United States and Mexico are c and C, respectively; that neither country is experiencing substantial long-term unemployment; and that labor quality in the two countries is the same.

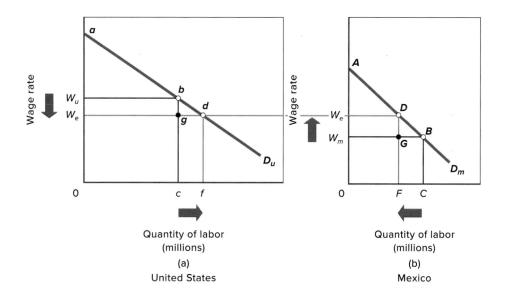

FIGURE 25.3
A simple immigration model.

(a) The migration of low-wage Mexican labor by the amount cf to the United States increases U.S. domestic output by $cbdf$, reduces the U.S. wage rate from W_u to W_e, and increases U.S. business income by W_eW_ubd.
(b) The out-migration of labor of CF from Mexico reduces Mexican domestic output by $FDBC$, raises the wage rate from W_m to W_e, and lowers Mexican business income by W_mW_eDB. Because the U.S. gain in domestic output of $cbdf$ exceeds Mexico's loss of domestic output of $FDBC$, the migration depicted increases economic efficiency and produces a net gain of world output.

Stars and Stripes

Immigrants have contributed mightily to the vitality and growth of the U.S. economy in recent decades. Since 1990, U.S. immigrants have founded 1 of every 4 public companies backed by venture capital. Yahoo!, Intel, eBay, Google, and Tesla all have one or more immigrant founders. About half the engineers and people with computer science doctorates

Dan Thornberg/EyeEm/Getty Images

in the United States are foreign-born. One-fourth of U.S. major league baseball players were born abroad. Children of immigrants often dominate U.S. math and science competitions. And our list could go on.

If we further suppose that migration (1) has no cost, (2) occurs solely in response to wage differentials, and (3) is unimpeded by law in both countries, then workers will migrate from Mexico to the United States until wage rates in the two countries are equal at W_e. At that level, $C - F$ (equals $f - c$) workers will have migrated from Mexico to the United States. Although the U.S. wage level will fall from W_u to W_e, U.S. domestic output (the sum of the marginal revenue products of the entire workforce) will increase from $0abc$ to $0adf$. This domestic output is the total output produced within the borders of the United States and equals U.S. domestic income.

In Mexico, the wage rate will rise from W_m to W_e, but domestic output will decline from $0ABC$ to $0ADF$. The gain in domestic output $cbdf$ in the United States exceeds the loss of domestic output $FDBC$ in Mexico. Thus, the migration from Mexico to the United States has clearly increased the world's output and income.

The elimination of barriers to the international flow of labor tends to create worldwide **efficiency gains from migration.** The same number of workers—rearranged among countries—produces greater total output and income after migration than before migration. The world gains output (and income) because the freedom to migrate enables people to move to countries where they can contribute more to world production. Economic migration not only provides a positive investment return to the mover, it also produces an overall efficiency gain. Migration enables the world to produce a larger output with its currently available resources. Therefore, labor mobility joins capital mobility and international trade in enhancing the world's standard of living. The nearby Consider This story discusses the large positive impact made by immigrants across many sectors of the economy.

> **efficiency gains from migration** The increases in total worldwide output that take place if the additions to output from *immigration* in the destination nation exceed the loss of output from *emigration* in the origin nation.

Income Shares

With personal gains and overall productivity gains, why would anyone oppose immigration? Our graphical model helps answer that question. There are specific groups of gainers and losers from immigration in both nations.

In Figure 25.3, as workers move from Mexico to the United States in search of higher wages, U.S. output increases while Mexican output decreases. The increase in U.S. output partly explains why the United States encourages a relatively high level of immigration through high annual quotas. This also explains why some countries try to discourage outflows of labor from their countries. In particular, countries are rightfully concerned about the emigration of highly educated workers, particularly when those citizens received subsidized education at home. Such undesirable outflows are commonly called **brain drains.**

> **brain drains** The exit or *emigration* of highly educated, highly skilled workers from a country.

Figure 25.3 reveals a second consequence of immigration on income shares. The decline in the wage rate from W_u to W_e in the United States reduces the wage income of native-born U.S. workers from $0W_ubc$ to $0W_egc$. The opposite outcome occurs in Mexico, where the average wage for the native-born workers who do not migrate rises.

Although we can specify income gains and losses to domestic-born workers, we cannot say what will happen to the total wage income (= domestic-born wage income + immigrant wage income) in each country. The final result depends on the elasticities of labor demand. For example, if labor demand is elastic, the wage decrease in the United States will increase total wage income. If labor demand is inelastic, the same wage decrease will cause total wage income to fall.

The immigration-caused decline in wage income for native-born U.S. workers is a major reason that many U.S. labor unions oppose increasing immigration quotas. Unions tend to resist policies that reduce the wages of their current membership or undercut their bargaining power by creating larger pools of potential workers for nonunion firms. In direct contrast, the increase in wages in the outflow country is a possible reason why labor groups in Mexico show little concern about the large-scale outflow of Mexican labor to the United States.

Finally, Figure 25.3 shows that immigration enhances business income in the United States while reducing it in Mexico. The before-immigration domestic output and income in the United States is represented by area $0abc$. Total wage income is $0W_ubc$—the wage rate multiplied by the number of workers. The remaining triangular area W_uab shows business income before immigration. The same reasoning applies to Mexico, where the triangle W_mAB represents before-immigration business income.

Unimpeded immigration increases business income from W_uab to W_ead in the United States and reduces it from W_mAB to W_eAD in Mexico. Other things equal, owners of U.S. businesses benefit from immigration, and owners of Mexican businesses are hurt by emigration. These outcomes are what we would expect intuitively; the United States is gaining "cheap" labor and Mexico is losing "cheap" labor. This conclusion is consistent with the historical fact that U.S. employers have often actively recruited immigrants and have generally supported higher immigration quotas, liberal guest-worker programs, and expanded specialized work visas such as H1-Bs.

Complications and Modifications

Our model is a purposeful simplification of the much more complex reality. Relaxing some of our assumptions and introducing the omitted factors may affect our conclusions.

Costs of Migration Our model has assumed that the movement of workers from Mexico to the United States is without personal cost, but we know that migrants incur the explicit, out-of-pocket costs of physically moving and the implicit opportunity costs of forgone income during the move and transition.

In Figure 25.3, the presence of migration costs means that the flow of labor from Mexico to the United States will stop short of that required to close the wage differential entirely. Wage rates will remain somewhat higher in the United States than in Mexico, and that wage-rate difference will not encourage further migration to close the wage gap. At some point, the remaining earnings gap between the two countries will not be sufficient to cover the marginal cost of migration. Migration will end, and the total output and income gain from migration will be less because wages have not equalized.

Remittances and Backflows Although most immigrants intend to relocate permanently, some migrants see their moves as temporary. They move to a more highly developed country; accumulate some wealth, training, or education through hard work and frugality; and return home to establish their own enterprises. During their time in the new country, these and other migrants frequently make sizable **remittances** to their families at home. These money transfers to the home country redistribute the net gain from migration between the countries involved.

In Figure 25.3, remittances by Mexican workers in the United States to their relatives in Mexico will cause the gain in U.S. income retained in the United States to be less than the domestic output and income gain shown. Similarly, the loss of income available in Mexico will be less than the domestic output and income loss shown. The World Bank estimates that $53 billion of remittances—an amount equal to roughly 4 percent of Mexico's GDP—flowed to Mexico from other countries in 2021. Most of these remittances originate in the United States and are a major reason Mexico favors liberal U.S. immigration laws and generally opposes U.S. policies to stem the flow of unauthorized immigrants across the U.S. border.

Global Perspective 25.2 shows that many developing countries receive large volumes of remittances from emigrants living and working in other countries.

remittances Payments by *immigrants* to family members and others located in the immigrants' home countries.

GLOBAL PERSPECTIVE 25.2

EMIGRANT REMITTANCES, SELECTED DEVELOPING COUNTRIES, 2021

Highly populated developing countries like India and Mexico that have sent millions of immigrants abroad are the largest recipients of emigrant remittances in absolute amounts, as can be seen in the bar chart. But because their economies are so large, those remittances are small relative to the size of their economies. India's remittances, for example, are only 3 percent the size of its domestic economic output. By contrast, the remittances received by smaller countries can exceed 20 percent of their respective economic outputs. These countries included Honduras (27 percent), El Salvador (26 percent), Jamaica (24 percent), and Guatemala (18 percent).

Source: The World Bank Group.

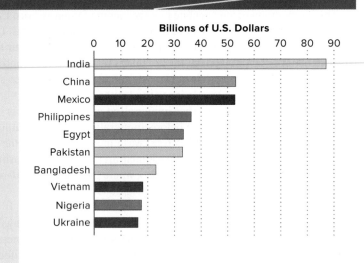

Billions of U.S. Dollars

Along with remittances, backflows of migrants to their home countries might also alter gains and losses through time. For example, if some Mexican workers who migrated to the United States acquire substantial labor market or managerial skills and then return home, their enhanced human capital might contribute substantially to economic development in Mexico. Further, some of the more successful U.S. immigrants eventually may use their expertise and wealth to help build new businesses in Mexico. Both will eventually increase labor demand in Mexico and raise wage rates there.

Complementary versus Substitute Resources Although the average wage rate of domestic-born workers may decline because of immigration, not all such workers will see their wages fall. Many immigrant workers and domestic-born workers are **complementary resources** rather than **substitute resources.** When that is the case, the lower wage rate resulting from large-scale immigration reduces production costs, creating an output effect that raises labor demand for certain domestic-born workers. For example, the large number of immigrants working in the home building industry lowers construction wages and reduces the cost of home building. That outcome in turn increases the number of houses built and sold, which increases the demand for domestic-born residents who help manufacture drywall, plumbing products, major appliances, and other home products.

complementary resources
Productive inputs that are used jointly with other inputs in the production process; resources for which a decrease in the *price* of one leads to an increase in the demand for the other.

substitute resources
Productive inputs that can be used instead of other inputs in the production process; resources for which an increase in the *price* of one leads to an increase in the demand for the other.

Expansion of Capital Long-run effects on capital also help to explain why native-born citizens may not be permanently harmed to the extent suggested by the simple immigration model. The stock of capital is implicitly constant in both countries in Figure 25.3, fixing the demand curves in place. But the rise in business income in the United States relative to the stock of capital produces a higher rate of return on capital. The higher rate of return stimulates overall investment, which in the long run adds to the nation's capital stock. Normally, the addition of new capital such as plant and equipment raises labor productivity, lowers production costs, and reduces product prices. As a result, wages and salaries rise because of increased demand for labor.

On the other hand, the inflow of unauthorized workers into certain low-wage occupations such as field harvesting may stifle R&D, technological advance, and investment in some industries. The easy availability of inexpensive legal or unauthorized immigrant labor provides little incentive to mechanize or otherwise economize on the use of labor. In this regard, economists note that the temporary slowing of the flow of unauthorized agricultural workers after the terrorist attacks of September 11, 2001, increased the purchase of mechanical harvesting equipment such as tree-trunk shakers used to harvest oranges.

Full Employment versus Unemployment Our model conveniently assumes full employment in both countries. Mexican workers presumably leave low-paying jobs to take higher-paying jobs in the United States (more or less immediately). However, in many circumstances, the factor that pushes immigrants from their homelands is not simply low wages but rather chronic unemployment or underemployment. Many developing countries have large populations and surplus labor. A sizable number of workers are either unemployed or so grossly underemployed that their contribution to domestic output is zero or near zero.

If we allow for this possibility, then Mexico would gain rather than lose by emigration. Unemployed Mexicans are making no or little contribution to Mexico's domestic output and must be sustained by transfers from the rest of the labor force. The remaining Mexican labor force will be better off by the amount of the transfers after the unemployed workers have migrated to the United States.

The unemployed workers moving to the United States from Mexico may reflect **negative self-selection,** in which movers are less capable and perhaps less motivated than similarly educated people who did not immigrate. Negative self-selection may combine with higher domestic (Mexican) wages and large remittances as an explanation of why Mexico generally opposes stronger border enforcement by the United States.

Conversely, if the Mexican immigrant workers are unable to find jobs in the United States and are sustained through transfers from employed U.S. workers, then the after-tax income of working Americans will decline. This fear explains why many Americans oppose immigration of low-education, low-skilled workers to the United States.

negative self-selection As it relates to international migration, the idea that those who choose to move to another country have poorer *wage* opportunities in the origin country than those with similar skills who choose not to *emigrate*.

Fiscal Impacts

What effects do immigrants have on tax revenues and government spending in the United States? Do they contribute to U.S. GDP, as our model suggests, or do they go on welfare and drain the government treasury?

Before the 1970s, the immigrant population was less likely to receive public assistance than people born in the United States. Migrants were typically young, single men with significant education and job training. They were readily employable in average-paying jobs and therefore were net contributors to the tax-expenditure system.

The situation reversed between the 1970s and 1990s, when immigrants began to use the welfare system proportionately more than natives. The changing mix of immigrants from relatively skilled workers toward unskilled workers explained the turnabout. Critics claimed that U.S. welfare programs were drawing unskilled (and often unauthorized) workers to the United States from some of the world's poorest nations. Immigrants made up more than 10 percent of Supplemental Security Income (SSI) rolls in 1998 compared to only 3.3 percent a decade before.

As a result of this trend, a major overhaul of the U.S. welfare system was passed into law in 1996. It denied welfare benefits to new legal immigrants for their first five years in the United States. As a result, between 1996 and 2006, cash welfare payments to immigrants declined by 73 percent, food stamps by 39 percent, and SSI payments by 20 percent.

Nonetheless, rates of welfare utilization continued to be higher among immigrants than nonimmigrants. For instance, a survey conducted by the Census Bureau indicated that in 2014, 55 percent of immigrant households used at least one form of welfare as compared with only 35 percent of nonimmigrant households. Among households headed by an unauthorized immigrant, the percentage stood at 63 percent.

In addition to utilizing welfare at high rates, low-income immigrants impose costs on state and local governments by enrolling children in public schools, using emergency health care facilities, and adding to the total volume of cases that must pass through the criminal justice system. For low-income immigrants, these fiscal burdens substantially exceed taxes paid. We will say more about this later.

Research Findings

All economists agree that U.S. immigration increases U.S. domestic output and income and that highly educated immigrants and successful entrepreneurs add to the vitality of American enterprise. But in light of the complications just discussed, no single generalization is possible as to the impact of immigration on the wages of native-born U.S. workers.

The best evidence indicates that immigration reduces the wages of native-born workers who have low levels of education. Immigration also may reduce the salaries of some highly trained native-born workers. For example, studies show that immigration reduces the wages of native-born Americans who do not have high school diplomas, native-born African American men, and native-born holders of doctorate degrees.

The overall effect of immigration on the average American wage is much less clear. Scholarly estimates on that effect range from minus 3 percent to plus 2 percent.

▶ Other things equal, immigration reduces the average wage rate, increases domestic output, lowers the total wage income of native-born workers, and bolsters business income in the destination nation; it has the opposite effects in the origin nation.

▶ Assessing the impacts of immigration is complicated by such factors as remittances and backflows, complementary versus substitute labor, investment impacts, unemployment, and fiscal effects.

The Unauthorized Immigration Debate

>> **LO25.4** Describe unauthorized immigration's effects on employment, wages, and state and local budgets.

Much recent concern about immigration has focused on unauthorized immigration, not immigration per se. Economists point out that a strong inflow of undocumented workers to some extent reflects the increasing scarcity of domestic unskilled labor in the United States. Only about 12 percent of the native-born U.S. workforce has less than a high-school diploma today, compared to about 50 percent in 1960. That scarcity has created significant employment opportunities for unskilled unauthorized immigrants. Unauthorized workers make up roughly 26 percent of all agricultural workers, 23 percent of all cleaning workers, 20 percent of all employees in clothing manufacturing, and 14 percent of all construction workers.

Many Americans fear that unauthorized immigrants and their families depress wage rates in these and other already low-wage U.S. occupations and also burden American citizens through their use of public services such as emergency medical care and public schools. Are these concerns justified?

Employment Effects

Two extreme views on unauthorized immigration are often expressed. Some observers suggest that the employment of unauthorized workers decreases the employment of legal workers on a one-for-one basis. They erroneously suggest that the economy has only a fixed number of jobs at any time. Supposedly, every job taken by an unauthorized worker deprives a legal resident of that job. At the other extreme is the claim that unauthorized workers accept only work that legal residents will not perform. This claim leads to the erroneous conclusion that unauthorized workers displace no legal residents from their jobs. Both views are misleading. Consider Figure 25.4, which illustrates a market for unskilled field workers in agriculture. The downward sloping curve D is the labor demand curve for field workers. The upward sloping supply curve S_d is the labor supply of domestic-born workers, while curve S_t reflects the combined total supply of domestic-born workers and unauthorized immigrants. The horizontal distances between S_t and S_d at the various wage rates measure the number of unauthorized immigrants offering their labor services at those wage rates.

With unauthorized workers present, as implied by curve S_t, the equilibrium wage and level of employment in this labor market are W_t and Q_t. At the low wage of W_t, only ab domestic-born workers are willing to work as field hands. The other workers—bd—are unauthorized immigrants. The low employment of domestic-born workers presumably is caused by better wage opportunities and working conditions in alternative occupations or by the availability of government transfer payments. Recall that unauthorized workers are not eligible for most welfare benefits.

Can we therefore conclude from Figure 25.4 that unauthorized workers have filled field jobs that most U.S.-born workers do not want? The answer is

FIGURE 25.4
The impacts of unauthorized workers in a low-wage labor market.

Unauthorized workers in a low-wage labor market shift the labor supply curve, as from S_d to S_t and reduce the market wage from W_d to W_t. At wage W_t, ab workers are domestic-born (or legal residents) and bd workers are unauthorized immigrants. If all the unauthorized workers were deported, however, Q_d American workers would be employed. To say that unauthorized workers do jobs that Americans are not willing to do (at any wage rate), therefore, is somewhat misleading. Similarly misleading is the conclusion that the deportation of unauthorized workers would boost the employment of American workers on a one-for-one basis.

"yes," but only with the proviso: "at wage rate W_t." With fewer unauthorized immigrants in this labor market, labor supply would be less than that shown by curve S_t. The wage rate would be higher than W_t, and more legal residents would offer their services as field hands. For example, if the United States cut off the full inflow of unauthorized workers to this market, the relevant supply curve would be S_d and the wage rate would rise to W_d. Then Q_d domestic-born workers (as opposed to ab workers) would work as field hands. The critical point is that the willingness of Americans to work at any particular job depends significantly on the wage rate being paid. A sufficiently high **compensating wage differential** (wage premium to compensate for undesirable work) will attract U.S. workers to otherwise undesirable work.

The opposite argument, that unauthorized workers reduce the employment of Americans by an amount equal to the employment of unauthorized workers, is also misleading. Figure 25.4 reveals that the unauthorized workers increase the total number of jobs in the labor market. With unauthorized workers, the number of jobs is Q_t. Without those workers, it is only Q_d. The deportation of the unauthorized workers would not increase domestic employment on a one-for-one basis. Native-born employment will increase by the amount bc in this specific labor market, not by bd.

Generally, unauthorized immigration causes some substitution of unauthorized workers for domestic workers, but the amount of displacement is less than the total employment of the unauthorized workers. Unauthorized immigration—just like legal immigration—increases total employment in the United States.

Wage Effects

Large flows of unauthorized workers into specific low-wage labor markets reduce wage rates in those markets. Note in Figure 25.4 that the greater supply of field workers reduces their wage rate from W_d to W_t. Some U.S. wages—including those of field laborers, food preparers, and house cleaners—are lower than otherwise because of unauthorized immigration.

As discussed previously, the overall effect of unauthorized immigration on the average wage rate in the economy is either a smaller decline or even positive. As with legal immigrants, some unauthorized workers are complementary inputs to domestic-born workers, not substitutes. An example is the unauthorized fruit pickers and the domestic-born truck drivers who deliver the fruit to grocery stores. The lower price of the fruit increases the amount of fruit demanded and thus the amount of it that needs to be delivered. As a result, the labor demand increases for the complementary truck drivers, whose wage rates rise.

Only where unauthorized workers and legal workers are substitute resources will the increase in labor supply reduce other workers' wages. Ironically, studies show that newly arrived unauthorized immigrants have a larger negative impact on the wages of previous immigrants than on the wages of native-born workers.

Unauthorized immigration has very little effect on the average level of wages in the United States. That average wage level depends mainly on the nation's overall level of labor productivity, which unauthorized immigration does not appreciably affect.

Price Effects

Because unauthorized immigrants work at lower pay than would be necessary to attract native-born workers, the prices of goods and services that unauthorized workers produce are lower than they would be otherwise. The extent of such price reduction depends on several factors, including how much of the total cost of producing and delivering a product involves the services performed by unauthorized immigrants. In industries where unauthorized immigrants are heavily used—for example, construction, agriculture, landscaping, home cleaning, restaurant meals, and lodging—the presence of unauthorized workers may have a discernible downward price effect. Lower prices raise the standard of living of all Americans and their families.

Fiscal Impacts on Local and State Governments

One major and very legitimate concern about unauthorized immigration is its negative fiscal impact on local and state governments. Cities and states with high concentrations of unauthorized immigrants bear the main burden. The federal government receives the payroll taxes and income taxes withheld from the earnings of some unauthorized immigrants, but the state and local governments bear most of the costs of their presence. Immigrants place their children in local schools, use local emergency medical care, and add to the cost of the criminal justice system, most of

compensating wage differences Differences in the *wages* received by workers in different jobs to compensate for the nonmonetary differences between the jobs.

Immigration, Aussie Style

Immigration Reform Has Been a Hot Topic. Could the Australian and Canadian Immigration Systems Serve as a Model for U.S. Immigration Reform?

Australia and Canada have immigration systems that are much more focused on job skills and education levels than is the current U.S. immigration system. As you know from reading this chapter, nearly 70 percent of immigrants legally admitted to the United States each year are family sponsored. That is, they are granted permanent residency not because they have job skills or educational backgrounds that are good fits for their new country but simply because they happen to have relatives in the United States who are willing to sponsor them. The vastly larger pool of potential immigrants who do not have U.S. relatives must apply for residency through the much smaller diversity lottery program.

This tilt toward family sponsorship has attracted criticism on economic grounds. Many of the sponsored relatives are elderly or even retired, for instance, so that they will make little or no payroll tax contributions before becoming eligible to receive government health care subsidies. Many others have job skills and educational backgrounds that make it difficult for them to find employment in the United States. Yet others are unable to work effectively from the get-go because of a lack of proficiency in English.

Australia and Canada avoid these problems by opting instead for immigration systems that are heavily tilted toward jobs skills and work experience. The application process is similar in both countries. Applicants take a quiz online, answering questions about their age, job skills, educational attainment, work experience, language skills, whether they have studied or worked in Australia or Canada, and whether they already have a job offer waiting for them in Australia or Canada. Applicants get more or fewer points on each question depending on what they answer (and they know that they should answer truthfully because anything they claim will be scrutinized later on).

Immigration officials in both countries set the number of points awarded for each question and each type of answer based on the needs of the local economy. Thus, for instance, if the Australian territory of New South Wales has a shortage of dentists, then anyone taking the quiz who indicates that they are a certified dentist with a desire to move to New South Wales will get more points than a person whose skills and location preference are not aligned with local needs.

A crucial point about these skill-based immigration systems is that they are not biased toward the highly educated or toward immigrants from particular countries. If there are already plenty of dentists in New South Wales, then a Dutch dentist wanting to move to New South Wales will get far fewer points than would, say, a Nigerian bus driver willing to move to a territory that has a shortage of bus drivers. In Australia there are currently shortages of, among other

Justin Sullivan/Getty Images

things, carpenters, electricians, cooks, livestock farmers, restaurant managers, and agricultural laborers.

Both countries do allow family sponsorship, but only immediate family members can be sponsored and there are numerical limits in place so that skills-based immigration will continue to dominate. Canada, for instance, allows citizens and legal permanent residents to sponsor parents and grandparents for permanent residency. But only 10,000 sponsorships are awarded each year and the recipients are selected by lottery.

Proponents of skills-based immigration argue that many of the problems that the United States is currently experiencing with respect to its immigration system would be resolved by switching to a system that matches immigrants with the needs of the U.S. economy. Among other things, every immigrant would have an easy time finding work and Americans would not have to worry about a tsunami of immigrants driving down wages. There would also be less financial burden placed on social services because the vast majority of immigrants would be working-aged adults paying taxes.

Opponents counter that America has done quite well with its emphasis on family reunification, a major benefit being that sponsored family members already have relatives in the United States who may be able to speed their assimilation, job prospects, and language acquisition through existing social and community networks.

Switching to a skills-based immigration system would be a major policy change and almost every major policy change involves extensive (and sometimes heated) discussion and debate. The immigration debate and how it unfolds should be interesting to watch.

which is provided by state and local governments. Immigrants do, however, pay state sales taxes and taxes on gasoline, and they indirectly pay property taxes built into rent.

The average net fiscal burden (government benefits minus taxes paid) on state and local government for each low-skilled immigrant household may be as high as $19,500 per household per year. In 2016, about 40 percent of the 4.5 million households falling into this low-skilled category were headed by unauthorized immigrants. One recent estimate of the fiscal burden for these households as a group is nearly $55 billion annually.

Other Concerns

Critics of unauthorized immigration point to other reasons for concern. First, they say that allowing immigrants to enter the United States unlawfully undermines general respect for the law. If immigration laws can be broken, why can't other laws also be broken? The success of many immigrants in entering the United States and working for employers illegally rests on other criminal activity such as the creation of fake birth certificates, Social Security cards, and driver's licenses. Also, some unauthorized immigrants engage in illegal activities such as drug smuggling, identity theft, and insurance fraud. Although legal U.S. immigrants have considerably lower incarceration rates than the native-born U.S. population, the crime rate for unauthorized immigrants is much higher than that of the native-born U.S. population.

Second, critics of the ineffective enforcement of border and employment laws point out that illegal immigration is highly unfair to the thousands of people enduring the expense and long waits associated with the process for legally gaining the right to live and work in the United States.

Finally, some observers see national defense as the greatest long-term risk from porous borders. Unlawful entry into the United States is clearly at odds with the goal of homeland security. Ineffective border enforcement against unauthorized immigrants allows career criminals and even terrorists to enter the United States undetected.

Conclusions

Overall, economic analysis suggests that immigration can either benefit or harm a nation, depending on the number of immigrants; their education, skills, and work ethic; and the rate at which they can be absorbed into the economy without disruption.

From a strictly economic perspective, immigration should be expanded until its marginal benefit equals its marginal cost. The MB = MC conceptual framework explicitly recognizes that there can be too few immigrants, just as there can be too many. Moreover, it recognizes that from a strictly economic standpoint, not all immigrants are alike. Some immigrants generate more benefits to the U.S. economy than others; and some immigrants impose more costs on taxpayers than others. The immigration of, say, a highly educated scientist obviously has a different net economic impact than does the immigration of a long-term welfare recipient.

Summary

LO25.1 Describe the extent of immigration into the United States.
Legal immigrants may be either permanent immigrants (green card holders) or temporary immigrants who are legally in the country until a specific date. The United States admitted 1,031,765 legal permanent residents in 2019. About 54 percent of these immigrants were women; 46 percent were men.

Unauthorized immigrants (also called undocumented workers or illegal aliens) are people who enter the country unlawfully or overstay their prescribed exit dates. An estimated 11.4 million unauthorized immigrants live in the United States. Forty-seven percent come from Mexico.

LO25.2 Discuss why economists view economic immigration as increasing the market value of human capital.
An economic migrant's decision to move to another country can be viewed as an investment, in which present sacrifices (explicit and implicit costs) are incurred to obtain larger lifetime gains (higher

earnings). Other things equal, the shorter the distance of the move and the younger the potential economic migrant, the more likely they will be to move to another country.

LO25.3 Explain how immigration affects average wages, resource allocation, domestic output, and group income.

The simple immigration model suggests that, for a high-wage country, the movement of migrants from a low-wage country (a) increases domestic output (= domestic income), (b) reduces the average wage rate, (c) reduces the total wage income of native-born workers, and (d) increases business income. The opposite effects occur in the low-wage country. Because the domestic output gains in the high-wage country exceed the domestic output losses in the low-wage country, labor resources are more efficiently allocated globally and world output rises.

The outcomes of immigration predicted by the simple immigration model become more complicated when considering (a) the costs of moving, (b) the possibility of remittances and backflows, (c) complementary rather than substitute labor, (d) impacts on investment, (e) the levels of unemployment in each country, and (f) the fiscal impact on the taxpayers of each country.

LO25.4 Describe unauthorized immigration's effects on employment, wages, and state and local budgets.

Legal U.S. residents who have less than a high school education seem to bear the brunt of the wage impact of immigration, although some highly educated workers are also affected. Immigration has little discernible effect on the overall average wage rate in the U.S. economy, with estimates ranging from minus 3 percent to plus 2 percent.

Undocumented workers in the United States reduce wage rates in narrowly defined low-wage labor markets, but they do not reduce native-born employment by the full extent of the employment of the unauthorized workers. American workers whose job skills are complementary to those of unauthorized immigrant labor may experience an increase in the demand for their services and wages because of illegal immigration.

Undocumented workers may increase the overall rate of return on capital, thus promoting greater national investment. However, large numbers of unauthorized workers in specific industries may reduce the incentive for those industries to mechanize. A legitimate concern is that unauthorized immigrant workers and their families impose greater fiscal costs on state and local governments than they contribute in tax revenues to those jurisdictions.

Terms and Concepts

economic immigrants

legal immigrants

unauthorized immigrants

H1-B provision

human capital

beaten paths

backflows

skill transferability

self-selection

efficiency gains from migration

brain drains

remittances

complementary resources

substitute resources

negative self-selection

compensating wage differential

Discussion Questions

McGraw Hill **connect**

1. Which of the following statements are true? Which are false? Explain why the false statements are untrue. **LO25.1**
   a. More immigrants arrive to the United States each year illegally than legally.
   b. The majority of legal immigrants are men.
   c. Over half the new legal immigrants to the United States each year come from Mexico.
   d. Most legal immigrants to the United States gain their legal status through employment-based preferences.

2. In what respect is the economic decision to move across international borders an investment decision? Why do economic migrants move to some countries but not to others? Cite an example of an explicit cost of moving and an implicit cost of moving. How do distance and age affect the migration decision? How does the presence of a large number of previous movers to a country affect the projected costs and benefits of subsequent movers? **LO25.2**

3. Suppose that the projected lifetime earnings gains from migration exceed the costs of moving. Explain how the decision to move might be reversed when a person considers present value. **LO25.2**

4. How might the output and income gains from immigration shown by the simple immigration model be affected by

(a) unemployment in the originating nation, (b) remittances by immigrants to the home country, and (c) backflows of migrants to the home country? **LO25.3**

5. Suppose initially that immigrant labor and native-born labor are complementary resources. Explain how substantial immigration might change the demand for native-born workers, altering their wages. (Review the relevant portion of Chapter 16 if necessary.) Next, suppose that new immigrant labor and previous immigrant labor (not native-born) are substitute resources. Explain how substantial immigration of new workers might affect the demand for previous immigrants, altering their wages. **LO25.3**

6. What is a "brain drain" as it relates to international migration? If emigrants are highly educated and received greatly subsidized education in the home country, is there any justification for that country to levy a "brain drain" tax on them? Do you see any problems with this idea? **LO25.3**

7. In September 2018, *The Wall Street Journal (WSJ)* reported that a growing shortage of labor in Eastern European countries such as Hungary was driving up wages and reducing business income. The reason for the shortages was a large migration of Eastern European workers to Western European countries. Use the simple immigration model to demonstrate the key elements of the *WSJ* story as just described. **LO25.3**

8. Why is each of these statements somewhat misleading? (*a*) "Unauthorized immigrants take only jobs that no American wants." (*b*) "Deporting 100,000 undocumented immigrants would create 100,000 job openings for Americans." **LO25.4**

9. Why are so many state and local governments greatly concerned about the federal government's allegedly lax enforcement of the immigration laws and congressional proposals to grant legal status (amnesty) to unlawful immigrants in the United States? How might an amnesty program affect the flow of future border crossings? **LO25.4**

10. If someone favors the free movement of labor within the United States, is it inconsistent for that person to also favor restrictions on the international movement of labor? Why or why not? **LO25.4**

11. **LAST WORD** What is the relative importance of family sponsorship (of permanent residency applications) in the United States as compared with Australia and Canada? What factor do Australia and Canada emphasize when selecting legal immigrants? What are the positives and negatives of emphasizing that factor?

Review Questions

1. Each year, the number of legal immigrants to the United States is _____ the number of unauthorized immigrants. **LO25.1**
   a. less than
   b. equal to
   c. greater than
   d. less than (but only in *most* years, not every year)

2. The primary reason people immigrate to the United States is: **LO25.2**
   a. to escape political or religious oppression back home.
   b. to reunite with family members.
   c. to improve earnings and living standards.
   d. none of the above.

3. True or False: Because older adults have more human capital, they are more likely to migrate to another country than younger adults. **LO25.2**

4. Use the accompanying tables for Neon and Zeon to answer the questions that follow. Assume that the wage rate shown equals hourly output and income. Also assume that the accumulated output and income are the sum of the marginal revenue products (MRPs) of each worker. **LO25.3**

Neon

Workers	Wage Rate = MRP	Domestic Output and Income
1	$21	$ 21
2	19	40 (= 21 + 19)
3	17	57 (= 21 + 19 + 17)
4	15	72
5	13	85
6	11	96
7	9	105

Zeon

Workers	Wage Rate = MRP	Domestic Output and Income
1	$15	$15
2	13	28 (= 15 + 13)
3	11	39 (= 15 + 13 + 11)
4	9	48
5	7	55
6	5	60
7	3	63

a. Which country has the greater stock of capital and technological prowess? How can you tell?

b. Suppose the equilibrium wage rate is $19 in Neon and $7 in Zeon. What is the domestic output (= domestic income) in the two countries?

c. Assuming zero migration costs and initial wage rates of $19 in Neon and $7 in Zeon, how many workers will move to Neon? Why will more than that number of workers not move to Neon?

d. After the move of workers, what will be the equilibrium wage rate in each country? What will be the domestic output after the migration? What is the amount of the combined gain in domestic output produced by the migration? Which country will gain output? Which will lose output? How will the income of native-born workers be affected in each country?

5. Migration between North Korea and South Korea has been prohibited since the end of the Korean War in 1953. South Korea is now much richer than North Korea and has a much higher marginal product of labor and a much higher wage rate than North Korea. If workers could migrate from North Korea to South Korea, we would expect: **LO25.3**
   a. output to fall in South Korea but rise in North Korea.
   b. output to rise in each country.
   c. total combined output in the two countries to fall.
   d. total combined output in the two countries to rise.

6. True or False: Research indicates that immigration causes large decreases in the average American wage. **LO25.3**

7. True or False: The MB = MC level of immigration is likely to be achieved if we simply let in every person who wishes to immigrate to the United States. **LO25.4**

Problems

1. Mexico has labor laws that specify a daily (rather than hourly) minimum wage. In 2022, the daily minimum wage in Mexico was about 173 pesos per day, and the exchange rate between Mexican pesos and U.S. dollars was about 20 pesos per dollar. **LO25.3**

   a. In 2022, what was the Mexican minimum daily wage in terms of dollars?

   b. Given that Mexican employees typically work 8-hour days, about how much per hour is the Mexican minimum wage in terms of U.S. dollars?

   c. In 2022, the federal minimum wage in the United States was $7.25 per hour. How many times larger was the hourly U.S. federal minimum wage than the hourly Mexican minimum wage?

   d. If unskilled workers have a tendency to migrate to where they can obtain the highest compensation for their labor, which country is more likely to receive low-skilled immigrants?

2. Differences in productivity are usually the major force behind differences in wages and unit labor costs. Suppose that a single unskilled worker at a pottery factory in Mexico can produce 1 mug per hour. By comparison, suppose that a single unskilled worker at a pottery factory in the United States can produce 14 mugs per hour because more and better machinery generates higher labor productivity. The Mexican mugs and the American mugs are identical in quality and durability and sell for the same price. **LO25.3**

   a. If unskilled pottery workers are paid the local minimum wage in both countries, how much is the labor cost *per mug* for mugs produced in Mexico? For mugs produced in the United States? (Use the minimum wages from problem 1 and make all calculations in dollars.)

   b. With regard to mug production, how much higher are labor costs *per hour* in the United States?

   c. With regard to mug production, how much higher are labor costs *per unit* in Mexico?

   d. Do higher labor costs per hour always imply higher labor costs per unit?

   e. If firms with lower labor costs per unit expand, while those with higher labor costs per unit contract, in which country will mug-making firms be increasing in size and hiring more employees? If unskilled pottery workers relocate to where they can find jobs, to which country will they be moving?

3. There is evidence that, other things equal, a 10 percent increase in the number of workers with a particular skill level leads to about a 4 percent decline in wages for workers with that skill level. In addition, this 10-to-4 ratio appears to hold true whether the increase in labor supply is caused by domestic changes in labor supply or by an influx of immigrants workers. **LO25.3**

   a. Suppose that 42,000 computer programmers work in Silicon Valley. If the number of computer programmers in Silicon Valley increases by 1,260 because of a change in U.S. immigration laws, by how many percentage points would you expect the wage of computer programmers to fall in Silicon Valley?

   b. Suppose that 8,000 full-time cooks work in restaurants in the Denver area. If Denver becomes popular both with U.S. citizens and with foreigners such that 400 full-time cooks move to Denver from other parts of the United States while 80 full-time cooks move to Denver from other countries, by how much would you expect the wages of full-time cooks to fall in Denver?

4. In 2022, an estimated 7.7 million Mexican-born immigrants were employed in the United States. **LO25.3**

   a. If 60 percent of the Mexican-born immigrants remitted money to family members in Mexico in 2022, and if they each sent $100 per month, how much money did they remit in total in 2022?

   b. If, instead, 100 percent of the Mexican-born immigrants remitted money to family members in Mexico in 2022, and if they each sent $250 per month, how much money did they remit in total in 2022?

   c. The actual amount remitted to Mexico in 2017 by Mexican-born immigrants living in the United States was about $53 billion. If we assume that 75 percent of the Mexican-born immigrants remitted money to Mexico that year and if we further assume that each of those immigrants remitted an equal amount each month, how much per month did each of those immigrants have to remit to total $53 billion for the year?

An Introduction to Macroeconomics

>> LEARNING OBJECTIVES

LO26.1 Explain why economists use GDP, inflation, and unemployment to assess the economy's health.

LO26.2 Discuss why sustained increases in living standards are historically recent.

LO26.3 Identify why saving and investment promote higher living standards.

LO26.4 Explain why shocks and sticky prices are responsible for short-run fluctuations in output and employment.

LO26.5 Characterize the degree to which various prices are sticky.

LO26.6 Explain why economists use different macroeconomic models for different time horizons.

Macroeconomics focuses on national economies while seeking answers to large-scale economic questions, including: Why are some countries really rich while others are deeply impoverished? Why do all countries—even the richest—go through alternating boom and bust periods? Can governments do anything to improve living standards or fight recessions?

Because this chapter is an introduction, it will answer these questions only in brief. Subsequent chapters provide the highly interesting details.

Performance and Policy

Macroeconomics studies the behavior of the economy as a whole. It is primarily concerned with two topics: long-run economic growth and the short-run fluctuations in output and employment that comprise the **business cycle.** These phenomena are closely related. Most economies enjoy a distinct growth trend that leads to higher output and higher standards of living in the long run. But the rate of growth is not constant. Sometimes it proceeds rapidly, sometimes slowly, and sometimes it even turns negative for while, a situation known as a *recession.*

To understand how economies operate and how to improve their performance, economists collect and analyze economic data, including the amount of new construction taking place each month, how many ships laden with cargo arrive at U.S. ports each year, and how many new inventions have been patented in the last few weeks. That said, macroeconomists tend to focus on three key statistics when assessing an economy's health and development.

Real GDP

Real GDP, or **real gross domestic product,** measures the value of the final goods and services produced within a country's borders during a specific period of time, typically a year. This statistic is very

>> **LO26.1** Explain why economists use GDP, inflation, and unemployment to assess the economy's health.

business cycle Recurring increases and decreases in the level of economic activity over periods of years; consists of peak, recession, trough, and expansion phases.

real gross domestic product (GDP) *Gross domestic product* adjusted for *inflation;* gross domestic product in a year divided by the GDP *price index* for that year, the index expressed as a decimal. Compare with *nominal GDP.*

useful because it tells us whether an economy's output is growing. For instance, if U.S. real GDP in one year is larger than in the previous year, we know that U.S. output increased from the first year to the second.

nominal gross domestic product (GDP) *GDP* measured in terms of *the price level* at the time of measurement; *GDP* not adjusted for *inflation*. Compare with *real gross domestic product (real GDP)*.

To calculate the value of real GDP, government statisticians first calculate **nominal GDP,** which is the dollar value of all goods and services produced within a country's borders using their prices during the year they were produced. Nominal GDP suffers from a major problem: It can increase from one year to the next even if there is no increase in output. To see how, consider a commercial blacksmith who produced 10 iron spiral staircases last year and 10 identical staircases this year. Clearly, the blacksmith's output did not change. But if the market price of a staircase rose from $10,000 last year to $20,000 this year, nominal GDP will have increased from $100,000 (= 10 × $10,000) to $200,000 (= 10 × $20,000). Without knowing about the price increase, we might incorrectly conclude that the output of staircases had doubled.

Real GDP avoids this problem by accounting for price changes. As a result, we can compare real GDP numbers from one year to the next and really know if there is a change in output (rather than a change in prices).

Because more output means more consumption possibilities—including not only fun things like more movies and more vacations, but also serious things like better health care and safer roads—economists and policymakers are deeply committed to encouraging a large and growing real GDP.

Unemployment

unemployment The failure to use all available *economic resources* to produce desired *goods* and *services*; the failure of the economy to fully employ its *labor force*.

Unemployment occurs when a person cannot get a job despite being willing to work and actively seeking work. High unemployment rates are undesirable because they indicate that a nation is not using a large portion of its most important resource—the talents and skills of its people. Unemployment is wasteful because we lose all the goods and services that unemployed workers could have produced if they had been working. Researchers have also drawn links between higher unemployment rates and major social problems such as higher crime rates, greater political unrest, and higher rates of depression and heart disease among unemployed people.

Inflation

inflation A rise in the general level of *prices* in an economy; an increase in an economy's *price level*.

Inflation is an increase in the overall level of prices. As an example, consider all the goods and services that a typical family buys over the course of one year. If the economy is experiencing inflation, the family will spend more money to buy those goods and services this year than it spent on those same goods and services last year. This can be troublesome for several reasons. First, if the family's income does not rise as fast as prices do, the family won't be able to purchase as much as it used to, and its standard of living will fall. In addition, a surprise jump in inflation reduces the purchasing power of people's savings. Their savings will buy less than expected due to the higher-than-expected prices.

Preview

Because real GDP, unemployment, and inflation are the standards by which economists keep track of long-run growth and short-run fluctuations, we spend a substantial amount of time in the next few chapters examining how these statistics are computed, how they affect people's well-being, and how they vary both across countries and over time.

We then build on that understanding by developing macroeconomic models of both long-run growth and short-run fluctuations to help you understand how policymakers attempt to maximize growth while minimizing unemployment and inflation.

**QUICK REVIEW
26.1**

▶ Macroeconomics studies long-run economic growth and short-run economic fluctuations.

▶ Macroeconomists focus their attention on three key economic statistics: real GDP, unemployment, and inflation.

▶ Macroeconomic models help to clarify many important questions about government economic policy.

The Miracle of Modern Economic Growth

Rapid and sustained economic growth is a modern phenomenon. Before the Industrial Revolution began in the late 1700s in England, standards of living showed virtually no growth over hundreds or even thousands of years. For instance, the standard of living of the average Roman peasant was virtually the same at the start of the Roman Empire around the year 500 B.C. as it was at the end of the Roman Empire 1,000 years later. Similarly, historians have estimated that the average Chinese peasant's standard of living was essentially the same in the year A.D. 1800 as it was in the year A.D. 100.

That is not to say that the Roman and Chinese economies did not expand over time. They did. In fact, their total output of goods and services increased many times over. However, as their output increased, their populations increased by similar proportions so that the amount of output *per person* remained virtually unchanged.

This pattern continued until the start of the Industrial Revolution, which ushered in not only factory production and automation but also constantly improving production technologies thanks to an emphasis on research and development. As a result, output began to grow faster than population, so that living standards rose as the amount of output per person increased.

In countries experiencing **modern economic growth,** output per person rises. Under modern economic growth, the annual increase in output per person is often not large, perhaps 2 percent per year in countries such as England that were the first to industrialize. But when compounded over time, an annual growth rate of 2 percent adds up rapidly. Indeed, it implies that the standard of living will double every 35 years. Thus, if the average citizen of a country enjoying 2 percent growth begins this year with an income of $10,000, in 35 years that person will have an income of $20,000. Then, 35 years after that, income will double again, so that her income 70 years from now will be $40,000. And 35 years after that, the average citizen's income will double again, to $80,000. Such high rates of growth are amazing when compared to the period before modern economic growth when standards of living remained unchanged for centuries.

Today, the citizens of the world's richest nations enjoy material standards of living that are on average more than 50 times higher than those experienced by citizens of the world's lowest-income nations, as shown in Global Perspective 26.1, which compares GDP per capita (per person) for

>> **LO26.2** Discuss why sustained increases in living standards are historically recent.

modern economic growth The historically recent phenomenon in which nations for the first time have experienced sustained increases in *real GDP per capita.*

GLOBAL PERSPECTIVE 26.1

GDP PER PERSON, SELECTED COUNTRIES

Average income per person—which by definition equals gross domestic product (GDP) per person—varies massively from country to country, even after adjusting for differences in the cost of living. This is best seen by comparing the average income per person in one of the world's richest countries, Switzerland, with that in one of the world's poorest, Burundi. In 2020, Switzerland's GDP per person of $71,352 was 93 times larger than Burundi's $771 per person.

Country	GDP per Person, 2020 (U.S. dollars based on purchasing power parity)
Switzerland	$71,352
United States	63,544
Germany	53,694
Canada	48,072
Saudi Arabia	46,763
United Kingdom	44,916
Japan	42,197
Russia	28,213
Mexico	18,333
China	17,312
India	6,454
Nigeria	5,187
Afghanistan	2,088
Somalia	875
Burundi	771

Source: The World Bank Group, data.worldbank.org.

the world's wealthiest and poorest countries. Those vast differences in living standards are almost entirely the result of the fact that different countries began modern economic growth at different dates. The countries that have been at it the longest have ended up far richer than those that began modern economic growth only recently.

▶ Before the Industrial Revolution, living standards did not show any sustained increases over time because any increase in output was usually offset by an equally large increase in population.

▶ Since the Industrial Revolution, many nations have experienced *modern economic growth* in which output grows faster than population—so that living standards rise over time.

>> LO26.3 Identify why saving and investment promote higher living standards.

saving The flow of money that is generated when *personal consumption expenditures* are less than *disposable income*. Compare with *savings*.

investment Expenditures that increase the volume of physical *capital* (roads, factories, wireless networks) and intangible ideas (formulas, processes, algorithms) that help to produce goods and services. Also known as *economic investment*. Not to be confused with *financial investment*.

financial investment The purchase of a financial asset (such as a *stock, bond,* or *mutual fund*) or real asset (such as a house, land, or factories) in the expectation of financial gain. Compare with economic investment.

Saving, Investment, and Choosing between Present and Future Consumption

To raise living standards over time, an economy must devote at least some part of its current output to increasing future output. This process requires both saving and investment.

- **Saving** occurs when current consumption is less than current income; the difference between them is savings.

- **Investment** happens when resources are directed toward increasing future output—either by paying for research to develop more efficient production technologies or by paying for the production of newly created capital goods (such as machinery, tools, and infrastructure) that will increase future output.

When thinking about why saving and investment are so important for economic growth, the key point is that the amount of investment is ultimately limited by the amount of saving. The only way that more output can be directed at investment activities is if saving increases. But that, in turn, implies that individuals and society as a whole must make trade-offs between current and future consumption. This is true because the only way to pay for more investment—and the higher levels of future consumption that more investment can generate—is to increase present saving. But increased saving can only come at the price of reduced current consumption. Individuals and society as a whole must therefore wrestle with a choice between present consumption and future consumption. They must decide how to balance the reductions in current consumption required to fund current investment against the increases in future consumption that the added current investment will make possible.

The nearby Consider This story explains the crucial difference between economic investment and financial investment. When economists say "investment," they mean economic investment.

CONSIDER THIS . . .

Economic versus Financial Investment

Economics students often are confused by the word "investment" because the ordinary usage of the word refers to a *financial investment* whereas economists use the word to refer to *economic investment*, which is an entirely different concept.

Financial investment captures what ordinary people mean when they say investment, namely, the purchase of assets like stocks, bonds, and real estate in the hope of reaping a financial gain. By contrast, when economists say "investment," they are referring to **economic investment**, which relates to the expansion of the economy's

Stephen Brashear/Getty Images

productive capacity. So economic investment includes, for example, spending that pays for the production of newly created capital goods like factories and wireless networks as well as the costs of developing new technologies like solar-powered helicopters or a cure for cancer.

For economists, purely financial transactions, such as swapping cash for a stock or a bond, are not "investment." Neither are the purchases of capital goods built in previous years. These transactions simply transfer the ownership of existing assets from one party to another. They do not increase the economy's productive capacity. And so they are not considered "investments" by economists.

Banks and Other Financial Institutions

Households are the principal source of savings, but businesses are the main economic investors. So how does the pool of savings generated by households get transferred to businesses? Banks and other financial institutions (such as mutual funds, pension plans, and insurance companies) act as intermediaries between households and businesses. These institutions collect households' savings, rewarding savers with interest, dividends, or capital gains (increases in asset values). They then lend the funds to businesses, which invest in equipment, factories, and other capital goods as well as research and development.

Macroeconomics devotes considerable attention to money, banking, and financial institutions because a well-functioning financial system promotes economic growth and stability by encouraging saving and by directing that saving into the most productive possible investments. In contrast, a poorly functioning financial system can create serious problems for an economy.

economic investment Spending for the production and accumulation of *capital,* additions to *inventories,* or the research and development of new goods or services, including funds spent on the creation of new works of music, literature, or software. Compare with *financial investment.*

▶ An economy can only grow if it invests, and it can only invest if it saves some of its current output. Thus, saving is crucial to increasing investment and, consequently, future output.

▶ Banks and other financial institutions channel household savings toward businesses, which invest in equipment, factories, and other capital goods as well as in the development of new productive technologies.

QUICK REVIEW
26.3

Uncertainty, Expectations, and Shocks

Decisions about savings and investment are complicated by the fact that the future is uncertain. Investment projects sometimes produce disappointing results or fail totally. As a result, firms spend considerable time trying to predict future trends so that they invest only in projects that are likely to succeed. For this reason, macroeconomics must take into account **expectations** about the future.

>> **LO26.4** Explain why shocks and sticky prices are responsible for short-run fluctuations in output and employment.

The Importance of Expectations and Shocks

Expectations are important for two reasons. The more obvious reason involves the effects of changing expectations on current behavior. If firms grow more pessimistic about the future returns that they expect from current investments, they will invest less today than they would if they were more optimistic. Expectations therefore have a large effect on economic growth because increased pessimism leads to less current investment and, subsequently, less future consumption.

The less-obvious reason that expectations are so important concerns what happens when expectations are unmet. Firms are often forced to cope with **shocks**—situations in which they were expecting one thing to happen but something else happened instead. For instance, consider a situation in which a firm decides to build a high-speed railroad that will shuttle passengers between Los Angeles and Las Vegas. The firm expects it to be very popular and make a handsome profit. But what if the railroad turns out to be unpopular and loses money? The firm will need to figure out how to respond to the unexpected bad news. Should it go out of business completely? Should it try to turn a profit by hauling cargo instead of passengers? Should it borrow $30 million to pay for a massive advertising campaign? These sorts of decisions are necessitated by the shock and surprise of having to deal with an unexpected situation.

Economies experience both demand shocks and supply shocks. **Demand shocks** are unexpected changes in the demand for goods and services. **Supply shocks** are unexpected changes in the supply of goods and services. Note that the word *shock* reveals only that something unexpected has happened. It does not tell us whether what has happened is unexpectedly good or unexpectedly bad. For this reason, economists use more specific terms. For instance, a *positive demand shock* refers to a situation in which actual demand is higher than expected, while a *negative demand shock* refers to a situation in which actual demand is lower than expected.

expectations The anticipations of consumers, *firms,* and others about future economic conditions.

shocks Sudden, unexpected changes in *demand* (or *aggregate demand*) or supply (or *aggregate supply*).

demand shocks Sudden, unexpected changes in demand.

supply shocks Sudden, unexpected changes in *aggregate supply.*

Demand Shocks and Sticky Prices

Economists believe that most short-run fluctuations in GDP and the business cycle are the result of demand shocks. Supply shocks do happen in some cases and are very important when they do occur. But we will focus most of our initial attention in this chapter and subsequent chapters on demand shocks, how they affect the economy, and how government policy may be able to help the economy adjust to them.

But why are demand shocks such a big problem? Why would we have to consider calling in the government to help deal with them? And why can't firms deal with demand shocks on their own?

The answer to these questions is that the prices of many goods and services are inflexible (slow to change, or "sticky") in the short run. As we will explain, this implies that price changes do not quickly equalize the quantities demanded of such goods and services with their respective quantities supplied. Instead, because prices are inflexible, the economy is forced to respond in the short run to demand shocks primarily through changes in output and employment rather than through changes in prices.

Example: A Single Firm Dealing with Demand Shocks and Sticky Prices

Although an entire economy is vastly more complex than a single firm, an analogy that uses a single car factory is helpful in explaining why demand shocks and inflexible prices help to explain most short-run fluctuations in output and employment. Consider a car manufacturing company named Buzzer Auto. Like most companies, Buzzer Auto is in business to make a profit. Part of turning a profit involves developing accurate expectations about future market conditions. Consequently, Buzzer constantly conducts market research to estimate future demand conditions so that it will design and build cars that people want to buy.

Setting Expectations After extensive market research, Buzzer concludes that it can earn a modest profit if it builds and staffs an appropriately sized factory to build an environmentally friendly SUV, which it decides to call the Proton. Buzzer's marketing economists collaborate with Buzzer's engineers and conclude that expected profits will be maximized if the firm builds a factory whose optimal (least cost) output rate is 900 cars per week. If the factory operates at this rate, it can produce a Proton for only $36,500 per vehicle. This cost per vehicle is good news because the firm's estimates for demand indicate that a supply of 900 vehicles per week can be sold at a price of $37,000 per vehicle. So, if everything goes according to plan, Buzzer Auto should make an accounting profit of $500 on each Proton that it produces and sells. Expecting these future conditions, Buzzer decides to build the factory, staff it, and begin making Protons.

Examine **Figure 26.1 (Key Graph)**, which shows the market for Protons when the vertical supply curve for Protons is fixed at the factory's optimal output rate of 900 cars per week. Notice that we have drawn in three possible demand curves. D_L corresponds to low demand for Protons, D_M corresponds to the medium level of demand that Buzzer's marketing economists expect to materialize, and D_H corresponds to high demand for Protons.

Figure 26.1a can be used to illustrate what will happen if everything goes according to the firm's expectations: If all goes according to plan and the actual demand that materializes is D_M, the equilibrium price will in fact be $37,000 per Proton, and the equilibrium quantity demanded will be 900 cars per week. Thus, if all goes according to expectations, the factory will have exactly the right capacity to meet the expected quantity demanded at the sales price of $37,000 per vehicle. In addition, the firm's books will show a profit of $500 per vehicle on each of the 900 vehicles that it builds and expects to sell each week at that price.

Full Employment with No Shocks If its expectations are always fulfilled, Buzzer Auto will never contribute to any of the short-run fluctuations in output and unemployment that affect real-world economies. First, if everything always goes according to plan and Buzzer Auto's expectations always come true, then the factory will always produce and sell at its optimal output rate of 900 cars per week. Thus, it would never experience any fluctuations in output—either in the short run or in the long run. At the same time, because producing a constant output of 900 cars each week will always require the same number of workers, the factory's labor demand and employment should never vary. So, if everything always goes according to plan, Buzzer Auto will never have any effect on unemployment because it will always hire a constant number of workers.

These facts imply that the short-run fluctuations in output and unemployment that we see in the real world must be the result of shocks—of things *not* going according to plan. In particular, business cycle fluctuations typically arise because actual demand ends up being either lower or higher than what businesses were expecting. In those cases, some adjustments are necessary to bring quantity demanded and quantity supplied back into alignment.

Price Changes If There Are Demand Shocks *and* Flexible Prices Figure 26.1a can also be used to illustrate how the market for Protons will adjust to unexpected changes in demand if prices are

...Il KEY GRAPH

FIGURE 26.1 The effect of demand shocks under flexible and fixed prices.

(a) If prices are flexible, then no matter what demand turns out to be, Buzzer Auto can continue to sell its optimal (least cost) output of 900 cars per week since the equilibrium price will adjust to equalize the quantity demanded with the quantity supplied. (b) By contrast, if Buzzer Auto sticks with a fixed-price policy, then the quantity demanded will vary with the level of demand. At the fixed price of $37,000 per vehicle, the quantity demanded will be 700 cars per week if demand is D_L, 900 cars per week if demand is D_M, and 1,150 cars per week if demand is D_H.

QUICK QUIZ FOR FIGURE 26.1

1. Comparing what happens in Figures 26.1a and 26.1b, the equilibrium price, if demand D_H happens, will be higher if:
   a. the price per vehicle is fixed.
   b. the price per vehicle is free to vary.
   c. the automaker's optimal output rate increases from 900 cars per week to 1,150 cars per week.
   d. demand shifts back down to D_M.

2. In Figure 26.1a, increased demand:
   a. raises price.
   b. lowers price.
   c. stabilizes price.
   d. none of the above.

3. In Figure 26.1b, increased demand:
   a. increases price.
   b. increases output.
   c. decreases price.
   d. decreases output.

4. At what level of demand will the same number of cars be sold regardless of whether price per vehicle is fixed or flexible?
   a. D_L
   b. D_M
   c. D_H
   d. all of the above

Answers: 1. b; 2. a; 3. b; 4. b

flexible. If demand is unexpectedly low at D_L, the market price will adjust downward to $35,000 per vehicle so that the quantity demanded at that price still equals the factory's optimal output rate of 900 cars per week. However, if demand is unexpectedly high at D_H, the market price will adjust upward to $40,000 per vehicle so that the quantity demanded still equals the factory's optimal output rate of 900 cars per week. These adjustments imply that if the price of Protons is free to quickly adjust in response to unexpected changes in demand, the factory can always operate at its optimal output rate of 900 cars per week. Only the amount of profit or loss will vary with demand.

Applying this logic to the economy as a whole, if the prices of goods and services can always adjust quickly to unexpected changes in demand, then the economy can always produce at its optimal capacity because prices will adjust to ensure that the quantity demanded of each good and service always equals the quantity supplied. If prices are fully flexible, there will be no short-run fluctuations in output. Production levels will remain constant, and unemployment levels will not change because firms will always need the same number of workers to produce the same amount of output.

Output Changes If There Are Demand Shocks *and* Sticky Prices In reality, many prices in the economy are inflexible and do not change rapidly when demand changes unexpectedly. Consider the extreme case shown in Figure 26.1b, in which the price of Protons is totally inflexible, fixed at $37,000 per Proton. Here, if demand unexpectedly falls from D_M to D_L, the quantity demanded at the fixed price of $37,000 will be only 700 cars per week, which is 200 cars fewer than the factory's optimal output of 900 cars per week. On the other hand, if demand is unexpectedly high at D_H, the quantity demanded at the fixed price of $37,000 will be 1,150 cars per week, which is 250 cars more than the factory's optimal output of 900 cars per week.

One way to deal with these unexpected shifts in quantity demanded is to try to adjust the factory's output to match them. That is, during weeks of low demand, Buzzer Auto could attempt to produce only 700 Protons, while during weeks of high demand it could try to produce 1,150 Protons. But this flexible output strategy is very expensive because factories operate at their lowest costs when they are producing constantly at their optimal output levels. Operating at either a higher or a lower production rate results in higher per-unit production costs.

inventories Goods that have been produced but remain unsold.

Manufacturing firms typically attempt to deal with unexpected changes in demand by maintaining an **inventory,** which is a stock of output that has been produced but not yet sold. Inventories are useful because companies can allow them to grow or decline in periods when demand is unexpectedly low or high—thereby allowing production to proceed smoothly and constantly at the optimal output level even when demand is variable. In our example, Buzzer Auto would maintain an inventory of unsold Protons. In weeks when demand is unexpectedly low, the inventory will increase by 200 Protons as the quantity demanded falls 200 vehicles short of the factory's optimal output. During weeks when demand is unexpectedly high, the inventory will decrease as the quantity demanded exceeds the factory's optimal output by 250 cars. By allowing inventory levels to fluctuate, Buzzer Auto can respond to unexpected shifts in demand by adjusting inventory levels rather than output levels. With any luck, the overall inventory level will stay roughly constant over time as unexpected increases and decreases in demand cancel each other out.

But consider what will happen if the firm experiences many successive weeks of unexpectedly low demand. Each week, the firm's inventory of unsold Protons will increase by 200 cars. If inventory continues to increase for many weeks, then Buzzer's managers will be forced to cut production because, among other things, there will simply be no place to park so many unsold vehicles. More importantly, holding large numbers of unsold cars in inventory is unprofitable: While the company incurs costs to build an unsold car, an unsold car obviously brings in no revenue. Constantly rising inventories hurt profits, and management will want to reduce output if it sees inventories rising week after week due to unexpectedly low demand. As output falls, the firm will have to lay off workers, and unemployment will increase.

Generalizing from a Single Firm to the Entire Economy

This simplified story about a single car company explains why economists believe that a combination of unexpected changes in demand and inflexible prices are the key to understanding the short-run fluctuations that affect real-world economies. Generalizing this story to the economy as a whole, if demand falls off for many goods and services across the entire economy for an extended period of time, then the firms that make those goods and services will be forced to cut production. As both manufacturing and service output decline, real GDP will fall and unemployment will rise.

On the other hand, if demand is unexpectedly high for a prolonged period of time, the economy will boom and unemployment will fall. In the case of our Proton example, for each week that demand is unexpectedly high, inventories will fall by 250 cars. If inventories continue to decrease week after week, they will eventually fall to zero. Buzzer will have to react by increasing production to more than the optimal output rate of 900 cars per week so that orders do not go unfilled. GDP will increase as more cars per week are produced, and unemployment will fall because the factory will need to hire more workers to produce the larger number of cars. (The nearby Consider This applies the lessons of Buzzer Auto to the COVID-19 recession of 2020, which involved both a demand shock *and* a supply shock.)

CONSIDER THIS . . .

Double Whammy!

The COVID-19 recession of 2020 was incredibly interesting from a macroeconomic perspective because it led to both a demand shock and a supply shock *simultaneously*.

The U.S. economy had been doing very well in the late 2010s, with low unemployment, subdued inflation, steadily rising wages, and a booming stock market. But then the pandemic arrived and governments around the world imposed "lockdowns" during which most businesses were forced to close and virtually all workers were ordered to stay at home to try to slow the spread of the coronavirus.

MOLPIX/Shutterstock

That unexpected turn of events was a shock. But it was one that generated both a decrease in the demand for goods and services (a negative demand shock) as well as a decrease in the supply of goods and services (a negative supply shock) because workers stuck at home not getting paid spent less on goods and services while firms shut down by the government could not produce any output.

That "double whammy" was one of the reasons that governments responded to the pandemic very aggressively, with the largest economic relief programs in history. We'll detail those policies and how they worked in coming chapters.

- Economic shocks occur when events unfold in ways that people or businesses are not expecting.

- Demand and supply shocks take place when demand or supply ends up being either higher or lower than expected.

- Real-world prices are often inflexible or "sticky" in the short run.

- When prices are sticky, the economy adjusts to demand shocks mostly through changes in output and employment (rather than through changes in prices).

QUICK REVIEW

26.4

How Sticky Are Prices?

We have just shown that **inflexible prices**—or "*sticky prices*" as economists often call them—help to explain how unexpected changes in demand lead to the fluctuations in GDP and employment that occur over the course of the business cycle. But not all prices are sticky. Indeed, the markets for many commodities and raw materials such as corn, oil, and natural gas feature extremely **flexible prices** that react within seconds to changes in supply and demand. By contrast, the prices of most consumer products are rather sticky, with the average good or service going 4.3 months between price changes.

To better appreciate how price stickiness varies by product or service, look at Table 26.1, which gives the average number of months between price changes in various industries, including manufacturing and retail. Service industry prices go nearly a year on average between updates while prices in the retail sector are updated on average every 4.6 months. The prices of specific products can change much more rapidly, including gasoline (two to three weeks) and airline tickets (hourly). By contrast, haircuts and newspapers average more than two years between price changes.

In later chapters, we identify and discuss several factors that cause short-run price stickiness. To keep the current discussion brief, let's focus on just two factors here. First, companies selling consumer products know that consumers prefer stable, predictable prices that do not fluctuate rapidly with changes in demand. Consumers would be annoyed if the same bottle of soda or shampoo cost one price one day, a different price the next day, and yet another price a week later. Volatile prices make planning more difficult. In addition, consumers who come in to buy the product on a day when the price happens to be high will likely feel that they are being taken advantage of. Thus, most retailers try to maintain stable prices as much as they can. Such firms do hold sales from time to time, but on the whole they try to keep prices stable and predictable—the result being price inflexibility.

>> **LO26.5** Characterize the degree to which various prices are sticky.

inflexible prices Product *prices* that remain in place (at least for a while) even though *supply* or *demand* has changed; stuck prices or sticky prices.

flexible prices Product *prices* that freely move upward or downward when product demand or supply changes.

Industry	Months
Services	11.3
Manufacturing	8.1
Finance	7.1
Utilities	4.7
Retail	4.6
Agriculture	3.2

TABLE 26.1

Average Number of Months between Price Changes in Selected Industries

Source: Yuriy Gorodnichenko and Michael Weber, "Are Sticky Prices Costly? Evidence from the Stock Market," *American Economic Review,* January 2016, pp. 165–99.

Second, in certain situations, a firm may fear that cutting its price will be counterproductive because its rivals might simply match the price cut—a situation often referred to as a "price war." This possibility is common among firms that have only one or two major rivals. Consider Coca-Cola and Pepsi. If Coca-Cola faces unexpectedly low demand for its product, it might be tempted to reduce its price in the hope that it can steal business away from Pepsi. But such a strategy will work only if Pepsi leaves its price alone when Coca-Cola cuts its price. In reality, if Coca-Cola cuts its price, Pepsi will very likely cut its price in retaliation, doing its best to make sure that Coca-Cola doesn't steal away its customers. If Pepsi retaliates, Coca-Cola will be made worse off by its decision to cut its price: It will not pick up much more business (because Pepsi also cut its price), and it will also be receiving less money for each bottle of Coke that it sells. Thus, firms that face the possibility of price wars often have sticky prices.

Categorizing Macroeconomic Models Using Price Stickiness

>> **LO26.6** Explain why economists use different macroeconomic models for different time horizons.

Price stickiness moderates over time. Firms that choose to use a fixed-price policy in the short run do not have to stick with that policy permanently. If unexpected changes in demand begin to look permanent, many firms will allow their prices to change so that price changes (in addition to quantity changes) can help to equalize quantities supplied with quantities demanded.

For this reason, economists speak of "sticky prices" rather than "stuck prices." Only in the very short run are prices totally inflexible. As time passes and prices are revised, the world looks much more like Figure 26.1a, in which prices are fully flexible, than Figure 26.1b, in which prices are totally inflexible. Indeed, the totally inflexible case shown in Figure 26.1b can be viewed as the extremely short-run response to an unexpected change in demand, while the fully flexible case shown in Figure 26.1a can be viewed as the long-run response that will take place as prices become fully flexible.

This insight is very useful in categorizing and understanding the differences between the various macroeconomic models that we will be presenting in subsequent chapters. For instance, the aggregate expenditures model presented in Chapter 31 is a short-run model that assumes perfectly inflexible prices. By contrast, the aggregate demand–aggregate supply model presented in Chapter 32 allows for flexible prices and is therefore useful for understanding how the economy behaves over longer periods of time.

As you study these various models, keep in mind that we need different models precisely because the economy behaves so differently depending on how much time has passed after a demand shock. The differences in behavior result from the fact that prices go from completely stuck immediately after a shock to fully flexible in the long run. Using different models for different stages in this process gives us much better insights into not only how economies actually behave but also how various government and central bank policies may have different effects in the short run (when prices are fixed) versus the long run (when prices are flexible).

Where will we go from here? In the remainder of Part 7, we examine how economists measure GDP and why GDP has expanded over time. Then, we discuss the terminology of business cycles and explore the measurement and types of unemployment and inflation. At that point you will be well prepared to examine the economic models, monetary considerations, and stabilization policies that lie at the heart of macroeconomics.

QUICK REVIEW
26.5

▶ Many commodity prices are extremely flexible and change constantly, but other prices in the economy change only infrequently.

▶ Some prices are inflexible in order to please retail customers, others because rival firms are afraid that price changes may trigger a price war.

▶ Prices tend to become more flexible over time, so that as time passes, the economy can react to demand shocks with price changes as well as with output and employment changes.

▶ Different macroeconomics models are required for the short run, during which prices are inflexible (so that demand shocks lead almost exclusively to output and employment changes), and for longer periods, during which prices become increasingly flexible (so that demand shocks lead more to price changes than output and employment changes).

The Behavioral Economics of Sticky Prices

Employee Psychology Appears to Play a Key Role in Price Stickiness.

This chapter discussed two reasons for sticky output prices: consumers preferring predictable prices and businesses fearing price wars. Another major cause of sticky output prices is the stickiness of a particular input price—the price of labor, that is, wages and salaries.

To understand why "sticky wages" can have such a large impact on the stickiness of output prices, we have to begin with the fact that wages and salaries make up about 70 percent of the average firm's costs. This means that firms will have difficulty cutting their per-unit output prices unless they can figure out a way to slash per-unit labor costs. Substantial efficiencies may be possible with respect to other production costs—such as rent and raw materials—but with labor costs comprising 70 percent of all costs, firms will be hard pressed to cut their per-unit selling prices by any substantial percentage unless they can figure out a way to cut their per-unit labor costs substantially.

As it turns out, reductions in per-unit labor costs are typically self-defeating due to psychological and cultural factors that constrain the relationship between a company and its employees. These factors are best explained by applying insights from behavioral economics, which is the subfield of economics that incorporates psychology and culture into the study of economic behavior. The key insight is that workers tend to get quite upset if their wages or salaries are cut. A firm that is facing reduced demand due to a recession may explain to its workers that it would like to cut costs in order to reduce its selling price and thereby recoup some of its lost sales. But workers whose pay is cut will feel that they are being taken advantage of by their employer since they are being asked to do the same amount of work for less money.

This resentment is counterproductive for firms because workers typically retaliate when their wages or salaries are reduced. Business people who have imposed pay cuts report that employee retaliation can take many forms. Workers may stop showing up on time. They often put in less effort while at work and also call in sick much more often. They begin to organize unions. And they may even go so far as to start stealing supplies or even vandalizing equipment. Taking these factors into account, firms have found that pay cuts often *increase* per-unit production costs.

Knowing that workers react so poorly to wage and salary cuts, most managers are loath to even propose such cuts. But at the same time, a reduction in demand that is caused by a recession means that either (1) per-unit costs must be cut in order to lower selling prices and thereby revive sales, or (2) a firm's output level must be reduced at the original price level in order to bring quantity supplied into alignment with the reduced level of quantity demand. Faced with this dilemma, most firms resort to layoffs that

VGstockstudio/Shutterstock

reduce total employment and thus total production (option 2) rather than pay cuts that keep everyone working but at a lower wage (option 1).

As an example, consider a typical firm, one whose labor costs constitute 70 percent of all of its costs. If a recession reduces the firm's sales by 20 percent, it may pursue option 2 by laying off 20 percent of its workforce but keeping wages and salaries unchanged for the 80 percent of workers who remain employed at the firm. The workers who were laid off will likely be resentful. But their negative feelings will not translate into higher costs or lower productivity for the firm. What is important for management is to avoid pay cuts for the workers who remain. By keeping their wages and salaries fixed, the firm will not engender any retaliation. Morale and productivity may even rise because the workers who remain employed may be grateful to still have paying jobs while many millions of workers across the economy are plunged into unemployment as a result of the recession.

A key point to understand, though, is that the layoffs will not change the firm's per-unit production costs. The firm's workforce will become 20 percent smaller, and thus its total labor bill will fall by 20 percent. But at the same time, a 20-percent smaller labor force will produce 20 percent less output, other things equal. This implies that the firm's labor cost per unit of output will remain unchanged. As a result, the firm will find it difficult to cut its price per unit. Unless the firm can find ways of making deep cuts in its nonlabor costs, its output price will tend to be sticky if not stuck. In this way, the stickiness of wages and salaries translates into price stickiness.

There are of course other causes of price stickiness in the economy, but this story of workers reacting badly to pay cuts is considered to be a leading contributor by most macroeconomists. When recessions hit, firms cut labor costs by firing workers rather than lowering wages and salaries.

Summary

LO26.1 Explain why economists use GDP, inflation, and unemployment to assess the economy's health.

Macroeconomics studies long-run economic growth and short-run economic fluctuations.

Macroeconomists focus their attention on three key economic statistics: real GDP, unemployment, and inflation. Real GDP measures the value of all final goods and services produced in a country during a specific period of time. The unemployment rate measures the percentage of all workers who are not able to find paid employment despite being willing and able to work at currently available wages. The inflation rate measures the extent to which the overall level of prices is rising in the economy.

LO26.2 Discuss why sustained increases in living standards are historically recent.

Before the Industrial Revolution, living standards did not show any sustained increases over time. Economies grew, but any increase in output was offset by an equally large increase in the population, so that the amount of output per person did not rise. By contrast, since the Industrial Revolution began in the late 1700s, many nations have experienced modern economic growth in which output grows faster than population—so that standards of living rise over time.

LO26.3 Identify why saving and investment promote higher living standards.

A key to modern economic growth is the promotion of saving and investment. Investment activities (such as funding research or increasing the amount of physical capital) increase the economy's future potential output level. But investment must be funded by savings, which accumulate only if people are willing to reduce current consumption below current income. Consequently, individuals and society face a trade-off between current consumption and future consumption.

Banks and other financial institutions help to convert saving into investment by lending the savings generated by households to businesses that wish to make investments.

LO26.4 Explain why shocks and sticky prices are responsible for short-run fluctuations in output and employment.

Expectations have an important effect on the economy because if people and businesses are more positive about the future, they will save and invest more. However, expectations are not always fulfilled. Individuals and firms must sometimes adjust to shocks—situations in which the future does not turn out as expected.

If prices are inflexible, or "sticky," shocks to demand or supply can result in disequilibrium situations in which quantity demanded does not equal quantity supplied. In such situations, the only way for the economy to adjust in the short run (the time horizon over which prices remain sticky) is through changes in output, employment, and inventories.

LO26.5 Characterize the degree to which various prices are sticky.

Prices are inflexible in the short run for various reasons. One reason is that firms often attempt to maintain stable prices to please consumers, who tend to prefer predictable prices. Second, a firm with just a few competitors may be reluctant to cut its price due to the fear of starting a price war.

LO26.6 Explain why economists use different macroeconomic models for different time horizons.

Price stickiness moderates over time. As a result, economists have found it sensible to build separate economic models for different time horizons. For instance, some models reflect the high degree of price inflexibility that occurs in the immediate short run, while other models reflect the high degree of price flexibility that occurs in the long run.

Terms and Concepts

business cycle	saving	demand shocks
real GDP (real gross domestic product)	investment	supply shocks
nominal GDP	financial investment	inventory
unemployment	economic investment	inflexible prices ("sticky prices")
inflation	expectations	flexible prices
modern economic growth	shocks	

Discussion Questions

McGraw Hill connect

1. Why do you think macroeconomists focus on just a few key statistics when trying to understand the health and trajectory of an economy? Would it be better to try to examine all possible data? Why or why not? **LO26.1**

2. Consider a nation in which the volume of goods and services is growing by 5 percent per year. What is the likely impact of this high rate of growth on the power and influence of its government relative to other countries experiencing slower rates of growth? How will this 5 percent growth rate likely affect the nation's living standards? Will the standard of living grow by 5 percent per year, given population growth? Why or why not? **LO26.2**

3. Has economic output always grown faster than the population? When did modern economic growth begin? Have all of the world's nations experienced the same extent of modern economic growth? **LO26.2**

4. Why is there a trade-off between the amount of consumption that people can enjoy today and the amount of consumption that they can enjoy in the future? Why can't people enjoy more of both? How does saving relate to investment and thus to economic growth? What role do banks and other financial institutions play in aiding the economic growth process? **LO26.3**

5. How does investment as defined by economists differ from investment as defined by the general public? What would happen

to the amount of economic investment made today if firms expect the future returns to such investment to be very low? What would happen to the amount of economic investment today if firms expect future returns to be very high? **LO26.4**

6. Why, in general, do shocks force people to make changes? Give at least two examples from your own experience. **LO26.4**

7. Catalog companies are committed to selling at the prices printed in their catalogs. If a catalog company finds its inventory of sweaters rising, what does that tell you about the demand for sweaters? Was it unexpectedly high, unexpectedly low, or as expected? If the company could change the price of sweaters, would it raise the price, lower the price, or keep the price the same? Given that the company cannot change the price of sweaters, however, consider the number of sweaters it orders each month from the company that manufactures the sweaters.

If inventories become very high, will the catalog company increase orders, decrease orders, or keep orders the same? Given what the catalog company does with its orders, what is likely to happen to employment and output at the sweater manufacturer? **LO26.4**

8. Are all prices in the economy equally inflexible? Which ones show large amounts of short-run flexibility? Which ones show a great deal of inflexibility over months or years? **LO26.5**

9. Why do many firms strive to maintain stable prices? **LO26.5**

10. Do prices tend to become more flexible or less flexible as time passes? Explain. **LO26.6**

11. **LAST WORD** Are labor costs a major fraction of the typical firm's overall production costs? How does wage stickiness cause price stickiness? Discuss why firms are averse to cutting wages and salaries during a business downturn.

Review Questions

1. An increase in _____ GDP guarantees that more goods and services are being produced by an economy. **LO26.1**
   a. nominal
   b. real

2. True or False: The term *economic investment* includes purchases of stocks, bonds, and real estate. **LO26.3**

3. If an economy has sticky prices, and demand unexpectedly increases, you would expect the economy's real GDP to: **LO26.4**
   a. increase.
   b. decrease.
   c. remain the same.

4. If an economy has fully flexible prices and demand unexpectedly increases, you would expect the economy's real GDP to: **LO26.4**

a. increase.
b. decrease.
c. remain the same.

5. If the demand for a firm's output unexpectedly decreases, you would expect its inventory to: **LO26.4**
   a. increase.
   b. decrease.
   c. remain the same.
   d. increase or remain the same, depending on whether or not prices are sticky.

6. True or False: Because price stickiness matters only in the short run, economists are comfortable using just one macroeconomic model for all situations. **LO26.6**

Problems

1. Suppose that the annual rates of growth of real GDP in Econoland over a five-year period were sequentially as follows: 3 percent, 1 percent, −2 percent, 4 percent, and 5 percent. What was the average of these growth rates in Econoland over these five years? What term would economists use to describe what happened in year 3? If the growth rate in year 3 had been a positive 2 percent rather than a negative 2 percent, what would have been Econoland's average growth rate over the five years? **LO26.1**

2. Suppose that Glitter Gulch, a gold mining firm, increased its sales revenues on newly mined gold from $100 million to $200 million between one year and the next. Assuming that the price of gold increased by 100 percent over the same period, by what numerical amount did Glitter Gulch's real output change? If the price of gold had not changed, what would have been the change in Glitter Gulch's real output? **LO26.1**

3. A mathematical approximation called the rule of 70 tells us how long it will take for something to double in size if it grows at a constant rate. The doubling time is approximately equal to the number 70 divided by the percentage rate of growth. Thus, if Oman's real GDP per person is growing at 7 percent per year, it will take about 10 years (= 70/7) to double. Apply the rule of 70 to solve the following problem: Real GDP per person in Oman in 2020 was about $15,000 per person, while it was about

$60,000 per person in the United States. If real GDP per person in Oman grows at the rate of 5 percent per year, about how long will it take Oman's real GDP per person to reach the level that the United States enjoyed in 2020? (Hint: How many times would Oman's 2020 real GDP per person have to double to reach the United States' 2020 real GDP per person?) **LO26.2**

4. Assume that a national restaurant chain called BBQ builds 10 new restaurants at a cost of $1 million per restaurant. It outfits each restaurant with an additional $200,000 of equipment and furnishings. To help partially defray the cost of this expansion, BBQ issues and sells 200,000 shares of stock at $30 per share. What is the amount of economic investment that has resulted from BBQ's actions? How much purely financial investment took place? **LO26.3**

5. Refer to Figure 26.1b and assume that price is fixed at $37,000 and that Buzzer Auto needs 5 workers for every 1 automobile produced. If demand is D_M and Buzzer wants to perfectly match its output and sales, how many cars will Buzzer produce, and how many workers will it hire? If, instead, demand unexpectedly falls from D_M to D_L, how many fewer cars will Buzzer sell? How many fewer workers will it need if it decides to match production to these lower sales? **LO26.4**

CHAPTER

27

Measuring Domestic Output and National Income

>> LEARNING OBJECTIVES

LO27.1 Define and measure gross domestic product (GDP).

LO27.2 Determine GDP by summing all expenditures on final goods and services.

LO27.3 Determine GDP by summing all incomes received for providing resources.

LO27.4 Describe the relationships among GDP, net domestic product, national income, personal income, and disposable income.

LO27.5 Distinguish between nominal GDP and real GDP.

LO27.6 Explain some limitations of the GDP measure.

"Disposable Income Flat." "Personal Consumption Surges." "GDP Up 4 Percent." These headlines, typical of cable TV news reports or *The Wall Street Journal,* give knowledgeable readers valuable information on the state of the economy. This chapter will help you interpret such headlines and understand the stories reported under them. More specifically, you will become familiar with the vocabulary and methods of national income accounting.

Assessing the Economy's Performance

>> **LO27.1** Define and measure gross domestic product (GDP).

national income accounting The techniques used to measure the overall production of a country's economy as well as other related variables.

gross domestic product (GDP) The total market value of all *final goods* and *services* produced annually within the boundaries of a nation.

National income accounting measures the economy's overall performance. The Bureau of Economic Analysis (BEA), an agency of the U.S. Commerce Department, compiles the National Income and Product Accounts (NIPA) for the U.S. economy. This accounting helps economists and policymakers:

- Assess the economy's health by monitoring production and employment levels.
- Track the economy's long-run growth trajectory.
- Adjust economic policies to safeguard and improve the economy's health.

Gross Domestic Product

The primary measure of an economy's performance is its *aggregate output*, or total output, of goods and services. There are several ways to measure aggregate output. The one favored by the Bureau of Economic Analysis is **gross domestic product (GDP),** or the dollar value of all final goods and services produced within a country's borders during a specific period of time, typically a year or a quarter.

Final Products Only Note that GDP only counts the value of **final goods and services,** that is, products that are purchased by their end (final) users. GDP excludes **intermediate goods and services** that are purchased for resale or as inputs used to produce other products. Thus, a loaf of bread that is purchased by a family for a camping trip is counted in GDP (because the family is the end user) while an identical loaf that is purchased by a sandwich shop is not counted in GDP (because the sandwich shop will be using the loaf of bread as an input to the production of its final product, sandwiches).

final goods and services Products that have been purchased for final use (rather than for resale or further processing or manufacturing).

Domestic Output Only GDP includes only the value of final goods and services produced within a nation's boundaries. Thus, the value of the cars produced at a Japanese-owned Toyota factory in Ohio would count as part of U.S. GDP (because the factory is located in the United States) but the value of the trucks produced at an American-owned Ford factory in Canada would not (because the factory lies outside the borders of the United States). What matters for GDP is where the final output is produced, not who makes it or who consumes it.

intermediate goods and services Products that are purchased for resale or further processing or manufacturing.

A Monetary Measure There's an old expression that says, "You can't add apples and oranges." That expression is true because apples and oranges are measured in different units. Apples are measured as 1 apple, 2 apples, 3 apples, 4 apples, and so forth. Oranges are measured as 1 orange, 2 oranges, 3 oranges, 4 oranges, etc. Thus it would make no sense to ask, "What is 2 apples plus 4 oranges?" You would get nowhere because the correct answer is "2 apples plus 4 oranges," which simply restates the question.

To add dissimilar items like apples and oranges together, they must share a common unit of measurement. When it comes to apples and oranges, one way to do this is by adding together pounds of apples and pounds of oranges. That can be done because both items (pounds of apples and pounds of oranges) now share a common unit of measurement (pounds).

Another strategy is to add together the dollar values of apples and oranges—and, by extension, the dollar values of any group of items. This is the method used to calculate GDP. Statisticians sum up the *monetary values* of all the final goods and services produced in the economy.

Consider the example presented in Table 27.1, where the economy produces three sofas and two computers in year 1 and two sofas and three computers in year 2. Because sofas and computers lack a common unit of measurement, there is no way to add them together. But we *can* add together the number of dollars of sofas and the number of dollars of computers. At $500 per sofa and $2,000 per computer, the market value (dollar value) of the economy's output in year 1 is $5,500 while the monetary value of the economy's output in year 2 is $7,000. It is consequently clear that aggregate output has increased by $1,500.

The higher valuation for aggregate output in year 2 is not at all obvious if you are merely told the numbers of sofas and computers produced in each year. Only by measuring individual outputs in the common unit of dollars can you understand that aggregate output has in fact increased.

Using dollars as the common unit of measurement for calculating GDP has an additional benefit. Because people put higher dollar values on things they like, we can infer that higher levels of GDP imply higher levels of satisfaction, all other things equal. It is for this reason that policy-makers are deeply concerned with how to increase GDP.

Value Added

GDP counts only final goods and services. But final goods and services are the result of a long chain of intermediate production steps. As an example, consider Table 27.2 and the multiple stages of production needed to manufacture a wool coat and get it to a final consumer. Firm A, a sheep ranch, sells $120 worth of raw wool to firm B, a wool processor. Firm B takes that raw wool and combines it with land, labor, capital, and entrepreneurship to produce $180 of processed wool that it sells to Firm C, a coat manufacturer. Firm C, the manufacturer, sells the coat to firm D, a wholesaler, which sells it to firm E, a retailer. Finally, a consumer, the final user, buys the coat for $350 from the retailer.

TABLE 27.1 Comparing Heterogeneous Output by Using Money Prices

Year	Annual Output	Market Value
1	3 sofas and 2 computers	3 at $500 + 2 at $2,000 = $5,500
2	2 sofas and 3 computers	2 at $500 + 3 at $2,000 = $7,000

TABLE 27.2 Value Added in a Five-Stage Production Process

(1) Stage of Production	(2) Sales Value of Materials or Product	(3) Value Added
	$ 0	
Firm A, sheep ranch	120	$120 (= $120 − $ 0)
Firm B, wool processor	180	60 (= 180 − 120)
Firm C, coat manufacturer	220	40 (= 220 − 180)
Firm D, clothing wholesaler	270	50 (= 270 − 220)
Firm E, retail clothier	**350**	80 (= 350 − 270)
Total sales values	$1,140	
Value added (total income)		**$350**

Because GDP counts only final goods and services, GDP in this example must be $350, the price that the final consumer pays Firm E for the final product (the wool coat). But there is another way to calculate the $350 dollar value of GDP that shines some light on the intermediate stages of production. It involves measuring and cumulating the *value added* at each stage of production.

value added The value of a product sold by a *firm* less the value of the products (materials) purchased and used by the firm to produce that product.

Value added is the market value of a firm's output *less* the value of the inputs the firm has bought. As Column 3 of Table 27.2 indicates, the value added by firm B is $60, the difference between the $180 value of its output, processed wool, and the $120 it paid to firm A for raw wool. Similarly, the value added by firm C is $40, or the difference between the $220 market value of its output, a finished coat, and the $180 it paid to firm B for processed wool.

Note that if you add together all of the value-added numbers in Column 3, they sum to $350, which is the same as the value of GDP that we calculated by looking only at the $350 market price paid by the final user. This is no coincidence. A final product's GDP value can always be calculated *either* as the market value paid by the final user *or* as the sum of the values added at each stage of the production process.

Gross Output and Multiple Counting

gross output (GO) The dollar value of the economic activity taking place at every stage of production and distribution. By contrast, *gross domestic product* (GDP) only accounts for the value of final output.

Gross output (GO) sums together the sales values received by firms at each stage of production. In Table 27.2, gross output is $1,140, or the sum of the sales values received by firms A through E.

Note that gross output is always larger than GDP because it includes not only the value of the final product but also the values of all of the earlier "business to business" transactions involving intermediate goods. Thus, in Table 27.2, we see that the GO of $1,140 is much larger than the GDP of $350.

multiple counting Wrongly including the value of *intermediate goods* in the *gross domestic product*; counting the same *good* or *service* more than once.

That large difference points out why we must do our best to avoid *multiple counting* when calculating GDP. **Multiple counting** is the mistake of including the sales values of intermediate goods in GDP. That is a mistake because GDP should only include the sales value of final products.

The most direct way of avoiding multiple counting is by making sure that you are adding together the sales values of final products only. The other is to calculate GDP by summing together values added. That method avoids multiple counting because the value added that is calculated at each stage of production subtracts off the input costs incurred at earlier stages of production. By subtracting them off, they do not get counted multiple times. The only thing that gets counted is each firm's unique contribution to the value of the final product.

GDP Excludes Nonproduction Transactions

Although many monetary transactions in the economy involve final goods and services, many others do not. These nonproduction transactions must be excluded from GDP because they have nothing to do with the production of final goods.

There are two types of *nonproduction transactions* that must be excluded from GDP: purely financial transactions and secondhand sales.

Financial Transactions Purely financial transactions include the following:

- *Public transfer payments* These are the social security payments, welfare payments, and veterans' payments that the government makes directly to households. Because the recipients contribute nothing to current production in return, including such payments in GDP would overstate the year's output.

- *Private transfer payments* These payments include, for example, allowance money given by parents to children and cash gifts given during the holidays. They produce no output. They simply transfer funds from one private individual to another and consequently do not enter into GDP.

- *Financial asset transactions* The buying and selling of stocks, bonds, and other financial assets is just a matter of transferring the ownership of existing financial assets from one person to another. Such transactions create nothing in the way of current production and are not included in GDP. Payments for the services provided by a stockbroker are included, however, because their services are currently provided and are thus a part of the economy's current output of goods and services.

Secondhand Sales Secondhand sales contribute nothing to current production and are therefore excluded from GDP. Suppose you sell your 2015 Ford Mustang to a friend. That transaction will not be counted in this year's GDP because it generates no current production.

Two Ways of Looking at GDP: Spending and Income

Let's look again at how the market value of total output—or of any single unit of total output—is measured. Given the data listed in Table 27.2, how can we measure the market value of a coat?

The first approach is to see how much the final user paid for it. That will tell us the market value of the final product. Or we can add up the entire wage, rent, interest, and profit incomes that were created in producing the coat. The second approach is the value-added method demonstrated in Table 27.2.

The final-product approach and the value-added approach are two ways of looking at the same thing. What is spent on making a product is income to those who helped make it. If $350 is spent on manufacturing a coat, then $350 is the total income derived from its production.

We can look at GDP in the same two ways. We can view GDP as the sum of all the money spent in buying it. That is the *output approach*, or **expenditures approach.** Or we can view GDP in terms of the income derived or created from producing it. That is the *earnings, allocations,* or **income approach.**

As illustrated in Figure 27.1, we can determine GDP for a particular year either by adding up all the money that was spent to buy total output *or* by adding up all the money that was derived as income from its production. Buying (spending money) and selling (receiving income) are two aspects of the same transaction. On the expenditures side of GDP, all final goods produced by the economy are bought either by the three domestic sectors (households, businesses, and

expenditures approach
The method that adds all expenditures made for *final goods* and final *services* to measure the *gross domestic product.*

income approach The method that adds all the *income* generated by the production of *final goods* and final *services* to measure the *gross domestic product.*

FIGURE 27.1 **The expenditures and income approaches to GDP.**

There are two general approaches to measuring gross domestic product. We can determine GDP as the value of output by summing all expenditures on that output. Alternatively, with some modifications, we can determine GDP by adding up all the components of income arising from the production of that output.

Expenditures, or output, approach

Consumption expenditures by households
plus
Investment expenditures by businesses
plus
Government purchases of goods and services
plus
Expenditures by foreigners

= GDP =

Income, or allocations, approach

Wages
plus
Rents
plus
Interest
plus
Profits
plus
Statistical adjustments

TABLE 27.3 Accounting Statement for the U.S. Economy Using the Expenditures (Output) Approach, 2021 (in Billions)

	Billions
Sum of:	
Personal consumption expenditures (C)	$15,742
Gross private domestic investment (I_g)	4,120
Government purchases (G)	4,053
Net exports (X_n)	−918
Equals:	
Gross domestic product	**$22,996**

Source: U.S. Bureau of Economic Analysis.

TABLE 27.4 Accounting Statement for the U.S. Economy Using the Income (Allocations) Approach, 2021 (in Billions)*

	Billions
Sum of:	
Compensation of employees	$12,581
Rents	726
Interest	686
Proprietors' income	1,822
Corporate profits	2,806
Taxes on production and imports	1,299
Equals:	
National income	**$19,920**
Less: Net foreign factor income	252
Plus: Consumption of fixed capital	3,848
Plus: Statistical discrepancy	−520
Equals:	
Gross domestic product	**$22,996**

*Some of the items in this table combine related categories that appear in the more detailed accounts. All data are subject to government revision.

Source: U.S. Bureau of Economic Analysis.

government) or by foreign buyers. On the income side (once certain statistical adjustments are made), the total receipts acquired from the sale of that total output are allocated to the suppliers of resources as wages, rents, interest, and profit.

Table 27.3 shows U.S. GDP for 2021 totaled up using the expenditures approach. Table 27.4 shows U.S. GDP for 2021 totaled up using the income approach. Both methods lead to the same result: U.S. GDP in 2021 was $22,996 billion.

QUICK REVIEW

27.1

▶ Gross domestic product (GDP) is a measure of the total market value of all final goods and services produced domestically in a specific quarter or year.

▶ GDP can be obtained by adding together the market selling prices of all final goods and services or by adding up the values added at each stage of production.

▶ GDP can be calculated as either the sum of all the money spent purchasing final goods and services (expenditures approach) or as the sum of all the incomes earned from providing the resources that went into producing those final goods and services (income approach).

The Expenditures Approach

>> **LO27.2** Determine GDP by summing all expenditures on final goods and services.

To determine GDP using the expenditures approach, we add up all the spending on final goods and services that has taken place throughout the year. National income accountants have developed precise definitions for each of the types of spending listed on the left side of Figure 27.1.

Personal Consumption Expenditures (*C*)

personal consumption expenditures (C) The expenditures of *households* for both durable and nondurable *consumer goods.*

durable good A consumer good with an expected life (use) of three or more years.

nondurable good A *consumer good* with an expected life (use) of less than three years.

service An (intangible) act or use for which a consumer, *firm*, or government is willing to pay.

What we have called "consumption expenditures by households" is what the national income accountants call **personal consumption expenditures (*C*).** This category covers all expenditures by households on goods and services. In a typical year, roughly 10 percent of personal consumption expenditures are on **durable goods**—products that have expected lives of 3 years or more. Such goods include new automobiles, furniture, and refrigerators. **Nondurable goods**—products with less than 3 years of expected life—make up 30 percent of personal consumption expenditures. Included in this category are food, clothing, and gasoline. About 60 percent of personal consumption expenditures is for **services**—the work done by lawyers, hair stylists, doctors, mechanics, and other service providers. Because of this high percentage, economists sometimes refer to the U.S. economy as a *service economy.* National income accounting combines the household spending on durable goods, nondurable goods, and services and uses the symbol *C* to designate the personal consumption expenditures component of GDP.

Gross Private Domestic Investment (*I_g*)

Gross private domestic investment (*I_g*) includes the following items:

- All final purchases of machinery, equipment, and tools used by business enterprises.
- Residential construction.

- Expenditures on the research and development (R&D) of new productive technologies.

- Money spent on the creation of new works of art, music, writing, film, and software.

- Changes in inventories.

Investment—or, more correctly, *economic investment*—refers to activities that increase the nation's stock of capital, which is the collection of human-made resources that help to produce goods and services. Those human-created resources can be divided into two broad categories that we can informally refer to as "tools" and "recipes."

Tools are tangible physical objects that help to produce goods and services. Recipes are the intangible methods, techniques, and management practices necessary to produce goods and services. A well-stocked kitchen requires both cooking equipment (tools) and an understanding of how to cook (recipes). A productive economy requires both tangible physical capital (factories, wireless networks, infrastructure) and intangible intellectual capital (knowing when to plant a crop, understanding how to fly a plane, comprehending the best way to organize a factory).

The first two items fall into the tools category. Final purchases of plant, machinery, and equipment increase the amount of physical capital available to produce future output. In a similar fashion, residential construction generates a future flow of output—housing services—that will keep people productive by keeping them healthy and sheltered.

The next two items fall into the recipes category. Spending on R&D increases the intangible stock of methods and techniques that we can use to produce output. Spending that funds the creation of new works of art, music, writing, and film increases the flow of entertainment and educational services, while spending that pays for new or improved software increases the productivity of everything from cell phones to self-driving cars.

Finally, please note that increases in inventories (unsold goods) are considered investments because they represent, in effect, "unconsumed output," or output that will increase the future supply of final goods and services when it is sold out of inventory and consumed in future periods. For economists, all new output that is not consumed is, by definition, capital. So an increase in inventories is registered as an addition (although perhaps temporary) to the economy's stock of capital goods (i.e., physical objects that increase future consumption).

Positive and Negative Changes in Inventories We need to look at changes in inventories more closely. Inventories can either increase or decrease over some period. Suppose they increased by $10 billion between December 31, 2026, and December 31, 2027. Therefore, in 2027, the economy produced $10 billion more output than people purchased. We want to count all output produced in 2027 as part of that year's GDP, even though some of it remained unsold at the end of the year. We do so by including the $10 billion increase in inventories as part of year 2027's investment. That way, the expenditures in 2027 correctly measure the output produced that year.

Alternatively, suppose that inventories decreased by $10 billion in 2027. This "drawing down of inventories" means that the economy sold $10 billion more of output in 2027 than it produced that year. It did so by selling goods produced in prior years—goods already counted as GDP in those years. Unless corrected, expenditures in 2027 will overstate GDP for 2027. So in 2027 we consider the $10 billion decline in inventories as "negative investment" and subtract it from total investment that year.

Excluding Financial Investment Please note that economists and NIPA accountants are careful to distinguish between *economic investment* and *financial investment*.

- Economic investment involves the creation of new productive capital, either new tools (plant, equipment, infrastructure) or new recipes (methods, systems, applications). As far as the national income and product accounts are concerned, economic investment is the only investment that matters and the only investment that should be included in the NIPA tables.

- By contrast, financial investment, like purchasing stocks or buying a bond, merely transfers the ownership of existing assets; it does not produce new capital goods. Thus, financial investment is *not* included in GDP.

So be careful to remember that while ordinary people in daily life do not distinguish between economic investment and financial investment, the only "investment" that is reported in the national income and product accounts is economic investment—the creation of new capital assets.

gross private domestic investment (I_g) Expenditures that increase the nation's stock of capital, which is the collection of physical objects and intangible ideas that help to produce goods and services. Includes spending on final purchases of plant, machinery, and equipment by business enterprises; residential construction; changes in *inventories*; expenditures on the *research and development (R&D)* of new productive technologies; and money spent on the creation of new works of art, music, writing, film, and software.

FIGURE 27.2
Gross investment, depreciation, net investment, and the stock of capital.

When gross investment exceeds depreciation during a year, net investment occurs. This net investment expands the stock of private capital from the beginning of the year to the end of the year by the amount of the net investment. Other things equal, the economy's production capacity expands.

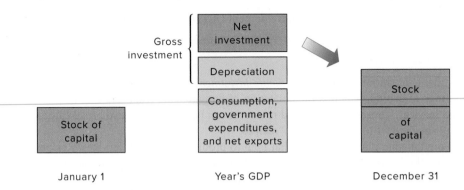

Gross Investment versus Net Investment When we speak of *gross private domestic investment*, the words "private" and "domestic" mean that we are speaking of investment spending by private businesses, not by government, and that the investment is taking place inside the country, not abroad.

The word "gross" means that we are referring to *all* investment goods—both those that replace machinery, equipment, and buildings that were used up (worn out or made obsolete) in producing the current year's output *as well as* any net additions to the economy's capital stock.

net private domestic investment *Gross private domestic investment* less *consumption of fixed capital;* the addition to the nation's stock of *capital* during a year.

Net private domestic investment measures only the *net* additions to the economy's total stock of capital. It is calculated by taking the economy's gross amount of investment and subtracting off the amount of capital that is used up over the course of a year, a quantity that is referred to as *depreciation:*

$$\text{Net investment} = \text{gross investment} - \text{depreciation}$$

In typical years, gross investment exceeds depreciation. Thus net investment is positive and the nation's capital stock rises by the amount of net investment. As Figure 27.2, illustrates, the capital stock at the end of a typical year exceeds the capital stock at the beginning of the year by the amount of net investment.

Gross investment does not always exceed depreciation, however. When gross investment and depreciation are *equal*, net investment is zero and there is no change in the size of the capital stock. When gross investment is *less* than depreciation, net investment is negative. In that case, the economy is *disinvesting*—using up more capital than it is producing—and the nation's stock of capital shrinks, which is exactly what happened during the Great Depression of the 1930s.

National income accountants use the symbol I for private domestic investment spending. To differentiate between gross investment and net investment, they add either the subscript g or the subscript n. But it is gross investment, I_g, that they use when tallying up GDP—not net investment (I_n).

Government Purchases (G)

government purchases (G) Expenditures by government for *goods* and *services* that government consumes in providing public services as well as expenditures for publicly owned capital that has a long lifetime; the expenditures of all governments in the economy for those *final goods* and final *services.*

The third category of expenditures in the national income accounts is **government purchases,** officially labeled "government consumption expenditures and gross investment." These expenditures have three components: (1) expenditures for goods and services that the government consumes in providing public services; (2) expenditures for *publicly owned capital* such as schools and highways, which have long lifetimes; and (3) government expenditures on R&D and other activities that increase the economy's stock of know-how.

These purchases include all government expenditures (federal, state, and local) on final goods as well as all direct purchases of resources, including labor. They do *not* include government transfer payments because, as we have seen, such payments merely transfer money to certain households and generate no production. National income accountants use the symbol G to signify government purchases.

Net Exports (X_n)

International trade transactions are a significant item in national income accounting. But when calculating U.S. GDP, we must keep in mind that we want to total up only those expenditures that are used to purchase goods and services produced *within the borders of the United States.*

Thus, we must add in the value of exports, X, because the money that people in other countries spend purchasing U.S. exports is by definition spending on goods and services produced within the United States.

Don't be confused by the fact that it is foreigners who buy our exports. The definition of GDP does not specify *who* is buying U.S.-made goods and services—only that the goods and services that they buy are made within U.S. borders. Thus, foreign spending on U.S. exports *must* be included in U.S. GDP.

At this point, you might incorrectly think that GDP should equal the sum of $C + I_g + G + X$. But C, I_g, and G include not only expenditures on domestically produced goods and services but also goods and services produced outside the United States. So to correctly calculate gross domestic product, we must subtract off the spending that goes to imports, M. That subtraction yields the correct formula for calculating gross domestic product: $GDP = C + I_g + G + X - M$.

Accountants simplify this formula for GDP by defining **net exports,** X_n, to be equal to exports minus imports:

net exports (X_n) *Exports minus imports.*

$$\text{Net exports}(X_n) = \text{exports}(X) - \text{imports}(M)$$

Using this definition of net exports, gross domestic product can be defined as the sum of household consumption expenditures, gross private domestic investment, government purchases, and net exports. In algebra:

$$GDP = C + I_g + G + X_n$$

Table 27.3 shows that in 2021 Americans spent $918 billion more on imports than foreigners spent on U.S. exports. That is, net exports in 2021 were a *minus* $918 billion.

Putting It All Together: GDP $= C + I_g + G + X_n$

Taken together, the four categories of expenditures provide a measure of the market value of a specific year's total output—its GDP. Table 27.3 indicates that 2021 U.S. GDP (in billions) totaled:

$$GDP = \$15{,}742 + \$4{,}120 + \$4{,}053 - \$918$$

Global Perspective 27.1 lists the GDPs of several countries in U.S. dollars.

🌐 GLOBAL PERSPECTIVE 27.1

COMPARATIVE GDPs IN TRILLIONS OF U.S. DOLLARS, SELECTED NATIONS, 2020

The United States, China, and Japan have the world's highest GDPs when local, domestic-currency GDPs are converted into U.S. dollars using international exchange rates. That method of comparing national incomes does not account for differences between countries in the cost of living. But it does demonstrate how countries compare in terms of being able to purchase and sell on international markets, which is a major concern for international trade and economic development.

GDP in Trillions of U.S. Dollars

Country	GDP
United States	~21
China	~15
Japan	~5
Germany	~4
United Kingdom	~3
India	~3
Italy	~2
Canada	~2
South Korea	~2
Russia	~1.5
Brazil	~1.5
Spain	~1.5
Mexico	~1
Nigeria	~0.5
Egypt	~0.4

Source: The World Bank Group, data.worldbank.org.

The Income Approach

>> **LO27.3** Determine GDP by summing all incomes received for providing resources.

Table 27.4 shows how 2021's expenditures of $22,996 billion were allocated as income to those responsible for producing that year's output. It would be convenient if we could say that the entire amount of expenditures flowed back to them in the form of wages, rent, interest, and profit. But some expenditures flow to other recipients (such as the government) or to other uses (such as paying to replace the capital goods that have worn out while producing this year's GDP). These items must be taken into account in order for the income approach and the expenditures approach to arrive at the same value for GDP. We will begin by looking at the items that make up *national income* in Table 27.4.

Compensation of Employees

By far the largest share of national income—$12,581 billion in 2021—was paid as wages and salaries by business and government to their employees. That figure also includes wage and salary supplements, including payments by employers into social insurance and into a variety of private pension, health, and welfare funds for workers.

Rents

Rents consist of the income received by the households and businesses that supply property resources. They include the monthly payments tenants make to landlords and the lease payments corporations pay for the use of office space. The figure used in the national accounts is *net* rent—gross rental income minus depreciation of the rental property.

Interest

Interest consists of the money paid by private businesses to the suppliers of loans used to purchase capital. It also includes the interest that households receive on savings deposits, certificates of deposit (CDs), and corporate bonds.

Proprietors' Income

The national income accounts divide "profits" into two accounts: *proprietors' income*, which consists of the net income of sole proprietorships, partnerships, and other unincorporated businesses; and *corporate profits*.

Corporate Profits

Corporate profits are the earnings of corporations. National income accountants subdivide corporate profits into three categories:

- *Corporate income taxes* These taxes are levied on corporations' profits. They flow to the government.
- *Dividends* Dividends are the part of after-tax profits that corporations choose to pay out, or distribute, to their stockholders. They thus flow to households, which are the ultimate owners of all corporations.
- *Undistributed corporate profits* Any after-tax profits that are not distributed to shareholders are saved, or retained, by corporations to pay for subsequent investment. Undistributed corporate profits are also called *retained earnings*.

taxes on production and imports A *national income accounting* category that includes such taxes as *sales, excise,* business property taxes, and *tariffs* that *firms* treat as costs of producing a product and pass on (in whole or in part) to buyers by charging a higher *price*.

Taxes on Production and Imports

The account called **taxes on production and imports** includes general sales taxes, excise taxes, business property taxes, license fees, and customs duties. Why do national income accountants add these indirect business taxes to wages, rent, interest, and profits in determining national income? The answer is: "to account for expenditures that are diverted to the government." Consider an item that would otherwise sell for $1 but costs $1.05 because the government has imposed a

5 percent sales tax. When this item is purchased, consumers spend $1.05 to buy it. But only $1 will go to the seller (who then distributes it as income in the form of wages, rent, interest, and profit). The remaining 5 cents flow as revenue to the government. The GDP accountants place the extra 5 cents into the category called "Taxes on Production and Imports" and loosely consider these taxes to be "income" to government.

From National Income to GDP

Expenditures on final goods and services flow either as income to private citizens or as "income" to government. As a result, **national income** is the total of all sources of private income (employee compensation, rents, interest, proprietors' income, and corporate profits) plus government revenue from taxes on production and imports. National income is all the income that flows to U.S.-supplied resources, whether here or abroad, plus taxes on production and imports.

Notice that the figure for national income shown in Table 27.4—$19,920 billion—is less than GDP as determined by the expenditures approach in Table 27.3. The two versions of the national accounting statement—the expenditures version and the income version—are brought into balance by subtracting one item from national income and adding two others.

national income Total *income* earned by *resource* suppliers for their contributions to *gross domestic product* plus *taxes on production and imports;* the sum of wages and salaries, *rent, interest, profit, proprietors' income*, and such taxes.

Net Foreign Factor Income First, we need to make a slight adjustment to account for the difference between "national income" and "domestic income." National income includes the total income of Americans, whether it was earned in the United States or abroad. But GDP is a measure of *domestic* output—total output produced within the United States regardless of the nationality of those who provide the resources. So, in moving from national income to GDP, we must take out the income Americans gain from supplying resources abroad and add in the income that people living in other countries gain by supplying resources in the United States. That process yields *net foreign factor income.*

In 2021, net foreign factor income was $252 billion, meaning that American-owned resources earned $252 billion more in other countries than foreign-owned resources earned in the United States. Because this $252 billion reflects the earnings of Americans, it is included in U.S. national income. But this income is not part of U.S. domestic income because it reflects earnings from output produced in other nations. It is part of those nations' domestic income, derived from the production of their domestic output. Thus, we subtract net foreign factor income from U.S. national income to determine the value of U.S. *domestic output* (output produced within U.S. borders).

Consumption of Fixed Capital Next, we must recognize that the useful lives of private capital equipment (such as cell phone towers or automobile assembly lines) extend far beyond the year in which they were produced. To avoid understating profit and income in the year of purchase and to avoid overstating profit and income in succeeding years, the cost of such capital must be allocated over its lifetime. The amount allocated is an estimate of how much of the capital is being used up, or depreciated, each year.

The economywide amount of depreciation is called **consumption of fixed capital** because it accounts for capital that has been "consumed" in producing the year's GDP. It is the portion of GDP that is set aside to pay for the ultimate replacement of the capital goods that have suffered depreciation and is consequently *not* available to flow to households as income. For that reason, it is not counted as part of national income.

On the other hand, depreciation *is* a cost of production and thus must be included in the gross value of output. We must therefore add the amount set aside for the consumption of fixed capital to national income in Table 27.4 to correctly calculate the economy's expenditures on output.

consumption of fixed capital An estimate of the amount of *capital* worn out or used up (consumed) in producing the *gross domestic product;* also called depreciation.

Statistical Discrepancy As you know, it should be possible to calculate GDP either by totaling up expenditures or by summing up incomes. Either method should give the same result.

In practice, however, it is not possible for NIPA accountants to measure every amount with total precision. Difficulties arise due to a wide range of factors, including people misreporting their incomes on tax returns and the difficulty involved with accurately estimating depreciation.

As a result, the GDP number produced by the income method always differs by a small percentage from the GDP number produced by the expenditures method.

To account for this difference, NIPA accountants add a statistical discrepancy to national income. The addition of that number equalizes the GDP totals produced by the two methods. As Table 27.4 shows, in 2021 the discrepancy value was negative $520 billion, or about 2.3 percent of GDP.

▶ The expenditures approach to GDP sums the total spending on final goods and services: GDP = C + I_g + G + X_n.

▶ The economy's stock of private capital expands when net investment is positive; stays constant when net investment is zero; and declines when net investment is negative.

▶ The income approach to GDP sums compensation to employees, rent, interest, proprietors' income, corporate profits, and taxes on production and imports to obtain national income, and then subtracts net foreign factor income and adds consumption of fixed capital and a statistical discrepancy to obtain GDP.

Other National Accounts

>> LO27.4 Describe the relationships among GDP, net domestic product, national income, personal income, and disposable income.

Several other national accounts provide additional useful information about the economy's performance.

Net Domestic Product

net domestic product (NDP) *Gross domestic product* less the part of the year's output that is needed to replace the *capital goods* worn out in producing the output; the nation's total output available for consumption or additions to the *capital stock*.

Because GDP is a measure of total output, it does not make allowances for replacing the capital goods used up in each year's production. As a result, it does not tell us how much output is available (for either consumption or *net* additions to the capital stock) after we set aside funds to pay for depreciation. To determine that amount, we must subtract consumption of fixed capital (depreciation) from GDP. The result is called **net domestic product (NDP):**

$$\text{NDP} = \text{GDP} - \text{consumption of fixed capital (depreciation)}$$

For the United States in 2021:

	Billions
Gross domestic product	$22,996
Less: Consumption of fixed capital	3,848
Equals: Net domestic product	$19,148

NDP is simply GDP adjusted for depreciation. It measures the total annual output that the entire economy—households, businesses, government, and foreigners—can consume without impairing its capacity to produce in ensuing years.

National Income

Recall that U.S. *national income* (NI) includes all income earned through the use of American-owned resources, whether they are located at home or abroad. It also includes taxes on production and imports.

To derive NI from NDP, we must subtract the statistical discrepancy from NDP and add net foreign factor income, because the latter is income earned by Americans overseas minus income earned by foreigners in the United States.

For the United States in 2021:

	Billions
Net domestic product	$19,148
Less: Statistical discrepancy	−520
Plus: Net foreign factor income	252
Equals: National income	$19,920

An alternative but equally valid method for adding up national income is to apply the income approach and sum together employee compensation, rent, interest, proprietors' income, corporate profit, and taxes on production and imports. That's what we did in the top half of Table 27.4.

Personal Income

Personal income (PI) includes all income received by households, whether earned or unearned. The starting point for calculating personal income is national income, which accounts for all the income *earned* by households for providing resources. But then, to calculate the total amount of income that was actually *received* by households, we must subtract off the value of business taxes, payroll taxes, and retained corporate profits before adding in the value of transfer payments.

We need to subtract off business taxes, payroll taxes, and retained corporate profits because households do not receive all of the income that they earn by providing resources. Taxes on production and imports, Social Security taxes (payroll taxes), corporate income taxes, and undistributed corporate profits flow either to the government or are retained by firms. They do not flow to households as personal income.

On the other hand, households receive trillions of dollars of government transfer payments that they collect, unearned, without having to provide any resources. These transfer payments include Social Security payments, unemployment compensation payments, welfare payments, disability and education payments to veterans, and private pension payments. To arrive at a correct value for personal income, we must add in the value of these transfer payments.

Thus, in moving from national income to personal income, we must subtract the income that is earned but not received and add the income that is received but not earned. For the United States in 2021:

personal income (PI) The earned and unearned *income* available to resource suppliers and others before the payment of personal *taxes.*

	Billions
National income	$19,920
Less: Taxes on production and imports	1,148
Less: Corporate income taxes	381
Less: Social Security contributions	1,591
Less: Undistributed corporate profits	1,006
Plus: Transfer payments	5,284*
Equals: Personal income	$21,077

*Includes statistical discrepancy, rounding error, and items that appear in more detailed accounts.

Disposable Income

Disposable income (DI) is the amount of income that households are free to dispose of (spend or save) after meeting all their legal tax obligations. Disposable income is equal to personal income less personal taxes, including personal income taxes, personal property taxes, and inheritance taxes. Households are free to divide their disposable income between consumption (C) and saving (S) as they see fit. Algebraically:

disposable income (DI) *Personal income* less personal taxes; income available for *personal consumption expenditures* and *personal saving.*

$$DI = C + S$$

For the United States in 2021:

	Billions
Personal income	$21,077
Less: Personal taxes	2,583
Equals: Disposable income	$18,495

Table 27.5 summarizes the relationship among GDP, NDP, NI, PI, and DI.

TABLE 27.5 The Relationships among GDP, NDP, NI, PI, and DI in the United States, 2021*

	Billions
Gross domestic product (GDP)	$22,996
Less: Consumption of fixed capital	3,848
Equals: Net domestic product	$19,148
Net domestic product (NDP)	$19,148
Less: Statistical discrepancy	−520
Plus: Net foreign factor income	252
Equals: National income (NI)	$19,920
National income (NI)	$19,920
Less: Taxes on production and imports	1,148
Less: Corporate income taxes	381
Less: Social Security contributions	1,591
Less: Undistributed corporate profits	1,006
Plus: Transfer payments	5,284*
Equals: Personal income (PI)	$21,077
Personal income (PI)	$21,077
Less: Personal taxes	2,583
Equals: Disposable income (DI)	$18,495

*Some of the items combine categories that appear in the more detailed accounts.

Source: Bureau of Economic Analysis, www.bea.gov.

The Circular Flow Revisited

Figure 27.3 is an elaborate flow diagram that shows the economy's four main sectors (households, businesses, government, and foreign) along with the flows of expenditures and allocations that determine GDP, NDP, NI, and PI. The orange arrows represent the spending flows—$C + I_g + G + X_n$—that together measure gross domestic product. To the right of the GDP rectangle are green arrows that show first the allocations of GDP and then the adjustments needed to derive NDP, NI, PI, and DI.

The diagram illustrates the adjustments necessary to determine each of the national income accounts. For example, net domestic product is smaller than GDP because consumption of fixed capital flows away from GDP in determining NDP. Also, disposable income is smaller than personal income because personal taxes flow away from PI (to government).

Note the three domestic sectors of the economy: households, government, and businesses. The household sector has an inflow of disposable income and outflows of consumption spending and savings. The government sector has an inflow of revenue from various types of taxes and an outflow of disbursements in the form of purchases and transfers. The business sector has inflows from three major sources of funds for business investment and an outflow of investment expenditures.

Also, take a look at the foreign sector (all other countries) in the flow diagram. Spending by foreigners on U.S. exports adds to U.S. GDP, but some of U.S. consumption, government, and investment expenditures buys imported products. The flow from the foreign sector shows that we handle this complication by calculating net exports (U.S. exports minus U.S. imports). The net export flow may be a positive or negative amount, adding to or subtracting from U.S. GDP.

Finally, you need to be aware that the flows shown in Figure 27.3 are dynamic entities and generally expand in size over time as the economy grows. But not always! Case in point: The COVID-19 recession of 2020—which is described in a Consider This story in Chapter 26—produced a pronounced slowing of the main spending and income flows. Specifically, U.S. businesses greatly reduced investment expenditures while households modestly reduced personal consumption expenditures. Consequently, GDP, NDP, NI, and PI all significantly declined.

FIGURE 27.3 U.S. domestic output and the flows of expenditure and income. This figure is an elaborate circular flow diagram that fits the expenditures and allocations sides of GDP to one another. The expenditures flows are shown in orange; the allocations or income flows are shown in green. You should trace through the income and expenditures flows, relating them to the five basic national income accounting measures.

▸ Net domestic product (NDP) is the market value of GDP minus consumption of fixed capital (depreciation).

▸ National income (NI) is all income earned through the use of American-owned resources, whether located at home or abroad. NI also includes taxes on production and imports.

▸ Personal income (PI) is all income received by households, whether earned or not.

▸ Disposable income (DI) is all income received by households minus personal taxes.

Nominal GDP versus Real GDP

>> **LO27.5** Distinguish between nominal GDP and real GDP.

Recall that GDP is a measure of the market or money value of all final goods and services produced by the economy in a given year. We use money or nominal values as a common denominator to sum that heterogeneous output into a meaningful total. But, as alluded to in Chapter 26, that creates a problem: How can we compare the market values of GDP from year to year if the value of money itself changes in response to inflation (rising prices) or deflation (falling prices)?

As an example of what can go wrong, consider the fact that the same McDonald's hamburger that sold for 18 cents in 1967 cost $1.69 in 2021. The hamburger was the same in both years and the utility that people got from it was the same, but its nominal GDP value was over nine times higher in 2021 because the price of a hamburger had increased from 18 cents to $1.69.

The way around this problem is to *deflate* GDP when prices rise and to *inflate* GDP when prices fall. This is accomplished by choosing a reference year and then using the output prices that prevailed in that reference year to value the quantities of output produced in other years.

Adjustment Process in a One-Product Economy

nominal gross domestic product (GDP) *GDP* measured in terms of the *price level* at the time of measurement; *GDP* not adjusted for *inflation*. Compare with *real gross domestic product* (*real GDP*).

real GDP *Gross domestic product* adjusted for *inflation*; gross domestic product in a year divided by the GDP *price index* for that year, the index expressed as a decimal. Compare with *nominal GDP*.

A GDP based on the prices that prevailed when output was produced is called unadjusted GDP, or **nominal GDP.** A GDP that has been deflated or inflated to reflect changes in the price level is called adjusted GDP, or **real GDP.**

There are two ways we can obtain real GDP from nominal GDP. One involves combining nominal GDP with a *price index*. The other calculates real GDP by breaking down nominal GDP into physical quantities of output on the one hand and prices on the other.

To see how they work, let's imagine an economy that produces only one good, pizza, in the amounts indicated in Table 27.6 for years 1, 2, and 3. Suppose that we measure each year's nominal GDP (= the money value of the pizzas produced each year) by gathering revenue data directly from the financial reports of the economy's pizza businesses.

After completing our effort, we will have determined nominal GDP for each year, as shown in column 4 of Table 27.6. But we will have no way of knowing to what extent the increases or decreases in nominal GDP that we observe are the result of changes in prices, changes in output, or some combination of those two factors. To figure that out, we need to calculate real GDP.

GDP Price Index Our first method for calculating real GDP proceeds in three stages. First, we assemble data on the price changes that occurred over various years (column 2). Then we use those price changes to establish an overall price index for the entire period (column 3). Finally, we use the index value for a particular year to adjust that year's nominal GDP into that year's real GDP (columns 4 and 5).

TABLE 27.6 Calculating Real GDP (Base Year = Year 1)

Year	(1) Units of Output	(2) Price of Pizza per Unit	(3) Price Index (Year 1 = 100)	(4) Unadjusted, or Nominal, GDP, (1) × (2)	(5) Adjusted, or Real, GDP
1	5	$10	100	$ 50	$50
2	7	20	200	140	70
3	8	25	250	200	80
4	10	30	—	—	—
5	11	28	—	—	—

A **price index** is a measure of the price of a specified collection of goods and services, called a "market basket," in a given year as compared to the price of an identical (or highly similar) collection of goods and services in a reference year. That point of reference, or benchmark, is known as the base period, **base year,** or, simply, the reference year. More formally,

$$\text{Price index in given year} = \frac{\text{price of market basket in specific year}}{\text{price of same market basket in base year}} \times 100 \quad (1)$$

By convention, the price ratio between a given year and the base year is multiplied by 100 to facilitate computation. For example, a price ratio of $2/1 (= 2)$ is expressed as a price index of 200. A price ratio of $1/3 (= 0.33)$ is expressed as a price index of 33.

In our pizza-only example, our market basket consists of only one product. Column 2 of Table 27.6 reveals that the price of pizza was $10 in year 1, $20 in year 2, and $25 in year 3. Let's select year 1 as our base year. Now we can express the prices of our market basket in years 2 and 3 relative to the price of the market basket in year 1:

$$\text{Price index, year 2} = \frac{\$20}{\$10} \times 100 = 200$$

$$\text{Price index, year 3} = \frac{\$25}{\$10} \times 100 = 250$$

For year 1 the index has to be 100, because that year and the base year are identical.

The index numbers tell us that the price of pizza rose from year 1 to year 2 by 100 percent $\{= [(200 - 100)/100] \times 100\}$ and from year 1 to year 3 by 150 percent $\{= [(250 - 100)/100] \times 100\}$.

Dividing Nominal GDP by the Price Index We can now use the index numbers shown in column 3 to deflate the nominal GDP figures in column 4. The simplest and most direct method of deflating is to divide nominal GDP by the corresponding index number expressed in hundredths (decimal form). Doing so gives us real GDP:

$$\text{Real GDP} = \frac{\text{nominal GDP}}{\text{price index (in hundredths)}} \quad (2)$$

Column 5 shows the results. These figures for real GDP measure the market value of the output of pizza in years 1, 2, and 3 as if the price of pizza had been a constant $10 throughout the 3-year period. In short, real GDP reveals the market value of each year's output measured in terms of dollars that have the same purchasing power that dollars had in the base year.

To test your understanding, extend Table 27.6 to years 4 and 5, using equations 1 and 2. Then run through the entire deflating procedure, using year 3 as the base period. (Hint: You will have to inflate some of the nominal GDP data. Use the same procedure as we used in the examples.)

An Alternative Method

The second method for calculating real GDP involves gathering data on physical outputs (as in column 1 of Table 27.6) and their prices (as in column 2). With those values in hand, we can calculate what the market value of output would have been in successive years if the base-year price ($10) had prevailed every year. In year 2, for instance, the 7 units of pizza would have had a value of $70 (= 7 units × $10). As column 5 confirms, that $70 worth of output is year 2's real GDP. Similarly, we could determine the real GDP for year 3 by multiplying the 8 units of output that year by the $10 price in the base year.

Once we have determined real GDP through this method, we can identify the price index for a given year by dividing the nominal GDP by the real GDP for that year:

$$\text{Price index (in hundredths)} = \frac{\text{nominal GDP}}{\text{real GDP}} \quad (3)$$

Example: In year 2 we get a price index of 200—or, in hundredths, 2.00—which equals the nominal GDP of $140 divided by the real GDP of $70.

Note that equation 3 is simply a rearrangement of equation 2.

price index An index number that shows how the weighted-average *price* of a "market basket" of goods changes over time relative to its price in a specific *base year.*

TABLE 27.7 Steps for Deriving Real GDP from Nominal GDP

Method 1

1. Find nominal GDP for each year.

2. Compute a GDP price index.

3. Divide each year's nominal GDP by that year's price index (in hundredths) to determine real GDP.

Method 2

1. Break down nominal GDP into physical quantities of output and prices for each year.

2. Find real GDP for each year by determining the dollar amount that each year's physical output would have sold for if base-year prices had prevailed. (The GDP price index can then be found by dividing nominal GDP by real GDP.)

Table 27.7 summarizes the two methods of determining real GDP in our single-good economy.

Real-World Considerations and Data

In the real world of *many* goods and services, determining GDP and constructing a reliable price index are far more complex matters than in our pizza-only economy. The government accountants must assign a "weight" to each of several categories of goods and services based on the relative proportion of each category in total output. They update the weights annually as expenditure patterns change and roll the base year forward year by year using a moving average of expenditure patterns. The GDP price index used in the United States is called the *chain-type annual-weights price index*—which hints at its complexity. We spare you the details.

Table 27.8 shows some of the relationships among nominal GDP, real GDP, and the GDP price index for the U.S. economy. Here the base year is 2012, where the value of the index is set at 100. Because the U.S. price level has been rising over the long run, the pre-2012 values of real GDP (column 3) are higher than the nominal values of GDP for those years (column 2). This upward adjustment acknowledges that prices were lower in the years before 2012, and thus nominal GDP understates the real output of those years when they are measured in terms of year 2012 prices. Since these pre-2012 values understate real GDP relative to 2012, they must be inflated to show the correct relationship to other years.

Conversely, the rising price level of the post-2012 years caused nominal GDP figures for those years to overstate real output relative to 2012 prices. So the statisticians deflate those figures to determine what real GDP would have been in other years if 2012 prices had prevailed. Doing so reveals that real GDP has been less than nominal GDP since 2012.

By inflating the nominal pre-2012 GDP data and deflating the post-2012 data, government accountants determine each year's real GDP, which can then be compared with the real GDP of any other year in the series. Consequently, the real GDP values in column 3 are directly comparable with one another.

Once we have determined nominal GDP and real GDP, we can compute the price index. And once we have determined nominal GDP and the price index, we can calculate real GDP. Example: Nominal GDP in 2015 was $18,206.0 billion and real GDP was $17,390.3 billion. So the price level in 2015 was 104.7 (= [$18,206.0/$17,390.3] × 100), or 4.7 percent higher than in 2012. If we knew the nominal GDP and the price level only, we could find the real GDP for 2015 by dividing the nominal GDP of $18,206.0 by the 2015 price index, expressed in hundredths (1.047).

To test your understanding of the relationships between nominal GDP, real GDP, and the price level, determine the values of the price index for 2000 in Table 27.8 and determine real GDP for 2005 and 2012. We have left those figures out on purpose.

TABLE 27.8 Nominal GDP, Real GDP, and GDP Price Index for the United States, Selected Years

Source: U.S. Bureau of Economic Analysis. All data subject to government revision.

(1) Year	(2) Nominal GDP, Billions of $	(3) Real GDP, Billions of $	(4) GDP Price Index (2012 = 100)
2000	10,251.0	13,138.0	_____
2005	13,039.2	_____	87.5
2010	15,049.0	15,649.0	96.2
2012	16,254.0	_____	100.0
2015	18,206.0	17,390.3	104.7
2020	20,893.7	18,384.7	113.6

▶ Nominal GDP is output valued at current prices. Real GDP is output valued at constant base-year prices.

▶ The GDP price index compares the price (market value) of all the goods and services included in

GDP in a given year to the price of the same market basket in a reference year.

▶ Nominal GDP can be transformed into real GDP by dividing nominal GDP by the GDP price index expressed in hundredths.

QUICK REVIEW

27.4

Shortcomings of GDP

GDP is a reasonably accurate and highly useful measure of how well or how poorly the economy is performing. But it has several shortcomings as a measure of both total output and well-being (utility).

>> **LO27.6** Explain some limitations of the GDP measure.

Nonmarket Activities

Certain productive activities do not take place in any market—the services of stay-at-home parents, for example, and the labor of carpenters who repair their own homes. Such activities do not show up in GDP because government accountants receive data only on economic transactions involving *market activities*—that is, transactions in which output or resources are traded for money. Consequently, GDP understates a nation's total output because it does not count *unpaid work*. There is one exception: The portion of farmers' output that farmers consume themselves is estimated and included in GDP.

Leisure and Psychic Income

The average workweek (excluding overtime) in the United States has declined since the beginning of the 1900s—from about 53 hours to about 35 hours. Moreover, workers today have more paid vacations, holidays, and leave time. This increase in leisure time has clearly had a positive effect on overall well-being. But our system of national income accounting understates well-being by ignoring leisure's value. Nor does the system accommodate the satisfaction—the "psychic income"—that many people derive from their work.

Improved Product Quality

Because GDP is quantitative rather than qualitative, it fails to capture the full value of improvements in product quality. For example, an $800 smartphone purchased today is of much higher quality than a smartphone that cost $800 a decade ago.

Quality improvement obviously has a great effect on economic well-being, an effect that goes above and beyond any increase in the quantity of output. Although the BEA adjusts GDP for the quality improvements of selected items, the vast majority of quality improvements are not yet reflected in GDP. (See this chapter's Last Word for more on this subject.)

The Underground Economy

Embedded in our economy is a flourishing, productive underground sector. Some of the people who conduct business there are bookies, smugglers, "fences" of stolen goods, and drug dealers. They have good reason to conceal their incomes.

Most participants in the underground economy, however, engage in perfectly legal activities but choose illegally not to report their full incomes to the Internal Revenue Service (IRS). A barista at a coffee shop may report just a portion of the tips received from customers. Storekeepers may report only a portion of their sales receipts. Workers who want to hold onto their unemployment compensation benefits may take an "off-the-books" or "cash-only" job. A brick mason may agree to rebuild a neighbor's fireplace in exchange for the neighbor's repairing his boat engine. None of these transactions show up in GDP.

Global Perspective 27.2 presents estimates of how big the underground economy is in various countries. Since underground transactions amount to about 7 percent of U.S. GDP, we can estimate that U.S. GDP was understated by about $1.6 trillion in 2021.

GDP and the Environment

The growth of GDP is sometimes accompanied by an increase in "gross domestic by-products," including dirty air and polluted water, toxic waste, congestion, and noise. The social costs of the

GLOBAL PERSPECTIVE 27.2

THE UNDERGROUND ECONOMY AS A PERCENTAGE OF GDP, SELECTED NATIONS

Underground economies vary in size worldwide. Three factors that help explain the variation are (1) the extent and complexity of regulation, (2) the type and degree of taxation, and (3) the effectiveness of law enforcement.

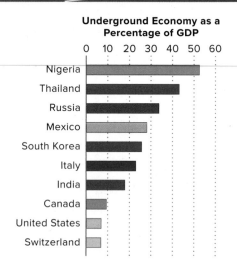

Underground Economy as a Percentage of GDP

Source: Leandro Medina and Friedrich Schneider, *Shadow Economies Around the World: What Did We Learn Over the Last 20 Years?* International Monetary Fund (IMF), 2018.

negative by-products reduce our economic well-being. Because those costs are not deducted from total output, GDP overstates our national well-being. Ironically, when money is spent to clean up pollution and reduce congestion, those expenses *are* added to GDP!

Composition and Distribution of Output

The composition of output is undoubtedly important for well-being, but GDP does not tell us whether the currently produced mix of goods and services is enriching or potentially detrimental to society. GDP assigns equal weight to an assault rifle and a laptop computer, as long as both sell for the same price. Moreover, GDP reveals nothing about the distribution of output. Does 90 percent of the output go to 10 percent of the households, for example, or is output more evenly distributed? The distribution of output may make a big difference for society's overall well-being.

Noneconomic Sources of Well-Being

Finally, just as a household's income does not measure its total happiness, a nation's GDP does not measure its total well-being. Many things could make a society better off without necessarily raising GDP: a reduction of crime and violence, peaceful relations with other countries, people's greater civility toward one another, better understanding between parents and children, or a reduction of drug and alcohol abuse.

The Importance of Intermediate Output

Because GDP focuses on final output, it ignores all of the business-to-business economic activity that takes place in the economy at earlier stages of production and distribution. That omission is worrisome because many people's jobs and many firms' profitability depend on economic activity at earlier stages.

We can get a sense of what is going on at those earlier stages by examining *gross output* (GO), which sums together the sales values received by firms at *every* stage of production. As you learned earlier in this chapter, GO is always larger than GDP because GO includes every stage of production while GDP only accounts for the final stage of production. In 2021, GO was $41.2 trillion in the United States while GDP was $23.0 trillion.

GO is particularly useful when attempting to gauge the magnitude of business cycle fluctuations. During the 2007–2009 recession, real GDP fell by 4.2 percent, while real GO fell by 8.6 percent. Thus, total economic activity fell by more than twice as much as final output. That substantial difference goes some way toward explaining why employment fell so dramatically during the Great Recession.

Measuring Quality to Price the Priceless

The Bureau of Economic Analysis (BEA) Faces a Difficult Task as It Attempts to Measure GDP and Inflation in the Digital Age.

GDP attempts to measure the value of an economy's output by summing together the dollar values of all final goods and services. That strategy for measuring the value of an economy's output has become significantly more challenging over the past twenty years. There are two basic problems. First, it is difficult to properly account for quality improvements, which are rapid for Digital Age products like electronics, software, and video games. Second, many Internet products—for instance, Google searches and driving directions—are provided free of charge.

Suppose that the price of an iPhone is the same now as it was last year, even though this year's iPhone is better than last year's iPhone. With the price fixed, the contribution of an iPhone to GDP will remain unchanged, even though the utility (satisfaction) that people get from purchasing an iPhone has increased. GDP will miss that increase in value. Similarly, if a service like Google is priced at zero, GDP will miss the value that users receive from Google searches.

Rapid quality improvements have also made inflation calculations more difficult. If this year's most popular video game delivered twice as much entertainment as last year's top-selling video game but their prices were both $60, how much of a contribution did those games make toward the economy's overall level of inflation? Viewed from a perspective of "the price of a top video game remained constant at $60," the contribution was zero. Viewed from a perspective of "how much money does it cost to purchase one unit of entertainment?" the contribution was negative 50 percent since the same dollar expenditure delivers twice as much enjoyment today as it did last year.

The statisticians at the BEA who compile the National Income and Product Accounts have decided to look at things from the latter perspective. Quality improvements matter and should be accounted for in GDP and inflation to the extent possible. The procedure for doing so is called hedonic adjustment (hedonic means "relating to pleasure"). It involves looking at a product as a collection of separate characteristics or services for which people are willing to pay money. Viewed this way, an iPhone is not a single item but a collection of, among other things, a camera, a web browser, a video game platform, a telephone, a compass, a map, a flashlight, and a way of accessing social media platforms.

Once an iPhone is thought of as a collection of attributes or services, inflation in the economy will depend not on the price of iPhones themselves, but on how the prices of the underlying attributes or services vary over time. For example, if this year's iPhone is identical in all ways to last year's iPhone but costs 3 percent less, then the value of one or more of the underlying characteristics or services must have gone down. It's up to national income accountants to figure out which ones changed, and by how much. Once they complete the fancy math, they can get a better handle on inflation.

Alex Potemkin/E+/Getty Images

By one estimate, properly accounting for hedonic adjustments reduces reported inflation by about 0.6 percent, which is a big deal since inflation is usually around 2 to 3 percent.

A different approach has to be taken when trying to account for the value of free products like Facebook and Google. When a product's price is zero, how do you account for the value that consumers receive from the product? One suggestion has been to value free services by putting a dollar value on the time that users spend using the service. If Safiyya spends 3.5 hours on Facebook each day and we estimate the value of her time to be worth $10 per hour, then we can place a value of $35 (= 3.5 hours × $10 per hour) on the services that she receives from Facebook.

The need to place a value on free services also matters because consumers have been transitioning from paid versions to free versions of various products. Consider maps. People used to pay for printed road maps. But now they can get electronic maps for free on their mobile devices. The money spent on printed maps was counted in GDP. But there is nothing to count with respect to digital maps. So, GDP will decline if we fail to capture the value that people receive from digital maps. The same is true for free music and video streamed over the Internet, storage space for photo albums, stock and bond prices, news and weather reports, and so on. These products are still valuable, so we would like to include them in GDP.

QUICK REVIEW
27.5

▶ GDP is a reasonably accurate and very useful indicator of a nation's economic performance but should not be interpreted as a comprehensive measure of well-being.

▶ The major limitations of GDP as an indicator of well-being are that it fails to account for nonmarket and illegal transactions, changes in leisure and in product quality, the composition and distribution of output, the environmental effects of pollution, and economic activity at earlier stages of production and distribution.

Summary

LO27.1 Define and measure gross domestic product (GDP).
Gross domestic product (GDP), a basic measure of an economy's economic performance, is the market value of all final goods and services produced within a nation's borders in a year.

Final goods are those purchased by end users, whereas intermediate goods are those purchased for resale or for further processing or manufacturing. Intermediate goods, nonproduction transactions, and secondhand sales are excluded in calculating GDP.

LO27.2 Determine GDP by summing all expenditures on final goods and services.
GDP may be calculated by summing total expenditures on all final output or by summing the income derived from the production of that output.

By the expenditures approach, GDP is determined by adding consumer purchases of goods and services, gross investment spending by businesses, government purchases, and net exports: $GDP = C + I_g + G + X_n$.

Personal consumption expenditures consist of expenditures on goods (durable goods and nondurable goods) and services. About 60 percent of consumer expenditures in the United States are on services, leading economists to refer to the U.S. economy as a *service economy*.

Gross investment is divided into (*a*) replacement investment (required to maintain the nation's stock of capital at its existing level) and (*b*) net investment (the net increase in the stock of capital). In most years, net investment is positive, and therefore the economy's stock of capital and production capacity increase.

LO27.3 Determine GDP by summing all incomes received for providing resources.
By the income, or allocations, approach, GDP is calculated as the sum of compensation to employees, rents, interest, proprietors' income, corporate profits, and taxes on production and imports, *minus* net foreign factor income, *plus* consumption of fixed capital and a statistical discrepancy.

LO27.4 Describe the relationships among GDP, net domestic product, national income, personal income, and disposable income.
Net domestic product (NDP) is GDP minus the consumption of fixed capital. National income (NI) is total income earned by a nation's resource suppliers plus taxes on production and imports; it is found by subtracting a statistical discrepancy from NDP and adding net foreign factor income to NDP. Personal income (PI) is the total income paid to households before they pay personal taxes. Disposable income (DI) is personal income after households have paid personal taxes. DI measures the amount of income available to households to consume or save.

LO27.5 Distinguish between nominal GDP and real GDP.
Nominal (current-dollar) GDP measures each year's output valued in terms of the prices prevailing in that year. Real (constant-dollar) GDP measures each year's output in terms of the prevailing prices in a selected base year. Because real GDP is adjusted for price-level changes, differences in real GDP are due only to differences in production activity. Economists use a GDP price index to convert nominal GDP to real GDP.

LO27.6 Explain some limitations of the GDP measure.
GDP is a reasonably accurate and very useful indicator of a nation's economic performance, but it has its limitations. It fails to account for nonmarket and illegal transactions, changes in leisure and in product quality, the composition and distribution of output, the environmental effects of pollution, noneconomic sources of well-being, and economic activity at earlier stages of production and distribution.

Terms and Concepts

national income accounting	personal consumption expenditures (*C*)	national income
gross domestic product (GDP)	durable good	consumption of fixed capital
final goods and services	nondurable good	net domestic product (NDP)
intermediate goods and services	service	personal income (PI)
value added	gross private domestic investment (I_g)	disposable income (DI)
gross output (GO)	net private domestic investment	nominal GDP
multiple counting	government purchases (*G*)	real GDP
expenditures approach	net exports (X_n)	price index
income approach	taxes on production and imports	base year

Discussion Questions

1. In what ways are national income statistics useful? **LO27.1**
2. Why do national income accountants compare the market value of the total outputs in various years rather than actual physical volumes of production? What problem is posed by any comparison over time of the market values of various total outputs? How is this problem resolved? **LO27.1**
3. Which of the following goods are usually intermediate goods and which are usually final goods: running shoes, cotton fibers, watches, textbooks, coal, sunscreen lotion, lumber? **LO27.1**
4. Why do economists include only final goods and services when measuring GDP? Why don't they include the value of the stocks and bonds bought and sold? Why don't they include the value of the used furniture bought and sold? **LO27.1**
5. Explain why an economy's output, in essence, is also its income. **LO27.1**
6. Provide three examples of each: consumer durable goods, consumer nondurable goods, and services. **LO27.2**
7. Why are changes in inventories included as part of investment spending? Suppose inventories decline by $1 billion during 2025. How would this $1 billion decrease affect the size of gross private domestic investment and gross domestic product in 2025? Explain. **LO27.2**
8. What is the difference between gross private domestic investment and net private domestic investment? If you were to determine net domestic product (NDP) through the expenditures approach, which of these two measures of investment spending would be appropriate? Explain. **LO27.2**
9. Use the concepts of gross investment and net investment to distinguish between an economy that has a rising capital stock and one that has a falling capital stock. Explain: "Though net investment can be positive, negative, or zero, it is impossible for gross investment to be less than zero." **LO27.2**
10. Define net exports. How are net exports determined? Explain why net exports might be a negative amount. **LO27.2**

11. Contrast nominal GDP and real GDP. Why is one more reliable than the other for comparing changes in the standard of living over a series of years? What is the GDP price index, and what is its role in differentiating nominal GDP and real GDP? **LO27.5**
12. Which of the following are included in this year's GDP? Which are excluded? Explain your answers. **LO27.6**
    a. Interest received on an AT&T corporate bond.
    b. Social Security payments received by a retired factory worker.
    c. Unpaid services of a family member who painted the family home.
    d. Income of a dentist from the dental services she provided.
    e. A monthly allowance that a college student receives from home.
    f. Money received by Josh when he resells his nearly brand-new Honda automobile to Kim.
    g. The publication and sale of a new college textbook.
    h. An increase in leisure resulting from a 2-hour decrease in the length of the workweek, with no reduction in pay.
    i. A $2 billion increase in business inventories.
    j. The purchase of 100 shares of Alphabet (the parent company of Google) stock.
13. Why is gross output a better measure of overall economic activity than GDP is? How could you construct a new statistic that focuses only on nonfinal economic activity? Given what you know about the behavior of GO and GDP during the Great Recession, would you expect your new statistic to show more or less volatility than GO and GDP? Why? How would you rank the three in terms of volatility? **LO27.6**
14. **LAST WORD** How do "free" products make the calculation of GDP more difficult? What are hedonic adjustments and why are they necessary? Will inflation tend to be overstated or understated if quality improvements are not accounted for? Explain.

Review Questions

1. Satoshi walks into Vitalik's sporting goods store and buys a punching bag for $100. That $100 payment counts as _____ for Satoshi and _____ for Vitalik. **LO27.1**
   a. income; expenditure
   b. value added; multiple counting
   c. expenditure; income
   d. rents; profits
2. Which of the following transactions are counted in GDP? **LO27.1**
   *Select **one or more** answers from the choices shown.*
   a. Kerry buys a new sweater to wear this winter.
   b. Patricia receives a Social Security check.
   c. Roberto gives his daughter $50 for her birthday.
   d. Nayana sells $1,000 of General Electric stock.
   e. Nick buys a new car.
   f. Patrick buys a used car.

3. A small economy starts the year with $1 million in capital. During the course of the year, gross investment is $150,000 and depreciation is $50,000. What is the economy's capital stock at the end of the year? **LO27.2**
   a. $1,150,000
   b. $1,100,000
   c. $1,000,000
   d. $850,000
   e. $800,000
4. Suppose that this year a small country has a GDP of $100 billion. Also assume that $I_g = \$30$ billion, $C = \$60$ billion, and $X_n = -\$10$ billion. What is the value of G? **LO27.3**
   a. $0
   b. $10 billion
   c. $20 billion
   d. $30 billion

5. Suppose that California imposes a sales tax of 10 percent on all goods and services. A Californian named Ralph then goes into a home improvement store in the state capital of Sacramento and buys a leaf blower that is priced at $200. With the 10 percent sales tax, his total comes to $220. How much of the $220 paid by Ralph is in the national income and product accounts as private income (employee compensation, rents, interest, proprietor's income, and corporate profits)? **LO27.3**
   a. $220
   b. $200
   c. $180
   d. none of the above

6. Suppose GDP is $16 trillion, with $10 trillion coming from consumption, $2 trillion coming from gross investment, $3.5 trillion coming from government expenditures, and $500 billion coming from net exports. Also suppose that across the whole economy, depreciation (consumption of fixed capital) totals $1 trillion. From these figures, we see that net domestic product equals: **LO27.4**
   a. $17.0 trillion.
   b. $16.0 trillion.
   c. $15.5 trillion.
   d. none of the above.

7. Suppose GDP is $15 trillion, with $8 trillion coming from consumption, $2.5 trillion coming from gross investment, $3.5 trillion coming from government expenditures, and $1 trillion coming from net exports. Also suppose that across the whole economy, personal income is $12 trillion. If the government collects $1.5 trillion in personal taxes, then disposable income is: **LO27.4**
   a. $13.5 trillion.
   b. $12.0 trillion.

c. $10.5 trillion.
d. none of the above.

8. Suppose that this year's nominal GDP is $16 trillion. To account for the effects of inflation, we construct a price-level index in which an index value of 100 represents the price level 5 years ago. Using that index, we find that this year's real GDP is $15 trillion. Given those numbers, we can conclude that the current value of the index is: **LO27.5**
   a. higher than 100.
   b. lower than 100.
   c. still 100.

9. Which of the following items are included in official U.S. GDP statistics? **LO27.6**
   *Select **one or more** answers from the choices shown.*
   a. Revenue generated by illegal marijuana growers.
   b. Money spent to clean up a toxic waste site in Ohio.
   c. Revenue generated by legal medical marijuana sales in California.
   d. The dollar value of the annoyance felt by local citizens living near a noisy airport in Georgia.
   e. Andre paying Ted for a haircut in Chicago.
   f. Emily and Aliya trading an hour of dance lessons for a haircut in Dallas.

10. Suppose GDP is $5.0 trillion, depreciation is $1 trillion, and gross output (GO) is $17.25 trillion. **LO27.6**
   a. What is the value of all stages of production and distribution *except for* final sales of goods and services?
   b. What is the dollar value of the economic activity taking place at every stage of production and distribution?

Problems

McGraw Hill connect

1. Suppose that annual output in year 1 in a three-good economy is 3 quarts of ice cream, 1 bottle of shampoo, and 3 jars of peanut butter. In year 2, the output mix changes to 5 quarts of ice cream, 2 bottles of shampoo, and 2 jars of peanut butter. If the prices in both years are $4 per quart for ice cream, $3 per bottle of shampoo, and $2 per jar of peanut butter, what was the economy's GDP in year 1? What was its GDP in year 2? **LO27.1**

2. Assume that a grower of flower bulbs sells its annual output of bulbs to an Internet retailer for $70,000. The retailer, in turn, brings in $160,000 from selling the bulbs directly to final customers. What amount would these two transactions add to personal consumption expenditures and thus to GDP during the year? **LO27.1**

3. If in some country personal consumption expenditures in a specific year are $50 billion, purchases of stocks and bonds are $30 billion, net exports are −$10 billion, government purchases are $20 billion, sales of secondhand items are $8 billion, and gross investment is $25 billion, what is the country's GDP for the year? **LO27.2**

4. The nearby table contains a list of domestic output and national income figures for a certain year. All figures are in billions. The questions that follow ask you to determine the major national income measures by both the expenditures and income approaches. The results you obtain with the different methods should be the same. **LO27.4**

Personal consumption expenditures	$245
Net foreign factor income	4
Transfer payments	12
Rents	14
Consumption of fixed capital (depreciation)	27
Statistical discrepancy	8
Social Security contributions	20
Interest	13
Proprietors' income	33
Net exports	11
Dividends	16
Compensation of employees	223
Taxes on production and imports	18
Undistributed corporate profits	21
Personal taxes	26
Corporate income taxes	19
Corporate profits	56
Government purchases	72
Net private domestic investment	33
Personal saving	20

a. Using the above data, determine GDP by both the expenditures approach and the income approach. Then determine NDP.

b. Now determine NI in two ways: first, by making the required additions or subtractions from NDP; and second, by adding up the types of income and taxes that make up NI.

c. Adjust NI (from part *b*) as required to obtain PI.

d. Adjust PI (from part *c*) as required to obtain DI.

5. Using the following national income accounting data, compute (*a*) GDP, (*b*) NDP, and (*c*) NI. All figures are in billions. **LO27.4**

Compensation of employees	$194.2
U.S. exports of goods and services	17.8
Consumption of fixed capital	11.8
Government purchases	59.4
Taxes on production and imports	14.4
Net private domestic investment	52.1
Transfer payments	13.9
U.S. imports of goods and services	16.5
Personal taxes	40.5
Net foreign factor income	2.2
Personal consumption expenditures	219.1
Statistical discrepancy	0.0

6. Suppose that in 2014 the total output in a single-good economy was 7,000 buckets of chicken. Also suppose that in 2014 each bucket of chicken was priced at $10. Finally, assume that in 2025 the price per bucket of chicken was $16 and that 22,000 buckets were produced. Determine the GDP price index for 2014, using 2025 as the base year. By what percentage did the price level, as measured by this index, rise between 2014 and 2025? What were the amounts of real GDP in 2014 and 2025? **LO27.5**

7. The following table shows nominal GDP and an appropriate price index for a group of selected years. Compute real GDP. Indicate in each calculation whether you are inflating or deflating the nominal GDP data. **LO27.5**

Year	Nominal GDP, Billions	Price Index 2005 = 100	Real GDP, Billions
1978	2,293.8	40.40	$_____
1988	5,100.4	66.98	$_____
1998	8,793.5	85.51	$_____
2008	14,441.4	108.48	$_____
2018	20,501.0	128.59	$_____

8. Assume that the total value of the following items is $600 billion in a specific year for Upper Mongoose: net exports = $50 billion; value of new goods and services produced in the underground economy = $75 billion; personal consumption expenditures = $300 billion; value of the services of stay-at-home parents = $25 billion; gross domestic investment = $100 billion; government purchases = $50 billion. What is Upper Mongoose's GDP for the year? What is the size of the underground economy as a percentage of GDP? By what percentage would GDP increase if the value of the services of stay-at-home spouses were included in GDP? **LO27.6**

CHAPTER

28

Economic Growth

LO28.1 Explain two ways to measure economic growth.

LO28.2 Describe the institutional structures necessary for modern economic growth.

LO28.3 Identify the supply, demand, and efficiency forces that lead to economic growth.

LO28.4 Describe the specific factors accounting for U.S. economic growth.

LO28.5 Explain how U.S. productivity growth has fluctuated since 1973.

LO28.6 Discuss whether economic growth is desirable and sustainable.

Economic growth is arguably the most revolutionary and powerful force in world history. Until a couple of hundred years ago, poverty, disease, and starvation were the normal lot of people throughout the world. As just one example, France during the 17th century suffered a famine about once every five or six years, with the severe famine of 1693 killing 7 percent of the population just by itself.

Today, by contrast, much of the world's population lives with luxuries that were unknown to our ancestors—hot running water, sewers, automobiles, televisions, antibiotics, wi-fi, fast food, air conditioning, and free public schools. Famine is rare. Life expectancy at birth has increased from 30 years to nearly 73 worldwide. And measured in constant 1990 dollars, the average annual income per capita worldwide has increased from about $600 five hundred years ago to about $10,600 today.

But not every part of the world has enjoyed economic growth; many places are still extremely poor. So economists feel compelled to investigate the causes of economic growth, the institutional structures that appear to promote economic growth, and the controversies surrounding the benefits and costs of economic growth.

>> **LO28.1** Explain two ways to measure economic growth.

economic growth (1) An outward shift in the *production possibilities curve* that results from an increase in resource supplies or quality or an improvement in *technology;* (2) an increase of real output (*gross domestic product*) or real output per capita.

Economic Growth

Economists define **economic growth** as either:

- An increase in *real GDP* over some time period.
- An increase in *real GDP per capita* over some time period.

With either definition, economic growth is calculated as a percentage rate of growth per quarter (3-month period) or per year. For the first definition, for example, real GDP in the United States (measured in constant 2012 dollars) was $18,384.7 billion in 2020 and $19,427.3 in 2021. So the real (inflation-adjusted) U.S. economic growth rate for 2021 was 5.7 percent {= [(19,427.3 billion − $18,384.7 billion)/$18,384.7 billion] × 100}. Growth rates are usually, but not always, positive. In recession year 2009, for instance, the U.S. rate of economic growth was *minus* 2.4 percent. Also note that the growth rate for 2021 was unusually high, due to the U.S. economy snapping back sharply after the short but extremely severe 2020 recession that was caused by the COVID-19 pandemic. Since 1970, the annual U.S. growth rate for real GDP has only exceeded 5 percent per year six times and the 2021 growth rate was the highest observed since real GDP grew at a 7.2 percent annual rate in 1984.

The second definition of economic growth takes into consideration the size of the population. **Real GDP per capita** (or *per capita output*) is the amount of real output per person in a country. It is calculated as follows:

$$\text{Real GDP per capita} = \frac{\text{Real GDP}}{\text{Population}}$$

real GDP per capita *Inflation*-adjusted output per person; *real GDP/* population.

For example, in 2020, real GDP in the United States was $18,384.7 billion and the population was 331.8 million. Therefore, real GDP per capita in that year was $55,409 (= $18,384.7 billion divided by 331.8 million). In 2021, real GDP per capita increased to $58,481 (= $19,427.3 billion divided by 2018's population of 332.2 million). So the growth rate of real GDP per capita in 2021 was 5.4 percent {= [($58,418 − $55,409)/$55,409] × 100}. By way of comparison, real GDP per capita fell by 3.5 percent in recession year 2009.

For measuring the expansion of military potential or political prominence, the growth of real GDP is more useful than the growth of real GDP per capita. Unless specified otherwise, the growth rates reported in the news and by international agencies refer to the growth rates of real GDP rather than real GDP per capita. For comparing living standards, however, the growth rate of real GDP per capita is superior. While China's GDP in 2020 was $14,722 billion compared with Denmark's $356 billion, Denmark's GDP per capita was $61,063 compared with China's strikingly lower $10,435.

In some cases, real GDP growth statistics can be misleading. For example, the African nation of Eritrea had real GDP growth of 1.3 percent per year from 2000 to 2008. But over the same period its annual population growth rate was 3.8 percent per year, resulting in a 2.5 percent per year decline in real GDP per capita.

Growth as a Goal

Growth is a widely held economic goal. The expansion of total output relative to population results in rising real wages and incomes and thus higher standards of living. An economy that is experiencing economic growth is better able to meet people's wants and resolve socioeconomic problems. Rising real wages and income provide more opportunities to individuals and families–a vacation trip, a personal computer, tuition–without sacrificing other opportunities and pleasures. A growing economy can undertake new programs to alleviate poverty, cultivate the arts, and protect the environment without impairing existing levels of consumption, investment, and public goods production.

In short, *growth lessens the burden of scarcity*. Unlike a static economy, a growing economy can consume more today while increasing its capacity to produce more in the future. By easing the burden of scarcity–by relaxing society's constraints on production–economic growth helps a nation attain its economic goals and undertake new endeavors.

Arithmetic of Growth

Economists pay so much attention to small changes in the rate of economic growth because those small changes in growth rates have large effects on the volume of output. For the United States, with a current nominal GDP of about $23 trillion, the difference between a 3 percent and a 4 percent growth rate is about $230 billion of output each year. For a poor country, a difference of one-half of a percentage point in the growth rate may mean the difference between hunger and starvation.

The mathematical approximation called the **rule of 70** helps us understand the effect of economic growth. According to the rule of 70, we can find the number of years it will take for some measure to double by dividing the number 70 by the measure's annual percentage rate of growth. For real GDP:

$$\text{Approximate number of years required to double real GDP} = \frac{70}{\text{annual percentage rate of growth}}$$

rule of 70 A method for determining the number of years it will take for some measure to double, given its annual percentage increase. Example: To determine the number of years it will take for the *price level* to double, divide 70 by the annual rate of *inflation*.

TABLE 28.1 U.S. Real GDP and Real GDP per Capita, Selected Years, 1950–2021

(1) Year	(2) Real GDP, Billions of 2012 $	(3) Population, Millions	(4) Real GDP, per Capita, 2012 $ (2) ÷ (3)
1950	$ 2,291	151.7	$15,102
1960	3,262	180.8	18,042
1970	4,954	205.1	24,154
1980	6,764	227.7	29,706
1990	9,372	250.2	37,458
2000	13,138	282.4	46,523
2010	15,649	309.8	50,513
2020	18,385	331.8	55,410
2021	19,427	332.2	58,480

Source: U.S. Bureau of Economic Analysis and U.S. Census Bureau.

Examples: A 3 percent annual growth rate will double real GDP in about 23 (= 70 ÷ 3) years. Growth of 8 percent per year will double real GDP in about 9 (= 70 ÷ 8) years. When compounded over many years, an apparently small difference in the growth rate thus becomes highly significant. Suppose China and Italy start with identical GDPs, but then China grows at 8 percent yearly, while Italy grows at 2 percent. China's GDP would double in about 9 years, while Italy's GDP would double in 35 years.

Growth in the United States

Table 28.1 gives an overview of economic growth in the United States since 1950. Column 2 reveals strong growth as measured by increases in real GDP. Note that between 1950 and 2021, real GDP increased more than eightfold.

The U.S. population also increased over that time period. Nevertheless, column 4 shows that real GDP per capita rose nearly fourfold over these years.

How quickly has U.S. GDP grown since 1950? Real GDP grew at an average annual rate of about 3.0 percent per year while real GDP per capita increased on average at roughly 1.9 percent per year. Those are very respectable growth rates, but we must qualify how we interpret them:

- *Improved products and services* Because the numbers in Table 28.1 do not fully account for improvements in products and services, they understate the growth of economic well-being. Such purely quantitative data do not fully compare an era of vacuum tube computers and low-efficiency V8 hot rods with an era of digital cell phone networks and fuel-sipping, hybrid-drive vehicles.

- *Added leisure* The increases in real GDP and per capita GDP in Table 28.1 were accomplished despite increases in leisure. The average workweek, once 50 hours, is now about 35 hours (excluding overtime hours). Again the raw growth numbers understate the gain in economic well-being.

- *Other impacts* These measures of growth do not account for the effects of growth on the environment and the quality of life. If growth debases the physical environment, excessively warms the planet, and creates a stressful work environment, the bare growth numbers will overstate the gains in well-being that result from growth. In contrast, if growth leads to stronger environmental protections or a more secure and stress-free lifestyle, GDP growth statistics will understate the gains in well-being.

QUICK REVIEW
28.1

- Economists measure economic growth as either (a) an increase in real GDP over time or (b) an increase in real GDP per capita over time.

- Real GDP in the United States has grown by about 3.0 percent annually since 1950, while real GDP per capita has grown by roughly 1.9 percent annually over the same period.

- Real GDP fails to fully account for quality improvements, excludes the dollar value of leisure activities, and does not account for the effects of growth on the environment.

Modern Economic Growth

Before the Industrial Revolution of the late 1700s, living standards were virtually constant over long periods of time. Greek peasants living in the year 300 B.C. had, for example, about the same material standard of living as Greek peasants living in the year A.D. 1500. By contrast, our current era of **modern economic growth** is characterized by sustained and ongoing increases in material prosperity that yield dramatic increases in the standard of living within less than a single human lifetime.

Economic historians informally date the start of the Industrial Revolution to the year 1776, when the Scottish inventor James Watt perfected an efficient steam engine that could power not only steamships and steam locomotives, but also factory equipment. Nearly all manufacturing shifted from items produced by hand by local craftsmen to items mass-produced in distant factories. New steamships and steam locomotives meant that resources flowed easily to factories and that factory output could be shipped to distant consumers at low cost. The result was a huge increase in long-distance trade and a major population shift as people left farms to work in the towns and cities where the new industrial factories were concentrated.

Many more inventions followed Watt's steam engine. These included electric power, railroads, motorized vehicles, telephones, airplanes, container ships, computers, and the Internet. The key point is that the last 250 years of history have been fundamentally different from anything that went before.

Modern economic growth has deeply affected cultural, social, and political arrangements.

- Culturally, the vast increases in wealth and living standards have given ordinary people significant time for leisure activities and the arts.

- Socially, countries experiencing modern economic growth have abolished feudalism, instituted universal public education, and largely eliminated ancient social norms and legal restrictions against women and minorities doing certain jobs or holding certain positions.

- Politically, countries experiencing modern economic growth have tended to move toward democracy, a form of government that was extremely rare before the Industrial Revolution.

In addition, the average human lifespan has more than doubled, from less than 30 years before modern economic growth began in the late 1700s to a worldwide average of over 72 years today. These and other changes speak to the truly revolutionary power of economic growth and naturally lead economists to consider the causes of economic growth and what policies can be pursued to sustain and promote it. Their desire is intensified by the reality that economic growth has been distributed so unevenly around the globe.

The Uneven Distribution of Growth

Modern economic growth spread slowly from its British birthplace. It first advanced to France, Germany, and other parts of Western Europe in the early 1800s before spreading to the United States, Canada, and Australia by the mid-1800s. Japan began to industrialize in the 1870s, but the rest of Asia did not follow until the early to mid-1900s. At that time, large parts of Central America, South America, and the Middle East also began to experience modern economic growth. Most recent has been Africa, which for the most part did not begin to experience modern economic growth until the last half-century.

The different starting dates for modern economic growth in various parts of the world are the main cause of the vast differences in today's per capita GDP levels. Figure 28.1 shows how GDP per capita has evolved since 1820 in the United States, Western Europe, Latin America, Asia, and Africa.

To make the comparisons easier in Figure 28.1, income levels in all places and at all times have been converted into 2011 U.S. dollars. Thus, it is clear that in 1820 per capita incomes in all areas were quite similar. The richest area in the world in 1820, Western Europe, had an average per capita income of $2,307, while the poorest area of the world at that time, Africa, had an average per capita income of $800. Thus, in 1820, average incomes in the richest area in the world were only about three times larger than those in the poorest area.

But because Western Europe and the United States started experiencing modern economic growth earlier than other areas, they are now vastly richer than most other areas. As just one example, per capita GDP in 2021 was $58,480 in the United States but only about $3,532 in

>> **LO28.2** Describe the institutional structures necessary for modern economic growth.

modern economic growth
The historically recent phenomenon in which nations for the first time have experienced sustained increases in *real GDP per capita*.

FIGURE 28.1
The great divergence in standards of living.

Income levels around the world were very similar in 1820. But they are now very different because certain areas, including the United States and Western Europe, began experiencing modern economic growth much earlier than other areas.

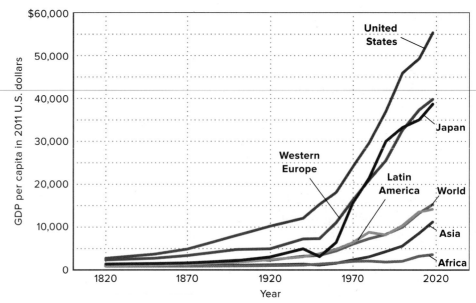

Source: Maddison Historical Statistics, The Maddison Project, University of Groningen.

Africa. Because modern economic growth has occurred for so much longer in the United States, U.S. living standards are nearly 17 times higher than those in Africa, on average.

Catching Up Is Possible

The countries that began modern economic growth more recently are not doomed to be permanently poorer than the countries that began modern economic growth earlier. Why? Because people can adopt technology more quickly than they can invent it.

The world's richest countries are rich mostly because they employ the most advanced productive technology. But because they already utilize the most advanced technology, they must invent new technology to get even richer. Because inventing and implementing new technology is slow and costly, real GDP per capita in the richest **leader countries** like the United States and Japan typically grows by just 2 to 3 percent per year.

By contrast, poorer **follower countries** can grow much faster because they can adopt, rather than reinvent, existing technologies. For instance, in many countries in Africa, the first telephones that most people ever used were mobile phones. These countries did not bother to install the copper wires necessary for land-line telephones, which use nineteenth-century technology. Instead, they chose to jump directly to Internet-capable mobile networks, which employ twenty-first-century technology. In doing so, these countries skipped past many stages of technology that the United States and other leader countries took over a century to invent and implement.

By skipping directly to the most advanced modern technology, follower countries can experience extremely rapid **catch-up growth.** South Korea, for example, averaged 8.8 percent annual growth in real GDP between 1960 and 2020—a pace of growth that transformed South Korea from one of the poorest countries in the world into a rich leader country that is on the cutting edge of technology in several areas, including electronics and automobiles.

China grew even more rapidly after it undertook market-oriented economic reforms starting in the late 1970s. Between 1980 and 2020, China's real GDP grew at an average annual rate of 9.9 percent per year. That rate of growth lifted hundreds of millions out of abject poverty and raised China to great power status in political and military relations.

China is now, however, near the "technological frontier" at which it will no longer be able to grow rapidly simply by borrowing established technologies from other countries. As with other countries that have pulled close to the technological frontier, its growth rate is slowing rapidly since it must now invest significant resources into invention and innovation. Once it becomes a leader country across all types of technology, its growth rate can be expected to decrease down to the 2 to 3 percent rate typical of established technological leader countries like Japan and the United States.

leader countries As it relates to *economic growth,* countries that develop and use the most advanced technologies, which then become available to *follower countries.*

follower countries As it relates to *economic growth,* countries that adopt advanced technologies that previously were developed and used by *leader countries.*

catch-up growth The rapid increases in real GDP per capita that can be achieved when a poor *follower country* adopts, rather than reinvents, cutting edge technologies that took *leader countries* decades to invent and implement.

Institutional Structures That Promote Modern Economic Growth

How does a country start the process of modern economic growth? And once it has started modern economic growth, how does it keep the process going?

Economic historians have identified several institutional structures that promote and sustain modern economic growth. Some institutions increase the savings and investment that are needed to fund the construction and maintenance of the factories and infrastructure required to run modern economies. Other institutions promote the development of new technologies. Still others ensure that resources flow efficiently to their most productive uses. These growth-promoting institutional structures include:

- *Strong property rights* Strong property rights are essential for promoting rapid and sustained economic growth. People will not invest if they believe that thieves, bandits, or a rapacious and tyrannical government will steal their investments or their expected returns.

- *Patents and copyrights* Before patents and copyrights were first issued and enforced, inventors and authors usually saw their ideas stolen before they could profit from them. By giving inventors and authors the exclusive right to market and sell their creations, patents and copyrights provide a strong financial incentive to invent and create (as is discussed in the nearby Consider This story about drug prices).

- *Efficient financial institutions* These institutions channel household savings toward the businesses, entrepreneurs, and inventors that do most of society's investing and inventing. Banks, along with stock and bond markets, appear to be crucial to modern economic growth.

- *Literacy and widespread education* Without highly educated scientists and inventors, new technologies do not get developed. And without a highly educated workforce, it is impossible to put those technologies to productive use.

- *Free trade* Free trade promotes economic growth by allowing countries to specialize. With specialization, various types of output are produced in the countries where they can be made at the lowest opportunity cost. Free trade also promotes the rapid spread of new ideas so that innovations made in one country quickly spread to other countries.

CONSIDER THIS . . .

Patents and Innovation

It costs U.S. and European drug companies about $1 billion to research, patent, and safety-test a new drug because literally thousands of candidate drugs fail for each drug that succeeds. The only way to recover these costs is by relying on patent protections that give a drug's developer the exclusive monopoly right to market and sell the new drug for 20 years. The revenues over that time period will hopefully be enough to cover the drug's development costs and—if the drug is popular—generate a profit for the drug company.

Photodisc Collection/EyeWire/Getty Images

Leader and follower countries have gotten into heated disputes over patented drugs, however, because the follower countries have often refused to recognize the patents granted to pharmaceutical companies in rich countries. India, for instance, has allowed local drug companies to copy and sell drugs that were developed by U.S.

companies and are still under patent protection in the United States.

That policy benefits Indian consumers because competition among the local drug companies drives down the price to below the monopoly price that would be charged by the patent owner. But the weak patent protections in India have a side effect. They make it completely unprofitable for local drug producers to try to develop innovative new drugs. Local rivals would simply copy the new drugs and sell them at very low prices. So India has recently moved to strengthen its patent protections to try to provide financial incentives to transform its local drug companies from copycats into innovators.

But note that the innovative new drugs that may result from the increased patent protections will not arrive without an opportunity cost. As patent protections in India are improved, inexpensive local drugs copied from the leader countries will no longer be available to Indian consumers.

- *A competitive market system* Under a market system, prices and profits serve as the signals that tell firms what and how much to make. Rich leader countries vary substantially in terms of how much government regulation they impose on markets, but in all cases, firms have substantial autonomy to follow market signals in determining their production and investment decisions.

Several other difficult-to-measure factors also influence a nation's capacity for economic growth. The overall social-cultural-political environment of the United States, for example, has encouraged economic growth. The United States has a stable political system characterized by democratic principles, internal order, the right of property ownership, the legal status of enterprise, and the enforcement of contracts. Economic freedom and political freedom have been "growth friendly."

In addition, there are virtually no social or moral taboos on production and material progress in the United States. The nation's social philosophy has embraced wealth creation as an attainable and desirable goal, and the inventor, the innovator, and the businessperson are given high degrees of prestige and respect. Finally, Americans have a positive attitude toward work and risk taking, resulting in an ample supply of willing workers and innovative entrepreneurs. A flow of enterprising immigrants has greatly augmented that supply.

The nearby Consider This shows how follower countries sometimes alter their institutional structures as they draw closer to the technological frontier.

**QUICK REVIEW
28.2**

▶ Large differences in standards of living exist today because technological leader countries like the United States have experienced up to 250 years of modern economic growth while technological follower countries have enjoyed modern economic growth for only a few decades.

▶ Poor follower countries can catch up to the living standards of rich leader countries by adopting the cutting-edge technologies and institutions already developed by rich leader countries.

▶ Institutional structures that promote growth include strong property rights, patents, efficient financial institutions, education, and a competitive market system.

Determinants of Growth

>> LO28.3 Identify the supply, demand, and efficiency forces that lead to economic growth.

We now focus on six factors that directly affect the rate and quality of economic growth. These determinants of economic growth can be grouped into four supply factors, one demand factor, and one efficiency factor.

Supply Factors

The first four determinants of economic growth relate to relaxing the physical and technical limits that constrain economic expansion. They are:

supply factors (in growth)
The four determinants of an economy's physical ability to achieve *economic growth* by increasing *potential output* and shifting out the *production possibilities curve*. The four determinants are improvements in technology plus increases in the quantity and quality of natural resources, human resources, and the stock of capital goods.

- Increases in the quantity and quality of natural resources
- Increases in the quantity and quality of human resources
- Increases in the supply (stock) of capital goods
- Improvements in technology

Any increases or improvements in these **supply factors** will increase the *potential* size of an economy's GDP. The remaining two factors (that is, the demand factor and the efficiency factor) are necessary for that potential to be fulfilled.

Demand Factor

The fifth determinant of economic growth is the **demand factor:**

demand factor (in growth)
The requirement that *aggregate demand* increase as fast as *potential output* if *economic growth* is to proceed as quickly as possible.

- To achieve the higher production potential created when the supply factors increase or improve, households, businesses, and the government must also expand their purchases of goods and services so as to provide a market for all the new output that can potentially be produced.

When this demand condition is met, there will be no unplanned increases in inventories, and resources will remain fully employed. The demand factor acknowledges that economic growth requires increases in total spending to realize the output gains made possible by increased production capacity.

Efficiency Factor

The first five determinants affect the quantity of economic output. The sixth determinant, the **efficiency factor,** deals with the quality of economic output:

- An economy must achieve economic efficiency in addition to full employment if it is to maximize the amount of satisfaction or utility that can be derived from its scarce resources.

To maximize well-being, the economy must use its resources in the least costly way (productive efficiency) to produce the specific mix of goods and services that maximizes people's utility (allocative efficiency). The ability to expand production, together with the full use of available resources, is not sufficient for achieving welfare-maximizing growth. To maximize well-being, those resources must be employed efficiently, as well.

The supply, demand, and efficiency factors in economic growth are related. Unemployment caused by insufficient total spending (the demand factor) may lower the rate of new capital accumulation (a supply factor) and delay expenditures on research (also a supply factor). Conversely, low spending on investment (a supply factor) may cause insufficient spending (the demand factor) and unemployment. Widespread inefficiency in the use of resources (the efficiency factor) may translate into higher costs of goods and services and thus lower profits, which in turn may slow innovation and reduce the accumulation of capital (supply factors).

Production Possibilities Analysis

To put the six factors affecting the rate of economic growth into better perspective, let's apply the production possibilities analysis introduced in Chapter 1.

Growth and Production Possibilities Recall that a curve like *AB* in Figure 28.2 is a production possibilities curve. It indicates the various *maximum* combinations of products an economy can produce with its fixed quantity and quality of natural, human, and capital resources and its current stock of technological knowledge. An improvement in any of the supply factors will push the production possibilities curve outward, as from *AB* to *CD*.

But the demand factor reminds us that the economy needs an increase in total spending to move from a point like *a* on curve *AB* to any of the points on the higher curve *CD*. And the efficiency factor reminds us that we need least-cost production and an optimal location on *CD* for the resources to make their maximum possible contribution to total output and human welfare. Recall from Chapter 1 that this "best allocation" is determined by expanding the production of each good until its marginal benefit equals its marginal cost. Here, we assume that this optimal combination of capital and consumer goods occurs at point *b*. If the efficiency factor is in full effect, then the economy will produce at point *b* rather than at any other point along curve *CD*.

Example: The net increase in the size of the U.S. labor force in recent decades has been 1 to 1.5 million workers per year. That increase raises the economy's production capacity. But obtaining the extra output that these added workers can produce depends on their success in finding jobs. It also depends on whether jobs are available in firms and industries where the workers' talents are fully and optimally used. Society does not want new labor-force entrants to be unemployed. Nor does it want pediatricians working as plumbers or pediatricians producing pediatric services for which marginal costs exceed marginal benefits.

Normally, increases in total spending match increases in production capacity, and the economy moves from a point on the previous production possibilities curve to a point on the expanded curve. Moreover, the

efficiency factor (in growth) The capacity of an economy to achieve *allocative* and *productive efficiency* and thereby fulfill the potential for growth that the *supply factors (of growth)* make possible; the capacity of an economy to achieve *economic efficiency* and thereby reach the optimal point on its *production possibilities curve.*

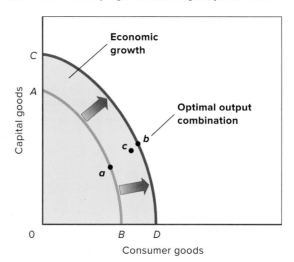

FIGURE 28.2
Economic growth and the production possibilities curve.

Economic growth is made possible by the four supply factors that shift the production possibilities curve outward, as from *AB* to *CD*. Economic growth is realized when the demand factor and the efficiency factor move the economy from points such as *a* and *c* that are inside *CD* to the optimal output point, which is assumed to be point *b* in this figure.

FIGURE 28.3
The supply determinants of real output.

Real GDP is usefully viewed as the product of the quantity of labor inputs (hours of work) multiplied by labor productivity.

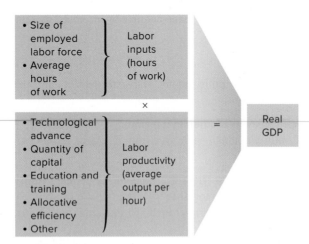

competitive market system tends to drive the economy toward productive and allocative efficiency. Occasionally, however, the economy ends up at some point such as *c* in Figure 28.2. That outcome occurred in the United States during the COVID-19 recession of 2020. Real output fell substantially below the amount of output that the economy could have produced if it had achieved full employment and operated on its production possibilities curve.

Labor and Productivity Society can increase its real output and income in two fundamental ways: (1) by increasing its inputs of resources and (2) by raising the productivity of those inputs. Figure 28.3 concentrates on the input of *labor* and provides a useful framework for discussing the role of supply factors in growth. A nation's real GDP in any year depends on the input of labor (measured in hours of work) multiplied by **labor productivity** (measured as real output per hour of work):

$$\text{Real GDP} = \text{hours of work} \times \text{labor productivity}$$

labor productivity Total output (GDP) divided by the quantity of labor (hours of work) employed to produce it; the *average product* of labor, or output per hour of work.

From this perspective, a nation's economic growth from one year to the next depends on its increase in labor inputs (if any) and its increase in labor productivity (if any).

Illustration: Assume that the hypothetical economy of Ziam has 10 workers in year 1, each working 2,000 hours per year (= 50 weeks at 40 hours per week). The total input of labor therefore is 20,000 hours. If productivity (average real output per hour of work) is $20, then real GDP in Ziam will be $400,000 (= 20,000 × $20). If work hours rise to 20,200 and labor productivity rises to $21 per hour, Ziam's real GDP will increase to $424,200 in year 2. Ziam's rate of economic growth will be about 6 percent [= ($424,200 − $400,000)/$400,000] for the year.

Hours of Work What determines the number of hours worked each year? As Figure 28.3 shows, the hours of labor input depend on the size of the employed labor force and the length of the average workweek. Labor-force size depends on the size of the working-age population and the **labor-force participation rate**—the percentage of the working-age population actually in the labor force. The length of the average workweek is governed by legal and institutional considerations and by collective bargaining agreements negotiated between unions and employers.

labor-force participation rate The percentage of the working-age population that is actually in the *labor force.*

Labor Productivity Figure 28.3 tells us that labor productivity is determined by technological progress, the quantity of capital goods available to workers, the quality of labor inputs, and the efficiency with which inputs are allocated, combined, and managed. Productivity rises when the health, training, education, and motivation of workers improve; when workers have more and better machinery and natural resources to work with; when production is better organized and managed; and when labor is reallocated from less-efficient industries to more-efficient industries.

Accounting for Growth

>> **LO28.4** Describe the specific factors accounting for U.S. economic growth.

The President's Council of Economic Advisers uses a system called **growth accounting** to assess the relative importance of the supply-side elements that contribute to changes in real GDP. This system groups these elements into two main categories:

growth accounting The bookkeeping of the supply-side elements such as productivity and labor inputs that contribute to changes in *real GDP* over some specific time period.

- Increases in hours of work
- Increases in labor productivity

Labor Inputs versus Labor Productivity

Table 28.2 provides the relevant data for the United States for five periods. The symbol "Q" in the table stands for "quarter" of the year. The beginning points for the first four periods are business-cycle peaks, and the last period includes future projections by the Council of Economic Advisers.

TABLE 28.2 Accounting for the Growth of U.S. Real GDP, 1953–2019, plus Projection from 2019 to 2032 (Average Annual Percentage Changes)

Item	Actual				Projected
	1953 Q2 to 1973 Q4	1973 Q4 to 1995 Q2	1995 Q2 to 2007 Q4	2007 Q4 to 2019 Q4	2019 Q4 to 2032 Q4
Increase in real GDP	3.6	2.8	3.2	1.7	2.2
Increase in quantity of labor	1.1	1.3	0.5	0.3	0.4
Increase in labor productivity	2.5	1.5	2.7	1.4	1.8

Source: Economic Report of the President, 2008 and 2019; U.S. Bureau of Economic Analysis; and U.S. Bureau of Labor Statistics.

The table clearly shows that increases in the quantity of labor and increases in labor productivity are both important sources of economic growth.

- Between 1953 and 2021, the labor force increased from 63.1 million to 161.2 million workers. Over that period, the average length of the workweek remained relatively stable. Falling birthrates slowed the growth of the native population, but increased immigration partly offset that slowdown. Of particular significance was a surge of women's participation in the labor force. Partly as a result, U.S. labor-force growth averaged about 1.4 million workers per year over those 71 years.

- The growth of labor productivity has also been important to economic growth. In fact, productivity growth has usually been more significant than labor force growth. For example, between 2007 and 2019, labor inputs increased by just 0.3 percent per year. As a result, 82 percent of the 1.7 percent average annual growth rate of GDP over that period was due to increases in labor productivity. The final column of Table 28.2 indicates that this trend is expected to continue; productivity growth is projected to account for 82 percent of the growth of real GDP between 2019 and 2032.

Because increases in labor productivity are so important to economic growth, economists investigate and assess the relative importance of the factors that contribute to productivity growth. There are five factors that appear to explain changes in productivity growth rates: technological advance, the amount of capital per worker, education and training, economies of scale, and resource allocation. We will examine each factor in turn, noting how much each factor contributes to productivity growth.

Technological Advance

The largest contributor to productivity growth is technological advance, which is thought to account for about 40 percent of productivity growth. As Nobel Laureate Paul Romer stated, "Human history teaches us that economic growth springs from better recipes, not just from more cooking."

Technological advance includes not only innovative production techniques but also new managerial methods and new forms of business organization that improve the production process. Technological advance is generated by the discovery of new knowledge, which allows resources to be combined in improved ways that increase output. Once discovered and implemented, new knowledge soon becomes available to entrepreneurs and firms at relatively low cost. Technological advance therefore eventually spreads through the entire economy, boosting productivity and economic growth.

Technological advance and capital formation (investment) are closely related, because technological advance usually promotes investment in new machinery and equipment. In fact, technological advance is often *embodied* within new capital (for example, new computers and autonomous drones).

Technological advance has been both rapid and profound. Gas and diesel engines, conveyor belts, and assembly lines are significant developments of the past. So, too, are fuel-efficient commercial aircraft, integrated microcircuits, personal computers, and containerized shipping. More recently, technological advance has exploded, particularly in the areas of computers, wireless communications, artificial intelligence, and the Internet. Other fertile areas of recent innovation are medicine and biotechnology.

Quantity of Capital per Worker

A second major contributor to productivity growth is increased capital, which explains roughly 30 percent of productivity growth. More and better plant and equipment make workers more productive. A nation acquires more capital by saving some of its income and using that savings to invest in plant and equipment.

Although some capital substitutes for labor, most capital is complementary to labor—it makes labor more productive. A key determinant of labor productivity is the amount of capital goods available *per worker*. If both the aggregate stock of capital goods and the size of the labor force increase over a given period, the individual worker is not necessarily better equipped, and productivity will not necessarily rise. Fortunately, the quantity of capital (machinery and buildings) available per U.S. worker has increased greatly over time. (In 2020 it was about $255,870 per worker.)

infrastructure The interconnected network of large-scale *capital goods* (such as roads, sewers, electrical grids, railways, ports, and the Internet) needed to operate a technologically advanced economy.

U.S. public investment in **infrastructure** (highways and bridges, public transit systems, wastewater treatment facilities, airports, educational facilities, and so on) has also grown over the years. This publicly owned capital complements private capital. Public investments in new highways, for instance, can promote private investments in new factories and retail stores along their routes.

Private investment in infrastructure also plays a large role in economic growth. One example is the tremendous growth of private capital relating to communications systems over the years.

Education and Training

human capital The knowledge and skills that make a person productive.

Ben Franklin once said, "He that hath a trade hath an estate," meaning that education and training contribute to a worker's stock of **human capital**—the knowledge and skills that make a worker productive. Investment in human capital includes not only formal education but also on-the-job training. Like investment in physical capital, investment in human capital is an important means of increasing labor productivity and earnings. An estimated 15 percent of productivity growth derives from investments in people's education and skills.

One measure of a nation's quality of labor is its level of educational attainment. Figure 28.4 shows large gains in education attainment over the past several decades. In 1960, only 44 percent of the U.S. population age 25 or older had at least a high school education, and only 8 percent had a college or post-college education. By 2020, those numbers had increased to 91 percent and 38 percent, respectively. More people are receiving more education than ever before.

But all is not upbeat with education in the United States. Many observers think that the quality of education in the United States has declined. For example, U.S. students perform poorly on science and math tests relative to students in many other nations, as can be seen in Global Perspective 28.1. And the United States has been producing fewer engineers and scientists, a problem that may trace back to inadequate training in math and science in elementary school, middle school, and high school. For these reasons, much recent public policy discussion and legislation has focused on improving the quality of the U.S. education and training system.

FIGURE 28.4
Changes in the educational attainment of the U.S. adult population.

The percentage of the U.S. adult population, age 25 or older, completing high school and college has been rising over recent decades.

Source: U.S. Census Bureau.

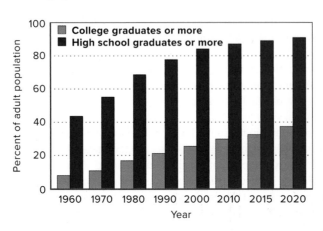

Economies of Scale and Resource Allocation

Economies of scale and improved resource allocation are the fourth and fifth sources of productivity growth; together, they explain about 15 percent of all productivity growth.

Economies of Scale Reductions in per-unit production costs that

GLOBAL PERSPECTIVE 28.1

AVERAGE TEST SCORES OF EIGHTH-GRADE STUDENTS IN MATH AND SCIENCE, TOP 12 TEST-TAKING COUNTRIES

The average performance of U.S. eighth-grade students did not compare favorably with that of eighth-graders in several other nations in the Seventh International Math and Science Study (2019).

Mathematics		Science	
Rank	Score	Rank	Score
1 Singapore	616	1 Singapore	608
2 Taiwan	612	2 Taiwan	574
3 South Korea	607	3 Japan	570
4 Japan	594	4 South Korea	561
5 Hong Kong	578	5 Russia	543
6 Russia	543	6 Finland	542
7 Ireland	524	7 Lithuania	534
8 Lithuania	520	8 Hungary	530
9 Israel	519	9 Australia	528
10 Australia	517	10 Ireland	523
11 Hungary	517	11 United States	522
12 United States	515	12 Sweden	521

Source: National Science Foundation.

---

result from increases in output levels are called **economies of scale.** Markets have grown over time, allowing firms to increase output levels and thereby achieve production advantages associated with greater size. As firms expand their size and output, they are able to use larger, more productive equipment and employ methods of manufacturing and delivery that increase productivity. They also are better able to recoup substantial investments in developing new products and production methods.

Examples: A large manufacturer of autos can use elaborate assembly lines with computerization and robotics, while smaller producers must compensate for less-advanced technologies by using more labor inputs. Large pharmaceutical firms greatly reduce the average amount of labor (researchers, production workers) needed to produce each pill as they increase the number of pills produced. Accordingly, economies of scale generate more real output and thus contribute to economic growth. Economies of scale account for about 7 percent of all productivity growth.

Improved Resource Allocation Thanks to improved resource allocation, workers have moved from low-productivity employment to high-productivity employment. Historically, many workers shifted from agriculture, where labor productivity is low, to manufacturing, where it is high. More recently, labor has shifted away from some manufacturing industries to even higher-productivity industries such as computer software, business consulting, and pharmaceuticals. As a result of such shifts, the average productivity of U.S. workers has increased.

Also, discrimination in education and the labor market has historically deterred some women and minorities from entering high-productivity jobs. With the decline of such discrimination over time, many members of those groups have shifted from lower-productivity jobs to higher-productivity jobs. The result has been higher overall labor productivity and higher real GDP.

Finally, tariffs, import quotas, and other barriers to international trade tend to relegate resources to relatively unproductive pursuits. The long-run movement toward liberalized international trade through international agreements has improved the allocation of resources, increased

economies of scale The situation when a firm's *average total cost* of producing a product decreases in the *long run* as the firm increases the size of its *plant* (and, hence, its output).

labor productivity, and expanded real output, both here and abroad. Improved resource allocation accounts for about 8 percent of all productivity growth.

To solidify your memory, make a pie chart of the percentage contributions made by each of the five factors that contribute to productivity growth (technological advance, the amount of capital per worker, education and training, economies of scale, and resource allocation).

**QUICK REVIEW
28.3**

▶ The determinants of economic growth include four supply factors (increases in the quantity and quality of natural resources, increases in the quantity and quality of human resources, increases in the stock of capital goods, and improvements in technology), one demand factor (increases in total spending), and one efficiency factor (allocative and productive efficiency).

▶ Improved technology, more capital per worker, greater education and training, economies of scale, and better resource allocation have been the main contributors to U.S. productivity growth and thus to U.S. economic growth.

Recent Fluctuations in Average Productivity Growth

>> LO28.5 Explain how U.S. productivity growth has fluctuated since 1973.

Figure 28.5 shows the growth of labor productivity (as measured by changes in the index of labor productivity) in the United States from 1973 to 2021, along with separate trend lines for 1973–1995, 1995–2010, and 2010–2021. Labor productivity in the business sector grew by an average of 1.5 percent per year over the 1973–1995 period. But productivity growth nearly doubled to 2.8 percent per year between 1995 and 2010 before decelerating to just 1.2 percent per year between 2010 and 2021.

Robust productivity growth is important because real output, real income, and real wages are linked to labor productivity. To see why, suppose that you are alone on an uninhabited island. The number of fish you can catch or coconuts you can pick per hour—your productivity—is your real wage (or real income) per hour. By *increasing your* productivity, you can improve your standard of living because you can gather more fish or more coconuts (goods) for each hour of work.

So it is for the economy as a whole: Over long periods, the economy's labor productivity determines its average real hourly wage. Thus, productivity growth is the economy's main route for improving living standards.

FIGURE 28.5   **Growth of labor productivity in the United States, 1973–2021.**

U.S. labor productivity (here, for the business sector) increased at an average annual rate of 1.5 percent from 1973 to 1995. But between 1995 and 2010, it rose at an annual rate of 2.8 percent before slowing to just 1.2 percent per year between 2010 and 2021.

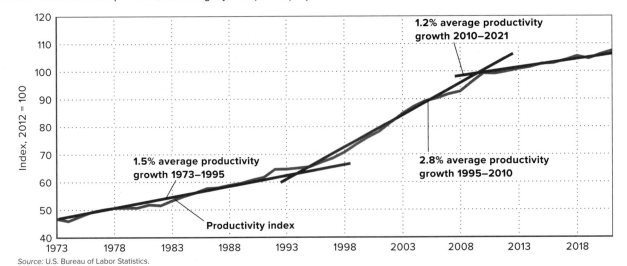

Source: U.S. Bureau of Labor Statistics.

Reasons for the Rise in Average Productivity Growth Between 1995 and 2010

Why did productivity growth increase rapidly between 1995 and 2010?

The Microchip and Information Technology The core element of the productivity speedup between 1995 and 2010 was an explosion of entrepreneurship and innovation based on the microprocessor, or *microchip*, which bundles transistors on a piece of silicon. Some observers liken the invention of the microchip to that of electricity, the automobile, air travel, the telephone, and television in importance and scope.

The microchip has found its way into thousands of applications. It has helped create a wide array of new products and services and new ways of doing business. Its immediate results were the pocket calculator, the bar-code scanner, the personal computer, and more powerful business computers. The miniaturization of electronic circuits also advanced the development of many other products, including cell phones, the global positioning system, Doppler radar, and gene sequencing equipment.

Perhaps of greatest significance, the widespread availability of personal and laptop computers stimulated the desire to tie them together. That desire promoted the rapid development of the Internet and its many manifestations, such as business-to-household and business-to-business electronic commerce (e-commerce). The combination of the computer, fiber-optic cable, wireless technology, and the Internet constitutes a spectacular advance in **information technology,** which now connects almost all parts of the world.

Start-ups Hundreds of new **start-up firms** advanced various aspects of the new information technology. Many of these firms created more "hype" than goods and services and quickly fell by the wayside. But a number of firms flourished, including Intel (microchips); Apple and Dell (personal computers); Microsoft and Oracle (computer software); Cisco Systems (Internet switching systems); Yahoo and Google (Internet search); and eBay, PayPal, and Amazon.com (electronic commerce). There are scores more! Most of these firms were either nonexistent or just a small blip on the radar 30 years ago. Today each of them has a large annual revenue and employs thousands of workers.

Increasing Returns Many of the successful information technology start-ups enjoyed **increasing returns,** which is what happens when a given percentage increase in the amount of inputs used by a firm leads to a larger percentage increase in the amount of output produced by the firm.

As an illustration, suppose that a company called Techco decides to double the size of its operations to meet the growing demand for its services.

- After doubling its plant and equipment and doubling its workforce, say, from 100 workers to 200 workers, it finds that its total output has tripled, from 8,000 units to 24,000 units.

- Techco has experienced increasing returns; its output has increased by 200 percent, while its inputs have increased by only 100 percent.

- Techco's labor productivity has also gone up from 80 units per worker ($= 8,000$ units/ 100 workers) to 120 units per worker ($= 24,000$ units/200 workers).

Increasing returns boost labor productivity and reduce per-unit production costs. Because these cost reductions result from increased output levels, increasing returns are an example of *economies of scale,* which occur when a firm's per-unit production cost declines as its output volume increases.

Both emerging firms and established firms were able to exploit several different sources of increasing returns and economies of scale during the so-called tech boom:

- *More specialized inputs* Firms were able to use more specialized and thus more productive capital and workers as they expanded their operations. A growing e-commerce business located in Silicon Valley, for example, could purchase highly specialized inventory management systems and hire specialized personnel such as accountants, marketing managers, and system maintenance experts.

- *Spreading of development costs* Firms were able to spread high product development costs over greater output. For example, suppose that a new software product cost $100,000 to

information technology New and more efficient methods of delivering and receiving information through the use of computers, wi-fi networks, wireless phones, and the Internet.

start-up firm A new *firm* focused on creating and introducing a particular new product or employing a specific new production or distribution method.

increasing returns An increase in a *firm's* output by a larger percentage than the percentage increase in its inputs.

develop but only $2 per unit to manufacture and sell. If the firm sold 1,000 units of the software, its per-unit cost was $102.00 [= ($100,000 + $2,000)/1,000], but if it sold 500,000 units, that cost dropped to only $2.20 [= ($100,000 + $1 million)/500,000].

- *Simultaneous consumption* Many technology products were able to satisfy large numbers of customers at the same time. Unlike a gallon of gas that needs to be produced for each buyer, a software program needs to be produced only once. It can then be made available at very low expense to thousands or even millions of buyers. The same was true of books delivered to electronic reading devices, movies distributed through streaming services, and information disseminated through the Internet.

- *Network effects* The domestic and global expansion of the Internet, wireless networks, and social media produced enormous network effects that magnified the value of output well beyond the cost of inputs. **Network effects** occur when a product's value to each user increases as more users use it. To see the power of network effects, imagine that you are the only one in the world with an Instagram account. That would be pretty pointless as the whole point is to share content and connect with people. But if there were a few thousand people also using Instagram, you would suddenly be able to derive significant benefits from your Instagram account. And if the number of users continued to increase, your benefit would continue to grow as there would be even more people to interact with. The larger the network of people using the service, the more beneficial it becomes to each individual user. Since the Internet is the largest network ever created, it's not surprising that it has generated the largest network effects ever seen and, along with them, extremely large economies of scale. You only have to build Instagram once. As the network grows, the cost per user falls, fast.

- *Learning by doing* Finally, the start-ups that produced new products or pioneered new ways of doing business were often able to experience increasing returns through **learning by doing.** Tasks that initially may have taken firms hours may take them only minutes once the methods are perfected. The more they produce, the more efficient they become.

> **network effects** Increases in the value of a product to each user, including existing users, as the total number of users rises.

> **learning by doing** Achieving greater *productivity* and lower *average total cost* through gains in knowledge and skill that accompany repetition of a task; a source of *economies of scale.*

Whatever the particular source of increasing returns, the result was higher productivity, which tended to reduce the per-unit cost of producing and delivering technology products during the 1995 to 2010 period.

Global Competition As with today's economy, the economy between 1995 and 2010 was characterized not only by information technology and increasing returns but also by heightened global competition. The market liberalization in China and the collapse of the socialist economies in the early 1990s led to a reawakening of capitalism throughout the world. New information technologies "shrank the globe" and made it imperative for all firms to lower their costs and innovate in order to remain competitive. Free-trade zones such as NAFTA and the European Union (EU), along with trade liberalization through the World Trade Organization (WTO), increased international competition by removing trade barriers. The larger geographic markets, in turn, enabled firms to expand beyond their national borders. Countries had to compete if they wanted to grow. (The nearby Global Perspective lists the 10 highest-ranked countries in terms of international economic competitiveness.)

Implications for Economic Growth

Other things equal, stronger productivity growth and heightened global competition allowed the economy to achieve a higher rate of economic growth during the 1995 to 2010 period. A glance back at Figure 28.2 will help make this point. Suppose that the shift of the production possibilities curve from *AB* to *CD* reflects annual changes in potential output before the increase in growth rates observed during the 1995 to 2010 period. Then the higher growth rates of that period would be depicted by a *larger* outward shift of the economy's production possibilities from *AB* to a curve beyond *CD*. When coupled with economic efficiency and increased total spending, the economy's real GDP was able to rise by even more than what is shown.

The Recent Productivity Slowdown

It is not clear whether the dramatic slowdown in productivity growth that took place after the Great Recession is permanent or transitory. Some economists have argued that the high

GLOBAL PERSPECTIVE 28.2

WORLD COMPETITIVENESS RANKINGS

The World Competitiveness Ranking, published annually by the International Institute for Management Development in Switzerland, measures each country's potential for economic growth. The index uses various factors—such as innovativeness, the capability to transfer technology among sectors, the efficiency of the financial system, rates of investment, and the degree of economic integration with the rest of the world—to measure a country's ability to achieve economic growth over time.

Country	Global Competitiveness Ranking, 2021
Switzerland	1
Sweden	2
Denmark	3
Netherlands	4
Singapore	5
Norway	6
Hong Kong	7
Taiwan	8
United Arab Emirates	9
United States	10

Source: IMD World Competitiveness Yearbook 2021, International Institute for Management Development.

productivity growth rates of 1995–2010 were a one-time anomaly due to the information technology revolution. But even if information technology caused an unusual burst of growth for 15 years, it is still surprising that post-2010 productivity growth rates have been so very low, much lower in fact than the rates observed before the information technology revolution.

Several possible explanations have been put forward to explain why productivity growth rates have fallen so low. One possible culprit is the high debt levels that accumulated before the Great Recession. Under this hypothesis, individuals and firms were too busy paying down debts after the Financial Crisis of 2007–2009 to make a lot of productive investments. At the same time, entrepreneurs who might have been able to improve productivity were perhaps unable to obtain loans because banks became reluctant to lend after having made so many bad loans prior to the Great Recession.

Overcapacity may be another explanation for the productivity slowdown. During the boom that preceded the Great Recession, worldwide productive capacity increased massively as many new factories were built. But the additional capacity may have been excessive relative to consumer demand. If so, firms would have been reluctant to install newer, more productive equipment or build newer, more productive factories because they already had more than enough production capacity. Under this hypothesis, productivity stagnated because producers continued to rely on aging machinery and equipment.

Another possible explanation points to the fact that many recent products—especially Internet apps—do not generate much of a measurable effect on GDP. Consider Facebook, YouTube, and Instagram. They are for the most part totally free to consumers. So measured output will hardly increase even if billions of people are using them. That being said, measured output isn't everything. The new products are undoubtedly generating a huge amount of consumer satisfaction; we just can't see those benefits in the GDP and productivity statistics.

Finally, it is possible that technological progress itself may have stalled. Under this hypothesis, productivity growth will remain slow until invention and innovation speed up again. Time will tell.

- Over long time periods, labor productivity growth determines an economy's growth of real wages and its standard of living.

- U.S. labor productivity grew at an average annual rate of 1.5 percent from 1973 to 1995, 2.8 percent from 1995 to 2010, and 1.2 percent from 2010 to 2021.

- The high labor productivity growth rate observed between 1995 and 2010 is attributed to the information technology revolution, start-ups, increasing returns, and heightened global competition.

- Possible explanations for the low productivity growth rate after 2010 include high debt levels, overcapacity, the rise of "free" Internet products, and a slowdown in technological progress.

QUICK REVIEW

28.4

Is Growth Desirable and Sustainable?

>> **LO28.6** Discuss whether economic growth is desirable and sustainable.

Economists usually take for granted that economic growth is desirable and sustainable. But not everyone agrees.

The Antigrowth View

Critics of growth say industrialization and growth result in pollution, climate change, species extinction, and other environmental problems. These adverse negative externalities occur because inputs in the production process reenter the environment as some form of waste. The more rapid our growth and the higher our standard of living, the more waste the environment must absorb—or attempt to absorb. In an already wealthy society, further growth usually means satisfying increasingly trivial wants at the cost of mounting threats to the ecological system.

Critics of growth also argue that there is little compelling evidence that economic growth has solved social problems such as poverty, homelessness, and discrimination. Consider poverty: In the antigrowth view, U.S. poverty is a problem of distribution, not production. Solving the problem requires a firm commitment to redistribute wealth and income, not further increases in output.

Antigrowth sentiment also says that while growth may permit us to "make a better living," it does not give us "the good life." We may be producing more and enjoying less, focused too much on materialism and not enough on families, friendship, and community. Growth means zero work-life balance, employee burnout, and worker alienation. In addition, the changing technology at the core of growth poses new anxieties and new sources of insecurity for workers. Both high-level and low-level workers face the prospect of having their hard-earned skills and experience rendered obsolete by onrushing technology. High-growth economies are high-stress economies, which may impair our physical and mental health.

Finally, critics of high rates of growth doubt that they are sustainable. The earth has finite amounts of natural resources, and they are being consumed at alarming rates. Higher rates of economic growth simply speed up the degradation and depletion of the earth's resources. In this view, slower, environmentally sustainable economic growth is preferable to faster growth.

In Defense of Economic Growth

Those who support economic growth believe that it is the path to the greater material abundance and higher living standards desired by the vast majority of people. Growth also enables society to improve the nation's infrastructure, enhance the care of the sick and elderly, provide greater access for the disabled, and provide more police and fire protection.

Economic growth may also be the only realistic way to reduce poverty, because there is only limited political support for greater redistribution of income. The proponents of growth argue that the best way to improve the economic position of the poor is to increase household incomes through higher productivity and faster economic growth. Also, a no-growth policy among industrial nations might severely limit growth in poor nations. Foreign investment and development assistance in those nations would fall, keeping the world's poor in poverty longer.

Economic growth has not made labor more unpleasant or hazardous, as critics suggest. In fact, growth advocates say, new machinery is usually less taxing and less dangerous than the machinery it replaces. Air-conditioned workplaces are more pleasant than steamy workshops. Furthermore, there is no guarantee that an end to economic growth will reduce materialism or worker alienation. The loudest protests against materialism are heard in those nations that now enjoy the highest levels of material abundance! The high standard of living that growth provides has increased our leisure and given us more time for reflection and self-fulfillment.

Economic growth need not threaten the environment, say growth proponents. Pollution is not so much a by-product of growth as it is a "problem of the commons." Much of the environment—streams, lakes, oceans, the air—is treated as common property, with insufficient or no restrictions on its use. The commons have become our dumping grounds; we have overused and debased them. Environmental pollution is a case of negative externalities, and correcting this problem involves regulatory legislation, pollution taxes, or market-based

Ladies First

The Substantial Rise in the Number of Women in the Paid Workforce in the United States Has Been One of the Major Labor Market Trends of the Past Six Decades.

In 1960, about 40 percent of American women worked full-time or part-time in paid jobs. Today, that number is about 60 percent. What's more, almost half of the U.S. workforce is now female. Let's examine some of the causes and consequences of this historically unprecedented increase in labor force participation.

American women have greatly increased their productivity in the workplace by becoming better educated and professionally trained. Women have earned the majority of bachelor's degrees since 1982, the majority of master's degrees since 1987, and the majority of doctoral degrees since 2008.

This decades-long dominance in educational attainment means that as of 2020, women constituted 53 percent of American workers with a bachelor's degree or higher. Since 1982, women have cumulatively earned 13 million more bachelor's, master's, and doctoral degrees than men. That translates to 131 female degrees for every 100 male degrees.

That superiority in educational attainment appears set to continue for at least another couple of generations. In 2018, women earned 141 bachelor's, master's, and doctoral degrees for every 100 earned by men. And, looking forward, the U.S. Department of Education projects that in 2027 women will earn 151 bachelor's, master's, or doctoral degrees for every 100 earned by men. This implies that the large majority of highly educated workers will be women for at least the next few decades.

Rising productivity has also increased women's wage rates. Those higher wages have, in turn, raised the opportunity costs—the forgone wage earnings—of staying at home. Women have therefore substituted employment in the labor market for what were once traditional home activities. This substitution has been particularly pronounced among married women. (Single women have always had substantial labor-force participation rates.)

Furthermore, changing lifestyles and the widespread availability of birth control have freed up time for greater labor-force participation by women. Women not only have fewer children, but those children are spaced closer together in age. Thus women who leave their jobs during their children's early years return to the labor force sooner.

Greater access to jobs by women has also raised their labor-force participation. Service industries—teaching, nursing, and office work, for

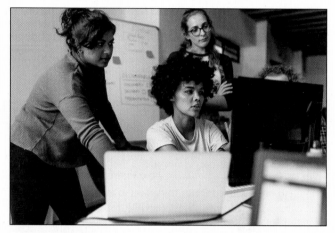

Jacob Lund/Shutterstock

instance—that traditionally have employed many women have expanded rapidly in the past several decades. Also, the population in general has shifted from farms and rural regions to urban areas, where jobs for women are more abundant and more geographically accessible. Additionally, discrimination and other occupational barriers to professions have greatly eroded, resulting in many more women becoming business managers, lawyers, professors, physicians, and entrepreneurs.

Concerns about discrimination persist. While there are relatively few examples of male and female colleagues with equal experience, tenure, and training being paid differently for doing the same job, women continue to enter lower-paid professions like education and home health care in larger numbers than men. They also tend to opt for more part-time as opposed to full-time work, and to fall behind equally educated male peers because women take more and longer career breaks to engage in child rearing.

When it comes to earnings, these factors offset the educational advantage held by women. Across all jobs and all earnings, women take home about 78 cents for every dollar earned by men. This has prompted calls for laws mandating paid maternity leave and legal guarantees that women who take time off from their careers to raise children not be demoted when they return to paid employment.

incentives. In addition, economic growth has allowed economies to preserve wilderness, create national parks and monuments, and clean up hazardous waste, while still enabling rising household incomes.

Is growth sustainable? Yes, say the proponents of growth. If we were depleting natural resources faster than we discover them, we would see the prices of those resources rise. That has not been the case for most natural resources; in fact, the prices of most of them have declined. And if one natural resource becomes too expensive, another resource will be substituted for it.

Moreover, say growth advocates, economic growth has to do with the expansion and application of human knowledge and information, not extractable natural resources. In this view, economic growth is limited only by human imagination.

QUICK REVIEW
28.5

▶ Critics of growth argue that it degrades the environment, increases human stress, and exhausts the earth's finite supply of natural resources.

▶ Defenders of growth say that it is the primary path to higher living standards, that it need not debase the environment, and that there are no indications that we are running out of resources.

▶ Defenders of growth argue that growth is sustainable because it is based on the expansion and application of human knowledge, which is limited only by human imagination.

Summary

LO28.1 Explain two ways to measure economic growth.

A nation's economic growth is measured either as an increase in real GDP over time or as an increase in real GDP per capita over time. Real GDP in the United States has grown at an average annual rate of about 3.0 percent since 1950; real GDP per capita has grown at roughly 1.9 percent annually over that same period.

LO28.2 Describe the institutional structures necessary for modern economic growth.

Sustained increases in real GDP per capita did not happen until the past two or so centuries, when England and then other countries began to experience modern economic growth, which is characterized by institutional structures that encourage savings, investment, and the development of new technologies. Institutional structures that promote growth include strong property rights, patents, efficient financial institutions, education, and a competitive market system.

Because technological leader countries have enjoyed up to two and a half centuries of modern economic growth, they now have much high standards of living compared with technological follower countries that have only recently begun to experience modern economic growth.

To continue raising living standards, rich leader countries must invent and apply new technologies; that limits their per-capita growth rates to about 2 percent per year. By contrast, poor follower countries can experience much faster catch-up growth by adopting, rather than reinventing, the institutions and cutting-edge technologies already developed by technological leader countries.

LO28.3 Identify the supply, demand, and efficiency forces that lead to economic growth.

The determinants of economic growth include four supply factors (changes in the quantity and quality of natural resources, changes in the quantity and quality of human resources, changes in the stock of capital goods, and improvements in technology), one demand factor (changes in total spending), and one efficiency factor (changes in how well an economy achieves allocative and productive efficiency).

The growth of a nation's capacity to produce output can be illustrated graphically by an outward shift of its production possibilities curve.

LO28.4 Describe the specific factors accounting for U.S. economic growth.

Growth accounting attributes increases in real GDP either to increases in the amount of labor being employed or to increases in the productivity of the labor being employed.

U.S. real GDP growth has been driven by increases in the productivity of labor. Those increases in labor productivity can be attributed to technological progress, increases in the quantity of capital per worker, improvements in the education and training of workers, the exploitation of economies of scale, and improvements in the allocation of labor across different industries.

LO28.5 Explain how U.S. productivity growth has fluctuated since 1973.

Over long time periods, the growth of labor productivity underlies an economy's growth of real wages and its standard of living. U.S. productivity rose by 1.5 percent annually between 1973 and 1995, 2.8 percent annually between 1995 and 2010, and just 1.2 percent annually from 2010 to 2021.

The 1995 to 2010 increase in the average rate of productivity growth was based on (a) rapid technological change in the form of the microchip and information technology, (b) new firms, increasing returns, and lower per-unit costs, and (c) heightened global competition that holds down prices.

The main sources of increasing returns are (a) the use of more specialized inputs as firms grow, (b) the spreading of development costs, (c) simultaneous consumption by consumers, (d) network effects, and (e) learning by doing. Increasing returns mean higher productivity and lower per-unit production costs.

Possible explanations for the slow productivity growth rate after the Great Recession of 2007–2009 include high debt levels, overcapacity, the rise of "free" Internet products, and a slowdown in technological innovation.

LO28.6 Discuss whether economic growth is desirable and sustainable.

Critics of rapid growth say that it degrades the environment, increases human stress, and depletes the earth's finite supply of natural resources. Defenders of rapid growth say that it is the primary path to the high and rising material standard of living that most people desire, that it need not debase the environment, and that there are no indications that we are running out of resources. Defenders argue that there are no natural limits to sustainable, environmentally friendly growth because growth is based on the expansion and application of human knowledge, which is limited only by human imagination.

Terms and Concepts

economic growth	supply factors (in growth)	human capital
real GDP per capita	demand factor (in growth)	economies of scale
rule of 70	efficiency factor (in growth)	information technology
modern economic growth	labor productivity	start-up firms
leader countries	labor-force participation rate	increasing returns
follower countries	growth accounting	network effects
catch-up growth	infrastructure	learning by doing

Discussion Questions

1. How is economic growth measured? Why is economic growth important? Why could the difference between a 2.5 percent and a 3 percent annual growth rate be of great significance over several decades? **LO28.1**

2. When and where did modern economic growth first happen? What are the major institutional factors that form the foundation for modern economic growth? What do they have in common? **LO28.2**

3. Why are some countries today much poorer than other countries? Are today's poor countries destined to always be poorer than today's rich countries? If so, explain why. If not, explain how today's poor countries can catch up to or even pass today's rich countries. **LO28.2**

4. What are the four supply factors of economic growth? What is the demand factor? What is the efficiency factor? Illustrate these factors in terms of the production possibilities curve. **LO28.3**

5. Suppose that Alpha and Omega have identically sized working-age populations but that total annual hours of work are much greater in Alpha than in Omega. Provide two possible reasons for this difference. **LO28.3**

6. What is growth accounting? To what extent have increases in U.S. real GDP resulted from more labor inputs? From greater labor productivity? Rearrange the following contributors to the growth of productivity in order of their quantitative importance: economies of scale, quantity of capital per worker, improved

resource allocation, education and training, and technological advance. **LO28.4**

7. True or False. If false, explain why: **LO28.4**
   a. Technological advance, which to date has played a relatively small role in U.S. economic growth, is destined to play a more important role in the future.
   b. Many public capital goods are complementary to private capital goods.
   c. Immigration has slowed economic growth in the United States.

8. Explain why there is such a close relationship between changes in a nation's rate of productivity growth and changes in its average real hourly wage. **LO28.5**

9. Relate each of the following to the 1995–2010 increase in the trend rate of productivity growth: **LO28.5**
   a. information technology
   b. increasing returns
   c. network effects
   d. global competition

10. What, if any, are the benefits and costs of economic growth, particularly as measured by real GDP per capita? **LO28.6**

11. **LAST WORD** Has female labor force participation increased or decreased in recent decades? What is the distribution of higher education degrees like across genders? Aside from discrimination, what are the reasons that women earn less than men on average, despite having higher levels of educational attainment?

Review Questions

1. If real GDP grows at 7 percent per year, then real GDP will double in approximately _____ years. **LO28.1**
   a. 70
   b. 14
   c. 10
   d. 7

2. In 1820, living standards in various places around the globe were _____ they are today. **LO28.2**
   a. more widely varying than
   b. just as widely varying as
   c. less widely varying than

3. True or False: Countries that currently have a low real GDP per capita are destined to always have lower living standards

than countries that currently have a high real GDP per capita. **LO28.2**

4. Identify each of the following situations as something that either promotes growth or inhibits growth. **LO28.2**
   a. Increasing corruption allows government officials to steal people's homes.
   b. A nation introduces patent laws for the first time.
   c. A court order shuts down all banks permanently.
   d. A poor country extends free public schooling from 8 years to 12 years.
   e. A nation adopts a free-trade policy.
   f. A formerly communist country adopts free markets.

5. Real GDP equals _____ times _____. **LO28.4**
   a. average hours of work; quantity of capital
   b. average hours of work; allocative efficiency
   c. labor input; labor productivity
   d. natural resources; improvements in technology

6. Suppose that just by doubling the amount of output that it produces each year, a firm's per-unit production costs fall by 30 percent. This result is an example of: **LO28.4**
   a. economies of scale.
   b. improved resource allocation.
   c. technological advance.
   d. the demand factor.

7. True or False: Computers and increased global competition have inhibited economic growth in recent decades. **LO28.5**

8. Identify the following arguments about economic growth as either antigrowth or pro-growth. **LO28.6**
   a. Growth means worker burnout and frantic schedules.
   b. Rising incomes allow people to buy more education, medical care, and recreation.
   c. Earth has only finite amounts of natural resources.
   d. Even the richest countries still have poverty, homelessness, and discrimination.
   e. Richer countries spend more money protecting the environment.
   f. Natural resource prices have fallen rather than increased over time.

Problems

1. Suppose an economy's real GDP is $30,000 in year 1 and $31,200 in year 2. What is the growth rate of its real GDP? Assume that the population is 100 in year 1 and 102 in year 2. What is the growth rate of real GDP per capita? **LO28.1**

2. What annual growth rate is needed for a country to double its output in 7 years? In 35 years? In 70 years? In 140 years? **LO28.1**

3. Assume that a leader country has real GDP per capita of $40,000, whereas a follower country has real GDP per capita of $20,000. Next suppose that the growth of real GDP per capita falls to zero percent in the leader country and rises to 7 percent in the follower country. If these rates continue for long periods of time, how many years will it take for the follower country to catch up to the living standard of the leader country? **LO28.2**

4. Refer to Figure 28.2 and assume that the values for points a, b, and c are $10 billion, $20 billion, and $18 billion, respectively. If the economy moves from point a to point b over a 10-year period, what must have been its annual rate of economic growth? If, instead, the economy was at point c at the end of the 10-year period, by what percentage did it fall short of its production capacity? **LO28.3**

5. Suppose that work hours in New Zombie are 200 in year 1, and productivity is $8 per hour worked. What is New Zombie's real GDP? If work hours increase to 210 in year 2 and productivity rises to $10 per hour, what is New Zombie's rate of economic growth? **LO28.4**

6. The per-unit cost of an item is its average total cost (= total cost/ quantity). Suppose that a new smartphone app costs $100,000 to develop and only $0.50 per unit to deliver to each smartphone customer. What will be the per-unit cost of the app if it sells 100 units? 1,000 units? 1 million units? **LO28.5**

Business Cycles, Unemployment, and Inflation

>> **LEARNING OBJECTIVES**

LO29.1 Describe the phases of the business cycle.

LO29.2 Measure unemployment and explain the different types of unemployment.

LO29.3 Measure inflation and distinguish between cost-push inflation and demand-pull inflation.

LO29.4 Explain how unanticipated inflation can redistribute real income.

LO29.5 Describe how inflation may affect the economy's level of real output.

The United States has experienced remarkable economic growth over time. But this growth has not been smooth, steady, and predictable from year to year. At various times the United States has experienced recessions, high unemployment, and high inflation. For example, U.S. unemployment rose by 17 million workers and the unemployment rate increased from 3.5 percent to 14.8 percent at the start of the COVID-19 pandemic in 2020. Other nations have also suffered from high unemployment or substantial inflation in recent years. For example, the Greek unemployment rate exceeded 17 percent in 2019 and Venezuela's inflation rate soared to 1.4 *million* percent in 2018 before slowing to a relatively small 2,000 percent in 2022.

In this chapter, we examine the concepts, terminology, and facts relating to macroeconomic instability. Specifically, we discuss the business cycle, unemployment, and inflation.

The Business Cycle

In the United States, real GDP grows by about 3 percent per year, *on average*. So the long-run trend is up, as illustrated by the upsloping line labeled "Growth Trend" in Figure 29.1. There is, however, a lot of variation around the average growth trend. That's because the U.S. economy demonstrates a pattern of alternating rises and declines in the rate of economic activity.

Economists refer to this cyclical pattern as the **business cycle.** Individual cycles (one "up" followed by one "down") vary substantially in duration and intensity. So while each cycle has similar stages, no two are identical.

>> **LO29.1** Describe the phases of the business cycle.

business cycle Recurring increases and decreases in the level of economic activity over periods of years; consists of peak, recession, trough, and expansion phases.

FIGURE 29.1
The business cycle.

Economists distinguish four phases of the business cycle; the duration and strength of each phase may vary.

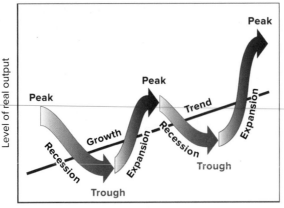

Phases of the Business Cycle

Figure 29.1 shows the four phases of a generalized business cycle:

- At a **peak,** business activity has reached a temporary maximum. Here the economy is near or at full employment, and the level of real output is at or very close to the economy's capacity. The price level is likely to rise during this phase.

- A **recession** is a period of decline in total output, income, and employment that lasts at least six months. Recessions generate a widespread contraction of business activity in many sectors of the economy. Along with a decline in real GDP, unemployment increases significantly. Table 29.1 documents the duration and intensity of the 11 recessions that the United States experienced between 1950 and 2020.

- In the **trough** of the recession or depression, output and employment "bottom out" at their lowest levels. The trough phase may be either short-lived or quite long.

- A recession is usually followed by a recovery and **expansion,** a period in which real GDP, income, and employment rise. At some point, the economy again approaches full employment. If spending then expands faster than production capacity, the prices of nearly all goods and services will rise, thereby generating a bout of inflation.

peak The point in a *business cycle* at which business activity has reached a temporary maximum; the point at which an *expansion* ends and a *recession* begins. At the peak, the economy is near or at *full employment* and the level of real output is at or very close to the economy's capacity.

recession A period of declining *real GDP*, accompanied by lower *real income* and higher *unemployment*.

Although all business cycles pass through the same phases, they vary greatly in duration and intensity. Many economists prefer to talk of business fluctuations rather than business cycles because the word cycles implies regularity while the term fluctuations does not.

The Great Depression of the 1930s resulted in a 27 percent decline in U.S. real GDP over a 3-year period and seriously impaired business activity for a decade. By comparison, the more recent recessions detailed in Table 29.1 were less severe in both intensity and duration.

The Business Cycle Dating Committee of the National Bureau of Economic Research (NBER) declares the start and end of recessions in the United States. Citing evidence of declining real output and falling employment, the NBER officially declared that the pandemic recession of 2020—the shortest and sharpest on record—lasted from February to April of 2020, when the COVID-19 lockdowns shuttered businesses, causing output and employment to plummet.

Recessions occur in other countries, too. Nearly all industrial nations and many developing nations suffer recessions in any given decade. In addition, it should be pointed out that the worldwide COVID-19 pandemic was highly unusual in that it put all of the world's economies into recession simultaneously. Normally, recessions are only loosely correlated across countries, with many countries showing growth even as some others enter or exit recessions.

Causation: A First Glance

A key question in macroeconomics is why the economy experiences business cycle fluctuations rather than slow, smooth growth. In terms of Figure 29.1, why does output move up and down rather than just staying on the smooth trend line?

TABLE 29.1
U.S. Recessions between 1950 and 2020

Period	Duration, Months	Depth (Decline in Real Output)
1953–54	10	−2.6%
1957–58	8	−3.7
1960–61	10	−1.1
1969–70	11	−0.2
1973–75	16	−3.2
1980	6	−2.2
1981–82	16	−2.9
1990–91	8	−1.4
2001	8	−0.4
2007–09	18	−4.3
2020	2	−10.1

Source: National Bureau of Economic Research (NBER).

The most prominent theory is that business cycle fluctuations are the result of sticky prices interacting with economic shocks. As discussed in Chapter 26, economic shocks are events that unexpectedly shift demand or supply. If prices were fully flexible, markets could always adjust very quickly to unexpected shifts in demand or supply because market prices would rapidly adjust to equalize the quantities demanded and quantities supplied of every product in the economy. But the prices of many goods and services are, in fact, sticky (barely able to adjust) or stuck (completely unable to adjust) in the weeks and months after a shock occurs. As a result, the economy is forced to respond to shocks primarily through changes in output and employment rather than through changes in prices.

With these factors in mind, economists cite several sources for the demand and supply shocks that cause most business cycles.

- *Political events* Unexpected political events, such as peace treaties, new wars, or terrorist attacks, can create economic opportunities or strains. In adjusting to these shocks, the economy may experience upswings or downswings.

- *Financial instability* Unexpected financial bubbles (rapid asset price increases) or bursts (abrupt asset price decreases) can spill over to the general economy. They may expand or contract lending, and they may boost or erode the confidence of consumers and businesses. Booms and busts in the rest of the economy may follow.

- *Irregular innovation* Significant new products or production methods, such as those associated with railroads, automobiles, computers, and the Internet, can rapidly spread through the economy, sparking sizable increases in investment, consumption, output, and employment. After the economy has largely absorbed the new innovation, the economy may for a time slow down or even decline. Because such innovations occur irregularly and unexpectedly, they may contribute to the variability of economic activity.

- *Productivity changes* When productivity—output per unit of input—unexpectedly increases, the economy booms; when productivity unexpectedly decreases, the economy recedes. These changes in productivity can result from unexpected changes in resource availability (of, say, oil or agricultural commodities) or from unexpected changes in the general rate of technological advance.

- *Monetary factors* Some economists see business cycles as purely monetary phenomena. When a nation's central bank shocks the economy by creating more money than people were expecting, an inflationary boom in output occurs. By contrast, printing less money than people were expecting triggers an output decline and, eventually, a decrease in the price level.

The COVID-19 recession of 2020 was very unusual in that it was caused by a public health crisis rather than by a shock to one of the above factors. But do note that the onset of the pandemic was itself a shock since both the U.S. economy and much of the world economy had been growing handsomely during the prior few years and were expected to continue growing robustly before the pandemic struck.

Whatever the source of economic shocks, most economists agree that unexpected changes in the level of total spending cause the majority of cyclical fluctuations. If total spending unexpectedly sinks and firms cannot lower prices, firms sell fewer units of output (because with prices fixed, lower spending implies fewer items purchased). Slower sales cause firms to cut back on production. As they do, GDP falls. And because fewer workers are needed to produce less output, employment also falls. The economy contracts and enters a recession.

By contrast, if the level of spending unexpectedly rises, then output, employment, and incomes rise. With prices sticky, the increased spending means that consumers buy more goods and services (because, with prices fixed, more spending means more items purchased). Firms respond by increasing output, which increases GDP. And because firms need to hire more workers to produce the larger volume of output, employment also increases. The economy booms and enjoys an expansion. Eventually, as time passes and prices become more flexible, prices also rise due to the increased spending.

Cyclical Impact: Durables and Nondurables

Although the business cycle is felt throughout the economy, it affects different sectors in different ways and to different degrees.

Firms and industries producing *capital goods* (for example, housing, communications satellites, and heavy equipment) and *consumer durables* (for example, automobiles, personal computers, and refrigerators) are affected most by the business cycle. Within limits, firms can postpone the purchase

trough The point in a *business cycle* at which business activity has reached a temporary minimum; the point at which a *recession* ends and an *expansion* (recovery) begins. At the trough, the economy experiences substantial *unemployment* and *real GDP* is less than *potential output*.

expansion The phase of the *business cycle* in which *real GDP, income,* and employment rise.

of capital goods. When a recession strikes, firms patch up their old equipment and make do rather than replace the old equipment. As a result, investment in capital goods declines sharply. The pattern is much the same for consumer durables such as cars and refrigerators. When recession occurs and households must trim their budgets, they often defer their purchases of these goods. Families repair their old cars and appliances rather than buy new ones, and the firms producing these products suffer. (However, producers of capital goods and consumer durables also benefit most from expansions.)

In contrast, *service* industries and industries that produce *nondurable consumer goods* are somewhat insulated from the recession's most severe effects. People find it difficult to cut back on needed medical and legal services, for example. And a recession actually helps some service firms, such as pawnbrokers and law firms that specialize in bankruptcy. Nor are the purchases of many nondurable goods, such as food and clothing, easy to postpone. As a result, the quantity and quality of the nondurable goods that are purchased will decline, but not by as much as the quantity and quality of the capital goods and consumer durables that are purchased.

QUICK REVIEW
29.1

▶ The typical business cycle goes through four phases: peak, recession, trough, and expansion.

▶ Fluctuations in output and employment are caused by economic shocks combined with sticky prices.

▶ Sources of shocks include irregular innovation, productivity changes, monetary factors, political

events, financial instability, and major public health emergencies (like the COVID-19 pandemic).

▶ During a recession, industries that produce capital goods and consumer durables normally suffer greater output and employment declines than industries that produce services or nondurable consumer goods.

Unemployment

>> **LO29.2** Measure unemployment and explain the different types of unemployment.

Two problems that arise over the course of the business cycle are unemployment and inflation. Let's look at unemployment first.

Measurement of Unemployment

The U.S. Bureau of Labor Statistics (BLS) conducts a nationwide random survey of some 60,000 households each month to determine who is employed and who is not. It asks which members of the household are working, unemployed and looking for work, not looking for work, and so on. From the answers, it determines the nation's unemployment rate for the month.

Figure 29.2 explains the mathematics.

To construct Figure 29.2, the BLS divides the total U.S. population into four groups:

FIGURE 29.2
The U.S. labor force, employment and unemployment, 2021.

The labor force consists of persons 16 years of age or older who are not in institutions and who are (1) employed or (2) unemployed but seeking employment.

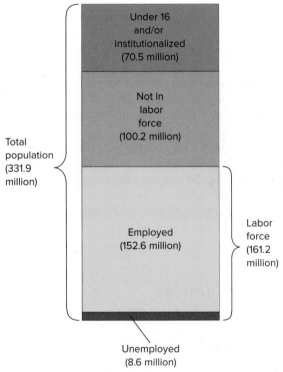

Total population (331.9 million)

Under 16 and/or institutionalized (70.5 million)

Not in labor force (100.2 million)

Employed (152.6 million)

Labor force (161.2 million)

Unemployed (8.6 million)

Source: U.S. Bureau of Labor Statistics.

- ***Under 16 and/or institutionalized*** is composed of people under 16 years of age, active duty military personnel, and individuals who are living in psychological hospitals, correctional institutions, or skilled nursing facilities. These people are assumed to be unemployable in the private sector either because of child labor laws, military obligations, or the circumstances that accompany institutionalization.

- ***Not in labor force*** is composed of noninstitutionalized people 16 years of age or older who are neither employed nor seeking work. They include stay-at-home parents, full-time students, and retirees.

- *Employed* consists of noninstitutionalized people age 16 and older who have jobs. These are people who both want to work *and* have a job.

- *Unemployed* consists of every noninstitutionalized person age 16 or older who is not employed but who wants to work and is actively seeking employment. (Please note that to be classified as unemployed, a person has to not only want a job but also be *actively seeking employment*. A person who claims to want a job but who isn't bothering to look for work is classified as "not in labor force.")

The **labor force** consists of the latter two groups—the employed plus the unemployed. The labor force includes anyone who has a job plus anyone lacking a job who is actively seeking employment.

The **unemployment rate** is the percentage of the labor force that is unemployed:

$$\text{Unemployment rate} = \frac{\text{unemployed}}{\text{labor force}} \times 100$$

The statistics underlying the rounded numbers in Figure 29.2 show that in 2021 the unemployment rate averaged

$$\frac{8,600,000}{161,200,000} \times 100 = 5.3\%$$

Despite the use of scientific sampling and interviewing techniques, the data collected by the monthly BLS surveys are subject to the following criticisms:

- *Part-time employment* The BLS lists all part-time workers as fully employed. In 2021 about 28 million people worked part-time as a result of personal choice. But another 5 million part-time workers either (1) wanted to work full-time and could not find a full-time job or (2) worked fewer part-time hours than desired. By counting them as fully employed, critics say, the BLS understates the unemployment rate.

- *Discouraged workers* You must be actively seeking work to be counted as unemployed. But many jobless people who actively search for employment become discouraged after a period of unsuccessful efforts. They stop actively searching for employment and get reclassified as "not in the labor force." According to critics, that reclassification understates the unemployment problem. The discouraged workers still want jobs, but are missing entirely in the official unemployment statistics. The number of such **discouraged workers** was roughly 463,000 in 2021, down from 657,000 in 2020.

Types of Unemployment

There are three types of unemployment: frictional, structural, and cyclical.

Frictional Unemployment At any given time some workers are "between jobs." Some of them are moving voluntarily from one job to another. Others have been fired and are seeking reemployment. Still others have been laid off because they work seasonal jobs and the season just changed. In addition to those between jobs, there are always many young workers searching for their first job.

As these unemployed people find jobs or are called back from temporary layoffs, other job seekers and laid-off workers replace them in the "unemployment pool." While the pool itself persists because newly unemployed workers are always flowing into it, most workers do not stay in the unemployment pool for very long. Indeed, when the economy is strong, most unemployed workers find new jobs within a couple of months. We should be careful not to confuse the permanence of the pool itself with the false idea that the pool's membership is permanent, too. That being said, there are workers who do remain unemployed and in the unemployment pool for many months or even several years.

Economists use the term **frictional unemployment,** or search unemployment, for workers who are unemployed as they actively search for a job. The word "frictional" reflects the fact that the labor market does not operate perfectly and instantaneously (without friction) in matching workers and jobs.

Frictional unemployment is inevitable and, at least in part, desirable. Many workers who are voluntarily between jobs are moving from low-paying, low-productivity jobs to higher-paying, higher-productivity positions. Their new jobs mean greater income for the workers, a better allocation of labor resources, and a larger real GDP for the economy.

Structural Unemployment Frictional unemployment blurs into **structural unemployment.** Changes over time in consumer demand and in technology alter the "structure" of the total demand for labor, both occupationally and geographically.

labor force Persons 16 years of age and older who are not in institutions and who are employed or are unemployed and seeking work.

unemployment rate The percentage of the *labor force* unemployed at any time.

discouraged workers Employees who have left the *labor force* because they have not been able to find employment.

frictional unemployment A type of unemployment caused by workers voluntarily changing jobs and by temporary layoffs; unemployed workers between jobs.

structural unemployment *Unemployment* of workers whose skills are not demanded by employers, who lack sufficient skill to obtain employment, or who cannot easily move to locations where jobs are available.

Occupationally, the demand for certain skills (for example, sewing clothes or working on farms) may decline or even vanish. The demand for other skills (for example, designing software or maintaining computer networks) will intensify. Structural unemployment occurs because the composition of the labor force does not respond immediately or completely to the new structure of job opportunities. Workers whose skills and experience have become obsolete or unneeded thus find that they have no marketable talents. They are structurally unemployed until they develop skills that employers want.

Geographically, the demand for labor also changes over time. An example is the migration of industry and thus of employment opportunities from the Snowbelt to the Sunbelt over the past few decades. Another example is the *offshoring* of jobs that occurs when the demand for a particular type of labor shifts from domestic firms to foreign firms. As job opportunities shift from one place to another, some workers become structurally unemployed.

The distinction between frictional and structural unemployment is hazy. The key difference is that *frictionally* unemployed workers have marketable skills and either live in areas where jobs exist or are able to move to areas that have job opportunities. *Structurally* unemployed workers find it hard to obtain new jobs without retraining, additional education, or moving to a new area. Frictional unemployment is short-term; structural unemployment is more likely to be long-term and consequently more serious.

cyclical unemployment A type of *unemployment* caused by insufficient total spending (insufficient *aggregate demand*) and which typically begins in the *recession* phase of the *business cycle.*

Cyclical Unemployment Unemployment that is caused by a decline in total spending is called **cyclical unemployment.** It typically begins in the recession phase of the business cycle. As the demand for goods and services decreases, employment falls and unemployment rises. Cyclical unemployment results from insufficient demand for goods and services and is exacerbated by the downward stickiness of wages in the economy, as discussed in the nearby Consider This story. The 25 percent unemployment rate in the depth of the Great Depression in 1933 reflected mainly cyclical unemployment.

We will say more about the high costs of cyclical unemployment later, but first we need to define "full employment."

CONSIDER THIS . . .

Downwardly Sticky Wages and Unemployment

Labor markets have an important quirk that helps to explain why unemployment goes up so much during a recession.

The quirk is that wages are flexible upward but sticky downward.

On the one hand, workers are perfectly happy to accept wage increases. So when the economy is booming and firms start bidding for the limited supply of labor, wages rise—often quite rapidly.

On the other hand, workers deeply resent pay cuts. So if the economy goes into a recession and firms need to reduce labor costs, managers almost never cut wages because doing so would only lead to disgruntled employees, low productivity, and—in extreme cases—workers stealing supplies or actively sabotaging their own firms.

Instead, managers usually opt for layoffs. The workers who are let go obviously don't like being unemployed. But those who remain get to keep their old wages. As a result, they keep on being as productive and cooperative as they were before.

The preference that managers show for layoffs over wage cuts results in downwardly sticky wages and an informal price floor that help to explain why unemployment goes up so much during a recession. The problem is that when the demand for labor falls during a recession, the informal

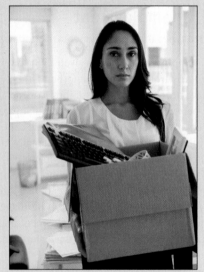

Jamie Grill/JGI/Blend Images/Getty Images

price floor prevents wages from falling. As a result, there is no way for falling wages to help entice at least some firms to hire a few more workers. Thus, when a recession hits, employment falls more precipitously than it would have if wages had been downwardly flexible.

Definition of Full Employment

Because frictional and structural unemployment are largely unavoidable in a dynamic economy, *full employment* is something less than 100 percent employment of the labor force. Economists say that the economy is "fully employed" when it is experiencing only frictional and structural unemployment. That is, full employment occurs when there is no cyclical unemployment.

Economists label the unemployment rate that is consistent with full employment as the **full-employment rate of unemployment,** or the **natural rate of unemployment (NRU).** At the NRU, the economy is said to be producing its **potential output,** the real GDP that occurs when the labor force and other inputs are "fully employed."

Note that a fully employed economy does not mean zero unemployment. Even when the economy is fully employed, the NRU is some positive percentage because it takes time for frictionally unemployed job seekers to find jobs. Also, it takes time for the structurally unemployed to achieve the skills needed for reemployment.

"Natural" does not mean that the economy will always operate at the NRU and thus realize its potential output. When cyclical unemployment occurs, the economy has much more unemployment than it would at the NRU. Moreover, the economy can operate for a while at an unemployment rate *below* the NRU. At times, the demand for labor may be so great that firms take a stronger initiative to hire and train the structurally unemployed. Also, some parents, teenagers, college students, and retirees who were casually looking for just the right part-time or full-time jobs may quickly find them. Thus the unemployment rate temporarily falls below the natural rate.

Also note that the NRU can vary over time as demographic factors, job-search methods, and public policies change. In the 1980s, the NRU was about 6 percent. Today, it is estimated to be between 3 and 4 percent.

Economic Cost of Unemployment

High unemployment involves heavy economic and social costs.

The GDP Gap The basic economic cost of unemployment is forgone output. When the economy fails to create enough jobs for all who are able and willing to work, potential production is irretrievably lost. Unemployment above the natural rate means that society is operating at some point inside its production possibilities curve. Economists call this sacrifice of output a **GDP gap**—the difference between actual and potential GDP. That is:

$$\text{GDP gap} = \text{actual GDP} - \text{potential GDP}$$

The GDP gap can be either negative or positive:

- When unemployment is above the natural rate of unemployment, the GDP gap will be negative (actual GDP < potential GDP) because only a smaller amount of output can be produced when employing a smaller amount of labor.

- By contrast, when unemployment is below the natural rate, the GDP gap will be positive (actual GDP > potential GDP) because the large quantity of labor being utilized allows the economy to produce more than the full-employment level of output.

To calculate potential GDP at any point in time, the BLS estimates what the economy's output would be at that instant if the actual unemployment rate equaled the natural rate of unemployment. Figure 29.3a shows the U.S. GDP gap for recent years while Figure 29.3b shows the actual unemployment rate over the same time period. Please note the close correlation between the actual unemployment rate (Figure 29.3b) and the GDP gap (Figure 29.3a). The higher the unemployment rate, the larger the GDP gap.

Okun's Law Arthur Okun was the first macroeconomist to quantify the inverse relationship between the actual unemployment rate and the GDP gap. He noticed that, on average:

$$\text{GDP gap} = -2.0 \times (\text{actual unemployment rate} - \text{natural unemployment rate})$$

This relationship came to be known as **Okun's law.** With respect to recessions, it implies that for every 1 percentage point by which the actual unemployment rate exceeds the natural rate, a GDP gap of about negative 2.0 percent will occur.

---

full-employment rate of unemployment The *unemployment rate* at which there is no *cyclical unemployment* of the *labor force;* equal to around 4 percent (rather than zero percent) in the United States because *frictional* and *structural unemployment* are unavoidable.

natural rate of unemployment (NRU) The *full-employment rate of unemployment;* the *unemployment rate* occurring when there is no cyclical unemployment and the economy is achieving its *potential output;* the unemployment rate at which actual *inflation* equals expected inflation.

potential output The real output (*GDP*) an economy can produce when it fully employs its available resources.

GDP gap Actual *gross domestic product* minus *potential output;* may be either a positive amount (a *positive GDP gap*) or a negative amount (a *negative GDP gap*).

Okun's law The generalization that any 1-percentage-point rise in the *unemployment rate* above the *full-employment rate of unemployment* is associated with a rise in the *negative GDP gap* by 2 percent of *potential output* (potential *GDP*).

FIGURE 29.3 Actual and potential real GDP and the unemployment rate.

(a) The difference between actual and potential GDP is the GDP gap. A negative GDP gap measures the output the economy sacrifices when actual GDP falls short of potential GDP. A positive GDP gap indicates that actual GDP is above potential GDP. (b) A high unemployment rate means a large GDP gap (negative), and a low unemployment rate means a small or even positive GDP gap.

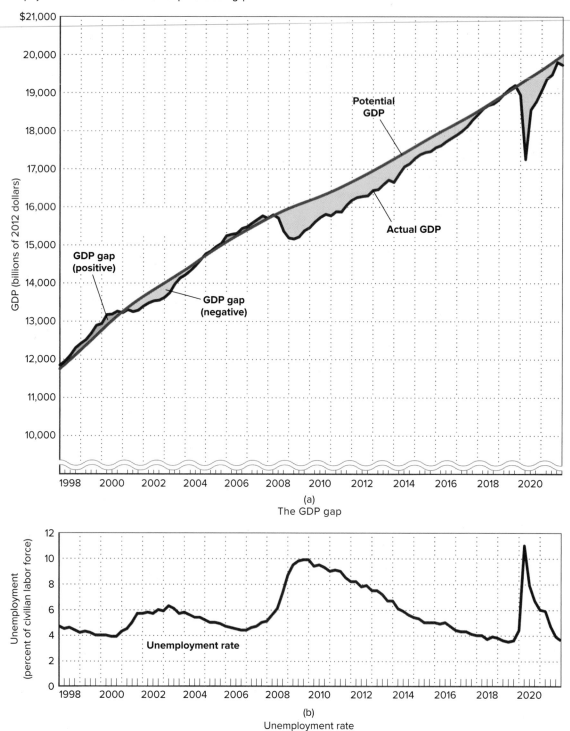

(a)
The GDP gap

(b)
Unemployment rate

Sources: Congressional Budget Office; Bureau of Economic Analysis; and Bureau of Labor Statistics.

By applying Okun's law, we can calculate the absolute loss of output associated with any above-natural unemployment rate. For example, in 2020 the average monthly unemployment rate was 8.1 percent, or 4.6 percentage points above that period's 3.5 percent natural rate of unemployment. Multiplying this 4.6 percent by Okun's negative 2.0 indicates that 2020's GDP gap was approximately negative 9.2 percent of potential GDP (in real terms). Applying this 9.2 percent loss of output to 2020's potential GDP of $19,344 billion, we find that the economy sacrificed $1,780 billion of real output.

As Figure 29.3 shows, sometimes the economy's actual output exceeds its potential or full-employment output. An unusually strong economic expansion in 1999 and 2000, for example, caused actual GDP to exceed potential GDP, thereby generating a positive GDP gap for those two years. You should note, though, that while actual GDP can exceed potential GDP for a time, positive GDP gaps create strong demand-pull inflationary pressures and cannot be sustained indefinitely.

Unequal Burdens An increase in the unemployment rate from, say, 5 percent to 9 or 10 percent might be more tolerable to society if every worker's hours and income were reduced proportionally. But this is not the case. The burden of unemployment is unequally distributed. Some workers retain their hours and income, while others become unemployed and earn nothing.

Table 29.2 examines unemployment rates for both the overall labor force and various demographic subgroups. We look at the years 2019 and 2020 as a way of investigating how unemployment varies over the course of the business cycle. In 2019, for example, the business cycle reached a peak, with the unemployment rate averaging 3.7 percent over the year. The economy then receded quickly in the spring of 2020 when the COVID-19 lockdowns began. The unemployment rate increased, with the average monthly unemployment rate equaling 8.1 percent during 2020.

TABLE 29.2
Unemployment Rates by Demographic Group: Full Employment (2019) and Recession (2020)*

	Unemployment Rate	
Demographic Group	2019	2020
Overall	3.7%	8.1%
Occupation:		
Management and professional occupations	2.0	4.5
Production occupations	3.9	9.0
Age:		
16–19	12.7	17.9
African American, 16–19	20.8	24.8
White, 16–19	11.5	17.0
Female, 20+	3.3	8.0
Male, 20+	3.4	7.4
Race and ethnicity:		
African American	6.1	11.4
Hispanic	4.3	10.4
Asian	2.7	8.7
White	3.3	7.3
Gender:		
Women	3.6	8.4
Men	3.7	7.8
Education:†		
Less than high school diploma	5.4	11.7
High school diploma only	3.7	9.0
College degree or more	2.1	4.8
Duration:		
15 or more weeks	2.8	4.2

*Civilian labor force data.
†People age 25 or over.

Sources: *Economic Report of the President 2019*, Bureau of Labor Statistics, Census Bureau.

By observing the large differences in unemployment rates in 2019 and 2020 for different demographic subgroups, we can generalize as follows:

- *Occupation* Workers in lower-skilled occupations (for example, laborers) have higher unemployment rates than workers in higher-skilled occupations (for example, professionals). Lower-skilled workers have more and longer spells of structural unemployment than higher-skilled workers. They also are less likely to be self-employed than are higher-skilled workers. Manufacturing, construction, and mining workers tend to be particularly hard-hit, but businesses generally retain most of their higher-skilled workers, in whom they have invested the expense of training.

- *Age* Teenagers have much higher unemployment rates than adults. Teenagers have lower skill levels, quit their jobs more frequently, are more frequently fired, and have less geographic mobility than adults. Many unemployed teenagers are new in the labor market, searching for their first jobs. Male African American teenagers, in particular, have very high unemployment rates. The unemployment rate for all teenagers rises during recessions.

- *Race and ethnicity* The unemployment rates of African Americans and Hispanics exceed the white unemployment rate at all stages of the business cycle. The causes include lower rates of educational attainment, greater concentration in lower-skilled occupations, and discrimination in the labor market. In general, the unemployment rate for African Americans is about twice that of whites and rises by about twice as many percentage points during most recessions.

- *Gender* The unemployment rates for men and women normally are very similar. But during the 2020 recession, the unemployment rate of women exceeded that of men, a fact attributable at least in part to women leaving the labor force in greater numbers than men to either care for sick family members or to provide at-home supervision for children whose schools switched from in-person instruction to distance learning during the pandemic.

- *Education* Less-educated workers, on average, have higher unemployment rates than workers with more education. Less education is usually associated with lower-skilled, less-permanent jobs; more time between jobs; and jobs that are more vulnerable to cyclical layoff.

- *Duration* The number of persons unemployed for long periods—15 weeks or more—as a percentage of the labor force is much lower than the overall unemployment rate. But that percentage rises significantly during recessions. Notice that it rose from 2.8 percent of the labor force in 2019 to 4.2 percent in 2020.

Noneconomic Costs

Policymakers are deeply concerned with unemployment rates and how to minimize the length and depth of business cycle downturns as a way of moderating the harm caused by unemployment. Their attention is warranted because severe cyclical unemployment is more than an economic malady; it is a social catastrophe.

- At the individual level, research links high unemployment to increases in suicide, homicide, heart attacks, strokes, and mental illness. The unemployed lose skills and self-respect. Morale plummets and families disintegrate. Widespread joblessness increases poverty, reduces hope for material advancement, and heightens ethnic tensions.

- At the social level, severe unemployment can lead to rapid and sometimes violent political upheaval. Witness Adolph Hitler's ascent to power against a background of unemployment in Germany.

QUICK REVIEW
29.2

▶ There are three types of unemployment: frictional, structural, and cyclical.

▶ The natural rate of unemployment (frictional plus structural) is presently around 3.5 percent in the United States.

▶ A positive GDP gap occurs when actual GDP exceeds potential GDP; a negative GDP gap occurs when actual GDP falls short of potential GDP.

▶ According to Okun's law, for each 1 percentage point of unemployment above the natural rate, the U.S. economy suffers an additional 2 percent decline in real GDP below potential GDP.

▶ Lower-skilled workers, teenagers, African Americans and Hispanics, and less-educated workers bear a disproportionate burden of unemployment.

Inflation

Inflation is a rise in the general level of prices. When inflation occurs, each dollar of income buys fewer goods and services than before. Inflation reduces the "purchasing power" of money. But inflation does not mean that all prices are rising. Even during periods of rapid inflation, some prices may be relatively constant, while others may even fall. For example, although the United States experienced high rates of inflation in the 1970s and early 1980s, the prices of video recorders, digital watches, and personal computers declined.

>> LO29.3 Measure inflation and distinguish between cost-push inflation and demand-pull inflation.

inflation A rise in the general level of *prices* in an economy; an increase in an economy's *price level*.

Measurement of Inflation

The **Consumer Price Index (CPI)** is the main measure of inflation in the United States. The government uses this index to report inflation rates each month and each year. It also uses the CPI to adjust Social Security benefits and income tax brackets for inflation. The CPI reports the price of a "market basket" of some 300 consumer goods and services that are purchased by typical urban consumers.

The composition of the market basket for the CPI is based on spending patterns of urban consumers in a specific period, presently 2013–2014. The BLS updates the composition of the market basket every few years so that it reflects the most recent patterns of consumer purchases and captures current inflation.

The BLS arbitrarily sets the CPI equal to 100 for 1982–1984. So the CPI for any particular year is calculated as follows:

$$CPI = \frac{\text{price of the most recent market basket in the particular year}}{\text{price estimate of the market basket in 1982–1984}} \times 100$$

Consumer Price Index (CPI) An index that measures the prices of a fixed "market basket" of some 300 goods and services bought by a "typical" consumer.

The inflation rate is equal to the percentage growth of CPI from one year to the next. For example, the CPI was 278.8 in 2021, up from 260.5 in 2020. So the rate of inflation for 2021 is calculated as follows:

$$\text{Rate of inflation} = \frac{278.8 - 260.5}{260.5} \times 100 = 7.0\%$$

In rare cases, the CPI declines from one year to the next. For example, the CPI fell from 215.3 in 2008 to 214.5 in 2009. So the rate of inflation for 2009 was −0.4 percent. A decline in the price level is called **deflation.**

In Chapter 28, we discussed the *rule of 70,* which tells us that we can find the number of years it will take for some measure to double, assuming that it grows at a constant annual percentage rate. To do so, we divide the number 70 by the annual percentage growth rate. Inflation is the growth rate of the price level. So a 3 percent annual rate of inflation will double the price level in about 23 (= 70 ÷ 3) years. Inflation of 8 percent per year will double the price level in about 9 (= 70 ÷ 8) years.

deflation A decline in the general level of *prices* in an economy; a decline in an economy's *price level*.

Facts of Inflation

Figure 29.4 shows December-to-December rates of annual inflation in the United States between 1960 and 2021. Observe that inflation reached double-digit rates in the 1970s and early 1980s

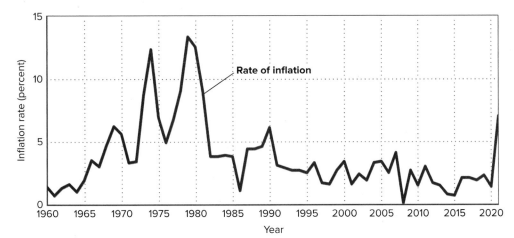

Source: U.S. Bureau of Labor Statistics.

FIGURE 29.4

Annual inflation rates in the United States, 1960–2021 (December-to-December changes in the CPI).

Since 1960, the major periods of rapid inflation in the United States were in the 1970s, early 1980s, and in the wake of the COVID-19 pandemic.

GLOBAL PERSPECTIVE 29.1

INFLATION RATES IN FIVE INDUSTRIAL NATIONS, 2010–2021

Inflation rates in the United States in recent years were neither extraordinarily high nor extraordinarily low relative to rates in other industrial nations, but did spike higher than the inflation rates of many other countries when the COVID-19 pandemic struck in 2020.

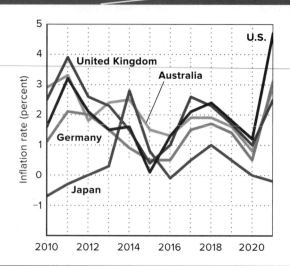

Source: International Monetary Fund.

Note: These are annual average inflation rates, which do not align directly with the December-to-December inflation rates shown in Figure 29.4 for the United States.

before declining. It remained muted during the decade or so following the Great Recession of 2007–2009 but then popped up to 7.0 percent in 2021 as the result of the COVID-19 pandemic, the ensuing supply chain disruptions, and how the federal government responded to the crisis in terms of generously distributing anti-recessionary stimulus funds.

Although the U.S. inflation rate spiked upward toward 10 percent after the COVID-19 pandemic, it was still the case that the U.S. inflation rate has been neither unusually high nor unusually low relative to the inflation rates typical of industrial nations, which saw a similar spike in inflation after the COVID-19 pandemic (see Global Perspective 29.1). By contrast, some other nations (not shown) have had extremely high annual rates of inflation in recent years independent of the COVID-19 pandemic. In 2020, for example, the annual inflation rate in Zimbabwe was 557 percent; Venezuela, 255 percent; Lebanon, 155 percent; and Sudan, 150 percent.

Types of Inflation

Nearly all prices in the economy are set by supply and demand. So if the overall price level is rising, we need to look for an explanation in terms of supply and demand.

Demand-Pull Inflation Usually, increases in the price level are caused by an excess of total spending beyond the economy's capacity to produce. Where inflation is rapid and sustained for long periods, the cause is invariably an overissuance of money by the central bank (the Federal Reserve in the United States) that leads to excessive spending and demand. When resources are already fully employed, the business sector cannot respond to that excess demand by expanding output. The excess demand bids up the prices of the limited output, producing **demand-pull inflation.** This type of inflation is characterized by "too much spending chasing too few goods."

demand-pull inflation
Increases in the *price level* (*inflation*) resulting from increases in *aggregate demand*.

As we will explain in detail in coming chapters, the generous stimulus checks that Congress sent to businesses and workers to help them weather the shutdowns and work disruptions caused by the COVID-19 pandemic were a source of demand-pull inflation until they ended in the fall of 2021. In particular, tens of millions of workers who had been idled by the pandemic received more income each month from enhanced unemployment benefits than they would have received in wages and salaries had they been working. That increase in spending power increased the demand for goods and services, thereby generating inflationary pressures of the demand-pull variety.

Cost-Push Inflation Inflation also may arise on the supply, or cost, side of the economy. During some periods in U.S. economic history, including the mid-1970s, the price level increased even though total spending was not excessive. In these periods, output and employment were both *declining* (evidence that total spending was not excessive) while the general price level was *rising*.

The theory of **cost-push inflation** explains rising output prices in terms of factors that raise **per-unit production costs** at each level of spending. Rising per-unit production costs squeeze profits and reduce the amount of output firms are willing to supply at the existing price level. As a result, the economy's supply of goods and services declines, and the price level rises.

$$\text{Per-unit production cost} = \frac{\text{total input cost}}{\text{units of output}}$$

In this scenario, costs are *pushing* the price level upward, whereas in demand-pull inflation demand is *pulling* it upward.

The major source of cost-push inflation has been *supply shocks*. Specifically, abrupt increases in the costs of productive inputs have occasionally driven up per-unit production costs and thus product prices. The rocketing prices of imported oil in 1973–1974 and again in 1979–1980 are good illustrations. As energy prices surged upward during these periods, the costs of producing and transporting virtually every product in the economy rose. Cost-push inflation ensued.

The COVID-19 pandemic caused supply shocks in the form of disruptions to the *supply chain* by which raw materials get transformed into finished products that must then be distributed to consumers. With employees locked down at home in various countries for various lengths of time, the economy's normal flow of production and distribution was disrupted. Shortages of labor and other inputs increased per-unit production costs. Inflation erupted in economies around the world in 2021 as cost-push inflation (caused by supply chain disruptions) reinforced demand-pull inflation (generated by stimulus spending).

Core Inflation

The inflation statistics calculated by the BLS are supposed to reflect the general trend in overall prices. That general trend can be obscured, though, by the rapid up and down price movements typical of energy and food products like wheat, gasoline, corn, and natural gas.

To avoid being misled by these rapid but temporary price changes, BLS employees calculate a measure of inflation called **core inflation** that excludes food and energy items.

If core inflation is low and stable, policymakers may be satisfied with current policy even though changes in the overall CPI index may be suggesting a rising inflation rate. But policymakers become greatly concerned when core inflation is high and rising, and they take deliberate measures to try to halt it.

We discuss these policy actions in detail in later chapters, but at this point it is important to add that the Federal Reserve (the U.S. central bank) has set a 2-percent inflation target since 2012, with the promise that it will adjust monetary policy as necessary to keep the U.S. inflation rate at or near 2 percent per year.

> **cost-push inflation**
> Increases in the *price level* (*inflation*) resulting from an increase in resource costs (for example, raw-material prices) and hence in *per-unit production costs;* inflation caused by reductions in *aggregate supply.*

> **per-unit production cost**
> The average production cost of a particular level of output; total input cost divided by units of output.

> **core inflation** The underlying increases in the *price level* after volatile food and energy *prices* are removed.

> ► Inflation is a rising general level of prices and is measured as a percentage change in a price index such as the CPI; deflation is a decline in the general level of prices.
>
> ► Demand-pull inflation occurs when total spending exceeds the economy's ability to provide goods and services at the existing price level; total spending *pulls* the price level upward.

> ► Cost-push inflation occurs when factors such as rapid increases in the prices of imported raw materials drive up per-unit production costs; higher costs *push* the price level upward.
>
> ► Core inflation is the underlying inflation rate after volatile food and energy prices have been removed.

> **QUICK REVIEW**
> # 29.3

Redistribution Effects of Inflation

Inflation redistributes real income. This redistribution helps some people, hurts other people, and leaves yet others largely unaffected. Who gets hurt? Who benefits? Who is unaffected? Before we can answer those questions, we need some terminology.

Nominal and Real Income

There is a difference between money (nominal) income and real income. **Nominal income** is the number of dollars received as wages, rent, interest, or profit. **Real income** measures the amount of

> **>> LO29.4** Explain how unanticipated inflation can redistribute real income.

> **nominal income** The number of dollars received by an individual or group for its *resources* during some period of time.

real income The amount of *goods* and *services* that can be purchased with *nominal income* during some period of time; nominal income adjusted for *inflation*.

goods and services that nominal income can buy; it is the purchasing power of nominal income, or income adjusted for inflation, and it is calculated as follows:

$$\text{Real income} = \frac{\text{nominal income}}{\text{price index (in hundredths)}}$$

Inflation need not alter an economy's overall real income—its total purchasing power. The above equation makes it clear that real income will remain the same when nominal income rises at the same percentage rate as the price index.

But when inflation occurs, not everyone's nominal income rises at the same pace as the price level. Therein lies the potential for a redistribution of real income. If the change in the price level differs from the change in a person's nominal income, his or her real income will be affected. The following approximation (shown by the $\cong$ sign) tells us roughly how much real income will change:

$$\begin{matrix} \text{Percentage} \\ \text{change in} \\ \text{real income} \end{matrix} \cong \begin{matrix} \text{percentage} \\ \text{change in} \\ \text{nominal income} \end{matrix} - \begin{matrix} \text{percentage} \\ \text{change in} \\ \text{price level} \end{matrix}$$

For example, suppose that the price level rises by 6 percent. If Bob's nominal income rises by 6 percent, his real income will *remain unchanged*. But if his nominal income instead rises by 10 percent, his real income will increase by about 4 percent. If Bob's nominal income rises by only 2 percent, his real income will *decline* by about 4 percent.

Anticipations

The redistribution effects of inflation depend on whether or not it is expected:

unanticipated inflation An increase of the *price level* (*inflation*) at a rate greater than expected.

anticipated inflation Increases in the *price level* (*inflation*) that occur at the expected rate.

- We will first discuss situations involving **unanticipated inflation,** which causes real income and wealth to be redistributed, harming some and benefiting others.

- We will then discuss situations involving **anticipated inflation,** in which people see an inflation coming. With the ability to plan ahead, people are able to avoid or lessen the redistribution effects of inflation.

Who Is Hurt by Inflation?

Unanticipated inflation hurts fixed-income recipients, savers, and creditors. It redistributes real income away from them and toward others.

Fixed-Income Receivers People whose incomes are fixed see their real incomes fall when unanticipated inflation occurs. The classic case is the elderly couple living on a private pension or annuity that provides a fixed amount of nominal income each month. They may have retired in, say, 2004 on what appeared to be an adequate pension. However, by 2022, they would have discovered that inflation had cut the annual purchasing power of that pension—their real income—by one-third.

Similarly, landlords who receive lease payments of fixed dollar amounts are hurt by inflation as they receive dollars of declining value over time. Likewise, public sector workers whose incomes are based on fixed pay schedules may see a decrease in their purchasing power. The fixed "steps" (the upward yearly increases) in their pay schedules may not keep up with inflation. Minimum-wage workers and families living on fixed welfare incomes are also hurt by inflation.

Savers Unanticipated inflation hurts savers. As prices rise, the real value (purchasing power) of accumulated savings deteriorates. Paper assets such as savings accounts, insurance policies, and annuities that were once adequate to meet rainy-day contingencies or provide for a comfortable retirement decline in real value. The simplest case is the person who hoards cash. A $1,000 cash balance lost about 20 percent of its real value between 2012 and 2022. Of course, most forms of savings earn interest. But the value of savings will still decline if the inflation rate exceeds the interest rate.

Creditors Unanticipated inflation harms creditors (lenders). Suppose Chase Bank lends Bob $1,000, to be repaid in two years. If in that time the price level doubles, the $1,000 that Bob repays will possess only half the purchasing power of the $1,000 he borrowed. As prices go up, the purchasing power of the dollar goes down. So the borrower pays back less-valuable dollars than those received from the lender. The owners of Chase Bank suffer a loss of real income.

Who Is Unaffected or Helped by Inflation?

Not everyone is hurt by unanticipated inflation.

Flexible-Income Receivers People who have flexible incomes may escape inflation's harm or even benefit from it. For example, individuals who derive their incomes solely from Social Security are largely unaffected by inflation because Social Security payments are *indexed* to the CPI. Nominal benefits automatically increase when the CPI increases, thus preventing inflation from eroding their purchasing power. Some union workers also get automatic **cost-of-living adjustments (COLAs)** in their pay when the CPI rises, although such increases rarely equal the full percentage rise in inflation.

In addition, some flexible-income receivers are helped by unanticipated inflation. The strong product demand and labor shortages implied by rapid demand-pull inflation may cause some nominal incomes to spurt ahead of the price level, thereby enhancing real incomes. For some, the 3 percent increase in nominal income that occurs when inflation is 2 percent may become a 7 percent increase when inflation is 5 percent. As an example, property owners faced with an inflation-induced real estate boom may be able to boost rents by more than the inflation rate. Also, some business owners may benefit from inflation. If product prices rise faster than resource prices, business revenues will increase more rapidly than costs.

Debtors Unanticipated inflation benefits debtors (borrowers). In our earlier example, Chase Bank's loss of real income from inflation is Bob's gain of real income. Debtor Bob borrows "dear" dollars but, because of inflation, pays back the principal and interest with "cheap" dollars whose purchasing power has been eroded by inflation. Real income is redistributed away from the owners of Chase Bank toward borrowers such as Bob.

The federal government, which had amassed over $29 trillion of public debt through 2021, has also benefited from inflation. Historically, the federal government has regularly paid off loans by taking out new loans. Inflation allows the Treasury to pay off loans with dollars of less purchasing power than the dollars originally borrowed. Nominal national income and therefore tax collections rise with inflation; the amount of public debt owed does not. Thus, inflation reduces the real burden of the public debt.

Anticipated Inflation

The redistribution effects of inflation are less severe or eliminated altogether if people anticipate inflation and can adjust their future nominal incomes to reflect expected increases in the price level. The prolonged inflation that began in the late 1960s prompted many labor unions in the 1970s to insist on labor contracts that provided cost-of-living adjustments.

Similarly, if inflation is anticipated, the redistribution of income from lender to borrower may be altered. Suppose a lender (perhaps a commercial bank) and a borrower (a household) both agree that 5 percent is a fair rate of interest on a 1-year loan provided the price level is constant. But assume that inflation has been occurring and is expected to be 6 percent over the next year. If the bank lends the household $100 at 5 percent interest, the borrower will pay the bank $105 at the end of the year. But if 6 percent inflation occurs during that year, the purchasing power of the $105 will have been reduced to about $99. The lender will, in effect, have paid the borrower $1 for the use of the lender's money for a year.

The lender can avoid this subsidy by charging an *inflation premium*—that is, by raising the interest rate by 6 percent, the amount of the anticipated inflation. By charging 11 percent interest, the lender will receive back $111 at the end of the year. Adjusted for the 6 percent inflation, that amount will have roughly the same purchasing power as $105 worth of today's money. The result then will be a mutually agreeable transfer of purchasing power from borrower to lender of $5, or 5 percent, for the use of $100 for one year.

Our example reveals the difference between the real interest rate and the nominal interest rate. The **real interest rate** is the percentage increase in *purchasing power* that the borrower pays the

cost-of-living adjustment (COLA) An automatic increase in the incomes (*wages*) of workers when *inflation* occurs; often included in *collective bargaining* agreements between *firms* and *unions*. Cost-of-living adjustments are also guaranteed by law for *Social Security* benefits and certain other government *transfer payments*.

real interest rate The *interest rate* expressed in dollars of constant value (adjusted for *inflation*) and equal to the *nominal interest rate* less the expected rate of inflation.

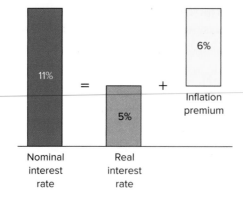

lender. In our example, the real interest rate is 5 percent. The **nominal interest rate** is the percentage increase in *money* that the borrower pays the lender, including that resulting from the built-in expectation of inflation, if any. In equation form:

Nominal interest rate = real interest rate + inflation premium (the expected rate of inflation)

As Figure 29.5 shows, the nominal interest rate in our example is 11 percent.

Other Redistribution Issues

nominal interest rate The *interest rate* expressed in terms of annual amounts currently charged for *interest* and not adjusted for *inflation*.

We end our discussion of the redistribution effects of inflation by making three final points:

- *Deflation* The effects of unanticipated deflation—declines in the price level—are the reverse of those of inflation. People with fixed nominal incomes will find their real incomes enhanced. Creditors will benefit at the expense of debtors. And savers will discover that the purchasing power of their savings has grown because of the falling prices.

- *Mixed effects* A person who is simultaneously an income earner, a holder of financial assets, and a debtor will probably find that the redistribution impact of unanticipated inflation is cushioned. If the person owns fixed-value monetary assets (savings accounts, bonds, and insurance policies), inflation will lessen their real value. But that same inflation may produce an increase in the person's nominal wage. Also, if the person holds a fixed-interest-rate mortgage, the real burden of that debt will decline. In short, many individuals are simultaneously hurt and helped by inflation. All these effects must be considered before we can conclude that any particular person's net position is better or worse because of inflation.

- *Arbitrariness* The redistribution effects of inflation occur regardless of society's goals and values. Inflation lacks a social conscience. It takes from some and gives to others, whether they are rich, poor, young, old, healthy, or infirm.

▶ Inflation harms those who receive relatively fixed nominal incomes and either leaves unaffected or helps those who receive flexible nominal incomes.

▶ Unanticipated inflation hurts savers and creditors while benefiting debtors.

▶ The nominal interest rate equals the real interest rate plus the inflation premium (the expected inflation rate).

Does Inflation Affect Output?

>> **LO29.5** Describe how inflation may affect the economy's level of real output.

Thus far, our discussion has focused on how inflation redistributes a specific level of total real income. But inflation also may affect an economy's level of real output (and thus its level of real income).

Cost-Push Inflation and Real Output

Recall that abrupt and unexpected increases in the prices of key resources such as oil can drive up overall production costs and generate cost-push inflation. As prices rise, the quantity demanded of goods and services falls. Firms respond by producing less output, and unemployment goes up.

Economic events of the 1970s provide an example of how inflation can reduce real output. In late 1973, the Organization of Petroleum Exporting Countries (OPEC) managed to quadruple the price of oil by unexpectedly restricting supply. The resulting cost-push inflation generated rapid price-level increases in the 1973–1975 period. At the same time, the U.S. unemployment rate rose from slightly less than 5 percent in 1973 to 8.5 percent in 1975. Similar outcomes occurred in 1979–1980 in response to a second OPEC oil supply shock.

Like other forms of unexpected inflation, cost-push inflation redistributes income and output. But cost-push inflation is unique in that it reduces the overall quantity of real output that gets divided. Prices rose for everybody during the 1973–1975 period, but OPEC members experienced higher incomes while unemployed workers in oil importing countries like the United States lost their incomes entirely.

Demand-Pull Inflation and Real Output

Economists do not fully agree on the effects of mild inflation (less than 3 percent) on real output.

The Case for Zero Inflation Some economists believe that even low levels of inflation reduce real output because inflation diverts time and effort toward activities designed to hedge against inflation. For example:

- Businesses incur the cost of changing millions of prices on their shelves and in their computers simply to keep up with inflation.

- Households and businesses spend considerable time and effort obtaining the information they need to distinguish between real and nominal prices, wages, and interest rates.

These economists argue that without inflation, more time and effort would be spent producing valuable goods and services. Proponents of "zero inflation" bolster their case by pointing to cross-country studies indicating that lower inflation rates are associated with higher rates of economic growth. Even mild inflation, say these economists, is detrimental to economic growth.

The Case for Mild Inflation Other economists note that full employment and economic growth depend on strong levels of total spending.

- They argue that strong spending creates high profits, a strong demand for labor, and a powerful incentive for firms to expand their plants and equipment. In this view, the mild inflation that is a by-product of strong spending is a small price to pay for full employment and continued economic growth.

- A low but steady rate of inflation also makes it easier for firms to adjust real wages downward when the level of total spending declines. That is helpful to the overall economy because if real wages can be cut during a recession, firms can afford to hire more workers. To see why having some inflation matters, note that with mild inflation, firms can reduce real wages by holding nominal wages steady. That is a good strategy for firms because workers tend to focus on what happens to nominal, rather than real, wages. Their real wages will in fact be falling because of the inflation, but they will continue to work just as hard because their nominal wages remain unchanged. By contrast, if inflation were zero, the only way to reduce real wages would be by cutting nominal wages and thereby angering employees, who would likely retaliate by putting in less effort and agitating for higher pay.

The defenders of mild inflation argue that it is much better for an economy to err on the side of strong spending, full employment, economic growth, and mild inflation than on the side of weak spending, unemployment, recession, and deflation.

Hyperinflation

A **hyperinflation** occurs when a country's inflation rate exceeds 50 percent per month. Compounded over a year, that is equivalent to an annual rate of about 13,000 percent.

Adverse Effects Unlike mild inflation, which has its fans, hyperinflation is roundly condemned by all economists because it has devastating impacts on real output and employment.

- As prices shoot up during a hyperinflation, normal economic relationships are disrupted. Business owners do not know what to charge for their products. Consumers do not know what to pay.

- Production declines because businesses, anticipating further price increases, find that it makes more financial sense to hoard (rather than use) materials, and to stockpile (rather than sell) finished products. Why sell today when the same product will fetch more money tomorrow?

hyperinflation An extremely high rate of *inflation*, usually defined as an inflation rate in excess of 50 percent per month.

The Great Resignation

The First Two Years of the COVID Pandemic Generated a Wide Variety of Firsts in U.S. Labor Markets—Everything from Mass Unemployment to Mass Resignations.

When the COVID-19 pandemic spread worldwide in the first months of 2020, most governments opted for lockdowns to slow the spread of the disease. In the United States, essential businesses such as grocery stores and hospitals were allowed to remain open, but the vast majority of firms had to shut their doors and send their employees home.

Since most businesses cannot operate using remote labor, output fell toward zero at the majority of businesses, which implied little or no money to pay workers. The situation was especially grave because it was not clear in the early spring of 2020 how long the lockdowns would last.

As thing turned out, most states ended their lockdowns within a couple of months, so that most businesses started recalling employees back to work by the late spring of 2020. But before that occurred, congress had already voted unprecedentedly generous unemployment benefits that would end up being available in most states through the summer of 2021.

What ensued was a historically unprecedented situation in which massive labor shortages arose largely because the enhanced unemployment benefits were so generous that 68 percent of the workers eligible to receive them could get more money collecting unemployment benefits than they could earn if they returned to work.

Given those options, millions of workers chose to remain unemployed even after jobs became plentiful again. The resulting shortage of workers was acute in many industries, including restaurants and food service, which had been hurt badly by the lockdowns and subsequent restrictions on indoor dining, but then, just a few months later, faced a situation in which they could not get enough workers even after most of their customers had returned.

Other huge labor market changes were also afoot as a result of the pandemic. Millions of white collar workers who had been allowed to work remotely using Zoom and other tools were reluctant to go back to offices even after offices had reopened. Managers had to scramble to see if they could accommodate those employees, some of whom were afraid to return to the office due to health concerns (especially before vaccines became widely available in the spring of 2021) but also because they had found that they liked working at home and not having to commute.

Many firms began to respond to the new situation by considering remote work to be a permanent feature of operations, some firms going so far as to cancel leases of office space because they were planning on having much, or even all, of their workforce working remotely from then on.

At the same time, the ongoing labor shortages gave employees leverage to ask for everything from wage increases to different work schedules. By the summer of 2021, numerous news articles reported the labor shortages and speculated on how long they would last. A

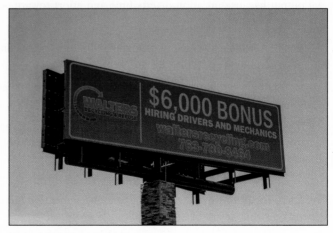

Michael Siluk/Alamy Stock Photo

common assumption was that things might go back to normal after the enhanced unemployment benefits ended in September 2021.

But then another surprising thing happened. Even after the generous unemployment benefits ended and even though there were still firms begging for workers and even though average wages had risen by 10 percent, the number of people working either full time or part time in the fall of 2021 was still 4 million fewer than before the pandemic.

By early 2022, the unemployment rate had fallen to under 4 percent, about where it had been before the pandemic. But the size of the labor force (which, as a reminder, includes both people who have jobs as well as unemployed people who are actively seeking work) was 3 million less than it was before the pandemic—meaning that even if everyone who in early 2022 was unemployed and seeking work joined those who were already working, the economy would have to get by with 3 million fewer workers than before the pandemic.

Once consequence of that dearth of workers was that anyone who *was* working had unprecedented opportunities to quit jobs that they didn't like and immediately get hired for jobs they liked better. This phenomenon became known as the Great Resignation, and by early 2022, nearly 5 million people a month were voluntarily quitting one job for another, by far the highest rate ever recorded.

But what had happened to the millions of people who had not come back to work by early 2022 despite what was arguably the best job market ever? More than half were probably older people near retirement age who had decided to retire a bit earlier than they had previously planned, assisted by retirement accounts rising rapidly due to a booming stock market. Others included younger people who had decided to live off of savings and not work for a while, and couples who had decided that they could get by on one income rather than two. •

- Investment also declines as savers refuse to extend loans to businesses, knowing that the loans will be repaid with rapidly depreciating money.

- Many people give up on money altogether and revert to barter, causing production and exchange to drop further as people spend literally hours every day trading and bartering instead of working and producing.

- The net result is economic collapse and, often, political chaos.

Examples Examples of hyperinflation include Germany after the First World War and Japan after the Second World War. In Germany, "prices increased so rapidly that waiters changed the prices on the menu several times during the course of a lunch. Sometimes customers had to pay double the price listed on the menu when they ordered."[1] In postwar Japan in 1947, "fishermen and farmers . . . used scales to weigh currency and change, rather than bothering to count it."[2]

Causation Hyperinflations are *always* caused by governments instituting highly imprudent expansions of the money supply. The rocketing money supply produces frenzied total spending and severe demand-pull inflation. Zimbabwe's 14.9 billion percent inflation rate in 2008 is the worst example. Venezuela in 2018 and several dozen other countries over the last century have caused inflation rates of 1 million percent per year or more.

Motivation Because hyperinflation causes so much harm, you may be asking why governments are sometimes willing to engage in the reckless money printing that invariably generates hyperinflation. The answer is that governments sometimes find themselves in a situation in which they cannot obtain enough revenue through either taxation or borrowing to cover the government's desired level of spending.

This is often the case during or immediately after a war, when government expenses skyrocket but tax revenues stagnate or even decline due to a depressed wartime or postwar economy. Unwilling or unable to slash spending down to a level that could be paid for by taxes plus borrowing, the government resorts to the printing press and prints up whatever amount of money is needed to cover its funding gap. The by-product is hyperinflation. The government maintains its rate of spending, but crashes the economy as a side effect.

Termination Hyperinflations end when governments cut their spending down to or below the amount of revenue that they can obtain through taxes and borrowing. Because the collateral damage is so great, most bouts of hyperinflation last 12 months or less. On the other hand, Greece in the 1940s and Nicaragua in the late 1980s each experienced over four years of continuous hyperinflation.

► Cost-push inflation reduces real output and employment.

► Economists argue about the effects of demand-pull inflation. Some argue that even mild demand-pull inflation (1 to 3 percent) reduces the economy's real output. Other say that mild inflation may be a

necessary by-product of the high and growing spending that produces high levels of output, full employment, and economic growth.

► Hyperinflation, caused by highly imprudent expansions of the money supply, may undermine the monetary system and severely decrease real output.

**QUICK REVIEW
29.5**

---

[1]Theodore Morgan, *Income and Employment,* 2nd ed. (Englewood Cliffs, NJ: Prentice Hall, 1952), p. 361.

[2]Rayburn M. Williams, *Inflation! Money, Jobs, and Politicians* (Arlington Heights, IL: AHM Publishing, 1980), p. 2.

Summary

LO29.1 Describe the phases of the business cycle.

The United States and other industrial economies have gone through periods of fluctuations in real GDP, employment, and the price level. Although they have certain phases in common—peak, recession, trough, expansion—business cycles vary greatly in duration and intensity.

Although economists explain the business cycle in terms of underlying causal factors such as major innovations, productivity shocks, money creation, and financial crises, they generally agree that changes in the level of total spending are the immediate causes of fluctuating real output and employment.

The business cycle affects all sectors of the economy, though in varying ways and degrees. The cycle has greater effects on output and employment in the capital goods and durable consumer goods industries than in the services and nondurable goods industries.

LO29.2 Measure unemployment and explain the different types of unemployment.

Economists distinguish among frictional, structural, and cyclical unemployment. The full-employment or natural rate of unemployment, which is composed of frictional and structural unemployment, is currently between 3 and 4 percent. The presence of part-time and discouraged workers makes it difficult to measure unemployment accurately.

The GDP gap, which can be either a positive or a negative value, is found by subtracting potential GDP from actual GDP. The economic cost of unemployment, as measured by the GDP gap, consists of the goods and services forgone by society when its resources are involuntarily idle. Okun's law suggests that every 1-percentage-point increase in the actual unemployment rate above the natural rate of unemployment causes an additional 2 percent negative GDP gap.

LO29.3 Measure inflation and distinguish between cost-push inflation and demand-pull inflation.

Inflation is a rise in the general price level and is measured in the United States by the Consumer Price Index (CPI). When inflation occurs, each dollar of income buys fewer goods and services than before. That is, inflation reduces the purchasing power of money. Deflation is a decline in the general price level.

Economists identify both demand-pull and cost-push (supply-side) inflation. Demand-pull inflation results from an excess of total spending relative to the economy's capacity to produce. The main source of cost-push inflation is abrupt and rapid increases in the prices of key resources. These supply shocks push up per-unit production costs and ultimately raise the prices of consumer goods.

LO29.4 Explain how unanticipated inflation can redistribute real income.

Unanticipated inflation arbitrarily redistributes real income at the expense of fixed-income receivers, creditors, and savers. If inflation is anticipated, individuals and businesses may be able to take steps to lessen or eliminate adverse redistribution effects.

When inflation is anticipated, lenders add an inflation premium to the interest rate charged on loans. The nominal interest rate thus reflects the real interest rate plus the inflation premium (the expected inflation rate).

LO29.5 Describe how inflation may affect the economy's level of real output.

Cost-push inflation reduces real output and employment. Proponents of zero inflation argue that even mild demand-pull inflation (1 to 3 percent) reduces the economy's real output. Other economists say that mild inflation may be a necessary by-product of the high and growing spending that produces high levels of output, full employment, and economic growth. A mild inflation also makes it easier for firms to adjust real wages downward when the level of total spending declines. They can do so by keeping nominal wages fixed while inflation reduces the purchasing power of every dollar received by employees.

Hyperinflation, caused by highly imprudent expansions of the money supply, may undermine the monetary system and severely decrease real output.

Terms and Concepts

business cycle	full-employment rate of unemployment	core inflation
peak	natural rate of unemployment (NRU)	nominal income
recession	potential output	real income
trough	GDP gap	unanticipated inflation
expansion	Okun's law	anticipated inflation
labor force	inflation	cost-of-living adjustments (COLAs)
unemployment rate	Consumer Price Index (CPI)	real interest rate
discouraged workers	deflation	nominal interest rate
frictional unemployment	demand-pull inflation	hyperinflation
structural unemployment	cost-push inflation	
cyclical unemployment	per-unit production costs	

Discussion Questions

Mc Graw Hill **connect**

1. What are the four phases of the business cycle? How long do business cycles last? Why does the business cycle affect output and employment in capital goods industries and consumer durable goods industries more severely than in industries producing consumer nondurables? **LO29.1**

2. How can a financial crisis lead to a recession? How can a major new invention lead to an expansion? **LO29.1**

3. How is the labor force defined, and who measures it? How is the unemployment rate calculated? Does an increase in the unemployment rate necessarily mean a decline in the size of the labor

force? Why is a positive unemployment rate—more than zero percent—fully compatible with full employment? **LO29.2**

4. How do unemployment rates vary by race and ethnicity, gender, occupation, and education? Why does the average length of time people are unemployed rise during a recession? **LO29.2**

5. Why is it difficult to distinguish among frictional, structural, and cyclical unemployment? Why is unemployment an economic problem? What are the consequences of a negative GDP gap? What are the noneconomic effects of unemployment? **LO29.2**

6. Even though the United States has an unemployment compensation program that provides income for those out of work, why should we worry about unemployment? **LO29.2**

7. What is the Consumer Price Index (CPI), and how is it determined each month? How does the Bureau of Labor Statistics calculate the inflation rate from one year to the next? How does inflation affect the purchasing power of a dollar? How does it explain differences between nominal and real interest rates? How does deflation differ from inflation? **LO29.3**

8. Distinguish between demand-pull inflation and cost-push inflation. Which of the two types is more likely to be associated with a negative GDP gap? Which is more likely to be associated with a positive GDP gap, in which actual GDP exceeds potential GDP? What is core inflation? Why is it calculated? **LO29.3**

9. Explain how an increase in your nominal income and a decrease in your real income might occur simultaneously. Who loses from inflation? Who gains? **LO29.4**

10. Explain how hyperinflation might lead to a severe decline in total output. **LO29.5**

11. **LAST WORD** How did the enhanced unemployment benefits approved by congress in the early days of the pandemic affect paid employment over the following year and a half? Why did some firms cancel leases? What role did older people play in the reduced size of the labor force?

Review Questions

1. Place the phases of the business cycle in order, starting with the highest level of GDP: recession, trough, peak, expansion. **LO29.1**

2. Most economists agree that the immediate cause of most cyclical changes in real output and employment is an unexpected change in _____. **LO29.1**
   a. the level of total spending
   b. the value of the stock market
   c. the value of the trade deficit
   d. the unemployment rate

3. Suppose that a country has 9 million people working full-time. It also has 1 million people who are actively seeking work but are currently unemployed, along with 2 million discouraged workers who have given up looking for work and are currently unemployed. What is this country's unemployment rate? **LO29.2**
   a. 10 percent
   b. 15 percent
   c. 20 percent
   d. 25 percent

4. Label each of the following scenarios as either frictional unemployment, structural unemployment, or cyclical unemployment. **LO29.2**
   a. Mariam just graduated from college and is looking for a job.
   b. A recession causes a local factory to lay off 30 workers.
   c. Thousands of bus and truck drivers permanently lose their jobs to self-driving vehicles.
   d. Hundreds of New York legal jobs permanently disappear when a lot of legal work gets outsourced to lawyers in India.

5. The unemployment rate that is consistent with full employment is _____. **LO29.2**
   a. the natural rate of unemployment
   b. the unnatural rate of unemployment
   c. the status quo rate of unemployment
   d. cyclical unemployment
   e. Okun's rate of unemployment

6. A country's current unemployment rate is 11 percent. Economists estimate that its natural rate of unemployment is 6 percent. About how large is this economy's negative GDP gap? **LO29.2**
   a. 1 percent
   b. 3 percent
   c. 6 percent
   d. 10 percent

7. Cost-push inflation occurs in the presence of _____. **LO29.3**
   a. excess inventory
   b. a trade deficit
   c. rising per-unit production costs
   d. excess demand for goods and services

8. Zion's nominal income will go up by 10 percent next year. Inflation is expected to be −2 percent next year. By approximately how much will Zion's real income change next year? **LO29.3**
   a. −2 percent
   b. 8 percent
   c. 10 percent
   d. 12 percent

9. Kaitlin has $10,000 of savings that she may deposit with her local bank. Kaitlin wants to earn a real rate of return of at least 4 percent, and she is expecting inflation to be exactly 3 percent. What is the lowest nominal interest rate that Kaitlin would be willing to accept from her local bank? **LO29.4**
   a. 4 percent
   b. 5 percent
   c. 6 percent
   d. 7 percent

10. True or False: Lenders are helped by unanticipated inflation. **LO29.4**

11. Economists agree that _____ inflation reduces real output. **LO29.5**
    a. cost-push
    b. demand-pull
    c. push-pull

Problems

1. Suppose that a country's annual growth rates were 5, 3, 4, −1, −2, 2, 3, 4, 6, and 3 percent in yearly sequence over a 10-year period. What was the country's trend rate of growth over this period? Which set of years most clearly demonstrates an expansionary phase of the business cycle? Which set of years best illustrates a recessionary phase of the business cycle? **LO29.1**

2. Assume the following data for a country: total population, 500; population under 16 years of age or institutionalized, 120; not in the labor force, 150; unemployed, 23; part-time workers looking for full-time jobs, 10. What is the size of the labor force? What is the official unemployment rate? **LO29.2**

3. Suppose that the natural rate of unemployment in a particular year is 5 percent and the actual unemployment rate is 9 percent. Use Okun's law to determine the size of the GDP gap in percentage-point terms. If potential GDP is $500 billion in that year, how much output is forgone because of cyclical unemployment? **LO29.2**

4. If the CPI was 110 last year and is 121 this year, what is this year's inflation rate? In contrast, suppose that the CPI was 110 last year and is 108 this year. What is this year's inflation rate? What term do economists use to describe this second outcome? **LO29.3**

5. How long would it take for the price level to double if inflation persisted at (*a*) 2 percent per year, (*b*) 5 percent per year, and (*c*) 10 percent per year? **LO29.3**

6. If your nominal income rises by 5.3 percent and the price level rises by 3.8 percent in some year, by what percentage will your real income (approximately) increase? If your nominal income rises by 2.8 percent and your real income rises by 1.1 percent in some year, what is the (approximate) inflation rate? **LO29.4**

7. Suppose that the nominal inflation rate is 4 percent and the inflation premium is 2 percent. What is the real interest rate? Alternatively, assume that the real interest rate is 1 percent and the nominal interest rate is 6 percent. What is the inflation premium? **LO29.4**

8. If the inflation premium is 2 percent and the nominal interest rate is 1 percent, what is the real interest rate? What is the real interest rate if the inflation premium is 3 percent while the nominal interest rate is 0.5 percent? **LO29.4**

Pavel Bobrovskiy/Shutterstock

Basic Macroeconomic Relationships*

>> **LEARNING OBJECTIVES**

LO30.1 Describe how changes in income affect consumption and saving.

LO30.2 List and explain factors other than income that can affect consumption.

LO30.3 Explain how changes in real interest rates affect investment.

LO30.4 Identify and explain factors other than the real interest rate that can affect investment.

LO30.5 Illustrate how changes in investment and the other components of total spending can multiply real GDP.

This chapter examines the basic relationships between three different pairs of economic aggregates. (Recall that "aggregate" means "total" or "combined.") Specifically, this chapter looks at the relationships between:

- Income and consumption (and income and saving).
- The interest rate and investment.
- Changes in spending and changes in output.

The Income-Consumption and Income-Saving Relationships

The direct (positive) relationship between income and consumption is one of the best-established relationships in macroeconomics. In examining this other-things-equal relationship, we are also exploring the relationship between income and saving. Recall that economists define *personal saving* as "not spending" or as "that part of disposable (after-tax) income not consumed." Saving (*S*) equals disposable income (DI) *minus* consumption (*C*).

Many factors determine a nation's levels of consumption and saving, but the most significant is disposable income. Consider some recent historical data for the United States. In Figure 30.1 each dot represents consumption and disposable income for one year since 2002. The line *C* that loosely fits these points shows that consumption is, normally, directly (positively) related to disposable income. Moreover, households spend most of their disposable income.

The **45°(degree) line** is a reference line. Because it bisects the 90° angle formed by the two axes of the graph, each point on it is equidistant from the two axes. At each point on the 45° line, consumption equals disposable income, or *C* = DI. Therefore, the vertical distance between the

>> **LO30.1** Describe how changes in income affect consumption and saving.

45° (degree) line The reference line in a two-dimensional graph that shows equality between the variable measured on the *horizontal axis* and the variable measured on the *vertical axis*. In the *aggregate expenditures model*, the line along which the value of output (measured horizontally) is equal to the value of *aggregate expenditures* (measured vertically).

*Note to the Instructor: If you wish to bypass the aggregate expenditures model (Keynesian cross model) covered in full in Chapter 31, assigning the present chapter will provide a seamless transition to the AD–AS model of Chapter 32 and the chapters beyond. If you want to cover the aggregate expenditures model, this present chapter provides the necessary building blocks.

FIGURE 30.1
Consumption and disposable income, 2002–2021.

Each dot in this figure shows consumption and disposable income in a specific year. The line *C*, which generalizes the relationship between consumption and disposable income, indicates a direct relationship and shows that households consume most of their after-tax incomes.

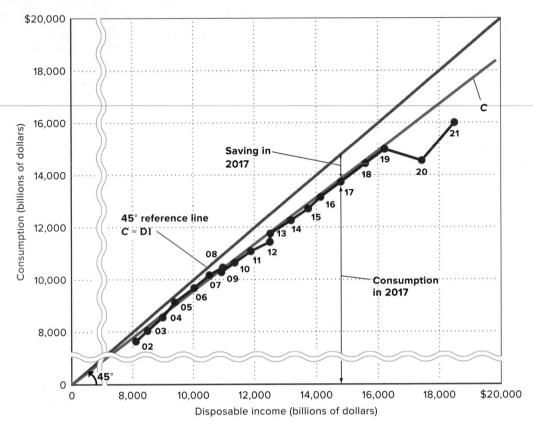

Source: Bureau of Economic Analysis.

45° line and any point on the horizontal axis measures either consumption or disposable income. If we use it to measure disposable income, then the vertical distance between it and the consumption line labeled *C* represents the amount of saving (*S*) in that year.

Saving is the amount by which actual consumption in any year falls short of the 45° line (*S* = DI − *C*). In 2017, for instance, disposable income was $14,801 billion and consumption was $13,725 billion, so saving was $1,076 billion (= $14,801 billion − $13,725 billion). Observe that the vertical distance between the 45° line and line *C* increases as we move rightward along the horizontal axis and decreases as we move leftward. Like consumption, saving typically varies directly with disposable income.

Consumption, Savings, and Disposable Income During the COVID-19 Pandemic

As you examine Figure 30.1, notice that the dots for 2002 through 2019 lie nearly atop line *C*, reflecting that, for each of those successive years, increases in disposable income (measured on the horizontal axis) were accompanied by increases in consumption (measured on the vertical axis). By contrast, if you compare the dots for 2019 and 2020, you will notice that while disposable income increased by $1,213 billion between 2019 and 2020, consumption *fell* by $437 billion between those two years. That is, an increase in disposable income between 2019 and 2020 resulted in a *decrease* in consumption between 2019 and 2020.

What accounts for that highly unusual anomaly in which consumption varied inversely, rather than directly, with disposable income? The answer will probably not surprise you. The anomaly was caused by the COVID-19 pandemic and how the public reacted to the various government stimulus programs which were enacted to fight the pandemic.

As mentioned in earlier chapters, the U.S. government began issuing massive stimulus payments during the spring of 2020 to fight the economic downturn caused by the pandemic. Those payments dramatically increased U.S. disposable income in 2020 and 2021. But Americans were very worried about the future even after those payments started to arrive because nobody could be sure just how long the pandemic might last or how large a toll it might take on the world economy and human health. As a result, people were not eager to spend down the large increase in disposable income that was generated by the stimulus payments. Fearing for the future, much of the windfall was saved, so much so that the personal savings rate increased from 7.6 percent of disposable income in late 2019 to 33.8 percent during the spring of 2020, immediately after lockdowns began.[1] That increase in savings more than offset the increase in disposable income, with the result being that consumption spending fell between 2019 and 2020 despite the sharp increase in disposable income.

If you compare the dots for 2020 and 2021, you will see that the inverse relationship between consumption and disposable income lasted only one year (between 2019 and 2020). Things were back to normal between 2020 and 2021, with higher disposable income (on the horizontal axis) being associated with higher consumption spending (on the vertical axis). That return to normalcy reflected growing confidence in the future as vaccines became available and the pandemic turned out to be less bad than initially feared. As that confidence increased, so did the willingness of individuals to consume, rather than save, out of disposable income.

The Consumption Schedule

The dots in Figure 30.1 represent historical data—the actual amounts of DI, C, and S in the United States over a period of years. But because we want to understand how the economy would behave under different possible scenarios, we need a hypothetical schedule showing the various amounts that households plan to consume at each level of disposable income that might prevail at some specific time. Columns 1 and 2 of Table 30.1, represented in **Figure 30.2a (Key Graph)**, show the hypothetical consumption schedule. This **consumption schedule** (or "consumption function") reflects the direct consumption–disposable income relationship suggested by the data in Figure 30.1. It is consistent with many household budget studies. In the aggregate, households increase their spending as their disposable income rises, and they spend a larger proportion of a small disposable income than of a large disposable income.

The Saving Schedule

It is relatively easy to derive a **saving schedule** (or "saving function"). Because saving equals disposable income less consumption ($S = DI - C$), we need only subtract consumption (Table 30.1, column 2) from disposable income (column 1) to find the amount saved (column 3) at each DI. Thus, columns 1 and 3 in Table 30.1 are the saving schedule, represented in Figure 30.2b. The

consumption schedule A table of numbers showing the amounts *households* plan to spend for *consumer goods* at different levels of *disposable income.*

saving schedule A table of numbers that shows the amounts *households* plan to save (plan not to spend for *consumer goods*), at different levels of *disposable income.*

TABLE 30.1 Consumption and Saving Schedules (in Billions) and Propensities to Consume and Save

(1) Level of Output and Income (GDP = DI)	(2) Consumption (C)	(3) Saving (S), (1) − (2)	(4) Average Propensity to Consume (APC), (2)/(1)	(5) Average Propensity to Save (APS), (3)/(1)	(6) Marginal Propensity to Consume (MPC), Δ(2)/Δ(1)*	(7) Marginal Propensity to Save (MPS), Δ(3)/Δ(1)*
(1) $370	$375	$−5	1.01	−.01		
					.75	.25
(2) 390	390	0	1.00	.00		
					.75	.25
(3) 410	405	5	.99	.01		
					.75	.25
(4) 430	420	10	.98	.02		
					.75	.25
(5) 450	435	15	.97	.03		
					.75	.25
(6) 470	450	20	.96	.04		
					.75	.25
(7) 490	465	25	.95	.05		
					.75	.25
(8) 510	480	30	.94	.06		
					.75	.25
(9) 530	495	35	.93	.07		
					.75	.25
(10) 550	510	40	.93	.07		

*The Greek letter Δ, delta, means "the change in."

---

[1] By comparison, the previous all-time high for the savings rate was 17.3 percent (in May of 1975).

..Il KEY GRAPH

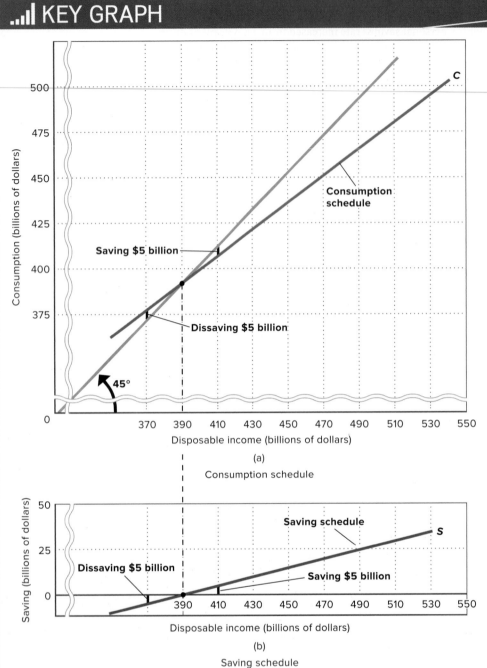

FIGURE 30.2 **Consumption and saving schedules.**

The two parts of this figure show the income-consumption and income-saving relationships in Table 30.1 graphically. (a) Consumption rises as income increases. Saving is negative (dissaving occurs) when the consumption schedule is above the 45° line, and saving is positive when the consumption schedule is below the 45° line. (b) Like consumption, saving increases as income goes up. The saving schedule is found by subtracting the consumption schedule in the top graph vertically from the 45° line. For these hypothetical data, saving is —$5 billion at $370 billion of income, zero at $390 billion of income, and $5 billion at $410 billion of income. Saving is zero where consumption equals disposable income.

QUICK QUIZ FOR FIGURE 30.2

1. **The slope of the consumption schedule in this figure is 0.75. Thus, the:**
   a. slope of the saving schedule is 1.33.
   b. marginal propensity to consume is 0.75.
   c. average propensity to consume is 0.25.
   d. slope of the saving schedule is also 0.75.

2. **In this figure, when consumption is a positive amount, saving:**
   a. must be a negative amount.
   b. must also be a positive amount.
   c. can be either a positive or a negative amount.
   d. is zero.

3. **In this figure:**
   a. the marginal propensity to consume is constant at all levels of income.
   b. the marginal propensity to save rises as disposable income rises.
   c. consumption is inversely (negatively) related to disposable income.
   d. saving is inversely (negatively) related to disposable income.

4. **When consumption equals disposable income:**
   a. the marginal propensity to consume is zero.
   b. the average propensity to consume is zero.
   c. consumption and saving must be equal.
   d. saving must be zero.

graph shows the direct relationship between saving and DI. It also shows that saving is a smaller proportion of a small DI than of a large DI. If households consume a smaller and smaller proportion of DI as DI increases, then they must be saving a larger and larger proportion of DI.

Remembering that at each point on the 45° line consumption equals DI, we see that *dissaving* (consuming in excess of after-tax income) will occur at relatively low DIs. For example, at $370 billion (row 1, Table 30.1), consumption is $375 billion. Households can consume more than their current incomes by liquidating (selling for cash) accumulated wealth or by borrowing. Graphically, dissaving is shown as the vertical distance of the consumption schedule above the 45° line or as the vertical distance of the saving schedule below the horizontal axis. We have marked the dissaving at the $370 billion level of income in Figures 30.2a and 30.2b. Both vertical distances measure the $5 billion of dissaving that occurs at $370 billion of income.

In our example, the **break-even income** is $390 billion (row 2, Table 30.1). At this income level, households plan to consume their entire incomes ($C =$ DI). Graphically, the consumption schedule cuts the 45° line, and the saving schedule cuts the horizontal axis (saving is zero) at the break-even income level.

At all higher incomes, households plan to save part of their incomes. Graphically, the vertical distance between the consumption schedule and the 45° line measures this saving (see Figure 30.2a), as does the vertical distance between the saving schedule and the horizontal axis (see Figure 30.2b). For example, at the $410 billion level of income (row 3, Table 30.1), both these distances indicate $5 billion of saving.

Average and Marginal Propensities

Columns 4 to 7 in Table 30.1 show additional characteristics of the consumption and saving schedules.

APC and APS The fraction, or percentage, of total income that is consumed is the **average propensity to consume (APC)**. The fraction of total income that is saved is the **average propensity to save (APS)**:

$$APC = \frac{consumption}{income}$$

and

$$APS = \frac{saving}{income}$$

For example, at $470 billion of income (row 6, Table 30.1), the APC is $\frac{450}{470} = \frac{45}{47}$, or about 0.96 ($= 96$ percent), while the APS is $\frac{20}{470} = \frac{2}{47}$, or about 0.04 ($= 4$ percent). Columns 4 and 5 in Table 30.1 show the APC and APS at each of the 10 levels of DI. The APC falls as DI increases, while the APS rises as DI goes up.

Because disposable income is either consumed or saved, the fraction of any DI consumed plus the fraction saved (not consumed) must exhaust that income. Mathematically, APC + APS = 1 at any level of disposable income, as columns 4 and 5 in Table 30.1 illustrate. So if 0.96 of the $470 billion of income in row 6 is consumed, 0.04 must be saved. That is why APC + APS = 1.

Global Perspective 30.1 shows APCs for several countries.

MPC and MPS The fact that households consume a certain proportion of a particular total income, for example, $\frac{45}{47}$ of a $470 billion disposable income, does not guarantee they will consume the same proportion of any *change* in income they might receive. The proportion, or fraction, of any change in income consumed is called the **marginal propensity to consume (MPC)**, "marginal" meaning "extra" or "a change in." Equivalently, the MPC is the ratio of a change in consumption to a change in the income that caused the consumption change:

$$MPC = \frac{change\ in\ consumption}{change\ in\ income}$$

The fraction of any change in income saved is the **marginal propensity to save (MPS)**. The MPS is the ratio of a change in saving to the change in income that brought it about:

$$MPS = \frac{change\ in\ saving}{change\ in\ income}$$

break-even income The level of *disposable income* at which *households* plan to consume (spend) all their income and to save none of it.

average propensity to consume (APC) Fraction (or percentage) of *disposable income* that *households* spend on *consumer goods*; consumption divided by *disposable income*.

average propensity to save (APS) Fraction (or percentage) of *disposable income* that *households* save; *saving* divided by *disposable income*.

marginal propensity to consume (MPC) The fraction of any change in *disposable income* spent for *consumer goods*; equal to the change in consumption divided by the change in disposable income.

marginal propensity to save (MPS) The fraction of any change in *disposable income* that *households* save; equal to the change in *saving* divided by the change in disposable income.

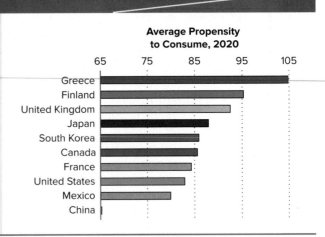

GLOBAL PERSPECTIVE 30.1

AVERAGE PROPENSITIES TO CONSUME, SELECTED NATIONS

There are surprisingly large differences in average propensities to consume (APCs) among nations. In 2020, Greece had an APC higher than 100 percent, indicating dissaving (negative saving). Most countries have APCs between 80 and 95 percent of disposable income. By contrast, China has a very high savings rate, leading to an APC of only 65 percent.

Source: Bureau of Economic Analysis.

If disposable income starts at $470 billion (row 6 horizontally in Table 30.1) and then rises by $20 billion to $490 billion (row 7), households will consume $\frac{15}{20}$, or $\frac{3}{4}$, and save $\frac{5}{20}$, or $\frac{1}{4}$, of that increase in income. In other words, the MPC is $\frac{3}{4}$ or 0.75, and the MPS is $\frac{1}{4}$ or 0.25, as shown in columns 6 and 7.

The sum of the MPC and the MPS for any change in disposable income must always be 1. Consuming or saving out of extra income is an either-or proposition; the fraction of any change in income not consumed is, by definition, saved. If 0.75 of extra disposable income is consumed, 0.25 must be saved. The fraction consumed (MPC) plus the fraction saved (MPS) must exhaust the whole change in income:

$$MPC + MPS = 1$$

FIGURE 30.3
The marginal propensity to consume and the marginal propensity to save.

In the two parts of this figure, the Greek letter delta (Δ) means "the change in." (a) The MPC is the slope ($\Delta C/\Delta DI$) of the consumption schedule. (b) The MPS is the slope ($\Delta S/\Delta DI$) of the saving schedule.

In our example, 0.75 plus 0.25 equals 1.

MPC and MPS as Slopes The MPC is the numerical value of the slope of the consumption schedule, and the MPS is the numerical value of the slope of the saving schedule. We know from the appendix to Chapter 1 that the slope of any line is the ratio of the vertical change to the horizontal change occasioned in moving from one point to another on that line.

Figure 30.3 measures the slopes of the consumption and saving lines, using enlarged portions of Figures 30.2a and 30.2b. Observe that consumption changes by $15 billion (the vertical change) for each $20 billion change in disposable income (the horizontal change). The slope of the consumption line is thus 0.75 (= $15/$20), which is the value of the MPC. Saving changes by $5 billion (shown as the vertical change) for every $20 billion change in disposable income (shown as the horizontal change). The slope of the saving line therefore is 0.25 (= $5/$20), which is the value of the MPS.

► Both consumption spending and saving rise when disposable income increases; both fall when disposable income decreases.

► The average propensity to consume (APC) is the fraction of any specific level of disposable income that is spent on consumer goods; the average propensity to save (APS) is the fraction of any specific level of disposable income that is saved. As disposable income increases, the APC falls and the APS rises.

► The marginal propensity to consume (MPC) is the fraction of a change in disposable income that is consumed, and it is the slope of the consumption schedule. The marginal propensity to save (MPS) is the fraction of a change in disposable income that is saved, and it is the slope of the saving schedule.

Nonincome Determinants of Consumption and Saving

Disposable income is the primary determinant of the amounts households will consume and save. But other determinants might prompt households to consume more or less at each possible level of income. Those other determinants are wealth, borrowing, expectations, and interest rates.

>> **LO30.2** List and explain factors other than income that can affect consumption.

- *Wealth* A household's wealth is the dollar amount of all the assets that it owns minus the dollar amount of its liabilities (its total debt). Households build wealth by saving money out of current income. The point of building wealth is to increase consumption possibilities. The larger a household's stock of wealth, the larger its present and future consumption possibilities.

  When events suddenly boost the value of existing wealth, households tend to increase their spending and reduce their saving. This **wealth effect** shifts the consumption schedule upward and the saving schedule downward. The schedules move in response to households taking advantage of the increased consumption possibilities granted by the sudden wealth increase. Examples: In the late 1990s, skyrocketing U.S. stock values expanded the value of household wealth by increasing the value of household assets. Predictably, households spent more and saved less. In contrast, a strong "reverse wealth effect" occurred in 2008. Plunging real estate and stock market prices joined to erase $11.2 trillion (yes, trillion) of household wealth. Consumers quickly reacted by reducing their consumption spending. The consumption schedule shifted downward.

wealth effect The tendency for people to increase their consumption spending when the value of their financial and real *assets* rises and to decrease their consumption spending when the value of those assets falls.

- *Borrowing* When a household borrows, it can increase current consumption beyond its disposable income. By allowing households to spend more, borrowing shifts the current consumption schedule upward.

  But note that there is no "free lunch." While borrowing in the present allows for higher consumption now, it necessitates lower consumption in the future when the debt must be repaid. Stated differently, increased borrowing increases debt (liabilities), which in turn reduces household wealth (because wealth = assets − liabilities). This reduction in wealth reduces future consumption possibilities.

- *Expectations* Household expectations about future prices and income may affect current spending and saving. For example, the expectation of higher prices tomorrow may cause households to buy more today while prices are still low. Thus, the current consumption schedule shifts up and the current saving schedule shifts down. In contrast, expectations of a recession and thus lower income in the future may lead households to reduce consumption and save more today. Greater present saving will help households build wealth that will help them ride out the expected bad times. The consumption schedule therefore shifts down and the saving schedule shifts up.

- *Real interest rates* When real interest rates (those adjusted for inflation) fall, households tend to borrow more, consume more, and save less. A lower real interest rate, for example, decreases monthly loan payments and induces consumers to purchase automobiles and other goods bought on credit. A lower real interest rate also diminishes the incentive to save because of the reduced interest "payment" to the saver. These effects on consumption and saving, however, are very modest. They mainly shift consumption toward some products (those bought on credit) and away from others. At best, lower real interest rates shift the consumption schedule slightly upward and the saving schedule slightly downward. Higher real interest rates do the opposite.

Other Important Considerations

We must make several additional important points regarding the consumption and saving schedules:

- *Switching to real GDP* When developing macroeconomic models, economists change their focus from the relationship between consumption (and saving) and *disposable income* to the relationship between consumption (and saving) and *real domestic output (real GDP)*. This modification is reflected in Figures 30.4a and 30.4b, where the horizontal axes measure real GDP.

- *Changes along schedules* The movement from one point to another on a consumption schedule (for example, from *a* to *b* on C_0 in Figure 30.4a) is a *change in the amount consumed* and is caused solely by a change in real GDP. On the other hand, an upward or downward shift of the entire schedule, for example, a shift from C_0 to C_1 or C_2 in Figure 30.4a, is a *shift of the consumption schedule* and is caused by changes in any one or more of the *nonincome* determinants of consumption just discussed.

  Similar terminology applies to the saving schedule in Figure 30.4b.

- *Simultaneous shifts* Changes in wealth, expectations, interest rates, and household debt shift the consumption schedule in one direction and the saving schedule in the opposite direction. If households decide to consume more at each possible level of real GDP, they must save less, and vice versa. (Even when they spend more by borrowing, they are, in effect, reducing their current saving by the amount borrowed because borrowing is, effectively, "negative saving.") Graphically, if the consumption schedule shifts upward from C_0 to C_1 in Figure 30.4a, the saving schedule shifts downward, from S_0 to S_1 in Figure 30.4b. Similarly, a downward shift of the consumption schedule from C_0 to C_2 means an upward shift of the saving schedule from S_0 to S_2.

- *Taxation* A change in taxes shifts the consumption and saving schedules in the same direction. Taxes are paid partly at the expense of consumption and partly at the expense of saving. So an increase in taxes reduces consumption *and* saving, thereby shifting downward both the consumption schedule in Figure 30.4a and the saving schedule in Figure 30.4b. Conversely, households partly consume and partly save any decrease in taxes. Both the consumption schedule and saving schedule shift upward.

- *Stability* The consumption and saving schedules usually are relatively stable unless altered by major tax increases or decreases. Their stability may come from the fact that consumption–saving decisions are strongly influenced by long-term considerations such as saving to meet emergencies or saving for retirement. In addition, changes in the nonincome determinants frequently work in opposite directions and therefore may be self-canceling.

FIGURE 30.4
Shifts of the (a) consumption and (b) saving schedules.

Normally, if households consume more at each level of real GDP, they are necessarily saving less. Graphically this means that an upward shift of the consumption schedule (C_0 to C_1) entails a downward shift of the saving schedule (S_0 to S_1). If households consume less at each level of real GDP, they are saving more. A downward shift of the consumption schedule (C_0 to C_2) is reflected in an upward shift of the saving schedule (S_0 to S_2). This pattern breaks down, however, when taxes change; then the consumption and saving schedules move in the *same* direction—opposite to the direction of the tax change.

(a)
Consumption schedule

(b)
Saving schedule

CONSIDER THIS . . .

The Pandemic Recession and the Paradox of Thrift

The Pandemic Recession of 2020 altered the prior consumption and saving behavior in the economy. Concerned about reduced wealth, high debt, and potential job losses, households increased their saving and reduced their consumption at each level of after-tax income (or each level of GDP). In Figure 30.4, this outcome is illustrated as the downward *shift* of the consumption schedule in the top graph and the upward *shift* of the saving schedule in the lower graph.

This change of behavior illustrates the so-called **paradox of thrift,** which refers to the possibility that a recession can be made worse when households become more thrifty and save in response to the downturn. The paradox of thrift rests on two major ironies. One irony is that saving more is *good* for the economy in the long run, as noted in Chapter 1 and Chapter 26. It finances investment and therefore fuels subsequent economic

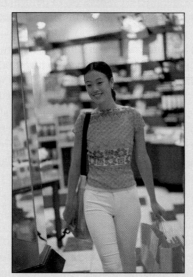

Digital Vision/Getty Images

growth. But saving more can be *bad* for the economy during a recession. Because firms are pessimistic about future sales, the increased saving is not likely to be matched by an equal amount of added investment. The extra saving simply reduces spending on currently produced goods and services. That means that even more businesses suffer, more layoffs occur, and people's incomes decline even more.

The paradox of thrift has a second irony related to the so-called *fallacy of composition:* Households as a group may inadvertently end up saving less when each individual household tries to save more during a recession. This is because each household's attempt to save more implies that it is also attempting to spend less. Across all households, that collective reduction in total spending in the economy creates additional job losses and further drives down total income. The decline in total income reduces the ability of households as a group to save as much as they did before their spending reduction and subsequent income decline.

The Interest-Rate–Investment Relationship

Recall that investment consists of expenditures on new plants, capital equipment, machinery, inventories, and so on. The investment decision is a marginal-benefit–marginal-cost decision: The marginal benefit from investment is the expected rate of return businesses hope to realize. The marginal cost is the interest rate that businesses must pay to borrow money. Businesses will invest in all projects for which the expected rate of return exceeds the real interest rate. Expected returns (profits) and the real interest rate therefore determine investment spending.

Expected Rate of Return

Investment spending is guided by the profit motive; businesses buy capital goods only when they think such purchases will be profitable. Suppose the owner of a small auto parts business is considering whether to invest in a new 3-D printer that costs $1,000 and has a useful life of only 1 year. The new machine will increase the firm's output and sales revenue. Suppose the net expected revenue from the machine (that is, revenue after subtracting operating costs such as electricity, labor, and certain taxes) is $1,100. After subtracting the $1,000 cost of the machine from the net expected revenue of $1,100, the firm will have an expected profit of $100. Dividing this $100 profit by the $1,000 cost of the machine, we find that the machine's **expected rate of return,** r, is 10 percent (= $100/$1,000). It is important to note that this rate of return is *expected*, not *guaranteed*. The investment may or may not generate as much revenue or as much profit as anticipated. Investment involves risk.

The Real Interest Rate

In our example, the interest cost of an investment is computed by multiplying the interest rate, i, by the $1,000 borrowed to buy the machine. If the interest rate is, say, 7 percent, the total interest cost will be $70. This amount compares favorably with the net expected return of $100, which equals a 10 percent expected rate of return. If the investment works out as expected, it will add $30 to the firm's profit.

>> **LO30.3** Explain how changes in real interest rates affect investment.

paradox of thrift The possibility that households trying to protect themselves against a recession by saving more may inadvertently worsen the recession and hurt themselves by reducing overall consumption and economic activity.

expected rate of return The increase in profit a *firm* anticipates it will obtain by purchasing capital or engaging in research and development (*R&D*); expressed as a percentage of the total cost of the investment (or R&D) activity.

We can generalize as follows: If the expected rate of return (10 percent) exceeds the interest rate (here, 7 percent), the investment should be undertaken. The firm expects the investment to be profitable. But if the interest rate (say, 12 percent) exceeds the expected rate of return (10 percent), the investment should not be undertaken because the firm expects the investment to be unprofitable.

The firm should undertake every investment project that it expects to be profitable. In other words, the firm should array its prospective investment projects from the highest expected rate of return, r, downward and then invest in all projects for which r exceeds i. The firm should invest to the point where $r = i$ because then it will have undertaken all investments for which r is greater than i.

The *real* interest rate, rather than the *nominal* rate, is crucial in making investment decisions. Recall from Chapter 29 that the nominal interest rate is expressed in dollars of current value, while the real interest rate is stated in constant or inflation-adjusted dollars. Also recall that the real interest rate is the nominal rate minus the inflation rate. In our 3-D printer illustration, our implicit assumption of a constant price level ensures that all our data, including the interest rate, are in real terms.

But what if inflation is occurring? Suppose a $1,000 investment is expected to yield a real (inflation-adjusted) return of 10 percent and the nominal interest rate is 15 percent. At first glance, we would say the investment would be unprofitable. But assume there is ongoing inflation of 10 percent per year. In that case, the investing firm will pay back dollars with approximately 10 percent less in purchasing power. While the nominal interest rate is 15 percent, the real rate is only 5 percent (= 15 percent − 10 percent). By comparing this 5 percent real interest rate with the 10 percent expected real rate of return, we find that the investment is potentially profitable and should be undertaken.

Investment Demand Curve

We now move from a single firm's investment decision to total demand for investment goods by the entire business sector. Assume that every firm has estimated the expected rates of return from all investment projects and has recorded those data. We can sum these data by asking: How many dollars' worth of investment projects have an expected rate of return of, say, 16 percent or more? How many have 14 percent or more? How many have 12 percent or more? And so on.

Suppose no prospective investments yield an expected return of 16 percent or more. But there are $5 billion of investment opportunities with expected rates of return between 14 and 16 percent; an additional $5 billion yielding between 12 and 14 percent; an additional $5 billion yielding between 10 and 12 percent; and an additional $5 billion in each successive 2 percent range of yield down to and including the 0 to 2 percent range.

To sum these figures for each rate of return, r, we add the amounts of investment that will yield each particular rate of return r or higher. Doing so provides the data table and the graph in **Figure 30.5 (Key Graph)**. In the table, the number opposite 12 percent, for example, means there are $10 billion of investment opportunities that will yield an expected rate of return of 12 percent or more. The $10 billion includes the $5 billion of investment expected to yield a return of 14 percent or more plus the $5 billion expected to yield between 12 and 14 percent.

Our example of the 3-D printer tells us that a firm will undertake an investment project whose expected rate of return, r, exceeds the real interest rate, i. Let's first suppose i is 12 percent. Businesses will undertake all investments for which r exceeds 12 percent. That is, they will invest until the 12 percent rate of return equals the 12 percent interest rate. Figure 30.5 reveals that $10 billion of investment spending will be undertaken at a 12 percent interest rate. In other words, $10 billion of investment projects have an expected rate of return of 12 percent or more.

Put another way: When the "price" of borrowing is 12 percent, firms will demand $10 billion of investment goods. If the interest rate is lower, say, 8 percent, the amount of investment for which r equals or exceeds i is $20 billion. Thus, firms will demand $20 billion of investment goods at an 8 percent real interest rate. At 6 percent, they will demand $25 billion of investment goods.

By applying the marginal-benefit–marginal-cost rule that firms should undertake investment projects up to the point where $r = i$, we see that we can add the real interest rate to the vertical axis in Figure 30.5. That is, the curve in Figure 30.5 not only shows rates of return; it also shows the quantity of investment demanded at each "price" i (interest rate) of investment. The vertical axis in Figure 30.5 shows the various possible real interest rates, and the horizontal axis shows the corresponding quantities of investment demanded. The inverse (downward sloping) relationship

..ıll KEY GRAPH

FIGURE 30.5   The investment demand curve.

The investment demand curve is constructed by arraying all potential investment projects in descending order of their expected rates of return. The curve slopes downward, reflecting an inverse relationship between the real interest rate (the financial "price" of each dollar of investing) and the quantity of investment demanded.

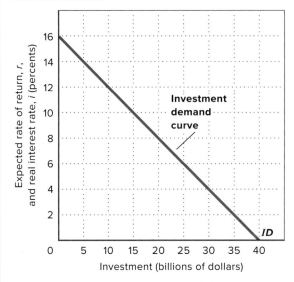

Real Interest Rate (*i*) and Expected Rate of Return (*r*)	Cumulative Amount of Investment Having this Rate of Return or Higher, Billions per Year
16%	$ 0
14	5
12	10
10	15
8	20
6	25
4	30
2	35
0	40

QUICK QUIZ FOR FIGURE 30.5

1. **The investment demand curve:**
   a. reflects a direct (positive) relationship between the real interest rate and investment.
   b. reflects an inverse (negative) relationship between the real interest rate and investment.
   c. shifts to the right when the real interest rate rises.
   d. shifts to the left when the real interest rate rises.

2. **In this figure:**
   a. greater cumulative amounts of investment are associated with lower real interest rates.
   b. lesser cumulative amounts of investment are associated with lower expected rates of return on investment.
   c. higher interest rates are associated with higher expected rates of return on investment, and therefore greater amounts of investment.
   d. interest rates and investment move in the same direction.

3. **In this figure, if the real interest rate falls from 6 to 4 percent:**
   a. investment will increase from 0 to $30 billion.
   b. investment will decrease by $5 billion.
   c. the expected rate of return will rise by $5 billion.
   d. investment will increase from $25 billion to $30 billion.

4. **In this figure, investment will be:**
   a. zero if the real interest rate is zero.
   b. $40 billion if the real interest rate is 16 percent.
   c. $30 billion if the real interest rate is 4 percent.
   d. $20 billion if the real interest rate is 12 percent.

Answers: 1. b; 2. a; 3. d; 4. c

---

between the interest rate (price) and the dollar quantity of investment demanded conforms to the law of demand discussed in Chapter 3. The curve *ID* in Figure 30.5 is the economy's **investment demand curve.** It shows the amount of investment at each real interest rate. The level of investment depends on the expected rate of return and the real interest rate.

investment demand curve
A curve that shows the amounts of *investment* demanded by an economy at a series of *real interest rates*.

▶ Changes in consumer wealth, consumer expectations, interest rates, household debt, and taxes can shift the consumption and saving schedules (as they relate to real GDP).

▶ A specific investment will be undertaken if the expected rate of return, *r*, equals or exceeds the real interest rate, *i*.

▶ The investment demand curve shows the total monetary amounts that will be invested by an economy at various possible real interest rates.

QUICK REVIEW

30.2

Shifts of the Investment Demand Curve

>> **LO30.4** Identify and explain factors other than the real interest rate that can affect investment.

Figure 30.5 shows the relationship between the real interest rate and the amount of investment demanded, other things equal. When other things change, the investment demand curve shifts. In general, any factor that leads businesses collectively to expect greater rates of return on their investments increases investment demand. That factor shifts the investment demand curve to the right, as from ID_0 to ID_1 in Figure 30.6. Any factor that leads businesses collectively to expect lower rates of return on their investments shifts the curve to the left, as from ID_0 to ID_2. What are those non-interest-rate determinants of investment demand?

- *Acquisition, maintenance, and operating costs* The initial costs of capital goods, and the estimated costs of operating and maintaining those items, affect the expected rate of return on investment. When these costs rise, the expected rate of return from prospective investment projects falls, and the investment demand curve shifts to the left. Example: Higher electricity costs associated with operating tools and machinery shift the investment demand curve to the left. Lower costs shift it to the right.

- *Business taxes* Firms look to expected returns *after taxes* in making their investment decisions. An increase in business taxes lowers the expected profitability of investments and shifts the investment demand curve to the left; a reduction of business taxes shifts it to the right.

- *Technological change* Technological progress—the development of new products, improvements in existing products, and the creation of new machinery and production processes—stimulates investment. The development of a more efficient machine, for example, lowers production costs or improves product quality and increases the expected rate of return from investing in the machine. Profitable new products (cholesterol medications, flying drones, self-driving cars, and so on) induce a flurry of investment as businesses tool up for expanded production. A rapid rate of technological progress shifts the investment demand curve to the right.

- *Stock of capital goods on hand* The stock of capital goods on hand, relative to output and sales, influences firms' investment decisions. When the economy is overstocked with production facilities and when firms have excessive inventories of finished goods, the expected rate of return on new investment declines. Firms with excess production capacity have little incentive to invest in new capital. Therefore, less investment is forthcoming at each real interest rate; the investment demand curve shifts leftward.

  When the economy is understocked with production facilities and when firms are selling their output as fast as they can produce it, the expected rate of return on new investment increases, and the investment demand curve shifts rightward.

- *Planned inventory changes* Recall from Chapter 27 that the definition of investment includes changes in inventories of unsold goods. An increase in inventories is a positive investment while a decrease in inventories is a negative investment. It is important to remember that some inventory changes are planned, while others are unplanned. Because the investment demand curve shows only planned investment, it is affected only by planned changes in

FIGURE 30.6
Shifts of the investment demand curve.

Increases in investment demand are shown as rightward shifts of the investment demand curve; decreases in investment demand are shown as leftward shifts of the investment demand curve.

firms' inventory levels. If firms plan to increase their inventories, the investment demand curve shifts to the right. If firms plan to decrease their inventories, the investment demand curve shifts to the left.

Firms make planned changes to their inventory levels mostly because they expect either faster or slower sales. A firm that expects its sales to double next year will want to keep more inventory in stock, thereby increasing its investment demand. By contrast, a firm that is expecting slower sales will plan to reduce its inventory, thereby reducing its overall investment demand. But because life often does not turn out as expected, firms often find that the actual amount of inventory investment that they end up making is either more or less than what they had planned. The size of the gap is the dollar amount of unplanned inventory changes.

- *Expectations* Most capital goods are durable, with a life expectancy of 10 or 20 years. Thus, the expected rate of return on capital investment depends on the firm's expectations of future sales, future operating costs, and future profitability of the product that the capital helps produce. These expectations are based on forecasts of future business conditions as well as on difficult-to-predict factors, such as changes in the domestic political climate, international relations, population growth, and consumer tastes. If executives become more optimistic about future sales, costs, and profits, the investment demand curve will shift to the right; a pessimistic outlook will shift the curve to the left.

Instability of Investment

Unlike consumption, investment is unstable; it rises and falls quite often. In fact, investment is the most volatile component of total spending—so much so that most fluctuations in output and employment result from demand shocks relating to unexpected increases and decreases in investment. Several interrelated factors explain the variability of investment.

- *Variability of expectations* Business expectations can change quickly when some event suggests a significant possible change in future business conditions. Changes in exchange rates, trade barriers, legislative actions, stock market prices, government economic policies, the outlook for war or peace, court decisions in key labor or antitrust cases, and a host of other considerations may substantially shift business expectations.

- *Durability* Within limits, purchases of capital goods are discretionary and therefore can be postponed. Firms can scrap or replace older equipment and buildings, or they can patch them up and use them for a few more years. Optimism about the future may prompt firms to replace their older facilities, and such modernizing will call for a high level of investment. A less optimistic view, however, may lead to smaller amounts of investment as firms repair older facilities and keep them in use.

- *Irregularity of innovation* New products and processes stimulate investment. Major innovations such as electricity, airplanes, automobiles, computers, and artificial intelligence induce vast upsurges or "waves" of investment spending that in time recede. But such innovations occur quite irregularly, adding to the volatility of investment.

- *Variability of profits* High current profits often generate optimism about the future profitability of new investments, whereas low current profits or losses spawn considerable doubt about the wisdom of new investments. Additionally, firms often save a portion of current profits as retained earnings and use these funds (as well as borrowed funds) to finance new investments. So current profits affect both the incentive and ability to invest. But profits themselves are highly variable from year to year, contributing to the volatility of investment.

The volatility of investment causes occasional and substantial unexpected shifts of the investment demand curve (as in Figure 30.6), which in turn generate significant changes in investment spending. These demand shocks can contribute to cyclical instability.

▶ The investment demand curve shifts when changes occur in (a) the costs of acquiring, operating, and maintaining capital goods, (b) business taxes, (c) technology, (d) the stock of capital goods on hand, and (e) business expectations.

▶ Investment is the most volatile component of total spending and most fluctuations in output and employment result from investment demand shocks.

▶ Investment volatility is driven by (a) changing expectations, (b) the flexibility that firms have to delay capital purchases, (c) the irregularity of innovation, and (d) fluctuations in profits, which affect the enthusiasm for investment and the money available to fund it.

QUICK REVIEW

30.3

The Multiplier Effect*

>> **LO30.5** Illustrate how changes in investment and the other components of total spending can multiply real GDP.

Assuming that the economy has room to expand—so that increases in spending do not lead to increases in prices—there is a direct (positive) relationship between changes in spending and changes in real GDP. More spending results in a higher real GDP; less spending results in a lower real GDP.

But there is much more to the relationship between these two aggregates. As an example, note that an initial change in investment spending can change output and income by a larger amount (that is, by an amount larger than the initial change in investment spending). That surprising result is called the multiplier effect: any initial change in a component of total spending can lead to a larger change in GDP.

multiplier The ratio of a change in *equilibrium GDP* to the change in *investment* or in any other component of *aggregate expenditures* or *aggregate demand;* the number by which a change in any such component must be multiplied to find the resulting change in equilibrium GDP.

The number known as the **multiplier** determines how much larger that change will be; it is the ratio of the change in GDP to the initial change in spending (in this case, investment). Stated algebraically,

$$\text{Multiplier} = \frac{\text{change in real GDP}}{\text{initial change in spending}}$$

By rearranging this equation, we can also say that the change in real GDP = multiplier × initial change in spending.

So if investment in an economy rises by $30 billion and GDP increases by $90 billion as a result, we know from the first version of that equation that the multiplier is 3 (= $90/$30).

Note these three points about the multiplier:

- The "initial change in spending" is usually associated with investment spending. But changes in consumption (unrelated to changes in income), net exports, and government purchases can also generate multiplier effects.

- The "initial change in spending" associated with investment spending results from a change in the real interest rate and/or a shift of the investment demand curve.

- The multiplier works in both directions. An initial increase in spending will create a "multiplied" increase in GDP, while an initial decrease in spending will create a "multiplied" decrease in GDP.

Rationale

The multiplier effect follows from two facts:

- First, the economy supports a continuous flow of expenditures and income through which dollars spent by Lee are received as income by Okafor and then spent by Okafor and received as income by Mendoza, and so on. (This chapter's Last Word presents this idea in a humorous way.)

- Second, any change in income changes both consumption and saving in the same direction as, and by a constant fraction of, the change in income.

It follows that an initial change in spending will start a "spending chain" throughout the economy—a chain in which each successive link is fractionally smaller than the previous link. That chain of spending will multiply the initial change in GDP. As a result, any initial change in spending will produce a magnified change in output and income.

The table in **Figure 30.7 (Key Graph)** illustrates the rationale underlying the multiplier effect. Suppose that a $5.00 billion increase in investment spending occurs. We assume that the MPC is 0.75, the MPS is 0.25, and prices remain constant. That is, neither the initial increase in spending nor any of the subsequent increases in spending cause prices to rise.

The initial $5.00 billion increase in investment spending generates an equal amount of wage, rent, interest, and profit income that will flow to households because spending and receiving

---

*Instructors who cover the full aggregate expenditures (AE) model (Chapter 31) rather than moving directly to aggregate demand and aggregate supply (Chapter 32) may choose to defer this discussion until after the analysis of equilibrium real GDP.

..ıll KEY GRAPH

FIGURE 30.7 The multiplier process (MPC = 0.75).

An initial change in investment spending of $5.00 billion creates an equal $5.00 billion of new income in round 1. Under our assumption that households have a marginal propensity to consume (MPC) equal to 0.75, households will spend $3.75 (= 0.75 × $5.00) billion of this new income, creating $3.75 billion of added income in round 2. Of this $3.75 billion of new income, households will spend $2.81 (= 0.75 × $3.75) billion, and income will rise by that amount in round 3. Such income increments over the entire process get successively smaller but eventually produce a total change in income and GDP of $20 billion. The multiplier therefore is 4 (= $20 billion/$5 billion).

	(1) Change in Income	(2) Change in Consumption (MPC = 0.75)	(3) Change in Saving (MPS = 0.25)
Increase in investment of **$5.00**	$5.00	$ 3.75	$1.25
Second round	3.75	2.81	0.94
Third round	2.81	2.11	0.70
Fourth round	2.11	1.58	0.53
Fifth round	1.58	1.19	0.39
All other rounds	4.75	3.56	1.19
Total	**$20.00**	$15.00	$5.00

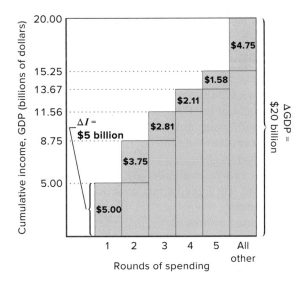

QUICK QUIZ FOR FIGURE 30.7

1. If the multiplier process stopped after two rounds, the cumulative change in income would be:
   a. $3.75.
   b. $5.00.
   c. $8.75.
   d. $20.00.

2. If the marginal propensity to consume (MPC) were larger than 0.75:
   a. the total change in income after all rounds would be less than $20.
   b. the marginal propensity to save would also increase.
   c. the total change in income after all rounds would still be $20.
   d. the multiplier would be larger than 4.

3. If the marginal propensity to save (MPS) were 0.40, the multiplier would be:
   a. less than 4.
   b. equal to 4.
   c. greater than 4.
   d. depends on what MPC equaled.

4. For the multiplier to be equal to 1, it would have to be the case that:
   a. MPC = 1.
   b. MPS = 1.
   c. MPS = 0.
   d. MPC = MPS = 1.

Answers: 1. c; 2. d; 3. a; 4. b

income are two sides of the same transaction. What businesses spend on investment, households will receive as income.

The $5.00 billion increase in household income will prompt an initial increase in consumption. How large will that initial increase in consumption be? We find the answer by applying the marginal propensity to consume of 0.75 to this change in income. The $5.00 billion increase in household income raises consumption by $3.75 (= 0.75 × $5) billion and saving by $1.25 (= 0.25 × $5) billion, as shown in columns 2 and 3 in the table.

Other households receive as income (second round) the $3.75 billion of consumption spending. Those households consume 0.75 of this $3.75 billion, or $2.81 billion, and save 0.25 of it, or $0.94 billion. The $2.81 billion that is consumed flows to still other households as income to be spent or saved (third round). And the process continues, with the added consumption and income becoming less in each round. The process ends when there is no more additional income to spend.

The bar chart in Figure 30.7 shows several rounds of this multiplier process, each bar corresponding to a row in the table. As shown by rounds 1 to 5 in the bar chart, each round adds a smaller and smaller blue block to national income and GDP. The process continues beyond the five rounds shown (for convenience we have simply cumulated the subsequent declining blocks into a single block labeled "All other"). The accumulation of the additional income in each round—the sum of the blue blocks—is the total change in income or GDP resulting from the initial $5.00 billion change in spending. Because the spending and responding effects of the increase in investment diminish with each successive round of spending, the cumulative increase in output and income eventually ends. In this case, the ending occurs when $20 billion of additional income accumulates. Thus, the multiplier is 4 (= $20 billion/$5 billion).

The Multiplier and the Marginal Propensities

You may have sensed from the table in Figure 30.7 that the fraction of any increase in income that is consumed (MPC) or saved (MPS) determines the size of the multiplier. That is true because the value of the MPC or MPS determines the size of each of the successive rounds of spending caused by any initial change in spending. The larger the MPC (smaller the MPS), the larger each successive round will be. The smaller the MPC (the larger the MPS), the smaller each successive round will be.

The MPC and the multiplier are directly related, while the MPS and the multiplier are inversely related. The formulas that summarize these multiplier relationships are presented in the next two equations.

The first equation presents the multiplier as a function of MPC:

$$\text{Multiplier} = \frac{1}{1 - \text{MPC}}$$

To understand the second equation, which presents the multiplier as a function of MPS, recall that MPC + MPS = 1. Therefore MPS = 1 − MPC, which means we can also write the multiplier formula as

$$\text{Multiplier} = \frac{1}{\text{MPS}}$$

This version of the multiplier formula indicates that the multiplier varies inversely with the MPS, so that a larger MPS implies a smaller multiplier, and vice versa. You can verify this inverse relationship for yourself by substituting particular MPS values into the formula. For instance, when the MPS is 0.25, as in our example, the multiplier is 4. If the MPS were 0.2, the multiplier would be 5. If the MPS were 0.33, the multiplier would be 3.

The intuition behind this inverse relationship between MPS and the multiplier has to do with how changes in the MPS affect the size of each round of the multiplier process. As we will demonstrate, the smaller the fraction of any change in income saved (that is, the smaller the MPS), the greater the amount of respending at each round and, therefore, the greater the multiplier.

To see why that is true, suppose that there is again a $5 billion increase in investment but this time assume that the MPS is 0.2 rather than 0.25. That lower MPS value of 0.2 implies a higher MPC value of 0.8 (since MPC = 1 − MPS). Taking that higher MPC of 0.8 into account, the first round of the table in Figure 30.7 will have consumption increasing by $4 billion (= MPC of 0.8 × $5 billion) rather than by $3.75 billion because saving will increase by $1 billion (= MPS of 0.2 × $5 billion) rather than $1.25 billion. The larger rise

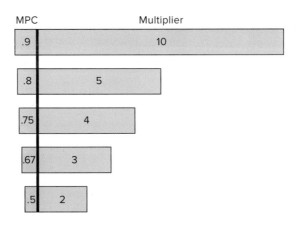

FIGURE 30.8
The MPC and the multiplier.

The larger the MPC, the greater the size of the multiplier.

in consumption in round 1 will produce a larger increase in income in round 2. The same will be true for all successive rounds. If we worked through all of the following rounds, we would find that the process ends when income has cumulatively increased by $25 billion, not the $20 billion shown in the table. When the MPS is 0.2 rather than 0.25, the multiplier is 5 (= $25 billion/ $5 billion) as opposed to 4 (= $20 billion/$5 billion). The smaller MPS has caused a larger multiplier.

By contrast, consider what happens if the MPS is increased to a larger value, say 0.33 rather than 0.25. That increase in the MPS to 0.33 implies a decrease in the MPC to 0.67 (since MPC = 1 − MPS). That smaller MPC of 0.67 means that each round's increase in consumption and income would be less than those in the table in Figure 30.7. Consequently, the multiplier process would end with a $15 billion increase in income rather than the $20 billion shown. When the MPS is 0.33 rather than 0.25, the multiplier is 3 (= $15 billion/$5 billion) as opposed to 4 (= $20 billion/$5 billion). The larger MPS has caused a smaller multiplier.

We can summarize these results in terms of MPC. A large MPC (small MPS) means the succeeding rounds of consumption spending shown in Figure 30.7 diminish slowly and thereby cumulate to a large total change in income. Conversely, a small MPC (a large MPS) causes the increases in consumption to decline quickly, so the cumulative change in income is small.

Figure 30.8 summarizes the direct (positive) relationship between the MPC and the multiplier; they get bigger together. To test your understanding, see if you can draw a similar graph that summarizes the inverse (negative) relationship between the MPS and the multiplier; when one gets bigger, the other gets smaller.

How Large Is the Actual Multiplier?

The multiplier that we have just described is based on simplifying assumptions. We have, for example, ignored taxes and imports. They matter because they reduce the amount by which the consumption of domestic output increases in each round of the multiplier process. When taxes and imports apply, households use some of the extra income that they receive in each round to purchase additional goods from abroad (imports) and to pay additional taxes. Buying imports and paying taxes drains off some of the additional consumption spending (on domestic output) created by each round's increase in income. So the multiplier effect is reduced, and the 1/MPS formula for the multiplier overstates the actual outcome. To correct this problem, we would need to change the multiplier equation to read "1 divided by the fraction of the change in income that is not spent on domestic output."

Also, an increase in spending may be partly dissipated as inflation rather than realized fully as an increase in real GDP. The multiplier process still happens, but it induces a much smaller change in real output because, at higher prices, any given amount of spending buys less real output.

Economists disagree on the size of the actual multiplier in the United States. Estimates range from as high as 2.5 to as low as zero. As you read subsequent chapters, keep in mind that the actual multiplier is much lower than the multipliers that we used here in this chapter for our simple explanatory examples of how the multiplier process works.

LAST WORD

Toppling Dominoes

A Humorous Look at the Multiplier

CLEVELAND—Yesterday, the local economy was plunged into a recession in less than 6 hours.

Many people are trying to explain the sudden change in local prospects. Here's one conjecture.

At precisely 9 a.m., Humbug, the Ford dealer, called Mr. Ajani, of Ajani's Men's Wear. "It's a great day, Mr. Ajani! The new models are in. Per your request, I've put in an order for you."

Agitated, Mr. Ajani responded, "That's not going to work Mr. Humbug. I just got hit with an unexpected tax bill. It's huge and I can't afford a new car right now. Sorry."

Humbug hung up. Two minutes later, his cell phone rang.

"This is Tanaka the landscaper. When do you want us to start working on your yard?"

"I'm sorry, Tanaka, but I can't do that right now," said Humbug.

Perplexed, Tanaka responded, "You were so excited about your new yard. What happened?"

"It's one of my customers. He canceled an order because he got hit with an unexpected tax bill."

Two hours later, Tanaka received a call from his wife, Samantha. "I'm so excited! Goldman's Electronics just received our new TV. They said they can install it tomorrow."

"We're going to have to send it back."

"Why?"

"Because Humbug isn't going to have that yard put in now that his customer Ajani can't buy a new car due to an unexpected tax assessment."

Ten minutes later, Samantha called Goldman's Electronics. "We don't need the TV."

Goldman frowned. He immediately called his travel agent, Gonzales. "Remember that trip to Spain that you scheduled for me?"

"Yes, everything is ready to go. We just need to run your credit card."

"It's impossible now. Mrs. Tanaka just canceled a TV order because Humbug didn't sell a car to Ajani because Ajani can't figure out how to pay his taxes."

Gonzalez got online and canceled Goldman's trip to Spain. He also went over to his local bank to talk to the lending officer, Tommy

Everything is stock/Shutterstock

Tightfist. "I can't make this month's loan payment because Goldman canceled his trip to Spain."

Tightfist got upset but knew that nothing could be done.

When Ms. Kozysic the baker came into the bank a bit later to ask for a loan, Tightfist shouted "No! How can I loan you money, Ms. Kozysic, when Gonzalez can't repay what he owes me?"

Dejected, Kozysic phoned up her general contractor, Bill Johnson, and said she couldn't remodel her storefront. Johnson laid off seven workers. It was a tough thing to tell them right after lunch.

At 2 p.m., Ford announced that it would be offering big rebates on all its new models.

Humbug phoned Ajani immediately, "I have great news. Unless that unexpected tax bill is massive, you are still going to be able to afford the car you wanted!"

"I don't have an expected tax bill," Ajani said. "My accountant made an error. It was all a mistake."

"Excellent!" exclaimed Humbug. "Now you can afford that lovely new car."

"Not possible," replied Ajani in a grim tone. "Business has been lousy."

"I'm sorry to hear that. What's going on?"

"I haven't seen Tanaka, Goldman, Gonzalez, Tightfist, or Kozysic for over a month. How can I survive if they don't patronize my shop?"

Source: Adopted from Art Buchwald, "Squaring the Economic Circle," *Cleveland Plain Dealer,* February 22, 1975.

QUICK REVIEW

30.4

▶ The multiplier effect reveals that an initial change in spending can cause a larger change in domestic income and output. The multiplier is the factor by which the initial change is magnified: multiplier = change in real GDP/initial change in spending.

▶ The higher the marginal propensity to consume (the lower the marginal propensity to save), the larger the multiplier [= $1/(1 - MPC)$ or $1/MPS$].

▶ Economists disagree on the size of the actual multiplier in the U.S. economy; estimates range all the way from zero to 2.5.

Summary

LO30.1 Describe how changes in income affect consumption and saving.

Other things equal, a direct (positive) relationship exists between income and consumption and between income and saving. The consumption and saving schedules show the various amounts that households intend to consume and save at the various income and output levels, assuming a fixed price level.

The *average* propensities to consume and save show the fractions of any total income that are consumed and saved; APC + APS = 1. The *marginal* propensities to consume and save show the fractions of any change in total income that are consumed and saved; MPC + MPS = 1.

LO30.2 List and explain factors other than income that can affect consumption.

Consumption and saving schedules (as they relate to real GDP) are determined by (*a*) the amount of wealth owned by households, (*b*) borrowing, (*c*) expectations of future prices and incomes, and (*d*) real interest rates and taxes. The consumption and saving schedules are relatively stable.

LO30.3 Explain how changes in real interest rates affect investment.

The immediate determinants of investment are (*a*) the expected rate of return and (*b*) the real interest rate. The economy's investment demand curve is found by cumulating investment projects, arraying them in descending order according to their expected rates of return, graphing the result, and applying the rule that firms should undertake investment up to the point at which the real interest rate, *i*, equals the expected rate of return, *r*. The investment demand curve reveals an inverse (negative) relationship between the real interest rate and the level of aggregate investment.

Either changes in real interest rates or shifts of the investment demand curve can change the level of investment.

LO30.4 Identify and explain factors other than the real interest rate that can affect investment.

Shifts of the investment demand curve can occur as the result of changes in (*a*) the acquisition, maintenance, and operating costs of capital goods; (*b*) business taxes; (*c*) technology; (*d*) the stocks of capital goods on hand; (*e*) planned inventory changes, and (*f*) expectations. Factors that contribute to the instability of investment spending include varying expectations, the durability of capital goods, the irregular occurrence of major innovations, and profit volatility.

LO30.5 Illustrate how changes in investment and the other components of total spending can multiply GDP.

Through the multiplier effect, an increase in investment spending (or consumption spending, government purchases, or net export spending) ripples through the economy, ultimately creating a magnified increase in real GDP. The multiplier equals the ultimate change in GDP divided by the initiating change in investment (or other component of spending).

The multiplier is equal to the reciprocal of the marginal propensity to save: The greater is the marginal propensity to save, the smaller is the multiplier. Also, the greater is the marginal propensity to consume, the larger is the multiplier.

Economists disagree on the size of the multiplier in the United States, with estimates ranging from 2.5 to 0. But all estimates of actual-economy multipliers are less than the multiplier in our purposefully simplified text illustrations.

Terms and Concepts

45° (degree) line

consumption schedule

saving schedule

break-even income

average propensity to consume (APC)

average propensity to save (APS)

marginal propensity to consume (MPC)

marginal propensity to save (MPS)

wealth effect

paradox of thrift

expected rate of return

investment demand curve

multiplier

Discussion Questions

1. Precisely how do the MPC and the APC differ? How does the MPC differ from the MPS? Why must the sum of the MPC and the MPS equal 1? **LO30.1**
2. Why does a downshift of the consumption schedule typically involve an equal upshift of the saving schedule? What is the exception to this relationship? **LO30.2**
3. Why will a reduction in the real interest rate increase investment spending, other things equal? **LO30.3**
4. In what direction will each of the following occurrences shift the investment demand curve, other things equal? **LO30.4**
   a. An increase in unused production capacity occurs.

   b. Business taxes decline.
   c. The cost of acquiring equipment falls.
   d. Widespread pessimism arises about future business conditions and sales revenues.
   e. A major new technological breakthrough creates prospects for a wide range of profitable new products.
5. How is it possible for investment spending to increase even in a period in which the real interest rate rises? **LO30.4**
6. Why is investment spending unstable? **LO30.4**
7. Is the relationship between changes in spending and changes in real GDP in the multiplier effect a direct (positive) relationship,

or is it an inverse (negative) relationship? How does the size of the multiplier relate to the size of the MPC? The MPS? What is the logic of the multiplier-MPC relationship? **LO30.5**

8. Why is the actual multiplier in the U.S. economy less than the multiplier in this chapter's example? **LO30.5**

9. **LAST WORD** What is the central economic idea humorously illustrated in the Last Word "Toppling Dominoes"? How does the central idea relate to economic recessions, on the one hand, and vigorous economic expansions, on the other?

Review Questions

1. What are the variables (the items measured on the axes) in a graph of the (*a*) consumption schedule and (*b*) saving schedule? Are the variables inversely (negatively) related, or are they directly (positively) related? What is the fundamental reason that the levels of consumption and saving in the United States are each higher today than they were a decade ago? **LO30.1**

2. In year 1, Anita earns $1,000 and saves $100. In year 2, Anita gets a $500 raise so that she earns a total of $1,500. Out of that $1,500, she saves $200. What is Anita's MPC out of her $500 raise? **LO30.1**
   a. 0.50
   b. 0.75
   c. 0.80
   d. 1.00

3. If the MPS rises, then the MPC will: **LO30.1**
   a. fall.
   b. rise.
   c. stay the same.

4. In what direction will each of the following occurrences shift the consumption and saving schedules, other things equal? **LO30.2**
   a. A large decrease in real estate values, including private homes.
   b. A sharp, sustained increase in stock prices.
   c. A 5-year increase in the minimum age for collecting Social Security benefits.
   d. An economywide expectation that a recession is over and that a robust expansion will occur.

e. A substantial increase in household borrowing to finance auto purchases.

5. Irving owns several frozen yogurt shops. He is considering whether he should build a new location downtown. The expected rate of return is 15 percent per year. He can borrow money at a 12 percent interest rate to finance the project. Should Irving proceed with this project? **LO30.3**
   a. Yes
   b. No

6. Which of the following scenarios will shift the investment demand curve right? *Select **one or more** answers from the choices shown.* **LO30.4**
   a. Business taxes increase.
   b. The expected return on capital increases.
   c. Firms have a lot of unused production capacity.
   d. Firms are planning on increasing their inventories.

7. True or False: Real GDP is more volatile (variable) than gross investment. **LO30.4**

8. If a $50 billion initial increase in spending leads to a $250 billion change in real GDP, how big is the multiplier? **LO30.5**
   a. 1.0
   b. 2.5
   c. 4.0
   d. 5.0

9. True or False: Larger MPCs imply larger multipliers. **LO30.5**

Problems

1. Refer to the table below. **LO30.1**
   a. Fill in the missing numbers in the table.
   b. What is the break-even level of income in the table? What is the term that economists use for the saving situation shown at the $240 level of income?

c. For each of the following items, indicate whether the value in the table is either constant or variable as income changes: the MPS, the APC, the MPC, the APS.

Level of Output and Income (GDP = DI)	Consumption	Saving	APC	APS	MPC	MPS
$240	$_____	$ −4	___	___		
260	_____	0	___	___	___	___
280	_____	4	___	___	___	___
300	_____	8	___	___	___	___
320	_____	12	___	___	___	___
340	_____	16	___	___	___	___
360	_____	20	___	___	___	___
380	_____	24	___	___	___	___
400	_____	28	___	___	___	___

2. Suppose that disposable income, consumption, and saving in some country are $200 billion, $150 billion, and $50 billion, respectively. Next, assume that disposable income increases by $20 billion, consumption rises by $18 billion, and saving goes up by $2 billion. What is the economy's MPC? Its MPS? What was the APC before the increase in disposable income? After the increase? **LO30.1**

3. **ADVANCED ANALYSIS** Suppose that the linear equation for consumption in a hypothetical economy is $C = 40 + 0.8Y$. Also suppose that income (Y) is $400. Determine ($a$) the marginal propensity to consume, (b) the marginal propensity to save, (c) the level of consumption, (d) the average propensity to consume, (e) the level of saving, and (f) the average propensity to save. **LO30.1**

4. **ADVANCED ANALYSIS** Linear equations for the consumption and saving schedules take the general form $C = a + bY$ and $S = -a + (1 - b)Y$, where C, S, and Y are consumption, saving, and national income, respectively. The constant a represents the vertical intercept, and b represents the slope of the consumption schedule. **LO30.1, LO30.2**

   a. Use the following data to substitute numerical values for a and b in the consumption and saving equations.

National Income (Y)	Consumption (C)
$ 0	$ 80
100	140
200	200
300	260
400	320

   b. What is the economic meaning of b? Of $(1 - b)$?
   c. Suppose that the amount of saving that occurs at each level of national income falls by $20 but that the values of b and $(1 - b)$ remain unchanged. Restate the saving and consumption equations inserting the new numerical values, and cite a factor that might have caused the change.

5. Use your completed table for problem 1 to solve this problem. Suppose the wealth effect is such that $10 changes in wealth produce $1 changes in consumption at each level of income. If real estate prices tumble such that wealth declines by $80, what will be the new level of consumption and saving at the $340 billion level of disposable income? The new level of saving? **LO30.2**

6. Suppose a handbill publisher can buy a new duplicating machine for $500 and the duplicator has a 1-year life. The machine is expected to contribute $550 to the year's net revenue. What is the expected rate of return? If the real interest rate at which funds can be borrowed to purchase the machine is 8 percent, will the publisher choose to invest in the machine? Will it invest in the machine if the real interest rate is 9 percent? If it is 11 percent? **LO30.3**

7. Assume there are no investment projects in the economy that yield an expected rate of return of 25 percent or more. But suppose there are $10 billion of investment projects yielding expected returns of between 20 and 25 percent; another $10 billion yielding between 15 and 20 percent; another $10 billion between 10 and 15 percent; and so forth. Cumulate these data and present them graphically, putting the expected rate of return (and the real interest rate) on the vertical axis and the amount of investment on the horizontal axis. What will be the equilibrium level of aggregate investment if the real interest rate is (a) 15 percent, (b) 10 percent, and (c) 5 percent? **LO30.3**

8. Refer to the table in Figure 30.5 and suppose that the real interest rate is 6 percent. Next, assume that some factor changes such that the expected rate of return declines by 2 percentage points at each prospective level of investment. Assuming no change in the real interest rate, by how much and in what direction will investment change? Which of the following might cause this change: (a) a decision to increase inventories; (b) an increase in excess production capacity? **LO30.4**

9. What will the multiplier be when the MPS is 0, 0.4, 0.6, and 1? What will it be when the MPC is 1, 0.90, 0.67, 0.50, and 0? How much of a change in GDP will result if firms increase their level of investment by $8 billion and the MPC is 0.80? If the MPC instead is 0.67? **LO30.5**

10. Suppose that an initial $10 billion increase in investment spending expands GDP by $10 billion in the first round of the multiplier process. If GDP and consumption both rise by $6 billion in the second round of the process, what is the MPC in this economy? What is the size of the multiplier? If, instead, GDP and consumption both rose by $8 billion in the second round, what would have been the size of the multiplier? **LO30.5**

CHAPTER 31

The Aggregate Expenditures Model

>> LEARNING OBJECTIVES

LO31.1 Explain the role of sticky prices in the aggregate expenditures model.

LO31.2 Derive an economy's investment schedule from the investment demand curve and an interest rate.

LO31.3 Combine consumption and investment to create an aggregate expenditures schedule for a private, closed economy and determine the economy's equilibrium level of output.

LO31.4 Discuss two alternate ways to characterize the equilibrium level of real GDP in a private closed economy.

LO31.5 Explain how the multiplier affects equilibrium real GDP.

LO31.6 Integrate the international sector into the aggregate expenditures model.

LO31.7 Integrate the public sector into the aggregate expenditures model.

LO31.8 Define equilibrium GDP, full-employment GDP, recessionary expenditure gaps, and inflationary expenditure gaps.

What determines a country's GDP, given its production capacity? What causes real GDP to rise in one period and to fall in another? To more thoroughly answer these two questions, we construct the aggregate expenditures model, which originated in the 1936 writings of British economist John Maynard Keynes (pronounced "Canes"). The basic premise of the aggregate expenditures model—also known as the "Keynesian cross" model—is that the amount of goods and services produced and the level of employment depend directly on the level of aggregate expenditures (total spending). Businesses will produce only a level of output that they think they can profitably sell. They will idle their workers and machinery when there are no markets for their goods and services.

Assumptions and Simplifications

>> **LO31.1** Explain the role of sticky prices in the aggregate expenditures model.

Keynes created the aggregate expenditures model in the middle of the Great Depression, hoping to explain both why the Great Depression had happened and how it might be ended.

A "Stuck Price" Model

The simplifying assumptions underpinning the aggregate expenditures model reflect the economic conditions that prevailed during the Great Depression. The most important assumption is that prices are fixed. The aggregate expenditures model is an extreme version of a sticky price model (Chapter 26). In fact, it is a stuck-price model because the price level cannot change at all.

Keynes made this simplifying assumption because he had observed that prices had not declined sufficiently during the Great Depression to boost spending and maintain output and employment at their pre-Depression levels. Macroeconomic theories popular before the Great Depression had predicted that prices would fall to equate quantity supplied and quantity demanded. But actual prices did not fall sufficiently during the Great Depression, and the economy sank far below its potential output. U.S. real GDP declined by 27 percent from 1929 to 1933, and the unemployment rate rose to 25 percent. Thousands of factories sat idle, gathering dust and producing nothing because there was insufficient demand for their output.

Unplanned Inventory Adjustments

To Keynes, the Great Depression's massive unemployment of labor and capital was caused by firms reacting in a predictable way to unplanned increases in inventory levels. Recall that inventory consists of goods that have been produced but which have not yet been sold. Firms may stock up on inventory in anticipation of rapid future sales. They may also intentionally decrease inventory levels if they believe that demand will decline in the future. But sometimes life does not go as planned. Sometimes inventories either rise or fall more than intended because demand is either unexpectedly high or unexpectedly low.

The Great Depression took everyone by surprise. Households and businesses unexpectedly reduced their spending, which caused inventories of unsold goods to unexpectedly surge. Unable or unwilling to slash their prices, firms could not sell output fast enough to prevent inventories from continuing to pile up. So they greatly reduced their rates of production, in some cases shutting down factories completely until inventory levels declined. Reduced production brought with it discharged workers, idle factory lines, and, in some cases, shuttered factories gathering dust. Keynes thought that economics needed a new model to explain these events. So he created the aggregate expenditures model that we study in this chapter.

The model's other key assumption—the one that allows it to achieve equilibrium—is that production decisions are made in response to unexpected changes in inventory levels. If inventories are unexpectedly rising (because sales unexpectedly lag production) firms will cut back on production so as to balance production with sales and prevent inventory levels from exceeding warehouse capacity. If inventories are unexpectedly falling (because sales unexpectedly exceed production) firms will increase production so as to take advantage of an unexpectedly good selling environment.

Current Relevance

The Keynesian aggregate expenditures model remains relevant today because many prices in the modern economy are inflexible downward over relatively short periods of time, as we discussed in Chapter 26. The aggregate expenditures model therefore helps us understand how the modern economy is likely to adjust to various economic shocks over shorter periods of time. For example, it provides insight into several aspects of the COVID-19 recession and recovery, including why unexpected initial declines in spending caused even larger declines in real GDP. It also illuminates the thinking underlying the various government stimulus programs—including tax cuts, government spending increases, and lower interest rates—that were implemented in response to the pandemic.

A Preview

We will build up the aggregate expenditures model in stages. As a first step, we examine aggregate expenditures and equilibrium GDP in a *private closed economy* that lacks both international trade and government. Then we will open the closed economy to exports and imports. We will also convert our "private" economy that has only private actors (businesses and households) into a more realistic "mixed" economy that includes the government sector. Doing so will allow us to analyze the effects of government expenditures and taxes.

Until we introduce taxes, we will assume that real GDP equals disposable income (DI). For instance, if $500 billion of output is produced as GDP, households will receive exactly $500 billion of disposable income that they can then consume or save.

Finally, unless specified otherwise, we will assume (as Keynes did) that the presence of excess production capacity and unemployed labor implies that an increase in aggregate expenditures will increase real output and employment without raising the price level.

Consumption and Investment Schedules

>> **LO31.2** Derive an economy's investment schedule from the investment demand curve and an interest rate.

planned investment The amount that *firms* plan or intend to invest.

In the private closed economy, the two components of aggregate expenditures are consumption, *C*, and gross investment, I_g. Because we examined the *consumption schedule* (Figure 30.2a) in the previous chapter, there is no need to repeat that analysis here. But to add the investment decisions of businesses to the consumption plans of households, we need to construct an investment schedule showing the amounts business firms collectively intend to invest—their **planned investment**—at each possible level of GDP. Such a schedule represents the investment plans of businesses in the same way the consumption schedule represents the consumption plans of households. In developing the investment schedule, we will assume that planned investment is independent of the level of current disposable income or real output.

TABLE 31.1
The Investment Schedule (in Billions)

investment schedule
A curve or schedule that shows the amounts that firms plan to invest at various possible values of *real gross domestic product* (real GDP).

(1) Level of Real Output and Income	(2) Investment (I_g)
$370	$20
390	20
410	20
430	20
450	20
470	20
490	20
510	20
530	20
550	20

Suppose the investment demand curve, *ID*, is as shown in Figure 31.1a and the current real interest rate is 8 percent. This means that firms will spend $20 billion on investment goods at both low and high levels of GDP. The line I_g in Figure 31.1b shows this graphically; it is the economy's **investment schedule.** You should not confuse this investment schedule I_g with the investment demand curve *ID* in Figure 31.1a. The investment schedule shows the amount of investment forthcoming at each level of GDP. As indicated in Figure 31.1b, the interest rate and investment demand curve together determine this amount ($20 billion). Table 31.1 shows the investment schedule in tabular form. Note that investment (I_g) in column 2 is $20 billion at all levels of real GDP.

FIGURE 31.1
(a) The investment demand curve and (b) the investment schedule.

(a) The level of investment spending (here, $20 billion) is determined by the real interest rate (here, 8 percent) together with the investment demand curve *ID*. (b) The investment schedule I_g relates the amount of investment ($20 billion) determined in (a) to the various levels of GDP. In this example, the amount of investment ($20 billion) is the same at all levels of GDP.

(a)
Investment demand curve

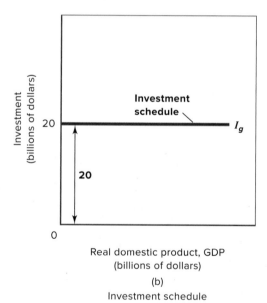

(b)
Investment schedule

QUICK REVIEW
31.1

▶ The aggregate expenditures model is a stuck-price model in which the amount of real output depends directly on the amount of total spending in the economy.

▶ Firms decide how much real output to produce in response to unexpected changes in inventory levels.

▶ If total spending is unexpectedly low in the economy, inventories will unexpectedly rise, causing firms to cut back on production. If total spending is unexpectedly high, inventories will unexpectedly fall, causing firms to increase production.

▶ The investment schedule I_g shows the amount of investment forthcoming at each level of GDP; I_g is different from the investment demand curve, *ID*, which shows how much investment firms plan to make at each interest rate.

Equilibrium GDP: $C + I_g = $ GDP

Now let's combine the consumption schedule of Chapter 30 with the investment schedule of the previous section to explain the equilibrium levels of output, income, and employment in the private closed economy.

Tabular Analysis

Columns 2 through 5 in Table 31.2 repeat the consumption and saving schedules of Table 30.1 and the investment schedule of Table 31.1.

Real Domestic Output Column 2 in Table 31.2 lists the various possible levels of total output—of real GDP—that the private sector might produce. Firms are willing to produce any one of these 10 levels of output just as long as the revenue that they receive from selling any particular amount of output equals or exceeds the costs of producing it. Those costs are the factor payments needed to obtain the required amounts of land, labor, capital, and entrepreneurship. For example, firms are willing to produce $370 billion of output if the costs of production (wages, rents, interest, and the normal profit needed to attract entrepreneurship) do not exceed the $370 billion in revenue that they will get from selling the output.

Aggregate Expenditures In the private closed economy of Table 31.2, aggregate expenditures consist of consumption (column 3) plus investment (column 5). Their sum is shown in column 6, which along with column 2 makes up the **aggregate expenditures schedule** for the private closed economy. This schedule shows the amount $(C + I_g)$ that will be spent at each possible output or income level.

At this point we are working with *planned investment*—the data in column 5 of Table 31.2. These data show the amounts that firms plan or intend to invest, not the amounts they actually will invest if there are unplanned changes in inventories. More about that shortly.

Equilibrium GDP Of the 10 possible levels of GDP in Table 31.2, which is the equilibrium level? Which total output is the economy capable of sustaining?

The equilibrium output is the output whose production creates total spending just sufficient to purchase that output. In other words, the **equilibrium GDP** occurs where the total quantity of goods produced (GDP) equals the total quantity of goods purchased $(C + I_g)$:

$$C + I_g = \text{GDP}$$

> **LO31.3** Combine consumption and investment to create an aggregate expenditures schedule for a private, closed economy and determine the economy's equilibrium level of output.

aggregate expenditures schedule A table of numbers showing the total amount spent on *final goods* and final *services* at different levels of *real gross domestic product* (*real GDP*).

equilibrium GDP The gross domestic product at which the total quantity of final goods and final services purchased (aggregate expenditures) is equal to the total quantity of final goods and services produced (the real domestic output); the real domestic output at which the aggregate demand curve intersects the aggregate supply curve. Also known as *equilibrium real output*.

TABLE 31.2 Determination of the Equilibrium Levels of Employment, Output, and Income: A Private Closed Economy

(1) Possible Levels of Employment, Millions	(2) Real Domestic Output (and Income) (GDP = DI)* Billions	(3) Consumption (C), Billions	(4) Saving (S), Billions	(5) Investment (I_g), Billions	(6) Aggregate Expenditures ($C + I_g$), Billions	(7) Unplanned Changes in Inventories, (+ or −)	(8) Tendency of Employment, Output, and Income
(1) 40	$370	$375	$−5	$20	$395	$−25	Increase
(2) 45	390	390	0	20	410	−20	Increase
(3) 50	410	405	5	20	425	−15	Increase
(4) 55	430	420	10	20	440	−10	Increase
(5) 60	450	435	15	20	455	−5	Increase
(6) 65	470	450	20	20	470	0	Equilibrium
(7) 70	490	465	25	20	485	+5	Decrease
(8) 75	510	480	30	20	500	+10	Decrease
(9) 80	530	495	35	20	515	+15	Decrease
(10) 85	550	510	40	20	530	+20	Decrease

*If we assume that depreciation and net foreign factor income are zero, government is ignored, and all saving occurs in the household sector of the economy, then GDP as a measure of domestic output is equal to NI, PI, and DI. This means that households receive a DI equal to the value of total output, real GDP.

If you look at the domestic output levels in column 2 and the aggregate expenditures levels in column 6, you will see that this equality exists only at $470 billion of GDP (row 6). That is the only output at which economywide spending precisely equals the amount needed to move that output off the shelves. At $470 billion of GDP, annual production and spending are in balance. There is no overproduction, which would result in excess inventories and consequently cutbacks in production. Nor is there an excess of total spending, which would draw down inventories of goods and prompt increases in production. In short, there is no reason for businesses to alter this rate of production; $470 billion is the equilibrium GDP.

Disequilibrium No level of GDP other than the equilibrium level of GDP can be sustained. At levels of GDP *less than* equilibrium, spending always exceeds GDP. If, for example, firms produced $410 billion of GDP (row 3 in Table 31.2), they would find it would yield $405 billion in consumer spending. Supplemented by $20 billion of planned investment, aggregate expenditures $(C + I_g)$ would be $425 billion, as shown in column 6. The economy would provide an annual rate of spending more than sufficient to purchase the $410 billion of annual production. Because buyers would be taking goods off the shelves faster than firms could produce them, an unplanned decline in business inventories of $15 billion would occur (column 7) if this situation continued. But businesses can adjust to such an imbalance between aggregate expenditures and real output by stepping up production. Greater output will increase employment and total income. This process will continue until the equilibrium level of GDP is reached ($470 billion).

The reverse is true at all levels of GDP *greater than* the $470 billion equilibrium level. Businesses will find that these total outputs fail to generate the spending needed to clear the shelves of goods. Being unable to recover their costs, businesses will cut back on production. To illustrate: At the $510 billion output (row 8), business managers would find spending is insufficient to permit the sale of all that output. Of the $510 billion of income that this output creates, $480 billion would be received back by businesses as consumption spending. Though supplemented by $20 billion of planned investment spending, total expenditures ($500 billion) would still be $10 billion below the $510 billion quantity produced. If this imbalance persisted, $10 billion of inventories would pile up (column 7). But businesses can adjust to this unintended accumulation of unsold goods by cutting back on the rate of production. The resulting decline in output would mean fewer jobs and a decline in total income.

Graphical Analysis

We can demonstrate our analysis graphically. In **Figure 31.2 (Key Graph)** the 45° line we developed in Chapter 30 takes on increased significance. At any point on this line, the value of what is measured on the horizontal axis (here, GDP) equals the value of what is measured on the vertical axis (here, aggregate expenditures, or $C + I_g$). Having discovered in our tabular analysis that the equilibrium level of domestic output occurs where $C + I_g$ equals GDP, we can say that the 45° line in Figure 31.2 is a graphical representation of that equilibrium condition.

Now we must graph the aggregate expenditures schedule onto Figure 31.2. To do so, we duplicate the consumption schedule *C* in Figure 30.2a and add to it vertically the constant $20 billion amount of investment I_g from Figure 31.1b. This $20 billion is the amount that firms plan to invest at all levels of GDP. Or, more directly, we can plot the $C + I_g$ data in column 6, Table 31.2.

In Figure 31.2, the aggregate expenditures line $C + I_g$ shows that total spending rises with income and output (GDP), but not as much as income rises. That condition holds true because the marginal propensity to consume—the slope of line *C*—is less than 1. A part of any increase in income will be saved rather than spent. And because the aggregate expenditures line $C + I_g$ is parallel to the consumption line *C*, the slope of the aggregate expenditures line also equals the MPC for the economy and is less than 1. For our particular data, aggregate expenditures rise by $15 billion for every $20 billion increase in real output and income because $5 billion of each $20 billion increment is saved. Therefore, the slope of the aggregate expenditures line is 0.75 (= $15/$20).

The equilibrium level of GDP occurs at the intersection of the aggregate expenditures schedule and the 45° line. This intersection locates the only point at which aggregate expenditures (on the vertical axis) are equal to GDP (on the horizontal axis). Because Figure 31.2 is based on the

.ıll KEY GRAPH

FIGURE 31.2 Equilibrium GDP in a private closed economy.

The aggregate expenditures schedule, $C + I_g$, is determined by adding the investment schedule I_g to the upsloping consumption schedule C. Since investment is assumed to be the same at each level of GDP, the vertical distances between C and $C + I_g$ do not change. Equilibrium GDP is determined where the aggregate expenditures schedule intersects the 45° line, in this case at $470 billion.

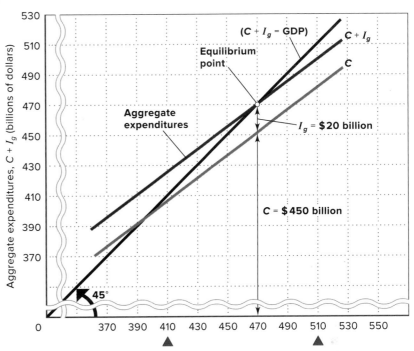

QUICK QUIZ FOR FIGURE 31.2

1. In this figure, the slope of the aggregate expenditures schedule $C + I_g$:
   a. increases as real GDP increases.
   b. falls as real GDP increases.
   c. is constant and equals the MPC.
   d. is constant and equals the MPS.

2. At all points on the 45° line:
   a. equilibrium GDP is possible.
   b. aggregate expenditures exceed real GDP.
   c. consumption exceeds investment.
   d. aggregate expenditures are less than real GDP.

3. The $490 billion level of real GDP is not an equilibrium because:
   a. investment exceeds consumption.
   b. consumption exceeds investment.
   c. planned $C + I_g$ exceeds real GDP.
   d. planned $C + I_g$ is less than real GDP.

4. The $430 billion level of real GDP is not an equilibrium because:
   a. investment exceeds consumption.
   b. consumption exceeds investment.
   c. planned $C + I_g$ exceeds real GDP.
   d. planned $C + I_g$ is less than real GDP.

Answers: 1. c; 2. a; 3. d; 4. c

data in Table 31.2, we once again find that equilibrium output is $470 billion. Observe that consumption at this output is $450 billion, and investment is $20 billion.

It is evident from Figure 31.2 that no levels of GDP *above* the equilibrium level are sustainable because at those levels $C + I_g$ falls short of GDP. In those situations, the aggregate expenditures schedule lies below the 45° line. At the $510 billion GDP level, for example, $C + I_g$ is only $500 billion. This underspending causes inventories to rise, prompting firms to adjust production downward, toward the $470 billion output level.

Conversely, at levels of GDP *below* $470 billion, the economy wants to spend in excess of what businesses are producing. Therefore, $C + I_g$ exceeds total output. Graphically, the aggregate expenditures schedule lies above the 45° line. At the $410 billion GDP level, for example, $C + I_g$ totals $425 billion. This excess spending causes inventories to fall below their planned level, prompting firms to adjust production upward, toward the $470 billion output level. Once production reaches that level, it will be sustained there indefinitely unless there is some change in the location of the aggregate expenditures line.

Other Features of Equilibrium GDP

>> **LO31.4** Discuss two alternate ways to characterize the equilibrium level of real GDP in a private closed economy.

We have seen that $C + I_g =$ GDP at equilibrium in the private closed economy. A closer look at Table 31.2 reveals two more characteristics of equilibrium GDP:

- Saving and *planned* investment are equal ($S = I_g$).
- There are no *unplanned* changes in inventories.

Saving Equals Planned Investment

As row 6 in Table 31.2 shows, saving and planned investment are both $20 billion at the $470 billion equilibrium level of GDP.

leakage (1) A withdrawal of potential spending from the income-expenditures stream via *saving,* tax payments, or *imports;* (2) a withdrawal that reduces the lending potential of the banking system.

Saving is a **leakage,** or a withdrawal, of spending from the economy's circular flow of income and expenditures. Saving causes consumption to be less than total output or GDP. Because of saving, consumption by itself is insufficient to remove domestic output from the shelves, apparently setting the stage for a decline in total output.

However, firms do not intend to sell their entire output to consumers. Some of that output will be capital goods sold to other businesses. Investment—that is, purchases of capital goods—is therefore an **injection** of spending into the income-expenditures stream. As an addition to consumption, investment is thus a potential replacement for the leakage of saving.

injection An addition of spending into the income-expenditure stream: any increment to *consumption, investment, government purchases,* or *net exports.*

If the leakage of saving at a certain level of GDP exceeds the injection of investment, then $C + I_g$ will be less than GDP and that level of GDP cannot be sustained. Any GDP for which saving exceeds investment is an above-equilibrium GDP. Consider GDP of $510 billion (row 8 in Table 31.2). Households save $30 billion, but firms plan to invest only $20 billion. This $10 billion excess of saving over planned investment reduces total spending to $10 billion below the value of total output. Specifically, aggregate expenditures will be $500 billion while real GDP is $510 billion. This spending deficiency will reduce real GDP.

Conversely, if the injection of investment exceeds the leakage of saving, then $C + I_g$ will be greater than GDP and drive GDP upward. Any GDP for which investment exceeds saving is a below-equilibrium GDP. For example, at a GDP of $410 billion (row 3 in Table 31.2), households save only $5 billion, but firms invest $20 billion. So investment exceeds saving by $15 billion. The larger injection of investment spending more than compensates for this small leakage of saving at this relatively low GDP level.

Only where $S = I_g$—where the leakage of saving of $20 billion is exactly offset by the injection of planned investment of $20 billion—will aggregate expenditures ($C + I_g$) equal real output (GDP). That $C + I_g =$ GDP equality defines the equilibrium GDP.

No Unplanned Changes in Inventories

unplanned changes in inventories Changes in *inventories* that *firms* did not anticipate; changes in inventories that occur because of unexpected increases or decreases of aggregate spending (or of *aggregate expenditures*).

As part of their investment plans, firms may decide to increase or decrease their inventories. But as line 6 of Table 31.2 confirms, there are no **unplanned changes in inventories** at equilibrium GDP. This fact, along with $C + I_g =$ GDP, and $S = I_g$, characterizes equilibrium GDP in the private closed economy.

Unplanned changes in inventories play a major role in achieving equilibrium GDP. For example, consider the $490 billion *above-equilibrium* GDP shown in row 7 of Table 31.2. What happens if firms produce that output, thinking they can sell it? Households save $25 billion of their $490 billion DI, so consumption is only $465 billion. Planned investment—which includes planned changes in inventories—is $20 billion (column 5). So aggregate expenditures ($C + I_g$) are $485 billion, and sales fall short of production by $5 billion. Firms retain that extra $5 billion of goods as an unplanned increase in inventories (column 7). That unplanned increase in inventories results from the failure of total spending to remove all of total output from the shelves.

Because changes in inventories are a part of investment, we note that *actual investment* is $25 billion. It consists of $20 billion of planned investment *plus* the $5 billion unplanned increase in inventories. Actual investment equals the saving of $25 billion, even though saving exceeds planned investment by $5 billion. Because firms cannot earn profits by accumulating unwanted inventories, the $5 billion unplanned increase in inventories prompts them to cut back employment and production. GDP falls to its equilibrium level of $470 billion, at which unplanned changes in inventories are zero.

Now look at the *below-equilibrium* $450 billion output (row 5, Table 31.2). Because households save only $15 billion of their $450 billion DI, consumption is $435 billion. Planned investment by firms is $20 billion, so aggregate expenditures are $455 billion. Sales exceed production by $5 billion because a $5 billion unplanned decrease in business inventories has occurred. Firms must *disinvest* $5 billion in inventories (column 7). Note again that actual investment is $15 billion ($20 billion planned *minus* the $5 billion decline in inventories) and is equal to the saving of $15 billion, even though planned investment exceeds saving by $5 billion. The unplanned decline in inventories, resulting from the excess of sales over production, encourages firms to expand production. GDP rises to $470 billion, at which unplanned changes in inventories are zero.

When economists say differences between investment and saving can occur and bring about changes in equilibrium GDP, they are referring to planned investment and saving. Equilibrium occurs only when planned investment and saving are equal. But when unplanned changes in inventories are taken into account, investment and saving are always equal, regardless of the level of GDP. Why? Actual investment consists of planned investment *and* unplanned investment (unplanned changes in inventories). Unplanned changes in inventories act as a balancing item that equates the actual amounts saved and invested in any period.

Changes in Equilibrium GDP and the Multiplier

In Chapter 30, we established that an initial change in spending can cause a greater change in real output through the multiplier effect. In equation form,

>> **LO31.5** Explain how the multiplier affects equilibrium real GDP.

$$\text{Multiplier} = \frac{\text{change in real GDP}}{\text{initial change in spending}}$$

Further, we discovered that the size of the multiplier depends on the size of the MPS in the economy:

$$\text{Multiplier} = \frac{1}{\text{MPS}}$$

We are about to apply those two versions of the multiplier to the aggregate expenditures model, but because the multiplier is such an important element of that model, we highly recommend that you quickly review Figure 30.7 **(Key Graph)** at this time.

Once you have reviewed Figure 30.7 **(Key Graph)**, note that in a private closed economy, $C + I_g = $ GDP when the economy is in equilibrium. So equilibrium GDP changes in response to changes in either the consumption schedule (C) or the investment schedule (I_g). Because changes in the investment schedule are the main sources of instability, we direct our attention toward them.

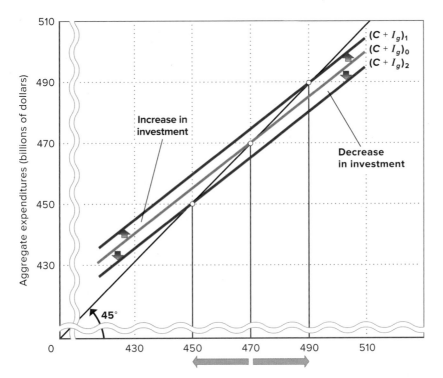

FIGURE 31.3
Changes in the aggregate expenditures schedule and the multiplier effect.

An upward shift of the aggregate expenditures schedule from $(C + I_g)_0$ to $(C + I_g)_1$ will increase the equilibrium GDP. Conversely, a downward shift from $(C + I_g)_0$ to $(C + I_g)_2$ will lower the equilibrium GDP. The extent of the changes in equilibrium GDP will depend on the size of the multiplier, which in this case is 4 (= 20/5). The multiplier is equal to 1/MPS (here, 4 = 1/.25).

Real domestic product, GDP (billions of dollars)

Figure 31.3 shows the effect of changes in investment spending on equilibrium real GDP. Suppose that the expected rate of return on investment rises or that the real interest rate falls such that investment spending increases by \$5 billion. That would be shown as an upward shift of the investment schedule in Figure 31.1b. In Figure 31.3, the \$5 billion increase of investment spending will increase aggregate expenditures from $(C + I_g)_0$ to $(C + I_g)_1$ and raise equilibrium real GDP from \$470 billion to \$490 billion.

If the expected rate of return on investment decreases or if the real interest rate rises, investment spending will decline by, say, \$5 billion. That would be shown as a downward shift of the investment schedule in Figure 31.1b and a downward shift of the aggregate expenditures schedule from $(C + I_g)_0$ to $(C + I_g)_2$ in Figure 31.3. Equilibrium GDP will fall from \$470 billion to \$450 billion.

In our examples, a \$5 billion change in investment spending leads to a \$20 billion change in output and income. So the *multiplier* is 4 (= \$20/\$5). The MPS is 0.25, meaning that for every \$1 billion of new income, \$0.25 billion of new saving occurs. Therefore, \$20 billion of new income is needed to generate \$5 billion of new saving. Once that increase in income and saving occurs, the economy is back in equilibrium, with $C + I_g = $ GDP; saving equal to planned investment; and no unplanned changes in inventories. You can see, then, why the multiplier is equal to 1/MPS and that the multiplier process is an integral part of the aggregate expenditures model.

QUICK REVIEW

31.2

▶ In a private closed economy, equilibrium GDP occurs where aggregate expenditures equal real domestic output ($C + I_g = $ GDP).

▶ At equilibrium GDP, saving equals planned investment ($S = I_g$) and unplanned changes in inventories are zero.

▶ Actual investment consists of planned investment plus unplanned changes in inventories (+ or −) and is always equal to saving in a private closed economy.

▶ Through the multiplier effect, an initial change in investment spending can cause a magnified change in domestic output and income.

Adding International Trade

>> **LO31.6** Integrate the international sector into the aggregate expenditures model.

net exports (X_n) *Exports minus imports.*

We now move from a private closed economy to a private open economy that incorporates exports (X) and imports (M). We focus on **net exports** (exports minus imports), which may be either positive or negative.

Net Exports and Aggregate Expenditures

Like consumption and investment, exports create domestic production, income, and employment for a nation. Although U.S. goods and services produced for export are sent abroad, foreign spending on those goods and services increases production and creates jobs and incomes in the United States. We must therefore include exports as a component of U.S. aggregate expenditures.

In addition, when an economy is open to international trade, it will spend part of its income on imports—goods and services produced abroad. To avoid overstating the value of domestic production, we must subtract the amount spent on imported goods because such spending generates production and income abroad rather than at home. So, to correctly measure aggregate expenditures for domestic goods and services, we must subtract expenditures on imports from total spending.

In short, for a private closed economy, aggregate expenditures are $C + I_g$. But for an open economy, aggregate expenditures are $C + I_g + (X - M)$. Or, recalling that net exports (X_n) equal $(X - M)$, we can say that aggregate expenditures for a private open economy are $C + I_g + X_n$.

The Net Export Schedule

A net export schedule lists the amount of net exports that occurs at each level of GDP. Table 31.3 shows two possible net export schedules for the hypothetical economy represented in Table 31.2. In net export schedule X_{n1} (columns 1 and 2), exports exceed imports by \$5 billion at each level of GDP. Perhaps exports are \$15 billion while imports are \$10 billion. In schedule X_{n2} (columns 1 and 3), imports are \$5 billion higher than exports. Perhaps imports are \$20 billion while exports are \$15 billion. To simplify our discussion, we assume in both schedules that net exports are independent of GDP.[1]

---

[1] In reality, although our exports depend on foreign incomes and are thus independent of U.S. GDP, our imports do vary directly with our own domestic national income. Just as our domestic consumption varies directly with our GDP, so do our purchases of foreign goods. As our GDP rises, U.S. households buy not only more Cadillacs and Harleys, but also more Mercedes and Kawasakis. However, for now we will ignore the complications of the positive relationship between imports and U.S. GDP.

Figure 31.4a represents the two net export schedules in Table 31.3. Schedule X_{n1} is above the horizontal axis and depicts positive net exports of $5 billion at all levels of GDP. Schedule X_{n2}, which is below the horizontal axis, shows negative net exports of $5 billion at all levels of GDP.

Net Exports and Equilibrium GDP

The aggregate expenditures schedule labeled $C + I_g$ in Figure 31.4b reflects the private closed economy. It shows the combined consumption and gross investment expenditures occurring at each level of GDP. With no foreign sector, the equilibrium GDP is $470 billion.

But in the private open economy, net exports can be either positive or negative. Let's see how each of the net export schedules in Figure 31.4a affects equilibrium GDP.

TABLE 31.3
Two Net Export Schedules (in Billions)

(1) Level of GDP	(2) Net Exports, X_{n1} ($X > M$)	(3) Net Exports, X_{n2} ($X < M$)
$370	$+5	$−5
390	+5	−5
410	+5	−5
430	+5	−5
450	+5	−5
470	+5	−5
490	+5	−5
510	+5	−5
530	+5	−5
550	+5	−5

Real domestic product, GDP (billions of dollars)

(a)

Net export schedule, X_n

Real domestic product, GDP (billions of dollars)

(b)

Aggregate expenditures schedule

FIGURE 31.4
Net exports and equilibrium GDP.

(a) Net exports can be either positive, as shown by the net export schedule X_{n1} or negative, as depicted by net export schedule X_{n2}. (b) Positive net exports elevate the aggregate expenditure schedule from the closed-economy level of $C + I_g$ to the open-economy level of $C + I_g + X_{n1}$. Negative net exports lower the aggregate expenditures schedule from the closed-economy level of $C + I_g$ to the open-economy level of $C + I_g + X_{n2}$.

Positive Net Exports Suppose the net export schedule is X_{n1}. We account for the $5 billion of additional net export expenditures by the rest of the world by adding that $5 billion to the $C + I_g$ schedule in Figure 31.4b. Aggregate expenditures at each level of GDP are then $5 billion higher than $C + I_g$ alone. The aggregate expenditures schedule for the open economy thus becomes $C + I_g + X_{n1}$. As a result, the equilibrium shifts to where $C + I_g + X_{n1}$ intersects the 45-degree line. In this case, international trade increases equilibrium GDP from $470 billion in the private closed economy to $490 billion in the private open economy. Adding net exports of $5 billion has increased GDP by $20 billion, in this case implying a multiplier of 4.

Generalization: Other things equal, positive net exports increase aggregate expenditures and GDP beyond what they would be in a closed economy.

Negative Net Exports Next, suppose that net exports are a negative $5 billion, as shown by X_{n2} in Figure 31.4a. In that case, our hypothetical economy is importing $5 billion more of goods than it is exporting. The aggregate expenditures schedule shown as $C + I_g$ in Figure 31.4b therefore overstates the expenditures on domestic output at each level of GDP. We must reduce the sum of expenditures by the $5 billion net amount spent on imported goods. We do that by subtracting the $5 billion of net imports from $C + I_g$.

The relevant aggregate expenditures schedule in Figure 31.4b becomes $C + I_g + X_{n2}$ and equilibrium GDP falls from $470 billion to $450 billion. Again, a change in net exports of $5 billion has produced a fourfold change in GDP, reminding us that the multiplier in this example is 4.

We therefore have a corollary to our first generalization: Other things equal, negative net exports reduce aggregate expenditures and GDP below what they would be in a closed economy. When imports exceed exports, the contractionary effect of the larger amount of imports outweighs the expansionary effect of the smaller amount of exports, so equilibrium real GDP decreases.

As Global Perspective 31.1 shows, net exports vary greatly among the major industrial nations.

 GLOBAL PERSPECTIVE 31.1

NET EXPORTS OF GOODS, SELECTED NATIONS, 2020

Some nations, such as China and Germany, have positive net exports; other countries, such as the United States and France, have negative net exports. For several decades, China has been the country with the largest positive net exports while the United States has been the country with the largest negative net exports.

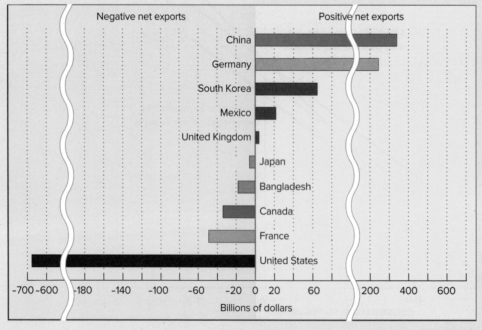

Source: The World Bank.

International Economic Linkages

Our analysis of net exports and real GDP suggests how circumstances or policies abroad can affect U.S. GDP.

Prosperity Abroad A rising level of real output and income among U.S. foreign trading partners enables the United States to sell more goods abroad, thus raising U.S. net exports and increasing U.S. real GDP (assuming initially there is excess capacity). There is good reason for Americans to be interested in our trading partners' prosperity. Their good fortune enables them to buy more U.S. exports, increasing our income and enabling us in turn to buy more foreign imports. These imported goods are the ultimate benefit of international trade. Trade transfers foreign prosperity to Americans.

Exchange Rates Depreciation (a decrease in the value) of the dollar relative to other currencies enables people abroad to obtain more dollars with each unit of their own currencies. The price of U.S. goods in terms of those currencies will fall, stimulating purchases of U.S. exports. Also, U.S. customers will find they need more dollars to buy foreign goods and, consequently, will reduce their spending on imports. If the economy has available capacity, the increased exports and decreased imports will increase U.S. net exports and expand the nation's GDP.

To check your understanding, think through the effects of an appreciation (increase in value) of the dollar on net exports and equilibrium GDP.

A Caution on Tariffs and Devaluations Because higher net exports increase real GDP, countries often look for ways to reduce imports and increase exports during recessions or depressions. Thus, a recession might tempt the U.S. federal government to increase tariffs and devalue the international value of the dollar (for instance, by supplying massive amounts of dollars in the foreign exchange market). Increasing net exports, the thinking goes, would expand domestic production, reduce domestic unemployment, and help the economy recover.

But this interventionist thinking is too simplistic. Suppose that the United States imposes high tariffs on foreign goods to reduce imports and thus increase our domestic production and employment. Our imports, however, are our trading partners' exports. So when we restrict our imports, we depress our trading partners' economies. They are likely to retaliate against us by imposing tariffs on our products. If they do so, our exports will decline, and our net exports may in fact fall. Thus imposing tariffs may decrease, not increase, our net exports.

That unfortunate possibility became a sad reality during the Great Depression of the 1930s, when various nations, including the United States, imposed trade barriers in an attempt to reduce their own domestic unemployment levels. The result was many rounds of retaliation that throttled world trade, worsened the depression, and increased domestic unemployment. Adding to the problem were some nations' attempts to increase their net exports by devaluing their currencies. Other nations then retaliated by devaluing their own currencies. The international exchange rate system collapsed, and world trade spiraled downward. Economic historians agree that tariffs and devaluations during the 1930s were huge policy mistakes.

▶ Positive net exports increase aggregate expenditures relative to the closed economy and, other things equal, increase equilibrium GDP.

▶ Negative net exports decrease aggregate expenditures relative to the closed economy and, other things equal, reduce equilibrium GDP.

▶ In the open economy, changes in (a) prosperity abroad, (b) tariffs, and (c) exchange rates can affect U.S. net exports and therefore U.S. aggregate expenditures and equilibrium GDP.

▶ Tariffs and deliberate currency depreciations are unlikely to increase net exports because other nations will retaliate.

QUICK REVIEW

31.3

Adding the Public Sector

Our final step in constructing the full aggregate expenditures model is to move the analysis from a private (no-government) open economy to an economy with a public sector (sometimes called a "mixed economy"). To do so, we must add government purchases and taxes to the model.

For simplicity, we assume that government purchases are independent of GDP and do not alter the consumption and investment schedules. Also, government's net tax revenues—total tax revenues less "negative taxes" in the form of transfer payments—are derived entirely from personal taxes. Finally, a fixed amount of taxes is collected regardless of the level of GDP.

>> **LO31.7** Integrate the public sector into the aggregate expenditures model.

TABLE 31.4 The Impact of Government Purchases on Equilibrium GDP

(1) Real Domestic Output and Income (GDP = DI), Billions	(2) Consumption (C), Billions	(3) Savings (S), Billions	(4) Investment (I_g), Billions	(5) Net Exports (X_n), Billions		(6) Government Purchases (G), Billions	(7) Aggregate Expenditures ($C + I_g + X_n + G$), Billions (2) + (4) + (5) + (6)
				Exports (X)	Imports (M)		
(1) $370	$375	$−5	$20	$10	$10	$20	$415
(2) 390	390	0	20	10	10	20	430
(3) 410	405	5	20	10	10	20	445
(4) 430	420	10	20	10	10	20	460
(5) 450	435	15	20	10	10	20	475
(6) 470	450	20	20	10	10	20	490
(7) 490	465	25	20	10	10	20	505
(8) 510	480	30	20	10	10	20	520
(9) 530	495	35	20	10	10	20	535
(10) 550	510	40	20	10	10	20	550

Government Purchases and Equilibrium GDP

Suppose the government decides to purchase $20 billion of goods and services regardless of the level of GDP and tax collections.

Tabular Example Table 31.4 shows the impact of this purchase on the equilibrium GDP. Columns 1 through 4 are carried over from Table 31.2 for the private closed economy, in which the equilibrium GDP was $470 billion. The only new items are exports and imports in column 5 and government purchases in column 6. (Observe in column 5 that net exports are always zero.) As column 7 shows, the addition of government purchases to private spending ($C + I_g + X_n$) yields a new, higher level of aggregate expenditures ($C + I_g + X_n + G$). Comparing columns 1 and 7, we find that aggregate expenditures and real output are equal at a higher level of GDP. Without government purchases, equilibrium GDP was $470 billion (row 6); *with* government purchases, aggregate expenditures and real output are equal at $550 billion (row 10). Increases in public spending, like increases in private spending, shift the aggregate expenditures schedule upward and produce a higher equilibrium GDP.

Note, too, that government spending is subject to the multiplier. A $20 billion increase in government purchases has increased equilibrium GDP by $80 billion (from $470 billion to $550 billion). The multiplier in this example is 4.

Note that this $20 billion increase in government spending is *not* financed by increased taxes.

Graphical Analysis In Figure 31.5, we vertically add $20 billion of government purchases, G, to the level of private spending, $C + I_g + X_n$. That added $20 billion raises the aggregate expenditures schedule (private plus public) to $C + I_g + X_n + G$, resulting in an $80 billion increase in equilibrium GDP, from $470 to $550 billion.

A decline in government purchases G will lower the aggregate expenditures schedule in Figure 31.5 and result in a multiplied decline in the equilibrium GDP. Verify in Table 31.4 that if government purchases decline from $20 billion to $10 billion, the equilibrium GDP will fall by $40 billion.

Taxation and Equilibrium GDP

lump-sum tax A tax that collects a constant amount (the tax revenue of government is the same) at all levels of *GDP*.

The government not only spends but also collects taxes. Suppose it imposes a **lump-sum tax**, which is a tax of a constant amount or, more precisely, a tax yielding the same amount of tax revenue at each level of GDP. Let's assume this tax is $20 billion, so that the government obtains $20 billion of tax revenue at each level of GDP regardless of the level of government purchases.

Tabular Example In Table 31.5, which continues our example, we find taxes in column 2, and we see in column 3 that disposable (after-tax) income is lower than GDP (column 1) by the $20 billion amount of the tax. Because households use disposable income both to consume and to save,

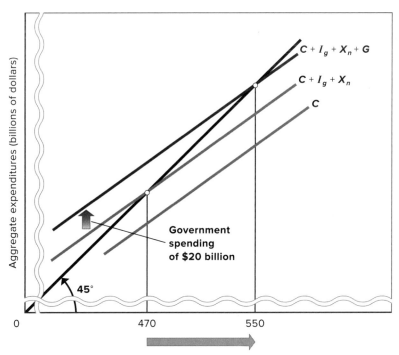

FIGURE 31.5
Government spending and equilibrium GDP.

The addition of government expenditures of G to our analysis raises the aggregate expenditures $(C + I_g + X_n + G)$ schedule and increases the equilibrium level of GDP, as would an increase in C, I_g, or X_n.

the tax lowers both consumption and saving. The MPC and MPS tell us how much consumption and saving will decline as a result of the $20 billion in taxes. Because the MPC is 0.75, the government tax collection of $20 billion will reduce consumption by $15 billion (= 0.75 × $20 billion). Because the MPS is 0.25, saving will drop by $5 billion (= 0.25 × $20 billion).

Columns 4 and 5 in Table 31.5 list the amounts of consumption and saving *at each level of GDP*. Note they are $15 billion and $5 billion smaller than those in Table 31.4. Taxes reduce disposable income relative to GDP by the amount of the taxes. This decline in DI reduces both consumption and saving at each level of GDP. The extent of the *C* and *S* reductions depends on the MPC and the MPS.

To find the effect of taxes on equilibrium GDP, we calculate aggregate expenditures again, as shown in column 9, Table 31.5. Aggregate spending is $15 billion less at each level of GDP than it

TABLE 31.5 Determination of the Equilibrium Levels of Employment, Output, and Income: Private and Public Sectors

(1) Real Domestic Output and Income (GDP = NI), Billions	(2) Taxes (T), Billions	(3) Disposable Income (DI), Billions (1) − (2)	(4) Consumption (Cₐ), Billions	(5) Savings (Sₐ), Billions (3) − (4)	(6) Investment (I_g), Billions	(7) Net Exports (Xₙ), Billions — Exports (X)	Imports (M)	(8) Government Purchases (G), Billions	(9) Aggregate Expenditures (Cₐ + I_g + Xₙ + G), Billions (4) + (6) + (7) + (8)
(1) $370	$20	$350	$360	$−10	$20	$10	$10	$20	$400
(2) 390	20	370	375	−5	20	10	10	20	415
(3) 410	20	390	390	0	20	10	10	20	430
(4) 430	20	410	405	5	20	10	10	20	445
(5) 450	20	430	420	10	20	10	10	20	460
(6) 470	20	450	435	15	20	10	10	20	475
(7) **490**	**20**	**470**	**450**	**20**	**20**	**10**	**10**	**20**	**490**
(8) 510	20	490	465	25	20	10	10	20	505
(9) 530	20	510	480	30	20	10	10	20	520
(10) 550	20	530	495	35	20	10	10	20	535

FIGURE 31.6
Taxes and equilibrium GDP.

If the MPC is 0.75, the $20 billion of taxes will lower the consumption schedule by $15 billion and cause a $60 billion decline in the equilibrium GDP. In the open economy with government, equilibrium GDP occurs where C_a(after-tax income) + $I_g + X_n + G$ = GDP. Here that equilibrium is $490 billion.

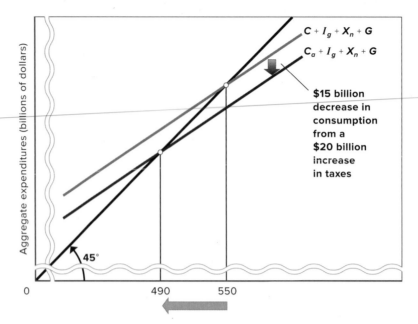

was in Table 31.4. The reason is that after-tax consumption, designated by C_a, is $15 billion less at each level of GDP. A comparison of real output and aggregate expenditures in columns 1 and 9 shows that the aggregate amounts produced and purchased are equal only at $490 billion of GDP (row 7). The $20 billion lump-sum tax has reduced equilibrium GDP by $60 billion, from $550 billion (row 10, Table 31.4) to $490 billion (row 7, Table 31.5).

Graphical Analysis   In Figure 31.6, the $20 billion increase in taxes shows up as a $15 (not $20) billion decline in the aggregate expenditures ($C_a + I_g + X_n + G$) schedule. This decline results solely from a decrease in the consumption C component of aggregate expenditures. Equilibrium GDP falls from $550 billion to $490 billion because of this tax-caused drop in consumption. With no change in government expenditures, tax increases lower the aggregate expenditures schedule relative to the 45° line and reduce equilibrium GDP.

In contrast, a *decrease* in existing taxes will raise the aggregate expenditures schedule in Figure 31.6 as a result of an increase in consumption at all GDP levels. You should confirm that a tax reduction of $10 billion (from the present $20 billion to $10 billion) will increase equilibrium GDP from $490 billion to $520 billion.

Injections, Leakages, and Unplanned Changes in Inventories   In the full model, it is still the case that injections into the income-expenditures stream equal leakages from the income stream. For the private closed economy, $S = I_g$. For the expanded economy, imports and taxes are added leakages. Saving, importing, and paying taxes are all uses of income that subtract from potential consumption. Consumption will now be less than GDP—creating a potential spending gap—in the amount of after-tax saving (S_a), imports (M), and taxes (T). But exports (X), government purchases (G), and investment (I_g), are injections into the income-expenditures stream. At the equilibrium GDP, the sum of the leakages equals the sum of injections. In symbols:

$$S_a + M + T = I_g + X + G$$

You should use the data in Table 31.5 to confirm this equality between leakages and injections at the equilibrium GDP of $490 billion. Also, substantiate that a lack of such equality exists at all other possible levels of GDP.

Although not directly shown in Table 31.5, the equilibrium characteristic of "no unplanned changes in inventories" will also be fulfilled at the $490 billion GDP. Because aggregate expenditures equal GDP, all the goods and services produced will be purchased. There will be no unplanned increase in inventories, so firms will have no incentive to reduce their employment and production. Nor will they experience an unplanned decline in their inventories, which would prompt them to expand their employment and output to replenish their inventories.

Equilibrium versus Full-Employment GDP

In the aggregate expenditures model, equilibrium GDP need not equal the economy's full-employment GDP. In fact, Keynes specifically designed the model to explain situations like the Great Depression, in which the economy appeared to be trapped in a bad equilibrium in which real GDP was far below potential output.

The fact that equilibrium and potential GDP in the aggregate expenditures model need not match reveals critical insights about the causes of demand-pull inflation. We will first examine the "expenditure gaps" that give rise to differences between equilibrium and potential GDP. Then we will see how the model helps to explain the COVID-19 recession of 2020 and preview the policies that the federal government used to try to halt and reverse it.

>> LO31.8 Define equilibrium GDP, full-employment GDP, recessionary expenditure gaps, and inflationary expenditure gaps.

Recessionary Expenditure Gap

Suppose that in **Figure 31.7 (Key Graph),** panel (a), the full-employment level of GDP is $510 billion and the aggregate expenditures schedule is AE_1. (For simplicity, we now dispense with the $C_a + I_g + X_n + G$ labeling.) This schedule intersects the 45° line to the left of the economy's full-employment output, so the economy's equilibrium GDP of $490 billion is $20 billion short of its full-employment output of $510 billion.

According to columns 1 and 2 of row 8 in Table 31.2, total employment at the full-employment GDP of $510 billion would be 75 million workers. But columns 1 and 2 of row 7 indicate that the economy depicted in Figure 31.7a is employing only 70 million workers at the equilibrium GDP of $490 billion. So 5 million available workers are not employed, and the economy is sacrificing $20 billion of output.

A **recessionary expenditure gap** is the amount by which aggregate expenditures *at the full-employment level of GDP* fall short of the amount required to achieve the full-employment level of GDP. Insufficient total spending contracts or depresses the economy. Table 31.5 shows that at the full-employment level of $510 billion (column 1), the corresponding level of aggregate expenditures is only $505 billion (column 9). The recessionary expenditure gap is thus $5 billion, the amount by which the aggregate expenditures curve would have to shift upward to realize equilibrium at the full-employment GDP. Graphically, the recessionary expenditure gap is the *vertical* distance (measured at the full-employment GDP) by which the actual aggregate expenditures schedule AE_1 lies below the hypothetical full-employment aggregate expenditures schedule AE_0. In Figure 31.7a, this recessionary expenditure gap is $5 billion. Because the multiplier is 4, there is a $20 billion differential (the recessionary expenditure gap of $5 billion times the multiplier of 4) between the equilibrium GDP and the full-employment GDP. This $20 billion difference is a negative *GDP gap*.

recessionary expenditure gap The amount by which *aggregate expenditures* at the *full-employment level of GDP* fall short of the amount required to achieve the full-employment level of GDP. In the aggregate expenditures model, the amount by which the *aggregate expenditures schedule* must shift upward to increase *real GDP* to its full-employment, noninflationary level.

Keynes's Solution to a Recessionary Expenditure Gap Keynes pointed to two different policies that a government might pursue to close a recessionary expenditure gap and achieve full employment. The first is to increase government spending. The second is to lower taxes. Both work by increasing aggregate expenditures.

Look back at Figure 31.5, which shows how an increase in government expenditures G will increase overall aggregate expenditures and, consequently, the equilibrium real GDP. Applying this strategy to the situation in Figure 31.7a, government could completely close the $20 billion negative GDP gap if it increased spending by the $5 billion amount of the recessionary expenditure gap. Given the economy's multiplier of 4, the $5 billion increase in G would create a $20 billion increase in equilibrium real GDP, bringing the economy to full employment.

Government also could lower taxes to close the recessionary expenditure gap and thus eliminate the negative GDP gap. Look back at Figure 31.6, in which an increase in taxes results in lower after-tax consumption spending and a smaller equilibrium real GDP. Keynes suggested a reversal of this process: Because an increase in taxes lowers equilibrium real GDP, a decrease in taxes will raise equilibrium GDP. The decrease in taxes will leave consumers with higher after-tax income, which will lead to higher consumption expenditures and an increase in equilibrium real GDP.

By how much should the government cut taxes? The answer is: By exactly $6.67 billion, because the MPC is 0.75. The tax cut of $6.67 billion will increase consumers' after-tax income by $6.67 billion. They will then increase consumption spending by 0.75 of that amount, or $5 billion. Aggregate expenditures will increase by the $5 billion needed to close the recessionary expenditure gap. The economy's equilibrium real GDP will rise to its potential output of $510 billion.

But a big warning is needed here: As the economy moves closer to its potential output, it becomes harder to justify Keynes's assumption that prices are stuck. As the economy closes its negative GDP

..ıll KEY GRAPH

FIGURE 31.7 Recessionary and inflationary expenditure gaps.

The equilibrium and full-employment GDPs may not coincide. (a) A recessionary expenditure gap is the amount (vertical distance) by which aggregate expenditures at the full-employment GDP level fall short of those needed to achieve full-employment. Here, the $5 billion recessionary expenditure gap that exists at the full-employment GDP level of $510 billion causes a $20 billion negative GDP gap by shifting the equilibrium level of GDP from $510 billion (where AE_0 intersects the 45-degree line) to $490 billion (where AE_1 intersects the 45-degree line). (b) An inflationary expenditure gap is the amount (vertical distance) by which aggregate expenditures at the full-employment GDP level exceed those just sufficient to achieve full-employment. Here, the inflationary expenditure gap is $5 billion. This $5 billion shifts the equilibrium level of GDP from $510 billion (where AE_0 intersects the 45-degree line) to $530 billion (where AE_2 intersects the 45-degree line). This overspending produces demand-pull inflation.

(a)
Recessionary expenditure gap

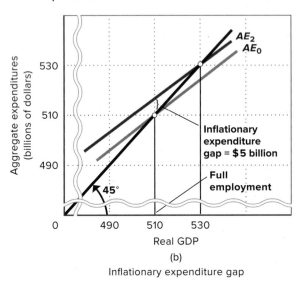

(b)
Inflationary expenditure gap

QUICK QUIZ FOR FIGURE 31.7

1. **In the economy depicted:**
   a. the MPS is 0.50.
   b. the MPC is 0.75.
   c. the full-employment level of real GDP is $530 billion.
   d. nominal GDP always equals real GDP.

2. **The inflationary expenditure gap depicted will cause:**
   a. demand-pull inflation.
   b. cost-push inflation.
   c. cyclical unemployment.
   d. frictional unemployment.

3. **The recessionary expenditure gap depicted will cause:**
   a. demand-pull inflation.
   b. cost-push inflation.
   c. cyclical unemployment.
   d. frictional unemployment.

4. **In the economy depicted, the $5 billion inflationary expenditure gap:**
   a. expands real GDP to $530 billion.
   b. leaves real GDP at $510 billion but causes inflation.
   c. could be remedied by equal $5 billion increases in taxes and government spending.
   d. implies that real GDP exceeds nominal GDP.

Answers: 1. b; 2. a; 3. c; 4. b

gap, nearly all workers are employed and nearly all factories are operating at or near full capacity. In that situation, there is no massive oversupply of productive resources to keep prices from rising. In fact, economists know from real-world experience that as GDP rises toward potential output, prices become increasingly flexible and inflationary in the medium run and the long run.

This fact is one of the major limitations of the aggregate expenditures model, and it is the reason we will develop the AD-AS model in the next chapter. That said, the aggregate expenditures model is still very useful because even an economy operating near full employment will show sticky or stuck prices in the short run. Over that shorter time horizon, the intuitions of the aggregate expenditures model will still hold true.

inflationary expenditure gap In the *aggregate-expenditures model*, the amount by which the *aggregate expenditures schedule* must shift downward to decrease the *nominal GDP* to its full-employment noninflationary level.

Inflationary Expenditure Gap

Economists use the term **inflationary expenditure gap** to describe the amount by which an economy's aggregate expenditures *at the full-employment level of GDP* exceed those just necessary to achieve the full-employment level of GDP. In Figure 31.7b, there is a $5 billion inflationary expenditure gap at the $510 billion full-employment GDP. This gap is shown by the vertical distance between the actual aggregate expenditures schedule AE_2 and the hypothetical schedule AE_0 that would be just sufficient to achieve the $510 billion full-employment GDP. Thus, the inflationary expenditure gap is the amount by which the aggregate expenditures schedule would have to shift downward to realize equilibrium at the full-employment level of GDP.

Why does the name "inflationary expenditure gap" contain the word *inflationary*? What does the situation depicted in Figure 31.7b have to do with inflation? The answer lies in the answer to a different question: *Can the economy achieve and maintain an equilibrium real GDP that is substantially above the full-employment output level?*

The unfortunate answer is no. If such a thing were possible, then the government could make real GDP as high as it wanted by simply increasing G to an arbitrarily high number. Graphically, it could raise the AE_2 curve in Figure 31.7b as far up as it wanted, thereby increasing equilibrium real GDP as high as it wanted. Living standards would skyrocket! But this outcome is not possible because, by definition, all the available workers in the economy are fully employed at the full-employment output level. Producing slightly more than the full-employment output level for a few months might be possible if employers can convince a sizable fraction of workers to work overtime day after day. But there simply is not enough labor for the economy to produce at much more than potential output for an extended period of time.

So what *does* happen in situations in which aggregate expenditures are so high that the model predicts an equilibrium level of GDP beyond potential output? The answer is twofold. First, the economy ends up producing either at potential output or just above potential output due to the limited supply of labor. Second, the economy experiences demand-pull inflation. With the supply of output limited by the supply of labor, high levels of aggregate expenditures drive up prices. Nominal GDP increases because of the higher price level, but real GDP does not. We will discuss this process in greater depth in the next chapter.

Application: The COVID Recession of 2020

In February 2020, the U.S. economy entered the shortest—but sharpest—recession on record as the COVID-19 pandemic prompted political leaders to impose lockdowns as a public health measure. We will defer discussion of the details of that recession until later chapters, but we can use the aggregate expenditures model to portray the ultimate effect of the crisis. We know that the AE_0 line in Figure 31.7a consists of the combined amount of after-tax consumption expenditures (C_a), gross investment expenditures (I_g), net export expenditures (X_n), and government purchases (G) planned at each level of real GDP. During the recession, both after-tax consumption and investment expenditures declined, with planned investment expenditures suffering the largest drop by far.

Aggregate expenditures thus declined, as from AE_0 to AE_1 in Figure 31.7a. The result was a multiple decline in real GDP, illustrated in the figure by the decline from $510 billion to $490 billion. In the language of the aggregate expenditures model, a recessionary expenditure gap produced one of the largest negative GDP gaps since the Great Depression. Employment nosedived by more than 22 million people, and the unemployment rate skyrocketed from 3.5 percent to almost 15 percent in just two months. As recessions go, it was a monster!

Policymakers undertook various macroeconomic stimulus policies to try to eliminate the recessionary expenditure gap as quickly as possible. The Federal Reserve lowered interest rates sharply to encourage investment and consumption while congress and the president passed several relief bills. The largest was the enormous, $2.2 trillion CARES Act that was designed to boost aggregate expenditures, reduce the recessionary expenditure gap, and, through the multiplier effect, increase real GDP and employment. Among other things, the CARES Act distributed $300 billion in one-time cash payments to individuals, funded $260 billion in increased unemployment benefits, lent or granted nearly $1 trillion to private businesses to keep them afloat, and distributed $340 billion to state and local governments whose tax collections were expected to collapse during the pandemic.

We defer discussion and further assessment of these stimulus attempts until Chapter 33, but Figure 31.7a clearly illuminates their purpose. If the government could drive up aggregate expenditures, such as from AE_1 to AE_0, the recession would come to an end and the recovery phase of the business cycle would begin.

Say's Law, the Great Depression, and Keynes

Aggregate Expenditure Theory Emerged as a Critique of Classical Economics and as a Response to the Great Depression.

Until the Great Depression of the 1930s, many prominent economists, including David Ricardo (1772–1823) and John Stuart Mill (1806–1873), believed that the market system would ensure full employment of an economy's resources. These so-called *classical economists* acknowledged that now and then abnormal circumstances such as wars, political upheavals, droughts, speculative crises, and gold rushes would occur, deflecting the economy from full-employment status. But they believed that when such deviations occurred, prices would automatically adjust so as to return the economy to full-employment output. For example, a slump in output and employment would result in lower prices, wages, and interest rates, which in turn would increase consumer spending, employment, and investment spending. Any excess supply of goods and workers would soon be eliminated.

Classical macroeconomists denied that the level of spending in an economy could be too low to bring about the purchase of the entire full-employment output. They based their denial of inadequate spending in part on *Say's law*, attributed to the nineteenth-century French economist J. B. Say (1767–1832). This law is the disarmingly simple idea that the very act of producing goods generates income equal to the value of the goods produced. The production of any output automatically provides the income needed to buy that output. In a nutshell, *supply creates its own demand.*

Say's law can best be understood in terms of a barter economy. A woodworker, for example, produces or supplies furniture as a means of buying or demanding the food and clothing produced by other workers. The woodworker's supply of furniture is the income that he will "spend" to satisfy his demand for other goods. The goods he buys (demands) will have a total value exactly equal to the goods he produces (supplies). And so it is for other producers and for the entire economy. Demand must be the same as supply!

Assuming that the composition of output is in accord with consumer preferences, all markets would be cleared of their outputs. It would seem that the only thing that firms need to do to sell the full-employment level of output is to produce that level of output. Say's law insists that there will be sufficient spending to purchase it all.

The Great Depression of the 1930s called Say's Law into question. In the United States, real GDP declined by 27 percent and the

Everett Historical/Shutterstock

unemployment rate rocketed to nearly 25 percent. Other nations experienced similar impacts. And cyclical unemployment lingered for a decade. An obvious inconsistency exists between a theory that says that unemployment is virtually impossible and the actual occurrence of a 10-year siege of substantial unemployment.

In 1936 British economist John Maynard Keynes (1883–1946) offered an explanation for cyclical unemployment and recessions. In his *General Theory of Employment, Interest, and Money*, Keynes attacked the foundations of classical theory and developed the ideas underlying the aggregate expenditures model. Keynes disputed Say's law, pointing out that income does not have to be spent in the same period that it is received. In fact, some income is always saved. In normal times, that saving is borrowed by businesses to buy capital goods—thereby boosting total spending in the economy. But if expectations about the future grow pessimistic, businesses will slash investment spending and a lot of that saving will not be put to use. The result will be insufficient total spending. Unsold goods will accumulate in producers' warehouses, and producers will respond by reducing their output and discharging workers. A recession or depression will result, and widespread cyclical unemployment will occur. Moreover, said Keynes, recessions are unlikely to be self-correcting. In contrast to the more laissez-faire view of the classical economists, Keynes argued that government should play an active role in stabilizing the economy.

QUICK REVIEW

31.4

▶ Government purchases shift the aggregate expenditures schedule upward and raise equilibrium GDP.

▶ Taxes reduce disposable income, lower consumption spending and saving, shift the aggregate expenditures schedule downward, and reduce equilibrium GDP.

▶ A recessionary expenditure gap is the amount by which an economy's aggregate expenditures schedule must shift upward to achieve the full-employment GDP; an inflationary expenditure gap is the amount by which the economy's aggregate expenditures schedule must shift downward to achieve full-employment GDP and eliminate demand-pull inflation.

Summary

LO31.1 Explain the role of sticky prices in the aggregate expenditures model.

The aggregate expenditures model views the total amount of spending in the economy as the primary factor determining the level of real GDP. The model assumes that the price level is fixed. Keynes made this assumption to reflect the general circumstances of the Great Depression, in which firms reduced output and employment, rather than prices, in response to a huge decline in their sales.

LO31.2 Derive an economy's investment schedule from the investment demand curve and an interest rate.

An investment schedule shows how much investment the firms in an economy are collectively planning to make at each possible level of GDP. In this chapter, we utilize a simple investment schedule in which investment is a constant value and therefore the same at all levels of GDP. That constant value is derived from the investment demand curve by determining what quantity of investment will be demanded at the economy's current real interest rate.

LO31.3 Combine consumption and investment to create an aggregate expenditures schedule for a private, closed economy and determine the economy's equilibrium level of output.

For a private closed economy, the equilibrium level of GDP occurs when aggregate expenditures and real output are equal or, graphically, where the $C + I_g$ line intersects the 45° line. At any GDP greater than equilibrium GDP, real output exceeds aggregate spending, resulting in unplanned investment in inventories and eventual declines in output and income (GDP). At any below-equilibrium GDP, aggregate expenditures will exceed real output, resulting in unplanned disinvestment in inventories and eventual increases in GDP.

LO31.4 Discuss two alternate ways to characterize the equilibrium level of real GDP in a private closed economy.

At equilibrium GDP, the amount households save (leakages) and the amount businesses plan to invest (injections) are equal. Any excess of saving over planned investment will lead to a shortfall of total spending, thus decreasing GDP. Any excess of planned investment over saving will cause an excess of total spending, thus increasing GDP. The change in GDP will in both cases correct the discrepancy between saving and planned investment.

At equilibrium GDP, there are no unplanned changes in inventories. When aggregate expenditures diverge from real GDP, an unplanned change in inventories occurs. Unplanned increases in inventories are followed by a cutback in production and a decline of real GDP. Unplanned decreases in inventories result in increased production and higher GDP.

Actual investment consists of planned investment plus unplanned changes in inventories and is always equal to saving.

LO31.5 Explain how the multiplier affects equilibrium real GDP.

A shift in the investment schedule (caused by changes in expected rates of return or changes in interest rates) shifts the aggregate expenditures curve and causes a new equilibrium level of real GDP. Real GDP changes by more than the amount of the initial change in investment. This multiplier effect (ΔGDP/ΔI_g) accompanies both increases and decreases in aggregate expenditures and also applies to changes in net exports (X_n) and government purchases (G).

LO31.6 Integrate the international sector into the aggregate expenditures model.

The net export schedule in the model of the open economy relates net exports (exports minus imports) to equilibrium GDP. For simplicity, we assume that the level of net exports is the same at all levels of real GDP.

Positive net exports increase aggregate expenditures to a higher level than they would be if the economy were "closed" to international trade. Negative net exports decrease aggregate expenditures relative to those in a closed economy, decreasing equilibrium real GDP by a multiple of their amount. Increases in exports or decreases in imports have an expansionary effect on real GDP, while decreases in exports or increases in imports have a contractionary effect.

LO31.7 Integrate the public sector into the aggregate expenditures model.

Government purchases in the model of the mixed economy shift the aggregate expenditures schedule upward and raise GDP.

Taxation reduces disposable income, lowers consumption and saving, shifts the aggregate expenditures curve downward, and reduces equilibrium GDP.

In the complete aggregate expenditures model, equilibrium GDP occurs where $C_a + I_g + X_n + G =$ GDP. At the equilibrium GDP, *leakages* of after-tax saving (S_a), imports (M), and taxes (T) equal *injections* of investment (I_g), exports (X), and government purchases (G): $S_a + M + T = I_g + X_n + G$. Also, there are no unplanned changes in inventories.

LO31.8 Define equilibrium GDP, full-employment GDP, recessionary expenditure gaps, and inflationary expenditure gaps.

Equilibrium GDP and full-employment GDP may differ.

A recessionary expenditure gap is the amount by which aggregate expenditures at the full-employment GDP fall short of those needed to achieve the full-employment GDP. This gap produces a negative GDP gap (= actual GDP minus potential GDP). An inflationary expenditure gap is the amount by which aggregate expenditures at the full-employment GDP exceed those just sufficient to achieve the full-employment GDP. This gap causes demand-pull inflation.

Keynes suggested that the solution to the large negative GDP gap during the Great Depression was for government to increase aggregate expenditures. It could do so by increasing its own expenditures (G) or by lowering taxes (T) to increase after-tax consumption expenditures (C_a) by households. Because the economy had millions of unemployed workers and massive amounts of unused production capacity, government could boost aggregate expenditures without worrying about creating inflation.

The stuck-price assumption of the aggregate expenditures model is not credible when the economy approaches or attains its full-employment output. With unemployment low and excess production capacity small or nonexistent, an increase in aggregate expenditures will cause inflation along with any increase in real GDP.

Terms and Concepts

planned investment	leakage	lump-sum tax
investment schedule	injection	recessionary expenditure gap
aggregate expenditures schedule	unplanned changes in inventories	inflationary expenditure gap
equilibrium GDP	net exports	

Discussion Questions

1. What is an investment schedule, and how does it differ from an investment demand curve? **LO31.2**
2. Why does equilibrium real GDP occur where $C + I_g$ = GDP in a private closed economy? What happens to real GDP when $C + I_g$ exceeds GDP? When $C + I_g$ is less than GDP? What two expenditure components of real GDP are purposely excluded in a private closed economy? **LO31.3**
3. Why is saving called a *leakage*? Why is planned investment called an *injection*? Why must saving equal planned investment at equilibrium GDP in a private closed economy? Are unplanned changes in inventories positive, negative, or zero at equilibrium GDP? Explain. **LO31.4**
4. Other things equal, what effect will each of the following changes independently have on the equilibrium level of real GDP in a private closed economy? **LO31.5**
   a. A decline in the real interest rate.
   b. An overall decrease in the expected rate of return on investment.
   c. A sizable, sustained increase in stock prices.
5. Depict graphically the aggregate expenditures model for a private closed economy. Now show a decrease in the aggregate expenditures schedule and explain why the decline in real GDP in your diagram is greater than the decline in the aggregate expenditures schedule. What term is used for the ratio of a decline in real GDP to the initial drop in aggregate expenditures? **LO31.5**
6. Assuming the economy is operating below its potential output, how does an increase in net exports affect real GDP? Why is it difficult, perhaps even impossible, for a country to boost its net exports by increasing its tariffs during a global recession? **LO31.6**
7. What is a recessionary expenditure gap? An inflationary expenditure gap? Which is associated with a positive GDP gap? A negative GDP gap? **LO31.8**
8. **LAST WORD** What is Say's law? How does it relate to the view held by classical economists that the economy generally will operate at a position on its production possibilities curve (Chapter 1)? Use production possibilities analysis to demonstrate Keynes's view on this matter.

Review Questions

1. True or False: The aggregate expenditures model assumes flexible prices. **LO31.1**
2. If total spending is just sufficient to purchase an economy's output, then the economy is: **LO31.3**
   a. in equilibrium.
   b. in recession.
   c. in debt.
   d. in expansion.
3. True or False: If spending exceeds output, real GDP will decline as firms cut back on production. **LO31.3**
4. If inventories unexpectedly rise, then production _____ sales and firms will respond by _____ output. **LO31.3**
   a. trails; expanding
   b. trails; reducing
   c. exceeds; expanding
   d. exceeds; reducing
5. If the multiplier is 5 and investment increases by $3 billion, equilibrium real GDP will increase by: **LO31.5**
   a. $2 billion.
   b. $3 billion.
   c. $8 billion.
   d. $15 billion.
   e. none of the above.
6. A depression abroad will tend to _____ our exports, which in turn will _____ net exports, which in turn will _____ equilibrium real GDP. **LO31.6**
   a. reduce; reduce; reduce
   b. increase; increase; increase
   c. reduce; increase; increase
   d. increase; reduce; reduce
7. Explain graphically the determination of equilibrium GDP for a private economy through the aggregate expenditures model. Now add government purchases (any amount you choose) to your graph, showing their impact on equilibrium GDP. Finally, add taxation (any amount of lump-sum tax that you choose) to your graph and show its effect on equilibrium GDP. Looking at your graph, determine whether equilibrium GDP has increased, decreased, or stayed the same given the sizes of the government purchases and taxes that you selected. **LO31.7**
8. The economy's current level of equilibrium GDP is $780 billion. The full-employment level of GDP is $800 billion. The multiplier is 4. Given those facts, we know that the economy faces _____ expenditure gap of _____. **LO31.8**
   a. an inflationary; $5 billion
   b. an inflationary; $10 billion
   c. an inflationary; $20 billion
   d. a recessionary; $5 billion
   e. a recessionary; $10 billion
   f. a recessionary; $20 billion
9. If an economy has an inflationary expenditure gap, the government could attempt to bring the economy back toward the full-employment level of GDP by _____ taxes or _____ government expenditures. **LO31.8**
   a. increasing; increasing
   b. increasing; decreasing
   c. decreasing; increasing
   d. decreasing; decreasing

Problems

1. Assuming the level of investment is $16 billion and independent of the level of total output, complete the following table and determine the equilibrium levels of output and employment in this private closed economy. What are the values of the MPC and MPS? **LO31.3**

Possible Levels of Employment, Millions	Real Domestic Output (GDP = DI), Billions	Consumption, Billions	Saving, Billions
40	$240	$244	$ ____
45	260	260	____
50	280	276	____
55	300	292	____
60	320	308	____
65	340	324	____
70	360	340	____
75	380	356	____
80	400	372	____

2. Using the consumption and saving data in problem 1 and assuming investment is $16 billion, what are saving and planned investment at the $380 billion level of domestic output? What are saving and actual investment at that level? What are saving and planned investment at the $300 billion level of domestic output? What are the levels of saving and actual investment? In which direction and by what amount will unplanned investment change as the economy moves from the $380 billion level of GDP to the equilibrium level of real GDP? From the $300 billion level of real GDP to the equilibrium level of GDP? **LO31.4**

3. By how much will GDP change if firms increase their investment by $8 billion and the MPC is 0.80? If the MPC is 0.67? **LO31.5**

4. Suppose that a certain country has an MPC of 0.9 and a real GDP of $400 billion. If its investment spending decreases by $4 billion, what will be its new level of real GDP? **LO31.5**

5. The data in columns 1 and 2 in the table below are for a private closed economy. **LO31.6**

   a. Use columns 1 and 2 to determine the equilibrium GDP for this hypothetical economy.

   b. Now open up this economy to international trade by including the export and import figures of columns 3 and 4. Fill in columns 5 and 6 and determine the equilibrium GDP for the

open economy. What is the change in equilibrium GDP caused by the addition of net exports?

   c. Given the original $20 billion level of exports, what would be net exports and the equilibrium GDP if imports were $10 billion greater at each level of GDP?

   d. What is the multiplier in this example?

6. Assume that, without taxes, the consumption schedule of an economy is as follows. **LO31.7**

GDP, Billions	Consumption, Billions
$100	$120
200	200
300	280
400	360
500	440
600	520
700	600

   a. Graph this consumption schedule and determine the MPC.

   b. Assume now that a lump-sum tax is imposed such that the government collects $10 billion in taxes at all levels of GDP. Graph the resulting consumption schedule and compare the MPC and the multiplier with those of the pretax consumption schedule.

7. Refer to columns 1 and 6 in the table for problem 5. Incorporate government into the table by assuming that it plans to tax and spend $20 billion at each possible level of GDP. Also assume that the tax is a personal tax and that government spending does not induce a shift in the private aggregate expenditures schedule. What is the change in equilibrium GDP caused by the addition of government? **LO31.7**

8. **ADVANCED ANALYSIS** Assume that the consumption schedule for a private open economy is such that consumption $C = 50 + 0.8Y$. Assume further that planned investment I_g and net exports X_n are independent of the level of real GDP and constant at $I_g = 30$ and $X_n = 10$. Recall also that, in equilibrium, the real output produced (Y) is equal to aggregate expenditures: $Y = C + I_g + X_n$. **LO31.7**

   a. Calculate the equilibrium level of income or real GDP for this economy.

   b. What happens to equilibrium Y if I_g changes to 10? What does this outcome reveal about the size of the multiplier?

(1) Real Domestic Output (GDP = DI), Billions	(2) Aggregate Expenditures, Private Closed Economy, Billions	(3) Exports, Billions	(4) Imports, Billions	(5) Net Exports, Billions	(6) Aggregate Expenditures, Private Open Economy, Billions
$200	$240	$20	$30	$ ____	$ ____
250	280	20	30	____	____
300	320	20	30	____	____
350	360	20	30	____	____
400	400	20	30	____	____
450	440	20	30	____	____
500	480	20	30	____	____
550	520	20	30	____	____

9. Refer to the accompanying table in answering the questions that follow: **LO31.8**

(1) Possible Levels of Employment, Millions	(2) Real Domestic Output, Millions	(3) Aggregate Expenditures $(C_a + I_g + X_n + G)$, Millions
90	$500	$520
100	550	560
110	600	600
120	650	640
130	700	680

a. If full employment in this economy is 130 million, will there be an inflationary expenditure gap or a recessionary expenditure gap? What will be the consequence of this gap? By how much would aggregate expenditures in column 3 have to change at each level of GDP to eliminate the inflationary expenditure gap or the recessionary expenditure gap? What is the multiplier in this example?

b. Will there be an inflationary expenditure gap or a recessionary expenditure gap if the full-employment level of output is $500 billion? By how much would aggregate expenditures in column 3 have to change at each level of GDP to eliminate the gap? What is the multiplier in this example?

c. Assuming that investment, net exports, and government expenditures do not change with changes in real GDP, what are the values of the MPC, the MPS, and the multiplier?

10. Answer the following questions, which relate to the aggregate expenditures model: **LO31.8**

a. If C_a is $100, I_g is $50, X_n is −$10, and G is $30, what is the economy's equilibrium GDP?

b. If real GDP in an economy is currently $200, C_a is $100, I_g is $50, X_n is −$10, and G is $30, will the economy's real GDP rise, fall, or stay the same?

c. Suppose that full-employment (and full-capacity) output in an economy is $200. If C_a is $150, I_g is $50, X_n is −$10, and G is $30, what will be the macroeconomic result?

Aggregate Demand and Aggregate Supply

>> LEARNING OBJECTIVES

LO32.1 Define aggregate demand (AD) and explain how its downward slope is the result of the real-balances effect, the interest-rate effect, and the foreign purchases effect.

LO32.2 Explain the factors that shift AD.

LO32.3 Define aggregate supply (AS) and explain how it differs in the immediate short run, the short run, and the long run.

LO32.4 Explain the factors that shift AS.

LO32.5 Explain how AD and AS determine an economy's equilibrium price level and real GDP.

LO32.6 Use the AD–AS model to explain demand-pull inflation, cost-push inflation, and recessions.

LO32.7 (Appendix) Relate the aggregate demand curve to the aggregate expenditures model.

During the sharp and sudden COVID recession of 2020, the terms *aggregate demand* and *aggregate supply* moved from the obscurity of economic blogs to the spotlight of national newspapers, cable television, and social media.

The news media and the general public had many questions: How could the government prevent a total collapse of aggregate demand? What might be done to offset the highest unemployment rate since the Great Depression? Would the federal government's $2.2 trillion CARES Act increase aggregate demand and reduce unemployment, as intended? Could a resurgence of the pandemic derail an economic expansion?

Aggregate demand and aggregate supply are the key elements of the **aggregate demand–aggregate supply model (AD–AS model),** the focus of this chapter. The aggregate expenditures model of the previous chapter is an immediate-short-run model in which prices are assumed to be fixed. In contrast, the AD–AS model in this chapter is a "variable price" model that allows both the price level and real GDP to change.

aggregate demand–aggregate supply (AD–AS) model The macroeconomic model that uses *aggregate demand* and *aggregate supply* to determine and explain the *price level* and real *domestic output* (real *gross domestic product*).

Aggregate Demand

aggregate demand A schedule or curve that shows the total quantity of *goods* and *services* that would be demanded (purchased) at various *price levels*.

In Chapter 29, we saw that the overall level of prices in the economy can be measured with a *price index* that shows how the nominal price of a "market basket" of goods and services changes over time relative to its price in a specific base year.

Aggregate demand is a schedule or curve that shows the amount of a nation's output (real GDP) that buyers collectively desire to purchase at each possible price level. These buyers include the nation's households, businesses, and government along with households, businesses, and governments located in other nations.

There is an inverse, or negative, relationship between the economy's overall price level (as measured by the price index) and the amount of real GDP that is demanded by households, businesses, and governments: When the price level rises, the quantity of real GDP demanded decreases; when the price level falls, the quantity of real GDP demanded increases.

Aggregate Demand Curve

The inverse relationship between the price level and real GDP is shown in Figure 32.1, where the aggregate demand curve AD slopes downward, as does the demand curve for an individual product.

Why the downward slope? The explanation is *not* the same as the explanation for why the demand for a single product slopes downward. That explanation centered on the *income effect* and the *substitution effect*:

- When the price of an *individual* product falls, the consumer's (constant) nominal income allows a larger purchase of the product; that's the income effect.

- At the same time, the consumer will want to buy more of the individual product because it becomes less expensive relative to other goods, whose prices have not changed; that's the substitution effect.

These explanations do not work for aggregate demand:

- In Figure 32.1, when the economy moves down its aggregate demand curve, it moves to a lower general price level. But our circular flow model tells us that when consumers pay lower prices for goods and services, less nominal income flows to resource suppliers in the form of wages, rents, interest, and profits. As a result, a decline in the price level does not necessarily mean an increase in the nominal income of the economy as a whole. Thus, a decline in the price level need not produce an income effect (in which more output is purchased because lower nominal prices leave buyers with greater real income).

- For similar reasons, there is no overall substitution effect in Figure 32.1. That's because prices *in general* are falling as we move down the aggregate demand curve. Consequently, there is no tendency for the price of any individual product to become cheaper relative to other products. When prices as a group are all falling together, the rationale for the substitution effect evaporates.

real-balances effect The tendency for increases in the *price level* to lower the real value (or *purchasing power*) of financial *assets* with fixed *money* value and, as a result, to reduce total spending and real output, and conversely for decreases in the *price level*.

FIGURE 32.1
The aggregate demand curve.

The downsloping aggregate demand curve AD indicates an inverse (or negative) relationship between the price level and the amount of real output purchased.

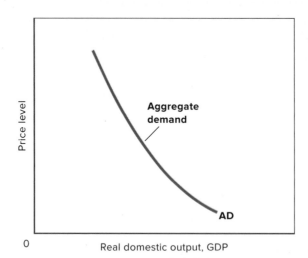

If the substitution and income effects do not explain the downward slope of the aggregate demand curve, what does? The explanation rests on three effects that follow from a price-level change.

Real-Balances Effect A change in the price level produces a **real-balances effect** in which consumer spending (*C*) varies inversely with changes in the price level. To understand how it works, begin by noting that when people refer to the "balances" in savings and other financial accounts, they are referring to *nominal balances*, which are simply the nominal dollar values in each account.

Because nominal balances are measured in money, they cannot by themselves tell us how much purchasing power a person possesses. That's because purchasing power also depends on prices. A nominal balance of $500 can purchase quite a bit if prices are low, but only a modest amount if prices are high.

The concept of real balances goes to the heart of the issue by using prevailing prices to convert nominal balances into real quantities. In particular, an individual's *real balances* are equal to the amount of real output that she could purchase at current prices if she liquidated (turned to cash) all of her assets and used the money to purchase goods and services. For any given amount of nominal balances, say $1,000, real balances will be higher if the price level falls and lower if the price level rises. For example, $1,000 will purchase more real output when prices are low than when they are high.

The fact that real balances (the purchasing power of nominal balances) vary inversely with the price level is the source of the real-balances effect. When the price level rises, real balances fall, purchasing power declines, and people demand less output. Conversely, when the price level falls, real balances increase, purchasing power rises, and people demand more output. So a higher price level means less consumption spending while a lower price level means more consumer spending.

Because consumer spending is a component of aggregate demand, the inverse relationship between the price level and consumption that is caused by the real-balances effect implies that the price level and aggregate demand must also be inversely related. As a result, the real-balances effect contributes to the downward slope of the AD curve.

Interest-Rate Effect The aggregate demand curve also slopes downward because of the **interest-rate effect,** under which an increase in the price level drives up the demand for money and thereby the interest rate, which in turn reduces investment spending (I) by businesses.

The interest rate is the price that must be paid for the use of (borrowed) money. The interest rate is determined by the interaction of the demand for money with the supply of money. Given a fixed supply of money, any increase in money demand will drive up the interest rate.

When we draw an aggregate demand curve, we assume that the supply of money in the economy is fixed. But when the price level rises, consumers need more money for purchases and businesses need more money to meet their payrolls and to buy other resources. A $10 bill will do when the price of an item is $10, but a $10 bill plus a $1 bill is needed when the item costs $11. In short, a higher price level increases the demand for money. Given our assumption that the supply of money is fixed, that increase in the demand for money will cause an increase in the interest rate.

Higher interest rates curtail investment spending and interest-sensitive consumption spending. A firm that expects a 6 percent rate of return on a potential purchase of capital will find that investment potentially profitable when the interest rate is, say, 5 percent. But the investment will be unprofitable and will not be made when the interest rate has risen to 7 percent. Similarly, consumers may decide not to purchase a new house or new automobile when the interest rate on loans goes up. So, by increasing the demand for money and consequently the interest rate, a higher price level reduces the amount of real output demanded.

Foreign Purchases Effect The final reason why the aggregate demand curve slopes downward is the **foreign purchases effect,** under which an increase in the price level results in a decrease in net exports (X_n). When the U.S. price level rises relative to foreign price levels, people living abroad will tend to buy fewer U.S. goods and Americans will tend to buy more foreign goods. The strength of these tendencies will depend on whether exchange rates adjust quickly and completely. But the general tendency will be for U.S. exports to fall and U.S. imports to rise. In short, the increase in the domestic price level will tend to cause net exports to decline.

These three effects, of course, work in the opposite direction for a decline in the price level. A decline in the price level increases consumption through the real-balances effect and interest-rate effect; increases investment through the interest-rate effect; and raises net exports by increasing exports and decreasing imports through the foreign purchases effect.

Changes in Aggregate Demand

Other things equal, a change in the price level will change the amount of aggregate spending and therefore change the amount of real GDP demanded by the economy. Movements along a fixed aggregate demand curve represent changes in the amount of real GDP demanded that occur in response to a change in the price level. However, if one or more of those "other things" change,

interest-rate effect The tendency for increases in the *price level* to increase the demand for money, raise interest rates, and, as a result, reduce total spending and real output in the economy (and the reverse for *price-level* decreases).

foreign purchases effect The inverse relationship between the *net exports* of an economy and its *price level* relative to foreign price levels.

>> **LO32.2** Explain the factors that shift AD.

FIGURE 32.2 Changes in aggregate demand.

A change in one or more of the listed determinants of aggregate demand will shift the aggregate demand curve. The rightward shift from AD$_1$ to AD$_2$ represents an increase in aggregate demand; the leftward shift from AD$_1$ to AD$_3$ shows a decrease in aggregate demand. The horizontal distances between AD$_1$ and the dashed lines represent initial changes in spending. The multiplier effect magnifies those initial changes in spending to produce the full shifts out to, respectively, AD$_2$ and AD$_3$.

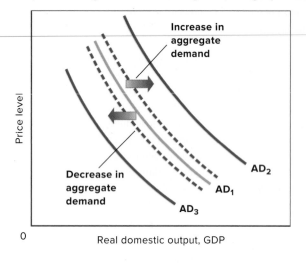

Determinants of Aggregate Demand: Factors That Shift the Aggregate Demand Curve

1. **Changes in consumer spending**
   a. Consumer wealth
   b. Consumer expectations
   c. Household borrowing
   d. Taxes

2. **Changes in investment spending**
   a. Interest rates
   b. Expected returns
      • Expected future business conditions
      • Technology
      • Degree of excess capacity
      • Business taxes

3. **Changes in government spending**

4. **Changes in net export spending**
   a. National income abroad
   b. Exchange rates

determinants of aggregate demand Factors such as consumption spending, *investment,* government spending, and *net exports* that, if they change, shift the aggregate demand curve.

the entire aggregate demand curve will shift. We refer to those other things as **determinants of aggregate demand** or, less formally, *aggregate demand shifters*. They are listed in Figure 32.2.

Changes (shifts) in aggregate demand can be broken down into two stages:

- A change in a determinant of aggregate demand that causes an initial change in the amount of real GDP demanded.

- A multiplier effect that magnifies that initial change in spending to produce a larger ultimate change in aggregate demand.

In Figure 32.2, the full rightward shift of the curve from AD$_1$ to AD$_2$ shows an increase in aggregate demand, separated into these two components.

The horizontal distance between AD$_1$ and the broken curve to its right illustrates an initial increase in spending—say, $5 billion of additional investment spending. If the economy's MPC is 0.75, then the simple multiplier is 4. So the aggregate demand curve shifts rightward from AD$_1$ to AD$_2$—four times the distance between AD$_1$ and the broken line. The multiplier process magnifies the $5 billion initial change in investment spending into successive rounds of additional consumption spending. After the shift, $20 billion (= $5 × 4) of additional real goods and services are demanded at each price level.

The leftward shift from AD$_1$ to AD$_3$ shows a decrease in aggregate demand, meaning that a smaller amount of real GDP is demanded at each price level. That shift begins with an initial decline in spending (shown as the horizontal distance between AD$_1$ and the dashed line to its left). That initial decline is then magnified by the multiplier effect into the full leftward shift, to AD$_3$.

Let's examine each determinant of aggregate demand listed in the table in Figure 32.2.

Consumer Spending

Even when the U.S. price level is constant, domestic consumers may alter their purchases of U.S.-produced real output. If those consumers decide to buy more output at each price level, the aggregate demand curve shifts to the right, as from AD$_1$ to AD$_2$ in Figure 32.2.

If they decide to buy less output, the aggregate demand curve shifts to the left, as from AD$_1$ to AD$_3$. Several factors other than a change in the price level may change consumer spending and therefore shift the aggregate demand curve. As Figure 32.2 shows, those factors are real consumer wealth, consumer expectations, household borrowing, and taxes.

Consumer Wealth Consumer wealth is the total dollar value of all assets owned by consumers less the dollar value of their liabilities (debts). Assets include stocks, bonds, and real estate. Liabilities include mortgages, student loans, and credit card balances.

Consumer wealth sometimes changes suddenly and unexpectedly due to surprising changes in asset values. An unforeseen increase in the stock market is a good example. The increase in wealth prompts pleasantly surprised consumers to save less and buy more. The resulting increase in consumer spending—the so-called *wealth effect*—shifts the aggregate demand curve to the right. In contrast, an unexpected decline in asset values causes an unanticipated reduction in consumer wealth at each price level. As consumers tighten their belts in response to the bad news, a "reverse wealth effect" sets in. Unpleasantly surprised consumers increase savings and reduce consumption, thereby shifting the aggregate demand curve to the left.

Consumer Expectations Changes in expectations about the future may alter consumer spending. When people expect their future real incomes to rise, they tend to spend more of their current incomes. Thus, current consumption spending increases (current saving falls), and the aggregate demand curve shifts to the right. Similarly, a widely held expectation of surging inflation in the near future may increase aggregate demand today because consumers will want to buy products before their prices escalate. Conversely, expectations of lower future income or lower future prices may reduce current consumption and shift the aggregate demand curve to the left.

Household Borrowing Consumers can increase their consumption spending by borrowing. Doing so shifts the aggregate demand curve to the right. By contrast, a decrease in borrowing for consumption purposes shifts the aggregate demand curve to the left. The aggregate demand curve also shifts to the left if consumers increase their savings to pay off their debts. With more money flowing to debt repayment, consumption expenditures decline, and the AD curve shifts left.

Personal Taxes A reduction in personal income tax rates raises take-home income and increases consumer purchases at each possible price level. Tax cuts shift the aggregate demand curve to the right. Tax increases reduce consumption spending and shift the aggregate demand curve to the left.

Investment Spending

Investment spending (the purchase of capital goods) is a second major determinant of aggregate demand. A decline in investment spending at each price level shifts the aggregate demand curve to the left. An increase in investment spending shifts it to the right. Investment spending depends on the real interest rate and the expected return from investment.

Real Interest Rates Other things equal, an increase in real interest rates will raise borrowing costs, lower investment spending, and reduce aggregate demand. We are not referring here to the "interest-rate effect" that results from a change in the price level. Instead, we are identifying a change in the real interest rate resulting from, say, a change in a nation's money supply. An increase in the money supply would lower the real interest rate, thereby increasing investment and aggregate demand. By contrast, a decrease in the money supply would raise the real interest rate, thereby reducing investment and decreasing aggregate demand.

Expected Returns Higher expected returns on investment projects increase the demand for capital goods and shift the aggregate demand curve to the right. Alternatively, declines in expected returns decrease investment and shift the aggregate demand curve to the left.

Expected returns are influenced by several factors:

- *Expectations about future business conditions* If firms are optimistic about future business conditions, they are more likely to forecast high rates of return on current investment and therefore may invest more today. If they think the economy will deteriorate in the future, they will forecast low rates of return and perhaps invest less today.

- *Technology* New and improved technologies enhance expected returns on investment and thus increase aggregate demand. For example, recent advances in gene-editing technology have motivated pharmaceutical companies to establish new labs and production facilities.

- *Degree of excess capacity* A rise in excess capacity—unused capital—reduces the expected return on new investment and hence decreases aggregate demand. Other things equal, firms operating factories at well below capacity have little incentive to build new factories. But when firms discover that their excess capacity is dwindling or has completely disappeared, their expected returns on new investment in factories and capital equipment rise. Thus, they increase their investment spending, and aggregate demand shifts to the right.

- *Business taxes* An increase in business taxes will reduce after-tax profits from capital investment and lower expected returns. As a result, investment and aggregate demand will decline. A decrease in business taxes has the opposite effects.

The variability of interest rates and expected returns makes investment highly volatile. Unlike consumption, investment spending rises and falls often, independent of changes in total income. Investment, in fact, is the least stable component of aggregate demand.

Government Spending

Government purchases are the third determinant of aggregate demand. An increase in government purchases (for example, more transportation projects) shifts the aggregate demand curve to the right, as long as tax collections and interest rates do not change as a result. In contrast, a reduction in government spending (for example, less military equipment) shifts the curve to the left.

Net Export Spending

The final determinant of aggregate demand is net export spending. Other things equal, higher U.S. *exports* mean an increased foreign demand for U.S. goods. So a rise in net exports (higher exports relative to imports) shifts the aggregate demand curve to the right. In contrast, a decrease in U.S. net exports shifts the aggregate demand curve to the left. (These changes in net exports are *not* those prompted by a change in the U.S. price level—those associated with the foreign purchases effect. The changes here are shifts of the AD curve, not movements along the AD curve.)

What might cause net exports to change, other than the price level? Two possibilities are changes in national income abroad and changes in exchange rates.

National Income Abroad Rising national income abroad encourages people living abroad to buy more products, some of which are made in the United States. U.S. net exports thus rise, and the U.S. aggregate demand curve shifts to the right. Declines in national income abroad do the opposite: They reduce U.S. net exports and shift the U.S. aggregate demand curve to the left.

Exchange Rates Changes in the dollar's exchange rate—the price of foreign currencies in terms of the U.S. dollar—may affect U.S. exports and therefore aggregate demand. Suppose the dollar depreciates in terms of the euro (meaning the euro appreciates in terms of the dollar). The new, relatively lower value of dollars and higher value of euros enables European consumers to obtain more dollars with each euro. From the perspective of Europeans, U.S. goods are now less expensive; it takes fewer euros to obtain them. So European consumers buy more U.S. goods, and U.S. exports rise. But U.S. consumers can now obtain fewer euros for each dollar. Because they must pay more dollars to buy European goods, Americans reduce their imports. U.S. exports rise, and U.S. imports fall. Conclusion: Dollar depreciation increases net exports (imports go down; exports go up) and therefore increases aggregate demand.

Dollar appreciation has the opposite effects: Net exports fall (imports go up; exports go down) and aggregate demand declines.

QUICK REVIEW
32.1

▶ Aggregate demand reflects an inverse relationship between the price level and the amount of real output demanded.

▶ Changes in the price level create real-balances, interest-rate, and foreign purchases effects that explain the downward slope of the aggregate demand curve.

▶ Changes in one or more of the determinants of aggregate demand (Figure 32.2) will shift the

aggregate demand curve by altering the amount of real GDP demanded at each price level.

▶ An increase in aggregate demand is shown as a rightward shift of the aggregate demand curve; a decrease, as a leftward shift of the curve.

▶ The multiplier effect magnifies initial changes in spending into larger changes in aggregate demand.

Aggregate Supply

Aggregate supply is a schedule or curve showing the relationship between a nation's price level and the amount of real domestic output that firms produce. This relationship varies depending on the time horizon and how quickly output prices and input prices can change. We will define three time horizons:

- In the *immediate short run*, both input prices and output prices are fixed.
- In the *short run*, input prices are fixed but output prices can vary.
- In the *long run*, both input prices and output prices can vary.

The relationship between the price level and total output is different in each of the three time horizons because input prices are stickier than output prices. Although both sets of prices become more flexible as time passes, output prices usually adjust more rapidly.

Aggregate Supply in the Immediate Short Run

Depending on the type of firm, the immediate short run can last anywhere from a few days to a few months. It lasts as long as *both* input prices and output prices stay fixed. Input prices are fixed in both the immediate short run and the short run by contractual agreements. In particular, 75 percent of the average firm's costs are wages and salaries—and these are almost always fixed by labor contracts for months or years at a time. As a result, they are usually fixed much longer than output prices, which can begin to change within a few days or a few months depending on the type of firm.

That said, output prices are also typically fixed in the immediate short run. Firms set fixed prices for their customers and then agree to supply whatever quantity demanded results at those fixed prices. For instance, once an appliance manufacturer sets its annual prices for refrigerators, stoves, and microwaves, it is obligated to supply as many appliances as customers want to buy at those prices. Similarly, a catalog company is obliged to sell however much customers want to buy of its products at the prices listed in its current catalog. And it is obligated to supply those quantities demanded until it sends out its next catalog.

With output prices fixed and firms selling however much customers want to purchase at those fixed prices, the **immediate-short-run aggregate supply curve** AS_{ISR} is a horizontal line, as Figure 32.3 shows. The AS_{ISR} curve is horizontal at the overall price level P_1, which is calculated from all of the individual prices set by the various firms in the economy. Its horizontal shape implies that the total amount of output supplied in the economy depends directly on the volume of spending that results at price level P_1. If total spending is low at price level P_1, firms will supply a small amount of output to match the low level of spending. If total spending is high at price level P_1, they will supply a high level of output to match the high level of spending. The resulting amount of output may be higher than or lower than the economy's full-employment output level Q_f.

Notice, however, that firms will respond in this manner to changes in total spending only as long as output prices remain fixed. As soon as firms can change their output prices, they will respond to changes in aggregate spending not only by increasing or decreasing output but also by raising or lowering prices. This situation leads to the upward sloping short-run aggregate supply curve that we discuss next.

Aggregate Supply in the Short Run

In macroeconomics, the short run begins after the immediate short run ends. More specifically, the short run is the period of time during which output prices are flexible but input prices are either totally fixed or highly inflexible.

>> **LO32.3** Define aggregate supply (AS) and explain how it differs in the immediate short run, the short run, and the long run.

aggregate supply A schedule or curve showing the total quantity of *goods* and *services* that would be supplied (produced) at various *price levels*.

immediate-short-run aggregate supply curve A horizontal *aggregate supply* curve that applies to time periods over which both input prices and output prices are fixed; an aggregate supply curve for which real output, but not the *price level*, changes when the *aggregate demand* curve shifts.

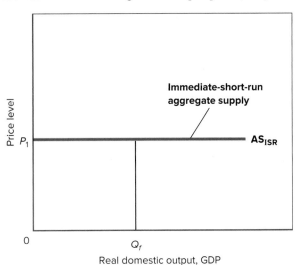

FIGURE 32.3
Aggregate supply in the immediate short run (ISR).

In the immediate short run, the aggregate supply curve AS_{ISR} is horizontal at the economy's current price level, P_1. With output prices fixed, firms collectively supply the level of output that is demanded at those prices. That level of output may differ from the economy's full-employment output level, Q_f.

FIGURE 32.4
The aggregate supply curve (short run).

The upsloping aggregate supply curve AS indicates a direct (or positive) relationship between the price level and the amount of real output that firms will offer for sale. The AS curve is relatively flat below the full-employment output because unemployed resources and unused capacity allow firms to respond to price-level rises with large increases in real output. It is relatively steep beyond the full-employment output because resource shortages and capacity limitations make it difficult to expand real output as the price level rises.

short-run aggregate supply curve An upward sloping *aggregate supply* curve relevant to time periods over which input prices are fixed but output prices are flexible; an aggregate supply curve for which real output and the price level both change when the *aggregate demand* curve shifts.

Some input prices are of course more flexible than others. Consider gasoline, which is an input for delivery firms like UPS. Because gasoline prices are quite flexible, UPS will have at least one very flexible input price. In contrast, wages at UPS are set by five-year labor contracts negotiated with its drivers' union, the Teamsters. Because wages are the firm's largest and most important input cost, UPS faces overall input prices that are inflexible for several years at a time. Thus, its "short run"—the period in which it can change its shipping prices but not its substantially fixed input prices—is actually quite long. Keep this example in mind as we derive the short-run aggregate supply for the entire economy. Its applicability does not depend on some arbitrary definition of how long the "short run" should be. Instead, the short run for which the model is relevant is any period of time during which output prices are flexible, but input prices are fixed or nearly fixed.

As Figure 32.4 shows, the **short-run aggregate supply curve** AS slopes upward because, with input prices fixed, changes in the price level will raise or lower firms' real profits. Consider an economy that has only a single multiproduct firm called Sahara whose owner must receive a real profit of $20 to produce the full-employment output of 100 units. Assume the owner's only input (aside from entrepreneurial talent) is 10 units of hired labor at $8 per worker, for a total wage cost of $80. Also assume that the 100 units of output sell for $1 per unit, so total revenue is $100. Sahara's nominal profit is $20 (= $100 − $80), and using the $1 price to designate the base-price index of 100, its real profit is also $20 (= $20/1.00). Well and good; the full-employment output is produced.

Next, consider what happens if the price of Sahara's output doubles. The doubling of the price level boosts total revenue from $100 to $200, but because we are discussing the short run during which input prices are fixed, the $8 nominal wage for each of the 10 workers remains unchanged so that total costs stay at $80. Nominal profit rises from $20 (= $100 − $80) to $120 (= $200 − $80). Dividing that $120 profit by the new price index of 200 (= 2.0 in hundredths), we find that Sahara's real profit is now $60. The rise in the real reward from $20 to $60 prompts the firm (economy) to produce more output. Conversely, price-level declines reduce real profits and cause the firm (economy) to reduce its output. So, in the short run, there is a direct, or positive, relationship between the price level and real output. When the price level rises, real output rises; and when the price level falls, real output falls. The result is an upward sloping short-run aggregate supply curve.

Notice, however, that the upward slope of the short-run aggregate supply curve is not constant. It is flatter at outputs below the full-employment output level Q_f and steeper at outputs above it. Why the difference?

- When the economy is operating below its full-employment output, it has large amounts of unused equipment and large numbers of unemployed workers. Firms can put these idle human and capital resources back to work with little upward pressure on per-unit production costs. And as output expands, few if any shortages of inputs will arise to raise per-unit production costs. Thus the slope of the short-run aggregate supply curve increases only slowly at output levels below the full-employment output level Q_f.

- In contrast, when the economy is operating beyond Q_f, the vast majority of its available resources are already employed. Adding more workers to a relatively fixed number of highly used capital resources such as plant and equipment creates congestion in the workplace and reduces the average efficiency of workers. Adding more capital, given the limited number of available workers, leaves equipment idle and reduces the efficiency of capital. Adding more land resources when capital and labor are highly constrained reduces the efficiency of land resources. Under these circumstances, total input costs rise more rapidly than total output. The result is rapidly rising per-unit production costs that give the short-run aggregate supply curve its rapidly increasing slope at output levels beyond Q_f.

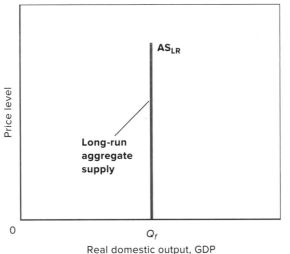

FIGURE 32.5
Aggregate supply in the long run.

The long-run aggregate supply curve AS_{LR} is vertical at the full-employment level of real GDP (Q_f) because in the long run wages and other input prices rise and fall to match changes in the price level. So price-level changes do not affect firms' profits and thus they create no incentive for firms to alter their output.

Aggregate Supply in the Long Run

In macroeconomics, the long run is the time horizon over which both input prices and output prices are flexible. It begins after the short run ends. The long run may last from a couple of weeks to several years, depending on the industry. But for the economy as a whole, it is the time horizon over which all output and input prices—including wage rates—are fully flexible.

The **long-run aggregate supply curve** AS_{LR} is vertical at the economy's full-employment output Q_f, as Figure 32.5 shows. The vertical curve means that in the long run the economy will produce the full-employment output level no matter what the price level is. How can this statement be true? Shouldn't higher prices cause firms to increase output? The explanation lies in the fact that in the long run, when both input prices and output prices are flexible, profit levels always adjust to give firms exactly the right profit incentive to produce exactly the full-employment output level, Q_f.

To see why, look back at the short-run aggregate supply curve AS in Figure 32.4. Suppose that the economy starts by producing at the full-employment output level Q_f and that the price level at that moment has an index value of $P = 100$. Now suppose that output prices double, so that the price index goes to $P = 200$. We previously demonstrated for our single-firm economy that this doubling of the price level will cause profits to rise in the short run and that the higher profits will motivate the firm to increase output.

This outcome, however, is dependent on the fact that input prices are fixed in the short run. Consider what will happen in the long run when they are free to change. Firms can produce beyond the full-employment output level only by running factories and businesses at extremely high rates. In doing so, they create a great deal of demand for the economy's limited supply of productive resources. In particular, labor is in great demand because the only way to produce beyond full employment is to have employees work overtime.

As time passes and input prices are free to change, the high level of resource demand will start to raise input prices. In particular, overworked employees will demand and receive raises as employers scramble to deal with the labor shortages that inevitably arise whenever the economy is producing above its full-employment output level. As input prices increase, firm profits begin to fall. As they decline, so does the motive that firms have to produce more than the full-employment output level.

This process of rising input prices and falling profits continues until the rise in input prices exactly matches the initial change in output prices (in our example, they both double). When that happens, firm profits in real terms return to their original level so that firms are once again motivated to produce at exactly the full-employment output level. This adjustment process means that in the long run, the economy will produce at full employment regardless of the price level (in our example, at either $P = 100$ or $P = 200$). Thus the long-run aggregate supply curve AS_{LR} is vertical above the full-employment output level. Every possible price level on the vertical axis is associated with the economy producing at the full-employment output level in the long run.

long-run aggregate supply curve A vertical *aggregate supply* curve relevant to time periods over which input prices and output prices are both fully flexible; an aggregate supply curve for which the *price level*, but not real output, changes when the *aggregate demand* curve shifts; a vertical aggregate supply curve that implies fully flexible *prices*.

Focusing on the Short Run

The immediate-short-run aggregate supply curve, the short-run aggregate supply curve, and the long-run aggregate supply curve are all important. Each curve is appropriate to situations that match their respective assumptions about the flexibility of input and output prices. But our focus in the rest of this chapter and the chapters that immediately follow will be on the short-run time horizon and, consequently, on short-run aggregate supply curves, such as the AS curve shown in Figure 32.4. Unless explicitly stated otherwise, all references to "aggregate supply" are to short-run aggregate supply, AS.

We are emphasizing the short-run aggregate supply curve because real-world economies typically manifest simultaneous changes in both their price levels and their levels of real output. The upward sloping short-run AS curve is the only version of aggregate supply that can handle simultaneous movements in both of these variables. By contrast, the price level is fixed in the immediate short run (Figure 32.3) and output is fixed in the long run (Figure 32.5). This renders these versions of aggregate supply unhelpful when it comes to understanding business cycles and macroeconomic policy. To analyze those issues correctly, we must employ the short-run aggregate supply curve, AS.

QUICK REVIEW
32.2

▶ The immediate-short-run aggregate supply curve is horizontal: given fixed input and output prices, producers will supply whatever quantity of real output is demanded at the current price level.

▶ The short-run aggregate supply curve slopes upward: given fixed resource prices, higher output prices raise profits and encourage firms to increase their output levels.

▶ The long-run aggregate supply curve is vertical: given sufficient time, wages and other input prices rise or fall to match any change in the price level.

Changes in Aggregate Supply

>> **LO32.4** Explain the factors that shift AS.

determinants of aggregate supply Factors such as input prices, *productivity*, and the legal-institutional environment that, if they change, shift the aggregate supply curve.

An aggregate supply curve identifies the relationship between the price level and real output, other things equal. But when one or more of those other things change, the curve shifts. The rightward shift of the curve from AS_1 to AS_2 in Figure 32.6 represents an increase in aggregate supply, indicating that firms are willing to produce and sell more real output at every price level. The leftward shift of the curve from AS_1 to AS_3 represents a decrease in aggregate supply. At each price level, firms produce less output than before.

Figure 32.6 lists the "other things" that shift the aggregate supply curve. Called the **determinants of aggregate supply** or *aggregate supply shifters*, they collectively position the aggregate supply

FIGURE 32.6 Changes in aggregate supply.

A change in one or more of the listed determinants of aggregate supply will shift the aggregate supply curve. The rightward shift of the aggregate supply curve from AS_1 to AS_2 represents an increase in aggregate supply; the leftward shift of the curve from AS_1 to AS_3 shows a decrease in aggregate supply.

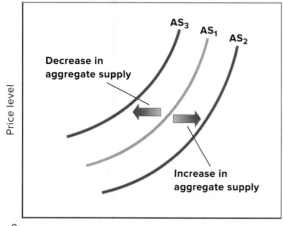

Determinants of Aggregate Supply: Factors That Shift the Aggregate Supply Curve

1. Changes in input prices
   a. Domestic resource prices
   b. Prices of imported resources

2. Changes in productivity

3. Changes in legal-institutional environment
   a. Business taxes and subsidies
   b. Government regulations

curve and shift the curve when they change. Changes in these determinants raise or lower per-unit production costs *at each price level*. These changes in per-unit production cost affect profits, leading firms to alter the amount of output they are willing to produce *at each price level*. Changes that increase profits cause firms to produce more, while changes that decrease profits cause firms to produce less.

As an example, firms may collectively offer $9 trillion of real output at a price level of 1.0 (100 in index value) when the supply shifters are all at particular values, but then only $8.8 trillion at that same price level if one or more of the supply shifters change. The point is that when one of the determinants listed in Figure 32.6 changes, the aggregate supply curve shifts to the right or left. Changes that reduce per-unit production costs shift the aggregate supply curve to the right, as from AS_1 to AS_2. Changes that increase per-unit production costs shift it to the left, as from AS_1 to AS_3.

The three aggregate supply determinants listed in Figure 32.6 require more discussion.

Input Prices

Input or resource prices—to be distinguished from the output prices that make up the price level—are a major ingredient of per-unit production costs and therefore a key determinant of aggregate supply. These resources can be either domestic or imported.

Domestic Resource Prices As stated earlier, wages and salaries make up about 75 percent of all business costs. Other things equal, decreases in wages increase profits by reducing per-unit production costs. So when wages fall, the aggregate supply curve shifts to the right. By contrast, increases in wages reduce profits by raising per-unit production costs. So when wages rise, the aggregate supply curve shifts to the left. Examples:

- Labor supply increases because of substantial immigration. Wages and per-unit production costs fall, shifting the AS curve to the right.

- Labor supply decreases because a rapid increase in pension income causes many older workers to opt for early retirement. Wage rates and per-unit production costs rise, shifting the AS curve to the left.

Similarly, the aggregate supply curve shifts when the prices of land or capital inputs change. Examples:

- The price of machinery and equipment falls because of declines in the prices of steel and electronic components. Per-unit production costs decline, and the AS curve shifts to the right.

- The supply of available land resources expands through discoveries of mineral deposits or technical innovations that transform "nonresources" (say, vast desert lands) into valuable resources (productive lands). The price of land declines, per-unit production costs fall, and the AS curve shifts to the right.

Prices of Imported Resources Resources imported from abroad (such as oil, tin, and copper) affect U.S. aggregate supply because added supplies of resources—whether domestic or imported—typically reduce resource prices and, consequently, per-unit production costs. Other things equal, a decrease in the price of imported resources will raise U.S. profits and increase U.S. aggregate supply. Conversely, an increase in the price of imported resources will lower U.S. profits and reduce U.S. aggregate supply, other things equal.

A good example of the major effect that changing resource prices can have on aggregate supply is the oil price hikes of the 1970s. At that time, the members of the Organization of Petroleum Exporting Countries (OPEC) worked in concert to decrease oil production and raise the price of oil. The tenfold increase in the price of oil that OPEC achieved during the 1970s drove per-unit production costs up and jolted the U.S. aggregate supply curve leftward.

Exchange-rate fluctuations may also alter the price of imported resources. Suppose that the dollar appreciates, enabling U.S. firms to obtain more foreign currency with each dollar. Domestic producers will now face a lower *dollar* price of imported resources. U.S. firms will respond by increasing their imports of foreign resources. By substituting cheap foreign resources for more expensive domestic resources, firms will lower their per-unit production costs at each level of output. Those falling per-unit production costs will shift the U.S. aggregate supply curve to the right.

A depreciation of the dollar has the opposite set of effects and shifts the aggregate supply curve to the left.

Productivity

productivity A measure of average output or real output per unit of input. For example, the productivity of labor is determined by dividing real output by hours of work.

The second major determinant of aggregate supply is **productivity,** which measures how much output can be produced from any given set of inputs. Mathematically, productivity is defined as average real output, or real output per unit of input:

$$\text{Productivity} = \frac{\text{total output}}{\text{total inputs}}$$

Higher productivity implies greater efficiency. An increase in productivity enables the economy to obtain more output from its limited resources.

An increase in productivity also implies a reduction in per-unit production costs. To see why that is true, let's work out an example of what productivity and per-unit production costs are before and after an increase in efficiency. Start by supposing that total output is 10 units, that 5 units of inputs are needed to produce that quantity, and that the price of each input unit is $2. Then,

$$\text{Productivity} = \frac{\text{total output}}{\text{total inputs}} = \frac{10}{5} = 2$$

meaning that we can produce two units of output for each unit of input. In addition, we see that:

$$\text{Productivity} = \frac{\text{total input cost}}{\text{total output}} = \frac{\$2 \times 5}{10} = \$1$$

which indicates that production costs are currently $1 per unit. (As an aside, note that we ascertained the total input cost by multiplying the per-unit input cost by the number of inputs used.)

Now suppose that productivity increases so that real output doubles to 20 units, while the price and quantity of input remain constant at $2 and 5 units, respectively. Using the above equations, we see that productivity rises from 2 to 4 and that the per-unit production cost of the output falls from $1 to $0.50. The doubled productivity has reduced the per-unit production cost by half.

By reducing per-unit production costs, an increase in productivity shifts the aggregate supply curve to the right. The main source of productivity advance is improved production technology, often embodied in new plant and equipment that replaces old plant and equipment. Other sources of productivity increases are a better-educated and better-trained workforce, improved forms of business enterprise, and the reallocation of labor resources from lower-productivity to higher-productivity uses.

Decreases in productivity are rare. But when they occur, they increase per-unit production costs and therefore reduce aggregate supply (shift the AS curve to the left).

Legal-Institutional Environment

Changes in the legal-institutional setting in which businesses operate are the final determinant of aggregate supply. Such changes may alter the per-unit costs of output and, in doing so, shift the aggregate supply curve. Two changes of this type are (1) changes in taxes and subsidies and (2) changes in the extent of regulation.

Business Taxes and Subsidies Higher business taxes, such as sales, excise, and payroll taxes, increase per-unit costs and reduce short-run aggregate supply. Higher business taxes shift aggregate supply to the left.

Similarly, a business subsidy—a payment or tax break by government to producers—lowers production costs and increases short-run aggregate supply. For example, the federal government subsidizes firms that blend ethanol (derived from corn) with gasoline to increase the U.S. gasoline supply. This reduces the per-unit production cost of making blended gasoline. To the extent that this and other subsidies are successful, the aggregate supply curve shifts rightward.

Government Regulation It is usually costly for businesses to comply with government regulations. More regulation therefore tends to increase per-unit production costs and shift the aggregate supply curve to the left. "Supply-side" proponents of deregulation of the economy have argued forcefully that, by increasing efficiency and reducing the paperwork associated with complex regulations, deregulation will reduce per-unit costs and shift the aggregate supply curve to the right. Other economists are less certain. Deregulation that results in accounting manipulations, monopolization, and business failures is likely to shift the AS curve to the left rather than to the right.

> **QUICK REVIEW**
> **32.3**

▶ Changes in one or more of the determinants of aggregate supply (Figure 32.6) will increase or decrease the aggregate amount of output supplied at each price level by either increasing or decreasing per-unit production costs.

▶ Decreases in per-unit production costs cause rightward shifts of the short-run aggregate supply curve while increases in per-unit production costs cause leftward shifts.

▶ Increases in productivity reduce per-unit production costs and shift the AS curve to the right, while decreases in productivity raise per-unit production costs and shift the AS curve to the left.

>> **LO32.5** Explain how AD and AS determine an economy's equilibrium price level and real GDP.

Equilibrium in the AD–AS Model

Of all the possible combinations of price levels and levels of real GDP, which combination will the economy gravitate toward, at least in the short run? **Figure 32.7 (Key Graph)** and its accompanying table provide the answer. Equilibrium occurs at the price level that equalizes the amounts of real output demanded and supplied. The intersection of the aggregate demand curve AD and the aggregate supply curve AS establishes the economy's **equilibrium price level** and **equilibrium real output.** Aggregate demand and aggregate supply *jointly* establish the price level and level of real GDP.

In Figure 32.7, the equilibrium price level and level of real output are 100 and $510 billion, respectively. To illustrate why those values constitute an equilibrium, suppose the price level is 92 rather than 100. We see from the table that the lower price level will encourage businesses to produce real output of $502 billion. This is shown by point *a* on the AS curve in the graph. But as revealed by the table and point *b* on the AD curve, buyers will want to purchase $514 billion of real output at price level 92. There will consequently be a $12 billion (= $514 billion demanded − $502 billion supplied) shortage of real output.

This shortage will not persist. Competition among buyers to purchase the limited ($502 billion) supply of real output will eliminate the shortage and drive the price level up from 92 to 100. The rise in the price level from 92 to 100 encourages producers to increase their real output from $502 billion to $510 billion and causes buyers to scale back their purchases from $514 billion to $510 billion. When equality occurs between the amounts of real output produced and purchased, as it does at price level 100, the economy will achieve equilibrium (here, at $510 billion of real GDP).

A final note: Although the equilibrium price level happens to be 100 in our example, nothing special is implied by that. Any price level can be an equilibrium price level.

equilibrium price level In the *aggregate demand–aggregate supply* (*AD–AS*) *model*, the *price level* at which *aggregate demand* equals *aggregate supply;* the price level at which the aggregate demand curve intersects the aggregate supply curve.

equilibrium real output (see *equilibrium real domestic output*) The *gross domestic product* at which the total quantity of *final goods* and final *services* purchased (*aggregate expenditures*) is equal to the total quantity of final goods and services produced (the real domestic output); the real domestic output at which the aggregate demand curve intersects the aggregate supply curve.

▅▃▂ KEY GRAPH

FIGURE 32.7 **The equilibrium price level and equilibrium real GDP.**

The intersection of the aggregate demand curve and the aggregate supply curve determines the economy's equilibrium price level. At the equilibrium price level of 100 (in index-value terms), the $510 billion of real output demanded matches the $510 billion of real output supplied. So the equilibrium GDP is $510 billion.

Real Output Demanded (Billions)	Price Level (Index Number)	Real Output Supplied (Billions)
$506	$108	$513
508	104	512
510	**100**	**510**
512	96	507
514	92	502

QUICK QUIZ FOR FIGURE 32.7

1. **The AD curve slopes downward because:**
   a. per-unit production costs fall as real GDP increases.
   b. the income and substitution effects are at work.
   c. changes in the determinants of AD alter the amounts of real GDP demanded at each price level.
   d. decreases in the price level give rise to real-balances effects, interest-rate effects, and foreign purchases effects that increase the amount of real GDP demanded.

2. **The AS curve slopes upward because:**
   a. per-unit production costs rise as real GDP expands toward and beyond its full-employment level.
   b. the income and substitution effects are at work.
   c. changes in the determinants of AS alter the amounts of real GDP supplied at each price level.
   d. increases in the price level give rise to real-balances effects, interest-rate effects, and foreign purchases effects that increase the amounts of real GDP supplied.

3. **At price level 92:**
   a. a GDP surplus of $12 billion occurs that drives the price level up to 100.
   b. a GDP shortage of $12 billion occurs that drives the price level up to 100.
   c. the aggregate amount of real GDP demanded is less than the aggregate amount of real GDP supplied.
   d. the economy is operating beyond its capacity to produce.

4. **Suppose real output demanded rises by $4 billion at each price level. The new equilibrium price level will be:**
   a. 108.
   b. 104.
   c. 96.
   d. 92.

Changes in Equilibrium

>> **LO32.6** Use the AD–AS model to explain demand-pull inflation, cost-push inflation, and recessions.

Now let's apply the AD–AS model to various situations. For simplicity, we will use *P* and *Q* symbols rather than actual numbers. Remember that these symbols represent, respectively, price index values and amounts of real GDP.

Increases in AD: Demand-Pull Inflation

Suppose the economy is operating at its full-employment output when businesses and government decide to increase their spending—actions that shift the aggregate demand curve to the right. Our list of determinants of aggregate demand (Figure 32.2) provides several reasons why this shift might occur. Perhaps firms boost their investment spending because they anticipate higher future profits from investments in new capital. And perhaps government increases spending to expand national defense.

As shown by the rise in the price level from P_1 to P_2 in Figure 32.8, the increase in aggregate demand beyond full-employment output causes inflation. This is demand-pull inflation because the price level is being pulled up by the increase in aggregate demand. Also observe that the increase in demand expands real output from the full-employment level Q_f to Q_1. The distance between Q_1 and Q_f is a positive, or "inflationary," GDP gap. Actual GDP exceeds potential GDP.

The classic American example of demand-pull inflation occurred in the late 1960s. The escalation of the war in Vietnam resulted in a 40 percent increase in defense spending between 1965 and 1967 and another 15 percent increase in 1968. The rise in government spending, on top of an already growing economy, shifted the economy's aggregate demand curve to the right, producing the worst inflation in two decades. Actual GDP exceeded potential GDP, thereby creating an inflationary GDP gap. Inflation jumped from 1.6 percent in 1965 to 5.7 percent by 1970.

Figure 32.8 reveals an interesting point concerning the multiplier effect. The increase in aggregate demand from AD_1 to AD_2 increases real output only to Q_1, not to Q_2, because part of the increase in aggregate demand is absorbed as inflation as the price level rises from P_1 to P_2. Had the price level remained at P_1, the shift of aggregate demand from AD_1 to AD_2 would have increased real output to Q_2. The full-strength multiplier effect would have occurred. But in Figure 32.8, inflation reduced the increase in real output—and thus the multiplier effect—by about one-half. Price-level flexibility weakens the realized multiplier effect.

Decreases in AD: Recession and Cyclical Unemployment

Decreases in aggregate demand result in recession and cyclical unemployment. For example, in 2020, U.S. investment spending greatly declined because the onset of the COVID-19 pandemic caused businesspeople to assume sharply lower expected returns on investment. In particular, businesspeople were worried about poor future business conditions and high degrees of unused production capacity. **Figure 32.9 (Key Graph)** shows the resulting decline in aggregate demand as a leftward shift from AD_1 to AD_2.

If prices were flexible in Figure 32.9, the economy's equilibrium would adjust from point *a* to point *c*, implying both a recession (since Q_2 is less than Q_f) and a decline in the price level. But we now add an important twist to the analysis: *Deflation*—a decline in the price level—is not the norm in the American economy. The U.S. price level is downwardly *in*flexible. This is illustrated in Figure 32.9 by the broken horizontal line at the initial price level P_1 that prevailed before aggregate demand shifted to the left. The broken horizontal line indicates that prices are stuck (completely inflexible) at price level P_1.

With the price level stuck at P_1, the economy moves from *a* to *b* along the broken horizontal line rather than from *a* to *c* along the short-run aggregate supply curve. The outcome is a decline of real output from Q_f to Q_1, with *no* change in the price level. It is as if the aggregate supply curve in Figure 32.9 is horizontal at P_1, to the left of point *a*, as indicated by the dashed line.

The decline of real output from Q_f to Q_1 constitutes a *recession*, and because fewer workers are needed to produce the lower output, *cyclical unemployment* arises. The distance between Q_1 and Q_f is a negative, or "recessionary," GDP gap—the amount by which actual output falls short of potential output.

Figure 32.9 also reveals that without a fall in the price level, the multiplier is at full strength. With the price level stuck at P_1, real GDP decreases by $Q_f - Q_1$, which matches the full leftward

FIGURE 32.8
An increase in aggregate demand that causes demand-pull inflation.

The increase of aggregate demand from AD_1 to AD_2 causes demand-pull inflation, shown as the rise in the price level from P_1 to P_2. It also causes an inflationary GDP gap of Q_1 minus Q_f. The rise of the price level reduces the size of the multiplier effect. If the price level had remained at P_1, the increase in aggregate demand from AD_1 to AD_2 would have increased output from Q_f to Q_2 and the multiplier would have been at full strength. But because of the increase in the price level, real output increases only from Q_f to Q_1 and the multiplier effect is reduced.

..ıl KEY GRAPH

FIGURE 32.9 A recession resulting from a leftward shift of aggregate demand when the price level is downwardly inflexible.

If the price level is downwardly inflexible at P_1, a decline of aggregate demand from AD_1 to AD_2 will move the economy leftward from a to b along the horizontal broken-line segment and reduce real GDP from Q_f to Q_1. Idle production capacity, cyclical unemployment, and a recessionary GDP gap (of $Q_1 - Q_f$) will result. If the price level were flexible downward, the decline in aggregate demand would move the economy depicted from a to c instead of from a to b.

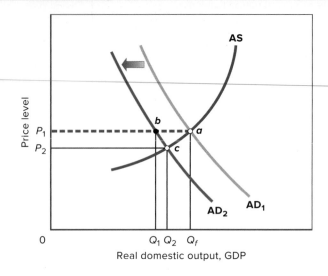

QUICK QUIZ FOR FIGURE 32.9

1. **If the price level remains stuck at P_1 and aggregate demand remains at AD_2, then:**
   a. the economy will be producing at full employment output.
   b. the price level will fall to P_2.
   c. the GDP gap will remain constant at $Q_1 - Q_f$.
   d. equilibrium will shift back to point a.

2. **Start from point b. If the price level becomes downwardly flexible, then:**
   a. the GDP gap will be reduced by the amount $Q_2 - Q_1$.
   b. the GDP gap will be reduced by the amount $Q_f - Q_1$.
   c. the GDP gap will be increased by the amount $Q_2 + Q_1$.
   d. the GDP gap will remain constant.

3. **Start from point b. For the economy to end up at point c would require:**
   a. upward price level flexibility.
   b. downward output flexibility.
   c. a downward shift of the AS curve.
   d. downward price flexibility.

4. **If prices were downwardly flexible, the equilibrium GDP and price level would be:**
   a. Q_f and P_1, respectively.
   b. Q_1 and P_1, respectively.
   c. Q_2 and P_1, respectively.
   d. Q_2 and P_2, respectively.

Answers: 1. c; 2. a; 3. d; 4. d

shift of the AD curve. The multiplier is at full strength because the reduction in aggregate demand occurs along what is, in effect, a horizontal segment of the AS curve. Because AS is effectively horizontal, none of the decrease in AD is dissipated as deflation, as some of it would be if prices were flexible and the economy shifted from a to c.

Note that this full-strength multiplier would also apply for an increase in aggregate demand from AD_2 to AD_1 along the broken line. The equilibrium would move from b to a, with GDP returning to Q_f and the price level remaining fixed at P_1. Thus, none of the increase in aggregate demand would be dissipated as inflation.

All recent recessions in the United States have generally mimicked the "GDP gap but no deflation" scenario shown in Figure 32.9. Consider the recession of 2007–2009, which resulted from chaos in the financial markets that quickly led to significant declines in spending by businesses and households. Aggregate demand declined dramatically, with actual GDP falling short of potential GDP by $1 trillion in 2009. At the same time, however, the price level barely budged, falling by only three-tenths of one percent in 2008 and in fact rising during 2009 as government stimulus efforts (lower taxes and higher spending) kicked in.

A similar thing happened during the pandemic recession of 2020. Actual GDP was 11 percent below potential GDP during the initial lockdown months, but the overall price level in the economy fell only slightly during those first few months before rising 1.3 percent over the entire year after government stimulus efforts kicked in.

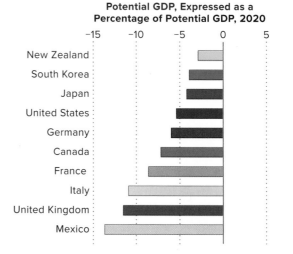

🌐 GLOBAL PERSPECTIVE 32.1

SIZE OF GDP GAPS, SELECTED COUNTRIES, 2020

A country's GDP gap between potential output and actual output can be expressed as a percentage of potential output. In 2020, GDP gaps were negative in countries around the world, reflecting the fact that the COVID-19 pandemic was a worldwide phenomenon. Please note, however, that inflation was positive in each of the countries listed, reflecting the strength of downward price stickiness even during deep recessions.

Source: OECD Economic Outlook, Organisation for Economic Co-operation and Development (OECD).

Global Perspective 32.1 lists the 2020 GDP gaps of 10 countries. None of them experienced a deflation, even though all of them experienced negative GDP gaps as a result of the COVID-19 pandemic.

Decreases in AS: Cost-Push Inflation

Suppose that a major terrorist attack on oil facilities severely disrupts world oil supplies and drives up oil prices by, say, 300 percent. Higher energy prices will spread throughout the economy, driving up production and distribution costs on a wide variety of goods and services. The U.S. aggregate supply curve would shift to the left, say, from AS_1 to AS_2 in Figure 32.10. The resulting increase in the price level would generate *cost-push inflation*.

Consistent with the behavior of the U.S. economy, we are assuming in Figure 32.10 that the price level is flexible upward. So when aggregate supply shifts leftward from AS_1 to AS_2, the economy's equilibrium moves upward from point *a* to point *b*, with the price level rising from P_1 to P_2 and real output declining from Q_f to Q_1.

The effects of the leftward shift in aggregate supply are doubly bad. Along with the rising price level and cost-push inflation, a recession (and negative GDP gap) occurs. The oil-price shock of the early 1970s is the most famous example of this double whammy. The members of OPEC slowed their production rates to drive up the price of crude oil, which nearly quadrupled between October of 1973 and January of 1974. That dramatic increase in the price of oil increased per-unit production costs throughout the economy, pushing AS sharply to the left. The result was the 1973–1974 recession that saw real GDP decline by over 3 percent while inflation spiked to an annualized rate of 12 percent per year.

Back in the 1970s, oil expenditures were about 10 percent of U.S. GDP compared to only about 3 percent today. So the U.S. economy is nowadays substantially less vulnerable to cost-push inflation arising from

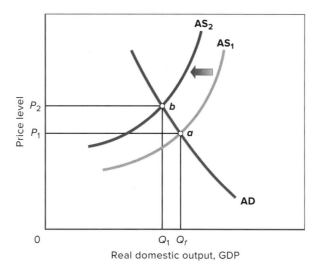

FIGURE 32.10
A decrease in aggregate supply that causes cost-push inflation.

A leftward shift of aggregate supply from AS_1 to AS_2 raises the price level from P_1 to P_2 and produces cost-push inflation. Real output declines and a recessionary GDP gap (of Q_1 minus Q_f) occurs.

oil shocks. That said, it is *not immune* from such shocks. A substantial supply shock caused by soaring oil prices would almost certainly cause U.S. aggregate supply to shift to the left by enough to again generate a decrease in output accompanied by significant cost-push inflation.

Increases in AS: Full Employment with Price-Level Stability

During the late 1990s, the United States experienced a combination of full employment, strong economic growth, and very low inflation. The unemployment rate fell to 4 percent and real GDP grew nearly 4 percent annually, *without igniting inflation.*

At first glance, this "macroeconomic bliss" seems to be incompatible with the AD–AS model. The aggregate supply curve suggests that increases in aggregate demand that strain the economy's production capacity will raise the price level (see Figure 32.8). Higher inflation, so it would seem, is the inevitable price paid for expanding output beyond the full-employment level.

But inflation remained very mild during the late 1990s. Figure 32.11 explains why. Thanks to the booming economy, aggregate demand increased from AD_1 to AD_2. Taken alone, that increase in aggregate demand would have moved the economy from *a* to *b*. Real output would have risen from full-employment output Q_1 to beyond-full-employment output Q_2. And the economy would have experienced significant inflation, shown by the increase in the price level from P_1 to P_3. Such inflation had in fact occurred during previous vigorous expansions of aggregate demand, including the expansion of the late 1980s.

Between 1990 and 2000, however, larger-than-usual increases in productivity occurred because of a burst of new technology relating to computers, the Internet, electronic commerce, and so on. In Figure 32.11, we represent this higher-than-usual productivity growth as the rightward shift from AS_1 to AS_2. The relevant aggregate demand and aggregate supply curves thus became AD_2 and AS_2, not AD_2 and AS_1. Instead of moving from *a* to *b*, the economy moved from *a* to *c*. Real output increased from Q_1 to Q_3, and the price level rose only modestly (from P_1 to P_2). The shift of the aggregate supply curve from AS_1 to AS_2 accommodated the rapid increase in aggregate demand and kept inflation mild.

But all good things come to an end. Aggregate demand eventually declined because of a substantial fall in investment spending, and in March 2001 the economy entered a recession. The terrorist attacks of September 11, 2001, further dampened private spending and prolonged the recession throughout 2001. The unemployment rate rose from 4.2 percent in January 2001 to 6.0 percent in December 2002. But consistent with downwardly flexible prices, the decline in aggregate demand did not cause a deflation. Inflation slowed, but remained positive. The price level did not fall.

The economy rebounded between 2002 and 2007, eventually re-achieving its earlier strong economic growth, low inflation, and low unemployment—until the housing bubble collapsed in 2006, and the so-called Great Recession started the following year.

FIGURE 32.11
Growth, full employment, and relative price stability.

Normally, an increase in aggregate demand from AD_1 to AD_2 would move the economy from *a* to *b* along AS_1. Real output would expand to Q_2, and inflation would result (P_1 to P_3). But in the late 1990s, significant increases in productivity shifted the aggregate supply curve, as from AS_1 to AS_2. The economy moved from *a* to *c* rather than from *a* to *b*. It experienced strong economic growth (Q_1 to Q_3), full employment, and only very mild inflation (P_1 to P_2) before receding in March 2001.

Price level / Real domestic output, GDP

QUICK REVIEW
32.4

▶ The equilibrium price level and amount of real output are determined at the intersection of the aggregate demand curve and the aggregate supply curve.

▶ Increases in aggregate demand beyond the full-employment level of real GDP cause demand-pull inflation.

▶ Decreases in aggregate demand cause recessions and cyclical unemployment, partly because the price level and wages tend to be inflexible in a downward direction.

▶ Decreases in aggregate supply cause cost-push inflation.

▶ Full employment, high economic growth, and price stability are compatible with one another if productivity-driven increases in aggregate supply are sufficient to balance growing aggregate demand.

The COVID-19 Inflation

In 2021, Supply Chain Disruptions, Combined with Strong Aggregate Demand, Led to an Inflation Caused by Simultaneous Shifts in both AD *and* AS.

In 2021, inflation in the United States ran at a 7.0 percent annual rate as measured by the Consumer Price Index (CPI). That was the highest rate of inflation in the United States since 1981—when inflation was 10.3 percent—and it came as a surprise to both consumers and economic forecasters, who had been expecting inflation to be 2.5 percent or lower during 2021.

Surprising events often have surprising causes, and 2021's unexpected surge in inflation was no exception. Most bouts of inflation are caused either by aggregate demand shifting right while aggregate supply remains essentially stationary, *or* by aggregate supply shifting left while aggregate demand remains essentially stationary. The former is more common, with one famous example from U.S. history occurring in the late 1960s when the federal government's decision to simultaneously spend more on both social services (Medicare and Medicaid started in 1965) and the Vietnam War massively increased government spending and pushed aggregate demand to the right very rapidly. As illustrated by Figure 32.8, the resulting demand-pull inflation caused the price level to rise by 5.8 percent in 1970.

The most famous example of the other situation (in which aggregate supply shifts left while aggregate demand remains stationary or nearly stationary) began in October 1973 when several Arab countries that were major oil exporters slashed their production by 25 percent and placed an embargo against selling their oil to the United States and several other nations as a protest against those countries having provided military supplies to Israel after Israel had been sneak-attacked on the religious holiday of Yom Kippur by Egypt and Syria. Although the war itself lasted only three weeks, the oil embargo lasted until April 1974, by which time the world price of oil had quadrupled, from $2.90 per barrel to $11.65 per barrel. Since oil was a major productive input, the AS curve shifted left, thereby plunging the world into an inflationary recession, as illustrated in Figure 32.10.

The unexpected inflation of 2021 combined a rightward shift of AD and a leftward shift of AS. It consequently featured both cost-push inflation and demand-pull inflation operating simultaneously. The increase in aggregate demand came from the massive amount of government spending that congress and the president approved to fight the negative economic effects of the COVID-19 pandemic. The annualized rate of federal expenditures, including transfer payments, went from about $4.9 trillion per year just prior to the pandemic to a peak of about $9.1 trillion per year in mid-2020 before falling down to a still-high annualized rate of about $7.0 trillion per year during 2021. That surge of spending pushed the AD curve *sharply* to the right.

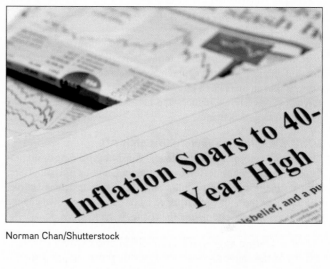

Norman Chan/Shutterstock

At the same time, a litany of supply chain disruptions shifted the AS curve to the left. These included everything from a shortage of computer chips to a dearth of unloading capacity at U.S. ports to factory shutdowns in various countries for various lengths of time due to anti-COVID lockdowns. All of those supply-reducing factors were augmented by labor shortages in the United States as older workers retired early and many younger workers decided to remain unemployed because they could make more collecting anti-pandemic unemployment benefits than they could working.

A key thing to keep in mind, however, was that real GDP had grown steadily throughout 2021, even after the various anti-pandemic stimulus programs had expired one by one. So as 2022 began, the focus was not on a threat of recession but rather on the high rate of inflation and what could be done to decrease it, especially because real wages had begun to decline due to the fact that consumer prices were going up faster than nominal wages.

As people looked to the future, supply chain problems were still apparent and the millions of older workers who had retired early seemed to be firm in their decision, implying that AS was not likely to start shifting rightward in any significant fashion any time soon. Consequently, prudence dictated that policymakers would have to be nimble if they wanted to return the economy to the mild inflation and steady growth witnessed in the late 2010s just prior to the pandemic. Any further leftward shifts of AS might have to be countered by rightward shifts of AD to prevent a recurrence of recession, but in a time of inflation, any rightward shifts of AD would only make the inflation problem worse.

Summary

LO32.1 Define aggregate demand (AD) and explain how its downward slope is the result of the real-balances effect, the interest-rate effect, and the foreign purchases effect.

The aggregate demand curve shows the level of real output that the economy demands at each price level.

The aggregate demand curve slopes downward because of the real-balances effect, the interest-rate effect, and the foreign purchases effect. The real-balances effect indicates that inflation reduces the real value or purchasing power of fixed-value financial assets held by households, causing cutbacks in consumer spending. The interest-rate effect means that, with a specific supply of money, a higher price level increases the demand for money, thereby raising the interest rate and reducing investment purchases. The foreign purchases effect suggests that an increase in one country's price level relative to other countries' price levels reduces the net export component of that nation's aggregate demand.

LO32.2 Explain the factors that shift AD.

The determinants of aggregate demand consist of spending by domestic consumers, by businesses, by government, and by foreign buyers. Changes in these groups' spending shift the aggregate demand curve. The extent of the shift is determined by the size of the initial change in spending and the strength of the economy's multiplier.

LO32.3 Define aggregate supply (AS) and explain how it differs in the immediate short run, the short run, and the long run.

The aggregate supply curve shows the levels of real output that businesses will produce at various possible price levels. The slope of the aggregate supply curve depends upon the flexibility of input and output prices.

The *immediate-short-run aggregate supply curve* assumes that both input prices and output prices are fixed. With output prices fixed, the aggregate supply curve is a horizontal line at the current price level. The *short-run aggregate supply curve* assumes nominal wages and other input prices remain fixed while output prices vary. The aggregate supply curve generally slopes upward because per-unit production costs, and hence the prices that firms receive, rise as real output expands. The aggregate supply curve is relatively steep to the right of the full-employment output level and relatively flat to the left of it.

The *long-run aggregate supply curve* assumes that nominal wages and other input prices fully match any change in the price level. The curve is vertical at the full-employment output level.

Because the short-run aggregate supply curve is the only version of aggregate supply that can handle simultaneous changes in the price level and real output, it serves well as the core aggregate supply curve for analyzing the business cycle and economic policy.

LO32.4 Explain the factors that shift AS.

The determinants of aggregate supply are input prices, productivity, and the legal-institutional environment. A change in any of these factors will change per-unit production costs at each output level and shift the aggregate supply curve.

LO32.5 Explain how AD and AS determine an economy's equilibrium price level and real GDP.

The intersection of the aggregate demand and aggregate supply curves determines an economy's equilibrium price level and real GDP. At the intersection, the quantity of real GDP demanded equals the quantity of real GDP supplied.

LO32.6 Use the AD–AS model to explain demand-pull inflation, cost-push inflation, and recessions.

Increases in aggregate demand to the right of the full-employment output cause inflation and positive GDP gaps (actual GDP exceeds potential GDP). An upward-sloping aggregate supply curve weakens the multiplier effect of an increase in AD because a portion of the increase in aggregate demand dissipates as inflation.

Shifts of the aggregate demand curve to the left of the full-employment output cause recession, negative GDP gaps, and cyclical unemployment. The price level may not fall during recessions because of downwardly inflexible prices and wages. When the price level is fixed, changes in aggregate demand produce full-strength multiplier effects.

Leftward shifts of the aggregate supply curve reflect increases in per-unit production costs and cause cost-push inflation, with accompanying negative GDP gaps. Rightward shifts of the aggregate supply curve, caused by large improvements in productivity, help explain the simultaneous achievement of full employment, economic growth, and price stability that occurred in the United States between 1996 and 2000.

Terms and Concepts

aggregate demand–aggregate supply (AD–AS) model

aggregate demand

real-balances effect

interest-rate effect

foreign purchases effect

determinants of aggregate demand

aggregate supply

immediate-short-run aggregate supply curve

short-run aggregate supply curve

long-run aggregate supply curve

determinants of aggregate supply

productivity

equilibrium price level

equilibrium real output

Discussion Questions

McGraw Hill **connect**

1. Why is the aggregate demand curve downsloping? Specify how your explanation differs from the explanation for the downsloping demand curve for a single product. What role does the multiplier play in shifts of the aggregate demand curve? **LO32.1**

2. Distinguish between "real-balances effect" and "wealth effect," as the terms are used in this chapter. How does each relate to the aggregate demand curve? **LO32.1**

3. What assumptions cause the immediate-short-run aggregate supply curve to be horizontal? Why is the long-run aggregate supply

curve vertical? Explain the shape of the short-run aggregate supply curve. Why is the short-run aggregate supply curve relatively flat to the left of the full-employment output and relatively steep to the right? **LO32.3**

4. Explain how an upsloping aggregate supply curve weakens the realized multiplier effect from an initial change in investment spending. **LO32.6**

5. Why does a reduction in aggregate demand in the actual economy reduce real output, rather than the price level? Why might a full-strength multiplier apply to a decrease in aggregate demand? **LO32.6**

6. Explain: "Unemployment can be caused by a decrease of aggregate demand or a decrease of aggregate supply." In each case, specify the price-level outcomes. **LO32.6**

7. Use shifts of the AD and AS curves to explain (*a*) the U.S. experience of strong economic growth, full employment, and price

stability in the late 1990s and early 2000s and (*b*) how a strong negative wealth effect from, say, a precipitous drop in house prices could cause a recession even though productivity is surging. **LO32.6**

8. In early 2020, the anti-pandemic lockdowns caused both consumption spending and the amount of labor employed by firms to sharply decline. Use AD–AS analysis to describe the two impacts on real GDP. **LO32.6**

9. **LAST WORD** What was so unusual about the bout of inflation that the United States experienced in 2021? Since real GDP kept on growing during 2021, what do we know about the relative sizes of the rightward shift of AD as compared with the leftward shift of AS? If AS had shifted further left, would it have been possible to offset that leftward shift of AS with a rightward shift in AD without further increasing the price level?

Review Questions

Mc Graw Hill **connect**

1. Which of the following help to explain why the aggregate demand curve slopes downward? **LO32.1**
   a. When the domestic price level rises, our goods and services become more expensive to people living abroad.
   b. When government spending rises, the price level falls.
   c. There is an inverse relationship between consumer expectations and personal taxes.
   d. When the price level rises, the real value of financial assets (like stocks, bonds, and savings account balances) declines.

2. Which of the following will shift the aggregate demand curve to the left? **LO32.2**
   a. The government reduces personal income taxes.
   b. Interest rates rise.
   c. The government raises corporate profit taxes.
   d. There is an economic boom overseas that raises the incomes of foreign households.

3. Label each of the following descriptions as being either an immediate-short-run aggregate supply curve, a short-run aggregate supply curve, or a long-run aggregate supply curve. **LO32.3**
   a. A vertical line.
   b. The price level is fixed.
   c. Output prices are flexible, but input prices are fixed.
   d. A horizontal line.
   e. An upsloping curve.
   f. Output is fixed.

4. Which of the following will shift the aggregate supply curve to the right? **LO32.4**
   a. A new networking technology increases productivity all over the economy.
   b. The price of oil rises substantially.
   c. Business taxes fall.
   d. The government passes a law doubling all manufacturing wages.

5. At the current price level, producers supply $375 billion of final goods and services while consumers purchase $355 billion of final goods and services. The price level is: **LO32.5**
   a. above equilibrium.
   b. at equilibrium.
   c. below equilibrium.
   d. more information is needed.

6. What effects would each of the following have on aggregate demand or aggregate supply, other things equal? In each case, use a diagram to show the expected effects on the equilibrium price level and the level of real output, assuming that the price level is flexible both upward and downward. **LO32.5**
   a. A widespread fear by consumers of an impending economic depression.
   b. A new national tax on producers based on the value added between the costs of the inputs and the revenue received from their output.
   c. A reduction in interest rates.
   d. A major increase in spending for health care by the federal government.
   e. The general expectation of coming rapid inflation.
   f. The complete disintegration of OPEC, causing oil prices to fall by one-half.
   g. A 10 percent across-the-board reduction in personal income tax rates.
   h. A sizable increase in labor productivity (with no change in nominal wages).
   i. A 12 percent increase in nominal wages (with no change in productivity).
   j. An increase in exports that exceeds an increase in imports (not due to tariffs).

7. True or False: Decreases in AD normally lead to decreases in both output and the price level. **LO32.6**

8. Assume that (*a*) the price level is flexible upward but not downward and (*b*) the economy is currently operating at its full-employment output. Other things equal, how will each of the following affect the equilibrium price level and equilibrium level of real output in the short run? **LO32.6**
   a. An increase in aggregate demand.
   b. A decrease in aggregate supply, with no change in aggregate demand.
   c. Equal increases in aggregate demand and aggregate supply.
   d. A decrease in aggregate demand.
   e. An increase in aggregate demand that exceeds an increase in aggregate supply.

9. True or False: If the price of oil suddenly increases by a large amount, AS will shift left, but the price level will not rise thanks to price inflexibility. **LO32.6**

Problems

1. Suppose that consumer spending initially rises by $5 billion for every 1 percent rise in household wealth and that investment spending initially rises by $20 billion for every 1 percentage point fall in the real interest rate. Also assume that the economy's multiplier is 4. If household wealth falls by 5 percent because of declining house values, and the real interest rate falls by 2 percentage points, in what direction and by how much will the aggregate demand curve initially shift at each price level? In what direction and by how much will it eventually shift? **LO32.2**

2. Answer the following questions on the basis of the following three sets of data for the country of North Vaudeville: **LO32.4**

(A)		(B)		(C)	
Price Level	Real GDP	Price Level	Real GDP	Price Level	Real GDP
110	275	100	200	110	225
100	250	100	225	100	225
95	225	100	250	95	225
90	200	100	275	90	225

a. Which set of data illustrates aggregate supply in the immediate short run in North Vaudeville? The short run? The long run?

b. Assuming no change in hours of work, if real output per hour of work increases by 10 percent, what will be the new levels of real GDP in the right column of A? Do the new data reflect an increase in aggregate supply or do they indicate a decrease in aggregate supply?

3. Suppose that the table presented below shows an economy's relationship between real output and the inputs needed to produce that output: **LO32.4**

Input Quantity	Real GDP
150.0	$400
112.5	300
75.0	200

a. What is productivity in this economy?

b. What is the per-unit cost of production if the price of each input unit is $2?

c. Assume that the input price increases from $2 to $3 with no accompanying change in productivity. What is the new per-unit cost of production? In what direction would the $1 increase in input price push the economy's aggregate

supply curve? What effect would this shift of aggregate supply have on the price level and the level of real output?

d. Suppose that the increase in input price does not occur but, instead, that productivity increases by 100 percent. What would be the new per-unit cost of production? What effect would this change in per-unit production cost have on the economy's aggregate supply curve? What effect would this shift of aggregate supply have on the price level and the level of real output?

4. Suppose that the aggregate demand and aggregate supply schedules for a hypothetical economy are as shown in the following table. **LO32.5**

Amount of Real GDP Demanded, Billions	Price Level (Price Index)	Amount of Real GDP Supplied, Billions
$100	300	$450
200	250	400
300	200	300
400	150	200
500	100	100

a. Use the data above to graph the aggregate demand and aggregate supply curves. What are the equilibrium price level and the equilibrium level of real output in this hypothetical economy? Is the equilibrium real output also necessarily the full-employment real output?

b. If the price level in this economy is 150, will quantity demanded equal, exceed, or fall short of quantity supplied? By what amount? If the price level is 250, will quantity demanded equal, exceed, or fall short of quantity supplied? By what amount?

c. Suppose that buyers desire to purchase $200 billion of extra real output at each price level. Sketch in the new aggregate demand curve as AD_1. What are the new equilibrium price level and level of real output?

5. Refer to the data in the table that accompanies problem 2. Suppose that the present equilibrium price level and level of real GDP are 100 and $225, and that data set B represents the relevant aggregate supply schedule for the economy. **LO32.6**

a. What must be the current amount of real output demanded at the 100 price level?

b. If the amount of output demanded declined by $25 at the 100 price level shown in B, what would be the new equilibrium real GDP? In business cycle terminology, what would economists call this change in real GDP?

The Relationship of the AD Curve to the Aggregate Expenditures Model

LO32.7 Relate the aggregate demand curve to the aggregate expenditures model.

The aggregate demand curve of this chapter and the aggregate expenditures model of Chapter 31 are intricately related.

Deriving the AD Curve from the Aggregate Expenditures Model

We can directly connect the downward sloping AD curve to the aggregate expenditures model by relating various possible price levels to corresponding equilibrium GDPs. In Figure 1 we have stacked the aggregate expenditures model (Figure 1a) and the aggregate demand curve (Figure 1b) vertically. We can do so because the horizontal axes of both models measure real GDP. Now let's derive the AD curve in three distinct steps. (Throughout this discussion, keep in mind that price level P_1 is lower than price level P_2, which is lower than price level P_3.)

- First suppose that the economy's price level is P_1 and its aggregate expenditures schedule is AE_1, the top schedule in Figure 1a. The equilibrium GDP is then Q_1 at point 1. So, in Figure 1b, we can plot the equilibrium real output Q_2 and the corresponding price level P_1. Doing so gives us point 1′ in Figure 1b.
- Now assume the price level rises from P_1 to P_2. Other things equal, this higher price level will (1) decrease the value of real balances (wealth), decreasing consumption expenditures; (2) increase the interest rate, reducing investment and interest-sensitive consumption expenditures; and (3) increase imports and decrease exports, reducing net export expenditures. The aggregate expenditures schedule falls from AE_1 to AE_2 in Figure 1a, giving us equilibrium Q_2 at point 2. In Figure 1b we plot this new price-level–real-output combination, P_2 and Q_2, as point 2′.
- Finally, suppose the price level rises from P_2 to P_3. The value of real balances falls, the interest rate rises, exports fall, and imports rise. Consequently, the consumption, investment, and net export schedules fall, shifting the aggregate expenditures schedule downward from AE_2 to AE_3, which gives us equilibrium Q_3 at point 3. In Figure 1b, we plot point 3′, where the price level is P_3 and real output is Q_3.

FIGURE 1 Deriving the aggregate demand curve from the aggregate expenditures model.

(a) Rising price levels from P_1 to P_2 to P_3 shift the aggregate expenditures curve downward from AE_1 to AE_2 to AE_3 and reduce real GDP from Q_1 to Q_2 to Q_3. (b) The aggregate demand curve AD is derived by plotting the successively lower real GDPs from the upper graph against the P_1, P_2, and P_3 price levels.

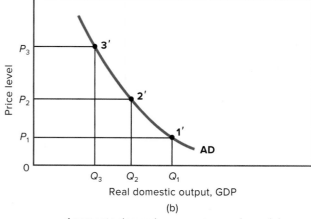

In summary, increases in the economy's price level successively shift its aggregate expenditures schedule downward and reduce real GDP. The resulting price-level–real-GDP combinations yield various points such as 1′, 2′, and 3′ in Figure 1b.

Together, such points locate the downward sloping aggregate demand curve for the economy.

Aggregate Demand Shifts and the Aggregate Expenditures Model

The determinants of aggregate demand listed in Figure 32.2 are the components of the aggregate expenditures model discussed in Chapter 31. When one of the determinants of aggregate demand changes, the aggregate expenditures schedule shifts upward or downward. We can easily link such shifts of the aggregate expenditures schedule to shifts of the AD curve.

Let's suppose that the price level is constant. In Figure 2 we begin with the aggregate expenditures schedule at AE_1 in the top diagram, yielding equilibrium real output Q_1. Assume now that investment increases in response to more optimistic business expectations, so the aggregate expenditures schedule rises from AE_1 to AE_2. (The notation "at P_1" reminds us that the price level is assumed constant.) The result will be a multiplied increase in equilibrium real output from Q_1 to Q_2.

In Figure 2b the increase in investment spending is reflected in the horizontal distance between AD_1 and the broken curve to its right. The immediate effect of the increase in investment is an increase in aggregate demand by the exact amount of the new spending. But then the multiplier process magnifies the initial increase in investment into successive rounds of consumption spending and an ultimate multiplied increase in aggregate demand from AD_1 to AD_2. Equilibrium real output rises from Q_1 to Q_2, the same multiplied increase in real GDP as that in the top graph. The initial increase in investment in the top graph has shifted the AD curve in the lower graph by a horizontal distance equal to the change in investment times the multiplier. This particular change in real GDP is still associated with the constant price level P_1. To generalize,

Shift of AD curve = initial change in spending × multiplier

FIGURE 2 Shifts of the aggregate expenditures schedule and of the aggregate demand curve.

(a) A change in some determinant of consumption, investment, or net exports (other than the price level) shifts the aggregate expenditures schedule upward from AE_1 to AE_2. The multiplier increases real output from Q_1 to Q_2. (b) The counterpart of this change is an initial rightward shift of the aggregate demand curve by the amount of initial new spending (from AD_1 to the broken curve). This leads to a multiplied rightward shift of the curve to AD_2, which is just sufficient to show the same increase of real output as that in the aggregate expenditures model.

(a)
Aggregate expenditures model

(b)
Aggregate demand–aggregate supply model

Appendix Summary

LO32.7 Relate the aggregate demand curve to the aggregate expenditures model.
A change in the price level alters the location of the aggregate expenditures schedule through the real-balances, interest-rate, and foreign purchases effects. We derive the AD curve from the aggregate expenditures model by allowing the price level to change and observing the effect on the aggregate expenditures schedule and thus on equilibrium GDP.

With the price level held constant, increases in consumption, investment, government, and net export expenditures shift the aggregate expenditures schedule upward and the AD curve to the right. Decreases in these spending components produce the opposite effects.

Appendix Discussion Questions

1. Explain carefully: "A change in the price level shifts the aggregate expenditures curve but not the aggregate demand curve." **LO32.7**
2. Suppose that the price level is constant and that investment decreases sharply. How would you show this decrease in the aggregate expenditures model? What is the outcome for real GDP? How would you show this fall in investment in the AD-AS model, assuming the economy is operating in what is, in effect, a horizontal section of the AS curve? **LO32.7**

Appendix Review Questions

1. True or False: A higher price level increases aggregate expenditures. **LO32.7**

2. If the government decreases expenditures, the *AE* curve will shift _____ and the AD curve will shift _____. **LO32.7**
   a. down; left
   b. down; right
   c. up; left
   d. up; right

Appendix Problems

1. Refer to Figures 1a and 1b in this Appendix. Assume that Q_1 is 300, Q_2 is 200, Q_3 is 100, P_3 is 120, P_2 is 100, and P_1 is 80. If the price level increases from P_1 to P_3 in Figure 1b, in what direction and by how much will real GDP change? If the slopes of the *AE* lines in Figure 1a are 0.8 and equal to the MPC, in what direction will the aggregate expenditures schedule in Figure 1a need to shift to produce the previously determined change in real GDP? What is the size of the multiplier in this example? **LO32.7**

2. Refer to Figure 2 in this Appendix and assume that Q_1 is \$400 and Q_2 is \$500, the price level is stuck at P_1, and the slopes of the *AE* lines in Figure 2a are 0.75 and equal to the MPC. In what direction and by how much does the aggregate expenditures schedule in Figure 2a need to shift to move the aggregate demand curve in Figure 2b from AD_1 to AD_2? What is the multiplier in this example? Given the multiplier, what must be the distance between AD_1 and the broken line to its right at P_1? **LO32.7**

Pavel Bobrovskiy/Shutterstock

CHAPTER

33

Fiscal Policy, Deficits, and Debt

In Chapter 31, we saw that an excessive increase in aggregate demand can cause demand-pull inflation and that a significant decline in aggregate demand can cause recession and cyclical unemployment. For these reasons, the federal government sometimes tries to "stimulate the economy" or "rein in inflation." Such countercyclical **fiscal policy** consists of deliberate changes in government spending and tax collections designed to achieve full employment, control inflation, and encourage economic growth. (The adjective "fiscal" simply means "financial.")

We begin this chapter by examining the logic behind fiscal policy, its current status, and its limitations. Then we examine a closely related topic: the U.S. public debt.

> **fiscal policy** Changes in government spending and tax collections designed to achieve full employment, price stability, and economic growth; also called *discretionary fiscal policy*.

Fiscal Policy and the AD–AS Model

>> **LO33.1** Identify the purposes, tools, and limitations of fiscal policy.

Fiscal policy consists of changes in government spending and tax collections designed to achieve full employment, price stability, and economic growth. Fiscal policy can be either discretionary or nondiscretionary:

- **Discretionary fiscal policy** refers to changes in government spending and taxes that are *at the option of* the federal government. They do not occur automatically. The current congress must pass a discretionary spending or tax bill and the president must sign it into law.

- **Nondiscretionary fiscal policy** refers to changes in spending and taxes that occur automatically, or passively, without the need for current congressional action. They occur as the result of spending and tax provisions put into law by earlier congresses.

> **Council of Economic Advisers (CEA)** A group of three persons that advises and assists the president of the United States on economic matters (including the preparation of the annual *Economic Report of the President*).

Discretionary fiscal policy is often initiated on the advice of the president's **Council of Economic Advisers (CEA),** a group of three economists who provide expertise and assistance on economic matters. Various congressional committees have final say, however, on the contents of any discretionary spending or tax bill that is sent to the president.

..ıll KEY GRAPH

FIGURE 33.1 Expansionary fiscal policy with the multiplier effect.

If the price level is downwardly inflexible at P_1, a decrease of aggregate demand from AD_1 to AD_2 will reduce real GDP from $510 billion (full employment) to $490 billion. Expansionary fiscal policy (increases in government spending or decreases in taxes) can be used to push this economy out of recession. A $5 billion increase in government spending or a $6.67 billion decrease in personal taxes (producing a $5 billion initial increase in consumption) will shift aggregate demand rightward from AD_2 to the downward sloping dashed curve. Assuming an MPC of 0.75, this economy would have a multiplier of 4. So the initial $5 billion rightward shift provided by the government would be magnified into a total rightward shift of $20 billion (= 4 times $5 billion), returning aggregate demand back to AD_1 and real GDP back to $510 billion.

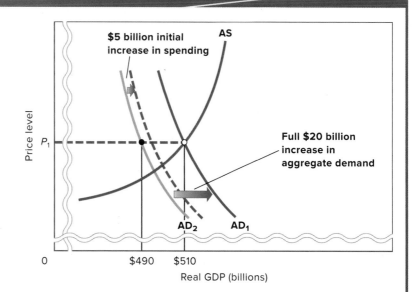

QUICK QUIZ FOR FIGURE 33.1

1. Suppose the government finds out too late that the MPC in the economy is 0.90 rather than 0.75, so that the multiplier is 10 instead of 4. The initial $5 billion stimulus would cause:
   a. the price level to rise higher than P_1.
   b. real GDP to fall short of $510 billion.
   c. the price level to fall below P_1.
   d. real GDP to fall short of $490 billion.

2. If the marginal propensity to save in the economy were 1, then the initial $5 government stimulus would result in a real GDP of:
   a. $460 billion.
   b. $485 billion.
   c. $490 billion.
   d. $495 billion.

3. Under the assumption that MPC = 0.75, an initial government stimulus of $7 billion (rather than $5 billion) would be:
   a. deflationary.
   b. recessionary.
   c. inflationary.
   d. discretionary.

4. Suppose that the government is expecting the aggregate supply curve AS to shift upward (left). If MPC = 0.75 and the government wishes to restore full employment output, then the government should provide an initial amount of stimulus that is:
   a. less than $5 billion.
   b. equal to $5 billion.
   c. greater than $5 billion.
   d. it depends on MPS.

Answers: 1. a; 2. d; 3. c; 4. c

Expansionary Fiscal Policy

When a recession occurs, the government may initiate an **expansionary fiscal policy** that is designed to increase aggregate demand and therefore raise real GDP. Consider **Figure 33.1 (Key Graph)**, where lower profit expectations cause a sharp decline in investment spending that shifts the economy's aggregate demand curve to the left from AD_1 to AD_2. (Disregard the arrows and dashed downward sloping line for now.)

Suppose the economy's potential or full-employment output is $510 billion in Figure 33.1. If the price level is inflexible downward at P_1, the broken horizontal line becomes relevant to the analysis. The aggregate demand curve moves leftward and reduces real GDP from $510 billion to $490 billion. The result is a GDP gap of negative $20 billion (= $490 billion − $510 billion). Unemployment increases because fewer workers are needed to produce the reduced level of output. In short, the economy is suffering both recession and cyclical unemployment.

What fiscal policy should the federal government use to stimulate the economy? It has three main options: (1) increase government spending, (2) reduce taxes, or (3) use some combination of the two. If the federal budget is balanced at the outset, expansionary fiscal policy will create a government **budget deficit**—government spending in excess of tax revenues.

expansionary fiscal policy An increase in *government purchases* of *goods* and *services*, a decrease in *net taxes*, or some combination of the two for the purpose of increasing *aggregate demand* and expanding real output.

budget deficit The amount by which expenditures exceed revenues in any year.

Increased Government Spending As an overall strategy, the government will want to shift the aggregate demand curve back where it came from, thereby returning the economy to producing $510 billion of real GDP at the intersection of AD_1 and AS. One way for the government to accomplish that goal is by initiating $5 billion of new spending on highways, education, and health care. We represent this new $5 billion of government spending as the horizontal distance between AD_2 and the dashed downward sloping line immediately to its right. At each price level, the amount of real output that is demanded is now $5 billion greater than that demanded before government spending increased. So aggregate demand will shift rightward, from AD_2 to the dashed downward sloping line immediately to its right.

The initial increase in aggregate demand is not the end of the story. Through the multiplier effect, the aggregate demand curve will shift farther, all the way to AD_1, a distance that exceeds the amount represented by the originating $5 billion increase in government purchases. This greater shift occurs because the multiplier process magnifies the initial change in spending into successive rounds of new consumption spending. If the economy's MPC is 0.75, then the simple multiplier is 4. Thus the aggregate demand curve shifts rightward by four times the $5 billion distance between AD_2 and the dashed downward sloping line. Because this *particular* increase in aggregate demand occurs along the horizontal dashed-line segment, real output rises by the full extent of the multiplier. Real output rises to $510 billion, up $20 billion from its recessionary level of $490 billion. Unemployment falls as firms increase their employment to the full-employment level that existed before the recession. Mission accomplished.

Tax Reductions Alternatively, the government could reduce taxes to shift the aggregate demand curve rightward from AD_2 to AD_1. Suppose the government cuts personal income taxes by $6.67 billion, which increases disposable income by the same amount. Consumption will rise by $5 billion (= MPC of 0.75 × $6.67 billion), and saving will go up by $1.67 billion (= MPC of 0.25 × $6.67 billion). In this case, the horizontal distance between AD_2 and the dashed downward sloping line in Figure 33.1 represents only the $5 billion initial increase in consumption spending. Again, we call it "initial" consumption spending because the multiplier process yields successive rounds of increased consumption spending. The aggregate demand curve eventually shifts rightward by four times the $5 billion initial increase in consumption produced by the tax cut. Real GDP rises by $20 billion, from $490 billion to $510 billion, implying a multiplier of 4. Employment increases accordingly.

You may have noted that a tax cut must be somewhat larger than an increase in government spending to achieve the same amount of rightward shift in the aggregate demand curve. Why? Part of a tax reduction increases saving, rather than consumption. To increase initial consumption by a specific amount, the government must reduce taxes by more than that amount. When the MPC is 0.75, taxes must fall by $6.67 billion to increase consumption by $5 billion because $1.67 billion of the $6.67 billion tax reduction is saved (not consumed). The smaller the MPC, the greater the tax cut needed to accomplish a specific initial increase in consumption.

Combined Government Spending Increases and Tax Reductions The government may combine spending increases and tax cuts to produce the desired initial increase in spending and the eventual increase in aggregate demand and real GDP. For example, the government might increase its spending by $1.25 billion while reducing taxes by $5 billion. As an exercise, you should explain why this combination will produce the targeted $5 billion initial increase in new spending.

Contractionary Fiscal Policy

contractionary fiscal policy A decrease in *government purchases* of *goods* and *services*, an increase in *net taxes*, or some combination of the two, for the purpose of decreasing *aggregate demand* and thus controlling *inflation*.

When demand-pull inflation occurs, a restrictive or **contractionary fiscal policy** may help control it. Look at Figure 33.2, where the full-employment level of real GDP is $510 billion. The economy starts at equilibrium at point *a*, where the initial aggregate demand curve AD_3 intersects aggregate supply curve AS. Suppose that after going through the multiplier process, a $5 billion initial increase in investment and net export spending shifts the aggregate demand curve to the right by $20 billion, from AD_3 to AD_4. (Ignore the downward sloping dashed line for now.) Given the upward sloping AS curve, the equilibrium GDP does not rise by the full $20 billion, however. It rises by only $12 billion, to $522 billion, thereby creating an inflationary GDP gap of $12 billion (= $522 billion − $510 billion). The upward slope of the AS curve means that some of the rightward movement of the AD curve ends up causing demand-pull inflation rather than increased output. The price level rises from P_1 to P_2, and the equilibrium moves to point *b*.

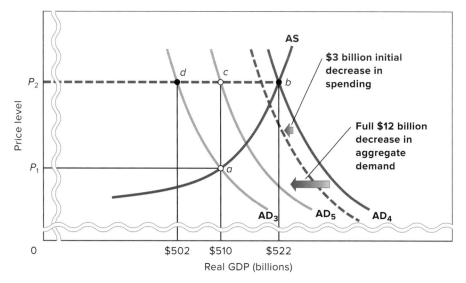

FIGURE 33.2
Contractionary fiscal policy.

Contractionary fiscal policy uses decreases in government spending, increases in taxes, or both, to reduce demand-pull inflation. Here, an increase in aggregate demand from AD_3 to AD_4 has driven the economy to point b and ratcheted the price level up to P_2, where it becomes inflexible downward. If the economy's MPC is 0.75 and the multiplier therefore is 4, the government can either reduce its spending by $3 billion or increase its taxes by $4 billion (which will decrease consumption by $3 billion) to eliminate the inflationary GDP gap of $12 billion (= $522 billion − $510 billion). Aggregate demand will shift leftward, first from AD_4 to the dashed downsloping curve to its left, and then to AD_5. With the price level remaining at P_2, the economy will move from point b to point c and the inflationary GDP gap will disappear.

Without a government response, the inflationary GDP gap will cause further inflation (as input prices rise in the long run to meet the increase in output prices). If the government looks to fiscal policy to eliminate the inflationary GDP gap, it can (1) decrease government spending, (2) raise taxes, or (3) use some combination of those two policies. When the economy faces demand-pull inflation, fiscal policy should move toward a government **budget surplus**—tax revenues in excess of government spending.

Decreased Government Spending To control demand-pull inflation, the government can decrease aggregate demand by reducing government spending. Look at Figure 33.2 and consider what would happen if the government attempted to design a spending-reduction policy to eliminate the inflationary GDP gap. Because the $12 billion gap was caused by the $20 billion rightward movement of the aggregate demand curve from AD_3 to AD_4, the government might naively think that it could solve the problem by causing a $20 billion leftward shift that would put the aggregate demand curve back in its original position. It could reduce government spending by $5 billion and then allow the multiplier effect to expand that initial decrease into a $20 billion decline in aggregate demand, thus shifting the aggregate demand curve leftward by $20 billion, putting it back at AD_3.

This policy would work fine if prices were flexible. The economy's equilibrium would move back from point b to point a, with equilibrium GDP returning to the full-employment level of $510 billion and the price level falling from P_2 back to P_1.

But this scenario is not what will actually happen. Instead, the price level is stuck at P_2, so that the dashed horizontal line at price level P_2 becomes important to the analysis. The fixed price level means that when the government reduces spending by $5 billion to shift the aggregate demand curve back to AD_3, it will actually cause a recession! The new equilibrium will not be at point a. It will be at point d, where aggregate demand curve AD_3 crosses the dashed horizontal line. At point d, real GDP is only $502 billion, $8 billion below the full-employment level of $510 billion.

The problem is that, with the price level downwardly inflexible at P_2, the $20 billion leftward shift of the aggregate demand curve causes a full $20 billion decline in real GDP. None of the change in aggregate demand can be dissipated as a decline in the price level. As a result, equilibrium GDP declines by the full $20 billion, falling from $522 billion to $502 billion, which is $8 billion below potential output. By failing to account for the inflexible price level, the government has overdone the decrease in government spending, replacing a $12 billion inflationary GDP gap with an $8 billion recessionary GDP gap. This was clearly not its goal.

Here's how it can avoid this scenario. The government first determines the size of the inflationary GDP gap. It is $12 billion. Second, it knows that with the price level fixed, the multiplier will be in full effect. Thus, it knows that any decline in government spending will be multiplied by a factor of 4. It then reasons that government spending will have to decline by only $3 billion rather than $5 billion. Why? Because the $3 billion initial decline in government spending will be

budget surplus The amount by which the revenues of the federal government exceed its expenditures in any year.

multiplied by 4, creating a $12 billion decline in aggregate demand. Under the circumstances, a $3 billion decline exactly offsets the $12 billion GDP gap.

Please note that the inflationary GDP gap is the problem that government wants to eliminate in Figure 33.2. To succeed, it doesn't have to undo the full $20 billion increase in aggregate demand that caused the inflation in the first place. With the price level stuck at P_2, the government only has to move the AD curve leftward by $12 billion.

Graphically, the horizontal distance between AD_4 and the dashed downward sloping line to its left represents the $3 billion decrease in government spending. Once the multiplier process is complete, this spending cut shifts the aggregate demand curve leftward by $12 billion, from AD_4 to AD_5. With the price level fixed at P_2, the economy will come to equilibrium at point c. The economy operates at its potential output of $510 billion, and the inflationary GDP gap is eliminated. Furthermore, the government will not accidentally push the economy into a recession by decreasing government spending by too much.

Increased Taxes Just as government can use tax cuts to increase consumption spending, it can use tax *increases* to *reduce* consumption spending. If the economy in Figure 33.2 has an MPC of 0.75, the government must raise taxes by $4 billion to achieve its fiscal policy objective. The $4 billion tax increase reduces saving by $1 billion (= the MPS of 0.25 × $4 billion). This $1 billion reduction in saving is, by definition, a reduction in savings, not spending. But the $4 billion tax increase also reduces consumption spending by $3 billion (= the MPC of 0.75 × $4 billion), as shown by the distance between AD_4 and the dashed downward sloping line to its left in Figure 33.2. After the multiplier process is complete, this initial $3 billion decline in consumption spending causes aggregate demand to shift leftward at each price level by $12 billion (= multiplier of 4 × $3 billion). With the economy moving to point c, the inflationary GDP gap is closed and the inflation is halted.

Combining Government Spending Decreases with Tax Increases The government may choose to combine spending decreases and tax increases in order to reduce aggregate demand and control inflation. To check your understanding, determine why a $1.5 billion decline in government spending combined with a $2 billion increase in taxes will shift the aggregate demand curve from AD_4 to AD_5.

▶ Discretionary fiscal policy is the purposeful change of government expenditures and tax collections by government to promote full employment, price stability, and economic growth.

▶ Expansionary fiscal policy consists of increases in government spending, reductions in taxes, or both, and is designed to expand real GDP by increasing aggregate demand.

▶ Contractionary fiscal policy entails decreases in government spending, increases in taxes, or both, and is designed to reduce aggregate demand and slow or halt demand-pull inflation.

▶ To be implemented correctly, contractionary fiscal policy must properly account for the ratchet effect and the fact that the price level will not fall as the government shifts the aggregate demand curve leftward.

Built-In Stability

Tax Collections and the Business Cycle

>> **LO33.2** Explain how built-in stabilizers moderate business cycles.

Under normal circumstances, government tax revenues change automatically over the course of the business cycle in ways that stabilize the economy. This automatic response, or built-in stability, constitutes what is commonly referred to as nondiscretionary (or "passive" or "automatic") budgetary policy. We did not include this built-in stability in the discussion about fiscal policy that we had in the last section because we implicitly assumed that the same amount of tax revenue was being collected at each level of GDP. But the actual U.S. tax system is such that *net tax revenues* vary directly with GDP. (Net taxes are tax revenues less transfers and subsidies. From here on, we will use "taxes" to mean "net taxes.")

Virtually any tax will yield more tax revenue as GDP rises. In particular, personal income taxes have progressive rates and thus generate more-than-proportionate increases in tax revenues as GDP expands. Furthermore, as GDP rises and more goods and services are purchased, revenues from corporate income taxes and from sales taxes and excise taxes also increase. And, similarly, revenues from payroll taxes rise as economic expansion creates more jobs. Conversely, when GDP declines, tax receipts from all these sources also decline.

Transfer payments (or "negative taxes") behave in the opposite way from tax revenues. Unemployment compensation payments and welfare payments decrease during economic expansion and increase during economic contraction.

FIGURE 33.3
Built-in stability.

Tax revenues, T, vary directly with GDP, while government spending, G, is assumed to be independent of GDP. As GDP falls in a recession, deficits occur automatically and help alleviate the recession. As GDP rises during expansion, surpluses occur automatically and help offset possible inflation.

Automatic or Built-In Stabilizers

A **built-in stabilizer** is anything that increases the government's budget deficit (or reduces its budget surplus) during a recession and increases its budget surplus (or reduces its budget deficit) during an expansion without requiring explicit action by policymakers. As Figure 33.3 reveals, this is precisely what the U.S. tax system does. Government expenditures G are fixed and assumed to be independent of the level of GDP. Congress decides on a particular level of spending, but it does not determine the magnitude of tax revenues. Instead, it establishes tax rates, and the tax revenues then vary directly with the level of GDP that the economy achieves. Line T represents that direct relationship between tax revenues and GDP.

Economic Importance The economic importance of the direct relationship between tax receipts and GDP becomes apparent when we consider that:

- Taxes reduce spending and aggregate demand.
- Reductions in spending are desirable when the economy is moving toward inflation, whereas increases in spending are desirable when the economy is slumping.

As shown in Figure 33.3, tax revenues automatically increase as GDP rises during prosperity, and since taxes reduce household and business spending, they restrain the economic expansion. That is, as the economy moves toward a higher GDP, tax revenues automatically rise and move the budget from deficit toward surplus. In Figure 33.3, observe that the high and perhaps inflationary income level GDP$_3$ automatically generates a contractionary budget surplus.

Conversely, as GDP falls during recession, tax revenues automatically decline, increasing spending by households and businesses and thus cushioning the economic contraction. With a falling GDP, tax receipts decline and move the government's budget from surplus toward deficit. In Figure 33.3, the low level of income GDP$_1$ will automatically yield an expansionary budget deficit.

Tax Progressivity Figure 33.3 reveals that the size of the automatic budget deficits or surpluses—and therefore built-in stability—depends on the responsiveness of tax revenues to changes in GDP. If tax revenues change sharply as GDP changes, the slope of line T in the figure will be steep and the vertical distances between T and G (the deficits or surpluses) will be large. If tax revenues change very little when GDP changes, the slope will be gentle and built-in stability will be low.

The steepness of T in Figure 33.3 depends on the tax system itself:

- In a **progressive tax** system, the average tax rate (= tax revenue/GDP) rises with GDP.
- In a **proportional tax** system, the average tax rate remains constant as GDP rises.
- In a **regressive tax** system, the average tax rate falls as GDP rises.

The progressive tax system has the steepest tax line T of the three. However, tax revenues will rise with GDP under both the progressive and the proportional tax systems, and they may rise, fall, or stay the same under a regressive tax system. The main point is this: The more progressive the tax system, the greater the economy's built-in stability.

built-in stabilizer A mechanism that increases government's budget deficit (or reduces its surplus) during a recession and increases government's budget surplus (or reduces its deficit) during an expansion without any action by policymakers. The tax system is one such mechanism.

progressive tax At the individual level, a *tax* whose *average tax rate* increases as the taxpayer's *income* increases. At the national level, a *tax* for which the *average tax rate* (= tax revenue/*GDP*) rises with *GDP*.

proportional tax At the individual level, a *tax* whose *average tax rate* remains constant as the taxpayer's *income* increases or decreases. At the national level, a *tax* for which the *average tax rate* (= tax revenue/*GDP*) remains constant as *GDP* rises or falls.

regressive tax At the individual level, a *tax* whose *average tax rate* decreases as the taxpayer's *income* increases. At the national level, a *tax* for which the *average tax rate* (= tax revenue/*GDP*) falls as *GDP* rises.

The built-in stability provided by the U.S. tax system has reduced the severity of business fluctuations, perhaps by as much as 8 to 10 percent of the change in GDP that otherwise would have occurred.[1] In recession-year 2009, for example, revenues from the individual income tax fell by a staggering 22 percent. This decline helped keep household spending and real GDP from falling even more than they did. But built-in stabilizers can only dampen, not counteract, swings in real GDP. Discretionary fiscal policy (changes in tax rates and expenditures) or monetary policy (central bank–caused changes in interest rates) therefore may be needed to try to counter a recession or an inflation of any appreciable magnitude.

Evaluating How Expansionary or Contractionary Fiscal Policy Is Determined

>> **LO33.3** Describe how the cyclically adjusted budget reveals the status of U.S. fiscal policy.

How can we determine whether a government's discretionary fiscal policy is expansionary, neutral, or contractionary? We cannot simply examine the actual budget deficits or surpluses that take place under the current policy because they will necessarily include the automatic changes in tax revenues that accompany every change in GDP. In addition, the expansionary or contractionary strength of any change in discretionary fiscal policy depends not on its absolute size but on how large it is relative to the size of the economy. So, in evaluating the status of fiscal policy, we must adjust deficits and surpluses to eliminate automatic changes in tax revenues and also compare the sizes of the adjusted budget deficits and surpluses to the level of potential GDP.

Cyclically Adjusted Budget

cyclically adjusted budget The estimated annual budget deficit or surplus that would occur under existing tax rates and government spending levels if the economy were to operate at its *full-employment* level of GDP for a year; the *full-employment* budget deficit or surplus.

Economists use the **cyclically adjusted budget** (also called the *full-employment budget*) to adjust actual federal budget deficits and surpluses to account for the changes in tax revenues that happen automatically whenever GDP changes. The cyclically adjusted budget measures what the federal budget deficit or surplus would have been under existing tax rates and government spending levels if the economy had achieved its full-employment level of GDP (its potential output). The idea essentially is to compare *actual* government expenditures with the tax revenues *that would have occurred* if the economy had achieved full-employment GDP. That procedure removes budget deficits or surpluses that arise simply because of cyclical changes in GDP and thus tell us nothing about whether the government's current discretionary fiscal policy is fundamentally expansionary, contractionary, or neutral.

Consider Figure 33.4a, where line G represents government expenditures and line T represents tax revenues. In full-employment year 1, government expenditures of $500 billion equal tax revenues of $500 billion, as indicated by the intersection of lines G and T at point a. The cyclically adjusted budget deficit in year 1 is zero—government expenditures equal the tax revenues forthcoming at the full-employment output GDP_1. Obviously, the cyclically adjusted deficit *as a percentage of potential GDP* is also zero. The government's fiscal policy is neutral.

Now suppose that a recession occurs and GDP falls from GDP_1 to GDP_2, as shown in Figure 33.4a. Let's also assume that the government takes no discretionary action, so lines G and T remain as shown in the figure. Tax revenues automatically fall to $450 billion (point c) at GDP_2, while government spending remains unaltered at $500 billion (point b). A $50 billion budget deficit (represented by distance bc) arises. But this **cyclical deficit** is simply a by-product of the economy's slide into recession, not the result of discretionary fiscal actions by the government. We would be wrong to conclude from this deficit that the government is engaging in an expansionary fiscal policy. The government's fiscal policy has not changed. It is still neutral.

cyclical deficit Federal *budget deficit* that is caused by a recession and the consequent decline in tax revenues.

That fact is highlighted when we remove the cyclical part of the deficit and thus consider the cyclically adjusted budget deficit for year 2 in Figure 33.4a. The $500 billion of government expenditures in year 2 is shown by b on line G. And, as shown by a on line T, $500 billion of tax revenues would have occurred if the economy had achieved its full-employment GDP. Because both b and a represent $500 billion, the cyclically adjusted budget deficit in year 2 is zero, as is this deficit as a percentage of potential GDP. Since the cyclically adjusted deficits are zero in both years, we know that government did not change its discretionary fiscal policy, even though a recession occurred and an actual deficit of $50 billion resulted.

---

[1]Alan J. Auerbach and Daniel Feenberg, "The Significance of Federal Taxes as Automatic Stabilizers," *Journal of Economic Perspectives,* Summer 2000, p. 54.

FIGURE 33.4 Cyclically adjusted deficits.

(a) In the left-hand graph, the cyclically adjusted deficit is zero at the full-employment output GDP$_1$. But it is also zero at the recessionary output GDP$_2$ because the $500 billion of government expenditures at GDP$_2$ equals the $500 billion of tax revenues that would be forthcoming at the full-employment GDP$_1$. There has been no change in fiscal policy. (b) In the right-hand graph, discretionary fiscal policy, as reflected in the downward shift of the tax line from T_1 to T_2, has increased the cyclically adjusted budget deficit from zero in year 3 (before the tax cut) to $25 billion in year 4 (after the tax cut). This is found by comparing the $500 billion of government spending in year 4 with the $475 billion of taxes that would accrue at the full-employment GDP$_3$. Such a rise in the cyclically adjusted deficit (as a percentage of potential GDP) identifies an expansionary fiscal policy.

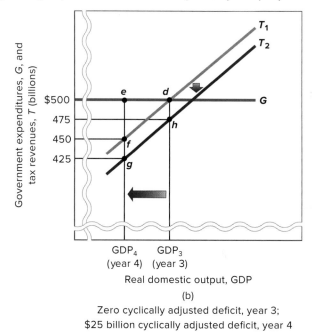

Next, consider Figure 33.4b. Suppose that real output declined from full-employment GDP$_3$ in year 3 to GDP$_4$ in year 4. Also suppose that government responded to the recession by reducing tax rates in year 4, as represented by the downward shift of the tax line from T_1 to T_2. What will have happened to the size of the cyclically adjusted deficit?

Government expenditures in year 4 are $500 billion, as shown by e. Compare that amount of spending with the $475 billion of tax revenues that would occur if the economy achieved potential output level GDP$_1$. That is, compare the amount of spending at position e on line G with the amount of tax revenue that would be collected at position h if the economy were still operating at full employment. The $25 billion by which spending at e exceeds full-employment tax collections at h is the cyclically adjusted budget deficit for year 4.

As a percentage of potential GDP, the cyclically adjusted budget deficit has increased from zero in year 3 (before the tax-rate cut) to some positive percent [= ($25 billion/GDP$_3$) × 100] in year 4. This increase in the relative size of the full-employment deficit between the two years reveals that the new fiscal policy is *expansionary*.

In contrast, if we observed a cyclically adjusted deficit (as a percentage of potential GDP) of zero in one year, followed by a cyclically adjusted budget surplus in the next, we could conclude that fiscal policy has changed from being neutral to being contractionary. Because the cyclically adjusted budget adjusts for automatic changes in tax revenues, the increase in the cyclically adjusted budget surplus reveals that government either decreased its spending (G) or increased tax rates such that tax revenues (T) increased. These changes in G and T are precisely the discretionary actions that we have identified as elements of a *contractionary* fiscal policy.

► Automatic changes in net taxes (taxes minus transfers) add a degree of built-in stability to the economy.

► Cyclical deficits arise from declines in net tax revenues that automatically occur as the economy recedes and incomes and profits fall.

► The cyclically adjusted budget eliminates cyclical effects on net tax revenues; it compares actual levels of government spending to the projected levels of net taxes that would occur if the economy were achieving its full-employment output.

QUICK REVIEW

33.2

Recent and Projected U.S. Fiscal Policy

>> **LO33.4** Summarize recent U.S. fiscal policy.

Table 33.1 lists actual federal budget deficits and surpluses (column 2) as a percentage of actual GDP, and cyclically adjusted deficits and surpluses (column 3) as a percentage of potential GDP. Note that:

- Cyclically adjusted deficits are generally smaller than actual deficits because the actual deficits include cyclical deficits, whereas the cyclically adjusted deficits eliminate them.
- Only cyclically adjusted surpluses and deficits as percentages of potential GDP (column 3) provide the information needed to determine whether fiscal policy is expansionary, contractionary, or neutral.

Fiscal Policy before the Great Recession

Take a look at the data in Table 33.1 for the years 2005 to 2007. The economy reached full employment over those three years after taking several years to gradually recover from the 2001 recession that was precipitated by the September 11th terrorist attacks. By 2007, full employment had been restored, although a −1.2 percent cyclically adjusted budget deficit still remained.

Fiscal Policy during and after the Great Recession

In the summer of 2007, a crisis in the market for mortgage loans flared up and then quickly exploded through every part of the financial system. Banks went bankrupt, major corporations like General Motors hurtled toward bankruptcy, and the stock market fell almost 50 percent. As the crisis worsened, general pessimism spread beyond the financial markets to the overall economy. Businesses and households curtailed spending, and in December 2007, the economy entered what was later termed "the Great Recession." To simulate the economy, Congress passed a $152 billion economic stimulus package in 2008 that focused primarily on sending checks of up to $600 each to taxpayers, veterans, and Social Security recipients.

TABLE 33.1 Federal Deficits (−) and Surpluses (+) as Percentages of GDP, 2005–2021

(1) Year	(2) Actual Deficit − or Surplus +	(3) Cyclically Adjusted Deficit − or Surplus +*
2005	−2.5	−2.3
2006	−1.8	−1.9
2007	−1.1	−1.2
2008	−3.1	−2.9
2009	−9.3	−7.5
2010	−8.3	−6.4
2011	−8.1	−6.3
2012	−6.5	−5.1
2013	−4.0	−2.6
2014	−2.7	−1.7
2015	−2.4	−1.8
2016	−3.1	−2.6
2017	−3.4	−3.1
2018	−3.8	−3.9
2019	−4.7	−4.9
2020	−14.9	−14.3
2021	−12.4	−12.5

*As a percentage of potential GDP.

Source: Budget and Economic Data, Congressional Budget Office.

As a percentage of GDP, the *actual* federal budget deficit jumped from −1.1 percent in 2007 to −3.1 percent in 2008. This increase resulted from an automatic drop-off of tax revenues during the recession, along with the fiscal stimulus checks paid out in 2008. As Table 33.1 shows, the *cyclically adjusted* budget deficit rose from −1.2 percent of potential GDP in 2007 to −2.9 percent in 2008. This increase in the cyclically adjusted budget deficit reveals that fiscal policy in 2008 was in fact expansionary.

The government had hoped that those receiving checks would spend the money and thus boost consumption and aggregate demand. But households either saved the money or used it to pay down credit card loans. Spending remained low and the economy continued to founder.

In response, Congress enacted the American Recovery and Reinvestment Act of 2009. This gigantic $787 billion program consisted of tax rebates, plus large spending increases on infrastructure, education, and health care. The idea was to flood the economy with additional spending to try to boost aggregate demand and get people back to work.

Unlike the lump-sum stimulus checks of 2008, the 2009 tax rebates showed up as small increases in workers' monthly payroll checks. By giving workers smaller amounts per month rather than a single large check, the government hoped that people would spend rather than save the bulk of their enhanced income.

The recession officially ended during the summer of 2009, but the economy did not rebound vigorously. Unemployment remained high and tax collections were low due to a stagnant economy. As a result, policymakers decided to continue with large amounts of fiscal stimulus. Annual actual (not cyclically adjusted) budget deficits amounted to −4.0, −2.7, and −2.4 percent of GDP, respectively, in 2013, 2014, and 2015. The cyclically adjusted budget deficits for those years were, respectively, −2.6, −1.7, and −1.8 percent of potential GDP. Fiscal stimulus was diminishing, but remained noticeably stimulatory.

The final years of the 2010s saw a continued use of fiscal stimulus, as evidenced by the fact that the cyclically adjusted deficit rose to almost −5.0 percent in 2019 after tax cuts were paired with increased spending. These were, however, full-employment years. As a result, quite a few economists questioned whether the government should have been applying so much stimulus at a time when the economy's resources were fully employed. In their reckoning, that much stimulus would only lead to inflation. Other economists countered that strong fiscal stimulus was still needed to counter lingering problems in the financial sector.

Inflation was 2.1 percent in 2017, 2.4 percent in 2018, and 1.8 percent in 2019. Both groups of economists claimed that those figures supported their own position. The group worried about inflation pointed out that inflation was higher than the Federal Reserve's 2-percent inflation target in two out of those three years. To them, this indicated that the economy was overheating and inflation would accelerate. The other group argued that with inflation under 3 percent in all three years, overheating was unlikely.

Fiscal Policy during and after the Pandemic Recession of 2020

After enjoying several years of full employment at the end of the 2010s, the U.S. economy was hammered by the COVID-19 pandemic in the spring of 2020. The policymakers who imposed anti-pandemic lockdowns at the start of the crisis were acutely aware of the enormous economic damage likely to result from shutting down most private businesses for weeks or months. Thus, only two weeks after lockdowns started, Congress passed the $2.2 trillion Coronavirus Aid, Relief, and Economic Security, or CARES, Act to provide massive stimulus to both individuals and businesses.

That stimulus package and several subsequent stimulus bills caused the *actual* federal budget deficit to balloon to −14.9 percent of potential GDP, thereby bestowing on 2020 the distinction of having had the highest federal deficit ever recorded in peacetime. (Only the deficits of World War I and World War II were larger, with, for instance, 1943 witnessing a deficit of −26.8 percent of GDP as the United States battled Italy, Japan, and Germany simultaneously.)

An interesting fact, though, was that the cyclically adjusted deficit for 2020 was, at −14.3 percent, only slightly smaller than the actual deficit of −14.9 percent. That implied, accurately, that despite all of the economic chaos caused by COVID-19, the economy was, thanks to all the stimulus, operating relatively close to full employment. By the first quarter of 2021, the GDP gap was only negative 2.8 percent after plummeting as low as negative 10.7 percent during March 2020, the first month of lockdowns.

On the one hand, that small GDP gap as 2021 began indicated a success for the massive amounts of fiscal stimulus that had been applied during 2020. On the other hand, Congress had already approved various stimulus programs that would extend well into 2021. Speculation quickly ensued as to whether that massive amount of stimulus was going to turn out to be excessive. When inflation began to rise rapidly in the spring of 2021, that debate only intensified, with one side saying that it was too early to "take the foot off the gas" and the other arguing that the U.S. economy was starting to "speed out of control."

By March 2022, the inflation rate was running at 8.5 percent per year while the economy was operating near full employment. Thus, attention began to focus almost entirely on the high and rising inflation rate, since it was clear that there was no longer any need for additional stimulus. In addition, it was argued that the large deficit spending that was continuing to take place was very likely at least partly responsible for the high rate of inflation, since expansionary budget deficits are excessively stimulatory for economies operating near potential output.

Problems, Criticisms, and Complications of Implementing Fiscal Policy

>> **LO33.5** Discuss the problems that governments may encounter in enacting and applying fiscal policy.

Governments may encounter a number of significant problems in enacting and applying fiscal policy.

Problems of Timing

Several problems of timing may arise in connection with fiscal policy:

- *Recognition lag* is the time between the beginning of recession or inflation and the certain awareness that it is actually happening. This lag arises because the economy does not move smoothly through the business cycle. Even during good times, the economy has slow months interspersed with months of rapid growth and expansion. Recognizing a recession is difficult because several slow months will have to happen in succession before people can conclude with any confidence that the good times are over and a recession has begun.

  The same is true with inflation. Even periods of moderate inflation have months of high inflation—so that several high-inflation months must come in sequence before people can confidently conclude that inflation has moved to a higher level.

  Due to recognition lags, the economy is often 4 to 6 months into a recession or inflation before the situation is clearly discernible in the relevant statistics. As a result, the economic downslide or inflation may become more serious than it would have if the situation had been identified and acted on sooner.

- *Administrative lag* is the time between when policymakers recognize the need for a fiscal action and when that fiscal action is actually taken. The wheels of democratic government turn slowly. Following the terrorist attacks of September 11, 2001, the U.S. Congress was stalemated for five months before passing a compromise economic stimulus law in March 2002.

- *Operational lag* is the delay between the time fiscal action is ordered and the time that it actually begins to affect output, employment, or the price level. Tax changes have very short operational lags because they can be lowered instantly and have immediate impacts on household and business spending. By contrast, government spending on public works— new dams, interstate highways, and so on—requires long planning periods and even longer periods of construction. Such spending is of questionable use in offsetting short (for example, 6- to 12-month) periods of recession. Consequently, discretionary fiscal policy has increasingly relied on tax changes rather than on changes in spending so as to reduce or eliminate operational lag.

Please note that the fiscal policy response to the COVID-19 recession was highly unusual in that there was essentially zero recognition lag since policymakers understood that a recession would be an unavoidable side effect of imposing lockdowns. There was also almost zero administrative lag because congress finished debate over and approved the CARES Act less than two weeks after lockdowns were first imposed in mid-March of 2020. And the operational lag was also extremely short because relief money started flowing to individuals and businesses only about a month after the CARES Act was approved. But normal recessions are much harder to discern, and thus fiscal policy normally encounters substantial recognition, administrative, and operational lags.

Political Considerations

Fiscal policy is conducted in the political arena. That environment may not only slow the enactment of fiscal policy but also generate situations in which political considerations override economic considerations. Politicians are human—they want to get reelected. A strong economy at election time will certainly help them. So they may favor large tax cuts under the guise of expansionary fiscal policy even though that policy is economically inappropriate. Similarly, they may rationalize increased government spending on popular items such as farm subsidies, highways, education, and homeland security. At the extreme, elected officials and political parties might collectively "hijack" fiscal policy for political purposes, cause inappropriate changes in aggregate demand, and thereby cause (rather than avert) economic fluctuations. In short, elected officials may cause so-called **political business cycles**—swings in overall economic activity and real GDP resulting from election-motivated fiscal policy, rather than from a desire to offset volatility in the private sector. Political business cycles are difficult to document and prove, but there is little doubt that political considerations weigh heavily in the formulation of fiscal policy.

political business cycles Fluctuations in the economy caused by the alleged tendency of Congress to destabilize the economy by reducing taxes and increasing government expenditures before elections and to raise taxes and lower expenditures after elections.

Future Policy Reversals

Fiscal policy may fail to achieve its objectives if households expect future reversals of policy. Consider a tax cut, for example. If taxpayers believe the tax reduction is temporary, they may save a large portion of their tax cut, reasoning that rates will return to their previous level in the future. They save more now so that they will be able to draw on their extra savings in the future when taxes rise again. So a tax reduction thought to be temporary may not increase present consumption spending and aggregate demand by as much as our simple model (Figure 33.1) suggests.

The opposite may be true for a tax increase. If taxpayers think it is temporary, they may reduce their saving to pay the tax while maintaining their present consumption. They may reason they can restore their saving when the tax rate again falls. So the tax increase may not reduce current consumption and aggregate demand by as much as policymakers intended.

To the extent that *consumption smoothing* occurs over time, fiscal policy will lose some of its strength.

Offsetting State and Local Finance

The fiscal policies of state and local governments are frequently *pro-cyclical*, meaning that they worsen rather than correct recession or inflation. Unlike the federal government, most state and local governments face constitutional or other legal requirements to balance their budgets. Like households and private businesses, state and local governments increase their expenditures during prosperity and cut them during recession.

During the Great Depression of the 1930s, most of the increase in federal spending was offset by decreases in state and local spending. During and immediately following the recession of 2001, many state and local governments offset lower tax revenues by raising tax rates, imposing new taxes, and reducing spending.

The $2.2 trillion CARES Act of 2020 made a special effort to reduce this problem by giving $340 billion to state and local governments. Because of that sizable federal aid, state and local governments did not have to increase taxes or reduce expenditure as much as they would have had to otherwise. Thus their collective fiscal actions did not offset the federal stimulus by nearly as much as would have been the case if states had not received the aid money.

Crowding-Out Effect

Another potential flaw of fiscal policy is the **crowding-out effect:** An expansionary fiscal policy (deficit spending) may increase the interest rate and reduce investment spending, thereby weakening or canceling the stimulus of the expansionary policy. The rising interest rate might also

crowding-out effect A rise in interest rates and a resulting decrease in *planned investment* caused by the federal government's increased borrowing to finance budget deficits and refinance debt.

potentially crowd out interest-sensitive consumption spending (such as purchasing automobiles on credit). But because investment is the most volatile component of GDP, the crowding-out effect focuses on investment and whether the stimulus provided by deficit spending may be partly or even fully neutralized by an offsetting reduction in investment spending.

To see the potential problem, realize that whenever the government borrows money (which it must do to engage in deficit spending), it increases the overall demand for money. If the monetary authorities are holding the money supply constant, this increase in demand will raise the price paid for borrowing money: the interest rate. Because investment spending varies inversely with the interest rate, some investment will be choked off or "crowded out."

Crowding out is likely to be less of a problem when the economy is in recession because investment demand tends to be weak. The reason: Output purchases slow during recessions, and therefore most businesses end up with substantial excess capacity. As a result, they do not have much incentive to add new machinery or build new factories. After all, why should they add capacity when some of their existing capacity is lying idle?

With investment demand weak during a recession, the crowding-out effect is likely to be very small. Simply put, there is not much investment for the government to crowd out. Even if deficit spending does increase the interest rate, the effect on investment may be fully offset by the improved investment prospects that businesses expect from the fiscal stimulus.

By contrast, when the economy is operating at or near full capacity, investment demand is likely to be quite strong, and crowding out will probably be a much more serious problem. When the economy is booming, factories will be running at or near full capacity, and firms will have high investment demand for two reasons. First, equipment running at full capacity wears out fast, so firms will be investing substantial amounts to replace worn-out machinery and equipment. Second, the economy is likely to be growing overall, so firms will be investing heavily in order to increase their production capacity and thereby take advantage of the economy's increasing demand for goods and services.

QUICK REVIEW
33.3

▶ The United States government ran the largest peacetime budget deficit in U.S. history—14.9 percent of GDP—as the result of the massive fiscal stimulus expended to offset the COVID-19 recession of 2020.

▶ Time lags, political problems, expectations, and state and local finances complicate fiscal policy.

▶ The crowding-out effect indicates that an expansionary fiscal policy may increase the interest rate and reduce investment spending.

The U.S. Public Debt

>> **LO33.6** Discuss the size, composition, and consequences of the U.S. public debt.

public debt The total amount owed by the federal government to the owners of government *securities;* equal to the sum of past government *budget deficits* less government *budget surpluses.*

The U.S. national debt, or **public debt,** is the accumulation of all past federal deficits and surpluses. The deficits have greatly exceeded the surpluses and have emerged mainly from war financing, recessions, and fiscal policy. As of January 2022, the total public debt was $29.7 trillion—$23.2 trillion held by the public, and $6.5 trillion held by federal agencies and the Federal Reserve.

To provide some historical perspective, please understand that the public debt was much smaller prior to the 2007–2009 recession. In 2006, it was $8.5 trillion. It then more than doubled, to $18.2 trillion by 2015, as large budget deficits were run to fight the Great Recession and aid the subsequent recovery.

The debt continued to rise during the late 2010s despite the economy returning to full employment in 2017. That ongoing rise despite full employment generated a large amount of consternation and concern that we will discuss and analyze in this section. As with much else in economics, the public debt brings with it both costs and benefits. Just before the COVID-19 pandemic hit in early 2020, the debt stood at $23.2 trillion. Over the next three months, as the CARES Act went into effect, it jumped to $26.5 trillion—which reflected $3.3 trillion of additional debt in just 90 days!

Ownership

U.S. government securities U.S. Treasury bills, notes, and *bonds* used to finance *budget deficits;* the components of the *public debt.*

The total public debt of over $29.7 trillion represents the total amount of money owed by the federal government to the holders of **U.S. government securities:** financial instruments issued by the federal government to borrow money to finance expenditures that exceed tax revenues. U.S. government securities (loan instruments) are of four types: *Treasury bills* (short-term securities), *Treasury notes* (medium-term securities), *Treasury bonds* (long-term securities), and *U.S. savings bonds* (long-term, nonmarketable bonds).

Figure 33.5 shows that the public, not including the Federal Reserve, held 58 percent of the federal debt in 2021 and that federal government agencies and the Federal Reserve held the remaining 42 percent. Citizens of foreign countries held about 26 percent of the total U.S. public debt in 2021, meaning that most of the U.S. public debt is held internally and not externally. Americans owed 74 percent of the public debt to Americans. Of the $7.7 trillion of debt held by foreigners, the top three holders were Japan, with 17 percent; China, with 14 percent; and the United Kingdom, with 8 percent.

A simple statement of the absolute size of the U.S. national debt ignores the fact that the wealth and productive ability of the U.S. economy is also vast. A wealthy, highly productive nation such as the United States can carry a large public debt much more easily than a low-income nation can. Thus, it is highly informative to examine the ratio of the public debt relative to GDP.

Figure 33.6 indicates that in 2021, the portion of the U.S. public debt that was held by the public (rather than by the Federal Reserve or government agencies) was 101 percent of that year's GDP.

Figure 33.6 also shows that the ratio of debt to GDP rose dramatically starting in 2008. That rapid increase occurred because of massive annual budget deficits that increased the ratio's

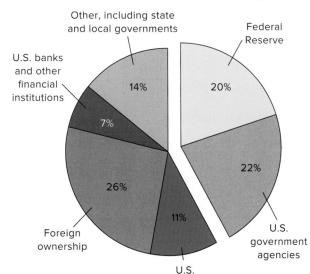

Debt held outside the federal government and Federal Reserve (58%)

Debt held by the federal government and Federal Reserve (42%)

Total debt: $29.7 trillion

FIGURE 33.5
Ownership of U.S. public debt, 2021.

The $29.7 trillion of public debt owed by the United States federal government in 2021 can be divided into the 58 percent held by the public (excluding the Federal Reserve), and the proportion held by federal agencies and the Federal Reserve System (42 percent). Of the total debt, 26 percent is foreign-owned.

Sources: Economic Report of the President 2022 and Treasury Bulletin, April 2022, U.S. Treasury.

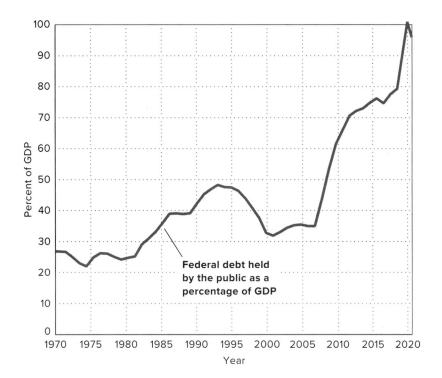

FIGURE 33.6
Federal debt held by the public, excluding the Federal Reserve, as a percentage of GDP, 1970–2021.

As a percentage of GDP, the federal debt held by the public increased steadily over the 1980–1995 period before declining significantly between 1995 and 2001. Since 2001, the percentage has gone up nearly every year, first jumping sharply after 2007–2009 recession and again in 2020 as the federal government borrowed sharply to fund anti-pandemic stimulus efforts. While the debt itself continued to rise in 2021, the debt-to-GDP ratio fell that year thanks to strong GDP growth.

Source: Federal Reserve Bank of St. Louis and U.S. Office of Management and Budget.

GLOBAL PERSPECTIVE 33.1

PUBLIC DEBT: INTERNATIONAL COMPARISONS

Although the United States has the world's largest public debt in absolute size, a number of other nations have public debts that are much larger fractions of their respective GDPs. In 2021, Venezuela had a public debt equal to over 300 percent of its annual GDP, while the U.S. public debt amounted to about 133 percent of U.S. GDP that year.

Public Sector Debt as Percentage of GDP, 2021

Country	
Venezuela	
Japan	
Greece	
Italy	
United States	
France	
Canada	
United Kingdom	
Brazil	
Germany	
Australia	
Mexico	

Scale: 0 50 100 150 200 250 300 350

Source: IMF Datamapper, International Monetary Fund.

numerator (debt) faster than annual economic growth increased the ratio's denominator (GDP). The debt-to-GDP ratio then spiked dramatically in 2020 due to a simultaneous increase in the numerator (caused by massive borrowing to fund pandemic relief efforts) and decrease in the denominator (caused by GDP falling as a result of the pandemic). By contrast, the debt-to-GDP ratio fell in 2021 not because the debt declined in absolute terms but because strong GDP growth generated an increase in the denominator of the ratio that more than offset the increase in the numerator caused by that year's additional debt.

International Comparisons

It is not uncommon for countries to have sizable public debts. As Global Perspective 33.1 shows, the public debt as a percentage of real GDP in the United States is on the higher end for industrially advanced nations, but still below that of Japan, Italy, and Greece.

Interest Charges

Many economists conclude that the primary burden of the debt is the annual interest charge accruing on the government notes and bonds sold to finance the debt. In 2021, interest on the total public debt was $352 billion. Although this amount is sizable in absolute terms, it was only 1.5 percent of GDP for 2021. In other words, the federal government had to collect taxes equal to 1.5 percent of GDP to service the total public debt. This percentage was virtually unchanged from 2000 despite the much higher total public debt, mostly because the Federal Reserve kept interest rates low in the wake of the Great Recession.

False Concerns

You may wonder if the large public debt might bankrupt the United States or place a tremendous burden on your children and grandchildren. Fortunately, these are largely false concerns. People were wondering the same things 50 years ago!

Bankruptcy

The large U.S. public debt does not threaten to bankrupt the federal government or leave it unable to meet its financial obligations. There are two main reasons: refinancing and taxation.

Refinancing As long as lenders view the U.S. public debt as manageable and sustainable, the public debt is easily refinanced. As portions of the debt come due each month, the government does not cut expenditures or raise taxes to provide the funds required. Rather, it refinances the debt by selling new bonds and using the proceeds to pay off the maturing bonds. The new bonds are in strong demand because lenders obtain a tradable security that (unlike other assets such as stocks, corporate debt, and real estate) is considered nearly riskless since there is virtually zero chance that the U.S. government would default on its debt payments.

Of course, refinancing could become an issue with a high enough debt-to-GDP ratio. Some countries, including Greece, have encountered this problem. High and rising ratios in the United States might raise fears that the U.S. government might be unable to pay back loans as they come due. But this is a false concern for the United States, given the U.S. economy's strong long-term growth prospects and how modest the U.S. debt-to-GDP ratio is as compared with those of other countries (see Global Perspective 33.1).

Taxation Financially distressed private households and corporations cannot extract themselves from their financial difficulties by taxing the public. If their incomes or sales revenues fall short of their expenses, they can indeed go bankrupt. But the federal government *does* have the option of imposing new taxes or increase existing tax rates to finance its debt. Such tax hikes may be politically unpopular and may weaken incentives to work and invest, but they *are* a means of raising funds to finance the debt.

Burdening Future Generations

In 2021, public debt per capita was $83,885. Was each child born in 2021 handed a $83,885 bill from the federal government? Not really. The public debt does not impose as much of a burden on future generations because the United States owes a substantial portion of the public debt to itself. U.S. citizens and institutions (banks, businesses, insurance companies, governmental agencies, and trust funds) own about 73 percent of the U.S. government securities. Although that part of the public debt is a liability to Americans (as taxpayers), it is simultaneously an asset to Americans (as holders of Treasury bills, Treasury notes, Treasury bonds, and U.S. savings bonds).

To eliminate the American-owned part of the public debt would require a gigantic transfer payment from Americans to Americans. Taxpayers would pay higher taxes, and debt holders would receive an equal amount for their U.S. government securities. Purchasing power in the United States would not change. Only the repayment of the 27 percent of the public debt owned by foreigners would negatively impact U.S. purchasing power.

The public debt increased sharply during the Second World War. But the decision to finance military purchases through the sale of government bonds did not shift the economic burden of the war to future generations. The economic cost of the Second World War consisted of the civilian goods society had to forgo in shifting scarce resources to war goods production. Regardless of whether society financed this reallocation through higher taxes or through borrowing, the real economic burden of the war would have been the same. That burden was borne almost entirely by those who lived during the war. They were the ones who did without a multitude of consumer goods to enable the United States to arm itself and its allies.

The next generation inherited the debt from the war, but it also inherited an equal amount of government bonds that would pay them cash in future years. In addition, it inherited the enormous benefits from the victory—namely, preserved political and economic systems at home and the "export" of those systems to Germany, Italy, and Japan. Those outcomes enhanced postwar U.S. economic growth and helped raise the standard of living for future generations of Americans.

Substantive Issues

Although the preceding issues relating to the public debt are false concerns, several actual concerns do exist.

Income Distribution

The ownership of government securities is highly uneven. Some people own much more than the $83,885-per-person portion of government securities; other people own less or none at all. In general, the ownership of the public debt is concentrated among wealthier groups. While the overall federal tax system is progressive, interest payments on the public debt do mildly increase income inequality. Income is transferred from people who, on average, have lower incomes to the higher-income bondholders. If greater income equality is one of society's goals, then this redistribution is undesirable.

Incentives

The current public debt necessitates annual interest payments of $352 billion. With no increase in the size of the debt, that interest charge must be paid out of tax revenues. Higher taxes may dampen incentives to bear risk, to innovate, to invest, and to work. So, in this indirect way, a large public debt may impair economic growth and therefore impose a burden of reduced output (and income) on future generations.

Foreign-Owned Public Debt

The 26 percent of the U.S. debt held by foreign citizens, foreign businesses, and foreign governments (including foreign central banks) is an economic burden to Americans. Because we do not owe that portion of the debt "to ourselves," the payment of interest and principal on this **external public debt** enables foreigners to buy some of our output. In return for the benefits derived from the borrowed funds, the United States transfers goods and services to foreign lenders. However, Americans also own debt issued by foreign governments, so payment of principal and interest by those governments transfers some of their goods and services to Americans.

external public debt
The portion of the public debt owed to foreign citizens, *firms,* and institutions.

Crowding-Out Effect Revisited

A potentially more serious problem is the financing (and continual refinancing) of the large public debt, which can transfer a real economic burden to future generations by passing onto them a smaller stock of capital goods. This possibility involves the previously discussed crowding-out effect: the idea that public borrowing drives up real interest rates, thereby reducing private investment spending. If public borrowing happened only during recessions, crowding out would not likely be much of a problem. Because private investment demand tends to be weak during recessions, any increase in interest rates during a recession would at most cause only a small reduction in investment spending.

In contrast, the need to continuously finance a large public debt may be more troublesome. Continuous financing implies having to borrow large amounts of money when the economy is near or at full employment. Because private investment spending is strong near economic peaks, any increase in interest rates at or near a peak may result in a substantial decline in private investment spending. If the amount of current investment crowded out is extensive, future generations will inherit an economy with a smaller production capacity and, other things equal, a lower standard of living.

Public Investments and Public-Private Complementarities But even with crowding out, two factors could partly or fully offset the net economic burden shifted to future generations. First, just as private expenditures may involve either consumption or investment, so it is with public goods. Part of the government spending enabled by the public debt is for public investment outlays (for example, highways, mass transit systems, and electric power facilities) and human capital (for example, investments in education, job training, and health). Like private expenditures on machinery and equipment, these **public investments** increase the economy's future production capacity by increasing the stock of public capital passed on to future generations. That greater stock of public capital may offset the diminished stock of private capital resulting from the crowding-out effect, thereby leaving the economy's overall production capacity unimpaired.

public investments
Government expenditures on public capital (such as roads, highways, bridges, mass-transit systems, and electric power facilities) and on *human capital* (such as education, training, and health).

Public-private complementarities may also reduce the crowding-out effect. Some public and private investments are complementary. Thus, a public investment financed through debt could spur some private-sector investment by increasing its expected rate of return. For example, the presence of a newly built federal building in a particular city may encourage private investment in the form of nearby office buildings, shops, and restaurants. Through this complementary effect, government spending on public capital may shift the private investment

The Social Security and Medicare Time Bombs

As the Population Ages, Social Security and Medicare Face Gigantic Funding Shortfalls.

The percentage of the U.S. population age 62 or older will rise substantially over the next several decades. As a result, fewer workers will be paying taxes into the Social Security system (income during retirement) and the Medicare system (medical care during retirement). Simultaneously, however, the "greying of the population" will result in many more retirees. The number of workers per Social Security and Medicare beneficiary was roughly 5:1 in 1960. Today it is a little less than 3:1, and by 2040 it will be only 2:1. As that ratio continues to fall, it will become impossible at current tax rates to fulfill the benefits promised under current law. Either taxes must rise, or benefits must be cut.

The Social Security Shortfall Social Security is the major public retirement program in the United States. The program costs $1.2 trillion annually and is financed by a 12.4 percent tax on earnings up to a set level of earnings ($147,000 in 2022). Half the tax (6.2 percent) is paid by the worker; the other half by the employer. Social Security is largely an annual "pay-as-you-go" plan, meaning that most of the current revenues from the Social Security tax are paid to current Social Security retirees.

Until 2009, however, annual Social Security tax revenues exceeded annual Social Security retirement payouts. That excess annual inflow was used to buy U.S. Treasury securities that were credited to a government account called the Social Security Trust Fund. But starting in 2009, annual Social Security revenues fell below annual Social Security payouts and the system started shifting money from the trust fund to make up the difference. As a result, the trust fund is expected to be exhausted in 2034. For each year thereafter, annual tax revenues will cover only 75 percent of promised benefits.

The Medicare Shortfall The Medicare program is the U.S. health care program for people age 65 and older in the United States. The program costs $926 billion per year and has been growing at about 9 percent annually since 1980. Like Social Security, it also is a pay-as-you-go plan, meaning that current medical benefits for people age 65 or older are being funded by current tax revenues. Like the Social Security tax, half the Medicare earnings tax is paid by the employer (1.45 percent) and half by the employee (1.45 percent). Unlike Social Security, though, the Medicare tax is paid on all earnings, not just those up to an annual cap.

The financial status of Medicare is even worse than that of Social Security. To begin with, the Medicare Trust Fund will be depleted in 2026, 8 years before the Social Security Trust Fund is expected to be depleted. Then, in subsequent years, the percentage of scheduled Medicare benefits covered by the current Medicare tax will decline from 97 percent in 2025 to 72 percent in 2035 and 69 percent in 2080.

The Unpleasant Options To restore long-run balance to Social Security and Medicare, the federal government must either reduce benefits or increase revenues. It's as simple—and as complicated—as that! The Social Security Administration concludes that bringing projected Social Security revenues and payments into balance over the

Kim Reinick/123RF

next 75 years would require a 16 percent permanent reduction in Social Security benefits, a 13 percent permanent increase in tax revenues, or some combination of the two. To bring projected Medicare revenues and expenses into long-run balance would require an increase in the Medicare payroll tax by 122 percent, a 51 percent reduction of Medicare payments from their projected levels, or some combination of each.

The options for closing all or part of the Social Security and Medicare funding gaps involve difficult economic trade-offs and dangerous political risks. Here are just a few examples:

- Increasing the retirement age for collecting Social Security or Medicare benefits will upset preretirement workers, who will start collecting benefits at older ages.

- Subjecting a larger portion of total earnings to the Social Security tax would constitute a gigantic tax increase on the earnings of the country's highest trained and educated individuals. This might reduce the incentive for younger people to obtain education and advance in their careers.

- Disqualifying wealthy individuals from receiving Social Security and Medicare benefits would tilt the programs toward becoming redistribution programs, rather than insurance programs. This would undermine the broad existing political support for the programs.

- Redirecting legal immigration toward high-skilled, high-earning entrants and away from low-skilled, low-earning immigrants to raise Social Security and Medicare revenues would also raise the ire of some native-born high-skilled workers and the proponents of immigration based on family reunification.

- Placing the payroll tax revenues into accounts that individuals, not the government, would own, maintain, and bequeath would transform the Social Security and Medicare programs from guaranteed "defined benefit plans" into much riskier "defined contribution plans." The high short-run volatility of the stock market might leave some unlucky people destitute in old age.

The problem is huge and will not go away. The federal government and the American people will eventually have to face up to the overpromising-underfunding problem and find ways to resolve it.

demand curve to the right. Even if the government borrowing needed to build the new federal building boosts the interest rate, total private investment need not fall. However, the increase in private investment might be smaller than anticipated. If it is, then the crowding-out effect will not be fully offset.

QUICK REVIEW

33.4

▶ The U.S. public debt—$29.7 trillion in 2021—is the total accumulation of all past federal budget deficits and surpluses; about 26 percent of the U.S. public debt is held by foreigners.

▶ The U.S. public debt held by the public (excluding the Federal Reserve) was 101 percent of GDP in 2021, up from 33 percent in 2000.

▶ The federal government is in no danger of going bankrupt because it needs only to refinance (not retire) the public debt and it can raise revenues, if needed, through higher taxes.

▶ The borrowing and interest payments associated with the public debt may (a) increase income inequality; (b) require higher taxes, which may dampen incentives; and (c) impede the growth of the nation's stock of capital through crowding out of private investment.

Summary

LO33.1 Identify the purposes, tools, and limitations of fiscal policy.

Fiscal policy consists of deliberate changes in government spending, taxes, or both to promote full employment, price-level stability, and economic growth. Fiscal policy requires increases in government spending, decreases in taxes, or both (a budget deficit) to increase aggregate demand and push an economy from a recession. Decreases in government spending, increases in taxes, or both (a budget surplus) are appropriate fiscal policy for decreasing aggregate demand to try to slow or halt demand-pull inflation.

LO33.2 Explain how built-in stabilizers moderate business cycles.

Built-in stability arises from net tax revenues, which vary directly with the level of GDP. During recession, the federal budget automatically moves toward a stabilizing deficit; during expansion, the budget automatically moves toward an anti-inflationary surplus. Built-in stability lessens, but does not fully correct, undesired changes in real GDP.

LO33.3 Describe how the cyclically adjusted budget reveals the status of U.S. fiscal policy.

Actual federal budget deficits can go up or down because of changes in GDP, changes in fiscal policy, or both. Deficits caused by changes in GDP are called cyclical deficits. The cyclically adjusted budget removes cyclical deficits from the budget and therefore measures the budget deficit or surplus that would occur if the economy operated at its full-employment output throughout the year. Changes in the cyclical budget deficit or surplus provide meaningful information as to whether the government's fiscal policy is expansionary, neutral, or contractionary. Changes in the actual budget deficit or surplus do not, because such deficits or surpluses can include cyclical deficits or surpluses.

LO33.4 Summarize recent U.S. fiscal policy.

The final years of the 2010s saw significant cyclically adjusted budget deficits of around 4 to 5 percent of GDP despite the U.S. economy operating at full employment. The amount of fiscal stimulus then multiplied in response to the COVID-19 pandemic, with the cyclically adjusted budget deficit peaking in 2020 at −14.3 percent of potential GDP.

LO33.5 Discuss the problems that governments may encounter in enacting and applying fiscal policy.

Certain problems complicate the enactment and implementation of fiscal policy. They include (a) timing problems associated with recognition, administrative, and operational lags; (b) the potential for misuse of fiscal policy for political rather than economic purposes; (c) the fact that state and local finances tend to be pro-cyclical; (d) potential ineffectiveness if households expect future policy reversals; and (e) the possibility of fiscal policy crowding out private investment.

LO33.6 Discuss the size, composition, and consequences of the U.S. public debt.

The public debt is the total accumulation of all past federal government deficits and surpluses. In 2021 the U.S. public debt was $29.7 trillion, or $83,885 per person. The public holds 58 percent of that federal debt; the Federal Reserve and federal agencies hold the other 42 percent. Foreigners hold 26 percent of the federal debt. Interest payments as a percentage of GDP were about 1.5 percent in 2021.

Because of large annual deficits, the U.S. public debt more than tripled between 2008 and 2021, rising from $9.2 trillion in 2008 to $27.9 trillion in 2021. The concern that a large public debt may bankrupt the U.S. government is generally a false worry because (a) the debt needs only to be refinanced rather than retired and (b) the federal government has the power to increase taxes to make interest payments on the debt.

In general, the public debt is not a vehicle for shifting economic burdens to future generations. Americans inherit not only most of the public debt (a liability) but also most of the U.S. government securities (an asset) that finance the debt.

More substantive problems associated with public debt include the following: (a) Payment of interest on the debt may increase income inequality. (b) Interest payments on the debt require higher taxes, which may impair incentives. (c) Paying interest or principal on the portion of the debt held by foreign nationals means a transfer of real output abroad. (d) Government borrowing to refinance or pay interest on the debt may increase interest rates and crowd out private investment spending, leaving future generations with a smaller stock of capital than they would have had otherwise.

The increase in investment in public capital that may result from debt financing may partly or wholly offset the crowding-out effect of the public debt on private investment. Also, the added public investment may stimulate private investment, where the two are complements.

Terms and Concepts

fiscal policy	built-in stabilizer	political business cycles
Council of Economic Advisers (CEA)	progressive tax	crowding-out effect
expansionary fiscal policy	proportional tax	public debt
budget deficit	regressive tax	U.S. government securities
contractionary fiscal policy	cyclically adjusted budget	external public debt
budget surplus	cyclical deficit	public investments

Discussion Questions   Mc Graw Hill connect

1. What is the role of the Council of Economic Advisers (CEA) as it relates to fiscal policy? Use an Internet search to find the names and university affiliations of the present members of the CEA. **LO33.1**

2. What are government's fiscal policy options for ending severe demand-pull inflation? **LO33.1**

3. (For students who were assigned Chapter 31) Use the aggregate expenditures model to show how government fiscal policy could eliminate either a recessionary expenditure gap or an inflationary expenditure gap (Figure 31.7). Explain how equal-size increases in *G* and *T* could eliminate a recessionary gap and how equal-size decreases in *G* and *T* could eliminate an inflationary gap. **LO33.1**

4. Some politicians have suggested that the United States enact a constitutional amendment requiring that the federal government balance its budget annually. Explain why such an amendment, if strictly enforced, would force the government to enact a contractionary fiscal policy whenever the economy experiences a severe recession. **LO33.1**

5. Explain how built-in (automatic) stabilizers work. What are the differences between proportional, progressive, and regressive tax systems as they relate to an economy's built-in stability? **LO33.2**

6. Define the cyclically adjusted budget, explain its significance, and state why it may differ from the actual budget. Suppose the full-employment, noninflationary level of real output is GDP$_3$ (not GDP$_2$) in the economy depicted in Figure 33.3. If the economy is operating at GDP$_2$ instead of GDP$_3$, what is the status of its cyclically adjusted budget? The status of its current fiscal policy? What change in fiscal policy would you recommend? How would you accomplish that in terms of the *G* and *T* lines in the figure? **LO33.3**

7. Briefly state and evaluate the problem of time lags in enacting and applying fiscal policy. Explain the idea of a political business cycle. How might expectations of a near-term policy reversal weaken fiscal policy based on changes in tax rates? What is

the crowding-out effect, and why might it be relevant to fiscal policy? **LO33.5**

8. How do economists distinguish between the absolute and relative sizes of the public debt? Why is the distinction important? Distinguish between refinancing the debt and retiring (repaying) the debt. How does an internally held public debt differ from an externally held public debt? Contrast the effects of retiring an internally held debt and retiring an externally held debt. **LO33.6**

9. True or false? If false, explain why. **LO33.6**
   a. The total public debt is more relevant to an economy than the public debt as a percentage of GDP.
   b. An internally held public debt is like a debt of the left hand owed to the right hand.
   c. The Federal Reserve and federal government agencies hold more than three-fourths of the public debt.
   d. As a percentage of GDP, the total U.S. public debt is the highest such debt among the world's advanced industrial nations.

10. Why might economists be quite concerned if the annual interest payments on the U.S. public debt sharply increased as a percentage of GDP? **LO33.6**

11. Trace the cause-and-effect chain through which financing and refinancing of the public debt might affect real interest rates, private investment, the capital stock, and economic growth. How might investment in public capital and public-private complementarities alter the outcome of the cause-effect chain? **LO33.6**

12. **LAST WORD** What do economists mean when they say Social Security and Medicare are "pay-as-you-go" plans? What are the Social Security and Medicare trust funds, and how long will they have money left in them? What is the key long-run problem of both Social Security and Medicare? To fix the problem, do you favor increasing taxes or do you prefer reducing benefits?

Review Questions   Mc Graw Hill connect

1. Which of the following would help a government reduce an inflationary output gap? **LO33.1**
   a. Raising taxes.
   b. Lowering taxes.
   c. Increasing government spending.
   d. Decreasing government spending.

2. The economy is in a recession. A congresswoman suggests increasing spending to stimulate aggregate demand and raising

taxes simultaneously to pay for the increased spending. Her suggestion to combine higher government expenditures with higher taxes is: **LO33.1**
   a. the worst possible combination of tax and expenditure changes.
   b. the best possible combination of tax and expenditure changes.
   c. a mediocre and contradictory combination of tax and expenditure changes.

3. During the recession of 2007–2009, the U.S. federal government's tax collections fell from about $2.6 trillion down to about $2.1 trillion while GDP declined by about 4 percent. Does the U.S. tax system appear to have built-in stabilizers? **LO33.2**
   a. Yes
   b. No

4. Last year, while a hypothetical economy was in a recession, government spending was $595 billion, and government revenue was $505 billion. Economists estimate that if the economy had been at its full-employment level of GDP last year, government spending would have been $555 billion and government revenue would have been $550 billion. Which of the following statements about this government's fiscal situation are true? **LO33.3**
   a. The government has a non–cyclically adjusted budget deficit of $595 billion.
   b. The government has a non–cyclically adjusted budget deficit of $90 billion.
   c. The government has a non–cyclically adjusted budget surplus of $90 billion.
   d. The government has a cyclically adjusted budget deficit of $555 billion.
   e. The government has a cyclically adjusted budget deficit of $5 billion.
   f. The government has a cyclically adjusted budget surplus of $5 billion.

5. Label each of the following scenarios as an example of a recognition lag, administrative lag, or operational lag. **LO33.5**
   a. To fight a recession, congress has passed a bill to increase infrastructure spending—but the legally required environmental-impact statement for each new project will take at least two years to complete before any building can begin.
   b. Distracted by a war that is going badly, politicians take no notice until inflation reaches 8 percent.
   c. Politicians recognize a sudden recession, but it takes many months of political deal making before they finally approve a stimulus bill.
   d. To fight a recession, the president orders federal agencies to get rid of petty regulations that burden private businesses—but the federal agencies begin by spending a year developing a set of regulations on how to remove petty regulations.

6. In January, the interest rate is 5 percent and firms borrow $50 billion per month for investment projects. In February, the federal government doubles its monthly borrowing from $25 billion to $50 billion, driving the interest rate up to 7 percent. As a result, firms cut back their borrowing to only $30 billion per month. Which of the following is true? **LO33.6**
   a. There is no crowding-out effect because the government's increase in borrowing exceeds firms' decrease in borrowing.
   b. There is a crowding-out effect of $20 billion.
   c. There is no crowding-out effect because both the government and firms are still borrowing a lot.
   d. There is a crowding-out effect of $25 billion.

Problems

McGraw Hill connect

1. Assume that a hypothetical economy with an MPC of .8 is experiencing a severe recession. By how much would government spending have to rise to shift the aggregate demand curve rightward by $25 billion? How large a tax cut would be needed to achieve the same increase in aggregate demand? Determine one possible combination of a government spending increase and a simultaneous tax increase that would accomplish the same goal. **LO33.1**

2. Refer back to the table in Figure 32.7 in the previous chapter. Suppose that aggregate demand increases such that the amount of real output demanded rises by $7 billion at each price level. By what percentage will the price level increase? Will this inflation be demand-pull inflation, or will it be cost-push inflation? If potential real GDP (that is, full-employment GDP) is $510 billion, what will be the size of the positive GDP gap after the change in aggregate demand? If government wants to use fiscal policy to counter the resulting inflation without changing tax rates, would it increase government spending or decrease it? **LO33.1**

3. (For students who were assigned Chapter 31) Assume that, without taxes, the consumption schedule for an economy is as shown below: **LO33.2**

GDP, Billions	Consumption, Billions
$100	$120
200	200
300	280
400	360
500	440
600	520
700	600

a. Graph this consumption schedule. What is the size of the MPC?
b. Assume that a lump-sum (regressive) tax of $10 billion is imposed at all levels of GDP. Calculate the tax rate at each level of GDP. Graph the resulting consumption schedule and compare the MPC and the multiplier with those of the pretax consumption schedule.
c. Now suppose a proportional tax with a 10 percent tax rate is imposed instead of the regressive tax. Calculate and graph the new consumption schedule, and calculate the MPC and the multiplier.
d. Finally, impose a progressive tax such that the tax rate is 0 percent when GDP is $100, 5 percent at $200, 10 percent at $300, 15 percent at $400, and so forth. Determine and graph the new consumption schedule, noting the effect of this tax system on the MPC and the multiplier.
e. Use a graph similar to Figure 33.3 to show why proportional and progressive taxes contribute to greater economic stability, while a regressive tax does not.

4. Refer to the following table for Waxwania: **LO33.2**

Government Expenditures, G	Tax Revenues, T	Real GDP
$160	$100	$500
160	120	600
160	140	700
160	160	800
160	180	900

What is the marginal tax rate in Waxwania? The average tax rate? Which of the following describes the tax system: proportional, progressive, or regressive?

5. Refer to the table for Waxwania in problem 4. Suppose that Waxwania is producing $600 of real GDP, whereas the potential real GDP (or full-employment real GDP) is $700. How large is its budget deficit? Its cyclically adjusted budget deficit? Its cyclically adjusted budget deficit as a percentage of potential real GDP? Is Waxwania's fiscal policy expansionary, or is it contractionary? **LO33.3**

6. Suppose that a country has no public debt in year 1 but experiences a budget deficit of $40 billion in year 2, a budget surplus of $10 billion in year 3, and a budget deficit of $2 billion in year 4.

What is the absolute size of its public debt in year 4? If its real GDP in year 4 is $104 billion, what is this country's public debt as a percentage of real GDP in year 4? **LO33.6**

7. Suppose that the investment demand curve in a certain economy is such that investment declines by $100 billion for every 1 percentage point increase in the real interest rate. Also, suppose that the investment demand curve shifts rightward by $150 billion at each real interest rate for every 1 percentage point increase in the expected rate of return from investment. If stimulus spending (an expansionary fiscal policy) by government increases the real interest rate by 2 percentage points, but also raises the expected rate of return on investment by 1 percentage point, how much investment, if any, will be crowded out? **LO33.6**

isak55/Shutterstock

Money, the Federal Reserve, and Interest Rates

>> **LEARNING OBJECTIVES**

LO34.1 Explain the functions of money.

LO34.2 Describe the components of the U.S. money supply.

LO34.3 Describe what "backs" the money supply.

LO34.4 Discuss the structure of the Federal Reserve.

LO34.5 Identify the functions and responsibilities of the Federal Reserve.

LO34.6 Explain the fractional reserve system used by U.S. banks and why the Fed might wish to influence their creation of checkable-deposit money.

LO34.7 Explain how the equilibrium interest rate is determined and why interest rates and bond prices vary inversely.

Money is a fascinating aspect of the economy:

> Money bewitches people. They fret for it, and they sweat for it. They devise most ingenious ways to get it, and most ingenuous ways to get rid of it. Money is the only commodity that is good for nothing but to be gotten rid of. It will not feed you, clothe you, shelter you, or amuse you unless you spend it or invest it. It imparts value only in parting. People will do almost anything for money, and money will do almost anything for people. Money is a captivating, circulating, masquerading puzzle.[1]

In this chapter and the next, we unmask the critical role of money in the economy. A well-operating monetary system helps the economy achieve both full employment and the efficient use of resources. A malfunctioning monetary system distorts the allocation of resources and creates severe fluctuations in output, employment, and prices.

>> **LO34.1** Explain the functions of money.

medium of exchange Any item sellers generally accept and buyers generally use to pay for a *good* or *service; money;* a convenient means of exchanging goods and *services* without engaging in *barter*.

The Functions of Money

What exactly is money? There is an old saying that "money *is* what money *does*." Generally, anything that performs the functions of money is money. Here are those functions:

- *Medium of exchange* First and foremost, money is a **medium of exchange** that is used for buying and selling goods and services. A bakery worker does not want to be paid 200 bagels per week. Nor does the bakery owner want to receive, say, halibut in exchange for bagels. Money

[1] *Creeping Inflation: The Pickpocket Prosperity.* Federal Reserve Bank of Philadelphia, 1957.

is a social invention with which resource suppliers and producers can be paid, and it can be used to buy any item in the marketplace. As a medium of exchange, money allows society to escape the complications of barter. And because it provides a convenient way of exchanging goods, money enables society to gain the advantages of geographic and human specialization.

- *Unit of account* Money is also a **unit of account.** Society uses monetary units—dollars, in the United States—to measure the relative worth of a wide variety of goods, services, and resources. Just as we measure distance in miles or kilometers, we gauge the value of goods in dollars.

  With money as an acceptable unit of account, the price of each item needs to be stated only in terms of the monetary unit. We need not state the price of cows in terms of corn, crayons, and cranberries. Money aids rational decision making by enabling buyers and sellers to easily compare the relative values of goods, services, and resources by simply examining their respective money prices. It also permits us to define debt obligations, determine taxes owed, and calculate the nation's GDP.

- *Store of value* Money also serves as a **store of value** that enables people to transfer purchasing power from the present to the future. People normally do not spend their entire paychecks on the day they receive them. To buy things later, they store some of their wealth as money. The money you place in a safe or a checking account will still be available to you a few weeks or months from now. When inflation is nonexistent or mild, holding money is a relatively risk-free way to store your wealth.

> **unit of account** A standard unit in which *prices* can be stated and the value of *goods* and *services* can be compared; one of the three functions of *money.*

> **store of value** An asset set aside for future use; one of the three functions of *money.*

People can choose to hold some or all of their wealth in a wide variety of assets besides money. These assets include real estate, stocks, bonds, precious metals such as gold, and even collectible items like fine art or comic books. But a key advantage that money has over all other assets is its *liquidity*, or spendability.

An asset's **liquidity** is the ease with which it can be converted quickly with little or no loss of purchasing power into either physical cash (bills and coins) or cash balances held in electronic systems like PayPay and Venmo that transfer cash around electronically. The more liquid an asset is, the more quickly it can be converted into physical or electronic cash and used to purchase goods, services, and other assets.

Levels of liquidity vary greatly. By definition, cash is perfectly liquid. By contrast, a house is highly illiquid for two reasons. First, it may take several months before a willing buyer is found and a sale negotiated. Second, there is a loss of purchasing power when the house is sold because numerous fees must be paid to real estate agents and other individuals to complete the sale.

> **liquidity** The degree to which an asset can be converted quickly into cash with little or no loss of purchasing power. *Money* is said to be perfectly liquid, whereas other assets have lesser degrees of liquidity.

As we are about to discuss, our economy uses several different types of money including cash, coins, checking account deposits, savings account deposits, and even more exotic things like deposits in money market mutual funds. As we describe the various forms of money in detail, take the time to compare their relative levels of liquidity—both with each other and as compared to other assets like stocks, bonds, and real estate. Cash is perfectly liquid. Other forms of money are highly liquid, but less liquid than cash.

The Components of the Money Supply

Societies have used many items as money, including whales' teeth, circular stones, elephant-tail bristles, gold coins, furs, and pieces of paper. Anything that is widely accepted as a medium of exchange can serve as money. In the United States, currency (cash) is not the only form of money. For example, certain debts of government and financial institutions also are used as money. Thus, the total quantity, or stock, of money depends upon what forms of money (cash, checkable deposits, etc.) are included in the tally.

> >> **LO34.2** Describe the components of the U.S. money supply.

In the United States, the two best-known tallies are known as $M1$ and $M2$. $M1$ contains the most immediately spendable (liquid) categories of money. $M2$ includes all the categories in $M1$ *plus* two additional categories of slightly less spendable money.

Money Definition *M*1

The narrowest definition of the U.S. money supply is called *M***1.** It consists of three components:

- *Currency* (coins and paper money) in the hands of the public.

- *Checkable deposits at commercial banks*, on which checks of any size can be drawn, at any time and as often as desired.

> *M***1** The most narrowly defined money supply, equal to *currency* in the hands of the public, *checkable deposits*, and *savings deposits* held at *commercial banks* and thrifts.

FIGURE 34.1

Components of money supply *M*1 and money supply *M*2, in the United States.

(a) *M*1 is a narrow definition of the money supply that includes currency (in circulation) and checkable deposits. (b) *M*2 is a broader definition that includes *M*1 along with two other categories of relatively liquid account balances, retail money market funds and small-denominated time deposits.

Source: Board of Governors of the Federal Reserve System.

- *Other liquid deposits*, including checkable deposits held at credit unions and other so-called thrift institutions *plus* savings deposits held at either commercial banks or thrift institutions.[2]

The supplies of coins and paper money are determined by the U.S. Department of the Treasury and the Federal Reserve System (the U.S. *central bank*). Commercial banks ("banks") and savings institutions ("thrifts") provide checkable deposits. Figure 34.1 shows that in November 2021, *M*1 was $20.3 trillion and *M*2 was $21.4 trillion. Thus, *M*2 was only $1.1 trillion, or about 5 percent, larger than *M*1.

Currency: Coins + Paper Money U.S. currency consists of metal coins and paper money. The metal coins are issued by the U.S. Treasury while the paper money consists of **Federal Reserve Notes** issued by the Federal Reserve System. The coins are minted by the U.S. Mint, while the paper money is printed on behalf of the Federal Reserve by the Bureau of Engraving and Printing. Both the U.S. Mint and the Bureau of Engraving and Printing are part of the U.S. Department of the Treasury.

As with the currencies of other countries, the currency of the United States is **token money.** That is, the face value of any piece of currency is unrelated to its *intrinsic value*—the value of the physical material (metal or paper and ink) from which that piece of currency is constructed. Governments make sure that face values exceed intrinsic values to discourage people from deconstructing coins and bills in order to resell the material that they are made out of as scrap metal or scrap paper. For instance, if 50-cent pieces each contained 75 cents' worth of metal, then it would be profitable to melt them down and sell the metal. Fifty-cent pieces would disappear from circulation very quickly!

Figure 34.1 shows that currency (coins and paper money) represents about 10.3 percent of *M*1 and about 9.8 percent of *M*2.

Checkable Deposits The safety and convenience of checks has made **checkable deposits** a large component of the *M*1 money supply. You would not think of stuffing a large amount of currency—say, $2,396 in bills—into an envelope and then dropping that envelope into a mailbox to pay a debt. But writing and mailing a check for a large sum is commonplace, as is swiping, tapping, or inserting a "debit card" that automatically pulls money out of a checking account to make a payment.

Federal Reserve Note Paper money issued by the *Federal Reserve Banks.*

token money Bills or coins for which the amount printed on the *currency* bears no relationship to the value of the paper or metal embodied within it; for currency still circulating, *money* for which the face value exceeds the commodity value.

checkable deposit Any deposit in a *commercial bank* or *thrift institution* against which a check may be written.

[2]Prior to May 2020, the "savings deposits held at either commercial banks or thrift institutions" component of the money supply was excluded from *M*1 but included in *M*2. As a result, *M*1 used to be substantially smaller and the non-*M*1 parts of *M*2 substantially larger.

In terms of checks, the person cashing a check must endorse it (sign it on the reverse side); the writer of the check subsequently receives a record of the cashed check as a receipt. Similarly, because you must sign your checks, the theft or loss of your checkbook is not nearly as calamitous as losing a large amount of currency. Finally, it is more convenient to swipe a debit card or write a check than to transport and count out large sums of currency. For all these reasons, checkable deposits are a large component of the money stock in the United States. About 23 percent of $M1$ and 22 percent of $M2$ are in the form of checkable deposits, on which checks can be drawn and debit card payments processed.

It might seem strange that checking account balances are regarded as part of the money supply. But the reason is clear: Checks and debit card payments are simply a way to transfer the ownership of bank deposits, and they are generally acceptable as a medium of exchange. Although checks are less generally accepted than currency or debit card payments for many small purchases, most sellers willingly accept checks as payment for major purchases. Moreover, people can convert checkable deposits into paper money and coins on demand; checks drawn on those deposits are thus the equivalent of currency.

In addition, cash-transfer systems like PayPal and Venmo are often set up to be able to draw money out of checking accounts. Thus, another reason that checkable deposits are considered money is because they can be converted almost instantaneously into spendable electronic cash balances in systems like PayPal and Venmo.

To summarize:

Money, $M1$ = currency + checkable deposits at commercial banks + other liquid deposits.

Institutions That Offer Checkable Deposits In the United States, a variety of financial institutions allow customers to write checks on the funds they have deposited. **Commercial banks** are the primary depository institutions. They accept the deposits of households and businesses, keep the money safe until it is withdrawn via checks or debit card activity, and in the meantime use it to make a wide variety of loans. Commercial bank loans provide short-term financial capital to businesses, and they finance consumer purchases of automobiles and other durable goods.

Savings and loan associations (S&Ls), mutual savings banks, and credit unions supplement the commercial banks. Collectively, these institutions are called **thrift institutions,** or simply "thrifts." *Savings and loan associations* and *mutual savings banks* accept the deposits of households and businesses and then use the funds to finance home mortgages and to provide other loans. *Credit unions* accept deposits from and lend to "members," who usually are a group of people who work for the same company.

The checkable deposits of banks and thrifts are known variously as demand deposits, NOW (negotiable order of withdrawal) accounts, ATS (automatic transfer service) accounts, and share draft accounts. Depositors can write checks on all of these accounts whenever, and in whatever amount, they choose.

Two Qualifications We must qualify our discussion in two important ways. First, currency held by the U.S. Treasury, the Federal Reserve banks, commercial banks, and thrift institutions is excluded from $M1$ and other measures of the money supply. A paper dollar or four quarters in the wallet of, say, Emma Buck obviously constitutes just $1 of the money supply. But if we counted currency held by banks as part of the money supply, the same $1 would count for $2 of money supply if Emma deposited the currency into her checking account. By excluding currency held by banks when determining the total money supply, we avoid this problem of double counting.

Also *excluded* from the money supply are any checkable deposits of the government (specifically, the U.S. Treasury) or the Federal Reserve that are held by commercial banks or thrift institutions. This exclusion enables a better assessment of the amount of money available *to the private sector* for potential spending. The amount of money available to households and businesses is of keen interest to the Federal Reserve in conducting its monetary policy (which we discuss in Chapter 35).

Money Definition *M2*

A second and broader definition of money includes all the categories of highly spendable money contained in $M1$ plus two near-monies. **Near-monies** are certain highly liquid financial assets that do not function directly or fully as a medium of exchange but can be readily converted into currency or checkable deposits. The *M2* definition of money includes two categories of near-monies.

---

commercial bank A *firm* that engages in the business of banking (accepts deposits, offers checking accounts, and makes loans).

thrift institution A *savings and loan association, mutual savings bank,* or *credit union.*

near-money Financial *assets* that are not themselves a *medium of exchange* but that have extremely high *liquidity* and thus can be readily converted into *money.* Includes noncheckable *savings accounts, time deposits,* and short-term *U.S. government securities* plus savings bonds.

M2 A more broadly defined *money supply,* equal to *M1* plus small *time deposits* (of less than $100,000) and individual *money market mutual fund* balances.

time deposit An interest-earning deposit in a *commercial bank* or *thrift institution* that the depositor can withdraw without penalty after the end of a specified period.

- *Small-denominated (less than $100,000) time deposits* Funds from **time deposits** become available at their maturity. For example, a person can convert a 6-month time deposit (usually referred to as a *certificate of deposit*, or CD) to currency without penalty 6 months or more after depositing it. In return for this withdrawal limitation, financial institutions pay a higher interest rate on time deposits than on ordinary checking or savings deposits (which can be withdrawn at any time without penalty). Note that while CD holders can in fact "cash in" CDs before their maturity dates, they would have to bear severe penalties if they did so. Because those early-withdrawal penalties discourage CD holders from spending their CD balances as readily as they would spend currency or checking account balances, funds held in time deposits are excluded from $M1$.

money market mutual funds (MMMFs) *Mutual funds* that invest in short-term *securities*. Depositors can write checks in minimum amounts or more against their accounts.

- *Retail money market funds (i.e., money market mutual funds held by individuals)* By making a telephone call, using the Internet, or writing a check for $500 or more, a depositor can redeem shares in a **money market mutual fund (MMMF)** offered by a mutual fund company. Such companies use the combined funds of individual shareholders to buy interest-bearing short-term credit instruments such as CDs and U.S. government securities. By holding those interest-earning assets, the funds can in turn offer interest payments on the balances held by shareholders in their MMMF accounts. The MMMFs in $M2$ include only the MMMF accounts held by individuals; those held by businesses and other institutions are excluded. The fact that MMMF checks must be for $500 or more (rather than for any amount) is why MMMFs are not included in $M1$.

Note that $M2$ is defined such that it encompasses the immediate medium-of-exchange items (currency and checkable deposits) that constitute $M1$ plus two near-monies that can be easily converted into currency and checkable deposits. $M2$ is, consequently, a measure of the portion of the money supply that is highly spendable.

In equation form:

$$\text{Money, } M2 = M1 + \text{small-denominated time deposits} + \text{MMMFs held by individuals}$$

In Figure 34.1, we see that the addition of the two categories that are unique to $M2$ implies a measure of money supply that is only slightly larger than the narrower $M1$ money supply. The nearby Consider This story explains why credit cards payments are not money.

CONSIDER THIS . . .

Are Credit Cards Money?

You may wonder why we have ignored credit cards such as Visa and Master-Card in our discussion of how the money supply is defined. After all, credit cards are a convenient way to buy things and account for about 27 percent of the dollar value of all transactions in the United States. The answer is that a credit card is not money. Rather, it is a convenient means of obtaining a short-term loan from the financial institution that issued the card.

What happens when you purchase an item with a credit card? The bank that issued the card will reimburse the seller by making a money payment and charging the establishment a transaction fee. Then, later, you will reimburse the bank for its loan to you by also making a money payment. Rather than reduce your cash or checking account balance with each purchase, you bunch your payments once a month (i.e., when your credit card bill comes due). You may have to pay an annual

Adam Crowley/Getty Images

fee for the services provided, and if you pay the bank in installments, you will pay a sizable interest charge on the loan. Credit cards are merely a means of deferring or postponing payment for a short period. Your checking account balance that you use to pay your credit card bill *is* money; the credit card is *not* money.*

Although credit cards are not money, they allow individuals and businesses to "economize" in the use of money. Credit cards enable people to hold less currency in their billfolds and, prior to payment due dates, fewer checkable deposits in their bank accounts. Credit cards also help people coordinate the timing of their expenditures with their receipt of income.

---

*A bank debit card, however, is very similar to a check in your checkbook. Unlike a purchase with a credit card, a purchase with a debit card creates a direct "debit" (a subtraction) from your checking account balance. That checking account balance is money—it is part of $M1$.

▸ Money serves as a medium of exchange, a unit of account, and a store of value.

▸ The *M1* definition of money includes currency held by the public, checkable deposits in commercial banks, and other liquid deposits, including savings deposits and checkable deposits held at thrifts.

▸ Thrift institutions, as well as commercial banks, offer accounts on which checks can be written.

▸ The *M2* definition of money includes *M1* plus small-denominated (less than $100,000) time deposits and money market mutual fund balances held by individuals.

What "Backs" the Money Supply?

The money supply in the United States essentially is "backed" (guaranteed) by the government's ability to keep the value of money relatively stable. Nothing more!

>> **LO34.3** Describe what "backs" the money supply.

Money as Debt

The major components of the money supply—paper money and checkable deposits—are debts, or promises to pay. In the United States, paper money is the circulating debt of the Federal Reserve Banks. Checkable deposits are the debts of commercial banks and thrift institutions.

Paper currency and checkable deposits have no intrinsic value. A $5 bill is just an inscribed piece of paper. A checkable deposit is merely a bookkeeping entry. And coins, we know, have less intrinsic value than their face value. Nor will government redeem the paper money you hold for anything tangible, such as gold.

To many people, it seems shady that the government does not back its currency with anything tangible. But the decision not to back the currency with anything tangible was made for a very good reason. If the government backed the currency with something tangible like gold, then the money supply would vary with the availability of gold. By not backing the currency, the government grants itself the freedom to provide as much or as little money as may be needed to best suit the country's economic needs. By choosing not to back the currency, the government gives itself the ability to freely "manage" the nation's money supply. Its monetary authorities are free to provide whatever amount of money is needed to promote full employment, price-level stability, and economic growth.

Value of Money

So why are currency and checkable deposits money, whereas, say, Monopoly (the game) money is not? What gives a $20 bill or a $100 check its value? The answer to these questions has three parts.

Acceptability Currency and checkable deposits are money because people accept them as money. By virtue of long-standing business practice, currency and checkable deposits perform the most essential function of money: They are acceptable as a medium of exchange. We accept paper money and checkable deposits because we are confident that they can be exchanged for goods, services, and resources.

Legal Tender Our confidence in the acceptability of paper money is strengthened because the government has designated currency as **legal tender.** Specifically, each bill contains the statement, "This note is legal tender for all debts, public and private." In other words, paper money is a valid and legal means of paying any debt that was contracted in dollars.

Note, however, that payments for goods and services are not payments of debts. Thus, private firms are under no legal obligation to accept cash in exchange for goods and services. It is perfectly legal for them to require customers to pay for products in noncash forms, such as cashier's checks or money orders. People selling goods and services can also legally refuse to take small coins or large bills.

The general acceptance of paper currency by society is more important than the government's decree that it serve as legal tender. This can be understood by the fact that checks function as money despite never having been designated as legal tender by the government. That being said, the Federal Deposit Insurance Corporation (FDIC) and the National Credit Union Administration (NCUA) enhance our willingness to use checks as a medium of exchange by insuring checking account deposits held at, respectively, commercial banks and thrifts.

Relative Scarcity The value of money, like the economic value of anything else, depends on its supply and demand. Money derives its value from its scarcity relative to its *utility* (its want-satisfying

legal tender Any form of *currency* that by law must be accepted by creditors (lenders) for the settlement of a financial debt; a nation's official currency is legal tender within its own borders.

power). The utility of money lies in its capacity to be exchanged for goods and services, now or in the future. The economy's demand for money thus depends on the total dollar volume of transactions in any period plus the amount of money that individuals and businesses want to hold for future transactions. With a reasonably constant demand for money, the supply of money provided by the monetary authorities will determine the domestic value or "purchasing power" of the monetary unit (dollar, yen, euro, and so forth).

Money and Prices

The purchasing power of money is the amount of goods and services a unit of money will buy.

The Purchasing Power of the Dollar The amount a dollar will buy varies inversely with the price level. That is, a reciprocal relationship exists between the general price level and the dollar's purchasing power. When the consumer price index or "cost-of-living" index goes up, the value of the dollar goes down, and vice versa. Higher prices decrease the dollar's value because people need more dollars to buy a particular amount of goods, services, or resources. For example, if the price level doubles, the value of the dollar declines by one-half, or 50 percent.

Conversely, lower prices increase the dollar's purchasing power because people need fewer dollars to obtain a specific quantity of goods and services. If the price level falls by, say, 50 percent, then the purchasing power of the dollar doubles.

In equation form, the relationship looks like this:

$$\$V = 1/P$$

To find the value of the dollar, $\$V$, divide 1 by the price level P expressed as an index number (in hundredths). If the price level is 1, then the value of the dollar is 1. If the price level rises to, say, 1.20, $\$V$ falls to $1/1.2 = 0.833$; thus, a 20 percent increase in the price level reduces the value of the dollar by 16.67 percent. Check your understanding of this reciprocal relationship by determining the value of $\$V$ and its percentage rise when P falls by 20 percent, from 1 to 0.80.

Inflation and Acceptability In Chapter 29, we noted situations in which a nation's currency becomes worthless and unacceptable in exchange. These instances of runaway inflation, or *hyperinflation*, happen when a government issues so many pieces of paper currency that the purchasing power of each of those units of money becomes almost totally undermined. The infamous post-World War I hyperinflation in Germany is an example. In December 1919, there were about 50 billion marks in circulation. Four years later, there were 496,585,345,900 billion marks in circulation! The result? The German mark in 1923 was worth an infinitesimal fraction of its 1919 value.

Runaway inflation may significantly depreciate the value of money between the time it is received and the time it is spent. Rapid declines in the value of a currency may cause it to cease being used as a medium of exchange. Businesses and households may refuse to accept paper money in exchange because they do not want to bear the loss in its value that will occur while it is in their possession. (All this despite the fact that the government says that paper currency is legal tender!) Without an acceptable domestic medium of exchange, the economy may simply revert to barter. Alternatively, more stable currencies such as the U.S. dollar or European euro may come into widespread use. At the extreme, a country may adopt a foreign currency as its own official currency as a way to end its economy's dependence on a hyperinflating local currency.

Similarly, people will use money as a store of value only as long as there is no sizable deterioration in the value of that money because of inflation. An economy can effectively employ money as a unit of account only when its purchasing power is relatively stable. A monetary "yardstick" that has shrunk to some length shorter than a yard (in terms of purchasing power) does not permit buyers and sellers to establish the terms of trade clearly. When the value of money is declining rapidly, sellers do not know what to charge and buyers do not know what to pay.

Stabilizing Money's Purchasing Power

Rapidly rising price levels (rapid inflation)—and the consequent erosion of money's purchasing power—typically result from imprudent economic policies, especially rapid increases in the money supply.

Because money's purchasing power varies inversely with the price level, stabilizing the purchasing power of a nation's money requires stabilizing the nation's price level. Such price-level stability (2 to 3 percent annual inflation) can be achieved through intelligent management of the nation's money supply and interest rates (*monetary policy*). It also requires appropriate *fiscal policy* that supports the efforts of the nation's monetary authorities to hold down inflation.

In the United States, a combination of legislation, government policy, and social practice tends to inhibit imprudent expansions of the money supply. The critical role of U.S. monetary authorities in maintaining the dollar's purchasing power is the subject of Chapter 36. For now, simply note that the monetary authorities make available a particular quantity of money, such as *M*2 in Figure 34.1, and can change that amount through their policy tools.

QUICK REVIEW

34.2

▶ In the United States, money consists of the debts of government, commercial banks, and thrift institutions.

▶ These debts efficiently perform the functions of money as long as their value, or purchasing power, is relatively stable.

▶ The value of money is rooted not in specified quantities of precious metals such as gold, but in the amounts of goods, services, and resources that money will purchase.

▶ The value of the dollar (its domestic purchasing power) is inversely related to the price level.

▶ Stabilizing the purchasing power of the monetary unit calls for (a) effective control over the supply of money by the monetary authorities and (b) the application of appropriate fiscal policies by the president and congress.

The Federal Reserve and the Banking System

In the United States, the "monetary authorities" are the members of the Board of Governors of the **Federal Reserve System** (the "Fed"). As Figure 34.2 shows, the Board directs the activities of the 12 Federal Reserve Banks, which in turn control the lending activity of the nation's banks and thrift institutions. The Fed's major goal is to control the money supply. Because checkable deposits in banks and thrifts are such a large part of the money supply, its duties also involve ensuring the stability of the banking system, including not only commercial banks but also savings and loans associations, mutual savings banks, and credit unions.

Historical Background

Early in the twentieth century, Congress decided that centralization and public control were essential for an efficient banking system. Decentralized, unregulated banking had fostered the inconvenience and confusion of numerous private bank notes being used as currency. It also had

>> **LO34.4** Discuss the structure of the Federal Reserve.

Federal Reserve System
The U.S. central bank, consisting of the *Board of Governors* of the Federal Reserve and the 12 *Federal Reserve Banks*, which controls the lending activity of the nation's banks and thrifts and thus the *money supply*; commonly referred to as the "Fed."

FIGURE 34.2
Framework of the Federal Reserve System and its relationship to the public.

The Board of Governors makes the basic policy decisions that provide monetary control of the U.S. money and banking systems. The 12 Federal Reserve Banks implement these decisions. Both the Board of Governors and the 12 Federal Reserve Banks are aided by the Federal Open Market Committee (FOMC).

resulted in occasional episodes of monetary mismanagement such that the money supply was inappropriate to the economy's needs. Sometimes "too much" money precipitated rapid inflation; other times "too little money" stunted the economy's growth by hindering the production and exchange of goods and services.

Furthermore, acute problems in the banking system occasionally erupted when banks either closed down or insisted on immediate repayment of loans to prevent their own failure. At such times, a banking crisis could emerge, with individuals and businesses that had lost confidence in their banks attempting to withdraw all of their money simultaneously—thereby further weakening the banks.

An unusually acute banking crisis in 1907 motivated Congress to create a National Monetary Commission to study the economy's monetary and banking problems and to propose a course of action for Congress. The result was the Federal Reserve Act of 1913.

Let's examine the various parts of the Federal Reserve System and their relationship to one another.

Board of Governors

Board of Governors The seven-member group that supervises and controls the money and banking system of the United States; the Board of Governors of the *Federal Reserve System;* the Federal Reserve Board.

The central authority of the U.S. money and banking system is the **Board of Governors** of the Federal Reserve System. The U.S. president, with the confirmation of the Senate, appoints the seven Board members. Terms are 14 years and staggered so that one member is replaced every 2 years. In addition, new members are appointed when resignations occur. The president selects the chairperson and vice chairperson of the Board from among the members. Those officers serve 4-year terms and can be reappointed to new 4-year terms by the president. The long-term appointments provide the Board with continuity, experienced membership, and independence from political pressures that could result in inflation.

The 12 Federal Reserve Banks

Federal Reserve Banks The 12 banks chartered by the U.S. government that collectively act as the *central bank* of the United States. They set monetary policy and regulate the private banking system under the direction of the *Board of Governors* and the *Federal Open Market Committee.* Each of the 12 is a *quasi-public bank* and acts as a *banker's bank* in its designated geographic region.

The 12 **Federal Reserve Banks,** which blend private and public control, collectively serve as the U.S. "central bank." They also serve as "bankers' banks."

Central Bank Most nations have a single central bank—for example, the United Kingdom's Bank of England or Japan's Bank of Japan. The U.S. central bank consists of 12 banks whose policies are coordinated by the Fed's Board of Governors. The 12 Federal Reserve Banks accommodate the geographic size and economic diversity of the United States as well as the large number of commercial banks and thrifts that are spread across the country.

Figure 34.3 shows the location of the 12 Federal Reserve Banks and the district that each serves. These banks implement the Board of Governors' basic policies.

FIGURE 34.3
The 12 Federal Reserve Districts.

The Federal Reserve System divides the United States into 12 districts, each having one central bank and, in some instances, one or more branches of the central bank.

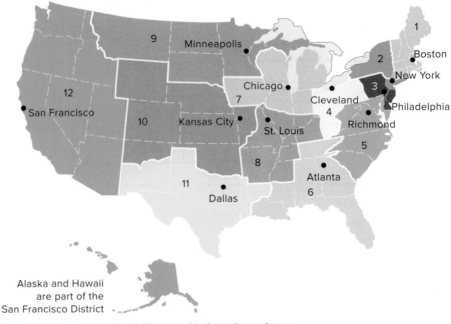

Alaska and Hawaii are part of the San Francisco District

Source: Federal Reserve Bulletin, Board of Governors of the Federal Reserve System.

Quasi-Public Banks The 12 Federal Reserve Banks are quasi-public banks that blend private ownership and public control. Each Federal Reserve Bank is owned by the private commercial banks in its district. (Federally chartered banks are required to purchase shares of stock in the Federal Reserve Bank in their district.) But the Board of Governors, a government body, sets the basic policies that the Federal Reserve Banks pursue.

Despite their private ownership, the Federal Reserve Banks are in practice public institutions. Unlike private firms, they are not motivated by profit. The policies they follow are designed by the Board of Governors to promote the well-being of the economy as a whole. Thus, the Fed's activities are frequently at odds with the profit motive. Also, the Federal Reserve Banks do not compete with commercial banks. In general, they do not deal with the public. Rather, they interact with the government on the one hand and commercial banks and thrifts on the other.

Bankers' Banks The Federal Reserve Banks are "bankers' banks" that perform essentially the same functions for banks and thrifts as those institutions perform for the public. Just as banks and thrifts accept deposits from, and make loans to, the public, so the central banks accept the deposits of, and make loans to, banks and thrifts. The funds that commercial banks and thrifts keep on deposit with the Fed are known as **reserve balances,** which is why the Fed's full name—the Federal Reserve Bank—contains the word "reserve."

> **reserve balances** Funds that *commercial banks* and *thrift institutions* hold on deposit at the *central bank.*

In noncrisis situations, the vast majority of reserve balances are the result of ongoing commercial bank and thrift operations, including taking deposits from individuals and businesses and receiving funds as borrowers repay loans. On those normal, noncrisis days, less than $150 million of reserve balances are the result of banks or thrifts borrowing from the Fed. But during financial crises, when the Fed acts as the "lender of last resort" to the banking system, the Federal Reserve Banks can lend out as much money as is needed to ensure that commercial banks and thrifts can meet their cash payment obligations.

Those emergency loans come in the form of reserve balances that the Fed deposits into the Federal reserve accounts of the banks and thrifts receiving emergency loans. During the initial lockdown phase of the COVID-19 pandemic in the spring of 2020, for example, the Fed lent $129 billion of reserve balances to banks and thrifts in just three weeks in order to make sure that the panicky mood that was evident on both Wall Street and Main Street did not precipitate a nationwide banking crisis.

The Federal Reserve Banks also have a third function, which banks and thrifts do not perform: They issue currency. In particular, Congress has authorized the Federal Reserve Banks to create and put into circulation Federal Reserve Notes, which constitute the U.S. economy's paper money supply.

FOMC

The **Federal Open Market Committee (FOMC)** aids the Board of Governors in conducting monetary policy. The FOMC is made up of 12 individuals:

- The seven members of the Board of Governors.
- The president of the New York Federal Reserve Bank.
- Four presidents selected from the remaining Federal Reserve Banks, each serving on a one-year rotating basis.

> **Federal Open Market Committee (FOMC)** The 12-member group within the *Federal Reserve System* that decides U.S. *monetary policy* and how it is executed through *open-market operations* (in which the Fed buys and sells U.S. government securities to adjust the *money supply*).

The FOMC meets regularly to direct the purchase and sale of government securities (bills, notes, bonds) in the "open market" in which such securities are bought and sold daily. The FOMC also makes decisions about the extent to which the Fed borrows and lends government securities in the open market. These *open-market operations* that help to control the nation's money supply and interest rates are conducted mostly by Federal Reserve Bank of New York, which is located in the heart of New York City's financial district, just a couple of blocks from Wall Street.

Commercial Banks and Thrifts

There are about 4,300 commercial banks in the United States. All of these banks are private corporations. They are, however, sometimes mistaken for being government entities because each of these banks can be categorized as being either a "state" bank, or as a "national" or "federal" bank.

THE WORLD'S 12 LARGEST COMMERCIAL BANKS, 2021

The world's 12 largest private sector banks are head-quartered in just five countries: China, France, Japan, the United Kingdom, and the United States.

Assets (trillions of U.S. dollars)

- ICBC (China)
- China Construction Bank (China)
- Agricultural Bank of China (China)
- Bank of China (China)
- Mitsubishi UFJ (Japan)
- HSBC (U.K.)
- BNP Paribas (France)
- JPMorgan Chase (U.S.)
- Bank of America (U.S.)
- Sumitomo Mitsui (Japan)
- Citigroup (U.S.)
- Wells Fargo (U.S.)

Source: "The World's Largest Public Companies 2021," Forbes.

Those terms are correct, but refer to whether a bank has a state or a federal charter, not whether it is owned or controlled by a state government or the federal government.

- Roughly three-fourths of the 4,300 commercial banks are state banks. These private banks are chartered (authorized) by individual states to operate within their respective borders.

- The remaining one-fourth of commercial banks are chartered by the federal government to operate nationally; these private banks are referred to as national, or federal, banks.

Some of the national banks are very large, ranking among the world's largest financial institutions (see Global Perspective 34.1).

The 7,000 or so thrift institutions—most of which are credit unions—are regulated by agencies separate and apart from the Board of Governors and the Federal Reserve Banks. The financial operations of credit unions are, for example, closely monitored by the National Credit Union Administration (NCUA).

That being said, thrift institutions are just as subject to monetary control by the Federal Reserve System as commercial banks, as is illustrated in Figure 34.2. Decisions concerning monetary policy affect thrifts as well as commercial banks.

Fed Functions, Responsibilities, and Independence

>> LO34.5 Identify the functions and responsibilities of the Federal Reserve.

The Fed performs several functions:

- ***Issuing currency*** The Federal Reserve Banks issue Federal Reserve Notes, the paper currency used in the United States. (The Federal Reserve Bank that issued a particular bill is identified in black in the upper left of new bills. "A1," for example, identifies the Boston bank, "B2" the New York bank, and so on.)

- ***Holding reserves and setting reserve requirements*** The Federal Reserve System is a banker's bank that allows commercial banks and thrifts to deposit currency with the Fed. Those deposits are known as *reserve balances* and the Fed has the legal power to set *reserve requirements,* which are percentages of individual checking account balances that banks and thrifts may be required to maintain as *bank reserves* to facilitate withdrawals by customers.[3]

---

[3]Please note that the Fed eliminated reserve requirements in 2020 and has stated that it has no intention of bringing them back. Whereas in previous decades the Fed viewed reserve requirements as a sensible way to help ensure the financial stability of the banking system, its current policy is to rely instead on bank capital requirements, which provide for financial stability by requiring bank and thrift shareholders to provide large enough reserves of financial capital to carry those institutions through all but the most extreme financial crises.

- *Lending to financial institutions and serving as an emergency lender of last resort* The Federal Reserve makes routine short-term loans to banks and thrifts and charges them an interest rate called the *discount rate*. During financial emergencies, the Fed also serves as the lender of last resort for not only banks and thrifts but also other sorts of financial firms (like insurance companies and money market funds) whose stability is considered essential to the health of the U.S. economy.

- *Providing for check collection* The Fed provides the banking system with a means for collecting on checks. If Suzannah writes a check on her Miami bank to Jobohán, who deposits it in his Dallas bank, how does the Dallas bank collect the money represented by the check drawn against the Miami bank? The Fed solves the problem ("clears checks") by adjusting the reserves (deposits) that the two banks hold at the Fed. In this example, the Miami bank's reserves are decreased by the amount of Suzannah's check while the Dallas bank's reserves are increased by the amount of Suzannah's check. The Dallas bank can then transfer that money into Jobohán's account.

- *Acting as the federal government's fiscal agent* The Fed acts as the fiscal agent (provider of financial services) for the federal government, which collects huge sums through taxation, spends equally large amounts on goods and services, and both sells and redeems its own bonds. To carry out those activities, the federal government employs the Federal Reserve.

- *Supervising banks* The Fed supervises the operations of banks. It periodically assesses bank profitability, ensures that banks perform according to the regulations, and seeks to uncover questionable practices or fraud.

- *Controlling the money supply* The Fed's most famous responsibility is to manage the money supply (and thus interest rates) according to the economy's needs. The Fed's goal is to make an amount of money available that is consistent with (1) full employment in the labor markets and (2) a stable price level. While most of the Fed's other functions are routine, managing the nation's money supply requires policy decisions that must be made when and if needed, and tailored as necessary to meet the circumstances, which sometimes include major financial and economic crises, such as dealing with the COVID-19 pandemic. (We will discuss how the Fed handles decisions about the money supply and interest rates in detail in Chapter 35.)

Federal Reserve Independence

Congress purposely established the Federal Reserve System as an independent agency of the federal government. The objective was to protect the Fed from political pressures so that it could effectively control the money supply and maintain price stability. Political pressures on Congress and the executive branch may at times result in inflationary fiscal policies, including tax cuts and special-interest spending. If Congress and the executive branch also controlled the nation's monetary policy, citizens and lobbying groups would undoubtedly pressure elected officials to keep interest rates low even though at times high interest rates are necessary to reduce aggregate demand and thus control inflation. An independent monetary authority (the Fed) can take actions to increase interest rates when higher rates are needed to stem inflation. Studies show that countries that have independent central banks like the Fed have lower rates of inflation, on average, than countries that have little or no central bank independence.

▶ The U.S. banking system consists of (a) the Board of Governors of the Federal Reserve System, (b) the 12 Federal Reserve Banks, and (c) some 4,300 commercial banks and 7,000 thrift institutions (mainly credit unions).

▶ The 12 Federal Reserve Banks are simultaneously (a) central banks, (b) quasi-public banks, and (c) bankers' banks.

▶ The major functions of the Fed are to (a) issue Federal Reserve Notes, (b) set reserve requirements, (c) lend money to financial institutions and serve as the lender of last resort in national financial emergencies, (d) provide for the rapid collection of checks, (e) act as the fiscal agent for the federal government, (f) supervise the operations of the banks, and (g) regulate the supply of money in the best interests of the economy.

QUICK REVIEW
34.3

Fractional Reserve Banking and the Money Supply

>> **LO34.6** Explain the fractional reserve system used by U.S. banks and why the Fed might wish to influence their creation of checkable-deposit money.

As noted earlier, *M*1 and *M*2 include both currency (coins and Federal Reserve Notes) as well as checkable deposits. As mentioned earlier, the U.S. Mint produces the coins and the U.S. Bureau of Engraving and Printing creates the Federal Reserve Notes.

But who creates the checkable deposits that are also part of *M*1 and *M*2? Surprisingly, it is loan officers!

Although that may sound like something a congressional committee should investigate, the monetary authorities are well aware that banks and thrifts create checkable deposits. In fact, the Federal Reserve relies *entirely* on banks and thrifts to create this vital component of the nation's money supply.

The Fractional Reserve Banking System

fractional reserve banking system A system in which *commercial banks* and *thrift institutions* hold less than 100 percent of their checkable-deposit liabilities as reserves of *currency* held in bank vaults or as deposits at the *central bank*.

The ability of loan officers at banks and thrifts to create checkable-deposit money is the result of the United States having a **fractional reserve banking system** in which only a portion (fraction) of checkable deposits are backed by reserves of currency either (1) stored on-site in the vaults of commercial bank and thrifts or (2) kept as *reserve balances* on deposit at the central bank. Our goal is to explain this system, which is used by nearly every country in the world, and show how commercial banks and thrifts create checkable deposits by issuing loans.

Illustrating the Idea: The Goldsmiths Here is the history behind the idea of the fractional reserve system.

When early traders began to use gold in making transactions, they soon realized that it was both unsafe and inconvenient to carry gold and to have it weighed and assayed (judged for purity) every time they negotiated a transaction. So by the sixteenth century they had begun to deposit their gold with goldsmiths, who would store it in vaults for a fee. On receiving a gold deposit, the goldsmith would issue a receipt to the depositor. Soon people were paying for goods with goldsmiths' receipts, which served as one of the first types of paper money.

At this point the goldsmiths—embryonic bankers—used a 100 percent reserve system; they backed their circulating paper money receipts fully with the gold that they held "in reserve" in their vaults. But because of the public's acceptance of the goldsmiths' receipts as paper money, the goldsmiths soon realized that owners rarely redeemed the gold they had in storage. In fact, the goldsmiths observed that the amount of gold being deposited with them in any week or month was likely to exceed the amount that was being withdrawn.

Then some clever goldsmith hit on the idea that their circulating paper money receipts could be issued in excess of the amount of gold held. Goldsmiths would put these receipts, which were redeemable in gold, into circulation by making interest-earning loans to merchants, manufacturers, and even governments. A borrower might, for instance, borrow $10,000 worth of gold receipts today with the promise to repay $10,500 worth of gold receipts in one year (a 5 percent interest rate). Borrowers were willing to accept loans in the form of gold receipts because the receipts were accepted as a medium of exchange in the marketplace.

This was the beginning of the fractional reserve system of banking, in which reserves in bank vaults are a fraction of the total money supply. If, for example, the goldsmith issued $1 million in receipts for actual gold in storage and another $1 million in receipts as loans, then the total value of paper money in circulation would be $2 million—twice the value of the gold. Gold reserves would be a fraction (one-half) of outstanding paper money.

Significant Characteristics of Fractional Reserve Banking The goldsmith story highlights two significant characteristics of fractional reserve banking. First, banks can create money through lending. In fact, goldsmiths created money when they made loans that were not fully backed by gold reserves. The quantity of such money goldsmiths could create depended on the amount of reserves they deemed prudent to have available. The smaller the amount of reserves thought necessary, the larger the amount of paper money the goldsmiths could create. Today, gold is no longer used as bank reserves. Instead, currency itself serves as bank reserves so that the creation of checkable-deposit money by banks (via their lending) is limited by the amount of currency reserves (either cash in vaults or *reserve balances* at the Fed) that the banks feel prudent, or are required by law, to keep. As we will see in the next chapter, one way that the Fed can influence bank lending—and, thus, the total volume of checkable-deposit money in the economy—is by changing the total amount of currency reserves in the banking system through what are referred to as "open-market" purchases and sales of government bonds. The more reserves banks have, the more likely they are to lend, all other things equal.

A second reality is that banks operating on the basis of fractional reserves are vulnerable to "panics" or "runs." A goldsmith who issued paper money equal to twice the value of his gold reserves would be unable to convert all that paper money into gold in the event that all the holders of that money appeared at his door at the same time demanding their gold. In fact, many European and U.S. banks were once ruined by this unfortunate circumstance. However, a bank panic is highly unlikely if the banker's reserve and lending policies are prudent. Indeed, one reason why banking systems are highly regulated industries is to prevent runs on banks.

This is also why the United States has the system of deposit insurance that we mentioned earlier. By guaranteeing deposits, deposit insurance helps to prevent the sort of bank runs that used to happen so often before deposit insurance was available. In those situations, rumors would spread that a bank was about to go bankrupt and that it only had a small amount of reserves left in its vaults. Bank runs are called "bank runs" because depositors would literally run to the bank trying to be one of the lucky few to withdraw their money while the bank had any reserves left. The rumors were usually totally unfounded. But, unfortunately, a bank could still go bankrupt even if it began the day with its normal amount of reserves. With so many customers withdrawing money simultaneously, it would run out of reserves and be forced to default on its obligations to its remaining depositors. By guaranteeing depositors that they will always get their money back, deposit insurance removes the incentive to try to withdraw one's deposit before anyone else can. It thus forestalls most bank runs.

Finally, it should be noted that while the making of new loans creates checkable-deposit money, the repayment of old loans destroys checkable-deposit money. Thus, *the overall volume of checkable-deposit money circulating in the economy depends upon the total outstanding volume of loans that have been extended by banks and thrifts at any point in time.*

Fed Influence over Lending and the Money Supply

Because bank and thrift loan officers create money through lending, the Federal Reserve is extremely attentive to the incentives and restrictions that it places on banks and thrifts with regard to their lending decisions. By modulating those incentives and restrictions, the Fed has at its disposal a powerful mechanism for altering the money supply and, as a result, influencing interest rates and economic activity.

In the next chapter, we will provide a detailed description of the various tools that the Fed uses to influence bank lending behavior. For now, just understand that from the perspective of individuals and businesses, Fed policy changes that prompt banks to increase their lending will result in easier access to credit, both in terms of the sheer volume of loans made available to the public as well as those loans being made available at lower interest rates. Both can spur spending in the economy, in particular greater investment spending on the part of businesses and increased consumption spending on the part of households and consumers.

The opposite is also true. If the Fed institutes policy changes that prompt banks to decrease their lending, individuals and firms will have a harder time accessing credit, both in terms of a lesser volume of loans made available to them and in terms of those loans charging higher interest rates. Both will tend to reduce spending in the economy, with firms borrowing and spending less on investment goods and individuals and households spending less on housing, automobiles, and other forms of consumption for which borrowing is common.

Thus, any decision by the Fed that influences bank lending will tend to change: (1) the total amount of checkable-deposit money in the economy; (2) the overall money supply; (3) interest rates; and (4) overall economic activity. It is for that reason that the Fed was established by congress as the primary supervisor of the banking system in addition to being the primary supervisor of the overall U.S. monetary system. The Fed would be far less effective at managing the money supply, interest rates, and economic activity if it were not also the nation's central bank and thus in a position to directly influence bank and thrift lending.

► Under the fractional reserve banking system, only a portion (fraction) of checkable deposits are backed by currency, which makes the system vulnerable to banking panics.

► Loan officers create checkable-deposit money any time they extend a loan.

► The overall volume of checkable-deposit money circulating in the economy depends upon the total outstanding volume of loans.

► The Fed can alter the money supply and thereby affect interest rates and economic activity by altering the incentives and restrictions that it places on bank lending and bank money creation.

Interest Rates

>> **LO34.7** Explain how the equilibrium interest rate is determined and why interest rates and bond prices vary inversely.

interest The payment made for the use of (borrowed) *money.*

The Fed influences the economy primarily through its ability to change the money supply ($M1$ and $M2$) and therefore affect interest rates and economic activity. **Interest** is the price paid for the use of money. It is the price that borrowers must pay lenders for transferring purchasing power to the future, the price that borrowers must pay lenders to compensate them for not being able to use their money until it is repaid, and the price that borrowers must pay to use $1 for 1 year. Although there are many different interest rates, we will simply speak of *the* interest rate unless we state otherwise.

Let's see how the interest rate is determined. Because it is a price, we again turn to demand-and-supply analysis for the answer.

The Demand for Money

The public wants to hold some of its wealth as money for two main reasons:

- To facilitate purchases (transactions).
- To hold as an asset (store of value).

These two sources of money demand are named, respectively, the transactions demand for money and the asset demand for money. Let's discuss them in sequence.

transactions demand for money The amount of money people want to hold for use as a *medium of exchange* (to make payments); varies directly with *nominal GDP.*

Transactions Demand, D_t The first reason people hold money is because it is convenient for purchasing goods and services. Households usually are paid once a week, every 2 weeks, or monthly, but their expenditures are less predictable and typically more frequent. Thus households must have enough money on hand to buy groceries and pay mortgage and utility bills. Businesses, too, need to have money available to pay for labor, materials, and other inputs. The demand for money as a medium of exchange is called the **transactions demand for money.**

Nominal GDP is the main determinant of the amount of money demanded for transactions. The larger the total money value of all the goods, services, and resources exchanged in the economy, the larger the amount of money needed to facilitate those transactions. The transactions demand for money varies directly with nominal GDP. We specify *nominal* GDP because households, firms, and financial institutions will want more money for transactions if prices rise or if real output increases. In both instances, a larger dollar volume is needed to accomplish the desired transactions.

In **Figure 34.4a (Key Graph),** we graph the quantity of money demanded for transactions against the interest rate. For simplicity, we assume that the quantity demanded depends exclusively on nominal GDP and is therefore independent of the interest rate. Our simplifying assumption allows us to graph the transactions demand D_t as a vertical line. This demand curve is positioned at $100 billion, on the assumption that nominal GDP is $300 billion and each dollar held for transactions purposes is spent an average of three times per year. Thus the public needs $100 billion (= $300 billion/3) to purchase that amount of nominal GDP.

asset demand for money The amount of *money* people want to hold as a *store of value;* this amount varies inversely with the *interest rate.*

Asset Demand, D_a The second reason for holding money derives from money's function as a store of value. People may hold their wealth either in tangible assets like real estate or in a variety of financial assets, including stocks, bonds, and money. To the extent they want to hold money as an asset, there is an **asset demand for money.**

To understand why people have an asset demand for money, you must compare money with other financial assets, such as bonds. Bonds make regular, substantial interest payments, while

..ıl KEY GRAPH

FIGURE 34.4 **The demand for money, the supply of money, and the equilibrium interest rate in the market for money.**

The total demand for money D_m is determined by horizontally adding the transactions demand for money D_t to the asset demand for money D_a. The transactions demand is vertical because it is assumed to depend on nominal GDP rather than on the interest rate. The asset demand varies inversely with the interest rate because of the opportunity cost involved in holding currency and checkable deposits that pay no interest or very low interest. Combining the money supply (stock) S_m with the total money demand D_m portrays the market for money and determines the equilibrium interest rate i_e.

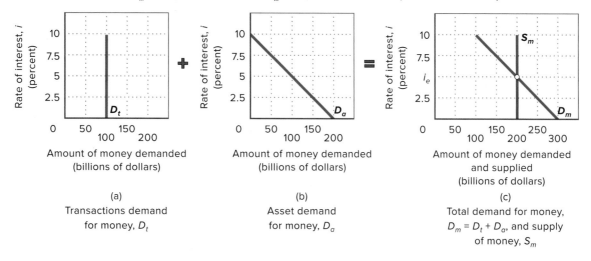

(a)
Transactions demand
for money, D_t

(b)
Asset demand
for money, D_a

(c)
Total demand for money,
$D_m = D_t + D_a$, and supply
of money, S_m

QUICK QUIZ FOR FIGURE 34.4

1. **In this graph, at the interest rate i_e (5 percent):**
   a. the amount of money demanded as an asset is $50 billion.
   b. the amount of money demanded for transactions is $200 billion.
   c. bond prices will decline.
   d. $100 billion is demanded for transactions, $100 billion is demanded as an asset, and the money supply is $200 billion.

2. **In this graph, at an interest rate of 10 percent:**
   a. no money will be demanded as an asset.
   b. total money demanded will be $200 billion.
   c. the Federal Reserve will supply $100 billion of money.
   d. there will be a $100 billion shortage of money.

3. **Curve D_a slopes downward because:**
   a. lower interest rates increase the opportunity cost of holding money.
   b. lower interest rates reduce the opportunity cost of holding money.

c. the asset demand for money varies directly (positively) with the interest rate.
d. the transactions-demand-for-money curve is perfectly vertical.

4. **Suppose the supply of money declines to $100 billion. The equilibrium interest rate would:**
   a. fall, the amount of money demanded for transactions would rise, and the amount of money demanded as an asset would decline.
   b. rise, while the amounts of money demanded both for transactions and as an asset would fall.
   c. fall, while the amounts of money demanded both for transactions and as an asset would increase.
   d. rise, the amount of money demanded for transactions would be unchanged, and the amount of money demanded as an asset would decline.

Answers: 1. d; 2. a; 3. b; 4. d

money earns either zero interest (currency) or extremely low interest (checking account deposits). Thus, from that perspective, bonds are a more attractive financial asset.

But that's not the end of the story. Bonds, stocks, and other financial assets are also riskier than money. Bond prices, for example, sometimes fall, generating *capital losses* for their owners. By contrast, the value of money is quite steady unless inflation is strong. So while money pays zero interest, it holds its value much better than bonds and other financial assets under normal circumstances. This gives people a reason to demand money as an asset.

Another reason that people demand money as an asset is because money can be used to purchase other assets when good "buying opportunities" arise. Money will hold its value when the stock market crashes 20 percent; so anyone holding money can jump in and buy stocks at low, post-crash prices. The only way to "buy the dips" is to have money on hand when the prices of other assets decline.

Knowing these advantages and disadvantages, the public must decide how much of its financial assets to hold as money. Their decision depends primarily on the interest rate. When a household or business holds money, it incurs the opportunity cost of the interest it could have received if it had used that money to purchase bonds. If bonds pay 6 percent interest, for example, then holding $100 as cash or in a noninterest checking account would cost $6 per year of forgone income.

The amount of money demanded as an asset therefore varies inversely with the interest rate (which is the opportunity cost of holding money as an asset). When the interest rate rises, being liquid and avoiding capital losses becomes more costly. So the public reacts by reducing its quantity demanded of money. By contrast, when the interest rate falls, the cost of being liquid and avoiding capital losses declines. The public therefore increases the quantity of financial assets that it wants to hold as money. This inverse relationship just described is shown by D_a in Figure 34.4b.

Also note that when we speak of the "public" here, we mean anyone and everyone outside the Federal Reserve. That includes businesses, the government, and financial institutions, including banks. Thus, the asset demand for money also includes the demand that banks and thrifts have for currency held as reserves against loan losses and withdrawals. The higher the interest rate, the less money banks want to hold as bank reserves, all other things equal.

total demand for money
The sum of the *transactions demand for money* and the *asset demand for money*.

Total Money Demand, D_m   As Figure 34.4 shows, we find the **total demand for money,** D_m, by horizontally adding the asset demand for money to the transactions demand for money. The result is the downward sloping line in Figure 34.4c, which represents the total amount of money the public wants to hold, both for transactions and as an asset, at each possible interest rate.

Recall that the transactions demand for money depends on nominal GDP. A change in nominal GDP will, consequently, shift the total demand for money curve D_m by altering the transactions demand for money. Consider an increase in nominal GDP. That will increase the transactions demand for money, and that extra transactions demand will shift the total money demand curve to the right. In contrast, a decline in nominal GDP shifts the total money demand curve to the left. As an example, suppose nominal GDP increases from $300 billion to $450 billion, and the average dollar held for transactions is still spent three times per year. Then the transactions demand curve will shift from $100 billion (= $300 billion/3) to $150 billion (= $450 billion/3). The total money demand curve will then lie $50 billion farther to the right at each possible interest rate.

The Equilibrium Interest Rate

We can combine the demand for money with the supply of money to determine the equilibrium interest rate. In Figure 34.4c, the vertical line S_m represents the money supply. It is a vertical line because the monetary authorities and financial institutions have provided the economy with some particular stock of money. Here, it is $200 billion.

Just as in a product market or a resource market, the intersection of demand and supply determines the equilibrium price in the market for money. In Figure 34.4, this equilibrium price is the equilibrium interest rate, i_e. At this interest rate, the quantity of money demanded (= $200 billion) equals the quantity of money supplied (= $200 billion).

As you have just seen, changes in the demand for money, the supply of money, or both can change the equilibrium interest rate. We are, however, most interested in changes in the money supply since the Fed can affect the money supply. To that end, please remember this important generalization: *An increase in the money supply will lower the equilibrium interest rate, while a decrease in the money supply will raise the equilibrium interest rate.*

Interest Rates and Bond Prices

Interest rates and bond prices are inversely related. When the interest rate increases, bond prices fall; when the interest rate decreases, bond prices rise. Why?

First understand that bonds are bought and sold in financial markets, with the price of bonds being determined by the interaction of bond demand with bond supply. As an example, suppose

Cryptocurrencies

The Blockchain Technology Behind Bitcoin Allows Private Citizens to Issue Digital "Cryptocurrencies." But Will Central Bank Digital Currencies Eventually Dominate?

In 2008, a secretive computer programmer who used the name Satoshi Nakamoto as an alias began recruiting other programmers to help him develop the "blockchain" technology that now underpins all of the world's digital currencies, including the two most popular, Bitcoin and Ether.

A blockchain is a sequence, or chain, of updates made to an electronic document known as a distributed ledger. Each updated version of the ledger is referred to as a block and the key insight developed by Nakamoto was that a blockchain could be used to keep track of property rights, including the ownership of digital money.

A key problem, historically, with any system of property rights is figuring out with certainty who owns what. Consider a 2-acre plot of land that you find for sale just north of Las Vegas, Nevada. There may be several people who will tell you that they own all or part of that plot—but what if only one of them says it's for sale?

Would you dare to buy the plot from that guy? And would anybody else recognize you as the rightful owner if you paid him his asking price?

The solution, traditionally, to these sorts of "who owns what" problems has been for the government to maintain centralized records of property ownership. Thus, for instance, there are official government records about who owns every square inch of land in and around Las Vegas. Anyone interested in buying property in Las Vegas can consult those records to see who owns what land and thus who has the right to sell any particular piece of land to someone else.

What Satoshi Nakamoto realized was that blockchain technology would allow private individuals, rather than the government, to maintain records about property rights that everybody involved would agree were both accurate and up-to-date. That is accomplished by a "consensus mechanism" by which any update to a blockchain has to be agreed upon by a majority of users. That certification system is almost perfectly secure against tampering because the resources that would be needed to fake a majority vote would cost billions of dollars on a large blockchain like Bitcoin. In addition, any rigged vote would be discovered quickly and almost immediately undone by a subsequent (non-rigged) vote.

One of the things that a blockchain can keep track of is the ownership of digital currencies, such as Bitcoin or Ether, which at their most fundamental levels are just strings of serial numbers recorded on a blockchain. Thus, for example, if you wanted to pay me a bitcoin for a used car, we would record that transaction on the Bitcoin blockchain by updating it so that the ownership of that particular bitcoin passed from your name to my name.

Blockchain-based digital currencies like Bitcoin and Ether are often referred to as **cryptocurrencies** because part of their consensus mechanism involves the use of cryptography, which is the branch of mathematics that studies how to create secure records and communication.

Travis Wolfe/Shutterstock

As of late 2022, there were over 21,000 cryptocurrencies trading in the world with a combined market value of just under $1 trillion. But it was also the case that no cryptocurrency had yet become widely used as a method of payment for goods and services. For that, official government-issued currencies were still overwhelmingly dominant throughout the world.

At the same time, 10 national central banks—including those of China, Nigeria, and Jamaica—had by late 2022 issued their own blockchain-based digital currencies in parallel with their respective traditional (paper) currencies. More than forty other central banks have indicated that they might also follow suit and issue their own CBDC, or central bank digital currency.

Thus, one possibility for the future of digital payments is that private cryptocurrencies like Bitcoin and Ether may never become very popular for transactions, with people instead using central bank digital currencies to pay for most goods and services. If that turns out to be the case, CBDCs could also revolutionize monetary and fiscal policy because when a recession happens, a government or central bank could choose to stimulate the economy by simply gifting additional currency units into the "cryptowallets" of each and every citizen, thereby providing them with more money to save, spend, or invest.

Satoshi Nakamoto's goal was to create digital money that was independent of government control. But it may turn out to be national governments and their central banks that have the last laugh when it comes to popularizing digital money.

---

cryptocurrency A digital money that uses blockchain technology to keep track of the ownership of particular pieces of digital currency.

that a bond with no expiration date pays a fixed $50 annual interest payment and is selling for its face value of $1,000. The "interest yield" on this bond is 5 percent:

$$\frac{\$50}{\$1,000} = 5\% \text{ interest yield}$$

Now suppose that the interest rate in the economy rises to $7\frac{1}{2}$ percent from 5 percent. Newly issued bonds will pay $75 per $1,000 loaned. Older bonds paying only $50 will not be sellable at their $1,000 face value. To compete with the $7\frac{1}{2}$ percent bond, the price of those older bonds must fall to $667 to remain competitive. The $50 fixed annual interest payment will then yield $7\frac{1}{2}$ percent to whoever buys the bond:

$$\frac{\$50}{\$667} = 7\frac{1}{2}\%$$

Next, suppose that the interest rate falls to $2\frac{1}{2}$ percent from the original 5 percent. Newly issued bonds will pay $25 on $1,000 loaned. A bond paying $50 will be highly attractive. Bond buyers will bid up its price to $2,000, where the yield will equal $2\frac{1}{2}$ percent:

$$\frac{\$50}{\$2,000} = 2\frac{1}{2}\%$$

These three examples demonstrate that bond prices fall when the interest rate rises and rise when the interest rate falls. *There is an inverse relationship between the interest rate and bond prices.*

If you are a visual learner, there is a simple image that captures this inverse relationship. Imagine two friends at a park riding a seesaw. At one end is Mr. Bond, and at the other is his friend, Mr. Rate. When Mr. Bond goes up, Mr. Rate goes down, and vice versa.

Another way of understanding why bond prices and interest rates move in opposite directions is to look back at the three examples above and notice that the annual payment is always fixed at $50. So the more you pay for the right to receive that $50 payment, the lower your rate of return (yield). Here are a few other examples to drive that point home.

- Pay $100 for the bond, and your rate of return is 50 percent ($= \$50/\$100 \times 100$)
- Pay $500 for the bond, and your rate of return is 10 percent ($= \$50/\$500 \times 100$)
- Pay $5,000 for the bond, and your rate of return is 1 percent ($= \$50/\$5000 \times 100$)

The more you pay today for a fixed future amount, the lower your percentage return. Test yourself by calculating what the yield would be on this bond at a price of $900 and at a price of $1,250. Verify that the higher price generates a lower yield.

▶ The total demand for money is the sum of the transactions demand for money and the asset demand for money.

▶ The equilibrium interest rate is determined where total money demand intersects money supply.

▶ Interest rates and bond prices are inversely related.

Summary

LO34.1 Explain the functions of money.
Money is anything that serves simultaneously as (*a*) a medium of exchange, (*b*) a unit of monetary account, and (*c*) a store of value.

LO34.2 Describe the components of the U.S. money supply.
There are two major definitions of the money supply, *M*1 and *M*2.

*M*1 consists of currency, checkable deposits at banks, and other liquid deposits, such as savings deposits at banks and checkable deposits held at thrifts.

*M*2 consists of *M*1 *plus* small-denominated (less than $100,000) time deposits and money market mutual fund balances held by individuals.

LO34.3 Describe what "backs" the money supply.
The money supply in the United States is "backed" (guaranteed) by the government's ability to keep the value of money relatively stable, which in turn depends largely on the government's effectiveness in managing the money supply.

LO34.4 Discuss the structure of the Federal Reserve
The U.S. banking system consists of (*a*) the Board of Governors of the Federal Reserve System, (*b*) the 12 Federal Reserve Banks, and (*c*) some 4,600 commercial banks and 7,000 thrift institutions (mainly credit unions). The Board of Governors is the basic policy-making body for the entire banking system. The directives of the Board and the Federal Open Market Committee (FOMC) are

implemented through the 12 Federal Reserve Banks, which are simultaneously (*a*) central banks, (*b*) quasi-public banks, and (*c*) bankers' banks.

LO34.5 Identify the functions and responsibilities of the Federal Reserve.

The major functions of the Fed are to (*a*) issue Federal Reserve Notes, (*b*) hold reserves deposited by banks and thrifts (and set reserve requirements, if any), (*c*) lend money to financial institutions and serve as the lender of last resort in national financial emergencies, (*d*) provide for the rapid collection of checks, (*e*) act as the fiscal agent for the federal government, (*f*) supervise the operations of the banks, and (*g*) regulate the supply of money in the economy's best interests.

The Fed is essentially an independent institution, controlled neither by the president nor by Congress. This independence shields the Fed from political pressure and allows it to raise and lower interest rates (via changes in the money supply) as needed to promote full employment, price stability, and economic growth.

LO34.6 Explain the fractional reserve system used by U.S. banks and why the Fed might wish to influence their creation of checkable-deposit money.

Under a fractional reserve banking system, only a portion (fraction) of checkable deposits are backed by currency. That fractional backing implies that a U.S. banks are vulnerable to bank panics. To mitigate that risk, the U.S. banking system employs deposit insurance. The Fed also stands ready to make emergency loans to banks experiencing bank runs.

Under a fractional reserve system, banks and thrifts create checkable-deposit money any time they extend a loan. Contrariwise, checkable-deposit money is destroyed (ceases to exist) whenever a bank or thrift loan is repaid.

The Fed can alter the money supply and affect interest rates and economic activity by altering the incentives and restrictions that it places on bank lending and bank money creation. Any decision by the Fed that influences bank lending will tend to change: the total amount of checkable-deposit money, the overall money supply, the total volume of lending, interest rates, and overall economic activity.

LO34.7 Explain how the equilibrium interest rate is determined and why interest rates and bond prices vary inversely.

The total demand for money consists of the transactions demand for money plus the asset demand for money. The amount of money demanded for transactions varies directly with nominal GDP; the amount of money demanded as an asset varies inversely with the interest rate. The market for money combines the total demand for money (= transaction demand + asset demand) with money supply to determine equilibrium interest rates.

The Fed can alter the interest rate by increasing or decreasing the money supply. When it does so, it affects some interest rates more than others. Those that are more (less) strongly affected are those paid on loans of low (high) risk and short (long) duration.

Interest rates and bond prices are inversely related.

Terms and Concepts

medium of exchange	thrift institution	reserve balances
unit of account	near-money	Federal Open Market Committee (FOMC)
store of value	*M*2	fractional reserve banking system
liquidity	time deposits	interest
*M*1	money market mutual fund (MMMF)	transactions demand for money
Federal Reserve Notes	legal tender	asset demand for money
token money	Federal Reserve System	total demand for money
checkable deposits	Board of Governors	cryptocurrency
commercial bank	Federal Reserve Banks	

Discussion Questions

McGraw Hill connect

1. What are the three basic functions of money? Describe how rapid inflation can undermine money's ability to perform each of the three functions. **LO34.1**
2. Which two of the following financial institutions offer checkable deposits included within the *M*1 money supply: mutual fund companies; insurance companies; commercial banks; securities firms; thrift institutions? Which of the following items is *not* included in either *M*1 or *M*2: currency held by the public; checkable deposits; money market mutual fund balances; small-denominated (less than $100,000) time deposits; currency held by banks; savings deposits? **LO34.2**
3. What are the components of the *M*1 money supply? What is the largest component? Which of the components of *M*1 is legal

tender? Why is the face value of a coin greater than its intrinsic value? What near-monies are included in the *M*2 money supply? **LO34.2**
4. Explain and evaluate the following statements: **LO34.2**
   a. The invention of money is one of the great achievements of humanity, for without it the enrichment that comes from broadening trade would have been impossible.
   b. Money is whatever society says it is.
   c. In the United States, the debts of government and commercial banks are used as money.
   d. People often say they would like to have more money, but what they usually mean is that they would like to have more goods and services.

e. When the price of everything goes up, it is not because everything is worth more but because the currency is worth less.

f. Any central bank can create money; the trick is to create enough, but not too much, of it.

5. What "backs" the money supply in the United States? What determines the value (domestic purchasing power) of money? How does the purchasing power of money relate to the price level? In the United States, who is responsible for maintaining money's purchasing power? **LO34.3**

6. How is the chairperson of the Federal Reserve System selected? Describe the relationship between the Board of Governors of the Federal Reserve System and the 12 Federal Reserve Banks. What is the purpose of the Federal Open Market Committee (FOMC)? What is its makeup? **LO34.4**

7. The following are two hypothetical ways in which the Federal Reserve Board might be appointed. Would you favor either of these two methods over the present method? Why or why not? **LO34.4**

a. Upon taking office, the U.S. president appoints seven people to the Federal Reserve Board, including a chair. Each appointee must be confirmed by a majority vote of the Senate, and each serves the same 4-year term as the president.

b. Congress selects seven members from its ranks (four from the House of Representatives and three from the Senate) to serve at congressional pleasure as the Board of Governors of the Federal Reserve System.

8. What do economists mean when they say that the Federal Reserve Banks are central banks, quasi-public banks, and bankers' banks? **LO34.4**

9. Why do economists nearly uniformly support an independent Fed rather than one beholden directly to either the president or Congress? **LO34.5**

10. Identify three functions of the Federal Reserve, other than its main role of controlling the supply of money. **LO34.5**

11. Explain why merchants accepted gold receipts as a means of payment even though the receipts were issued by goldsmiths, not the government. What risk did goldsmiths introduce into the payments system by issuing loans in the form of gold receipts? **LO34.6**

12. Why is the banking system in the United States referred to as a fractional reserve banking system? What is the role of deposit insurance in a fractional reserve system? **LO34.6**

13. What is the basic determinant of (*a*) the transactions demand and (*b*) the asset demand for money? Explain how to combine these two demands graphically to determine total money demand. How is the equilibrium interest rate in the money market determined? Use a graph to show how an increase in the total demand for money affects the equilibrium interest rate (no change in money supply). Use your general knowledge of equilibrium prices to explain why the previous interest rate is no longer sustainable. **LO34.7**

14. **LAST WORD** What is a blockchain and how can it be used to keep track of property rights? Have any cryptocurrencies become popular with consumers for buying goods and services? How could a central bank use its CBDC to apply fiscal stimulus during a recession?

Review Questions

1. The three functions of money are: **LO34.1**
   a. liquidity, store of value, and gifting.
   b. medium of exchange, unit of account, and liquidity.
   c. liquidity, unit of account, and gifting.
   d. medium of exchange, unit of account, and store of value.

2. Suppose that a small country currently has $4 million of currency in circulation, $6 million of checkable deposits, $200 million of savings deposits, $40 million of small-denominated time deposits, and $30 million of money market mutual fund deposits. From these numbers we see that this small country's *M*1 money supply is _____, while its *M*2 money supply is _____. **LO34.2**
   a. $10 million; $280 million
   b. $10 million; $270 million
   c. $210 million; $280 million
   d. $250 million; $270 million

3. Recall the formula that states that $V = 1/P$, where *V* is the value of the dollar and P is the price level. If the price level falls from 1 to 0.75, what will happen to the value of the dollar? **LO34.3**
   a. It will rise by a third (33.3 percent).
   b. It will rise by a quarter (25 percent).
   c. It will fall by a quarter (−25 percent).
   d. It will fall by a third (−33.3 percent).

4. Which group votes on the open-market operations that are used to control the U.S. money supply and interest rates? **LO34.4**
   a. Federal Reserve System
   b. The 12 Federal Reserve Banks
   c. Board of Governors of the Federal Reserve System
   d. Federal Open Market Committee (FOMC)

5. An important reason why members of the Federal Reserve's Board of Governors are each given extremely long, 14-year terms is to: **LO34.4**
   a. insulate members from political pressures that could result in inflation.
   b. help older members avoid job searches before retiring.
   c. attract younger people with lots of time left in their careers.
   d. avoid the trouble of constantly having to deal with new members.

6. Which of the following is *not* a function of the Fed? **LO34.5**
   a. Setting reserve requirements for banks
   b. Advising Congress on fiscal policy
   c. Regulating the supply of money
   d. Serving as a lender of last resort

7. A goldsmith has $2 million of gold in his vaults. He issues $5 million in gold receipts. His gold holdings are what fraction of the paper money (gold receipts) he has issued? **LO34.6**
   a. 1/10
   b. 1/5
   c. 2/5
   d. 5/5

8. Suppose that last year $30 billion in new loans were extended by banks while $50 billion in old loans were paid off by borrowers. What happened to the money supply? **LO34.6**
   a. Increased
   b. Decreased
   c. Stayed the same

9. When bond prices go up, interest rates go _____. **LO34.7**
   a. up
   b. down
   c. nowhere

10. If nominal GDP increases and the money supply remains fixed, the interest rate will, other things equal, go _____. **LO34.7**
  a. up
  b. down
  c. nowhere

11. If the asset demand for money increases at the same time that the money supply decreases, the interest rate will _____, other things held equal. **LO34.7**
  a. rise
  b. fall
  c. remain unchanged

Problems

McGraw Hill connect

1. Assume that the following asset values (in millions of dollars) exist in Ironmania: Federal Reserve Notes in circulation = $700; Money market mutual funds (MMMFs) held by individuals = $400; Corporate bonds = $300; Iron ore deposits = $50; Currency in commercial banks = $100; Savings deposits = $140; Checkable deposits = $1,500; Small-denominated (less than $100,000) time deposits = $100; Coins in circulation = $40. **LO34.2**
  a. What is M1 in Ironmania?
  b. What is M2 in Ironmania?

2. Assume that Jimmy Cash has $2,000 in his checking account at Folsom Bank and uses his checking account debit card to withdraw $200 of cash from the bank's ATM machine. By what dollar amount did the M1 money supply change as a result of this single, isolated transaction? **LO34.2**

3. Suppose the price level and value of the U.S. dollar in year 1 are 1 and $1, respectively. If the price level rises to 1.25 in year 2, what is the new value of the dollar? If, instead, the price level falls to 0.50, what is the value of the dollar? **LO34.3**

4. Assume that the following data characterize the hypothetical economy of Trance: money supply = $200 billion; quantity of money demanded for transactions = $150 billion; quantity of money demanded as an asset = $10 billion at 12 percent interest, increasing by $10 billion for each 2-percentage-point fall in the interest rate. **LO34.7**
  a. What is the equilibrium interest rate in Trance?
  b. At the equilibrium interest rate, what are the quantity of money supplied, the quantity of money demanded, the amount of money demanded for transactions, and the amount of money demanded as an asset in Trance?

5. Suppose a bond with no expiration date has a face value of $10,000 and annually pays $800 in fixed interest. In the table provided below, calculate and enter either the interest rate that the bond would yield to a bond buyer at each of the bond prices listed or the bond price at each of the interest yields shown. What generalization can you draw from the completed table? **LO34.7**

Bond Price	Interest Yield, %
$ 8,000	_____
_____	8.9
$10,000	_____
$11,000	_____
_____	6.2

CHAPTER

35

Monetary Policy, GDP, and the Price Level

>> **LEARNING OBJECTIVES**

LO35.1 Explain the tools of monetary policy, including open-market operations, forward guidance, and the administered rates.

LO35.2 Relate how the Fed's tools and strategies have evolved over the past several decades.

LO35.3 Define the Fed's dual mandate and explain how conflicts can arise between meeting the inflation target and the unemployment target.

LO35.4 Explain how monetary policy affects real GDP and the price level.

LO35.5 Explain the advantages and shortcomings of monetary policy.

LO35.6 Describe how the various components of macroeconomic theory and stabilization policy fit together.

LO35.7 (Appendix) State the Taylor Rule and explain how it balances the two parts of the Fed's dual mandate.

monetary policy Actions or communications by a *central bank* intended to help it achieve its macroeconomic policy objectives, which for the U.S. *Federal Reserve* are full employment of the labor force and a stable *price level.*

Some newspaper commentators have stated that the chair of the Federal Reserve Board (Jerome Powell in 2022) is the second most powerful person in the United States, after the President. That statement is an exaggeration, but there is no doubt about the chair's influence, nor about the importance of the Federal Reserve and the **monetary policy** that it conducts. Such policy consists of deliberate changes in the money supply to influence interest rates and thus the total level of spending in the economy. The goal of monetary policy is to achieve and maintain price-level stability, full employment, and economic growth. The chair has some big responsibilities!

Tools of Monetary Policy

>> **LO35.1** Explain the tools of monetary policy, including open-market operations, forward guidance, and the administered rates.

The Federal Reserve employs a wide variety of "monetary policy tools" to help it manage the U.S. money supply and thereby affect interest rates and economic activity.

Open-Market Operations

The Fed has the legal right to buy and sell financial assets as part of its efforts to manage the money supply and interest rates. The only assets that the Fed normally buys or sells are U.S. government bonds (issued by the U.S. Treasury to finance the federal debt) or bonds issued by various federal agencies (like the Federal National Mortgage Association, which issues bonds to help finance home mortgages). There are major public markets in which these types of bonds are purchased and sold. Because these markets are said to be "open" to the public, the Fed's transactions in these markets are known as **open-market operations.**

The Fed's purchases and sales of bonds are made in large quantities so as to influence the equilibrium price of bonds and, consequently, their interest rates. In addition, the Fed's purchases and sales also affect the supply of money in the hands of the public, which is why the Fed's policy actions are referred to as monetary policy.

Buying Bonds to Decrease an Interest Rate As a concrete example of how open-market operations affect interest rates and the money supply, suppose that the Fed wishes to decrease the interest rate on 20-year U.S. Treasury bonds.

As we explained in the last chapter, a bond's price and its interest rate are inversely related; thus, when a bond's price goes up, its interest rate goes down, and vice versa. The Fed uses that inverse relationship to decide whether to purchase or sell a particular type of bond. Since the Fed wants, in this example, to decrease the interest rate on 20-year government bonds, it will know that it will have to increase their price. Thus, it will buy lots of 20-year Treasury bonds, knowing that the increase in demand generated by its purchases will raise the equilibrium price of those bonds and therefore decrease their equilibrium interest rate.

That purchase of bonds by the Fed will also automatically increase the money supply because the Fed will pay for those bonds by creating new money, which it hands over to the sellers of the bonds to pay them for the bonds that they just sold to the Fed.

open-market operations
The purchases and sales of U.S. government *securities* that the *Federal Reserve System* undertakes in order to influence *interest rates* and the *money supply;* one method by which the *Federal Reserve* implements *monetary policy.*

Selling Bonds to Increase an Interest Rate The Fed could also reverse the transactions just described if it wanted to achieve the opposite result, a higher interest rate on 20-year government bonds. In that case, the Fed would know that it would need to decrease the price of those bonds (since a lower bond price will imply a higher interest rate). To accomplish that goal, the Fed will go into its inventory of bonds (that it has built up over the years by purchasing bonds in the open markets) and find some 20-year Treasury bonds to sell. It will then sell those bonds on the open market, thereby increasing the supply of 20-year Treasury bonds and lowering their equilibrium price. That price decrease will automatically raise their interest rate while also decreasing the economy's money supply, since all the money paid by the buyers of those bonds to the Fed will be taken out of circulation by the Fed once the Fed receives those funds.

Table 35.1 summarizes the effects that open-market bond purchases and sales have on bond interest rates and the money supply.

Administered Rates

The Federal Reserve has three **administered rates,** or interest rates that are set (administered) by the Fed to influence the lending and borrowing decisions of financial institutions. The key point about these rates is that they are directly controlled by the Federal Reserve and, thus, not a

administered rate An *interest rate* set by a *central bank* to help it manage market-determined *interest rates.*

TABLE 35.1 The Effects of Open-Market Operations on the Money Supply, Bond Prices, and Interest Rates

Fed Action	Effect on Money Supply	Effect on Bond Price	Effect on Bond Interest Rate
The Fed buys bonds	The money supply increases because the Fed creates new money to pay for the bonds.	Fed buying increases bond *demand*, driving up the equilibrium bond price.	Bond interest rate decreases as equilibrium bond price increases.
The Fed sells bonds	The money supply decreases because the Fed removes from circulation the money that it receives for the bonds.	Fed selling increases bond *supply*, driving down the equilibrium bond price.	Bond interest rate increases as equilibrium bond price decreases.

product of market forces. That is very useful because their independence from market forces implies that they can serve as decisive outside influences on a wide variety of market equilibrium interest rates.

Two of the administered rates—the *interest rate on reserve balances* and the *overnight reverse repo rate*—are set, or administered, by the Fed to influence market equilibrium interest rates in the so-called money market. The term **money market** is an umbrella term that refers to a wide variety of short-term lending markets that involve commercial and financial loans that range in duration from overnight to 1 year. The money market includes the markets for U.S. Treasury bills, bank certificates of deposit, commercial paper (short-term promissory notes, or IOUs, issued by businesses), interbank loans (loans between banks and thrifts), money market mutual funds, and lending-and-repurchase agreements, or "repos," in which a valuable financial asset (usually a U.S. Treasury bond) serves as collateral.

money market The financial *markets* in which short-term, low-risk debt *securities* are traded, including U.S. Treasury bills, overnight loans of bank reserves, and commercial paper.

The money market offers those with funds to lend—banks, money managers, and individual investors—safe, liquid, short-term lending opportunities, and it offers borrowers—banks, securities dealers, hedge funds, and nonfinancial corporations—access to low-interest loans since the interest rates on low-risk/short-term loans are typically much lower than the interest rates on higher-risk/longer-term loans due to the fact that lenders demand less compensation (lower interest rates) for short-term loans of low risk than they do for longer-term loans of higher risk. The money market is very important because it accounts for about one-third of all lending and credit in the U.S. economy.

The Interest Rate on Reserve Balances (IORB) In 2020, the Fed ended its previous practice of requiring each bank (and thrift) to keep a minimum amount of currency reserves on deposit at their regional Federal Reserve Bank. Since that time, banks have been legally free to decide for themselves how big their reserves against withdrawals and bank runs will be. They have also been free to decide how large a fraction of those reserves they will keep in the form of currency as opposed to investments in highly liquid short-term debt assets (like Treasury bills and commercial paper) that can be sold almost instantly in the money market to raise cash to fund withdrawals or to fend off bank runs.

interest rate on reserve balances (IORB) The *interest rate* that the Federal Reserve pays *banks* and thrifts on any money that they deposit at (loan to) a Federal Reserve Bank on an overnight basis; one of the three *administered rates* set by the Federal Reserve.

The **interest rate on reserve balances (IORB)** is the administered rate that the Fed offers to commercial banks on any currency that they choose to keep on deposit overnight as reserve balances at one of the twelve Federal Reserve Banks. Since any such deposits are paid the IORB rate, they are functionally equivalent to loans and, in some cases, it is easiest to think of the IORB rate as the rate that banks receive for any money that they choose to lend to the Fed.

The IORB rate is very powerful because if the Fed sets the IORB rate higher than the interest rates available in the money market, banks will know that they can earn a higher interest rate (the IORB rate) by parking currency at their local Federal Reserve Bank than they can by investing their reserve funds into Treasury bills, commercial paper, or other money market loans.

That ability to modulate the willingness of banks to lend money into the money market gives the Fed substantial control over equilibrium interest rates in the money market. As a concrete example, suppose that the Fed sets the IORB rate at 2 percent. In that case, banks will not be interested in any money market investment opportunities that pay less than 2 percent since they could obviously do better by keeping their funds on deposit overnight at the Fed and receiving the 2-percent IORB rate. To compete for the attention of banks, those other lending opportunities will have to offer interest rates of at least 2 percent per year. Thus, by setting the IORB rate at 2 percent, the Fed has the ability to nudge money market interest rates into being near to or above 2 percent, as well.

In actual practice, some money market rates will remain a bit lower, since there are other lenders in the money markets besides banks. But by being able to control the interest rate at which banks are willing to lend into the money markets, the Fed can in large measure control money-market interest rates and thus all the business and financial activity in the economy that is affected by money-market rates.

Finally, please note that changes in the IORB rate also affect the size of the economy's overall money supply and thus influence the overall level of interest rates in the economy, too, as per Figure 34.4. That is true because whatever amount of money is lent by banks to the Fed at the IORB rate is money that sits in the Fed's vaults rather than circulating through the economy. Thus, when the Fed raises the IORB rate, it decreases the overall money supply and puts upward pressure on interest rates in general (not just on money-market interest rates).

The Overnight Reverse Repo Rate (ON RRP) The **overnight reverse repo rate (ON RRP)** is the administered rate that the Fed offers to nonbank financial companies on any currency that they choose to lend to the Fed on an overnight basis. Those loans are transacted by means of a reverse version of a "lending and repurchase," or "repo," agreement. Under such a "reverse repo" transaction, the Fed sells a U.S. Treasury security to a lender at a price just below the bond's current market price while also promising to buy the bond back the next morning at the full market price. This "sell then buy back" arrangement is equivalent to an overnight loan from the lender to the Fed in which the bond serves as collateral in the case of default. That is true because if the Fed were to fail to buy the bond back the next morning as promised, the lender could sell the bond at full value to get their money back. On the other hand, if the Fed does buy the bond back the next morning as promised, then the difference between the slightly-below-market price at which the Fed sold the bond to the lender and the full market price at which the Fed buys the bond back will provide a monetary gain to the lender that is functionally equivalent to interest.

The Fed administers the *overnight reverse repo rate* separately from the *interest rate on reserve balances* for two reasons. First, the Fed is only legally allowed to pay interest on reserve balances to banks and other depository institutions that take checkable deposits. Thus, only depository institutions can receive the IORB rate on money that they leave on deposit overnight at the Fed. That matters because depository institutions are not the only financial firms that participate in the money market. Thus, if the Fed is to have even stronger control over money-market interest rates, it needs a way to influence the behavior of the nonbanks that operate in the money market. The *overnight reverse repo rate* satisfies that need because it allows the Fed to offer nonbanks an alternative to money market investments. Just as the availability of the IORB rate implies that banks will not want to invest in the money market at any rate below the IORB rate, the availability of the ON RRP rate ensures that nonbanks will not want to invest in the money market at any rate below the ON RRP rate.

Thus, between the IORB rate offered to depository institutions like banks and the ON RRP rate offered to nondepository financial firms like money market mutual funds, the Fed has strong control over money-market interest rates. In fact, one way to think about the IORB and ON RRP rates is that they give the Fed the ability to "put a floor" under money-market rates, meaning a level below which money-market rates are unlikely to go. As an example, suppose that the Fed sets the IORB rate at 1.75 percent and the ON RRP rate at 1.65 percent. Then there would be hardly any participants in the money market that would lend money for less than 1.65 percent per year. The banks will not lend for anything less than the 1.75 percent IORB rate that they can get by loaning money to the Fed, and the nonbanks will not lend for anything less than the 1.65 percent ON RRP rate that they can get for loaning money to the Fed. Thus, it is highly likely that nearly every interest rate in the money market will end up being near to or above 1.65 percent.

The Fed has consistently set the ON RRP rate about 0.10 percentage points below the IORB rate rather than, for instance, setting them at equal rates. That gap allows the Fed to manage the money-market lending behavior of banks and nonbanks independently of each other, rather than give both groups of financial firms exactly the same incentives with regard to lending to the Fed or lending into the money market (as would be the case if the Fed set the ON RRP and IORB rates at equal levels).

Finally, please note that changes in the ON RRP rate also affect the size of the economy's overall money supply and thus influence the overall level of interest rates in the economy, as well, as per Figure 34.4. That is true because whatever amount of money is lent by nonbanks to the Fed

overnight reverse repo rate (ON RRP) The *interest rate* that the Federal Reserve pays eligible nonbank financial firms for any money that they loan to a Federal Reserve Bank overnight using a reverse *repo* transaction; one of the three *administered rates* set by the *Federal Reserve.*

at the ON RRP rate is money that sits in the Fed's vaults rather than circulating in the economy. Thus, when the Fed raises the ON RRP rate, it decreases the overall money supply and puts upward pressure on interest rates in general (not just on money-market interest rates).

The Discount Rate The so-called *discount rate* is the third and final of the Fed's three administered interest rates. Unlike the IORB and ON RRP rates, which are both rates at which financial institutions can lend money *to* the Fed, the **discount rate** is an interest rate at which depository institutions can borrow money *from* the Fed. Any such loans must be collateralized, meaning that the Fed will loan a bank money at the discount rate but only if the bank posts U.S. Treasury securities or other low-risk bonds as collateral that the Fed will get to keep if the bank does not repay the loan.

> **discount rate** The interest rate that the *Federal Reserve Banks* charge on the loans they make to *commercial banks* and *thrifts;* one of the three *administered rates* set by the *Federal Reserve.*

The point of the discount rate is to give banks a backup source of low-cost (that is, low-interest-rate) liquidity if they are unable to obtain funds in the money market. Normally that is not an issue, but if a specific bank is hit with a bank run, then it may not be able to find anyone in the money market willing to lend it the money that it needs to calm the bank run by demonstrating that it has the ability to fulfill each and every request from depositors to withdraw funds. In such a situation, the bank can go to the Fed and borrow the currency it needs to calm the panic. The rate that it will pay on that loan is the discount rate, and the currency that is borrowed from the Fed will come in the form of newly created reserve balances that the Fed will deposit into the bank's account at the Fed.

Another situation in which the discount rate is useful is during major financial crises. During such crises, part or all of the money market may freeze up, so that even the highest quality borrowers with perfect credit ratings cannot borrow money. That happened during the financial crisis in 2008, but the banking system was not hit with any widespread bank runs because people knew that even if a bank panic started, the banks involved could borrow whatever money they might need to pay depositors and calm the panic from the Fed at the discount rate.

The Fed always sets the discount rate higher than the IORB rate because if the discount rate (at which banks can borrow *from* the Fed) were lower than the IORB rate (at which banks can lend *to* the Fed), banks would have access to an infinitely large and totally unearned profit opportunity, since they could, for instance, borrow some money at, say, 1.5 percent from the Fed and then turn right around and lend that money back to the Fed at a higher interest rate, like 2.5 percent. To prevent that sort of *arbitrage* situation from ever arising, the Fed always sets the discount rate higher than the IORB rate.

Table 35.2 summarizes the three administered rates and gives their respective values in January 2020, before the COVID-19 pandemic, and January 2022, after the Fed had aggressively lowered the administered rates to help fight the negative economic consequences of the pandemic.

The Fed's Ability to Enforce the Administered Rates A key point about the three administered rates is that the Fed has 100 percent credibility in enforcing them, due to the Fed's ability to create as much new money as it wants, any time it wants.

TABLE 35.2 The Federal Reserve's Three Administered Interest Rates, January 2020 and January 2022

Name	Eligible Entities	Description	Purpose	Percentage Rate in January 2020	Percentage Rate in January 2022
Discount rate	Depository institutions (banks and thrifts)	Interest rate paid *to* the Fed for currency reserves borrowed against collateral	Low-cost emergency liquidity for depository institutions	2.25	0.25
Interest on reserve balances (IORB)	Depository institutions (banks and thrifts)	Interest rate paid *by* the Fed on currency deposits held at Federal Reserve Banks	Control of money-market interest rates	1.55	0.15
Overnight reverse repo rate (ON RRP)	Select nondepository financial firms, including money market funds	Interest rate paid *by* the Fed on collateralized loans	Control of money-market interest rates	1.45	0.05

Consider the two rates that the Fed uses to control interest rates in the money market. The IORB and ON RRP rates involve the Fed paying interest on money that is loaned to it overnight by, respectively, banks and nonbanks. The Fed's promise to pay interest on those loans is fully credible because the Fed can create the money necessary to pay that interest any time it wants and in any amount it wants. Thus, nobody on Wall Street ever doubts the ability of the Fed to use IORB and ON RRP to incentivize banks and nonbanks to lend to the Fed at those rates rather than into the money market at lower rates.

Similarly, consider the money that banks are eligible to borrow from the Fed at the discount rate. That lending facility is intended to calm financial markets if there is a bank run or a financial crisis. It is fully credible in those situations because the Fed can create however much money as may be needed to satisfy every single request that the Fed may receive from banks to borrow at the discount rate. Thus, the Fed's ability to use the discount rate to calm bank panics is also unlimited.

Forward Guidance

Another powerful tool that the Fed has at its disposal is **forward guidance,** or intentionally and clearly communicating to the public exactly how the Federal Reserve sees the state of the economy and, on that basis, how the Fed intends to conduct monetary policy going forward. Those communications are influential because individuals and businesses will use what the Fed says to help shape their own spending and investment decisions. In fact, forward guidance may be strong enough to alter the economy's macroeconomic trajectory just by itself.

If, for example, the Fed says that the economy seems to be slipping into a recession and, as a result, it plans to lower interest rates over the following six months to stimulate the economy, businesses that might have otherwise decided to cut back on investment spending (because they feared a deep recession and collapsing sales) may now decide to go ahead and invest in new plant and equipment (because they can see that the Fed shares their fears and is going to take strong steps to try to partly preclude—or even fully avert—the looming recession). Thus, as long as the Fed has credibility with the public, its ability to shape public expectations with forward guidance is itself a powerful monetary policy tool that can be used in conjunction with the Fed's other monetary policy tools.

Along those lines, it should be noted that forward guidance can affect the economy's overall money supply. That is true because, as you will recall from the previous chapter, part of the economy's money supply is *checkable deposits* held at banks and thrifts. That is important to remember with respect to forward guidance because when banks and thrifts issue new loans, they do so by creating new checkable-deposit money that gets deposited into borrowers' checking accounts.

- If the Fed's forward guidance is optimistic, or "positive," about the economy's prospects, then loan officers and potential borrowers will likely feel more positive about the economy's prospects, too, and thus more likely to want to borrow and lend. If the dollar volume of new loans being granted exceeds the dollar value of old loans being paid off, the total amount of checkable-deposit money will increase, thereby increasing the overall size of the money supply, all other things equal.
- Contrariwise, if the Fed's forward guidance is pessimistic, or "negative," about the economy's prospects, then it will be likely that fewer loans will be demanded and granted. If the dollar volume of new loans being granted ends up being less than the dollar value of old loans being paid off, the total amount of checkable-deposit money will decrease, thereby reducing the overall size of the money supply, all other things equal.

The Federal Funds Rate Many central banks have a **policy rate** that they use as part of their forward guidance efforts. The policy rate helps to communicate to the public, in a very brief and easy to understand format, the bank's **monetary policy stance,** that is, whether the bank's current outlook with respect to monetary policy is expansionary, restrictive, or neutral.

The Federal Reserve's policy rate is known as the **federal funds rate,** and, like all policy rates, it is an interest rate on a specific type of short-term, low-risk loan. In some countries, the policy rate is the interest rate on overnight loans of currency that are negotiated between commercial

forward guidance Public communications made by a *central bank* to describe (1) how it perceives the state of the *economy* and (2) how it intends to manage *monetary policy.*

policy rate A short-term *interest rate* that a *central bank* manages to help communicate the stance of *monetary policy* as well as to achieve its *monetary policy* goals.

monetary policy stance A *central bank's* disposition regarding how it sees the current and future state of the economy and, thus, whether its current monetary policy actions will be consistent with an *expansionary monetary policy,* a *restrictive monetary policy,* or a *neutral monetary policy.*

federal funds rate The *interest rate* that U.S. banks and other nonbank financial firms charge one another on overnight loans of *currency* held on deposit at one of the twelve *Federal Reserve Banks;* the Federal Reserve's *policy rate.*

federal funds market The financial *market* in which *banks* and other financial firms negotiate overnight loans of *currency* ("federal funds") held on deposit at one of the twelve *Federal Reserve Banks*.

federal funds target range The 0.25-percent-wide range within which the *Federal Reserve* guides its *policy rate,* the *effective federal funds rate*. Also a key part of the Federal Reserve's *forward guidance* communications.

effective federal funds rate The equilibrium *interest rate* determined in the *federal funds market;* the interest rate that U.S. banks and other depository institutions charge one another for overnight loans of currency held on deposit at one of the twelve *Federal Reserve Banks*.

banks. In the United States, the policy rate is the overnight lending rate that large financial firms and government agencies charge each other to borrow currency held on deposit at one of the Federal Reserve Banks. That *federal funds rate* is determined in the **federal funds market,** whose participants include U.S. commercial banks and thrifts, U.S. branches of foreign banks, savings and loan organizations, and government-sponsored enterprises, such as the Federal National Mortgage Association (Fannie Mae), as well as securities firms and agencies of the federal government.

It should be noted, however, that while the *federal funds market* is indeed a competitive market in which supply and demand determine an equilibrium price, it is nevertheless a highly constrained and aggressively managed market. At any moment in time, the Fed sets a **federal funds target range** for the federal funds rate. This target range is usually only a quarter-of-a-percent wide. Thus, for example, the upper limit of the federal funds target range may be set at 2.00 percent per year while the bottom limit is set at 1.75 percent per year. At other times, the target range may be set so that the upper limit is 0.25 percent per year while the bottom limit is 0.00 percent per year. In almost all cases, the gap between the upper and lower limits is exactly 0.25 percent.

The Fed then adjusts the IORB rate available to depository institutions and the ON RRP rate available to nondepository financial firms to ensure that the equilibrium interest rate in the federal funds market—the **effective federal funds rate**—always ends up being within the *federal funds target range*. That level of control over the equilibrium interest rate in the federal funds market is possible because the federal funds market is part of the overall money market and, as you know, the Fed can guide all of the interest rates within the money market by adjusting the IORB rate and the ON RRP rate either higher or lower. If the Fed wants the equilibrium *effective federal funds rate* to fall, it will lower the IORB and ON RRP rates. And if the Fed wants the equilibrium *effective federal funds rate* to rise, it will raise the IORB and ON RRP rates.

One of the great benefits to the Fed of publicly announcing the federal funds target range is simplicity. The general public is largely unaware of the existence of the administered rates, how open-market operations work, or that the Fed is constantly taking steps to guide short-term interest rates by influencing the money market. But the Fed is able to convey in an uncomplicated fashion the overall stance of monetary policy by simply announcing the current target range for the federal funds rate and whether it expects to raise or lower the target range in the future based on current and projected macroeconomic conditions. Individuals and businesses can then gather most of what they need to know from simple headlines, such as, "The Fed Raises Target Range to Fight Inflation" or "Fearing Recession, FOMC Lowers Federal Funds Target Range."

Finally, please note that changing the federal funds target range and then using IORB and ON RRP to guide the effective federal funds rate into the target range changes the economy's money supply because, as we mentioned above, changes in IORB and ON RRP directly alter the amount of money in the hands of the public. When the IORB and ON RRP interest rates are increased, financial firms lend more money to the Fed, thereby reducing the amount of money held by the public outside the Fed. And contrariwise, when the IORB and ON RRP interest rates are decreased, financial firms lend less money to the Fed, thereby increasing the amount of money held by the public outside the Fed. Those changes in the economy's overall money supply in turn affect the overall level of interest rates in the economy, as per Figure 34.4.

QUICK REVIEW
35.1

▶ The Fed has three main tools of monetary control: (a) open-market operations, (b) changing the administered interest rates, and (c) forward guidance.

▶ The three administered interest rates are the interest rate on reserve balances (IORB) at which banks and other depository institutions can loan money to the Fed; the overnight reverse repo rate (ON RRP) at which nondepository financial institutions can loan money to the Fed;

and the discount rate at which banks and other depository institutions can borrow money from the Fed.

▶ The Fed uses the federal funds target range to signal its monetary policy stance to the public.

▶ Open-market operations, changes in the administered rates, and forward guidance alter the money supply.

The Evolution of the Fed's Tools and Strategies

A good way to understand how the Federal Reserve System uses its current set of monetary policy tools to influence the macroeconomy is to study how its set of tools, and its strategies for employing those tools, have evolved over the past 30 years, mostly as a result of the major challenges the Fed faced during the financial crisis of 2007–2008.

>> **LO35.2** Relate how the Fed's tools and strategies have evolved over the past several decades.

From Conventional to Unconventional

Before the extremely severe financial crisis of 2007–2008, the Fed employed a smaller collection of monetary policy tools. It was not yet, for example, paying IORB or ON RRP, and thus could not use them to control the effective federal funds rate or other money-market interest rates.

The Fed did, however, set targets for the federal funds rate back then just as it does today. But the way that the Fed achieved those targets was not by adjusting the IORB or ON RRP rates (which did not yet exist). Instead, the Fed used open-market operations to guide the effective federal funds rate toward its target.

To do that, the Fed would first announce a change in its target for the federal funds rate and then buy or sell short-term U.S. Treasury securities from banks to alter the amounts of money (in the form of *reserve balances*) that the banks held at the Fed. Those changes in the amounts of money held by banks would cause those institutions to lend more or less money in the federal funds market and thus alter the equilibrium federal funds rate that is determined in that market.

The financial crisis of 2007–2008 was so severe, however, that the Fed felt it necessary to slash the federal funds rate from 5.25 percent in July 2007 down to nearly zero percent in December 2008. That was deeply problematic because, as the federal funds rate approached zero, the Fed appeared to be "out of ammunition" with respect to being able to apply further stimulus to an economy that was experiencing its worst recession since the Great Depression of the 1930s.

That pessimism was based on the fact that, up to that point in time, the Fed's primary way of stimulating the U.S. economy when it was experiencing a business downturn was to stimulate investment spending by lowering the federal funds rate and thereby guiding other interest rates lower, too. Money-market rates invariably fell when the federal funds rate fell, and longer-term interest rates would also typically decline at least somewhat when the federal funds rate was reduced. But with the effective federal funds rate already reduced to just 0.16 percent in late 2008, there appeared to be no way for the Fed to generate any further monetary policy stimulus since it didn't seem possible for the Fed to reduce the federal funds rate by any substantial additional amount since doing so would result in a negative interest rate. If zero was the limit, the Fed's ability to simulate the economy was maxed out.

The Zero Lower Bound By cutting the effective federal funds rate to nearly zero, the Fed had been forced to confront the **zero lower bound problem,** which refers to the fact that once short-term interest rates are at zero percent, any further rate cuts will probably cause more harm than good. To understand why, first note that further rate cuts are indeed possible. That may sound strange, but the Fed is very much capable of forcing short-term interest rates below zero, into negative territory.

As an example, consider a 1-year bond that will pay its owner $103 in a year. If you bought that bond today for $100 and held it for a year, you would get a positive 3 percent return since you would, in a year's time, receive three dollars more than the $100 that you paid today. But suppose the Fed buys so many of this type of bond that its price today rises to $105. Then if you bought it today for $105 and held it for a year, you would end up with a *negative* rate of return because what you would get for it in a year ($103) would be less than what you are paying for it today ($105).

From this example, it is clear that the Fed could always, if it wanted to, drive bond prices up high enough to cause their interest rates to turn negative. Indeed, the Fed's legal authority to print money guarantees it the ability to drive bond prices up however high it would like and thus generate negative interest rates to whatever degree it might like.

zero lower bound problem The constraint placed on the ability of a *central bank* to stimulate the economy through lower short-term *interest rates* by the fact that short-term *interest rates* cannot be driven lower than zero without causing depositors to withdraw funds from the banking system.

The Fed, however, has never seen fit to follow such a strategy. That is because negative interest rates might discourage, rather than encourage, spending in the economy. In particular, if the Fed were to force the federal funds rate into negative territory, then interest rates on checking accounts and money-market funds would likely go negative, too. That is a big problem because many people who hold checking accounts and money-market accounts would withdraw all of their money from those accounts in favor of cash, which by definition has neither a positive nor a negative interest rate. That is, they would prefer getting zero interest on physical cash as compared with negative rates on deposit accounts (whose balances, due to those negative rates, would necessarily shrink over time as the negative rates ate away at their value).

Those withdrawals would amount to a slow-motion bank panic that would drain loanable funds from the banking system. In addition, the overall rate of consumption spending might also decline due to the fact that we live in the age of e-commerce, in which so much economic activity is transacted electronically. If a negative interest rate caused people to convert checking account balances that are easily accessed electronically into physical cash that cannot be spent online, there might be less economic activity overall, all other things equal.

On the other hand, some economists have conjectured that negative interest rates might possibly stimulate economic activity, their hypothesis being that negative interest rates on checking account balances might cause people to try to spend their money more rapidly, before the negative rates reduced the spending power of those balances.

After considering the various theoretical conjectures that economists were making about the possible economic effects of negative interest rates, the Fed concluded that negative interest rates were too risky to try, since nobody actually knew if negative rates would make the economy's recessionary situation better or worse. But with negative rates being a "no go," the Fed needed to figure out some other way to try to stimulate the economy.

Quantitative Easing The Fed's pre-crisis strategy of focusing almost entirely on the federal funds rate and other short-term interest rates had been the standard, or "conventional," approach to monetary policy for many decades. But with further reductions of short-term rates not being an option during the 2007–2009 financial crisis due to the zero lower bound problem, the Fed needed to come up with a new, "unconventional" approach that could be used to apply additional stimulus after it had already slashed the federal funds rate down to nearly zero. The Fed's solution was to keep the federal funds rate and other short-term interest rates at a low level (through the use of IORB and ON RRP) while pioneering the use of open-market operations that would lower the longer-term interest rates that drive many business investment decisions.

As background, please understand that economists believe that most decisions by businesses about whether to invest in new capital equipment or spend money on R&D depend on long-term interest rates. That is because businesses wish to synchronize the monetary returns that they hope will be generated by those investments with the debt payments needed to repay the loans that were used to fund those investments. As a simple example, consider a farmer who wishes to plant a new grove of orange trees. It will take at least five years before those trees are mature enough to generate full harvests. Thus, if the farmer is investigating various loan options to fund the planting of those trees, he will prefer a long-term loan that won't be due or require monthly payments for at least five years. That way, by the time he has to make loan payments, the trees will be mature and producing not only fruit but also revenue, some of which can be used to pay back the loan.

Many business investments take at least a year or two to start generating revenue. Certain ones, like R&D for innovative new medicines, may not pay off for ten or twenty years. Thus, when it comes to influencing business investment decisions, longer-term interest rates are very important. It was with that in mind that the Fed initiated the program that would end up being called *quantitative easing,* or QE.

The Fed put this new strategy into effect by purchasing hundreds of billions of dollars' worth of 10-year and 20-year U.S. Treasury bonds as well as equally large amounts of long-duration bonds issued by federal agencies. Those purchases raised the prices of those particular long-duration federally issued bonds, thereby reducing their interest rates. But the Fed was aiming for wider effects because it knew that by lowering the interest rates on longer-duration government bonds, it would also tend to lower the interest rates on the longer-duration bonds that private companies issue to fund investment spending. Those spillover effects were expected to occur because bonds of similar duration compete with each other for the economy's limited supply of loanable funds. By lowering the interest rates on longer-term *federally issued* debt, the Fed would be able to put downward pressure on longer-term *privately issued* debt, much of which is used, as we just mentioned, to fund business investment spending.

This strategy of using open-market bond purchases to try to drive down all sorts of longer-term interest rates came to be known as **quantitative easing, or QE,** because the Fed would always pre-announce the *quantity* of money that it was going to create and spend on a particular round of bond buying in order to generate an *easing* of the borrowing conditions (interest rates) facing companies that wished to borrow by issuing longer-term bonds.

The Fed's first round of quantitative easing started in November 2008 when the Fed pre-announced that it was going to buy $800 billion of mortgage-backed securities from federal agencies like the Federal Home Loan Mortgage Corporation (Freddie Mac). Later rounds of quantitative easing included a pre-announced commitment to buy $600 billion of U.S. Treasury bonds by June 30, 2011, as well as a pre-announced commitment that the Fed would, starting in December of 2012, purchase $85 billion per month of various types of long-term Treasury and agency bonds until it felt that the economy had recovered enough that such purchases were no longer needed.

Forward Guidance Another key innovation after the financial crisis was the Fed's expanded use of forward guidance. As just mentioned, during the financial crisis, the Fed started to pre-announce each round of quantitative easing. It did so to indicate to the public not only that it was concerned about the lingering effects of the 2007–2009 recession but that, in addition to lowering short-term interest rates down to extremely low levels, it was going to take an additional concrete step—quantitative easing—to help the economy recover as quickly as possible.

The Fed also put more emphasis on making clear statements about the federal funds target range and making it crystal clear to the public just how the FOMC members felt at any point in time about the current state of the economy and its future prospects. This was done by issuing an official statement after each FOMC meeting that summarized exactly how the FOMC members saw the current macroeconomic situation and what current and future actions they anticipated taking.

All of this forward guidance was done deliberately to help instill a feeling of confidence on the part of the public. The Fed's message was: "Hey, everybody! We are *not* out of ammunition. Short-term interest rates may be near zero, but we have innovative new ways to stimulate the economy, including trillions of dollars' worth of quantitative easing that will put downward pressure on longer-term interest rates."

quantitative easing (QE)
An *open-market operation* in which a *central bank* pre-announces that it will spend a fixed quantity of *money* purchasing long-term bonds so as to lower long-term *interest rates* and thereby ease *credit* conditions for long-horizon investors, such as *businesses* borrowing to purchase *capital goods*.

CONSIDER THIS . . .

Picking Winners

It might have occurred to you to wonder why the Fed limits its open-market operations to purchases and sales of government debt. If the Fed's goal is to affect economic activity, why shouldn't it also purchase a wider variety of financial assets, such as corporate bonds, corporate stock, real estate, or even industrial commodities like oil and lumber?

The simplest answer is that purchasing most of those assets would be illegal because congress has not yet passed a law that would allow the Fed to buy or sell those assets. More important, however, is *why* congress has not given the Fed that latitude.

Congress does not want the Fed creating favoritism or inefficiencies in the private sector. If the Fed, for instance,

Design Pics

announced that it would be purchasing a lot of Tesla bonds and thereby lowering the interest rate at which Tesla corporation can borrow, it would give Tesla a competitive advantage over its auto-making competitors whose bonds the Fed would not be buying. And if the Fed regularly purchased or sold industrial commodities like oil, copper, and aluminum, the equilibrium quantities and prices in those markets would not reflect the social optimum where MB = MC. Instead, the Fed would likely cause over- or under-production that would generate dead-weight *efficiency losses* to society.

To avoid those sorts of problems, the Fed sticks to government bonds.

Evaluating the New Normal

By the mid-2010s, the economy had recovered enough that the Fed began to taper down its quantitative-easing efforts. A couple of years later, as the economy recovered even more, the Fed began to reverse QE with a policy that came to be known as **quantitative tightening, or QT.** Instead of buying long-term government bonds to lower their interest rates, the Fed began to sell them in order to raise their interest rates. That made good sense because a robustly growing economy clearly did not need the stimulus provided by artificially low long-term interest rates.

quantitative tightening (QT)
The opposite of *quantitative easing*. An *open-market operation* in which a *central bank* pre-announces that it will sell a fixed quantity of long-term bonds so as to raise long-term *interest rates* and thereby tighten *credit* conditions for long-horizon investors, such as *businesses* borrowing to purchase *capital goods*.

An open question, however, was whether the Fed should (1) return to the conventional monetary policy it had practiced before the financial crisis or (2) treat the unconventional monetary policy that it had developed during the crisis as the "new normal."

One argument in favor of making unconventional monetary policy the new normal was that it seemed to have worked pretty well during and after the financial crisis. A second Great Depression had been averted, and by the late 2010s the economy was enjoying full employment and low inflation. Thus, many asked whether there would be any benefit to going back to the old ways of doing things. Had not the old ways been incapable of dealing with the zero lower bound? And how much worse might the crisis have been if the Fed had not been willing to innovate?

Along those lines, proponents of the new normal asked rhetorical questions like: Wasn't it a good thing that the Fed had learned to control short-term interest rates with IORB and ON RRP rather than open-market operations? Wasn't it good that the Fed had started doing QE and QT so that it could affect long-term interest rates as well as short-term interest rates and thereby allow itself the opportunity to add further stimulus to the economy even when short-term interest rates were up against the zero lower bound? And, in addition to all that, wasn't it a positive thing that the Fed could now control short-term and long-term interest rates independently of one another?

One counterargument was that the artificially low long-term interest rates created by QE may have encouraged congress to run larger budget deficits than it otherwise would have, thereby making it more likely that, to repay that additional debt, some future congress would feel compelled to impose sharply higher tax rates that would then slow economic growth by removing from the private sector trillions of dollars that would otherwise have gone toward consumer spending or business investment.

Another fear was that the trillions of dollars of reserves that the Fed had created to finance its QE bond purchases might end up generating a huge inflation if those massive quantities of bank reserves were ever used to vastly increase bank lending and the amount of checkable account deposit money that was circulating in the economy. A notable fact about IORB and ON RRP, however, is that they can be used to mitigate that inflationary threat.

That is true because whenever the Fed raises the IORB and ON RRP rates, it encourages banks and other financial firms to lend reserves to the Fed rather than using them to back new loans and thereby create new checkable deposit money. The higher the IORB and ON RRP rates, the greater the quantity of reserves that banks will lend to the Fed, thereby reducing their ability to create new checkable deposit money, all other things equal.

Figuratively speaking, IORB and ON RRP transform the Fed's own vaults into a giant "money sponge" that the Fed can use to reduce the overall money supply, thereby reducing inflationary pressures, all other things equal. It was indeed the case that when inflation unexpectedly shot up to 7.0 percent per year in 2021, one of the Fed's first policy moves was to signal that it would begin raising the IORB and ON RRP rates as part of its efforts to try to get inflation back under control.

These debates will continue. But for the time being, the Fed has announced that unconventional monetary policy is the new normal, and that it will continue to make use of the tools and strategies that it developed during the financial crisis.

QUICK REVIEW
35.2

▶ The severity of the 2007–2008 financial crisis caused the Fed to slash short-term interest rates down to nearly zero.

▶ To get around the zero lower bound problem, the Fed introduced several unconventional monetary policies, including the use of quantitative easing, or

QE, to lower the longer-term interest rates that have the greatest effect on business investment and R&D spending.

▶ The Fed also increased its use of forward guidance and began using the IORB and ON RRP rates to control short-term interest rates.

The Dual Mandate

Now that you understand the Fed's monetary policy tools, it's time to study how the Fed uses those tools to comply with the dual mandate given to it by congress in 1977.

The **dual mandate** states that the Fed's two highest objectives should be full employment and stable prices. To that end, the Fed has set itself two concrete targets that it pursues simultaneously:

1. Achieving the *full-employment rate of unemployment*, which is currently around 3 to 4 percent of the labor force.

2. Achieving the Fed's *target rate of inflation*, which is currently set at 2 percent per year.

The Fed's Unemployment Target

The **full-employment rate of unemployment,** or *natural rate of unemployment*, is the unemployment rate that exists in an economy when it is producing at potential output (full employment). At full employment, every person who wants a job is employed, so that there is zero *cyclical unemployment*. Structural and frictional unemployment do remain, however, as there will still be some people either between jobs (*frictional unemployment*) or in need of retraining after their old jobs were eliminated due to changes in consumer preferences, evolving production technologies, or offshoring (*structural unemployment*). Thus, the full-employment rate of unemployment is not zero unemployment, but, rather, a modest positive number that reflects frictional and structural unemployment.

The full-employment rate of unemployment also reflects changes in government industrial policy and labor force regulations, the size of labor force growth relative to the growth rate of the demand for labor, and a wide variety of other factors that affect how much labor is necessary to produce the full-employment level of output, how much labor is available to produce it, and how quickly the frictionally and structurally unemployed return to work. These factors change over time, thereby causing the full-employment rate of unemployment to change over time, too.

The full-employment rate of unemployment is currently estimated to lie somewhere between 3 and 4 percent of the labor force. In December 2021, for example, the median estimate made by Federal Reserve board members and Federal Reserve bank presidents was 3.5 percent. In practice, this estimate serves as the FOMC's **target rate of unemployment.**

- If the actual unemployment rate rises appreciably higher than 3.5 percent, the Fed will be inclined, other things equal, toward assuming that the economy is decelerating and consequently in need of an **expansionary monetary policy** (or "easy money" policy) under which the Fed would increase the money supply and lower interest rates to encourage investment and consumption spending.

- Contrariwise, if the actual unemployment rate falls appreciably below 3.5 percent, the Fed will be inclined, other things equal, toward assuming that the economy will soon experience a burst of inflation as firms bid up resource prices in an attempt to produce more than the full-employment level of output. That presumption will suggest a **restrictive monetary policy** (or "tight money" policy) under which the Fed would reduce the money supply and increase interest rates to restrain investment and consumption spending.

- Finally, if the actual unemployment rate is exactly at, or very close to, 3.5 percent, the Fed would be inclined toward a **neutral monetary policy** under which the Fed would leave the money supply and interest rates alone unless the economy were experiencing a significant inflation or deflation, in which case the Fed might adjust the money supply and interest rates to deal with those price-level problems.

The Fed's Inflation Target

As just indicated, the unemployment rate cannot *by itself* determine whether monetary policy should be expansionary, restrictive, or neutral. The Fed must also consider whether inflation is above or below the Fed's **target rate of inflation,** which has been set at 2 percent per year since 2012.[1]

---

[1]Prior to 2012, the Fed had a general, but unspecific, goal with respect to inflation, which was to "maintain price stability." Setting a specific inflation target in 2012 was an example of the Fed using forward guidance to try to help the public understand what the Fed's motivations were and thus what the Fed would be likely to do with respect to its monetary policy stance at any point in the future.

>> LO35.3 Define the Fed's dual mandate and explain how conflicts can arise between meeting the inflation target and the unemployment target.

dual mandate The 1977 congressional directive that the Federal Reserve System's highest priorities should be *full employment* and price level stability. In practice, the Fed aims for the *full-employment rate of unemployment* and an *inflation rate* of 2 percent per year.

full-employment rate of unemployment The *unemployment rate* at which there is no *cyclical unemployment* of the *labor force;* equal to around 4 percent (rather than zero percent) in the United States because *frictional* and *structural unemployment* are unavoidable.

target rate of unemployment The Fed's desired *unemployment rate,* equal to the *full-employment rate of unemployment,* which is estimated to be between 4 and 5 percent for the U.S. economy.

expansionary monetary policy *Central bank* actions to increase the *money supply,* lower *interest rates,* and expand *real GDP.* Implemented when the economy is operating below *potential output.* Also known as an "easy money" policy.

restrictive monetary policy *Central bank* actions to reduce the *money supply,* increase *interest rates,* and reduce *inflation.* Implemented when the economy is operating above *potential output.* Also known as a "tight money" policy.

neutral monetary policy
A *monetary policy* in which the *money supply* and *interest rates* are left as they are by the *central bank* because the economy appears to be operating at *potential output,* with stable *prices* and a low level of *unemployment.* Compare with *expansionary monetary policy* and *restrictive monetary policy.*

target rate of inflation The publicly announced annual *inflation* rate that a *central bank* attempts to achieve through *monetary policy* actions if it is following an *inflation-targeting* monetary policy.

Why 2 Percent? There are several reasons why 2 percent was selected as the Fed's inflation target, rather than, say, 10 percent or zero percent.

Compensating for Upward Measurement Bias There is a consensus among economists that the *Consumer Price Index* (CPI) and other measures of inflation have an upward bias, meaning that they tend to say that inflation is higher than it actually is.

The upward bias in inflation measurement is estimated to be around half a percent, or 0.5 percent, per year. That fact implies that it would be dangerous for the Fed to have an inflation target of less than 0.5 percent. To see why, imagine that the Fed sets an inflation target of zero and then uses contractionary monetary policy to guide measured inflation down to that target rate. In that situation, the fact that measured inflation has a half-percent upward bias will imply that actual (unbiased) inflation will be about a half a percent lower, or negative 0.5 percent. That is deeply problematic because deflations (periods of negative inflation) usually only happen if the economy is in a severe recession, like the Great Depression of the 1930s or the severe recession of 2007–2009. Thus, to avoid accidentally putting the economy into a recession by conducting an overly contractionary monetary policy, the Fed must set an inflation target of *at least* positive 0.5 percent.

Protecting Savers On the other hand, the Fed does not want to set too high an inflation target because it will want to avoid any substantial loss of purchasing power on the part of savers, creditors, and people on fixed incomes who fail to anticipate the inflation created by the Fed. An inflation rate of 10 percent or even 5 percent would cause noticeable harm to those who are caught unaware. It is also the case that individuals and businesses begin to complain about inflation when it reaches 4 or 5 percent per year. Knowing these facts, the Fed has opted for a 2-percent inflation target as a way of balancing the need to have a target greater than 0.5 percent with the need to not let inflation get uncomfortably high.

Assisting Downward Wage Flexibility A low but positive rate of inflation also helps to overcome the downward inflexibility of real wages by giving firms the ability to lower real wages by simply keeping nominal wages fixed as the 2-percent rate of inflation chips away at the purchasing power of those fixed nominal wages. This matters because it is *real* (inflation-adjusted) wages that determine real labor costs and, thus, the willingness of employers to hire additional employees. By making it easier for real wages to decline, the Fed makes it more likely that when a recession strikes and millions are unemployed, real wages can adjust downward and thereby increase the number of workers that firms want to hire. (See the Consider This piece in Chapter 29 for details.)

Avoiding the Zero Lower Bound A target rate of 2 percent should also help the Fed avoid the *zero lower bound problem* in which any nominal interest rate lower than zero will cause people to withdraw money from their checking accounts, thereby putting contractionary pressure on the economy because (1) banks will have a reduced ability to extend loans and (2) people who've switched to cash may spend less than they did back when they previously had ready access to electronic payments drawn from checking account balances.

inflationary expectations
The public's forecast about likely future *inflation* rates; influenceable by central bank policy actions, including a credible *target rate of inflation.*

The 2-percent target rate helps to avoid those problems by helping the public form its **inflationary expectations.** Just as long as the Fed is believed to be credible in its pronouncements, people will believe that it will use its control over the money supply to correct any deviation away from its 2-percent inflation target. That, in turn, will ensure that the nominal interest rates facing businesses and consumers should normally be at least 3 or 4 percent per year.

We know that such should be the case because of the equation presented in Chapter 29 that tells us that *the nominal interest rate = real interest rate + expected inflation.* If people believe that the Fed will always follow through on its commitment to maintaining an inflation rate at or near its target rate of 2 percent, then expected inflation on the right-hand side of that equation will be 2 percent. That will mean that the left-hand side, the nominal interest rate, will also have to be at least 2 percent. In fact, it should be even higher by the amount of the real interest rate (on the right-hand side of the equation) that lenders demand as compensation for the use of their money. Since that real rate of interest is likely to be at least 1 to 2 percent, the nominal interest rate should be at least 3 or 4 percent, which is high enough that if the economy were to enter into a recession, the Fed would have plenty of room to cut interest rates and stimulate the economy before having to worry about the zero lower bound problem.

Balancing Inflation and Unemployment Other things equal, the Fed will be more inclined toward a restrictive monetary policy if the actual rate of inflation is above the target rate of inflation, and more inclined toward an expansionary monetary policy if the actual rate of inflation is

..ıll KEY GRAPH

FIGURE 35.1 **The dual-mandate bullseye chart.**

The Federal Reserve's 2-percent inflation target and 3.5-percent unemployment target provide the "crosshairs" that define the center of the dual-mandate bullseye. For comparison, the red dot indicates where actual unemployment and actual inflation were in January 2022. The closer the Fed can get to hitting the center of the bullseye, the closer it is to achieving its dual mandate.

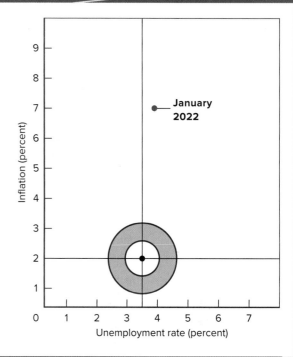

QUICK QUIZ FOR FIGURE 35.1

1. In the figure, the Fed's dual-mandate target is illustrated by:
   a. the red dot.
   b. the vertical cross-hairs line.
   c. the origin point where the vertical and horizontal axes intersect.
   d. the black dot.

2. Points that lie northwest (up and to the left) of the center of the bullseye indicate that the Fed should:
   a. definitely tighten monetary policy.
   b. definitely loosen monetary policy.
   c. definitely be neutral with monetary policy and make no changes.
   d. reflect on the mixed signals that it is receiving.

3. If the Fed's inflation target increased from 2 percent to 3 percent and its unemployment target increased from 3.5 percent to 5 percent, then:
   a. the red dot would move up and to the right.
   b. the black dot would move up and to the right.
   c. both crosshairs would move down and to the left.
   d. the red dot would move down and to the left.

4. Points that lie northeast (up and to the right) of the center of the bullseye indicate that the Fed should:
   a. raise its inflation target and increase its unemployment target.
   b. reflect on the mixed signals that it is receiving.
   c. definitely loosen monetary policy.
   d. definitely tighten monetary policy.

Answers: 1. d; 2. a; 3. b; 4. b

below the target rate of inflation. But it must also consider whether the unemployment rate is above or below the full-employment rate of unemployment. The two parts of the dual mandate must be pursued in tandem.

The Bullseye Chart

To help you visualize how the Fed pursues the dual mandate, consider **Figure 35.1 (Key Graph),** which presents the Federal Reserve's dual-mandate "bullseye chart" as of January 2022. The red dot indicates where the actual unemployment rate and actual inflation rate stood in January 2022. By contrast, the center of the bullseye plots the Fed's two target rates.

The position of the red dot relative to the center of the bullseye indicates the amounts by which actual unemployment and actual inflation differed from the Fed's target rates for unemployment and inflation in January 2022. As an exercise, look up the current unemployment and inflation rates and plot the spot that represents them. Is that spot close to the center of the bullseye? And in what direction does it lie relative to the center of the bullseye? To the northwest? Directly south? To the southeast? Keep that relative position in mind as you read the next section.

Adjusting Policy to Target the Bullseye

What should the Fed do when actual inflation and actual unemployment differ from the center of the dual-mandate bullseye?

It depends on where the red dot lies relative to the center of the bullseye.

Northwest and Southeast: No Conflicts If the red dot that plots actual inflation and unemployment is located to the northwest or southeast of the center of the bullseye, the Fed will have no confusion as to the stance of monetary policy. In those two quadrants, the actual inflation and unemployment rates will both suggest the same policy stance.

The Northwest Quadrant—Restrictive Policy Required If the current combination of actual employment and actual inflation is to the northwest of the center of the bullseye (that is, at any point where actual inflation exceeds 2 percent and actual unemployment is less than 3.5 percent), the economy is probably overheating and a restrictive monetary policy is in order. Higher interest rates will reduce aggregate demand, thereby putting downward pressure on prices while simultaneously cooling off the labor market. The actual inflation rate should fall downward, toward the 2-percent inflation target. The actual unemployment rate should rise upward, toward the 3.5 percent estimate of the full-employment rate of unemployment. If the restrictive monetary policy works as intended, the red dot will migrate toward the black dot at the center of the bullseye.

The Southeast Quadrant—Expansionary Policy Needed Now consider the situation for points to the southeast of the center of the bullseye. For those points, actual inflation is less than 2 percent while actual unemployment is higher than 3.5 percent. Any such combination suggests an economy operating below potential output. For these points, an expansionary monetary policy is appropriate. Lower interest rates will stimulate aggregate demand, thereby reducing the unemployment rate down toward the 3.5 percent estimate of the full-employment rate of unemployment while simultaneously raising the inflation rate up toward the Fed's 2-percent target. If the expansionary monetary policy works as intended, the red dot will migrate toward the black dot at the center of the bullseye.

Southwest and Northeast: Conflicts Things are not clear-cut in the other two quadrants. As you are about to see, the Fed will not easily know what to do in those locations because the inflation rate and unemployment rate will be suggesting *opposite* policy stances.

The Southwest Quadrant—Conflicting Signals To the southwest of the center of the bullseye (actual inflation less than 2 percent, actual unemployment less than 3.5 percent), the Fed will have a policy predicament. The fact that the actual unemployment rate is below the full-employment rate of unemployment will suggest that the Fed should be inclined toward a restrictive monetary policy. But the fact that the inflation rate is below 2 percent will suggest that an expansionary policy is in order.

The Northeast Quadrant—Conflicting Signals The opposite problem exists in the northeast quadrant (actual inflation greater than 2 percent, actual unemployment higher than 3.5 percent). There, the unemployment rate will be suggesting an expansionary monetary policy (to reduce the unemployment rate down to the 3.5 percent target) while the inflation rate will be suggesting a contractionary monetary policy (to reduce the inflation rate down to the 2-percent inflation target).

Putting Policy Weights on Inflation and Unemployment Complicating matters even further is the fact that very few policymakers are likely to give equal weight to inflation and unemployment. Indeed, if inflation remains mild, there may not be much harm if it exceeds the 2-percent target. By contrast, every bit of cyclical unemployment represents not only personal misery for those left unemployed but also permanently foregone output that cannot be recovered. Thus, most economists assume that FOMC members will give more weight to meeting the full-employment target.

One famous macroeconomic model, the so-called *Taylor rule*, goes so far as to assume that the FOMC will care *twice* as much about achieving the full-employment rate of unemployment as it will about meeting the 2-percent inflation target. Because this model has at times made accurate predictions about the FOMC's behavior with regard to setting an expansionary or restrictive monetary policy, its assumption that the FOMC cares twice as much about unemployment may be roughly correct. That being said, the FOMC is free to set monetary policy however it wishes, and has no allegiance to the Taylor Rule or any other system that tries to suggest how the Fed should weigh the trade-offs that may arise in specific situations between meeting one target or the other. The point of Figure 35.1 is not to predict exactly what the Fed will do in any given situation but rather to point out how its commitment to the dual mandate will tend to influence its decisions.

▶ The dual mandate states that the Fed's top two goals should be full employment and stable prices.

▶ In pursuing the dual mandate, the Fed aims for an inflation rate of 2 percent and an unemployment rate equal to its best estimate of the full-employment rate of unemployment. In the early

2020s, Fed officials believed that value to be around 3.5 percent of the labor force.

▶ The actual unemployment and inflation rates may give the Fed conflicting signals about whether monetary policy should be expansionary, restrictive, or neutral.

Monetary Policy, Real GDP, and the Price Level

We have identified and explained the tools of expansionary and restrictive monetary policy. We now want to explain how monetary policy affects investment, aggregate demand, real GDP, and the price level.

>> **LO35.4** Explain how monetary policy affects real GDP and the price level.

Cause-Effect Chain

The four diagrams in **Figure 35.2 (Key Graph)** will help you understand how monetary policy works toward achieving its goals.

The Market for Money   Figure 35.2a represents the "market for money" that we studied in Chapter 34.[2] It brings together the demand curve for money D_m as well as three supply curves for money: S_{m1}, S_{m2}, and S_{m3}.

Recall from the previous chapter that the total demand for money is composed of the transactions demand for money plus the asset demand for money. Demand curve D_m represents that sum.

Each of the three money supply curves is represented by a vertical line. That's because each line represents a different amount of money supply determined by the Fed. Since the Fed can set whatever supply of money it wants independently of the interest rate, each money supply curve plots as a vertical line (indicating that the quantity of money is independent of the interest rate).

The equilibrium interest rate is the rate at which the amount of money demanded equals the amount supplied. If the supply of money is $125 billion ($S_{m1}$), the equilibrium interest rate is 10 percent. With a money supply of $150 billion ($S_{m2}$), the equilibrium interest rate is 8 percent; with a money supply of $175 billion ($S_{m3}$), the equilibrium interest rate is 6 percent.

You know from Chapter 30 that the real (rather than the nominal) interest rate is critical for investment decisions. So here we assume that Figure 35.2a portrays the real interest rate.

Investment   These 10, 8, and 6 percent real interest rates are carried rightward to the investment demand curve in Figure 35.2b. This curve shows the inverse relationship between the interest rate—the cost of borrowing to invest—and the amount of investment spending. At the 10 percent interest rate, it will be profitable for the nation's businesses to invest $15 billion; at 8 percent, $20 billion; at 6 percent, $25 billion.

Changes in the interest rate mainly affect the investment component of total spending, although they also affect spending on durable consumer goods (such as autos) that are purchased on credit. Changes in the real interest rate greatly affect investment spending because of the large cost and long-term nature of capital purchases. Capital equipment, factory buildings, and warehouses are tremendously expensive. In absolute terms, interest charges on funds borrowed for these purchases are considerable. So the lower the interest rate, the more firms are willing to invest.

Similarly, the interest cost on a house purchased with a home mortgage loan is quite large. A 0.5 percent increase in the interest rate could amount to tens of thousands of dollars over the duration of the loan.

In brief, the impact of changing interest rates is mainly on investment (and, through that, on aggregate demand, output, employment, and the price level). Moreover, as Figure 35.2b shows, investment spending varies inversely with the real interest rate, so that if the real interest rate increases, investment spending declines, and vice versa.

Equilibrium GDP   Figure 35.2c shows the impact that our three real interest rates (and their corresponding levels of investment spending) have on aggregate demand. Aggregate demand curve AD_1 is associated with the $15 billion level of investment spending, AD_2 with the $20 billion level

---

[2]Please note that this "market for money" in which the demand for and supply of money determine an equilibrium interest rate has nothing at all to do with the wide variety of short-term lending markets for business and government loans that are collectively referred to as "the money market."

..ıll KEY GRAPH

FIGURE 35.2   Monetary policy and equilibrium GDP.

An expansionary monetary policy that shifts the money supply curve rightward from S_{m1} to S_{m2} in (a) lowers the interest rate from 10 to 8 percent in (b). As a result, investment spending increases from \$15 billion to \$20 billion, shifting the aggregate demand curve rightward from AD_1 to AD_2 in (c) so that real output rises from the recessionary level of \$880 billion to the full-employment level $Q_f =$ \$900 billion along the horizontal dashed line. In (d), the economy at point a has an inflationary output gap of \$10 billion because it is producing at \$910 billion, which is \$10 billion above the full-employment output level. A restrictive monetary policy that shifts the money supply curve leftward in (a) from $S_{m3} =$ \$175 billion to \$162.5 billion will increase the interest rate from 6 percent to 7 percent. Investment spending thus falls by \$2.5 billion, from \$25 billion to \$22.5 billion in (b). This initial decline is multiplied by 4 by the multiplier process so that the aggregate demand curve shifts leftward in (d) by \$10 billion from AD_3 to AD_4, moving the economy along the horizontal dashed line to equilibrium b. This returns the economy to full-employment output and eliminates the inflationary output gap.

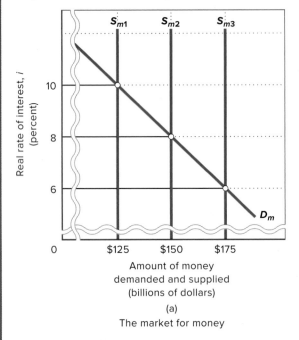

(a)
The market for money

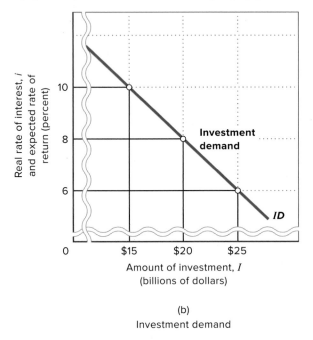

(b)
Investment demand

QUICK QUIZ FOR FIGURE 35.2

1. **The ultimate objective of an expansionary monetary policy is depicted by:**
   a. an increase in the price level from P_2 to P_3.
   b. a reduction of the interest rate from 8 to 6 percent.

   c. an increase in investment from \$20 billion to \$25 billion.
   d. an increase in real GDP from Q_1 to Q_f.

---

of investment spending, and AD_3 with the \$25 billion level of investment spending. Other things equal, higher investment spending shifts the aggregate demand curve to the right.

Suppose the money supply in Figure 35.2a is \$150 billion (S_{m2}), producing an equilibrium interest rate of 8 percent. In Figure 35.2b, we see that this 8 percent interest rate will bring about \$20 billion of investment spending. This \$20 billion of investment spending joins with consumption spending, net exports, and government spending to yield aggregate demand curve AD_2 in Figure 35.2c. The equilibrium levels of real output and prices are $Q_f =$ \$900 billion and P_2, as determined by the intersection of AD_2 and the aggregate supply curve AS.

To test your understanding of these relationships, explain why each of the other two levels of money supply in Figure 35.2a results in a different interest rate, level of investment, aggregate demand curve, and equilibrium real output.

Effects of an Expansionary Monetary Policy

Recall that real-world price levels tend to be downwardly inflexible. Thus, with our economy starting from the initial equilibrium where AD_2 intersects AS, the price level will be downwardly inflexible at P_2 so that aggregate supply will be horizontal for values of real output to the left of Q_f. Thus,

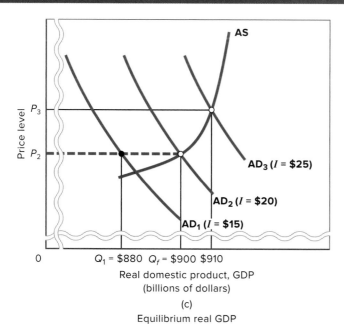

(c)
Equilibrium real GDP
and the price level

(d)
Equilibrium real GDP
and the price level

2. A successful restrictive monetary policy is evidenced by a shift in the money supply curve from:

a. S_{m3} to a point halfway between S_{m2} and S_{m3}, a decrease in investment from $25 billion to $22.5 billion, and a decline in aggregate demand from AD_3 to AD_4.

b. S_{m1} to S_{m2}, an increase in investment from $20 billion to $25 billion, and an increase in real GDP from Q_1 to Q_f.

c. S_{m3} to S_{m2}, a decrease in investment from $25 billion to $20 billion, and a decline in the price level from P_3 to P_2.

d. S_{m3} to S_{m2}, a decrease in investment from $25 billion to $20 billion, and an increase in aggregate demand from AD_2 to AD_3.

3. The Federal Reserve could increase the money supply from S_{m1} to S_{m2} by:

a. increasing the discount rate.

b. reducing taxes.

c. purchasing bonds as part of quantitative easing (QE).

d. selling bonds as part of quantitative tightening (QT).

4. If the spending-income multiplier is 4 in the economy depicted, an increase in the money supply from $125 billion to $150 billion will:

a. shift the aggregate demand curve rightward by $20 billion.

b. increase real GDP by $25 billion.

c. increase real GDP by $100 billion.

d. shift the aggregate demand curve leftward by $5 billion.

Answers: 1. d; 2. a; 3. c; 4. a

if aggregate demand decreases, the economy's equilibrium moves leftward along the dashed horizontal line shown in Figure 35.2c.

Such a decline would happen if the money supply fell to $125 billion ($S_{m1}$), shifting the aggregate demand curve leftward to AD_1 in Figure 35.2b. The result is a real output of $880 billion, $20 billion less than the economy's full-employment output level of $900 billion. The economy will be experiencing recession, a negative GDP gap, and substantial unemployment. The Fed therefore should institute an expansionary monetary policy.

The FOMC will take some combination of the following expansionary monetary policy actions: (1) utilize positive forward guidance by announcing a lower federal funds target range; (2) lower the IORB and ON RRP rates as necessary to guide the effective federal funds rate down into the new federal funds target range; and/or (3) engage in quantitative easing by purchasing longer-term government bonds. The intended outcome is lower short-term and long-term interest rates that will increase investment, aggregate demand, and equilibrium GDP.

Those lower rates can be achieved by the Fed because its expansionary monetary policy actions will all tend to expand the money supply: (1) Positive forward guidance backed by a lower effective federal funds rate will cause an increase in checkable-deposit money as more loans are extended by depository institutions due to increased optimism about future economic prospects;

(2) the lower IORB and ON RRP rates will increase the amount of money circulating in the economy outside the Fed's vaults as financial firms react to the lower IORB and ON RRP rates by lending less reserves to the Fed; and (3) purchases of government bonds as part of QE will increase the money supply as the Fed creates new money to pay for those bond purchases.

Suppose that the Fed's expansionary actions increase the money supply from $125 billion to $150 billion ($S_{m1}$ to S_{m2}). That reduces the interest rate from 10 to 8 percent in Figure 35.2a, which in turn boosts investment spending from $15 billion to $20 billion in Figure 35.2b. This $5 billion increase in investment shifts the aggregate demand curve rightward by more than the increase in investment because of the multiplier effect. If the economy's MPC is 0.75, the multiplier will be 4, meaning that the $5 billion increase in investment shifts the AD curve rightward by $20 billion ($= 4 \times \$5$ billion) at each price level. Specifically, aggregate demand shifts from AD_1 to AD_2, as Figure 35.2c shows. This rightward shift in the aggregate demand curve along the dashed horizontal line will eliminate the negative GDP gap by increasing GDP from $880 billion to the full-employment GDP of $Q_f = \$900$ billion.[3]

Column 1 in Table 35.3 summarizes the chain of events associated with an expansionary monetary policy.

Effects of a Restrictive Monetary Policy

Next we consider restrictive monetary policy. We will use graphs *a*, *b*, and *d* of Figure 35.2 to demonstrate the effects of a restrictive monetary policy. Figure 35.2d represents exactly the same economy as Figure 35.2c but adds some extra curves that relate only to restrictive monetary policy. You should consequently ignore Figure 35.2c as we go through this section.

To see how restrictive monetary policy works, first consider a situation in which the economy moves from operating at a full-employment equilibrium to operating at more than full employment, so that inflation is a problem and restrictive monetary policy is appropriate. Assume that the economy begins at the full-employment equilibrium where AD_2 and AS intersect. At this equilibrium, $Q_f = \$900$ billion, and the price level is P_2.

Next, assume that the money supply expands from $150 billion to $175 billion ($S_{m3}$) in Figure 35.2a. The result is an interest rate of 6 percent, investment spending of $25 billion rather than $20 billion, and aggregate demand AD_3. As the AD curve shifts to the right from AD_2 to AD_3 in Figure 35.2d, the economy moves along the upward sloping AS curve until it reaches an equilibrium at point *a*, where AD_3 intersects AS. At the new equilibrium, the price level has risen to P_3 and the equilibrium level of real GDP has increased to $910 billion, indicating an inflationary GDP gap of $10 billion ($= \$910$ billion $- \$900$ billion). Aggregate demand AD_3 is excessive relative to the economy's full-employment level of real output $Q_f = \$900$ billion. To rein in spending, the Fed will institute a restrictive monetary policy.

TABLE 35.3 Monetary Policies for Recession and Inflation

(1) Expansionary Monetary Policy	(2) Restrictive Monetary Policy
Problem: unemployment and recession	*Problem:* inflation
↓	↓
Positive forward guidance, a lower federal funds target range, reductions in IORB and ON RRP, and/or quantitative easing	Negative forward guidance, a higher federal funds target range, increases in IORB and ON RRP, and/or quantitative tightening
↓	↓
Money supply rises	Money supply falls
↓	↓
Interest rates fall	Interest rates rise
↓	↓
Investment spending increases	Investment spending decreases
↓	↓
Aggregate demand increases	Aggregate demand decreases
↓	↓
Real GDP rises	Inflation declines

---

[3]To keep things simple, we are assuming that the increase in real GDP does not increase the demand for money. In reality, the transactions demand for money would rise along with real GDP, thereby slightly increasing interest rates in the economy and slightly offsetting the decline of the interest rate from 8 to 6 percent that was engineered by the Fed.

The FOMC will undertake some combination of the following restrictive monetary policy actions: (1) utilize negative forward guidance by announcing a higher federal funds target range; (2) raise the IORB and ON RRP rates as necessary to guide the effective federal funds rate up into the new federal funds target range; and/or (3) engage in quantitative tightening by selling longer-term government bonds. The intended outcome is higher short-term and long-term interest rates that will decrease investment, aggregate demand, and equilibrium GDP.

Those higher rates can be achieved by the Fed because its restrictive monetary policy actions will all tend to decrease the money supply: (1) Negative forward guidance backed by a higher effective federal funds rate will cause a decrease in the total amount of checkable-deposit money as fewer new loans are extended due to decreased optimism about future economic prospects; (2) the higher IORB and ON RRP rates will increase the amount of money locked away in the Fed's vaults as financial firms react to the higher IORB and ON RRP rates by lending more reserves to the Fed; and (3) sales of longer-term government bonds as part of QT will decrease the money supply as the Fed stores away in its vaults, completely out of public circulation, all of the money paid to it by the purchasers of those bonds.

The Fed must be careful, though, about just *how much* to decrease the money supply. The problem is that prices are inflexible at price level P_3. As a result, the dashed horizontal line to the left of point a in Figure 35.2d becomes relevant, and the Fed cannot simply lower the money supply to S_{m2} in Figure 35.2a. If it were to do that, investment demand would fall to $20 billion in Figure 35.2b, and the AD curve would shift to the left from AD_3 back to AD_2. But because of inflexible prices, the economy's equilibrium would move to point c, where AD_2 intersects the horizontal dashed line that represents aggregate supply to the left of point a. This would put the economy into a recession, with equilibrium output below the full-employment output level $Q_f = \$900$ billion.

What the Fed needs to do to achieve full employment is to move the AD curve back only from AD_3 to AD_4, so that the economy will come to equilibrium at point b. This will require a $10 billion decrease in aggregate demand, so that equilibrium output falls from $910 billion at point a to $Q_f = \$900$ billion at point b. The Fed can achieve this shift by setting the supply of money in Figure 35.2a at $162.5 billion.

To see how this works, draw in a vertical money supply curve in Figure 35.2a at $162.5 billion and label it as S_{m4}. It will be exactly halfway between money supply curves S_{m2} and S_{m3}. Notice that the intersection of S_{m4} with the money demand curve D_m results in a 7 percent interest rate. In Figure 35.2b, this 7 percent interest rate results in investment spending of $22.5 billion (halfway between $20 billion and $25 billion). Thus, by setting the money supply at $162.5 billion, the Fed can reduce investment spending by $2.5 billion, lowering it from the $25 billion associated with AD_3 down to only $22.5 billion. This decline in investment spending initially shifts the AD curve only $2.5 billion to the left of AD_3. But then the multiplier process works its magic. Because the multiplier is 4 in our model, the AD curve ends up moving by a full $10 billion ($= 4 \times \$2.5$ billion) to the left, to AD_4. This shift moves the economy to equilibrium b, returning output to the full-employment level and eliminating the inflationary GDP gap.[4]

Column 2 in Table 35.3 summarizes the cause-effect chain of a restrictive money policy.

▶ The Fed engages in an expansionary monetary policy when it increases the money supply to reduce interest rates and increase investment spending and real GDP.

▶ The Fed engages in a restrictive monetary policy when it reduces the money supply to increase interest rates and reduce investment spending and inflation.

▶ When pursuing a restrictive monetary policy, the Fed must be careful to take into account downward price stickiness and its effect on the size of the multiplier.

QUICK REVIEW

35.4

Monetary Policy: Evaluation and Issues

Monetary policy has become the dominant component of U.S. national stabilization policy. It has two key advantages over fiscal policy:

- Speed and flexibility.
- Isolation from political pressure.

>> **LO35.5** Explain the advantages and shortcomings of monetary policy.

---

[4]Again, we assume for simplicity that the decrease in GDP does not feed back to reduce the demand for money and thus the interest rate. In reality, this would occur, slightly offsetting the increase in the interest rate that was engineered by the Fed.

Compared with fiscal policy, monetary policy can be quickly altered. Recall that congressional deliberations may delay the application of fiscal policy for months. In contrast, the FOMC is free to update monetary policy on a daily basis if necessary.

Also, because the members of the Board of Governors serve 14-year terms, they are relatively isolated from political lobbying and need not worry about retaining their popularity with voters. Thus, the Board, more readily than congress, can engage in politically unpopular policies (such as higher interest rates) that may be necessary for the economy's long-term health.

In addition, monetary policy is subtler and more politically neutral than fiscal policy. Changes in government spending and taxes directly affect the allocation of resources, and are sometimes so narrowly targeted that they bring benefits only to a single firm or a single congressional district. By contrast, because monetary policy works broadly and indirectly, it is more politically palatable.

Recent U.S. Monetary Policy

The Federal Reserve has been very busy over the last two decades.

The Mortgage Default Crisis The 2007–2008 financial crisis was precipitated by a huge wave of home-mortgage defaults that began in 2006. The Fed responded with several actions as the crisis became severe in the summer of 2007. In August 2007, it lowered the discount rate by half a percentage point. Then, between September 2007 and April 2008, it lowered the effective federal funds rate from 5.25 percent to 2.00 percent. The Fed also took a series of extraordinary actions to prevent the failure of key financial firms that would otherwise have been overwhelmed by withdrawal requests on the part of depositors and investors.

By late 2008, it was clear that the U.S. economy faced a crisis unequaled since the Great Depression of the 1930s. The Fed responded with a series of innovative monetary policy initiatives.

zero interest rate policy (ZIRP) A *monetary policy* in which a *central bank* sets *nominal interest rates* at or near zero percent per year in order to stimulate the economy.

The Fed began by moving toward a **zero interest rate policy,** or **ZIRP,** in December 2008. Under ZIRP, the Fed aimed to keep short-term interest rates near zero to stimulate the economy. It lowered the federal funds target range to just zero to 0.25 percent and acted aggressively as a lender of last resort, lending freely at the discount rate. The Fed also took the highly unusual step of acting as a "buyer of last resort," purchasing debt securities from financial firms at pre-crisis prices so that those firms would not have to sell those assets at the low, panic prices then prevailing in the bond markets.

The crisis was resolved by late 2009, after which the Fed no longer had to act as a lender or buyer of last resort. But with the unemployment rate rising toward 10 percent, the Fed had to figure out a way to continue stimulating the economy even though ZIRP meant that short-term interest rates were as low as they could go without encountering the zero lower bound problem.

As explained earlier, the Fed's solution was to keep short-term interest rates low with IORB and ON RRP while initiating its first quantitative easing, or QE, program to lower longer-term interest rates.

The 2010s Recovery By the close of 2015, the Fed felt that various economic indicators were signaling that monetary stimulus could end. For example, the unemployment rate had fallen back to just 5 percent in 2015, which was well below its 2009 peak of 10 percent. On that basis, the FOMC decided that the Fed could abandon ZIRP and QE while raising interest rates back up toward normal levels using forward guidance, a higher federal funds target range, increases in IORB and ON RRP, and quantitative tightening. Over the next five years, interest rates gradually increased and the economy continued to improve.

By early 2020, the U.S. economy was operating at full employment, with a 3.5-percent unemployment rate that exactly equaled the Fed's unemployment target and a 2.3-percent inflation rate that was only slightly higher than the Fed's inflation target. Given that the economy was operating almost exactly at the center of the Fed's bullseye target, it seemed that the Fed might have very little to do for the next few years.

The 2020 COVID Recession When COVID-19 struck in the spring of 2020 and governments all over the world ordered lockdowns, it was clear that the economic damage might be severe. The Fed responded with every tool at its disposal. It used forward guidance to make it clear to the public that it understood that the crisis was severe and needed an aggressive response. It lowered the federal funds target range down to the lowest possible non-negative range, 0 to 0.25 percent. It used the administered rates to not only get the effective federal funds rate into the new target range but to also guide all of the other money-market rates to very low levels. And it reinitiated QE by purchasing $3 trillion of longer-term bonds to lower longer-term interest rates.

Thanks in large part to the Fed's aggressive actions, the COVID recession was the shortest on record and the economy was back to producing at potential output by the fall of 2021, just 18 months after lockdowns were initiated in March 2020.

Problems and Complications

U.S. monetary policy faces both limitations and complications.

Recognition and Operational Lags Recall from Chapter 33 that fiscal policy is hindered by three delays, or lags—a recognition lag, an administrative lag, and an operational lag. By contrast, while monetary policy also usually faces a recognition lag and an operational lag, the FOMC's ability to alter its monetary policy stance on a daily, or even hourly, basis implies that monetary policy is *not* subject to an administrative lag.

With respect to the Fed's recognition lag, the COVID pandemic was perhaps the only instance in U.S. history where monetary policy was *not* subject to a recognition lag. That was true because the implementation of lockdowns and workplace closures made it obvious to everyone that a recession was going to happen. Under more typical circumstances, however, monetary policy *does* face a recognition lag because the many random fluctuations in economic activity and the rate of inflation that occur over the course of the business cycle make it difficult for the Fed to quickly recognize when the economy is *truly* starting to recede or when inflation is *really* starting to taking off.

With respect to the Fed's operational lag, changes in interest rates typically involve an operational lag of at least 3 to 6 months because that much time is required for interest-rate changes to have any substantial impacts on investment, aggregate demand, real GDP, or the price level. By contrast, the effects of forward guidance on individual and firm behavior can be nearly instantaneous. The same is true of the Fed's ability to calm a financial panic by showing that it will act as a lender of last resort.

Cyclical Asymmetry and the Liquidity Trap As a general matter, monetary policy may be highly effective in slowing expansions and controlling inflation but much less reliable in pulling the economy out of a severe recession. As a result, economists sometimes say that monetary policy is subject to a **cyclical asymmetry.** The metaphor of "pushing on a string" is often invoked to capture this dichotomy, or difference.

To understand the metaphor, imagine that the FOMC is standing on the left-hand side of Figure 35.2c, holding one end of a monetary-policy string. And then imagine that the other end of the monetary-policy string is tied to the AD curve. Because the string would go taut if pulled on, monetary policy may be useful in pulling aggregate demand to the left. But because the string would go limp if pushed on, monetary policy will be ineffective at pushing aggregate demand to the right.

The reason for this asymmetry, or difference, is the asymmetric way in which people act in response to higher interest rates. If pursued vigorously, a restrictive monetary policy can, for example, make banks feel that the extension of new business loans is very unattractive compared to other lending options made available by the Fed. Why, for example, would a bank want to extend risky businesses loans at 5 percent if the Fed, via IORB, is offering them a risk-free rate of 5.5 percent? The result is less lending, less investment, and reduced aggregate demand. Consequently, the Fed can almost certainly achieve a restrictive goal with the policy tools at its disposal.

By contrast, the Fed cannot be certain of achieving an expansionary goal by lowering interest rates. That's because it may encounter a **liquidity trap,** in which the lower interest rates and larger amounts of bank reserves (liquidity) that the Fed provides to fight a recession have little or no effect on lending, borrowing, investment, or aggregate demand. For example, the Fed's response to the 2007–2009 financial crisis involved lowering short-term rates to nearly zero and purchasing so many government bonds from the public that the perfectly liquid reserve balances held by banks and thrifts soared from just $44 billion before the crisis to over $1.1 trillion in 2009.

cyclical asymmetry The idea that *monetary policy* may be more successful in slowing expansions and controlling *inflation* than in extracting the economy from severe recession.

liquidity trap A situation in a severe *recession* in which the *central bank's* injection of additional currency (liquidity) into the financial system has little or no additional positive impact on lending, borrowing, *investment,* or *aggregate demand.*

A New Inflationary Era?

As the Fed Decided How Aggressively to Raise Interest Rates to Fight the Post-Pandemic Inflation, It Had to Consider Whether the World Economy Had Permanently Transitioned to a More Inflationary Era.

When inflation spiked after the COVID-19 pandemic, both Wall Street and Main Street wondered how, exactly, the Fed would react, both in the short run and in the long run. A crucial consideration was whether the U.S. economy—and indeed the entire world economy—had shifted from an era during which inflation fighting was easy to one in which inflation fighting would be more difficult due to permanent changes in resource supplies and production processes.

Consider labor force growth. The U.S. labor force grew rapidly starting in the 1960s as the very large Baby Boom generation entered the labor force, as the U.S. massively expanded legal immigration, and as legal and cultural changes facilitated women's entering the labor force in huge numbers for the first time.

As a result of those massive and ongoing increases in the supply of labor, wage growth was suppressed relative to what it would have been had the labor force not grown as rapidly. From the perspective of employers, labor was relatively inexpensive, which in turn pushed the aggregate supply curve rightward relative to where it would have been if labor costs had been higher.

The net effect was downward pressure on the price level, all other things equal. And that meant that the Fed was operating in an economic environment that enjoyed constant downward price pressures due to strong labor force growth.

That all started to change after the 2007–2008 recession as immigration to the United States slowed. The change accelerated sharply when over a million older workers decided to retire early during the COVID pandemic. And it was kicked up yet another notch when over a million prime-age workers did not return to employment after the pandemic ended. The net result was a U.S. labor force that was about 2.5 million workers smaller at the end of 2022 than it would have been had pre-pandemic labor-force growth trends continued.

That smaller pool of available workers generated widespread labor shortages across many industries, thereby driving up the cost of labor and shifting the aggregate supply curve leftward. And because the U.S. birth rate plunged during the pandemic, it became more likely that the long-run growth rate of the U.S. labor force might fall significantly over the coming decades, even after accounting for future immigration. Such a scenario would, all other things equal, generate higher labor costs and, thus, higher inflationary pressures.

A second economywide factor that could be permanently inflationary is the reversal of globalization that was observed in the aftermath of the pandemic. After international supply chains were repeatedly snarled during the pandemic, many corporate managers reacted by reorganizing their production processes so as to have components and inputs produced less far away. That, though, drives up costs because "on-shoring" and "near-shoring" almost always involve the use of suppliers who are more expensive, sometimes significantly so. If that trend continues and becomes permanent, it will put upward pressure on inflation that did not exist when components

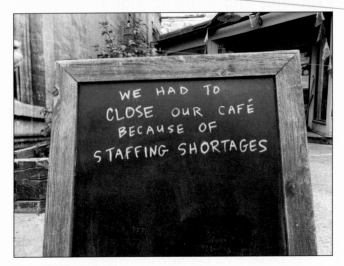

Michael Vi/Shutterstock

and raw materials were sourced to the very cheapest producer anywhere in the world.

A third factor that suggests that the world economy may be permanently moving into a higher-cost, more inflationary era is the fact that energy costs look likely to rise going forward for both geopolitical and environmental reasons. In terms of geopolitics, sanctions against Russia for invading the Ukraine in early 2022 meant less Russian oil and natural gas being sold onto the world energy market, driving up their price. In addition, many governments are passing laws to move away from lower-cost but more-polluting energy sources like coal and oil toward wind, solar, and renewables. Unfortunately, many of those "green energy" sources come with higher price tags, either for dealing with their intermittency (the sun does not shine at night; the wind often fails to blow) or for having to build out a lot of new infrastructure (such as for delivering more electricity across electrical grids if all vehicles switch from gasoline and diesel to electric). The net result may be higher energy prices throughout the economy and thus constant inflationary pressures that central banks will have to deal with.

For central bankers, several possibilities are raised by the prospect of a new era that has stronger inflationary pressures. If such an era is indeed upon us, central banks might, for example, have to raise interest rates more aggressively than they did before the pandemic to keep inflation equally under control. Alternatively, perhaps it might be better to not try very hard to fight the new inflationary trends if doing so would generate high unemployment. If that were the eventual consensus, then the Fed might settle for, say, a 4-percent inflation target rather than a 2-percent inflation target and only raise interest rates aggressively if inflation rose appreciably higher than 4 percent. Time will tell.

Nevertheless, despite all of that liquidity, commercial bank lending fell by 25 percent during the recession and remained weak over the following five years. Banks were fearful that loans would not be paid back. So they opted to make fewer loans. The result was low investment spending and low aggregate demand despite the much lower interest rates and much greater liquidity that had been engineered by the Fed.

Finally, it should be pointed out that the Fed has continued to maintain high amounts of liquidity in the banking system by purchasing massive amounts of government bonds from the public through various forms of open-market operations, including QE and reverse-repo transactions. The Fed refers to that high-liquidity policy as the "ample reserves regime" and has stated that it intends to continue with an ample reserves regime for the foreseeable future. As a result, bank and thrift reserve balances are expected to remain at very high levels, and indeed totaled over $3.8 trillion at the start of 2022.

Other Issues and Concerns The liquidity trap scenario demonstrates that the Fed is not omnipotent. An expansionary monetary policy can suffer from a "you can lead a horse to water, but you can't make it drink" problem. As we just explained, the Fed can lower interest rates, but it cannot guarantee that banks will want to make additional loans. Households and businesses can frustrate the Fed, too, by not wanting to borrow. And when the Fed buys securities from the public, the sellers may save the money they receive from the Fed, rather than increasing their spending on goods and services.

The liquidity trap that occurred during the 2007–2009 crisis was a primary reason why congress acted so forcefully with respect to *fiscal* policy in the spring of 2009. With monetary policy maxed out, Congress approved the gargantuan American Recovery and Redevelopment Act, which authorized the infusion of $787 billion of tax cuts and government spending in 2009 and 2010. This spending helped to ensure a rightward shift of AD even after interest rates had fallen toward zero and banks were sitting on reserves rather than lending.

Fiscal policy was also used aggressively during the COVID-19 crisis, since it was not clear that banks would lend or that borrowers would borrow despite the Fed's herculean efforts to lower both short-term and long-term interest rates. The Paycheck Protection Program and the CARES Act got cash directly into the hands of unemployed workers and struggling businesses. The result was a highly potent dose of fiscal stimulus at a time when monetary policy was very likely "maxed out" and hobbled by a liquidity trap.

The fiscal stimulus was in fact so effective and so long lasting that it contributed significantly to the jump in the U.S. inflation rate from 1.4 percent in the first year of the pandemic, 2020, to 7.0 percent the next year. As you know, that extremely large increase in the inflation rate occurred because the massive fiscal stimulus enacted by congress to fight the pandemic combined with supply chain problems caused by the pandemic to simultaneously shift AD to the right and AS to the left, thereby generating the highest U.S. inflation rate since 1981.

▶ Monetary policy has several major advantages over fiscal policy, including isolation from political pressures and the absence of an administrative lag.

▶ To help stimulate the economy after the Great Recession, the Federal Reserve implemented the zero interest rate policy (ZIRP) and quantitative easing (QE).

▶ The main weaknesses of monetary policy are cyclical asymmetry, the liquidity trap, and the recognition and operational lags.

**QUICK REVIEW
35.5**

The "Big Picture"

Figure 35.3 (Key Graph) brings together the analytical and policy aspects of macroeconomics discussed in this and the seven preceding chapters. This "big picture" shows how the many concepts and principles that we have covered relate to one another and how they constitute a coherent theory of the price level and real output in a market economy.

Study this diagram and you will see that the price level, output, employment, and income all result from the interaction of aggregate supply and aggregate demand. The items shown in red relate to public policy.

>> **LO35.6** Describe how the various components of macroeconomic theory and stabilization policy fit together.

⣿⣿ KEY GRAPH

FIGURE 35.3 **The AD–AS theory of the price level, real output, and stabilization policy.**

This figure integrates the various components of macroeconomic theory and stabilization policy. Components that either constitute public policy or are strongly influenced by public policy are shown in red.

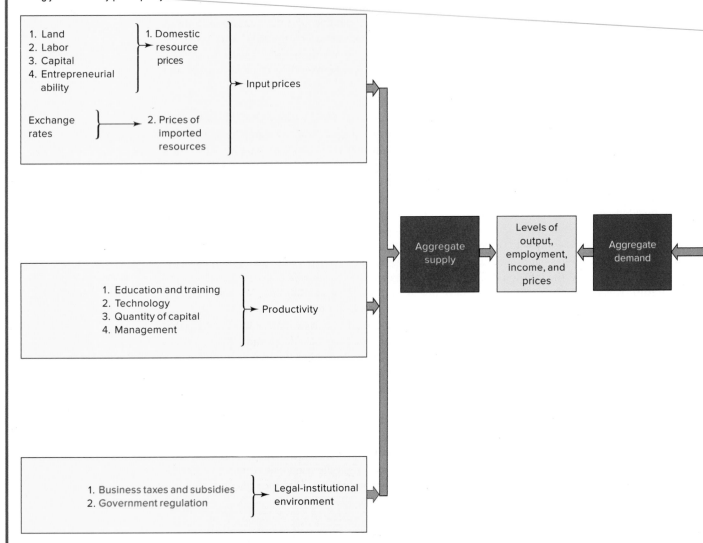

QUICK QUIZ FOR FIGURE 35.3

1. **All else equal, an increase in domestic resource availability will:**
   a. increase input prices, reduce aggregate supply, and increase real output.
   b. raise labor productivity, reduce interest rates, and lower the international value of the dollar.
   c. increase net exports, increase investment, and reduce aggregate demand.
   d. reduce input prices, increase aggregate supply, and increase real output.

2. **All else equal, an expansionary monetary policy during a recession will:**
   a. lower the interest rate, increase investment, and reduce net exports.
   b. lower the interest rate, increase investment, and increase aggregate demand.
   c. increase the interest rate, increase investment, and reduce net exports.
   d. reduce productivity, aggregate supply, and real output.

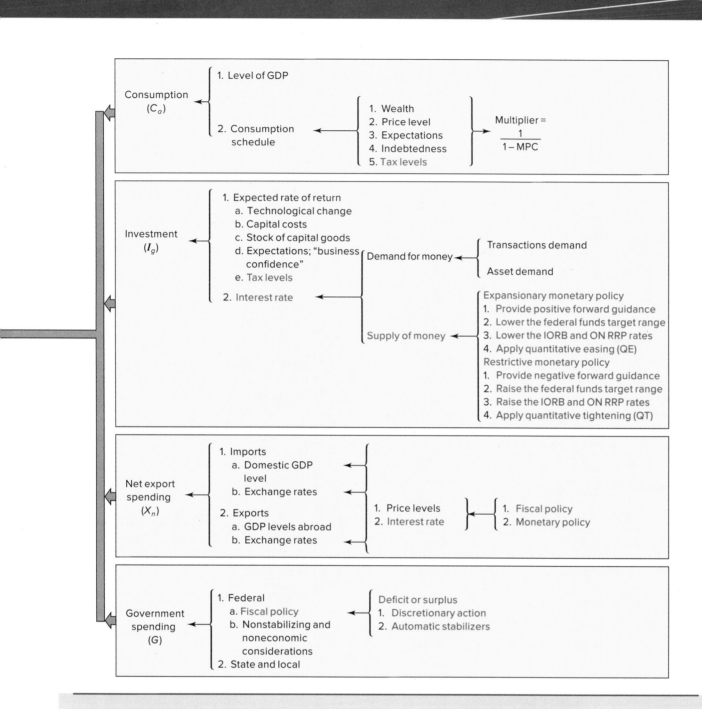

3. A personal income tax cut, combined with a reduction in corporate income and excise taxes, would:

   a. increase consumption, investment, aggregate demand, and aggregate supply.

   b. reduce productivity, raise input prices, and reduce aggregate supply.

   c. increase government spending, reduce net exports, and increase aggregate demand.

   d. increase the supply of money, reduce interest rates, increase investment, and expand real output.

4. An appreciation of the dollar would:

   a. reduce the price of imported resources, lower input prices, and increase aggregate supply.

   b. increase net exports and aggregate demand.

   c. increase aggregate supply and aggregate demand.

   d. reduce consumption, investment, net export spending, and government spending.

Summary

LO35.1 Explain the tools of monetary policy, including open-market operations, forward guidance, and the administered rates.

The main tools of monetary policy are (a) open-market operations, (b) the administered interest rates, and (c) forward guidance.

The three administered rates are the *interest rate on reserve balances* (IORB) at which depository institutions (banks and thrifts) can lend the Fed money; the *overnight reverse repo rate* (ON RRP) at which nondepository financial firms can lend the Fed money; and the *discount rate* at which depository institutions can borrow money from the Fed.

The Federal Reserve's policy rate is the *effective federal funds rate,* for which it publicly announces a target range as part of its forward guidance efforts.

The Fed adjusts the IORB and ON RRP rates to control the effective federal funds rate as well as other money market interest rates.

LO35.2 Relate how the Fed's tools and strategies have evolved over the past several decades.

Before the 2007–2008 financial crisis, the Federal Reserve used open-market operations exclusively for raising and lowering the effective federal funds rate.

The crisis was so severe, though, that the Fed had to lower the effective federal funds rate to nearly zero, which, due to the zero lower bound problem, meant that the Fed needed additional ways to stimulate the economy.

One solution was quantitative easing, or the pre-announced purchase of a specific dollar amount (quantity) of longer-term government bonds to lower (ease) interest rates on longer-term government debt. The Fed also began to use IORB, ON RRP, and forward guidance. Together, these policy tools constitute the "new normal" of monetary policy in the United States.

LO35.3 Define the Fed's dual mandate and explain how conflicts can arise between meeting the inflation target and the unemployment target.

Congress has instructed the Federal Reserve to simultaneously pursue two goals, or targets: the full-employment rate of unemployment (which is currently estimated to be around 3 to 4 percent of the labor force) and the target rate of inflation (which the Fed has set at 2 percent per year).

The Dual Mandate Bullseye chart illustrates how the Fed may sometimes receive "mixed signals" about whether it should pursue an expansionary, restrictive, or neutral monetary policy. It is assumed by many economists that, in such situations, the Fed will put more emphasis on full employment in the labor force than on meeting its inflation target.

LO35.4 Explain how monetary policy affects real GDP and the price level.

Monetary policy affects the economy through a complex chain of causation: (a) forward guidance, including any change to the federal funds target range, helps to shape the spending, saving, and investment decisions of both individuals and firms; (b) changes to the IORB and ON RRP rates alter short-term interest rates in the money market, including the effective federal funds rate; (c) quantitative easing or tightening shift longer-term interest rates; (d) changes in both short-term and longer-term interest rates affect investment; (e) changes in investment affect aggregate demand; (f) changes in aggregate demand affect real GDP and the price level. Table 35.3 summarizes all of the basic ideas relevant to the use of monetary policy.

LO35.5 Explain the advantages and shortcomings of monetary policy.

The advantages of monetary policy include its flexibility and political acceptability. In the late 2000s and 2010s, the Fed used monetary policy to help stabilize the financial sector in the wake of the 2007–2009 financial crisis and to promote recovery from the Great Recession of 2007–2009. The Fed also acted swiftly to promote financial stability and rapid recovery when the COVID crisis struck in 2020. Today, nearly all economists view monetary policy as a significant stabilization tool.

Monetary policy has two major limitations: (1) the recognition and operational lags complicate the timing of monetary policy; and (2) in a severe recession, the reluctance of banks to lend—and of firms and households to borrow—may contribute to a liquidity trap that limits the effectiveness of an expansionary monetary policy.

LO35.6 Describe how the various components of macroeconomic theory and stabilization policy fit together.

The economy's *aggregate supply* of final goods and services is determined by input prices, productivity, and the legal-institutional environment.

The economy's *aggregate demand* for final goods and services is determined by the factors that influence consumption spending, investment expenditures, net export spending, and government expenditures.

Terms and Concepts

monetary policy	federal funds rate	expansionary monetary policy
open-market operations	federal funds market	restrictive monetary policy
administered rate	federal funds target range	neutral monetary policy
money market	effective federal funds rate	target rate of inflation
interest rate on reserve balances (IORB)	zero lower bound problem	inflationary expectations
overnight reverse repo rate (ON RRP)	quantitative easing (QE)	zero interest rate policy (ZIRP)
discount rate	quantitative tightening (QT)	cyclical asymmetry
forward guidance	dual mandate	liquidity trap
policy rate	full-employment rate of unemployment	
monetary policy stance	target rate of unemployment	

Discussion Questions

1. What are open-market operations, and how do they affect interest rates and the money supply? **LO35.1**

2. What are the Federal Reserve's three administered rates and which of them involve the Fed borrowing as opposed to lending? Which one is most important in terms of helping to mitigate or avoid bank runs? **LO35.1**

3. Why does the Fed employ forward guidance? How does the federal funds target range relate to the Fed's forward-guidance efforts? **LO35.1**

4. What is the zero lower bound? What bad things might happen if the Fed lowered short-term interest rates below zero? **LO35.2**

5. What is the difference between quantitative tightening and quantitative easing? Why did the Fed feel that it was necessary to start using quantitative easing for the first time during the financial crisis? **LO35.2**

6. What are the two parts of the Fed's dual mandate? How does the dual mandate relate to the bullseye chart? Which quadrants of the bullseye chart give conflicting signals to the Fed and what is the source of the confusion in each case? **LO35.3**

7. How does the Fed's 2-percent inflation target help with downward wage flexibility? **LO35.3**

8. Explain the links between changes in a nation's money supply, interest rate, investment spending, aggregate demand, real GDP, and price level. **LO35.4**

9. Suppose that the FOMC chair makes an official public statement that (1) substantially increases investor expectations for faster economic growth but which (2) does *not* change the administered rates or what the Fed has been doing with respect to quantitative easing, open-market operations, and other monetary policy actions. What will be the effect on the investment demand curve? (Hint: Recall the difference between a movement along a curve and a shift of a curve.) **LO35.4**

10. Why was the Fed designed to be insulated from political pressure? What might go wrong with monetary policy if it were not insulated from political pressure? Explain. **LO35.5**

11. What do economists mean when they say that monetary policy can exhibit cyclical asymmetry? How does the idea of a liquidity trap relate to cyclical asymmetry? Why is the possibility of a liquidity trap significant to policymakers? **LO35.5**

12. What component of aggregate demand is influenced by technological change? What about for aggregate supply? How would improvements in productivity affect investment spending? Other things equal, how would improvements in the productivity of capital affect the interest rate? **LO35.6**

13. **LAST WORD** Why would slower growth of the labor force put upward pressure on inflation? What are "on-shoring" and "near-shoring" and how do they affect inflationary pressures in the economy? How might the Fed react to an era of higher inflationary pressures? Explain.

Review Questions

1. If the effective federal funds rate is 2.14 percent, which of the following is most likely to be the Fed's target range for the federal funds rate? **LO35.1**
   a. 0.00 to 0.25 percent
   b. 1.00 to 1.25 percent
   c. 2.00 to 2.25 percent
   d. none of the above

2. If the IORB rate is 4.25 percent, the effective federal funds rate is 4.18 percent, and the ON RRP rate is 4.00 percent, which group might lend money in the federal funds market? **LO35.1**
   a. Commercial banks
   b. Nonbank financial companies
   c. The Federal Reserve

3. A commercial bank sells a Treasury bond to the Federal Reserve for $100,000. The money supply: **LO35.1**
   a. increases by $100,000.
   b. decreases by $100,000.
   c. is unaffected by the transaction.

4. How did the Federal Reserve control the federal funds rate before the 2007–2009 financial crisis? **LO35.2**
   a. Quantitative easing
   b. Open-market operations
   c. Forward guidance
   d. All of the above

5. Which policy would be the most helpful in lowering long-term interest rates? **LO35.2**
   a. Numerical neutrality
   b. Quantitative easing
   c. Raising the administered rates
   d. Lowering the federal funds target range

6. The dual mandate tells the Fed that its two highest priorities should be stable prices and _____. **LO35.3**
   a. economic growth
   b. high wages
   c. low inequality
   d. low unemployment

7. Which combination would give the FOMC conflicting signals about the stance of monetary policy? **LO35.3**
   a. Inflation and unemployment both below target
   b. Inflation and unemployment both on target
   c. Inflation above target and unemployment below target
   d. Inflation below target and unemployment above target

8. In which situation does the Fed have to worry most about downward price stickiness? **LO35.4**
   a. When applying expansionary monetary policy
   b. When applying restrictive monetary policy
   c. When continuing a neutral monetary policy
   d. All of the above

9. Other things equal, a lower real interest rate will cause: **LO35.4**
   a. the AS curve to shift left.
   b. the AD curve to shift right.
   c. the AS curve to shift right.
   d. the AD curve to shift left.

10. The metaphor most commonly invoked to capture the idea that an expansionary monetary policy might not work due to borrowers not wanting to borrow or lenders not wanting to lend is: **LO35.5**
    a. pulling on a rope.
    b. hovering over a slope.
    c. pushing on a string.
    d. pouring through a sieve.

11. True or False: A liquidity trap occurs when expansionary monetary policy fails to work because a decrease in interest rates does not cause an increase in lending and borrowing. **LO35.5**

12. True or False: In the United States, monetary policy has two key advantages over fiscal policy: (1) isolation from political pressure and (2) speed and flexibility. **LO35.5**

Problems

1. Draw two separate demand-and-supply diagrams that illustrate, respectively, bond purchases and bond sales by the Fed. In each figure, the price of bonds is the vertical axis variable while the quantity of bonds demanded or supplied is the horizontal axis variable. In each of the two figures, show the initial equilibrium before the Fed action and the new equilibrium after the Fed has (1) increased the demand for bonds in the first figure and (2) increased the supply of bonds in the second figure. Note which way the equilibrium bond price moves in each figure, and then use the fact that "bond prices and interest rates move inversely" to infer in which direction interest rates move in each situation. **LO35.1**

2. Draw and label your own Dual-Mandate Bullseye chart. First draw and label the two axes. Then draw in the crosshairs and the bullseye, indicating with tick marks and descriptive labels the numerical values of the inflation target and the unemployment target. Then label the four quadrants by their compass positions (Northeast, Southeast, Southwest, Northwest). Next, for each quadrant, write whether points in that quadrant are above or below each target value (for instance, the labels for the Northeast would be: "inflation > 2-percent target," and, "unemployment > 3.5 percent target"). Then add a label to each quadrant that indicates whether the Fed is getting "consistent signals" or "inconsistent signals" about whether to engage in either a restrictive, expansionary, or neutral monetary policy. Next, for any quadrant where the Fed is getting *consistent signals*, write down what the Fed's monetary policy stance should be for that quadrant (i.e., restrictive, expansionary, or neutral). **LO35.3**

3. Examine the nearby Dual-Mandate Bullseye chart that shows where the U.S. economy was exactly one year before the COVID-19 lockdowns began. Write a brief essay of just a

paragraph or two explaining how an FOMC member might have reacted to this information, including whether the Fed was getting mixed signals and what policies they might have recommended to move the red dot toward the center of the bullseye. (Note that at that time, the Fed believed the full-employment rate of unemployment to be about 4.2 percent of the labor force.) **LO35.3**

4. Refer to the table for Moola below to answer the following questions. What is the equilibrium interest rate in Moola? What is the level of investment at the equilibrium interest rate? Is there either a recessionary output gap (negative GDP gap) or an inflationary output gap (positive GDP gap) at the equilibrium interest rate and, if either, what is the amount? Given money demand, by how much would the Moola central bank need to change the money supply to close the output gap? What is the expenditure multiplier in Moola? **LO35.4**

Money Supply	Money Demand	Interest Rate	Investment at Interest (Rate Shown)	Potential Real GDP	Actual Real GDP at Interest (Rate Shown)
$500	$800	2%	$50	$350	$390
500	700	3	40	350	370
500	600	4	30	350	350
500	500	5	20	350	330
500	400	6	10	350	310

The Taylor Rule

LO35.7 State the Taylor Rule and explain how it balances the two parts of the Fed's dual mandate.

Weighing Unemployment against Inflation

When deciding whether monetary policy should be expansionary, restrictive, or neutral at any given point in time, the Federal Open Market Committee (FOMC) has to do its best to abide by the dual mandate's requirement that the Fed attempt to maintain full employment and stable prices simultaneously. As the monetary policy bullseye chart makes clear, however, the Fed may end up receiving conflicting signals from the unemployment rate and the inflation rate as to whether monetary policy should be expansionary, contractionary, or neutral and, thus, whether interest rates may have to be raised, lowered, or left alone.

As economists have attempted to model the Fed's decision making with regard to setting interest rates, they have done their best to take that dilemma into account. The most famous such model, the so-called *Taylor rule*, does so by assuming that the FOMC will care more about meeting the unemployment part of the dual mandate than the inflation part of the dual mandate.

The Taylor Rule

The stance of monetary policy is a matter of policy discretion by the members of the FOMC. At each of their meetings, committee members assess whether the current monetary policy stance—expansionary, restrictive, or neutral—remains appropriate for achieving the twin goals of stable prices and full employment. If the majority of FOMC members conclude that a change is needed, the FOMC adjusts how it is handling the monetary policy tools at its disposal.

A rule of thumb suggested by economist John Taylor roughly matches the FOMC's actual policy decisions about the *effective federal funds rate* during many time periods. It is based on economists' widely held belief that central bankers are willing to tolerate above-target inflation if doing so helps to achieve full employment.

To capture that preference, the **Taylor rule** takes into account both the Fed's 2-percent inflation target as well as its 3.5-percent unemployment rate target. It does so by assuming

---

Taylor rule A *monetary rule* proposed by economist John Taylor that would stipulate exactly how much the *Federal Reserve System* should change *real interest rates* in response to divergences of *real GDP* from potential GDP and divergences of actual rates of *inflation* from a target rate of inflation.

---

that the two major components of the Fed's interest-rate targeting decisions will be:

- The **inflation gap** (= current actual inflation rate − 2 percent target inflation rate)
- The **unemployment gap** (= current actual unemployment rate − 3.5 percent target unemployment rate)

There are several ways to express the Taylor rule mathematically.[1] The most intuitive version is:

$$
\begin{aligned}
\text{Fed target interest rate} = \ &\text{real risk-free interest rate} \\
&+ \text{current actual inflation rate} \\
&+ 0.5 \times (\text{inflation gap}) \\
&- 1.0 \times (\text{unemployment gap})
\end{aligned}
$$

The real risk-free interest rate is the minimum real rate of return that lenders demand for the use of their money. Based on historical data, the real risk-free interest rate is normally about 2 percent per year. Substituting that value into the Taylor rule gives us:

$$
\begin{aligned}
\text{Fed target interest rate} = \ &2 + \text{current actual inflation rate} \\
&+ 0.5 \times (\text{inflation gap}) \\
&- 1.0 \times (\text{unemployment gap})
\end{aligned}
$$

Predicting Fed Policy with the Taylor Rule

We can use the Taylor rule to predict the Fed's interest rate target for the effective federal funds rate and, thus, whether it will pursue an expansionary monetary policy (by lowering the effective federal funds rate from its current level) or a restrictive monetary policy (by raising the effective federal funds rate from its current level).

- Suppose, for example, that the current actual inflation rate is 3 percent and the current actual unemployment rate is 2.5 percent. Then the inflation gap is 1 percent (= 3 percent actual inflation − 2 percent target inflation) and the unemployment gap is negative 1 percent

---

inflation gap The difference between the current actual rate of *inflation* and the central bank's *target rate of inflation;* a key component of the *Taylor Rule.*

unemployment gap The difference between the actual rate of *unemployment* and the *full-employment rate of unemployment,* which is believed to be between 3 and 4 percent for the U.S. economy; a key component of the *Taylor rule.*

---

[1]The version of the Taylor rule that we present uses Okun's law to convert deviations of actual GDP from full-employment GDP into deviations of the actual unemployment rate from the full-employment rate of unemployment.

(= 2.5 percent actual unemployment rate − 3.5 percent target unemployment rate). Substituting those values into our equation, we find that the Fed's target interest rate will be 6.5 percent [= 2 percent real risk-free rate + 3 percent current actual inflation rate + 0.5 × inflation gap of 1 percent − 1.0 × unemployment gap of minus 1 percent].

- Similarly, let's suppose that the Fed is hitting the dual-mandate bullseye dead center. In that case, actual inflation is equal to the target rate of 2 percent and actual unemployment is equal to the target rate of 3.5 percent. Substituting those values into the Taylor rule tells us that when the economy is operating at the Fed's dual-mandate sweet spot, the Fed will want to target an interest rate of 4 percent [= 2 percent real-risk free rate + 2 percent current actual inflation rate + 0.5 × inflation gap of zero − 1.0 × unemployment gap of zero].

Favoring the Unemployment Gap over the Inflation Gap

Note that in the Taylor rule equation, the coefficient on the inflation gap is 0.5 while the coefficient on the unemployment gap is 1.0. This reflects the fact that policymakers are assumed to care more about the unemployment gap than about the inflation gap. In fact, they are assumed to care precisely twice as much about the unemployment gap because the unemployment gap's coefficient of 1.0 is twice as large as the inflation gap's coefficient of 0.5.

Those differing weights give us a hint as to how the real-world FOMC may deal with situations in which the economy is operating in either the southwest or northeast quadrants of the bullseye chart. Those are the quadrants in which inflation and unemployment give contradictory signals about monetary policy. The Taylor rule's coefficient weights on the unemployment gap and the inflation gap tell us that the Fed will resolve the contradictory signals by targeting an effective federal funds rate that puts twice as much weight on closing the unemployment gap as it does on closing the inflation gap.

The Taylor Rule and Quantitative Easing

One of the ways that the Taylor rule is of great interest is because it can be used to demonstrate why the Fed felt it necessary to initiate quantitative easing to help the economy recover from the Great Recession of 2007–2009.

Consider the economic situation in 2009. Actual inflation was −0.36 percent and actual unemployment was 10.0 percent. If we assume an inflation target of 2.0 percent and a natural rate of unemployment of 3.5 percent, then the effective federal funds rate suggested by the Taylor Rule turns out to be *negative* 6.04 percent [= 2 − 0.36 + 0.5 × (−0.36 − 2.0) − 1.0 × (10.0 − 3.5)].

That's a nice suggestion, but it's also a dangerous suggestion because the zero lower bound problem implies that any negative interest rate would very likely end up generating more harm than help. Long before the Fed could even get to negative 2.0 percent—let alone negative 6.04 percent!—people would begin removing deposits from the banking system in order to convert their money into cash that would not be subject to a negative rate of return. That conversion could, in turn, cause all sorts of economic problems, including decreased spending by consumers.

What the Fed's then-chair Ben Bernanke understood at the time was that the recession of 2007–2009 was so severe that the Fed was in uncharted territory. Whereas all of the downturns between the Great Depression of the 1930s and the Great Recession of 2007–2009 had been mild enough that they could be handled with reductions in short-term interest rates, getting out of the Great Recession would have required reductions in longer-term interest rates, too. The result was quantitative easing and the Fed's decision to purchase large amounts of longer-term government bonds in order to lower longer-term interest rates and thereby provide additional economic stimulus after the Fed had already lowered short-term interest rates down to nearly zero.

Appendix Summary

LO35.7 State the Taylor Rule and explain how it balances the two parts of the Fed's dual mandate.
The Taylor rule attempts to model how the Federal Reserve and other central banks will set their policy rates if they feel that there is a trade-off between meeting their goals with respect to inflation on the one hand and employment on the other hand.

When applied to the U.S. economy, the Taylor rule suggests that the Federal Reserve's target for its policy rate, the effective federal funds rate, will equal the sum of the real risk-free interest rate of 2 percent + the current rate of inflation + 1/2 times the inflation gap − 1.0 times the unemployment gap.

Appendix Terms and Concepts

Taylor rule   inflation gap   unemployment gap

Appendix Discussion Questions

1. Does the Taylor Rule put a higher weight on resolving the unemployment gap or the inflation gap? Explain. **LO35.7**

Appendix Review Questions

1. The Taylor Rule puts _____ as much weight on closing the unemployment gap as it does on closing the inflation gap. **LO35.7**
   a. just
   b. twice
   c. half
   d. ten times

2. In 2020, near the start of the COVID crisis, the annualized inflation rate briefly hit −5.9 percent while the unemployment rate briefly soared to 14.7 percent. If the target inflation rate was 2.0 percent and the full-employment rate of unemployment was 3.5 percent, what value does the Taylor Rule predict for the Fed's target interest rate back then? Would that rate have been possible given the zero lower bound problem? **LO35.7**
   a. Negative 3.35 percent; not possible.
   b. Positive 1.95 percent; possible.
   c. Negative 19.5 percent; not possible.
   d. Positive 3.35; possible.

Appendix Problems

1. In 1980, the U.S. inflation rate was 13.5 percent and the unemployment rate reached 7.8 percent. Suppose that the target rate of inflation was 3 percent back then and that the full-employment rate of unemployment was 6 percent at that time. What value does the Taylor rule predict for the Fed's target interest rate? Would you be surprised to learn that the effective federal funds rate reached 18.9 percent in December 1980? Explain why or why not. **LO35.7**

2. Suppose that actual inflation is 3 percentage points, the Fed's inflation target is 2 percentage points, and unemployment is 1 percentage point below the Fed's unemployment target. According to the Taylor rule, what value will the Fed want to set for its target interest rate? **LO35.7**

CHAPTER
36

Financial Economics

>> LEARNING OBJECTIVES

LO36.1 Distinguish between economic investment and financial investment.

LO36.2 Explain the time value of money and calculate the present value of money.

LO36.3 Distinguish among the most common financial investments: stocks, bonds, and mutual funds.

LO36.4 Explain how percentage rates of return provide a common framework for comparing assets.

LO36.5 Define arbitrage.

LO36.6 Define risk and distinguish between diversifiable and nondiversifiable risk.

LO36.7 Explain the factors that determine investment decisions.

LO36.8 Explain why arbitrage will tend to move all investments onto the Security Market Line.

Financial economics studies investor preferences and how they affect the trading and pricing of financial assets like stocks, bonds, and real estate. The two most important investor preferences are a desire for high rates of return and a dislike of risk and uncertainty. This chapter explains how these preferences interact to produce a strong positive relationship between risk and return: The riskier an investment, the higher its rate of return. This positive relationship compensates investors for bearing risk.

Financial Investment

>> **LO36.1** Distinguish between economic investment and financial investment.

economic investment Spending for the production and accumulation of *capital*, additions to *inventories*, or the research and development of new goods or services, including funds spent on the creation of new works of music, literature, or software. Compare with *financial investment*.

Financial economics focuses on the investments that individuals and firms make in the wide variety of assets available to them in our modern economy. Before proceeding, it is important for you to understand the difference between economic investment and financial investment.

Economic investment refers either to paying for *new* additions to the capital stock or for *new* replacements for capital stock that has worn out. Thus, *new* factories, houses, retail stores, construction equipment, and wireless networks are all good examples of economic investments. So are purchases of office computers to replace computers that have become obsolete as well as purchases of new commercial airplanes to replace planes that have served out their useful lives. Economic investment also includes research and development spending and spending to produce new intellectual assets like books, films, and music. Economic investment pays for things that will increase the economy's ability to produce desired goods and services.

Financial investment is a far broader, much more inclusive concept. It includes economic investment and a whole lot more. **Financial investment** refers to either buying or building an asset with the expectation of financial gain. It does not distinguish between *new* assets and *old* assets. Purchasing an old house or an old factory is just as much a financial investment as purchasing a new house or a new factory. For financial investment, it does not matter if the purchase of an asset adds to the capital stock, replaces the capital stock, or does neither.

Investing in old comic books is just as much a financial investment as building a new oil refinery. Finally, unlike economic investment, financial investment can involve either *financial assets* (such as stocks, bonds, and futures contracts) or *real assets* (such as land, factories, and retail buildings).

When bankers, entrepreneurs, corporate executives, retirement planners, and ordinary people use the word investment, they almost always mean financial investment. In fact, the ordinary meaning of the word investment *is* financial investment. So, for this chapter, we use the word investment in its ordinary sense of "financial investment" rather than in the far narrower sense of "economic investment," which we have used throughout most of the rest of this book. In addition, much of our focus will be on tradable financial assets like stocks and bonds that are collectively known as **securities** under U.S. law.

financial investment The purchase of a financial asset (such as a *stock, bond,* or *mutual fund*) or real asset (such as a house, land, or factories) in the expectation of financial gain. Compare with economic investment.

securities Financial assets such as stocks and bonds that are tradable in organized financial markets, such as the New York Stock Exchange (NYSE).

Present Value

Because a specific amount of money is more valuable to a person the sooner it is received, people are going to want to be compensated if you ask them to wait to receive it. The amount that you must compensate them for having to wait is the *time value of money* (also known as the time value of delay).

The time value of money underlies one of the fundamental ideas in financial economics: **present value,** which is the present-day value of returns or costs that are expected to arrive in the future. Present value is especially useful when investors wish to determine the proper current price to pay for an asset. In fact, the proper current price for any risk-free investment *is* the present value of its expected future returns. And while some adjustments have to be made when determining the proper price of a risky investment, the process is entirely based on the logic of present value. Thus we begin our study of finance by explaining present value and how we use it to price risk-free assets. Next, we turn our attention to risk and how the financial markets determine the prices of risky assets by taking into account investor preferences regarding the trade-off between potential return and potential risk.

>> **LO36.2** Explain the time value of money and calculate the present value of money.

present value Today's value of some amount of *money* that is to be received at a particular future date.

Compound Interest

The best way to understand present value is by first understanding compound interest. **Compound interest** explains how quickly an investment increases in value when interest is paid, or *compounded,* not only on the original amount invested but also on all interest payments that have been previously made.

As an example of compound interest in action, consider Table 36.1, which shows the amount of money that $100 invested today becomes if it increases, or compounds, at an 8 percent annual interest rate, i, for various numbers of years. *To simplify, we will express annual interest rates as decimals.* So the 8 percent annual interest rate can be expressed as $i = 0.08$. The key to understanding compound interest is to realize that 1 year's worth of growth at interest rate i will always result in $(1 + i)$ times as much money at the end of a year as there was at the beginning of the year. Consequently, if the first year begins with $100 and if $i = 0.08$, then $(1 + 0.08)$ or 1.08 times as much money–$108–will be available at the end of the year.

We show the computation for the first year in column 2 of Table 36.1 and display the $108 outcome in column 3. The same logic also applies to other initial amounts. If a year begins with $500, there will be 1.08 times more money after 1 year, or $540. Algebraically, let X_0 denote the amount of money at the start of the first year and X_1 the amount after 1 year's worth of growth. Then we see that any given number of dollars X_0 at the start of the first year grows into $X_1 = (1 + i)X_0$ dollars after 1 year's worth of growth.

compound interest *Interest* that is paid both on an original sum of money and on interest that has already been paid on that sum.

Next, consider what happens if the initial investment of $100 that grew into $108 after 1 year continues to grow at 8 percent interest for a second year. The $108 available at the beginning of the second year will grow into an amount of

(1) Years of Compounding	(2) Compounding Computation	(3) Value at Year's End
1	$100 (1.08)	$108.00
2	100 (1.08)^2	116.64
3	100 (1.08)^3	125.97
4	100 (1.08)^4	136.05
5	100 (1.08)^5	146.93
17	100 (1.08)^{17}	370.00

TABLE 36.1
Compounding: $100 at 8 Percent Interest

money that is 1.08 times larger by the end of the second year. That amount, as shown in Table 36.1, is $116.64. Notice that we make the computation in the table by multiplying the initial $100 by $(1.08)^2$. We do so because the original $100 is compounded by 1.08 into $108, and then the $108 is again compounded by 1.08. More generally, the second year begins with $(1 + i)X_0$ dollars, which will grow to $(1 + i)(1 + i)X_0 = (1 + i)^2X_0$ dollars by the end of the second year.

Similar reasoning shows that the amount of money at the end of 3 years has to be $(1 + i)^3X_0$ because the amount of money at the beginning of the third year, $(1 + i)^2X_0$, gets multiplied by $(1 + i)$ to convert it into the amount of money at the end of the third year. In terms of Table 36.1, that amount is $125.97, which is $(1.08)^3$100.

As you can see, we now have a fixed pattern. The $100 that is invested at the beginning of the first year becomes $(1 + i)$100 after 1 year, $(1 + i)^2$100 after 2 years, $(1 + i)^3$100 after 3 years, and so on. It therefore is clear that the amount of money after t years will be $(1 + i)^t$100. This pattern always holds true, regardless of the size of the initial investment. Thus, investors know that if they invest X_0 dollars today and earn compound interest at the rate i, then X_0 dollars will grow into exactly $(1 + i)^tX_0$ dollars after t years. Economists express that fact with the following formula:

$$X_t = (1 + i)^tX_0 \qquad (1)$$

Equation 1 captures the idea that if investors have the opportunity to invest X_0 dollars today at interest rate i, then they have the ability to transform X_0 dollars today into $(1 + i)^tX_0$ dollars in t years.

But notice that the logic of the equality also works in reverse, in that it also shows that $(1 + i)^tX_0$ dollars in t years can be transformed into X_0 dollars today. That may seem very odd, but it is exactly what happens when people take out loans. For instance, consider a situation in which an investor named Roberto takes out a loan for $100 today, a loan that will accumulate interest at 8 percent per year for 5 years. Under such an arrangement, the amount Roberto owes will grow with compound interest into $(1.08)^5$100 = $146.93 in 5 years. This means that Roberto can convert $146.93 in 5 years (the amount required to pay off the loan) into $100 today (the amount he borrows today).

Consequently, the compound interest formula given in equation 1 defines not only the rate at which present amounts of money can be converted to future amounts of money but also the rate at which future amounts of money can be converted into present amounts of money.

The Present Value Model

The present value model simply rearranges equation 1 to make it easier to transform future amounts of money into present amounts of money. To derive the formula used to calculate the present value of a future amount of money, we divide both sides of equation 1 by $(1 + i)^t$ to obtain

$$\frac{X_t}{(1 + i)^t} = X_0 \qquad (2)$$

The logic of equation 2 is identical to that of equation 1. Both allow investors to convert present amounts of money into future amounts of money and vice versa. However, equation 2 makes it much easier to convert a given number of dollars in the future into their present-day equivalent. In fact, it says that X_t dollars in t years converts into exactly $X_t/(1 + i)^t$ dollars today. This may not seem important, but it is actually very powerful because it allows investors to easily calculate how much they should pay for any particular asset.

To understand why, realize that an asset's owner obtains the right to receive one or more future payments. If an investor is considering buying an asset, her problem is to try to determine how much she should pay today to buy the asset and receive those future payments. Equation 2 makes this task very easy. If she knows how large a future payment will be (X_t dollars), when it will arrive (in t years), and what the interest rate is (i), then she can apply equation 2 to determine the payment's present value: that is, its value in present-day dollars. If she does this for each of the future payments that the asset in question is expected to make, she will be able to calculate the overall present value of all of the asset's future payments by simply summing together the present values of each of those individual payments. This will allow her to determine the price she should pay for the asset. *The asset's current price should exactly equal the sum of the present values of all of the asset's future payments.*

As a simple example, suppose that Cecilia has the chance to buy an asset that is guaranteed to return a single payment of exactly $370.00 in 17 years. Again let's assume the interest rate is 8 percent per year. Then Cecelia can use equation 2 to determine the present value of that future payment: $370.00/(1 + 0.8)^{17} = $370.00/(1.08)^{17} = $100 today. This is confirmed in the row for year 17 in Table 36.1.

To see why Cecilia should be willing to pay a price that is *exactly* equal to the $100 present value of the asset's single future payment of $370.00 in 17 years, consider the following thought experiment. What would happen if she were to invest $100 today in an alternative investment that guarantees to compound her money for 17 years at 8 percent per year? How large would her investment in this alternative become? Equation 1 and Table 36.1 tell us that the answer is exactly $370.00.

This is very important because it shows that Cecilia and other investors have two different ways of purchasing the right to receive $370.00 in 17 years. They can either:

- Purchase the asset in question for $100.
- Invest $100 in the alternative asset that pays 8 percent per year.

Because either investment will deliver the same future benefit, both investments are in fact identical. Consequently, they should have identical prices. Each should cost precisely $100 today.

A good way to understand why this must be the case is to consider how the presence of the alternative investment affects the behavior of both the potential buyers and the potential sellers of the asset in question. First, notice that Cecilia and other potential buyers would never pay more than $100 for the asset in question because they know that they can get the same future return of $370.00 in 17 years by investing $100 in the alternative asset. At the same time, the people selling the asset in question would not sell it to Cecilia or other potential buyers for anything less than $100 since they know that the only other way for Cecilia and other potential investors to get a future return of $370.00 in 17 years is by paying $100 for the alternative investment. Since Cecilia and the other potential buyers will not pay more than $100 for the asset in question and its sellers will not accept less than $100 for the asset in question, the result will be that the asset in question and the alternative investment will have exactly the same price of $100 today.

- Financial investment refers to buying an asset with the hope of financial gain.

- The time-value of money is the idea that a specific amount of money is more valuable to a person the sooner it is received because of the potential for compound interest.

- Compound interest is the payment of interest not only on the original amount invested but also on any interest payments previously made; X_0 dollars today growing at interest rate i will become $(1 + i)^t X_0$ dollars in t years.

- The present value formula facilitates transforming future amounts of money into present-day amounts of money; X_t dollars in t years converts into exactly $X_t/(1 + i)^t$ dollars today.

- An investment's proper current price is equal to the sum of the present values of all the future payments that it is expected to make.

QUICK REVIEW
36.1

Applications

Present value has many everyday applications. Let's examine two of them.

Take the Money and Run? The winners of state lotteries typically receive their winnings in equal installments spread out over 20 years. For instance, suppose that Zoe gets lucky and wins a $100 million jackpot. She will not receive $100 million all at once. Rather, she will receive $5 million per year for 20 years, for a total of $100 million.

Zoe may object to this installment payment system for a variety of reasons. For one thing, she may be very old, so that she is not likely to live long enough to collect all of the payments. Therefore, she might prefer to receive her winnings immediately so that she can make large immediate donations to her favorite charities or large immediate investments in a business project. And, of course, she may just be impatient and want to buy a lot of really expensive consumption goods sooner rather than later.

Fortunately for Zoe, if she does wish to receive her winnings sooner rather than later, several private financial companies are ready and willing to help her. They do so by arranging swaps. Lottery winners sell the right to receive their installment payments in exchange for a single lump sum that they get immediately. The people who hand over the lump sum receive the right to collect the installment payments.

Present value is crucial to arranging these swaps because the financial companies use it to determine the value of the lump sum that lottery winners like Zoe will receive in exchange for giving up their installment payments. The lump sum is equal to the sum of the present values of each of the future payments. Assuming an interest rate of 5 percent per year, the sum of the present values of each of Zoe's 20 installment payments of $5 million is $62,311,051.71. So, depending on her preferences, Zoe can either receive that amount immediately or $100 million spread out over 20 years.

Salary Caps and Deferred Compensation Another example of present value comes directly from the sporting news. Many professional sports leagues worry that richer teams, if not held in check, will outbid poorer teams for the best players. The result would be a situation in which only the richer teams have any real chance of doing well and winning championships.

To prevent that outcome from happening, many leagues have instituted salary caps. These are upper limits on the total amount of money that each team can spend on salaries during a given season. For instance, one popular basketball league has a salary cap of about $120 million per season, which means that each team's total wage bill for all its players has to be no more than $120 million each year.

Typically, however, the salary contracts that are negotiated between individual players and their teams are for multiple seasons. So, during negotiations, players are often asked to help their team stay under the current season's salary cap by agreeing to receive more compensation in later years. For instance, suppose that a team's current payroll is $100 million, and it would like to add a superstar named HiTop to a two-year contract. HiTop, however, is used to earning $30 million per year. This is a major problem for the team because the $120 million salary cap means that the most that the team can pay HiTop for the current season is $20 million.

A common solution is for HiTop to agree to receive only $20 million the first season in order to help the team stay under the salary cap. In exchange for this concession, the team agrees to pay HiTop more than the $30 million he would normally demand for the second season. The team uses the present-value formula to figure out how large his second-season salary should be. HiTop, too, can use the present-value formula to figure out that if the interest rate is 8 percent per year, he should be paid a total of $40.8 million during his second season, because this amount will equal the $30 million he wants for the second season plus $10.8 million to make up for the $10 million reduction in his salary during the first season. That is, the present value of the $10.8 million of delayed compensation that he will receive during the second season precisely equals the $10 million that he agrees to give up during the first season.

Some Popular Investments

>> **LO36.3** Distinguish among the most common financial investments: stocks, bonds, and mutual funds.

The number and types of financial "instruments" in which one can invest are numerous, amazingly creative, and highly varied. Most are much more complicated than the investments we used to explain compounding and present value. But, fortunately, all investments share three features:

- They require that investors pay some price—determined in the market—to acquire them.
- They give their owners the chance to receive future payments.
- The future payments are typically risky.

These features allow us to treat all assets in a unified way. Three of the most popular investments are stocks, bonds, and mutual funds. In 2019, the median value of stock holdings for U.S. families that held stocks was $25,000; the median value for bonds was $121,000; and the median value for "pooled funds" (mainly mutual funds) was $110,000.[1]

Stocks

stock (corporate) An ownership share in a corporation.

Recall that **stocks** are ownership shares in a corporation. If an investor owns 1 percent of a corporation's shares, she gets 1 percent of the votes at the annual shareholders' meeting that selects the company's managers, and she is also entitled to 1 percent of any future profit distributions. There is no guarantee, however, that a company will be profitable.

---

[1] Federal Reserve, "Changes in U.S. Family Finances from 2016 to 2019; Evidence from the Survey of Consumer Finances," p. 16.

Firms often lose money and sometimes even go **bankrupt,** meaning that they are unable to make timely payments on their debts. In the event of a bankruptcy, control of a corporation's assets goes to a bankruptcy judge, whose job is to enforce the legal rights of the people who loaned money to the company. The judge will try to ensure that the company's debtors are repaid. Typically, repaying debtors involves selling off the corporation's assets (factories, real estate, patents, and so on) to raise money to pay off the company's debts.

The money raised by selling the firm's assets may be greater than or less than the amount of the firm's debts. If it is greater than the value of the firm's debts, any remaining money is divided equally among shareholders. If it is less than the firm's debts, the shareholders get nothing at all while the lenders have to accept less than what they are owed. If, for instance, they are collectively owed $100 million but the bankruptcy court's "fire sale" yields only $80 million, then each lender will get back only 80 cents for each dollar they were owed by the firm. In Wall Street slang, the lenders "have to take a haircut."

The maximum amount of money that shareholders can lose is what they pay for their shares. If the company goes bankrupt owing more than the value of the firm's assets, shareholders do not have to make up the difference. This **limited liability rule** limits the risk involved in investing in corporations by capping investors' potential losses at the amount that they paid for their shares. Investors can lose money, but no more than what they paid to purchase their shares.

When firms are profitable, however, investors can look forward to gaining financially in either or both of two possible ways. The first is through **capital gains,** meaning that they sell their shares for more money than they paid for them. The second is by receiving **dividends,** which are equal shares of any current or future profits that are paid out by a company to its shareholders. As we will soon explain, a corporation's current share price is determined by the size of the capital gains and dividends that investors expect the corporation to generate in the future.

Bonds

Bonds are debt contracts that are issued most frequently by governments and corporations. They typically work as follows: An initial investor lends the government or the corporation a certain amount of money, say $1,000, for a certain period of time, say 10 years. In exchange, the government or corporation promises to make a series of semiannual payments in addition to returning the $1,000 at the end of the 10 years. The semiannual payments constitute interest on the loan. For instance, the bond agreement may specify that the borrower will pay $30 every six months. The bond therefore generates $60 per year in payments, which is equal to a 6 percent interest rate on the initial $1,000 loan.

The initial investor is free to sell the bond at any time to other investors, who then gain the right to receive any of the remaining semiannual payments as well as the final $1,000 payment when the bond comes due after 10 years. As we will soon demonstrate, the price at which the bond sells to another investor depends on the current rates of return available on other investments offering a similar stream of future payments and facing a similar level of risk.

The primary risk a bondholder faces is the possibility that the corporation or government that issues the bond will **default** on, or fail to make, the bond's promised payments. This risk is much greater for corporations, but default risk is also possible with respect to local and state governments. They sometimes default when (1) they cannot raise enough tax revenue to make their bond payments or (2) when defaulting on bond payments is politically easier than making budget cuts. The U.S. federal government, however, has never defaulted on its bond payments and is very unlikely to ever default because it has access to huge amounts of current and potential tax revenue and can sell U.S. securities to the Fed as a way to obtain money.

Bonds are much more predictable than stocks. Unless a bond goes into default, its owner knows the size of its future payments and exactly when they will arrive. By contrast, stock prices and dividends are highly volatile because they depend on profits, which vary greatly depending on the overall business cycle and on factors specific to individual firms and industries—things such as changing consumer preferences, variations in the costs of inputs, and changes in the tax code. The fact that bonds are typically more predictable (and thus less risky) than stocks explains why they generate lower average rates of return than stocks. Indeed, this difference in rates of return has been very large historically. From 1926 to 2021, stocks on average returned about 10 percent per year worldwide, while bonds on average returned only roughly 6 percent per year worldwide.

bankrupt A legal situation in which an individual or *firm* finds that it cannot make timely interest payments on money it has borrowed. In such cases, a bankruptcy judge can order the individual or firm to liquidate (turn into cash) its assets in order to pay lenders at least some portion of the amount they are owed.

limited liability rule A law that limits the potential losses that an investor in a *corporation* may suffer to the amount that she paid for her shares in the corporation. Encourages *financial investment* by limiting risk.

capital gain The gain realized when *securities* other *assets* are sold for a *price* greater than the price paid for them.

dividends Payments by a corporation of all or part of its profit to its stockholders (the corporate owners).

bond A financial contract that obligates a borrower to make coupon (interest) payments for a specified period of time before also paying back the principal amount that was initially borrowed.

defaults Situations in which borrowers stop making loan payments or do not pay back loans that they took out and are now due.

mutual funds Investment companies that pool money from numerous individual investors in order to purchase *portfolios* of *stocks* or *bonds;* includes both *index funds* as well as *actively managed funds.*

portfolio A specific collection of *stocks, bonds,* or other *financial investments* held by an individual or a *mutual fund.*

index funds *Mutual funds* whose *portfolios* exactly match a stock or bond index (a collection of *stocks* or *bonds* meant to capture the overall behavior of a particular category of investments) such as the Standard & Poor's 500 Index or the Russell 3000 Index.

actively managed funds *Mutual funds* that have portfolio managers who constantly buy and sell *assets* in an attempt to generate high returns.

passively managed funds *Mutual funds* whose *portfolios* are not regularly updated by a fund manager attempting to generate high returns. Rather, once an initial portfolio is selected, it is left unchanged so that investors receive whatever return that unchanging portfolio subsequently generates. *Index funds* are a type of passively managed fund.

TABLE 36.2 The 10 Largest Mutual Funds, October 2021

Fund Name*	Assets under Management, Billions
Vanguard 500 Index Admiral Shares	$411.0
SPDR S&P 500 ETF	386.4
Fidelity 500 Index Fund	350.3
Vanguard Total Stock Index Admiral Shares	315.5
iShares Core S&P 500	287.0
Vanguard Total Stock Index Institutional Plus	269.7
Vanguard Total Stock Market Index ETF	263.0
Vanguard 500 Index ETF	247.0
Vanguard Total Stock Market Index Institutional	230.8
Fidelity Government Cash Reserves	210.0

Source: "The 25 Largest Mutual Funds," MarketWatch.com.

Mutual Funds

A **mutual fund** is a company that maintains a professionally managed **portfolio,** or collection, of either stocks or bonds. The company purchases the portfolio by pooling the money of many investors. Because these investors provide the money to purchase the portfolio, they own it, and any gains or losses generated by the portfolio flow directly to them. Table 36.2 lists the 10 largest U.S. mutual funds based on their assets under management.

Most of the more than 9,300 mutual funds currently operating in the United States choose to maintain portfolios that invest in specific categories of bonds or stocks. For instance, some fill their portfolios exclusively with the stocks of small tech companies, while others buy only bonds issued by certain state or local governments. In addition, there are **index funds** whose portfolios exactly match a stock index or bond index. Stock and bond indexes follow the performance of a particular group of stocks or bonds to gauge how well a particular category of investments is doing. For instance, the Standard & Poor's 500 Index contains the 500 largest stocks trading in the United States to capture how the stocks of large corporations vary over time.

There is an important distinction between actively managed and passively managed mutual funds. **Actively managed funds** have portfolio managers who constantly buy and sell assets in an attempt to generate high returns. By contrast, index funds are **passively managed funds** because the assets in their portfolios are chosen to exactly match whatever stocks or bonds are contained in their respective underlying indexes.

Later in this chapter, we discuss the relative merits of actively managed funds and index funds, but for now we point out that both types are very popular and that, overall, U.S. households held $34.4 trillion in mutual funds and corporate equities at the end of 2020. By way of comparison, U.S. GDP in 2020 was $20.9 trillion, and the estimated value of all the financial assets held by households in 2020 (including everything from individual stocks and bonds to checking account deposits) was about $100.7 trillion.

QUICK REVIEW 36.2

▶ Three popular forms of financial investments are stocks, bonds, and mutual funds.

▶ Stocks are ownership shares in corporations and bestow upon their owners a proportional share of any future profit.

▶ Bonds are debt contracts that promise to pay a fixed series of payments in the future.

▶ Mutual funds are pools of investor money used to buy portfolios of stocks or bonds.

Calculating Investment Returns

>> **LO36.4** Explain how percentage rates of return provide a common framework for comparing assets.

Investors buy assets to obtain one or more future payments. The simplest case is purchasing an asset for resale. For instance, an investor may buy a house for $300,000 with the hope of selling it for $360,000 one year later. On the other hand, she could also rent out the house for $3,000 per month and thereby receive a stream of future payments. Or she could do a little of both, paying

$300,000 for the house now, renting it out for five years, and then selling it. In that case, she is expecting a stream of smaller payments followed by a large one.

Percentage Rates of Return

Economists have developed a common framework for evaluating the gains or losses of assets that make only one future payment as well as those that make many future payments. They state the gain or loss as a **percentage rate of return,** by which they mean the percentage gain or loss (relative to the buying price) over a given period of time, typically a year. For instance, if Noelle buys a rare comic book today for $100 and sells it in 1 year for $125, she makes a 25 percent per year rate of return. She determines this rate of return by dividing the gain of $25 by the purchase price of $100. By contrast, if she sold the comic book for only $92, then she would make a loss of 8 percent per year (which she calculates by dividing the $8 loss by the purchase price of $100).

A similar calculation is made for assets that deliver a series of payments. For instance, an investor who buys a house for $300,000 and expects to rent it out for $3,000 per month is expecting to make a 12 percent per year rate of return because he divides his $36,000 per year of rent collections by the $300,000 purchase price of the house.

percentage rate of return The percentage gain or loss, relative to the buying *price,* of an *economic investment* or *financial investment* over some period of time.

The Inverse Relationship between Asset Prices and Rates of Return

A fundamental concept in financial economics is that, other things equal, *an investment's rate of return is inversely related to its price. The higher the price paid for an asset, the lower its rate of return will be, all other things equal.* To understand why, consider a bond that pays $24,000 of interest each year. If an investor pays $100,000 for the bond, he will earn a 24 percent per year rate of return (the $24,000 annual interest payment divided by the $100,000 purchase price of the bond).

But suppose that the purchase price of the bond rises to $200,000. In that case, the investor will earn only a 12 percent per year rate of return, because the $24,000 annual interest payment is divided by the much larger purchase price of $200,000. Consequently, as the price of the bond goes up, the rate of return from buying it goes down.

The same relationship holds for other investments, such as rental property. The higher the price of a rental property, given its monthly rent, the lower the rate of return. The underlying cause of this general relationship is the fact that the future payments are held constant while one varies the current price. The fact that the future payments are held constant implies that there is an upper limit to the financial rewards of owning the asset. As a result, the more an investor pays for the asset now, the smaller those future payments will be relative to the amount paid to obtain them. Thus, higher asset prices imply lower rates of return.

CONSIDER THIS . . .

Corporate Ownership

The rise of mutual funds has radically changed the way corporations are controlled. Before the 1970s, corporations knew that the vast majority of their shares were owned by individuals, the large majority of whom were interested in holding their shares for the long run. Those long-run individual investors paid close attention to what corporate officers were doing and would reprimand bad decisions at annual shareholder meetings.

By contrast, neither actively nor passively managed funds have much incentive to care about the long-run success of the companies whose shares they buy and sell. Consider actively managed funds. Their managers lack an incentive to care about long-term

Chris Stein/Stone/Getty Images

performance because they are paid bonuses that depend almost entirely on quarterly performance rather than long-term performance. At the same time, the managers of passively managed funds have no incentive to care about corporate management or policy initiatives because they simply buy whatever stocks are included in their funds' respective underlying indexes.

Critics worry that the decline of close scrutiny by individual shareholders has helped to exacerbate a variety of problems, including corporate managers being paid excessive salaries and CEOs being overly focused on accounting gimmicks that offer a short-run boost to company share prices rather than good management decisions that will pay off only after many years have passed.

Arbitrage

arbitrage The activity of selling one asset and buying an identical or nearly identical asset to benefit from temporary differences in *prices* or *rates of return;* the practice that equalizes prices or returns on similar financial instruments and thus eliminates further opportunities for riskless financial gains.

Arbitrage is the term that financial economists use for the buying and selling process that leads profit-seeking investors to equalize the average expected rates of return generated by identical or nearly identical assets. Arbitrage happens when investors try to profit from situations where two identical or nearly identical assets have different rates of return. They do so by simultaneously selling the asset with the lower rate of return and buying the asset with the higher rate of return. For instance, consider what will happen in a case where two very similar t-shirt companies start with different rates of return despite the fact that they are equally profitable and have equally good future prospects. To make things concrete, suppose that a company called T4me starts out with a rate of return of 10 percent per year while TSTG (T-Shirts to Go) starts out with a rate of return of 15 percent per year.

Because both companies are basically identical and have equally good prospects, investors in T4me will want to shift over to TSTG, which offers higher rates of return for the same amount of risk. As they begin to shift over, however, the prices of the two companies' stocks will change—and with them, the two companies' rates of return. Because so many investors will be selling the shares of the lower-return company, T4me, the supply of its shares trading on the stock market will increase, thereby causing T4me's share price to decline. But because asset prices and rates of return are inversely related, the lower share price will cause T4me's rate of return to rise.

At the same time, the rate of return on the higher-return company, TSTG, will begin to fall. As investors switch from T4me to TSTG, the increased demand for TSTG's shares will drive up their price. And as the price of TSTG goes up, its rate of return must fall.

This arbitrage process will continue—with the rate of return on the higher-return company falling and the rate of return on the lower-return company rising—until both companies have the same rate of return. This convergence happens because as long as the rates of return on the two companies are not identical, there will always be some investors who will want to sell the shares of the lower-return company so they can buy the shares of the higher-return company. As a result, arbitrage will continue until the rates of return are equal.

Generally, only a very short period of time is needed for prices to equalize. In fact, for highly traded assets like stocks and bonds, arbitrage often forces the rates of return on identical or nearly identical investments to converge within a matter of minutes or sometimes even within a matter of seconds. This convergence is very helpful to small investors who do not have a large amount of time to study the thousands of potential investment opportunities available in the financial markets. Thanks to arbitrage, they can invest with the confidence that assets with similar characteristics will have similar rates of return.

QUICK REVIEW
36.3

- ▶ Stating gains or losses as percentage rates of return provides a common framework for comparing different assets.

- ▶ Asset prices and percentage rates of return are inversely related.

- ▶ Arbitrage refers to the buying and selling that takes place to equalize the percentage rates of return on identical or nearly identical assets.

Risk

risk The uncertainty as to the future returns of a particular *financial investment* or *economic investment.*

Investors purchase assets to obtain one or more future payments. As used by financial economists, the word **risk** refers to investors' uncertainty regarding the eventual size of those future payments.

The underlying problem is that the future is uncertain. Many factors affect an investment's future payments, and each of these may turn out better or worse than expected. As a simple example, consider buying a farm. Suppose that in an average year, the farm will generate a profit of $100,000. But if a freak hailstorm damages the crops, the profit will fall to only $60,000. If weather conditions turn out to be perfect, the farm's profit will rise to $120,000. Because there is no way to tell in advance what will happen, investing in the farm is risky.

When financial economists use the word *risk*, they do not use it in the casual way that refers only to potentially bad outcomes (as in, "there is a risk that this experimental medicine may kill you"). In financial economics, the word *risk* means that an outcome—good or bad, major or minor, likely or unlikely—lacks certainty. Some outcome will occur, but you cannot be sure what it will be. For instance, suppose that you are given a raffle ticket that will pay you either $10, $100, or $1,000 when a drawing is made in one month. There are no bad outcomes in this particular case, only good ones. But because you do not know with certainty which outcome will occur, the situation is, by our definition, risky. However, the word *risk* in financial economics certainly does not preclude negative outcomes. If you buy shares of common stock in some company, your stock may go up in value. But the company could also go bankrupt, in which case you may lose your entire investment.

Diversification

Investors have many options regarding their portfolios, or collections of investments. For example, they can choose to concentrate their wealth in just one or two investments or spread it out over a large number of investments. **Diversification** is the strategy of investing in a large number of investments to reduce the overall risk to the entire portfolio. It is the process of not putting all of your eggs in one basket.

diversification The strategy of investing in a large number of investments in order to reduce the overall risk to an entire investment *portfolio*.

Diversification generally succeeds in reducing risk. If an investor's portfolio consists of only one investment—say, one stock—then if anything awful happens to that stock, the investor's entire portfolio will suffer greatly. By contrast, if the investor spreads his wealth over many stocks, then a bad outcome for any one particular stock will cause only a small amount of damage to the overall portfolio. In addition, it is typically the case that if something bad is happening to one part of the portfolio, something good will be happening to another part of the portfolio, and the two effects will tend to offset each other. Thus, diversification reduces the risk to the overall portfolio.

Even though diversification can reduce a portfolio's risks, it cannot eliminate them entirely. Even if an investor has placed each of his eggs into different baskets, all of the eggs may still end up broken if all of the different baskets get dropped simultaneously. That is, even if an investor has created a well-diversified portfolio, all of the investments still have a chance to do badly simultaneously. As an example, consider the COVID-19 recession of 2020. With economic activity declining and consumer spending falling, nearly all companies faced reduced sales and lowered profits, a fact that caused their stock prices to decline simultaneously. Consequently, even if investors had diversified their portfolios across numerous stocks, their portfolios still declined in value because nearly all of their investments performed poorly simultaneously.

Financial economists divide an individual investment's overall risk into two components, diversifiable risk and nondiversifiable risk. **Diversifiable risk** (or *idiosyncratic risk*) is the risk that is specific to a given investment and that can be eliminated by diversification. For instance, a soda pop maker faces the risk that the demand for its product may suddenly decline because people want to drink mineral water instead of soda pop. But this risk does not matter to an investor if she has a diversified portfolio that contains stock in the soda pop maker as well as stock in a mineral water company. While the stock price of the soda pop maker falls due to the change in consumer preferences, the stock price of the mineral water company is going up—so that, as far as the overall portfolio is concerned, the two effects will offset each other.

diversifiable risk Investment *risk* that investors can reduce via *diversification*; also called idiosyncratic risk.

By contrast, **nondiversifiable risk** (or *systemic risk*) pushes all investments in the same direction at the same time so that there is no possibility of using good effects to offset bad effects. The best example of a nondiversifiable risk is the business cycle. If the economy does well, then corporate profits rise and nearly every stock does well. But if the economy does badly, then corporate profits fall and nearly every stock does badly. As a result, even if one builds a well-diversified portfolio, the business cycle will still affect that portfolio because nearly every asset in the portfolio will move in the same direction at the same time whenever the economy improves or worsens.

nondiversifiable risk Investment *risk* that investors are unable to reduce via *diversification*; also called systemic risk.

That said, creating a diversified portfolio is still an investor's best strategy because doing so at least eliminates diversifiable risk. Indeed, for investors who have successfully created diversified portfolios, all diversifiable risks will be eliminated, so that the only remaining source of risk is nondiversifiable risk.

Thus, when investors consider whether to add a particular investment to a portfolio that is already diversified, they can ignore the investment's diversifiable risk. They can ignore it because, as part of a diversified portfolio, the investment's diversifiable risk will be "diversified away." Indeed, the only risk left is the amount of nondiversifiable risk that the investment carries. Investors can therefore base their decisions about whether to add a potential new investment to their portfolios by comparing the potential investment's level of nondiversifiable risk with its potential returns. If they find this trade-off attractive, they will add the investment, whereas if it seems unattractive, they will not.

Global Perspective 36.1 shows that investment risk varies significantly across countries due to underlying differences in political, economic, and financial risks.

GLOBAL PERSPECTIVE 36.1

INTERNATIONAL DIFFERENCES IN RISK

The International Country Risk Guide attempts to distill the political, economic, and financial risks facing 140 countries into a single "composite risk rating" for each country, with higher numbers indicating less risk. The table below presents the ranks and rating numbers for 15 countries, including the three least risky (ranked 1 through 3) and the three most risky (ranked 138 through 140). Risk ratings numbers above 80 are considered *very low risk;* 70–80 are considered *low risk;* 60–70 *moderate risk;* 50–60 *high risk;* and below 50 *very high risk.*

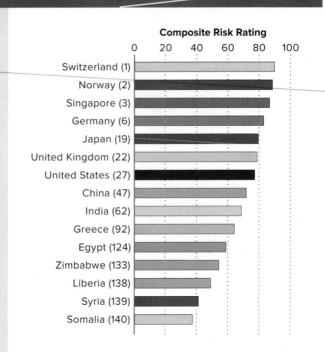

Composite Risk Rating

Source: "International Country Risk Guide," PRS Group.

QUICK REVIEW

36.4

▶ An asset is risky if its future payments are uncertain.

▶ Diversification is an investment strategy in which savers invest in a large number of different investments in order to reduce the overall risk to their entire portfolio.

▶ Risks that can be canceled out by diversification are called diversifiable risks; risks that cannot be canceled out by diversification are called nondiversifiable risks.

Comparing Risky Investments

>> **LO36.7** Explain the factors that determine investment decisions.

Economists believe that the two most important factors affecting investment decisions are returns and risks—specifically nondiversifiable risks. But for investors to compare different investments on the basis of returns and risks, they need ways to measure returns and risks. The two standard measures are, respectively, the average expected rate of return and the beta statistic.

Average Expected Rate of Return

average expected rate of return The *probability-weighted average* of an investment's possible future returns.

probability-weighted average Each of the possible future rates of return from an investment multiplied by its respective probability (expressed as a decimal) of happening.

Each investment's **average expected rate of return** is the probability-weighted average of the investment's possible future rates of return. The term **probability-weighted average** simply means that each of the possible future rates of return is multiplied by its probability expressed as a decimal (so that a 50 percent probability is 0.50 and a 23 percent probability is 0.23) before being added together to obtain the average. For instance, if an investment has a 75 percent probability of generating 11 percent per year and a 25 percent probability of generating 15 percent per year, then its average expected rate of return will be 12 percent = (0.75 × 11 percent) + (0.25 × 15 percent). By weighting each possible outcome by its probability, this process ensures that the resulting average gives more weight to outcomes that are more likely to happen (unlike the normal averaging process, which would treat every outcome the same).

Once investors have calculated the average expected rates of return for all the assets they are interested in, there will naturally be some impulse to simply invest in those assets with the highest rates of return. But while that strategy might satisfy investor cravings for high rates of return, it would not take proper account of the fact that investors dislike risk and uncertainty. To quantify their dislike, investors require a statistic that measures each investment's risk level.

Beta

One popular statistic that measures risk is called beta. **Beta** is a *relative* measure of nondiversifiable risk. It measures how the nondiversifiable risk of a given asset or portfolio of assets compares with that of the **market portfolio,** which is the name given to a portfolio that contains every asset available in the financial markets. The market portfolio is a useful standard of comparison because it is as diversified as possible. In fact, because it contains every possible asset, each and every diversifiable risk will be diversified away. As a result, the market portfolio's risk and volatility must be due entirely to nondiversifiable risk. Consequently, the market portfolio can serve as a useful benchmark against which to measure any particular asset's level of nondiversifiable risk.

Such comparisons are very simple because the beta statistic is standardized such that the market portfolio's level of nondiversifiable risk is set equal to 1.0. Consequently, an asset with beta = 0.5 has a level of nondiversifiable risk that is one-half of that possessed by the market portfolio, while an asset with beta = 2.0 has twice as much nondiversifiable risk as the market portfolio. In addition, investors can use beta numbers to compare various assets. For instance, an asset with beta = 2.0 has four times more exposure to nondiversifiable risk than an asset with beta = 0.5.

Beta can be calculated not only for individual assets but also for portfolios. Indeed, it can be calculated for portfolios no matter how many or how few assets they contain and no matter what those assets are. Thus mutual fund investors can use beta to quickly see how the nondiversifiable risk of any given fund's portfolio compares with that of other potential investments that they may be considering.

In summary: The beta statistic is used along with average expected rates of return to give investors standard measures of risk and return that allow them to sensibly compare different investment opportunities.

beta A relative measure of *nondiversifiable risk* that measures how the non-diversifiable risk of a given *asset* or *portfolio* compares with that of the *market portfolio* (the portfolio that contains every asset available in the financial markets).

market portfolio The portfolio consisting of every financial asset (including every *stock* and *bond*) traded in the financial markets. Used to calculate *beta* (a measure of the degree of riskiness) for specific stocks, bonds, and mutual funds.

Relationship between Risk and Average Expected Rate of Return

The fact that investors dislike risk has a profound effect on asset prices and average expected rates of return. In particular, their dislike of risk and uncertainty causes investors to pay higher prices for less-risky assets and lower prices for more-risky assets. But because asset prices and average expected rates of return are inversely related, less-risky assets will have lower average expected rates of return than more-risky assets.

Stated another way: *Risk levels and average expected rates of return are positively related.* The more risky an investment is, the higher its average expected rate of return will be. A great way to understand this relationship is to think of higher average expected rates of return as a form of compensation. Because investors dislike risk, they demand higher levels of compensation the more risky an asset is. The higher levels of compensation come in the form of higher average expected rates of return.

Be sure to note that this phenomenon affects all assets. Regardless of whether the assets are stocks, bonds, real estate, or anything else, assets with higher levels of risk always end up with higher average expected rates of return to compensate investors for the higher levels of risk involved. No matter what the investment opportunity is, investors examine its possible future payments, determine how risky they are, and then select a price that reflects those risks. Because less-risky investments command higher prices, they end up with lower rates of return, whereas more-risky investments end up with lower prices and, consequently, higher rates of return.

The Risk-Free Rate of Return

We have just demonstrated that there is a positive relationship between risk and returns, with higher returns compensating investors for higher levels of risk. One investment, however, is considered to be risk-free for all intents and purposes. That investment is short-term U.S. government bonds.

These bonds are short-term loans to the U.S. government, with the duration of the loans ranging from 4 weeks to 26 weeks. They are essentially risk-free because there is almost no chance that the U.S. government will not be able to repay these loans on time and in full. To pay its debt, it can shift funds within its enormous budget, raise taxes, or borrow newly created money from the Fed. Although it is true that the U.S. government may eventually be destroyed or disabled to such an extent that it will not be able to repay some of its loans, the chances of such a calamity happening within 4 or even 26 weeks are essentially zero. Consequently, because it is a near certainty that the bonds will be repaid in full and on time, investors think of them as risk-free.

This leads us to another consideration. Because higher levels of risk lead to higher rates of return, and vice versa, a person might be tempted to assume—incorrectly—that because government bonds are risk-free, they should earn a zero percent rate of return. The problem with this line of thinking is that it mistakenly assumes that risk is the only thing that rates of return compensate for. The truth is, however, that rates of return compensate not only for risk but also for something else that economists call *time preference*.

time preference The human tendency, because of impatience, to prefer to spend and consume in the present rather than save and wait to spend and consume in the future; this inclination varies in strength among individuals.

Time preference refers to the fact that because people tend to be impatient, they typically prefer to consume things in the present rather than in the future. For example, most people, if given the choice between a serving of their favorite dessert immediately or a serving of their favorite dessert in five years, will choose to consume the serving immediately.

This time preference for consuming sooner rather than later affects the financial markets because people want to be compensated for delayed consumption. In particular, if Dave asks Oprah to lend him $1 million for one year, he is implicitly asking Oprah to delay consumption for a year because if she lends Dave the $1 million, she will not be able to spend that money herself for at least a year. If Oprah is like most people and prefers to spend her $1 million sooner rather than later, the only way Dave will be able to convince Oprah to loan him $1 million is to offer her some form of compensation. The compensation comes in the form of an interest payment that will allow Oprah to consume more in the future than she can now. For instance, Dave can offer to pay Oprah $1.1 million in one year in exchange for $1 million today. That is, Oprah will get back the $1 million she lends to Dave today as well as an extra $100,000 to compensate her for being patient.

Notice that this type of interest payment has nothing to do with risk. It is purely compensation for being patient and must be paid even if there is no risk involved and 100 percent certainty that Dave will fulfill his promise to repay.

Because short-term U.S. government bonds are for all intents and purposes completely risk-free and 100 percent likely to repay as promised, their rates of return are *purely* compensation for time preference and the fact that people must be compensated for delaying their own consumption opportunities when they lend money to the government. Therefore, the rate of return earned by short-term U.S. government bonds is often called the **risk-free interest rate,** or i^f, to indicate that their rate of return is not in any way a compensation for risk.

risk-free interest rate The *interest rate* earned on short-term U.S. government *bonds*.

Keep in mind, however, that the Fed has the power to change the risk-free interest rate generated by short-term U.S. government bonds. As discussed in Chapter 35, the Fed can use open-market operations to lower or raise interest rates by making large purchases or sales of U.S. securities in the bond market. These open-market operations affect the money supply, which affects all interest rates, including the rates on short-term U.S. government bonds. Thus the Fed indirectly determines the risk-free interest rate and, consequently, the compensation that investors receive for being patient.

QUICK REVIEW
36.5

▶ The average expected rate of return is the probability-weighted average of an investment's possible future returns.

▶ Beta measures the nondiversifiable risk of an investment relative to the amount of nondiversifiable risk facing the market portfolio, which is the portfolio containing every asset available in the financial markets.

▶ Because investors dislike risk, riskier investments must offer higher rates of return to compensate investors for bearing more risk.

▶ Average expected rates of return compensate investors for both risk and time preference, which is the preference most people have to consume sooner rather than later.

The Security Market Line

>> **LO36.8** Explain why arbitrage will tend to move all investments onto the Security Market Line.

Security Market Line (SML) A line that shows the *average expected rate of return* of all *financial investments* at each level of *nondiversifiable risk*, the latter measured by *beta*.

Investors must be compensated for time preference as well as for the amount of nondiversifiable risk that an investment carries with it. This section introduces a simple model called the **Security Market Line,** which indicates how this compensation is determined for tradable financial assets (securities) no matter what their respective risk levels happen to be.

The underlying logic of the model is this: Any investment's average expected rate of return has to be the sum of two parts—one that compensates for time preference and another that compensates for risk. That is,

$$\text{Average expected} = \text{rate that compensates for}$$
$$\text{rate of return} \quad \text{time preference}$$
$$+ \text{ rate that compensates for risk}$$

As noted earlier, the compensation for time preference is equal to the risk-free interest rate, i^f, that is paid on short-term government bonds. As a result, this equation can be simplified to

$$\text{Average expected rate of return} = i^f + \text{rate that compensates for risk}$$

Finally, because economists typically refer to the rate that compensates for risk as the **risk premium**, this equation can be simplified even further to

$$\text{Average expected rate of return} = i^f + \text{risk premium}$$

risk premium The rate of return in excess of the *risk-free interest rate* that compensates a lender or investor for *risk*.

Naturally, the size of the risk premium that compensates for risk will vary depending on how risky an investment happens to be. In particular, it will depend on how big or small the investment's beta is. Investments with large betas and lots of nondiversifiable risk will require larger risk premiums than investments that have small betas and low levels of nondiversifiable risk. And, in the most extreme case, risk-free assets that have betas equal to zero will require no compensation for risk at all since they have no risk to compensate for.

This logic is translated into Figure 36.1. The horizontal axis of Figure 36.1 measures risk levels using beta; the vertical axis measures average expected rates of return. As a result, any investment can be plotted on Figure 36.1 just as long as we know its beta and its average expected rate of return. We have plotted two investments in Figure 36.1. The first is a risk-free short-term U.S. government bond, which is indicated by the lower-left dot in the figure. The second is the market portfolio, which is indicated by the dot in the middle of the figure.

The lower dot is located where it is because every risk-free asset has a beta = 0 and an expected return equal to i^f. These values place the lower dot i^f percentage points up the vertical axis, as shown in Figure 36.1. Note that this location conveys the logic that because this asset has no risk, its average expected rate of return only has to compensate investors for time preference—which is why its average expected rate of return is equal to precisely i^f and no more.

The market portfolio, by contrast, is risky, so that its average expected rate of return must compensate investors not only for time preference but also for the level of risk to which the market portfolio is exposed, which by definition is beta = 1.0. This implies that the vertical distance from the horizontal axis to the upper dot is equal to the sum of i^f and the market portfolio's risk premium.

The straight line connecting the risk-free asset's lower dot and the market portfolio's upper dot is called the Security Market Line, or SML. The SML is extremely important because it defines the relationship between average expected rates of return and risk levels that must hold for all assets and all portfolios trading in the financial markets. The SML illustrates the idea that every asset's average expected rate of return is the sum of a rate of return that compensates for time preference and a rate of return that compensates for risk.

As we explained earlier, the precise location of the intercept at any given time is determined by the Federal Reserve's monetary policy and how it affects the rate of return on short-term U.S. government bonds. The slope of the SML, however, is determined by investors' feelings about risk and how much compensation they require for dealing with it. If investors greatly dislike risk, then the SML will have to be very steep, so that any given increase in risk on the horizontal axis will result in a very large increase in compensation as measured by average expected rates of return on the vertical axis. On the other hand, if investors dislike risk only moderately, then the SML will be relatively flat since any given increase in risk on the horizontal axis would require only a moderate increase in compensation as measured by average expected rates of return on the vertical axis.

FIGURE 36.1
The Security Market Line.

The Security Market Line shows the relationship between average expected rates of return and risk levels that must hold for every asset or portfolio trading in the financial markets. Each investment's average expected rate of return is the sum of the risk-free interest rate that compensates for time preference as well as a risk premium that compensates for the investment's level of risk. The Security Market Line's upward slope reflects the fact that investors must be compensated for higher levels of risk with higher average expected rates of return.

FIGURE 36.2
Risk levels determine average expected rates of return.

The Security Market Line can be used to determine an investment's average expected rate of return based on its risk level. In this figure, investments having a risk level of beta = X will have an average expected rate of return of Y percent per year. This average expected rate of return will compensate investors for time preference in addition to providing them exactly the right-sized risk premium to compensate them for dealing with a risk level of beta = X.

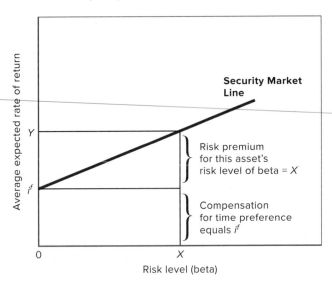

FIGURE 36.3
Arbitrage and the Security Market Line.

Arbitrage pressures will tend to move any asset or portfolio that lies off the Security Market Line back onto the line. Since asset A, for instance, begins with a rate of return higher than the rate Y which is sufficient to compensate investors for risk level X, investors will buy asset A eagerly, driving up its price and decreasing its average expected rate of return. And they will continue to do so until asset A moves down vertically to point B on the SML and earns exactly the rate of return Y that is necessary to compensate investors for risk level X. The opposite happens with asset C, whose initial rate of return is not enough to compensate investors for risk level X. Investors will sell asset C and cause its price to fall until its rate of return rises up to Y on the SML. Therefore, all assets with risk level X end up on the Security Market Line at point B.

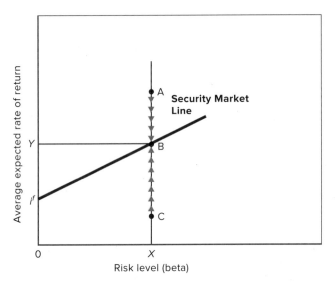

It is important to realize that once investor preferences about risk have determined the slope of the SML and monetary policy has determined its vertical intercept, *the SML plots out the precise relationship between risk levels and average expected rates of return that should hold for every asset.* Consider Figure 36.2, where there is an asset whose risk level on the horizontal axis is beta = X. The SML tells us that every asset with that risk level should have an average expected rate of return equal to Y on the vertical axis. This average expected rate of return exactly compensates for both time preference and the fact that the asset in question is exposed to a risk level of beta = X.

Finally, it should be pointed out that arbitrage will ensure that all investments having an identical level of risk also will have an identical rate of return—the return given by the SML. This is illustrated in Figure 36.3, where the three assets A, B, and C all share the same risk level of beta = X but initially have three different average expected rates of return. Since asset B lies on the SML, it has the average expected rate of return Y that precisely compensates investors for time preference and risk level X. Asset A, however, has a higher average expected rate of return that overcompensates investors for risk level X while asset C has a lower average expected rate of return that undercompensates investors for risk level X.

Arbitrage pressures will quickly eliminate these over- and under-compensations. For instance, consider what will happen to asset A. Investors will be hugely attracted to its overly high rate of return and will rush to buy it. That will drive up its price. But because average expected rates of return and prices are inversely related, the increase in A's price will cause its average expected rate of return to fall. So asset A will move vertically downward in Figure 36.3 until it reaches point B. It must fall to the same position as asset B because at any point higher than B, asset A will earn an excessive return that will cause people to continue to bid up its price (and thus lower its rate of return). Only when the price of A has been driven up far enough such that its rate of return falls to Y will the buying pressures stop.

A similar process will also move asset C back to the SML. Investors will dislike the fact that its average expected rate of return is so low. This will cause them to sell it, driving down its price. Since average expected rates of return and prices are inversely related, this will cause its average expected rate of return to rise, thereby causing C to ascend vertically in Figure 36.3.

Note that C will continue to rise until it reaches the SML, since only then will it have the average expected rate of return Y that properly compensates investors for time preference and risk level X. At that rate of return, the arbitrage pressures will stop since investors will be receiving exactly the compensation required for them to be just willing to own asset C.

Security Market Line: Applications

The SML analysis is highly useful in clarifying why investors scrutinize the intentions and actions of the Federal Reserve and change their behaviors during financial crises.

An Increase in the Risk-Free Rate by the Fed We have just explained how the position of the Security Market Line is fixed by two factors. The vertical intercept is set by the risk-free interest rate while the slope is determined by the amount of compensation investors demand for bearing nondiversifiable risk. As a result, changes in either factor can shift the SML and thereby cause large changes in both average expected rates of return and asset prices.

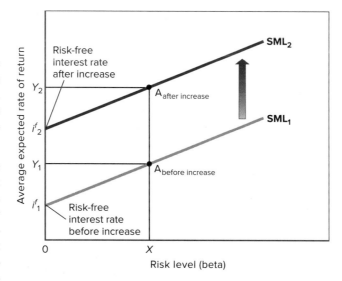

Risk-free interest rate after increase

$A_{\text{after increase}}$

SML_2

SML_1

$A_{\text{before increase}}$

Risk-free interest rate before increase

Risk level (beta)

Average expected rate of return

Y_2

i^f_2

Y_1

i^f_1

0 X

FIGURE 36.4
An increase in risk-free interest rates causes the SML to shift up vertically.

The risk-free interest rate set by the Federal Reserve is the Security Market Line's vertical intercept. Consequently, if the Federal Reserve increases the risk-free interest rate, the Security Market Line's vertical intercept will move up. This rise in the risk-free interest rate will result in a decline in all asset prices and thus an increase in the average expected rate of return on all assets. So the Security Market Line will shift up parallel from SML_1 to SML_2. Here, asset A with risk level beta $= X$ sees its average expected rate of return rise from Y_1 to Y_2.

As an example, consider what happens to the SML if the Federal Reserve changes policy and uses open-market operations (described in Chapter 35) to increase the risk-free interest rate that is paid on short-term government bonds. Since the risk-free interest rate is the SML's vertical intercept, the Fed's action will move the SML's vertical intercept upward, as illustrated in Figure 36.4. The result is a parallel upward shift of the SML from SML_1 to SML_2. (The shift is parallel because nothing has happened that would affect the SML's slope, which is determined by the amount of compensation that investors demand for bearing risk.)

Notice what this upward shift implies. Not only does the rate of return on short-term U.S. government bonds increase when the Federal Reserve changes policy, but the rate of return on risky assets increases as well. For instance, consider asset A, which originally has rate of return Y_1. After the SML shifts upward, asset A ends up with the higher rate of return Y_2. There is a simple intuition behind this increase. Risky assets must compete with risk-free assets for investor money. When the Federal Reserve increases the rate of return on risk-free short-term U.S. government bonds, they become more attractive to investors. But to get the money to buy more risk-free bonds, investors have to sell risky assets. This drives down their prices and—because prices and average expected rates of return are inversely related—causes their average expected rates of return to increase. The result is that asset A moves up vertically in Figure 36.4, its average expected rate of return increasing from Y_1 to Y_2 as investors reallocate their wealth from risky assets like asset A to risk-free bonds.

This process explains why investors are so watchful of the Federal Reserve and keenly interested in its policies. Any increase in the risk-free interest rate leads to a decrease in asset prices that directly reduces investors' wealth.

The Fed's power to change asset prices through monetary policy stems entirely from the fact that changes in the risk-free rate shift the SML and thus totally redefine the investment opportunities available in the economy. As the set of options changes, investors modify their portfolios to obtain the best possible combination of risk and returns from the new set of investment options. In doing so, they engage in massive amounts of buying and selling to get rid of assets they no longer want and acquire assets that they now desire. These massive changes in supply and demand for financial assets are what cause their prices to change so drastically when the Federal Reserve alters the risk-free interest rate.

The Security Market Line during the COVID Pandemic The premium demanded by investors to take on risk may vary from one period to another depending upon economic circumstances. The special circumstances of the financial markets during the early days of the COVID-19 recession of 2020 provide an excellent illustration of so-called *time-varying risk premiums* and thus the impact that Federal Reserve actions had during the crisis.

Index Funds versus Actively Managed Funds

Do Actively Managed Funds Outperform Index Funds?

It might seem obvious to you that actively managed funds would generate higher rates of return than index funds. After all, active fund managers are paid to "beat the market," while an index fund manager does virtually nothing, his portfolio earning whatever the underlying index earns. Surprisingly, however, the exact opposite is true. Once costs are taken into account, index funds trounce managed funds by well over 1 percent per year. Now, 1 percent per year may not sound like a lot, but the compound interest formula of equation 1 near the start of this chapter shows that $10,000 growing for 30 years at 10 percent per year becomes $170,449.40, whereas that same amount of money growing at 11 percent for 30 years becomes $220,892.30. For anyone saving for retirement, an extra 1 percent per year is a very big deal.

Why do actively managed funds do so much worse than index funds? The answer is twofold. First, arbitrage makes it virtually impossible for actively managed funds to select portfolios that will do any better than index funds that have similar levels of risk. As a result, *before taking costs into account,* actively managed funds and index funds produce very similar returns. Second, actively managed funds charge their investors much higher fees than do passively managed funds. So, *after taking costs into account,* actively managed funds do worse by about 1 percent per year.

Let's discuss each of these factors in more detail. The reason that actively managed funds cannot do better than index funds before taking costs into account has to do with the power of arbitrage to ensure that investments having equal levels of risk also have equal average expected rates of return. As we explained above with respect to Figure 36.3, investments that deviate from the Security Market Line (SML) are very quickly forced back onto the SML by arbitrage so that investments with equal levels of risk have equal average expected rates of return. This implies that index funds and actively managed funds with equal levels of risk will end up with identical average expected rates of return despite the best efforts of actively managed funds to produce superior returns.

The reason actively managed funds charge much higher fees than index funds is because they run up much higher costs while

Sirtravelalot/Shutterstock

trying to produce superior returns. Not only do they have to pay large salaries to active managers, but they also have to pay for the massive amounts of trading that those managers engage in. The costs of running an index fund are, by contrast, very small since changes are made to an index fund's portfolio only on the rare occasions when the fund's underlying index changes. As a result, trading costs are low and there is no need to pay for an active manager. The overall result is that while the largest and most popular index fund currently charges its investors only 0.04 percent per year for its services, the typical actively managed fund charges about 0.71 percent per year.

So why are actively managed funds still in business? The answer may well be that index funds are boring. Because they are set up to mimic indexes that are in turn designed to show what average performance levels are, index funds are by definition stuck with average rates of return and absolutely no chance of exceeding average rates of return. For investors who want to try to beat the average, actively managed funds are the only way to go.

When the pandemic hit and the economy slowed dramatically due to lockdowns, the Federal Reserve used expansionary monetary policy to lower interest rates, including the interest rates of short-term U.S. government bonds. Because the risk-free interest rate earned by these securities determines the vertical intercept of the Securities Market Line, the actual SML for the economy shifted downward from that shown in Figure 36.1 as short-term U.S. government bond rates fell. This decline would be portrayed as the opposite of the upward shift shown in Figure 36.4.

But wouldn't we expect stock market prices to rise when the risk-free rate of return falls? That certainly did *not* happen during the short but sharp recession. Yes, stock market prices normally rise when the risk-free interest rate falls. But during this unusual period, investors became very fearful about losses from investments in general and began to look for any place of financial safety. As their appetite for risk decreased, they demanded a much higher rate of compensation for taking on any particular level of risk. In terms of Figure 36.4, the slope of the SML greatly increased. Thus, between the Fed's deliberate reduction of the risk-free rate and investors' diminished appetite for risk, two things happened at once to the SML: (1) Its intercept (the risk-free rate) fell but (2) the SML became much steeper. In Figure 36.1, these two effects would be shown by a much steeper SML emanating from a lower point on the vertical axis.

The increase in the slope of the SML overwhelmed the decline in the intercept. Investors sold off stocks, which greatly reduced stock prices, even though the risk-free interest rate fell simultaneously. The net effect was a stock market crash during the first month of the pandemic.

But when it became clear after a few weeks that the pandemic would be less awful than initially feared, investors' appetite for risk began to grow again, implying that the slope of the SML started to flatten. The Fed was still holding the risk-free interest rate very low, but the increasingly flat slope of the SML drove up stock prices steadily, so that major stock market indexes like the S&P 500 had regained their pre-COVID peaks within six months of the "COVID crash."

Summary

LO36.1 Distinguish between economic investment and financial investment.

Financial economics focuses on investor preferences and how they affect the trading and pricing of the wide variety of financial assets available in the modern economy, including stocks, bonds, and real estate.

LO36.2 Explain the time value of money and calculate the present value of money.

The compound-interest formula states that if X_0 dollars are invested today at interest rate i and allowed to grow for t years, the original investment will become $(1 + i)^t X_0$ dollars in t years. The present-value formula rearranges the compound-interest formula. It tells investors the current number of dollars that they have to invest today to receive X_t dollars in t years. A risk-free investment's proper current price is the sum of the present values of each of the investment's expected future payments.

LO36.3 Distinguish among the most common financial investments: stocks, bonds, and mutual funds.

Stocks give shareholders the right to share in any future profits that corporations may generate. Bonds provide bondholders with the right to receive a fixed stream of future payments that serve to repay a loan. Mutual funds own and manage portfolios of bonds and stocks; fund investors get the returns generated by those portfolios.

LO36.4 Explain how percentage rates of return provide a common framework for comparing assets.

Investors can use percentage rates of return as a common framework for comparing different assets, even when those various assets have a wide variety of current prices and a large diversity of future payment

amounts. The percentage rate of return generated by an asset is inversely related to its price.

LO36.5 Define arbitrage.

Arbitrage is the process whereby investors equalize the average expected rates of return generated by identical or nearly identical assets. If two identical assets have different rates of return, investors will sell the asset with the lower rate of return and buy the asset with the higher rate of return. Because investment prices and investment returns move inversely, the returns of the higher-returning asset will fall while the returns of the lower-returning asset will rise. This will continue until the rates of return on the two assets have been equalized.

LO36.6 Define risk and distinguish between diversifiable and nondiversifiable risk.

An asset is risky if its future payments are uncertain. Risks that can be canceled out by diversification are called diversifiable risks. Risks that cannot be canceled out by diversification are called nondiversifiable risks.

LO36.7 Explain the factors that determine investment decisions.

Investors can estimate a risky investment's proper current value by calculating its average expected rate of return, which uses a probability-weighted average to place more weight on outcomes that are more likely to happen.

Beta measures the nondiversifiable risk of an investment relative to the amount of nondiversifiable risk facing the market portfolio, which, by definition, has a beta equal to 1.0.

Investors must be compensated for the delayed use of their money (time preference) and risk. Because a well-diversified portfolio has zero diversifiable risk, investors need to be compensated only for the portfolio's nondiversifiable risk.

An asset's average expected rate of return is the sum of the return that compensates for delay (time preference) plus the return that compensates for nondiversifiable risk.

LO36.8 Explain why arbitrage will tend to move all investments onto the Security Market Line.
The Security Market Line (SML) is a straight upsloping line showing how the average expected rates of return on assets and portfolios in the economy vary with their respective levels of nondiversifiable risk as measured by beta. Arbitrage ensures that every asset in the economy should plot onto the SML.

The slope of the SML reflects the investors' dislike for nondiversifiable risk, with steeper slopes reflecting greater dislike for that risk. The vertical intercept of the SML equals the risk-free interest rate that compensates for delay (time preference).

Terms and Concepts

economic investment	defaults	nondiversifiable risk
financial investment	mutual funds	average expected rate of return
securities	portfolio	probability-weighted average
present value	index funds	beta
compound interest	actively managed funds	market portfolio
stock	passively managed funds	time preference
bankrupt	percentage rate of return	risk-free interest rate
limited liability rule	arbitrage	Security Market Line
capital gain	risk	risk premium
dividends	diversification	
bond	diversifiable risk	

Discussion Questions

connect

1. Suppose that the city of New York issues bonds to raise money to pay for a new tunnel linking New Jersey and Manhattan. An investor named Susan buys one of the bonds on the same day that the city of New York pays a contractor for completing the first stage of construction. Is Susan making an economic or a financial investment? What about the city of New York? **LO36.1**

2. What is compound interest? How does it relate to the formula $X_t = (1 + i)^t X_0$? What is present value? How does it relate to the formula $X_t/(1 + i)^t = X_0$? **LO36.2**

3. How do stocks and bonds differ in terms of the future payments that they are expected to make? Which type of investment (stocks or bonds) is considered to be more risky? Given what you know, which investment (stocks or bonds) do you think commonly goes by the nickname "fixed income"? **LO36.3**

4. What are mutual funds? What different types of mutual funds are there? And why do you think they are so popular with investors? **LO36.3**

5. Corporations often distribute profits to their shareholders in the form of dividends, which are quarterly payments sent to shareholders. Suppose that you have the chance to buy a share in a fashion company called Rogue Designs for $35 and that the company will pay dividends of $2 per year on that share. What is the annual percentage rate of return? Next, suppose that you and other investors could get a 12 percent per year rate of return on the stocks of other very similar fashion companies. If investors care only about rates of return, what should happen to the share price of Rogue Designs? (Hint: This is an arbitrage situation.) **LO36.5**

6. Why is it reasonable to ignore diversifiable risk and care only about nondiversifiable risk? What about investors who put all their money into only a single risky stock? Can they properly ignore diversifiable risk? **LO36.6**

7. If we compare the betas of various investment opportunities, why do the assets that have higher betas also have higher average expected rates of return? **LO36.7**

8. The U.S. government issues longer-term bonds with horizons of up to 30 years. Why do 20-year bonds issued by the U.S. government have lower rates of return than 20-year bonds issued by corporations? And which do you think has the higher rate of return, longer-term U.S. government bonds or short-term U.S. government bonds? Explain. **LO36.7**

9. What determines the vertical intercept of the Security Market Line (SML)? What determines its slope? And what will happen to an asset's price if it initially plots onto a point above the SML? **LO36.8**

10. Suppose that the Federal Reserve thinks that a stock market bubble is occurring and wants to reduce stock prices. What should it do to interest rates? **LO36.8**

11. Consider another situation involving the SML. Suppose that the risk-free interest rate stays the same, but that investors' dislike of risk grows more intense. Given this change, will average expected rates of return rise or fall? Next, compare what will happen to the rates of return on low-risk and high-risk investments. Which will have a larger increase in average expected rates of return, investments with high betas or investments with low betas? And will high-beta or low-beta investments show larger percentage changes in their prices? **LO36.8**

12. **LAST WORD** Why is it so hard for actively managed funds to generate higher rates of return than passively managed index funds having similar levels of risk? Is there a simple way for an actively managed fund to increase its average expected rate of return?

Review Questions

1. Identify each of the following investments as either an economic investment or a financial investment. **LO36.1**
   a. A company builds a new factory.
   b. A pension plan buys some Space X stock.
   c. A mining company sets up a new gold mine.
   d. A merchant buys a 100-year-old farmhouse in the countryside.
   e. A bus driver buys a newly built home in the city.
   f. A company buys an old factory.

2. It is a fact that $(1 + 0.12)^3 = 1.40$. Knowing that to be true, what is the present value of $140 received in three years if the annual interest rate is 12 percent? **LO36.2**
   a. $1.40
   b. $12
   c. $100
   d. $112

3. Asset X is expected to deliver 3 future payments. They have present values of, respectively, $1,000, $2,000, and $7,000. Asset Y is expected to deliver 10 future payments, each having a present value of $1,000. Which of the following statements correctly describes the relationship between the current price of Asset X and the current price of Asset Y? **LO36.2**
   a. Asset X and Asset Y should have the same current price.
   b. Asset X should have a higher current price than Asset Y.
   c. Asset X should have a lower current price than Asset Y.

4. Tamar can buy an asset this year for $1,000. She is expecting to sell it next year for $1,050. What is the asset's anticipated percentage rate of return? **LO36.4**
   a. 0 percent
   b. 5 percent
   c. 10 percent
   d. 15 percent

5. Sammy buys stock in a suntan-lotion maker and also stock in an umbrella maker. One stock does well when the weather is good; the other does well when the weather is bad. Sammy's portfolio indicates that "weather risk" is a _____ risk. **LO36.6**
   a. diversifiable
   b. nondiversifiable
   c. automatic

6. An investment has a 50 percent chance of generating a 10 percent return and a 50 percent chance of generating a 16 percent return. What is the investment's average expected rate of return? **LO36.7**
   a. 10 percent
   b. 11 percent
   c. 12 percent
   d. 13 percent
   e. 14 percent
   f. 15 percent
   g. 16 percent

7. If an investment has 35 percent more nondiversifiable risk than the market portfolio, its beta will be: **LO36.7**
   a. 35
   b. 1.35
   c. 0.35

8. The interest rate on short-term U.S. government bonds is 4 percent. The risk premium for any asset with a beta = 1.0 is 6 percent. What is the average expected rate of return on the market portfolio? **LO36.8**
   a. 0 percent
   b. 4 percent
   c. 6 percent
   d. 10 percent

9. Suppose that an SML indicates that assets with a beta = 1.15 should have an average expected rate of return of 12 percent per year. If a particular stock with a beta = 1.15 currently has an average expected rate of return of 15 percent, what should we expect to happen to its price? **LO36.8**
   a. Rise.
   b. Fall.
   c. Stay the same.

10. If the Fed increases interest rates, the SML will shift _____ and asset prices will _____. **LO36.8**
    a. down; rise
    b. down; fall
    c. up; rise
    d. up; fall

Problems

1. Suppose that you invest $100 today in a risk-free investment and let the 4 percent annual interest rate compound. Rounded to full dollars, what will be the value of your investment 4 years from now? **LO36.2**

2. Suppose that you desire to get a lump-sum payment of $100,000 two years from now. Rounded to full dollars, how many current dollars will you have to invest today at 10 percent interest to accomplish your goal? **LO36.2**

3. Suppose that a risk-free investment will make three future payments of $100 in 1 year, $100 in 2 years, and $100 in 3 years. If the Federal Reserve has set the risk-free interest rate at 8 percent, what is the proper current price of this investment? What is the price of this investment if the Federal Reserve raises the risk-free interest rate to 10 percent? **LO36.2**

4. Suppose initially that two assets, A and B, will each make a single guaranteed payment of $100 in 1 year. But asset A has a current price of $80 while asset B has a current price of $90. **LO36.5**
   a. What are the rates of return of assets A and B at their current prices? Given these rates of return, which asset should investors buy and which asset should they sell?
   b. Assume that arbitrage continues until A and B have the same expected rate of return. When arbitrage ends, will A and B have the same price?
   Next, consider another pair of assets, C and D. Asset C will make a single payment of $150 in one year, while D will make a single payment of $200 in one year. Assume that the current price of C is $120 and that the current price of D is $180.

c. What are the rates of return of assets C and D at their current prices? Given these rates of return, which asset should investors buy and which asset should they sell?

d. Assume that arbitrage continues until C and D have the same expected rate of return. When arbitrage ends, will C and D have the same price?

Compare your answers to questions *a* through *d* before answering question *e*.

e. We know that arbitrage will equalize rates of return. Does it also guarantee to equalize prices? In what situations will it equalize prices?

5. Consider an asset that costs $120 today. You are going to hold it for 1 year and then sell it. Suppose that there is a 25 percent chance that it will be worth $100 in a year, a 25 percent chance that it will be worth $115 in a year, and a 50 percent chance that it will be worth $140 in a year. What is its average expected rate of return? Next, figure out what the investment's average expected rate of return would be if its current price were $130 today. Does the increase in the current price increase or decrease the asset's average expected rate of return? At what price would the asset have a zero average expected rate of return? **LO36.7**

6. **ADVANCED ANALYSIS** Suppose that the equation for the SML is $Y = 0.05 + 0.04X$, where Y is the average expected rate of return, 0.05 is the vertical intercept, 0.04 is the slope, and X is the risk level as measured by beta. What is the risk-free interest rate for this SML? What is the average expected rate of return at a beta of 1.5? What is the value of beta at an average expected rate of return of 7 percent? **LO36.8**

Sushiman/Shutterstock

Extending the Analysis of Aggregate Supply

>> LEARNING OBJECTIVES

LO37.1 Explain the relationship between short-run aggregate supply and long-run aggregate supply.

LO37.2 Apply the extended (short-run/long-run) AD–AS model to inflation, recessions, and economic growth.

LO37.3 Explain the short-run trade-off between inflation and unemployment (the Phillips Curve).

LO37.4 Explain why there is no long-run trade-off between inflation and unemployment.

LO37.5 Explain the relationships among tax rates, tax revenues, and aggregate supply.

During the early years of the Great Depression, many economists suggested that the economy would correct itself in the *long run* without government intervention. Economist John Maynard Keynes responded, "In the long run we are all dead!"

For several decades following the Great Depression, macroeconomists understandably focused on refining fiscal policy and monetary policy to smooth business cycles and address the problems of unemployment and inflation. The main emphasis was on short-run problems and policies associated with the business cycle.

But over people's lifetimes, and from generation to generation, the long run is tremendously important for economic well-being. For that reason, macroeconomists have refocused attention on long-run macroeconomic adjustments, processes, and outcomes. The renewed emphasis on the long run has produced significant insights about aggregate supply, economic growth, and economic development. We will also see in the next chapter that it has renewed historical debates over the causes of macro instability and the effectiveness of stabilization policy.

Our goals in this chapter are to extend the analysis of aggregate supply to the long run, examine the inflation-unemployment relationship, and evaluate the effect of taxes on aggregate supply. The latter is a key concern of so-called *supply-side economics*.

From Short Run to Long Run

>> **LO37.1** Explain the relationship between short-run aggregate supply and long-run aggregate supply.

short run (macroeconomics)
In *macroeconomics,* the relatively short period of time (typically, weeks to months) in which *nominal wages* and other input *prices* do not change in response to a change in a nation's *price level.*

long run (macroeconomics)
In *macroeconomics,* a period of time sufficiently long for *nominal wages* and other input *prices* to change in response to a change in a nation's *price level.*

In Chapter 32, we noted that in macroeconomics the flexibility of input prices defines the difference between the **short run** and the **long run.** Input prices are inflexible or even totally fixed in the short run but fully flexible in the long run. By contrast, output prices are flexible in both the short run and the long run.

The assumption that input prices are flexible only in the long run leads to large differences in the shape and position of the short-run aggregate supply curve and the long-run aggregate supply curve. As Chapter 32 explained, the short-run aggregate supply curve is an upward sloping line, whereas the long-run aggregate supply curve is a vertical line at the economy's full-employment output level, Q_f.

We will begin this chapter by discussing how aggregate supply transitions from the short run to the long run. Once that is done, we will combine the long-run and short-run aggregate supply curves with the aggregate demand curve to form a single model that can provide insights into how the economy adjusts to economic shocks as well as changes in monetary and fiscal policy in both the short run and the long run. That will lead us to discuss how economic growth relates to long-run aggregate supply and how inflation and aggregate supply are related in the long run and the short run. We will conclude with a discussion of a particular set of economic policies that may help increase both short-run aggregate supply and long-run aggregate supply.

Short-Run Aggregate Supply

Our immediate objective is to demonstrate the relationship between short-run aggregate supply and long-run aggregate supply. We begin by briefly reviewing short-run aggregate supply.

Consider the short-run aggregate supply curve AS_1 in Figure 37.1a. This curve is based on three assumptions: (1) The initial price level is P_1, (2) firms and workers have established nominal wages on the expectation that this price level will persist, and (3) the price level is flexible both upward and downward. Observe from point a_1 that at price level P_1 the economy is operating at its full-employment output Q_f. This output is the real production forthcoming when the economy is operating at its natural rate of unemployment (or potential output).

Now let's review the short-run effects of a change in the price level, say, from P_1 to P_2 in Figure 37.1a. The higher output prices associated with price level P_2 increase firms' revenues, and because their nominal wages and other input prices remain unchanged, their profits rise. Those higher profits

FIGURE 37.1 **Short-run and long-run aggregate supply.**

(a) In the short run, nominal wages and other input prices do not respond to price-level changes and are based on the expectation that price level P_1 will continue. An increase in the price level from P_1 to P_2 increases profits and output, moving the economy from a_1 to a_2; a decrease in the price level from P_1 to P_3 reduces profits and real output, moving the economy from a_1 to a_3. The short-run aggregate supply curve therefore slopes upward. (b) In the long run, a rise in the price level results in higher nominal wages and other input prices and thus shifts the short-run aggregate supply curve to the left. Conversely, a decrease in the price level reduces nominal wages and shifts the short-run aggregate supply curve to the right. After such adjustments, the economy obtains equilibrium at points such as b_1 and c_1. Thus, the long-run aggregate supply curve is vertical at the full-employment output.

(a)
Short-run aggregate supply

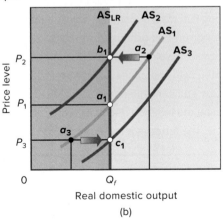
(b)
Long-run aggregate supply

lead firms to increase their output from Q_f to Q_2, and the economy moves from a_1 to a_2 on aggregate supply AS_1. At output Q_2 the economy is operating beyond its full-employment output. The firms make this possible by extending the work hours of part-time and full-time workers, enticing new workers such as homemakers and retirees into the labor force, and hiring and training the structurally unemployed. Thus, the nation's unemployment rate declines below its natural rate.

How will the firms respond when the price level *falls*, say, from P_1 to P_3 in Figure 37.1a? Because the prices they receive for their products are lower while workers' nominal wages remain unchanged, firms discover that their revenues and profits have diminished or disappeared. They reduce their production and employment, and, as shown by the movement from a_1 to a_3, real output falls to Q_3. A higher unemployment rate accompanies the decline in real output. At output Q_3 the unemployment rate is greater than the natural rate of unemployment associated with output Q_f.

Long-Run Aggregate Supply

The outcomes are different in the long run. To explain why, we need to account for changes in nominal wages that occur in response to changes in the price level. Doing so allows us to derive the economy's long-run aggregate supply curve.

We illustrate the implications for aggregate supply in Figure 37.1b. Again, suppose that the economy is initially at point a_1 (P_1 and Q_f). As we've seen, an increase in the price level from P_1 to P_2 will move the economy from point a_1 to point a_2 along the short-run aggregate supply curve AS_1. At a_2, the economy is producing more than its potential output. The demand for productive inputs is very high, so input prices will begin to rise. In particular, the high demand for labor will drive up nominal wages, which will increase per-unit production costs. That increase in marginal production costs will squeeze profit margins. Producers will respond by producing less. So the short-run supply curve will shift leftward from AS_1 to AS_2, which now reflects the higher price level P_2 and the new expectation that P_2, not P_1, will continue. The leftward shift in the short-run aggregate supply curve to AS_2 moves the economy from a_2 to b_1. Real output falls back to its full-employment level Q_f, and unemployment rises to its natural rate.

What is the long-run outcome of a *decrease* in the price level? Assuming eventual downward wage flexibility, a decline in the price level from P_1 to P_3 in Figure 37.1b works in the opposite way from a price-level increase. At first the economy moves from point a_1 to a_3 on AS_1. Profits are squeezed or eliminated because prices have fallen but nominal wages and other input costs have not. But this movement along AS_1 is the short-run supply response that results only while input prices remain constant. As time passes, input prices will begin to fall because the economy is producing below its full-employment output level. With so little output being produced, the demand for inputs will be low, and their prices will begin to decline. In particular, the low demand for labor will drive down nominal wages, reduce per-unit production costs, and raise profit margins. Lower nominal wages therefore shift the short-run aggregate supply curve rightward from AS_1 to AS_3 because at any given price level P, firms will want to produce more units of output. After short-run aggregate supply shifts to AS_3, real output returns to its full-employment level of Q_f at point c_1.

By tracing a line between the long-run equilibrium points b_1, a_1, and c_1, we obtain a long-run aggregate supply curve. Observe that it is vertical at the full-employment level of real GDP. After long-run adjustments in nominal wages and other nominal input prices have been completed, real output is Q_f regardless of the specific price level.

Long-Run Equilibrium in the AD–AS Model

Figure 37.2 helps us understand long-run equilibrium in the AD–AS model, which we just extended to encompass both short-run and long-run aggregate supply. (Hereafter, we refer to this model as the extended AD–AS model, with "extended" referring to the inclusion of both the short-run and the long-run aggregate supply curves.)

In the short run, equilibrium occurs where the downward sloping aggregate demand curve and upward sloping short-run aggregate supply

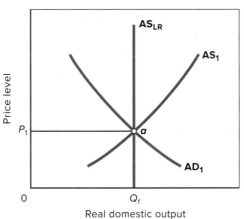

FIGURE 37.2
Equilibrium in the long-run AD–AS model.

The long-run equilibrium price level P_1 and level of real output Q_f occur at the intersection of the aggregate demand curve AD_1, the long-run aggregate supply curve AS_{LR}, and the short-run aggregate supply curve AS_1.

curve intersect. Equilibrium can occur at any level of output, not only the full-employment level. Either a negative GDP gap or a positive GDP gap is possible in the short run.

In the long run, however, the short-run aggregate supply curve adjusts as we just described. After those adjustments, long-run equilibrium occurs where the aggregate demand curve, vertical long-run aggregate supply curve, and short-run aggregate supply curve all intersect. Figure 37.2 shows the long-run outcome. Equilibrium occurs at point a, where AD_1 intersects both AS_{LR} and AS_1, and the economy achieves its full-employment (or potential) output, Q_f. At long-run equilibrium price level P_1 and output level Q_f, neither a negative GDP gap nor a positive GDP gap occurs. The economy's *natural rate of unemployment* prevails, meaning that the economy achieves full employment.

In the United States, output Q_f in Figure 37.2 implies a 4 to 5 percent unemployment rate. The natural rate of unemployment can vary from one time period to another and can differ between countries. But whatever the rate happens to be, it defines the level of potential output and establishes the location of the long-run AS curve.

▶ The short-run aggregate supply curve slopes upward because nominal wages and other input prices are fixed in the short run while output prices change, thereby increasing (as output prices rise) or decreasing (as output prices fall) firm profits and the incentive to produce output.

▶ The long-run aggregate supply curve is vertical because input prices eventually rise in response to changes in output prices.

▶ The long-run equilibrium GDP and price level occur at the intersection of the aggregate demand curve, the long-run aggregate supply curve, and the short-run aggregate supply curve.

▶ In long-run equilibrium, the economy achieves its natural rate of unemployment and its full-potential real output.

Applying the Extended AD–AS Model

>> LO37.2 Apply the extended (short-run/long-run) AD–AS model to inflation, recessions, and economic growth.

The extended AD–AS model helps clarify the long-run aspects of demand-pull inflation, cost-push inflation, and recession.

Demand-Pull Inflation in the Extended AD–AS Model

Recall that demand-pull inflation occurs when an increase in aggregate demand pulls up the price level. Earlier, we depicted this inflation by shifting an aggregate demand curve rightward along a stable aggregate supply curve (see Figure 32.8).

In our extended AD–AS model, an increase in the price level that is associated with GDP exceeding the full employment level eventually leads to an increase in nominal wages and thus a leftward shift of the short-run aggregate supply curve. In Figure 37.3, we initially suppose the price level is P_1 at the intersection of aggregate demand curve AD_1, short-run supply curve AS_1, and long-run aggregate supply curve AS_{LR}. The economy is achieving its full-employment real output Q_f at point a.

Now consider the effects of an increase in aggregate demand as represented by the rightward shift from AD_1 to AD_2. This shift might result from any one of a number of factors, including an increase in investment spending or a rise in net exports. Whatever its cause, the increase in aggregate demand boosts the price level from P_1 to P_2 and expands real output from Q_f to Q_2 at point b. There, a positive GDP gap of $Q_2 - Q_f$ occurs.

So far, none of this is new to you. But now the distinction between short-run aggregate supply and long-run aggregate supply becomes important. With the economy producing above potential output, inputs will be in high demand. Input prices including nominal wages will rise. As they do, the short-run aggregate supply curve will ultimately shift leftward such that it intersects long-run aggregate supply at point c. There, the economy has reestablished a long-run equilibrium, with the price level and real output now P_3 and Q_f, respectively. Only at point c does the new aggregate demand curve AD_2 intersect both the short-run aggregate supply curve AS_2 and the long-run aggregate supply curve AS_{LR}.

FIGURE 37.3
Demand-pull inflation in the extended AD–AS model.

An increase in aggregate demand from AD_1 to AD_2 drives up the price level and increases real output in the short run. But in the long run, nominal wages rise and the short-run aggregate supply curve shifts leftward, as from AS_1 to AS_2. Real output then returns to its prior level, and the price level rises even more. In this scenario, the economy moves from a to b and then eventually to c.

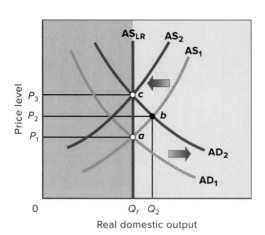

In the short run, demand-pull inflation drives up the price level and increases real output. In the long run, only the price level rises. In the long run, the initial increase in aggregate demand moves the economy along its vertical aggregate supply curve AS_{LR}. For a while, an economy can operate beyond its full-employment level of output. But the demand-pull inflation eventually causes adjustments of nominal wages that return the economy to its full-employment output Q_f.

FIGURE 37.4
Cost-push inflation in the extended AD–AS model.

Cost-push inflation occurs when the short-run aggregate supply curve shifts leftward, as from AS_1 to AS_2. If government counters the decline in real output by increasing aggregate demand to the broken line, the price level rises even more. That is, the economy moves in steps from *a* to *b* to *c*. In contrast, if government allows a recession to occur, nominal wages eventually fall and the aggregate supply curve shifts back rightward to its original location. The economy moves from *a* to *b* and eventually back to *a*.

Cost-Push Inflation in the Extended AD–AS Model

Cost-push inflation arises from factors that increase the cost of production at each price level, shifting the aggregate supply curve leftward and raising the equilibrium price level. Previously (Figure 32.10), we considered cost-push inflation using only the short-run aggregate supply curve. Now we want to analyze that type of inflation in its long-run context.

Analysis Look at Figure 37.4, in which we again assume that the economy is initially operating at price level P_1 and output level Q_f (point *a*). Suppose that international oil producers agree to reduce the supply of oil to boost its price by, say, 100 percent. As a result, the per-unit production cost of producing and transporting goods and services rises substantially in the economy represented by Figure 37.4. This increase in per-unit production costs shifts the short-run aggregate supply curve to the left, as from AS_1 to AS_2, and the price level rises from P_1 to P_2 (as seen by comparing points *a* and *b*). In this case, the leftward shift of the aggregate supply curve is not a *response* to a price-level increase, as it was in our previous discussions of demand-pull inflation. Rather, it is the *cause* of the price-level increase.

Policy Dilemma Cost-push inflation creates a dilemma for policymakers. Without some expansionary stabilization policy, aggregate demand in Figure 37.4 remains in place at AD_1 and real output declines from Q_f to Q_2. Government can counter this recession, negative GDP gap, and high unemployment by using fiscal policy and monetary policy to increase aggregate demand to AD_2. But there is a potential policy trap here: An increase in aggregate demand to AD_2 will further raise inflation by increasing the price level from P_2 to P_3 (a move from point *b* to point *c*).

Suppose the government recognizes this policy trap and decides not to increase aggregate demand from AD_1 to AD_2 (you can now disregard the dashed AD_2 curve) and instead decides to allow a cost-push-created recession to run its course. How will that happen? Widespread layoffs, plant shutdowns, and business failures eventually occur. At some point the demand for oil, labor, and other inputs will decline so much that oil prices, nominal wages, and other input prices will decline. When that happens, the initial leftward shift of the short-run aggregate supply curve will reverse itself. That is, the declining per-unit production costs caused by the recession shift the short-run aggregate supply curve rightward from AS_2 to AS_1. The price level returns to P_1, and the full-employment level of output is restored at Q_f (point *a* on the long-run aggregate supply curve AS_{LR}).

This analysis yields two generalizations:

- If the government attempts to maintain full employment when there is cost-push inflation, even more inflation will occur.

- If the government takes a hands-off approach to cost-push inflation, the recession will linger. Although falling input prices will eventually undo the initial rise in per-unit production costs, the economy in the meantime will experience high unemployment and a loss of real output. There will also be a deflation as the economy adjusts back from *b* to *a*.

The nearby Consider This feature discusses how supply shocks contributed to the COVID-19 inflation.

CONSIDER THIS . . .

Cost-Push Contagion

In late 2019, the U.S. economy was enjoying rapid, noninflationary growth. The unemployment rate was just 3.5 percent, real GDP was growing robustly at 2.6 percent per year, and inflation was muted at just 1.8 percent per year. Even better, all forecasts were for the strong growth and low inflation to continue.

But then the COVID-19 virus spread worldwide, causing governments around the world to impose strict lockdowns during the spring of 2020 for at least a month or two, with various lesser restrictions, such as social distancing, continuing through the next two years.

The lockdowns acted as a major negative supply shock since tens of millions of people were prevented from going

Andrey_Popov/Shutterstock

to work. The general slowdown in spending—despite massive fiscal stimulus by the Federal government—also caused tens of thousands of businesses to go bankrupt, especially in the food service and hospitality industries. Those reductions in productive capacity shifted aggregated supply even further leftward. The result was a sharp initial decrease in real GDP in the spring of 2020 followed over the next year by steadily increasing consumer prices, so that by the summer of 2021 inflation was running at a 5.4 percent annual rate. COVID-19 had infected the economy as well as human beings. Cost-push inflation had arrived and looked ready to stay a while. By the summer of 2022, inflation was running at 9.1 percent per year.

A Controversy: Recessions and Stimulus in the Extended AD–AS Model

By far the most controversial application of the extended AD–AS model is its application to recession (or depression) caused by decreases in aggregate demand. We will look at this controversy in detail in Chapter 38; here we simply identify the key point of contention.

Suppose in Figure 37.5 that aggregate demand initially is AD_1 and that the short-run and long-run aggregate supply curves are AS_1 and AS_{LR}, respectively. Therefore, as shown by point a, the price level is P_1 and output is Q_f. Now suppose that investment spending declines dramatically, reducing aggregate demand to AD_2. Observe that real output declines from Q_f to Q_1, indicating that a recession has occurred. But if we make the controversial assumption that prices and nominal wages are flexible downward, the price level falls from P_1 to P_2. With the economy producing below potential output at point b, demand for inputs will be low. Eventually, nominal wages and input prices fall; when that happens, the short-run aggregate supply curve shifts rightward from AS_1 to AS_2. The negative GDP gap evaporates without the need for expansionary fiscal or monetary policy since real output expands from Q_1 (point b) back to Q_f (point c). The economy is again located on its long-run aggregate supply curve AS_{LR}, but now at lower price level P_3.

There is much disagreement about this hypothetical scenario. The key point of dispute revolves around the degree to which both input and output prices may be downwardly inflexible and how long it would take in the actual economy for the necessary downward price and wage adjustments to occur to regain the full-employment level of output. For now, suffice it to say that most economists believe that if such adjustments are forthcoming, they will occur only after the economy has experienced a relatively long-lasting recession with its accompanying high unemployment and large loss of output. The severity and length of the major recession of 2007–2009 has strengthened this view. Therefore, economists recommend active monetary policy, and perhaps fiscal policy, to counteract recessions.

Economic Growth with Ongoing Inflation

We have seen how demand and supply shocks can cause, respectively, demand-pull inflation and cost-push inflation. In these previous cases, the extent of the inflation was *finite* because the

FIGURE 37.5
Recession in the extended AD–AS model.

A recession occurs when aggregate demand shifts leftward, as from AD_1 to AD_2. If prices are downwardly flexible, the price level falls from P_1 to P_2 as the economy moves from point a to point b. With the economy in recession at point b, nominal wages will fall, shifting the aggregate supply curve from AS_1 to AS_2. The price level declines to P_3, and real output returns to Q_f. The economy moves from a to b to c.

size of the initial movement in either the AD curve or the AS curve was *limited*. For instance, in Figure 37.3, the aggregate demand curve shifts right by a limited amount, from AD_1 to AD_2. As the economy's equilibrium moves from a to b to c, the price level rises from P_1 to P_2 to P_3. During this transition, inflation obviously occurs because the price level is rising. But once the economy reaches its new equilibrium at point c, the price level remains constant at P_3 and no further inflation takes place. That is, the limited movement in aggregate demand causes a limited amount of inflation that ends when the economy returns to full employment.

But the modern economy almost always experiences continuous, but usually mild, positive rates of inflation. That can happen only with ongoing shifts in either the aggregate demand or long-run aggregate supply curve because any single, finite shift will cause inflation of limited magnitude and duration. This insight is crucial to understanding why modern economies usually experience ongoing inflation while achieving economic growth. Both aggregate demand and long-run aggregate supply increase over time in the actual economy. The ongoing, positive, and mild rates of inflation that we observe in the actual economy happen because the increases in aggregate demand generally exceed the increases in long-run aggregate supply. It will be helpful to examine this point graphically.

Increases in Long-Run Aggregate Supply As discussed in Chapter 28, economic growth is driven by supply factors such as improved technologies and access to more or better resources. Economists illustrate economic growth as either an outward shift of an economy's production possibilities curve or as a rightward shift of its long-run aggregate supply curve. As Figure 37.6 shows, the outward shift of the production possibilities curve from AB to CD in graph a is equivalent to the rightward shift of the economy's long-run aggregate supply curve from AS_{LR1} to AS_{LR2} in graph b.

Let's simply transfer this rightward shift of the economy's long-run aggregate supply curve to Figure 37.7, which depicts U.S. economic growth in the context of the extended aggregate demand–aggregate supply model. Suppose the economy's long-run aggregate supply curve initially is AS_{LR1}, while its aggregate demand curve and short-run aggregate supply curve are AD_1 and AS_1, as shown. The equilibrium price level is P_1 and the equilibrium level of real output is Q_1.

Now let's assume that economic growth driven by changes in supply factors (quantity and quality of resources and technology) shifts the long-run aggregate supply curve rightward from AS_{LR1} to AS_{LR2} while the economy's aggregate demand curve remains at AD_1. Also, suppose that product and resource prices are flexible downward. The economy's potential output will expand, as reflected by the increase of available real output from Q_1 to Q_2. With aggregate demand constant at AD_1, the

FIGURE 37.6 Production possibilities and long-run aggregate supply.

(a) Economic growth driven by supply factors (such as improved technologies or the use of more or better resources) shifts an economy's production possibilities curve outward, as from *AB* to *CD*. (b) The same factors shift the economy's long-run aggregate supply curve to the right, as from AS_{LR1} to AS_{LR2}.

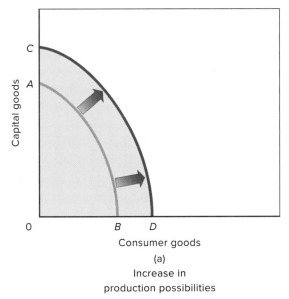

(a)

Increase in
production possibilities

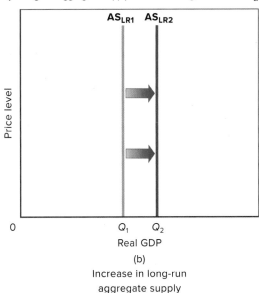

(b)

Increase in long-run
aggregate supply

FIGURE 37.7
Depicting U.S. growth via the extended AD–AS model.

Long-run aggregate supply and short-run aggregate supply have increased over time, as from AS_{LR1} to AS_{LR2} and AS_1 to AS_2. Simultaneously, aggregate demand has shifted rightward, as from AD_1 to AD_2. The actual outcome of these combined shifts has been economic growth, shown as the increase in real output from Q_1 to Q_2, accompanied by mild inflation, shown as the rise in the price level from P_1 to P_2.

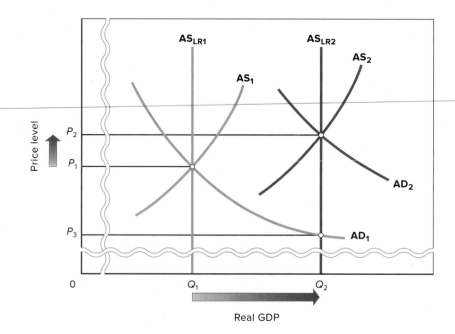

rightward shift of the long-run aggregate supply curve will lower the price level from P_1 to P_3. *Taken alone, expansions of long-run aggregate supply in the economy are deflationary.*

Increases in Aggregate Demand and Inflation But a decline in the price level, such as the one from P_1 to P_3 in Figure 37.7, is not part of the long-run U.S. growth experience. Why not? Because the U.S. central bank—the Federal Reserve—engineers ongoing increases in the nation's money supply to create rightward shifts of the aggregate demand curve. These increases in aggregate demand would be highly inflationary without the increases in long-run aggregate supply. But because the Fed usually ensures that the inflationary rightward shifts of the aggregate demand curve proceed only slightly faster than the deflationary rightward shifts of the aggregate supply curve, only mild inflation occurs along with economic growth.

We illustrate this outcome in Figure 37.7, where aggregate demand shifts to the right from AD_1 to AD_2 at the same time long-run aggregate supply shifts rightward from AS_{LR1} to AS_{LR2}. Real output expands from Q_1 to Q_2 and the price level increases from P_1 to P_2. At the higher price level P_2, the economy confronts a new short-run aggregate supply curve AS_2. Figure 37.7 describes the actual U.S. experience: economic growth, accompanied by mild inflation. Since the early 1980s, real output has increased on average at about 2.5 percent annually while inflation has averaged roughly 2.6 percent a year.

Of course, other long-term outcomes besides that depicted are possible. Whether deflation, zero inflation, mild inflation, or rapid inflation accompanies economic growth depends on the extent to which aggregate demand increases relative to long-run aggregate supply. Over long periods, any inflation that accompanies economic growth is exclusively the result of aggregate demand increasing more rapidly than long-run aggregate supply. The expansion of long-run aggregate supply—of potential real GDP—never causes inflation. Holding all other things equal, the expansion of long-run aggregate supply causes deflation, not inflation.

QUICK REVIEW

37.2

▸ In the short run, demand-pull inflation raises both the price level and real output. In the long run, nominal wages rise, the short-run aggregate supply curve shifts to the left, and only the price level increases.

▸ Cost-push inflation creates a policy dilemma for the government: If it engages in an expansionary policy to increase output, additional inflation will occur; if it does nothing, the recession will linger until input prices have fallen by enough to return the economy to producing at potential output.

▸ In the short run, a decline in aggregate demand reduces real output (creates a recession). In the long run, if input and output prices are downwardly flexible, input prices will fall, the short-run aggregate supply curve will shift to the right, and real output will return to its full-employment level.

▸ The economy has ongoing inflation because the Fed uses monetary policy to shift the AD curve to the right faster than the supply factors of economic growth shift the long-run AS curve to the right.

The Inflation-Unemployment Relationship

We have just seen that the Fed can determine how much inflation occurs in the economy by how much it causes aggregate demand to shift relative to aggregate supply. Given that low inflation and low unemployment rates are the Fed's major economic goals, its ability to control inflation brings up at least two interesting policy questions: Are low unemployment and low inflation compatible goals or conflicting goals? How do we explain situations in which high unemployment and high inflation coexist?

The extended AD–AS model supports three significant generalizations relating to these questions:

- Under normal circumstances, there is a short-run trade-off between the inflation rate and the unemployment rate.

- Aggregate supply shocks can cause both higher inflation rates and higher unemployment rates.

- There is no significant trade-off between inflation and unemployment over long periods of time.

Let's examine each of these generalizations.

The Phillips Curve

We can demonstrate the short-run trade-off between the inflation rate and the unemployment rate through the **short-run downward sloping Phillips Curve,** named after A. W. Phillips, who developed the idea in Great Britain. This curve, shown in Figure 37.8a, suggests an inverse relationship between the inflation rate and the unemployment rate. Lower unemployment rates (measured as leftward movements on the horizontal axis) are associated with higher rates of inflation (measured as upward movements on the vertical axis).

The underlying rationale of the Phillips Curve becomes apparent when we view the short-run aggregate supply curve in Figure 37.9 and perform a simple mental experiment. Suppose that in some short-run period aggregate demand expands from AD_0 to AD_2, either because firms decide to buy more capital goods or because the government decides to increase its expenditures. Whatever the cause, the short-run price level rises from P_0 to P_2 and real output rises from Q_0 to Q_2. As real output rises, the unemployment rate falls.

Now let's compare what would have happened if the increase in aggregate demand had been larger, say, from AD_0 to AD_3. The equilibrium at P_3 and Q_3 indicates that the amount of inflation and the growth of real output would both have been greater (and that the unemployment rate would have been lower). Similarly, suppose aggregate demand during the year had increased only modestly, from AD_0 to AD_1. Compared with our shift from AD_0 to AD_2, the amount of inflation and the growth of real output would have been smaller (and the unemployment rate higher).

>> **LO37.3** Explain the short-run trade-off between inflation and unemployment (the Phillips Curve).

short-run downward sloping Phillips Curve A downward sloping line illustrating the inverse relationship that A.W. Phillips theorized should exist between the *unemployment rate* (on the horizontal axis) and the *inflation rate* (on the vertical axis). Believed by many mainstream economists to hold in the *short run* but not in the *long run*.

(a)
The concept

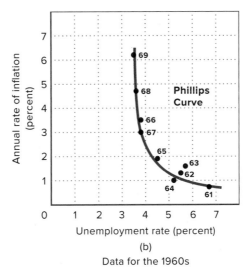

(b)
Data for the 1960s

FIGURE 37.8
The Phillips Curve: concept and empirical data.

(a) The Phillips Curve relates annual rates of inflation and annual rates of unemployment for a series of years. Because this is an inverse relationship, there presumably is a trade-off between unemployment and inflation. (b) Data points for the 1960s seemed to confirm the Phillips Curve concept. (Note: The unemployment rates are annual averages and the inflation rates are on a December-to-December basis.)

FIGURE 37.9
The short-run effect of changes in aggregate demand on real output and the price level.

Comparing the effects of various possible increases in aggregate demand leads to the conclusion that the larger the increase in aggregate demand, the higher the rate of inflation and the greater the increase in real output. Because real output and the unemployment rate move in opposite directions, we can generalize that, given short-run aggregate supply, high rates of inflation should be accompanied by low rates of unemployment.

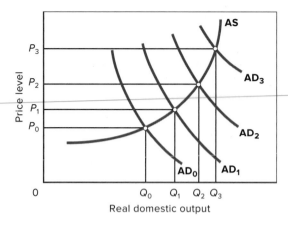

The generalization we draw from this mental experiment is this: *Assuming a constant short-run aggregate supply curve,* high inflation rates are accompanied by low unemployment rates, and low inflation rates are accompanied by high unemployment rates. Other things equal, the expected relationship should look something like Figure 37.8a.

Figure 37.8b reveals that the annual values for U.S. inflation and unemployment during the 1960s fit the theory nicely. On the basis of that evidence and evidence from other countries, most economists working at the end of the 1960s concluded there was a stable, predictable trade-off between unemployment and inflation. Moreover, U.S. macroeconomic policy was built on that supposed trade-off. Economists believed that it was impossible to achieve "full employment without inflation." Manipulation of aggregate demand through fiscal and monetary measures would move the economy along the Phillips Curve. An expansionary fiscal and monetary policy that boosted aggregate demand and lowered the unemployment rate would simultaneously increase inflation. The government could use a restrictive fiscal and monetary policy to reduce the inflation rate, but only at the cost of a higher unemployment rate and more forgone production. Society had to choose between the incompatible goals of price stability and full employment; it had to decide where to locate on its Phillips Curve.

For reasons that we will soon explain, today's economists reject the idea of a stable, unmoving Phillips Curve. Nevertheless, they agree there is a short-run trade-off between unemployment and inflation: *Given short-run aggregate supply, increases in aggregate demand increase real output and reduce the unemployment rate.* As the unemployment rate dips below the natural rate, a demand-pull inflation will be generated. Conversely, when recession sets in and the unemployment rate increases, the weak aggregate demand that caused the recession also leads to lower inflation rates.

Periods of time during which we see both exceptionally low unemployment *and* exceptionally low inflation do occur, but only under special sets of economic circumstances. One such period was the late 1990s, when faster productivity growth increased aggregate supply and fully blunted the inflationary impact of rapidly rising aggregate demand (review Figure 32.11).

Aggregate Supply Shocks and the Phillips Curve

The unemployment-inflation experience of the 1970s and early 1980s demolished the idea of an always-stable Phillips Curve. In Figure 37.10, we show the Phillips Curve for the 1960s in blue and then add the data points for 1970 through 2015. Observe that in most of the years of the 1970s and early 1980s, the economy experienced both higher inflation rates *and* higher unemployment rates than it did in the 1960s. In fact, inflation and unemployment rose simultaneously in some of those years. This condition is called **stagflation**—a media term that combines the words "stagnation" and "inflation." If there still was any such thing as a Phillips Curve, it had clearly shifted outward, perhaps as shown.

Adverse Aggregate Supply Shocks Contradict the Phillips Curve The data points for the 1970s and early 1980s support our second generalization: Aggregate supply shocks can cause inflation rates and unemployment rates to rise *simultaneously*. A series of adverse **aggregate supply shocks**—sudden, large increases in resource costs that jolt an economy's short-run aggregate supply curve leftward—hit the economy in the 1970s and early 1980s. The most significant of these shocks was a quadrupling of oil prices in 1973 by the Organization of Petroleum Exporting Countries (OPEC). Consequently, the cost of producing and distributing virtually every product and service rose rapidly. (Other factors working to increase U.S. costs during this period included major agricultural shortfalls, a greatly depreciated dollar, and wage hikes previously held down by wage and price controls.)

These shocks shifted the aggregate supply curve to the left and were therefore not likely to cause the inverse relationship between inflation and unemployment that is generated by shifts

stagflation *Inflation* accompanied by stagnation in the rate of growth of output and an increase in *unemployment* in the economy; simultaneous increases in the *inflation* rate and the *unemployment rate.*

aggregate supply shocks Sudden, large changes in resource costs that shift an economy's aggregate supply curve.

FIGURE 37.10 Inflation rates and unemployment rates, 1960–2021.

A series of aggregate supply shocks in the 1970s resulted in higher rates of inflation *and* higher rates of unemployment. So data points for the 1970s and 1980s tended to be above and to the right of the blue Phillips Curve for the 1960s. In the 1990s, the inflation-unemployment data points slowly moved back (down and to the left) toward the position of the 1960s Phillips Curve; so the points for the late 1990s and 2000s are somewhat similar to those from the 1960s. However, the data point for 2009 (9.3 percent unemployment, −0.34 percent inflation) was located dramatically lower and much farther to the right relative to the data point for 2008 (5.8 percent unemployment, 3.8 percent inflation). That movement reflected negative inflation accompanied by much higher unemployment during 2009. As the economy slowly mended after the Great Recession, the data points for 2011 through 2016 (highlighted in blue) showed inflation and unemployment falling simultaneously—a pattern inconsistent with moving along a single fixed Philips curve.

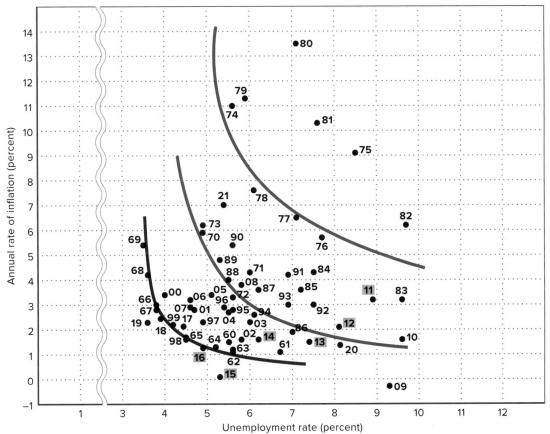

Source: U.S. Bureau of Labor Statistics.

of the AD curve along a fixed AS curve (as in Figure 37.9). Indeed, the cost-push inflation model shown in Figure 37.4 tells us that we should expect to see exactly the opposite relationship between inflation and unemployment when a supply shock shifts the AS curve to the left. That's because a leftward shift of the short-run aggregate supply curve in Figure 37.4 increases the price level and reduces real output, thereby increasing the unemployment rate at the same time inflation is also increasing.

This scenario, say most economists, is what happened during two periods in the 1970s. The U.S. unemployment rate shot up from 4.9 percent in 1973 to 8.5 percent in 1975, reflecting a significant decline in real GDP. In the same period, the U.S. price level rose by 21 percent. The stagflation scenario recurred in 1978, when OPEC increased oil prices by more than 100 percent. The U.S. price level rose by 26 percent over the 1978–1980 period, while unemployment increased from 6.1 to 7.2 percent.

Stagflation's Demise in the 1980s Another look at Figure 37.10 reveals a generally inward movement of the inflation-unemployment points between 1982 and 1989. One precursor to this favorable trend of lower unemployment accompanied by lower inflation was the deep recession of 1981–1982, largely caused by a restrictive monetary policy aimed at reducing double-digit inflation. Other factors were at work, too. Foreign competition throughout this period held down wage and price hikes in several basic industries such as automobiles and steel. Deregulation of the airline and trucking industries also resulted in wage reductions. A significant decline in OPEC's monopoly power and a greatly reduced reliance on oil in the production process produced a stunning fall in the price of oil and its derivative products, such as gasoline.

All these factors combined to reduce per-unit production costs and to shift the short-run aggregate supply curve rightward (as from AS_2 to AS_1 in Figure 37.4). By 1989, inflation had decreased from a peak of 13.4 percent down to 4.8 percent while the unemployment rate had fallen from a peak of 9.7 percent down to 5.3 percent. Stagflation was at an end.

Post–Great Recession Evidence against a Stable Phillips Curve It also appeared for a while that the Phillips curve might be making a comeback because the inflation-unemployment points for the late 1990s and 2000s in Figure 37.10 are closer to the points associated with the Phillips Curve of the 1960s than to the points that plot the data for the late 1970s and early 1980s. But the severe recession of 2007–2009 led to shifts in unemployment and inflation that were inconsistent with a stable Phillips curve along which there was a predictable inverse relationship between inflation and unemployment. In particular, the points for 2011 through 2016 moved substantially down and to the left as the economy experienced an ongoing pattern of falling inflation coinciding with falling unemployment as it recovered from the Great Recession. That movement represented a positive relationship between unemployment and inflation, exactly the opposite of the inverse relationship between those two variables that you would expect to find along a stable Phillips Curve.

The Misery Index The media sometimes express the sum of the unemployment rate and the inflation rate as a rough gauge of the economic discomfort that inflation and unemployment jointly impose on an economy in a particular year. The sum of the two rates is the *misery index*. For example, a nation with a 5 percent unemployment rate and a 5 percent inflation rate has a misery index number of 10, as does a nation with an 8 percent unemployment rate and a 2 percent inflation rate.

Global Perspective 37.1 shows the misery index for several nations between 2010 and 2021. The U.S. misery index number has been neither exceptionally low nor exceptionally high relative to the misery index numbers for the other major economies shown. However, economists do not put much stock in the misery index because they do not view the national discomfort associated with a 1 percent change in inflation and a 1 percent change in unemployment as necessarily equivalent. In particular, the misery index can greatly disguise the extent of hardship during a recession. The rise in the unemployment rate in these circumstances causes a huge loss of national output and income (and a great increase in misery!), even if lower inflation partially or fully offsets the higher unemployment rate.

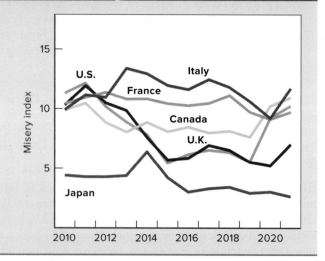

GLOBAL PERSPECTIVE 37.1

THE MISERY INDEX, SELECTED NATIONS, 2010–2021

The U.S. misery index number (the sum of its unemployment rate and inflation rate) has generally been in the midrange of such numbers relative to other major economies in recent years.

Source: The World Bank (data.worldbank.org) and International Labour Organization (ilo.org). Inflation rates and unemployment rates are both on an average annual basis.

The Long-Run Phillips Curve

The overall set of data points in Figure 37.10 supports our third generalization relating to the inflation-unemployment relationship: There is no apparent *long-run* trade-off between inflation and unemployment. Economists point out that when decades (as opposed to a few years) are considered, any rate of inflation is consistent with the natural rate of unemployment. We know from Chapter 29 that the natural rate of unemployment is the unemployment rate that occurs when cyclical unemployment is zero; it is the full-employment rate, or the rate of unemployment when the economy achieves its potential output.

>> **LO37.4** Explain why there is no long-run trade-off between inflation and unemployment.

Why is there a short-run inflation-unemployment trade-off but not a long-run trade-off? Figure 37.11 provides an answer.

Short-Run Phillips Curve

Consider Phillips Curve PC_1 in Figure 37.11. Suppose the economy initially is experiencing a 3 percent inflation rate and a 5 percent natural rate of unemployment. Such short-term curves as PC_1, PC_2, and PC_3 (drawn as straight lines for simplicity) exist because the actual inflation rate is not always the same as the expected rate.

Establishing an additional point on Phillips Curve PC_1 will clarify this conclusion. We begin at a_1, where we assume nominal wages are set on the assumption that the 3 percent inflation rate will continue. That is, because workers expect output prices to rise by 3 percent per year, they negotiate wage contracts that feature 3 percent per year increases in nominal wages so that their nominal wage increases exactly offset the expected increase in prices and thereby keep their real wages the same.

But suppose that the inflation rate rises to 6 percent, perhaps because the Fed has decided to move the AD curve to the right even faster than it had been moving it before. With a nominal wage rate set on the expectation of a 3 percent inflation rate, the higher product prices raise business profits. Firms respond to the higher profits by hiring more workers and increasing output. In the short run, the economy moves to b_1, which, unlike a_1, involves a lower unemployment rate (4 percent) and a higher inflation rate (6 percent). The move from a_1 to b_1 is consistent both with an upward sloping aggregate supply curve and with the inflation-unemployment trade-off implied by the Phillips Curve. But this short-run Phillips Curve simply is a manifestation of the following principle: *When the actual inflation rate is higher than expected, profits temporarily rise and the unemployment rate temporarily falls.*

Long-Run Vertical Phillips Curve

Point b_1 is not a stable equilibrium. Workers will recognize that their nominal wages have not increased as fast as inflation and will therefore renegotiate their labor contracts, demanding faster increases in nominal wages. These faster increases in nominal wages make up for the higher inflation rate and restore the workers' lost purchasing power. As these new labor contracts kick in, business profits fall to their prior level. The reduction in profits means that the original motivation to employ more workers and increase output has disappeared.

Unemployment then returns to its natural level at point a_2. Note, however, that the economy now faces both a higher actual inflation rate as well as a higher expected inflation rate—6 percent rather than 3 percent. Because wages are a production cost, the 6 percent increase in wage rates that was negotiated in response to inflation rising from 3 to 6 percent implies faster future increases in output prices as firms are forced to raise prices more rapidly (6 percent per year rather than 3 percent per year) to

FIGURE 37.11
The long-run vertical Phillips Curve.

Increases in aggregate demand beyond those consistent with full-employment output may temporarily boost profits, output, and employment (as from a_1 to b_1). But nominal wages eventually will catch up so as to sustain real wages. When they do, profits will fall, negating the previous short-run stimulus to production and employment (the economy now moves from b_1 to a_2). Consequently, there is no trade-off between the rates of inflation and unemployment in the long run; that is, the long-run Phillips Curve is roughly a vertical line at the economy's natural rate of unemployment.

make up for the 6 percent rate of wage growth that was just negotiated. In other words, the initial increase in inflation will become *persistent* because it leads to renegotiated labor contracts that perpetuate the increase in the inflation rate from 3 percent to 6 percent. In addition, because the new labor contracts are public, the higher inflation rates that they cause will be *expected* by everyone rather than being a surprise.

In view of the higher 6 percent expected inflation rate, the short-run Phillips Curve shifts upward from PC_1 to PC_2 in Figure 37.11. An "along-the-Phillips-Curve" kind of movement—as from a_1 to b_1 on PC_1—is merely a short-run or transient occurrence. In the long run, after nominal wage contracts catch up with increases in the inflation rate, unemployment returns to its natural rate at a_2, and there is a new short-run Phillips Curve PC_2 that has the higher expected inflation rate (6 percent) at the natural rate of unemployment (5 percent).

The scenario repeats if aggregate demand continues to increase more rapidly than expected. Prices rise momentarily ahead of nominal wages, profits expand, and employment and output increase (as with the movement from a_2 to b_2 along PC_2). But in time, the rate at which nominal wages increase accelerates to match the higher (9 percent) rate of inflation at b_2. Profits then fall to their original level, pushing unemployment back to its natural rate at a_3. The economy's "reward" for temporarily lowering the unemployment rate below the natural rate is to lock in a still-higher (9 percent) inflation rate.

Movements along a given short-run Phillips curve that lead to higher inflation and a below-natural rate of unemployment (such as the movement from a_1 to b_1 on PC_1) cause the short-run curve to shift rightward, to a less favorable position (such as PC_2) at which the expected and actual inflation rates are higher. A stable Phillips Curve with a consistent, inverse relationship between the unemployment rate and the inflation rate simply does not exist in the long run. Instead, the economy is characterized in the long run by the **long-run vertical Phillips Curve,** defined in Figure 37.11 by the vertical line (PC_{LR}) that runs through a_1, a_2, and a_3. Along that vertical long-run Phillips Curve, *any* rate of inflation is consistent with the 5 percent natural rate of unemployment. Thus, the thinking goes, society ought to choose a low inflation rate rather than a high one.

Disinflation

The distinction between the short-run Phillips Curve and the long-run Phillips Curve also helps to explain **disinflation**—by which we mean reductions in the rate of inflation. Suppose that in Figure 37.11 the economy starts at a_3, where the inflation rate is 9 percent. And suppose that a decline in the rate at which aggregate demand shifts to the right faster than aggregate supply (as happened during the 1981–1982 recession) reduces inflation below the 9 percent expected rate, say, to 6 percent. Business profits fall because output prices are rising less rapidly than nominal wages (which would have been negotiated on the assumption that the 9 percent inflation rate would continue). In response to declining profits, firms reduce their employment, and consequently the unemployment rate rises. The economy temporarily slides downward from point a_3 to c_3 along short-run Phillips Curve PC_3.

We can summarize this sequence of events by noting that *when the actual inflation rate ends up being lower than the expected inflation rate, profits temporarily fall and the unemployment rate temporarily rises.* This is the same thing as saying that a stable short-run Phillips curve exists and does not move in the short run. But it will only exist and remain fixed in one location in the short run.

In the long run, firms and workers will adjust their expectations to the new 6 percent inflation rate. In particular, negotiated wage increases will be set at 6 percent rather than 9 percent. Profits will be restored, employment will rise, and the unemployment rate will fall back to its natural rate of 5 percent at a_2. That implies that the short-run Phillips curve shifts leftward to PC_2, along which a 6-percent inflation rate is associated with the 5-percent natural rate of unemployment.

If the rate at which aggregate demand shifts to the right faster than aggregate supply declines even more, the scenario will continue. Inflation declines from 6 percent to, say, 3 percent, moving the economy from a_2 to c_2 along PC_2. The lower-than-expected inflation rate squeezes profits and reduces employment. But in the long run, firms respond to the lower profits by negotiating lower nominal wage increases. Profits are restored and unemployment returns to its natural rate at a_1 as the short-run Phillips Curve shifts leftward from PC_2 to PC_1. Meanwhile, the long-run Phillips Curve remains vertical at the 5-percent natural rate of unemployment.

long-run vertical Phillips Curve The *Phillips Curve* after all *nominal wages* and other input prices have adjusted to changes in the rate of *inflation;* a line emanating straight upward at the economy's *natural rate of unemployment.*

disinflation A reduction in the rate of *inflation.*

▶ As implied by the upward sloping short-run aggregate supply curve, there may be a short-run trade-off between the inflation rate and the unemployment rate. This trade-off is reflected in the Phillips Curve.

▶ Aggregate supply shocks that produce severe cost-push inflation can cause stagflation—a simultaneous increase in the inflation rate and the unemployment rate. Such stagflation occurred

from 1973 to 1975 and from 1978 to 1980, producing Phillips Curve data points above and to the right of the Phillips Curve for the 1960s.

▶ After all nominal wage adjustments responding to increases and decreases in the inflation rate have occurred, the economy ends up back at its full-employment level of output and its natural rate of unemployment. The long-run Phillips Curve therefore is vertical at the natural rate of unemployment.

Taxation and Aggregate Supply

A final topic in our discussion of aggregate supply is taxation, a key aspect of **supply-side economics.** "Supply-side economists" or "supply-siders" stress that changes in aggregate supply are an active force in determining the levels of inflation, unemployment, and economic growth. Government policies can either impede or promote rightward shifts of the short-run and long-run aggregate supply curves shown in Figure 37.2. One such policy is taxation.

These economists argue that the enlargement of the U.S. tax system has impaired incentives to work, save, and invest. In this view, high tax rates impede productivity growth and hence slow the expansion of long-run aggregate supply. By reducing the after-tax rewards of workers and producers, high tax rates reduce the financial attractiveness of working, saving, and investing.

>> **LO37.5** Explain the relationships among tax rates, tax revenues, and aggregate supply.

supply-side economics A view of *macroeconomics* that emphasizes the role of costs and *aggregate supply* in explaining *inflation, unemployment,* and *economic growth.*

Taxes and Incentives to Work, Save, and Invest

Supply-siders focus their attention on *marginal tax rates*—the rates on extra dollars of income—because those rates affect the benefits from working, saving, or investing more. In 2021, marginal federal income tax rates varied from 10 to 37 percent.

Supply-siders believe that lower marginal tax rates cause people to work more, thereby increasing aggregate inputs of labor. In particular, lower marginal tax rates increase the after-tax wage rate, making leisure more expensive and work more attractive. So lower income tax rates should increase the supply of labor and, along with it, GDP.

Saving, remember, is the prerequisite of investment and the returns that come from investment. Thus, supply-side economists recommend lower marginal tax rates on investments as a way of encouraging saving and investing. They argue that higher investment is desirable because it will equip workers with more and technologically superior machinery and equipment. Labor productivity will rise. Long-run aggregate supply will shift to the right at a faster pace. Unemployment and inflation should both decrease.

The Laffer Curve

According to supply-siders, reductions in marginal tax rates increase the nation's aggregate supply and can leave the nation's tax revenues unchanged or even enlarge them. Thus, tax cuts need not produce federal budget deficits.

This conclusion is based on the **Laffer Curve,** named after Arthur Laffer, the economist who popularized it. The Laffer Curve in Figure 37.12 depicts the relationship between tax rates and tax revenues. As tax rates increase from 0 to 100 percent, tax revenues increase from zero to some maximum level (at *m*) and then fall to zero. Tax revenues decline beyond some point because higher tax rates discourage economic activity, thereby shrinking the tax base (domestic output and income). This outcome is easiest to see at the extreme, where the tax rate is 100 percent. Tax revenues here are, in theory, reduced to zero because the 100 percent confiscatory tax rate has halted production. A 100 percent tax rate applied to a tax base of zero yields no revenue.

Laffer Curve A curve relating government tax rates and tax revenues and on which a particular tax rate (between zero and 100 percent) maximizes tax revenues.

**FIGURE 37.12
The Laffer Curve.**

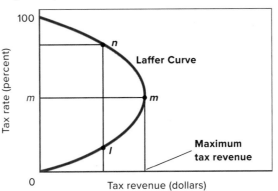

The Laffer Curve suggests that up to point *m* higher tax rates will result in larger tax revenues. But tax rates higher than *m* will adversely affect incentives to work and produce, reducing the size of the tax base (output and income) to the extent that tax revenues will decline. It follows that if tax rates are above *m*, reductions in tax rates will produce increases in tax revenues.

In the early 1980s, Laffer suggested that the United States was at a point such as *n* on the curve in Figure 37.12. At *n*, tax rates are so high that production is discouraged to the extent that tax revenues are below the maximum at *m*. If the economy is at *n*, then reducing the tax rate can increase tax revenues or leave them unchanged. For example, lowering the tax rate from point *n* to point *m* will increase tax revenues, while lowering the tax rate further, to point *l*, will bring in the same total tax revenue as before at point *n*.

Laffer's reasoning was that lower tax rates stimulate incentives to work, save and invest, innovate, and accept business risks, thus triggering an expansion of real output and income. That enlarged tax base sustains tax revenues even though tax rates are lowered. Indeed, between points *n* and *m*, a lower tax rate results in *increased* tax revenue.

Also, when taxes are lowered, tax avoidance (which is legal) and tax evasion (which is not) decline. High marginal tax rates prompt taxpayers to avoid taxes through various legal tax shelters, such as buying municipal bonds, on which the interest earned is legally tax-free. High rates also encourage some taxpayers to illegally evade income taxes by hiding income from the Internal Revenue Service. Supply-siders note that lower tax rates reduce the inclination to engage in either tax avoidance or tax evasion.

The Laffer curve also implies that for any amount of tax revenue that the government can possibly collect, there will be both a high tax rate at which that amount of revenue can be collected as well as a low tax rate at which that amount of revenue can be collected. As an example, compare points *n* an *l* in Figure 37.12. Point *n* has a high tax rate and point *l* has a low tax rate, but they both collect the same amount of tax revenue. So if the government's major goal when setting tax rates is simply to collect a particular total amount of tax revenue, Laffer argued that the government should always opt for the lower tax rate. By doing so, the government will collect the revenue it desires while impinging as little as possible on the private economy.

Criticisms of the Laffer Curve

The Laffer Curve and its supply-side implications have been subject to severe criticism.

Taxes, Incentives, and Time A fundamental criticism concerns the sensitivity of economic incentives to changes in tax rates. Skeptics say ample empirical evidence shows that a tax cut's impact on incentives is small, of uncertain direction, and relatively slow to emerge. For example, studies indicate that decreases in tax rates lead some people to work more but lead others to work less. Those who work more are enticed by the higher after-tax pay; they substitute work for leisure because the opportunity cost of leisure has increased. But other people work less because the higher after-tax pay enables them to "buy more leisure." With the tax cut, they can earn the same level of after-tax income while working fewer hours.

Inflation or Higher Real Interest Rates Most economists think that the demand-side effects of a tax cut are more immediate and certain than longer-term supply-side effects. Thus, tax cuts undertaken when the economy is at or near full employment may produce increases in aggregate demand that overwhelm any increase in aggregate supply. The likely result is inflation or a restrictive monetary policy to prevent inflation. If the latter occurs, real interest rates will rise and investment will decline, which defeats the purpose of the supply-side tax cuts.

Position on the Curve Some skeptics argue that the Laffer Curve is merely a logical necessity. They agree with Laffer that there must be *some* tax rate between 0 and 100 percent at which tax revenue will be maximized. Indeed, economists of all persuasions agree with that conclusion. But the issue of *where* a particular economy is located on its Laffer Curve is not at all obvious. If the economy is at a point like *n* in Figure 37.12, then a lower tax rate will *increase* tax revenue. But if the economy is at any point on the curve below point *m,* a tax cut will *reduce* tax revenue.

Evaluation

Today, there is general agreement that the U.S. economy is operating at a point below *m*—rather than above *m*—on the Laffer Curve in Figure 37.12. In this zone, higher personal tax rates increase tax revenues, while lower personal tax rates reduce tax revenues.

At the same time, economists also recognize that, other things being equal, changes in tax rates do result in *some* supply-side effects, especially in terms of altering certain taxpayers' behavior. These feedback effects imply that cuts in tax rates reduce tax revenues in percentage terms by less

Do Tax Increases Reduce Real GDP?*

Determining the Relationship between Changes in Taxes and Changes in GDP Is Fraught with Complexity. Christina Romer and David Romer Devised a Novel Way to Approach the Topic. Their Findings Suggest that Tax Increases Reduce Real GDP.'

How do changes in the level of taxation affect the level of economic activity? The simple positive correlation between taxation and economic activity shows that, on average, when economic activity rises more rapidly, tax revenues also rise more rapidly. But this correlation almost surely does not reflect a positive effect of tax increases on output. Rather, under our tax system, any positive shock to output raises tax revenues by increasing income.

In "The Macroeconomic Effects of Tax Changes: Estimates Based on a New Measure of Fiscal Shocks," Christina Romer and David Romer observe that this difficulty is just one of many manifestations of a more general problem. Changes in taxes occur for many reasons. And because the factors that give rise to tax changes often are correlated with other developments in the economy, disentangling the effects of tax changes from the effects of those other factors is inherently difficult.

To address this problem, Romer and Romer use the narrative record—presidential speeches, executive branch documents, congressional reports, and so on—to identify the size, timing, and principal motivation for all major tax policy actions in the post–World War II United States. This narrative analysis allows them to separate revenue changes resulting from legislation from changes occurring for other reasons. It also allows them to classify legislated changes according to their primary motivation.

Romer and Romer find that despite the complexity of the legislative process, significant tax changes have been motivated by one of four factors: counteracting other influences in the economy; paying for increases in government spending; addressing inherited budget deficits; or promoting long-run growth.

They then argue that tax changes that were legislated to counteract other influences on the economy, or to pay for increases in government spending, are very likely to be correlated with other factors affecting the economy. As a result, these observations are likely to lead to unreliable estimates of the effects of tax changes.

But tax changes that are made to promote long-run growth, or to reduce an inherited budget deficit, are undertaken for reasons essentially unrelated to other factors influencing output. Thus, examining the behavior of output following these sorts of tax changes is likely to provide reliable estimates of the output effects of tax changes. The results of this more reliable test indicate that tax changes have very large effects: a tax increase equal to 1 percent of real GDP lowers real GDP by roughly 2 to 3 percent.

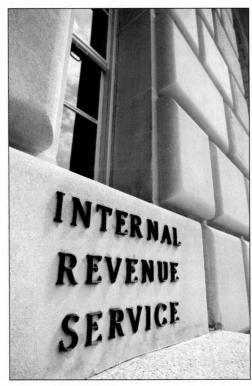

Thinkstock/Stockbyte/Getty Images

Romer and Romer also find that the output effect of a tax change is much more closely tied to actual changes in tax policy as opposed to news or gossip about potential future tax changes. Investment, in particular, falls sharply in response to actual tax changes. Indeed, the strong response of investment helps to explain why the output consequences of tax increases are so large.

Romer and Romer additionally find suggestive evidence that tax increases that were legislated to reduce an inherited budget deficit have much smaller output costs than other tax increases. This is consistent with the idea that deficit-driven tax increases may have important expansionary effects through improved expectations, lower long-term interest rates, or improved confidence regarding the economy's prospects.

than the tax-rate reductions themselves. Similarly, tax-rate increases do not raise tax revenues by as much in percentage terms as the tax-rate increases. These effects are driven by the fact that changes in marginal tax rates alter taxpayer behavior and thus affect taxable income. Although these effects seem to be relatively modest, they need to be considered in designing tax policy—and, in fact, the federal government's Office of Tax Policy created a special division in 2007 devoted to estimating the magnitude of such effects for proposed changes in U.S. tax laws.

As discussed in this chapter's Last Word, this new division's forecasting challenges are made even more difficult by the fact that the effects of a tax-rate change appear to depend not only on how large the rate change happens to be but also on *why* the tax rate is being modified.

QUICK REVIEW
37.4

▶ Supply-side economists focus their attention on government policies, such as high taxation, that may impede the expansion of aggregate supply.

▶ The Laffer Curve relates tax rates to levels of tax revenue and suggests that, under some circumstances, cuts in tax rates will expand the tax base (output and income) and increase tax revenues.

▶ Most economists believe that the United States is currently operating along the portion of the Laffer Curve where tax rates and tax revenues move in the same, not opposite, directions.

▶ Today's economists recognize the importance of considering supply-side effects in designing optimal fiscal policy.

Summary

LO37.1 Explain the relationship between short-run aggregate supply and long-run aggregate supply.

In macroeconomics, the short run is the period in which nominal wages do not respond to changes in the price level. The long run is the period in which nominal wages fully respond to changes in the price level.

The short-run aggregate supply curve slopes upward. Because nominal wages are unresponsive to price-level changes, increases in the price level (prices received by firms) increase profits and real output. Conversely, decreases in the price level reduce profits and real output. However, the long-run aggregate supply curve is vertical. With sufficient time for adjustment, nominal wages rise and fall with the price level, moving the macroeconomic equilibrium up and down along the vertical long-run aggregate supply curve at the economy's full-employment output level.

LO37.2 Apply the extended (short-run/long-run) AD–AS model to inflation, recessions, and economic growth.

In the short run, demand-pull inflation raises the price level and real output. Once nominal wages rise to match the increase in the price level, the temporary increase in real output is reversed.

In the short run, cost-push inflation raises the price level and lowers real output. Unless the government expands aggregate demand, nominal wages eventually decline under conditions of recession, and the short-run aggregate supply curve shifts back to its initial location. Prices and real output eventually return to their original levels.

If prices and wages are flexible downward, a decline in aggregate demand lowers output and the price level. The decline in the price level eventually lowers nominal wages and shifts the short-run aggregate supply curve rightward. Full-employment output is thus restored.

One-time changes in aggregate demand (AD) and aggregate supply (AS) can cause only limited bouts of inflation. Ongoing mild inflation occurs because the Fed purposely increases AD slightly faster than the expansion of long-run AS that is driven by the supply factors of economic growth.

LO37.3 Explain the short-run trade-off between inflation and unemployment (the Phillips Curve).

Assuming a stable, upward sloping short-run aggregate supply curve, rightward shifts of the aggregate demand curve yield the generalization that higher inflation rates are associated with lower unemployment rates, and vice versa. This inverse relationship is known as the Phillips Curve, and empirical data for the 1960s were consistent with it. Since the 1960s, however, the data have only sometimes been consistent with an inverse relationship between unemployment and inflation. So while there is evidence supporting an inverse relationship in the short run during certain periods of time, no stable long-run relationship between inflation and unemployment seems to exist.

LO37.4 Explain why there is no long-run trade-off between inflation and unemployment.

Although there may be a short-run trade-off between inflation and unemployment, there is no long-run trade-off. Workers adapt their expectations to new inflation realities, and when they do, the unemployment rate returns to the natural rate. So the long-run Phillips Curve is vertical at the natural rate, meaning that higher rates of inflation do not permanently "buy" the economy less unemployment.

LO37.5 Explain the relationships among tax rates, tax revenues, and aggregate supply.

Supply-side economists focus attention on government policies, such as high taxation, that impede the expansion of aggregate supply. The Laffer Curve relates tax rates to levels of tax revenue and suggests that under some circumstances, cuts in tax rates will expand the tax base (output and income) and increase tax revenues. Most economists believe that the United States is currently operating in the range of the Laffer Curve where tax rates and tax revenues move in the same, not opposite, direction. However, today's economists do recognize the importance of considering supply-side effects in designing optimal fiscal policy.

Terms and Concepts

short run	stagflation	disinflation
long run	aggregate supply shocks	supply-side economics
short-run downward sloping Phillips Curve	long-run vertical Phillips Curve	Laffer Curve

Discussion Questions

1. Distinguish between the short run and the long run as they relate to macroeconomics. Why is the distinction important? **LO37.1**
2. Which of the following statements are true? Which are false? Explain why the false statements are untrue. **LO37.1**
   a. Short-run aggregate supply curves reflect an inverse relationship between the price level and the level of real output.
   b. The long-run aggregate supply curve assumes that nominal wages are fixed.
   c. In the long run, an increase in the price level will result in an increase in nominal wages.
3. Suppose the government misjudges the natural rate of unemployment to be much lower than it actually is, and thus undertakes expansionary fiscal and monetary policies to lower it. Use the concept of the short-run Phillips Curve to explain why these policies might at first succeed. Use the concept of the long-run Phillips Curve to explain these policies' long-run outcome. **LO37.4**

4. What do the distinctions between short-run aggregate supply and long-run aggregate supply have in common with the distinction between the short-run Phillips Curve and the long-run Phillips Curve? Explain. **LO37.4**
5. What is the Laffer Curve, and how does it relate to supply-side economics? Why is determining the economy's location on the curve so important in assessing tax policy? **LO37.5**
6. Why might one person work more, earn more, and pay more income tax when his or her tax rate is cut, while another person will work less, earn less, and pay less income tax under the same circumstance? **LO37.5**
7. **LAST WORD** On average, does an increase in taxes raise or lower real GDP? If taxes as a percentage of GDP go up by 1 percent, by how much does real GDP typically change? Are the decreases in real GDP caused by tax increases temporary or permanent? Does the intention of a tax increase matter?

Review Questions

1. Suppose the full-employment level of real output (Q) for a hypothetical economy is $250 and the price level (P) initially is 100. Use the short-run aggregate supply schedules below to answer the questions that follow: **LO37.1**

AS (P_{100})		AS (P_{125})		AS (P_{75})	
P	**Q**	**P**	**Q**	**P**	**Q**
125	$280	125	$250	125	$310
100	250	100	220	100	280
75	220	75	190	75	250

   a. What is the level of real output in the short run if the price level unexpectedly rises from 100 to 125 because of an increase in aggregate demand? What happens if the price level unexpectedly falls from 100 to 75 because of a decrease in aggregate demand? Explain each situation, using numbers from the table.
   b. What is the level of real output in the long run when the price level rises from 100 to 125? When it falls from 100 to 75? Explain each situation.
   c. Illustrate the circumstances described in parts a and b on graph paper, and derive the long-run aggregate supply curve.
2. Suppose that AD and AS intersect at an output level that is higher than the full-employment output level. After the economy adjusts back to equilibrium in the long run, the price level will be _____. **LO37.2**
   a. higher than it is now
   b. lower than it is now
   c. the same as it is now

3. Suppose that an economy begins in long-run equilibrium before the price level and real GDP both decline simultaneously. If those changes were caused by only one curve shifting, then those changes are best explained as the result of: **LO37.2**
   a. the AD curve shifting right.
   b. the AS curve shifting right.
   c. the AD curve shifting left.
   d. the AS curve shifting left.
4. Identify the two descriptions below as being the result of either cost-push inflation or demand-pull inflation. **LO37.2**
   a. Real GDP is below the full-employment level and prices have risen recently.
   b. Real GDP is above the full-employment level and prices have risen recently.
5. Use graphical analysis to show how each of the following will affect the economy, first in the short run and then in the long run. Assume that the United States is initially operating at its full-employment level of output, that prices and wages are eventually flexible both upward and downward, and that there is no counteracting fiscal or monetary policy. **LO37.2**
   a. Because of a war abroad, the oil supply to the United States is disrupted, sending oil prices rocketing upward.
   b. Construction spending on new homes rises dramatically, greatly increasing total U.S. investment spending.
   c. Economic recession occurs abroad, significantly reducing foreign purchases of U.S. exports.
6. Between 2000 and 2020, the U.S. price level rose by about 50 percent while real output increased by about 42 percent. Use the aggregate demand–aggregate supply model to illustrate these outcomes graphically. **LO37.2**

7. Assume there is a particular short-run aggregate supply curve for an economy and the curve is relevant for several years. Use AD–AS analysis to show graphically why higher rates of inflation over this period will be associated with lower rates of unemployment, and vice versa. What is this inverse relationship called? **LO37.3**

8. Aggregate supply shocks can cause _____ inflation rates that are accompanied by _____ unemployment rates. **LO37.3**
   a. higher; higher
   b. higher; lower
   c. lower; higher
   d. lower; lower

9. Suppose that firms are expecting 6 percent inflation while workers are expecting 9 percent inflation. How much of a pay raise will workers demand if their goal is to maintain the purchasing power of their incomes? **LO37.4**
   a. 3 percent
   b. 6 percent
   c. 9 percent
   d. 12 percent

10. Suppose that firms were expecting inflation to be 3 percent, but it actually turned out to be 7 percent. Other things equal, firm profits will be: **LO37.4**
    a. smaller than expected.
    b. larger than expected.

Problems

McGraw Hill **connect**

1. Use the nearby figure to answer the following questions. Assume that the economy initially is operating at price level 120 and real output level $870. This output level is the economy's potential (full-employment) level of output. Next, suppose that the price level rises from 120 to 130. By how much will real output increase in the short run? In the long run? Instead, now assume that the price level drops from 120 to 110. Assuming flexible product and resource prices, by how much will real output fall in the short run? In the long run? What is the long-run level of output at each of the three price levels shown? **LO37.1**

2. **ADVANCED ANALYSIS** Suppose that the equation for a particular short-run AS curve is $P = 20 + 0.5Q$, where P is the price level and Q is real output in dollar terms. What is Q if the price level is 120? Suppose that the Q in your answer is the full-employment level of output. By how much will Q increase *in the short run* if the price level unexpectedly rises from 120 to 132? By how much will Q increase *in the long run* due to the price-level increase? **LO37.1**

3. Suppose that over a 30-year period Buskerville's price level increased from 72 to 138, while its real GDP rose from $1.2 trillion to $2.1 trillion. Did economic growth occur in Buskerville? If so, by what average yearly rate in percentage terms (rounded to one decimal place)? Did Buskerville experience inflation? If so, by what average yearly rate in percentage terms (rounded to one decimal place)? Which shifted rightward faster in Buskerville: its long-run aggregate supply curve (AS_{LR}) or its aggregate demand curve (AD)? **LO37.2**

4. Suppose that for years East Confetti's short-run Phillips Curve was such that each 1 percentage point increase in its unemployment rate was associated with a 2 percentage point decline in its inflation rate. Then, during several recent years, the short-run pattern changed such that its inflation rate rose by 3 percentage points for every 1 percentage point drop in its unemployment rate. Graphically, did East Confetti's Phillips Curve shift upward or did it shift downward? Explain. **LO37.3**

Current Issues in Macro Theory and Policy

>> LEARNING OBJECTIVES

LO38.1 Describe alternative perspectives on the causes of macroeconomic instability.

LO38.2 Explain why new classical economists believe the economy will self-correct from aggregate demand and aggregate supply shocks.

LO38.3 Describe the rules versus discretion debate regarding stabilization policy.

As any academic discipline evolves, it naturally evokes a number of internal disagreements. Economics is no exception. In this chapter, we examine a few alternative perspectives on macro theory and policy. We focus on the disagreements regarding three interrelated questions: (1) What causes instability in the economy? (2) Is the economy self-correcting? (3) Should government adhere to *rules* or use *discretion* in setting economic policy?

What Causes Macro Instability?

Capitalist economies experienced considerable instability during the twentieth century. The United States, for example, experienced the Great Depression, numerous recessions, inflation, and deflation. Instability has continued in the twenty-first century, with the U.S. experiencing a tech-bubble recession in 2001, a real-estate financial-crisis recession from 2007 to 2009, and a pandemic recession in 2020.

Economists have different perspectives about the causes of macroeconomic instability.

>> **LO38.1** Describe alternative perspectives on the causes of macroeconomic instability.

Mainstream View

For simplicity, we will use the term "mainstream view" to characterize the prevailing macroeconomic perspective of the majority of economists. According to the mainstream view, instability arises from two sources: (1) price stickiness and (2) unexpected shocks to either aggregate demand or aggregate supply.

As we explained in Chapter 37, in the long run, when input prices and output prices are fully flexible and have time to adjust to changes in aggregate demand or short-run aggregate supply, the economy always returns to producing at potential output. In the shorter run, however, stickiness in either input or output prices means that any shock to either aggregate demand or aggregate supply will result in changes in output and employment.

Changes in Aggregate Demand Mainstream macroeconomics focuses on aggregate spending and its components. Recall that the basic equation underlying aggregate expenditures is

$$C_a + I_g + X_n + G = \text{GDP}$$

That is, the aggregate amount of after-tax consumption, gross investment, net exports, and government spending determines the total amount of goods and services produced and sold. In equilibrium, $C_a + I_g + X_n + G$ (aggregate expenditures) equals GDP (real output). A decrease in the price level increases equilibrium GDP and thus allows us to trace out a downward sloping aggregate demand curve for the economy (see the Chapter 32 appendix). Any change in one of the spending components in the aggregate expenditures equation shifts the aggregate demand curve. The result is a change in equilibrium real output, the price level, or both.

Investment spending in particular is subject to wide "booms" and "busts." Significant increases in investment spending are multiplied into even greater increases in aggregate demand and thus can produce demand-pull inflation. Significant declines in investment spending are multiplied into even greater decreases in aggregate demand and thus can cause recessions.

Adverse Aggregate Supply Shocks In the mainstream view, the second source of macroeconomic instability arises on the supply side. Occasionally, such external events as wars or an artificial supply restriction of a key resource can boost resource prices and significantly raise per-unit production costs. The result is a sizable decline in a nation's aggregate supply, which destabilizes the economy by simultaneously causing cost-push inflation and recession.

Monetarist View

monetarism The macroeconomic view that the main cause of changes in aggregate output and the *price level* is fluctuations in the *money supply;* espoused by advocates of a *monetary rule.*

Monetarism (1) focuses on the money supply, (2) holds that markets are highly competitive, and (3) says that a competitive market system gives the economy a high degree of macroeconomic stability. Monetarists argue that the price and wage flexibility provided by competitive markets should cause fluctuations in aggregate demand to alter product and resource prices rather than output and employment. Thus, monetarists say, the market system would provide substantial macroeconomic stability *were it not for government interference in the economy*.

The problem, as monetarists see it, is that government is to blame for downward wage and price inflexibility because government has implemented minimum-wage laws, pro-union legislation, guaranteed prices for certain farm products, and pro-business monopoly legislation. They argue that government interference has undermined the market's natural ability to provide macroeconomic stability. Moreover, monetarists believe that the Fed's attempts to use monetary policy to mitigate business cycles have backfired, so that its monetary policy actions intensify (rather than dampen) the business cycle.

equation of exchange $MV = PQ$, in which M is the supply of *money*, V is the *velocity* of money, P is the *price level,* and Q is the physical volume of *final goods* and final *services* produced.

Equation of Exchange The fundamental equation of monetarism is the **equation of exchange:**

$$MV = PQ$$

where M is the supply of money; V is the **velocity** of money, that is, the average number of times per year a dollar is spent on final goods and services; P is the price level or, more specifically, the average price at which each unit of physical output is sold; and Q is the physical volume of all goods and services produced.

The left side of the equation of exchange, MV, represents the total amount spent by purchasers of output, while the right side, PQ, represents the total amount received by sellers of that output. The nation's money supply (M) multiplied by the number of times it is spent each year (V) must equal the nation's nominal GDP ($= P \times Q$). The dollar value of total spending must equal the dollar value of total output.

velocity The number of times per year that the average dollar in the *money supply* is spent for *final goods* and final *services;* *nominal gross domestic product (GDP)* divided by the *money supply.*

Stable Velocity Official statistics show that the velocity of money changes over time. Monetarists argue that these changes in velocity are mostly gradual, which they say is to be expected because the underlying factors that affect velocity are themselves slow to change, so that changes in velocity from one year to the next can be readily anticipated. Monetarists also hold that velocity does not change in response to changes in the money supply itself. Instead, people have a stable desire to hold money relative to holding other financial assets, holding real assets, and buying current output. The factors that determine the amount of money the public wants to hold depend mainly on the level of nominal GDP, and those factors in turn determine money velocity.

Example: Assume that when nominal GDP is $400 billion, the public desires $100 billion of money to purchase that output. That means that V is 4 ($= $400 billion of nominal GDP/$100 billion of money). If we further assume that the actual money supply is $100 billion, the economy will be in equilibrium with respect to money because the actual amount of money supplied ($100 billion) will equal the amount the public wants to hold ($100 billion).

If velocity is stable, the equation of exchange suggests that there is a predictable relationship between the money supply and nominal GDP (= PQ). An increase in the money supply of, say, $10 billion will upset equilibrium in our example because the public will find itself holding more money or liquidity than it wants. That is, the actual amount of money held ($110 billion) will exceed the amount of holdings desired ($100 billion). In that case, the reaction of the public (households and businesses) is to restore its desired balance of money relative to other items, such as stocks and bonds, factories and equipment, houses and automobiles, and clothing and toys. But the spending of money by individual households and businesses will leave more cash in the checkable deposits or billfolds of other households and firms. And they too will try to "spend down" their excess cash balances. But, overall, the $110 billion money supply cannot be spent down because a dollar spent is a dollar received.

Instead, the collective attempt to reduce cash balances will increase aggregate demand, thereby boosting nominal GDP. Because velocity in our example is 4—that is, each dollar is spent, on average, four times per year—nominal GDP rises from $400 billion to $440 billion. At that higher nominal GDP, the money supply of $110 billion equals the amount of money desired ($440 billion/ 4 = $110 billion), so that equilibrium is reestablished.

The $10 billion increase in the money supply thus eventually increases nominal GDP by $40 billion. Spending on goods, services, and assets expands until nominal GDP has gone up enough to restore the original 4-to-1 equilibrium relationship between nominal GDP and the money supply.

Note that the relationship GDP/M defines V. So a stable relationship between nominal GDP and M implies a stable value for V, and vice versa. With V stable, any change in M will cause a proportionate change in nominal GDP. Thus, monetarists say that changes in the money supply have a predictable effect on nominal GDP (= $P \times Q$). An increase in M increases P or Q, or some combination of both. A decrease in M reduces P or Q, or some combination of both.

Monetary Causes of Instability Monetarists say that inappropriate monetary policy is the single most important cause of macroeconomic instability. An increase in the money supply directly increases aggregate demand. Under conditions of full employment, that increase in aggregate demand raises the price level. For a time, higher prices cause firms to increase their real output, and the unemployment rate falls below its natural rate. But after nominal wages rise to reflect the higher prices and thus to restore real wages, real output moves back to its full-employment level and the unemployment rate returns to its natural rate. The inappropriate increase in the money supply leads to inflation, together with instability of real output and employment.

Conversely, a decrease in the money supply reduces aggregate demand. Real output temporarily falls, and the unemployment rate rises above its natural rate. Eventually, nominal wages fall and real output returns to its full-employment level. The inappropriate decline in the money supply leads to deflation, together with instability of real GDP and employment.

Here, the contrast between mainstream macroeconomists and monetarists comes into sharp focus. Mainstream macroeconomists view the instability of investment as the main cause of macroeconomic instability, and they consider monetary policy to be a stabilizing factor because changes in the money supply can be used to raise or lower interest rates as needed, thereby smoothing out the swings in investment that drive macroeconomic instability. In contrast, monetarists view changes in the money supply as the main cause of instability in the economy. For example, they say that the Great Depression occurred largely because the Fed allowed the money supply to fall by roughly one-third during that period. Monetarists acknowledge that investment *did* collapse during the Great Depression, but they view that decline as an effect of bad monetary policy rather than as one of the driving factors behind the downturn.

Real-Business-Cycle View

A third view holds that business cycles are caused by real factors that affect aggregate supply, rather than by monetary, or spending, factors that cause fluctuations in aggregate demand. In **real-business-cycle theory,** business fluctuations result from significant changes in technology and resource availability. Those changes affect productivity and thus the long-run growth trend of aggregate supply.

An example focusing on recession will clarify this thinking. Suppose productivity (output per worker) declines sharply because of a large increase in oil prices, which makes it prohibitively expensive to operate certain types of machinery. That decline in productivity implies a reduction

real-business-cycle theory A theory that *business cycles* result from changes in *technology* and *resource* availability, which affect *productivity* and thus increase or decrease long-run *aggregate supply.*

FIGURE 38.1
Real-business-cycle theory.

In real-business-cycle theory, a decline in resource availability shifts the nation's long-run aggregate supply curve to the left from AS_{LR1} to AS_{LR2}. The decline in real output from Q_1 to Q_2, in turn, reduces money demand (less is needed) and money supply (fewer loans are taken out) such that aggregate demand shifts leftward from AD_1 to AD_2. The result is a recession in which the price level remains constant.

in the economy's ability to produce real output. The result will be a decrease in the economy's long-run aggregate supply curve, as represented by the leftward shift from AS_{LR1} to AS_{LR2} in Figure 38.1.

As real output falls from Q_1 to Q_2, the public needs less money to buy the reduced volume of goods and services. So the demand for money falls. Moreover, the slowdown in business activity means that businesses need to borrow less from banks, reducing the part of the money supply that banks create through their lending. Thus, the supply of money also falls. In this controversial scenario, changes in the supply of money respond to changes in the demand for money. The decline in the money supply then reduces aggregate demand, as from AD_1 to AD_2 in Figure 38.1. The outcome is a decline in real output from Q_1 to Q_2, with no change in the price level.

Conversely, a large increase in aggregate supply (not shown) caused by, say, major innovations in the production process will shift the long-run aggregate supply curve rightward. Real output will increase, and so will money demand and money supply. Aggregate demand will shift rightward by an amount equal to the rightward shift of long-run aggregate supply. Real output will increase without driving up the price level.

Conclusion: In real-business-cycle theory, macro instability arises on the aggregate supply side of the economy. That stands in sharp contrast to the belief held by both mainstream economists and monetarists that aggregate demand fluctuations are responsible for most business cycle fluctuations.

The nearby Consider This story explains why the Great Recession of 2007–2009 is better explained by the mainstream view than by real-business-cycle theory.

CONSIDER THIS . . .

Too Much Money?

The severe recession of 2007–2009 fits the mainstream view that recessions are caused by AD shocks rather than the real-business-cycle view that they are caused by AS shocks. In particular, the recession began with an unexpected financial crisis that caused significant reductions in investment and consumption that significantly reduced aggregate demand. Additionally, the price level was sticky downward, with the leftward shift of the aggregate demand curve generating mostly declines in output and income rather than lower prices and deflation.

Economists with monetarist leanings, however, cite monetary factors as the main cause of the financial crisis that led to the initial declines in aggregate demand. They argue that the Federal Reserve flooded the economy with too much money and held interest rates too low for too long in promoting recovery from the 2001

Baron Wolman/The Image Bank/ Getty Images

recession. In this line of reasoning, the excess money and low interest rates contributed to the pre-recession price bubble in the housing market. When that bubble burst, the resulting mortgage defaults set in motion the forces that produced the decline in AD and therefore the recession.

All economists agree that the bursting of the housing bubble led to the recession. And too-loose monetary policy may have contributed to the bubble. But mainstream economists also cite the role of the very large international flows of foreign savings into the United States during this period. These inflows drove down interest rates and helped to fuel the housing bubble. Other factors such as "pass-the-risk" lending practices, government policies promoting home ownership, and poorly designed and enforced financial regulations certainly came into play. The mainstream view is that causes of the financial crisis and recession were numerous and complex.

Coordination Failures

A fourth and final view of macroeconomic instability relates to **coordination failures,** which occur when people fail to reach a mutually beneficial equilibrium because they lack a way to coordinate their actions.

As an example, let's consider a recession. Suppose that individual firms and households expect other firms and consumers to cut back on investment and consumption. As a result, each firm and household will anticipate a reduction of aggregate demand. Firms therefore reduce their own investment spending because they anticipate that their future production capacity will become excessive. Households also reduce their own consumption spending because they anticipate that they will experience reduced work hours, possible layoffs, and falling incomes in the future.

Aggregate demand will indeed decline and the economy will indeed experience a recession in response to what amounts to a self-fulfilling prophecy. Moreover, the economy will stay at a below-full-employment level of output because, once there, producers and households have no individual incentive to increase spending. If all producers and all households could agree to increase their investment and consumption spending simultaneously, then aggregate demand would rise, and real output and real income would increase. Each producer and each consumer would be better off. However, this outcome will not occur because there is no mechanism for firms and households to agree on such a joint spending increase.

In this case, the economy is stuck in an *unemployment equilibrium* because of a coordination failure. With a different set of expectations, a coordination failure might leave the economy in an *inflation equilibrium*. The economy therefore has a number of such potential equilibrium positions, some good and some bad, depending on people's mix of expectations. Macroeconomic instability, then, reflects the economy's movement from one such equilibrium position to another as expectations change.

> **coordination failure** A situation in which people do not reach a mutually beneficial outcome because they lack some way to jointly coordinate their actions; a possible cause of macroeconomic instability.

> **QUICK REVIEW**
> ## 38.1

▶ Mainstream economists say that macroeconomic instability usually stems from swings in investment spending and, occasionally, from adverse aggregate supply shocks.

▶ Monetarists view the economy through the equation of exchange ($MV = PQ$). If velocity V is stable, changes in the money supply M lead directly to changes in nominal GDP ($= P \times Q$). For monetarists, changes in M caused by inappropriate monetary policy are the single most important cause of macroeconomic instability.

▶ In the real-business-cycle theory, significant changes in "real" factors such as technology, resource availability, and productivity change the economy's long-run aggregate supply, causing macroeconomic instability.

▶ Macroeconomic instability can result from coordination failures—less-than-optimal equilibrium positions that occur because businesses and households lack a way to coordinate their actions.

Does the Economy "Self-Correct"?

Just as there are disputes over the causes of macroeconomic instability, there are disputes over whether or not the economy will correct itself when instability does occur. Economists also disagree on how long it will take for any such self-correction to take place. The points of disagreement can be understood by examining how *new classical economics* approaches macroeconomic self-correction.

New Classical View of Self-Correction

New classical economists tend to be either monetarists or adherents of **rational expectations theory,** which assumes that people will do their logical (rational) best to correctly anticipate future events as much as possible so as to minimize the likelihood of ever being caught off guard. To the degree that they are able to understand and anticipate future events or the future consequences of current events, they will be able to make better current decisions with respect to maximizing both personal utility and business profits. Examples: (1) Before driving up into the mountains, you check the weather news hourly so you can develop an accurate sense about likely weather hazards. (2) You study macroeconomics so that you will know the best places to invest your money if the Fed decides to loosen monetary policy. (3) Knowing how bad this year's flu virus is, you wash your hands several times per day in order to reduce your chances of becoming infected.

> **>> LO38.2** Explain why new classical economists believe the economy will self-correct from aggregate demand and aggregate supply shocks.

> **rational expectations theory** A hypothesis that assumes that people develop logical (rational) models that attempt to correctly anticipate future events (expectations) as much as possible so as to make better current decisions given what is likely to happen in the future. Can cause individuals and firms to take actions that offset monetary and fiscal policy initiatives.

FIGURE 38.2 The new classical view of self-correction.

(a) An *unanticipated* increase in aggregate demand from AD₁ to AD₂ first moves the economy from *a* to *b*, and the economy then self-corrects to *c*. By contrast, an *anticipated* increase in aggregate demand from AD₁ to AD₂ moves the economy directly from *a* to *c*. (b) An *unanticipated* decrease in aggregate demand from AD₁ to AD₃ moves the economy from *a* to *d*, and the economy then self-corrects to *e*. By contrast, an anticipated decrease in aggregate demand from AD₁ to AD₃ moves the economy directly from *a* to *e*. (Mainstream economists, however, say that if the price level remains at P_1, the economy will move from *a* to *f*, and even if the price level falls to P_4, the economy may remain at *d* because of downward wage inflexibility.)

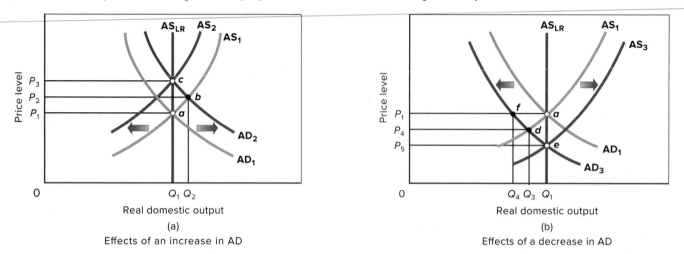

(a)
Effects of an increase in AD

(b)
Effects of a decrease in AD

new classical economics
The theory that, although unanticipated *price-level* changes may create macroeconomic instability in the short run, the economy will return to and stabilize at the full-employment level of domestic output in the long run because *prices* and *wages* adjust automatically to correct movements away from the full-employment output level.

New classical economics contends that when the economy diverges from its full-employment output, internal mechanisms within the economy automatically move it back to that output. So policymakers should stand back and let the automatic correction occur, rather than engage in active fiscal and monetary policy. This perspective is often associated with the vertical long-run Phillips Curve, which we discussed in Chapter 37. But we will analyze it here using the extended AD–AS model that was also developed in Chapter 37.

Examples of Macroeconomic Self-Correction Figure 38.2a demonstrates the new classical idea that the economy is capable of self-correction. Specifically, an increase in aggregate demand, say, from AD₁ to AD₂, moves the economy upward along its short-run aggregate supply curve AS₁ from *a* to *b*. The price level rises and real output increases. With the economy producing beyond potential output, high resource demand drives up the prices of labor and other productive inputs. Per-unit production costs increase and the short-run aggregate supply curve shifts leftward, eventually from AS₁ to AS₂. The economy moves from *b* to *c*, and real output returns to its full-employment level, Q_1. This level of output dictates the position of the economy's vertical long-run aggregate supply curve, AS$_{LR}$.

Conversely, a decrease in aggregate demand from AD₁ to AD₃ in Figure 38.2b first moves the economy downward along its short-run aggregate supply curve AS₁ from point *a* to *d*. The price level declines, as does the level of real output. With the economy producing below potential output, low resource demand drives down the prices of labor and other productive inputs. When that happens, per-unit production costs decline and the short-run aggregate supply curve shifts to the right, eventually from AS₁ to AS₃. The economy moves to *e*, where it again achieves its full-employment level, Q_1. As in Figure 38.2a, the economy in Figure 38.2b has automatically self-corrected to its full-employment output and its natural rate of unemployment.

Rational Expectations Theory and the Speed of Self-Correcting Adjustments There is some disagreement among new classical economists on how long it will take for self-correction to occur. Monetarists usually hold the *adaptive expectations* view that people form their expectations by extrapolating from present and past conditions. As a result, they only gradually change their expectations as experience unfolds, which means that the shifts in the short-run aggregate supply curves shown in Figure 38.2 may not occur for two or three years, or even longer, if people are assumed to have adaptive expectations. By contrast, other new classical economists believe that people have *rational expectations*, meaning that they are forward looking and do their best to rationally and accurately anticipate future outcomes. Under the assumption of rational expectations, price-level changes that are fully anticipated will be changes that people adjust to quickly, or even instantaneously.

Although many areas of economics (including finance and game theory) have incorporated rational expectations theory, our interest here is with the new classical version of rational expectations theory as it relates to macroeconomic adjustments. This application of rational expectations theory (hereafter, RET) is based on two assumptions:

- People behave rationally, gathering and intelligently processing information to form expectations about things that are economically important to them. They adjust those expectations quickly as new developments affecting future economic outcomes occur. Where there is adequate information, people's beliefs about future economic outcomes will accurately reflect the likelihood that those outcomes will occur. For example, if it is clear that a certain policy will cause inflation, people will recognize that fact and adjust their economic behavior in anticipation of inflation.

- RET economists assume that all product and resource markets are highly competitive and that prices and wages are flexible both upward and downward. But the RET economists go further, assuming that new information is quickly (in some cases, instantaneously) taken into account in market demand and supply curves. The upshot is that equilibrium prices and quantities should adjust *rapidly* to unforeseen events like unexpected technological advances or unexpected aggregate supply shocks. And they adjust *instantaneously* to events that have known outcomes—for example, changes in fiscal or monetary policy.

Unanticipated Price-Level Changes RET implies not only that the economy is self-correcting but also that self-correction occurs quickly even in response to unexpected macroeconomic shocks. According to RET, unanticipated changes in the price level—called **price-level surprises**—*do* cause temporary changes in real output. As an example, suppose that an unanticipated increase in foreign demand for U.S. goods increases U.S. aggregate demand from AD_1 to AD_2 in Figure 38.2a. The immediate result that we actually observe is an unexpected increase in the price level from P_1 to P_2 and an unexpected increase in GDP to a level higher than full employment.

But now an interesting question arises. If wages and prices are fully flexible, as assumed in RET, why doesn't the higher price level cause wages and other input prices to rise *immediately*? If they did rise immediately, the aggregate supply curve would instantaneously shift leftward from AS_1 to AS_2, so that any increase in real output would last only a brief moment or two. The economy would jump almost directly from point *a* to point *c*.

As we have already noted, the macroeconomic adjustments that we actually observe after a positive demand shock like the movement from AD_1 to AD_2 don't move anywhere nearly as rapidly as that. So RET proponents need to provide us with an explanation as to why the economy moves first (as it does) from point *a* to *b* along AS_1 before having to wait months or even years for aggregate supply to shift left so as to return the economy to full employment at point *c*. If firms have rational expectations, they should know that they are going to end up back at point *c*, producing no more output than they did at point *a*. So why would they as rational agents ever bother increasing their output levels above full employment?

The RET explanation is that firms increase output from Q_1 to Q_2 because of misperceptions about the rising prices that they observe for their own products. They mistakenly confuse the general increase in the price level that is actually taking place across the entire economy for a specific increase in the price of their own product. They mistakenly think that their own selling price is increasing *relative to* the prices of other products. That makes them think that their profit margins are going to increase, which in turn spurs them to increase output beyond the full-employment level.

The truth, of course, is that *all* prices, including the price of labor (nominal wages), are going to rise in response to the unexpected demand shock. Once firms see that *all* prices and wages are rising, they will decrease their production to previous levels. But that will only happen once they realize their mistake about confusing the general increase in the price level for a specific increase in the price of their own product. That realization could take a while. And so RET theorists have an explanation for why the economy only slowly adjusts from *a* to *b* to *c* even when people are assumed to utilize rational expectations.

The same analysis in reverse applies to an unanticipated price-level decrease. In Figure 38.2b, firms at first misunderstand why the prices of their own products are falling from *a* to *b* after aggregate demand unexpectedly shifts left from AD_1 to AD_3. They mistakenly believe that their own respective prices are falling due to decreases in the demand for their own products relative to the demand for other products. Not understanding that aggregate demand has decreased all across

price-level surprises
Unanticipated changes in the *price level*.

the economy, they mistakenly anticipate declines in their own respective profits and consequently cut production. The collective result of those individual reductions is a decrease in real output that will persist until firms see what is really happening with aggregate demand. Once firms see what is really happening—that *all* prices and wages are dropping, not just their own—they will increase their respective outputs. When they do, the short-run aggregate supply curve in Figure 38.2b will shift rightward from AS_1 to AS_3, and the economy will "self-correct" by moving from *d* to *e*.

Fully Anticipated Price-Level Changes In RET, *fully anticipated* price-level changes do not change real output, even for short periods. In Figure 38.2a, again consider the increase in aggregate demand from AD_1 to AD_2. Businesses immediately recognize that the higher prices being paid for their products are part of the inflation they had anticipated. They also understand that the same forces that are causing the inflation will result in higher nominal wages, leaving their profits unchanged. The economy therefore moves directly from *a* to *c*. The price level rises as expected, and output remains at its full-employment level Q_1, also as expected.

Similarly, a *fully anticipated* price-level decrease will leave real output unchanged. Firms anticipate that nominal wages will decline by the same percentage amount as the declining price level, leaving profits unchanged. The economy represented by Figure 38.2b therefore moves directly from *a* to *e*. Deflation occurs, but the economy continues to produce its full-employment output Q_1. The anticipated decline in aggregate demand causes no change in real output.

Mainstream View of Self-Correction

While mainstream economists have incorporated some aspects of RET into their own models, most economists strongly disagree with RET on the question of downward price and wage flexibility. While the stock market, foreign exchange market, and certain commodity markets experience day-to-day or minute-to-minute price changes, including price declines, the same is not true of many product markets and most labor markets. There is ample evidence, say mainstream economists, that many prices and wages are inflexible downward for long periods. As a result, it may take years for the economy to move from recession back to full-employment output, unless it gets help from fiscal and monetary policy.

Downward Wage Inflexibility There are several reasons why firms may not be able to, or may not want to, lower nominal wages. Firms may not be able to cut wages because of wage contracts and the legal minimum wage. And firms may not want to lower wages if they fear potential problems with morale, effort, and efficiency.

efficiency wage An above-market (above-equilibrium) *wage* that minimizes wage costs per unit of output by encouraging greater effort or reducing turnover.

Efficiency Wage Theory An **efficiency wage** is an above-market-equilibrium wage that minimizes a firm's labor cost per unit of output. Normally, we would think that the market wage is the efficiency wage because it is the lowest wage at which a firm can obtain a particular type of labor. But where the cost of supervising workers is high or where worker turnover is great, firms may discover that paying more than the market wage lowers their wage cost per unit of output.

Example: Suppose a firm's workers, on average, produce 8 units of output at a $9 market wage but 10 units of output at a $10 above-market wage. The efficiency wage is $10, not the $9 market wage. At the $10 wage, the labor cost per unit of output is only $1 (= $10 wage/10 units of output), compared with $1.12 (= $9 wage/8 units of output) at the $9 wage.

How can a higher wage result in greater efficiency?

- *Greater work effort* The above-market wage raises the cost to workers of losing their jobs as a result of poor performance. Because workers have a strong incentive to retain their relatively high-paying jobs, they are more likely to provide greater work effort. In other words, workers are more reluctant to shirk (neglect or avoid work) because the higher wage makes job loss more costly to them. Consequently, the above-market wage can be the efficient wage; it can enhance worker productivity so much that the higher wage more than pays for itself.

- *Lower supervision costs* With less incentive among workers to shirk, the firm needs fewer supervisory personnel to monitor work performance. Lower supervisory costs, too, can lower the firm's overall wage cost per unit of output.

- *Reduced job turnover* The above-market pay discourages workers from voluntarily leaving their jobs. The lower turnover rate in turn reduces the firm's cost of hiring and training workers. It also gives the firm a more experienced, more productive workforce.

The key implication for macroeconomic instability is that efficiency wages add to the downward inflexibility of wages. Firms that pay efficiency wages will be reluctant to cut wages when aggregate demand declines, because such cuts may encourage shirking, require more supervisory personnel, and increase turnover. In other words, wage cuts that reduce productivity and raise per-unit labor costs are self-defeating.

▶ New classical economists believe that the economy "self-corrects" when unanticipated events divert it from its full-employment level of real output.

▶ In rational expectations theory (RET), unanticipated price-level changes cause changes in real output in the short run but not in the long run.

▶ According to RET, market participants immediately change their actions in response to anticipated

price-level changes such that no change in real output occurs.

▶ Mainstream economists say that the economy can get mired in recession for several months or more because of downward price and wage inflexibility. Sources of downward wage inflexibility include minimum wages, labor contracts, and efficiency wages.

QUICK REVIEW
38.2

Rules or Discretion?

The different views on the causes of instability and on the speed of self-correction have led to vigorous debate. Should the government adhere to policy rules that prohibit it from causing instability in an economy that is otherwise stable? Or should it use discretionary fiscal and monetary policy, when needed, to stabilize a sometimes-unstable economy?

>> **LO38.3** Describe the rules versus discretion debate regarding stabilization policy.

In Support of Policy Rules

Monetarists and other new classical economists believe that policy rules will reduce instability in the economy. They believe that such rules will prevent government from trying to "manage" aggregate demand. That outcome is desirable because, in their view, such management is likely to *cause* more instability than it cures.

Monetary Rules Because inappropriate monetary policy is the major source of macroeconomic instability, say monetarists, the enactment of a **monetary rule** would make sense. One such rule would be a requirement that the Fed expand the money supply each year at the same annual rate as the typical growth rate of the economy's productive capacity. That fixed-rate expansion of the money supply would occur whatever the state of the economy. The Fed's sole monetary role would be to use its tools (open-market operations, the discount rate, interest on reserves, and reserve requirements) to ensure that the nation's money supply grew steadily by, say, 3 to 5 percent a year. According to Milton Friedman, a prominent monetarist,

> Such a rule . . . would eliminate . . . the major cause of instability in the economy—the capricious and unpredictable impact of countercyclical monetary policy. As long as the money supply grows at a constant rate each year, be it 3, 4, or 5 percent, any decline into recession will be temporary. The liquidity provided by a constantly growing money supply will cause aggregate demand to expand. Similarly, if the supply of money does not rise at a more than average rate, any inflationary increase in spending will burn itself out for lack of fuel.[1]

Figure 38.3 illustrates the rationale for a monetary rule. Suppose the economy represented there is operating at its full-employment real output, Q_1. Also suppose the nation's long-run aggregate supply curve shifts rightward, as from AS_{LR1} to AS_{LR2}, each year, signifying the average annual increase in potential real output. As you know, such annual increases in "potential GDP" result from added resources, improved resources, and improved technology.

Monetarists argue that a monetary rule would tie increases in the money supply to the typical rightward shift of long-run aggregate supply. Due to the direct link between changes in the money supply and aggregate demand, the monetary rule would ensure that the AD curve shifts rightward, as from AD_1 to AD_2, each year. As a result, while GDP increases from Q_1 to Q_2, the price level will remain constant at P_1. A monetary rule, in short, will promote steady growth of real output along with price stability.

monetary rule (1) A set of guidelines to be followed by a *central bank* that wishes to adjust monetary policy over time to achieve goals such as promoting *economic growth*, encouraging *full employment*, and maintaining a stable *price level*. (2) The guidelines for conducting monetary policy suggested by *monetarism*. As traditionally formulated, the *money supply* should be expanded each year at the same annual rate as the potential rate of growth of *real gross domestic product;* the supply of money should be increased steadily between 3 and 5 percent per year. (Also see *Taylor rule*.)

---

[1] Lawrence S. Ritter and William L. Silber, *Money* (Basic Books, 1984).

FIGURE 38.3
Rationale for a monetary rule.

A monetary rule that required the Fed to increase the money supply at an annual rate linked to the long-run increase in potential GDP would shift aggregate demand rightward, as from AD₁ to AD₂, at the same pace as the shift in long-run aggregate supply, here, AS$_{LR1}$ to AS$_{LR2}$. Thus the economy would experience growth without inflation or deflation.

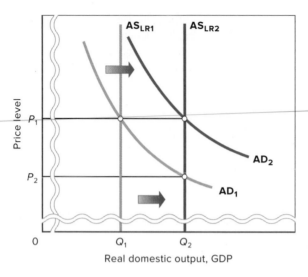

Generally, rational expectations economists also support a monetary rule. They conclude that an expansionary or restrictive monetary policy will alter the inflation rate but not real output. Suppose, for example, the Fed implements an easy money policy to reduce interest rates, expand investment spending, and boost real GDP. On the basis of past experience and economic knowledge, the public will anticipate that this policy is inflationary and will take protective actions. Workers will press for higher nominal wages; firms will raise their product prices; and lenders will increase their nominal interest rates on loans.

All these responses are designed to prevent inflation from having adverse effects on the real income of workers, businesses, and lenders. But collectively they would immediately raise wage and price levels. So the increase in aggregate demand brought about by the expansionary monetary policy would be completely dissipated in higher prices and wages. Real output and employment would not be increased by the easy money policy. Only higher prices and inflation would result.

In this view, the combination of rational expectations and instantaneous market adjustments dooms discretionary monetary policy to ineffectiveness. If discretionary monetary policy produces only inflation (or deflation), say the RET economists, then it makes sense to limit the Fed's discretion and to require that Congress enact a monetary rule consistent with either price-level stability or inflation-rate stability.

Inflation Targeting In recent decades, the call for a Friedman-type monetary rule has faded. In 2012, the Fed did, however, adopt a flexible version of another type of monetary rule. Under **inflation targeting**, the Fed commits to adjusting monetary policy as necessary to achieve a publicly announced inflation rate. The Fed's choice for its **target rate of inflation** was 2 percent per year, in line with the target rates chosen around the same time by the European Central Bank and the Bank of Japan.

Strictly interpreted, inflation targeting would focus the Fed's attention nearly exclusively on controlling inflation and deflation, rather than on counteracting business fluctuations. Proponents of strict inflation targeting generally believe the economy will have fewer, shorter, and less severe business cycles if the Fed adheres to the rule "Set a known inflation goal and achieve it." The Fed, however, reserves the right to use monetary policy as necessary to smooth the business cycle even if doing so might cause inflation to deviate from the target rate of 2 percent.

Global Perspective 38.1 lists the inflation targets of several national and regional central banks. Some countries, like Mexico, have a target *range* for inflation—such as 2 percent to 4 percent per year—rather than a single target number. In those cases, the middle value of the target range is presented.

inflation targeting The declaration by a *central bank* of a goal for a specific range of *inflation* in a future year, coupled with *monetary policy* designed to achieve the goal.

target rate of inflation The publicly announced annual *inflation* rate that a *central bank* attempts to achieve through *monetary policy* actions if it is following an *inflation targeting* monetary policy.

Balanced Budget Monetarists and new classical economists also question the effectiveness of *fiscal* policy. At the extreme, a few of them favor a constitutional amendment requiring the federal government to balance its budget annually. Others suggest that government adopt a "passive" fiscal policy, not intentionally creating budget deficits or surpluses. They believe that deficits and surpluses caused by recession or inflationary expansion will eventually correct themselves as the economy self-corrects to its full-employment output level.

Monetarists are particularly strong in their opposition to expansionary fiscal policy. They believe that the deficit spending accompanying such a policy has a strong tendency to "crowd out" private investment. Suppose government runs a budget deficit by printing and selling U.S. securities— that is, by borrowing from the public. By engaging in such borrowing, the government is competing with private businesses for funds. The borrowing increases the demand for money, which then raises the interest rate and crowds out a substantial amount of private investment that would otherwise have been profitable. The net effect of a budget deficit on aggregate demand therefore is unpredictable and, at best, modest.

GLOBAL PERSPECTIVE 38.1

CENTRAL BANK INFLATION TARGETS, SELECTED CENTRAL BANKS, 2021

Not all central banks use inflation targets. But among those that do, the target rates vary substantially. Areas that have enjoyed low inflation rates over the past few decades usually have target rates of 2 percent—as is the case for Japan and the United States. By contrast, countries that have experienced high rates of inflation in recent decades typically have higher inflation targets. Those higher targets are often part of a long-term strategy to use a series of incremental reductions of the target rate, spread out over many years, to gradually squeeze inflation down to a low level like 2 percent.

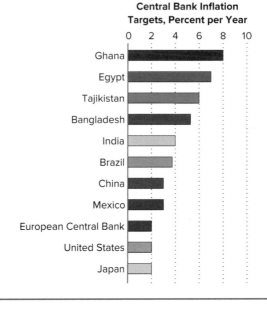

Central Bank Inflation Targets, Percent per Year

Source: Various central bank websites.

RET economists reject discretionary fiscal policy for the same reason they reject active monetary policy: They don't think it can work. Business and labor will immediately adjust their behavior in anticipation of the price-level effects of a change in fiscal policy. The economy will move directly to the anticipated new price level. Like monetary policy, say the RET theorists, fiscal policy can move the economy along its vertical long-run aggregate supply curve. But because its effects on inflation are fully anticipated, fiscal policy cannot alter real GDP even in the short run. The best course of action for government is to balance its budget.

In Defense of Discretionary Stabilization Policy

Mainstream economists oppose both a strict, Friedman-style monetary rule and a balanced-budget requirement. They believe that monetary policy and fiscal policy are important tools for achieving and maintaining full employment, price stability, and economic growth.

Discretionary Monetary Policy In supporting discretionary monetary policy, mainstream economists argue that the rationale for the Friedman monetary rule is flawed. While there is indeed a close relationship between the money supply and nominal GDP over long periods, over shorter periods the relationship breaks down. The reason is that the velocity of money has proved to be more variable and unpredictable than monetarists contend. Arguing that velocity is variable both cyclically and over time, mainstream economists contend that a constant annual rate of increase in the money supply might not eliminate fluctuations in aggregate demand. In terms of the equation of exchange, a steady rise of M does not guarantee a steady expansion of aggregate demand because V—the rate at which money is spent—can change.

Look again at Figure 38.3, in which we demonstrated the Friedman-style monetary rule that the Fed should expand the money supply annually by a fixed percentage, regardless of the state of the economy. During the period in question, optimistic business expectations might create a boom in investment spending and thus shift the aggregate demand curve to some location to the right of AD_2. (You may want to pencil in a new AD curve, labeling it AD_3.) The price level will then rise above P_1; that is, demand-pull inflation will occur. In this case, the monetary rule will not accomplish its goal of maintaining price stability. Mainstream economists say that the Fed can use a restrictive monetary policy to reduce the excessive investment spending and thereby hold the rightward shift of aggregate demand to AD_2, thus avoiding inflation.

Now suppose instead that investment declines because of pessimistic business expectations. Aggregate demand will then increase by some amount less than the increase from AD_1 to AD_2 in Figure 38.3. Again, the monetary rule fails the stability test: The price level sinks below P_1 (deflation occurs). Or if the price level is inflexible downward at P_1, the economy will not achieve its full-employment output (unemployment rises). An expansionary monetary policy can help avoid each outcome.

Mainstream economists quip that the trouble with the monetary rule is that it tells the policy-maker, "Don't do something; just stand there."

Discretionary Fiscal Policy Mainstream economists support the use of fiscal policy to keep recessions from deepening or to keep mild inflation from becoming severe inflation. They recognize the possibility of crowding out but do not think it is a serious problem when business borrowing is depressed, which is usually the case in a recession. Because politicians can abuse fiscal policy, most economists feel that it should be held in reserve for situations where monetary policy appears to be ineffective or working too slowly.

As indicated earlier, mainstream economists oppose requirements to balance the budget annually. Tax revenues fall sharply during recessions and rise briskly during periods of demand-pull inflation. Therefore, a law or a constitutional amendment mandating an annually balanced budget would require the government to increase tax rates and reduce government spending during recession and reduce tax rates and increase government spending during economic booms. The first set of actions would worsen recession, and the second set would fuel inflation.

Policy Successes

Finally, mainstream economists point out several specific policy successes in the past four decades:

- A tight money policy dropped inflation from 13.5 percent in 1980 to 3.2 percent in 1983.
- An expansionary fiscal policy reduced the unemployment rate from 9.7 percent in 1982 to 5.5 percent in 1988.
- An easy money policy helped the economy recover from the 1990–1991 recession.
- Judicious tightening of monetary policy in the mid-1990s, and then again in the late 1990s, helped the economy remain on a noninflationary, full-employment growth path.
- In late 2001 and 2002, expansionary fiscal and monetary policy helped the economy recover from a series of economic blows, including the collapse of numerous Internet startup firms; a severe decline in investment spending; the impacts of the terrorist attacks of September 11, 2001; and a precipitous decline in stock values.
- In 2007 the Fed vigorously responded to a crisis in the mortgage market by ensuring monetary liquidity in the banking system. Besides aggressively lowering the federal funds rate from 5.25 percent in the summer of 2007 to just 2 percent in April 2008, the Fed greatly increased the reserves of the banking system. It also undertook other lender-of-last-resort actions to unfreeze credit and prevent a possible collapse of the entire financial system. During the Great Recession of 2007–2009, the Fed lowered the federal funds rate further, holding it in the 0 to 0.25 percent range to break the economy's downward slide and to promote economic recovery.
- To help prevent the world economy from sliding into a financial crisis when the COVID-19 pandemic began to bite, the Fed injected nearly $4 trillion of liquidity (cash) into the world financial system between February and June 2020 through either asset purchases (mostly government bonds) or by making dollar loans to major financial institutions and other central banks. The Fed also lowered the Federal funds rate very aggressively, from 1.59 percent to just 0.05 percent, between March 3 and April 3 of 2020. Those decisive actions resulted in the shortest U.S. recession on record (just two months) and a quick return to a positive outlook among business-people and investors, with, for example, the stock market regaining its pre-pandemic highs by mid-August of 2020, just six months after the crisis began to affect financial markets.

QUICK REVIEW 38.3

▸ Mainstream economists disagree with monetarists and rational expectations economists as to whether the Fed should use monetary rules or discretion.

▸ Monetarist and rational expectations economists oppose discretion because they believe that discretion adds more instability to the business cycle than it cures.

▸ Mainstream economists oppose strict monetary rules and defend both monetary and fiscal policy discretion because they believe that both theory and evidence suggest that discretionary policies are helpful in achieving full employment, price stability, and economic growth.

Market Monetarism

Market Monetarists Call for a New Monetary Rule That Would Institutionalize Fed Policy Responses to Changes in Real Output and Inflation.

In the aftermath of the Great Recession of 2007–2008, a new breed of "market monetarists" suggested that the Fed and other central banks should use prediction markets to adjust monetary policy.

In prediction markets, people can place bets on how likely it is that a particular political or financial outcome will end up happening. There are, for example, many commodities futures markets where people can bet on things like the price of corn next January or the price of oil in five years.

Extensive studies have shown that prediction markets make by far the most accurate predictions about the future—much better than those made by individual experts or even groups of experts attempting to pool their many decades of expertise. The superior prognosticating performance of prediction markets appears to be due to the fact that they incorporate the knowledge and insights of everyone who participates. As a result, even information that is only known to a few nonexperts can improve the prediction.

Prediction markets are not perfect. They do make mistakes—for instance predicting the wrong candidate to win the presidential election or predicting that the price of oil will be $46 per barrel in July whereas the actual price ends up being $53 per barrel. But because prediction markets are the best available tool for predicting future outcomes, market monetarists want to piggyback on their predictive accuracy to help the Fed set monetary policy. In particular, they argue that the Fed should set up a prediction market for nominal GDP and then use the predictions generated by that market to adjust monetary policy.

As you know, nominal GDP can grow for two reasons: inflation or increases in real GDP. Market monetarists point out that if you look back over many decades of data, nominal GDP growth in the United States has averaged about 5 percent per year. Of that amount, about 3 percent per year has on average been due to real GDP growth while the remaining 2 percent has been caused by inflation.

The Fed's goal would be for the prediction market to always be predicting 5 percent growth in nominal GDP. If the prediction ever deviated from that 5 percent target, the Fed would loosen or tighten monetary policy in whatever direction would be needed for the prediction to adjust back to 5 percent.

To see how this monetary rule would work, suppose that the prediction market for nominal GDP is forecasting only 4 percent nominal GDP growth next year (rather than the desired rate of 5 percent). Because prediction markets make the most accurate forecasts, this 4 percent prediction will be our best available information on what is likely to happen with the economy next year. And since what is likely to happen is less than the target rate of 5 percent, stimulus will

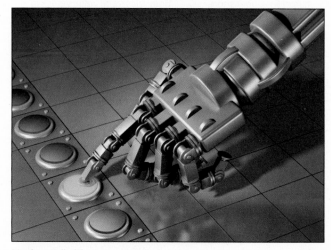

Matthias Kulka/The Image Bank/Getty Images

be called for. Market monetarists would want the Fed to loosen monetary policy and stimulate the economy until the participants in the nominal GDP prediction market are "voting with their pocketbooks" that nominal GDP will grow by 5 percent next year. When the predicted growth rate reaches 5 percent, the Fed can stop stimulating.

On the flip side, if the prediction market were forecasting 7 percent nominal GDP growth next year rather than the desired 5 percent, market monetarists would want the Fed to tighten monetary policy until the market's prediction fell back down to the 5 percent target rate. That way, contractionary monetary policy would only be applied if and when the prediction market is indicating that the economy is overheating (relative to the 5 percent target growth rate for nominal GDP). Once the prediction market is indicating that the economy is on target again, contractionary actions can end and the Fed can switch to a neutral policy stance (i.e., neither expansionary nor contractionary).

Market monetarism has prompted a vigorous debate. Some opponents argue that "targeting the forecast" would overly constrain the Fed's discretion when reacting to severe crises while others point out that a 5 percent target for nominal GDP growth would prevent real GDP growth from ever exceeding 5 percent per year. So while market monetarism has garnered several prominent proponents, including Nobel Laureate Paul Krugman and former Council of Economic Advisors Chair Christina Romer, the debate over an optimal monetary policy rule will continue.

TABLE 38.1 Summary of Alternative Macroeconomic Views

Issue	Mainstream Macroeconomics	New Classical Economics	
		Monetarism	**Rational Expectations**
View of the private economy	Potentially unstable	Stable in long run at natural rate of unemployment	Stable in long run at natural rate of unemployment
Cause of the observed instability of the private economy	Investment plans unequal to saving plans (changes in AD); AS shocks	Inappropriate monetary policy	Unanticipated AD and AS shocks in the short run
Assumptions about short-run price and wage stickiness	Both prices and wages stuck in the immediate short run; in the short run, wages sticky while prices inflexible downward but flexible upward	Prices flexible upward and downward in the short run; wages sticky in the short run	Prices and wages flexible both upward and downward in the short run
Appropriate macro policies	Active fiscal and monetary policy	Monetary rule	Monetary rule
How changes in the money supply affect the economy	By changing the interest rate, which changes investment and real GDP	By directly changing AD, which changes GDP	No effect on output because price-level changes are anticipated
View of the velocity of money	Unstable	Stable	No consensus
How fiscal policy affects the economy	Changes AD and GDP via the multiplier process	No effect unless money supply changes	No effect because price-level changes are anticipated
View of cost-push inflation	Possible (AS shock)	Impossible in the long run in the absence of excessive money supply growth	Impossible in the long run in the absence of excessive money supply growth

Summary of Alternative Views

Table 38.1 summarizes the fundamental ideas and policy implications of the three schools of macroeconomic theory that we have discussed: mainstream macroeconomics, monetarism, and rational expectations.

These different perspectives have obliged mainstream economists to rethink some of their fundamental principles and to revise many of their positions. Although considerable disagreement remains, mainstream macroeconomists agree with monetarists that "money matters" and that excessive growth of the money supply is the major cause of long-lasting, rapid inflation. They also agree with RET proponents and advocates for coordination failures that expectations matter. If government can create expectations of price stability, full employment, and economic growth, households and firms will tend to act in ways to make them happen.

In closing this chapter, let us note that it is thanks to ongoing challenges to conventional wisdom that macroeconomics continues to evolve. Do not presume that any of these schools of thought will have the last laugh. Much remains to be discovered.

Summary

LO38.1 Describe alternative perspectives on the causes of macroeconomic instability.

The mainstream view holds that macro instability is caused by a combination of price stickiness and shocks to aggregate demand or aggregate supply. With prices inflexible in the short run, changes in aggregate demand or short-run aggregate supply result in changes in output and employment. In the long run when input prices and output prices are fully flexible, the economy will produce at potential output.

Monetarism focuses on the equation of exchange: $MV = PQ$. Because velocity V is thought to be stable, changes in M (the money supply) create changes in nominal GDP ($= PQ$). Monetarists believe that the most significant cause of macroeconomic instability has

been inappropriate monetary policy. Rapid increases in M cause inflation; insufficient growth of M causes recession.

Real-business-cycle theory identifies changes in resource availability and technology (real factors), which alter productivity, as the main causes of macroeconomic instability. In this theory, shifts of the economy's long-run aggregate supply curve change real output.

A coordination failure occurs when people lack a way to coordinate their actions in order to achieve a mutually beneficial equilibrium. Depending on people's expectations, the economy can come to rest at either a good equilibrium (noninflationary full-employment output) or a bad equilibrium (less-than-full-employment output or demand-pull inflation).

Rational expectations theory rests on two assumptions: (1) With sufficient information, people's beliefs about future economic outcomes accurately reflect the likelihood that those outcomes will occur; and (2) markets are highly competitive, and prices and wages are flexible both upward and downward.

LO38.2 Explain why new classical economists believe the economy will self-correct from aggregate demand and aggregate supply shocks.

New classical economists (monetarists and rational expectations theorists) see the economy as automatically correcting itself when disturbed from its full-employment level of real output. In RET, unanticipated changes in aggregate demand change the price level, which in the short run leads firms to change output. But once the firms realize that all prices are changing (including nominal wages) as part of general inflation or deflation, they restore their output to the previous level. By contrast, anticipated changes in aggregate demand produce only changes in the price level, not changes in real output.

Mainstream economists reject the new classical view that all prices and wages are flexible downward. They contend that nominal wages, in particular, are inflexible downward because of several factors, including minimum-wage laws, labor contracts, and efficiency wages. Thus declines in aggregate demand lower real output, not only wages and prices.

LO38.3 Describe the rules versus discretion debate regarding stabilization policy.

Monetarist and rational expectations economists say the Fed should adhere to some form of policy rule, rather than rely exclusively on discretion. The Friedman rule would direct the Fed to increase the money supply at a fixed annual rate equal to the long-run growth of potential GDP. In 2012, the Fed took another path, however, and adopted an inflation target of 2 percent per year, thereby committing itself to adjusting monetary policy to reach that goal except in extreme cases where a different inflation rate might be necessary to smooth the business cycle.

Monetarists and rational expectations theorists also support maintaining a "neutral" fiscal policy, as opposed to using discretionary fiscal policy to create budget deficits or budget surpluses. A few monetarists and rational expectations economists favor a constitutional amendment requiring the federal government to balance its budget annually.

Mainstream economists oppose strict, Friedman-style monetary rules and a balanced-budget requirement, and they defend discretionary monetary and fiscal policies. They say that both theory and evidence suggest that such policies are helpful in achieving full employment, price stability, and economic growth.

Terms and Concepts

monetarism	coordination failure	efficiency wage
equation of exchange	rational expectations theory	monetary rule
velocity	new classical economics	inflation targeting
real-business-cycle theory	price-level surprises	target rate of inflation

Discussion Questions

McGraw Hill **connect**

1. According to mainstream economists, what is the usual cause of macroeconomic instability? What role does the spending-income multiplier play in creating instability? How might adverse aggregate supply factors cause instability, according to mainstream economists? **LO38.1**
2. Briefly describe the difference between a so-called real business cycle and a more traditional "spending" business cycle. **LO38.1**
3. Craig and Kris were walking directly toward each other in a congested store aisle. Craig moved to his left to avoid Kris, and at the same time Kris moved to his right to avoid Craig. They bumped into each other. What concept does this example illustrate? How does this idea relate to macroeconomic instability? **LO38.1**
4. State and explain the basic equation of monetarism. What is the major cause of macroeconomic instability, as viewed by monetarists? **LO38.1**
5. Use the equation of exchange to explain the rationale for a monetary rule. Why will such a rule run into trouble if V unexpectedly falls because of, say, a drop in investment spending by businesses? **LO38.1**
6. What is an efficiency wage? How might payment of an above-market wage reduce shirking by employees and reduce worker turnover? How might efficiency wages contribute to downward wage inflexibility, at least for a time, when aggregate demand declines? **LO38.2**
7. Explain the difference between "active" discretionary fiscal policy advocated by mainstream economists and "passive" fiscal policy advocated by new classical economists. Explain: "The problem with a balanced-budget amendment is that it would, in a sense, require active fiscal policy—but in the wrong direction—as the economy slides into recession." **LO38.3**
8. You have just been elected president of the United States, and the present chair of the Federal Reserve Board has resigned. You need to appoint a new person to this position, as well as a person to chair your Council of Economic Advisers. Using Table 38.1 and your knowledge of macroeconomics, identify the views on macro theory and policy you would want your appointees to hold. Remember, the economic health of the entire nation—and your chances for reelection—may depend on your selection. **LO38.3**
9. **LAST WORD** Compare and contrast the market monetarist 5-percent target for nominal GDP growth with the older, simpler monetary rule advocated by Milton Friedman.

1. If prices are sticky and the number of dollars of gross investment unexpectedly increases, the _____ curve will shift _____. **LO38.1**
   a. AD; right
   b. AD; left
   c. AS; right
   d. AS; left

2. First, imagine that both input prices and output prices are fixed in the economy. What does the aggregate supply curve look like? If AD decreases in this situation, what will happen to equilibrium output and the price level? Next, imagine that input prices are fixed, but output prices are flexible. What does the aggregate supply curve look like? In this case, if AD decreases, what will happen to equilibrium output and the price level? Finally, if both input prices and output prices are fully flexible, what does the aggregate supply curve look like? In this case, if AD decreases, what will happen to equilibrium output and the price level? (To check your answers, review Figures 32.3, 32.4, and 32.5 in Chapter 32.) **LO38.1**

3. Suppose that the money supply is $1 trillion and money velocity is 4. Then the equation of exchange would predict nominal GDP to be: **LO38.1**
   a. $1 trillion.   c. $5 trillion.
   b. $4 trillion.   d. $8 trillion.

4. If the money supply fell by 10 percent, a monetarist would expect nominal GDP to _____. **LO38.1**
   a. rise
   b. fall
   c. stay the same

5. An economy is producing at full employment when AD unexpectedly shifts to the left. A new classical economist would assume that as the economy adjusts back to producing at full employment, the price level will _____. **LO38.2**
   a. increase
   b. decrease
   c. stay the same

6. Use an AD–AS graph to demonstrate and explain the price-level and real-output outcome of an anticipated decline in aggregate demand, as viewed by RET economists. (Assume that the economy initially is operating at its full-employment level of output.) Then demonstrate and explain on the same graph the outcome as viewed by mainstream economists. **LO38.2**

7. Place "MON," "RET," or "MAIN" beside the statements that most closely reflect monetarist, rational expectations, or mainstream views, respectively: **LO38.3**
   a. Anticipated changes in aggregate demand affect only the price level; they have no effect on real output.
   b. Downward wage inflexibility means that declines in aggregate demand can cause long-lasting recession.
   c. Changes in the money supply M increase PQ; at first only Q rises, because nominal wages are fixed, but once workers adapt their expectations to new realities, P rises and Q returns to its former level.
   d. Fiscal and monetary policies smooth out the business cycle.
   e. The Fed should increase the money supply at a fixed annual rate.

1. Suppose that the money supply and the nominal GDP for a hypothetical economy are $96 billion and $336 billion, respectively. What is the velocity of money? How will households and businesses react if the central bank reduces the money supply by $20 billion? By how much will nominal GDP have to fall to restore equilibrium, according to the monetarist perspective? **LO38.1**

2. Assume the following information for a hypothetical economy in year 1: money supply = $400 billion; the long-term average annual growth rate of potential GDP = 3 percent; velocity = 4. Assume that the banking system initially has no excess reserves and that the reserve requirement is 10 percent. Also suppose that velocity is constant and that the economy initially is operating at its full-employment real output. **LO38.3**
   a. What is the level of nominal GDP in year 1?
   b. Suppose the Fed adheres to a monetary rule that says that the money supply should grow at the same rate as potential GDP. How big will the money supply have to be in year 2 to meet its monetary rule? And by how much will the money supply have to increase between year 1 and year 2 to meet its monetary rule?

PART 11

Andrew F. Kazmierski/Shutterstock

International Trade

>> **LEARNING OBJECTIVES**

LO39.1 List several key facts about international trade.

LO39.2 Define comparative advantage and explain how specialization and trade add to a nation's output.

LO39.3 Explain why differences between world prices and domestic prices lead to exports and imports.

LO39.4 Analyze the economic effects of tariffs and quotas.

LO39.5 Critique the most frequently presented arguments for protectionism.

LO39.6 Explain the objectives of the WTO, EU, NAFTA, and USMCA, and discuss offshoring and trade adjustment assistance.

Backpackers in the wilderness like to think they are "leaving the world behind," but, like Atlas, they carry the world on their shoulders. Much of their equipment is imported—knives from Switzerland, rain gear from South Korea, cameras from Japan, aluminum pots from England, sleeping bags from China, and compasses from Finland.

International trade and the global economy affect all of us daily, whether we are hiking in the wilderness, driving our cars, buying groceries, or working at our jobs. We cannot "leave the world behind." We are enmeshed in a global web of economic relationships.

This chapter focuses on the trading of goods and services. In later chapters, we examine the U.S. balance of payments, exchange rates, U.S. trade deficits, and the economics of developing nations.

Some Key Trade Facts

The following are important facts relating to international trade.

>> **LO39.1** List several key facts about international trade.

- U.S. exports and imports have more than doubled as percentages of GDP since 1980.

- A *trade deficit* occurs when imports exceed exports. The United States has a trade deficit in goods. In 2021, U.S. imports of goods exceeded U.S. exports of goods by $1,091 billion.

- A *trade surplus* occurs when exports exceed imports. The United States has a trade surplus in services (such as air transportation services and financial services). In 2021, U.S. exports of services exceeded U.S. imports of services by $230 billion.

- Principal U.S. exports include chemicals, agricultural products, consumer durables, aircraft, and computer software and services (think Microsoft and Google).

- The United States is also a large exporter of educational services since all the money spent on tuition at U.S. schools by foreign students counts as a U.S. service export. During the 2019/2020 academic year the U.S. hosted over one million foreign students and reported $41 billion in education exports.

GLOBAL PERSPECTIVE 39.1

EXPORTS AS A SHARE OF GDP, SELECTED NATIONS, 2021

Some countries engage in much more international trade than other countries. The dollar value of exports exceeds 80 percent of the dollar value of GDP in Belgium and the Netherlands, which are both small European countries that do a lot of trade with large neighboring countries like France and Germany that have tens of millions of eager consumers ready to purchase Belgian and Dutch products. By contrast, exports are only 16 percent of GDP in Japan and just 10 percent in the United States, reflecting the fact that both of those countries have huge populations that are capable of consuming the large majority of output produced by domestic firms.

Source: Organisation for Economic Co-operation and Development (OECD).

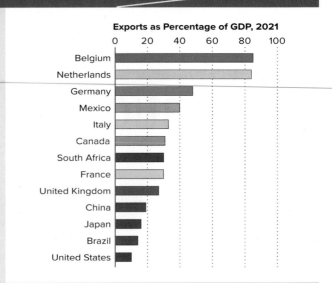

Exports as Percentage of GDP, 2021

- Principal U.S. imports include petroleum, automobiles, metals, household appliances, and computers.
- Like other advanced industrial nations, the United States imports many goods that are in the same categories as the goods that it exports. Examples include automobiles, computers, chemicals, semiconductors, and petroleum.
- Canada is the United States' most important trading partner as measured by the dollar value of trade. In 2021, about 12 percent of U.S. exported goods and services were sold to Canadians, who in turn provided 11 percent of imported U.S. goods and services.
- The United States has a sizable trade deficit in goods with China. In 2021 it was $355 billion.
- Starting in 2012, the hydraulic fracking boom greatly reduced U.S. dependence on foreign oil. In 2018, the U.S. become a net exporter of oil for the first time in 75 years as well as the world's largest producer of oil, ahead of Russia and Saudi Arabia.
- The United States leads the world in the combined volume of exports and imports, as measured in dollars.
- China, the United States, Germany, Japan, and the United Kingdom (in that order) were the top five exporters by dollars in 2020.
- Currently, the United States provides about 9.5 percent of the world's exports.
- Exports of goods and services make up about 10 percent of total U.S. output. That percentage is much lower than the percentage in many other nations, including Belgium, the Netherlands, Germany, Mexico, Canada, South Africa, and Brazil. (See Global Perspective 39.1.)
- China has become a major international trader, with an estimated $2.7 trillion of exports in 2020. Other Asian economies—including South Korea, Taiwan, and Singapore—are also active in international trade. Their combined exports exceed those of France, Britain, or Italy.
- International trade links the world's economies together. Through trade, changes in economic conditions in one place on the globe can quickly affect other places.
- International trade is often at the center of debates over economic policy, both within the United States and internationally.

With this information in mind, let's turn to the economics of international trade.

The Economic Basis for Trade

The simple answer to the question "Why do nations **trade**?" is "They trade because it is beneficial." The benefits that emerge relate to three underlying facts:

- The distribution of natural, human, and capital resources among nations is uneven; nations differ in their endowments of economic resources.

- Efficient production of various goods requires different technologies, and not all nations have the same level of technological expertise.

- Products are differentiated as to quality and other attributes, and some people may prefer certain goods imported from abroad rather than similar goods produced domestically.

To understand the interaction of these three facts, think of China, which has an abundance of inexpensive labor. As a result, China can produce efficiently (at low cost of other goods forgone) a variety of **labor-intensive goods,** such as textiles, electronics, apparel, toys, and sporting goods.

In contrast, Australia has vast amounts of land with which it can inexpensively produce such **land-intensive goods** as beef, wool, and meat. Mexico, meanwhile, has the soil, tropical climate, rainfall, and ready supply of unskilled labor that allow for the low-cost production of vegetables. And industrially advanced economies such as the United States and Germany that have relatively large amounts of capital can inexpensively produce **capital-intensive goods** such as airplanes, automobiles, agricultural equipment, machinery, and chemicals.

Also, regardless of their resource intensities, nations can develop individual products that are in demand worldwide because of their special qualities. Examples: fashions from Italy, chocolates from Belgium, software from the United States, and watches from Switzerland.

The distribution of resources, technology, and product distinctiveness among nations is relatively stable over short time periods but can change dramatically over longer time periods. When that distribution changes, the relative efficiency and success that nations have in producing and selling goods also change. As national economies evolve, the size and quality of their labor forces may change, the volume and composition of their capital stocks may shift, new technologies may develop, and even the quality of land and the quantity of natural resources may change. In short, as economists say, comparative advantage can change.

Comparative Advantage

If a country's borders are open to international trade, that country is said to have an open economy. By contrast, when a country's borders are closed to international trade, a country is said to have a closed economy.

When a country has an open economy, it will produce more of certain goods (exports) and fewer of other goods (imports) than it would if its borders were closed to international trade. That happens because an open economy will shift the use of its labor and other productive resources toward export industries and away from import industries. For example, in the presence of international trade, the United States uses more resources to make commercial aircraft and to grow wheat, and fewer resources to make television sets and to sew clothes. So we ask: Do such shifts of resources make economic sense? Do they enhance the U.S. standard of living?

The answers are affirmative. International trade and specialization increase the productivity of U.S. resources and allow the United States to obtain greater total output than otherwise would be possible. These benefits are the result of exploiting both *absolute advantage* and *comparative advantage*.

Because these concepts are often confused, let's take a moment to explain that the key difference between *absolute advantage* and *comparative advantage* lies in how a person conceptualizes what the word "efficiency" means and thus what it means for a country to be "efficient" at producing a specific product. Pay close attention in what follows to the fact that one definition has to do with inputs, while the other has to do with outputs.

>> **LO39.2** Define comparative advantage and explain how specialization and trade add to a nation's output.

trade The voluntary exchange of goods, services, or assets between two or more parties.

labor-intensive goods Products requiring relatively large amounts of *labor* to produce.

land-intensive goods Products requiring relatively large amounts of land to produce.

capital-intensive goods Products that require relatively large amounts of *capital* to produce.

- One way to think about efficiency is the way that an engineer does, in terms of how much of the product the country can make from a given amount of resource *inputs*.
- The other is to think of efficiency the way an economist does, in terms of how much of other types of *output* must be foregone to produce one unit of the product in question.

Let's use steel as an example.

absolute advantage A situation in which a person or country can produce more of a particular product from a specific quantity of resource inputs than some other person or country.

comparative advantage A situation in which a person or country can produce a specific product at a lower *opportunity cost* in terms of other types of *output* foregone than some other person or country; the basis for specialization and trade.

- A country is said to have an **absolute advantage** over other countries in the production of steel if it can produce more steel than any other country from an identical set of resource inputs.
- By contrast, a country is said to have a **comparative advantage** over other countries in the production of steel if it can produce steel at a lower *opportunity cost* in terms of alternative types of output (for instance, hamburgers or yoga lessons) that must be foregone in order to free up the resources necessary to produce one unit of steel.

In 1776, Adam Smith used the concept of absolute advantage to argue for international specialization and trade. He noted that nations will be better off if each specializes in the production of those products in which it has an absolute advantage and is therefore the most efficient producer in the engineering sense:

> It is the maxim of every prudent master of a family, never to attempt to make at home what it will cost him more to make than to buy. The taylor does not attempt to make his own shoes, but buys them of the shoemaker. The shoemaker does not attempt to make his own clothes, but employs a taylor. The farmer attempts to make neither the one nor the other, but employs those different artificers. . . .
>
> What is prudence in the conduct of every private family, can scarce be folly in that of a great kingdom. If a foreign country can supply us with a commodity cheaper than we can make it, better buy it of them with some part of the produce of our own industry, employed in a way in which we have some advantage.[1]

Adam Smith's invocation of absolute advantage as the basis of international trade struck everyone as decidedly reasonable because it lined up with engineering efficiency: each country would specialize in whatever it could produce at the lowest cost in terms of resource inputs.

But several decades later, David Ricardo realized that what matters isn't a product's cost measured in terms of the amount of inputs needed to make it but, rather, in terms of alternative products foregone to make it. If the whole purpose of production is to produce goods and services that people want to consume, then the correct way to think about the opportunity cost of producing 10 tons of steel is not "How much labor, coal, and iron ore are required to produce 10 tons of steel?" but, rather, "What other valuable consumption products have to be foregone in order to produce 10 tons of steel?" That is, the correct way to think about the opportunity cost of 10 tons of steel is not to measure the raw materials that went into producing it but, rather, all of the other products that could have been made from those same inputs.

As Ricardo pointed out, this "foregone-consumption perspective" implies that a nation does not need Smith's absolute advantage (i.e., total superiority in the engineering efficiency with which it produces products) to benefit from specialization and trade. It only needs a comparative advantage, meaning the ability to produce a product at a lower opportunity cost in terms of other consumption goods and services forgone.

Ricardo also demonstrated an even more startling fact about international trade. He showed that it is also advantageous for a country to specialize and trade with other countries even if it is *less* productive (in the engineering sense) in *all* economic activities relative to other nations. A nation with an absolute *dis*advantage in all products does not have to despair. It can also benefit from trade just as long as it has a comparative advantage in at least one product (which in practice is always the case).

The nearby Consider This story (A CPA and a House Painter) provides a simple, two-person illustration of Ricardo's principle of comparative advantage. Be sure to read it now because it will greatly help you understand the graphical analysis that follows.

---

[1]Adam Smith, *The Wealth of Nations* (originally published, 1776; New York: Modern Library, 1937), p. 424.

CONSIDER THIS . . .

A CPA and a House Painter

Suppose that Madison, a certified public accountant (CPA), is a swifter painter than Mason, the professional painter she is thinking of hiring. Also assume that Madison can earn $50 per hour as an accountant but would have to pay Mason $15 per hour. And suppose that Madison would need 30 hours to paint her house but Mason would need 40 hours.

Should Madison take time away from her accounting to paint her own house, or should she hire the painter? Madison's opportunity cost of painting her house is $1,500 (= 30 hours of sacrificed CPA time × $50 per CPA hour). The cost of hiring Mason is only $600 (= 40 hours of painting × $15 per hour of painting). Although Madison is better at both accounting and painting, she will get her house painted at lower cost by specializing in accounting

Kim Steele/Digital Vision/Getty Images

and using some of her earnings from accounting to hire a house painter.

Similarly, Mason can reduce his cost of obtaining accounting services by specializing in painting and using some of his income to hire Madison to prepare his income tax forms. Suppose Mason would need 10 hours to prepare his tax return, while Madison could handle the task in 2 hours. Mason would sacrifice $150 of income (= 10 hours of painting time × $15 per hour) to do something he could hire Madison to do for $100 (= 2 hours of CPA time × $50 per CPA hour). By specializing in painting and hiring Madison to prepare his tax return, Mason lowers the cost of getting his tax return prepared.

We will see that what is true for our CPA and house painter is also true for nations. Specializing on the basis of comparative advantage enables nations to reduce the cost of obtaining the goods and services they desire.

▶ International trade enables nations to specialize, increase productivity, and increase the amount of output available for consumption.

▶ A country is said to have an *absolute advantage* over the other producers of a product if it can produce the product more efficiently, by which we mean that it can produce more of the product from any given amount of resource inputs than can any other producer.

▶ A country is said to have a *comparative advantage* over the other producers of a product if it can produce the product at a lower opportunity cost, by which we mean that it must forgo less of the output of alternative products when allocating resources to producing the product in question.

QUICK REVIEW

39.1

Two Isolated Nations

Our goal is to place the idea of comparative advantage into the context of trading nations. Our method is to build a simple model that relies on the familiar concept of the production possibilities curve. Suppose the world consists of just two nations, the United States and Mexico. For simplicity, suppose that the labor forces in the United States and Mexico are of equal size. Each nation can produce both beef and raw (unprocessed) vegetables but at different levels of economic efficiency. Suppose the U.S. and Mexican domestic production possibilities curves for beef and vegetables are those shown in Figure 39.1a and Figure 39.1b. Note three realities relating to the production possibilities curves in the two graphs:

- *Constant costs* The curves derive from the data in Table 39.1 and are drawn as straight lines, in contrast to the bowed-outward production possibilities frontiers we examined in Chapter 1. We have therefore replaced the law of increasing opportunity costs with the assumption of constant costs. This substitution simplifies our discussion but does not impair the validity of our analysis and conclusions.

- *Different costs* The production possibilities curves of the United States and Mexico reflect different resource mixes and differing levels of technology. Specifically, the differing slopes of the two curves reflect the numbers in the figures and reveal that the opportunity costs of producing beef and vegetables differ between the two nations.

FIGURE 39.1
Production possibilities for the United States and Mexico.

The two production possibilities curves show the combinations of vegetables and beef that the United States and Mexico can produce domestically. The curves for both countries are straight lines because we are assuming constant opportunity costs. (a) As reflected by the slope of *VB* in the left graph, the opportunity-cost ratio in the United States is 1 vegetable ≡ 1 beef. (b) The production possibilities curve *vb* in the right graph has a steeper slope, reflecting the different opportunity-cost ratio in Mexico of 2 vegetables ≡ 1 beef. The difference in the opportunity-cost ratios between the two countries defines their comparative advantages and is the basis for specialization and international trade.

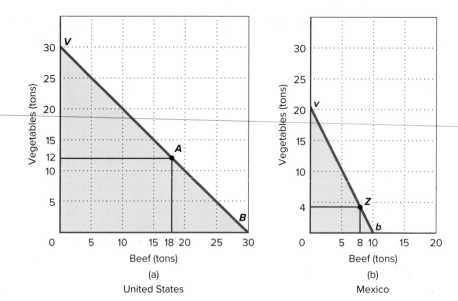

(a)
United States

(b)
Mexico

• **U.S. absolute advantage in both products** A producer (an individual, firm, or country) has an absolute advantage over another producer if it can produce more of a product than the other producer using the same amount of resources. Because of our convenient assumption that the U.S. and Mexican labor forces are the same size, the two production possibilities curves show that the United States has an absolute advantage in producing both products. If the United States and Mexico use their entire (equal-size) labor forces to produce either vegetables or beef, the United States can produce more of either than Mexico can. The United States, using the same number of workers as Mexico, has greater production possibilities. Output per worker—labor productivity—in the United States exceeds that in Mexico in producing both products.

Opportunity-Cost Ratio in the United States In Figure 39.1a, with full employment, the United States will operate at some point on its production possibilities curve. On that curve, it can increase its output of beef from 0 tons to 30 tons by forgoing 30 tons of vegetables. The *absolute value* of the slope of the production possibilities curve is 1 (= 30 vegetables/30 beef), meaning that the United States must sacrifice 1 ton of vegetables for each extra ton of beef. In the United States, the **opportunity-cost ratio** (domestic exchange ratio) for the two products is 1 ton of vegetables (V) for 1 ton of beef (B), or

United States: $1V \equiv 1B$ (The "≡" sign simply means "equivalent to")

Within its borders, the United States can "exchange" a ton of vegetables for a ton of beef. Our constant-cost assumption means that this exchange or opportunity-cost relationship prevails for all possible moves from one point to another along the U.S. production possibilities curve.

Opportunity-Cost Ratio in Mexico Mexico's production possibilities curve in Figure 39.1b represents a different full-employment opportunity-cost ratio. Mexico must give up 20 tons of

opportunity-cost ratio An equivalency showing the number of units of two products that can be produced with the same *resources;* the equivalency 1 corn ≡ 3 olives shows that the resources required to produce 3 units of olives must be shifted to corn production to produce 1 unit of corn.

TABLE 39.1 International Specialization According to Comparative Advantage and the Gains from Trade

Country	(1) Outputs before Specialization	(2) Outputs after Specialization	(3) Amounts Exported (−) and Imported (+)	(4) Outputs Available after Trade	(5) Gains from Specialization and Trade (4) − (1)
United States	18 beef	30 beef	−10 beef	20 beef	2 beef
	12 vegetables	0 vegetables	+15 vegetables	15 vegetables	3 vegetables
Mexico	8 beef	0 beef	+10 beef	10 beef	2 beef
	4 vegetables	20 vegetables	−15 vegetables	5 vegetables	1 vegetables

vegetables to obtain 10 tons of beef. The absolute value of the slope of the production possibilities curve is 2 ($= 20$ vegetables/10 beef). So, in Mexico, the opportunity-cost ratio for the two goods is 2 tons of vegetables for 1 ton of beef, or

$$\text{Mexico: } 2V \equiv 1B$$

Self-Sufficiency Output Mix If the United States and Mexico are isolated and self-sufficient, then each country must choose an output mix on its own production possibilities curve. Each will select the mix that provides it with the greatest total utility or satisfaction. Let's assume that point A in Figure 39.1a is the optimal mix in the United States. That is, society deems the combination of 18 tons of beef and 12 tons of vegetables preferable to any other combination of the goods available along the production possibilities curve. Mexico's optimal product mix is 8 tons of beef and 4 tons of vegetables, as indicated by point Z in Figure 39.1b. The two countries' choices are reflected in column 1 of Table 39.1.

Specializing Based on Comparative Advantage

A producer (an individual, firm, or nation) has a *comparative advantage* in producing a particular product if it can produce that product at a lower opportunity cost than other producers. Comparative advantage is the key determinant in whether or not nations can gain from specialization and trade. In fact, absolute advantage turns out to be irrelevant.

In our example, for instance, the United States has an absolute advantage over Mexico in producing both vegetables and beef. Still, the United States can gain from specialization and trade with Mexico because what actually matters is whether the opportunity costs of producing the two products (beef and vegetables) differ in the two countries. If they do, then each nation will enjoy a comparative advantage in one of the products. As a result, total output can increase if each country specializes in the production of the good in which it has the lower opportunity cost.

The **principle of comparative advantage** says that total output will be greatest when each good is produced by the nation that has the lowest domestic opportunity cost for producing that good. In our two-nation illustration, the United States has the lower domestic opportunity cost for beef. The United States must forgo only 1 ton of vegetables to produce 1 ton of beef, whereas Mexico must forgo 2 tons of vegetables for 1 ton of beef. The United States has a comparative (opportunity cost) advantage in beef and should specialize in beef production. The "world" (that is, the United States and Mexico) in our example would clearly not be economizing in the use of its resources if a high-cost producer (Mexico) produced a specific product (beef) when a low-cost producer (the United States) could have produced it. Having Mexico produce beef means that the world economy would have to give up more vegetables than is necessary to obtain a ton of beef.

Mexico has the lower domestic opportunity cost for vegetables. It must sacrifice only $\frac{1}{2}$ ton of beef to produce 1 ton of vegetables, while the United States must forgo 1 ton of beef to produce 1 ton of vegetables. Mexico has a comparative advantage in vegetables and should specialize in vegetable production. Again, the world would not be employing its resources economically if vegetables were produced by a high-cost producer (the United States) rather than by a low-cost producer (Mexico). If the United States produced vegetables, the world would be giving up more beef than necessary to obtain each ton of vegetables. Table 39.2 summarizes the situation.

A comparison of columns 1 and 2 in Table 39.1 verifies that specialized production enables the world to obtain more output from its fixed amount of resources. By specializing completely in beef, the United States can produce 30 tons of beef and no vegetables. Mexico, by specializing

> **principle of comparative advantage** The proposition that an individual, region, or nation will benefit if it specializes in producing goods for which its own *opportunity costs* are lower than the opportunity costs of a trading partner, and then exchanging some of the products in which it specializes for other desired products produced by others.

TABLE 39.2 Comparative-Advantage Example: A Summary

Beef	Vegetables
Mexico: Must give up 2 tons of vegetables to get 1 ton of beef.	**Mexico:** Must give up $\frac{1}{2}$ ton of beef to get 1 ton of vegetables.
United States: Must give up 1 ton of vegetables to get 1 ton of beef.	**United States:** Must give up 1 ton of beef to get 1 ton of vegetables.
Comparative advantage: United States	**Comparative advantage:** Mexico

completely in vegetables, can produce 20 tons of vegetables and no beef. These figures exceed the yields generated without specialization: 26 tons of beef (= 18 in the United States + 8 in Mexico) and 16 tons of vegetables (= 12 in the United States + 4 in Mexico) As a result, the world ends up with 4 more tons of beef (= 30 tons − 26 tons) and 4 more tons of vegetables (= 20 tons − 16 tons) than it would with self-sufficiency and unspecialized production.

Terms of Trade

terms of trade The rate at which units of one product can be exchanged for units of another product; the *price* of a *good* or *service;* the amount of one good or service that must be given up to obtain 1 unit of another good or service.

We have just seen that specialization in production will allow the largest possible amounts of both beef and vegetables to be produced. But with each country specializing in the production of only one item, how will the vegetables produced by Mexico and the beef produced by the United States be divided between consumers in the two countries? The key turns out to be the **terms of trade,** the exchange ratio at which the United States and Mexico trade beef and vegetables.

Crucially, the terms of trade also establish whether each country will find it worthwhile to bother specializing at all. Why? The terms of trade determine whether each country can "get a better deal" by specializing and trading than it could if it opted instead for self-sufficiency. For example, note that because $1B \equiv 1V (= 1V \equiv 1B)$ in the United States, it must get more than 1 ton of vegetables for each 1 ton of beef exported; otherwise, it will not benefit from exporting beef in exchange for Mexican vegetables. The United States must get a better "price" (more vegetables) for its beef through international trade than it can get domestically. Otherwise, no gain from trade exists and such trade will not occur.

Similarly, because $1B \equiv 2V (= 2V \equiv 1B)$ in Mexico, Mexico must obtain 1 ton of beef by exporting less than 2 tons of vegetables to get it. Mexico must be able to pay a lower "price" for beef in the world market than it must pay domestically. Otherwise, it will not want to trade. The international exchange ratio or terms of trade must therefore lie somewhere between

$$1B \equiv 1V \text{(United States' cost conditions)}$$

and

$$1B \equiv 2V \text{(Mexico's cost conditions)}$$

Where between these limits will the exchange ratio fall? The United States will prefer a rate close to $1B \equiv 2V$, say, $1B \equiv 1\frac{3}{4}V$. The United States wants to obtain as many vegetables as possible for each 1 ton of beef it exports. Mexico wants a rate near $1B \equiv 1V$, say, $1B \equiv 1\frac{1}{4}V$ because Mexico wants to export as few vegetables as possible for each 1 ton of beef it receives in exchange.

The actual exchange ratio (= terms of trade) depends on world supply and demand for the two products. If overall world demand for vegetables is weak relative to its supply and if the demand for beef is strong relative to its supply, the price of vegetables will be lower and the price of beef will be higher. The exchange ratio will settle nearer the $1B \equiv 2V$ terms that the United States prefers. If overall world demand for vegetables is great relative to their supply and if the demand for beef is weak relative to its supply, the ratio will settle nearer the $1B \equiv 1V$ level favorable to Mexico.

Gains from Trade

trading possibilities line A line that shows the different combinations of two products that an economy is able to obtain (consume) when it specializes in the production of one product and trades (exports) it to obtain the other product.

Suppose the international terms of trade are $1B \equiv 1\frac{1}{2}V$. The possibility of trading on these terms permits each nation to augment its domestic production possibilities curve with a trading possibilities line (or curve), as shown in **Figure 39.2 (Key Graph).** Just as a production possibilities curve shows the amounts of these products that a full-employment economy can obtain by shifting resources from one to the other, a **trading possibilities line** shows the amounts of the two products that a nation can obtain by specializing in one product and trading for the other. The trading possibilities lines in Figure 39.2 reflect the assumption that both nations specialize on the basis of comparative advantage: The United States specializes completely in beef (at point *B* in Figure 39.2a), and Mexico specializes completely in vegetables (at point *v* in Figure 39.2b).

Improved Alternatives With specialization and trade, the United States is no longer constrained by its domestic production possibilities line, which requires it to give up 1 ton of beef for every

..ıll KEY GRAPH

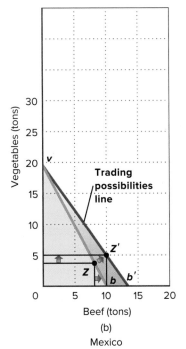

FIGURE 39.2 Trading possibilities lines and the gains from trade.

As a result of specialization and trade, both the United States and Mexico can have higher levels of output than the levels attainable on their domestic production possibilities curves. (a) The United States can move from point *A* on its domestic production possibilities curve to, say, *A'* on its trading possibilities line. (b) Mexico can move from *Z* to *Z'*.

QUICK QUIZ FOR FIGURE 39.2

1. **The production possibilities curves in graphs (a) and (b) imply:**
   a. increasing domestic opportunity costs.
   b. decreasing domestic opportunity costs.
   c. constant domestic opportunity costs.
   d. first decreasing, then increasing domestic opportunity costs.

2. **Before specialization, the domestic opportunity cost of producing 1 unit of beef is:**
   a. 1 unit of vegetables in both the United States and Mexico.
   b. 1 unit of vegetables in the United States and 2 units of vegetables in Mexico.
   c. 2 units of vegetables in the United States and 1 unit of vegetables in Mexico.
   d. 1 unit of vegetables in the United States and $\frac{1}{2}$ unit of vegetables in Mexico.

3. **After specialization and international trade, the world output of beef and vegetables is:**
   a. 20 tons of beef and 20 tons of vegetables.
   b. 45 tons of beef and 15 tons of vegetables.
   c. 30 tons of beef and 20 tons of vegetables.
   d. 10 tons of beef and 30 tons of vegetables.

4. **After specialization and international trade:**
   a. the United States can obtain units of vegetables at less cost than it could before trade.
   b. Mexico can obtain more than 20 tons of vegetables, if it so chooses.
   c. the United States no longer has a comparative advantage in producing beef.
   d. Mexico can benefit by prohibiting vegetables imports from the United States.

Answers: 1. c; 2. b; 3. c; 4. a

---

1 ton of vegetables. Instead, through trade with Mexico, the United States can get $1\frac{1}{2}$ tons of vegetables for every ton of beef that it exports to Mexico, as long as Mexico has vegetables to export. Trading possibilities line *BV'* thus represents the $1B \equiv 1\frac{1}{2}V$ trading ratio.

Similarly, Mexico no longer has to move down its domestic production possibilities curve, giving up 2 tons of vegetables for each ton of beef. It can now export just $1\frac{1}{2}$ tons of vegetables for each 1 ton of beef that it wants by moving down its trading possibilities line *vb'*.

Specialization and trade create a new exchange ratio between beef and vegetables, and each nation's trading possibilities line reflects that ratio. For both nations, this exchange ratio is superior to the unspecialized (domestic only) exchange ratio embodied in their respective production possibilities curves. In both countries, self-sufficiency is inefficient and therefore undesirable.

▶ The principle of comparative advantage says that total world output will be greatest when each good is produced by the nation that has the lowest domestic opportunity cost.

▶ The rate at which countries can trade units of one product for units of another product is referred to as the terms of trade.

▶ A trading possibilities line shows the amounts of two products that a nation can obtain by specializing in the production of one product and then trading for the other.

gains from trade The extra output that trading partners obtain through specialization of production and exchange of *goods* and *services*.

Greater Output Specialization according to comparative advantage results in a more efficient allocation of world resources, and larger outputs of both products are therefore available to both nations.

Suppose that at the $1B \equiv 1\frac{1}{2}V$ terms of trade, the United States exports 10 tons of beef to Mexico and, in return, Mexico exports 15 tons of vegetables to the United States. How do the new quantities of beef and vegetables available to the two nations compare with the optimal product mixes that existed before specialization and trade? Point A in Figure 39.2a reminds us that the United States chose 18 tons of beef and 12 tons of vegetables originally. But by producing 30 tons of beef and no vegetables and by trading 10 tons of beef for 15 tons of vegetables, the United States can obtain 20 tons of beef and 15 tons of vegetables. This new, superior combination of beef and vegetables is indicated by point A′ in Figure 39.2a. The United States' **gains from trade** are 2 tons of beef *and* 3 tons of vegetables.

Similarly, recall that Mexico's optimal product mix was 4 tons of vegetables and 8 tons of beef (point Z) before specialization and trade. Now, after specializing in vegetables and trading for beef, Mexico can have 5 tons of vegetables and 10 tons of beef. It accomplishes that by producing 20 tons of vegetables and no beef and exporting 15 tons of its vegetables in exchange for 10 tons of American beef. This new position is indicated by point Z′ in Figure 39.2b. Mexico's gains from trade are 1 ton of vegetables *and* 2 tons of beef.

Points A′ and Z′ in Figure 39.2 are superior economic positions to points A and Z. This fact is enormously important! We know that a nation can expand its production possibilities boundary either by (1) expanding the quantity and improving the quality of its resources or by (2) implementing technological improvements. We have now established that international trade enables a nation to circumvent the output constraint illustrated by its production possibilities curve. An economy can grow by expanding international trade. The outcome of international specialization and trade is equivalent to having more and better resources or discovering and implementing improved production techniques.

Table 39.1 summarizes the transactions and outcomes in our analysis. Please give it one final careful review.

Trade with Increasing Opportunity Costs

To explain the basic principles underlying international trade, we simplified our analysis in several ways. For example, we limited discussion to two products and two nations. But multiproduct and multinational analysis yield the same conclusions. We also assumed constant opportunity costs (linear production possibilities curves), which is a more substantive simplification. Let's consider the effect of allowing increasing opportunity costs (concave-to-the-origin production possibilities curves) to enter the picture.

Suppose that the United States and Mexico are initially at positions on their concave production possibilities curves where their domestic cost ratios are $1B \equiv 1V$ and $1B \equiv 2V$, as they were in our constant-cost analysis. As before, comparative advantage indicates that the United States should specialize in beef and Mexico in vegetables. But now, as the United States begins to expand beef production, its cost of beef will rise; it will have to sacrifice more than 1 ton of vegetables to get 1 additional ton of beef. Resources are no longer perfectly substitutable between alternative uses, as the constant-cost assumption implied. Resources less and less suitable to beef production must be allocated to the U.S. beef industry in expanding beef output, and that means increasing costs—the sacrifice of larger and larger amounts of vegetables for each additional ton of beef.

Similarly, suppose that Mexico expands vegetable production starting from its $1B \equiv 2V$ cost ratio position. As production increases, it will find that its $1B \equiv 2V$ cost ratio begins to rise. Sacrificing 1 ton of beef will free resources that are capable of producing only something less than 2 tons of vegetables because those transferred resources are less suitable to vegetable production.

As the U.S. cost ratio falls from $1B \equiv 1V$ and the Mexican ratio rises from $1B \equiv 2V$, a point will be reached where the cost ratios are equal in the two nations, perhaps at $1B \equiv 1\frac{3}{4}V$. At this point, the underlying basis for further specialization and trade—differing cost ratios—has disappeared, and further specialization is therefore uneconomical. And, most important, this point of equal cost ratios may be reached while the United States is still producing some vegetables along with its beef and Mexico is still producing some beef along with its vegetables. The primary effect of increasing opportunity costs is less-than-complete specialization. For this reason, we often find domestically produced products competing directly against identical or similar imported products within a particular economy.

The Case for Free Trade

The case for free trade can be reduced to one compelling argument: Through free trade based on the principle of comparative advantage, the world economy can achieve a more efficient allocation of resources and a higher level of material well-being than it can without free trade.

Because the resource mixes and technological knowledge of the world's nations are all somewhat different, each nation can produce particular commodities at different opportunity costs. Each nation should produce goods for which its domestic opportunity costs are lower than the domestic opportunity costs of other nations, and it should exchange those goods for products for which its domestic opportunity costs are higher than those of other nations. If every nation follows this guideline, the world will realize the advantages of geographic and human specialization. The world and each free-trading nation will obtain a larger real income from its fixed supplies of resources.

Government trade barriers lessen or eliminate gains from specialization. If nations cannot trade freely, they must shift resources from efficient (low-cost) to inefficient (high-cost) uses to satisfy their diverse wants. A recent study estimates household income in the United States to be about $18,000 per year higher than it would otherwise be thanks to the massive decline in tariff rates since the end of World War II.[2] To put that figure in perspective, note that median household income in the United States in 2020 was a little under $70,000 per year. Thus, around a quarter of today's median household income can be attributed to falling tariff rates and the benefits that derive from international specialization and trade.

One side benefit of free trade is that it promotes competition and deters monopoly. The increased competition from foreign firms forces domestic firms to find and use the lowest-cost production techniques. It also compels them to be innovative with respect to both product quality and production methods, thereby contributing to economic growth. In addition, free trade gives consumers a wider range of product choices. Finally, free trade links national interests and breaks down national animosities. Confronted with political disagreements, trading partners tend to negotiate rather than make war.

[2]Gary Clyde Hufbauer and Zhiyao (Lucy) Lu, "The Payoff to America from Globalization: A Fresh Look with a Focus on Costs to Workers," Peterson Institute for International Economics, *Policy Brief 17-16,* May 2017 (updated).

QUICK REVIEW 39.3

▶ International trade enables nations to specialize, increase productivity, and increase output available for consumption.

▶ Comparative advantage means total world output will be greatest when each good is produced by the nation that has the lowest domestic opportunity cost.

▶ Specialization is less than complete among nations because opportunity costs normally rise as any specific nation produces more of a particular good.

Supply and Demand Analysis of Exports and Imports

Supply and demand analysis reveals how equilibrium prices and quantities of exports and imports are determined. The amount of a good or a service that a nation will export or import depends on differences between the equilibrium world price and the equilibrium domestic price. The interaction of *world* supply and demand determines the equilibrium **world price**—the price that equates the quantities supplied and demanded globally through international trade. By contrast, the interaction of *domestic* supply and demand determines the equilibrium **domestic price**—the price that would prevail in a closed economy that does not engage in international trade. The domestic price equates quantity supplied and quantity demanded domestically.

In the absence of trade, the domestic prices in a closed economy may or may not equal the world equilibrium prices. When economies are opened for international trade, differences between

>> **LO39.3** Explain why differences between world prices and domestic prices lead to exports and imports.

world price The international market *price* of a *good* or *service*, determined by world demand and supply.

domestic price The *price* of a *good* or *service* within a country, determined by domestic demand and supply.

world and domestic prices encourage exports or imports. To understand why, consider the international effects of price differences in a simple two-nation world, consisting of the United States and Canada, which are both producing aluminum. We assume there are no trade barriers, such as tariffs and quotas, and no international transportation costs.

Supply and Demand in the United States

Figure 39.3a shows the domestic supply curve S_d and the domestic demand curve D_d for aluminum in the United States, which for now is a closed economy. The intersection of S_d and D_d determines the equilibrium domestic price of $1 per pound and the equilibrium domestic quantity of 100 million pounds. Domestic suppliers produce 100 million pounds and sell them all at $1 a pound. There are no domestic surpluses or shortages of aluminum. But what would happen if the U.S. economy is opened to trade and the world price of aluminum is above or below this $1 domestic price?

U.S. Export Supply If the aluminum price in the rest of the world (that is, Canada) exceeds $1, U.S. firms will produce more than 100 million pounds and will export the excess domestic output. First, consider a world price of $1.25. We see from the supply curve S_d that U.S. aluminum firms will produce 125 million pounds of aluminum at that price. The demand curve D_d tells us that U.S. consumers will purchase only 75 million pounds at $1.25. The outcome is a domestic surplus of 50 million pounds of aluminum. U.S. producers will export those 50 million pounds at the $1.25 world price.

What if the world price is $1.50? The supply curve shows that U.S. firms will produce 150 million pounds of aluminum, while the demand curve tells us that domestic consumers will buy only 50 million pounds. So U.S. producers will export the domestic surplus of 100 million pounds.

In the upper half of Figure 39.3b, we plot the domestic surpluses—the U.S. exports—that occur at world prices above the $1 domestic equilibrium price. When the world and domestic prices are equal (= $1), the quantity of exports supplied is zero (point a) because there is no surplus of domestic output available to export at that price. When the world price is $1.25, U.S. firms export 50 million pounds of surplus aluminum (point b). At a $1.50 world price, the domestic surplus of 100 million pounds is exported (point c).

FIGURE 39.3 **U.S. export supply and import demand.**

(a) Domestic supply S_d and demand D_d set the domestic equilibrium price of aluminum at $1 per pound. At world prices above $1, there are domestic surpluses of aluminum. At prices below $1, there are domestic shortages. (b) Surpluses are exported (top curve), and shortages are met by importing aluminum (lower curve). The export supply curve shows the direct relationship between world prices and U.S. exports; the import demand curve portrays the inverse relationship between world prices and U.S. imports.

(a)
U.S. domestic aluminum market

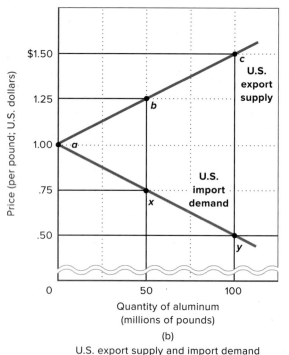

(b)
U.S. export supply and import demand

The U.S. **export supply curve,** found by connecting points *a*, *b*, and *c*, shows the amount of aluminum that U.S. producers will export at each world price above $1. This curve *slopes upward*, indicating a direct or positive relationship between the world price and the amount of U.S. exports. As world prices increase relative to domestic prices, U.S. exports rise.

U.S. Import Demand If the world price is below the domestic $1 price, the United States will import aluminum. Consider a $0.75 world price. The supply curve in Figure 39.3a reveals that at that price U.S. firms produce only 75 million pounds of aluminum. But the demand curve shows that the United States wants to buy 125 million pounds at that price. The result is a domestic shortage of 50 million pounds. To satisfy that shortage, the United States will import 50 million pounds of aluminum.

At an even lower world price, $0.50, U.S. producers will supply only 50 million pounds. Because U.S. consumers want to buy 150 million pounds at that price, there is a domestic shortage of 100 million pounds. Imports will flow to the United States to make up the difference. That is, at a $0.50 world price U.S. firms will supply 50 million pounds, and 100 million pounds will be imported.

In the lower half of Figure 39.3b, we plot the U.S. **import demand curve** from these data. This *downward sloping curve* shows the amounts of aluminum that the United States will import at world prices below the $1 U.S. domestic price. The relationship between world prices and imported amounts is inverse or negative. At a world price of $1, domestic output will satisfy U.S. demand; imports will be zero (point *a*). At $0.75, the United States will import 50 million pounds of aluminum (point *x*); at $0.50, the United States will import 100 million pounds (point *y*). Connecting points *a*, *x*, and *y* yields the *downward sloping* U.S. import demand curve. It reveals that as world prices fall relative to U.S. domestic prices, U.S. imports increase.

export supply curve An upward sloping curve that shows the amount of a product that domestic *firms* will export at each *world price* that is above the *domestic price*.

import demand curve A downsloping curve showing the amount of a product that an economy will import at each *world price* below the *domestic price*.

Supply and Demand in Canada

We repeat our analysis in Figure 39.4, this time from Canada's viewpoint. (We have converted Canadian dollar prices to U.S. dollar prices via the exchange rate.) Note that the domestic supply curve S_d and the domestic demand curve D_d for aluminum in Canada yield a domestic price of $0.75, which is $0.25 lower than the $1 U.S. domestic price.

FIGURE 39.4 Canadian export supply and import demand.

(a) At world prices above the $0.75 domestic price, production in Canada exceeds domestic consumption. At world prices below $0.75, domestic shortages occur. (b) Surpluses result in exports, and shortages result in imports. The Canadian export supply curve and import demand curve depict the relationships between world prices and exports or imports.

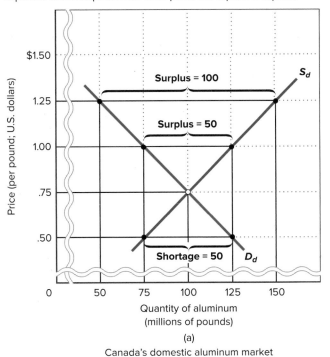

(a)
Canada's domestic aluminum market

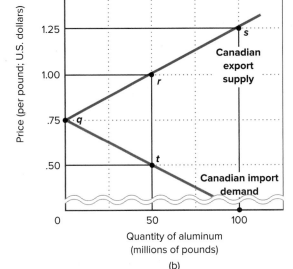

(b)
Canada's export supply and import demand

The analysis proceeds exactly as above except that the domestic price is now the Canadian price. If the world price is $0.75, Canadians will neither export nor import aluminum (giving us point *q* in Figure 39.4b). At world prices above $0.75, Canadian firms will produce more aluminum than Canadian consumers will buy. Canadian firms will export the surplus. When the world price is $1, Figure 39.4b tells us that Canada will have (and will export) a domestic surplus of 50 million pounds (yielding point *r*). At $1.25, it will have (and will export) a domestic surplus of 100 million pounds (point *s*). Connecting these points yields the upward sloping Canadian export supply curve, which reflects the domestic surpluses (and hence the exports) that occur when the world price exceeds the $0.75 Canadian domestic price.

At world prices below $0.75, domestic shortages occur in Canada. When the world price is $0.50, Figure 39.4a shows that Canadian consumers want to buy 125 million pounds of aluminum, but Canadian firms will produce only 75 million pounds. The shortage will bring 50 million pounds of imports to Canada (point *t* in Figure 39.4b). The Canadian import demand curve in that figure shows the Canadian imports that will occur at all world aluminum prices below the $0.75 Canadian domestic price.

Equilibrium World Price, Exports, and Imports

equilibrium world price
The *price* of an internationally traded product that equates the quantity of the product demanded by importers with the quantity of the product supplied by exporters; the price determined at the intersection of the export supply curve and the import demand curve.

We now have the tools for determining the **equilibrium world price** of aluminum and the equilibrium world levels of exports and imports when the world is opened to trade. Figure 39.5 combines the U.S. export supply curve and import demand curve shown in Figure 39.3b with the Canadian export supply curve and import demand curve that we derived in Figure 39.4b. The two U.S. curves proceed rightward from the $1 U.S. domestic price; the two Canadian curves proceed rightward from the $0.75 Canadian domestic price.

International equilibrium occurs in this two-nation model where one nation's import demand curve intersects another nation's export supply curve. In this case, the U.S. import demand curve intersects Canada's export supply curve at *e*. There, the world price of aluminum is $0.88. The Canadian export supply curve indicates that Canada will export 25 million pounds of aluminum at this price. Also at this price the United States will import 25 million pounds from Canada, indicated by the U.S. import demand curve. The $0.88 world price equates the quantity of imports demanded and the quantity of exports supplied (25 million pounds). Thus, there will be world trade of 25 million pounds of aluminum at $0.88 per pound.

After trade, the single $0.88 world price will prevail in both Canada and the United States. Only one price for a standardized commodity can persist in a highly competitive world market. With trade, all consumers can buy a pound of aluminum for $0.88, and all producers can sell it for that price. This world price means that Canadians will pay more for aluminum with trade ($0.88) than without it ($0.75). The increased Canadian output caused by trade raises Canadian per-unit production costs and therefore raises the price of aluminum in Canada. The United States, however, pays less for aluminum with trade ($0.88) than without it ($1). The U.S. gain comes from Canada's comparative cost advantage in producing aluminum.

Why would Canada willingly send 25 million pounds of its aluminum output to the United States for U.S. consumption? After all, producing this output uses up scarce Canadian resources and drives up the price of aluminum for Canadians. Canadians are willing to export aluminum to the United States because

FIGURE 39.5
Equilibrium world price and quantity of exports and imports.

In a two-nation world, the equilibrium world price (= $0.88) is determined by the intersection of one nation's export supply curve and the other nation's import demand curve. This intersection also decides the equilibrium volume of exports and imports. Here, Canada exports 25 million pounds of aluminum to the United States.

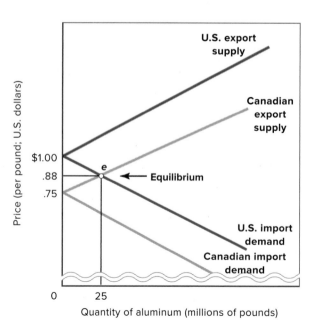

Quantity of aluminum (millions of pounds)

Canadians gain the means—the U.S. dollars—to import other goods, say, computer software, from the United States. Canadian exports enable Canadians to acquire imports that have greater value to Canadians than the exported aluminum. Canadian exports to the United States finance Canadian imports from the United States.

▶ A nation will export a particular product if the world price exceeds the domestic price; it will import the product if the world price is less than the domestic price.

▶ In a two-country world model, equilibrium world prices and equilibrium quantities of exports and imports occur where one nation's export supply curve intersects the other nation's import demand curve.

**QUICK REVIEW
39.4**

Trade Barriers and Export Subsidies

While a nation as a whole gains from trade, trade may harm particular domestic industries and their workers. Those industries might seek to preserve their economic positions by persuading their respective governments to protect them from imports—perhaps through tariffs, import quotas, or other trade barriers.

Indeed, the public may be won over by the apparent plausibility ("Cut imports and prevent domestic unemployment") and the patriotic ring ("Buy American!") of the arguments. The alleged benefits of tariffs are immediate and clear-cut to the public, but the adverse effects cited by economists are obscure and dispersed over the entire economy. When political deal-making is added in—"You back tariffs for the apparel industry in *my* state, and I'll back tariffs for the auto industry in *your* state"—the outcome can be a politically robust network of trade barriers. These impediments to free international trade can take several forms.

Tariffs are excise taxes or "duties" on the dollar values or physical quantities of imported goods. They may be imposed to obtain revenue or to protect domestic firms. A **revenue tariff** is usually applied to a product that is not being produced domestically, for example, tin, coffee, or bananas in the case of the United States. Revenue tariffs are designed to provide the federal government with revenue, and their rates tend to be modest. A **protective tariff** is implemented to shield domestic producers from foreign competition. These tariffs impede free trade by increasing the prices of imported goods and therefore shifting sales toward domestic producers. Although protective tariffs are usually not high enough to stop the importation of foreign goods, they put foreign producers at a competitive disadvantage. A tariff on imported auto tires, for example, will make domestically produced tires more attractive to consumers.

An **import quota** is a government-imposed limit on the quantities or total values of specific items that are imported in some period. Once a quota is filled, further imports of that product are prohibited. Import quotas are more effective than tariffs in impeding international trade. With a tariff, a product can go on being imported in large quantities. But with an import quota, all imports are prohibited once the quota is filled.

A **voluntary export restriction (VER)** is a trade barrier by which foreign firms "voluntarily" limit the amount of their exports to a particular country. VERs have the same effect as import quotas. Exporters agree to them to avoid more stringent tariffs or quotas. In the late 1990s, for example, Canadian producers of softwood lumber (fir, spruce, cedar, pine) agreed to a VER on exports to the United States under the threat of a permanently higher U.S. tariff.

Nontariff barriers (NTBs) include onerous licensing requirements, unreasonable standards pertaining to product quality, or simply bureaucratic hurdles and delays in customs procedures. Some nations require importers of foreign goods to obtain licenses and then restrict the number of licenses issued. Japan and several European countries require domestic importers of several types of foreign goods to obtain licenses. By restricting the number of licenses, governments can limit imports.

An **export subsidy** is a government payment to a domestic producer of export goods designed to aid that producer in attracting foreign buyers for its output. By offsetting some of a firm's production costs, the subsidies enable the domestic firm to charge a lower price and thus to sell more exports in world markets. For example, the United States and other nations have subsidized domestic farmers to boost the domestic food supply. These subsidies have artificially lowered the export prices of U.S. agricultural exports.

>> **LO39.4** Analyze the economic effects of tariffs and quotas.

tariff A *tax* imposed by a nation on an imported good.

revenue tariff A *tariff* designed to produce *income* for the federal government.

protective tariff A *tariff* designed to shield domestic producers of a *good* or *service* from the competition of foreign producers.

import quota A limit imposed by a nation on the quantity (or total value) of a good that may be imported during some period of time.

voluntary export restrictions (VER) Voluntary limitations by countries or *firms* of their exports to a particular foreign nation; undertaken to avoid the enactment of formal trade barriers by the foreign nation.

nontariff barriers (NTBs) All barriers other than *protective tariffs* that nations erect to impede international trade, including *import quotas*, licensing requirements, unreasonable product-quality standards, unnecessary bureaucratic detail in customs procedures, and so on.

export subsidy A government payment to a domestic producer to enable the *firm* to reduce the *price* of a *good* or *service* to foreign buyers.

..ıll KEY GRAPH

FIGURE 39.6 **The economic effects of protective tariffs and import quotas.**

This economy is initially closed to international trade, so that the equilibrium price and quantity are determined by the intersection of domestic demand D_d and domestic supply S_d. When the economy is opened to trade, the domestic price falls to the world price P_w, with domestic consumers purchasing d units and domestic suppliers producing a units. A tariff that increases the price of the product from P_w to P_t will reduce domestic consumption from d to c. Domestic producers will be able to sell more output (b rather than a) at a higher price (P_t rather than P_w). Foreign exporters are injured because they sell less output (bc rather than ad). The yellow area indicates the amount of tariff paid by domestic consumers. An import quota of $Q = bc$ units causes the supply curve to shift right by bc units to $S_d + Q$, thereby shifting the equilibrium to where domestic demand D_d intersects $S_d + Q$. The import quota of bc units has the same effects as the tariff, with one exception: The amount represented by the yellow area will go to foreign producers rather than to the domestic government.

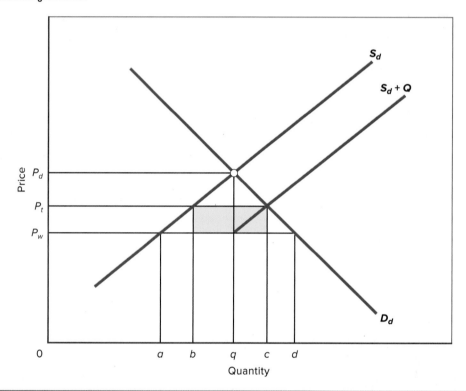

QUICK QUIZ FOR FIGURE 39.6

1. **If the government set the import quota at *ad* units instead of *bc* units, the supply curve $S_d + Q$ would intersect domestic demand D_d at:**
   a. the domestic price P_d, and imports would equal zero.
   b. the tariff price P_t, and imports would equal *bc*.
   c. the tariff price P_t, and imports would equal *ad*.
   d. the world price P_w, and imports would equal *ad* units.

2. **If the government set an import quota greater than zero but less than *bc*, the price would be:**
   a. higher than P_d.
   b. between P_t and P_d.
   c. between P_w and P_t.
   d. less than P_w.

3. **If the government cuts the tariff in half, domestic producers will see their sales:**
   a. increase
   b. decrease.
   c. fall by half.
   d. double.

4. **If the government sets the tariff equal to $P_d - P_w$ dollars, the trade deficit will:**
   a. increase to *ab*.
   b. decrease to zero
   c. increase to $P_d - P_t$.
   d. remain steady at *bc*.

Answers: 1. d; 2. b; 3. b; 4. b

Economic Impact of Tariffs

We will confine our in-depth analysis of the effects of trade barriers to the two most common types of trade barriers: tariffs and quotas. Once again, we turn to supply-and-demand analysis for help. Curves D_d and S_d in **Figure 39.6 (Key Graph)** show domestic demand and supply for a product in which a nation, say, the United States, does *not* have a comparative advantage—for example, smartphones. (Disregard curve $S_d + Q$ for now.) Without world trade, the domestic price and output will be P_d and q, respectively.

Assume now that the domestic economy is opened to world trade and that China, which *does* have a comparative advantage in smartphones, begins to sell its smartphones in the United States. We assume that with free trade the domestic price cannot differ from the world price, which here is P_w. At P_w, domestic consumption is d and domestic production is a. The horizontal distance between the domestic supply and demand curves at P_w represents imports of ad. Thus far, our analysis is similar to the analysis of world prices in Figure 39.3.

Direct Effects Suppose now that the United States imposes a tariff on each imported smartphone. The tariff, which raises the price of imported smartphones from P_w to P_t, has four effects:

- *Decline in consumption* Consumption of smartphones in the United States declines from d to c as the higher price moves buyers up and to the left along their demand curve. The tariff prompts consumers to buy fewer smartphones and reallocate a portion of their expenditures to less-desired substitute products. U.S. consumers are clearly injured by the tariff, because they pay $P_t - P_w$ more for each of the c units they buy at price P_t.

- *Increased domestic production* U.S. producers—which are not subject to the tariff—receive the higher price P_t per unit. Because this new price is higher than the pretariff world price P_w, the domestic smartphone industry moves up and to the right along its supply curve S_d, increasing domestic output from a to b. Domestic producers thus enjoy both a higher price *and* expanded sales, which explains why domestic producers lobby for protective tariffs. From a social point of view, however, the increase in domestic production from a to b means that the tariff permits domestic producers of smartphones to bid resources away from other, more efficient, U.S. industries.

- *Decline in imports* Chinese producers are hurt. Although the sales price of each smartphone that they sell in the United States is higher by $P_t - P_w$, that amount accrues to the U.S. government, not to Chinese producers. The after-tariff world price, or the per-unit revenue to Chinese producers, remains at P_w, but the volume of U.S. imports (Chinese exports) falls from ad to bc.

- *Tariff revenue* The yellow rectangle represents the amount of revenue the tariff yields. Total revenue from the tariff is determined by multiplying the tariff, $P_t - P_w$ per unit, by the number of smartphones imported, bc. This tariff revenue is a transfer of income from consumers to government and does not represent any net change in the nation's economic well-being. The result is that government gains this portion of what consumers lose by paying more for smartphones.

Indirect Effect Tariffs have a subtle effect beyond what our supply and demand diagram can show. Because China sells fewer smartphones in the United States, it earns fewer dollars and so must buy fewer U.S. exports. U.S. export industries must then cut production and release resources. These are highly efficient industries, as we know from their comparative advantage and their ability to sell goods in world markets.

Tariffs directly promote the expansion of inefficient industries that do not have a comparative advantage. They also indirectly cause the contraction of relatively efficient industries that do have a comparative advantage. Put bluntly, tariffs shift resources in the wrong direction—and that is not surprising. We know that specialization and world trade lead to more efficient use of world resources and greater world output. But protective tariffs reduce world trade. Therefore, tariffs also reduce efficiency and the world's real output.

Economic Impact of Quotas

Quotas have the same economic impact as a tariff, with one big difference: While tariffs generate revenue for the domestic government, a quota transfers that revenue to foreign producers.

Suppose in Figure 39.6 that, instead of imposing a tariff, the United States prohibits any imports of Chinese smartphones in excess of bc units. In other words, an import quota of bc smartphones is imposed on China. We deliberately chose the size of this quota to be the same amount as imports would be under a $P_t - P_w$ tariff so that we can compare "equivalent" situations. As a consequence of the quota, the supply of smartphones is $S_d + Q$ in the United States. This supply consists of the domestic supply plus the fixed amount bc ($= Q$) that importers will provide at each domestic price. The supply curve $S_d + Q$ does not extend below price P_w because Chinese producers will not export any smartphones to the United States at any price below P_w. Instead, they would sell them to other countries at the world market price of P_w.

Most of the economic results are the same as those with a tariff. Prices of smartphones are higher (P_t instead of P_w) because imports have been reduced from ad to bc. Domestic consumption of smartphones is down from d to c. U.S. producers enjoy both a higher price (P_t rather than P_w) and increased sales (b rather than a).

The difference between tariffs and quotas is that the price increase of $P_t - P_w$ paid by U.S. consumers on imports of bc—the yellow area—no longer goes to the U.S. Treasury as tariff (tax) revenue but flows to the Chinese firms that have acquired the quota rights to sell smartphones in the United States. For consumers in the United States, a tariff produces a better economic outcome than a quota, other things being the same. A tariff generates government revenue that can be used to cut other taxes or to finance public goods and services that benefit the United States. In contrast, the higher price created by quotas results in additional revenue for foreign producers.

**QUICK REVIEW
39.5**

▶ A tariff on a product increases its price, reduces its consumption, increases its domestic production, reduces its imports, and generates tariff revenue for the government.

▶ An import quota does the same, except a quota generates revenue for foreign producers rather than for the government imposing the quota.

Net Costs of Tariffs and Quotas

Study after study finds that the costs of tariffs and quotas to consumers substantially exceed the gains to producers and government. A sizable net cost or efficiency loss to society arises from trade protection. Furthermore, industries employ large amounts of economic resources to influence Congress to pass and maintain protectionist laws. Because these rent-seeking efforts divert resources away from more socially desirable purposes, trade restrictions impose these additional costs on society as well.

Conclusion: The gains that U.S. trade barriers create for protected industries and their workers come at the expense of much greater losses for the entire economy. The result is economic inefficiency, reduced consumption, and lower standards of living.

The Case for Protection: A Critical Review

>> **LO39.5** Critique the most frequently presented arguments for protectionism.

Despite the logic of specialization and trade, protectionists still exist in some union halls, corporate boardrooms, and political conference rooms. What arguments do protectionists make to justify trade barriers? How valid are those arguments?

Military Self-Sufficiency Argument

The argument here is not economic but political-military: Protective tariffs can preserve or strengthen industries that produce the materials essential for national defense. In an uncertain world, political-military objectives (self-sufficiency) sometimes must take precedence over economic goals (efficiency in the use of world resources).

Unfortunately, it is difficult to measure and compare the benefit of increased national security against the cost of economic inefficiency when protective tariffs are imposed. Economists can only point out that when a nation levies tariffs to increase military self-sufficiency, it incurs economic costs.

All people in the United States would agree that relying on hostile nations for necessary military equipment is not a good idea, yet the self-sufficiency argument is open to serious abuse. Nearly every industry can claim that it makes direct or indirect contributions to national security and hence deserves protection from imports.

Diversification-for-Stability Argument

Highly specialized economies such as Saudi Arabia (based on oil) and Cuba (based on sugar) are dependent on international markets for their income. In these economies, wars, international political developments, recessions abroad, and random fluctuations in world supply and demand for one or two particular goods can cause deep declines in export revenues and therefore in domestic income. Tariff and quota protections are allegedly needed in such nations to enable greater industrial diversification and greater domestic stability.

There is some truth in this diversification-for-stability argument. But the argument has little or no relevance to the United States and other advanced economies with highly diversified economies.

Infant Industry Argument

The infant industry argument contends that protective tariffs can allow new domestic industries to establish themselves. Temporarily shielding young domestic firms from the severe competition of more mature and more efficient foreign firms gives infant industries a chance to develop and become efficient producers. Tariff protection for such infant industries will correct for a misallocation of world resources that was caused by historically different levels of economic development between domestic and foreign industries.

There are some logical problems with the infant industry argument. For instance, it is difficult to determine which infant industries are capable of achieving economic maturity and therefore deserve protection. Also, protective tariffs may persist even after industrial maturity has been realized.

Most economists believe that if infant industries are to be subsidized, there are better means than tariffs for doing so. Direct subsidies, for example, have the advantage of making explicit which industries are being aided and to what degree.

Protection-Against-Dumping Argument

The protection-against-dumping argument contends that tariffs can protect domestic firms from "dumping" by foreign producers. **Dumping** is the sale of a product in a foreign country at prices either below cost or below the prices commonly charged at home. Foreign companies may dump their goods to drive their competitors out of business. If that company is a monopoly in the home country, it may dump its good for a lower price in foreign countries in order to achieve the per-unit cost savings associated with large-scale production.

dumping The sale of a product in a foreign country at *prices* either below cost or below the prices commonly charged at home.

Because dumping is an "unfair trade practice," most nations prohibit it. For example, where dumping is shown to injure U.S. firms, the federal government imposes tariffs called *antidumping duties* on the goods in question. But relatively few documented cases of dumping occur each year, and specific instances of unfair trade do not justify widespread, permanent tariffs. Moreover, antidumping duties can be abused. Often, what is alleged to be dumping is simply comparative advantage at work.

Increased Domestic Employment Argument

Arguing for a tariff to "save U.S. jobs" becomes fashionable when the economy encounters a recession. In an economy that engages in international trade, exports involve residents of foreign countries spending their money to purchase domestically produced output, while imports reflect domestic residents spending their money to obtain output produced in foreign countries. So, according to this argument, reducing imports will divert spending that is currently being used to purchase another nation's output toward purchases of domestically produced output. Thus, domestic output and employment will rise.

This "increased domestic employment" argument has several shortcomings. First, while imports may eliminate some U.S. jobs, they create others. Thus, while imports have indeed eliminated the jobs of some U.S. steel and textile workers in recent decades, other workers have gained jobs unloading ships, flying imported aircraft, and selling imported electronic equipment. Import restrictions alter the composition of employment, but they may have little or no effect on the overall volume of employment.

Smoot-Hawley Tariff Act Legislation passed in 1930 that established very high *tariffs*. Its objective was to reduce *imports* and stimulate the domestic economy, but it resulted only in retaliatory tariffs by other nations.

Second, nations adversely affected by tariffs and quotas are likely to retaliate, causing a "trade war" (more precisely, a *trade barrier war*) that chokes off trade and makes all nations worse off. The **Smoot-Hawley Tariff Act** of 1930 is a classic example. Although that act was meant to reduce imports and stimulate U.S. production, its high tariffs prompted adversely affected nations to retaliate with their own equally high tariffs. International trade fell, lowering the output and income of all nations. Economic historians generally agree that the Smoot-Hawley Tariff Act contributed to both the length and severity of the Great Depression.

Finally, forcing an excess of exports over imports cannot succeed in raising domestic employment over the long run. It is through U.S. imports that foreign nations earn dollars to buy U.S. exports. In the long run, a nation must import in order to export. The long-run impact of tariffs is not an increase in domestic employment but, at best, a reallocation of workers away from export industries and toward protected domestic industries. This shift implies a less efficient allocation of resources.

Cheap Foreign Labor Argument

The cheap foreign labor argument says that domestic firms and workers must be shielded from the ruinous competition of countries where wages are low. If protection is not provided, cheap imports will flood U.S. markets, and the prices of U.S. goods—along with the wages of U.S. workers—will be pulled down. That is, domestic living standards in the United States will be reduced.

The cheap foreign labor argument suggests that, to maintain its standard of living, the United States should not trade with low-wage Mexico. But what would actually happen if the United States did not trade with Mexico? Would wages and living standards actually rise in the United States as a result? No. To obtain vegetables, the United States will have to reallocate a portion of its labor from its relatively more-efficient beef industry to its relatively less-efficient vegetable industry. As a result, the average productivity of U.S. labor will fall, as will real wages and living standards. Both countries' labor forces will have diminished standards of living because without specialization and trade they will have less output available to them. Compare column 4 with column 1 in Table 39.1 or points A' and Z' with A and Z in Figure 39.2 to confirm this point.

The cheap foreign labor argument incorrectly focuses on labor costs *per hour*. As an example, suppose that a U.S. factory pays its workers $20 per hour while a factory in a developing country pays its workers $4 per hour. The proponents of the cheap foreign labor argument look at these numbers and conclude—incorrectly—that it is impossible for the U.S. factory to compete with the factory in the developing country. But this conclusion fails to take into account two crucial facts:

- What actually matters are labor costs *per unit of output*, not labor costs *per hour of work*.
- Differences in productivity typically mean that labor costs *per unit of output* are often nearly identical between high-wage and low-wage countries despite huge differences in hourly wage rates.

To see why these points matter, let's take the productivity of the two factories into account. Because the U.S. factory uses much more sophisticated technology, better-trained workers, and much more capital per worker, one worker in one hour can produce 20 units of output. Because the U.S. workers get paid $20 per hour, the U.S. factory's labor cost per unit of output is $1. The factory in the developing country is much less productive because it uses less efficient technology, and its relatively untrained workers have much less machinery and equipment to work with. A worker there produces only 4 units per hour. Given the foreign wage of $4 per hour, the labor cost per unit of output at the factory in the developing country is also $1. Thus, the lower wage rate per hour at the factory in the developing country does not translate into lower labor costs per unit—meaning that it won't be able to undersell its U.S. competitor just because its workers get paid lower wages per hour.

In short, firms in developing countries only *sometimes* have an advantage in terms of labor costs per unit of output. Whether they do in any specific situation varies by industry and firm and depends on differences in productivity as well as differences in labor costs per hour. For many goods, labor productivity in high-wage countries like the United States is so much higher than labor productivity in low-wage countries that it is actually cheaper *per unit of output* to manufacture those goods in high-wage countries. That is why, for instance, Intel still makes microchips in the United States and why most automobiles are still produced in the United States, Japan, and Europe rather than in low-wage countries.

▶ Most rationales for trade protections are special-interest requests that, if followed, would create gains for protected industries and their workers at the expense of greater losses for the economy.

▶ The cheap foreign labor argument against international trade fails because its proponents forget to take into account differences in productivity between high-wage and low-wage countries.

QUICK REVIEW
39.6

Multilateral Trade Agreements and Free-Trade Zones

Aware of the detrimental effects of trade wars and the general weaknesses of arguments for trade protections, nations have worked to lower tariffs worldwide.

General Agreement on Tariffs and Trade

In 1947, 23 nations, including the United States, signed the **General Agreement on Tariffs and Trade (GATT).** GATT was based on three principles: (1) equal, nondiscriminatory trade treatment for all member nations; (2) the reduction of tariffs by multilateral negotiation; and (3) the elimination of import quotas. Basically, GATT provided a forum for the multilateral negotiation of reduced trade barriers.

Since the Second World War, member nations have completed eight "rounds" of GATT negotiations to reduce trade barriers. The eighth round of negotiations began in Uruguay in 1986. After seven years of complex discussions, in 1993 a new agreement was reached by GATT's 128 member nations. The Uruguay Round agreement took effect on January 1, 1995, and its provisions were phased in through 2005.

Under this agreement, tariffs on thousands of products were eliminated or reduced, with overall tariffs dropping by 33 percent. The agreement also liberalized government rules that in the past impeded a global market for services such as advertising, accounting, legal services, tourist services, and financial services. Quotas on imported textiles and apparel were phased out and replaced with tariffs. Other provisions reduced agricultural subsidies paid to farmers and protected intellectual property (patents, trademarks, and copyrights) against piracy.

World Trade Organization

The Uruguay Round agreement established the **World Trade Organization (WTO)** as GATT's successor. Some 164 nations belonged to the WTO in 2021. The WTO oversees trade agreements reached by its member nations, and it rules on trade disputes between members. It also provides forums for further rounds of trade negotiations. The ninth and latest round of negotiations—the **Doha Development Agenda**—was launched in Doha, Qatar, in late 2001. (The trade rounds occur over several years in several venues but are named after the city or country of origination.) The negotiations are aimed at further reducing tariffs and quotas, as well as agricultural subsidies that distort trade.

GATT and the WTO have been positive forces in the trend toward liberalized world trade. The trade rules agreed upon by the member nations provide a strong bulwark against the protectionism called for by the special-interest groups in the various member nations.

The WTO is quite controversial. Critics are concerned that rules crafted to expand international trade and investment enable firms to circumvent national laws that protect workers and the environment. Critics ask: What good are minimum-wage laws, worker-safety laws, collective-bargaining rights, and environmental laws if firms can easily shift their production to nations that have weaker laws or if consumers can buy goods produced in those countries?

Proponents of the WTO respond that labor and environmental protections should be pursued directly by the nations so affected, and via international organizations other than the WTO. These

>> LO39.6 Explain the objectives of the WTO, EU, NAFTA, and USMCA, and discuss offshoring and trade adjustment assistance.

General Agreement on Tariffs and Trade (GATT) The international agreement reached in 1947 in which 23 nations agreed to eliminate *import quotas*, negotiate reductions in *tariff* rates, and give each other equal and nondiscriminatory treatment. It now includes most nations and has become the *World Trade Organization.*

World Trade Organization (WTO) An organization of 164 nations (as of 2021) that oversees the provisions of the current world trade agreement, resolves trade disputes stemming from it, and holds forums for further rounds of trade negotiations.

Doha Development Agenda The latest, uncompleted (as of late 2021) sequence of trade negotiations by members of the *World Trade Organization;* named after Doha, Qatar, where the set of negotiations began. Also called the Doha Round.

issues should not be linked to the process of trade liberalization, which confers widespread economic benefits across nations. Moreover, say WTO proponents, many environmental and labor concerns are greatly overblown. Most world trade is among advanced industrial countries, not between them and countries with lower environmental and labor standards. Moreover, the free flow of goods and resources raises output and income in the developing nations. Historically, such increases in living standards have eventually resulted in stronger, not weaker, protections for the environment and for workers.

The European Union

European Union (EU) An association of 28 European nations (as of mid-2019) that has eliminated tariffs and quotas among them, established common tariffs for imported goods from outside the member nations, eliminated barriers to the free movement of capital, and created other common economic policies.

Countries have also sought to reduce tariffs by creating regional free-trade zones. The most prominent example is the **European Union (EU).** Initiated in 1958 as the Common Market, the EU was initially composed of just six European nations. As of 2021, it had 27 members.

The EU has abolished tariffs and import quotas on nearly all products traded among the participating nations and established a common system of tariffs applicable to all goods received from nations outside the EU. It has also liberalized the movement of capital and labor within the EU and has created common policies in other economic matters of joint concern, such as agriculture, transportation, and business practices.

EU integration has achieved for Europe what the U.S. constitutional prohibition on tariffs by individual states has achieved for the United States: increased regional specialization, greater productivity, greater output, and faster economic growth. The free flow of goods and services has created large markets for EU industries. The resulting economies of large-scale production have enabled these industries to achieve much lower costs than they could have achieved in their small, single-nation markets.

eurozone The 19 nations (as of 2019) of the 28-member (as of 2019) *European Union* that use the *euro* as their common *currency*. The eurozone countries are Austria, Belgium, Cyprus, Estonia, Finland, France, Germany, Greece, Ireland, Italy, Luxembourg, Malta, the Netherlands, Portugal, Slovakia, Slovenia, and Spain.

One of the most significant accomplishments of the EU was the establishment of the so-called **eurozone** or euro area in the early 2000s. As of 2018, 19 members of the EU (Austria, Belgium, Cyprus, Estonia, Finland, France, Germany, Greece, Ireland, Italy, Latvia, Lithuania, Luxembourg, Malta, the Netherlands, Portugal, Slovenia, Slovakia, and Spain) use the euro as a common currency. But the United Kingdom, Denmark, and Sweden have opted not to use the common currency, at least for now.

Economists believe that the adoption of the euro raised the standard of living in eurozone nations. By ending the inconvenience and expense of exchanging currencies, the euro has enhanced the free flow of goods, services, and resources among eurozone members. Companies that previously sold products in only one or two European nations have found it easier to price and sell their products in all 19 eurozone countries. The euro has also allowed consumers and businesses to more easily comparison shop for outputs and inputs, which has increased competition, reduced prices, and lowered costs.

North American Free Trade Agreement

North American Free Trade Agreement (NAFTA) The 1993 treaty that established an international free-trade zone composed of Canada, Mexico, and the United States.

In 1993 Canada, Mexico, and the United States created a major free-trade zone. The **North American Free Trade Agreement (NAFTA)** established a free-trade area that has about the same combined output as the EU but encompasses a much larger geographic area. NAFTA has eliminated tariffs and other trade barriers among Canada, Mexico, and the United States for most goods and services.

Critics of NAFTA feared that it would cause a massive loss of U.S. jobs as firms moved to Mexico to take advantage of lower wages and weaker regulations on pollution and workplace safety. Also, they were concerned that Japan and South Korea would build plants in Mexico and transport goods tariff-free to the United States, further hurting U.S. firms and workers.

In retrospect, critics were much too pessimistic. Since the passage of NAFTA in 1993, employment in the United States has increased by more than 38 million workers. NAFTA has increased trade among Canada, Mexico, and the United States and has enhanced the standard of living in all three countries.

In late 2018, negotiations were completed for a trade treaty that is intended to be the successor to NAFTA. Known as the United States-Mexico-Canada Agreement (or USMCA), the treaty cannot go into effect until after it is ratified by the governments of all three countries. The document leaves most elements of NAFTA in place but calls for stronger environmental and labor protections while also insisting on higher minimum wages in Mexican export industries as well as additional protections for intellectual property.

Trade Adjustment Assistance

The **Trade Adjustment Assistance Act** of 2002 introduced some innovative policies to help those hurt by shifts in international trade patterns. The law provides cash assistance (beyond unemployment insurance) for up to 78 weeks for workers displaced by imports or the relocation of U.S. manufacturing plants to other countries. To obtain the assistance, workers must participate in job searches, training programs, or vocational education. Also provided are relocation allowances to help displaced workers move to new jobs within the United States. Refundable tax credits for health insurance help workers maintain their insurance coverage during the retraining and job-search period. Workers who are 50 years of age or older are eligible for "wage insurance," which replaces some of the difference in pay (if any) between their old and new jobs. Many economists support trade adjustment assistance because it not only helps workers hurt by international trade but also helps create the political support necessary to reduce trade barriers and export subsidies.

However, not all economists favor trade adjustment assistance. Loss of jobs from imports, sending work abroad, and plant relocations to other countries account for only a small fraction (about 4 percent in recent years) of total job losses in the economy each year. Many workers also lose their jobs because of changing patterns of demand, changing technology, bad management, and other dynamic aspects of a market economy. Some critics ask, "What makes losing one's job to international trade worthy of such treatment, compared to losing one's job to, say, technological change or domestic competition?"

Offshoring of Jobs

Some U.S. jobs lost because of international trade are lost because of the ongoing globalization of resource markets, especially the market for labor. In recent years, U.S. firms have found the outsourcing of work abroad to be increasingly profitable. Economists call this business activity **offshoring**—shifting work previously done by U.S. workers to workers located in other nations. Offshoring is not a new practice, but traditionally it involved components for U.S. manufacturing goods. For example, Boeing has long offshored the production of major airplane parts for its "American" aircraft.

Recent advances in computer and communications technology have enabled U.S. firms to offshore service jobs such as data entry, book composition, software coding, call-center operations, medical transcription, and claims processing to countries such as India and the Philippines. Where offshoring occurs, some of the value added in the production process accrues to foreign countries rather than to the United States. Therefore part of the income generated from the production of U.S. goods is paid to foreigners, not to American workers.

Offshoring is a wrenching experience for many Americans who lose their jobs, but it is not necessarily bad for the overall economy. Offshoring simply reflects growing specialization and international trade in services or "tasks." As with trade in goods, trade in services reflects comparative advantage and is beneficial to both trading parties. Moreover, the United States has a sizable trade surplus with other nations in services. The United States gains by specializing in high-valued services such as transportation services, accounting services, legal services, and advertising services, where it maintains a comparative advantage. It then "trades" to obtain lower-valued services such as call-center and data-entry work, for which comparative advantage lies abroad.

Offshoring also increases the demand for complementary jobs in the United States. Jobs that are close substitutes for existing U.S. jobs are lost, but the number of complementary jobs in the United States grows. For example, the lower price of writing software code in India may mean a lower cost of software sold in the United States and abroad. That lower cost, in turn, may create more jobs for U.S.-based workers such as software designers, marketers, and distributors. Moreover, offshoring may encourage domestic investment and the expansion of firms in the United States by reducing their production costs and keeping them competitive worldwide. In some instances, "offshoring jobs" may equate to "importing competitiveness." Entire firms that might otherwise disappear abroad may remain profitable in the United States only because they can offshore some of their work.

Trade Adjustment Assistance Act A U.S. law passed in 2002 that provides cash assistance, education and training benefits, health care subsidies, and *wage* subsidies (for persons age 50 or older) to workers displaced by *imports* or relocations of U.S. *plants* to other countries.

offshoring The practice of shifting work previously done by domestic workers to workers located abroad.

Petition of the Candlemakers, 1845

French Economist Frédéric Bastiat (1801–1850) Devastated the Proponents of Protectionism by Satirically Extending Their Reasoning to Its Logical and Absurd Conclusions.

Petition of the Manufacturers of Candles, Waxlights, Lamps, Candlesticks, Street Lamps, Snuffers, Extinguishers, and of the Producers of Oil Tallow, Rosin, Alcohol, and, Generally, of Everything Connected with Lighting.

TO MESSIEURS THE MEMBERS OF THE CHAMBER OF DEPUTIES.

Gentlemen—You are on the right road. You reject abstract theories, and have little consideration for cheapness and plenty. Your chief care is the interest of the producer. You desire to emancipate him from external competition, and reserve the national market for national industry.

We are about to offer you an admirable opportunity of applying your—what shall we call it? your theory? No; nothing is more deceptive than theory; your doctrine? your system? your principle? but you dislike doctrines, you abhor systems, and as for principles, you deny that there are any in social economy: we shall say, then, your practice, your practice without theory and without principle.

We are suffering from the intolerable competition of a foreign rival, placed, it would seem, in a condition so far superior to ours for the production of light, that he absolutely inundates our national market with it at a price fabulously reduced. The moment he shows himself, our trade leaves us—all consumers apply to him; and a branch of native industry, having countless ramifications, is all at once rendered completely stagnant. This rival . . . is no other than the Sun.

What we pray for is, that it may please you to pass a law ordering the shutting up of all windows, skylights, dormer windows, outside and inside shutters, curtains, blinds, bull's-eyes; in a word, of all openings, holes, chinks, clefts, and fissures, by or through which the light of the sun has been in use to enter houses, to the prejudice of the meritorious manufacturers with which we flatter ourselves we have accommodated our country—a country which, in gratitude, ought not to abandon us now to a strife so unequal.

If you shut up as much as possible all access to natural light, and create a demand for artificial light, which of our French

Malcolm Fife/Pixtal/age fotostock

manufacturers will not be encouraged by it? If more tallow is consumed, then there must be more oxen and sheep; and, consequently, we shall behold the multiplication of artificial meadows, meat, wool, hides, and, above all, manure, which is the basis and foundation of all agricultural wealth.

The same remark applies to navigation. Thousands of vessels will proceed to the whale fishery; and, in a short time, we shall possess a navy capable of maintaining the honor of France, and gratifying the patriotic aspirations of your petitioners, the undersigned candlemakers and others.

Only have the goodness to reflect, Gentlemen, and you will be convinced that there is, perhaps, no Frenchman, from the wealthy coalmaster to the humblest vender of lucifer matches, whose lot will not be ameliorated by the success of this our petition.

Source: Frédéric Bastiat, *Economic Sophisms* (The Foundation for Economic Education, 1996).

QUICK REVIEW
39.7

▶ The General Agreement on Tariffs and Trade (GATT) of 1947 reduced tariffs and quotas and established a process for numerous subsequent rounds of multinational trade negotiations.

▶ The World Trade Organization (WTO)—GATT's current successor—rules on trade disputes.

▶ The European Union (EU) and the North American Free Trade Agreement (NAFTA) established multinational free-trade zones.

▶ The offshoring of jobs has prompted programs like trade adjustment assistance to help displaced workers transition to new jobs.

Summary

LO39.1 List several key facts about international trade.

The United States leads the world in the combined volume of exports and imports. Other major trading nations are Germany, Japan, the western European nations, and the Asian economies of China, South Korea, Taiwan, and Singapore. The United States' principal exports include chemicals, agricultural products, consumer durables, aircraft, and computer software and services; its principal imports include petroleum, automobiles, metals, household appliances, and computers.

LO39.2 Define comparative advantage and explain how specialization and trade add to a nation's output.

World trade is based on three considerations: the uneven distribution of economic resources among nations, the fact that efficient production of various goods requires particular techniques or combinations of resources, and the differentiated products produced among nations.

Mutually advantageous specialization and trade are possible between any two nations if they have different domestic opportunity-cost ratios for any two products. By specializing on the basis of comparative advantage, nations can obtain larger real incomes with fixed amounts of resources. The terms of trade determine how the trading nations share this increase in world output.

LO39.3 Explain why differences between world prices and domestic prices lead to exports and imports.

A nation's export supply curve shows the quantities of a product the nation will export at world prices that exceed the domestic price (the price in a closed, no-international-trade economy). A nation's import demand curve reveals the quantities of a product it will import at world prices below the domestic price.

In a two-nation model, the equilibrium world price and the equilibrium quantities of exports and imports occur where one nation's export supply curve intersects the other nation's import demand curve. A nation will export a particular product if the world price exceeds the domestic price; it will import the product if the world price is less than the domestic price. The country with the lower costs of production will be the exporter and the country with the higher costs of production will be the importer.

LO39.4 Analyze the economic effects of tariffs and quotas.

Trade barriers take the form of protective tariffs, quotas, nontariff barriers, and voluntary export restrictions. Export subsidies also distort international trade. Supply-and-demand analysis demonstrates that protective tariffs and quotas increase the prices and reduce the quantities demanded of the affected goods. Sales by foreign exporters diminish; domestic producers, however, gain higher prices and more sales. Consumer losses from trade restrictions greatly exceed producer and government gains, creating an efficiency loss to society.

LO39.5 Critique the most frequently presented arguments for protectionism.

The strongest arguments for protection are the infant industry and military self-sufficiency arguments. Most other arguments for protection are interest-group appeals or reasoning fallacies that emphasize producer interests over consumer interests or stress the immediate effects of trade barriers while ignoring long-run consequences. The cheap foreign labor argument for protection fails because it focuses on labor costs per hour rather than on what really matters: labor costs per unit of output.

LO39.6 Explain the objectives of the WTO, EU, NAFTA, and USMCA, and discuss offshoring and trade adjustment assistance.

In 1947 the General Agreement on Tariffs and Trade (GATT) was formed to encourage nondiscriminatory treatment for all member nations, to reduce tariffs, and to eliminate import quotas.

GATT's successor, the World Trade Organization (WTO), had 164 member nations in 2021. It implements trade agreements, rules on trade disputes between members, and provides forums for continued discussions on trade liberalization.

Free-trade zones liberalize trade within regions. Two examples of free-trade arrangements are the 27-member European Union (EU) and the North American Free Trade Agreement (NAFTA), comprising Canada, Mexico, and the United States.

The Trade Adjustment Assistance Act of 2002 provides cash assistance, education and training benefits, health care subsidies, and wage subsidies to qualified workers displaced by imports or relocations of plants from the United States to abroad.

Offshoring is the practice of shifting work previously done by Americans in the United States to workers located in other nations. Although offshoring eliminates some U.S. jobs, it lowers production costs and expands sales, and it therefore may create other U.S. jobs. Less than 4 percent of all job losses in the United States each year are caused by imports, offshoring, or plant relocations abroad.

Terms and Concepts

trade	trading possibilities line	protective tariff
labor-intensive goods	gains from trade	import quota
land-intensive goods	world price	voluntary export restriction (VER)
capital-intensive goods	domestic price	nontariff barrier (NTB)
absolute advantage	export supply curve	export subsidy
comparative advantage	import demand curve	dumping
opportunity-cost ratio	equilibrium world price	Smoot-Hawley Tariff Act
principle of comparative advantage	tariff	General Agreement on Tariffs and Trade (GATT)
terms of trade	revenue tariff	

World Trade Organization (WTO)

Doha Development Agenda

European Union (EU)

eurozone

North American Free Trade Agreement (NAFTA)

Trade Adjustment Assistance Act

offshoring

Discussion Questions

Mc Graw Hill connect

1. Quantitatively, how important is international trade to the United States relative to the importance of trade to other nations? What country is the United States' most important trading partner, quantitatively? With what country does the United States have the largest trade deficit? **LO39.1**

2. Distinguish among land-, labor-, and capital-intensive goods, citing an example of each without resorting to the examples in the text. How do these distinctions relate to international trade? How do distinctive products, unrelated to resource intensity, relate to international trade? **LO39.2**

3. Explain: "The United States can make certain toys with greater productive efficiency than China can. Yet we import those toys from China." Relate your answer to the ideas of Adam Smith and David Ricardo. **LO39.2**

4. Suppose Big Country can produce 80 units of X by using all its resources to produce X or 60 units of Y by devoting all its resources to Y. Comparable figures for Small Nation are 60 units of X and 60 units of Y. Assuming constant costs, in which product should each nation specialize? Explain why. What are the limits of the terms of trade between these two countries? **LO39.2**

5. What is an export supply curve? What is an import demand curve? How do such curves relate to the determination of the equilibrium world price of a tradable good? **LO39.3**

6. Why is a quota more detrimental to an economy than a tariff that results in the same level of imports as the quota? What is the net outcome of either tariffs or quotas for the world economy? **LO39.4**

7. "The potentially valid arguments for tariff protection—military self-sufficiency, infant industry protection, and diversification for stability—are also the most easily abused." Why are these arguments susceptible to abuse? **LO39.4**

8. Evaluate the effectiveness of artificial trade barriers, such as tariffs and import quotas, as a way to achieve and maintain full employment throughout the U.S. economy. How might such policies reduce unemployment in one U.S. industry but increase it in another U.S. industry? **LO39.4**

9. In 2018, manufacturing workers in the United States earned average compensation of $21.86 per hour. That same year, manufacturing workers in Mexico earned average compensation of $3.20 per hour. How can U.S. manufacturers possibly compete? Why isn't all manufacturing done in Mexico and other low-wage countries? **LO39.4**

10. How might protective tariffs reduce both the imports and the exports of the nation that levies tariffs? How might import competition lead to quality improvements and cost reductions by U.S. firms? **LO39.4**

11. Identify and state the significance of each of the following trade-related entities: (*a*) the WTO, (*b*) the EU, (*c*) the eurozone, and (*d*) NAFTA. **LO39.6**

12. What form does trade adjustment assistance take in the United States? How does such assistance promote political support for free-trade agreements? Do you think workers who lose their jobs because of changes in trade laws deserve special treatment relative to workers who lose their jobs because of other changes in the economy, say, changes in patterns of government spending? **LO39.6**

13. What is offshoring of white-collar service jobs, and how does it relate to international trade? Why has offshoring increased over the past few decades? Give an example (other than that in the text) of how offshoring can eliminate some U.S. jobs while creating other U.S. jobs. **LO39.6**

14. **LAST WORD** What central point was Bastiat trying to make in his fictional petition of the candlemakers?

Review Questions

Mc Graw Hill connect

1. In Country A, a worker can make 5 bicycles per hour. In Country B, a worker can make 7 bicycles per hour. Which country has an absolute advantage in making bicycles? **LO39.2**
   a. Country A
   b. Country B

2. In Country A, the production of 1 bicycle requires using resources that could otherwise be used to produce 11 lamps. In Country B, the production of 1 bicycle requires using resources that could otherwise be used to produce 15 lamps. Which country has a comparative advantage in making bicycles? **LO39.2**
   a. Country A
   b. Country B

3. True or False: If Country B has an absolute advantage over Country A in producing bicycles, it will also have a comparative advantage over Country A in producing bicycles. **LO39.2**

4. Suppose that the opportunity-cost ratio for sugar and almonds is $4S \equiv 1A$ in Hawaii but $1S \equiv 2A$ in California. Which state has the comparative advantage in producing almonds? **LO39.2**
   a. Hawaii
   b. California
   c. Neither

5. Suppose that the opportunity-cost ratio for fish and lumber is $1F \equiv 1L$ in Canada but $2F \equiv 1L$ in Iceland. Then _____ should specialize in producing fish while _____ should specialize in producing lumber. **LO39.2**
   a. Canada; Iceland
   b. Iceland; Canada

6. Suppose that the opportunity-cost ratio for watches and cheese is $1C \equiv 1W$ in Switzerland but $1C \equiv 4W$ in Japan. At which of the following international exchange ratios (terms of trade) will

Switzerland and Japan be willing to specialize and engage in trade with each other? **LO39.2**

Select one or more answers from the choices shown.

a. $1C \equiv 3W$
b. $1C \equiv \frac{1}{2}W$
c. $1C \equiv 5W$
d. $\frac{1}{2}C \equiv 1W$
e. $2C \equiv 1W$

7. Which of the following are benefits of international trade? **LO39.2**

Choose one or more answers from the choices shown.

a. A more efficient allocation of resources
b. A higher level of material well-being
c. Gains from specialization
d. Promoting competition
e. Deterring monopoly
f. Reducing the threat of war

8. We see quite a bit of international trade in the real world. And trade is driven by specialization. So why don't we see full specialization—for instance, all cars in the world being made in South Korea, or all the mobile phones in the world being made in China? Choose the best answer from among the following choices. **LO39.2**

a. High tariffs
b. Extensive import quotas
c. Increasing opportunity costs
d. Increasing returns

9. True or False: If a country is open to international trade, the domestic price of a product can differ from the international price of that product. **LO39.3**

10. Suppose that the current international price of wheat is $6 per bushel and that the United States is currently exporting 30 million bushels per year. If the United States suddenly became a closed economy with respect to wheat, would the domestic price of wheat in the United States end up higher or lower than $6? **LO39.3**

a. Higher
b. Lower
c. It will stay the same.

11. Suppose that if Iceland and Japan were both closed economies, the domestic price of fish would be $100 per ton in Iceland and $90 per ton in Japan. If the two countries decided to open up to international trade with each other, which of the following could be the equilibrium international price of fish once they begin trading? **LO39.3**

a. $75
b. $85
c. $95
d. $105

12. Draw a domestic supply-and-demand diagram for a product in which the United States does not have a comparative advantage. What impact do foreign imports have on domestic price and quantity? On your diagram show a protective tariff that eliminates approximately one-half of the assumed imports. What are the price-quantity effects of this tariff on (*a*) domestic consumers, (*b*) domestic producers, and (*c*) foreign exporters? How would the effects of a quota that creates the same amount of imports differ? **LO39.4**

13. American apparelmakers complain to Congress about competition from China. Congress decides to impose either a tariff or a quota on apparel imports from China. Which policy would Chinese apparel manufacturers prefer? **LO39.4**

a. Tariff
b. Quota

Problems

1. Assume that the comparative-cost ratios of two products—baby formula and tuna fish—are as follows in the nations of Canswicki and Tunata:

   > Canswicki: 1 can baby formula $\equiv$ 2 cans tuna fish
   > Tunata: 1 can baby formula $\equiv$ 4 cans tuna fish

   In what product should each nation specialize? Which of the following terms of trade would be acceptable to both nations: (a) 1 can baby formula $\equiv 2\frac{1}{2}$ cans tuna fish; (b) 1 can baby formula $\equiv$ 1 can tuna fish; (c) 1 can baby formula $\equiv$ 5 cans tuna fish? **LO39.2**

2. The accompanying hypothetical production possibilities tables are for New Zealand and Spain. Each country can produce apples and plums. Plot the production possibilities data for each of the two countries separately. Referring to your graphs, answer the following: **LO39.2**

New Zealand's Production Possibilities Table (Millions of Bushels)

Product	Production Alternatives			
	A	B	C	D
Apples	0	20	40	60
Plums	15	10	5	0

Spain's Production Possibilities Table (Millions of Bushels)

Product	Production Alternatives			
	R	S	T	U
Apples	0	20	40	60
Plums	60	40	20	0

a. What is each country's opportunity cost ratio of producing plums and apples?
b. Which nation should specialize in each product?
c. Show the trading possibilities lines for each nation if the actual terms of trade are 1 plum for 2 apples. (Plot these lines on your graph.)
d. Suppose the optimum product mixes before specialization and trade were alternative B in New Zealand and alternative S in Spain. What would be the gains from specialization and trade?

3. The following hypothetical production possibilities tables are for China and the United States. Assume that before specialization and trade, the optimal product mix for China is alternative B and for the United States is alternative U. **LO39.2**

a. Are comparative-cost conditions such that the two countries should specialize? If so, what product should each produce?

b. What is the total gain in apparel and chemical output that would result from such specialization?

c. What are the limits of the terms of trade? Suppose that the *actual* terms of trade are 1 unit of apparel for 1.5 tons of chemicals and that the *actual* amount traded is 4 units of apparel for 6 tons of chemicals. What are the gains from specialization and trade for each nation?

Product	China Production Possibilities					
	A	**B**	**C**	**D**	**E**	**F**
Apparel (in thousands)	30	24	18	12	6	0
Chemicals (in tons)	0	6	12	18	24	30

Product	U.S. Production Possibilities					
	R	**S**	**T**	**U**	**V**	**W**
Apparel (in thousands)	10	8	6	4	2	0
Chemicals (in tons)	0	4	8	12	16	20

4. Refer to Figure 3.6. Assume that the graph depicts the U.S. domestic market for corn. How many bushels of corn, if any, will the United States export or import at a world price of $1, $2, $3, $4, and $5? Use this information to construct the U.S. export supply curve and import demand curve for corn. Suppose that the only other corn-producing nation is France, where the domestic price is $4. Which country will export corn, and which country will import it? **LO39.3**

The Balance of Payments, Exchange Rates, and Trade Deficits

>> LEARNING OBJECTIVES

LO40.1 Explain the two types of international financial transactions.

LO40.2 Define and explain the two components of the balance of payments: the current account and the capital and financial account.

LO40.3 Explain how exchange rates are determined.

LO40.4 Distinguish between flexible and fixed exchange rates.

LO40.5 Explain the current system of managed floating exchange rates.

LO40.6 Identify the causes and consequences of recent U.S. trade deficits.

LO40.7 (Appendix) Explain how exchange rates worked under the gold standard and Bretton Woods.

On May 6, 2022, 1 U.S. dollar could buy 1.41 Australian dollars, 0.81 British pounds, 1.29 Canadian dollars, 0.95 European euros, 130.57 Japanese yen, or 20.18 Mexican pesos. What explains this seemingly haphazard array of exchange rates?

In Chapter 39 we examined comparative advantage as the underlying economic basis of world trade. Now we introduce and explain the highly important monetary and financial aspects of international trade.

International Financial Transactions

International financial transactions fall into two broad categories:

- **International trade** encompasses all cross-border purchases and sales of currently produced goods and services. Examples include an Egyptian firm exporting cotton to the United States and a U.S. company hiring an Indian call center to answer its phones.
- **International asset transactions** include all cross-border purchases and sales of real or financial assets in which the property rights to those assets are transferred from a citizen of one country to a citizen of another country. International asset transactions include selling a business to foreign investors and purchasing a vacation home in another country from a local citizen.

>> **LO40.1** Explain the two types of international financial transactions.

international trade The exchange (trade) of goods and services across international borders.

international asset transactions The sale, trade, or transfer of ownership rights to either real or financial assets, including currency, across international borders.

These two categories of international financial transactions reflect the fact that whether they live in different countries or the same country, individuals and firms can only exchange two things: currently produced goods and services or assets.

Money is by far the most commonly exchanged asset. Money flows from the buyers of the goods, services, or assets to the sellers of the goods, services, or assets. Importers are buyers and exporters are sellers. As a result, *imports cause outflows of money while exports cause inflows of money.*

When the buyers and sellers are both from places that use the same currency, there is no confusion about what type of money to use. Americans from California and Wisconsin will use their common currency, the dollar. People from France and Germany will use their common currency, the euro. However, when the buyers and sellers are from places that use different currencies, an *intermediate* asset transaction has to take place: The buyers must convert their own currency into the currency that the sellers use and accept.

Consider the case of an English software company that wants to buy an artificial intelligence supercomputer made by a U.S. company. The U.S. company sells these high-powered machines for $300,000. To pay for the machine, the English company has to convert some of its money (British pounds) into the money that the U.S. company will accept (U.S. dollars). This process is not difficult. As we will soon explain, there are many easy-to-use foreign exchange markets in which those who need to sell pounds and buy dollars can interact with people who want to do just the opposite (buy pounds and sell dollars). The demand and supply created by these two groups will determine the equilibrium exchange rate between the two currencies. That exchange rate will, in turn, determine how many pounds the English company must pay for the supercomputer. For instance, if the exchange rate is £1 = $2, then the English company will have to convert £150,000 to obtain the $300,000 necessary to purchase the computer.

QUICK REVIEW
40.1

▸ International financial transactions involve trade either in currently produced goods and services or assets.

▸ While imports of goods, services, and assets cause outflows of money, exports of goods, services, and assets create inflows of money.

▸ If buyers and sellers use different currencies, then foreign exchange transactions take place so that the seller (exporter) can be paid in its own currency.

The Balance of Payments

>> **LO40.2** Define and explain the two components of the balance of payments: the current account and the capital and financial account.

balance of payments A summary of all the financial transactions that take place between the individuals, *firms,* and governmental units of one nation and those of all other nations during a year.

A nation's **balance of payments** is the sum of all the financial transactions that take place between its residents and the residents of foreign nations. Most of these transactions fall into the two main categories that we just discussed: international trade and international asset transactions. But the balance of payments also includes international transactions that fall into other categories. They include expenditures made by tourists, interest and dividends received or paid abroad, debt forgiveness, and remittances made by immigrants to their relatives back home.

The Bureau of Economic Analysis at the U.S. Department of Commerce compiles a balance-of-payments statement each year. This statement summarizes all of the billions of payments that U.S. individuals and firms receive from foreigners as well as all of the billions of payments that U.S. individuals and firms make to foreigners. It shows inward flows of money *to* the United States and outward flows of money *from* the United States. For convenience, all of these money payments are stated in U.S. dollars, even though many of the payments were made using foreign currencies.

Table 40.1 is a simplified balance-of-payments statement for the United States in 2021. It is organized into two broad categories: the *current account* and the *capital and financial account.*

Current Account

current account The section in a nation's *international balance of payments* that records its exports and imports of *goods* and *services,* its net *investment income,* and its net *transfers.*

The top portion of Table 40.1 is called the **current account.** It mainly summarizes U.S. trade in currently produced goods and services. Items 1 and 2 show U.S. exports and imports of goods in 2021. U.S. exports have a *plus* (+) sign because they generate flows of money into the United States. U.S. imports have a *minus* (−) sign because they cause flows of money out of the United States.

TABLE 40.1 The U.S. Balance of Payments, 2021 (in Billions)

CURRENT ACCOUNT	
(1) U.S. goods exports	$+1,762
(2) U.S. goods imports	−2,853
(3) *Balance on goods*	$−1,091
(4) U.S. exports of services	+771
(5) U.S. imports of services	−541
(6) *Balance on services*	+230
(7) *Balance on goods and services*	−861
(8) Net investment income	+174*
(9) Net transfers	−135
(10) **Balance on current account**	−822
CAPITAL AND FINANCIAL ACCOUNT	
Capital account	
(11) *Balance on capital account*	−2
Financial account	
(12) Foreign purchases of assets located in the United States	+1,948†
(13) U.S. purchases of assets located abroad	−1,124†
(14) *Balance on financial account*	+824
(15) **Balance on capital and financial account**	+822
	$ 0

*Includes other, less significant, categories of income.
†Includes one-half of a $137 billion statistical discrepancy as well as one-half of $42 billion in net financial derivatives transactions.

Source: Bureau of Economic Analysis, U.S. Department of Commerce. Preliminary 2021 data. The export and import data are on a "balance-of-payment basis" and usually vary from the data on exports and imports reported in the National Income and Product Accounts.

Balance on Goods Items 1 and 2 in Table 40.1 reveal that in 2021, U.S. goods exports of $1,762 billion were less than U.S. goods imports of $2,853 billion. A country's *balance of trade on goods* is the difference between its exports and its imports of goods. If exports exceed imports, the result is a trade surplus on the balance of goods. If imports exceed exports, the result is a trade deficit on the balance of goods. We note in item 3 that, in 2021, the United States incurred a trade deficit on goods of $1,091 billion.

Balance on Services The United States exports not only goods, such as airplanes and oil, but also services, such as insurance contracting, business consulting, air travel, and investment advice. Item 4 in Table 40.1 shows that these service "exports" totaled $771 billion in 2021. These exports generated flows of money into the United States, thus the + sign. Item 5 indicates that the United States also imports services from foreigners. Those service imports totaled $541 billion in 2021, and because they generate flows of money out of the United States, they carry a − sign. Summed together, items 4 and 5 indicate that the balance on services (item 6) in 2021 was $230 billion.

The **balance on goods and services** shown as item 7 is the difference between U.S. exports of goods and services (items 1 and 4) and U.S. imports of goods and services (items 2 and 5). In 2021, U.S. imports of goods and services exceeded U.S. exports of goods and services by $861 billion. So a **trade deficit** of that amount is said to have occurred on the U.S. balance of goods and services. In contrast, a **trade surplus** on the balance of goods and services will occur whenever exports of goods and services exceed imports of goods and services.

Item 7, the overall U.S. trade balance, is equal to the sum of the trade deficits or trade surpluses that the United States has with each country in the world. To give you a sense of how large those surpluses and deficits are, and by how much they vary from country to country, Global Perspective 40.1 indicates the size of the U.S. trade deficit or surplus with particular nations. The U.S. trade deficit with China is particularly large.

Balance on Current Account Items 8 and 9 do not relate directly to international trade in goods and services. They are listed as part of the current account because they are international financial flows that account for certain international financial transactions that *look like* international trade in goods or services. For instance, item 8, *net investment income*, represents the

balance on goods and services The exports of *goods* and *services* of a nation less its imports of goods and services in a year.

trade deficit The amount by which a nation's *imports* of goods (or goods and *services*) exceed its *exports* of goods (or goods and *services*).

trade surplus The amount by which a nation's *exports* of goods (or goods and *services*) exceed its *imports* of goods (or goods and *services*).

🌐 **GLOBAL PERSPECTIVE 40.1**

U.S. TRADE BALANCES IN GOODS AND SERVICES, SELECTED NATIONS, 2021

The United States has large trade deficits in goods and services with several nations, in particular, China, Mexico, Germany, and Japan.

Source: Bureau of Economic Analysis.

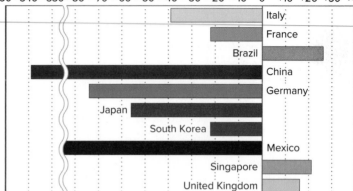

difference between (a) the interest and dividend payments that foreigners pay to U.S. citizens and companies for the services provided by U.S. capital invested abroad ("exported" capital) and (b) the interest and dividends that U.S. citizens and companies pay to foreigners for the services provided by foreign capital invested here ("imported" capital). In 2021, U.S. net investment income was a positive $174 billion.

Item 9 shows net transfers, both public and private, between the United States and the rest of the world. Included here are foreign aid, pensions paid to U.S. citizens living abroad, and remittances by immigrants to relatives abroad. These $135 billion of transfers are net U.S. outpayments (and therefore listed as a negative number in Table 40.1). They are listed as part of the current account because they can be considered the financial flows that accompany the granting of gifts and the importing of "thank you notes."

balance on current account
The exports of *goods* and *services* of a nation less its imports of goods and services plus its *net investment income* and *net transfers* in a year.

By adding all of the transactions in the current account, we obtain the **balance on current account** shown in item 10. In 2021 the United States had a current account deficit of $822 billion. In other words, U.S. current account transactions generated more money flows out of the United States than money flows into the United States.

Capital and Financial Account

capital and financial account
The section of a nation's *international balance of payments* that records (1) debt forgiveness by and to foreigners and (2) foreign purchases of assets in the United States and U.S. purchases of assets abroad.

The bottom portion of Table 40.1 summarizes U.S. international asset transactions. It is called the **capital and financial account** and consists of two separate accounts: the *capital account* and the *financial account*.

Capital Account The capital account mainly measures debt forgiveness—which is an asset transaction because the person forgiving a debt essentially hands the IOU back to the borrower. It is a "net" account (one that can be either + or −). The negative $2 billion listed in line 11 tells us that in 2021 U.S. citizens forgave $2 billion more of debt owed to them by foreigners than foreigners forgave debt owed to them by Americans. The − sign indicates a debit; it is an "on-paper" outpayment (asset transfer) equal to the net amount of debt forgiven.

Financial Account The financial account summarizes international asset transactions, that is, international purchases and sales of real or financial assets. Line 12 lists the amount of foreign purchases of assets in the United States. It has a + sign because any purchase of a U.S.-owned asset by a foreigner generates a flow of money toward the American who sells the asset. Line 13 lists U.S. purchases of assets abroad. This item has a − sign because such purchases generate a flow of money from the Americans who buy foreign assets toward the foreigners who sell them those assets.

Items 12 and 13, added together, yield a positive $824 billion balance on the financial account for 2021 (line 14). In 2021 the United States "exported" $1,948 billion of ownership of its real and financial assets and "imported" $1,124 billion. In other words, this surplus in the financial account brought in income of $824 billion to the United States. The **balance on capital and financial account** (line 15) is $822 billion. It is the sum of the $2 billion debit on the capital account and the $824 billion surplus on the financial account.

Observe that the $822 billion surplus in the capital and financial account equals the $822 billion deficit in the current account. In fact, the two numbers always equal—or "balance." Let's see why.

balance on capital and financial account The sum of the *capital account balance* and the *financial account balance.*

Why the Balance?

The balance on the current account and the balance on the capital and financial account must always sum to zero because any deficit or surplus in the current account automatically creates an offsetting entry in the capital and financial account. People can trade only two things: currently produced goods and services or preexisting assets (including money). Therefore, if trading partners have an imbalance in their trade of currently produced goods and services, the only way to make up for that imbalance is with a net transfer of assets from one party to the other.

To understand why, suppose that Finley (a U.S. citizen) makes shoes and Henri (a Swiss citizen) makes watches and that the two trade only with each other. Assume that their financial assets consist entirely of money, with each beginning the year with $1,000 in their own bank account. Suppose that this year Finley exports $300 of shoes to Henri and imports $500 of watches from Henri. Finley therefore ends the year with a $200 goods deficit with Henri.

However, Finley and Henri's goods transactions also result in asset exchanges that cause a net transfer of assets from Finley to Henri that are exactly equal in value to Finley's $200 goods deficit with Henri. Why? Henri pays Finley $300 for her shoes while Finley pays Henri $500 for his watches. The *net* result of these opposite-direction asset movements is that $200 of Finley's initial assets of $1,000 are transferred to Henri. This transfer is unavoidable because the $300 that Finley receives from her exports of shoes pays for only the first $300 of her $500 of imports of watches. The only way for Finley to pay for the remaining $200 of watch imports is for her to transfer $200 of her initial asset holdings to Henri. Consequently, Finley's assets decline by $200, from $1,000 to $800, while Henri's assets rise by $200, from $1,000 to $1,200.

Consider how the transaction between Finley and Henri affects the U.S. balance-of-payments statement (Table 40.1), other things equal. Finley's $200 goods deficit with Henri shows up in the U.S. current account as a −$200 entry in the balance on goods account (line 3) and carries down to a −$200 entry in the balance on current account (line 10).

In the capital and financial account, this $200 is recorded as +$200 in the account labeled *foreign purchases of assets located in the United States* (line 12). This +$200 then carries down to the balance on capital and financial account (line 15).

For a slightly different perspective, consider the entries this way: Henri has used $200 worth of watches to purchase $200 of Finley's initial $1,000 of assets. The +$200 entry in line 12 simply recognizes this fact. This +$200 entry exactly offsets the −$200 in the current account.

Thus, the balance of payments always balances. Any current account deficit or surplus in the top half of the statement automatically generates an offsetting international asset transfer that shows up in the capital and financial account in the bottom half of the statement. That is, current account deficits generate transfers of assets *to* foreigners, while current account surpluses generate transfers of assets *from* foreigners.

▶ A nation's balance-of-payments statement summarizes all of the international financial transactions that take place between its residents and the residents of all foreign nations. It includes the current account balance and the capital and financial account balance.

▶ The current account balance is a nation's exports of goods and services less its imports of goods and services plus its net investment income and net transfers.

▶ The capital and financial account balance includes the net amount of the nation's debt forgiveness as well as the nation's sale of real and financial assets to people living abroad less its purchases of real and financial assets from foreigners.

▶ The current account balance and the capital and financial account balance always sum to zero because any current account imbalance automatically generates an offsetting international asset transfer.

QUICK REVIEW

40.2

Flexible Exchange Rates

>> **LO40.3** Explain how exchange rates are determined.

flexible exchange rate A *rate of exchange* that is determined by the international demand for and supply of a nation's money and that is consequently free to rise or fall because it is not subject to *currency interventions*. Also referred to as a "floating exchange rate."

Exchange-rate systems come in two varieties:

- In a **flexible- or floating-exchange-rate** system, demand and supply determine exchange rates without government intervention.

- In a **fixed-exchange-rate** system, a government sets the exchange rates for its currency and adjusts monetary and fiscal policy as necessary to maintain those rates.

We begin by looking at flexible exchange rates. Let's examine the rate, or price, at which U.S. dollars might be exchanged for British pounds in the market for foreign currency. In **Figure 40.1 (Key Graph)** we show demand D_1 and supply S_1 of pounds. Note that both the demand for and supply of pounds are expressed in terms of U.S. dollars. They interact to determine the equilibrium price for pounds, which is expressed in terms of how many dollars are required to purchase one pound.

The *demand-for-pounds curve* D_1 slopes downward because all British goods and services will be cheaper to Americans if pounds become less expensive. That is, at lower dollar prices for pounds, Americans can obtain more pounds and therefore more British goods and services per dollar. To buy those cheaper British goods, U.S. consumers will increase the quantity of pounds they demand.

..ıll KEY GRAPH

FIGURE 40.1 **The market for foreign currency (pounds).**

The intersection of the demand-for-pounds curve D_1 and the supply-of-pounds curve S_1 determines the equilibrium dollar price of pounds, here, $2. That means that the exchange rate is $2 = £1. Not shown: An increase in demand for pounds or a decrease in supply of pounds will increase the dollar price of pounds and thus cause the pound to appreciate. Also not shown: A decrease in the demand for pounds or an increase in the supply of pounds will reduce the dollar price of pounds, meaning that the pound has depreciated.

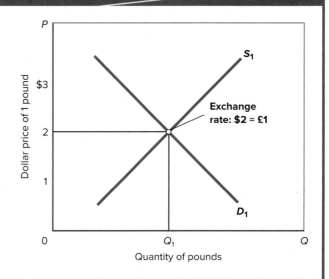

QUICK QUIZ FOR FIGURE 40.1

1. **Which of the following statements is true?**
   a. The quantity of pounds demanded falls when the dollar appreciates.
   b. The quantity of pounds supplied declines as the dollar price of the pound rises.
   c. At the equilibrium exchange rate, the pound price of $1 is $£\frac{1}{2}$.
   d. The dollar appreciates if the demand for pounds increases.

2. **At the price of $2 for £1 in this figure:**
   a. the dollar-pound exchange rate is unstable.
   b. the quantity of pounds supplied equals the quantity demanded.
   c. the dollar price of £1 equals the pound price of $1.
   d. U.S. goods exports to Britain must equal U.S. goods imports from Britain.

3. **Other things equal, a leftward shift of the demand curve in this figure:**
   a. would depreciate the dollar.
   b. would create a shortage of pounds at the previous price of $2 for £1.

   c. might be caused by a major recession in the United States.
   d. might be caused by a significant rise of real interest rates in Britain.

4. **Other things equal, a rightward shift of the supply curve in this figure would:**
   a. depreciate the dollar and might be caused by a significant rise of real interest rates in Britain.
   b. depreciate the dollar and might be caused by a significant fall of real interest rates in Britain.
   c. appreciate the dollar and might be caused by a significant rise of real interest rates in the United States.
   d. appreciate the dollar and might be caused by a significant fall of real interest rates in the United States.

As a concrete example, suppose that you are a U.S. citizen on vacation in London. If it takes only 50 cents to buy 1 pound, you will end up wanting to purchase many more souvenirs than if it cost $1.50 to buy 1 pound. The lower the dollar price of purchasing a pound, the less expensive British goods and services appear to you and the more dollars you want to sell for pounds in order to buy "cheap" British products. So the demand curve for pounds slopes downward.

The *supply-of-pounds curve* S_1 slopes upward because the British will purchase more U.S. goods as the dollar price of a pound rises (that is, as the pound price of a dollar falls). The more dollars the British can get in exchange for £1, the less expensive U.S. products will look to them and, hence, the more pounds they will want to supply so as to get the dollars they need to purchase "cheap" U.S. products.

The intersection of the supply curve and the demand curve determine the dollar price of pounds. In Figure 40.1, that price (exchange rate) is $2 for £1. At this exchange rate, the quantities of pounds supplied and demanded are equal; neither a shortage nor a surplus of pounds occurs.

fixed exchange rate A *rate of exchange* that is pegged by a government or central bank at a particular ratio (for instance, $1 = 6 yuan) rather than being allowed to vary with changes in demand and supply.

Depreciation and Appreciation

An exchange rate determined by market forces can, and often does, change constantly, just as stock and bond prices do.

- When the dollar price of pounds *rises*, for example, from $2 = £1 to $3 = £1, the dollar has *depreciated* relative to the pound (and the pound has appreciated relative to the dollar). When a currency depreciates, more units of it (dollars) are needed to buy a single unit of the other currency (the pound).

- When the dollar price of pounds *falls*, for example, from $2 = £1 to $1 = £1, the dollar has *appreciated* relative to the pound (and the pound has depreciated relative to the dollar). When a currency appreciates, fewer units of it (dollars) are needed to buy a single unit of the other currency (pounds).

Note that a depreciation of the dollar implies an appreciation of the pound, and vice versa. When the dollar price of a pound jumps from $2 = £1 to $3 = £1, the pound has appreciated relative to the dollar because it takes fewer pounds to buy $1. At $2 = £1, it took £$\frac{1}{2}$ to buy $1; at $3 = £1, it takes only £$\frac{1}{3}$ to buy $1. Conversely, when the dollar appreciates relative to the pound, the pound depreciates relative to the dollar. More pounds are needed to buy a dollar.

In general, the relevant terminology and relationships between the U.S. dollar and another currency are as follows (where the "≡" sign means "is equivalent to").

- Dollar price of foreign currency *increases* ≡ dollar depreciates relative to the foreign currency ≡ foreign currency price of dollar decreases ≡ foreign currency appreciates relative to the dollar.

- Dollar price of foreign currency *decreases* ≡ dollar appreciates relative to the foreign currency ≡ foreign currency price of dollar increases ≡ foreign currency depreciates relative to the dollar.

Determinants of Flexible Exchange Rates

What factors cause a nation's currency to appreciate or depreciate in the market for foreign exchange? Here are three generalizations:

- If the demand for a nation's currency increases, that currency will appreciate. If the demand declines, that currency will depreciate.

- If the supply of a nation's currency increases, that currency will depreciate. If the supply decreases, that currency will appreciate.

- If a nation's currency appreciates, some foreign currency depreciates relative to it.

With these generalizations in mind, let's examine the determinants of exchange rates—the factors that shift the demand or supply curve for a certain currency. As we do so, keep in mind that the other-things-equal assumption is always in force.

Changes in Tastes Any change in consumer tastes or preferences for the products of a foreign country may alter the demand for that nation's currency and change its exchange rate. If technological advances in U.S. aircraft make them more attractive to British consumers and businesses, then the British will supply more pounds in the exchange market to purchase more U.S. airplanes. The supply-of-pounds curve shifts to the right, causing the pound to depreciate and the dollar to appreciate.

In contrast, the U.S. demand-for-pounds curve shifts to the right if British woolen apparel becomes more fashionable in the United States. The pound will appreciate and the dollar will depreciate.

Relative Income Changes A nation's currency is likely to depreciate if its growth of national income is more rapid than that of other countries. Here's why: A country's imports vary directly with its income level. As national income rises in the United States, Americans will buy both more domestic goods and more foreign goods. If the U.S. economy is expanding rapidly and the British economy is stagnant, U.S. imports of British goods, and therefore U.S. demands for pounds, will increase. The dollar price of pounds will rise, so the dollar will depreciate.

Relative Inflation Rate Changes Other things equal, changes in the relative inflation rates of two nations change their relative price levels and alter the exchange rate between their currencies. The currency of the nation with the higher inflation rate—the more rapidly rising price level—tends to depreciate. Suppose, for example, that inflation is zero percent in Great Britain and 5 percent in the United States so that prices, on average, are rising by 5 percent per year in the United States while, on average, prices remain unchanged in Great Britain. U.S. consumers will seek out more of the now relatively lower-priced British goods, increasing the demand for pounds. British consumers will purchase less of the now relatively higher-priced U.S. goods, reducing the supply of pounds. This combination of increased demand for pounds and reduced supply of pounds causes the pound to appreciate and the dollar to depreciate.

According to **purchasing-power-parity theory,** exchange rates should eventually adjust such that they equate the purchasing power of various currencies. If a certain market basket of identical products costs $10,000 in the United States and £5,000 in Great Britain, the exchange rate should move to $2 = £1. That way, a dollar spent in the United States will buy exactly as much output as it would if it were first converted to pounds (at the $2 = £1 exchange rate) and then used to buy output in Great Britain.

In terms of our example, 5 percent inflation in the United States will increase the price of the market basket from $10,000 to $10,500, while the zero percent inflation in Great Britain will leave the market basket priced at £5,000. For purchasing power parity to hold, the exchange rate would have to move from $2 = £1 to $2.10 = £1. That means the dollar would depreciate and the pound would appreciate. In practice, however, exchange rates are often very slow to adjust to equate the purchasing power of various currencies and thereby achieve "purchasing power parity," even over long periods.

purchasing-power-parity theory The idea that if countries have *flexible exchange rates* (rather than *fixed exchange rates*), the exchange rates between national currencies will adjust to equate the purchasing power of various currencies. In particular, the exchange rate between any two national currencies will adjust to reflect the *price-level* differences between the two countries.

Relative Interest Rates Changes in relative interest rates between two countries may alter their exchange rate. Suppose that real interest rates rise in the United States but stay constant in Great Britain. British citizens will then find the United States a more attractive place in which to loan money directly or loan money indirectly by buying bonds. To make these loans, they have to supply pounds in the foreign exchange market to obtain dollars. The increase in the supply of pounds results in depreciation of the pound and appreciation of the dollar.

Changes in Relative Expected Returns on Stocks, Real Estate, and Production Facilities International investing extends beyond buying foreign bonds. It also includes international investments in stocks and real estate as well as foreign purchases of factories and production facilities. Other things equal, the extent of this foreign investment depends on relative expected returns. To make the investments, investors in one country must sell their own local currency to purchase the foreign currencies needed for their foreign investments.

For instance, suppose that investing in England suddenly becomes more popular due to a more positive outlook regarding expected returns on English stocks, real estate, and production facilities. U.S. investors therefore will sell U.S. assets to buy more assets in England. The U.S. assets will be sold for dollars, which will then be brought to the foreign exchange market and exchanged for pounds, which will in turn be used to purchase British assets. The increased demand for pounds in the foreign exchange market will cause the pound to appreciate and therefore the dollar to depreciate relative to the pound.

TABLE 40.2 Determinants of Exchange Rates: Factors That Change the Demand for or the Supply of a Particular Currency and Thus Alter the Exchange Rate

Determinant	Examples
Change in tastes	Japanese electronic equipment declines in popularity in the United States (Japanese yen depreciates; U.S. dollar appreciates).
	European tourists reduce visits to the United States (U.S. dollar depreciates; European euro appreciates).
Change in relative incomes	England encounters a recession, reducing its imports, while U.S. real output and real income surge, increasing U.S. imports (British pound appreciates; U.S. dollar depreciates).
Change in relative inflation rates	Switzerland experiences a 1% inflation rate compared to Canada's 5% rate (Swiss franc appreciates; Canadian dollar depreciates).
Change in relative real interest rates	The Federal Reserve drives up interest rates in the United States, while the Bank of England takes no such action (U.S. dollar appreciates; British pound depreciates).
Changes in relative expected returns on stocks, real estate, or production facilities	Corporate tax cuts in the United States raise expected after-tax investment returns in the United States relative to those in Europe (U.S. dollar appreciates; the euro depreciates).
Speculation	Currency traders believe South Korea will have much greater inflation than Taiwan (South Korean won depreciates; Taiwanese dollar appreciates).
	Currency traders think Norway's interest rates will plummet relative to Denmark's rates (Norway's krone depreciates; Denmark's krone appreciates).

Speculation *Currency speculators* buy and sell currencies with an eye toward reselling or repurchasing them at a profit. Suppose speculators expect the U.S. economy to (1) grow more rapidly than the British economy and (2) experience more rapid inflation than Britain. These expectations translate into an anticipation that the pound will appreciate and the dollar will depreciate. Speculators who are holding dollars will therefore try to convert them into pounds. This effort will increase the demand for pounds and cause the dollar price of pounds to rise (that is, cause the dollar to depreciate). A self-fulfilling prophecy occurs: The pound appreciates and the dollar depreciates because speculators act on the belief that these changes will in fact take place. In this way, speculation can cause changes in exchange rates.

Table 40.2 provides additional examples of the determinants of exchange rates; the table is worth careful study.

Disadvantages of Flexible Exchange Rates

Flexible exchange rates may cause several significant problems, all related to the fact that flexible exchange rates are often volatile and can change by a large amount in just a few weeks or months. In addition, they often take substantial swings that can last several years or more.

Uncertainty and Diminished Trade The risks and uncertainties associated with flexible exchange rates may discourage the flow of trade. Suppose a U.S. automobile dealer contracts to purchase 10 British cars for £150,000. At the current exchange rate of, say, $2 for £1, the U.S. importer expects to pay $300,000 for these automobiles. But if during the 3-month delivery period the exchange rate shifts to $3 for £1, the £150,000 payment contracted by the U.S. importer will become $450,000.

That increase in the dollar price of pounds may thus turn the U.S. importer's anticipated profit into a substantial loss. Aware of the possibly adverse change in the exchange rate, the U.S. importer may not be willing to assume the risks involved. The U.S. firm may confine its operations to domestic automobiles, thereby reducing the volume of international trade.

The same thing can happen with investments. Assume that when the exchange rate is $3 to £1, a U.S. firm invests $30,000 (or £10,000) in a British enterprise. It estimates a return of 10 percent; that is, it anticipates annual earnings of $3,000, or £1,000. Suppose these expectations prove correct in that the British firm earns £1,000 in the first year on the £10,000 investment. But suppose that during the year, the value of the dollar appreciates to $2 = £1. The absolute return is now only $2,000 (rather than $3,000), and the rate of return falls from the anticipated 10 percent to only $6\frac{2}{3}$ percent (= $2,000/$30,000).

Investment is always risky. But the risk of changing exchange rates affects only international investments, not domestic investments. That added risk may persuade the U.S. investor not to venture overseas.

Terms-of-Trade Changes A decline in the international value of its currency will worsen a nation's terms of trade. For example, an increase in the dollar price of a pound will mean that the United States must export more goods and services to finance a specific level of imports from Britain.

Instability Flexible exchange rates may destabilize the domestic economy because wide fluctuations in the exchange rate may stimulate and then depress domestic industries that produce exported goods. If the U.S. economy is operating at full employment and its currency depreciates, the results will be inflationary, for two reasons. (1) Foreign demand for U.S. goods may rise, increasing total spending and pulling up U.S. prices. Also, the prices of all U.S. imports will increase. (2) Conversely, appreciation of the dollar will lower U.S. exports and increase imports, possibly causing unemployment.

Flexible or floating exchange rates also may complicate the use of domestic stabilization policies that seek full employment and price stability, especially in nations whose exports and imports are large relative to their total domestic output.

▶ Under a flexible exchange rate system, exchange rates are determined by the demand for, and supply of, individual national currencies in the foreign exchange market.

▶ Determinants of flexible exchange rates (factors that shift currency supply and demand curves) include (a) changes in tastes; (b) relative national incomes; (c) relative inflation rates; (d) real interest rates; (e) relative expected returns on stocks, real estate, and production facilities; and (f) speculation.

▶ The volatility of flexible exchange rates may have several negative consequences, including discouraging international trade, worsening a nation's terms of trade, and destabilizing a nation's domestic economy by depressing export industries.

Fixed Exchange Rates

>> **LO40.4** Distinguish between flexible and fixed exchange rates.

To circumvent the disadvantages of flexible exchange rates, governments have at times fixed or "pegged" their exchange rates. Under a fixed exchange rate, the government stands ready to buy or sell as much of its own currency as is demanded or supplied at the constant (fixed) exchange rate that it announces.

Suppose that the U.S. government decides to fix the dollar-pound exchange rate at $2 = £1. To enforce that peg, the U.S. government must stand ready to exchange both pounds for dollars as well as dollars for pounds at the fixed ratio of $2 = £1. If Americans want to exchange $20 billion for pounds, the U.S. government will need to come up with 10 billion pounds (= the required number of pounds at the $2 = £1 exchange rate). And if Britons wish to exchange £6 billion for dollars, the U.S. government will have to come up with 12 billion dollars (= required number of dollars at the $2 = £1 exchange rate).

Foreign Exchange Market Replaced by Government Peg

As long as the U.S. government is able to come up with the necessary amounts of both dollars (to satisfy exchange requests for pounds) and pounds (to satisfy exchange requests for dollars), the fixed exchange rate will preempt the foreign exchange market. All buying and selling of pounds for dollars or dollars for pounds will take place with the U.S. government. The U.S. government will *become* the dollar-pound foreign exchange market.

There will be no other dollar-pound market because, as long as the U.S. government can maintain the peg, there will be no other exchange rate that buyers and sellers will both simultaneously prefer, and thus no possibility of a given buyer and a given seller ever voluntarily agreeing to exchange dollars for pounds at any other exchange rate. To understand why, consider an exchange rate like $3 = £1. British citizens wishing to convert pounds to dollars will prefer $3 = £1 to the $2 = £1 exchange rate being offered by the U.S. government because each of their pounds would convert into $3 rather than $2. But will British citizens be able to find anyone willing to take the opposite end of the deal and exchange dollars for pounds at a $3 = £1 exchange rate? The answer is no, because anyone wishing to convert dollars to pounds can go to the U.S. government and exchange money at the rate of $2 = £1, under which they will have to give up only $2 (rather than $3) to buy £1. So while British citizens prefer any exchange rate that gives them more dollars per pound than the $2 = £1 rate being offered by the U.S. government, they are not going to find anybody willing to exchange money at those rates. Thus anybody who wants to exchange pounds for dollars will end up dealing with the U.S. government and exchanging money at the $2 = £1 fixed rate.

You should take a moment to convince yourself that the reverse is also true: While Americans would prefer an exchange rate that requires them to give up less than $2 for each £1, no British citizen would willingly accept a rate lower than $2 = £1 because doing so would mean receiving fewer dollars for their pounds than if they exchanged their pounds at the $2 = £1 exchange rate being offered by the U.S. government. So everyone wishing to exchange dollars for pounds will also end up dealing with the U.S. government and exchanging money at the $2 = £1 fixed exchange rate.

Note, however, that if the U.S. government ever stops honoring its pledge to exchange dollars for pounds and pounds for dollars at the $2 = £1 exchange rate, a private market for foreign exchange will instantly pop back into existence to connect the buyers and sellers of dollars and pounds. Because the exchange rate will be determined by supply and demand once again, it may end up at an equilibrium value that is substantially different from the fixed exchange rate that the government abandoned.

Official Reserves

A government that opts for a fixed exchange rate typically places its central bank in charge of day-to-day operations. It thus becomes the central bank's task to exchange as much local currency for foreign currency and as much foreign currency for local currency as is necessary each day to maintain the peg.

Satisfying requests to exchange foreign currency for local currency is easy, as the central bank has the legal right to print as much local currency as it wants. But to satisfy requests to exchange local currency for foreign currency, the central bank must maintain a stock (inventory) of foreign currency because it can't legally create additional units of any other country's money.

The stock of the particular foreign currency that is used to maintain the fixed exchange rate is just one component of the **official reserves** that the central bank will maintain for the government. The official reserves will consist not only of stockpiles of various foreign currencies but also stockpiles of bonds issued by foreign governments, gold reserves, and special reserves held at the International Monetary Fund. The stockpiles of foreign currencies are called **foreign-exchange reserves,** or, less formally, FX reserves.

Defending a Peg by Altering Demand or Supply

Because a central bank that sets a fixed exchange rate must stand ready to buy and sell as much domestic and foreign currency as is demanded each day, it is possible that a central bank will run out of FX reserves. If that happens, the central bank will have to abandon its peg unless it (1) can get an emergency loan of foreign currency from the International Monetary Fund or (2) take drastic steps to alter or limit the quantities of currency demanded and supplied each day. Those drastic steps fall into three categories.

Trade Policies A nation that is pursuing a fixed exchange rate can undertake policies that alter the volume of international trade and finance as a way of helping to maintain a peg. The United States could try, for instance, to maintain the $2 = £1 exchange rate in the face of a shortage of pounds by discouraging imports (thereby reducing the demand for pounds) and encouraging exports (thus increasing the supply of pounds). Imports could be reduced by means of new tariffs or import quotas; special taxes could be levied on the interest and dividends U.S. financial investors receive from foreign investments. Also, the U.S. government could subsidize certain U.S. exports to increase the supply of pounds.

The fundamental problem is that these policies reduce the volume of world trade and change its makeup from what is economically desirable. When nations impose tariffs, quotas, and the like, they lose some of the economic benefits of a free flow of world trade. That loss should not be underestimated: Trade barriers by one nation lead to retaliatory responses from other nations, multiplying the loss.

Exchange Controls and Rationing Another option is to adopt rationing via exchange controls (which are also sometimes referred to as capital controls). Under **exchange controls,** the U.S.

official reserves Foreign *currencies* owned by the central bank of a nation.

foreign-exchange reserves Stockpiles of foreign currencies maintained by a nation's *central bank.* Obtained when the *central bank* sells local currency in exchange for foreign currency in the *foreign exchange market.*

exchange controls Restrictions that a government may impose over the quantity of foreign currency demand by its citizens and *firms* and over the *rate of exchange* as a way to limit the nation's quantity of *outpayments* relative to its quantity of *inpayments* (in order to eliminate a *payments deficit*).

government could handle the problem of a pound shortage by requiring that all pounds obtained by U.S. exporters be sold to the federal government. Then the government would allocate or ration this limited supply of pounds among various U.S. importers. This policy would restrict the value of U.S. imports to the amount of foreign exchange earned by U.S. exports. Assuming balance in the capital and financial account, there would then be no balance-of-payments deficit.

There are major objections to exchange controls:

- *Distorted trade* Like *trade controls* (tariffs, quotas, and export subsidies), exchange controls will distort the pattern of international trade away from the pattern suggested by comparative advantage.

- *Favoritism* The process of rationing scarce foreign exchange might lead to government favoritism toward selected importers (big contributors to reelection campaigns, for example).

- *Restricted choice* Controls will limit freedom of consumer choice. The U.S. consumers who prefer Volkswagens might have to buy Chevrolets. The business opportunities for some U.S. importers might be impaired if the government decides to limit imports.

- *Black markets* Enforcement problems are likely under exchange controls. U.S. importers might want foreign exchange badly enough to pay more than the $2 = £1$ official rate, setting the stage for black-market dealings between importers and illegal sellers of foreign exchange.

Domestic Macroeconomic Adjustments A final way to help maintain a fixed exchange rate is to use domestic stabilization policies (monetary policy and fiscal policy) to eliminate a shortage of foreign currency. Tax hikes, reductions in government spending, and a high-interest-rate policy will reduce total spending in the U.S. economy and, consequently, domestic income. Because the volume of imports varies directly with domestic income, demand for British goods, and therefore for pounds, will be restrained.

If these "contractionary" policies reduce the domestic price level relative to Britain's, U.S. buyers of consumer and capital goods will divert their demands from British goods to U.S. goods, reducing the demand for pounds. Moreover, the high-interest-rate policy will lift U.S. interest rates relative to those in Britain.

Lower prices on U.S. goods and higher U.S. interest rates will increase British imports of U.S. goods and increase British financial investment in the United States. Both developments will increase the supply of pounds. The combination of a decrease in the demand for and an increase in the supply of pounds will reduce or eliminate the original U.S. balance-of-payments deficit.

Maintaining fixed exchange rates by such means is hardly appealing. The "price" of exchange-rate stability for the United States will be a decline in output, employment, and price levels—in other words, a recession. Maintaining a peg and achieving domestic stability are both important national economic goals, but to sacrifice macroeconomic stability simply to defend a currency peg would be to let the tail wag the dog.

This chapter's Last Word discusses these concerns in the context of the so-called exchange rate trilemma, which points out that governments have to make hard choices when it comes to choosing an exchange rate policy.

QUICK REVIEW
40.4

- ▶ To circumvent the disadvantages of flexible exchange rates, at times nations have fixed or "pegged" their exchange rates.

- ▶ Under a system of fixed exchange rates, nations set their exchange rates and then maintain them by buying or selling official reserves of currencies, establishing trade barriers, employing exchange controls, or incurring inflation or recession.

- ▶ Under a fixed exchange rate, any increase (decrease) in foreign exchange reserves will automatically generate an accompanying increase (decrease) in the domestic money supply that can cause inflation (deflation) unless it is offset by other policy actions.

The Current Exchange Rate System: The Managed Float

>> **LO40.5** Explain the current system of managed floating exchange rates.

Over the past 140 years, the world's nations have used three different exchange-rate systems. From 1879 to 1934, most nations used a gold standard, which implicitly created fixed exchange rates. From 1944 to 1971, most countries participated in the Bretton Woods system, which was a fixed-exchange-rate system indirectly tied to gold. Since 1971, most countries have mixed mostly flexible exchange rates with occasional **currency interventions** during which a government buys or sells foreign exchange in order to stabilize short-term changes in exchange rates or to correct exchange rate imbalances that are negatively affecting the world economy.

Because the current exchange-rate system mixes mostly flexible exchange rates with occasional government intervention, it is thought of as generating **managed floating exchange rates.** Under this system, the major currencies such as dollars, euros, pounds, and yen fluctuate in response to changes in supply and demand. At the same time, some developing nations like China peg their currency to the U.S. dollar, and then allow their currency to fluctuate with it against other currencies. Also, some nations peg the value of their currencies to a "basket" or group of other currencies.

How well does the managed float work? It has both proponents and critics.

In Support of the Managed Float Proponents of the managed-float system argue that it has functioned far better than many experts anticipated. Skeptics had predicted that fluctuating exchange rates would reduce world trade and finance. But in real terms, world trade under the managed float has grown tremendously over the past several decades. Moreover, as supporters are quick to point out, currency crises, such as those in Turkey and Lebanon in 2021, were not the result of the floating-exchange-rate system itself. Rather, the abrupt currency devaluations and depreciations resulted from internal problems in those nations.

Proponents also point out that the managed float has weathered severe economic turbulence that might have caused a fixed-rate system to break down. Events including the OPEC oil embargoes of 1970s, major national recessions in the 1980s, and the collapse of the Soviet Bloc in the 1990s all caused substantial imbalances in international trade and finance, as did soaring U.S. budget deficits in the 2000s, the Great Recession of 2007–2009, and the European Debt Crisis of the mid-2010s. Flexible rates enabled the system to adjust to all these events, whereas the same events would have put unbearable pressure on a fixed-rate system.

Concerns with the Managed Float There is still much sentiment in favor of greater exchange-rate stability. Those favoring more stable exchange rates see problems with the current system. They argue that the excessive volatility of exchange rates under the managed float threatens the prosperity of economies that rely heavily on exports. Several financial crises in individual nations (including Mexico, South Korea, Indonesia, Thailand, Russia, and Brazil) were exacerbated by abrupt changes in exchange rates. These crises led to massive "bailouts" of those economies via loans from the International Monetary Fund (IMF). But the availability of IMF bailouts may spur moral hazard. Nations may undertake risky and inappropriate economic policies because they expect the IMF to bail them out if problems arise. Moreover, some exchange-rate volatility has occurred even when underlying economic and financial conditions were relatively stable, suggesting that speculation plays too large a role in determining exchange rates.

Skeptics say the managed float is basically a "nonsystem" because the guidelines as to what each nation may or may not do with its exchange rates are not specific enough to keep the system working in the long run. Nations inevitably will be tempted to intervene in the foreign exchange market, not merely to smooth out short-term fluctuations in exchange rates but also to prop up their currency if it is chronically weak, manipulate the exchange rate to achieve domestic stabilization goals, or utilize an artificially depreciated currency to give its exporters an unfair advantage in international trade.

So what are we to conclude? Flexible exchange rates have not worked perfectly, but they have not failed miserably. Thus far they have survived, and no doubt have eased, several major shocks to the international trading system. Meanwhile, the "managed" part of the float has given nations some sense of control over their collective economic destinies. On balance, most economists favor continuation of the present system of "almost" flexible exchange rates.

---

currency intervention
A government's buying and selling of its own currency or foreign currencies to alter international exchange rates.

managed floating exchange rate An *exchange rate* that is allowed to change (float) as a result of changes in *currency* supply and demand but at times is altered (managed) by governments via their buying and selling of particular currencies.

▶ The managed floating system of exchange rates (1971–present) relies on foreign exchange markets to establish equilibrium exchange rates.

▶ Under the system, nations can buy and sell official reserves of foreign currency to stabilize short-term changes in exchange rates or to correct exchange-rate imbalances that are negatively affecting the world economy.

▶ Proponents point out that international trade and investment have grown tremendously under the system. Critics say that it is a "nonsystem" and argue that the exchange rate volatility allowed under the managed float discourages international trade and investment. That is, trade and investment would be even larger if exchange rates were more stable.

QUICK REVIEW

40.5

Recent U.S. Trade Deficits

>> **LO40.6** Identify the causes and consequences of recent U.S. trade deficits.

As Figure 40.2a shows, the United States has experienced large and persistent trade deficits in recent decades. These deficits rose rapidly in the early 2000s, with the trade deficit on goods and services peaking at $764 billion in 2006. The trade deficit on goods and services then declined precipitously to just $395 billion in 2009 as consumers and businesses greatly curtailed their purchases of imports during the Great Recession of 2007–2009. As the economy recovered from that recession, the trade deficit on goods and services began rising again and reached $555 billion in 2011 before a series of annual deficits that ranged between $447 billion and $581 billion through 2019.

The strong stimulus spending enacted to fight the COVID-19 pandemic in 2020 and the strong rebound in U.S. economic growth during 2021 caused cash-rich U.S. consumers to increase their purchases of imports at the same time that many foreign consumers cut back on their purchases of U.S. exports (because their countries were experiencing slower recoveries from the COVID-19 recession than the United States was). The result was a massive $861 billion trade deficit in goods and services for the United States in 2021.

The current account deficit (Figure 40.2b) reached a then-record high of $817 billion in 2006, equivalent to about 6.0 percent of that year's GDP. The current account deficit subsequently declined to $380 billion—2.6 percent of GDP—in the recession year 2009. After the 2007–2009 recession ended, the current account deficit fluctuated but generally tended to increase, reaching $472 billion in 2019, or about 2.2 percent of that year's GDP. In 2021, however, the current account deficit soared to $822 billion, thereby exceeding 2006's previous record of $817 billion. But because U.S. GDP had grown 66 percent larger between 2006 and 2021, the $822 billion current account deficit of 2021 was only about 3.6 percent of that year's GDP, meaning that it was, as a percentage of GDP, substantially less than the $817 billion current account deficit recorded in 2006.

Causes of the Trade Deficits

The large U.S. trade deficits have had several causes. First, the U.S. economy expanded more rapidly between 2002 and 2007 than the economies of several U.S. trading partners. The strong U.S. income growth that accompanied that economic growth enabled Americans to greatly increase their purchases of imported products. In contrast, Japan and some European nations suffered recession or experienced relatively slow income growth over that same period. So consumers in those countries increased their purchases of U.S. exports much less rapidly than Americans increased their purchases of foreign imports.

FIGURE 40.2 U.S. trade deficits, 2005–2021.

(a) The United States experienced large deficits in *goods* and in *goods and services* between 2005 and 2021. (b) The U.S. current account, generally reflecting the goods and services deficit, was also in substantial deficit. The large current account and trade deficits are expected to continue for many years to come.

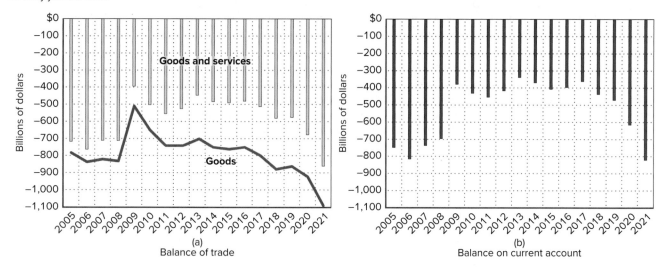

(a)
Balance of trade

(b)
Balance on current account

Source: Bureau of Economic Analysis.

Another factor explaining the large trade deficits is the enormous U.S. trade imbalance with China. In 2021 the United States imported $355 billion more of goods and services from China than it exported to China. Even in the recession year 2009, the trade deficit with China was $220 billion. The 2021 deficit with China was 50 percent larger than the combined deficits with Mexico ($108 billion), Germany ($70 billion), and Japan ($60 billion). The United States is China's largest export market, and although China has greatly increased its imports from the United States, its standard of living has not yet risen sufficiently for its households to afford large quantities of U.S. products. Adding to the problem, China's government has fixed the exchange rate of its currency, the yuan, to a basket of currencies that includes the U.S. dollar. Therefore, China's large trade surpluses with the United States have not caused the yuan to appreciate much against the U.S. dollar. Greater appreciation of the yuan would have made Chinese goods more expensive in the United States and reduced U.S. imports from China. In China, a stronger yuan would have reduced the dollar price of U.S. goods and increased Chinese purchases of U.S. exports. That combination—reduced U.S. imports from China and increased U.S. exports to China—would have reduced the large U.S. trade imbalance.

A declining U.S. saving rate (= saving/total income) also contributed to the large U.S. trade deficits. Up until the recession of 2007–2009, the U.S. saving rate declined substantially, while its investment rate (= investment/total income) increased. The gap between U.S. investment and U.S. saving was filled by foreign purchases of U.S. real and financial assets, which created a large surplus on the U.S. capital and financial account. Because foreign savers were willing to finance a large part of U.S. investment, Americans were able to save less and consume more. Part of that added consumption spending was on imported goods.

Finally, many foreigners simply view U.S. assets favorably because of the relatively high risk-adjusted rates of return they provide. The purchase of those assets provides foreign currency to Americans that enables them to finance their strong appetite for imported goods. The capital account surpluses, therefore, may partially cause the high U.S. trade deficits, not just result from those high deficits.

Implications of U.S. Trade Deficits

The prerecession U.S. trade deficits were the largest ever run by a major industrial nation. Whether the large trade deficits should be of significant concern to the United States and the rest of the world is debatable. Most economists see both benefits and costs to trade deficits.

Increased Current Consumption At the time a trade deficit or a current account deficit is occurring, American consumers benefit. A trade deficit means that the United States is receiving more goods and services as imports from abroad than it is sending out as exports. Taken alone, a trade deficit allows the United States to consume outside its production possibilities curve. It augments the domestic standard of living. But there is a catch: The gain in present consumption may come at the expense of reduced future consumption. When and if the current account deficit declines, Americans may have to consume less than before and perhaps even less than they produce.

Increased U.S. Indebtedness A trade deficit is considered unfavorable because it must be financed by borrowing from the rest of the world, selling off assets, or dipping into official reserves. Recall that current account deficits are financed by surpluses in the capital and financial accounts. Such surpluses require a net inflow of dollars to buy U.S. assets, including debt issued by Americans. Therefore, when U.S. exports are insufficient to finance U.S. imports, the United States increases both its debt to people abroad and the value of foreign claims against assets in the United States. Financing of the U.S. trade deficit has resulted in a larger foreign accumulation of claims against U.S. financial and real assets than the U.S. claim against foreign assets. In 2021, foreigners owned about $18 trillion more of U.S. assets (corporations, land, stocks, bonds, loan notes) than U.S. citizens and institutions owned of foreign assets.

If the United States wants to regain ownership of these domestic assets, at some future time it will have to export more than it imports. At that time, domestic consumption will be lower because the United States will need to send more of its output abroad than it receives as imports. Therefore, the current consumption gains delivered by U.S. current account deficits may mean permanent debt, permanent foreign ownership, or large sacrifices of future consumption.

We say "may mean" because the foreign lending to U.S. firms and foreign investment in the United States increases the U.S. capital stock. U.S. production capacity therefore might increase

The Exchange Rate Trilemma

Countries Cannot Achieve All Three of the Most Coveted Goals of Exchange Rate Policy Simultaneously. The Best They Can Do is "Two Out of Three."

Countries must choose between three possible Exchange Rate Policies. This three-way choice—or "trilemma"—is made more difficult by the fact that each Policy can achieve only two out three desirable Goals. Countries would love to be able to achieve all three goals at once. But only two out of three can be obtained at a time—which means that policymakers have to think very carefully about which two Goals they care about the most and, thus, which Policy they need to select in order to achieve those two Goals.

In the nearby triangular figure, each corner represents one of the three Goals.

- Goal A is *Exchange-Rate Stability*, meaning that a country's exchange rate with other currencies will remain stable (or even perfectly constant) over time.

- Goal B is *Free Financial and Trade Flows*, meaning that anyone can buy or sell as much of the country's currency as they would like in order to buy or sell assets anywhere in the world or to import or export goods to whatever extent they please.

- Goal C is an *Independent Monetary Policy* that can always be directed toward setting interest rates and monetary policy so as to best suit the needs of the country's own domestic economy and its own unique business cycle (rather than having to focus on other factors).

As we mentioned above, it is only possible for countries to achieve two out of the three Goals at a time. But countries do not choose exchange rate Goals; they choose exchange-rate Policies. As it turns out, there are exactly three exchange-rate Policies to choose from. In the figure, the three Policies are represented by the three sides of the triangle, with each side connecting the two Goals that it can achieve.

- Policy #1 is Exchange Controls, meaning rules set by the central bank as to how much money individuals and businesses can exchange per day or per month if there is a fixed exchange rate or a highly constrained dirty float. If a country opts for Policy #1 (Exchange Controls), then it can achieve Goal A (*Exchange Rate Stability*) and Goal C (an *Independent Monetary Policy*) but not Goal B (*Free Financial and Trade Flows*).

- By contrast, if a country opts for Policy #2 (a Fixed Exchange Rate), then it can achieve Goal A (*Exchange Rate Stability*) and Goal B (*Free Financial and Trade Flows*) but not Goal C (an *Independent Monetary Policy*).

- Finally, if a country opts for Policy #3 (a Floating Exchange Rate), then it can achieve Goal B (*Free Financial and Trade Flows*) and Goal C (an *Independent Monetary Policy*) but not Goal A (*Exchange Rate Stability*).

Note again that the side of the triangle that represents a particular Policy connects to the two Goals that that Policy can achieve. Also note that the side of the triangle that represents a particular policy lies *opposite* to the Goal that it cannot achieve. So, for example, the side of the triangle that is labeled Policy #2 (Fixed Exchange Rate) connects to the two goals that it can achieve (Goals A and B) while lying opposite to the goal that it cannot achieve (Goal C).

Let's give you some intuition about why countries can only achieve two out of the three Goals when they select a particular exchange-rate Policy. Consider Hong Kong, which uses Policy #2 (a Fixed Exchange Rate). In pursuing that Policy, Hong Kong must exchange as much or as little of its own currency as is necessary each day to maintain its fixed exchange rate with the U.S. dollar. But that means that its monetary policy is entirely devoted to maintaining its fixed exchange rate and thus cannot be used for expansive or restrictive monetary policy. By choosing to maintain a fixed exchange rate, Hong Kong loses the ability to maintain an *Independent Monetary Policy* (Goal C). Yet, at the same time, its choice of a Fixed Exchange Rate does ensure that it will achieve *Exchange Rate Stability* (Goal A) and *Free Financial and Trade Flows* (Goal B) since a fixed-exchange rate is by definition stable and the willingness of the Hong Kong central bank to exchange as much or as little of its own currency as is necessary to preserve its exchange rate peg means that there will always be as many Hong Kong dollars as people may want for international trade or international asset transactions.

To test yourself, see if you can explain why Policy #1 precludes Goal B and why Policy #3 precludes Goal A.

more rapidly than otherwise because of a large surplus on the capital and financial account. Faster increases in production capacity and real GDP enhance the economy's ability to service foreign debt and buy back real capital, if that is desired.

Trade deficits therefore are a mixed blessing. The long-term impacts of the record-high U.S. trade deficits are largely unknown. That "unknown" worries some economists, who are concerned that foreigners will lose financial confidence in the United States. If that happens, those foreigners will restrict their lending to American households and businesses and also reduce their purchases of U.S. assets. Both actions will decrease the demand for U.S. dollars in the foreign exchange market and cause the U.S. dollar to depreciate. A sudden, large depreciation of the U.S. dollar might disrupt world trade and negatively affect economic growth worldwide. Other economists, however, downplay this scenario. Because any decline in the U.S. capital and financial account surplus is automatically met with a decline in the current account deficit, U.S. net exports would rise and the overall impact on the American economy would be slight.

**QUICK REVIEW
40.6**

▶ The United States has had large trade deficits in recent decades.

▶ Causes include (a) more rapid income growth in the United States than in Japan and some European nations, resulting in expanding U.S. imports relative to exports; (b) the emergence of a large trade deficit with China; (c) continuing large trade deficits with oil-exporting nations; and (d) a large surplus in the capital and financial account, which enabled Americans to reduce their saving and buy more imports.

▶ The severe recession of 2007–2009 in the United States substantially lowered the U.S. trade deficit by reducing American spending on imports.

▶ U.S. trade deficits have produced current increases in the living standards of U.S. consumers but the accompanying surpluses on the capital and financial account have increased U.S. debt to the rest of the world and increased foreign ownership of assets in the United States.

Summary

LO40.1 Explain the two types of international financial transactions.

International financial transactions involve trade either in currently produced goods and services or in preexisting assets. Exports of goods, services, and assets create inflows of money, while imports cause outflows of money. If buyers and sellers use different currencies, then foreign exchange transactions take place so that exporters can be paid in their own currency.

LO40.2 Define and explain the two components of the balance of payments: the current account and the capital and financial account.

The balance of payments records all international trade and financial transactions taking place between a given nation and the rest of the world. The balance on goods and services (the trade balance) compares exports and imports of both goods and services. The current account balance includes not only goods and services transactions but also net investment income and net transfers.

The capital and financial account includes (*a*) the net amount of the nation's debt forgiveness and (*b*) the nation's sale of real and financial assets to people living abroad less its purchases of real and financial assets from foreigners.

The current account and the capital and financial account always sum to zero. A deficit in the current account is always offset by a surplus in the capital and financial account. Conversely, a surplus in the current account is always offset by a deficit in the capital and financial account.

LO40.3 Explain how exchange rates are determined.

Flexible or floating exchange rates between international currencies are determined by the demand for and supply of those currencies. Under flexible rates, a currency will depreciate or appreciate as a result of changes in tastes, relative income changes, relative changes in inflation rates, relative changes in real interest rates, and speculation. The exchange-rate fluctuations that occur under a flexible exchange rate system introduce uncertainty that can reduce the volume of international trade and destabilize the local economy.

LO40.4 Distinguish between flexible and fixed exchange rates.

Some countries have their central banks fix, or peg, their exchange rates to a particular value in order to eliminate the uncertainty about future exchange rates that arises under a floating exchange rate system. Because foreign currencies must be bought and sold to maintain a fixed exchange rate, the central bank will maintain reserves (stockpiles) of various foreign currencies. Those foreign exchange (FX) reserves are a subset of a nation's overall collection of official reserves, which can include gold, foreign bonds, and special reserves held with the International Monetary Fund in addition to its holdings of FX reserves.

To maintain a fixed exchange rate, a central bank will simultaneously stand ready to sell as much foreign currency as buyers demand at the fixed exchange rate and buy as much foreign currency as sellers wish to supply at the fixed exchange rate. If FX reserves fall continuously, they may become exhausted. In such situations, and assuming the country wishes to continue the peg, the country will have to invoke protectionist trade policies, engage in exchange controls, or endure undesirable domestic macroeconomic adjustments.

LO40.5 Explain the current system of managed floating exchange rates.

Since 1971, most of the world's major economies have used a system of managed floating exchange rates. Under a managed float, market forces generally set rates, although governments intervene with varying frequency to alter their exchange rates.

LO40.6 Identify the causes and consequences of recent U.S. trade deficits.

Between 1997 and 2007, the United States had large and rising trade deficits, which are projected to last well into the future. Causes of the trade deficits include (*a*) more rapid income growth in the United States than in Japan and some European nations, resulting in expanding U.S. imports relative to exports, (*b*) the emergence of a large trade deficit with China, and (*c*) a large surplus in the capital and financial account, which enabled Americans to reduce their saving and buy more imports.

U.S. trade deficits have produced current increases in the living standards of U.S. consumers. The accompanying surpluses on the capital and financial account have increased U.S. debt to the rest of the world and increased foreign ownership of assets in the United States. This greater foreign investment in the United States, however, has undoubtedly increased U.S. production possibilities.

Terms and Concepts

international trade	trade surplus	purchasing-power-parity theory
international asset transactions	balance on current account	official reserves
balance of payments	capital and financial account	foreign-exchange reserves
current account	balance on capital and financial account	exchange controls
balance on goods and services	flexible- or floating-exchange-rate system	currency interventions
trade deficit	fixed-exchange-rate system	managed floating exchange rates

Discussion Questions

Mc Graw Hill **connect**

1. Do all international financial transactions necessarily involve exchanging one nation's distinct currency for another? Explain. Could a nation that neither imports goods and services nor exports goods and services still engage in international financial transactions? **LO40.1**

2. Explain: "U.S. exports earn supplies of foreign currencies that Americans can use to finance imports." Indicate whether each of the following creates a demand for or a supply of European euros in foreign exchange markets: **LO40.1**

   a. A U.S. airline firm purchases several Airbus planes assembled in France.

   b. A German automobile firm decides to build an assembly plant in South Carolina.

   c. A U.S. college student decides to spend a year studying at the Sorbonne in Paris.

   d. An Italian manufacturer ships machinery from one Italian port to another on a Liberian freighter.

   e. The U.S. economy grows faster than the French economy.

   f. A U.S. government bond held by a Spanish citizen matures, and the loan amount is paid back to that person.

   g. It is widely expected that the euro will depreciate in the near future.

3. What do the plus signs and negative signs signify in the U.S. balance-of-payments statement? Which of the following items appear in the current account and which appear in the capital and financial account: U.S. purchases of assets abroad, U.S. services imports, foreign purchases of assets in the United States, U.S. goods exports, U.S. net investment income? Why must the current account and the capital and financial account sum to zero? **LO40.2**

4. "Exports pay for imports. Yet in 2021 the nations of the world exported about $861 billion more of goods and services to the United States than they imported from the United States." Resolve the apparent inconsistency of these two statements. **LO40.2**

5. Generally speaking, how is the dollar price of euros determined? Cite a factor that might increase the dollar price of euros. Cite a different factor that might decrease the dollar price of euros. Explain: "A rise in the dollar price of euros necessarily means a fall in the euro price of dollars." Illustrate and elaborate: "The dollar-euro exchange rate provides a direct link between the prices of goods and services produced in the eurozone and in the United States." Explain the purchasing-power-parity theory of exchange rates, using the euro-dollar exchange rate as an illustration. **LO40.3**

6. Suppose that a Swiss watchmaker imports watch components from Sweden and exports watches to the United States. Also suppose the dollar depreciates, and the Swedish krona appreciates, relative to the Swiss franc. Speculate as to how each would hurt the Swiss watchmaker. **LO40.3**

7. Explain why the U.S. demand for Mexican pesos slopes downward and the supply of pesos to Americans slopes upward. Assuming a system of flexible exchange rates between Mexico and the United States, indicate whether each of the following

will cause the Mexican peso to appreciate or depreciate, other things equal: **LO40.3**

a. The United States unilaterally reduces tariffs on Mexican products.

b. Mexico encounters severe inflation.

c. Deteriorating political relations reduce American tourism in Mexico.

d. The U.S. economy moves into a severe recession.

e. The United States engages in a high-interest-rate monetary policy.

f. Mexican products become more fashionable to U.S. consumers.

g. The Mexican government encourages U.S. firms to invest in Mexican oil fields.

h. The rate of productivity growth in the United States diminishes sharply.

8. Explain why you agree or disagree with the following statements. Assume other things equal. **LO40.3**

a. A country that grows faster than its major trading partners can expect the international value of its currency to depreciate.

b. A nation whose interest rate is rising more rapidly than interest rates in other nations can expect the international value of its currency to appreciate.

c. A country's currency will appreciate if its inflation rate is less than that of the rest of the world.

9. Is it accurate to think of a fixed exchange rate as a simultaneous price ceiling and price floor? Explain. **LO40.4**

10. What have been the major causes of the large U.S. trade deficits in recent years? What are the major benefits and costs associated with trade deficits? Explain: "A trade deficit means that a nation is receiving more goods and services from abroad than it is sending abroad." How can that situation be considered "unfavorable"? **LO40.6**

11. **LAST WORD** Explain why Policy #1 precludes the achievement of Goal B while promoting the success of Goals A and C. Then explain why Policy #3 makes it impossible for a country to achieve Goal A while simultaneously helping it to achieve Goals C and B.

Review Questions   connect

1. An American company wants to buy a television from a Chinese company. The Chinese company sells its TVs for 1,200 yuan each. The current exchange rate between the U.S. dollar and the Chinese yuan is $1 = 6 yuan. How many dollars will the American company have to convert into yuan to pay for the television? **LO40.1**

   a. $7,200
   b. $1,200
   c. $200
   d. $100

2. Suppose that a country has a trade surplus of $50 billion, a balance on the capital account of $10 billion, and a balance on the current account of −$200 billion. The balance on the capital and financial account is: **LO40.2**

   a. $10 billion.
   b. $50 billion.
   c. $200 billion.
   d. −$200 billion.

3. The exchange rate between the U.S. dollar and the British pound starts at $1 = £0.5. It then changes to $1 = £0.75. Given this change, we would say that the U.S. dollar has _____ while the British pound has _____. **LO40.3**

   a. depreciated; appreciated
   b. depreciated; depreciated
   c. appreciated; depreciated
   d. appreciated; appreciated

4. A meal at a McDonald's restaurant in New York costs $8. The identical meal at a McDonald's restaurant in London costs £4. According to the purchasing-power-parity theory of exchange rates, the exchange rate between U.S. dollars and British pounds should tend to move toward: **LO40.3**

   a. $2 = £1.
   b. $1 = £2.
   c. $4 = £1.
   d. $1 = £4.

5. Suppose that the Fed is fixing the dollar-pound exchange rate at $2.50 = £1. If the Fed's reserve of pounds falls by £500 million, by how much would the supply of dollars increase, all other things equal? **LO40.4**

6. Suppose that the government of China is currently fixing the exchange rate between the U.S. dollar and the Chinese yuan at a rate of $1 = 6 yuan. Also suppose that at this exchange rate, the people who want to convert dollars to yuan are asking to convert $10 billion per day of dollars into yuan, while the people who want to convert yuan into dollars are asking to convert 36 billion yuan per day into dollars. What will happen to the size of China's official reserves of dollars? **LO40.4**

   a. They will increase.
   b. They will decrease.
   c. They will stay the same.

7. Suppose that a country follows a managed-float policy but that its exchange rate is currently floating freely. In addition, suppose that it has a massive current account deficit. Other things equal, are its official reserves increasing, decreasing, or staying the same? If it decides to engage in a currency intervention to reduce the size of its current account deficit, will it buy or sell its own currency? As it does so, will its official reserves of foreign currencies get larger or smaller? **LO40.5**

8. If the economy booms in the United States while going into recession in other countries, the U.S. trade deficit will tend to _____. **LO40.6**

   a. increase
   b. decrease
   c. remain the same

9. Other things equal, if the United States continually runs trade deficits, foreigners will own _____ U.S. assets. **LO40.6**

   a. more and more
   b. less and less
   c. the same amount of

Problems

1. Alpha's balance-of-payments data for 2020 are shown below. All figures are in billions of dollars. What are the (*a*) balance on goods, (*b*) balance on goods and services, (*c*) balance on current account, and (*d*) balance on capital and financial account? **LO40.2**

Goods exports	$+40
Goods imports	−30
Service exports	+15
Service imports	−10
Net investment income	−5
Net transfers	+10
Balance on capital account	0
Foreign purchases of Alpha assets	+20
Alpha purchases of assets abroad	−40

2. China had a $49.1 billion overall current account surplus in 2018. Assuming that China's net debt forgiveness was zero in 2018 (its capital account balance was zero), by how much did Chinese purchases of financial and real assets abroad exceed foreign purchases of Chinese financial and real assets? **LO40.2**

3. Refer to the following table, in which Q_d is the quantity of loonies demanded, *P* is the dollar price of loonies, Q_s is the quantity of loonies supplied in year 1, and Q_s' is the quantity of loonies supplied in year 2. All quantities are in billions and the dollar-loonie exchange rate is fully flexible. **LO40.3**

Q_d	P	Q_s	Q_s'
10	125	30	20
15	120	25	15
20	115	20	10
25	110	15	5

a. What is the equilibrium dollar price of loonies in year 1?
b. What is the equilibrium dollar price of loonies in year 2?
c. Did the loonie appreciate or did it depreciate relative to the dollar between years 1 and 2?
d. Did the dollar appreciate or did it depreciate relative to the loonie between years 1 and 2?
e. Which one of the following could have caused the change in relative values of the dollar (used in the United States) and the loonie (used in Canada) between years 1 and 2: (1) More rapid inflation in the United States than in Canada, (2) an increase in the real interest rate in the United States but not in Canada, or (3) faster income growth in the United States than in Canada?

4. Suppose that the current Canadian dollar (CAD) to U.S. dollar exchange rate is $0.85 CAD = $1 US and that the U.S. dollar price of an iPhone is $300. What is the Canadian dollar price of an iPhone? Next, suppose that the CAD to U.S. dollar exchange rate moves to $0.96 CAD = $1 US. What is the new Canadian dollar price of an iPhone? Other things equal, would you expect Canada to import more or fewer iPhones at the new exchange rate? Explain. **LO40.3**

5. **ADVANCED ANALYSIS** Return to problem 3 and assume that the exchange rate is fixed at 110. In year 1, what is the minimum initial size of the U.S. reserve of loonies such that the United States can maintain the peg throughout the year? What is the minimum initial size that is necessary at the start of year 2? Next, consider only the data for year 1. What peg should the United States set if it wants the fixed exchange rate to increase the domestic money supply by $1.2 trillion? **LO40.4**

Previous International Exchange-Rate Systems

LO40.7 Explain how exchange rates worked under the gold standard and Bretton Woods.

This chapter explained the current system of managed floating exchange rates. But before this system began in 1971, the world had previously used two other exchange rate systems: the gold standard, which implicitly created fixed exchange rates, and the Bretton Woods system, which was an explicit fixed-rate system indirectly tied to gold. Because the features and problems of these two systems help explain why we have the current system, they are well worth knowing more about.

The Gold Standard: Fixed Exchange Rates

Between 1879 and 1934 the world's major nations adhered to a fixed-rate system called the **gold standard.** Under this system, each nation had to:

- Define its currency in terms of a quantity of gold.
- Maintain a fixed relationship between its stock of gold and its money supply.
- Allow gold to be freely exported and imported.

When each nation defines its currency in terms of gold, the various national currencies have fixed relationships with one another. For example, if the United States defines $1 as worth 25 grains of gold, and Britain defines £1 as worth 50 grains of gold, then a British pound is worth 2×25 grains, or $2. This exchange rate was fixed under the gold standard. The exchange rate did not change in response to changes in currency demand and supply.

Gold Flows If we ignore the costs of packing, insuring, and shipping gold between countries, under the gold standard the rate of exchange would not vary from this $2 = £1 rate. No one in the United States would pay more than $2 = £1 because 50 grains of gold could always be bought for $2 in the United States and sold for £1 in Britain. Nor would the British pay more than £1 for $2. Why should they when they could buy 50 grains of gold in Britain for £1 and sell it in the United States for $2?

Under the gold standard, the potential free flow of gold between nations resulted in fixed exchange rates.

Domestic Macroeconomic Adjustments When currency demand or supply changes, the gold standard requires domestic macroeconomic adjustments to maintain the fixed

exchange rate. To understand why, suppose that U.S. tastes change such that U.S. consumers want to buy more British goods. The resulting increase in the demand for pounds creates a shortage of pounds in the United States, implying a U.S. balance-of-payments deficit.

What will happen? Remember that the rules of the gold standard prohibit the exchange rate from moving from the fixed $2 = £1 rate. The rate cannot move to, say, a new equilibrium at $3 = £1 to correct the imbalance. Instead, gold will flow from the United States to Britain to correct the payments imbalance.

But recall that the gold standard requires participants to maintain a fixed relationship between their domestic money supplies and their quantities of gold. The flow of gold from the United States to Britain will require a reduction of the money supply in the United States. Other things equal, that outflow will reduce total spending in the United States and lower U.S. real domestic output, employment, income, and, perhaps, prices. Also, the decline in the money supply will boost U.S. interest rates.

The opposite will occur in Britain. The inflow of gold will increase the money supply, which will increase total spending in Britain. Domestic output, employment, income, and, perhaps, prices will rise. The British interest rate will fall.

Declining U.S. incomes and prices will reduce the U.S. demand for British goods and therefore reduce the U.S. demand for pounds. Lower interest rates in Britain will make it less attractive for U.S. investors to make financial investments there, also lessening the demand for pounds. For all these reasons, the demand for pounds in the United States will decline. In Britain, higher incomes, prices, and interest rates will make U.S. imports and U.S. financial investments more attractive. In buying these imports and making these financial investments, British citizens will supply more pounds in the exchange market.

In short, domestic macroeconomic adjustments in the United States and Britain, triggered by the international flow of gold, will produce new demand and supply conditions for pounds such that the $2 = £1 exchange rate is maintained. After all the adjustments are made, the United States will not have a payments deficit and Britain will not have a payments surplus.

Thus the gold standard has the advantage of maintaining stable exchange rates and correcting balance-of-payments deficits and surpluses automatically. However, its critical drawback is that nations must accept domestic adjustments in such distasteful forms as unemployment and falling incomes on the one hand, or inflation on the other hand. Under the gold standard, a nation's money supply is altered by changes in supply and demand in currency markets, and nations cannot establish their own monetary policy in their own national interest. If the United States, for example, were to experience declining

---

gold standard A historical system of fixed exchange rates in which nations defined their currencies in terms of gold, maintained fixed relationships between their stocks of gold and their money supplies, and allowed gold to be freely exported and imported.

output and income, the loss of gold under the gold standard would reduce the U.S. money supply. A reduced money supply would increase interest rates, decrease borrowing and spending, and produce further declines in output and income.

Collapse of the Gold Standard

The gold standard collapsed under the weight of the worldwide Depression of the 1930s. As domestic output and employment fell worldwide, the restoration of prosperity became the primary goal of afflicted nations. They responded by enacting protectionist measures to reduce imports. The idea was to get their economies moving again by promoting consumption of domestically produced goods. To make their exports less expensive abroad, many nations redefined their currencies at lower levels in terms of gold. For example, a country that had previously defined the value of its currency at 1 unit = 25 grains of gold might redefine it as 1 unit = 10 grains of gold. Such redefining is an example of **devaluation**—a deliberate action by a government to reduce the international value of its currency. A series of such devaluations in the 1930s meant that exchange rates were no longer fixed. The lack of fixed exchange rates violated a major tenet of the gold standard, and the system broke down.

The Bretton Woods System

The Great Depression and the Second World War left world trade and the world monetary system in shambles. To lay the groundwork for a new international monetary system, in 1944, the major nations held an international conference at Bretton Woods, New Hampshire. The conference produced a commitment to a modified fixed-exchange-rate system called an *adjustable-peg system,* or, simply, the **Bretton Woods system**. The new system sought to capture the advantages of the old gold standard (fixed exchange rate) while avoiding its disadvantages (painful domestic macroeconomic adjustments).

Furthermore, the conference created the **International Monetary Fund (IMF)** to make the new exchange-rate system feasible and workable. The new international monetary system managed through the IMF prevailed with modifications until 1971. (The IMF still plays a basic role in international finance; in recent decades it has performed a major role in providing loans to developing countries, nations experiencing financial crises, and nations making the transition from communism to capitalism.)

---

devaluation A decrease in the governmentally defined value of a currency.

Bretton Woods system The international monetary system developed after the Second World War in which *adjustable pegs* were employed, the *International Monetary Fund* helped stabilize foreign exchange rates, and gold and the dollar were used as *international monetary reserves.*

International Monetary Fund (IMF) The international association of nations that was formed after the Second World War to make loans of foreign monies to nations with temporary *balance of payments deficits* and, until the early 1970s, manage the international system of pegged exchange rates agreed upon at the Bretton Woods conference. It now mainly makes loans to nations facing possible defaults on private and government loans.

IMF and Pegged Exchange Rates

How did the adjustable-peg system of exchange rates work? First, as with the gold standard, each IMF member had to define its currency in terms of gold (or dollars), thus establishing rates of exchange between its currency and the currencies of all other members. In addition, each nation was obligated to keep its exchange rate stable with respect to every other currency. To do so, nations would have to use their official currency reserves to intervene in foreign exchange markets.

Assume again that the U.S. dollar and the British pound are "pegged" to each other at $2 = £1. And suppose again that the demand for pounds temporarily increases so that a shortage of pounds occurs in the United States (the United States has a balance-of-payments deficit). How can the United States keep its pledge to maintain a $2 = £1 exchange rate when the new equilibrium rate is, say, $3 = £1? As we noted previously, the United States can supply additional pounds to the exchange market, increasing the supply of pounds such that the equilibrium exchange rate falls back to $2 = £1.

Under the Bretton Woods system, there were three main sources of the needed pounds:

- *Official reserves* The United States might currently possess pounds in its official reserves as the result of past actions against a payments surplus.
- *Gold sales* The U.S. government might sell some of its gold to Britain for pounds. The proceeds would then be offered in the exchange market to augment the supply of pounds.
- *IMF borrowing* The needed pounds might be borrowed from the IMF. Nations participating in the Bretton Woods system were required to make contributions to the IMF based on the size of their national income, population, and trade volume. If necessary, the United States could borrow pounds on a short-term basis from the IMF by supplying its own currency as collateral.

Fundamental Imbalances: Adjusting the Peg

The Bretton Woods system recognized that from time to time a nation may be confronted with persistent and sizable balance-of-payments problems that cannot be corrected through the means listed above. In such cases, the nation would eventually run out of official reserves and be unable to maintain its current fixed exchange rate. The Bretton Woods remedy was correction by devaluation, that is, by an "orderly" reduction of the nation's pegged exchange rate. Also, the IMF allowed each member nation to alter the value of its currency by 10 percent, on its own, to correct a so-called fundamental (persistent and continuing) balance-of-payments deficit. Larger exchange-rate changes required the permission of the Fund's board of directors.

By requiring approval of significant rate changes, the Fund guarded against arbitrary and competitive currency devaluations by nations seeking only to boost output in their own countries at other countries' expense. In our example, devaluation of the dollar would increase U.S. exports and lower U.S. imports, helping to correct the United States' persistent payments deficit.

Demise of the Bretton Woods System

Under this adjustable-peg system, nations came to accept gold and the dollar as international reserves. The acceptability of gold as an international medium of exchange derived from its earlier use under the gold standard. Other nations accepted the dollar as international money because the United States had accumulated large quantities of gold, and between 1934 and 1971 it maintained a policy of buying gold from, and selling gold to, foreign governments at a fixed price of $35 per ounce. The dollar was convertible into gold on demand, so the dollar came to be regarded as a substitute for gold, or "as good as gold." The discovery of new gold was limited, but a growing volume of dollars helped facilitate the expanding volume of world trade during this period.

But a major problem arose. The United States had persistent payments deficits throughout the 1950s and 1960s. Those deficits were financed in part by U.S. gold reserves but mostly by payment of U.S. dollars. As the number of dollars held by foreigners soared and the U.S. gold reserves dwindled, other nations began to question whether the dollar was really "as

good as gold." The ability of the United States to continue to convert dollars into gold at $35 per ounce became increasingly doubtful, as did the role of dollars as international monetary reserves. Thus the dilemma was: To maintain the dollar as a reserve medium, the U.S. payments deficit had to be eliminated. But elimination of the payments deficit would remove the source of additional dollar reserves and thus limit the growth of international trade and finance.

The problem culminated in 1971 when the United States ended its 37-year-old policy of exchanging gold for dollars at $35 per ounce. It severed the link between gold and the international value of the dollar, thereby "floating" the dollar and letting market forces determine its value. The floating of the dollar withdrew U.S. support from the Bretton Woods system of fixed exchange rates and effectively ended the system. Nearly all major currencies began to float. The result has been the current regime of "managed floating exchange rates" described earlier in this chapter.

Appendix Summary

LO40.7 Explain how exchange rates worked under the gold standard and Bretton Woods.

Between 1879 and 1934, most major trading nations were on the gold standard, in which each nation fixed an exchange rate between its currency and gold. With each nation's currency fixed to gold, the system also implicitly set fixed exchange rates between different national currencies.

Any balance-of-payments imbalance would automatically lead to offsetting international flows of gold. These gold flows, in turn, led to automatically occurring domestic macroeconomic adjustments as the country exporting gold automatically encountered a decrease in its money supply while the country importing gold automatically experienced an increase in its money supply. When the Great Depression hit, many countries found these automatic adjustments too hard to bear, and they abandoned the gold standard.

The Bretton Woods system was implemented after the end of the Second World War and lasted until 1971. Under this system, the United States fixed the value of the U.S. dollar to gold at a rate of $35 per ounce. Other countries then set fixed exchange rates with the dollar so that their currencies were indirectly fixed to gold through the dollar.

The International Monetary Fund was created to administer the Bretton Woods system, which allowed countries some flexibility in adjusting their exchange rates to help offset balance-of-payments imbalances.

As the United States encountered increasingly large balance-of-payments imbalances in the 1960s and early 1970s, its ability to maintain its gold peg of $35 per ounce lost credibility. The United States abandoned the gold standard in 1971, thereby ending the Bretton Woods system. All major currencies then began the current regime of managed floating exchange rates.

Appendix Terms and Concepts

gold standard | devaluation | Bretton Woods system | International Monetary Fund (IMF)

Appendix Discussion Questions

1. Compare and contrast the Bretton Woods system of exchange rates with that of the gold standard. What caused the collapse of the gold standard? What caused the demise of the Bretton Woods system? **LO40.7**

Appendix Review Questions

1. Think back to the gold standard period. If the United States suffered a recession, to what degree could it engage in expansionary monetary policy? **LO40.7**

Appendix Problems

1. Suppose Zeeland pegs its currency, the zee, at 1 zee = 36 grains of gold. Aeeland pegs its currency, the aeellar, at 1 aeellar = 10 grains of gold. **LO40.7**
   a. What is the exchange rate between the zee and the aeellar?
   b. How many aeellars could you get for 7 zees?
   c. In terms of gold, would you rather have 14.5 zees or 53 aeellars?

Andrew F. Kazmierski/Shutterstock

CHAPTER

41

The Economics of Developing Countries

>> **LEARNING OBJECTIVES**

LO41.1 Distinguish between industrially advanced countries and developing countries.

LO41.2 List the obstacles to economic development.

LO41.3 Explain the vicious circle of poverty that afflicts low-income nations.

LO41.4 Describe the role of government in promoting economic development.

LO41.5 Explain how industrial nations attempt to aid low-income countries.

It is difficult for those of us in the United States, where per capita GDP in 2020 was about $63,544, to grasp the fact that about 700 million people, or about 10 percent of the world's population, live on $1.90 or less a day. Hunger and disease are the norm in many nations of the world.

In this chapter we identify the developing countries, discuss their characteristics, and explore the obstacles that impede their growth. We also examine the appropriate roles of the private sector and government in economic development. Finally, we look at policies that might help developing countries increase their growth rates.

The Rich and the Poor

>> **LO41.1 Distinguish between industrially advanced countries and developing countries.**

Just as there is considerable income inequality among families within a nation, so too is there great income inequality among nations. According to the United Nations, the richest 20 percent of the world's population receives more than 75 percent of the world's income; the poorest 20 percent receives less than 2 percent. The poorest 60 percent receives less than 6 percent of the world's income.

Classifications

industrially advanced countries High-income countries such as the United States, Canada, Japan, and the nations of western Europe that have highly developed *market economies* based on large stocks of technologically advanced *capital goods* and skilled labor forces.

The World Bank classifies countries into four income categories—high-income, upper-middle-income, lower-middle-income, and low-income—on the basis of national income per capita, as Figure 41.1 shows. The *high-income nations*, shown in dark green, are known as the **industrially advanced countries (IACs).** They include the United States, Japan, Canada, Australia, New Zealand, and most of western Europe. In general, these nations have well-developed market economies based on large stocks of capital goods, advanced production technologies, and well-educated workers. In 2020 this group of economies had an average per capita income of $46,036.

FIGURE 41.1 Groups of economies.

The world's nations are grouped into industrially advanced countries (IACs) and developing countries (DVCs). The IACs (shown in dark green) are high-income countries. The DVCs are upper-middle-income, lower-middle-income, and low-income countries (shown respectively in light green, yellow, and orange).

■ Low ($1,045 or less) □ Lower middle ($1,046–$4,095) □ Upper middle ($4,096–$12,695) ■ High ($12,696 or more) ■ No data

Source: The World Bank. Note that national income per capita is converted to U.S. dollars using the World Bank's Atlas Method, which adjusts national amounts to U.S. dollars using 3-year exchange rate averages.

developing countries Many countries of Africa, Asia, and Latin America that are characterized by lack of capital goods, use of nonadvanced technologies, low literacy rates, high unemployment, relatively rapid population growth, and labor forces heavily committed to agriculture.

The remaining nations are called **developing countries (DVCs).** They have wide variations of income per capita and are mainly located in Africa, Asia, and Latin America. The DVCs are a highly diverse group that can be divided into three groups:

- The *upper-middle-income nations*, shown in light green in Figure 41.1, include Brazil, Iraq, South Africa, Mexico, China, and Thailand. The per capita output of these nations ranged from $4,220 to $12,570 in 2020 and averaged $9,426.
- The *lower-middle-income nations*, shown in yellow, had per capita incomes ranging from $1,060 to $4,070 in 2020 with an average per capita income of $2,201. This category includes Tajikistan, India, Bangladesh, Kenya, Vietnam, and Samoa.
- The *low-income nations*, shown in orange, had a per capita income of $1,045 or less in 2020 and averaged only $811 of income per person. Sub-Saharan nations in Africa represented 23 of the 27 countries falling into this income category in 2020. Low-income DVCs have relatively low levels of industrialization. In general, literacy rates are low, unemployment is high, population growth is rapid, and exports consist largely of agricultural produce (such as cocoa, bananas, sugar, and raw cotton) and raw materials (such as copper, iron ore, natural rubber). Capital equipment is minimal, production technologies are simple, and labor productivity is very low. About 9 percent of the world's population lives in these low-income DVCs, all of which suffer widespread poverty.

Comparisons

Several comparisons will bring the differences in world income into sharper focus:

- In 2020, U.S. GDP was $20.9 trillion. The combined GDPs of the 125 DVCs in that year added up to $31.0 trillion.
- The United States, with only 4.2 percent of the world's population in 2020, produced 24.7 percent of the world's output.
- In 2020, U.S. per capita GDP was 117 times greater than per capita GDP in the Democratic Republic of the Congo, one of the world's poorest nations.
- The annual sales of the world's largest corporations exceed the national incomes of many DVCs. Walmart's annual world revenues of $559 billion in 2020 were greater than the national incomes of all but 21 nations.

Growth, Decline, and Income Gaps

Two other points relating to Figure 41.1 should be noted. First, nations have demonstrated considerable differences in their ability to improve their circumstances over time. On the one hand, DVCs such as Chile, China, India, Malaysia, and Thailand achieved high annual growth rates in their GDPs in recent decades. Consequently, their real output per capita increased severalfold. Several former DVCs, such as Singapore, Greece, and Hong Kong (now part of China), have achieved IAC status. In contrast, a number of DVCs in sub-Saharan Africa and the Middle East have recently been experiencing stagnant or even declining per capita GDPs.

Second, the absolute income gap between rich and poor nations has been widening. The DVCs must grow faster than the IACs for the gap to be narrowed.

A quick glance back at Figure 28.1 will confirm the "great divergence" in standards of living that emerged by the end of the twentieth century between the United States, Western Europe, and Japan relative to Africa, Latin America, and Asia (excluding Japan).

The Human Realities of Poverty

Development economist Michael Todaro points out that mere statistics conceal the human implications of the extreme poverty in the low-income DVCs:

> Let us examine a typical "extended" family in rural Asia. The Asian household is likely to comprise ten or more people, including parents, five to seven children, two grandparents, and some aunts and uncles. They have a combined annual income, both in money and in "kind" (i.e., they consume a share of the food they grow), of $250 to $300. Together they live in a poorly constructed one-room house as tenant farmers on a large agricultural estate. . . . The father, mother, uncle, and the older children must work all

TABLE 41.1 **Selected Socioeconomic Indicators of Development**

Country	(1) Per Capita Income, 2020*	(2) Life Expectancy at Birth, 2019	(3) Under-5 Mortality, Rate per 1,000, 2019	(4) Adult Illiteracy Rate, Percent, 2018	(5) Regular Internet Users, percent, 2020	(6) Per Capita Energy Consumption, 2018**
United States	$63,544	79	7	1	89	310
Japan	42,197	84	3	1	93	151
China	17,312	77	8	3	71	103
Brazil	14,836	76	14	7	74	61
India	6,454	70	34	26	41	23
Mauritania	5,257	65	73	47	21	12
Ethiopia	2,423	67	51	48	25	3
Mozambique	1,967	61	74	39	15	8

*Purchasing power parity basis (see World Bank website for definition and methodology).
**Millions of British Thermal Units (BTUs) per person per year.

Source: The World Bank's *World Development Indicators* (data.worldbank.org) and United States Energy Information Agency (eia.gov).

day on the land. None of the adults can read or write. . . . There is only one meal a day. . . . The house has no electricity, sanitation, or fresh water supply. There is much sickness, but qualified doctors and medical practitioners are far away in the cities attending to the needs of wealthier families. The work is hard, the sun is hot and aspirations for a better life are constantly being snuffed out. In this part of the world the only relief from the daily struggle for physical survival lies in the spiritual traditions of the people.[1]

Table 41.1 contrasts various socioeconomic indicators for selected DVCs with those for the United States and Japan.

Obstacles to Economic Development

The paths to economic development are essentially the same for developing countries and industrially advanced economies:

>> **LO41.2** List the obstacles to economic development.

- The DVCs must use their existing supplies of resources more efficiently. In other words, they must eliminate unemployment and underemployment, and they must combine labor and capital resources in a way that achieves lowest-cost production. They must also direct their scarce resources so that they will achieve allocative efficiency.

- The DVCs must expand the quantity and quality of their resources. By achieving greater supplies of raw materials, capital equipment, and productive labor, and by advancing their technological knowledge and human capital, DVCs can push their production possibilities curves outward.

All DVCs are aware of these two paths to economic development. Why, then, have some of them traveled those paths while others have lagged far behind? The differences lie in the nations' physical, human, and socioeconomic environments.

Natural Resources

The distribution of natural resources among the DVCs is extremely uneven. Some DVCs have valuable deposits of bauxite, tin, copper, tungsten, nitrates, and petroleum, and they have used their natural resource endowments to achieve rapid growth. For example, several members of the Organization of Petroleum Exporting Countries (OPEC), including Kuwait, have used oil experts to grow their economies. In other cases, multinational corporations of industrially advanced countries own or control a DVC's natural resources, often diverting much of the economic benefits of these resources abroad. Furthermore, world markets for many of the farm products and raw materials that the DVCs export are subject to large price fluctuations that contribute to the DVCs' instability.

---

[1]Michael P. Todaro, *Economic Development* (Pearson Education, 2000).

Other DVCs lack mineral deposits, have little arable land, and have few sources of power. Moreover, most of the low-income countries are situated in Central and South America, Africa, the Indian subcontinent, and southeast Asia, where tropical climates prevail. The heat and humidity hinder productive labor; human, crop, and livestock diseases are widespread; and weed and insect infestations plague agriculture.

A weak resource base can be a serious obstacle to growth. Real capital can be accumulated and the quality of the labor force improved through education and training. But it is not as easy to augment the natural resource base. It may be unrealistic for many of the DVCs to envision an economic destiny comparable with that of, say, the United States or Canada—both of which were endowed by nature with thick forests, rich soils, plenty of oil, and rich mineral deposits. But we must be careful in generalizing: Japan, for example, has achieved a high standard of living despite limited natural resources. It simply imports the large quantities of natural resources that it needs to produce goods for consumption at home and for export abroad.

Human Resources

Three statements describe many of the poorest DVCs with respect to human resources:

- Populations are large.
- Unemployment and underemployment are widespread.
- Educational levels and labor productivity are low.

Large Populations As equation (1) demonstrates, a nation's standard of living or real income per capita depends on the size of its total output (or income) relative to its total population:

$$\text{Standard of living} = \frac{\text{Total output (or income)}}{\text{Population}} \qquad (1)$$

Some of the DVCs with the most meager natural and capital resources have not only low total incomes but also large populations. These large populations often produce high population densities (population per square mile). In column 2 of Table 41.2, note the high population densities of the selected DVCs relative to the lower densities of the United States and the world.

The high population densities of many DVCs have resulted from decades of higher rates of population growth than most IACs. Column 3 of Table 41.2 shows the varying rates of population growth in selected countries over a recent period: 2019–2020. Although *total fertility rates*—the number of children per biological female's lifetime—are dramatically declining in most DVCs, the population growth rates of the DVCs remain considerably higher than those of the IACs. Between 2019 and 2020, the annual population growth rate was 2.7 percent for the low-income DVCs, 1.4 percent for the lower-middle income DVCS, and 1.0 for the upper-middle income DVCs. Those numbers are substantially higher than the 0.4 percent rate of population growth found in the IACs (with much of that being due to immigration into IACs; indeed, the total fertility rate in the large majority of IACs is now substantially less than the replacement rate necessary to keep their populations stable over time).

Because a large percentage of the world's population lives in DVCs, their population growth is the most significant component of worldwide population growth. Over the next 15 years, 9 out of every 10 people added to the world population are projected to be born in developing nations.

TABLE 41.2
Population Statistics, Selected Countries

(1) Country	(2) Population per Square Kilometer, 2020*	(3) Annual Rate of Population Increase, 2019–2020
United States	36	0.4
Pakistan	287	2.0
Bangladesh	1,265	1.0
Nigeria	226	2.5
India	464	1.0
China	149	0.3
Kenya	94	2.3
Philippines	368	1.3
Yemen	54	2.3
World	**60**	**1.0**

*1 square kilometer (km) = 0.386 square mile.

Source: *World Development Indicators 2021*, The World Bank (data.worldbank.org).

In some of the poorest DVCs, rapid population growth strains the levels of income growth so severely that per capita income remains stagnant or even falls toward subsistence levels. In the worst instances, death rates rise sharply as war, drought, and natural disasters cause severe malnutrition and disease.

Boosting the standard of living in countries that have subsistence or near-subsistence levels of income is a daunting task. When a DVC is just starting to modernize its economy, initial increases in real income can for a time increase population and short-circuit the process. If population increases are sufficiently large, they simply spread the higher level of total income among more people such that the original gain in per capita income disappears.

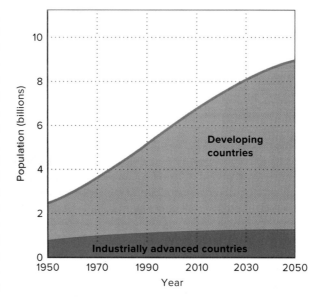

FIGURE 41.2
Population growth in developing countries and advanced industrial countries, 1950–2050.

The majority of the world's population lives in the developing nations, and those nations will account for most of the increase in population through the middle of the twenty-first century.

Source: United Nations.

The Demographic Transition Why might income gains in the poorest DVCs increase population growth, at least for a while? The answer is the **demographic transition,** or the period of several decades during which the population expands because it takes time to transition from a situation of high birth and death rates to a situation of low birth and death rates.

Before the Industrial Revolution and modern medicines and technology, the entire world was one in which both death rates and birthrates were high. There were no antibiotics to treat disease, no understanding of preventing diseases through immunization, and no understanding of food- and water-borne illnesses caused by bacteria and viruses. Given the high death rates that resulted from that ignorance, most families opted to have six or more children so that two or three might survive to adulthood. Thus, high birthrates accompanied high death rates.

When modern medicine and sanitation arrive in a country, death rates plunge quite rapidly. But people who are accustomed to high death rates will continue for several decades to have large families, thinking, out of habit, that large families are necessary for having at least a couple of children survive to adulthood. As people become used to lower death rates, they adjust downward the number of children they are having. That creates the situation of low death rates accompanied by low birth rates that is found today in almost every high income and middle income nation—that is, the nations that have already completed the demographic transition. But many poorer DVCs are still in the intermediate period where death rates have fallen while birthrates are yet to fall. Thus, their populations are growing quite rapidly because they experience many more births than deaths each year.

Most experts see birth control as a key strategy for hastening the demographic transition. But low literacy rates make it difficult to disseminate information about contraceptive devices. In addition, large families are a major source of labor in poor agricultural areas. Adults may also regard having many children as a kind of informal social security system: the more children they have, the greater the probability of having a relative to care for them in old age.

Chinese authorities took a harsh stance on fertility choices in 1980, when they instituted a "one child per family" law that imposed fines, removed social benefits, and in some cases forced abortions on any family that had, or attempted to have, more than one child. The law was widely credited with assisting in the dramatic increase in living standards that accompanied China's subsequent economic boom. But the policy may have been too effective over the long run because, by 2012, China's labor force was declining and the government faced a situation in which too few workers would be paying taxes to support too many retirees. As a result, the one child per family law was eliminated in late 2015 in hopes of encouraging Chinese families to have more children. In 2021, the Chinese government announced that it was going to begin encouraging families to have up to three children.

demographic transition The massive decline in birthrates that occurs once a developing country achieves higher standards of living because the perceived marginal cost of additional children begins to exceed the perceived marginal benefit.

Qualifications We need to qualify our focus on population growth as a major cause of low per-capita incomes. High population density does not consign a nation to poverty. China and India have immense populations and low incomes, but Japan, Singapore, and Hong Kong are densely populated and have high incomes. Moreover, the standard of living in many parts of China and India has rapidly increased in recent years.

Also, the population growth rate for the DVCs as a group has declined significantly in recent decades. The world's population may even begin to decline toward the later part of this century.

Development economists typically suggest a dual approach to development. The surest way for the poorest DVCs to break out of their poverty, they argue, is to implement policies that expand output and income while also increasing access to birth control information and methods. In terms of the standard of living equation (1) earlier in this section, a set of policies that raises the numerator (total income) and holds constant or lowers the denominator (population) will provide the biggest lift to a developing nation's standard of living.

Unemployment and Underemployment For many DVCs, employment-related data are either nonexistent or highly unreliable. But observation suggests that unemployment is high. There is also significant **underemployment,** which means that a large number of people are employed fewer hours per week than they want, work at jobs unrelated to their training, or spend much of the time on their jobs unproductively.

underemployment A situation in which workers are employed in positions requiring less education and skill than they have.

Many economists contend that unemployment may be as high as 15 to 20 percent in the rapidly growing urban areas of the DVCs. There has been substantial migration in most developing countries from rural to urban areas, motivated by the expectation of finding jobs with higher wage rates than are available in agricultural and other rural employment. But this huge migration to the cities reduces a migrant's chance of obtaining a job. In many cases, migration to the cities has greatly exceeded the growth of urban job opportunities, resulting in very high urban unemployment rates. Thus, rapid rural-urban migration has given rise to urban unemployment rates that are two or three times higher than rural rates.

In many of the poorer DVCs, rural agricultural labor is so abundant relative to capital and natural resources that a significant percentage of the labor contributes little or nothing to agricultural output. Similarly, many DVC workers are self-employed as proprietors of small shops, in handicrafts, or as street vendors. Unfortunately, however, many of them must endure long stretches of idle time at work due to a lack of demand. While they are not unemployed, they are clearly underemployed.

Some perspective is needed, however. The nearby Consider This story explains that, despite the unemployment problems that challenge DVCs, extreme poverty has fallen dramatically around the world in recent decades. This is good news, but much more could be done to increase employment opportunities—and thus living standards—in poorer countries.

CONSIDER THIS . . .

Faster, Please

The World Bank defines extreme poverty as an income of $1.90 per day or less, adjusted to local currency and accounting for differences in the cost of living and inflation. Under that definition, extreme poverty has plummeted in recent decades.

Between 1990 and 2017, the number of people living in extreme poverty declined from 1.9 billion to 698 million. That decline of about 1.2 billion people living in extreme poverty is especially impressive because the world's population increased from 5.3 billion to 7.5 billion over the

John Wollwerth/Shutterstock

same time horizon. If you work out the percentages, you will find that the extreme poverty rate fell from 35.9 percent of the world's population in 1990 to 9.3 percent in 2017.

That sharp decline in extreme poverty represents a massive decrease in human suffering. That is because people living in extreme poverty are typically unable to provide for basic human needs, such as sufficient food, safe drinking water, adequate sanitation facilities, proper health care, sturdy shelter, and education.

Low Labor Productivity DVCs have found it difficult to invest in physical capital. As a result, their workers are poorly equipped with machinery and tools and therefore are relatively unproductive. Remember that rapid population growth tends to reduce the amount of physical capital available per worker, and that reduction erodes labor productivity and decreases real per capita incomes.

Moreover, most poor countries have not been able to invest adequately in their human capital (see Table 41.1, columns 3 and 4). Consequently, expenditures on health and education have been meager. Low levels of literacy, high levels of malnutrition, lack of proper medical care, and insufficient educational facilities all contribute to populations that are ill equipped for industrialization and economic expansion. Also, a number of the poorest DVCs forgo vast amounts of productive human capital by denying or restricting educational and work opportunities to women.

Particularly vital is the absence of a vigorous entrepreneurial class willing to bear risks, accumulate capital, and provide the organizational requisites essential to economic growth. Closely related is the lack of labor trained to handle the routine supervisory functions basic to any program of development. Ironically, the higher-education systems of some DVCs emphasize the humanities and offer relatively few courses in business, engineering, and the sciences. Some DVCs are ruled by repressive governments, which create an environment hostile to thinking independently, taking initiatives, and assuming economic risks.

While migration from the DVCs to other countries has modestly offset rapid population growth, it has also deprived some DVCs of highly productive workers. Often the best-trained and most highly motivated workers, such as physicians, engineers, teachers, and nurses, leave the DVCs to better their circumstances in the IACs. This so-called "brain drain" contributes to the deterioration in the overall skill level and productivity of the labor force.

Capital Accumulation

The accumulation of capital goods is an important focal point of economic development. All DVCs have a relative lack of capital goods such as factories, machinery, equipment, and public utilities. Better-equipped labor forces would greatly enhance productivity and would help boost per capita output. There is a close relationship between output per worker (labor productivity) and real income per worker. A nation must produce more goods and services per worker as output to enjoy more goods and services per worker as income. One way of increasing labor productivity is to provide each worker with more tools and equipment.

Once initiated, the process of capital accumulation may be cumulative. If capital accumulation increases output faster than population growth, a margin of saving may arise that permits further capital formation. In a sense, capital accumulation feeds on itself.

Let's look more closely at domestic capital accumulation.

Domestic Capital Formation Like any other nation, a developing nation accumulates capital through saving and investing. A nation must save (refrain from consumption) to free some of its resources from the production of consumer goods. Investment spending must then absorb those released resources in the production of capital goods. But impediments to saving and investing are much greater in a low-income nation than they are in an advanced economy.

Savings Potential Consider first the savings side of the picture. Some of the lowest-income countries, such as Burundi, Chad, Ghana, Guinea, Liberia, Madagascar, Mozambique, and Sierra Leone, have negative saving or save only 0 to 7 percent of their GDPs. Their people are simply too poor to save a significant portion of their incomes. Interestingly, however, some middle-income countries save a larger percentage of their domestic outputs than do advanced industrial countries. In 2019 India and China saved 30 and 44 percent of their domestic outputs, respectively, compared to 27 percent for Japan, 28 percent for Germany, and 19 percent for the United States. The problem is that the DVCs' domestic outputs are so low that even when saving rates are larger than those of advanced nations, the total volume of saving is not large.

Capital Flight Some of the developing countries have suffered **capital flight,** the transfer of private DVC savings to accounts held in the IACs. (In this usage, "capital" is simply "money," "money capital," or "financial capital.") Many wealthy citizens of DVCs have used their savings to invest in the more economically advanced nations, enabling them to avoid high investment risks at home, which include the loss of savings or real capital from government expropriation, abrupt changes in taxation, potential hyperinflation, or high volatility of exchange rates. If a DVC's political climate is

capital flight The transfer of savings from *developing countries* to *industrially advanced countries* to avoid government expropriation, taxation, or higher rates of *inflation,* or simply to realize greater returns on *financial investments.*

unsettled, savers may shift their funds overseas to a "safe haven" in fear that a new government might confiscate their wealth. Rapid or skyrocketing inflation in a DVC will have similar detrimental effects. Transferring savings overseas may also be a means of evading high domestic taxes on interest income or capital gains. Finally, investors may send their money capital to the IACs to achieve higher interest rates or to take advantage of a greater variety of investment opportunities.

Whatever the motivation, the amount of capital flight from some DVCs is significant and offsets much of the IACs' lending and granting of financial aid to developing nations.

infrastructure The interconnected network of large-scale *capital goods* (such as roads, sewers, electrical grids, railways, ports, and the Internet) needed to operate a technologically advanced economy.

Investment Obstacles   The infrastructure (stock of public capital goods) in many DVCs is insufficient to enable private firms to achieve adequate returns on their investments. Poor roads and bridges, inadequate railways, little gas and electricity production, poor communications, unsatisfactory housing, and inadequate educational and public health facilities create an inhospitable environment for private investment. A substantial portion of any new private investment would have to be used to create the infrastructure needed by all firms. Rarely can firms provide an investment in infrastructure themselves and still earn a positive return on their overall investment.

How, then, can developing nations build up their infrastructure? The higher-income DVCs may be able to do so through taxation and public spending. But, in the lowest-income DVCs, there is little income to tax. Nevertheless, a poor DVC can accumulate capital by transferring surplus agricultural labor to the improvement of the infrastructure. If each agricultural village allocated its surplus labor to the construction of irrigation canals, wells, schools, sanitary facilities, and roads, significant amounts of capital might be accumulated at no significant sacrifice of consumer goods production. Such investment bypasses the problems inherent in the financial aspects of capital accumulation. It does not require consumers to save portions of their money income, nor does it presume the presence of an entrepreneurial class eager to invest. When leadership and cooperative spirit are present, this "in-kind" investment is a promising avenue for accumulating basic capital goods.

In some developing nations, the major obstacle to investment is the lack of entrepreneurs who are willing to assume the risks associated with investment. In addition, the incentive to invest may be weak even in the presence of substantial savings and a large number of willing entrepreneurs. Several factors may combine in a DVC to reduce investment incentives, including political instability, high inflation rates, and lack of economies of scale. A related problem in many countries is the high cost of legally registering a new business. As Global Perspective 41.1 indicates, those costs are prohibitive in many countries, amounting to more than twice what an average person makes in a year!

🌐 GLOBAL PERSPECTIVE 41.1

COST OF BUSINESS START-UP PROCEDURES AS A PERCENTAGE OF AVERAGE INCOME, 2019

In every country in the world, entrepreneurs have to complete paperwork and pay fees to register a new business with the local government. For each country, the World Bank's Doing Business Project publishes those costs as a percentage of average national income. Those percentages are startlingly high in several low-income countries, including Venezuela, Somalia, and Haiti. By contrast they are quite low in several developing nations, such as India and China, as well as in every industrially advanced country. In the United Kingdom, for instance, it costs just £12 (or about $17 dollars) to register a new business with the government.

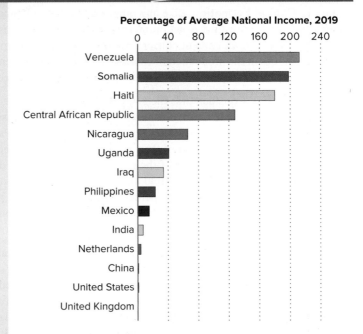

Percentage of Average National Income, 2019

Source: World Bank's Doing Business Project, The World Bank, doingbusiness.org.

Technological Advance

Given the rudimentary state of technology in the DVCs, they are far from the frontiers of technological advance. But the IACs have accumulated an enormous body of technological knowledge that the developing countries might adopt and apply without expensive research. Crop rotation and contour plowing require no additional capital equipment and would contribute significantly to productivity. By raising grain storage bins a few inches above ground, farmers could avoid a large amount of grain spoilage. Although such changes may sound trivial to people who live in advanced nations, the resulting gains in productivity might mean the difference between subsistence and starvation in some poverty-ridden nations.

The application of either existing or new technological knowledge often requires the use of new and different capital goods. But, within limits, a nation can obtain at least part of that capital without an increase in the rate of capital formation. If a DVC channels the annual flow of replacement investment from technologically inferior to technologically superior capital equipment, it can increase productivity even with a constant level of investment spending. Indeed, it can achieve some advances through **capital-saving technology** rather than **capital-using technology.** A new fertilizer, better adapted to a nation's topography and climate, might be cheaper than the fertilizer currently being used. A seemingly high-priced metal plow that lasts 10 years may be cheaper in the long run than an inexpensive but technologically inferior wooden plow that has to be replaced every year.

To what extent have DVCs adopted and effectively used available IAC technological knowledge? The picture is mixed. Such technological borrowing has been instrumental in the rapid growth of such Pacific Rim countries as Japan, South Korea, Taiwan, and Singapore. Similarly, the OPEC nations have benefited significantly from IAC knowledge of oil exploration, production, and refining.

Still, the transfer of advanced technologies to the poorest DVCs is not an easy matter. In IACs, technological advances usually depend on the availability of highly skilled labor and abundant capital. Such advances tend to be capital-using or, to put it another way, labor-saving. Developing economies require technologies appropriate to quite different resource endowments: abundant unskilled labor and very limited quantities of capital goods. Although labor-using and capital-saving technologies are appropriate to DVCs, much of the IACs' highly advanced technology is inappropriate for them. They must develop their own appropriate technologies. However, because technological change that fails may well mean hunger and malnutrition, there is a strong tendency to retain traditional production techniques.

capital-saving technology An improvement in *technology* that permits a greater quantity of a product to be produced with a specific amount of *capital* (or permits the same amount of the product to be produced with a smaller amount of capital).

capital-using technology An improvement in *technology* that requires the use of a greater amount of *capital* to produce a specific quantity of a product.

Sociocultural and Institutional Factors

Economic considerations alone do not explain why an economy does or does not grow. Substantial sociocultural and institutional readjustments are usually an integral part of the growth process. Economic development means not only changes in a nation's physical environment (new transportation and communications facilities, new schools, new housing, new plants and equipment) but also changes in the way people think, behave, and associate with one another. An openness to break from custom and tradition is frequently a prerequisite of economic development. A critical but intangible ingredient in that development is the **will to develop.** Economic growth may hinge on what individuals within DVCs want for themselves and their children. Do they want more material abundance? If so, are they willing to make the necessary changes in their institutions and ways of doing things?

will to develop The mental state of wanting *economic growth* strongly enough to change from old to new ways of doing things.

Sociocultural Obstacles Sociocultural impediments to growth are numerous and varied. In some DVCs, tribal and ethnic allegiances take precedence over national allegiance. Each tribe confines its economic activity to the tribal unit, eliminating any possibility for production-increasing specialization and trade. The desperate economic circumstances in Somalia, Sudan, Libya, Syria, and Afghanistan are due in no small measure to military and political conflicts among rival groups.

In countries with a formal or informal caste system, labor is allocated to occupations on the basis of status or tradition rather than on the basis of skill or merit. The result is a misallocation of human resources.

Religious beliefs and observances may seriously restrict the length of the workday and divert to ceremonial uses resources that might have been used for investment. Some religious and philosophical beliefs are dominated by the view that the universe is capricious, the idea that there is little or no correlation between an individual's activities and endeavors and that person's outcomes or experiences. The **capricious-universe view** leads to a fatalistic attitude. If "providence" rather than hard work, saving, and investing is the cause of one's lot in life, why save, work hard, and invest? Why engage in family planning? Why innovate?

Other attitudes and cultural factors may impede economic activity and growth: emphasis on the performance of duties rather than on individual initiative; focus on the group rather than on individual achievement; and the belief in reincarnation, which reduces the importance of one's current life.

Institutional Obstacles Political corruption and bribery are common in many DVCs. School systems and public service agencies are often ineptly administered, and petty politics frequently impairs their functioning. Tax systems are arbitrary, unjust, cumbersome, and detrimental to incentives to work and invest.

Because of the predominance of farming in DVCs, the problem of achieving an optimal institutional environment in agriculture is a vital consideration in any growth program. Specifically, the institutional problem of **land reform** demands attention in many DVCs. But the necessary reform may vary tremendously from nation to nation. In some DVCs the problem is excessive concentration of land ownership in the hands of a few wealthy families. This situation is demoralizing for tenants, weakens their incentive to produce, and typically does not promote capital improvements. At the other extreme is the situation in which each family owns and farms a piece of land far too small for the use of modern agricultural technology.

An important complication is that political considerations sometimes push reform in the direction of farms that are too small to achieve economies of scale.

Examples: Land reform in South Korea weakened the political control of the landed aristocracy and opened the way for the emergence of strong commercial and industrial middle classes, all to the benefit of the country's economic development. In contrast, the prolonged dominance of the landed aristocracy in the Philippines may have stifled economic development there.

capricious-universe view The view held by some people that fate and outside events, rather than hard work and enterprise, will determine their economic destinies.

land reform Policy changes aimed at creating a more efficient distribution of land ownership in developing countries. Can involve everything from government purchasing large land estates and dividing the land into smaller farms to consolidating tiny plots of land into larger, more efficient private farms.

**QUICK REVIEW
41.1**

▶ About 9 percent of the world's population lives in the low-income DVCs, which typically are characterized by scarce natural resources, inhospitable climates, large populations, high unemployment and underemployment, low education levels, and low labor productivity.

▶ For DVCs just beginning to modernize, high birthrates caused by improved medical care and sanitation can increase population faster than income growth, leading to lower living standards; but as development continues, the opportunity costs of having children rise and population growth typically slows.

▶ Low saving rates, capital flight, weak infrastructures, and lack of investors impair capital accumulation in many DVCs.

▶ Sociocultural and institutional factors are often serious impediments to economic growth in DVCs.

The Vicious Circle

>> **LO41.3** Explain the vicious circle of poverty that afflicts low-income nations.

vicious circle of poverty A problem common in some *developing countries* in which their low *per capita incomes* are an obstacle to realizing the levels of *savings* and *investment* needed to achieve rates of growth of output that exceed their rates of population growth.

Many DVCs are caught in a **vicious circle of poverty.** They stay poor because they are poor! Consider Figure 41.3. Common to most DVCs is low per capita income. A family that is poor has little ability or incentive to save. Furthermore, low incomes mean low levels of product demand. Thus, there are few available resources, on the one hand, and no strong incentives, on the other hand, for investment in physical or human capital. Consequently, labor productivity is low. And because output per person is real income per person, it follows that per capita income is low.

Many economists think that the key to breaking out of this vicious circle is to increase the rate of capital accumulation, to achieve an investment level of, say, 10 percent of national income. But Figure 41.3 reminds us that rapid population growth may partially or entirely undo the potentially beneficial effects of a higher rate of capital accumulation. Suppose that initially a DVC is realizing no growth in its real GDP but somehow manages to increase saving and investment to 10 percent of its GDP. As a result, real GDP begins to grow at, say, 2.5 percent per year. With a stable population, real GDP per capita will also grow at 2.5 percent per year. If that growth persists, the standard of living will double in about 28 years. But what if population also grows at the rate of 2.5 percent per year, as it does in parts of the Middle East, northern Africa, and sub-Saharan Africa? Then real income per person will remain unchanged and the vicious circle will persist.

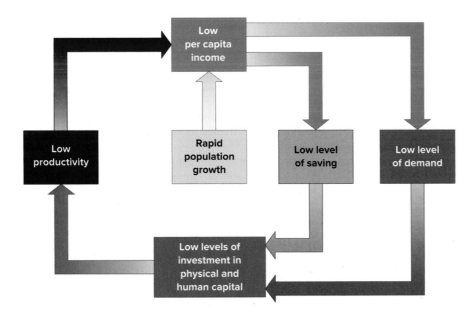

FIGURE 41.3
The vicious circle of poverty.

Low per capita incomes make it difficult for poor nations to save and invest, a condition that perpetuates low productivity and low incomes. Furthermore, rapid population growth may quickly absorb increases in per capita real income and thereby destroy the possibility of breaking out of the poverty circle.

But if population can be kept constant or limited to some growth rate significantly below 2.5 percent, real income per person will rise. Then the possibility arises of further enlargement of the flows of saving and investment, continuing advances in productivity, and the continued growth of per capita real income. If a nation can achieve a process of self-sustaining expansion of income, saving, investment, and productivity, then it can transform the self-perpetuating vicious circle of poverty into a self-regenerating, beneficent circle of economic progress. The challenge is to create effective policies and strategies that accomplish that transition.

The Role of Government

Economists suggest that developing nations have several avenues for fostering economic growth and improving their standards of living. Much of this is possible only if, however, a government has a sufficient amount of **state capacity,** meaning that a government has the ability to accomplish specific policy goals, such as providing public goods, enforcing property rights, and maintaining a monopoly on the legal use of force within its territory.

>> **LO41.4 Describe the role of government in promoting economic development.**

state capacity The ability of a government to achieve specific policy goals.

Unfortunately, some of the world's poorest countries lack state capacity because they are plagued by banditry and intertribal warfare that divert attention and resources from the task of development. A strong, stable national government is needed to establish domestic law and order and to achieve peace and unity. Research demonstrates that political instability (as measured by the number of revolutions and coups per decade) and slow economic growth go hand in hand.

A government that lacks state capacity is referred to as a fragile state or **failed state** and in such instances the practical power of the government to provide even basic government services such as elementary education, basic sanitation, and effective levels of law enforcement may be close to zero. In 2021, failed states included Yemen, Somalia, Syria, and South Sudan. Thus, our list of avenues that DVC governments have for fostering economic development begins with the achievement and maintenance of state capacity itself.

failed state A nation whose government lacks the *state capacity* to maintain even basic government functions like law enforcement and the provision of basic services like education and sanitation.

A Positive Role

Fortunately, most DVCs have significant amounts of state capacity that can be directed toward fostering economic development. But economists generally agree that as soon as sufficient state capacity has been achieved, government efforts must support private efforts, not substitute for them. That is not always the case in practice, however.

Establishing the Rule of Law Clearly defined and strictly enforced property rights bolster economic growth by ensuring that individuals receive and retain the fruits of their labor.

Because legal protections reduce investment risk, the rule of law encourages direct investments by firms in the IACs. Government itself must live by the law. The presence of corruption in the government sanctions criminality throughout the economic system. Such criminality discourages the growth of output because it lowers the returns available to honest workers and honest businesspeople.

Building Infrastructure Government is the only institution that is in a position to provide public infrastructure. But it need not do all the work through government entities. It can contract out much of the work to private enterprises.

Recall that DVCs (or *follower countries*) can adopt technologies that were developed at high cost in the more technologically advanced leader countries without paying any of those development costs. DVCs can often jump directly to the most modern and highly productive infrastructure without going through the long process of development and replacement that was required in the IACs. For example, many DVCs have developed Internet-capable wireless phone networks instead of using their scarce resources to build and expand landline systems.

Embracing Globalization Other things equal, open economies that participate in international trade grow faster than closed economies. Also, DVCs that welcome foreign direct investment enjoy greater growth rates than DVCs that view such investment suspiciously or even as exploitation and therefore put severe obstacles in its way.

Realistic exchange-rate policies by government also help. Exchange rates that are fixed at unrealistic levels invite balance-of-payments problems and speculative trading in currencies. Often, such trading forces a nation into an abrupt devaluation of its currency, sending shock waves throughout its economy. More flexible exchange rates enable more gradual adjustments and thus less susceptibility to major currency shocks and the domestic disruption they cause.

Building Human Capital Government programs that encourage literacy, education, and labor-market skills enhance economic growth by building human capital. In particular, policies that close the education gap between women and men spur economic growth in developing countries. Promoting the education of women pays off in terms of reduced fertility, greater productivity, and greater emphasis on educating children.

Promoting Entrepreneurship The lack of a sizable and vigorous entrepreneurial class in some DVCs means that private enterprise is not capable of spearheading the growth process. Government may have to take the lead, at least at first. But many DVCs would benefit by converting some of their state enterprises into private firms. State enterprises often are inefficient, more concerned with providing maximum employment than with introducing modern technology and delivering goods and services at minimum per-unit cost. Moreover, state enterprises are poor "incubators" for developing profit-focused, entrepreneurial persons who leave the firm to set up their own businesses.

Developing Credit Systems Banking systems in some of the poorest DVCs are nearly nonexistent, which makes it difficult for domestic savers and international lenders to lend money to DVC borrowers, who in turn wish to create capital goods. A first step toward developing effective credit systems is **microcredit,** in which groups of people pool their money and make small loans to budding entrepreneurs and owners of small businesses. People from the IACs can offer microcredit loans to entrepreneurs in DVCs, helping nurture the spirit of enterprise. The benefits of micro-lending accrue not only to the entrepreneurs receiving the micro loans but also to their nations as a whole because the micro loans that are invested successfully create jobs, expand output, and raise the standard of living.

microcredit Anti-poverty programs that lend small amounts of money to poor entrepreneurs.

Avoiding High Rates of Inflation At the national level, DVC governments must guard against excessive money creation and the high inflation that it brings. High inflation rates simply are not conducive to economic investment and growth because inflation lowers the real returns generated by investments. DVCs can help keep inflation in check by establishing independent central banks to maintain proper control over their money supplies. Studies indicate that DVCs that control inflation enjoy higher growth rates than those that do not.

Controlling Population Growth Government can provide information about birth control options. Families with fewer children consume less and save more; they also free up time for women to receive an education and participate in the labor market. As women participate in the labor market, they tend to reduce their fertility rate, which further helps to control population growth.

Making Peace with Neighbors Countries at war or in fear of war with neighboring nations divert scarce resources to armaments, rather than to private capital or public infrastructure. Sustained peace among neighboring nations eventually leads to economic cooperation and integration, broadened markets, and stronger economic growth.

Public-Sector Problems

Although the public sector can positively influence economic development, serious problems can and do arise with government-directed initiatives. Indeed, development experts are less enthusiastic about the role of government in the growth process than they were a few decades ago. Unfortunately, government misadministration and **corruption** are common in many DVCs, and government officials sometimes line their own pockets with foreign-aid funds. Moreover, political leaders often confer monopoly privileges on relatives, friends, and political supporters and grant exclusive rights to relatives or friends to produce, import, or export certain products. Such monopoly privileges lead to higher domestic prices and diminish the DVC's ability to compete in world markets.

Similarly, managers of state-owned enterprises are often appointed on the basis of cronyism rather than competence. Many DVC governments, particularly in Africa, have created "marketing boards" as the sole purchaser of agricultural products from local farmers. The boards buy farm products at artificially low prices and sell them at higher world prices; the "profit" ends up in the pockets of government officials. In recent years, the perception of government has shifted from that of catalyst and promoter of growth to that of a potential impediment to development. According to a recent ranking of 180 nations based on perceived corruption, the 40 nations at the bottom of the list (most corrupt) were DVCs. Global Perspective 41.2 shows the corruption scores for 16 selected nations, including the two least corrupt (New Zealand and Denmark) and the two most corrupt (South Sudan and Somalia).

corruption The misuse of government power, with which one has been entrusted or assigned, to obtain private gain; includes payments from individuals or companies to secure advantages in obtaining government contracts, avoiding government regulations, or obtaining inside knowledge about forthcoming policy changes.

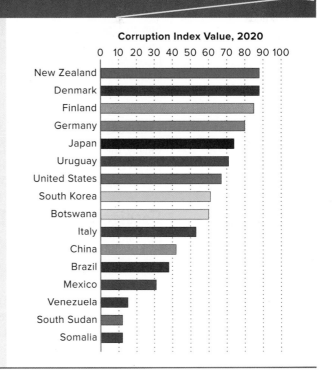

GLOBAL PERSPECTIVE 41.2

THE CORRUPTION PERCEPTIONS INDEX, SELECTED NATIONS, 2020*

The corruption perceptions index measures the degree of corruption existing among public officials and politicians as seen by businesspeople, risk analysts, and the general public. An index value of 100 is highly clean and 0 is highly corrupt. The highest ranking country was New Zealand with a score of 88, while the lowest ranking countries, tied with a score of 12, were South Sudan and Somalia.

Corruption Index Value, 2020

New Zealand, Denmark, Finland, Germany, Japan, Uruguay, United States, South Korea, Botswana, Italy, China, Brazil, Mexico, Venezuela, South Sudan, Somalia

*Index values are subject to change on the basis of election outcomes, military coups, and so on.

Source: Transparency International.

The Role of Advanced Nations

>> **LO41.5** Explain how industrial nations attempt to aid low-income countries.

How can the IACs help developing countries in their pursuit of economic growth? To what degree have IACs provided assistance?

Expanding Trade

Some authorities maintain that the simplest and most effective way for the industrially advanced nations to aid DVCs is to lower international trade barriers. Such action would enable DVCs to elevate their national incomes through increased trade. Trade barriers instituted by the IACs are often highest for labor-intensive manufactured goods, such as textiles, clothing, footwear, and processed agricultural products. These are precisely the sorts of products for which the DVCs have a comparative advantage. Also, many IACs' tariffs rise as the degree of product processing increases; for example, tariffs on chocolates are higher than those on cocoa. Tariffs therefore discourage DVCs from developing processing industries of their own.

Additionally, large agricultural subsidies in the IACs encourage excessive production of food and fiber in the IACs. The overproduction flows into world markets, where it depresses agricultural prices. DVCs, which typically do not subsidize farmers, therefore face artificially low prices for their farm exports. The IACs could greatly help DVCs by reducing farm subsidies along with tariffs.

But lowering trade barriers is certainly not a panacea. Some poor nations need only large foreign markets for their raw materials to achieve growth. But the problem for many poor nations is not to obtain markets in which to sell existing products or relatively abundant raw materials but rather to get the capital and technical assistance they need to produce products for domestic consumption.

Also, close trade ties with advanced nations entail certain disadvantages. Dependence by the DVCs on exports to the IACs leaves the DVCs highly vulnerable to recessions in the IACs. As firms cut back production in the IACs, the demand for DVC resources declines; and as income in the IACs declines, the demand for DVC-produced goods declines. By reducing the demand for DVC exports, recessions in the IACs can severely reduce the prices of raw materials exported by the DVCs. For example, during the recession of 2007–2009, the world price of zinc fell from $2.02 per pound to $0.49 per pound, and the world price of copper fell from $4.05 per pound to $1.40 per pound. These sorts of price declines severely reduce DVC export earnings when recessions strike IACs.

Admitting Temporary Workers

Some economists recommend that the IACs help the DVCs by accepting more seasonal or other temporary workers from the DVCs. Temporary migration provides an outlet for surplus DVC labor. Moreover, migrant remittances to families in the home country serve as a sorely needed source of income. The problem is that some temporary workers do not leave when their visas or work permits expire, which may not be in the IACs' long-run best interest.

Discouraging Arms Sales

Finally, the IACs can help the DVCs as a group by discouraging the sale of military equipment to the DVCs. Such purchases by the DVCs divert public expenditures from infrastructure and education and heighten tensions in DVCs that have long-standing disputes with neighbors.

Foreign Aid: Public Loans and Grants

Official development assistance (ODA), or simply "foreign aid," is another route through which IACs can help DVCs. Foreign aid that strengthens infrastructure could enhance the flow of private capital to the DVCs.

Direct Aid The United States and other IACs have assisted DVCs directly through a variety of programs designed to stimulate economic development. Over the past 10 years, U.S. loans and grants to the DVCs totaled $21 billion to $36 billion per year. The U.S. Agency for International Development (USAID) administers most of this aid, some of which consists of grants of surplus food under the Food for Peace program. Other advanced nations also have substantial foreign aid

GLOBAL PERSPECTIVE 41.3

OFFICIAL DEVELOPMENT ASSISTANCE AS A PERCENTAGE OF GDP, SELECTED NATIONS

The United States is the world's largest provider of official development assistance (ODA). In 2020, the United States provided $35.5 billion of ODA out of a worldwide total of $161.1 billion. But many industrialized nations contribute a larger percentage of their national incomes to development assistance than does the United States, as indicated by the bar chart.

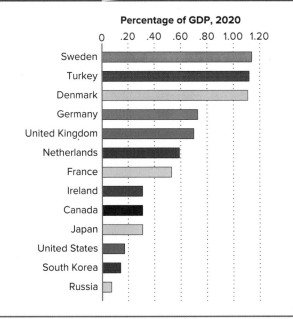

Percentage of GDP, 2020

Source: Organisation for Economic Co-operation and Development (OECD).

programs. In 2020 foreign aid from the IACs to the developing nations totaled $161.1 billion, or about one-fourth of 1 percent of the IACs' collective GDP that year. Global Perspective 41.3 illustrates that countries differ widely in how much development aid ("official development assistance") they award as a percentage of their respective GDPs.

A large portion of foreign aid is distributed on the basis of political and military considerations rather than strictly economic considerations. Egypt, Iraq, Israel, and Pakistan, for example, are major recipients of U.S. aid. Asian, Latin American, and African nations with lower standards of living receive less.

Only one-fourth of foreign aid goes to the 10 countries in which 70 percent of the world's poorest people live. The most affluent 40 percent of the DVC population receives over twice as much aid as the poorest 40 percent. Many economists argue that the IACs should shift foreign aid away from the middle-income DVCs and toward the poorest DVCs.

Some of the world's poorest nations do receive large amounts of foreign aid relative to their meager GDPs. For example, in 2019 foreign aid relative to GDP was 56 percent in Tuvalu, 38 percent in Somalia, 22 percent in Afghanistan, 20 percent in Tonga, and 16 percent in South Sudan.

These and many other low-income DVCs also receive large amounts of support from private donors in the IACs. In fact, in recent years the private giving to the DVCs by private U.S. universities, foundations (such as the Gates Foundation), voluntary organizations, and religious organizations has exceeded the foreign aid provided by the U.S. government.

The large accumulated debts of some of the poorest DVCs have become a severe roadblock to their growth. Therefore, some of the recent direct assistance by the IACs to the DVCs has taken the form of forgiving parts of the past IAC-government loans to low-income DVCs. In 2005 the G8 nations canceled $55 billion of debt owed by developing countries to the World Bank, the International Monetary Fund, and the African Development Bank. Of course, debt forgiveness creates a *moral hazard problem*. If current debt forgiveness creates an expectation of later debt forgiveness, a country has little incentive against running up a new debt. Therefore, future loans by the IACs must be extended cautiously in the future to nations that currently receive debt forgiveness.

By contrast, there were few worries about moral hazard when the G20 nations chose, in April 2020, to suspend the collection of debt payments owed by 73 developing countries to help them through the COVID-19 pandemic. Because those debt payments were suspended temporarily, rather than being forgiven permanently, the G20 action was expected to provide little to no temptation for any developing government to fall prey to moral hazard and borrow excessively in the hope of future debt forgiveness.

Microfinance and Cash Transfers

Development Efforts Have Increasingly Focused on Lending, Granting, or Gifting Money to Individuals.

For the most of the twentieth century, international development efforts focused on infrastructure projects, such as building roads, bridges, and electrical grids. Efforts aimed directly at individuals were relatively rare and poorly funded. That has changed drastically in the last few decades as development efforts have become increasingly focused on delivering cash directly to poor individuals. The results, however, have been mixed.

Microcredit In the mid-1970s, a Bangladeshi economics professor named Muhammad Yunus discovered that making small loans to poor villagers in his native Bangladesh could sometimes facilitate economic growth and advancement at the individual level. A group of women could, for instance, start a modest but profitable textile company if they could borrow amounts of money as small as $10 or $20 to purchase looms and other equipment.

The even more startling part was that these small loans, or *microcredit,* were nearly always paid back. Whereas the poor had often been thought of by development experts as being too uneducated or inexperienced to help themselves out of poverty, Yunus showed that the poor often had good business sense and were in some cases constrained not by ignorance but by a lack of capital.

In 1983, Yunus established the Grameen Bank (literally the "Village Bank") to provide microcredit throughout Bangladesh. The Grameen Bank later expanded beyond microcredit into banking and insurance services for the poor, a set of activities that came to be referred to as **microfinance.** Its individual-focused approach to development spawned hundreds of imitators in scores of nations and earned Yunus the 2006 Nobel Peace Prize.

Tim Gerard Barker/Lonely Planet Images/Getty Images

Unfortunately, development economists have found that microfinance does not offer a consistent way out of poverty by itself. Randomized experiments show that, on average, the households and individuals receiving microcredit usually do no better than nonrecipients on economic, health, and social outcomes such as family income, the total number of calories consumed, and rates of school attendance.

microfinance The provision of small loans and other financial services to low-income *entrepreneurs* and small-business owners in *developing countries*.

World Bank A bank that lends (and guarantees loans) to *developing countries* to assist them in increasing their *capital stock* and thus in achieving *economic growth*.

The World Bank Group The United States and other IACs also support the DVCs by participating in the **World Bank,** whose major objective is helping DVCs achieve economic growth by lending DVC governments the money that they need to complete specific development projects.

The World Bank was established in 1945, along with the International Monetary Fund (IMF). Supported by 189 member nations, the World Bank not only lends out of its capital funds but also sells bonds, lends the proceeds, and guarantees and insures private loans:

- The World Bank is a "last-resort" lending agency; its loans are limited to economic projects for which private funds are not readily available.

- The majority of World Bank loans are "hard loans" that are only issued to projects that are judged to be capable of generating returns sufficient to pay off them off.

- Many World Bank loans have been for basic development projects—dams, irrigation projects, health and sanitation programs, communications, and transportation facilities. The Bank has helped finance the infrastructure needed to encourage the flow of private capital.

- The Bank has provided technical assistance to the DVCs by helping them determine what avenues of growth seem appropriate for their economic development.

Two divisions of the World Bank focus on lending to the private sector and on concessional loans that function more like grants than the hard loans that the World Bank typically issues. The

Conditional cash transfers Conditional cash transfer programs provide poor families with transfers (grants) of cash if they send their children to school and participate in preventive health programs. As just one example, the Mexican government's *Oportunidades* program gives bi-weekly cash grants to poor families who keep their kids in school and participate in health screenings and nutritional programs.

Conditional cash transfer programs have been in place since the early 1990s, which makes them old enough for us to be able to draw some conclusions about their effectiveness. Some very positive outcomes are apparent. The programs have been shown to increase school enrollment by up to 30 percent and to improve health and nutrition so much that rates of illness among young children fall by more than 10 percent. Children enrolled in conditional cash transfer programs also end up taller than children who are not enrolled.

Unfortunately, the effectiveness of conditional cash transfers in relieving poverty in developing countries is limited by other factors. As just one example, school enrollment goes up but test scores stay the same, probably because the schools themselves are poorly funded and often ineffective. Similarly, the wages earned by the students who stay in school longer don't seem to be much higher than those of the students who dropped out earlier, probably because of the low quality of many schools as well as high rates of unemployment in many local labor markets.

Unconditional cash transfers The newest antipoverty initiatives targeted at individuals are known as **unconditional cash transfers** because they simply hand cash to poor adults with no conditions attached. They operate under the theory that many poor people are held back by a lack of either physical or human capital, and that if you were to give them no-strings-attached cash, they would use the money to pay for tools and training.

That assumption has proven true in early testing. As an example, a randomized study in Uganda that started in 2008 offered the chance to receive unconditional cash transfers to young people who were willing to submit essays detailing what they planned to do with any money received. Half of the participants were then randomly selected to receive the money, with it being made explicitly clear that nobody would be following up to see if the recipients actually spent the money on what they had written in their essays (which, for the most part, indicated a desire to spend cash transfers on vocational training and business equipment).

The researchers running the study found that the half who were randomly selected to receive unconditional cash transfers ended up "65 percent more likely to practice a skilled trade such as carpentry, metalworking, tailoring, or hairstyling" than those who did not receive unconditional cash transfers. Even better, the results were long lasting, with recipients earning salaries that were 41 percent higher four years later.

Because unconditional cash transfer programs are quite new, however, it is not yet clear whether their early promise can be replicated in other places or even why granting cash unconditionally seems to work better than either conditional cash transfers or microfinance. Experiments are under way to find out.

---

conditional cash transfers Anti-poverty programs in which households receive regular cash transfers (grants) as long as they keep their children in school and participate in preventative health care programs.

unconditional cash transfers Anti-poverty programs that give cash transfers (grants) to poor individuals with no strings attached in the hope that the recipients will improve their economic prospects by spending the money on either education or physical capital.

International Finance Corporation (IFC) loans money to private enterprises within DVCs. The *International Development Association (IDA)* grants money that does not have to be paid back to the poorest DVC governments in addition to issuing them "soft loans" that have generously low interest rates and extended payout periods.

Foreign Harm? The foreign-aid approach to helping DVCs has met with several criticisms.

Dependency and Incentives A basic criticism is that foreign aid may promote dependency rather than self-sustaining growth. Critics argue that injections of funds from the IACs encourage the DVCs to ignore the painful economic decisions, the institutional and cultural reforms, and the changes in attitudes toward thrift, industry, hard work, and self-reliance that are needed for economic growth. They say that, after some five decades of foreign aid, the DVCs' demand for foreign aid has increased rather than decreased. These aid programs should have withered away if they had been successful in promoting sustainable growth.

Bureaucracy and Centralized Government IAC aid is given to the governments of the DVCs, not to their residents or businesses. The consequence is that the aid typically generates massive, ineffective government bureaucracies and centralizes government power over the economy. The stagnation and collapse of the Soviet Union and communist countries of eastern Europe is evidence that highly bureaucratized economies are not very conducive to economic growth and development.

Furthermore, the bureaucratization of the DVCs often shifts the nation's focus from producing more output to bickering over how unearned "income" should be distributed.

Corruption and Misuse Some estimates suggest that from 10 to 20 percent of foreign aid is "diverted" to the private bank accounts of local government officials. Also, IAC-based aid consultants and multinational corporations are major beneficiaries of aid programs. Some economists contend that as much as one-fourth of each year's aid is spent on expert consultants. Furthermore, because IAC corporations manage many of the aid projects, they are major beneficiaries of, and lobbyists for, foreign aid.

Flows of Private Capital

foreign direct investment
Financial investments made to obtain a lasting ownership interest in *firms* operating outside the economy of the investor; may involve purchasing existing assets or building new production facilities.

The total flow of private capital to DVCs was $616 billion in 2020. The main private investors and lenders are now private IAC firms and individuals, not commercial banks. Also, more of the flow is in the form of **foreign direct investment** in DVCs, rather than loans to DVC governments. For example, General Motors or Ford might finance the construction of plants in Mexico or Brazil to assemble autos or produce auto parts. JPMorgan Chase or Bank of America might make loans to private firms operating in Argentina or China or to the governments of Thailand and Malaysia.

Whereas some DVCs once viewed foreign direct investment as "exploitation," many of them now seek out foreign direct investment as a way to expand their capital stock and improve their citizens' job opportunities and wages. Those wages are often very low by IAC standards but high by DVC standards. Another benefit of direct investment in DVCs is that management skills and technological knowledge often accompany the capital.

Unfortunately for the low-income DVCs, the strong flow of private capital to the DVCs has been very selective. The vast majority of IAC investment and lending has been directed toward China, India, Mexico, and other middle-income DVCs, with only small amounts flowing toward such extremely impoverished DVCs as those in Africa.

In fact, as we have indicated, many of the lowest-income countries face staggering debt burdens from previous government and private loans. Payment of interest and principal on this external debt is diverting expenditures away from maintenance of infrastructure, new infrastructure, education, and private investment.

Further, the flows of private capital to both the middle-income and low-income DVCs fell after the COVID-19 pandemic began in early 2020. It may be several years before foreign direct investment regains its momentum.

QUICK REVIEW
41.2

▶ The IACs can assist the DVCs through expanded trade, foreign aid, and flows of private capital.

▶ Many of the poorest DVCs have large external debts that pose an additional obstacle to economic growth.

▶ The worldwide COVID-19 recession reduced direct investment by IACs in DVCs.

Summary

LO41.1 Distinguish between industrially advanced countries and developing countries.
The majority of the world's nations are developing countries (low- and middle-income nations). While some DVCs have been realizing rapid growth rates in recent years, others have experienced little or no growth.

LO41.2 List the obstacles to economic development.
Scarcities of natural resources make it more challenging, but not impossible, for a nation to develop.

The large and rapidly growing populations in many DVCs contribute to low per capita incomes. Increases in per capita incomes frequently induce greater population growth, often reducing per capita incomes to near-subsistence levels. The demographic transition view, however, suggests that rising living standards must precede declining birthrates.

Most DVCs suffer from unemployment and underemployment. Labor productivity is low because of insufficient investment in physical and human capital.

In many DVCs, formidable obstacles impede both saving and investment. In some of the poorest DVCs, the savings potential is very low, and many savers transfer their funds to the IACs rather than invest them domestically. The lack of a vigorous entrepreneurial class and the weakness of investment incentives also impede capital accumulation.

Appropriate social and institutional changes and, in particular, the presence of the will to develop are essential ingredients in economic development.

LO41.3 Explain the vicious circle of poverty that afflicts low-income nations.

The vicious circle of poverty brings together many of the obstacles to growth, supporting the view that poor countries stay poor because of their poverty. Low incomes inhibit saving and the accumulation of physical and human capital, making it difficult to increase productivity and incomes. Overly rapid population growth may offset promising attempts to break the vicious circle.

LO41.4 Describe the role of government in promoting economic development.

The obstacles to growth—the absence of an entrepreneurial class, the dearth of infrastructure, the saving-investment dilemma, and the presence of social-institutional obstacles to growth—suggest that government should play a major role in initiating growth. Economists suggest that DVCs that have achieved basic levels of state capacity and the rule of law can make further development progress through such policies as building infrastructure, opening their economies to international trade, setting realistic exchange rates, encouraging foreign direct investment, building human capital, encouraging entrepreneurship, controlling population growth, and making peace with neighbors. However, the corruption and maladministration that are common to the public sectors of many DVCs suggest that government may not be very effective in instigating growth.

LO41.5 Explain how industrial nations attempt to aid low-income countries.

Advanced nations can encourage development in the DVCs by reducing IAC trade barriers and by directing foreign aid (official development assistance) to the neediest nations, providing debt forgiveness to the poorest DVCs, allowing temporary low-skilled immigration from the DVCs, and discouraging arms sales to the DVCs. Critics of foreign aid, however, say that it (*a*) creates DVC dependency, (*b*) contributes to the growth of bureaucracies and centralized economic control, and (*c*) is rendered ineffective by corruption and mismanagement.

In recent years the IACs have reduced foreign aid to the DVCs but have increased direct investment and other private capital flows to the DVCs. Little of the foreign direct investment, however, has gone to the poorest DVCs. Also, foreign direct investment plummeted during the worldwide recession of 2007–2009.

Terms and Concepts

industrially advanced countries (IACs)

developing countries (DVCs)

demographic transition

underemployment

capital flight

infrastructure

capital-saving technology

capital-using technology

will to develop

capricious universe view

land reform

vicious circle of poverty

state capacity

failed state

microcredit

corruption

World Bank

foreign direct investment

microfinance

conditional cash transfers

unconditional cash transfers

Discussion Questions

connect

1. What are the four categories used by the World Bank to classify nations on the basis of national income per capita? Identify any two nations of your choice for each of the four categories. **LO41.1**

2. Explain how the absolute per capita income gap between rich and poor nations might increase, even though per capita income (or output) is growing faster in DVCs than in IACs. **LO41.1**

3. Explain how each of the following can be obstacles to the growth of income per capita in the DVCs: lack of natural resources, large populations, low labor productivity, poor infrastructure, and capital flight. **LO41.2**

4. What is the demographic transition? Contrast the demographic transition view of population growth with the traditional view that slower population growth is a prerequisite for rising living standards in the DVCs. **LO41.2**

5. As it relates to the vicious circle of poverty, what is meant by the saying "Some DVCs stay poor because they are poor"? Change the box labels as necessary in Figure 41.3 to explain rapid economic growth in countries such as South Korea and Chile. What factors other than those contained in the figure might contribute to that growth? **LO41.3**

6. Because real capital is supposed to earn a higher return where it is scarce, how do you explain the fact that most international investment flows to the IACs (where capital is relatively abundant) rather than to the DVCs (where capital is very scarce)? **LO41.3**

7. What factors cause failed states? List and discuss five policies that DVC governments might undertake to promote economic development and expansion of income per capita in their countries. **LO41.4**

8. Do you think that the problems the DVCs face require a government-directed or a private-sector-directed development process? Explain your reasoning. **LO41.4**

9. Why do you think there is so much government corruption in some developing countries? **LO41.4**

10. What types of products do the DVCs typically export? How do those exports relate to the law of comparative advantage? How do tariffs by IACs reduce DVCs' standard of living? **LO41.5**

11. Do you favor debt forgiveness to all DVCs, just the poorest ones, or none at all? What incentive problem might debt relief create? Would you be willing to pay $20 a year more in personal income taxes for debt forgiveness? How about $200? How about $2,000? **LO41.5**

12. Do you think that IACs such as the United States should open their doors wider to the immigration of low-skilled DVC workers as a way to help DVCs develop? Do you think that it is appropriate for students from DVC nations to stay in IAC nations to work and build careers? **LO41.5**

13. **LAST WORD** Explain the differences among microcredit, conditional cash transfers, and unconditional cash transfers. Then explain how effective each policy has been.

Review Questions

1. True or False: The term *developing country* (DVC) is applied to rich nations like the United States and Germany because their economies are always growing quickly by developing new technologies. **LO41.1**

2. True or False: A DVC that has little in the way of natural resources is destined to remain poor. **LO41.2**

3. Suppose a country's total output is growing 10 percent per year, but its population is growing 11 percent per year. What will happen to living standards? **LO41.2**
   a. They will rise.
   b. They will fall.
   c. They will remain the same.

4. A DVC's population is growing 2 percent per year and its output is growing 3 percent per year. If the government wants to improve living standards over the coming decades, which of the following would probably be the best savings rate for the economy? **LO41.2**
   a. 0 percent
   b. 2 percent
   c. 5 percent
   d. 10 percent

5. Compare a hypothetical DVC with a hypothetical IAC. In the DVC, average per capita income is $500 per year. In the IAC, average per capita income is $40,000 per year. If both countries have a savings rate of 10 percent per year, the amount of savings per capita in the DVC will be _____ per person per year, while in the IAC it will be _____ per person per year. **LO41.3**
   a. $50; $4,000
   b. $5; $400
   c. $450; $36,000
   d. None of the above

6. Which of the following policies would economists consider to be actions by a DVC government that will *improve* growth prospects? **LO41.4**
   *Choose **one or more** answers from the choices shown.*
   a. Helping to extend the banking system to the rural poor.
   b. Passing high tariffs against foreign products.
   c. Constructing better ports, roads, and Internet networks.
   d. Charging high fees for public elementary schools.

7. True or False: Economists are unanimous that foreign aid greatly helps DVCs. **LO41.5**

8. True or False: Some economists argue that the single best thing that IACs could do for DVCs in terms of economic growth is to eliminate trade barriers between IACs and DVCs. **LO41.5**

Problems

1. Assume a DVC and an IAC currently have real per capita outputs of $500 and $50,000, respectively. If both nations have a 3 percent increase in their real per capita outputs, by how much will the per capita output gap change? **LO41.1**

2. Assume that a very tiny and very poor DVC has income per capita of $300 and total national income of $3 million. How large is its population? If its population grows by 2 percent in some year while its total income grows by 3 percent, what will be its new income per capita rounded to full dollars? If the population had not grown during the year, what would have been its income per capita? **LO41.2**

Historical Economic
Data Tables

Selected Economics Statistics for Various Years, 1929–1993

Statistics in rows 1–5 are in billions of dollars in the year specified. Numbers may not add to totals because of rounding.

GDP AND INCOME DATA	1929	1933	1940	1942	1944	1946	1950	1960	1970	1972
1 Gross domestic product (billions of nominal dollars)	104.6	57.2	102.9	166.0	224.4	227.5	299.8	542.4	1,073.3	1,279.1
1A Personal consumption expenditures	77.4	45.9	71.3	89.0	108.6	144.2	192.0	331.2	646.7	768.2
1B Gross private domestic investment	17.2	2.3	14.6	11.8	9.2	33.1	56.5	86.5	170.0	228.1
1C Government purchases	9.6	8.9	15.6	65.4	108.6	43.0	50.5	120.5	252.6	286.2
1D Net exports of goods and services	0.4	0.1	1.5	−0.3	−2.0	7.2	0.7	4.2	3.9	−3.4
2 Net domestic product	94.1	49.1	92.3	151.0	203.1	201.8	266.4	474.5	936.5	1,118.1
3 National income	94.2	48.9	91.5	152.4	200.9	201.3	266.6	478.9	937.5	1,119.5
3A Wages and salaries	51.4	29.8	52.7	88.0	124.3	122.5	158.3	301.3	623.3	731.3
3B Rent	6.1	2.9	3.8	5.5	6.3	6.9	8.8	16.5	20.7	22.7
3C Interest	4.6	4.0	3.3	3.2	2.4	1.8	3.1	10.3	39.5	48.0
3D Profits	10.8	−0.2	9.9	20.8	25.0	18.2	36.1	54.7	86.2	117.2
3E Proprietor's income	14.0	5.3	12.2	23.3	29.3	35.7	37.5	50.6	77.8	95.1
3F Taxes on production and imports*	7.3	7.1	9.6	11.6	13.6	16.2	22.8	45.5	90.0	105.2
4 Personal income	85.3	47.2	79.4	126.7	169.7	182.5	233.7	422.1	865.0	1,024.5
5 Disposable income	83.6	46.4	77.7	121.8	152.1	165.3	214.8	376.1	762.0	900.8
6 Disposable income per capita	686	369	588	903	1,099	1,169	1,416	2,080	3,715	4,291
7 Personal saving as a percent of disposable income	4.7	−0.7	6.8	26.2	27.9	11.8	9.3	10.1	12.8	12.4

OTHER STATISTICS	1929	1933	1940	1942	1944	1946	1950	1960	1970	1972
8 Real GDP (billions of 2012 dollars)	1,110.2	817.8	1,331.1	1,862.8	2,353.2	2,059.8	2,291.1	3,262.1	4,954.4	5,386.7
9 Economic growth rate (percent change in real GDP)	—	−1.2	8.8	18.9	8.0	−11.6	8.7	2.6	0.2	5.3
10 Consumer price index (1982–1984 = 100)	17.1	13.0	14.0	16.3	17.6	19.5	25.0	29.8	39.8	42.5
11 Rate of inflation (percent change in CPI)	0.0	−5.1	0.7	10.9	1.7	8.3	5.8	1.4	5.6	3.4
12 Money supply, M2 (billions of $)	—	—	—	—	—	—	—	312.4	626.5	802.3
13 Effective federal funds interest rate (%)	—	—	—	—	—	—	—	3.21	7.17	4.44
14 Prime interest rate (%)	5.50	1.50	1.50	1.50	1.50	1.50	2.07	4.82	7.90	5.25
15 Population (millions)	121.9	125.7	132.1	134.9	138.4	141.4	151.7	180.8	205.1	209.9
16 Real GDP per capita (in 2012 dollars)	9,107	6,506	10,076	13,809	17,003	14,567	15,103	18,043	24,156	25,663
17 Growth rate of real GDP per capita (%)	—	−1.8	7.9	17.6	6.7	−12.5	6.9	0.5	−1.0	4.1
18 Civilian labor force (millions)	49.2	51.6	55.6	56.4	54.6	57.5	62.1	69.7	82.8	87.0
18A Employment (millions)	47.6	38.8	47.5	53.8	54.0	55.3	58.9	65.8	78.7	82.1
18B Unemployment (millions)	1.6	12.8	8.1	2.7	0.7	2.3	3.2	3.9	4.1	4.9
19 Unemployment rate (%)	3.2	24.9	14.6	4.7	1.2	3.9	5.3	5.5	4.9	5.6
20 Productivity growth, business sector (%)	—	—	—	—	—	—	8.2	1.8	2.0	3.2
21 After-tax manufacturing profit per dollar of sales (cents)	—	—	—	—	—	—	7.1	4.4	4.5	4.4
22 Price of crude oil (U.S. average, dollars per barrel)	1.27	0.67	1.02	1.19	1.21	1.41	2.51	2.88	3.18	3.39
23 Federal budget surplus (+) or deficit (−) (billions of dollars)	0.7	−2.6	−2.9	−20.5	−47.6	−15.9	−3.1	0.3	−2.8	−23.4
24 Federal budget surplus (+) or deficit (−) as a percent of GDP	0.7	−4.5	−2.8	−12.4	−21.2	−7.0	−1.0	0.1	−0.3	−1.8
25 Public debt (billions of dollars)	16.9	22.5	50.7	79.2	204.1	271.0	256.9	290.5	389.2	448.5
26 Public debt as a percent of GDP	16.2	39.3	49.3	47.7	91.0	119.1	85.7	53.6	36.3	35.1
27 Balance on current account (billions of dollars)	—	—	—	—	—	4.9	−1.8	2.8	2.3	−5.8

*Combines items from smaller accounts.

1974	1976	1978	1980	1982	1984	1986	1988	1990	1991	1992	1993
1,545.2	1,873.4	2,351.6	2,857.3	3,343.8	4,037.6	4,579.6	5,236.4	5,963.1	6,158.1	6,520.3	6,858.6
930.2	1,147.7	1,422.3	1,750.7	2,071.3	2,492.3	2,886.3	3,330.0	3,809.0	3,943.4	4,197.6	4,452.0
274.5	323.2	478.4	530.1	581.0	820.1	849.1	937.0	993.4	944.3	1,013.0	1,106.8
341.4	404.2	476.3	589.6	711.5	827.9	976.1	1,078.9	1,238.6	1,299.0	1,344.5	1,364.9
−0.8	−1.6	−25.4	−13.1	−20.0	−102.7	−131.9	−109.4	−77.9	−28.6	−34.7	−65.2
1,338.3	1,613.2	2,024.4	2,428.9	2,806.8	3,439.2	3,894.3	4,451.9	5,074.6	5,225.7	5,560.1	5,855.1
1,346.4	1,609.4	2,022.7	2,418.6	2,834.5	3,433.9	3,831.2	4,471.6	5,013.8	5,164.4	5,475.2	5,730.3
887.7	1,048.3	1,316.8	1,622.2	1,893.0	2,215.9	2,542.1	2,948.0	3,340.4	3,450.5	3,668.2	3,817.3
23.2	20.3	16.5	19.0	23.8	24.7	18.3	22.5	28.2	38.6	60.6	90.1
71.7	87.4	114.8	182.2	274.8	330.2	353.1	377.9	433.4	391.8	365.6	353.1
125.7	174.3	238.6	223.6	229.9	337.9	324.4	414.5	417.7	452.6	477.2	524.6
112.2	131.0	166.0	171.6	171.2	228.2	256.5	325.5	353.2	354.2	400.2	428.0
125.9	148.1	170.0	200.0	241.8	297.0	336.8	383.2	440.9	476.7	503.4	517.2
1,251.8	1,502.6	1,863.7	2,323.6	2,791.6	3,292.7	3,733.1	4,283.4	4,913.8	5,084.9	5,420.9	5,657.9
1,100.8	1,330.0	1,634.1	2,024.1	2,436.9	2,914.8	3,295.3	3,777.5	4,319.1	4,496.0	4,808.1	5,009.2
5,146	6,098	7,340	8,888	10,494	12,330	13,691	15,414	17,264	17,734	18,714	19,245
13.3	11.6	10.7	11.1	12.0	11.3	8.8	8.5	8.4	8.8	9.4	7.9

1974	1976	1978	1980	1982	1984	1986	1988	1990	1991	1992	1993
5,660.1	5,952.8	6,572.8	6,763.5	6,810.1	7,637.7	8,231.7	8,872.2	9,371.5	9,361.3	9,691.1	9,957.7
−0.5	5.4	5.5	−0.3	−1.8	7.2	3.5	4.2	1.9	−0.1	3.5	2.8
51.9	58.4	67.9	86.4	97.7	105.5	110.8	120.7	134.2	138.2	142.3	146.3
12.1	5.0	9.0	12.4	3.8	4.0	1.2	4.4	6.3	3.0	3.0	2.8
902.1	1,152.0	1,366.0	1,599.8	1,905.9	2,306.4	2,728.0	2,988.2	3,271.8	3,372.2	3,424.7	3,474.5
10.51	5.05	7.94	13.35	12.24	10.23	6.80	7.57	8.10	5.69	3.52	3.02
10.80	6.84	9.05	15.28	14.85	12.06	8.32	9.32	10.01	8.46	6.25	6.00
213.9	218.1	222.6	227.7	232.2	236.4	240.7	245.1	250.2	253.5	256.9	260.3
26,461	27,294	29,527	29,704	29,329	32,308	34,199	36,198	37,456	36,928	37,723	38,255
−1.5	4.4	4.4	−1.4	−2.7	6.3	2.5	3.2	0.7	−1.4	2.2	1.4
92.0	96.2	102.2	107.0	110.2	113.5	117.8	121.7	125.9	126.4	128.1	129.2
86.8	88.8	96.0	99.3	99.5	105.0	109.6	115.0	118.8	117.7	118.5	120.3
5.2	7.4	6.2	7.7	10.7	8.5	8.2	6.7	7.1	8.6	9.6	8.9
5.6	7.7	6.1	7.1	9.7	7.5	7.0	5.5	5.6	6.8	7.5	6.9
−1.7	3.2	1.1	−0.2	−0.8	2.7	2.9	1.5	1.0	3.3	4.4	−0.6
6.4	5.5	5.3	5.6	4.4	4.8	4.6	6.6	4.8	4.1	3.1	3.7
6.87	8.19	9.00	21.59	28.52	25.88	12.51	12.58	20.03	16.54	15.99	14.25
−6.1	−73.7	−59.2	−73.8	−128.0	−185.4	−221.2	−155.2	−221.0	−269.2	−290.3	−255.1
−0.4	−3.9	−2.5	−2.6	−3.8	−4.6	−4.8	−3.0	−3.7	−4.4	−4.5	−3.7
492.7	653.5	789.2	930.2	1,197.1	1,663.0	2,214.8	2,684.4	3,364.8	3,801.7	4,177.0	4,535.7
31.9	34.9	33.6	32.6	35.8	41.2	48.4	51.3	56.4	61.7	64.1	66.1
2.0	4.3	−15.1	2.3	−5.5	−94.3	−147.2	−121.2	−79.0	2.9	−51.6	−84.8

Sources: Bureau of Economic Analysis; Bureau of Labor Statistics; Federal Reserve System; *Economic Report of the President 2022;* and U.S. Energy Information Administration.

Selected Economics Statistics for Various Years, 1994–2021

Statistics in rows 1–5 are in billions of dollars in the year specified. Numbers may not add to totals because of rounding.

GDP AND INCOME DATA	1994	1995	1996	1997	1998	1999	2000	2001	2002	2003	2004	2005	2006
1 Gross domestic product (billions of nominal dollars)	7,287.2	7,639.7	8,073.1	8,577.6	9,062.8	9,631.2	10,251.0	10,581.9	10,929.1	11,456.5	12,217.2	13,039.2	13,815.6
1A Personal consumption expenditures	4,721.0	4,962.6	5,244.6	5,536.8	5,877.2	6,283.8	6,767.2	7,073.8	7,348.9	7,740.7	8,232.0	8,769.1	9,277.2
1B Gross private domestic investment	1,256.5	1,317.5	1,432.1	1,595.6	1,736.7	1,887.1	2,038.4	1,934.8	1,930.4	2,027.1	2,281.3	2,534.7	2,701.0
1C Government purchases	1,402.3	1,449.4	1,492.8	1,547.1	1,611.6	1,719.9	1,826.4	1,950.0	2,089.5	2,210.6	2,338.1	2,475.3	2,623.8
1D Net exports of goods and services	−92.5	−89.8	−96.4	−102.0	−162.7	−259.6	−381.1	−376.7	−439.7	−522.0	−634.1	−739.9	−786.5
2 Net domestic product	6,231.6	6,517.4	6,897.8	7,338.2	7,753.1	8,232.2	8,739.7	8,982.4	9,271.1	9,737.4	10,395.4	11,068.2	11,691.5
3 National income	6,114.6	6,452.3	6,870.6	7,349.9	7,825.7	8,291.5	8,872.4	9,146.6	9,394.2	9,815.8	10,495.8	11,195.5	11,942.3
3A Wages and salaries	4,006.2	4,198.1	4,416.9	4,708.8	5,071.1	5,402.7	5,847.1	6,038.3	6,135.1	6,353.6	6,719.5	7,066.1	7,479.7
3B Rent	113.7	124.9	142.5	147.1	165.2	178.5	183.5	202.4	208.4	227.1	242.8	221.1	181.1
3C Interest	347.3	357.4	361.9	394.4	456.7	466.0	542.1	542.2	462.0	443.6	377.3	471.8	564.8
3D Profits	624.8	706.2	789.5	869.7	808.5	834.9	786.6	758.7	911.7	1,056.3	1,289.3	1,488.6	1,646.3
3E Proprietor's income	456.6	481.2	543.8	584.0	640.2	696.4	753.9	831.0	870.0	897.5	962.9	979.1	1,050.9
3F Taxes on production and imports*	566.0	584.5	616.0	645.9	684.0	713.0	759.2	774.0	807.0	837.7	904.0	968.8	1,019.5
4 Personal income	5,947.1	6,291.4	6,678.5	7,092.5	7,606.7	8,006.8	8,655.9	9,012.8	9,160.9	9,498.5	10,044.3	10,604.9	11,384.7
5 Disposable income	5,254.0	5,543.0	5,841.4	6,160.7	6,574.2	6,894.9	7,419.6	7,773.8	8,108.8	8,495.0	8,995.5	9,392.5	10,027.7
6 Disposable income per capita	19,943	20,792	21,658	22,570	23,806	24,684	26,274	27,255	28,160	29,230	30,674	31,732	33,558
7 Personal saving as a percent of disposable income	6.9	7.0	6.5	6.3	6.8	5.0	4.7	4.9	5.7	5.4	5.0	2.9	3.6

OTHER STATISTICS	1994	1995	1996	1997	1998	1999	2000	2001	2002	2003	2004	2005	2006
8 Real GDP (billions of 2012 dollars)	10,358.9	10,637.0	11,038.3	11,529.2	12,045.8	12,623.4	13,138.0	13,263.4	13,488.4	13,865.5	14,399.7	14,901.3	15,315.9
9 Economic growth rate (percent change in real GDP)	4.0	2.7	3.8	4.4	4.5	4.8	4.1	1.0	1.7	2.8	3.9	3.5	2.8
10 Consumer price index (1982–1984 = 100)	150.1	153.9	159.1	161.8	164.4	168.8	174.6	177.4	181.8	185.5	191.7	198.1	203.1
11 Rate of inflation (percent change in CPI)	2.6	2.5	3.4	1.7	1.6	2.7	3.4	1.6	2.5	2.0	3.3	3.3	2.5
12 Money supply, M2 (billions of $)	3,486.4	3,629.5	3,818.6	4,032.9	4,375.2	4,638.0	4,924.7	5,432.7	5,770.9	6,065.9	6,417.2	6,680.1	7,069.5
13 Effective federal funds interest rate (%)	4.21	5.83	5.30	5.46	5.35	4.97	6.24	3.88	1.67	1.13	1.35	3.22	4.97
14 Prime interest rate (%)	7.14	8.83	8.27	8.44	8.36	8.00	9.24	6.94	4.68	4.12	4.34	6.19	7.96
15 Population (millions)	263.5	266.6	269.7	273.0	276.2	279.3	282.4	285.2	288.0	290.6	293.3	296.0	298.8
16 Real GDP per capita (in 2012 dollars)	39,313	39,899	40,928	42,232	43,613	45,197	46,523	46,506	46,835	47,713	49,095	50,342	51,258
17 Growth rate of real GDP per capita (%)	2.8	1.5	2.6	3.2	3.3	3.6	2.9	0.0	0.7	1.9	2.9	2.5	1.8
18 Civilian labor force (millions)	131.0	132.3	134.0	136.3	137.7	139.4	142.6	143.8	144.9	146.5	147.4	149.3	151.4
18A Employment (millions)	123.1	124.9	126.7	129.6	131.5	133.5	136.9	136.9	136.5	137.7	139.2	141.7	144.4
18B Unemployment (millions)	8.0	7.4	7.2	6.7	6.2	5.9	5.7	6.8	8.4	8.8	8.1	7.6	7.0
19 Unemployment rate (%)	6.1	5.6	5.4	4.9	4.5	4.2	4.0	4.7	5.8	6.0	5.5	5.1	4.6
20 Productivity growth, business sector (%)	0.9	1.1	2.1	2.7	3.3	4.2	3.0	3.2	3.1	5.7	1.6	1.8	1.2
21 After-tax manufacturing profit per dollar of sales (cents)	5.5	6.0	6.5	6.7	6.0	6.4	6.9	0.8	3.2	5.4	7.1	7.4	8.1
22 Price of crude oil (U.S. average, dollars per barrel)	13.19	14.62	18.46	17.23	10.87	15.56	26.72	21.84	22.51	27.56	36.77	50.28	59.69
23 Federal budget surplus (+) or deficit (−) (billions of dollars)	−203.2	−164.0	−107.4	−21.9	69.3	125.6	236.2	128.2	−157.8	−377.6	−412.7	−318.3	−248.2
24 Federal budget surplus (+) or deficit (−) as a percent of GDP	−2.8	−2.1	−1.3	−0.3	0.8	1.3	2.3	1.2	−1.4	−3.3	−3.4	−2.4	−1.8
25 Public debt (billions of dollars)	4,800.2	4,988.7	5,323.2	5,502.4	5,614.2	5,776.1	5,662.2	5,943.4	6,405.7	6,998.0	7,596.1	8,170.4	8,680.2
26 Public debt as a percent of GDP	65.9	65.3	65.9	64.1	61.9	60.0	55.2	56.2	58.6	61.1	62.2	62.7	62.8
27 Balance on current account (billions of dollars)	−121.6	−113.6	−124.8	−140.7	−215.1	−286.6	−401.9	−394.1	−456.1	−522.3	−635.9	−749.2	−816.7

*Combines items from smaller accounts.

2007	2008	2009	2010	2011	2012	2013	2014	2015	2016	2017	2018	2019	2020	2021**
14,474.2	14,769.9	14,478.1	15,049.0	15,599.7	16,254.0	16,843.2	17,550.7	18,206.0	18,695.1	19,479.6	20,527.2	21,372.6	20,893.7	22,996.1
9,746.6	10,050.1	9,891.2	10,260.3	10,698.9	11,047.4	11,363.5	11,847.7	12,263.5	12,693.3	13,239.1	13,913.5	14,428.7	14,047.6	15,741.6
2,673.0	2,477.6	1,929.7	2,165.5	2,332.6	2,621.8	2,826.0	3,044.2	3,237.2	3,205.0	3,381.4	3,637.8	3,826.3	3,637.8	4,120.0
2,790.6	2,983.0	3,076.3	3,155.6	3,147.9	3,136.5	3,133.0	3,168.8	3,231.6	3,303.1	3,399.1	3,572.0	3,713.9	3,859.5	4,052.7
−735.9	−740.9	−419.2	−532.3	−579.6	−551.6	−479.4	−510.0	−526.2	−506.3	−539.9	−596.2	−596.3	−651.2	−918.2
12,221.4	12,411.0	12,106.6	12,658.0	13,125.3	13,678.0	14,162.0	14,735.7	15,294.6	15,708.0	16,361.5	17,253.7	17,937.0	17,317.8	19,148.2
12,297.3	12,359.3	12,054.8	12,781.1	13,375.5	14,099.6	14,507.1	15,228.1	15,749.5	16,033.4	16,774.9	17,673.3	18,273.1	17,710.7	19,920.2
7,878.5	8,056.8	7,759.0	7,925.4	8,226.2	8,567.4	8,835.0	9,250.2	9,699.4	9,966.1	10,426.1	10,959.5	11,447.7	11,572.2	12,580.9
186.3	290.3	347.6	433.7	506.5	534.5	577.4	602.7	609.5	626.6	652.7	681.9	692.1	711.6	726.4
637.3	673.4	544.7	471.0	449.6	494.0	459.2	504.8	591.1	567.3	612.5	598.7	558.2	618.8	686.1
1,533.2	1,285.8	1,386.8	1,728.7	1,809.8	1,997.4	2,010.7	2,120.2	2,060.5	2,037.7	2,128.9	2,305.0	2,367.8	2,243.8	2,805.8
995.5	959.7	937.6	1,107.3	1,227.4	1,346.4	1,402.2	1,445.6	1,420.8	1,423.3	1,505.8	1,580.4	1,598.9	1,650.0	1,821.9
1,066.5	1,093.3	1,079.1	1,115.0	1,156.0	1,159.9	1,222.6	1,304.6	1,368.2	1,412.4	1,448.9	1,547.8	1,608.4	914.3	1,299.1
12,021.4	12,477.6	12,080.4	12,594.5	13,339.3	14,014.3	14,193.6	14,976.6	15,685.2	16,096.9	16,850.2	17,706.0	18,424.4	19,627.6	21,077.2
10,528.9	10,970.1	10,928.0	11,356.9	11,885.6	12,504.8	12,517.3	13,192.0	13,745.3	14,138.7	14,801.2	15,629.7	16,219.3	17,432.0	18,494.5
34,899	36,021	35,568	36,654	38,059	39,732	39,474	41,276	42,672	43,556	45,283	47,536	49,073	52,544	55,671
3.3	4.6	5.9	6.2	6.8	8.6	6.1	7.1	7.5	7.0	7.3	7.6	7.6	16.6	12.3

2007	2008	2009	2010	2011	2012	2013	2014	2015	2016	2017	2018	2019	2020	2021**
15,623.9	15,643.0	15,236.3	15,649.0	15,891.5	16,254.0	16,553.3	16,932.1	17,390.3	17,680.3	18,079.1	18,606.8	19,032.7	18,384.7	19,427.3
2.0	0.1	−2.6	2.7	1.5	2.3	1.8	2.3	2.7	1.7	2.3	2.9	2.3	−3.4	5.7
211.4	211.4	217.3	220.5	227.2	231.2	234.7	236.3	237.8	242.6	247.8	252.6	258.3	261.6	280.1
4.1	0.0	2.8	1.4	3.1	1.8	1.5	0.7	0.6	2.1	2.1	1.9	2.3	1.3	7.1
7,469.4	8,189.7	8,493.1	8,799.4	9,657.7	10,457.0	11,026.1	11,678.7	12,341.0	13,210.6	13,853.0	14,376.9	15,337.9	19,154.9	21,553.1
5.02	1.92	0.16	0.18	0.10	0.14	0.11	0.09	0.13	0.39	1.00	1.83	2.16	0.37	0.08
8.05	5.07	3.25	3.25	3.25	3.25	3.25	3.25	3.26	3.51	4.10	4.90	5.29	3.53	3.25
301.7	304.5	307.2	309.8	312.3	314.7	317.1	319.6	322.1	324.6	326.9	328.8	330.5	331.8	332.2
51,786	51,373	49,597	50,513	50,885	51,649	52,202	52,979	53,990	54,468	55,305	56,590	57,588	55,409	58,481
1.0	−0.8	−3.5	1.8	0.7	1.5	1.1	1.5	1.9	0.9	1.5	2.3	1.8	−3.8	5.4
153.1	154.3	154.2	153.9	153.6	155.0	155.4	155.9	157.1	159.2	160.3	162.1	163.5	160.8	161.2
146.1	145.4	139.9	139.1	139.9	142.5	143.9	146.3	148.8	151.4	153.3	155.8	157.5	147.8	152.6
7.1	8.9	14.3	14.8	13.7	12.5	11.5	9.6	8.3	7.8	7.0	6.3	6.0	12.9	8.6
4.6	5.8	9.3	9.6	8.9	8.1	7.4	6.2	5.3	4.9	4.4	3.9	3.7	8.1	5.4
2.5	−0.1	6.1	1.7	−0.2	0.3	1.5	0.6	0.6	1.3	1.1	1.5	2.1	2.4	1.9
7.3	4.2	5.6	8.3	9.2	8.5	8.9	8.8	7.9	8.7	8.4	9.1	8.5	6.9	13.8
66.52	94.04	56.35	74.71	95.73	94.52	95.99	87.39	44.39	38.29	48.05	61.40	55.59	36.86	65.90
−160.7	−458.6	−1,412.7	−1,294.4	−1,299.6	−1,087.0	−680.0	−485.0	−439.0	−584.7	−665.4	−779.0	−983.6	−3,132.4	−2,775.3
−1.1	−3.1	−9.8	−8.6	−8.3	−6.7	−4.0	−2.8	−2.4	−3.1	−3.4	−3.8	−4.6	−15.0	−12.1
9,229.2	10,699.8	12,311.3	14,025.2	15,222.9	16,432.7	17,156.1	18,141.4	18,922.2	19,976.8	20,492.7	21,974.1	23,201.4	27,747.8	29,617.2
63.8	72.4	85.0	93.2	97.6	101.1	101.9	103.4	103.9	106.9	105.2	107.0	108.6	132.8	128.8
−736.6	−696.5	−379.7	−432.0	−455.3	−418.1	−339.5	−370.0	−408.9	−397.6	−361.7	−438.2	−472.2	−616.1	−821.6

**Data for 2021 and the years immediately prior are subject to change because of subsequent government data revisions.

Sources: Bureau of Economic Analysis; Bureau of Labor Statistics; Federal Reserve System; *Economic Report of the President 2022;* and U.S. Energy Information Administration.

Glossary

Note: Terms set in *italic type* are defined separately in this glossary.

45° (degree) line   The reference line in a two-dimensional graph that shows equality between the variable measured on the *horizontal axis* and the variable measured on the *vertical axis*. In the *aggregate expenditures model,* the line along which the value of output (measured horizontally) is equal to the value of *aggregate expenditures* (measured vertically).

ability-to-pay principle   The idea that those who have greater *income* (or *wealth*) should pay a greater proportion of it as taxes than those who have less income (or wealth).

absolute advantage   A situation in which a person or country can produce more of a particular product from a specific quantity of resource inputs than some other person or country.

absolute value   The magnitude of a number without regard to its sign. For any number *x*, the absolute value of *x* is denoted $|x|$, and $|x|$ = +*x* no matter whether *x* itself is a positive or negative number. Thus, $|-3| = +3$ and $|+3| = +3$.

accounting profit   The *total revenue* of a *firm* less its *explicit costs;* the profit (or net income) that appears on accounting statements and that is reported to the government for tax purposes.

acreage allotments   A pre-1996 government program that limited the total number of acres to be used in producing (reduced amounts of) various food and fiber products and allocated these acres among individual farmers. These farmers had to limit their plantings to the allotted number of acres to obtain *price supports* for their crops.

actively managed funds   *Mutual funds* that have portfolio managers who constantly buy and sell *assets* in an attempt to generate high returns.

administered rate   An *interest rate* set by a *central bank* to help it manage market-determined *interest rates.*

adverse selection problem   A problem arising when information known to one party to a contract or agreement is not known to the other party, causing the latter to incur major costs. Example: Individuals who have the poorest health are most likely to buy health insurance.

Affordable Care Act (ACA)   A major health care law passed by the federal government in 2010. Major provisions include an individual health insurance mandate, a ban on insurers refusing to accept patients with preexisting conditions, and federal (rather than state) regulation of health insurance policies.

AFL-CIO   An acronym for the American Federation of Labor-Congress of Industrial Organizations; the largest federation of *labor unions* in the United States.

agency shop   A place of employment where the employer may hire either *labor union* members or nonmembers but where those employees who do not join the union must either pay union dues or donate an equivalent amount of money to a charity.

aggregate   A collection of specific economic units treated as if they were one unit.

aggregate demand   A schedule or curve that shows the total quantity of *goods* and *services* that would be demanded (purchased) at various *price levels.*

aggregate demand–aggregate supply (AD-AS) model   The macroeconomic model that uses *aggregate demand* and *aggregate supply* to determine and explain the *price level* and real domestic output (*real gross domestic product*).

aggregate expenditures schedule   A table of numbers showing the total amount spent on *final goods* and final *services* at different levels of *real gross domestic product* (*real GDP*).

aggregate supply   A schedule or curve showing the total quantity of *goods* and *services* that would be supplied (produced) at various *price levels.*

aggregate supply shocks   Sudden, large changes in resource costs that shift an economy's aggregate supply curve.

agribusiness   The portion of the agricultural and food product industries that is dominated by large corporations.

Agricultural Act of 2018   The 2018 act that made minor changes to programs and policies of the Agricultural Act of 2014.

agricultural risk coverage   A form of crop insurance that pays out if the total revenue generated by all the farmers planting a given crop in a given county falls below a predetermined value.

Alcoa case   A 1945 case in which the courts ruled that the possession of monopoly power, no matter how reasonably that power had been used, was a violation of the antitrust laws; temporarily overturned the *rule of reason* applied in the *U.S. Steel case.*

allocative efficiency   The apportionment of resources among *firms* and industries to obtain the production of the products most wanted by society (consumers); the output of each product at which its *marginal cost* and *marginal benefit* are equal, and at which the sum of *consumer surplus* and *producer surplus* is maximized.

AT&T case   A major antitrust case decided in 1984 that broke up the American Telephone and Telegraph company (AT&T), which had run a domestic telephone monopoly across the entire United States for many decades, into 22 regional telephone operating companies.

anchoring   The tendency people have to unconsciously base, or "anchor," the valuation of an item they are currently thinking about on recently considered but logically irrelevant information.

anticipated inflation   Increases in the *price level* (*inflation*) that occur at the expected rate.

antitrust laws   Legislation (including the *Sherman Act* and *Clayton Act*) that prohibits anticompetitive business activities such as *price fixing,* bid rigging, monopolization, and *tying contracts.*

antitrust policy   The use of the *antitrust laws* to promote *competition* and *economic efficiency.*

aquaculture   The cultivation of aquatic animals and plants for food.

arbitrage   The activity of selling one *asset* and buying an identical or nearly identical asset to benefit from temporary differences in *prices* or *rates of return;* the practice that equalizes prices or returns on similar financial instruments and thus eliminates further opportunities for riskless financial gains.

asset demand for money   The amount of *money* people want to hold as a *store of value;* this amount varies inversely with the *interest rate.*

asymmetric information   A situation where one party to a market transaction has more information about a product or service than the other. The result may be an under- or overallocation of resources.

average expected rate of return   The *probability-weighted average* of an investment's possible future returns.

average fixed cost (AFC)   A *firm's* total *fixed cost* divided by output (the quantity of product produced).

average product (AP)   The total output produced per unit of a *resource* employed; equal to *total product* divided by the quantity of the employed resource.

average propensity to consume (APC)   Fraction (or percentage) of *disposable income* that *households* spend on *consumer goods;* consumption divided by *disposable income.*

average propensity to save (APS)   Fraction (or percentage) of *disposable income* that *households* save; *saving* divided by *disposable income.*

average revenue   Total revenue from the sale of a product divided by the quantity of the product sold (demanded); equal to the *price* at which the product is sold when all units of the product are sold at the same price.

average tax rate   Total tax paid divided by total *taxable income* or some other base (such as total income) against which to compare the amount of tax paid. Expressed as a percentage.

average total cost (ATC)   A firm's *total cost* divided by output (the quantity of product produced); equal to *average fixed cost* plus *average variable cost.*

average variable cost (AVC)   A firm's total *variable cost* divided by output (the quantity of product produced).

backflows   The return of workers to the countries from which they originally emigrated.

balance of payments   A summary of all the financial transactions that take place between the individuals, *firms,* and governmental units of one nation and those of all other nations during a year.

balance on capital and financial account   The sum of the *capital account balance* and the *financial account balance.*

balance on current account   The exports of *goods* and *services* of a nation less its imports of goods and services plus its *net investment income* and *net transfers* in a year.

balance on goods and services   The exports of *goods* and *services* of a nation less its imports of goods and services in a year.

bankrupt   A legal situation in which an individual or *firm* finds that it cannot make timely interest payments on money it has borrowed. In such cases, a bankruptcy judge can order the individual or firm to liquidate (turn into cash) its assets in order to pay lenders at least some portion of the amount they are owed.

barrier to entry   Anything that artificially prevents the entry of *firms* into an *industry.*

barter   The direct exchange of one *good* or *service* for another good or service.

base year   The year with which other years are compared when an index is constructed; for example, the base year for a *price index.*

beaten paths   Migration routes taken previously by family, relatives, friends, and other migrants.

behavioral economics   The branch of economic theory that combines insights from economics, psychology, and biology to make more accurate predictions about human behavior than conventional *neoclassical economics,* which is hampered by its core assumptions that people are fundamentally *rational* and almost entirely self-interested. Behavioral economics can explain *framing effects, anchoring, mental accounting,* the *endowment effect, status quo bias, time inconsistency,* and *loss aversion.*

behavioral remedy   A directive imposed by a regulator on an offending *monopoly* firm that seeks to resolve the firm's illegal monopoly behavior by requiring different actions be taken by the firm in the future, such as not engaging in price fixing or refraining from using tying contracts.

benefits-received principle   The idea that those who receive the benefits of *goods* and *services* provided by government should pay the taxes required to finance them.

beta   A relative measure of *nondiversifiable risk* that measures how the nondiversifiable risk of a given *asset* or *portfolio* compares with that of the *market portfolio* (the portfolio that contains every asset available in the financial markets).

bilateral monopoly   A market in which there is a single seller (*monopoly*) and a single buyer (*monopsony*).

Board of Governors   The seven-member group that supervises and controls the money and banking system of the United States; the Board of Governors of the *Federal Reserve System;* the Federal Reserve Board.

bond   A financial contract that obligates a borrower to make coupon (interest) payments for a specified period of time before also paying back the principal amount that was initially borrowed.

brain drains   The exit or *emigration* of highly educated, highly skilled workers from a country.

break-even income   The level of *disposable income* at which *households* plan to consume (spend) all their income and to save none of it.

break-even point   An output at which a *firm* makes a *normal profit* (*total revenue = total cost*) but not an *economic profit.*

Bretton Woods system   The international monetary system developed after the Second World War in which *adjustable pegs* were employed, the *International Monetary Fund* helped stabilize foreign exchange rates, and gold and the dollar were used as *international monetary reserves.*

British thermal unit (BTU)   The amount of energy required to raise the temperature of 1 pound of water by 1 degree Fahrenheit.

budget constraint   The limit that the size of a consumer's income (and the *prices* that must be paid for *goods* and *services*) imposes on the ability of that consumer to obtain goods and services.

budget deficit   The amount by which expenditures exceed revenues in any year.

budget line   A line that shows the different combinations of two products a consumer can purchase with a specific money income, given the products' *prices.*

budget surplus   The amount by which the revenues of the federal government exceed its expenditures in any year.

built-in stabilizer   A mechanism that increases government's budget deficit (or reduces its surplus) during a recession and increases government's budget surplus (or reduces its deficit) during an expansion without any action by policymakers. The tax system is one such mechanism.

business cycle   Recurring increases and decreases in the level of economic activity over periods of years; consists of peak, recession, trough, and expansion phases.

businesses   Economic entities (*firms*) that purchase resources and provide *goods* and *services* to the economy.

capital   Man-made physical objects (factories, roads) and intangible ideas (the recipe for cement) that do not directly satisfy human wants but which help to produce *goods* and *services* that do satisfy human wants. One of the four *economic resources.*

capital and financial account   The section of a nation's *international balance of payments* that records (1) debt forgiveness by and to foreigners and (2) foreign purchases of assets in the United States and U.S. purchases of assets abroad.

capital flight   The transfer of savings from *developing countries* to *industrially advanced countries* to avoid government expropriation, taxation, or higher rates of *inflation,* or simply to realize greater returns on *financial investments.*

capital gain   The gain realized when *securities* other *assets* are sold for a *price* greater than the price paid for them.

capital-intensive goods   Products that require relatively large amounts of *capital* to produce.

capital-saving technology   An improvement in *technology* that permits a greater quantity of a product to be produced with a specific amount of *capital* (or permits the same amount of the product to be produced with a smaller amount of capital).

capital-using technology   An improvement in *technology* that requires the use of a greater amount of *capital* to produce a specific quantity of a product.

capricious-universe view   The view held by some people that fate and outside events, rather than hard work and enterprise, will determine their economic destinies.

cartel   A formal agreement among *firms* (or countries) in an *industry* to set the *price* of a product and establish the outputs of the individual firms (or countries) or to divide the market for the product geographically.

catch-up growth   The rapid increases in real GDP per capita that can be achieved when a poor *follower country* adopts, rather than reinvents, cutting edge technologies that took *leader countries* decades to invent and implement.

cease-and-desist order   An order from a court or government agency to a corporation or individual to stop engaging in a specified practice.

Celler-Kefauver Act   The federal law of 1950 that amended the *Clayton Act* by prohibiting the acquisition of the assets of one *firm* by another firm when the effect would be less competition.

change in demand   A movement of an entire *demand curve* (or of the numerical entries in a demand schedule) such that the *quantity demanded* changes at every particular *price;* caused by a change in one or more of the *determinants of demand.*

change in quantity demanded   A change in the *quantity demanded* along a fixed *demand curve* (or within a fixed demand schedule) as a result of a change in the *price* of the product.

change in quantity supplied   A change in the *quantity supplied* of a product along a fixed *supply curve* (or within a fixed supply schedule) as a result of a change in the product's *price.*

change in supply   A movement of an entire *supply curve* (or of the numerical entries in a schedule) such that the *quantity supplied* changes at every particular *price;* caused by a change in one or more of the *determinants of supply.*

checkable deposit   Any deposit in a *commercial bank* or *thrift institution* against which a check may be written.

circular flow diagram   An illustration showing the flow of *resources* from *households* to *firms* and of products from firms to households. These flows are accompanied by reverse flows of *money* from firms to households and from households to firms.

Clayton Act   The federal antitrust law of 1914 that strengthened the *Sherman Act* by making it illegal for *firms* to engage in certain specified practices including *tying contracts, interlocking directorates,* and certain forms of *price discrimination.*

closed shop   A place of employment where only workers who are already members of a labor union may be hired.

Coase theorem   The idea, first stated by economist Ronald Coase, that some *externalities* can be resolved through private negotiations among the affected parties.

cognitive biases   Misperceptions or misunderstandings that cause *systematic errors.* Most result either (1) from *heuristics* that are prone to *systematic errors* or (2) because the brain is attempting to solve a type of problem (such as a calculus problem) for which it was not evolutionarily evolved and for which it has little innate capability.

coinsurance   The percentage of (say, health care) costs that an insured individual pays while the insurer pays the remainder.

collective bargaining   The negotiation of labor contracts between *labor unions* and *firms* or government entities.

collective demand for a public good   A schedule or a curve showing the collective willingness to pay of consumers for a public good. Can be found by vertically adding individual demand curves, which is equivalent to adding the respective maximum prices that individual consumers are willing to pay for the last unit of the public good at each possible quantity demanded.

collective-action problem   The difficulty of getting a large group of voters to organize against a policy when the costs of that policy are widely dispersed (so that none of them individually has much of a personal incentive to take action).

collusion   Cooperation or conspiracy in which *firms* act together (collude) to fix *prices,* divide a market, or otherwise restrict competition. Most collusion is illegal.

command system   A method of organizing an economy in which property resources are publicly owned and government uses *central economic planning* to direct and coordinate economic activities; *socialism;* communism. Compare with *market system.*

commercial bank   A *firm* that engages in the business of banking (accepts deposits, offers checking accounts, and makes loans).

comparative advantage   A situation in which a person or country can produce a specific product at a lower *opportunity cost* in terms of other types of *output* foregone than some other person or country; the basis for specialization and trade.

compensating wage differences   Differences in the *wages* received by workers in different jobs to compensate for the nonmonetary differences between the jobs.

competition   The effort and striving between two or more independent rivals to secure the business of one or more third parties by offering the best possible terms.

complementary goods   Products and *services* that are used together. When the *price* of one falls, the demand for the other increases (and conversely).

complementary resources   Productive inputs that are used jointly with other inputs in the production process; resources for which a decrease in the *price* of one leads to an increase in the demand for the other.

compound interest   *Interest* that is paid both on an original sum of money and on interest that has already been paid on that sum.

conditional cash transfers   Anti-poverty programs in which households receive regular cash transfers (grants) as long as they keep their children in school and participate in preventative health care programs.

conflict minerals Minerals (especially gold, tin, tantalum, and tungsten) that are minded and sold by combatants in war zones in Africa as a way to help finance their military activities.

conglomerate merger The merger of two *firms* operating in separate industries or separate geographic areas so that neither firm is a supplier, customer, or competitor of the other; any merger that is neither a *horizontal merger* nor a *vertical merger*.

constant returns to scale The situation when a firm's *average total cost* of producing a product remains unchanged in the *long run* as the firm varies the size of its *plant* (and, hence, its output).

constant-cost industry An *industry* in which the entry and exit of *firms* have no effect on the *prices* that firms in the industry must pay for resources and thus no effect on production costs.

consumer equilibrium In marginal utility theory, the combination of goods purchased that maximizes *total utility* by applying the *utility-maximizing rule*.

consumer goods Products and *services* that satisfy human wants directly.

Consumer Price Index (CPI) An index that measures the *prices* of a fixed "market basket" of some 300 *goods* and *services* bought by a "typical" consumer.

consumer sovereignty The determination by consumers of the types and quantities of *goods* and *services* that will be produced with the scarce resources of the economy; consumers' direction of production through their *dollar votes*.

consumer surplus The difference between the maximum *price* a consumer is (or consumers are) willing to pay for an additional unit of a product and its market price; the triangular area below the demand curve and above the market price.

consumption of fixed capital An estimate of the amount of *capital* worn out or used up (consumed) in producing the *gross domestic product*; also called depreciation.

consumption schedule A table of numbers showing the amounts *households* plan to spend for *consumer goods* at different levels of *disposable income*.

contestable industries Industries in which even dominant firms have to worry about competition because new entrants and existing competitors are able to compete successfully for market share and users.

contractionary fiscal policy A decrease in *government purchases* of *goods* and *services,* an increase in *net taxes,* or some combination of the two, for the purpose of decreasing *aggregate demand* and thus controlling *inflation*.

coordination failure A situation in which people do not reach a mutually beneficial outcome because they lack some way to jointly coordinate their actions; a possible cause of macroeconomic instability.

coordination problem The chronic failure of command economies to harmonize the economic activities of producers so as to efficiently satisfy consumer demands; caused by command economies eschewing economic coordination via markets, prices, and profits in favor of central planning.

copayment A fixed amount (such as $25 per office visit) that the insured individual must pay even after the annual deductible has been passed.

core inflation The underlying increases in the *price level* after volatile food and energy *prices* are removed.

corporate income tax A tax levied on the net income (accounting profit) of corporations.

corruption The misuse of government power, with which one has been entrusted or assigned, to obtain private gain; includes payments from individuals or companies to secure advantages in obtaining government contracts, avoiding government regulations, or obtaining inside knowledge about forthcoming policy changes.

cost-benefit analysis A method for deciding whether or not to provide a public good that involves a comparison of the total cost of providing that public good with its collective benefit (measured by collective willingness to pay).

cost-of-living adjustment (COLA) An automatic increase in the incomes (*wages*) of workers when *inflation* occurs; often included in *collective bargaining* agreements between *firms* and *unions*. Cost-of-living adjustments are also guaranteed by law for *Social Security* benefits and certain other government *transfer payments*.

cost-push inflation Increases in the *price level* (*inflation*) resulting from an increase in resource costs (for example, raw-material prices) and hence in *per-unit production costs;* inflation caused by reductions in *aggregate supply*.

Council of Economic Advisers (CEA) A group of three persons that advises and assists the president of the United States on economic matters (including the preparation of the annual *Economic Report of the President*).

countercyclical payments (CCPs) Cash *subsidies* paid to farmers when market *prices* for certain crops drop below targeted prices. Payments are based on previous production and are received regardless of the current crop grown.

creative destruction The hypothesis that the creation of new products and production methods destroys the market power of firms committed to existing products and older ways of doing business.

credible threat In a *sequential game* with two players, a statement made by Player 1 that truthfully (credibly) threatens a penalizing action against Player 2 if Player 2 does something that Player 1 does not want Player 2 to do. Opposite of *empty threat*.

crop insurance Insurance that farmers can purchase that will pay out if crop selling prices or crop revenues fall below predetermined values.

cross elasticity of demand The ratio of the percentage change in *quantity demanded* of one good to the percentage change in the *price* of some other good. A positive coefficient indicates the two products are *substitute goods;* a negative coefficient indicates they are *complementary goods*.

crowding-out effect A rise in interest rates and a resulting decrease in *planned investment* caused by the federal government's increased borrowing to finance budget deficits and refinance debt.

currency intervention A government's buying and selling of its own currency or foreign currencies to alter international exchange rates.

current account The section in a nation's *international balance of payments* that records its exports and imports of *goods* and *services,* its net *investment income,* and its *net transfers*.

cyclical asymmetry The idea that *monetary policy* may be more successful in slowing expansions and controlling *inflation* than in extracting the economy from severe recession.

cyclical deficit Federal *budget deficit* that is caused by a recession and the consequent decline in tax revenues.

cyclical unemployment A type of *unemployment* caused by insufficient total spending (insufficient *aggregate demand*) and which typically begins in the *recession* phase of the *business cycle*.

cyclically adjusted budget The estimated annual budget deficit or surplus that would occur under existing tax rates and government spending levels if the economy were to operate at its *full-employment* level of GDP for a year; the *full-employment* budget deficit or surplus.

deadweight loss A reduction in the total net benefit that society can obtain from its limited supply of resources. Caused by an underallocation or overallocation of resources to the production of a particular *good* or *service*. Also called *efficiency loss.*

decreasing-cost industry An *industry* in which expansion through the entry of *firms* lowers the *prices* that firms in the industry must pay for resources and therefore decreases their production costs.

deductible The dollar sum of (for example, health care) costs that an insured individual must pay before the insurer begins to pay.

defaults Situations in which borrowers stop making loan payments or do not pay back loans that they took out and are now due.

defensive medicine The recommendation by physicians of more tests and procedures than are warranted medically or economically as a way of protecting themselves against later malpractice suits.

deflation A decline in the general level of *prices* in an economy; a decline in an economy's *price level.*

demand A schedule or curve that shows the various amounts of a product that consumers are willing and able to purchase at each of a series of possible *prices* during a specified period of time.

demand curve A curve that illustrates the *demand* for a product by showing how each possible *price* (on the *vertical axis*) is associated with a specific *quantity demanded* (on the *horizontal axis*).

demand factor (in growth) The requirement that *aggregate demand* increase as fast as *potential output* if *economic growth* is to proceed as quickly as possible.

demand schedule A table of numbers showing the amounts of a *good* or *service* buyers are willing and able to purchase at various *prices* over a specified period of time.

demand shocks Sudden, unexpected changes in demand.

demand-pull inflation Increases in the *price level* (*inflation*) resulting from increases in *aggregate demand.*

demand-side market failures Underallocations of resources that occur when private demand curves understate consumers' full willingness to pay for a *good* or *service.*

demographers Scientists who study the characteristics of human populations.

demographic transition The massive decline in birthrates that occurs once a developing country achieves higher standards of living because the perceived marginal cost of additional children begins to exceed the perceived marginal benefit.

dependent variable A variable that changes as a consequence of a change in some other (independent) variable; the "effect" or outcome.

deregulation The removal of most or even all of the government regulation and laws designed to supervise an industry. Sometimes undertaken to combat *regulatory capture.*

derived demand The demand for a resource that depends on the demand for the products it helps to produce.

determinants of aggregate demand Factors such as consumption spending, *investment,* government spending, and *net exports* that, if they change, shift the aggregate demand curve.

determinants of aggregate supply Factors such as input prices, *productivity,* and the legal-institutional environment that, if they change, shift the aggregate supply curve.

determinants of demand Factors other than *price* that determine the quantities demanded of a *good* or *service.* Also referred to as "demand shifters" because changes in the determinants of demand will cause the *demand curve* to shift either right or left.

determinants of supply Factors other than *price* that determine the quantities supplied of a *good* or *service.* Also referred to as "supply shifters" because changes in the determinants of supply will cause the *supply curve* to shift either right or left.

devaluation A decrease in the governmentally defined value of a currency.

developing countries Many countries of Africa, Asia, and Latin America that are characterized by lack of capital goods, use of non-advanced technologies, low literacy rates, high unemployment, relatively rapid population growth, and labor forces heavily committed to agriculture.

diagnosis-related group (DRG) system Payments to doctors and hospitals under *Medicare* based on which of hundreds of carefully detailed diagnostic categories best characterize each patient's condition and needs.

dictator game A mutually anonymous behavioral economics game in which one person ("the dictator") unilaterally determines how to split an amount of money with the second player.

differentiated oligopoly An *oligopoly* in which *firms* produce a *differentiated product.*

diffusion The spread of an *innovation* through its widespread imitation.

digital platform An *Internet* website or software application (app) that facilitates interactions between two or more distinct but interdependent sets of users.

dilemma of regulation The trade-off faced by a *regulatory agency* in setting the maximum legal *price* a monopolist may charge: The *socially optimal price* is below *average total cost* (and either bankrupts the *firm* or requires that it be subsidized), while the higher, *fair-return price* does not produce *allocative efficiency.*

diminishing marginal utility The principle that as a consumer increases the consumption of a *good* or *service,* the *marginal utility* obtained from each additional unit of the good or service decreases.

direct controls Government policies that directly constrain activities that generate *negative externalities.* Examples include maximum emissions limits for factory smokestacks and laws mandating the proper disposal of toxic wastes.

direct network effect A *network effect* that involves only a single network of users connected to a *digital platform.* Compare with *indirect network effect.*

direct payments Cash subsidies paid to farmers based on past production levels; a permanent transfer payment unaffected by current crop *prices* and current production.

direct relationship The relationship between two variables that change in the same direction, for example, product *price* and quantity supplied; a positive relationship.

discount rate The interest rate that the *Federal Reserve Banks* charge on the loans they make to *commercial banks* and *thrifts;* one of the three *administered rates* set by the *Federal Reserve.*

discouraged workers Employees who have left the *labor force* because they have not been able to find employment.

discrimination The practice of according individuals or groups inferior treatment in hiring, occupational access, education and training, promotion, wage rates, or working conditions even though they have the same abilities, education, skills, and work experience as other workers.

discrimination coefficient A measure of the cost or disutility of prejudice; the monetary amount an employer is willing to pay to hire a preferred worker rather than a nonpreferred worker of the same ability.

diseconomies of scale The situation when a firm's *average total cost* of producing a product increases in the *long run* as the firm increases the size of its *plant* (and, hence, its output).

disinflation A reduction in the rate of *inflation*.

disposable income (DI) *Personal income* less personal taxes; income available for *personal consumption expenditures* and *personal saving*.

diversifiable risk Investment *risk* that investors can reduce via *diversification;* also called idiosyncratic risk.

diversification The strategy of investing in a large number of investments in order to reduce the overall risk to an entire investment *portfolio*.

dividends Payments by a corporation of all or part of its profit to its stockholders (the corporate owners).

division of labor The separation of the work required to produce a product into a number of different tasks that are performed by different workers; *specialization* of workers.

Doha Development Agenda The latest, uncompleted (as of late 2021) sequence of trade negotiations by members of the *World Trade Organization;* named after Doha, Qatar, where the set of negotiations began. Also called the Doha Round.

dollar votes The "votes" that consumers cast for the production of preferred products when they purchase those products rather than the alternatives that were also available.

domestic price The *price* of a *good* or *service* within a country, determined by domestic demand and supply.

dominant strategy In a strategic interaction (*game*) between two or more players, a course of action (strategy) that a player will wish to undertake no matter what the other players choose to do.

dual mandate The 1977 congressional directive that the Federal Reserve System's highest priorities should be *full employment* and price level stability. In practice, the Fed aims for the *full-employment rate of unemployment* and an *inflation rate* of 2 percent per year.

dumping The sale of a product in a foreign country at *prices* either below cost or below the prices commonly charged at home.

DuPont cellophane case The antitrust case brought against DuPont in which the U.S. Supreme Court ruled (in 1956) that while DuPont had a monopoly in the narrowly defined market for cellophane, it did not monopolize the more broadly defined market for flexible packaging materials. It was thus not guilty of violating the *Sherman Act*.

durable good A consumer good with an expected life (use) of three or more years.

earmarks Narrow, specially designated spending authorizations placed in broad legislation by senators and representatives for the purpose of providing benefits to *firms* and organizations within their constituencies. Earmarked projects are exempt from competitive bidding and normal evaluation procedures.

earned-income tax credit (EITC) A refundable federal *tax credit* for low-income working people designed to reduce poverty and encourage labor-force participation.

economic cost A payment that must be made to obtain and retain the *services* of a *resource;* the income a *firm* must provide to a resource supplier to attract the resource away from an alternative use; equal to the quantity of other products that cannot be produced when resources are instead used to make a particular product.

economic growth (1) An outward shift in the *production possibilities curve* that results from an increase in resource supplies or quality or an improvement in *technology;* (2) an increase of real output (*gross domestic product*) or real output per capita.

economic immigrants International migrants who have moved from one country to another to obtain economic gains such as better employment opportunities.

economic investment Spending for the production and accumulation of *capital,* additions to *inventories,* or the research and development of new goods or services, including funds spent on the creation of new works of music, literature, or software. Compare with *financial investment*.

economic perspective A viewpoint that envisions individuals and institutions making rational decisions by comparing the *marginal benefits* and *marginal costs* associated with their actions.

economic principle A widely accepted generalization about the economic behavior of individuals or institutions.

economic profit The return flowing to those who provide the economy with the *economic resource* of *entrepreneurial ability;* the *total revenue* of a *firm* less its *economic costs* (which include both *explicit costs* and *implicit costs*); also called "pure profit" and "above-normal profit."

economic rent Any payment to a resource provider or seller of output in excess of the *economic cost* (opportunity cost) of providing that resource or output.

economic resources The *land, labor, capital,* and *entrepreneurial ability* that are used to produce *goods* and *services*. Also known as the *factors of production*.

economic system A particular set of institutional arrangements and a coordinating mechanism for solving the *economizing problem;* a method of organizing an economy, of which the *market system* and the *command system* are the two general types.

economic, or pure, profit The return flowing to those who provide the economy with the *economic resource* of *entrepreneurial ability;* the *total revenue* of a *firm* less its *economic costs* (which include both *explicit costs* and *implicit costs*); also called "above-normal profit."

economics The social science concerned with how individuals, institutions, and society make optimal (best) choices under conditions of scarcity.

economies of scale The situation when a firm's *average total cost* of producing a product decreases in the *long run* as the firm increases the size of its *plant* (and, hence, its output).

economizing problem The choices necessitated because society's economic wants for *goods* and *services* are unlimited but the resources available to satisfy these wants are limited (scarce).

effective federal funds rate The equilibrium *interest rate* determined in the *federal funds market;* the interest rate that U.S. banks and other depository institutions charge one another for overnight loans of currency held on deposit at one of the twelve *Federal Reserve Banks*.

efficiency factor (in growth) The capacity of an economy to achieve *allocative* and *productive efficiency* and thereby fulfill the potential for growth that the *supply factors (of growth)* make possible; the capacity of an economy to achieve *economic efficiency* and thereby reach the optimal point on its *production possibilities curve*.

efficiency gains from migration The increases in total worldwide output that take place if the additions to output from *immigration* in the destination nation exceed the loss of output from *emigration* in the origin nation.

efficiency loss Reductions in combined consumer and producer surplus caused by an underallocation or overallocation of resources to the production of a *good* or *service*. Also called *deadweight loss.*

efficiency loss of a tax The loss of *net benefits* to society because a tax reduces the production and consumption of a taxed good below the level of *allocative efficiency*. Also called the *deadweight loss* of the tax.

efficiency wage An above-market (above-equilibrium) *wage* that minimizes wage costs per unit of output by encouraging greater effort or reducing turnover.

elastic demand Product or resource demand whose *price elasticity of demand* is greater than 1, so that any given percentage change in *price* leads to a larger percentage change in *quantity demanded*. As a result, quantity demanded is relatively sensitive to (elastic with respect to) price.

elasticity of resource demand A measure of the responsiveness of *firms* to a change in the *price* of a particular *resource* they employ or use; the percentage change in the quantity demanded of the *resource* divided by the percentage change in its *price.*

employer mandate The requirement under the *Patient Protection and Affordable Care Act* (*PPACA*) of 2010 that firms with 50 or more employees pay for insurance policies for their employees or face a fine of $2,000 per employee per year. Firms with fewer than 50 employees are exempt.

empty threat In a *sequential game* with two players, a noncredible (bluffing) statement made by Player 1 that threatens a penalizing action against Player 2 if Player 2 does something that Player 1 does not want Player 2 to do. Opposite of *credible threat.*

endowment effect The tendency people have to place higher valuations on items they possess (are endowed with) than on identical items that they do not possess; perhaps caused by *loss aversion.*

entitlement programs Government programs such as *social insurance, Medicare,* and *Medicaid* that guarantee (entitle) particular levels of transfer payments or noncash benefits to all who fit the programs' criteria.

entrepreneurial ability The human resource that combines the other *economic resources* of *land, labor,* and *capital* to produce new products or make innovations in the production of existing products; provided by *entrepreneurs.*

entrepreneurs Individuals who provide *entrepreneurial ability* to *firms* by setting strategy, advancing innovations, and bearing the financial risk if their firms do poorly.

equality-efficiency trade-off The decrease in *economic efficiency* that may accompany a decrease in *income inequality;* the presumption that some income inequality is required to achieve economic efficiency.

equation of exchange $MV = PQ$, in which M is the supply of *money,* V is the *velocity* of money, P is the *price level,* and Q is the physical volume of *final goods* and final *services* produced.

equilibrium GDP The gross domestic product at which the total quantity of final goods and final services purchased (aggregate expenditures) is equal to the total quantity of final goods services produced (the real domestic output); the real domestic output at which the aggregate demand curve intersects the aggregate supply curve. Also known as *equilibrium real output.*

equilibrium position In the indifference curve model, the combination of two goods at which a consumer maximizes his or her *utility* (reaches the highest attainable *indifference curve*), given a limited amount to spend (a *budget constraint*).

equilibrium price The *price* in a competitive market at which the *quantity demanded* and the *quantity supplied* are equal, there is neither a shortage nor a surplus, and there is no tendency for price to rise or fall.

equilibrium price level In the *aggregate demand–aggregate supply* (*AD-AS*) *model,* the *price level* at which *aggregate demand* equals *aggregate supply;* the price level at which the aggregate demand curve intersects the aggregate supply curve.

equilibrium quantity (1) The quantity at which the intentions of buyers and sellers in a particular market match at a particular *price* such that the *quantity demanded* and the *quantity supplied* are equal; (2) the profit-maximizing output of a *firm.*

equilibrium real output (see *equilibrium real domestic output*) The *gross domestic product* at which the total quantity of *final goods* and final *services* purchased (*aggregate expenditures*) is equal to the total quantity of final goods and services produced (the real domestic output); the real domestic output at which the aggregate demand curve intersects the aggregate supply curve.

equilibrium world price The *price* of an internationally traded product that equates the quantity of the product demanded by importers with the quantity of the product supplied by exporters; the price determined at the intersection of the export supply curve and the import demand curve.

European Union (EU) An association of 28 European nations (as of mid-2019) that has eliminated tariffs and quotas among them, established common tariffs for imported goods from outside the member nations, eliminated barriers to the free movement of capital, and created other common economic policies.

eurozone The 19 nations (as of 2019) of the 28-member (as of 2019) *European Union* that use the *euro* as their common *currency.* The eurozone countries are Austria, Belgium, Cyprus, Estonia, Finland, France, Germany, Greece, Ireland, Italy, Luxembourg, Malta, the Netherlands, Portugal, Slovakia, Slovenia, and Spain.

excess capacity *Plant* resources that are underused when imperfectly competitive *firms* produce less output than that associated with achieving minimum *average total cost.*

exchange controls Restrictions that a government may impose over the quantity of foreign currency demand by its citizens and *firms* and over the *rate of exchange* as a way to limit the nation's quantity of *outpayments* relative to its quantity of *inpayments* (in order to eliminate a *payments deficit*).

excise tax A tax levied on the production of a specific product or on the quantity of the product purchased.

excludability The characteristic displayed by those goods and services for which sellers are able to prevent nonbuyers from obtaining benefits.

exclusive unionism The policy, pursued by many *craft unions,* in which a *union* first gets employers to agree to hire only union workers and then excludes many workers from joining the union so as to restrict the supply of labor and drive up wages. Compare with *inclusive unionism.* The policies typically employed by a *craft union.*

exit mechanism The method of resolving workplace dissatisfaction by quitting one's job and searching for another.

expansion The phase of the *business cycle* in which *real GDP, income,* and employment rise.

expansionary fiscal policy An increase in *government purchases* of *goods* and *services*, a decrease in *net taxes*, or some combination of the two for the purpose of increasing *aggregate demand* and expanding real output.

expansionary monetary policy *Central bank* actions to increase the *money supply*, lower *interest rates*, and expand *real GDP*. Implemented when the economy is operating below *potential output*. Also known as an "easy money" policy.

expectations The anticipations of consumers, *firms,* and others about future economic conditions.

expected rate of return The increase in profit a *firm* anticipates it will obtain by purchasing capital or engaging in research and development (*R&D*); expressed as a percentage of the total cost of the investment (or R&D) activity.

expected-rate-of-return curve As it relates to research and development (*R&D*), a curve showing the anticipated gain in *profit*, as a percentage of R&D expenditure, from an additional dollar spent on R&D.

expenditures approach The method that adds all expenditures made for *final goods* and final *services* to measure the *gross domestic product*.

explicit cost The monetary payment made by a *firm* to an outsider to obtain a *resource*.

export subsidy A government payment to a domestic producer to enable the *firm* to reduce the *price* of a *good* or *service* to foreign buyers.

export supply curve An upward sloping curve that shows the amount of a product that domestic *firms* will export at each *world price* that is above the *domestic price*.

external public debt The portion of the public debt owed to foreign citizens, *firms,* and institutions.

externality A cost or benefit from production or consumption that accrues to someone other than the immediate buyers and sellers of the product being produced or consumed (see *negative externality* and *positive externality*).

extraction cost All costs associated with extracting a natural resource and readying it for sale.

factors of production The four *economic resources: land, labor, capital,* and *entrepreneurial ability.*

failed state A nation whose government lacks the *state capacity* to maintain even basic government functions like law enforcement and the provision of basic services like education and sanitation.

fair-return price For *natural monopolies* subject to rate (*price*) regulation, the price that would allow the regulated monopoly to earn a *normal profit*; a price equal to *average total cost*.

fairness A person's opinion as to whether a price, wage, or allocation is considered morally or ethically acceptable.

fallacy of composition The false notion that what is true for the individual (or part) is necessarily true for the group (or whole).

farm commodities Agricultural products such as grains, milk, cattle, fruits, and vegetables that are usually sold to processors, who use the products as inputs in creating *food products*.

fast-second strategy An approach by a dominant *firm* in which it allows other firms in its *industry* to bear the risk of innovation and then quickly becomes the second firm to offer any successful new product or adopt any improved production process.

federal funds market The financial *market* in which *banks* and other financial firms negotiate overnight loans of *currency* ("federal funds") held on deposit at one of the twelve *Federal Reserve Banks*.

federal funds rate The *interest rate* that U.S. banks and other non-bank financial firms charge one another on overnight loans of *currency* held on deposit at one of the twelve *Federal Reserve Banks*; the Federal Reserve's *policy rate*.

federal funds target range The 0.25-percent-wide range within which the *Federal Reserve* guides its *policy rate*, the *effective federal funds rate*. Also a key part of the Federal Reserve's *forward guidance* communications.

Federal Open Market Committee (FOMC) The 12-member group within the *Federal Reserve System* that decides U.S. *monetary policy* and how it is executed through *open-market operations* (in which the Fed buys and sells U.S. government securities to adjust the *money supply*).

Federal Reserve Banks The 12 banks chartered by the U.S. government that collectively act as the *central bank* of the United States. They set monetary policy and regulate the private banking system under the direction of the *Board of Governors* and the *Federal Open Market Committee*. Each of the 12 is a *quasi-public bank* and acts as a *banker's bank* in its designated geographic region.

Federal Reserve Note Paper money issued by the *Federal Reserve Banks*.

Federal Reserve System The U.S. central bank, consisting of the *Board of Governors* of the Federal Reserve and the 12 *Federal Reserve Banks*, which controls the lending activity of the nation's banks and thrifts and thus the *money supply*; commonly referred to as the "Fed."

Federal Trade Commission Act The federal law of 1914 that established the *Federal Trade Commission*.

fee for service In the health care *industry*, payment to physicians for each visit made or procedure performed.

final goods and services Products that have been purchased for final use (rather than for resale or further processing or manufacturing).

financial investment The purchase of a financial asset (such as a *stock, bond,* or *mutual fund*) or real asset (such as a house, land, or factories) in the expectation of financial gain. Compare with economic investment.

first-mover advantage In *game theory*, the benefit obtained by the party that moves first in a *sequential game*. A situation that occurs in a *sequential game* if the player who gets to move first has an advantage in terms of final outcomes over the player(s) who move subsequently.

fiscal policy Changes in government spending and tax collections designed to achieve full employment, price stability, and economic growth; also called *discretionary fiscal policy*.

fishery A stock of fish or other marine animal that is composed of a distinct group, for example, New England cod, Pacific tuna, or Alaskan crab.

fishery collapse A rapid decline in a *fishery*'s population because its fish are being harvested faster than they can reproduce.

fixed cost Any cost that in total does not change when the *firm* changes its output.

fixed exchange rate A *rate of exchange* that is pegged by a government or central bank at a particular ratio (for instance, $1 = 6 yuan) rather than being allowed to vary with changes in demand and supply.

flexible exchange rate A *rate of exchange* that is determined by the international demand for and supply of a nation's money and that is consequently free to rise or fall because it is not subject to *currency interventions*. Also referred to as a "floating exchange rate."

flexible prices Product *prices* that freely move upward or downward when product demand or supply changes.

follower countries As it relates to *economic growth,* countries that adopt advanced technologies that previously were developed and used by *leader countries.*

food products Processed *farm commodities* sold through grocery stores and restaurants. Examples: bread, meat, fish, chicken, pork, lettuce, peanut butter, and breakfast cereal.

foreign direct investment *Financial investments* made to obtain a lasting ownership interest in *firms* operating outside the economy of the investor; may involve purchasing existing assets or building new production facilities.

foreign purchases effect The inverse relationship between the *net exports* of an economy and its *price level* relative to foreign price levels.

foreign-exchange reserves Stockpiles of foreign currencies maintained by a nation's *central bank.* Obtained when the *central bank* sells local currency in exchange for foreign currency in the *foreign exchange market.*

forward guidance Public communications made by a *central bank* to describe (1) how it perceives the state of the *economy* and (2) how it intends to manage *monetary policy.*

four-firm concentration ratio The percentage of total *industry* sales accounted for by the top four *firms* in an industry.

fractional reserve banking system A system in which *commercial banks* and *thrift institutions* hold less than 100 percent of their checkable-deposit liabilities as reserves of *currency* held in bank vaults or as deposits at the *central bank.*

framing effects In *prospect theory,* changes in people's decision making caused by new information that alters the context, or "frame of reference," that they use to judge whether options are viewed as gains or losses relative to the *status quo.*

free-rider problem The inability of potential providers of an economically desirable *good* or *service* to obtain payment from those who benefit, because of *nonexcludability.*

freedom of choice The freedom of owners of property resources to employ or dispose of them as they see fit, of workers to enter any line of work for which they are qualified, and of consumers to spend their incomes in the manner that they prefer.

freedom of enterprise The freedom of *firms* to obtain economic resources, to use those resources to produce products of the firms' own choosing, and to sell their products in markets of their choice.

Freedom to Farm Act A law passed in 1996 that revamped 60 years of U.S. farm policy by ending *price supports* and *acreage allotments* for wheat, corn, barley, oats, sorghum, rye, cotton, and rice.

freemium pricing A pricing strategy in which an Internet business offers its core product for free but charges users for upgrades and special features that some users may be willing to pay for.

frictional unemployment A type of unemployment caused by workers voluntarily changing jobs and by temporary layoffs; unemployed workers between jobs.

full-employment rate of unemployment The *unemployment rate* at which there is no *cyclical unemployment* of the *labor force;* equal to around 4 percent (rather than zero percent) in the United States because *frictional* and *structural unemployment* are unavoidable.

future value The amount to which some current amount of *money* will grow if *interest* earned on the amount is left to compound over time. (*See compound interest.*)

gains from trade The extra output that trading partners obtain through specialization of production and exchange of *goods* and *services.*

game theory The study of how people behave in strategic situations in which individuals must take into account not only their own possible actions but also the possible reactions of others. Originally developed to analyze the best ways to play games like poker and chess.

GDP gap Actual *gross domestic product* minus *potential output;* may be either a positive amount (a *positive GDP gap*) or a negative amount (a *negative GDP gap*).

General Agreement on Tariffs and Trade (GATT) The international agreement reached in 1947 in which 23 nations agreed to eliminate *import quotas,* negotiate reductions in *tariff* rates, and give each other equal and nondiscriminatory treatment. It now includes most nations and has become the *World Trade Organization.*

Gini ratio A numerical measure of the overall dispersion of income among *households,* families, or individuals; found graphically by dividing the area between the diagonal line and the *Lorenz curve* by the entire area below the diagonal line.

gold standard A historical system of fixed exchange rates in which nations defined their currencies in terms of gold, maintained fixed relationships between their stocks of gold and their money supplies, and allowed gold to be freely exported and imported.

government failure Inefficiencies in resource allocation caused by problems in the operation of the *public sector* (government). Specific examples include the *principal-agent problem,* the *special-interest effect,* the *collective-action problem, rent seeking,* and *political corruption.*

government purchases (G) Expenditures by government for *goods* and *services* that government consumes in providing public services as well as expenditures for publicly owned capital that has a long lifetime; the expenditures of all governments in the economy for those *final goods* and final *services.*

gross domestic product (GDP) The total market value of all *final goods* and *services* produced annually within the boundaries of a nation.

gross output (GO) The dollar value of the economic activity taking place at every stage of production and distribution. By contrast, *gross domestic product* (GDP) only accounts for the value of final output.

gross private domestic investment (I_g) Expenditures that increase the nation's stock of capital, which is the collection of physical objects and intangible ideas that help to produce goods and services. Includes spending on final purchases of plant, machinery, and equipment by business enterprises; residential construction; changes in *inventories*; expenditures on the *research and development (R&D)* of new productive technologies; and money spent on the creation of new works of art, music, writing, film, and software.

growth accounting The bookkeeping of the supply-side elements such as productivity and labor inputs that contribute to changes in *real GDP* over some specific time period.

H1-B provision A provision of the U.S. immigration law that allows the annual entry of 65,000 high-skilled workers in "specialty occupations" such as science, *R&D,* and computer programming to work legally and continuously in the United States for six years.

health maintenance organizations (HMOs) Health care providers that contract with employers, insurance companies, labor unions, or government units to provide health care for their workers or others who are insured.

health savings accounts (HSAs)   Tax-free savings accounts into which people with high-deductible health insurance plans can place funds each year. Accumulated funds can be used to pay out-of-pocket medical expenses such as *deductibles* and *copayments*. Unused funds accumulate from year to year and can be used after retirement to supplement *Medicare*.

Herfindahl index   A measure of the concentration and competitive-ness of an *industry;* calculated as the sum of the squared percentage market shares of the individual *firms* in the industry.

heuristics   The brain's low-energy mental shortcuts for making deci-sions. They are "fast and frugal" and work well in most situations but in other situations result in *systematic errors.*

homogeneous oligopoly   An *oligopoly* in which *firms* produce a stan-dardized product.

horizontal axis   The "left-right" or "west-east" measurement line on a graph or grid.

horizontal merger   The merger into a single *firm* of two firms pro-ducing the same product and selling it in the same geographic market.

households   Economic entities (of one or more persons occupying a housing unit) that provide *resources* to the economy and use the *income* received to purchase *goods* and *services* that satisfy economic wants.

human capital   The knowledge and skills that make a person productive.

hyperinflation   An extremely high rate of *inflation,* usually defined as an inflation rate in excess of 50 percent per month.

imitation problem   The potential for a *firm's* rivals to produce a close variation of (imitate) a firm's new product or process, greatly reducing the originator's profit from *R&D* and *innovation.*

immediate market period   The length of time during which the produc-ers of a product are unable to change the quantity supplied in response to a change in price and in which there is a *perfectly inelastic supply.*

immediate-short-run aggregate supply curve   A horizontal *aggregate supply* curve that applies to time periods over which both input prices and output prices are fixed; an aggregate supply curve for which real output, but not the *price level,* changes when the *aggregate demand* curve shifts.

imperfect competition   All *market structures* except *pure competition;* includes *monopoly, monopolistic competition,* and *oligopoly.*

implicit cost   The monetary income a *firm* sacrifices when it uses a *resource* it owns rather than supplying the resource in the market; equal to what the resource could have earned in the best-paying alter-native employment; includes a *normal profit.*

import competition   The competition that domestic *firms* encounter from the products and *services* of foreign producers.

import demand curve   A downsloping curve showing the amount of a product that an economy will import at each *world price* below the *domestic price.*

import quota   A limit imposed by a nation on the quantity (or total value) of a good that may be imported during some period of time.

in-app purchases   A pricing strategy in which an internet business (that may or may not give away its core product for free) charges us-ers of its application software ("app") for items that enhance the user experience within the application.

incentive function   The inducement that an increase in the price of a commodity gives to sellers to make more of it available (and

conversely for a decrease in *price*), and the inducement that an in-crease in price offers to buyers to purchase smaller quantities (and conversely for a decrease in price).

incentive pay plan   A compensation structure that ties worker pay directly to performance. Such plans include piece rates, bonuses, *stock options,* commissions, and *profit-sharing plans.*

incentive problem   The difficulty common to command economies wherein the numerical production targets set by central planning boards cause managers to produce substandard or unwanted output.

inclusive unionism   The policy, pursued by *industrial unions,* in which a *union* attempts to include every worker in a given *industry* so as to be able to restrict the entire industry's labor supply and thereby raise wages. Compare with *exclusive unionism.*

income approach   The method that adds all the *income* generated by the production of *final goods* and final *services* to measure the *gross domestic product.*

income effect   A change in the quantity demanded of a product that results from the change in *real income (purchasing power)* caused by a change in the product's *price.*

income elasticity of demand   The ratio of the percentage change in the *quantity demanded* of a good to a percentage change in consumer *income;* measures the responsiveness of consumer purchases to income changes.

income inequality   The unequal distribution of an economy's total *income* among *households* or families.

income mobility   The extent to which *income* receivers move from one part of the income distribution to another over some period of time.

increasing returns   An increase in a *firm's* output by a larger percent-age than the percentage increase in its inputs.

increasing-cost industry   An *industry* in which expansion through the entry of new *firms* raises the *prices* that firms in the industry must pay for *resources* and therefore increases their production costs.

independent unions   U.S. unions that are not affiliated with the *AFL-CIO* or *Strategic Organizing Center.*

independent variable   The variable causing a change in some other (dependent) variable.

index funds   *Mutual funds* whose *portfolios* exactly match a stock or bond index (a collection of *stocks* or *bonds* meant to capture the overall behavior of a particular category of investments) such as the Standard & Poor's 500 Index or the Russell 3000 Index.

indifference curve   A curve showing the different combinations of two products that yield the same satisfaction or *utility* to a consumer.

indifference map   A set of *indifference curves,* each representing a different level of *utility,* that together show the preferences of a consumer.

indirect network effect   A *network effect* involving two or more *networks* connected by a *digital platform,* in which a change in the number of users within one network causes changes felt by the users of a different network which in turn boomerang back to the original network of users to affect the value of their network. Compare with *direct network effect.*

individual transferable quotas (ITQs)   Limits (quotas) set by a gov-ernment or a fisheries commission on the total number or total weight of a species that an individual fisher can harvest during some particular time period; fishers can sell (transfer) the right to use all or part of their respective individual quotas to other fishers.

industrial regulation The older and more traditional type of business or commercial regulation in which government is concerned with the *prices* charged and the *services* provided to the public in specific *industries*. Differs from *social regulation*.

industrially advanced countries High-income countries such as the United States, Canada, Japan, and the nations of western Europe that have highly developed *market economies* based on large stocks of technologically advanced *capital goods* and skilled labor forces.

inelastic demand Product or resource demand for which the *price elasticity of demand* is less than 1, so that any given percentage change in *price* leads to a smaller percentage change in *quantity demanded*. As a result, quantity demanded is relatively insensitive to (inelastic with respect to) price.

inferior good A *good* or *service* whose consumption declines as *income* rises, other things equal.

inflation A rise in the general level of *prices* in an economy; an increase in an economy's *price level*.

inflation gap The difference between the current actual rate of *inflation* and the central bank's *target rate of inflation*; a key component of the *Taylor Rule*.

inflation targeting The declaration by a *central bank* of a goal for a specific range of *inflation* in a future year, coupled with *monetary policy* designed to achieve the goal.

inflationary expectations The public's forecast about likely future *inflation* rates; influenceable by central bank policy actions, including a credible *target rate of inflation*.

inflationary expenditure gap In the *aggregate-expenditures model*, the amount by which the *aggregate expenditures schedule* must shift downward to decrease the *nominal GDP* to its full-employment noninflationary level.

inflexible prices Product *prices* that remain in place (at least for a while) even though *supply* or *demand* has changed; stuck prices or sticky prices.

information technology New and more efficient methods of delivering and receiving information through the use of computers, wi-fi networks, wireless phones, and the Internet.

infrastructure The interconnected network of large-scale *capital goods* (such as roads, sewers, electrical grids, railways, ports, and the Internet) needed to operate a technologically advanced economy.

injection An addition of spending into the income-expenditure stream: any increment to *consumption, investment, government purchases,* or *net exports*.

innovation The first commercially successful introduction of a new product, use of a new method of production, or creation of a new form of business organization.

insurable risk An eventuality for which both the frequency and magnitude of potential losses can be estimated with considerable accuracy. Insurance companies are willing to sell insurance against such risks.

insurance exchanges Government-regulated markets for health insurance in which individuals seeking to purchase health insurance to comply with the *personal mandate* of the *Patient Protection and Affordable Care Act* (*PPACA*) of 2010 will be able to comparison shop among insurance policies approved by regulators. Each state will have its own exchange.

interest The payment made for the use of (borrowed) *money*.

interest income The *income* received by the owners of *capital* for supplying capital to *businesses*.

interest rate on reserve balances (IORB) The *interest rate* that the Federal Reserve pays *banks* and thrifts on any money that they deposit at (loan to) a Federal Reserve Bank on an overnight basis; one of the three *administered rates* set by the Federal Reserve.

interest-rate cost-of-funds curve As it relates to research and development (*R&D*), a curve showing the *interest rate* a *firm* must pay to obtain any particular amount of funds to finance R&D.

interest-rate effect The tendency for increases in the *price level* to increase the demand for money, raise interest rates, and, as a result, reduce total spending and real output in the economy (and the reverse for *price-level* decreases).

interindustry competition The competition for sales between the products of one *industry* and the products of another industry.

interlocking directorate A situation where one or more members of the board of directors of a *corporation* are also on the board of directors of a competing corporation; illegal under the *Clayton Act*.

intermediate goods and services Products that are purchased for resale or further processing or manufacturing.

international asset transactions The sale, trade, or transfer of ownership rights to either real or financial assets, including currency, across international borders.

International Monetary Fund (IMF) The international association of nations that was formed after the Second World War to make loans of foreign monies to nations with temporary *balance of payments deficits* and, until the early 1970s, manage the international system of pegged exchange rates agreed upon at the Bretton Woods conference. It now mainly makes loans to nations facing possible defaults on private and government loans.

international trade The exchange (trade) of goods and services across international borders.

Internet The world-wide *network* of interconnected computers that can communicate and share data; also known as the world wide web, or www.

invention The conception of a new product or process combined with the first proof that it will work.

inventories Goods that have been produced but remain unsold.

inverse relationship The relationship between two variables that change in opposite directions, for example, product *price* and quantity demanded; a negative relationship.

inverted-U theory The idea that, other things equal, *R&D* expenditures as a percentage of sales rise with *industry* concentration, reach a peak at a *four-firm concentration ratio* of about 50 percent, and then fall as the ratio further increases.

investment Expenditures that increase the volume of physical *capital* (roads, factories, wireless networks) and intangible ideas (formulas, processes, algorithms) that help to produce goods and services. Also known as *economic investment*. Not to be confused with *financial investment*.

investment demand curve A curve that shows the amounts of *investment* demanded by an economy at a series of *real interest rates*.

investment schedule A curve or schedule that shows the amounts that firms plan to invest at various possible values of *real gross domestic product* (real GDP).

invisible hand The tendency of *competition* to cause individuals and firms to unintentionally but quite effectively promote the interests of society even when each individual or firm is only attempting to pursue its own interests.

kinked-demand curve   A *demand curve* that has a flatter slope above the current *price* than below the current price. Applies to a *noncollusive oligopoly* firm if its rivals will match any price decrease but ignore any price increase.

labor   Any mental or physical exertion on the part of a human being that is used in the production of a *good* or *service*. One of the four *economic resources*.

labor force   Persons 16 years of age and older who are not in institutions and who are employed or are unemployed and seeking work.

labor productivity   Total output (GDP) divided by the quantity of labor (hours of work) employed to produce it; the *average product* of labor, or output per hour of work.

labor-force participation rate   The percentage of the working-age population that is actually in the *labor force*.

labor-intensive goods   Products requiring relatively large amounts of *labor* to produce.

Laffer Curve   A curve relating government tax rates and tax revenues and on which a particular tax rate (between zero and 100 percent) maximizes tax revenues.

laissez-faire capitalism   A hypothetical *economic system* in which the government's economic role is limited to protecting private property and establishing a legal environment appropriate to the operation of *markets* in which only mutually agreeable transactions take place between buyers and sellers; sometimes referred to as "pure capitalism."

land   In addition to the part of the earth's surface not covered by water, this term refers to any and all natural resources ("free gifts of nature") that are used to produce *goods* and *services*. Thus, it includes the oceans, sunshine, coal deposits, forests, the electromagnetic spectrum, and *fisheries*. Note that land is one of the four *economic resources*.

land reform   Policy changes aimed at creating a more efficient distribution of land ownership in developing countries. Can involve everything from government purchasing large land estates and dividing the land into smaller farms to consolidating tiny plots of land into larger, more efficient private farms.

land-intensive goods   Products requiring relatively large amounts of land to produce.

law of demand   The principle that, other things equal, an increase in a product's *price* will reduce the quantity of it demanded, and conversely for a decrease in price.

law of diminishing marginal utility   The principle that as a consumer increases the consumption of a *good* or *service*, the *marginal utility* obtained from each additional unit of the good or service decreases.

law of diminishing returns   The principle that as successive increments of a variable *resource* are added to a fixed resource, the *marginal product* of the variable resource will eventually decrease.

law of increasing opportunity costs   The principle that as the production of a good increases, the *opportunity cost* of producing an additional unit rises.

law of supply   The principle that, other things equal, an increase in the *price* of a product will increase the quantity of it supplied, and conversely for a price decrease.

leader countries   As it relates to *economic growth*, countries that develop and use the most advanced technologies, which then become available to *follower countries*.

leakage   (1) A withdrawal of potential spending from the income-expenditures stream via *saving*, tax payments, or *imports;* (2) a withdrawal that reduces the lending potential of the banking system.

learning by doing   Achieving greater *productivity* and lower *average total cost* through gains in knowledge and skill that accompany repetition of a task; a source of *economies of scale*.

least-cost combination of resources   The quantity of each *resource* that a *firm* must employ in order to produce a particular output at the lowest total cost; the combination at which the ratio of the *marginal product* of a resource to its *marginal resource cost* (to its *price* if the resource is employed in a competitive market) is the same for the last dollar spent on each of the resources employed.

legal immigrant   A person who lawfully enters a country for the purpose of residing there.

legal tender   Any form of *currency* that by law must be accepted by creditors (lenders) for the settlement of a financial debt; a nation's official currency is legal tender within its own borders.

limited liability rule   A law that limits the potential losses that an investor in a *corporation* may suffer to the amount that she paid for her shares in the corporation. Encourages *financial investment* by limiting risk.

liquidity   The degree to which an asset can be converted quickly into cash with little or no loss of purchasing power. *Money* is said to be perfectly liquid, whereas other assets have lesser degrees of liquidity.

liquidity trap   A situation in a severe *recession* in which the *central bank's* injection of additional currency (liquidity) into the financial system has little or no additional positive impact on lending, borrowing, *investment,* or *aggregate demand*.

loanable funds theory of interest   The concept that the supply of and demand for *loanable funds* determine the equilibrium rate of *interest*.

lockout   A negotiating tactic in which a *firm* forbids its unionized workers to return to work until a new *collective bargaining* agreement is signed; a means of imposing costs (lost wages) on union workers.

logrolling   The trading of votes by legislators to secure favorable outcomes on decisions concerning the provision of *public goods* and *quasi-public goods*.

long run   In *microeconomics,* a period of time long enough to enable producers of a product to change the quantities of all the resources they employ, so that all resources and costs are variable and no resources or costs are fixed.

long run (macroeconomics)   In *macroeconomics,* a period of time sufficiently long for *nominal wages* and other input *prices* to change in response to a change in a nation's *price level*.

long-run aggregate supply curve   A vertical *aggregate supply* curve relevant to time periods over which input prices and output prices are both fully flexible; an aggregate supply curve for which the *price level,* but not real output, changes when the *aggregate demand* curve shifts; a vertical aggregate supply curve that implies fully flexible *prices*.

long-run supply   A schedule or curve showing the prices at which a purely competitive industry will make various quantities of its product available in the *long run*.

long-run vertical Phillips Curve   The *Phillips Curve* after all *nominal wages* and other input prices have adjusted to changes in the rate of *inflation;* a line emanating straight upward at the economy's *natural rate of unemployment*.

Lorenz curve   A curve showing the distribution of income in an economy. The cumulated percentage of families (income receivers) is measured along the horizontal axis and the cumulated percentage of income is measured along the vertical axis.

loss aversion In *prospect theory,* the property of most people's preferences that the pain generated by losses feels substantially more intense than the pleasure generated by gains.

lump-sum tax A tax that collects a constant amount (the tax revenue of government is the same) at all levels of *GDP.*

M1 The most narrowly defined money supply, equal to *currency* in the hands of the public, *checkable deposits,* and *savings deposits* held at *commercial banks* and thrifts.

M2 A more broadly defined *money supply,* equal to *M1* plus small *time deposits* (of less than $100,000) and individual *money market mutual fund* balances.

macroeconomics The part of *economics* concerned with the performance and behavior of the economy as a whole. Focuses on *economic growth,* the *business cycle, interest rates, inflation,* and the behavior of major economic *aggregates* such as the household, business, and government sectors.

managed floating exchange rate An *exchange rate* that is allowed to change (float) as a result of changes in *currency* supply and demand but at times is altered (managed) by governments via their buying and selling of particular currencies.

marginal analysis The comparison of *marginal* ("extra" or "additional") *benefits* and *marginal costs,* usually for decision making.

marginal cost (MC) The extra (additional) cost of producing 1 more unit of output; equal to the change in *total cost* divided by the change in output (and, in the short run, to the change in total *variable cost* divided by the change in output).

marginal cost-marginal benefit rule As it applies to *cost-benefit analysis,* the tenet that a government project or program should be expanded to the point where the *marginal cost* and *marginal benefit* of additional expenditures are equal.

marginal product (MP) The additional output produced when 1 additional unit of a resource is employed (the quantity of all other resources employed remaining constant); equal to the change in *total product* divided by the change in the quantity of a resource employed.

marginal productivity theory of income distribution The hypothesis that the *wage* rate paid to *labor* will tend to equal the *marginal revenue product* of labor.

marginal propensity to consume (MPC) The fraction of any change in *disposable income* spent for *consumer goods;* equal to the change in consumption divided by the change in disposable income.

marginal propensity to save (MPS) The fraction of any change in *disposable income* that *households* save; equal to the change in *saving* divided by the change in disposable income.

marginal rate of substitution (MRS) The rate at which a consumer is willing to substitute one good for another (from a given combination of goods) and remain equally satisfied (have the same *total utility);* equal to the slope of a consumer's *indifference curve* at each point on the curve.

marginal resource cost (MRC) The amount by which the total cost of employing a *resource* increases when a *firm* employs 1 additional unit of the resource (the quantity of all other resources employed remaining constant); equal to the change in the *total cost* of the resource divided by the change in the quantity of the resource employed.

marginal revenue The change in *total revenue* that results from the sale of 1 additional unit of a *firm's* product; equal to the change in total revenue divided by the change in the quantity of the product sold.

marginal revenue product (MRP) The change in a firm's *total revenue* when it employs 1 additional unit of a *resource* (the quantity of all other resources employed remaining constant); equal to the change in *total revenue* divided by the change in the quantity of the resource employed.

marginal tax rate The *tax* rate paid on an additional dollar of *income.*

marginal utility The extra *utility* a consumer obtains from the consumption of 1 additional unit of a *good* or *service;* equal to the change in *total utility* divided by the change in the quantity consumed.

market Any institution or mechanism that brings together buyers (demanders) and sellers (suppliers) of a particular *good* or *service.*

market failure The inability of a *market* to bring about the allocation of *resources* that best satisfies the wants of society; in particular, the overallocation or underallocation of resources to the production of a particular *good* or *service* because of *externalities* or *asymmetric information,* or because markets fail to provide desired *public goods.*

market portfolio The portfolio consisting of every financial asset (including every *stock* and *bond*) traded in the financial markets. Used to calculate *beta* (a measure of the degree of riskiness) for specific stocks, bonds, and mutual funds.

market structure The characteristics of an *industry* that define the likely behavior and performance of its *firms.* The primary characteristics are the number of firms in the industry, whether they are selling a *differentiated product,* the ease of entry, and how much control firms have over output prices. The most commonly discussed market structures are *pure competition, monopolistic competition, oligopoly,* pure *monopoly,* and *monopsony.*

market system (1) An *economic system* in which individuals own most *economic resources* and in which *markets* and *prices* serve as the dominant coordinating mechanism used to allocate those resources; *capitalism.* Compare with *command system.* (2) All the product and resource markets of a *market economy* and the relationships among them.

marketing loan program A federal farm subsidy under which certain farmers can receive a loan (on a per-unit-of-output basis) to plant a crop and then, depending on the harvest *price* of the crop, either pay back the loan with interest or keep the loan proceeds while forfeiting their harvested crop to the lender.

mechanism design The part of *game theory* concerned with designing the rules of a *game* so as to maximize the likelihood of players reaching a socially optimal outcome.

median-voter model The theory that under majority rule the median (middle) voter will be in the dominant position to determine the outcome of an election.

Medicaid A federal program that helps finance the medical expenses of individuals covered by the *Supplemental Security Income* (*SSI*) and *Temporary Assistance for Needy Families* (*TANF*) programs.

Medicare A federal program that provides for (1) compulsory hospital insurance for senior citizens, (2) low-cost voluntary insurance to help older Americans pay physicians' fees, and (3) subsidized insurance to buy prescription drugs. Financed by *payroll taxes.*

medium of exchange Any item sellers generally accept and buyers generally use to pay for a *good* or *service; money;* a convenient means of exchanging goods and *services* without engaging in *barter.*

mental accounting The tendency people have to create separate "mental boxes" (or "accounts") in which they deal with particular financial transactions in isolation, rather than dealing with them as part of an overall decision-making process that would consider how to best allocate their limited budgets across all possible options by using the *utility-maximizing rule.*

microcredit Anti-poverty programs that lend small amounts of money to poor entrepreneurs.

microeconomics The part of economics concerned with (1) decision making by individual units such as a *household,* a *firm,* or an *industry* and (2) individual markets, specific *goods* and *services,* and product and resource *prices.*

microfinance The provision of small loans and other financial services to low-income *entrepreneurs* and small-business owners in *developing countries.*

Microsoft case A 2002 antitrust case in which Microsoft was found guilty of violating the *Sherman Act* by engaging in a series of unlawful activities designed to maintain its *monopoly* in operating systems for personal computers; as a remedy the company was prohibited from engaging in a set of specific anticompetitive business practices.

midpoint formula A method for calculating *price elasticity of demand* or *price elasticity of supply* that averages the starting and ending *prices* and quantities when computing percentages.

minimum efficient scale (MES) The lowest level of output at which a *firm* can minimize long-run *average total cost.*

minimum wage The lowest *wage* that employers may legally pay for an hour of work.

modern economic growth The historically recent phenomenon in which nations for the first time have experienced sustained increases in *real GDP per capita.*

monetarism The macroeconomic view that the main cause of changes in aggregate output and the *price level* is fluctuations in the *money supply;* espoused by advocates of a *monetary rule.*

monetary policy Actions or communications by a *central bank* intended to help it achieve its macroeconomic policy objectives, which for the U.S. *Federal Reserve* are full employment of the labor force and a stable *price level.*

monetary policy stance A *central bank*'s disposition regarding how it sees the current and future state of the economy and, thus, whether its current monetary policy actions will be consistent with an *expansionary monetary policy,* a *restrictive monetary policy,* or a *neutral monetary policy.*

monetary rule (1) A set of guidelines to be followed by a *central bank* that wishes to adjust monetary policy over time to achieve goals such as promoting *economic growth,* encouraging *full employment,* and maintaining a stable *price level.* (2) The guidelines for conducting monetary policy suggested by *monetarism.* As traditionally formulated, the *money supply* should be expanded each year at the same annual rate as the potential rate of growth of *real gross domestic product;* the supply of money should be increased steadily between 3 and 5 percent per year. (Also see *Taylor rule.*)

money Any item that is generally acceptable to sellers in exchange for *goods* and *services.*

money market The financial *markets* in which short-term, low-risk debt *securities* are traded, including U.S. Treasury bills, overnight loans of bank reserves, and commercial paper.

money market mutual funds (MMMFs) *Mutual funds* that invest in short-term *securities.* Depositors can write checks in minimum amounts or more against their accounts.

monopolistic competition A *market structure* in which many *firms* sell a *differentiated product,* entry is relatively easy, each firm has some control over its product *price,* and there is considerable *nonprice competition.*

monopsony A *market structure* in which there is only a single buyer of a good, *service,* or *resource.*

moral hazard problem The possibility that individuals or institutions will behave more recklessly after they obtain insurance or similar contracts that shift the financial burden of bad outcomes onto others. Example: A bank whose deposits are insured against losses may make riskier loans and investments.

MR = MC rule The principle that a *firm* will maximize its profit (or minimize its loss) by producing the output at which *marginal revenue* and *marginal cost* are equal, provided product *price* is equal to or greater than *average variable cost.*

MRP = MRC rule The principle that to maximize profit (or minimize losses), a *firm* should employ the quantity of a resource at which its *marginal revenue product* (MRP) is equal to its *marginal resource cost* (MRC), the latter being the wage rate in a purely competitive labor market.

multi-homing The phenomenon that occurs when consumers use one or more competing Internet products simultaneously. Also called *multi-tenanting.*

multiple counting Wrongly including the value of *intermediate goods* in the *gross domestic product;* counting the same *good* or *service* more than once.

multiplier The ratio of a change in *equilibrium GDP* to the change in *investment* or in any other component of *aggregate expenditures* or *aggregate demand;* the number by which a change in any such component must be multiplied to find the resulting change in equilibrium GDP.

mutual funds Investment companies that pool money from numerous individual investors in order to purchase *portfolios* of *stocks* or *bonds;* includes both *index funds* as well as *actively managed funds.*

mutual interdependence A situation in which a change in *price* strategy (or in some other strategy) by one *firm* will affect the sales and profits of another firm (or other firms). Any firm that makes such a change can expect its rivals to react to the change.

myopia Refers to the difficulty human beings have with conceptualizing the more distant future. Leads to decisions that overly favor present and near-term options at the expense of more distant future possibilities.

Nash equilibrium The situation that occurs in some *simultaneous games* wherein every player is playing his or her *dominant strategy* at the same time and thus no player has any reason to change behavior.

national health insurance A program in which a nation's government provides a basic package of health care to all citizens at no direct charge or at a low cost-sharing level. Financing is out of general *tax* revenues.

national income Total *income* earned by *resource* suppliers for their contributions to *gross domestic product* plus *taxes on production and imports;* the sum of wages and salaries, *rent, interest, profit, proprietors' income,* and such taxes.

national income accounting The techniques used to measure the overall production of a country's economy as well as other related variables.

National Labor Relations Act (NLRA) The basic labor-relations law in the United States. Defines the legal rights of unions and management and identifies unfair union and management labor practices; established the *National Labor Relations Board*. Often referred to as the Wagner Act, after the legislation's sponsor, New York Senator Robert F. Wagner.

National Labor Relations Board (NLRB)   The board established by the *National Labor Relations Act* of 1935 to investigate unfair labor practices, issue *cease-and-desist orders,* and conduct elections among employees to determine if they wish to be represented by a *labor union.*

natural monopoly   An *industry* in which *economies of scale* are so great that a single *firm* can produce the industry's product at a lower average total cost than would be possible if more than one firm produced the product.

natural rate of unemployment (NRU)   The *full-employment rate of unemployment;* the *unemployment rate* occurring when there is no cyclical unemployment and the economy is achieving its *potential output;* the unemployment rate at which actual *inflation* equals expected inflation.

near-money   Financial *assets* that are not themselves a *medium of exchange* but that have extremely high *liquidity* and thus can be readily converted into *money.* Includes noncheckable *savings accounts, time deposits,* and short-term *U.S. government securities* plus savings bonds.

negative externality   A cost imposed without compensation on third parties by the production or consumption of sellers or buyers. Example: A manufacturer dumps toxic chemicals into a river, killing fish prized by sports fishers. Also known as an external cost or a spillover cost.

negative network effect   The phenomenon observed when the value of a *network* decreases as the size of a network (number of users) increases. Also referred to as a negative network *externality.*

negative self-selection   As it relates to international migration, the idea that those who choose to move to another country have poorer *wage* opportunities in the origin country than those with similar skills who choose not to *emigrate.*

negative-sum game   A strategic interaction (game) between two or more parties (players) in which the winners' gains are less than the losers' losses so that the gains and losses sum to a negative number.

neoclassical economics   The dominant and conventional branch of economic theory that attempts to predict human behavior by building economic models based on simplifying assumptions about people's motives and capabilities. These include that people are fundamentally *rational;* motivated almost entirely by *self-interest;* good at math; and unaffected by *heuristics, time inconsistency,* and *self-control problems.*

net benefits   The total benefits of some activity or policy less the total costs of that activity or policy.

net domestic product (NDP)   *Gross domestic product* less the part of the year's output that is needed to replace the *capital goods* worn out in producing the output; the nation's total output available for consumption or additions to the *capital stock.*

net exports (X_n)   *Exports* minus *imports.*

net private domestic investment   *Gross private domestic investment* less *consumption of fixed capital;* the addition to the nation's stock of *capital* during a year.

network   In *economics,* a group of people or objects that are connected to each other by a *service* or piece of *infrastructure* that facilitates flows of *goods,* services, or information.

network congestion   A *negative network effect* that occurs when a network's capacity limits are approached or exceeded and the quality of the network's services declines as a result.

network effect   The phenomenon whereby the value of a *network* depends on the size of the network (number of users).

network effects   Increases in the value of a product to each user, including existing users, as the total number of users rises.

network pollution   A *negative network effect* that occurs on social networks when the presence of too many connected users degrades the average quality of the information that users obtain from the network.

network switching cost   The cost that a user will have to incur in order to switch from one *network* product to a competing *network* product.

neutral monetary policy   A *monetary policy* in which the *money supply* and *interest rates* are left as they are by the *central bank* because the economy appears to be operating at *potential output,* with stable *prices* and a low level of *unemployment.* Compare with *expansionary monetary policy* and *restrictive monetary policy.*

new classical economics   The theory that, although unanticipated *price-level* changes may create macroeconomic instability in the short run, the economy will return to and stabilize at the full-employment level of domestic output in the long run because *prices* and *wages* adjust automatically to correct movements away from the full-employment output level.

nominal gross domestic product (GDP)   *GDP* measured in terms of the *price level* at the time of measurement; *GDP* not adjusted for *inflation.* Compare with *real gross domestic product* (*real GDP*).

nominal income   The number of dollars received by an individual or group for its *resources* during some period of time.

nominal interest rate   The *interest rate* expressed in terms of annual amounts currently charged for *interest* and not adjusted for *inflation.*

nominal wage   The amount of *money* received by a worker per unit of time (hour, day, etc.); money wage.

noncash transfer   A *government transfer payment* in the form of *goods* and *services* rather than *money,* for example, food stamps, housing assistance, and job training; also called *in-kind transfers.*

noncompeting groups   Collections of workers who do not compete with each other for employment because the skill and training of the workers in one group are substantially different from those of the workers in other groups.

nondiversifiable risk   Investment *risk* that investors are unable to reduce via *diversification;* also called systemic risk.

nondurable good   A *consumer good* with an expected life (use) of less than three years.

nonexcludability   The inability to keep nonpayers (free riders) from obtaining benefits from a certain good; a characteristic of a *public good.*

nonprice competition   Competition based on distinguishing one's product by means of *product differentiation* and then *advertising* the distinguished product to consumers.

nonrenewable natural resource   Things such as oil, natural gas, and metals, that are either in actual fixed supply or that renew so slowly as to be in virtual fixed supply when viewed from a human time perspective.

nonrivalry   The idea that one person's benefit from a certain *good* does not reduce the benefit available to others; a characteristic of a *public good.*

nontariff barriers (NTBs)   All barriers other than *protective tariffs* that nations erect to impede international trade, including *import quotas,* licensing requirements, unreasonable product-quality standards, unnecessary bureaucratic detail in customs procedures, and so on.

normal good   A *good* or *service* whose consumption increases when *income* increases and falls when income decreases, other things equal.

normal profit   The payment made by a *firm* to obtain and retain *entrepreneurial ability;* the minimum *income* that entrepreneurial ability must receive to induce *entrepreneurs* to provide their entrepreneurial ability to a firm; the level of *accounting profit* at which a firm generates an *economic profit* of zero after paying for entrepreneurial ability.

normative economics   The part of economics involving value judgments about what the economy should be like; focused on which economic goals and policies should be implemented; policy economics.

North American Free Trade Agreement (NAFTA)   The 1993 treaty that established an international free-trade zone composed of Canada, Mexico, and the United States.

occupational licensing   The laws of state or local governments that require that a worker satisfy certain specified requirements and obtain a license from a licensing board before engaging in a particular occupation.

occupational segregation   The crowding of women or minorities into less desirable, lower-paying occupations.

official reserves   Foreign *currencies* owned by the central bank of a nation.

offshoring   The practice of shifting work previously done by domestic workers to workers located abroad.

Okun's law   The generalization that any 1-percentage-point rise in the *unemployment rate* above the *full-employment rate of unemployment* is associated with a rise in the *negative GDP gap* by 2 percent of *potential output* (potential *GDP*).

oligopoly   A *market structure* in which a few *firms* sell either a *standardized* or *differentiated product,* into which entry is difficult, in which the firm has limited control over product *price* because of *mutual interdependence* (except when there is collusion among firms), and in which there is typically *nonprice competition.*

one-time game   A strategic interaction (*game*) between two or more parties (players) that all parties know will take place only once.

open shop   A place of employment in which the employer may hire nonunion workers and in which the workers need not become members of a *labor union.*

open-market operations   The purchases and sales of U.S. government *securities* that the *Federal Reserve System* undertakes in order to influence *interest rates* and the *money supply;* one method by which the *Federal Reserve* implements *monetary policy.*

opportunity cost   The amount of other products that must be forgone or sacrificed to produce a unit of a given product.

opportunity-cost ratio   An equivalency showing the number of units of two products that can be produced with the same *resources;* the equivalency 1 corn ≡ 3 olives shows that the resources required to produce 3 units of olives must be shifted to corn production to produce 1 unit of corn.

optimal amount of R&D   The level of *R&D* at which the *marginal benefit* and *marginal cost* of R&D expenditures are equal.

optimal reduction of an externality   The reduction of a *negative externality* such as pollution to the level at which the *marginal benefit* and *marginal cost* of reduction (abatement) are equal.

other-things-equal assumption   The assumption that factors other than those being considered are held constant. Also known as the *ceteris paribus* assumption.

output effect   The possibility that when the *price* of the first of a pair of *substitute resources* falls, the *quantity demanded* of both resources will rise because the reduction in the price of the first resource so greatly reduces production costs that the volume of output created with the two resources increases by so much that the quantity demanded of the second resource increases even after accounting for the *substitution effect.* (See the second definition listed in the entry for *substitution effect.*)

overnight reverse repo rate (ON RRP)   The *interest rate* that the Federal Reserve pays eligible nonbank financial firms for any money that they loan to a Federal Reserve Bank overnight using a reverse *repo* transaction; one of the three *administered rates* set by the *Federal Reserve.*

paradox of thrift   The possibility that households trying to protect themselves against a recession by saving more may inadvertently worsen the recession and hurt themselves by reducing overall consumption and economic activity.

paradox of voting   A situation where paired-choice voting by majority rule fails to provide a consistent ranking of society's preferences for *public goods* or *public services.*

parity concept   The idea that year after year the sale of a specific output of a farm product should enable a farmer to purchase a constant amount of nonagricultural *goods* and *services.*

parity ratio   The ratio of the *price* received by farmers from the sale of an agricultural commodity to the prices of other goods paid by them; usually expressed as a percentage; used as a rationale for *price supports.*

passively managed funds   *Mutual funds* whose *portfolios* are not regularly updated by a fund manager attempting to generate high returns. Rather, once an initial portfolio is selected, it is left unchanged so that investors receive whatever return that unchanging portfolio subsequently generates. *Index funds* are a type of passively managed fund.

patent   An exclusive right given to inventors to produce and sell a new product or machine for 20 years from the time of patent application.

payroll tax   A *tax* levied on employers of labor equal to a percentage of all or part of the *wages* and salaries paid by them and on employees equal to a percentage of all or part of the wages and salaries received by them.

peak   The point in a *business cycle* at which business activity has reached a temporary maximum; the point at which an *expansion* ends and a *recession* begins. At the peak, the economy is near or at *full employment* and the level of real output is at or very close to the economy's capacity.

per se violations   Collusive actions, such as attempts by *firms* to fix *prices* or divide a market, that are violations of the *antitrust laws,* even if the actions themselves are unsuccessful.

per-unit production cost   The average production cost of a particular level of output; total input cost divided by units of output.

percentage rate of return   The percentage gain or loss, relative to the buying *price,* of an *economic investment* or *financial investment* over some period of time.

perfectly elastic demand   Product or *resource* demand in which *quantity demanded* can be of any amount at a particular product or resource *price;* graphs as a horizontal *demand curve.*

perfectly inelastic demand Product or *resource* demand in which *price* can be of any amount at a particular quantity of the product or resource that is demanded; when the *quantity demanded* does not respond to a change in price; graphs as a vertical *demand curve*.

personal consumption expenditures (C) The expenditures of *households* for both durable and nondurable *consumer goods*.

personal income (PI) The earned and unearned *income* available to resource suppliers and others before the payment of personal *taxes*.

personal income tax A *tax* levied on the taxable income of individuals, *households,* and unincorporated *firms*.

personal mandate The requirement under the *Patient Protection and Affordable Care Act* (*PPACA*) of 2010 that all U.S. citizens and legal residents purchase health insurance unless they are already covered by employer-sponsored health insurance or government-sponsored health insurance (*Medicaid* or *Medicare*).

Pigovian tax A *tax* or charge levied on the production of a product that generates *negative externalities*. If set correctly, the tax will precisely offset the overallocation (overproduction) generated by the negative externality.

planned investment The amount that *firms* plan or intend to invest.

policy rate A short-term *interest rate* that a *central bank* manages to help communicate the stance of *monetary policy* as well as to achieve its *monetary policy* goals.

political business cycles Fluctuations in the economy caused by the alleged tendency of Congress to destabilize the economy by reducing taxes and increasing government expenditures before elections and to raise taxes and lower expenditures after elections.

political corruption The unlawful misdirection of government resources, or actions that occur when government officials abuse their entrusted powers for personal gain. (Also see *corruption*.)

portfolio A specific collection of *stocks, bonds,* or other *financial investments* held by an individual or a *mutual fund*.

positive economics The analysis of facts or data to establish scientific generalizations about economic behavior.

positive externality A benefit obtained without compensation by third parties from the production or consumption of sellers or buyers. Example: A beekeeper benefits when a neighboring farmer plants clover. Also known as an *external benefit* or a spillover benefit.

positive network effect The phenomenon observed when the value of a *network* increases as the size of the network (number of users) increases. Also called a positive network *externality*.

positive-sum game A strategic interaction (game) between two or more parties (players) in which the winners' gains exceed the losers' losses so that the gains and losses sum to something positive.

potential output The real output (*GDP*) an economy can produce when it fully employs its available resources.

poverty rate The percentage of the population with incomes below the official poverty income levels that are established by the federal government.

precommitments Actions taken ahead of time that make it difficult for the future self to avoid doing what the present self desires. See *time inconsistency* and *self-control problems*.

preferred provider organization (PPO) An arrangement in which doctors and hospitals agree to provide health care to insured individuals at rates negotiated with an insurer.

present value Today's value of some amount of *money* that is to be received at a particular future date.

price ceiling A legally established maximum *price* for a *good,* or *service*. Normally set at a price below the *equilibrium price*.

price discrimination The selling of a product to different buyers at different *prices* when the price differences are not justified by differences in cost.

price elasticity of demand The ratio of the percentage change in *quantity demanded* of a product or *resource* to the percentage change in its *price;* a measure of the responsiveness of buyers to a change in the price of a product or resource.

price elasticity of supply The ratio of the percentage change in *quantity supplied* of a product or *resource* to the percentage change in its *price;* a measure of the responsiveness of producers to a change in the price of a product or resource.

price floor A legally established minimum *price* for a *good,* or service. Normally set at a price above the *equilibrium price*.

price index An index number that shows how the weighted-average *price* of a "market basket" of goods changes over time relative to its price in a specific *base year*.

price leadership An informal method that *firms* in an *oligopoly* may employ to set the *price* of their product: One firm (the leader) is the first to announce a change in price, and the other firms (the followers) soon announce identical or similar changes.

price loss coverage A form of crop insurance that pays participating farmers if the market price of their output falls below a predetermined value.

price supports The term used to refer to *price floors* applied to *farm commodities;* the minimum *price* that the government allows farmers to receive for farm commodities like wheat or corn.

price taker A seller (or buyer) that is unable to affect the *price* at which a product or *resource* sells by changing the amount it sells (or buys).

price war Successive, competitive, and continued decreases in the *prices* charged by *firms* in an oligopolistic *industry*. At each stage of the price war, one *firm* lowers its price below its rivals' price, hoping to increase its sales and revenues at its rivals' expense. The war ends when the price decreases cease.

price-level surprises Unanticipated changes in the *price level*.

pricing power The ability of a firm to raise *price* without substantially reducing *quantity demanded;* increases as *demand* becomes increasingly *inelastic*.

principal-agent problem (1) At a *firm,* a conflict of interest that occurs when agents (workers or managers) pursue their own objectives to the detriment of the principals' (stockholders') goals. (2) In *public choice theory,* a conflict of interest that arises when elected officials (who are the agents of the people) pursue policies that are in their own interests rather than policies that would be in the better interests of the public (the principals).

principle of comparative advantage The proposition that an individual, region, or nation will benefit if it specializes in producing goods for which its own *opportunity costs* are lower than the opportunity costs of a trading partner, and then exchanging some of the products in which it specializes for other desired products produced by others.

prisoner's dilemma A famous *game* analyzed in *game theory* in which two players who could have reached a mutually beneficial outcome through cooperation will instead end up at a mutually inferior outcome as they pursue their own respective interests (instead of cooperating). Helps to explain why collusion can be difficult for *oligopoly* firms to achieve or maintain.

private good   A *good* or *service* that is individually consumed and that can be profitably provided by privately owned *firms* because they can exclude nonpayers from receiving the benefits.

private information   Facts known by one party to a market transaction but hidden from others; results in *asymmetric information.*

private property   The right of private persons and *firms* to obtain, own, control, employ, dispose of, and bequeath *land, capital,* and other property.

probability-weighted average   Each of the possible future rates of return from an investment multiplied by its respective probability (expressed as a decimal) of happening.

process innovation   The development and use of new or improved production or distribution methods.

producer surplus   The difference between the actual *price* a producer receives (or producers receive) and the minimum acceptable price; the triangular area above the *supply curve* and below the market price.

product differentiation   A strategy in which one *firm*'s product is distinguished from competing products by means of its design, related *services,* quality, location, or other attributes (except *price*).

product innovation   The development and sale of a new or improved product (or service).

product market   A market in which products are sold by *firms* and bought by *households.*

production possibilities curve   A curve showing the different combinations of two goods or *services* that can be produced in a *full-employment, full-production* economy where the available supplies of *resources* and technology are fixed.

productive efficiency   The production of a *good* in the least costly way; occurs when production takes place at the output level at which per-unit production costs are minimized.

productivity   A measure of average output or real output per unit of input. For example, the productivity of labor is determined by dividing real output by hours of work.

profit-maximizing combination of resources   The quantity of each *resource* a *firm* must employ to maximize its *profit* or minimize its loss; the combination of resource inputs at which the *marginal revenue product* of each resource is equal to its *marginal resource cost* (to its *price* if the resource is employed in a competitive market).

progressive tax   At the individual level, a *tax* whose *average tax rate* increases as the taxpayer's *income* increases. At the national level, a *tax* for which the *average tax rate* (= tax revenue/*GDP*) rises with *GDP.*

property tax   A *tax* on the value of property (*capital, land, stocks* and *bonds,* and other *assets*) owned by *firms* and *households.*

proportional tax   At the individual level, a *tax* whose *average tax rate* remains constant as the taxpayer's *income* increases or decreases. At the national level, a *tax* for which the *average tax rate* (= tax revenue/*GDP*) remains constant as *GDP* rises or falls.

prospect theory   A *behavioral economics* theory of preferences having three main features: (1) people evaluate options on the basis of whether they generate gains or losses relative to the *status quo;* (2) gains are subject to *diminishing marginal utility,* while losses are subject to diminishing marginal disutility; and (3) people are prone to *loss aversion.*

protective tariff   A *tariff* designed to shield domestic producers of a *good* or *service* from the competition of foreign producers.

public assistance programs   Government programs that pay benefits to those who are unable to earn *income* (because of permanent disabilities or because they have very low income and dependent children); financed by general *tax* revenues and viewed as public charity (rather than earned rights).

public choice theory   The economic analysis of government decision making, politics, and elections.

public debt   The total amount owed by the federal government to the owners of government *securities;* equal to the sum of past government *budget deficits* less government *budget surpluses.*

public good   A *good* or *service* that is characterized by *nonrivalry* and *nonexcludability.* These characteristics typically imply that no private *firm* can break even when attempting to provide such products. As a result, they are often provided by governments, who pay for them using general *tax* revenues.

public interest theory of regulation   The presumption that the purpose of the regulation of an *industry* is to protect the public (consumers) from abuse of the power possessed by *natural monopolies.*

public investments   Government expenditures on public capital (such as roads, highways, bridges, mass-transit systems, and electric power facilities) and on *human capital* (such as education, training, and health).

purchasing-power-parity theory   The idea that if countries have *flexible exchange rates* (rather than *fixed exchange rates*), the exchange rates between national currencies will adjust to equate the purchasing power of various currencies. In particular, the exchange rate between any two national currencies will adjust to reflect the *price-level* differences between the two countries.

pure monopoly   A *market structure* in which one *firm* sells a unique product, into which entry is blocked, in which the single firm has considerable control over product *price,* and in which *nonprice competition* may or may not be found.

pure rate of interest   The hypothetical *interest rate* that is completely *risk*-free and only compensates investors for their willingness to patiently forego alternative consumption and investment opportunities until their money is repaid.

pure, or perfect, competition   A *market structure* in which a very large number of *firms* sells a *standardized product,* into which entry is very easy, in which the individual seller has no control over the product *price,* and in which there is no nonprice competition; a market characterized by a very large number of buyers and sellers.

purely competitive labor market   A *resource market* in which many *firms* compete with one another in hiring a specific kind of *labor,* numerous equally qualified workers supply that labor, and no one controls the market *wage rate.*

quadratic voting system   A majority voting system in which voters can express strength of preference by purchasing as many votes as they like at a price equal to the square of the number of votes purchased. Quadratic voting is more likely (but not guaranteed) to result in economically efficient decisions than traditional one-person-one-vote (1p1v) majority voting systems.

quantitative easing (QE)   An *open-market operation* in which a *central bank* pre-announces that it will spend a fixed quantity of *money* purchasing long-term bonds so as to lower long-term *interest rates* and thereby ease *credit* conditions for long-horizon investors, such as *businesses* borrowing to purchase *capital goods.*

quantitative tightening (QT)   The opposite of *quantitative easing.* An *open-market operation* in which a *central bank* pre-announces that it will sell a fixed quantity of long-term bonds so as to raise long-term *interest rates* and thereby tighten *credit* conditions for long-horizon investors, such as *businesses* borrowing to purchase *capital goods.*

quasi-public good   A *good* or *service* to which *excludability* could apply but that has such a large *positive externality* that government sponsors its production to prevent an underallocation of resources.

rational   Behaviors and decisions that maximize a person's chances of achieving their goals. See *rational behavior*.

rational behavior   Human behavior based on comparison of *marginal costs* and *marginal benefits;* behavior designed to maximize *total utility*. See *rational*.

rational expectations theory   A hypothesis that assumes that people develop logical (rational) models that attempt to correctly anticipate future events (expectations) as much as possible so as to make better current decisions given what is likely to happen in the future. Can cause individuals and firms to take actions that offset monetary and fiscal policy initiatives.

real GDP   *Gross domestic product* adjusted for *inflation;* gross domestic product in a year divided by the GDP *price index* for that year, the index expressed as a decimal. Compare with *nominal GDP*.

real GDP per capita   *Inflation*-adjusted output per person; *real GDP*/population.

real gross domestic product (GDP)   *Gross domestic product* adjusted for *inflation;* gross domestic product in a year divided by the GDP *price index* for that year, the index expressed as a decimal. Compare with *nominal GDP*.

real income   The amount of *goods* and *services* that can be purchased with *nominal income* during some period of time; nominal income adjusted for *inflation*.

real interest rate   The *interest rate* expressed in dollars of constant value (adjusted for *inflation*) and equal to the *nominal interest rate* less the expected rate of inflation.

real wage   The amount of *goods* and *services* a worker can purchase with his or her *nominal wage;* the *purchasing power* of the *nominal wage*.

real-balances effect   The tendency for increases in the *price level* to lower the real value (or *purchasing power*) of financial *assets* with fixed *money* value and, as a result, to reduce total spending and real output, and conversely for decreases in the *price level*.

real-business-cycle theory   A theory that *business cycles* result from changes in *technology* and *resource* availability, which affect *productivity* and thus increase or decrease long-run *aggregate supply*.

recession   A period of declining *real GDP*, accompanied by lower *real income* and higher *unemployment*.

recessionary expenditure gap   The amount by which *aggregate expenditures* at the *full-employment level of GDP* fall short of the amount required to achieve the full-employment level of GDP. In the aggregate expenditures model, the amount by which the *aggregate expenditures schedule* must shift upward to increase *real GDP* to its full-employment, noninflationary level.

regressive tax   At the individual level, a *tax* whose *average tax rate* decreases as the taxpayer's *income* increases. At the national level, a *tax* for which the *average tax rate* (= tax revenue/*GDP*) falls as *GDP* rises.

regulatory agency   An agency, commission, or board established by the federal government or a state government to control the *prices* charged and the *services* offered by a *natural monopoly* or *public utility*.

regulatory capture   The situation that occurs when a governmental *regulatory agency* ends up being controlled by the industry that it is supposed to be regulating.

remittances   Payments by *immigrants* to family members and others located in the immigrants' home countries.

renewable natural resources   Things such as forests, water in reservoirs, and wildlife that are capable of growing back or building back up (renewing themselves) if they are harvested at moderate rates.

rent control   A law that sets a maximum price on the rents that a landlord can legally charge tenants for renting an apartment or a house.

rent-seeking behavior   Attempts by individuals, firms, or unions to use political influence to receive payments in excess of the minimum amount they would normally be willing to accept to provide a particular good or service.

repeated game   A strategic interaction (*game*) between two or more parties (players) that all parties know will take place repeatedly.

replacement rate   The *total fertility rate* necessary to offset deaths in a country and thereby keep the size of its population constant (without relying on immigration). For most countries, a total fertility rate of about 2.1 births per woman per lifetime.

reserve balances   Funds that *commercial banks* and *thrift institutions* hold on deposit at the *central bank*.

residual claimant   In a market system, the economic agent who receives (is claimant to) whatever profit or loss remains (is residual) at a firm after all other *input* providers have been paid. The residual is compensation for providing the economic input of *entrepreneurial ability* and flows to the firm's owners.

resource market   A market in which *households* sell and *firms* buy *resources* or the services of resources.

restrictive monetary policy   *Central bank* actions to reduce the *money supply,* increase *interest rates,* and reduce *inflation*. Implemented when the economy is operating above *potential output*. Also known as a "tight money" policy.

revenue tariff   A *tariff* designed to produce *income* for the federal government.

right-to-work law   A state law that makes it illegal to require that a worker join a *labor union* in order to retain his or her job; laws that make *union shops* and *agency shops* illegal.

risk   The uncertainty as to the future returns of a particular *financial investment* or *economic investment*.

risk premium   The rate of return in excess of the *risk-free interest rate* that compensates a lender or investor for *risk*.

risk-free interest rate   The *interest rate* earned on short-term U.S. government *bonds*.

rivalry   The characteristic displayed by certain goods and services that consumption by one person precludes consumption by others.

rule of 70   A method for determining the number of years it will take for some measure to double, given its annual percentage increase. Example: To determine the number of years it will take for the *price level* to double, divide 70 by the annual rate of *inflation*.

rule of reason   The rule stated and applied in the *U.S. Steel* case that only combinations and contracts unreasonably restraining trade are subject to actions under the antitrust laws and that size and possession of *monopoly* power are not by themselves illegal. Compare with *per se violation*.

sales tax   A *tax* levied on the cost (at retail) of a broad group of products.

saving   The flow of money that is generated when *personal consumption expenditures* are less than *disposable income*. Compare with *savings*.

saving schedule   A table of numbers that shows the amounts *households* plan to save (plan not to spend for *consumer goods*), at different levels of *disposable income*.

scarcity   The limits placed on the amounts and types of *goods* and *services* available for consumption as the result of there being only limited *economic resources* from which to produce output; the fundamental economic constraint that creates *opportunity costs* and that necessitates the use of *marginal analysis* (*cost-benefit analysis*) to make optimal choices.

scientific method   The procedure for the systematic pursuit of knowledge involving the observation of facts and the formulation and testing of hypotheses to obtain theories, principles, and laws.

securities   Financial assets such as stocks and bonds that are tradable in organized financial markets, such as the New York Stock Exchange (NYSE).

Security Market Line (SML)   A line that shows the *average expected rate of return* of all *financial investments* at each level of *nondiversifiable risk*, the latter measured by *beta*.

self-control problems   Refers to the difficulty people have in sticking with earlier plans and avoiding suboptimal decisions when finally confronted with a particular decision-making situation. A manifestation of *time inconsistency* and potentially avoidable by using *precommitments*.

self-interest   That which each *firm*, property owner, worker, and consumer believes is best for itself and seeks to obtain.

self-selection   As it relates to international migration, the idea that those who choose to move to a new country tend to have greater motivation for economic gain or greater willingness to sacrifice current consumption for future consumption than those with similar skills who choose to remain at home.

sequential game   A strategic interaction (*game*) between two or more parties (players) in which each party moves (makes a decision) in a predetermined order (sequence).

service   An (intangible) act or use for which a consumer, *firm*, or government is willing to pay.

Sherman Act   The federal antitrust law of 1890 that makes *monopoly* and conspiracies to restrain trade criminal offenses.

shocks   Sudden, unexpected changes in *demand* (or *aggregate demand*) or supply (or *aggregate supply*).

short run   In *microeconomics*, a period of time in which producers are able to change the quantities of some but not all of the *resources* they employ; a period in which some resources (usually *plant*) are fixed and some are variable.

short run (macroeconomics)   In *macroeconomics*, the relatively short period of time (typically, weeks to months) in which *nominal wages* and other input *prices* do not change in response to a change in a nation's *price level*.

short-run aggregate supply curve   An upward sloping *aggregate supply* curve relevant to time periods over which input prices are fixed but output prices are flexible; an aggregate supply curve for which real output and the price level both change when the *aggregate demand* curve shifts.

short-run downward sloping Phillips Curve   A downward sloping line illustrating the inverse relationship that A.W. Phillips theorized should exist between the *unemployment rate* (on the horizontal axis) and the *inflation rate* (on the vertical axis). Believed by many mainstream economists to hold in the *short run* but not in the *long run*.

short-run supply curve   A *supply curve* that shows the quantity of a product a *firm* in a purely competitive *industry* will offer to sell at various *prices* in the *short run*; the portion of the firm's short-run *marginal cost* curve that lies above its *average-variable-cost* curve.

shortage   The amount by which the *quantity demanded* of a product exceeds the *quantity supplied* at a particular (below-equilibrium) *price*.

simultaneous consumption   The same-time derivation of *utility* from some product by a large number of consumers.

simultaneous game   A strategic interaction (*game*) between two or more parties (players) in which every player moves (makes a decision) at the same time.

skill transferability   The ease with which people can shift their work talents from one job, region, or country to another job, region, or country.

slope of a straight line   The ratio of the vertical change (the rise or fall) to the horizontal change (the run) between any two points on a straight line. The slope of an upward-sloping line is positive, reflecting a direct relationship between two variables; the slope of a downward-sloping line is negative, reflecting an inverse relationship between two variables.

Smoot-Hawley Tariff Act   Legislation passed in 1930 that established very high *tariffs*. Its objective was to reduce *imports* and stimulate the domestic economy, but it resulted only in retaliatory tariffs by other nations.

social insurance programs   Programs that replace the earnings lost when people retire or are temporarily unemployed, that are financed by payroll *taxes*, and that are viewed as earned rights (rather than charity).

social regulation   Regulation in which government is concerned with the conditions under which *goods* and *services* are produced, their physical characteristics, and the impact of their production on society. Differs from *industrial regulation*.

Social Security   The social insurance program in the United States financed by federal *payroll taxes* on employers and employees and designed to replace a portion of the earnings lost when workers become disabled, retire, or die.

socially optimal price   The *price* of a product that results in the most efficient allocation of an economy's *resources* and that is equal to the *marginal cost* of the product.

special-interest effect   Any political outcome in which a small group ("special interest") gains substantially at the expense of a much larger number of persons who each individually suffers a small loss.

specialization   The use of the *resources* of an individual, a *firm*, a region, or a nation to concentrate production on one or a small number of *goods* and *services*.

stagflation   *Inflation* accompanied by stagnation in the rate of growth of output and an increase in *unemployment* in the economy; simultaneous increases in the *inflation rate* and the *unemployment rate*.

Standard Oil case   A 1911 antitrust case in which Standard Oil was found guilty of violating the *Sherman Act* by illegally monopolizing the petroleum *industry*. As a remedy the company was divided into several competing *firms*.

start-up firm   A new *firm* focused on creating and introducing a particular new product or employing a specific new production or distribution method.

startups Newly formed firms that are attempting to pioneer a new product or production method.

state capacity The ability of a government to achieve specific policy goals.

statistical discrimination The practice of judging an individual on the basis of the average characteristics of the group to which he or she belongs rather than on his or her own personal characteristics.

status quo The existing state of affairs; in *prospect theory,* the current situation from which gains and losses are calculated.

status quo bias The tendency most people have when making choices to select any option that is presented as the default (*status quo*) option. Explainable by *prospect theory* and *loss aversion.*

stock (corporate) An ownership share in a corporation.

store of value An *asset* set aside for future use; one of the three functions of *money.*

strategic behavior Self-interested economic actions that take into account the expected reactions of others.

Strategic Organizing Center (SOC) A loose federation of American unions that includes the Service Workers and Teamsters unions; the second largest union federation after the *AFL-CIO.*

strike The withholding of *labor* services by an organized group of workers (a *labor union*).

structural remedy A directive imposed by a regulator on an offending monopoly firm that seeks to resolve the firm's illegal monopoly behavior by changing the structure of the offending business, for instance by breaking it up into multiple competing firms.

structural unemployment *Unemployment* of workers whose skills are not demanded by employers, who lack sufficient skill to obtain employment, or who cannot easily move to locations where jobs are available.

substitute goods Products or *services* that can be used in place of each other. When the *price* of one falls, the *demand* for the other product falls; conversely, when the price of one product rises, the demand for the other product rises.

substitute resources Productive inputs that can be used instead of other inputs in the production process; resources for which an increase in the *price* of one leads to an increase in the demand for the other.

substitution effect (1) A change in the quantity demanded of a *consumer good* that results from a change in its relative expensiveness caused by a change in the good's own *price.* (2) The reduction in the *quantity demanded* of the second of a pair of *substitute resources* that occurs when the price of the first resource falls and causes *firms* that employ both resources to switch to using more of the first resource (whose price has fallen) and less of the second resource (whose price has remained the same).

subtractive versioning A pricing strategy in which an internet business offers customers the option of paying to remove an annoying feature (such as advertising) from its base offering.

Supplemental Nutrition Assistance Program (SNAP) A government program that provides food money to low-income recipients by depositing electronic money onto *Electronic Benefit Transfer* (*EBT*) *cards.* Formerly known as the food-stamp program.

Supplemental Security Income (SSI) A federally financed and administered program that provides a uniform nationwide minimum *income* for the aged, blind, and disabled who do not qualify for benefits under *Social Security* in the United States.

supply A schedule or curve that shows the various amounts of a product that producers are willing and able to make available for sale at each of a series of possible *prices* during a specified period of time.

supply curve A curve that illustrates the *supply* for a product by showing how each possible *price* (on the *vertical axis*) is associated with a specific *quantity supplied* (on the *horizontal axis*).

supply factors (in growth) The four determinants of an economy's physical ability to achieve *economic growth* by increasing *potential output* and shifting out the *production possibilities curve.* The four determinants are improvements in technology plus increases in the quantity and quality of natural resources, human resources, and the stock of capital goods.

supply schedule A table of numbers showing the amounts of a *good* or *service* producers are willing and able to make available for sale at each of a series of possible *prices* during a specified period of time.

supply shocks Sudden, unexpected changes in *aggregate supply.*

supply-side economics A view of *macroeconomics* that emphasizes the role of costs and *aggregate supply* in explaining *inflation, unemployment,* and *economic growth.*

surplus The amount by which the *quantity supplied* of a product exceeds the *quantity demanded* at a specific (above-equilibrium) *price.*

systematic errors Suboptimal choices that (1) are not *rational* because they do not maximize a person's chances of achieving his or her goals and (2) occur routinely, repeatedly, and predictably.

target rate of inflation The publicly announced annual *inflation* rate that a *central bank* attempts to achieve through *monetary policy* actions if it is following an *inflation targeting* monetary policy.

target rate of unemployment The Fed's desired *unemployment rate,* equal to the *full-employment rate of unemployment,* which is estimated to be between 4 and 5 percent for the U.S. economy.

tariff A *tax* imposed by a nation on an imported good.

taste-for-discrimination model A theory that views discrimination as a preference for which an employer is willing to pay.

tax incidence The degree to which a *tax* falls on a particular person or group.

tax subsidy A grant in the form of reduced *taxes* through favorable *tax* treatment. For example, employer-paid health insurance is exempt from federal *income taxes* and *payroll taxes.*

taxes on production and imports A *national income accounting* category that includes such taxes as *sales, excise,* business property taxes, and *tariffs* that *firms* treat as costs of producing a product and pass on (in whole or in part) to buyers by charging a higher *price.*

Taylor rule A *monetary rule* proposed by economist John Taylor that would stipulate exactly how much the *Federal Reserve System* should change *real interest rates* in response to divergences of *real GDP* from potential GDP and divergences of actual rates of *inflation* from a target rate of inflation.

technological advance (1) An improvement in the quality of existing products, the invention of entirely new products, or the creation of new or better ways of producing or distributing products. (2) Any improvement in the methods by which resources are combined such that the same quantity of inputs can be made to yield a combination of outputs that is preferred to any combination of outputs that was previously possible.

technological lock-in The unwillingness of users to switch to a better product or technology because so many people are already using an older technology that enjoys *positive network effects.*

Temporary Assistance for Needy Families (TANF) A state-administered and partly federally funded program in the United States that provides financial aid to poor families; the basic welfare program for low-income families in the United States; contains time limits and work requirements.

terms of trade The rate at which units of one product can be exchanged for units of another product; the *price* of a *good* or *service;* the amount of one good or service that must be given up to obtain 1 unit of another good or service.

The Agricultural Act of 2014 The agricultural law enacted in the United States in 2014 that eliminated *direct payments* and *countercyclical payments* in favor of two types of *crop insurance—price loss coverage* and *agricultural risk coverage.*

thrift institution A *savings and loan association, mutual savings bank,* or *credit union.*

time deposit An interest-earning deposit in a *commercial bank* or *thrift institution* that the depositor can withdraw without penalty after the end of a specified period.

time inconsistency The human tendency to systematically misjudge at the present time what will actually end up being desired at a future time.

time preference The human tendency, because of impatience, to prefer to spend and consume in the present rather than save and wait to spend and consume in the future; this inclination varies in strength among individuals.

time-value of money The idea that a specific amount of *money* is more valuable to a person the sooner it is received because the money can be placed in a financial account or *investment* and earn *compound interest* over time; the *opportunity cost* of receiving a sum of money later rather than earlier.

tipping point The size of a *network* beyond which further network growth becomes self-sustaining (due to the network's sheer size creating large enough *positive network effects* to attract additional users, whose participation further increases the size of the network's positive network effects, thereby attracting even more users, and so on).

token money Bills or coins for which the amount printed on the *currency* bears no relationship to the value of the paper or metal embodied within it; for currency still circulating, *money* for which the face value exceeds the commodity value.

total allowable catch (TAC) The overall limit set by a government or a fisheries commission on the total number of fish or tonnage of fish that fishers collectively can harvest during some particular time period. Used to set the fishing limits for *individual transferable quotas (ITQs).*

total cost The sum of *fixed cost* and *variable cost.*

total demand for money The sum of the *transactions demand for money* and the *asset demand for money.*

total fertility rate The average number of children per lifetime birthed by a nation's women.

total product (TP) The total output of a particular *good* or *service* produced by a *firm* (or a group of firms or the entire economy).

total revenue (TR) The total number of dollars received by a *firm* (or firms) from the sale of a product; equal to the total expenditures for the product produced by the firm (or firms); equal to the quantity sold (demanded) multiplied by the *price* at which it is sold.

total surplus The sum of consumer surplus and producer surplus; a measure of social welfare; also known as social surplus.

total utility The total amount of satisfaction derived from the consumption of a single product or a combination of products.

total-revenue test A test to determine *elasticity of demand.* Demand is elastic if *total revenue* moves in the opposite direction from a *price* change; it is inelastic when it moves in the same direction as a price change; and it is of unitary elasticity when it does not change when price changes.

trade The voluntary exchange of goods, services, or assets between two or more parties.

Trade Adjustment Assistance Act A U.S. law passed in 2002 that provides cash assistance, education and training benefits, health care subsidies, and *wage* subsidies (for persons age 50 or older) to workers displaced by *imports* or relocations of U.S. *plants* to other countries.

trade deficit The amount by which a nation's *imports* of goods (or goods and *services*) exceed its *exports* of goods (or goods and *services*).

trade surplus The amount by which a nation's *exports* of goods (or goods and *services*) exceed its *imports* of goods (or goods and *services*).

trading possibilities line A line that shows the different combinations of two products that an economy is able to obtain (consume) when it specializes in the production of one product and trades (exports) it to obtain the other product.

tragedy of the commons The tendency for commonly owned *natural resources* to be overused, neglected, or degraded because their common ownership gives nobody an incentive to maintain or improve them.

transactions demand for money The amount of money people want to hold for use as a *medium of exchange* (to make payments); varies directly with *nominal GDP.*

transfer payment A payment of *money* (or *goods* and *services*) by a government to a *household* or *firm* for which the payer receives no *good* or *service* directly in return.

trough The point in a *business cycle* at which business activity has reached a temporary minimum; the point at which a *recession* ends and an *expansion* (recovery) begins. At the trough, the economy experiences substantial *unemployment* and *real GDP* is less than *potential output.*

tying contract A requirement imposed by a seller that a buyer purchase another (or other) of its products as a condition for buying a desired product; a practice forbidden by the *Clayton Act.*

U.S. government securities U.S. Treasury bills, notes, and *bonds* used to finance *budget deficits;* the components of the *public debt.*

U.S. Steel case The antitrust action brought by the federal government against the U.S. Steel Corporation in which the courts ruled (in 1920) that only unreasonable restraints of trade were illegal and that size and the possession of monopoly power were not by themselves violations of the *antitrust laws.*

ultimatum game A *behavioral economics* game in which a mutually anonymous pair of players interact to determine how an amount of money is to be split. The first player suggests a division. The second player either accepts that proposal (in which case the split is made accordingly) or rejects it (in which case neither player gets anything).

unanticipated inflation An increase of the *price level* (*inflation*) at a rate greater than expected.

unauthorized immigrants   People who have entered a country unlawfully to reside there; also called undocumented workers, unauthorized workers, and illegal aliens.

unconditional cash transfers   Anti-poverty programs that give cash transfers (grants) to poor individuals with no strings attached in the hope that the recipients will improve their economic prospects by spending the money on either education or physical capital.

underemployment   A situation in which workers are employed in positions requiring less education and skill than they have.

unemployment   The failure to use all available *economic resources* to produce desired *goods* and *services;* the failure of the economy to fully employ its *labor force.*

unemployment gap   The difference between the actual rate of *unemployment* and the *full-employment rate of unemployment,* which is believed to be between 3 and 4 percent for the U.S. economy; a key component of the *Taylor rule.*

unemployment insurance   The social insurance program that in the United States is financed by state *payroll taxes* on employers and makes *income* available to workers who become unemployed and are unable to find jobs.

unemployment rate   The percentage of the *labor force* unemployed at any time.

uninsurable risk   An eventuality for which the frequency or magnitude of potential losses is unpredictable or unknowable. Insurance companies are not willing to sell insurance against such risks.

union shop   A place of employment where the employer may hire either *labor union* members or nonmembers but where nonmembers must become members within a specified period of time or lose their jobs.

unionization rate   The percentage of a particular population of workers that belongs to *labor unions;* alternatively, the percentage of a population of workers that is represented by one union or another in *collective bargaining.*

unit elasticity   *Demand* or *supply* for which the *elasticity coefficient* is equal to 1; means that the percentage change in the *quantity demanded* or *quantity supplied* is equal to the percentage change in *price.*

unit of account   A standard unit in which *prices* can be stated and the value of *goods* and *services* can be compared; one of the three functions of *money.*

unplanned changes in inventories   Changes in *inventories* that *firms* did not anticipate; changes in inventories that occur because of unexpected increases or decreases of aggregate spending (or of *aggregate expenditures*).

user cost   The *opportunity cost* of extracting and selling a *nonrenewable natural resource* today rather than waiting to extract and sell the resource in the future; the *present value* of the decline in future revenue that will occur because a nonrenewable natural resource is extracted and sold today rather than being extracted and sold in the future.

utility   The want-satisfying power of a *good* or *service;* the satisfaction or pleasure a consumer obtains from the consumption of a good or service (or from the consumption of a collection of *goods* and *services*).

utility-maximizing rule   The principle that to obtain the greatest *total utility,* a consumer should allocate *money income* so that the last dollar spent on each *good* or *service* yields the same *marginal utility* (MU). For two goods X and Y, with prices P_x and $P_y,$ total utility will be maximized by purchasing the amounts of X and Y such that $MU_x/P_x = MU_y/P_y$ for the last dollar spent on each good.

value added   The value of a product sold by a *firm* less the value of the products (materials) purchased and used by the firm to produce that product.

variable cost   A cost that increases when the *firm* increases its output and decreases when the firm reduces its output.

velocity   The number of times per year that the average dollar in the *money supply* is spent for *final goods* and final *services; nominal gross domestic product* (*GDP*) divided by the *money supply.*

venture capital   That part of household *savings* used to finance high-risk business enterprises in exchange for *stock* (and thus a share of any *profit* if the enterprises are successful).

vertical axis   The "up-down" or "north-south" measurement line on a graph or grid.

vertical intercept   The point at which a line meets the vertical axis of a graph.

vertical merger   The merger of one or more *firms* engaged in different stages of the production of a particular *final good.*

very long run   In microeconomics, a period of time long enough that *technology* can change and *firms* can introduce new products.

vicious circle of poverty   A problem common in some *developing countries* in which their low *per capita incomes* are an obstacle to realizing the levels of *savings* and *investment* needed to achieve rates of growth of output that exceed their rates of population growth.

voice mechanism   Communication by workers through their *union* to resolve grievances with an employer.

voluntary export restrictions (VER)   Voluntary limitations by countries or *firms* of their exports to a particular foreign nation; undertaken to avoid the enactment of formal trade barriers by the foreign nation.

wage   The *price* paid for the use or *services* of *labor* per unit of time (per hour, per day, and so on).

wage differential   The difference between the *wage* received by one worker or group of workers and that received by another worker or group of workers.

wealth effect   The tendency for people to increase their consumption spending when the value of their financial and real *assets* rises and to decrease their consumption spending when the value of those assets falls.

Wheeler-Lea Act   The federal law of 1938 that amended the *Federal Trade Commission Act* by prohibiting unfair and deceptive acts or practices of commerce (such as false and misleading advertising and the misrepresentation of products).

will to develop   The mental state of wanting *economic growth* strongly enough to change from old to new ways of doing things.

winner-take-all industries   Industries in which factors such as *economies of scale* and *positive network effects* might be expected to lead to *pure monopoly.*

World Bank   A bank that lends (and guarantees loans) to *developing countries* to assist them in increasing their *capital stock* and thus in achieving *economic growth.*

world price   The international market *price* of a *good* or *service,* determined by world demand and supply.

World Trade Organization (WTO) An organization of 164 nations (as of 2021) that oversees the provisions of the current world trade agreement, resolves trade disputes stemming from it, and holds forums for further rounds of trade negotiations.

X-inefficiency The production of output, whatever its level, at a higher average (and total) cost than is necessary for producing that level of output.

zero interest rate policy (ZIRP) A *monetary policy* in which a *central bank* sets *nominal interest rates* at or near zero percent per year in order to stimulate the economy.

zero lower bound problem The constraint placed on the ability of a *central bank* to stimulate the economy through lower short-term *interest rates* by the fact that short-term *interest rates* cannot be driven lower than zero without causing depositors to withdraw funds from the banking system.

zero-sum game A strategic interaction (game) between two or more parties (players) in which the winners' gains exactly offset the losers' losses so that the gains and losses sum to zero.

Index

Note: **Boldface** page numbers indicate definitions of key terms; page numbers followed by "n" indicate notes.

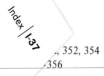